MW01625251

BIG IDEAS MATH®
Modeling Real Life

Grade 6
Common Core Edition

TEACHING EDITION

Ron Larson
Laurie Boswell

Erie, Pennsylvania
BigIdeasLearning.com

Big Ideas Learning, LLC
1762 Norcross Road
Erie, PA 16510-3838
USA

For product information and customer support, contact Big Ideas Learning at **1-877-552-7766** or visit us at ***BigIdeasLearning.com***.

Cover Image:
Valdis Torms, cobalt88/iStock/Getty Images Plus

Front Matter:
xxxvi Ryan McVay/DigitalVision/Getty Images; **xxxvii** Blackzheep/iStock/Getty Images Plus; **xxxviii** janulla/iStock/Getty Images Plus; **xxxix** Talaj/iStock/Getty Images Plus; **xli** scotto72/E+/Getty Images; **xlii** iZonda/iStock/Getty Images Plus; **xliii** Tal Inbar/Wikipedia; **xliv** NASA/Terry Virts; **xlv** damedeeso/iStock/Getty Images Plus

Printed in the U.S.A.

IBSN 13: 978-1-63708-745-9

2 3 4 5 6 7 8 9 10—25 24 23 22 21

One Voice from Kindergarten Through Algebra 2

Written by renowned authors, Dr. Ron Larson and Dr. Laurie Boswell, *Big Ideas Math* offers a seamless math pedagogy from elementary through high school. Together, Ron and Laurie provide a consistent voice that encourages students to make connections through cohesive progressions and clear instruction. Since 1992, Ron and Laurie have authored over 50 mathematics programs.

"Each time Laurie and I start working on a new program, we spend time putting ourselves in the position of the reader. How old is the reader? What is the reader's experience with mathematics? The answers to these questions become our writing guides. Our goal is to make the learning targets understandable and to develop these targets in a clear path that leads to student success."

Ron Larson

Ron Larson, Ph.D., is well known as lead author of a comprehensive and widely used mathematics program that ranges from elementary school through college. He holds the distinction of Professor Emeritus from Penn State Erie, The Behrend College, where he taught for nearly 40 years. He received his Ph.D. in mathematics from the University of Colorado. Dr. Larson engages in the latest research and advancements in mathematics education and consistently incorporates key pedagogical elements to ensure focus, coherence, rigor, and student self-reflection.

"My passion and goal in writing is to provide an essential resource for exploring and making sense of mathematics. Our program is guided by research around the learning and teaching of mathematics in the hopes of improving the achievement of all students. May this be a successful year for you!"

Laurie Boswell, Ed.D., is the former Head of School at Riverside School in Lyndonville, Vermont. In addition to authoring textbooks, she provides mathematics consulting and embedded coaching sessions. Dr. Boswell received her Ed.D. from the University of Vermont in 2010. She is a recipient of the Presidential Award for Excellence in Mathematics Teaching and later served as president of CPAM. Laurie has taught math to students at all levels, elementary through college. In addition, Laurie has served on the NCTM Board of Directors and as a Regional Director for NCSM. Along with Ron, Laurie has co-authored numerous math programs and has become a popular national speaker.

Contributors, Reviewers,

Big Ideas Learning would like to express our gratitude to the mathematics education and instruction experts who served as our advisory panel, contributing specialists, and reviewers during the writing of *Big Ideas Math: Modeling Real Life*. Their input was an invaluable asset during the development of this program.

Contributing Specialists and Reviewers

- **Sophie Murphy**, Ph.D. Candidate, Melbourne School of Education, Melbourne, Australia
  Learning Targets and Success Criteria Specialist and Visible Learning Reviewer
- **Linda Hall**, Mathematics Educational Consultant, Edmond, OK
  Advisory Panel and Teaching Edition Contributor
- **Michael McDowell**, Ed.D., Superintendent, Ross, CA
  Project-Based Learning Specialist
- **Kelly Byrne**, Math Supervisor and Coordinator of Data Analysis, Downingtown, PA
  Advisory Panel and Content Reviewer
- **Jean Carwin**, Math Specialist/TOSA, Snohomish, WA
  Advisory Panel and Content Reviewer
- **Nancy Siddens**, Independent Language Teaching Consultant, Las Cruces, NM
  English Language Learner Specialist
- **Nancy Thiele**, Mathematics Consultant, Mesa, AZ
  Teaching Edition Contributor
- **Kristen Karbon**, Curriculum and Assessment Coordinator, Troy, MI
  Advisory Panel and Content Reviewer
- **Kery Obradovich**, K–8 Math/Science Coordinator, Northbrook, IL
  Advisory Panel and Content Reviewer
- **Jennifer Rollins**, Math Curriculum Content Specialist, Golden, CO
  Advisory Panel
- **Becky Walker**, Ph.D., School Improvement Services Director, Green Bay, WI
  Advisory Panel
- **Anthony Smith**, Ph.D., Associate Professor, Associate Dean, University of Washington Bothell, Seattle, WA
  Reading/Writing Reviewer
- **Nicole Dimich Vagle**, Educator, Author, and Consultant, Hopkins, MN
  Assessment Reviewer
- **Jill Kalb**, Secondary Math Content Specialist, Arvada, CO
  Content Reviewer
- **Janet Graham**, District Math Specialist, Manassas, VA
  Response to Intervention and Differentiated Instruction Reviewer
- **Sharon Huber**, Director of Elementary Mathematics, Chesapeake, VA
  Universal Design for Learning Reviewer

Student Reviewers

- Jackson Currier
- Mason Currier
- Taylor DeLuca
- Ajalae Evans
- Malik Goodwine
- Majesty Hamilton
- Reilly Koch
- Kyla Kramer
- Matthew Lindemuth
- Greer Lippert
- Zane Lippert
- Jeffrey Lobaugh
- Riley Moran
- Zoe Morin
- Deke Patton
- Brooke Smith
- Dylan Throop
- Jenna Urso
- Madison Whitford
- Jenna Wigham

and Research

Research

Ron Larson and Laurie Boswell used the latest in educational research, along with the body of knowledge collected from expert mathematics instructors, to develop the *Modeling Real Life* series. By implementing the work of renowned researchers from across the world, *Big Ideas Math* offers at least a full year's growth within a full year's learning while also encouraging a growth mindset in students and teachers. Students take their learning from surface-level to deep-level, then transfer that learning by modeling real-life situations. For more information on how this program uses learning targets and success criteria to enhance teacher clarity, see pages xiv–xv.

The pedagogical approach used in this program follows the best practices outlined in the most prominent and widely accepted educational research, including:

- *Visible Learning*
  John Hattie © 2009
- *Visible Learning for Teachers*
  John Hattie © 2012
- *Visible Learning for Mathematics*
  John Hattie © 2017
- *Principles to Actions: Ensuring Mathematical Success for All*
  NCTM © 2014
- *Adding It Up: Helping Children Learn Mathematics*
  National Research Council © 2001
- *Mathematical Mindsets: Unleashing Students' Potential through Creative Math, Inspiring Messages and Innovative Teaching*
  Jo Boaler © 2015
- *What Works in Schools: Translating Research into Action*
  Robert Marzano © 2003
- *Classroom Instruction That Works: Research-Based Strategies for Increasing Student Achievement*
  Marzano, Pickering, and Pollock © 2001
- *Principles and Standards for School Mathematics*
  NCTM © 2000
- *Rigorous PBL by Design: Three Shifts for Developing Confident and Competent Learners*
  Michael McDowell © 2017
- Common Core State Standards for Mathematics National Governors Association Center for Best Practices and Council of Chief State School Officers © 2010
- *Universal Design for Learning Guidelines*
  CAST © 2011
- Rigor/Relevance Framework®
  International Center for Leadership in Education
- *Understanding by Design*
  Grant Wiggins and Jay McTighe © 2005
- Achieve, ACT, and The College Board
- *Elementary and Middle School Mathematics: Teaching Developmentally*
  John A. Van de Walle and Karen S. Karp © 2015
- *Evaluating the Quality of Learning: The SOLO Taxonomy*
  John B. Biggs & Kevin F. Collis © 1982
- *Unlocking Formative Assessment: Practical Strategies for Enhancing Students' Learning in the Primary and Intermediate Classroom*
  Shirley Clarke, Helen Timperley, and John Hattie © 2004
- *Formative Assessment in the Secondary Classroom*
  Shirley Clarke © 2005
- *Improving Student Achievement: A Practical Guide to Assessment for Learning*
  Toni Glasson © 2009

Focus and Coherence from

Instructional Design

A single authorship team from Kindergarten through Algebra 2 results in a logical progression of focused topics with meaningful coherence from course to course.

FOCUS

A focused program reflects the balance in grade-level standards while simultaneously supporting and engaging students to develop conceptual understanding of the major work of the grade.

The **Learning Target** and **Success Criteria** for each section focus the learning into manageable chunks, using clear teaching text and Key Ideas within the Student Edition.

2.1 Multiplying Integers

Learning Target: Find products of integers.

Success Criteria:
- I can explain the rules for multiplying integers.
- I can find products of integers with the same sign.
- I can find products of integers with different signs.

Ratios

Words A **ratio** is a comparison of two quantities. The **value of the ratio** a to b is the number $\frac{a}{b}$, which describes the multiplicative relationship between the quantities in the ratio.

Examples 2 snails *to* 6 fish

$\frac{1}{2}$ cup of milk *for every* $\frac{1}{4}$ cup of cream

Algebra The ratio of a to b can be written as $a : b$.

Laurie's Notes

Chapter 5 Overview

The study of ratios and proportions in this chapter builds upon and connects to prior work with rates and ratios in the previous course. Students should have an understanding of how ratios are represented and how ratio tables are used to find equivalent ratios. Tape diagrams and double number lines were also used to represent and solve problems involving equivalent ratios.

Laurie's Notes prepare you for the math concepts in each chapter and section and make connections to the threads of major topics for the course.

a Single Authorship Team

COHERENCE

A single authorship team built a coherent program that has intentional progression of content within each grade and between grade levels. Your students will build new understanding on foundations from prior grades and connect concepts throughout the course.

The authors developed content that progresses from prior chapters and grades to future ones. In addition to charts like this one, Laurie's Notes provide point of use insights about where your students have come from and where they are going in their learning progression.

Through the Grades

Grade 7	Grade 8	High School
• Use samples to draw inferences about populations. • Compare two populations from random samples using measures of center and variability. • Approximate the probability of a chance event and predict the approximate relative frequency given the probability.	• Construct and interpret scatter plots. • Find and assess lines of fit for scatter plots. • Use equations of lines to solve problems and interpret the slope and the y-intercept. • Construct and interpret a two-way table summarizing data. Use relative frequencies to describe possible association between the two variables.	• Classify data as quantitative or qualitative, choose and create appropriate data displays, and analyze misleading graphs. • Make and use two-way tables to recognize associations in data by finding marginal, relative, and conditional relative frequencies. • Interpret scatter plots, determine how well lines of fit model data, and distinguish between correlation and causation.

One author team thoughtfully wrote each course, creating a seamless progression of content from Kindergarten to Algebra 2.

See pages xxviii and xxix for the K–8 Progressions chart.

Gra			Grade 4	Grade 5	Grade 6	Grade 7	Grade 8
			Operations and Algebraic Thinking		Expressions and Equations		
oblems involving and subtraction 0. roperties of ns. ith addition and ion equations. *s 1–5, 10, 11*	Solve problems involving addition and subtraction within 20. Work with equal groups of objects. *Chapters 1–6, 15*	Solve problems involving multiplication and division within 100. Apply properties of multiplication. Solve problems involving the four operations, and identify and explain patterns in arithmetic. *Chapters 1–5, 8, 9, and 14*	Use the four operations with whole numbers to solve problems. Understand factors and multiples. Generate and analyze patterns. *Chapters 2–6, 12*	Write and interpret numerical expressions. Analyze patterns and relationships. *Chapters 2, 12*	Perform arithmetic with algebraic expressions. *Chapter 5* Solve one-variable equations and inequalities. *Chapters 6, 8* Analyze relationships between dependent and independent variables. *Chapter 6*	Write equivalent expressions. *Chapter 3* Use numerical and algebraic expressions, equations, and inequalities to solve problems. *Chapters 3, 4, 6*	Understand the connections between proportional relationships, lines, and linear equations. *Chapter 4* Solve linear equations and systems of linear equations. *Chapters 1, 5* Work with radicals and integer exponents. *Chapters 8, 9*
							Functions
							Define, evaluate, and compare functions, and use functions to model relationships between quantities.

You have used number lines to find sums of positive numbers, which involve movement to the right. Now you will find sums with negative numbers, which involve movement to the left.

Throughout each course, lessons build on prior learning as new concepts are introduced. Here the students are reminded of the use of number lines with positive numbers.

Using Number Lines to Find Sums

a. Find $4 + (-4)$.

Draw an arrow from 0 to 4 to represent 4. Then draw an arrow 4 units to the left to represent adding -4.

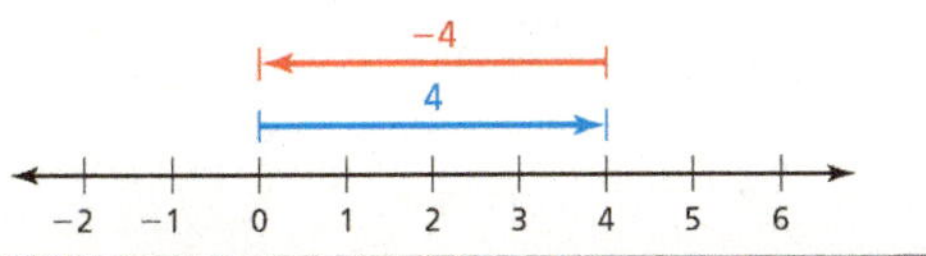

Rigor in Math: A Balanced Approach

Instructional Design

The authors wrote every chapter and every section to give you a meaningful balance of rigorous instruction.

RIGOR

A rigorous program provides a balance of three important building blocks.

- **Conceptual Understanding**
  Discovering why
- **Procedural Fluency**
  Learning how
- **Application**
  Knowing when to apply

Conceptual Understanding
Students have the opportunity to develop foundational concepts central to the *Learning Target* in each *Exploration* by experimenting with new concepts, talking with peers, and asking questions.

EXPLORATION 1 **Understanding Quotients Involving N**

Work with a partner.

a. Discuss the relationship between multiplication your partner.

b. **INDUCTIVE REASONING** Complete the table. Th for dividing (i) two integers with the same sign a different signs.

Expression	Type of Quotient	Quoti
$-15 \div 3$	Integers	
$12 \div (-6)$		
$10 \div (-2)$		

Conceptual Thinking
Ask students to think deeply with conceptual questions.

29. **MP NUMBER SENSE** Without solving, determine whether $\frac{x}{4} = \frac{15}{3}$ and $\frac{x}{15} = \frac{4}{3}$ have the same solution. Explain your reasoning.

EXAMPLE 1 **Graphing a Linear Equation in Standard Form**

Graph $-2x + 3y = -6$.

Step 1: Write the equation in slope-intercept form.

$-2x + 3y = -6$	Write the equation.
$3y = 2x - 6$	Add $2x$ to each side.
$y = \frac{2}{3}x - 2$	Divide each side by 3.

Step 2: Use the slope and the y-intercept to graph the equation.

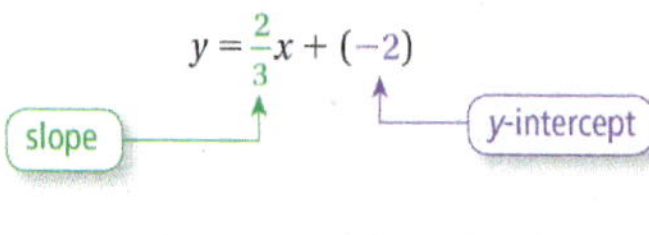

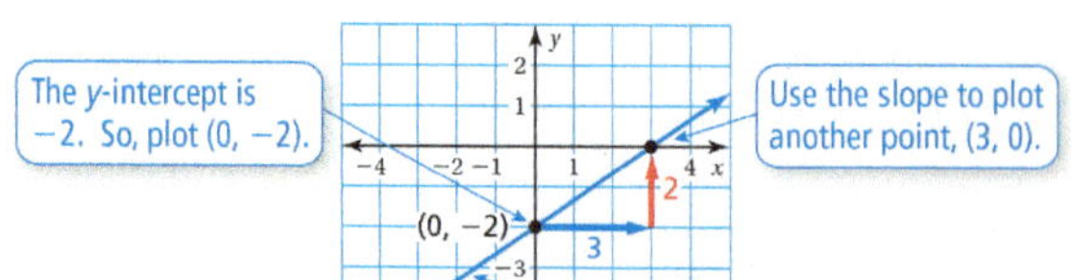

Procedural Fluency
Solidify learning with clear, stepped-out teaching and examples.

Then shift conceptual understanding into procedural fluency with *Try Its*, *Self-Assessments*, *Practice*, and *Review & Refresh*.

STEAM Applications

Students begin every chapter with a fun, engaging STEAM video to see how math applies to everyday life. Students apply what they learn in the chapter with a related *Performance Task*.

Name________________________ Date__________

Chapter 3 **Performance Task**

Chlorophyll in Plants

What is needed for photosynthesis? How can you use the amount of chlorophyll in a lake to determine the level of biological productivity?

Photosynthesis is the process by which plants acquire energy from the sun. Sunlight, carbon dioxide, and water are used by a plant to produce glucose and dioxygen.

1. You want to make models of the molecules involved in photosynthesis for a science fair project. The table shows the number of each element used for each molecule. Let *x*, *y*, and *z* represent the costs of a model carbon atom, model hydrogen atom, and

	Number of Atoms		
Molecule	**Carbon**	**Hydrogen**	**Oxygen**
Carbon Dioxide	1	0	2
Water	0	2	1

Daily Application Practice

Modeling Real Life, *Dig Deeper*, *Problem Solving*, and other non-routine problems help students apply surface-level skills to gain a deeper understanding. These problems lead students to independent problem-solving.

36. **DIG DEEPER!** The *girth* of a package is the distance around the perimeter of a face that does not include the length as a side. A postal service says that a rectangular package can have a maximum combined length and girth of 108 inches.

a. Write an inequality that represents the allowable dimensions for the package.

b. Find three different sets of allowable dimensions that are reasonable for the package. Find the volume of each package.

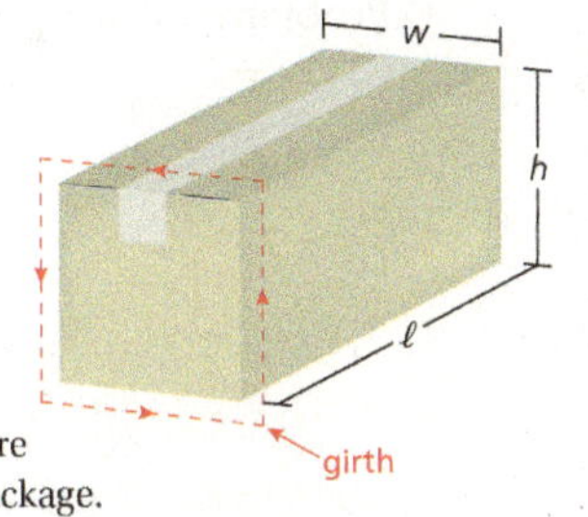

THE PROBLEM-SOLVING PLAN

1. **Understand the Problem**
   Think about what the problem is asking, what information you know, and how you might begin to solve.
2. **Make a Plan**
   Plan your solution pathway before jumping in to solve. Identify any relationships and decide on a problem-solving strategy.
3. **Solve and Check**
   As you solve the problem, be sure to evaluate your progress and check your answers. Throughout the problem-solving process, you must continually ask, "Does this make sense?" and be willing to change course if necessary.

Problem-Solving Plan

Walk students through the Problem-Solving Plan, featured in many examples, to help them make sense of problems with confidence.

Embedded Mathematical Practices

Encouraging Mathematical Mindsets

Developing proficiency in the **Mathematical Practices** is about becoming a mathematical thinker. Students learn to ask why, and to reason and communicate with others as they learn. Use this guide to communicate opportunities in your classroom for students to develop proficiency with the mathematical practices.

1

One way to **Make Sense of Problems and Persevere in Solving Them** is to use the Problem-Solving Plan. Students should take time to analyze the given information and what the problem is asking to help them plan a solution pathway.

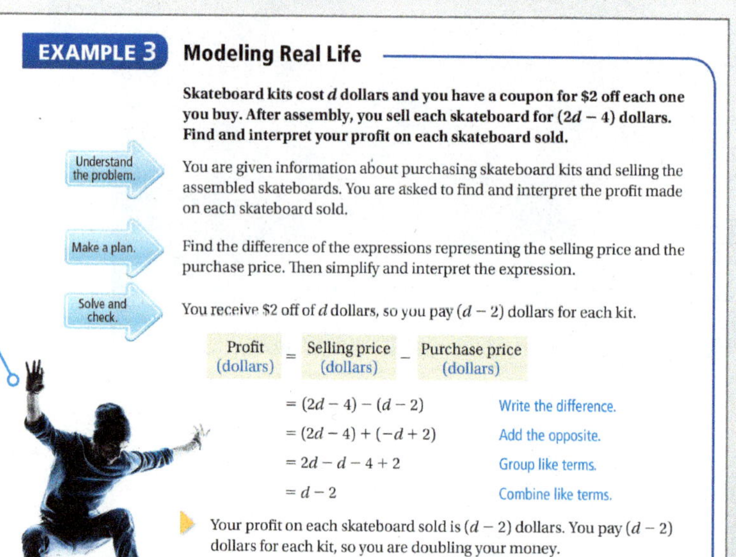

EXAMPLE 3 **Modeling Real Life**

Skateboard kits cost d dollars and you have a coupon for \$2 off each one you buy. After assembly, you sell each skateboard for $(2d - 4)$ dollars. Find and interpret your profit on each skateboard sold.

Understand the problem. You are given information about purchasing skateboard kits and selling the assembled skateboards. You are asked to find and interpret the profit made on each skateboard sold.

Make a plan. Find the difference of the expressions representing the selling price and the purchase price. Then simplify and interpret the expression.

Solve and check. You receive \$2 off of d dollars, so you pay $(d - 2)$ dollars for each kit.

Profit (dollars) = Selling price (dollars) − Purchase price (dollars)

$= (2d - 4) - (d - 2)$ Write the difference.

$= (2d - 4) + (-d + 2)$ Add the opposite.

$= 2d - d - 4 + 2$ Group like terms.

$= d - 2$ Combine like terms.

Your profit on each skateboard sold is $(d - 2)$ dollars. You pay $(d - 2)$ dollars for each kit, so you are doubling your money.

Look for labels such as:

- Explain the Meaning
- Find Entry Points
- Analyze Givens
- Make a Plan
- Interpret a Solution
- Consider Similar Problems
- Consider Simpler Forms
- Check Progress
- Problem Solving

2

Students **Reason Abstractly** when they explore a concrete example and represent it symbolically. Other times, students **Reason Quantitatively** when they see relationships in numbers or symbols and draw conclusions about a concrete example.

a. Represent each table in the same coordinate plane. Which graph represents a proportional relationship? How do you know?

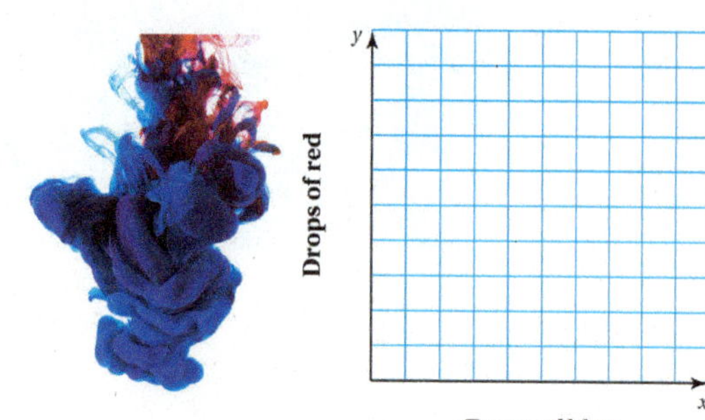

Look for labels such as:

- Make Sense of Quantities
- Use Equations
- Use Expressions
- Understand Quantities
- Use Operations
- Number Sense
- Reasoning

Math Practice

Reasoning

How is the graph of the proportional relationship different from the other graph?

b. Which property can you use to solve each of the equations modeled by the algebra tiles? Solve each equation and explain your method.

Math Practice

Make Conjectures
Can you use algebra tiles to solve any equation? Explain your reasoning.

46. MP LOGIC When you multiply or divide each side of an inequality by the same negative number, you must reverse the direction of the inequality symbol. Explain why.

3

When students **Construct Viable Arguments and Critique the Reasoning of Others**, they make and justify conclusions and decide whether others' arguments are correct or flawed.

Look for labels such as:

- Use Assumptions
- Use Definitions
- Use Prior Results
- Make Conjectures
- Build Arguments
- Analyze Conjectures
- Use Counterexamples
- Justify Conclusions
- Compare Arguments
- Construct Arguments
- Listen and Ask Questions
- You Be the Teacher
- Logic

36. MP APPLY MATHEMATICS You decide to make and sell bracelets. The cost of your materials is $84.00. You charge $3.50 for each bracelet.

a. Write a function that represents the profit P for selling b bracelets.

b. Which variable is independent? dependent? Explain.

c. You will *break even* when the cost of your materials equals your income. How many bracelets must you sell to break even?

Look for labels such as:

- Apply Mathematics
- Simplify a Solution
- Use a Diagram
- Use a Table
- Use a Graph
- Use a Formula
- Analyze Relationships
- Interpret Results
- Modeling Real Life

4

To **Model with Mathematics**, students apply the math they have learned to a real-life problem, and they interpret mathematical results in the context of the situation.

BUILDING TO FULL UNDERSTANDING

Throughout each course, students have opportunities to demonstrate specific aspects of the mathematical practices. Labels throughout the book indicate gateways to those aspects. Collectively, these opportunities will lead students to a full understanding of each mathematical practice. Developing these mindsets and habits will give meaning to the mathematics they learn.

Embedded Mathematical Practices (continued)

5

To **Use Appropriate Tools Strategically**, students need to know what tools are available and think about how each tool might help them solve a mathematical problem. When students choose a tool to use, remind them that it may have limitations.

Look for labels such as:

- Choose Tools
- Recognize Usefulness of Tools
- Use Other Resources
- Use Technology to Explore
- Using Tools

d. Enter the function $y = \left(\frac{1}{10}\right)^x$ into your graphing calculator. Use the *table* feature to evaluate the function for positive integer values of x until the calculator displays a y-value that is not in standard form. Do the results support your answer in part (c)? Explain.

X	Y1
1	.1
2	.01
3	.001
4	1E-4
5	1E-5
6	1E-6
7	1E-7

X=6

Math Practice

Use Technology to Explore

How can writing $\frac{1}{10}$ as a power of 10 help you understand the calculator display?

6

When students **Attend to Precision**, they are developing a habit of being careful in how they talk about concepts, label their work, and write their answers.

Look for labels such as:

- Communicate Precisely
- Use Clear Definitions
- State the Meaning of Symbols
- Specify Units
- Label Axes
- Calculate Accurately
- Precision

Add 1.459 + 23.7.

$$\begin{array}{r} {}^{1} \\ 1.459 \\ +\ 23.700 \\ \hline 25.159 \end{array}$$

Insert zeros so that both numbers have the same number of decimal places.

Math Practice

Calculate Accurately

Why is it important to line up the decimal points when adding or subtracting decimals?

49. MP **PRECISION** Consider the equation $c = ax - bx$, where a, b, and c are whole numbers. Which of the following result in values of a, b, and c so that the original equation has exactly one solution? Justify your answer.

$a - b = 1, c = 0$ $\quad$ $a = b, c \neq 0$ $\quad$ $a = b, c = 0$ $\quad$ $a \neq b, c = 0$

 **STRUCTURE** **Tell whether the triangles are similar. Explain.**

14. 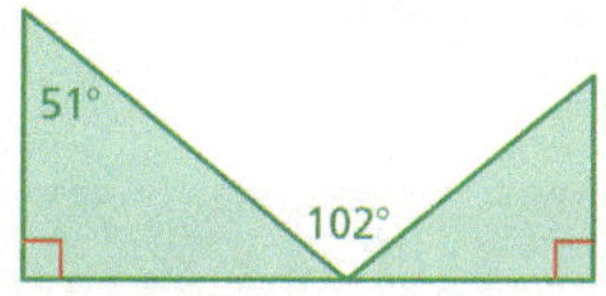

15. 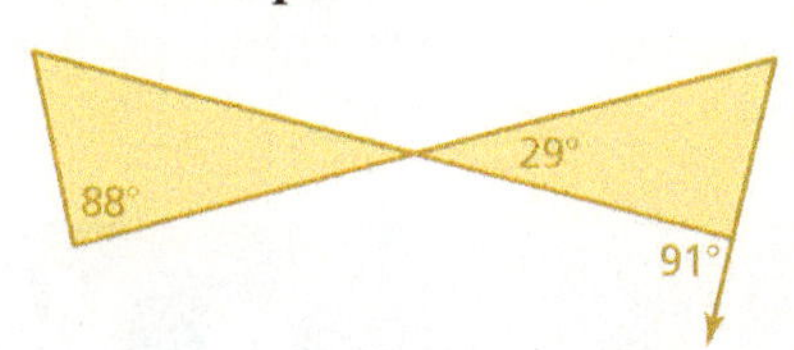

7

Students **Look For and Make Use of Structure** by looking closely to see structure within a mathematical statement, or stepping back for an overview to see how individual parts make one single object.

Find the sum of the areas of the faces.

Surface Area	=	Area of bottom	+	Area of a side	+	Area of a side	+	Area of a side	+	Area of a side	
S	=	49	+	35	+	35	+	35	+	35	= 189

Look for labels such as:
- Look for Structure
- Look for Patterns
- View as Components
- Structure
- Patterns

Math Practice

Look for Patterns
How can you find the surface area of a square pyramid by calculating the area of only two of the faces?

35.  **REPEATED REASONING** You have been assigned a nine-digit identification number.

a. Should you use the Fundamental Counting Principle or a tree diagram to find the total number of possible identification numbers? Explain.

b. How many identification numbers are possible?

8

When students **Look For and Express Regularity in Repeated Reasoning**, they can notice patterns and make generalizations. Remind students to keep in mind the goal of a problem, which will help them evaluate reasonableness of answers along the way.

Look for labels such as:
- Repeat Calculations
- Find General Methods
- Maintain Oversight
- Evaluate Results
- Repeated Reasoning

Visible Learning Through Learning Targets,

Making Learning Visible

Knowing the learning intention of a chapter or section helps learners focus on the purpose of an activity, rather than simply completing it in isolation. This program supports visible learning through the consistent use of Learning Targets and Success Criteria to ensure positive outcomes for all students.

Every chapter and section shows a **Learning Target** and related **Success Criteria**. These are purposefully integrated into each carefully written lesson.

4.4 Writing and Graphing Inequalities

Learning Target: Write inequalities and represent solutions of inequalities on number lines.

Success Criteria:
- I can write word sentences as inequalities.
- I can determine whether a value is a solution of an inequality.
- I can graph the solutions of inequalities.

Chapter Learning Target:
Understand equations and inequalities.

Chapter Success Criteria:
- I can identify key words and phrases to write equations and inequalities.
- I can write word sentences as equations and inequalities.
- I can solve equations and inequalities using properties.
- I can use equations and inequalities to model and solve real-life problems.

The **Chapter Review** reminds students to rate their understanding of the learning targets.

Chapter Self-Assessment

As you complete the exercises, use the scale below to rate your understanding of the success criteria in your journal.

1	2	3	4
I do not understand.	I can do it with help.	I can do it on my own.	I can teach someone else.

6.1 Writing Equations in One Variable *(pp. 245–250)*

Learning Target: Write equations in one variable and write equations that represent real-life problems.

Write the word sentence as an equation.

. The product of a number m and 2 is 8.

Students review each section with a reminder of that section's learning target.

Icons throughout **Laurie's Notes** suggest ways to target where students are in their learning.

Fist of Five: Ask students to indicate their understanding of the first and second success criterion. Then select students to explain each one.

QUESTIONS FOR LEARNERS

As students progress through a section, they should be able to answer the following questions.
- What are you learning?
- Why are you learning this?
- Where are you in your learning?
- How will you know when you have learned it?
- Where are you going next?

Success Criteria, and Self-Assessment

Self-Assessment for Problem Solving

Solve each exercise. Then rate your understanding of the success criteria in your journal.

24 in.

18. An emperor penguin is 45 inches tall. It is 24 inches taller than a rockhopper penguin. Write and solve an equation to find the height (in inches) of a rockhopper penguin. Is your answer reasonable? Explain.

19. **DIG DEEPER!** You get in an elevator and go up 2 floors and down 8 floors before exiting. Then you get back in the elevator and go up 4 floors before exiting on the 12th floor. On what floors did you enter the elevator?

Self-Assessments are included throughout every section, and in the **Chapter Review**, to help students take ownership of their learning and think about where to go next.

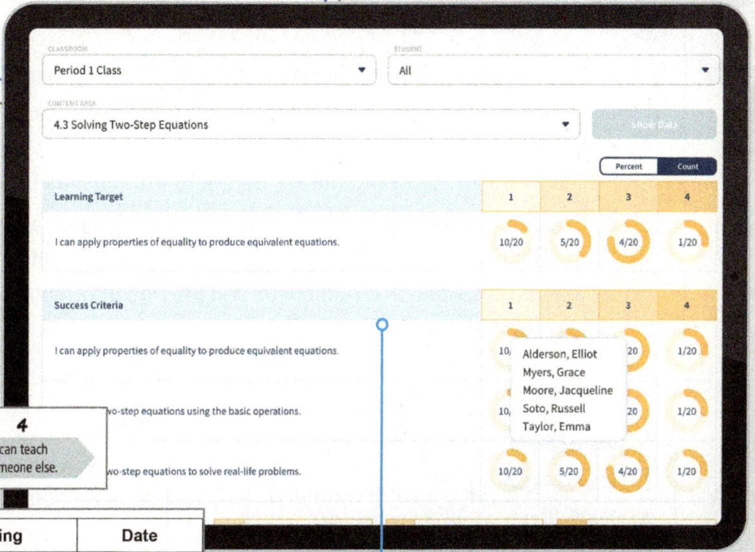

Period 1 Class

All

4.3 Solving Two-Step Equations

Percent | Count

Learning Target	1	2	3	4
I can apply properties of equality to produce equivalent equations.	10/20	5/20	4/20	1/20

Success Criteria	1	2	3	4
I can apply properties of equality to produce equivalent equations.	10/		20	1/20
…o-step equations using the basic operations.	10/		20	1/20
…o-step equations to solve real-life problems.	10/20	5/20	4/20	1/20

Alderson, Elliot
Myers, Grace
Moore, Jacqueline
Soto, Russell
Taylor, Emma

Students use a 4-point scale to rate their understanding of each success criterion. They can keep track of their learning on paper or online.

1	2	3	4
I do not understand.	I can do it with help.	I can do it on my own.	I can teach someone else.

	Rating	Date
1.1 Rational Numbers		
Learning Target: Understand absolute values and ordering of rational numbers.	1 2 3 4	
I can graph rational numbers on a number line.	1 2 3 4	
I can find the absolute value of a rational number.	1 2 3 4	
I can use a number line to compare rational numbers.	1 2 3 4	

When students use the online **Self-Assessment** tool to keep track of their learning, you can view easy-to-read live reports to inform your instruction.

Ensuring Positive Outcomes

John Hattie's *Visible Learning* research consistently shows that using Learning Targets and Success Criteria can result in two years' growth in one year, ensuring positive outcomes for student learning and achievement.

Sophie Murphy, M.Ed., wrote the chapter-level learning targets and success criteria for this program. Sophie is currently completing her Ph.D. at the University of Melbourne in Australia with Professor John Hattie as her leading supervisor. Sophie completed her Master's thesis with Professor John Hattie in 2015. Sophie has over 20 years of experience as a teacher and school leader in private and public school settings in Australia.

High-Impact Strategies

Purposeful Focus

Many of the things we do as educators have a positive effect on student learning, but which ones have the greatest impact? This program purposefully integrates **five key strategies** proven to have some of the highest impact on student achievement.

TEACHER CLARITY

Before starting a new topic, make clear the learning target. As students explore and learn, continue to connect their experiences back to the success criteria so they know where they are in their learning.

Self-Assessment for Concepts & Skills

- Identify the reasons for incorrect answers for Exercises 9–14. Are the errors computational? Do students complete Exercises 9–12 with ease but struggle with Exercises 13 and 14? Are the negative numbers the issue? Make sure students are aware of the reasons for their mistakes.
- Exercise 15 asks students to explain the relationship between using the Distributive Property to simplify an expression and to factor an expression. Students' responses will provide information about their level of understanding.

FEEDBACK

Actively listen as you probe for student understanding, being mindful of the feedback that you provide. When students provide you with feedback, you see where your students are in their learning and make instructional decisions for where to go next.

Try It

- These exercises provide a review of three additional data displays.
- **Turn and Talk:** Have students discuss their answers. Remind them of *Talk Moves* that they can use in their discussions. Then review the answers as a class.

CLASSROOM DISCUSSION

Encourage your students to talk together! This solidifies understanding while honing their ability to reason and construct arguments. Students benefit from hearing the reasoning of classmates and hearing peers critique their own reasoning.

Daily Support from a Master Educator

In Laurie's Notes, master educator Laurie Boswell uses her professional training and years of experience to help you guide your students to better understanding.

Laurie studied Professor John Hattie's research on *Visible Learning* and met with Hattie on multiple occasions to ensure she was interpreting his research accurately and embedding it effectively. Laurie's expertise continues with an ongoing collaboration with Sophie Murphy, who is pursuing her Ph.D. under Professor Hattie.

for Student Achievement

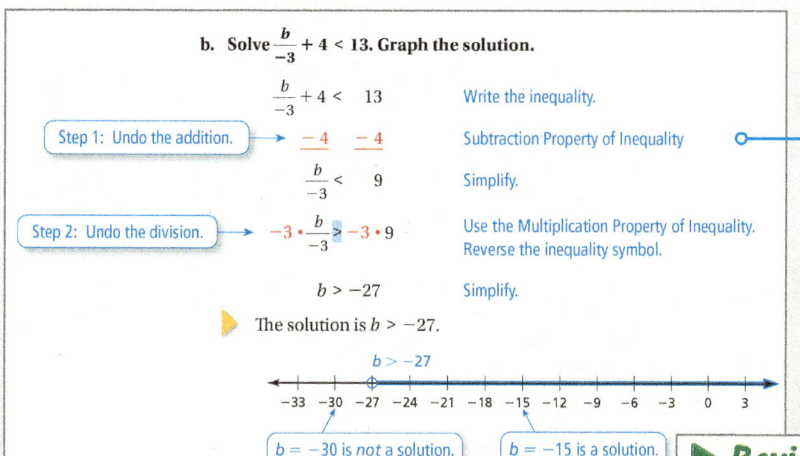

b. Solve $\frac{b}{-3} + 4 < 13$. Graph the solution.

	$\frac{b}{-3} + 4 < 13$	Write the inequality.
Step 1: Undo the addition.	$-4 \quad -4$	Subtraction Property of Inequality
	$\frac{b}{-3} < 9$	Simplify.
Step 2: Undo the division.	$-3 \cdot \frac{b}{-3} > -3 \cdot 9$	Use the Multiplication Property of Inequality. Reverse the inequality symbol.
	$b > -27$	Simplify.

The solution is $b > -27$.

DIRECT INSTRUCTION

Follow exploration and discovery with explicit instruction to build procedural skill and fluency. Teach with clear Key Ideas and powerful stepped-out examples that have been carefully designed to meet the success criteria.

Review & Refresh

Solve the inequality. Graph the solution.

1. $-3x \geq 18$ **2.** $\frac{2}{3}d > 8$ **3.** $2 \geq \frac{g}{-4}$

Find the missing values in the ratio table. Then write the equivalent ratios.

4.

Flutes	7		28
Clarinets	4	12	

5.

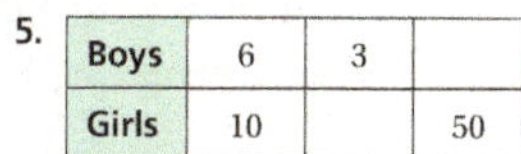

Boys	6	3	
Girls	10		50

6. What is the volume of the cube?

A. 8 ft^3 **B.** 16 ft^3

C. 24 ft^3 **D.** 32 ft^3

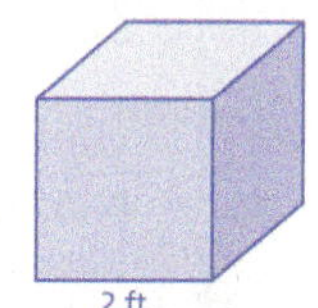

SPACED PRACTICE

Effective practice does not just focus on a single topic of new learning; students must revisit concepts over time so deeper learning occurs. This program cohesively offers multiple opportunities for students to build their conceptual understanding by intentionally revisiting and applying concepts throughout subsequent lessons and chapters. *Review & Refresh* exercises in every section also provide continual practice on the major topics.

We focus on **STRATEGIES** with some of the **HIGHEST IMPACT** on student achievement—up to 2 years of learning for a year of input.

Five Strategies for Purposeful Focus

Professor John Hattie, in his *Visible Learning* network, identified more than 250 influences on student learning, and developed a way of ranking them. He conducted meta-analyses and compared the influences by their **effect size**—the impact the factor had on student learning.

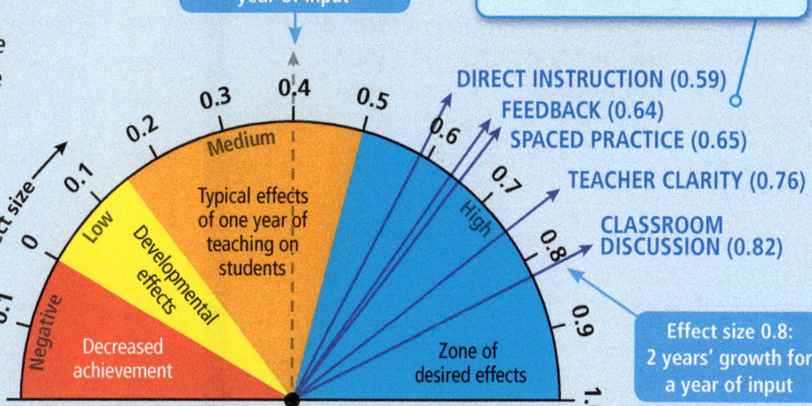

Barometer of Influences

How to Use This Program: Plan

Taking Advantage of Your Resources

You play an indispensable role in your students' learning. This program provides rich resources for learners of all levels to help you **Plan**, **Teach**, and **Assess**.

Plan every chapter and section with tools in the Teaching Edition such as **Suggested Pacing**, **Progression Tables**, and chapter and section **Overviews** written by Laurie Boswell.

Suggested Pacing

Chapter Opener	1 Day
Section 1	2 Days
Section 2	2 Days
Section 3	2 Days
Section 4	2 Days
Section 5	

Preparing to Teach

- Students should be familiar with organizing the results of an **experiment** in a table.
- **Model with Mathematics:** In this exploration, students will gain a conceptual sense of **probability** by performing activities to determine the likelihood of an **event**. They will pursue the concept of possible **outcomes**, which leads to describing the likelihood of an event.

Through the Chapter

Standard	7.1	7.2	7.3	7.4
8.F.A.1 Understand that a function is a rule that assigns to each input exactly one output. The graph of a function is the set of ordered pairs consisting of an input and the corresponding output.	●	★		
8.F.A.2 Compare properties of two functions each represented in a different way (algebraically, graphically, numerically in tables, or by verbal descriptions).			★	
8.F.A.3 Interpret the equation $y = mx + b$ as defining a linear function, whose graph is a straight line; give examples of functions that are not			●	★

Find Your Resources Digitally

Use the resources page that is available on your *BigIdeasMath.com* dashboard. Here, you can download, customize, and print these planning resources and many more. Use the filters to view resources specific to a chapter or section.

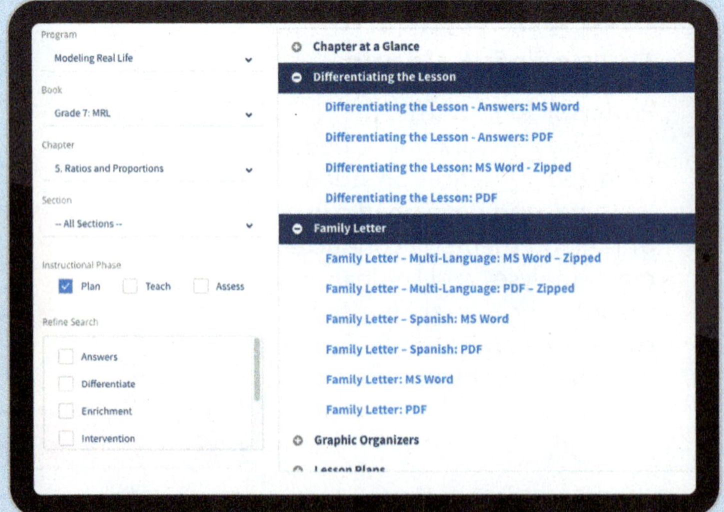

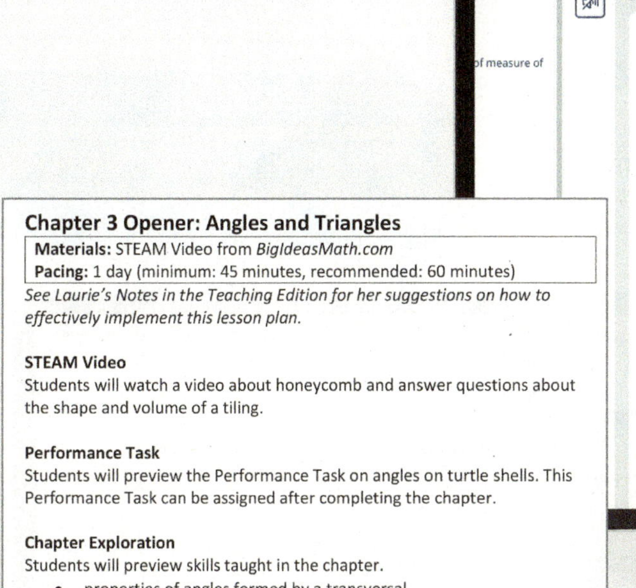

Chapter 3 Opener: Angles and Triangles

Materials: STEAM Video from *BigIdeasMath.com*
Pacing: 1 day (minimum: 45 minutes, recommended: 60 minutes)

See Laurie's Notes in the Teaching Edition for her suggestions on how to effectively implement this lesson plan.

STEAM Video
Students will watch a video about honeycomb and answer questions about the shape and volume of a tiling.

Performance Task
Students will preview the Performance Task on angles on turtle shells. This Performance Task can be assigned after completing the chapter.

Chapter Exploration
Students will preview skills taught in the chapter.

- properties of angles formed by a transversal

Access all planning resources of the Teaching Edition in the **Dynamic Classroom**. Use the customizable **Lesson Plans** to help teach each lesson to meet your specific classroom needs.

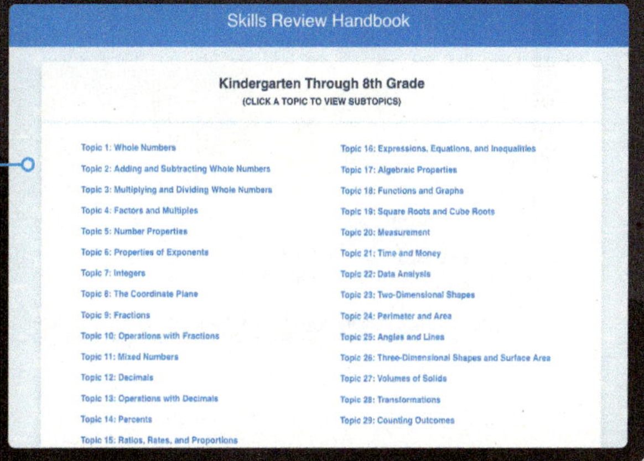

Review topics using the **Skills Review Handbook** to support students. Each topic includes a key concept and vocabulary and contains examples and exercises.

Plan Online

Remember as you are planning, that the *Dynamic Classroom* has the same interactive tools, such as the digital *Sketchpad*, that students will use to model concepts. Plan ahead by practicing these tools to guide students as they use these manipulatives and models.

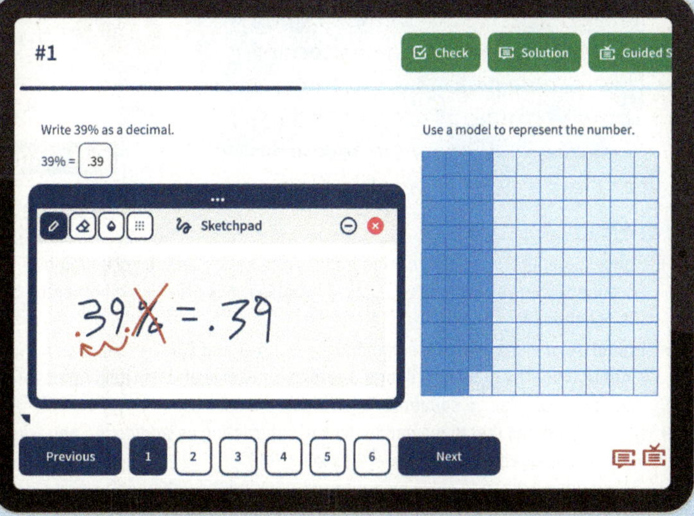

How to Use This Program: Teach

Multiple Pathways for Instruction

Big Ideas Learning provides everything at your fingertips to help you make the best instructional choices for your students.

Present all content digitally using the **Dynamic Classroom**. Send students a page link on-the-fly with **Flip-To** to direct where you want your students to go.

Have students think ahead about chapter concepts in the world around them with a **STEAM video**. Then, students transfer their learning in the **Connecting Concepts** and **Performance Task** at the end of the chapter.

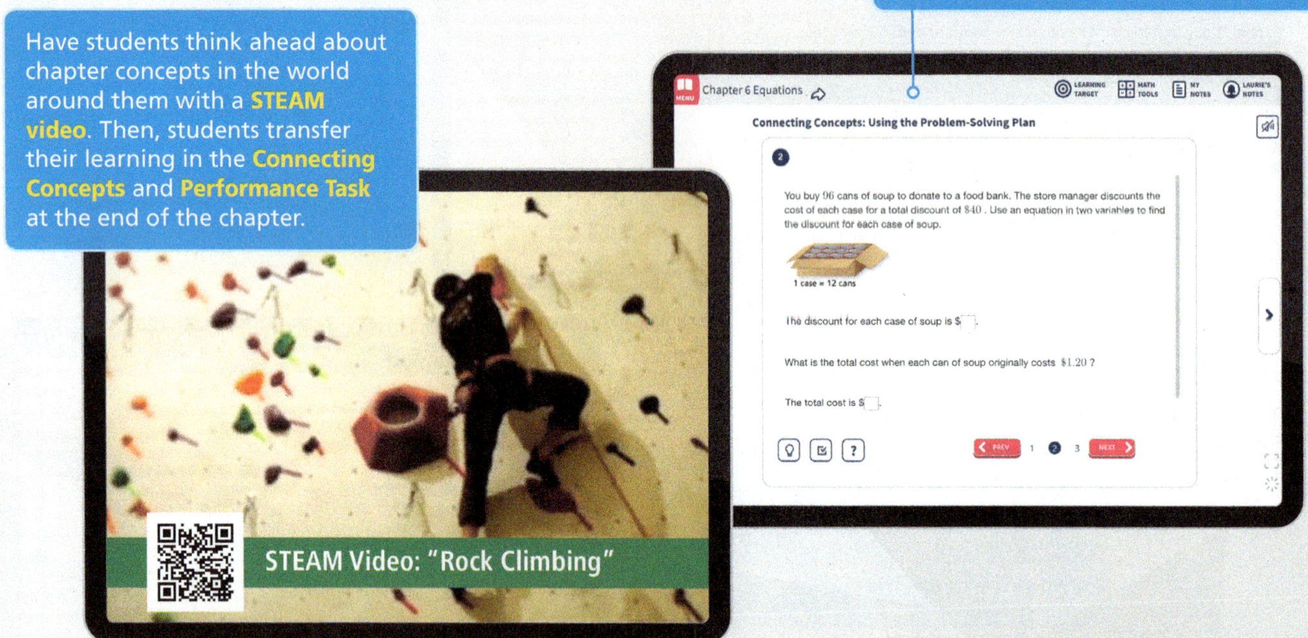

Engage students with a creative hook at the beginning of each section with **Motivate**. This activity, written by master educator Laurie Boswell, provides a conceptual introduction for the section. Then, encourage mathematical discovery with **Exploration**.

Motivate

- ? Show students a collection of algebra tiles and ask, "Can the collection be simplified? Can you remove zero pairs? What is the expression represented by the collection?"
- **Model:** As a class, model the equations $x + 3 = 7$ and $x + 2 = 5$ using algebra tiles. These do not require a zero pair to solve and will help remind students how to solve equations using algebra tiles.
- Remind students that they need to think of subtracting as *adding the opposite* when using algebra tiles (i.e., $x - 3$ as $x + (-3)$).
- ? "What does it mean to solve an equation?" To find the value of the variable that makes the equation true.

4.1 Solving Equations Using Addition or Subtraction

Learning Target: Write and solve equations using addition or subtraction.

Success Criteria:
- I can apply the Addition and Subtraction Properties of Equality to produce equivalent equations.
- I can solve equations using addition or subtraction.
- I can apply equations involving addition or subtraction to solve real-life problems.

EXPLORATION 1 Using Algebra Tiles to Solve Equations

Work with a partner.

a. Use the examples to explain the meaning of each property.

Addition Property of Equality: $x + 2 = 1$

$x + 2 + 5 = 1 + 5$

Subtraction Property of Equality: $x + 2 = 1$

$x + 2 - 1 = 1 - 1$

Are these properties true for equations involving negative numbers? Explain your reasoning.

b. Write the four equations modeled by the algebra tiles. Explain how you can use algebra tiles to solve each equation. Then find the solutions.

Lead students to procedural fluency with clear **Examples** and **Self-Assessment** opportunities for them to try on their own.

EXAMPLE 1 **Determining Whether Two Quantities are Proportional**

Tell whether x and y are proportional. Explain your reasoning.

a.

x	1	2	3	4
y	−2	0	2	4

Plot the points. Draw a line through the points.

The line does *not* pass through the origin. So, x and y are not proportional.

b.

x	0	2	4	6
y	0	2	4	6

Plot the points. Draw a line through the points.

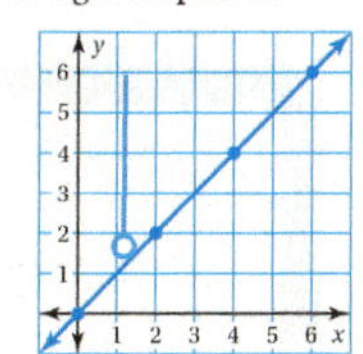

The line passes through the origin. So, x and y are proportional.

EXAMPLE 3 **Modeling Real Life**

The graph shows the area y (in square feet) that a robotic vacuum cleans in x minutes. Find the area cleaned in 10 minutes.

Robotic Vacuum

The graph is a line through the origin, so x and y are proportional. You can write an equation to represent the relationship between area and time.

Because the graph passes through the point (1, 16), the unit rate is 16 square feet per minute and the constant of proportionality is $k = 16$. So, an equation of the line is $y = 16x$. Substitute to find the area cleaned in 10 minutes.

$y = 16x$ — Write the equation.

$= 16(10)$ — Substitute 10 for x.

$= 160$ — Multiply.

So, the vacuum cleans 160 square feet in 10 minutes.

Help students apply and problem solve with **Modeling Real Life** applications, **Dig Deeper** problems, and **Math Practice** conceptual problems.

Let **Laurie's Notes** guide your teaching and scaffolding decisions at every step to support and deepen all students' learning. You may want to group students differently as they move in and out of these levels with each skill and concept. Student self-assessment and feedback help guide your instructional decisions about how and when to layer support.

Scaffolding Instruction

- In the exploration, students discussed various methods of solving proportions. They will continue this work in the lesson.
- **Emerging:** Students may be able to create a ratio table but may struggle to write and/or solve the proportion. Students will benefit from close examination of the examples.
- **Proficient:** Students can write and solve proportions using a variety of methods (including tables). Students should review Examples 4 and 5 before proceeding to the Self-Assessment exercises.

Name ________________ Date ________

Lesson 7.1 **Extra Practice**

You randomly choose one of the tiles shown.

1. How many possible outcomes are there?
2. What are the favorable outcomes of choosing a number greater than 6?
3. In how many ways can choosing a number divisible by 2 occur?

Differentiate and support your learners with **Differentiating the Lesson**, **Resources by Chapter**, **English Language Support**, and much more.

How to Use This Program: Assess

Powerful Assessment Tools

Gain insight into your students' learning with these powerful formative and summative assessment tools tailored to every learning target and standard.

Access real-time data and navigate easily through student responses with **Formative Check**.

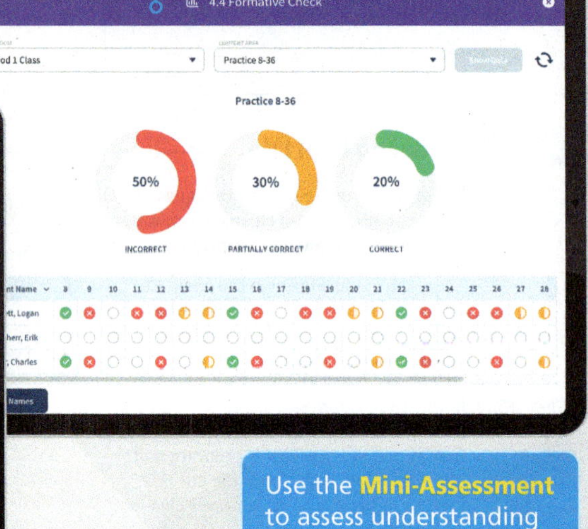

Use the **Mini-Assessment** to assess understanding of lesson concepts.

Mini-Assessment

Write the word sentence as an inequality.

1. A number a is at least 5. $a \geq 5$
2. Four times a number b is no more than -4.73. $4b \leq -4.73$
3. Tell whether -2 is a solution of $6g - 14 > -21$. not a solution
4. A rollercoaster is at most 45 meters high. Write and graph an inequality that represents the height of the ...

$h \leq 45$; 40 41 42 43 44

Scaffold **Practice** from the **Assignment Guide and Concept Check**. Assign print or digital versions, and project answers and solutions in class using the **Answer Presentation Tool**.

6.1 Practice

Review & Refresh

Find the missing dimension. Use the scale 1 : 15.

	Item	Model	Actual
1.	Figure skater	Height: ▭ in.	Height: 67.5 in.
2.	Pipe	Length: 5 ft	Length: ▭ ft

Simplify the expression.

3. $2(3p - 6) + 4p$

4. $5n - 3(4n + 1)$

Scaffold assignments to support all students in their learning progression. The suggested assignments are a starting point. Continue to assign additional exercises and revisit with spaced practice to move every student toward proficiency.

Assignment Guide and Concept Check

Level	Assignment 1	Assignment 2
Emerging	4, 8, 9, 10, 11, 14, 16, 17, 26, 27, 31	18, 19, 32, 33, 35, 36, 39, 40, 41, 42
Proficient	4, 8, 9, 10, 11, 17, 18, 19, 26, 28, 30, 32, 48	25, 33, 35, 37, 39, 40, 42, 43, 47
Advanced	4, 8, 9, 12, 13, 14, 23, 25, 26, 30, 32, 33, 48	38, 40, 45, 46, 47, 49, 50, 51

- Assignment 1 is for use after students complete the Self-Assessment for Concepts & Skills.
- Assignment 2 is for use after students complete the Self-Assessment for Problem Solving.
- The red exercises can be used as a concept check.

Assign **Quizzes** or **Chapter Tests** to assess understanding of section or chapter content or use **Alternative Assessments** and **Performance Tasks**, which include scoring rubrics.

Name______________________________ Date ________

Grade 7 **Course Benchmark 2**
For use after Chapter 5

Find the sum. Write your answer in simplest form.

1. $-\frac{1}{7}+\frac{1}{7}$

2. $-3.2+(-4.92)$

3. The table shows the change in the water level (in centimeters) of a reservoir for three months. Find the total change in the water level for the three-month period.

Month	1	2	3
Change in Water Level	$-\frac{1}{3}$	$-\frac{2}{21}$	$-\frac{16}{21}$

Find the difference. Write your answer in simplest form.

4. $-\frac{2}{5}-\left(-\frac{9}{5}\right)$

5. $-8.3-6.8$

6. At 4 P.M., the total snowfall is 3 centimeters. At 8P.M., the total snowfall is 14 centimeters. What is the mean hourly snowfall?

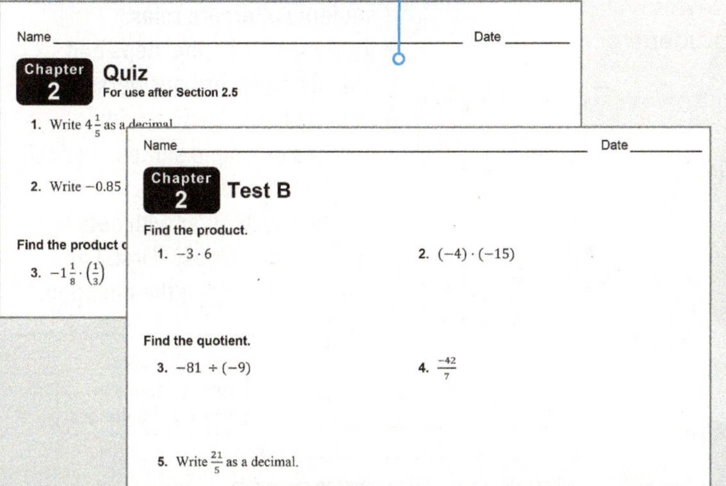

Name______________________________ Date ________

Chapter 2 **Quiz**
For use after Section 2.5

1. Write $4\frac{1}{5}$ as a decimal.

2. Write -0.85

Find the product

3. $-1\frac{1}{8}\cdot\left(\frac{1}{3}\right)$

Name______________________________ Date ________

Chapter 2 **Test B**

Find the product.

1. $-3\cdot 6$

2. $(-4)\cdot(-15)$

Find the quotient.

3. $-81\div(-9)$

4. $\frac{-42}{7}$

5. Write $\frac{21}{5}$ as a decimal.

Assess student learning of standards throughout the year with cumulative **Course Benchmark Tests** to measure progress. Use the results to help plan instruction and intervention.

Measure learning across grades with adaptive **Progression Benchmark Tests**.

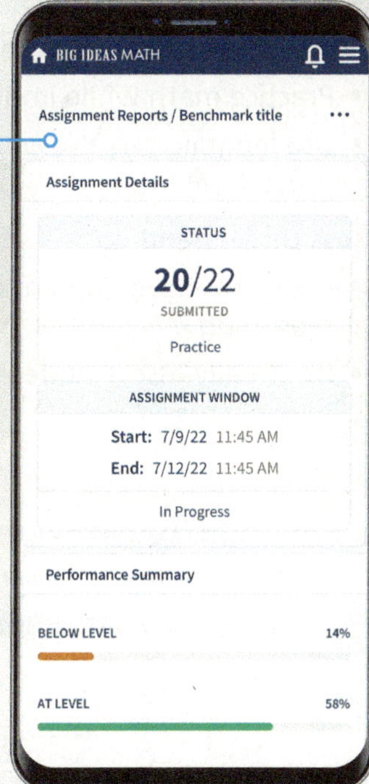

Use the **Assignment Builder** to assign digital versions of the print **Quizzes**, **Chapter Tests**, and **Course Benchmark Tests**. Receive immediate feedback through robust reporting.

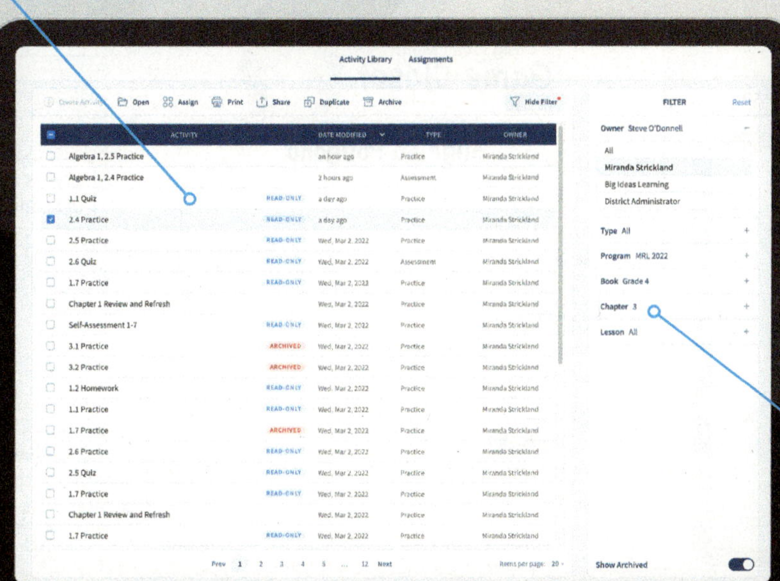

Assessment item point values are weighted. You can customize an item's total point value to fit your needs.

Strategic Support for All Learners

Support for English Language Learners

Big Ideas Learning supports English Language Learners (ELLs) with a blend of print and digital resources available in Spanish. Look to your Teaching Edition for opportunities to support all students with the language development needed for mathematical understanding.

Students' WIDA scores are a starting point. As the year progresses, students may move in and out of language levels with varying language demands of the content and as students change and grow.

Clarify, Connect, and Scaffold

- Clarify language that may be difficult or confusing for ELLs
- Connect new learning to something students already know
- Differentiate student comprehension while completing practice exercises
- Target Beginner, Intermediate, and Advanced ELLs, which correspond to **WIDA** reading, writing, speaking, and listening language mastery levels

Practice Language and Content

- Practice math while improving language skills
- Use language as a resource to develop procedural fluency

Assess Understanding

- Check for development of mathematical reasoning
- Informally assess student comprehension of concepts

ELL Support

After demonstrating Example 1, have students practice language by working in pairs to complete Try It Exercises 1–3. Have one student ask another, "What is the first step? Do you add or subtract? What is the solution?" Have students alternate roles.

WIDA 1: Entering
WIDA 2: Emerging → **Beginner:** Write the steps and provide one-word answers.

WIDA 3: Developing
WIDA 4: Expanding → **Intermediate:** Answer with phrases or simple sentences such as, "First, I add five."

WIDA 5: Bridging
WIDA 6: Reaching → **Advanced:** Answer with detailed sentences such as, "First, I add five to each side of the equation."

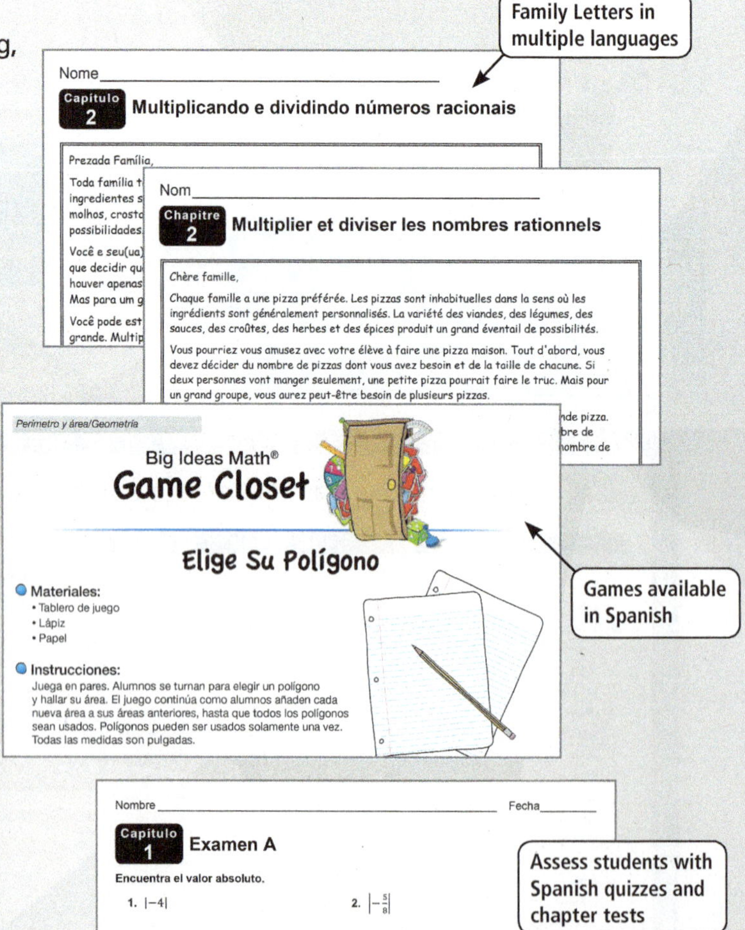

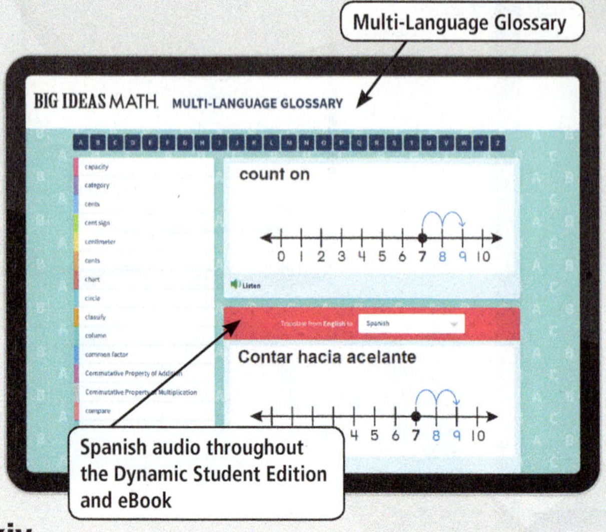

Students Get the Support They Need, When They Need It

There will be times throughout this course when students may need help. Whether students missed a section, did not understand the content, or just want to review, take advantage of the resources provided in the *Dynamic Student Edition*.

Students use the **Self-Assessment** tool to keep track of their understanding of the section's Learning Target and Success Criteria.

Students can take notes throughout the lesson using the **My Notes** function. These notes will be organized for them by chapter and section.

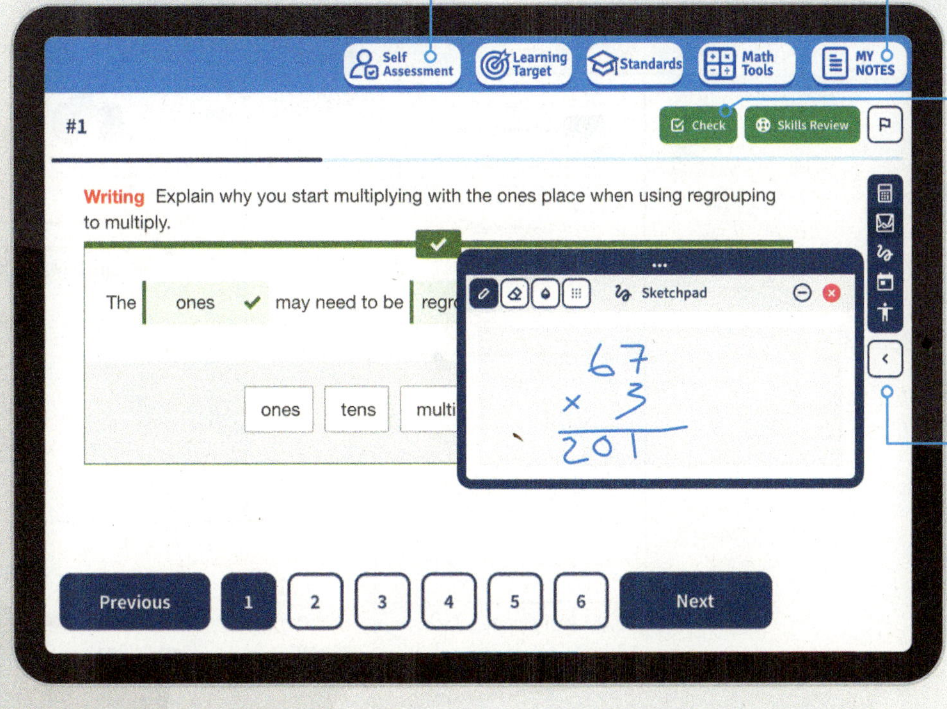

Self Assessment | Learning Target | Standards | Math Tools | MY NOTES

#1 | Check | Skills Review

Writing Explain why you start multiplying with the ones place when using regrouping to multiply.

The ones may need to be regr

ones | tens | multi

Sketchpad

67
× 3
201

Previous | 1 | 2 | 3 | 4 | 5 | 6 | Next

Students **Check** their answers to selected exercises as they work through the lesson. They can use the **Help** option to view the Digital Example and Tutorial Extra Example videos.

Support your students as they utilize the available **tools** to help clearly show their work and emphasize their math knowledge. Tools are easy to use and were created with accessibility and functionality in mind.

USE THESE QR CODES TO EXPLORE ADDITIONAL RESOURCES

Multi-Language Glossary
View definitions and examples of vocabulary words

Skills Trainer
Practice previously learned skills

Interactive Tools
Visualize mathematical concepts

Skills Review Handbook
A collection of review topics

Meeting the Needs of All Learners

Resources at Your Fingertips

This robust, innovative program utilizes a mixture of print and digital resources that allow for a variety of instructional approaches. The program encompasses hands-on activities, interactive explorations, videos, scaffolded instruction, learning support, and many more resources that appeal to students and teachers alike.

PRINT RESOURCES

Student Edition

Teaching Edition

Student Journal

Resources by Chapter

- Family Letter
- Warm-Ups
- Extra Practice
- Reteach
- Enrichment and Extension
- Chapter Self-Assessment
- Puzzle Time

Assessment Book

- Prerequisite Skills Practice
- Pre- and Post-Course Tests
- Course Benchmark Tests
- Quizzes
- Chapter Tests
- Alternative Assessments
- STEAM Performance Tasks

Rich Math Tasks

Skills Review Handbook

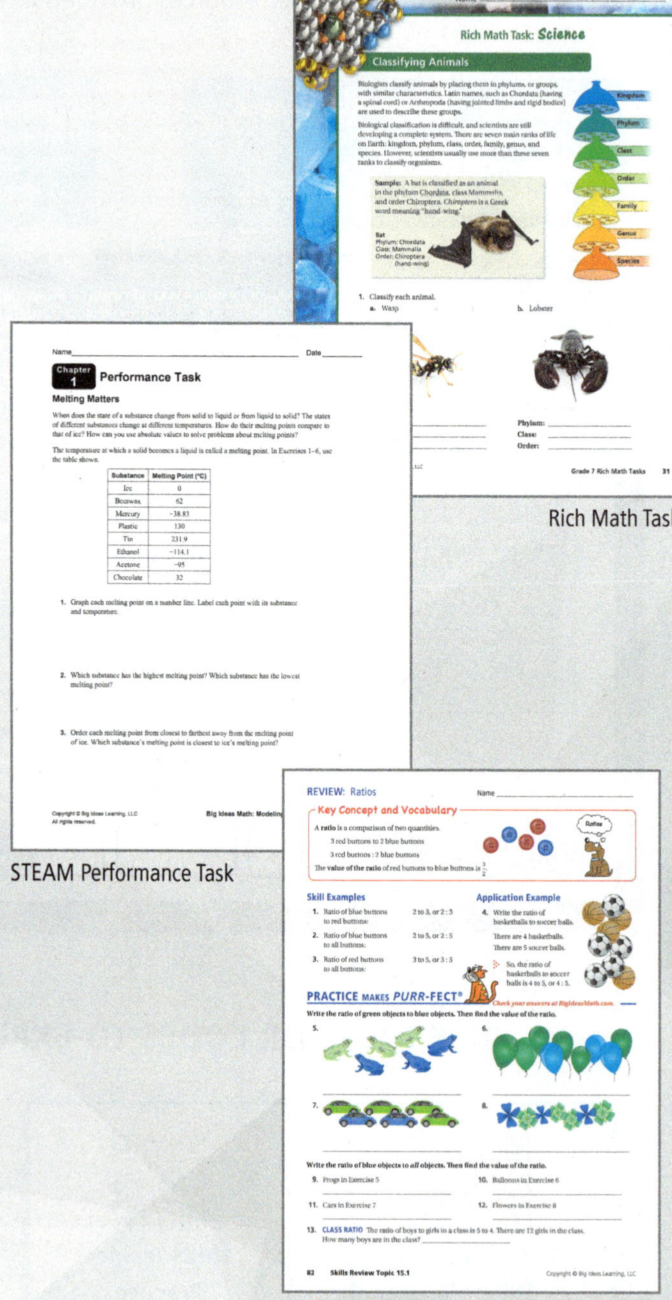

Name

Rich Math Task: Science

Classifying Animals

Biologists classify animals by placing them in phylums, or groups, with similar characteristics. Latin names, such as Chordata (having a spinal cord) or Arthropoda (having jointed limbs and rigid bodies) are used to describe these groups.

Biological classification is difficult, and scientists are still developing a complete system. There are seven main ranks of life on Earth: kingdom, phylum, class, order, family, genus, and species. However, scientists usually use more than these seven ranks to classify organisms.

Sample: A bat is classified as an animal in the phylum Chordata, class Mammalia, and order Chiroptera. *Chiroptera* is a Greek word meaning "hand-wing."

1. Classify each animal.
   a. Wasp
   b. Lobster

Phylum:
Class:
Order:

Grade 7 Rich Math Tasks 31

Rich Math Task

Name Date

Chapter 1 Performance Task

Melting Matters

When does the state of a substance change from solid to liquid or from liquid to solid? The states of different substances change at different temperatures. How do their melting points compare to that of ice? How can you use absolute values to solve problems about melting points?

The temperature at which a solid becomes a liquid is called a melting point. In Exercises 1–6, use the table shown.

Substance	Melting Point (°C)
Ice	0
Beeswax	62
Mercury	−38.83
Plastic	130
Tin	231.9
Ethanol	−114.1
Acetone	−95
Chocolate	32

1. Graph each melting point on a number line. Label each point with its substance and temperature.

2. Which substance has the highest melting point? Which substance has the lowest melting point?

3. Order each melting point from closest to farthest away from the melting point of ice. Which substance's melting point is closest to ice's melting point?

Copyright © Big Ideas Learning, LLC All rights reserved. Big Ideas Math: Modeling

STEAM Performance Task

REVIEW: Ratios Name

Key Concept and Vocabulary

A **ratio** is a comparison of two quantities.

3 red buttons to 2 blue buttons

3 red buttons : 2 blue buttons

The **value of the ratio** of red buttons to blue buttons is $\frac{3}{2}$.

Skill Examples

1. Ratio of blue buttons to red buttons: 2 to 3, or 2 : 3
2. Ratio of blue buttons to all buttons: 2 to 5, or 2 : 5
3. Ratio of red buttons to all buttons: 3 to 5, or 3 : 5

Application Example

4. Write the ratio of basketballs to soccer balls.

There are 4 basketballs.
There are 5 soccer balls.

So, the ratio of basketballs to soccer balls is 4 to 5, or 4 : 5.

PRACTICE MAKES PURR-FECT® Check your answers at BigIdeasMath.com.

Write the ratio of green objects to blue objects. Then find the value of the ratio.

5.
6.
7.
8.

Write the ratio of blue objects to *all* objects. Then find the value of the ratio.

9. Frogs in Exercise 5
10. Balloons in Exercise 6
11. Cars in Exercise 7
12. Flowers in Exercise 8
13. CLASS RATIO The ratio of boys to girls in a class is 5 to 4. There are 12 girls in the class. How many boys are in the class?

82 Skills Review Topic 15.1 Copyright © Big Ideas Learning, LLC

Skills Review Handbook

Through Program Resources

TECHNOLOGY RESOURCES

Dynamic Student Edition

- Interactive Tools
- Interactive Explorations
- Digital Examples
- Tutorial Extra Example Videos
- Self-Assessments

Dynamic Classroom

- Laurie's Notes
- Interactive Tools
- Interactive Explorations
- Digital Examples with PowerPoints
- Formative Check
- Flip-To
- Digital Warm-Ups and Closures
- Mini-Assessments

Resources

- Answer Presentation Tool
- Chapter at a Glance
- Complete Materials List
- Cross-Curricular Projects
- Skills Trainer
- Vocabulary Flash Cards
- STEAM Videos
- Game Library
- Multi-Language Glossary
- Lesson Plans
- Differentiating the Lesson
- Graphic Organizers
- Pacing Guides
- Worked-Out Solutions Key
- Math Tool Paper
- Family Letters
- Homework App
- Skills Review Handbook

Dynamic Assessment System

- Practice
- Assessments
- Progression Benchmark Tests
- Detailed Reports

Video Support for Teachers

- Life on Earth Videos
- Professional Development Videos
- Concepts and Tools Videos

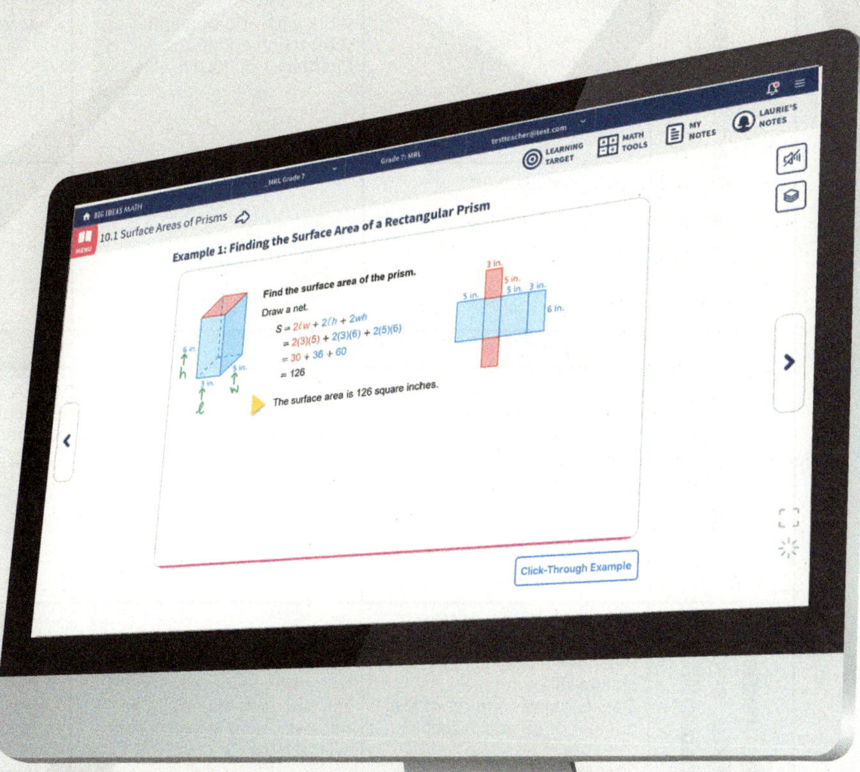

Cohesive Progressions

	Grade K	Grade 1	Grade 2	Grade 3
Number and Quantity	**Counting and Cardinality**			
	Know number names and the count sequence. Count to tell the number of objects. Compare numbers. *Chapters 1–4, 6, 8–10*			
	Number and Operations – Base Ten			
	Work with numbers 11–19 to gain foundations for place value. *Chapter 8*	Extend the counting sequence. Use place value and properties of operations to add and subtract. *Chapters 6–9*	Use place value and properties of operations to add and subtract. *Chapters 2–10, 14*	Use place value and properties of operations to perform multi-digit arithmetic. *Chapters 7–9, 12*
				Num. and Oper. – Fractions
				Understand fractions as numbers. *Chapters 10, 11, 14*
Algebra and Functions	**Operations and Algebraic Thinking**			
	Understand addition as putting together and adding to, and understand subtraction as taking apart and taking from. *Chapters 5–7*	Solve problems involving addition and subtraction within 20. Apply properties of operations. Work with addition and subtraction equations. *Chapters 1–5, 10, 11*	Solve problems involving addition and subtraction within 20. Work with equal groups of objects. *Chapters 1–6, 15*	Solve problems involving multiplication and division within 100. Apply properties of multiplication. Solve problems involving the four operations, and identify and explain patterns in arithmetic. *Chapters 1–5, 8, 9, and 14*
Geometry	**Geometry**			
	Identify and describe shapes. Analyze, compare, create, and compose shapes. *Chapters 11, 12*	Reason with shapes and their attributes. *Chapters 12, 14*	Reason with shapes and their attributes. *Chapter 15*	Reason with shapes and their attributes. *Chapters 10, 13*
Measurement, Data, and Probability	**Measurement and Data**			
	Describe and compare measurable attributes. Classify objects and count the number of objects in each category. *Chapters 4, 11, 13*	Measure lengths indirectly and by iterating length units. Tell and write time. Represent and interpret data. *Chapters 10–12*	Measure and estimate lengths in standard units. Relate addition and subtraction to length. Work with time and money. Represent and interpret data. *Chapters 11–14*	Solve problems involving measurement and estimation of intervals of time, liquid volumes, and masses of objects. Represent and interpret data. Understand the concepts of area and perimeter. *Chapters 6, 12, 14, 15*

Through the Grades

Grade 4	Grade 5	Grade 6	Grade 7	Grade 8
Number and Operations – Base Ten		**The Number System**		
Generalize place value understanding for multi-digit whole numbers. Use place value and properties of operations to perform multi-digit arithmetic. *Chapters 1–5*	Understand the place value system. Perform operations with multi-digit whole numbers and with decimals to hundredths. *Chapters 1, 3–7*	Perform operations with multi-digit numbers and find common factors and multiples. *Chapter 1* Divide fractions by fractions. *Chapter 2* Extend understanding of numbers to the rational number system. *Chapter 8*	Perform operations with rational numbers. *Chapters 1, 2*	Extend understanding of numbers to the real number system. *Chapter 9*
Number and Operations – Fractions		**Ratios and Proportional Relationships**		
Extend understanding of fraction equivalence and ordering. Build fractions from unit fractions. Understand decimal notation for fractions, and compare decimal fractions. *Chapters 7–11*	Add, subtract, multiply, and divide fractions. *Chapters 6, 8–11*	Use ratios to solve problems. *Chapters 3, 4*	Use proportional relationships to solve problems. *Chapters 5, 6*	
Operations and Algebraic Thinking		**Expressions and Equations**		
Use the four operations with whole numbers to solve problems. Understand factors and multiples. Generate and analyze patterns. *Chapters 2–6, 12*	Write and interpret numerical expressions. Analyze patterns and relationships. *Chapters 2, 12*	Perform arithmetic with algebraic expressions. *Chapter 5* Solve one-variable equations and inequalities. *Chapters 6, 8* Analyze relationships between dependent and independent variables. *Chapter 6*	Write equivalent expressions. *Chapter 3* Use numerical and algebraic expressions, equations, and inequalities to solve problems. *Chapters 3, 4, 6*	Understand the connections between proportional relationships, lines, and linear equations. *Chapter 4* Solve linear equations and systems of linear equations. *Chapters 1, 5* Work with radicals and integer exponents. *Chapters 8, 9*
				Functions
				Define, evaluate, and compare functions, and use functions to model relationships between quantities. *Chapter 7*
Geometry				
Draw and identify lines and angles, and classify shapes by properties of their lines and angles. *Chapters 13, 14*	Graph points on the coordinate plane. Classify two-dimensional figures into categories based on their properties. *Chapters 12, 14*	Solve real-world and mathematical problems involving area, surface area, and volume. *Chapter 7*	Draw, construct, and describe geometrical figures and describe the relationships between them. *Chapters 5, 9, 10* Solve problems involving angle measure, area, surface area, and volume. *Chapters 9, 10*	Understand congruence and similarity. *Chapters 2, 3* Use the Pythagorean Theorem. *Chapter 9* Solve problems involving volumes of cylinders, cones, and spheres. *Chapter 10*
Measurement and Data		**Statistics and Probability**		
Solve problems involving measurement and conversion of measurements from a larger unit to a smaller unit. Represent and interpret data. Understand angles and measure angles. *Chapters 10–13*	Convert measurement units within a given measurement system. Represent and interpret data. Understand volume. *Chapters 11, 13*	Develop understanding of statistical variability and summarize and describe distributions. *Chapters 9, 10*	Make inferences about a population, compare two populations, and use probability models. *Chapters 7, 8*	Investigate patterns of association in bivariate data. *Chapter 6*

Common Core State Standards for

Standard Code	Standard	Grade 6
Ratios and Proportional Relationships		
6.RP.A.1	Understand the concept of a ratio and use ratio language to describe a ratio relationship between two quantities.	**3.1, 3.2, 3.3, 3.4,** 3.5, 3.6, 4.4
6.RP.A.2	Understand the concept of a unit rate *a*/*b* associated with a ratio *a* : *b* with $b \neq 0$, and use rate language in the context of a ratio relationship.	**3.5,** 3.6
6.RP.A.3	Use ratio and rate reasoning to solve real-world and mathematical problems, e.g., by reasoning about tables of equivalent ratios, tape diagrams, double number line diagrams, or equations.	**3.1, 3.2, 3.3, 3.4, 3.5, 3.6, 4.4,** 6.4
	a. Make tables of equivalent ratios relating quantities with whole-number measurements, find missing values in the tables, and plot the pairs of values on the coordinate plane. Use tables to compare ratios.	**3.3, 3.4, 3.5,** 3.6, 4.4, 6.4
	b. Solve unit rate problems including those involving unit pricing and constant speed.	**3.5,** 3.6
	c. Find a percent of a quantity as a rate per 100 (e.g., 30% of a quantity means 30/100 times the quantity); solve problems involving finding the whole, given a part and the percent.	**4.4**
	d. Use ratio reasoning to convert measurement units; manipulate and transform units appropriately when multiplying or dividing quantities.	**3.6,** 7.1, 7.7
The Number System		
6.NS.A.1	Interpret and compute quotients of fractions, and solve word problems involving division of fractions by fractions, e.g., by using visual fraction models and equations to represent the problem.	**2.2, 2.3**
6.NS.B.2	Fluently divide multi-digit numbers using the standard algorithm.	**2.6,** 2.7, 7.1, 7.3, 7.7
6.NS.B.3	Fluently add, subtract, multiply, and divide multi-digit decimals using the standard algorithm for each operation.	**2.4, 2.5, 2.7,** 5.3, 6.2, 7.6, 8.8, 9.2, 9.3
6.NS.B.4	Find the greatest common factor of two whole numbers less than or equal to 100 and the least common multiple of two whole numbers less than or equal to 12. Use the distributive property to express a sum of two whole numbers 1–100 with a common factor as a multiple of a sum of two whole numbers with no common factor.	**1.4, 1.5, 5.5**
6.NS.C.5	Understand that positive and negative numbers are used together to describe quantities having opposite directions or values (e.g., temperature above/below zero, elevation above/below sea level, credits/debits, positive/negative electric charge); use positive and negative numbers to represent quantities in real-world contexts, explaining the meaning of 0 in each situation.	**8.1,** 8.2, **8.3,** 8.4, 8.5, 8.7, 8.8

Boldface indicates a lesson in which the standard is a primary focus.

Mathematical Content Correlated to Grade 6

Standard Code	Standard	Grade 6
6.NS.C.6	Understand a rational number as a point on the number line. Extend number line diagrams and coordinate axes familiar from previous grades to represent points on the line and in the plane with negative number coordinates.	
	a. Recognize opposite signs of numbers as indicating locations on opposite sides of 0 on the number line; recognize that the opposite of the opposite of a number is the number itself, e.g., $-(-3) = 3$, and that 0 is its own opposite.	**8.1, 8.3**
	b. Understand signs of numbers in ordered pairs as indicating locations in quadrants of the coordinate plane; recognize that when two ordered pairs differ only by signs, the locations of the points are related by reflections across one or both axes.	**8.5,** 8.6
	c. Find and position integers and other rational numbers on a horizontal or vertical number line diagram; find and position pairs of integers and other rational numbers on a coordinate plane.	**8.1, 8.2, 8.3,** 8.4, **8.5,** 8.6, 8.7, 8.8
6.NS.C.7	Understand ordering and absolute value of rational numbers.	
	a. Interpret statements of inequality as statements about the relative position of two numbers on a number line diagram.	**4.3, 8.2, 8.3,** 8.4, 8.7, 8.8
	b. Write, interpret, and explain statements of order for rational numbers in real-world contexts.	**4.3, 8.2, 8.3,** 8.4
	c. Understand the absolute value of a rational number as its distance from 0 on the number line; interpret absolute value as magnitude for a positive or negative quantity in a real-world situation.	**8.4**
	d. Distinguish comparisons of absolute value from statements about order.	**8.4**
6.NS.C.8	Solve real-world and mathematical problems by graphing points in all four quadrants of the coordinate plane. Include use of coordinates and absolute value to find distances between points with the same first coordinate or the same second coordinate.	3.4, 6.4, **8.5, 8.6**
Expressions and Equations		
6.EE.A.1	Write and evaluate numerical expressions involving whole-number exponents.	**1.1, 1.2,** 5.1
6.EE.A.2	Write, read, and evaluate expressions in which letters stand for numbers.	
	a. Write expressions that record operations with numbers and with letters standing for numbers.	**5.2,** 5.3, 5.4, 6.1, 6.2, 6.3, 6.4, 8.7, 8.8
	b. Identify parts of an expression using mathematical terms (sum, term, product, factor, quotient, coefficient); view one or more parts of an expression as a single entity.	1.3, 1.4, 1.5, **5.1,** 5.2, 5.3, **5.4, 5.5,** 6.1

Boldface indicates a lesson in which the standard is a primary focus.

Common Core State Standards for

Standard Code	Standard	Grade 6
	c. Evaluate expressions at specific values of their variables. Include expressions that arise from formulas used in real-world problems. Perform arithmetic operations, including those involving whole-number exponents, in the conventional order when there are no parentheses to specify a particular order (Order of Operations).	**5.1,** 5.2, 5.3, 5.4, 6.1, 6.2, 6.3, 6.4, **7.1, 7.2, 7.3,** 7.5, 7.7, 8.7, 8.8
6.EE.A.3	Apply the properties of operations to generate equivalent expressions.	**5.3, 5.4, 5.5**
6.EE.A.4	Identify when two expressions are equivalent (i.e., when the two expressions name the same number regardless of which value is substituted into them).	**5.3, 5.4, 5.5**
6.EE.B.5	Understand solving an equation or inequality as a process of answering a question: which values from a specified set, if any, make the equation or inequality true? Use substitution to determine whether a given number in a specified set makes an equation or inequality true.	**6.1, 6.2, 6.3,** 6.4, 7.1, 7.2, 7.3, 7.7, **8.7, 8.8**
6.EE.B.6	Use variables to represent numbers and write expressions when solving a real-world or mathematical problem; understand that a variable can represent an unknown number, or, depending on the purpose at hand, any number in a specified set.	**6.1, 6.2, 6.3, 6.4,** 7.1, 7.2, 7.3, 7.5, 7.7, **8.7, 8.8**
6.EE.B.7	Solve real-world and mathematical problems by writing and solving equations of the form $x + p = q$ and $px = q$ for cases in which p, q and x are all non-negative rational numbers.	**6.1, 6.2, 6.3,** 6.4, 7.1, 7.2, 7.7
6.EE.B.8	Write an inequality of the form $x > c$ or $x < c$ to represent a constraint or condition in a real-world or mathematical problem. Recognize that inequalities of the form $x > c$ or $x < c$ have infinitely many solutions; represent solutions of such inequalities on number line diagrams.	**8.7, 8.8**
6.EE.C.9	Use variables to represent two quantities in a real-world problem that change in relationship to one another; write an equation to express one quantity, thought of as the dependent variable, in terms of the other quantity, thought of as the independent variable. Analyze the relationship between the dependent and independent variables using graphs and tables, and relate these to the equation.	**6.4**
Geometry		
6.G.A.1	Find the area of right triangles, other triangles, special quadrilaterals, and polygons by composing into rectangles or decomposing into triangles and other shapes; apply these techniques in the context of solving real-world and mathematical problems.	**7.1, 7.2, 7.3,** 7.5, 7.6, 8.6
6.G.A.2	Find the volume of a right rectangular prism with fractional edge lengths by packing it with unit cubes of the appropriate unit fraction edge lengths, and show that the volume is the same as would be found by multiplying the edge lengths of the prism. Apply the formulas $V = lwh$ and $V = Bh$ to find volumes of right rectangular prisms with fractional edge lengths in the context of solving real-world and mathematical problems.	**7.7**

Boldface indicates a lesson in which the standard is a primary focus.

Mathematical Content Correlated to Grade 6

Standard Code	Standard	Grade 6
6.G.A.3	Draw polygons in the coordinate plane given coordinates for the vertices; use coordinates to find the length of a side joining points with the same first coordinate or the same second coordinate. Apply these techniques in the context of solving real-world and mathematical problems.	**8.6**
6.G.A.4	Represent three-dimensional figures using nets made up of rectangles and triangles, and use the nets to find the surface area of these figures. Apply these techniques in the context of solving real-world and mathematical problems.	**7.5, 7.6**
Statistics and Probability		
6.SP.A.1	Recognize a statistical question as one that anticipates variability in the data related to the question and accounts for it in the answers.	**9.1**, 9.2, 9.3, 10.1, 10.4
6.SP.A.2	Understand that a set of data collected to answer a statistical question has a distribution which can be described by its center, spread, and overall shape.	**9.1, 9.2, 9.3, 9.4, 9.5, 10.1, 10.3, 10.4, 10.5**
6.SP.A.3	Recognize that a measure of center for a numerical data set summarizes all of its values with a single number, while a measure of variation describes how its values vary with a single number.	**9.2, 9.3, 9.4, 9.5**,.10.1, 10.4, 10.5
6.SP.B.4	Display numerical data in plots on a number line, including dot plots, histograms, and box plots.	**9.1**, 9.2, 9.3, 9.4, 9.5, 10.1, **10.2**, **10.3**, 10.4, **10.5**
6.SP.B.5	Summarize numerical data sets in relation to their context, such as by:	
	a. Reporting the number of observations.	**9.1**, **9.2**, 9.3, 9.4, 9.5, 10.1, 10.2, 10.4
	b. Describing the nature of the attribute under investigation, including how it was measured and its units of measurement.	**9.1**
	c. Giving quantitative measures of center (median and/or mean) and variability (interquartile range and/or mean absolute deviation), as well as describing any overall pattern and any striking deviations from the overall pattern with reference to the context in which the data were gathered.	**9.2, 9.3, 9.4, 9.5**, 10.1, 10.4, **10.5**
	d. Relating the choice of measures of center and variability to the shape of the data distribution and the context in which the data were gathered.	**10.4**

Boldface indicates a lesson in which the standard is a primary focus.

Suggested Pacing

Chapters 1–10	155 Days

Chapter 1 (13 Days)

Chapter Opener	1 Day
Section 1.1	2 Days
Section 1.2	2 Days
Section 1.3	1 Day
Section 1.4	2 Days
Section 1.5	2 Days
Connecting Concepts	1 Day
Chapter Review	1 Day
Chapter Test	1 Day
Year-To-Date	**13 Days**

Chapter 2 (15 Days)

Chapter Opener	1 Day
Section 2.1	1 Day
Section 2.2	3 Days
Section 2.3	2 Days
Section 2.4	1 Day
Section 2.5	1 Day
Section 2.6	1 Day
Section 2.7	2 Days
Connecting Concepts	1 Day
Chapter Review	1 Day
Chapter Test	1 Day
Year-To-Date	**28 Days**

Chapter 3 (22 Days)

Chapter Opener	1 Day
Section 3.1	3 Days
Section 3.2	3 Days
Section 3.3	3 Days
Section 3.4	3 Days
Section 3.5	3 Days
Section 3.6	3 Days
Connecting Concepts	1 Day
Chapter Review	1 Day
Chapter Test	1 Day
Year-To-Date	**50 Days**

Chapter 4 (13 Days)

Chapter Opener	1 Day
Section 4.1	2 Days
Section 4.2	2 Days
Section 4.3	2 Days
Section 4.4	3 Days
Connecting Concepts	1 Day
Chapter Review	1 Day
Chapter Test	1 Day
Year-To-Date	**63 Days**

Chapter 5 (15 Days)

Chapter Opener	1 Day
Section 5.1	2 Days
Section 5.2	2 Days
Section 5.3	2 Days
Section 5.4	2 Days
Section 5.5	3 Days
Connecting Concepts	1 Day
Chapter Review	1 Day
Chapter Test	1 Day
Year-To-Date	**78 Days**

Chapter 6 (14 Days)

Chapter Opener	1 Day
Section 6.1	3 Days
Section 6.2	2 Days
Section 6.3	2 Days
Section 6.4	3 Days
Connecting Concepts	1 Day
Chapter Review	1 Day
Chapter Test	1 Day
Year-To-Date	**92 Days**

Chapter 7 (16 Days)

Chapter Opener	1 Day
Section 7.1	1 Day
Section 7.2	1 Day
Section 7.3	2 Days
Section 7.4	2 Days
Section 7.5	2 Days
Section 7.6	2 Days
Section 7.7	2 Days
Connecting Concepts	1 Day
Chapter Review	1 Day
Chapter Test	1 Day
Year-To-Date	**108 Days**

Chapter 8 (22 Days)

Chapter Opener	1 Day
Section 8.1	2 Days
Section 8.2	2 Days
Section 8.3	2 Days
Section 8.4	2 Days
Section 8.5	2 Days
Section 8.6	2 Days
Section 8.7	3 Days
Section 8.8	3 Days
Connecting Concepts	1 Day
Chapter Review	1 Day
Chapter Test	1 Day
Year-To-Date	**130 Days**

Chapter 9 (12 Days)

Chapter Opener	1 Day
Section 9.1	2 Days
Section 9.2	1 Day
Section 9.3	1 Day
Section 9.4	2 Days
Section 9.5	2 Days
Connecting Concepts	1 Day
Chapter Review	1 Day
Chapter Test	1 Day
Year-To-Date	**142 Days**

Chapter 10 (13 Days)

Chapter Opener	1 Day
Section 10.1	1 Day
Section 10.2	2 Days
Section 10.3	2 Days
Section 10.4	2 Days
Section 10.5	2 Days
Connecting Concepts	1 Day
Chapter Review	1 Day
Chapter Test	1 Day
Year-To-Date	**155 Days**

An editable version of the Pacing Guide is available in two forms (regular and block scheduling) at *BigIdeasMath.com*.

Numerical Expressions and Factors

■ Major Topic
■ Supporting Topic
■ Additional Topic

Fractions and Decimals

Ratios and Rates

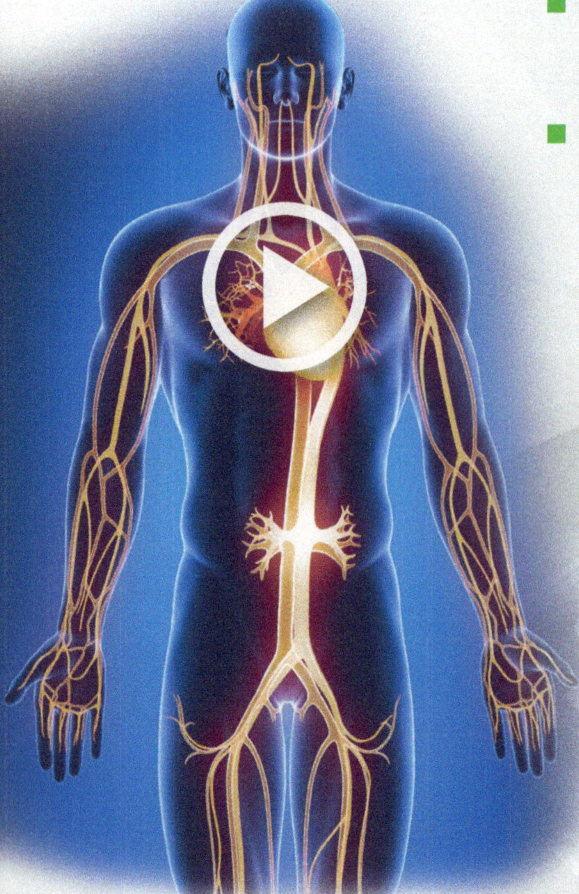

■ Major Topic
■ Supporting Topic
■ Additional Topic

Percents

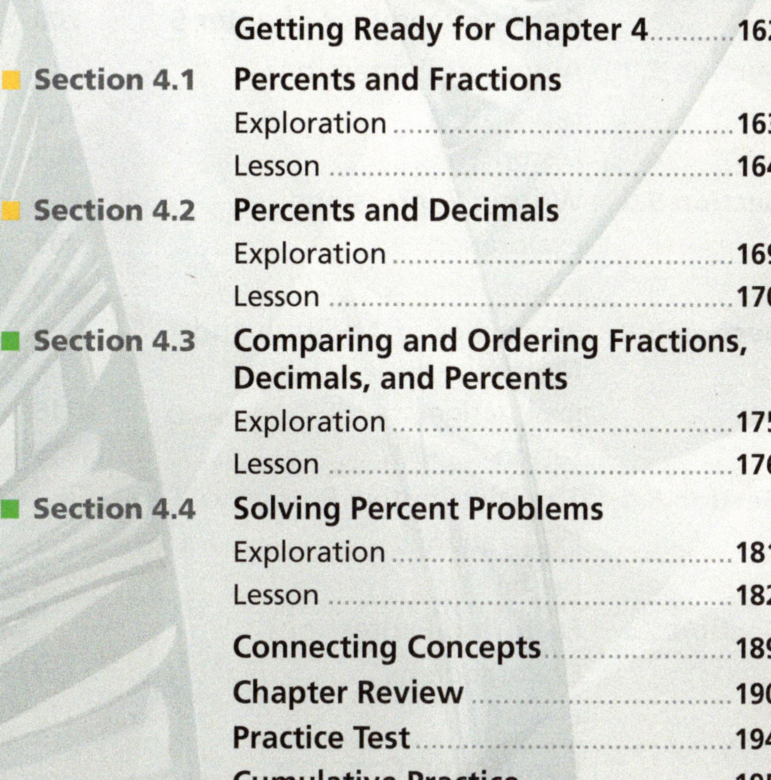

Algebraic Expressions and Properties

■ Major Topic
■ Supporting Topic
■ Additional Topic

Equations

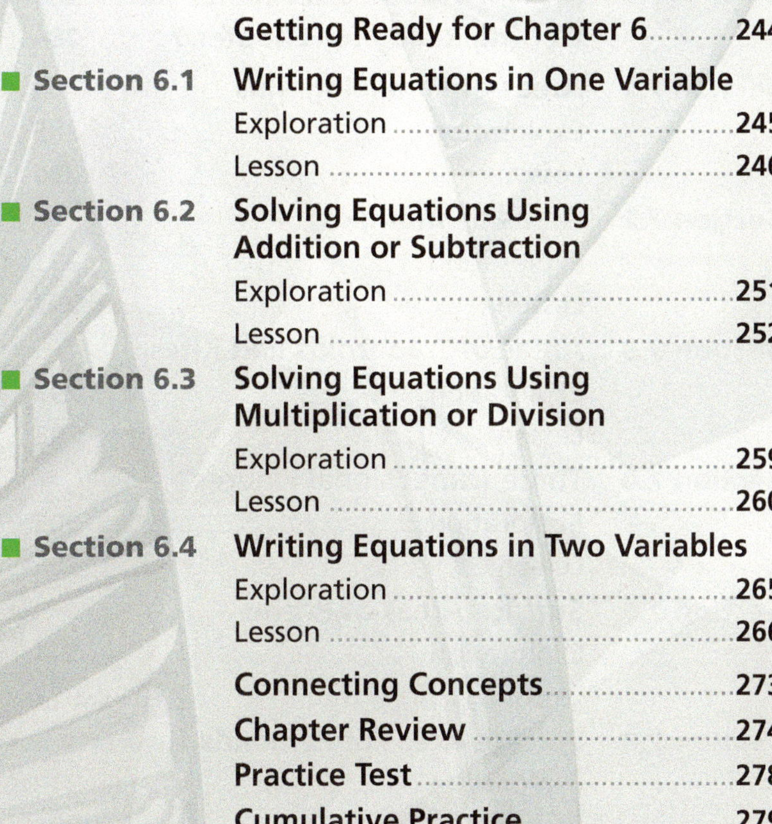

Area, Surface Area, and Volume

■ Major Topic
■ Supporting Topic
■ Additional Topic

Integers, Number Lines, and the Coordinate Plane

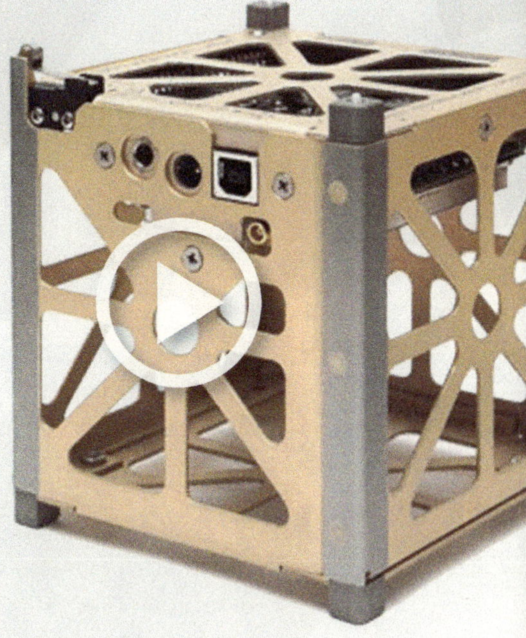

Statistical Measures

Major Topic
Supporting Topic
Additional Topic

Data Displays

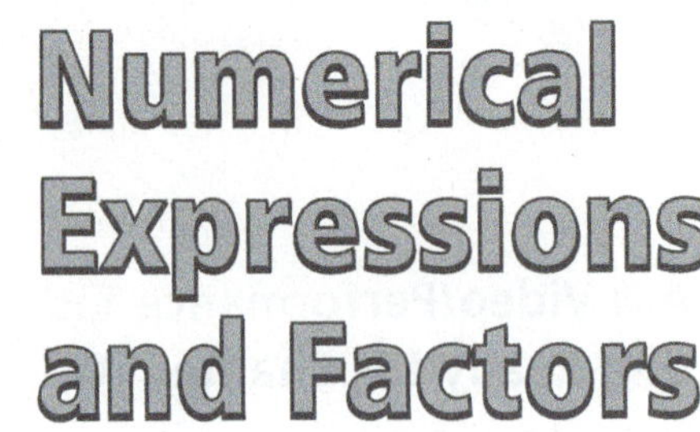

1 Numerical Expressions and Factors

Chapter Learning Target:
Understand factors.

Chapter Success Criteria:
- I can identify factors of a number.
- I can explain order of operations.
- I can solve a problem using factors.
- I can model different types of multiples of numbers.

STEAM Video: "Filling Piñatas"

Laurie's Notes

Chapter 1 Overview

The transition from fifth to sixth grade is a time when many students are feeling a range of emotions, particularly if they are entering a new school, or experiencing having multiple core teachers for the first time. Sharing what the classroom climate and culture will be, along with an overview of the first chapter, will help students form a positive mindset as they begin the year.

From the first day, you want to establish a norm in your classroom that each student will discuss mathematical problems with a partner or group. Explorations at the beginning of each lesson, and Formative Assessment Tips such as *Turn and Talk,* are explicit opportunities for student engagement. I hope you find the suggestions in Laurie's Notes to be helpful in promoting student dialogue and engagement.

In this chapter, students will extend their knowledge from prior courses. It is important for students to become secure in this content, so the foundation is set for completing computational work with fractions and decimals in the next chapter.

Chapter 1 includes the order of operations, which is an essential understanding for work in mathematics. The inclusion of exponents as they evaluate expressions is new to students. Take time to discuss the need for an agreed upon order in which operations are performed, just as North Americans agree to drive on the right side of the road. Some of the problems in the lessons integrate prior work with fractions and decimals. If students are not confident in these operations, you may need to review these prior skills.

Number theory concepts are presented in the second part of the chapter; a continuation of work that began in previous courses. Students should be familiar with prime and composite numbers, and know the difference between factors and multiples. It is common, however, for students to mix up these concepts. A factor tree is introduced as a tool for finding the prime factorization of a number. Prime factorizations will be used to find the greatest common factor (GCF) and the least common multple (LCM) of two numbers. Contextual applications of the GCF and the LCM will also be explored in this chapter.

Suggested Pacing

Chapter Opener	1 Day
Section 1	2 Days
Section 2	2 Days
Section 3	1 Day
Section 4	2 Days
Section 5	2 Days
Connecting Concepts	1 Day
Chapter Review	1 Day
Chapter Test	1 Day
Total Chapter 1	13 Days
Year-to-Date	13 Days

Chapter Learning Target

Understand factors.

Chapter Success Criteria

- Identify factors of a number.
- Explain order of operations.
- Solve a problem using factors.
- Model different types of multiples of numbers.

Chapter 1 Learning Targets and Success Criteria

Section	Learning Target	Success Criteria
1.1 Powers and Exponents	Write and evaluate expressions involving exponents.	• Write products of repeated factors as powers. • Evaluate powers.
1.2 Order of Operations	Write and evaluate numerical expressions using the order of operations.	• Explain why there is a need for a standard order of operations. • Evaluate numerical expressions involving several operations, exponents, and grouping symbols. • Write numerical expressions involving exponents to represent a real-life problem.
1.3 Prime Factorization	Write a number as a product of prime factors and represent the product using exponents.	• Find factor pairs of a number. • Explain the meanings of prime and composite numbers. • Create a factor tree to find the prime factors of a number. • Write the prime factorization of a number.
1.4 Greatest Common Factor	Find the greatest common factor of two numbers.	• Explain the meaning of factors of a number. • Use lists of factors to identify the greatest common factor of numbers. • Use prime factors to identify the greatest common factor of numbers.
1.5 Least Common Multiple	Find the least common multiple of two numbers.	• Explain the meaning of multiples of a number. • Use lists of multiples to identify the least common multiple of numbers. • Use prime factors to identify the least common multiple of numbers.

Progressions

Through the Grades		
Grade 5	**Grade 6**	**Grade 7**
• Use parentheses, brackets, or braces in numerical expressions. • Multiply and divide by powers of ten. Evaluate expressions with powers of ten and whole-number exponents.	• Find the GCF of two whole numbers. Find the LCM of two whole numbers. • Write and evaluate numerical expressions with whole-number exponents.	• Add, subtract, multiply, and divide rational numbers.

Through the Chapter					
Standard	**1.1**	**1.2**	**1.3**	**1.4**	**1.5**
6.NS.B.4 Find the greatest common factor of two whole numbers less than or equal to 100 and the least common multiple of two whole numbers less than or equal to 12. Use the distributive property to express a sum of two whole numbers 1–100 with a common factor as a multiple of a sum of two whole numbers with no common factor.			▲	●	●
6.EE.A.1 Write and evaluate numerical expressions involving whole-number exponents.	●	★			

Key

▲ = preparing ★ = complete

● = learning ■ = extending

STEAM Video

1. *Sample answer:* to see which factors are common factors
2. *Sample answer:* have 48 taffies, 12 kazoos, and 96 mints; no

Performance Task

Sample answer: no; If a party planner uses the greatest number of tables, there may not be many people at each table.

Mathematical Practices

Students have opportunities to develop aspects of the mathematical practices throughout the chapter. Here are some examples.

1. **Make Sense of Problems and Persevere in Solving Them**
   1.4 Math Practice note, *p. 21*
2. **Reason Abstractly and Quantitatively**
   1.2 Exercise 46, *p. 14*
3. **Construct Viable Arguments and Critique the Reasoning of Others**
   1.5 Exercise 32, *p. 31*
4. **Model with Mathematics**
   1.4 Exercise 37, *p. 25*
5. **Use Appropriate Tools Strategically**
   1.2 Math Practice note, *p. 9*
6. **Attend to Precision**
   1.1 Math Practice note, *p. 5*
7. **Look for and Make Use of Structure**
   1.3 Math Practice note, *p. 18*
8. **Look for and Express Regularity in Repeated Reasoning**
   1.3 Exercise 70, *p. 20*

Laurie's Notes

STEAM Video

Before the Video

- In this video, several types of party favors are divided into equal amounts to make the greatest number of piñatas for a fundraiser.
- To introduce the STEAM Video, read aloud the first paragraph of Filling Piñatas and discuss the questions.
- ? "Can you think of any situations in which you would want to separate objects into equal groups?"
- ? "Are there any common factors that may be more useful than others?"
- ? "Can you think of any other ways to use common factors?"

During the Video

- Pause the video at 1:54. The video shows a chart of the factors of 50.
- ? "What has happened in the video so far?" They have sorted the taffies into equal piles.
- ? "Why are they listing all the factors of 50?" To find how many ways the taffies can be divided equally to make identical piñatas.
- ? "What are they ultimately trying to find?" The greatest number of piñatas that they can make by dividing the different amounts of party favors into equal groups.
- Watch the remainder of the video.

After the Video

- Have students work with a partner to answer Questions 1 and 2.
- As students discuss the questions, listen for an understanding of factors and finding the greatest common factor.

Performance Task

- Use this information to spark students' interest and promote thinking about real-life problems.
- ? Ask, "When making arrangements for a party, should a party planner always use the greatest number of identical tables possible? Explain why or why not."
- After completing the chapter, students will have gained the knowledge needed to complete "Setting the Table."

STEAM Video

Filling Piñatas

Common factors can be used to make identical groups of objects. Can you think of any situations in which you would want to separate objects into equal groups? Are there any common factors that may be more useful than others? Can you think of any other ways to use common factors?

Watch the STEAM Video "Filling Piñatas." Then answer the following questions. The table below shows the numbers of party favors that Alex and Enid use to make piñatas.

Party Favor	Taffies	Key Chains	Kazoos	Bubbles	Mints
Number	50	12	16	24	100

1. When finding the number of identical piñatas that can be made, why is it helpful for Alex and Enid to list the factors of each number given in the table?

2. You want to create 6 identical piñatas. How can you change the numbers of party favors in the table to make this happen? Can you do this without changing the total number of party favors?

Performance Task

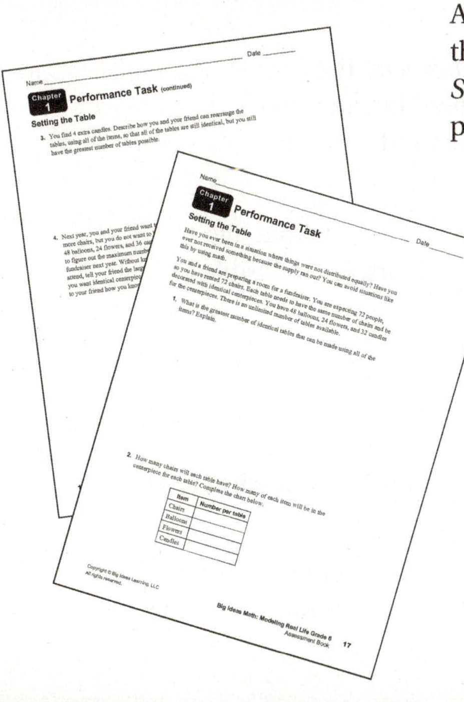

Name ______ Date ______

Chapter 1 **Performance Task**

Setting the Table

Have you ever been in a situation where things were not distributed equally? Have you ever not received something because the supply ran out? You can avoid situations like this by using math.

You and a friend are preparing a room for a fundraiser. You are expecting 72 people, so you have rented 72 chairs. Each table needs to have the same number of chairs and be decorated with identical centerpieces. You have 48 balloons, 24 flowers, and 32 candles for the centerpieces. There is an unlimited number of tables available.

1. What is the greatest number of identical tables that can be made using all of the items? Explain.

2. How many chairs will each table have? How many of each item will be in the centerpiece for each table? Complete the chart below.

Item	Number per table
Chairs	
Balloons	
Flowers	
Candles	

Big Ideas Math: Modeling Real Life Grade 6
Assessment Book 17

Name ______ Date ______

Chapter 1 **Performance Task** (continued)

Setting the Table

3. You find 4 extra candles. Describe how you and your friend can rearrange the tables, using all of the items, so that all of the tables are still identical, but you still have the greatest number of tables possible.

4. Next year, you and your friend want ... more chairs, but you do not want to ... 48 balloons, 24 flowers, and 36 ca... to figure out the maximum numb... fundraiser next year. Without kn... attend, tell your friend the larg... you want identical centerpiec... to your friend how you kno...

Setting the Table

After completing this chapter, you will be able to use the concepts you learned to answer the questions in the *STEAM Video Performance Task*. You will be asked to plan a fundraising event with the items below.

72 chairs

48 balloons

24 flowers

32 candles

You will find the greatest number of identical tables that can be prepared, and what will be in each centerpiece. When making arrangements for a party, should a party planner always use the greatest number of identical tables possible? Explain why or why not.

Getting Ready for Chapter 1

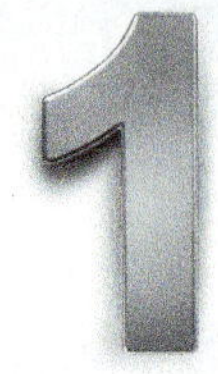

Chapter Exploration

Work with a partner. In Exercises 1–3, use the table.

	2	3	4	5	6	7	8	9	10
11	12	13	14	15	16	17	18	19	20
21	22	23	24	25	26	27	28	29	30
31	32	33	34	35	36	37	38	39	40
41	42	43	44	45	46	47	48	49	50
51	52	53	54	55	56	57	58	59	60
61	62	63	64	65	66	67	68	69	70
71	72	73	74	75	76	77	78	79	80
81	82	83	84	85	86	87	88	89	90
91	92	93	94	95	96	97	98	99	100

Eratosthenes
(c. 276–c. 194 B.C.)

This table is called the *Sieve of Eratosthenes*. Eratosthenes was a Greek mathematician who was the chief librarian at the Library of Alexandria in Egypt. He was the first person to calculate the circumference of Earth.

1. Cross out the multiples of 2 that are greater than 2. Do the same for 3, 5, and 7.
2. The numbers that are *not* crossed out are called *prime numbers*. The numbers that are crossed out are called *composite numbers*. In your own words, describe the characteristics of prime numbers and composite numbers.
3. **MP MODELING REAL LIFE** Work with a partner. Cicadas are insects that live underground and emerge from the ground after x or $x + 4$ years. Is it possible that both x and $x + 4$ are prime? Give some examples.

Vocabulary

The following vocabulary terms are defined in this chapter. Think about what each term might mean and record your thoughts.

exponent
numerical expression
order of operations
common factors
greatest common factor
common multiples
least common multiple

Laurie's Notes

Chapter Exploration

- In addition to being a Greek mathematician and historian, Eratosthenes was a geographer and astronomer. His calculations were remarkably accurate. Although Eratosthenes was influential to many fields of study, his critics called him *Beta* (the second letter of the Greek alphabet) because they believed he fell short of first place.
- The Sieve of Eratosthenes is an ancient algorithm for identifying smaller prime numbers. Multiples of prime numbers can be used to eliminate the composite numbers in the table.
- Students should be familiar with the terms *multiples, factor pairs, prime numbers,* and *composite numbers*. Reviewing these terms throughout the exercises will help ease the transition to the new material presented in the chapter.

ELL Support

Explain that the mathematics you use come from many different cultures, including Greek, Islamic, and Western European. Point out that in this context, the word *table* refers to a type of chart. Be sure to distinguish it from a type of furniture.

Vocabulary

- These terms represent some of the vocabulary that students will encounter in Chapter 1. Discuss the terms as a class.
- Where have students heard the term *common factors* outside of a math classroom? In what contexts? Students may not be able to write the actual definition, but they may write phrases associated with common factors.
- Allowing students to discuss these terms now will prepare them for understanding the terms as they are presented in the chapter.
- When students encounter a new definition, encourage them to write in their *Student Journals*. They will revisit these definitions during the Chapter Review.

Topics for Review

- Dividing Whole Numbers
- Factor Pairs
- Identifying Prime and Composite Numbers
- Multiples of Whole Numbers
- Order of Operations (no exponents)

Chapter Exploration

1.

	2	3	~~4~~	5	~~6~~	7	~~8~~	~~9~~	~~10~~
11	~~12~~	13	~~14~~	~~15~~	~~16~~	17	~~18~~	19	~~20~~
~~21~~	~~22~~	23	~~24~~	~~25~~	~~26~~	~~27~~	~~28~~	29	~~30~~
31	~~32~~	~~33~~	~~34~~	~~35~~	~~36~~	37	~~38~~	~~39~~	~~40~~
41	~~42~~	43	~~44~~	~~45~~	~~46~~	47	~~48~~	~~49~~	~~50~~
~~51~~	~~52~~	53	~~54~~	~~55~~	~~56~~	~~57~~	~~58~~	59	~~60~~
61	~~62~~	~~63~~	~~64~~	~~65~~	~~66~~	67	~~68~~	~~69~~	~~70~~
71	~~72~~	73	~~74~~	~~75~~	~~76~~	~~77~~	~~78~~	79	~~80~~
~~81~~	~~82~~	83	~~84~~	~~85~~	~~86~~	~~87~~	~~88~~	89	~~90~~
~~91~~	~~92~~	~~93~~	~~94~~	~~95~~	~~96~~	97	~~98~~	~~99~~	~~100~~

2. A prime number is a whole number that is *not* a multiple of any other whole numbers other than 1 and itself. A composite number is a whole number that is a multiple of two whole numbers other than 1 and itself.

3. yes; *Sample answer:* 3, 7; 7, 11; 13, 17; 19, 23

Learning Target

Write and evaluate expressions involving exponents.

Success Criteria

- Write products of repeated factors as powers.
- Evaluate powers.

Warm Up

Cumulative, vocabulary, and prerequisite skills practice opportunities are available in the *Resources by Chapter* or at *BigIdeasMath.com.*

ELL Support

Students may know the words *product* and *power* from everyday language. Explain that in the context of math, these words have very specific meanings. In everyday life, a product is something that is made to be sold. In math, a product is the result of multiplication. In common language, power means strength or force. In math, a power is a product of repeated factors.

Exploration 1

a–h. See Additional Answers.

i. 3 is the number being multiplied, 5 is how many times 3 is used as a factor.

Exploration 2

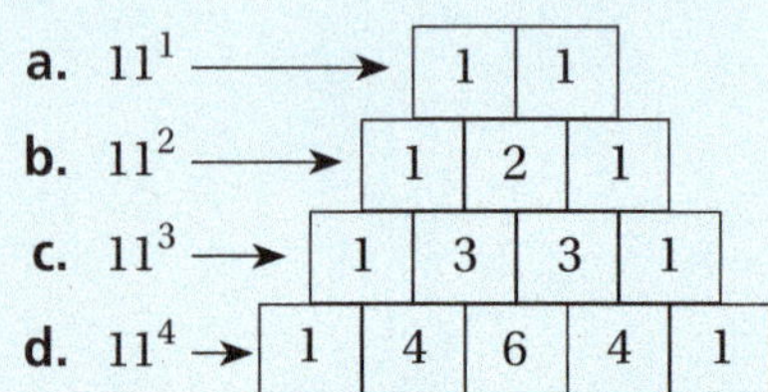

Sample answer: Each digit is a 1 or the sum of the two numbers above it.

Laurie's Notes

Preparing to Teach

- When students evaluate a **power**, they should consider which strategy is most appropriate: mental math, paper and pencil, or using a calculator.
- In prior courses, students evaluated whole-number powers of 10. In this lesson, they will begin to evaluate other **bases** as well.
- You want students to realize that exponents offer a more efficient way of representing repeated multiplication, and that the exponent tells the number of factors in the expression.

Motivate

? Ask, "Have you heard the St. Ives nursery rhyme?"

- The St. Ives nursery rhyme can be found online at *BigIdeasMath.com.*

? Have students work with a partner. Ask, "How many kits were met?" 2401 kits Have several students share their answers and reasoning.

- Discuss the idea that this pattern can continue, and explain that the explorations are also related to repeated multiplication.

Exploration 1

- Explain that in the notation 10^2, the 2 is called an **exponent**. Some students may be familiar with the notation and vocabulary. It will be made formal in the lesson. Discuss a sample before students work with a partner.
- Observe strategies students use for finding the values in the last column. Mental math strategies are important: in finding the product $3 \times 3 \times 3 \times 3$, some students will find 3×3, then 9×3, and then use paper and pencil to find 27×3. Show students that they can also find 3×3, and then 9×9.
- **MP8 Look for and Express Regularity in Repeated Reasoning:** Understanding how to represent repeated factors using an exponent requires students to recognize the pattern or structure of the expression.
- **Common Error:** Students often say 3^5 means multiply 3 five times. Actually, there are only four multiplications to perform. The number 3 is written five times, meaning there are five *factors* of 3.

Exploration 2

- Help students to find the exponent key on a calculator. Use the problems from Exploration 1 to determine how to evaluate powers.
- **FYI:** An entry point for all will be the beginning and ending 1. Groups may see patterns within the diagonals, across the rows, or addition from row to row.
- **Note:** This diagram begins like Pascal's Triangle, which is a rich investigation for interested students.

? **Extension:** Have students determine the next line in the diagram. Check by evaluating 11^5. Then ask, "If there was a box at the top, what number would be in it?" 1 "What power of 11 would the number represent?" 11^0

- **MP7 Look for and Make Use of Structure:** Help students see why the additive pattern in the diagram is related to the sum of the partial products when you multiply by 11.

$$\begin{array}{rl} 1331 & \\ \times \quad 11 & \\ \hline 1331 & \leftarrow 11^3 \\ +\ 13310 & \leftarrow 10 \times 11^3 \\ \hline 14641 & \leftarrow 11^4 \end{array}$$

1.1 Powers and Exponents

Learning Target: Write and evaluate expressions involving exponents.

Success Criteria:
- I can write products of repeated factors as powers.
- I can evaluate powers.

EXPLORATION 1

Writing Expressions Using Exponents

Work with a partner. Copy and complete the table.

Repeated Factors	Using an Exponent	Value
a. 10×10		
b. 4×4		
c. 6×6		
d. $10 \times 10 \times 10$		
e. $100 \times 100 \times 100$		
f. $3 \times 3 \times 3 \times 3$		
g. $4 \times 4 \times 4 \times 4 \times 4$		
h. $2 \times 2 \times 2 \times 2 \times 2 \times 2$		

i. In your own words, describe what the two numbers in the expression 3^5 mean.

Math Practice

Repeat Calculations

What patterns do you notice in the expressions? How does this help you write exponents?

EXPLORATION 2

Using a Calculator to Find a Pattern

Work with a partner. Copy the diagram. Use a calculator to find each value. Write one digit of the value in each box. Describe the pattern in the digits of the values.

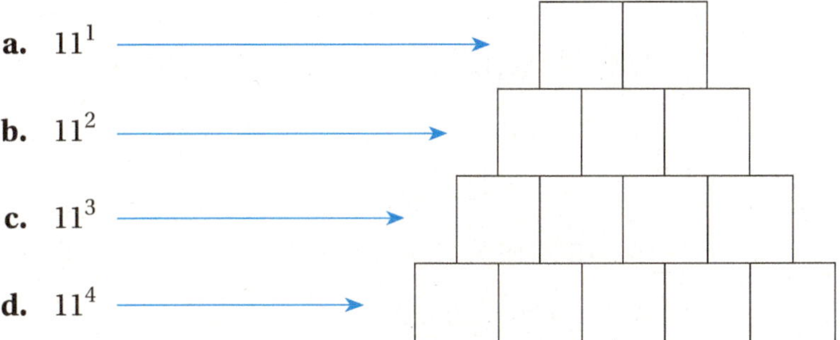

1.1 Lesson

Key Vocabulary
power, *p. 4*
base, *p. 4*
exponent, *p. 4*
perfect square, *p. 5*

A **power** is a product of repeated factors. The **base** of a power is the repeated factor. The **exponent** of a power indicates the number of times the base is used as a factor.

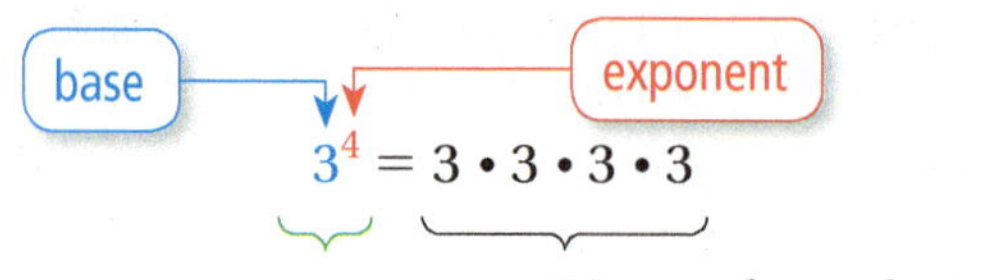

power   3 is used as a factor 4 times.

Remember

You can use the dot symbol • to indicate multiplication. For example, the product of 3 and 5 can be expressed as 3×5 or $3 \cdot 5$.

Power	Words
3^2	Three *squared*, or three to the second
3^3	Three *cubed*, or three to the third
3^4	Three to the fourth
3^5	Three to the fifth

EXAMPLE 1 Writing Expressions as Powers

Write each product as a power.

a. $7 \cdot 7 \cdot 7 \cdot 7 \cdot 7$

Because 7 is used as a factor 5 times, its exponent is 5.

So, $7 \cdot 7 \cdot 7 \cdot 7 \cdot 7 = 7^5$.

b. $12 \times 12 \times 12$

Because 12 is used as a factor 3 times, its exponent is 3.

So, $12 \times 12 \times 12 = 12^3$.

c. $100 \times 100 \times 100 \times 100 \times 100 \times 100$

Because 100 is used as a factor 6 times, its exponent is 6.

So, $100 \times 100 \times 100 \times 100 \times 100 \times 100 = 100^6$.

Try It **Write the product as a power.**

1. $2 \times 2 \times 2$
2. $6 \cdot 6 \cdot 6 \cdot 6 \cdot 6 \cdot 6$
3. $15 \times 15 \times 15 \times 15$
4. $20 \cdot 20 \cdot 20 \cdot 20 \cdot 20 \cdot 20 \cdot 20$

Laurie's Notes

Scaffolding Instruction

- Students explored how to write a product of repeated factors using an **exponent**, and how to evaluate a **power**, both with and without a calculator. Review the vocabulary terms for exponential expressions in the text. Examples 1 and 2 provide the opportunity for students to show an understanding of writing and evaluating powers.
- **Emerging:** For Examples 1 and 2, students may benefit from receiving guided instruction or working with a partner.
- **Proficient:** If students are confident in writing and evaluating powers, they can work with a partner to read through Example 3, and then check their understanding of **perfect squares** using the Try It exercises. Students can self-assess using the Self-Assessment for Concepts & Skills exercises.
- In Example 4, guided instruction may be needed for all students.

EXAMPLE 1

- Note that two different representations are used for multiplication (• and ×).
- Discuss with students the need to be careful. The dot may be mistaken as a decimal point (2.2 versus 2 • 2) and the × may be mistaken as a variable.

? "Are there other representations of multiplication you are familiar with?" Students may mention the use of parentheses. For instance, 3(4) = 12.

Try It

- Explain to students that the Try It exercises within the lesson provide an opportunity to check and build understanding. The goal is deep learning of the skill or concept, so that students are able to apply and transfer this knowledge to solve problems.
- Have students use whiteboards to work on the problems. Ask two volunteers to share by displaying their whiteboards. Discuss any differences in their answers.
- Have students use *Thumbs Up* to indicate their understanding of writing powers.

ELL Support

Have students work in groups to complete the exercises. Remind them to use the process described in Example 1 as they collaborate.
Beginner: Write out the equation. For example, $2 \times 2 \times 2 = 2^3$.
Intermediate: Describe the equation. For example, "Two times two times two equals two to the third power."
Advanced: Explain the functions of bases, exponents, and powers.

Scaffold instruction to support all students in their learning. Learning is individualized and you may want to group students differently as they move in and out of these levels with each skill and concept. Student self-assessment and feedback help guide your instructional decisions about how and when to layer support for all students to become proficient learners.

Formative Assessment Tip

Thumbs Up
This technique asks students to indicate the extent to which they understand a concept, procedure, or even the directions for an activity. It can be a quick way for students to communicate where their learning is with respect to a specific success criterion.

I get it

I don't get it

I'm not sure

Extra Example 1

Write each product as a power.

a. $6 \cdot 6 \cdot 6 \cdot 6$ 6^4

b. $14 \times 14 \times 14 \times 14 \times 14$ 14^5

c. $50 \cdot 50 \cdot 50$ 50^3

Try It

1. 2^3
2. 6^6
3. 15^4
4. 20^7

Extra Example 2

Find the value of each power.

a. 8^3 512 **b.** 13^2 169

Try It

5. 216 **6.** 81

7. 81 **8.** 324

Extra Example 3

Determine whether each number is a perfect square.

a. 50 not a perfect square

b. 9 perfect square

Try It

9. perfect square

10. not a perfect square

11. not a perfect square

12. perfect square

ELL Support

Check comprehension by having ELLs work in pairs to complete the Self-Assessment for Concepts & Skills exercises. Then have two pairs present their answers to each other and revise them if there is any disagreement.

Self-Assessment for Concepts & Skills

13. 64

14. 243

15. 1331

16–17. See Additional Answers.

18. $3 + 3 + 3 + 3 = 3 \times 4$; the others show powers as products of repeated factors.

Laurie's Notes

EXAMPLE 2

- Students should be able to evaluate some powers using mental math.
- To practice using precise language, ask a volunteer to read the problem and the answer. You should hear, "7 squared is 49" and "5 cubed is 125."
- A common error many students make is to multiply the exponent by the base. For example, saying $7^2 = 7 \times 2 = 14$ rather than $7 \times 7 = 49$. The simpler the problem, the more often they seem to make this error.
- Evaluating a power is the second success criterion. Connect the work students are doing with the success criterion so that they understand what success looks like. This is how their learning becomes visible.

Discuss

- As an introduction to the definition of a perfect square, write the following sequence on the board: 1, 4, 9, 16, 25, 36, . . .
- ? "What are the next three numbers in the sequence?" 49, 64, 81 "What is the pattern?" Square the whole numbers in order. Students will often answer that you add 3, add 5, add 7, and so on. This is also a correct pattern, so you may need to probe further to get students to recognize that the numbers in the sequence are squares of the whole numbers.
- **MP5 Use Appropriate Tools Strategically:** Define **perfect square**. Give students a pile of square tiles and ask them to make a larger square. If you don't have square tiles, students can color squares on grid paper of various sizes. How many tiles were used? The number will always be a perfect square. The square tiles are a tool to help students visualize square numbers.

1 tile 4 tiles 9 tiles

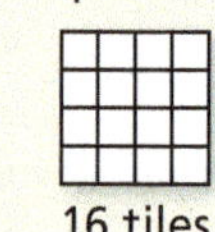

16 tiles

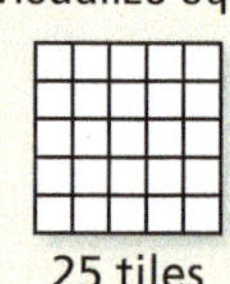

25 tiles

EXAMPLE 3

- Work through each part of the example.
- Give students 20 tiles and ask them to use all of the tiles to make a square. They will not be able to make a square because 20 is not a perfect square.

Try It

- Ask students to explain their answers either visually or verbally, so that others can understand the different strategies.
- Some students may reason that 99 is not a perfect square because $9^2 = 81$ and $10^2 = 100$. The base is between 9 and 10, so it is not a whole number.

Self-Assessment for Concepts & Skills

- Review the success criteria with students and have them complete the exercises. Discuss any common errors that may arise.
- The vocabulary in this lesson is important. Students should be able to explain the difference between exponents and powers, either by description or example.

The Success Criteria Self-Assessment chart can be found in the *Student Journal* or online at *BigIdeasMath.com*.

EXAMPLE 2 Finding Values of Powers

Find the value of each power.

a. 7^2

$7^2 = 7 \cdot 7$ Write as repeated multiplication.

$= 49$ Simplify.

b. 5^3

$5^3 = 5 \cdot 5 \cdot 5$

$= 125$

Try It **Find the value of the power.**

5. 6^3 **6.** 9^2 **7.** 3^4 **8.** 18^2

The square of a whole number is a **perfect square**.

EXAMPLE 3 Identifying Perfect Squares

Determine whether each number is a perfect square.

a. 64

Because $8^2 = 64$, 64 is a perfect square.

b. 20

No whole number squared equals 20. So, 20 is not a perfect square.

Math Practice

Communicate Precisely

How can you use $4^2 = 16$ and $5^2 = 25$ to explain why 20 is *not* a perfect square?

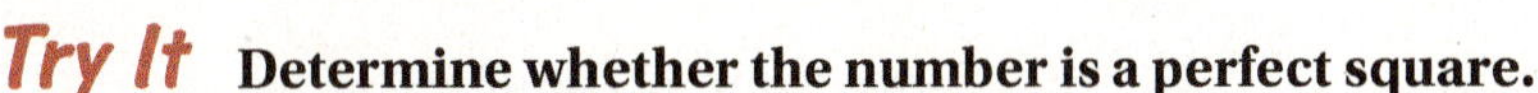

Try It **Determine whether the number is a perfect square.**

9. 25 **10.** 2 **11.** 99 **12.** 36

Self-Assessment for Concepts & Skills

Solve each exercise. Then rate your understanding of the success criteria in your journal.

FINDING VALUES OF POWERS **Find the value of the power.**

13. 8^2 **14.** 3^5 **15.** 11^3

16. **VOCABULARY** How are exponents and powers different?

17. **VOCABULARY** Is 10 a perfect square? Is 100 a perfect square? Explain.

18. **WHICH ONE DOESN'T BELONG?** Which one does *not* belong with the other three? Explain your reasoning.

$2^4 = 2 \times 2 \times 2 \times 2$

$3^2 = 3 \times 3$

$3 + 3 + 3 + 3 = 3 \times 4$

$5 \cdot 5 \cdot 5 = 5^3$

Remember

The *area* of a figure is the amount of surface it covers. Area is measured in square units.

You can use powers to find areas of squares. The area of a square is equal to its side length squared.

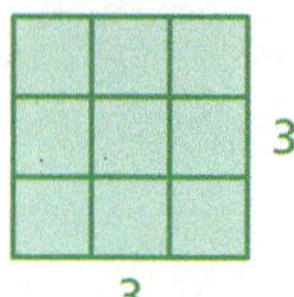

Area $= 3^2 = 9$ square units

EXAMPLE 4 Modeling Real Life

A life-size MONOPOLY® game board is a square with a side length of 11 yards. What is the area of the game board?

Use a verbal model to solve the problem.

$$\text{Area of game board} = (\text{Side length})^2$$

$= 11^2$ Substitute 11 for side length.

$= 121$ Multiply.

▶ The area of the game board is 121 square yards.

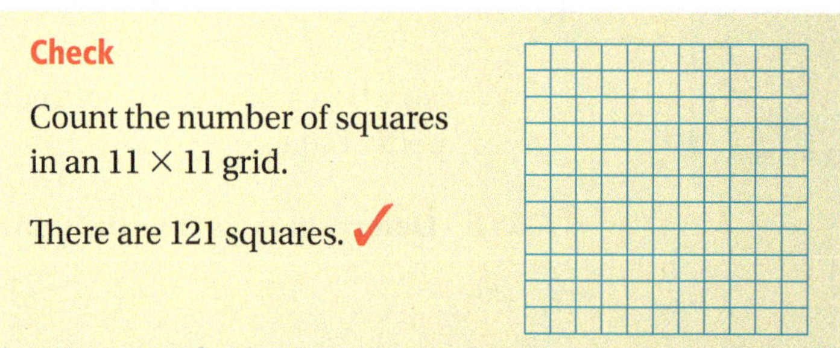

Check

Count the number of squares in an 11×11 grid.

There are 121 squares. ✓

Self-Assessment for Problem Solving

Solve each exercise. Then rate your understanding of the success criteria in your journal.

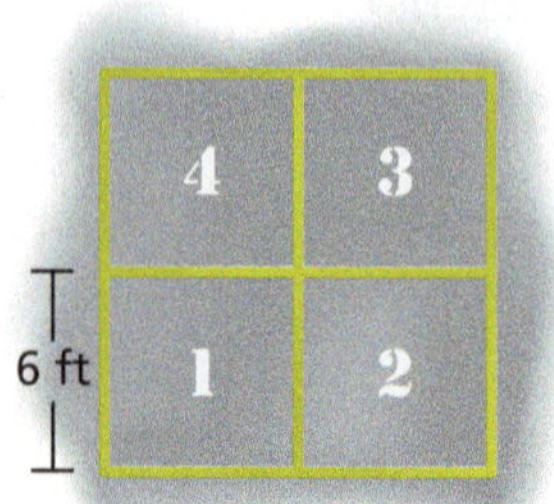

19. A square solar panel has an area of 16 square feet. Write the area as a power. Then find the side lengths of the panel.

20. The four-square court shown is a square made up of four identical smaller squares. What is the area of the court?

21. **DIG DEEPER!** Each face of a number cube is a square with a side length of 16 millimeters. What is the total area of all of the faces of the number cube?

Laurie's Notes

EXAMPLE 4

- **Teaching Tip:** The problems on the last page of each lesson can involve much of a class period. Having students work on the problems in class where you and other students can support their learning is more productive than solving application problems for homework and having little support.
- Explain that a verbal model is an equation. It uses words to state the formula or process that will be used to solve a problem.
- ? "How do you find the area of a square?" Square the side length. "Can you find the area of a chess or checkers board? Explain." Yes, if you know, or can measure, a side length, square it to find the area.
- **MP1 Make Sense of Problems and Persevere in Solving Them:** Students need to verbalize what the problem is asking, and how the picture helps them. Then students should be able to write down the mathematical process and explain their work. The squares they formed using tiles can help students visualize the MONOPOLY® board as well. Some students may need to draw an 11×11 grid to get started, but they will eventually see that $11 \times 11 = 121$ square yards is the answer.
- Refer students to the Remember note and remind them to label their answers with square units.

Extra Example 4

A baseball diamond is a square with a side length of 90 feet. What is the area of a baseball diamond? 8100 ft^2

Self-Assessment for Problem Solving

- The goal for all students is to feel comfortable with the problem-solving plan. It is important for students to problem-solve in class, where they may receive support from you and their peers. Keep in mind that some students may only be ready to understand the problem.
- Students should work independently or with a partner on these exercises. Support students with probing questions and by providing feedback.
- ? **Probing Questions:** "What resources do you have available? How can grid paper help you? Do your answers make sense? What are the units for your answers? Can you check your solution?"
- Coach students not to solve the problem for their partners. Model what guided questions sound like.
- There should have been several opportunities where students made a connection between the examples and the success criteria. Now they should record their understanding of the success criteria in their journals.

The Success Criteria Self-Assessment chart can be found in the *Student Journal* or online at *BigIdeasMath.com.*

Self-Assessment for Problem Solving

19. *Sample answer:* 4^2; 4 ft

20. 144 ft^2

21. 1536 mm^2

Closure

- You have a dozen boxes of a dozen protein bars each, and each protein bar has a dozen dark chocolate chips. Use an exponent to write and evaluate an expression for the total number of dark chocolate chips.
  12^3; 1728 dark chocolate chips

Learning Target

Write and evaluate expressions involving exponents.

Success Criteria

- Write products of repeated factors as powers.
- Evaluate powers.

Review & Refresh

1. 300
2. 1400
3. 369
4. 1359
5. $(5 + 8) \times 4$
6. $(11 - 7) \div 2$
7. 4.0
8. 12.90
9. 3
10. 20

Concepts, Skills, & Problem Solving

11. 8^2; 64
12. 4^3; 64
13. 9^4; 6561
14. 12^4; 20,736
15. 9^2
16. 13^2
17. 15^3
18. 2^5
19. 14^3
20. 8^4
21. 11^5
22. 7^6
23. 16^4
24. 43^5
25. 167^3
26. 245^4
27. 25
28. 64
29. 36
30. 1
31. 0
32. 4096
33. 16
34. 144
35. 343
36. 625
37. 32
38. 196
39. 117,649
40. 65,536
41. 20,736
42. 1,419,857

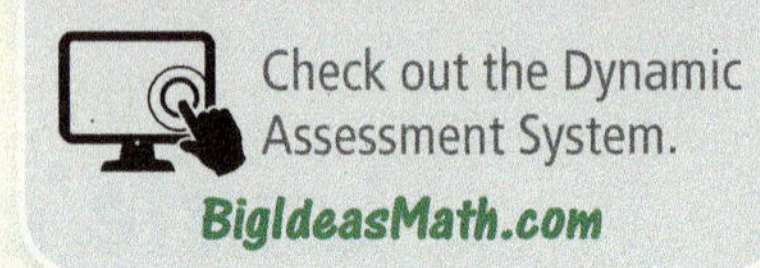

Assignment Guide and Concept Check

Scaffold assignments to support all students in their learning progression. The suggested assignments are a starting point. Continue to assign additional exercises and revisit with spaced practice to move every student toward proficiency.

Level	Assignment 1	Assignment 2
Emerging	4, 6, 8, 10, 13, 15, 18, 27, 28, 30, 31, 40, 44, 45	33, 41, 43, 46, 47, 52, 53, 54, 55
Proficient	4, 6, 8, 10, 13, 16, 22, 30, 31, 33, 34, 41, 46, 47	43, 50, 51, 53, 54, 55, 56, 57
Advanced	4, 6, 8, 10, 13, 24, 26, 30, 31, 36, 42, 50, 51	43, 54, 55, 56, 57, 58

- Assignment 1 is for use after students complete the Self-Assessment for Concepts & Skills.
- Assignment 2 is for use after students complete the Self-Assessment for Problem Solving.
- The red exercises can be used as a concept check.

Review & Refresh Prior Skills

Exercises 1–4 Multiplying Whole Numbers
Exercises 5 and 6 Writing Numerical Expressions
Exercises 7 and 8 Rounding Decimals
Exercises 9 and 10 Multiplying Whole Numbers and Fractions

Common Errors

- **Exercises 15–26** Students may miscount the number of factors. Remind them to be careful when counting the number of factors, and that the number of factors is the exponent.
- **Exercises 27–38** Students may make the same mistake that is illustrated in Exercise 43, that is, they may write the exponent as a factor. Remind them that the exponent is the number of times the base is used as a factor. You may want to demonstrate this point with a couple of quick examples. For instance, using Exercise 27, point out that $5^2 = 5 \times 5 = 25$ but $5 \times 2 = 10$.

1.1 Practice

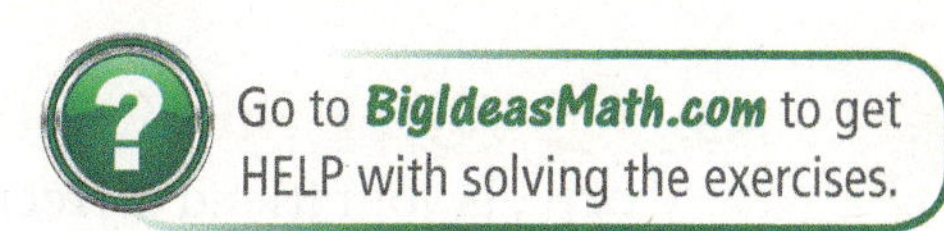

Review & Refresh

Multiply.

1. 150×2
2. 175×8
3. 123×3
4. 151×9

Write the sentence as a numerical expression.

5. Add 5 and 8, then multiply by 4.
6. Subtract 7 from 11, then divide by 2.

Round the number to the indicated place value.

7. 4.03785 to the tenths
8. 12.89503 to the hundredths

Complete the sentence.

9. $\frac{1}{10}$ of 30 is ▭.
10. $\frac{4}{5}$ of 25 is ▭.

Concepts, Skills, & Problem Solving

WRITING EXPRESSIONS USING EXPONENTS **Copy and complete the table.** (See Exploration 1, p. 3.)

Repeated Factors	Using an Exponent	Value
11. 8×8		
12. $4 \times 4 \times 4$		
13. $9 \times 9 \times 9 \times 9$		
14. $12 \times 12 \times 12 \times 12$		

WRITING EXPRESSIONS AS POWERS **Write the product as a power.**

15. 9×9
16. 13×13
17. $15 \times 15 \times 15$
18. $2 \cdot 2 \cdot 2 \cdot 2 \cdot 2$
19. $14 \times 14 \times 14$
20. $8 \cdot 8 \cdot 8 \cdot 8$
21. $11 \times 11 \times 11 \times 11 \times 11$
22. $7 \cdot 7 \cdot 7 \cdot 7 \cdot 7 \cdot 7$
23. $16 \cdot 16 \cdot 16 \cdot 16$
24. $43 \times 43 \times 43 \times 43 \times 43$
25. $167 \cdot 167 \cdot 167$
26. $245 \cdot 245 \cdot 245 \cdot 245$

FINDING VALUES OF POWERS **Find the value of the power.**

27. 5^2
28. 4^3
29. 6^2
30. 1^7
31. 0^3
32. 8^4
33. 2^4
34. 12^2
35. 7^3
36. 5^4
37. 2^5
38. 14^2

MP USING TOOLS **Use a calculator to find the value of the power.**

39. 7^6
40. 4^8
41. 12^4
42. 17^5

43. **YOU BE THE TEACHER** Your friend finds the value of 8^3. Is your friend correct? Explain your reasoning.

$8^3 = 8 \cdot 3 = 24$

IDENTIFYING PERFECT SQUARES **Determine whether the number is a perfect square.**

44. 8 **45.** 4 **46.** 81 **47.** 44

48. 49 **49.** 125 **50.** 150 **51.** 144

52. **MODELING REAL LIFE** On each square centimeter of a person's skin, there are about 39^2 bacteria. How many bacteria does this expression represent?

53. **REPEATED REASONING** The smallest figurine in a gift shop is 2 inches tall. The height of each figurine is twice the height of the previous figurine. What is the height of the tallest figurine?

54. **MODELING REAL LIFE** A square painting measures 2 meters on each side. What is the area of the painting in square centimeters?

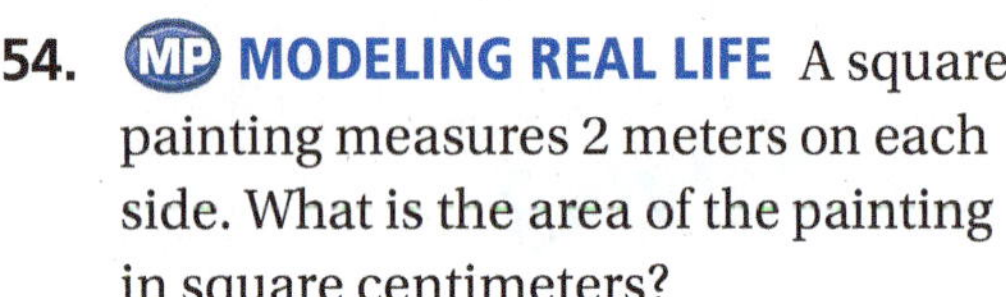

55. **NUMBER SENSE** Write three powers that have values greater than 120 and less than 130.

56. **DIG DEEPER!** A landscaper has 125 tiles to build a square patio. The patio must have an area of at least 80 square feet.

a. What are the possible arrangements for the patio?

b. How many tiles are not used in each arrangement?

12 in.

12 in.

57. **PATTERNS** Copy and complete the table. Describe what happens to the value of the power as the exponent decreases. Use this pattern to find the value of 4^0.

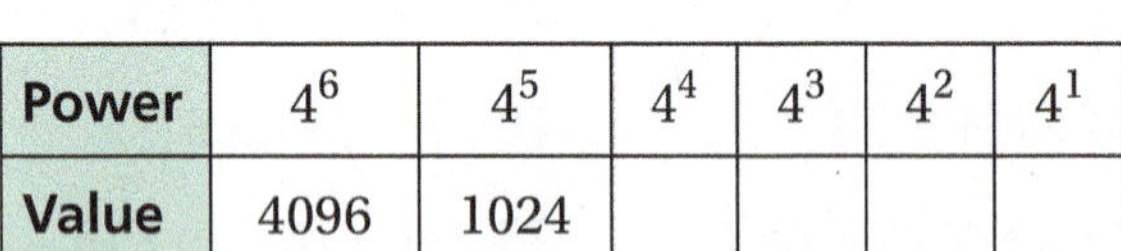

Power	4^6	4^5	4^4	4^3	4^2	4^1
Value	4096	1024				

58. **REPEATED REASONING** How many blocks do you need to add to Square 6 to get Square 7? to Square 9 to get Square 10? to Square 19 to get Square 20? Explain.

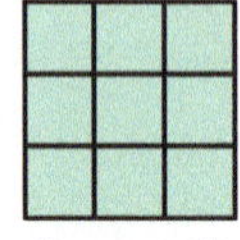
Square 3

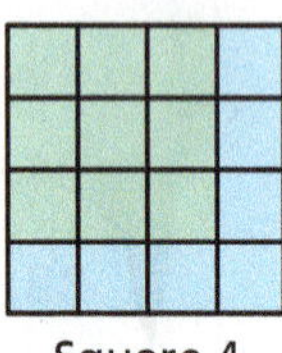
Square 4

Square 5

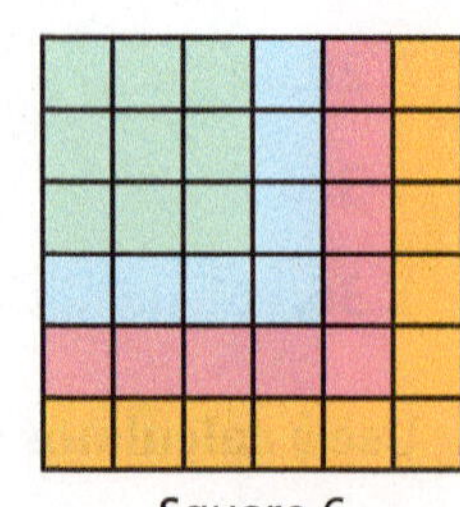
Square 6

Mini-Assessment

Write the product as a power. Then find the value of the power.

1. $3 \times 3 \times 3$ 3^3; 27
2. 2×2 2^2; 4
3. $5 \cdot 5 \cdot 5 \cdot 5 \cdot 5$ 5^5; 3125
4. $16 \cdot 16$ 16^2; 256
5. The number of students in a school is about 13^3. How many students does this expression represent? 2197 students

Section Resources

Surface Level	Deep Level
Resources by Chapter • Extra Practice • Reteach • Puzzle Time Student Journal • Self-Assessment • Practice Differentiating the Lesson Tutorial Videos Skills Review Handbook Skills Trainer	Resources by Chapter • Enrichment and Extension Graphic Organizers Dynamic Assessment System • Section Practice

Concepts, Skills, & Problem Solving

43. no; $8^3 = 8 \cdot 8 \cdot 8 = 512$

44. not a perfect square

45. perfect square

46. perfect square

47. not a perfect square

48. perfect square

49. not a perfect square

50. not a perfect square

51. perfect square

52. 1521

53. 16 in.

54. 40,000 cm^2

55. *Sample answer:* $11^2, 5^3, 2^7$

56. **a.** 9 by 9, 10 by 10, 11 by 11

b. 44; 25; 4

57.

Power	4^6	4^5	4^4
Value	4096	1024	256

Power	4^3	4^2	4^1
Value	64	16	4

The value of the power is divided by 4. $4^0 = 1$

58. 13; add $7^2 - 6^2$ blocks;
19; add $10^2 - 9^2$ blocks;
39; add $20^2 - 19^2$ blocks

Learning Target

Write and evaluate numerical expressions using the order of operations.

Success Criteria

- Explain why there is a need for a standard order of operations.
- Evaluate numerical expressions involving several operations, exponents, and grouping symbols.
- Write numerical expressions involving exponents to represent a real-life problem.

Warm Up

Cumulative, vocabulary, and prerequisite skills practice opportunities are available in the *Resources by Chapter* or at *BigIdeasMath.com.*

ELL Support

Students might know the word *operation* from a medical context. Explain that a doctor may perform an operation on a person. In the context of math, you may perform an operation on numbers or variables. Addition, subtraction, multiplication, and division are common operations. The order of operations is a set of rules that describe the order in which operations must be performed.

Exploration 1

a. 10; 7; no **b.** 45; 9; no

c. 62; 48; no **d.** 38; 48; no

Exploration 2

a. *Sample answer:* so expressions always have the same value

b. Multiply first, then add or subtract.

c–e. See Additional Answers.

Laurie's Notes

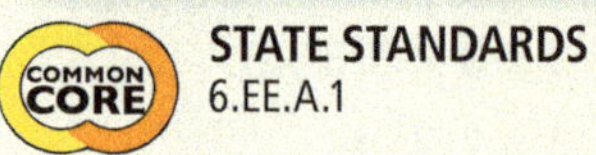

STATE STANDARDS
6.EE.A.1

Preparing to Teach

- In the previous course, students were introduced to the **order of operations**. They may only recall PEMDAS, or more currently GEMA, but they need to understand more about the order of operations than just remembering an acronym. One problem with relying upon the acronym, is that students often forget the left-to-right rule when multiplication and division (or addition and subtraction) occur in the same expression.
- It is important for students to know that the order in which operations are performed was a decision. If a decision was not made, it would be possible to get different values for the same expression, as demonstrated in the Motivate. This is the essence of the first success criterion.

Motivate

- **Model:** Place two calculators, one scientific and one non-scientific, under a document camera or give the calculators to a student. Press the same sequence of keys, $20 - 8 \times 2$ and then enter (or =), on each calculator.
- ? "What is the answer on each calculator?" The scientific calculator should display 4 and the non-scientific calculator should display 24.
- ? "Is it okay to have different values for the same expression? Explain." No, the value is 4. To obtain the correct value on the non-scientific calculator, perform the multiplication separately, and then subtract the result from 20.
- The non-scientific calculator performs the operations in order from left to right. The scientific calculator uses the agreed upon order of operations and performs the multiplication before the subtraction.

Exploration 1

- Introduce the exploration and have students work with partners to complete it.
- ? When students have finished, ask, "Did the order in which you performed the operations matter?" Yes, the order mattered in all of the problems. Have students discuss why, explicitly, an order of operations is needed.
- **Extension:** Write an expression involving two or more operations in which the order does not matter. *Sample answer:* $4 + 2 \times 1$

Exploration 2

- The goal of this exploration is that students use technology to determine the order in which to perform computations, exponents included.
- **Teaching Strategy:** Have students use the calculator on their phones, display a calculator under a document camera, or use a calculator on an interactive board. Students need to be familiar with their own technology.
- **Extension:** Use all of the symbols and numbers, in any order, to write an expression that has a value of 2. Use one of the given numbers as an exponent in your expression. Have students share and compare their expressions.

$$(\,), +, -, 1, 2, 3, 4$$

Sample answer: $1 + (4 - 3)^2$

1.2 Order of Operations

Learning Target: Write and evaluate numerical expressions using the order of operations.

Success Criteria:
- I can explain why there is a need for a standard order of operations.
- I can evaluate numerical expressions involving several operations, exponents, and grouping symbols.
- I can write numerical expressions involving exponents to represent a real-life problem.

EXPLORATION 1 Comparing Different Orders

Work with a partner. Find the value of each expression by using different orders of operations. Are your answers the same?

a. Add, then multiply. $3 + 2 \times 2$ | Multiply, then add. $3 + 2 \times 2$

b. Subtract, then multiply. $18 - 3 \cdot 3$ | Multiply, then subtract. $18 - 3 \cdot 3$

c. Multiply, then subtract. $8 \times 8 - 2$ | Subtract, then multiply. $8 \times 8 - 2$

d. Multiply, then add. $6 \cdot 6 + 2$ | Add, then multiply. $6 \cdot 6 + 2$

EXPLORATION 2 Determining Order of Operations

Work with a partner.

a. Scientific calculators use a standard order of operations when evaluating expressions. Why is a standard order of operations needed?

b. Use a scientific calculator to evaluate each expression in Exploration 1. Enter each expression exactly as written. For each expression, which order of operations is correct?

c. What order of operations should be used to evaluate $3 + 2^2$, $18 - 3^2$, $8^2 - 2$, and $6^2 + 2$?

d. Do $18 \div 3 \cdot 3$ and $18 \div 3^2$ have the same value? Justify your answer.

e. How does evaluating powers fit into the order of operations?

Math Practice

Use Technology to Explore
How does a scientific calculator help you explore order of operations?

1.2 Lesson

Key Vocabulary
numerical expression, *p. 10*
evaluate, *p. 10*
order of operations, *p. 10*

A **numerical expression** is an expression that contains numbers and operations. To **evaluate**, or find the value of, a numerical expression, use a set of rules called the **order of operations**.

Key Idea

Order of Operations

1. Perform operations in grouping symbols.
2. Evaluate numbers with exponents.
3. Multiply and divide from left to right.
4. Add and subtract from left to right.

EXAMPLE 1 Using Order of Operations

a. Evaluate $12 - 2 \times 4$.

$12 - 2 \times 4 = 12 - 8$ — Multiply 2 and 4.

$= 4$ — Subtract 8 from 12.

b. Evaluate $60 \div [(4 + 2) \times 5]$.

$60 \div [(4 + 2) \times 5] = 60 \div [6 \times 5]$ — Perform operation in parentheses.

$= 60 \div 30$ — Perform operation in brackets.

$= 2$ — Divide 60 by 30.

Try It Evaluate the expression.

1. $7 \cdot 5 + 3$
2. $(28 - 20) \div 4$
3. $[6 + (15 - 10)] \times 5$

EXAMPLE 2 Using Order of Operations with Exponents

Remember to multiply and divide from left to right. In Example 2, you should divide before multiplying because the division symbol comes first when reading from left to right.

Evaluate $30 \div (7 + 2^3) \times 6$.

$30 \div (7 + 2^3) \times 6 = 30 \div (7 + 8) \times 6$ — Evaluate power in parentheses.

$= 30 \div 15 \times 6$ — Perform operation in parentheses.

$= 2 \times 6$ — Divide 30 by 15.

$= 12$ — Multiply 2 and 6.

Try It Evaluate the expression.

4. $6 + 2^4 - 1$
5. $4 \cdot 3^2 + 18 - 9$
6. $16 + (5^2 - 7) \div 3$

Laurie's Notes

Scaffolding Instruction

- Students should have a sense of why a standard order of operations is necessary, as stated in the first success criterion. Exponents and grouping symbols are now included in the order of operations.
- **Emerging:** Students understand that there is an order in which operations must be performed, but they may make errors in computations or identifying the operations. Going through Examples 1 and 2, either independently or with guided instruction, will help students become proficient with the first two success criteria.
- **Proficient:** Students have a good understanding of the order of operations but need to practice working with multiple operations. The Try It exercises will help students assess their learning.
- All students should practice using order of operations with the Try It exercises, before applying their understanding to real-life problems.

Key Idea

- **FYI:** Students should recall the **order of operations** from the previous course. The order is now extended to include exponents in a **numerical expression**.
- **Common Error:** Students may forget the left-to-right rule for multiplication and division, or addition and subtraction. For instance, $24 - 10 + 6 = 20$, not 8.
- If you introduce the common acronym PEMDAS (or GEMA) as a memory tool for the order of operations, remind students that the left-to-right rules are important. When using PEMDAS, clarify that "P" represents all grouping symbols, not just parentheses.

EXAMPLE 1

- ? "How many operations are in the expression in part (a)?" 2 "Which operation should be performed first?" multiplication
- ? "Tell a partner how this example is different from those you have solved." There are two types of grouping symbols: parentheses and brackets. "How do you think this problem should be solved? Write your thoughts on a whiteboard."
- Give sufficient time for students to complete the example, and then have them discuss their results.
- **Teaching Strategy:** Have students use a calculator to check their answers.

EXAMPLE 2

- ? "How many operations are in this expression?" 4
- **MP3 Construct Viable Arguments and Critique the Reasoning of Others:** Ask a volunteer to explain the order in which the expression should be evaluated. Have other students critique the reasoning.
- Refer to the push-pin note to reinforce the left-to-right rule.

Try It

- Each student should work independently before checking his or her work with a neighbor. Encourage students to show their work instead of trying to evaluate the expressions in their heads.
- Have students display work on whiteboards so you can quickly assess where students are in their progress with the success criteria. Offer feedback as needed.

Scaffold instruction to support all students in their learning. Learning is individualized and you may want to group students differently as they move in and out of these levels with each skill and concept. Student self-assessment and feedback help guide your instructional decisions about how and when to layer support for all students to become proficient learners.

Teaching Strategy

Calculators are now, and will continue to be, a commonly used tool. Students should be familiar with calculator apps they have on their phones, tablets, or computers. It is important to understand how computations are performed. Is the app like a scientific calculator, which uses the order of operations? How are exponents evaluated? Can parentheses be used?
In many lessons, it is helpful for students to use the technology they already own. If access to technology is a problem for all students, pair students to share resources, or use a document camera (or interactive board) to display a calculator to the whole class. Familiarity with calculators is important.

Extra Example 1

a. Evaluate $16 + 5 \times 2$. 26

b. Evaluate $21 \times [32 \div (10 - 2)]$. 84

Extra Example 2

Evaluate $15 \times (12 - 3^2) \div 9$. 5

Try It

1. 38 **2.** 2

3. 55 **4.** 21

5. 45 **6.** 22

Extra Example 3

a. Evaluate $10 - \frac{1+3}{2}$. 8

b. Evaluate $7 + 5(8 - 6.5) \times 2^3$. 67

ELL Support

Review the order of operations before having students work in pairs to complete Try It Exercises 7–9.

Beginner: Write each step of the solution. For example, $\frac{8(2+5)}{7} = \frac{8 \times 7}{7} = \frac{56}{7} = 8$.

Intermediate: Describe each step. For example, "First, add two and five. Next, multiply eight and seven. Last, divide fifty-six by seven."

Advanced: Explain why each step was done in the order chosen.

Try It

7. 4
8. 24
9. 8

Self-Assessment for Concepts & Skills

10. 15
11. 4
12. 2

13. Using the order of operations, $12 - 8 \div 2 = 12 - 4 = 8$ and $(12 - 8) \div 2 = 4 \div 2 = 2$.

14. As illustrated below, perform the operation in parentheses, evaluate 3^2, divide 8 by 2, add 4 and 9.

$$8 \div (6 - 4) + 3^2$$
$$= 8 \div 2 + 3^2 = 8 \div 2 + 9$$
$$= 4 + 9 = 13$$

15. $(5^2 - 8) \times 2$; $(5^2 - 8) \times 2 = 34$, the other expressions have a value of 9.

Laurie's Notes

Discuss

- Discuss different ways multiplication can be represented. Share with students that another way to represent multiplication is to use parentheses. For example, 3 times 4 can be represented as 3×4, $3 \cdot 4$, 3(4), or (3)(4).
- Explain that $3(2 + 7)$ is the same as $3 \times (2 + 7)$. A number written next to, but outside of, a parenthesis implies multiplication.

EXAMPLE 3

- Have students work through each part of the example.
- Ask volunteers to share their work with the class. Students talking about their work is more engaging than a teacher telling students how to do the work.
- Remind students that the fraction bar means division. You can rewrite an expression that contains a fraction bar using division symbols and parentheses. The fraction bar can be thought of as a grouping symbol.

Try It

- These exercises will provide important feedback to you and your students. Are they confident in deciding which order the operations must be performed when evaluating numerical expressions? If so, they are showing proficiency with the second success criterion.
- **Teaching Tip:** You want to model that your classroom is a safe learning environment. If there are incorrect answers, state without judgment, "I've seen different answers to this problem. That will happen often this year. We can all learn from mistakes and learning is our goal, not just getting a correct answer."

Self-Assessment for Concepts & Skills

- Can students explain why there is a need for a standard order of operations?
- Exercise 14 is key to helping students assess their understanding of evaluating numerical expressions using the order of operations.
- **Note:** Students may be able to explain the order in which to perform operations, but then make a computational mistake. Be sure to analyze incorrect responses. Is the error computational, or a misunderstanding of the order of operations? Students should also be looking for this distinction.

ELL Support

Provide language practice while allowing students to check their own comprehension. Encourage ELLs to refer to the order of operations as needed. Allow time for students to complete the exercises independently, and then discuss their answers in a group. Ask group members to reach a consensus, but you may provide support if they cannot agree.

The Success Criteria Self-Assessment chart can be found in the *Student Journal* or online at *BigIdeasMath.com.*

The symbols $\times$ and $\bullet$ are used to indicate multiplication. You can also use parentheses to indicate multiplication. For example, $3(2 + 7)$ is the same as $3 \times (2 + 7)$.

EXAMPLE 3 Using Order of Operations

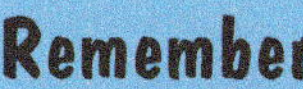

Remember

You can interpret a fraction as division of the numerator by the denominator.

$\frac{a}{b} = a \div b$

a. **Evaluate $9 + \frac{8-2}{3}$.**

$$9 + \frac{8-2}{3} = 9 + (8 - 2) \div 3$$ Rewrite fraction as division.

$$= 9 + 6 \div 3$$ Perform operation in parentheses.

$$= 9 + 2$$ Divide 6 by 3.

$$= 11$$ Add 9 and 2.

b. **Evaluate $10 - 8(13 + 7) \div 4^2$.**

$$10 - 8(13 + 7) \div 4^2 = 10 - 8(20) \div 4^2$$ Perform operation in parentheses.

$$= 10 - 8(20) \div 16$$ Evaluate 4^2.

$$= 10 - 160 \div 16$$ Multiply 8 and 20.

$$= 10 - 10$$ Divide 160 by 16.

$$= 0$$ Subtract 10 from 10.

Try It

Evaluate the expression.

7. $50 + 6(12 \div 4) - 8^2$ **8.** $5^2 - \frac{1}{5}(10 - 5)$ **9.** $\frac{8(2 + 5)}{7}$

Self-Assessment for Concepts & Skills

Solve each exercise. Then rate your understanding of the success criteria in your journal.

USING ORDER OF OPERATIONS **Evaluate the expression.**

10. $7 + 2 \bullet 4$ **11.** $8 \div 4 \times 2$ **12.** $3(5 + 1) \div 3^2$

13. **WRITING** Why does $12 - 8 \div 2 = 8$, but $(12 - 8) \div 2 = 2$?

14. MP **REASONING** Describe the steps in evaluating the expression $8 \div (6 - 4) + 3^2$.

15. **WHICH ONE DOESN'T BELONG?** Which expression does *not* belong with the other three? Explain your reasoning.

$5^2 - 8 \times 2$	$5^2 - (8 \times 2)$	$5^2 - 2 \times 8$	$(5^2 - 8) \times 2$

EXAMPLE 4 Modeling Real Life

The diagram shows landing zones for skydivers. Zone 1 is for experts. The remaining space is divided in half and designated as Zones 2 and 3 for tandem divers. What is the area of Zone 2?

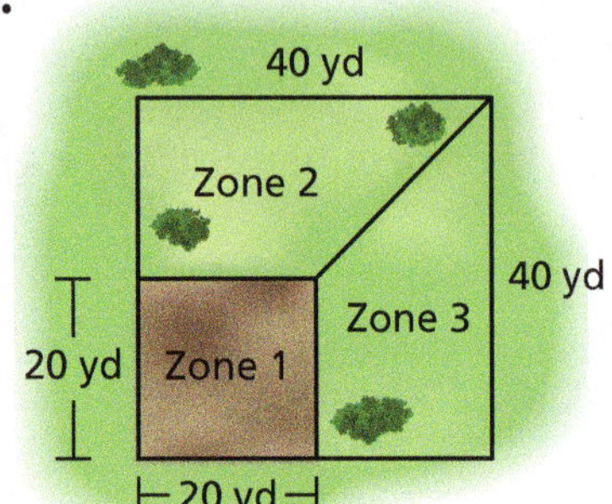

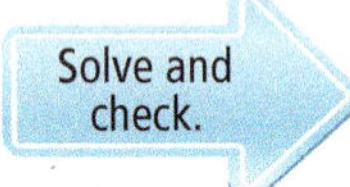

Understand the problem.

You are given the dimensions of landing zones and that the areas of Zones 2 and 3 are equal. You are asked to find the area of Zone 2.

Make a plan.

Use a verbal model to write an expression. Subtract the area of Zone 1 from the total area to find the combined area of Zones 2 and 3. Then multiply the combined area by one-half.

Solve and check.

Verbal Model One-half (Total area − Area of Zone 1)

Expression $\frac{1}{2}$ (40^2 − 20^2)

$$\frac{1}{2}(40^2 - 20^2) = \frac{1}{2}(1600 - 400) \quad \text{Evaluate powers in parentheses.}$$

$$= \frac{1}{2}(1200) \quad \text{Perform operation in parentheses.}$$

$$= 600 \quad \text{Multiply } \frac{1}{2} \text{ and 1200.}$$

The area of Zone 2 is 600 square yards.

Check Verify that the areas of the three zones have a sum equal to the total area.

$400 + 600 + 600 \overset{?}{=} 1600$

$1600 = 1600$ ✓

Self-Assessment for Problem Solving

Solve each exercise. Then rate your understanding of the success criteria in your journal.

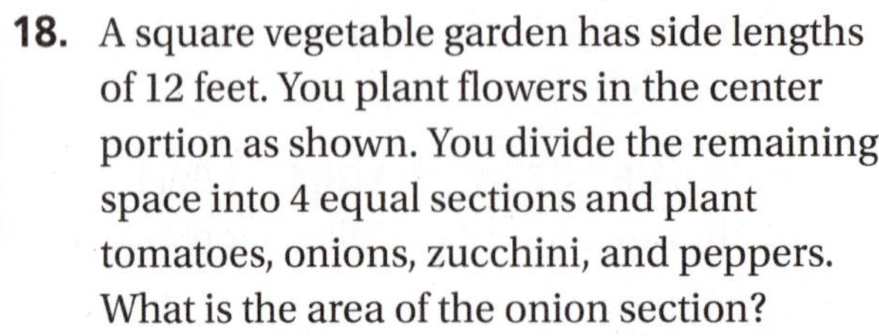

16. A square plot of land has side lengths of 40 meters. An archaeologist divides the land into 64 equal parts. What is the area of each part?

17. A glass block window is made of two different-sized glass squares. The window has side lengths of 40 inches. The large glass squares have side lengths of 10 inches. Find the total area of the small glass squares.

18. A square vegetable garden has side lengths of 12 feet. You plant flowers in the center portion as shown. You divide the remaining space into 4 equal sections and plant tomatoes, onions, zucchini, and peppers. What is the area of the onion section?

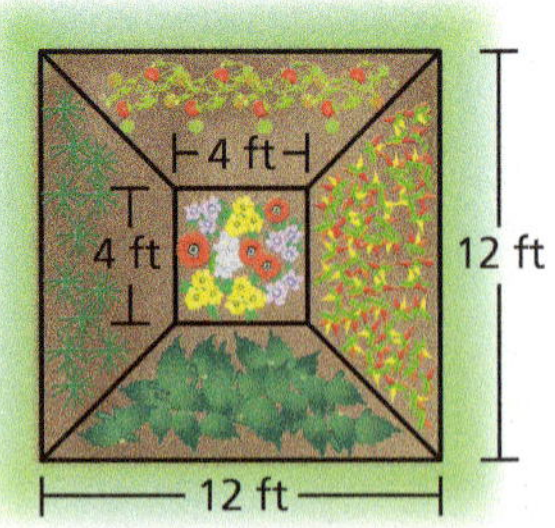

Laurie's Notes

EXAMPLE 4

- Draw or display the diagram. Have students *Turn and Talk* about what they know and what the problem is asking them to find.
- Give time for conversation and then use *Thumbs Up* to determine which students feel they can explain how to start this problem. Encourage students who are not confident to move next to a person with a thumb up. Students need practice explaining their thinking to someone who doesn't understand.
- **FYI:** There are different strategies that can be used to solve this problem. When de-briefing the problem, it is important to solicit multiple strategies.
- **MP6 Attend to Precision:** The question is asking students to find area. Check that students have labeled their answers with the correct units.

Self-Assessment for Problem Solving

- Encourage students to use a Four Square to complete the exercises. Until students become comfortable with the problem-solving plan, they may only be ready to complete the first square.

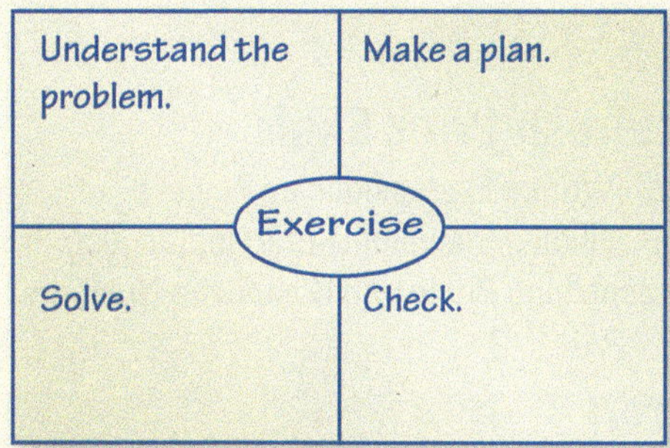

- Each of the exercises involves the concept of area. Discuss what area means and conservation of area, meaning a region does not change in area when it is subdivided into smaller parts.
- Students should begin by working independently, so they can assess their understanding of writing a numerical expression to represent a contextual problem. After the initial time working alone, allow students to move to different locations in the classroom to offer or solicit help. There may be multiple approaches to solving these problems.
- As students are working through the exercises, encourage them to assess their understanding of the learning target and success criteria, keeping the focus on the learning target.

The Success Criteria Self-Assessment chart can be found in the *Student Journal* or online at *BigIdeasMath.com.*

Closure

- **Exit Ticket:** Evaluate each expression.
  a. $18 + 4 \times 10$ 58 **b.** $12 \div 6 \times 2$ 4 **c.** $5^2 - 20 + 3(24 - 18)$ 23

Extra Example 4

The diagram shows stations in a classroom. The areas of Stations 1 and 3 are the same. What is the area of Station 3?

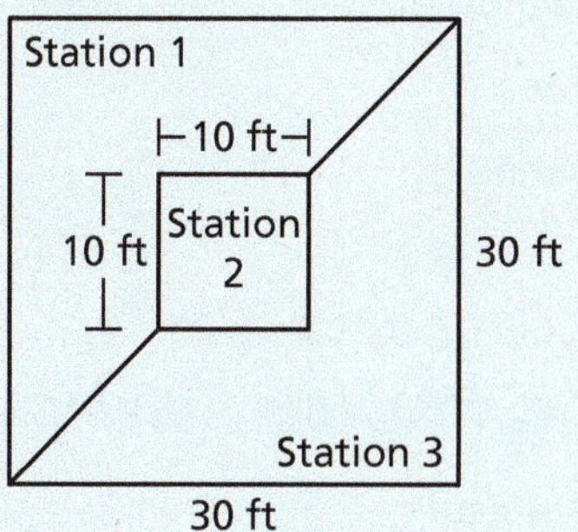

400 ft^2

Self-Assessment for Problem Solving

16. 25 m^2

17. 700 in.^{2}

18. 32 ft^2

Learning Target

Write and evaluate numerical expressions using the order of operations.

Success Criteria

- Explain why there is a need for a standard order of operations.
- Evaluate numerical expressions involving several operations, exponents, and grouping symbols.
- Write numerical expressions involving exponents to represent a real-life problem.

Review & Refresh

1. 11^4
2. 13^5
3. $h = 8$ in.
4. $\ell = 5$ m
5. composite
6. prime
7. prime

Concepts, Skills, & Problem Solving

8. 60; 40; no
9. 10; 22; no
10. 8
11. 5
12. 60
13. 24
14. 6
15. 88
16. 27
17. 13
18. 16
19. 41
20. 2
21. 24
22. 32
23. 204
24. 0.75
25. no; $9 + 3 \times 3^2 = 9 + 27 = 36$
26. no; $19 - 6 + 12 = 13 + 12 = 25$
27. 8

Assignment Guide and Concept Check

Check out the Dynamic Assessment System.
BigIdeasMath.com

Scaffold assignments to support all students in their learning progression. The suggested assignments are a starting point. Continue to assign additional exercises and revisit with spaced practice to move every student toward proficiency.

Level	Assignment 1	Assignment 2
Emerging	2, 4, 7, 9, 10, 13, 17, 20, 28, 29	25, 26, 27, 30, 35, 37, 40, 41, 43
Proficient	2, 4, 7, 9, 11, 15, 20, 23, 30, 37	25, 26, 33, 36, 38, 41, 42, 43
Advanced	2, 4, 7, 9, 12, 18, 22, 24, 33, 38	25, 26, 36, 42, 43, 44, 45, 46

- Assignment 1 is for use after students complete the Self-Assessment for Concepts & Skills.
- Assignment 2 is for use after students complete the Self-Assessment for Problem Solving.
- The red exercises can be used as a concept check.

Review & Refresh Prior Skills

Exercises 1 and 2 Writing Expressions as Powers
Exercises 3 and 4 Finding the Volume of a Rectangular Prism
Exercises 5–7 Identifying Prime and Composite Numbers

Common Errors

- **Exercises 12, 18, and 19** Students may want to evaluate multiplication before division in an expression (or a part of an expression) that contains division before multiplication from left to right. Remind students that multiplication and division are performed from left to right.

1.2 Practice

Go to *BigIdeasMath.com* to get HELP with solving the exercises.

Review & Refresh

Write the product as a power.

1. $11 \times 11 \times 11 \times 11$
2. $13 \times 13 \times 13 \times 13 \times 13$

Find the missing dimension of the rectangular prism.

3. 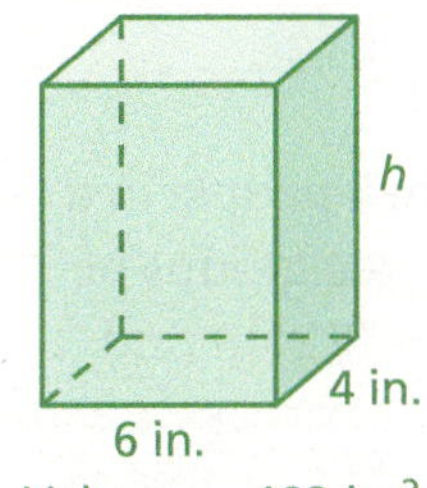

4. 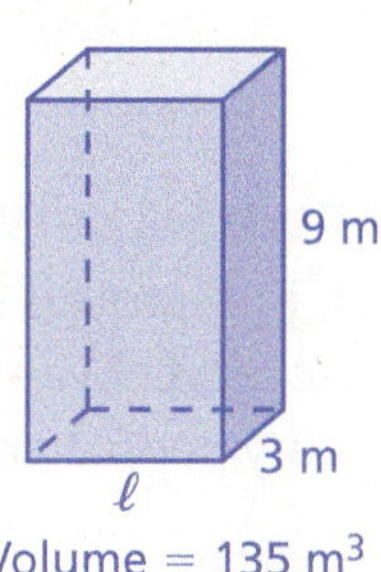

Tell whether the number is prime or composite.

5. 9
6. 11
7. 23

Concepts, Skills, & Problem Solving

COMPARING DIFFERENT ORDERS **Find the value of the expression by using different orders of operations. Are your answers the same?** (See Exploration 1, p. 9.)

8. Add, then multiply. $4 + 6 \times 6$ Multiply, then add. $4 + 6 \times 6$
9. Subtract, then multiply. $5 \times 5 - 3$ Multiply, then subtract. $5 \times 5 - 3$

USING ORDER OF OPERATIONS **Evaluate the expression.**

10. $5 + 18 \div 6$
11. $(11 - 3) \div 2 + 1$
12. $45 \div 9 \times 12$
13. $6^2 - 3 \cdot 4$
14. $42 \div (15 - 2^3)$
15. $4^2 \cdot 2 + 8 \cdot 7$
16. $(5^2 - 2) \times 1^5 + 4$
17. $4 + 2 \times 3^2 - 9$
18. $8 \div 2 \times 3 + 4^2 \div 4$
19. $3^2 + 12 \div (6 - 3) \times 8$
20. $(10 + 4) \div (26 - 19)$
21. $(5^2 - 4) \cdot 2 - 18$
22. $2 \times [(16 - 8) \times 2]$
23. $12 + 8 \times 3^3 - 24$
24. $6^2 \div [(2 + 4) \times 2^3]$

MP YOU BE THE TEACHER **Your friend evaluates the expression. Is your friend correct? Explain your reasoning.**

25. $9 + 3 \times 3^2 = 12 \times 9$
$= 108$

26. $19 - 6 + 12 = 19 - 18$
$= 1$

27. **MP PROBLEM SOLVING** You need to read 20 poems in 5 days for an English project. Each poem is 2 pages long. Evaluate the expression $20 \times 2 \div 5$ to find how many pages you need to read each day.

USING ORDER OF OPERATIONS **Evaluate the expression.**

28. $12 - 2(7 - 4)$

29. $4(3 + 5) - 3(6 - 2)$

30. $6 + \frac{1}{4}(12 - 8)$

31. $9^2 - 8(6 + 2)$

32. $4(3 - 1)^3 + 7(6) - 5^2$

33. $8\left[\left(1\frac{1}{6} + \frac{5}{6}\right) \div 4\right]$

34. $7^2 - 2\left(\frac{11}{8} - \frac{3}{8}\right)$

35. $8(7.3 + 3.7 - 8) \div 2$

36. $2^4(5.2 - 3.2) \div 4$

37. $\frac{6^2(3 + 5)}{4}$

38. $\frac{12^2 - 4(6) + 1}{11^2}$

39. $\frac{26 \div 2 + 5}{3^2 - 3}$

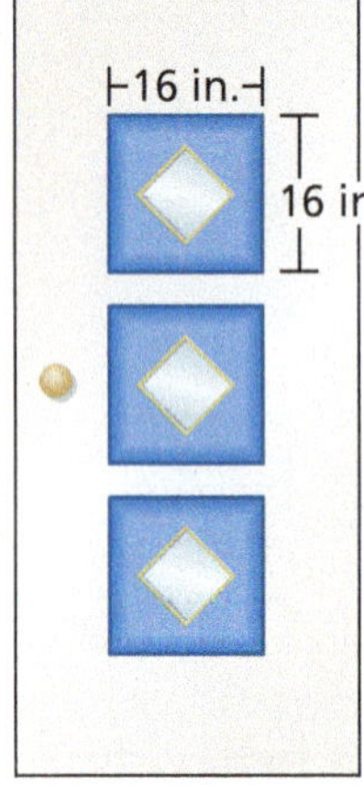

40. **MP PROBLEM SOLVING** Before a show, there are 8 people in a theater. Five groups of 4 people enter, and then three groups of 2 people leave. Evaluate the expression $8 + 5(4) - 3(2)$ to find how many people are in the theater.

41. **MP MODELING REAL LIFE** The front door of a house is painted white and blue. Each window is a square with a side length of 7 inches. What is the area of the door that is painted blue?

42. **MP PROBLEM SOLVING** You buy 6 notebooks, 10 folders, 1 pack of pencils, and 1 lunch box for school. After using a $10 gift card, how much do you owe? Explain how you solved the problem.

43. **OPEN-ENDED** Use all four operations and at least one exponent to write an expression that has a value of 100.

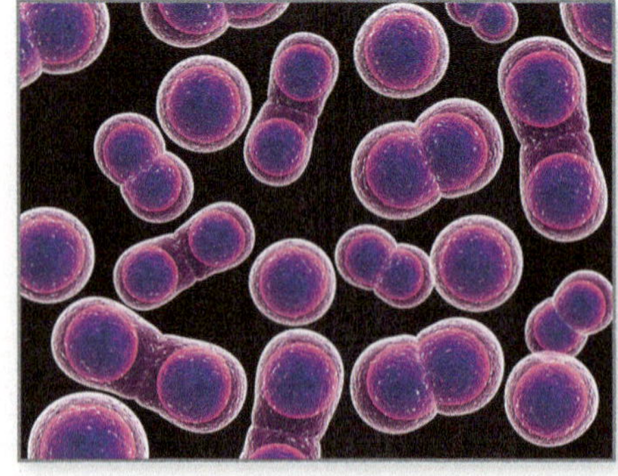

44. **MP REPEATED REASONING** A Petri dish contains 35 cells. Every day, each cell in the Petri dish divides into 2 cells in a process called *mitosis*. How many cells are there after 14 days? Justify your answer.

45. **MP REASONING** Two groups collect litter along the side of a road. It takes each group 5 minutes to clean up a 200-yard section. How long does it take both groups working together to clean up 2 *miles*? Explain how you solved the problem.

46. **MP NUMBER SENSE** Copy each statement. Insert +, −, ×, or ÷ symbols to make each statement true.

a. $27 \;\square\; 3 \;\square\; 5 \;\square\; 2 = 19$

b. $9^2 \;\square\; 11 \;\square\; 8 \;\square\; 4 \;\square\; 1 = 60$

c. $5 \;\square\; 6 \;\square\; 15 \;\square\; 9 = 24$

d. $14 \;\square\; 2 \;\square\; 7 \;\square\; 3 \;\square\; 9 = 10$

Common Errors

- **Exercises 28–36** Students may forget that parentheses can be used to indicate multiplication. Remind them of the various ways to indicate multiplication.
- **Exercises 37–39** Students may be unsure of how to evaluate these expressions. Remind them that the fraction bar means division. If necessary, have students rewrite the expressions using division symbols in place of the fraction bars. Be sure they insert additional parentheses if necessary.
- **Exercise 45** Students may not see the implication that the two groups are working *simultaneously* and they may end up with a time of 88 minutes instead of 44 minutes. Point out that the two groups are working at the same time, so together they are able to clean up 400 yards in 5 minutes.

Mini-Assessment

Evaluate the expression.

1. $4 + 12 \div 3$ 8
2. $20 - 4 \cdot 2^2$ 4
3. $(6^2 - 3) \times (2 + 8)$ 330
4. $4^3 \div 2 - \frac{1}{4}(7 - 5)^2$ 31
5. You have four $1 bills, three $5 bills, and two $10 bills in your wallet. How much money do you have in your wallet? $39

Section Resources

Surface Level	Deep Level
Resources by Chapter • Extra Practice • Reteach • Puzzle Time Student Journal • Self-Assessment • Practice Differentiating the Lesson Tutorial Videos Skills Review Handbook Skills Trainer	Resources by Chapter • Enrichment and Extension Graphic Organizers Dynamic Assessment System • Section Practice
Transfer Level	
Dynamic Assessment System • Mid-Chapter Quiz	Assessment Book • Mid-Chapter Quiz

Concepts, Skills, & Problem Solving

28. 6 **29.** 20

30. 7 **31.** 17

32. 49 **33.** 4

34. 47 **35.** 12

36. 8 **37.** 72

38. 1 **39.** 3

40. 22 **41.** 621 in.^{2}

42. $23; Add the prices of the items you buy. Then subtract the amount of the gift card from the total.

43. *Sample answer:* $(5^2 - 3 \times 5) \div 2 + 95$

44. 573,440; *Sample answer:* The cells double 14 times, and $35 \times 2^{14} = 573{,}440$.

45. 44 min; Two miles is 3520 yards. Each group can clean $200 \div 5 = 40$ yards each minute, so together the two groups can clean 80 yards each minute and $3520 \div 80 = 44$ minutes.

46. **a.** $27 \div 3 + 5 \times 2 = 19$

b. *Sample answer:* $9^2 + 11 - 8 \times 4 \div 1 = 60$

c. $5 \times 6 - 15 + 9 = 24$

d. $14 \times 2 \div 7 - 3 + 9 = 10$

Learning Target

Write a number as a product of prime factors and represent the product using exponents.

Success Criteria

- Find factor pairs of a number.
- Explain the meanings of prime and composite numbers.
- Create a factor tree to find the prime factors of a number.
- Write the prime factorization of a number.

Warm Up

Cumulative, vocabulary, and prerequisite skills practice opportunities are available in the *Resources by Chapter* or at *BigIdeasMath.com.*

ELL Support

Explain that the words *prime* and *factor* have special meanings in math. In everyday life, a factor is a circumstance that influences an outcome. Write the sentence, "She considers many factors before visiting her grandmother." Discuss what those factors may be. Tell students that in math, a factor is a whole number other than zero that when multiplied with another factor makes a product. The word *prime* means of the best quality, such as in the phrase *prime beef.* In math, however, a prime number is a whole number greater than 1 that can only be divided by 1 and itself.

Exploration 1

a. yes; $108 = 3 \cdot 3 \cdot 3 \cdot 2 \cdot 2$

b–c. See Additional Answers.

Laurie's Notes

COMMON CORE **STATE STANDARDS**
6.NS.B.4

Preparing to Teach

- In prior grades, students were introduced to **factor pairs** and prime numbers. They may have used a visual model to organize paired factors.

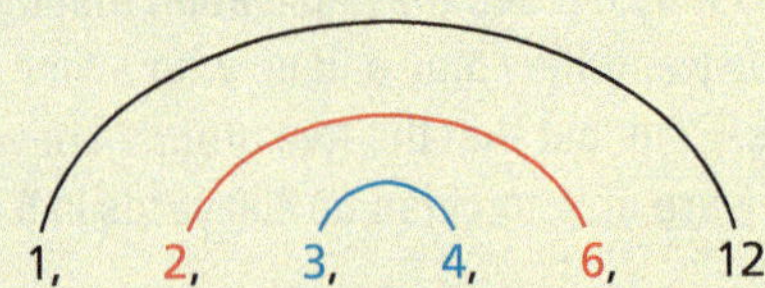

- This lesson builds on the basic skill of writing a number as the product of two factors. Now students will write a number as the product of its prime factors. This is known as the **prime factorization** of a number.
- Students need to know that **factor trees** for the same number may look different but will ultimately lead to the same prime factorization. A factor tree is an efficient way of investigating all the factors of a number.
- If your standards do not require prime factorization, you may skip this lesson and proceed to the next. If you choose to skip teaching prime factorization, be sure to use alternate methods when finding the GCF and LCM.

Motivate

- ? Write the number 2520 on the board. "What do you think is special about 2520?" Students may state that it is even, or that it ends in 0.
- ? "Because 2520 ends in 0, what number divides into it evenly?" 10
- ? "Because 2520 is an even number, what number divides into it evenly?" 2
- ? "What other numbers do you think divide into 2520 evenly?" Students may guess correctly that 2520 is divisible by all the numbers 1–10. This is a good time to check your students' knowledge of divisibility rules.

Exploration 1

- Students may be familiar with a fact family triangle. A factor tree is similar, but the branches continue to show additional fact families.

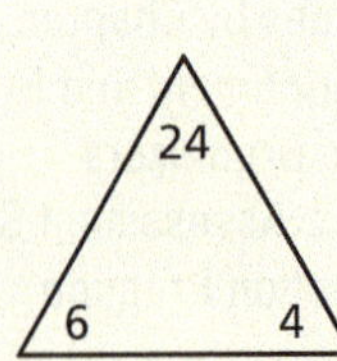

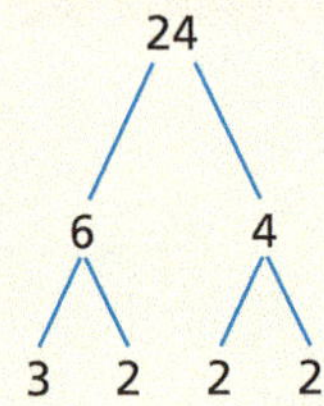

- The partial factor trees shown for 108 demonstrate that you need to know two factors of a number to begin the tree.
- Be sure that students understand how to correctly interpret a factor tree. For example, $108 = 2 \cdot 54$ can also be written as $108 = 2 \cdot 2 \cdot 27$ but cannot be written as $108 = 2 \cdot 54 \cdot 2 \cdot 27$. In other words, a number is not the product of all the numbers below it in the factor tree.
- In part (c), discuss students' observations.

1.3 Prime Factorization

Learning Target: Write a number as a product of prime factors and represent the product using exponents.

Success Criteria:
- I can find factor pairs of a number.
- I can explain the meanings of prime and composite numbers.
- I can create a factor tree to find the prime factors of a number.
- I can write the prime factorization of a number.

EXPLORATION 1 Rewriting Numbers as Products of Factors

Work with a partner. Two students use *factor trees* to write 108 as a product of factors, as shown below.

Student A

108

2 • 54

2 • 27

So, 108 = 2 • 2 • 27.

3 factors

Student B

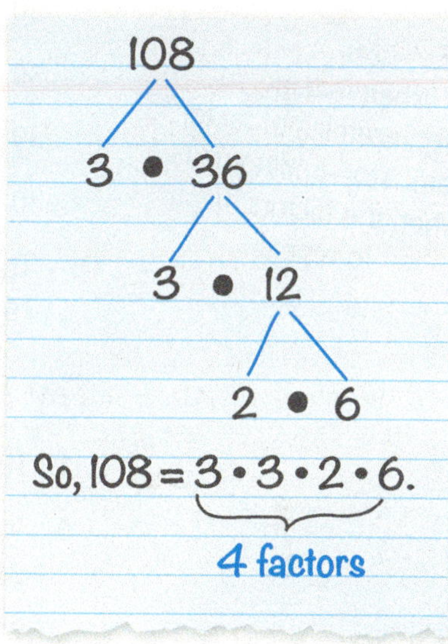

a. Without using 1 as a factor, can you write 108 as a product with more factors than each student used? Justify your answer.

Math Practice

Interpret Results
How do you know your answer makes sense?

b. Use factor trees to write 80, 162, and 300 as products of as many factors as possible. Do not use 1 as a factor.

c. Compare your results in parts (a) and (b) with other groups. For each number, identify the product with the greatest number of factors. What do these factors have in common?

1.3 Lesson

Because 2 is a factor of 10 and $2 \cdot 5 = 10$, 5 is also a factor of 10. The pair 2, 5 is called a **factor pair** of 10.

Key Vocabulary

factor pair, *p. 16*
prime factorization, *p. 16*
factor tree, *p. 16*

EXAMPLE 1 Finding Factor Pairs

The brass section of a marching band has 30 members. The band director arranges the brass section in rows. Each row has the same number of members. How many possible arrangements are there?

Use the factor pairs of 30 to find the number of arrangements.

$30 = 1 \cdot 30$ There could be 1 row of 30 or 30 rows of 1.

$30 = 2 \cdot 15$ There could be 2 rows of 15 or 15 rows of 2.

$30 = 3 \cdot 10$ There could be 3 rows of 10 or 10 rows of 3.

$30 = 5 \cdot 6$ There could be 5 rows of 6 or 6 rows of 5.

$30 = 6 \cdot 5$ The factors 5 and 6 are already listed.

There are 8 possible arrangements: 1 row of 30, 30 rows of 1, 2 rows of 15, 15 rows of 2, 3 rows of 10, 10 rows of 3, 5 rows of 6, or 6 rows of 5.

When making an organized list of factor pairs, stop finding pairs when the factors begin to repeat.

Try It **List the factor pairs of the number.**

1. 18 **2.** 24 **3.** 51

4. **WHAT IF?** The woodwinds section of the marching band has 38 members. Which has more possible arrangements, the brass section or the woodwinds section? Explain.

Key Idea

Prime Factorization

The **prime factorization** of a composite number is the number written as a product of its prime factors.

You can use factor pairs and a **factor tree** to help find the prime factorization of a number. The factor tree is complete when only prime factors appear in the product. A factor tree for 60 is shown.

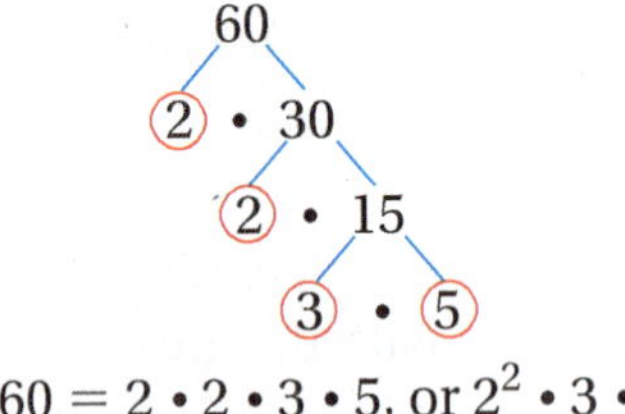

$60 = 2 \cdot 2 \cdot 3 \cdot 5$, or $2^2 \cdot 3 \cdot 5$

Remember

A *prime number* is a whole number greater than 1 with exactly two factors, 1 and itself. A *composite number* is a whole number greater than 1 with factors in addition to 1 and itself.

Laurie's Notes

Scaffolding Instruction

- Students have used their prior knowledge of prime numbers, and perhaps divisibility rules, to write a composite number as a product of its factors. After reviewing the vocabulary terms, students will progress from finding the factor pairs of a number to using a **factor tree** to find the prime factorization of a number.
- **Emerging:** Example 1 lays the foundation for understanding factor pairs and Example 2 provides more practice with prime factorization. Students may work through these examples using whiteboards, and then *Turn and Talk* with a partner.
- **Proficient:** After going through Example 1, students who are proficient with factor pairs, factor trees, and prime factorization can proceed to Self-Assessment Exercises 9–19.

Discuss

- Define a **factor pair** and give an example.
- ? "Can every number be written as a factor pair? Explain." Yes, every number can be written as 1 times itself.

EXAMPLE 1

- Pose the problem and have students share their work with a neighbor. The question of order, 2 • 15 versus 15 • 2, will likely arise.
- **Visual Model:** You can use 30 square tiles and ask how to form a rectangle using all of the tiles. The dimensions of the rectangles are factor pairs found in this example.
- In the context of the problem, 5 • 6 is a factor pair and it can be interpreted two ways: 5 rows of 6 or 6 rows of 5. It is still one factor pair.
- ? "How do you know that you have not forgotten or missed any factor pairs?" Listen for an understanding of the organized manner in which factor pairs are listed.

Try It

- **MP2 Reason Abstractly and Quantitatively:** Note that even though 38 > 30, 38 has fewer factor pairs than 30. Students should reason that the size of the number is not what determines the number of factor pairs.
- ⊙ When you have finished discussing the exercises, ask students to use *Thumbs Up* to indicate their understanding of the first success criterion.

Key Idea

- ? "What is a composite number?" a number greater than one that has more than two factors
- Write the definition of **prime factorization**.
- Work through the example shown, using the vocabulary terms: factors, prime, and composite.
- Remind students that 15 is odd, but not prime, and that the numbers 3 and 5 can be reversed. If time allows, ask students to name a factor pair of 60 that does not include a prime number. Then have them work in pairs to find the prime factorization and compare it to the example.

Scaffold instruction to support all students in their learning. Learning is individualized and you may want to group students differently as they move in and out of these levels with each skill and concept. Student self-assessment and feedback help guide your instructional decisions about how and when to layer support for all students to become proficient learners.

Extra Example 1

A technology classroom has 40 computers. The teacher arranges the computers in rows. Each row has the same number of computers. How many possible arrangements are there? 8

Try It

1. 1, 18; 2, 9; 3, 6
2. 1, 24; 2, 12; 3, 8; 4, 6
3. 1, 51; 3, 17
4. brass section; There are only 4 possible arrangements with the woodwinds section: 1 row of 38, 38 rows of 1, 2 rows of 19, or 19 rows of 2.

ELL Support

Explain to students that to find factor pairs, they can use the strategy of starting with 1 and working their way up the whole numbers. In other words, they ask, "Can the number be divided by 1? 2? 3? 4? 5? and so on." Have students work with a partner to complete Try It Exercises 1–4.

Beginner: Write the factor pairs.
Intermediate: Verbally describe the factor pairs.
Advanced: Explain how they found the answer.

Extra Example 2

Write the prime factorization of 45.

$3^2 \cdot 5$

Try It

5. $2^2 \cdot 5$
6. $2^3 \cdot 11$
7. $2 \cdot 3^2 \cdot 5$
8. $2 \cdot 3 \cdot 7 \cdot 11$

Self-Assessment for Concepts & Skills

9. $2 \cdot 7$
10. $2 \cdot 43$
11. $2^3 \cdot 5$
12. $2^2 \cdot 3 \cdot 43$
13. *Sample answer:* A composite number has whole number factors other than 1 and itself, but a prime number does not.
14. *Sample answer:* The factor pairs are repeated, so there are only 3 pairs.
15. 6, 9; The others are factor pairs of 56.

Laurie's Notes

EXAMPLE 2

- Ask students to name a factor pair of 48. Solicit at least two different ways in which the factor tree can be started.
- Work through two different versions of a factor tree for 48. As the push-pin note states, it is important for students to understand that the steps may be different, but the final prime factorization will be the same.
- ? "Why is 2 • 2 • 3 • 2 • 2 the same as 3 • 2 • 2 • 2 • 2?" Multiplication is commutative.
- ? "Why isn't 1 listed in the prime factorization of a number?" 1 is neither prime nor composite.
- When students finish, ask them to use *Thumbs Up* to indicate their understanding of starting a factor tree, as represented by the third success criterion. Students need to understand that how they start the factor tree maybe different, but the prime factorization will be the same.

Try It

- **Common Error:** In Exercise 5, students may begin to write a factor pair of 10 and 10. It is easy for them to forget that factor pairs must multiply to make the number, not add.
- In Exercise 8, encourage students to use divisibility rules to find the largest factor they can, using mental math, versus starting with 2 • 231.

Self-Assessment for Concepts & Skills

- Students have progressed from finding a factor pair of a number to finding its prime factorization, and writing the prime factorization using powers of primes. Are students comfortable with creating a factor tree? Can they approach a number differently from their peers and explain why they will arrive at the same prime factorization?
- Exercise 15 affords a view of the depth of student understanding of factor pairs by having to work backwards.
- Do students realize that they can check their prime factorizations by multiplying the factors?

ELL Support

Check student comprehension of Exercises 9–12. Allow students to work in pairs to complete the exercises. Have students write the prime factorization of each exercise and compare answers with another pair. Have groups discuss any differences and come to agreement on the prime factorization of each.

The Success Criteria Self-Assessment chart can be found in the *Student Journal* or online at *BigIdeasMath.com.*

EXAMPLE 2 Writing a Prime Factorization

Write the prime factorization of 48.

Choose any factor pair of 48 to begin the factor tree.

Notice that beginning with different factor pairs results in the same prime factorization. Every composite number has only one prime factorization.

Tree 1

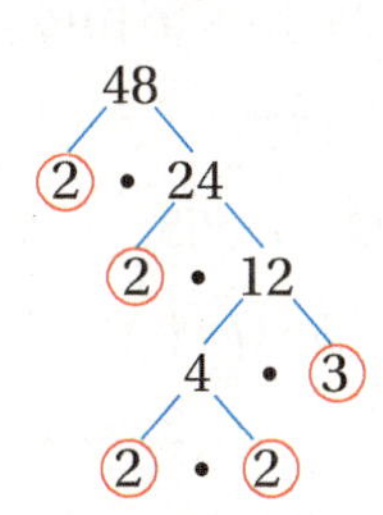

$48 = 2 \cdot 2 \cdot 3 \cdot 2 \cdot 2$

Find a factor pair and draw "branches."

Circle the prime factors as you find them.

Find factors until each branch ends at a prime factor.

Tree 2

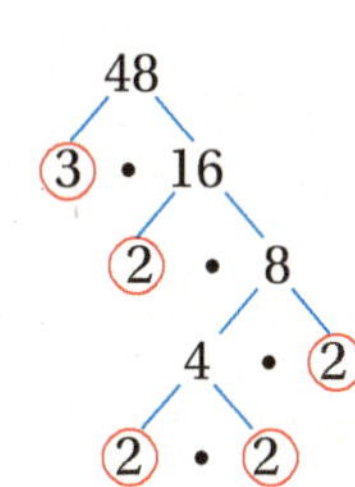

$48 = 3 \cdot 2 \cdot 2 \cdot 2 \cdot 2$

The prime factorization of 48 is $2 \cdot 2 \cdot 2 \cdot 2 \cdot 3$, or $2^4 \cdot 3$.

Try It **Write the prime factorization of the number.**

5. 20 **6.** 88 **7.** 90 **8.** 462

Self-Assessment for Concepts & Skills

Solve each exercise. Then rate your understanding of the success criteria in your journal.

WRITING A PRIME FACTORIZATION **Write the prime factorization of the number.**

9. 14 **10.** 86 **11.** 40 **12.** 516

13. **WRITING** Explain the difference between prime numbers and composite numbers.

14. **MP STRUCTURE** Your friend lists the following factor pairs and concludes that there are 6 factor pairs of 12. Explain why your friend is incorrect.

1, 12	2, 6	3, 4
12, 1	6, 2	4, 3

15. **WHICH ONE DOESN'T BELONG?** Which factor pair does *not* belong with the other three? Explain your reasoning.

2, 28 4, 14 6, 9 7, 8

EXAMPLE 3 Using a Prime Factorization

What is the greatest perfect square that is a factor of 1575?

Because 1575 has many factors, it is not efficient to list all of its factors and check for perfect squares. Use a factor tree to write the prime factorization of 1575. Then analyze the prime factors to find perfect square factors.

1575
25 • 63
(5) • (5) (7) • 9
(3) • (3)

$$1575 = 3 \cdot 3 \cdot 5 \cdot 5 \cdot 7$$

> **Math Practice**
>
> **View as Components**
>
> Explain how the prime factorization is used to identify 9, 25, and 225 as the only perfect square factors of 1575.

The prime factorization shows that 1575 has three factors other than 1 that are perfect squares.

$3 \cdot 3 = 9$

$5 \cdot 5 = 25$

$(3 \cdot 5) \cdot (3 \cdot 5) = 15 \cdot 15 = 225$

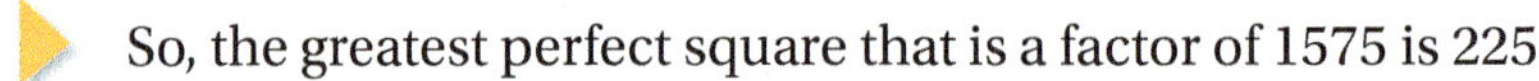

So, the greatest perfect square that is a factor of 1575 is 225.

Self-Assessment for Problem Solving

Solve each exercise. Then rate your understanding of the success criteria in your journal.

16. A group of 20 friends plays a card game. The game can be played with 2 or more teams of equal size. Each team must have at least 2 members. List the possible numbers and sizes of teams.

17. You arrange 150 chairs in rows for a school play. You want each row to have the same number of chairs. How many possible arrangements are there? Are all of the possible arrangements appropriate for the play? Explain.

18. What is the least perfect square that is a factor of 4536? What is the greatest perfect square that is a factor of 4536?

19. **DIG DEEPER!** The prime factorization of a number is $2^4 \times 3^4 \times 5^4 \times 7^2$. Is the number a perfect square? Explain your reasoning.

Laurie's Notes

EXAMPLE 3

- In this example, students have an opportunity to use prime factorization to investigate special characteristics of a number.
- Students need to find the prime factorization of 1575 to answer the question.
- Ask students which factor pair they will use to begin their factor trees of 1575. Have students use whiteboards to record and share their answers. Discuss similarity in answers. Expect to see 5 and 315, or 9 and 175. Ask why they know that 25 is a factor. Connect 25 to a quarter and 1575 to $15.75.

Self-Assessment for Problem Solving

- Allow time in class for students to practice using the problem-solving plan. Remember, some students may only be able to complete the first step.
- The first two exercises assess the meaning of factor pairs, and the last two are applications of prime factorizations.
- **MP4 Model with Mathematics:** Remind students to check to make sure their answers make sense in the context of the problem.
- Have students work independently. Give enough time for students to complete the four problems. When all students have completed the exercises, place students into groups of four to discuss their solutions, and reach a consensus. Can they check their solutions?
- If time allows, ask four groups to each explain one of the exercises. Be sure to choose groups that you know have the correct work and answer. If any groups are still using diagrams for Exercises 16 and 17, work with them separately so that they see the pattern without drawing the diagram.

The Success Criteria Self-Assessment chart can be found in the *Student Journal* or online at *BigIdeasMath.com.*

Learning Target

Write a number as a product of prime factors and represent the product using exponents.

Success Criteria

- Find factor pairs of a number.
- Explain the meanings of prime and composite numbers.
- Create a factor tree to find the prime factors of a number.
- Write the prime factorization of a number.

Closure

- **Exit Ticket:** The class ended and a student didn't finish finding the prime factorization. The student's first step was 8×24.
  a. What was the original number? 192
  b. Finish finding the prime factorization. $2^6 \times 3$

Extra Example 3

What is the greatest perfect square that is a factor of 675? 225

Self-Assessment for Problem Solving

16. 2 teams of 10, 4 teams of 5, 5 teams of 4, 10 teams of 2

17. 12; no; *Sample answer:* 150 rows with 1 chair each is not practical.

18. 1; 324

19. yes; $2^4 \times 3^4 \times 5^4 \times 7^2 = (2^2 \times 3^2 \times 5^2 \times 7) \times (2^2 \times 3^2 \times 5^2 \times 7)$

Formative Assessment Tip

Exit Ticket

This technique asks students to respond to a question at the end of a lesson, activity, or learning experience. The *Exit Ticket* allows you to collect evidence of student learning. I cut scrap paper into smaller pieces so that "exit tickets" can be distributed quickly to students.

The *Exit Ticket* is helpful in planning instruction. During the class there may be students you have not heard from. They may not have raised their hands, or they may have been less vocal when working with partners. The *Exit Ticket* helps you gauge the ability of all students to answer a particular type of question. Collect the *Exit Tickets* and use the responses to inform subsequent instruction.

Review & Refresh

1. 34
2. 44
3. 13

4–6. See Additional Answers.

7. 102; $408 \div 4 = (400 + 8) \div 4$
8. 314; $628 \div 2 = (600 + 20 + 8) \div 2$
9. 323; $969 \div 3 = (900 + 60 + 9) \div 3$
10. equilateral, equiangular, acute
11. isosceles, obtuse
12. isosceles, right

Concepts, Skills, & Problem Solving

13. $2 \cdot 2 \cdot 3 \cdot 5$
14. $3 \cdot 3 \cdot 7$
15. $2 \cdot 2 \cdot 2 \cdot 3 \cdot 5$
16. $2 \cdot 3 \cdot 5 \cdot 5$
17. 1, 15; 3, 5
18. 1, 22; 2, 11
19. 1, 34; 2, 17
20. 1, 39; 3, 13
21. 1, 45; 3, 15; 5, 9
22. 1, 54; 2, 27; 3, 18; 6, 9
23. 1, 59
24. 1, 61
25. 1, 100; 2, 50; 4, 25; 5, 20; 10, 10
26. 1, 58; 2, 29
27. 1, 25; 5, 5
28. 1, 76; 2, 38; 4, 19
29. 1, 52; 2, 26; 4, 13
30. 1, 88; 2, 44; 4, 22; 8, 11
31. 1, 71
32. 1, 91; 7, 13
33. 2^4
34. 5^2
35. $2 \cdot 3 \cdot 5$
36. $2 \cdot 13$
37. $2^2 \cdot 3 \cdot 7$
38. $2 \cdot 3^3$
39. $5 \cdot 13$
40. $7 \cdot 11$
41. $2 \cdot 23$
42. $3 \cdot 13$
43. $3^2 \cdot 11$
44. $2^3 \cdot 3$
45. $3^2 \cdot 5 \cdot 7$
46. $2 \cdot 5 \cdot 7^2$
47. $2^2 \cdot 5 \cdot 7$
48. $2^7 \cdot 5$
49. 180
50. 1575
51. 12,584

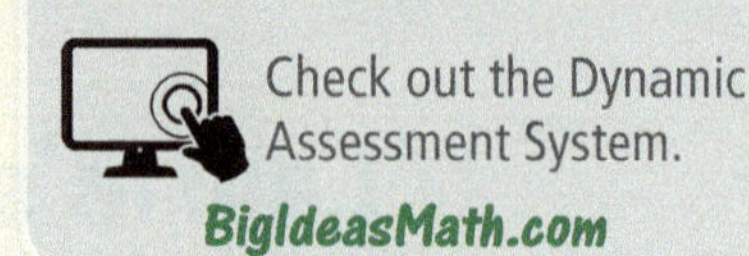

Assignment Guide and Concept Check

Scaffold assignments to support all students in their learning progression. The suggested assignments are a starting point. Continue to assign additional exercises and revisit with spaced practice to move every student toward proficiency.

Level	Assignment 1	Assignment 2
Emerging	3, 6, 9, 12, 16, 17, 20, 22, 33, 35, 49	25, 44, 50, 52, 53, 57, 65, 66
Proficient	3, 6, 9, 12, 16, 20, 25, 27, 35, 44, 50	46, 51, 52, 57, 59, 65, 66, 67, 68
Advanced	3, 6, 9, 12, 16, 25, 31, 32, 38, 46, 51	52, 64, 66, 67, 68, 69, 70, 71, 72

- Assignment 1 is for use after students complete the Self-Assessment for Concepts & Skills.
- Assignment 2 is for use after students complete the Self-Assessment for Problem Solving.
- The red exercises can be used as a concept check.

Review & Refresh Prior Skills

Exercises 1–3 Using Order of Operations
Exercises 4–6 Graphing Line Segments
Exercises 7–9 Using the Distributive Property
Exercises 10–12 Classifying Triangles

Common Errors

- **Exercises 33–48** Students may think that smaller numbers have fewer factors. Remind students to keep finding factors until all factors are prime numbers.
- **Exercises 49–51** Students may incorrectly write the exponent as a factor. Remind them that the exponent is the number of times the base is used as a factor. That is, $3^2 = 3 \cdot 3$, not $3 \cdot 2$.

1.3 Practice

Review & Refresh

Evaluate the expression.

1. $2 + 4^2(5 - 3)$

2. $2^3 + 4 \times 3^2$

3. $9 \times 5 - 2^4\left(\frac{5}{2} - \frac{1}{2}\right)$

Plot the points in a coordinate plane. Draw a line segment connecting the points.

4. (1, 1) and (4, 3)

5. (2, 3) and (5, 9)

6. (2, 5) and (4, 8)

Use the Distributive Property to find the quotient. Justify your answer.

7. $408 \div 4$

8. $628 \div 2$

9. $969 \div 3$

Classify the triangle in as many ways as possible.

10.

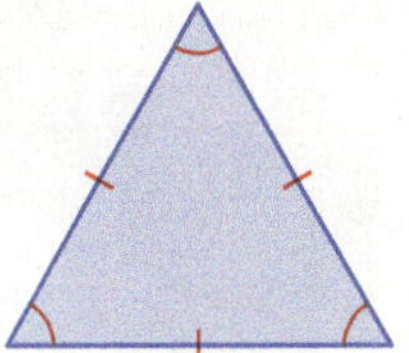

11.

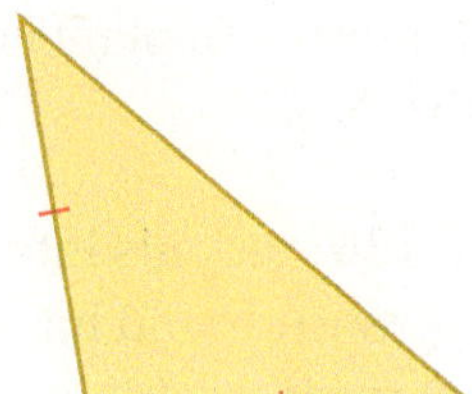

12.

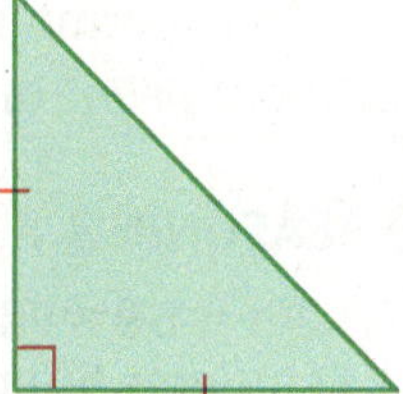

Concepts, Skills, & Problem Solving

REWRITING A NUMBER **Write the number as a product of as many factors as possible. Do not use 1 as a factor.** (See Exploration 1, p. 15.)

13. 60 **14.** 63 **15.** 120 **16.** 150

FINDING FACTOR PAIRS **List the factor pairs of the number.**

17. 15 **18.** 22 **19.** 34 **20.** 39

21. 45 **22.** 54 **23.** 59 **24.** 61

25. 100 **26.** 58 **27.** 25 **28.** 76

29. 52 **30.** 88 **31.** 71 **32.** 91

WRITING A PRIME FACTORIZATION **Write the prime factorization of the number.**

33. 16 **34.** 25 **35.** 30 **36.** 26

37. 84 **38.** 54 **39.** 65 **40.** 77

41. 46 **42.** 39 **43.** 99 **44.** 24

45. 315 **46.** 490 **47.** 140 **48.** 640

USING A PRIME FACTORIZATION **Find the number represented by the prime factorization.**

49. $2^2 \cdot 3^2 \cdot 5$

50. $3^2 \cdot 5^2 \cdot 7$

51. $2^3 \cdot 11^2 \cdot 13$

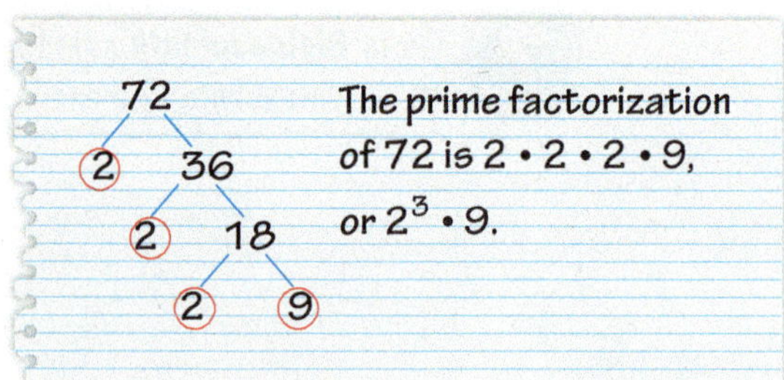

52. **YOU BE THE TEACHER** Your friend finds the prime factorization of 72. Is your friend correct? Explain your reasoning.

USING A PRIME FACTORIZATION Find the greatest perfect square that is a factor of the number.

53. 250	**54.** 275	**55.** 392	**56.** 338
57. 244	**58.** 650	**59.** 756	**60.** 1290
61. 2205	**62.** 1890	**63.** 495	**64.** 4725

65. **VOCABULARY** A botanist separates plants into equal groups of 5 for an experiment. Is the total number of plants in the experiment *prime* or *composite*? Explain.

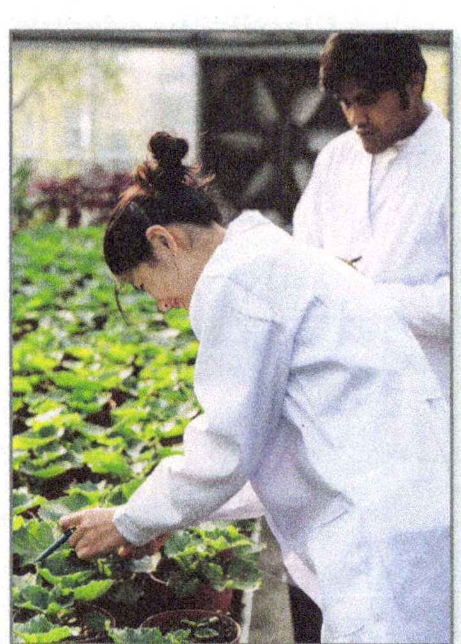

66. **MP REASONING** A teacher divides 36 students into equal groups for a scavenger hunt. Each group should have at least 4 students but no more than 8 students. What are the possible group sizes?

67. **CRITICAL THINKING** Is 2 the only even prime number? Explain.

68. **MP LOGIC** One table at a bake sale has 75 cookies. Another table has 60 cupcakes. Which table allows for more rectangular arrangements? Explain.

69. **PERFECT NUMBERS** A *perfect number* is a number that equals the sum of its factors, not including itself. For example, the factors of 28 are 1, 2, 4, 7, 14, and 28. Because $1 + 2 + 4 + 7 + 14 = 28$, 28 is a perfect number. What are the perfect numbers between 1 and 27?

70. **MP REPEATED REASONING** Choose any two perfect squares and find their product. Then multiply your answer by another perfect square. Continue this process. Are any of the products perfect squares? What can you conclude?

71. **MP PROBLEM SOLVING** The stage manager of a school play creates a rectangular stage that has whole number dimensions and an area of 42 square yards. String lights will outline the stage. What is the least number of yards of string lights needed to enclose the stage?

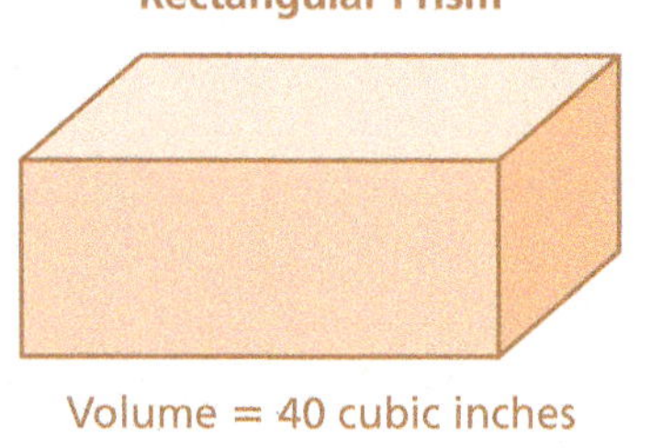

72. **DIG DEEPER!** Consider the rectangular prism shown. Using only whole number dimensions, how many different prisms are possible? Explain.

Common Errors

- **Exercise 69** Students may find the prime factorizations of the numbers between 1 and 27 instead of listing the factor pairs. Remind students to list all factor pairs.

Mini-Assessment

1. List the factor pairs of 36. 1, 36; 2, 18; 3, 12; 4, 9; 6, 6
2. Write the prime factorization of 78. $2 \cdot 3 \cdot 13$
3. Write the prime factorization of 40. $2^3 \cdot 5$
4. What is the greatest perfect square that is a factor of 192? 64

Section Resources

Surface Level	Deep Level
Resources by Chapter • Extra Practice • Reteach • Puzzle Time Student Journal • Self-Assessment • Practice Differentiating the Lesson Tutorial Videos Skills Review Handbook Skills Trainer	Resources by Chapter • Enrichment and Extension Graphic Organizers Dynamic Assessment System • Section Practice

Concepts, Skills, & Problem Solving

52. no; 9 is not prime.

53. 25 **54.** 25

55. 196 **56.** 169

57. 4 **58.** 25

59. 36 **60.** 1

61. 441 **62.** 9

63. 9 **64.** 225

65. composite; *Sample answer:* 5 is a factor of the total.

66. 9 groups of 4 students, 6 group of 6 students

67. yes; The rest of the even whole numbers have 2 as a factor.

68. cupcake table; Because 60 has more factors than 75, there are more rectangular arrangements.

69. 6

70. yes; The product of two perfect squares is a perfect square.

71. 26 yd

72. 6; There are 6 unique arrangements of length, width, and height using the factors of 40. (Note that $1 \times 1 \times 40$ names the same prism as $40 \times 1 \times 1$.); $1 \times 1 \times 40$, $1 \times 2 \times 20$, $1 \times 4 \times 10$, $1 \times 5 \times 8$, $2 \times 2 \times 10$, $2 \times 4 \times 5$

Learning Target

Find the greatest common factor of two numbers.

Success Criteria

- Explain the meaning of factors of a number.
- Use lists of factors to identify the greatest common factor of numbers.
- Use prime factors to identify the greatest common factor of numbers.

Warm Up

Cumulative, vocabulary, and prerequisite skills practice opportunities are available in the *Resources by Chapter* or at *BigIdeasMath.com.*

ELL Support

Explain the comparative and superlative word endings *–er* and *–est* by writing *small, smaller,* and *smallest* on the board. Ask a volunteer to draw a small circle. Then ask another student to draw a smaller circle. Ask, "Which one is smallest?" Explain that the word *great* means large, and that the greatest common factor is the largest of the factors that are shared by two or more numbers.

Exploration 1

a–d. See Additional Answers.

e. It is the greatest of the common factors; The greatest common factors are circled in diagrams for parts (a) through (d).

Exploration 2

a. 18 and 27, 180 and 55; $2 \cdot 3 \cdot 3 = 18, 3 \cdot 3 \cdot 3 = 27,$ $2 \cdot 2 \cdot 3 \cdot 3 \cdot 5 = 180, 5 \cdot 11 = 55$

b–d. See Additional Answers.

Laurie's Notes

STATE STANDARDS
6.NS.B.4

Preparing to Teach

- The ability to find all factors, including prime factors, is essential to finding the **greatest common factor** (GCF). **Common factors** and the GCF are useful when working with fractions, applications of division, and eventually algebraic rational expressions.
- Students should see that finding commonalities in two sets is not limited to sets of numbers, as demonstrated in the Motivate.
- **MP5 Use Appropriate Tools Strategically:** There are often different strategies or methods for solving a problem. A mathematically proficient student is able to assess which method will be more efficient, and why. Using lists of factors is more efficient for finding the GCF of 16 and 20, while using prime factorizations is more efficient for finding the GCF of 32, 48, and 120.

Motivate

- Introduce a **Venn diagram** to students by taking a survey of students who own a cat or a dog. Create and display a Venn diagram for the two sets. See the Teaching Strategy on page T-23.
- Use the survey to select several students that own a cat, a dog, and both a cat and a dog. Place the initials of each student in the appropriate location of the Venn diagram. The goal is for students to understand the characteristics of each region.

Exploration 1

- Expect that students will need to write, erase, and write again as they list the factors of each pair of numbers.
- **MP5 Use Appropriate Tools Strategically:** Calculators can be used to support students in finding factors.
- ? Have students share their work. Ask, "Will there always be at least one number in the overlap? Explain." Yes, 1 is always a common factor.
- **FYI:** Two numbers that only have 1 as a common factor are called *relatively prime.*
- **Connection:** Writing the factors in a Venn diagram is similar to using lists of factors for finding the GCF. A Venn diagram allows students to see that there can be several common factors but only one greatest common factor.

Exploration 2

- **MP1 Make Sense of Problems and Persevere in Solving Them:** Students must make sense of the structure of the Venn diagram, and how it visually represents the factors of two numbers. Each number in the overlap is a factor of both original numbers.
- **Note:** Part (b) is similar to part (a) in the first exploration, however, part (b) only asks for prime factors.
- Ask volunteers to share their reasoning about each part.
- In part (d), ask guiding questions so students recognize two methods for finding the GCF: using lists of factors and using prime factorizations.
- **Common Error:** Students may choose only the largest prime number in the overlap of the two circles. Guide those students through another example to clarify any misunderstanding.

1.4 Greatest Common Factor

Learning Target: Find the greatest common factor of two numbers.

Success Criteria:
- I can explain the meaning of factors of a number.
- I can use lists of factors to identify the greatest common factor of numbers.
- I can use prime factors to identify the greatest common factor of numbers.

A **Venn diagram** uses circles to describe relationships between two or more sets. The Venn diagram shows the factors of 12 and 15. Numbers that are factors of both 12 and 15 are represented by the overlap of the two circles.

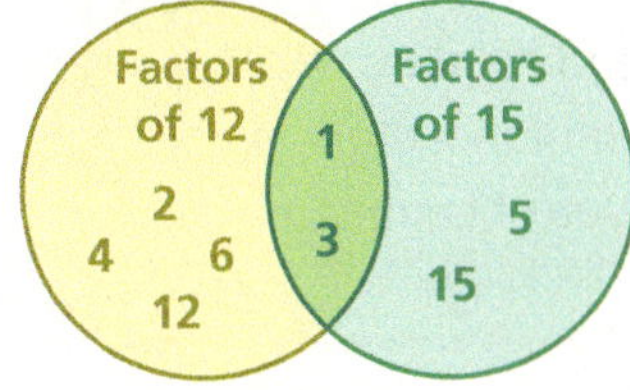

EXPLORATION 1

Identifying Common Factors

Work with a partner. In parts (a)–(d), create a Venn diagram that represents the factors of each number and identify any *common factors*.

a. 36 and 48

b. 16 and 56

c. 30 and 75

d. 54 and 90

e. Look at the Venn diagrams in parts (a)–(d). Explain how to identify the *greatest common factor* of each pair of numbers. Then circle it in each diagram.

EXPLORATION 2

Using Prime Factors

Work with a partner.

a. Each Venn diagram represents the prime factorizations of two numbers. Identify each pair of numbers. Explain your reasoning.

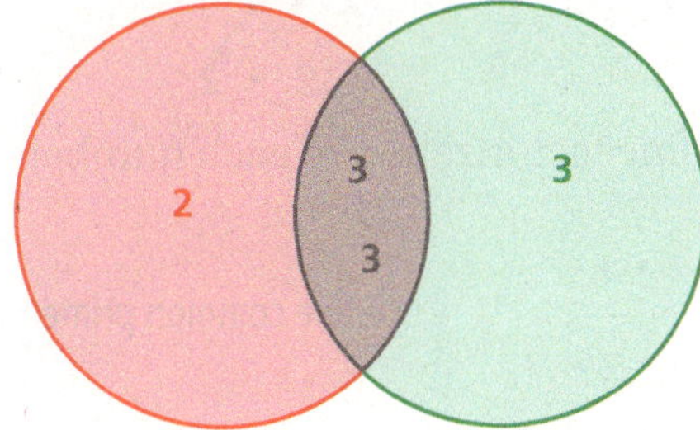

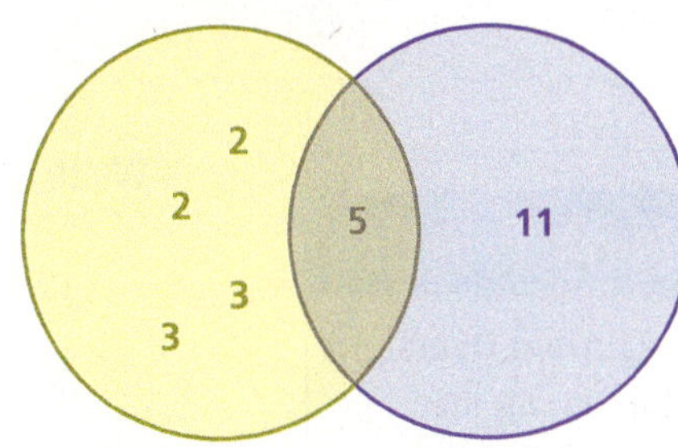

b. Create a Venn diagram that represents the prime factorizations of 36 and 48.

c. Repeat part (b) for the remaining number pairs in Exploration 1.

d. MP **STRUCTURE** Make a conjecture about the relationship between the greatest common factors you found in Exploration 1 and the numbers in the overlaps of the Venn diagrams you just created.

Math Practice

Interpret a Solution

What does the diagram representing the prime factorizations mean?

1.4 Lesson

Factors that are shared by two or more numbers are called **common factors**. The greatest of the common factors is called the **greatest common factor** (GCF). One way to find the GCF of two or more numbers is by listing factors.

Key Vocabulary
Venn diagram, *p. 21*
common factors, *p. 22*
greatest common factor, *p. 22*

EXAMPLE 1 Finding the GCF Using Lists of Factors

Find the GCF of 24 and 40.

List the factors of each number.

Factors of 24: 1, 2, 3, 4, 6, 8, 12, 24

Factors of 40: 1, 2, 4, 5, 8, 10, 20, 40

Circle the common factors.

The common factors of 24 and 40 are 1, 2, 4, and 8. The greatest of these common factors is 8.

So, the GCF of 24 and 40 is 8.

Try It **Find the GCF of the numbers using lists of factors.**

1. 8, 36 **2.** 18, 72 **3.** 14, 28, 49

Another way to find the GCF of two or more numbers is by using prime factors. The GCF is the product of the common prime factors of the numbers.

EXAMPLE 2 Finding the GCF Using Prime Factorizations

Find the GCF of 12 and 56.

Make a factor tree for each number.

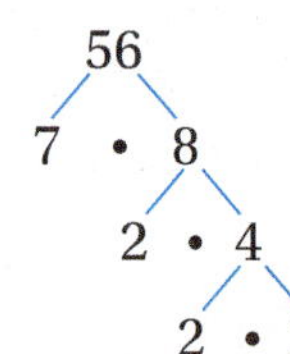

Write the prime factorization of each number.

$12 = 2 \cdot 2 \cdot 3$

$56 = 2 \cdot 2 \cdot 2 \cdot 7$

Circle the common prime factors.

$2 \cdot 2 = 4$

Find the product of the common prime factors.

So, the GCF of 12 and 56 is 4.

Math Practice

Maintain Oversight
Explain why the method used in Example 2 works.

Try It **Find the GCF of the numbers using prime factorizations.**

4. 20, 45 **5.** 32, 90 **6.** 45, 75, 120

Laurie's Notes

Scaffolding Instruction

- Students have used a powerful visual representation of **common factors** to find the **greatest common factor** (GCF). Now they will move on to more efficient methods: lists of factors and factor trees.
- **Emerging:** Students who want to continue using Venn diagrams, or who struggled with the two different approaches in the explorations, will benefit from guided instruction in Examples 1 and 2. The Try It exercises will allow you to assess their progress.
- **Proficient:** Students who were confident in both explorations, and were able to make the connection between the greatest common factor and common prime factors, can self-assess using the Try It exercises.

EXAMPLE 1

- Using lists of factors to find the GCF is similar to the method used in Exploration 1.
- ? "What are the factors of 24?" 1, 2, 3, 4, 6, 8, 12, 24
- ? "What are the factors of 40?" 1, 2, 4, 5, 8, 10, 20, 40
- ? "Which factors appear in both lists?" 1, 2, 4, 8
- **FYI:** Students should not just say, "The greatest common factor is 8." The complete answer is, "The greatest common factor of 24 and 40 is 8."

Try It

- **Neighbor Check:** Students should complete the exercises on their own, and then share their methods and answers with a partner or group. Listen to their reasoning in Exercises 2 and 3.
- ? "How do you find the GCF of three numbers?" Find all the common factors of all three numbers and choose the greatest.

EXAMPLE 2

- Using prime factorizations to find the GCF is similar to the method used in Exploration 2.
- ? "Which prime factors do 12 and 56 have in common?" two factors of 2
- The greatest common factor of two (or more) numbers is the product of the prime factors that they have in common. The greatest common factor of 12 and 56 is $2 \cdot 2$, or 4.
- The solution can be checked by the first method of using lists of factors.
- ? "Does it matter which method you use? Explain." No, each method will give you the correct answer.
- ? "How do you decide which method to use?" If the numbers have relatively few factors, use the lists of factors method. If the numbers have relatively large numbers of factors, use the prime factorizations method.

Try It

- Have students use whiteboards to complete the exercises. As they share their factor trees, encourage students to study other boards and compare their factor trees to other factor trees. This is a good opportunity to show that even though factor trees may differ, they result in the same prime factorization.

Scaffold instruction to support all students in their learning. Learning is individualized and you may want to group students differently as they move in and out of these levels with each skill and concept. Student self-assessment and feedback help guide your instructional decisions about how and when to layer support for all students to become proficient learners.

Extra Example 1

Find the GCF of 36 and 54 using lists of factors. 18

ELL Support

Have students work in pairs to complete Try It Exercises 1–3. Each partner should factor one of the given numbers by listing factors, as demonstrated in Example 1. Then partners should compare their lists and circle the common factors.
Beginner: State the greatest common factor.
Intermediate: Use a complete sentence to verbally identify the greatest common factor.
Advanced: Identify the greatest common factor, and explain the process they used to find it.

Try It

1. 4
2. 18
3. 7

Extra Example 2

Find the GCF of 40 and 48 using prime factorizations. 8

Try It

4. 5
5. 2
6. 15

Teaching Strategy

Using a Venn diagram allows students to visually organize sets of data and identify similarities or differences. Here is a Venn diagram based upon one set of numbers and two categories: even and multiples of 3.

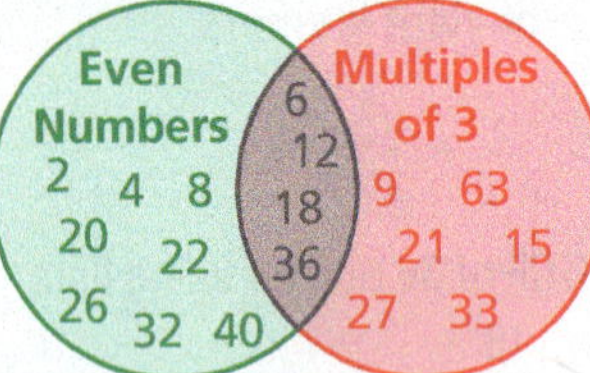

The goal is for students to understand the characteristics of each region. Use the model to discuss observations that can be made from the data, such as 6 represents both an even number and a multiple of 3.

Extra Example 3

Which pair of numbers has a GCF of 12?

A. 18, 30 **B.** 24, 36

C. 36, 72 **D.** 48, 54

B

Try It

7. *Sample answer:* 20, 30

Self-Assessment
for Concepts & Skills

8. 8

9. 7

10. 18

11. C; No whole number can be multiplied by 4 to get 10.

12. What is the greatest common prime factor of 24 and 32?; 2; 8

Laurie's Notes

EXAMPLE 3

- Pose the problem.
- **MP2 Reason Abstractly and Quantitatively:** Asking students questions where they need to explain constraints or parameters helps them to focus on and develop their reasoning skills.

? "Why can't a greater number be a factor of a lesser number?" The greater number can't divide into the lesser number evenly.

- **Big Idea:** The GCF of two numbers will always be less than or equal to the lesser of the two original numbers.
- Work through the remainder of the example as shown.

Try It

- **Reasoning:** In Exercise 7, students are given the GCF and need to find the two original numbers. Write the various solutions on the board and look for similarities in the answers.

Self-Assessment for Concepts & Skills

- Students can use these exercises to determine if they can use both methods of finding the GCF and immediately know if they have understood the success criteria for this lesson.
- Exercise 12 helps students to differentiate similar vocabulary terms. After students complete the assessment, have a whole-class discussion about the meaning of each question.

ELL Support

Have students check their comprehension by completing the exercises in groups. Remind them to use the methods they have learned. When they have completed Exercises 8–10, have groups compare answers and discuss any differences they encounter.

The Success Criteria Self-Assessment chart can be found in the *Student Journal* or online at *BigIdeasMath.com*.

EXAMPLE 3 Finding Two Numbers with a Given GCF

Which pair of numbers has a GCF of 15?

A. 10, 15 **B.** 30, 60 **C.** 21, 45 **D.** 45, 75

The number 15 cannot be a factor of the lesser number 10. So, you can eliminate Choice A.

The number 15 cannot be a factor of a number that does not have a 0 or 5 in the ones place. So, you can eliminate Choice C.

List the factors for Choices B and D. Then identify the GCF for each.

Choice B: **Factors of 30:** 1, 2, 3, 5, 6, 10, 15, 30

Factors of 60: 1, 2, 3, 4, 5, 6, 10, 12, 15, 20, 30, 60

The GCF of 30 and 60 is 30.

Choice D: **Factors of 45:** 1, 3, 5, 9, 15, 45

Factors of 75: 1, 3, 5, 15, 25, 75

The GCF of 45 and 75 is 15.

The correct answer is **D**.

Try It

7. Write a pair of numbers whose greatest common factor is 10.

Self-Assessment for Concepts & Skills

Solve each exercise. Then rate your understanding of the success criteria in your journal.

FINDING THE GCF **Find the GCF of the numbers.**

8. 16, 40 **9.** 35, 63 **10.** 18, 72, 144

11. **MULTIPLE CHOICE** Which number is *not* a factor of 10? Explain.

A. 1 **B.** 2 **C.** 4 **D.** 5

12. **DIFFERENT WORDS, SAME QUESTION** Which is different? Find "both" answers.

What is the greatest common factor of 24 and 32?

What is the greatest common divisor of 24 and 32?

What is the greatest common prime factor of 24 and 32?

What is the product of the common prime factors of 24 and 32?

EXAMPLE 4 Modeling Real Life

You are filling piñatas for your friend's birthday party. The list shows the gifts you are putting into the piñatas. You want identical groups of gifts in each piñata with no gifts left over. What is the greatest number of piñatas you can make?

*18 kazoos
*24 mints
*42 lollipops

The GCF of the numbers of gifts represents the greatest number of identical groups of gifts you can make with no gifts left over. So, to find the number of piñatas, find the GCF.

Write the prime factorization of each number.

$18 = 2 \cdot 3 \cdot 3$

$24 = 2 \cdot 3 \cdot 2 \cdot 2$ Circle the common prime factors.

$42 = 2 \cdot 3 \cdot 7$

$2 \cdot 3 = 6$ Find the product of the common prime factors.

The GCF of 18, 24, and 42 is 6.

So, you can make at most 6 piñatas.

Check Verify that 6 identical piñatas will use all of the gifts.

18 kazoos ÷ 6 piñatas = 3 kazoos per piñata

24 mints ÷ 6 piñatas = 4 mints per piñata

42 lollipops ÷ 6 piñatas = 7 lollipops per piñata ✓

Self-Assessment for Problem Solving

Solve each exercise. Then rate your understanding of the success criteria in your journal.

13. You use 30 sandwiches and 42 granola bars to make identical picnic baskets. You make the greatest number of picnic baskets with no food left over. How many sandwiches and how many granola bars are in each basket?

14. You fill bags with cookies to give to your friends. You bake 45 chocolate chip cookies, 30 peanut butter cookies, and 15 oatmeal cookies. You want identical groups of cookies in each bag with no cookies left over. What is the greatest number of bags you can make?

Laurie's Notes

EXAMPLE 4

- Students need to realize that a situation will rarely ask for a GCF; students will have to infer from the problem that they need the GCF to solve it.
- Ask a volunteer to read the problem. Discuss the list of gifts. Discuss what it means to have identical groups of the gifts in each piñata.
- ? "How can you distribute the 18 kazoos?" Put 1 kazoo in 18 different piñatas, put 2 kazoos in 9 different piñatas, put 3 kazoos in 6 different piñatas, and so on. Repeat the question for the mints and lollipops.
- **MP3 Construct Viable Arguments and Critique the Reasoning of Others:** It is important to ask students to justify their answers and communicate their reasoning to others.
- ? "Which method for finding the GCF should be used and why?" Using prime factorizations, because there are three numbers and finding the prime factorization of each is fairly quick.

Self-Assessment for Problem Solving

- Encourage students to use a Four Square to complete these exercises. Until students become comfortable with the problem-solving plan, they may only be ready to complete the first square.
- Students need to work independently so that they have time to read the problem, notice the word *greatest*, and begin solving.
- As students finish, ask them to justify their answers. Can they provide a method to check their answers? Choose students who can aid those still struggling and will help, not tell.
- Select at least one exercise for one or two volunteers to explain and verify to the class.

The Success Criteria Self-Assessment chart can be found in the *Student Journal* or online at *BigIdeasMath.com*.

Closure

- **Group Discussion:** Put students into small groups, and ask them to find at least four ways to answer the question and explain their reasoning. Which One Doesn't Belong?

  A. 4, 8 **B.** 21, 35 **C.** 24, 44 **D.** 28, 20

- This exercise includes entry points for all students, and promotes discussion. Because it is early in the school year, students need to practice having a discussion and validating all thoughts.
- Some possible answers and reasons are shown, but students may see others.
  Choice A, because it's the only pair with single digit numbers.
  Choice A, because it's the only pair without any numbers in the 20s.
  Choice B, because it's the only pair that has a GCF of 7 and all the others have a GCF of 4, or because it's the only pair that contains odd numbers.
  Choice D, because it's the only pair with numbers in descending order.
- After a few minutes into the discussion, tell the class that one of their choices must involve a GCF.
- If time allows, have a group explain their choice. Invite others to explain a choice that hasn't been mentioned and see how many different ways students view the numbers.

Extra Example 4

You are making appetizer platters for a party. There are 16 fruit kabobs, 32 cheese cubes, and 40 meatballs to put on the platters. You want identical groups of appetizers on each platter with no appetizers left over. What is the greatest number of platters you can make? 8

Self-Assessment for Problem Solving

13. 5 sandwiches, 7 granola bars

14. 15

Learning Target

Find the greatest common factor of two numbers.

Success Criteria

- Explain the meaning of factors of a number.
- Use lists of factors to identify the greatest common factor of numbers.
- Use prime factors to identify the greatest common factor of numbers.

Review & Refresh

1. 1, 20; 2, 10; 4, 5
2. 1, 16; 2, 8; 4, 4
3. 1, 56; 2, 28, 4, 14; 7, 8
4. 1, 87; 3, 29
5. sometimes
6. sometimes
7. always
8. never

Concepts, Skills, & Problem Solving

9. 6
10. 2
11. 12
12. 3
13. 14
14. 1
15. 13
16. 17
17. 1
18. 12
19. 4
20. 2
21. 15
22. 9
23. 9
24. 12
25. 1
26. 19
27. 15
28. 6
29. 21
30. 24
31. 1
32. 18
33. *Sample answer:* 10, 15
34. *Sample answer:* 24, 36
35. *Sample answer:* 37, 74
36. 23 packets
37. 8 arrangements

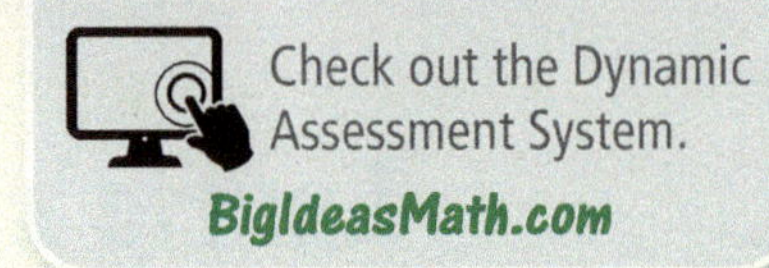

Assignment Guide and Concept Check

Scaffold assignments to support all students in their learning progression. The suggested assignments are a starting point. Continue to assign additional exercises and revisit with spaced practice to move every student toward proficiency.

Level	Assignment 1	Assignment 2
Emerging	4, 8, 11, 12, 13, 21, 23, 38, 41	26, 30, 33, 36, 37, 39, 44, 50
Proficient	4, 8, 11, 14, 15, 26, 28, 38, 44	34, 37, 39, 47, 49, 50, 51, 53
Advanced	4, 8, 11, 16, 20, 30, 31, 38, 48	35, 39, 49, 52, 53, 54, 55, 56

- Assignment 1 is for use after students complete the Self-Assessment for Concepts & Skills.
- Assignment 2 is for use after students complete the Self-Assessment for Problem Solving.
- The red exercises can be used as a concept check.

Review & Refresh Prior Skills

Exercises 1–4 Finding Factor Pairs
Exercises 5–8 Using Properties of Quadrilaterals

Common Errors

- **Exercises 9–11** Some students may struggle using a Venn diagram. Make sure they understand that the overlap of any (or all) circles can be used to find the GCF of the numbers represented by the circles.

1.4 Practice

Review & Refresh

List the factor pairs of the number.

1. 20 **2.** 16 **3.** 56 **4.** 87

Tell whether the statement is *always, sometimes,* or *never* true.

5. A rectangle is a rhombus.

6. A rhombus is a square.

7. A square is a rectangle.

8. A trapezoid is a parallelogram.

Concepts, Skills, & Problem Solving

USING A VENN DIAGRAM Use a Venn diagram to find the greatest common factor of the numbers. (See Exploration 1, p. 21.)

9. 12, 30 **10.** 32, 54 **11.** 24, 108

FINDING THE GCF Find the GCF of the numbers using lists of factors.

12. 6, 15 **13.** 14, 84 **14.** 45, 76

15. 39, 65 **16.** 51, 85 **17.** 40, 63

18. 12, 48 **19.** 24, 52 **20.** 30, 58

FINDING THE GCF Find the GCF of the numbers using prime factorizations.

21. 45, 60 **22.** 27, 63 **23.** 36, 81

24. 72, 84 **25.** 61, 73 **26.** 38, 95

27. 60, 75 **28.** 42, 60 **29.** 42, 63

30. 24, 96 **31.** 189, 200 **32.** 90, 108

OPEN-ENDED Write a pair of numbers with the indicated GCF.

33. 5 **34.** 12 **35.** 37

36. MP **MODELING REAL LIFE** A teacher is making identical activity packets using 92 crayons and 23 sheets of paper. What is the greatest number of packets the teacher can make with no items left over?

37. MP **MODELING REAL LIFE** You are making balloon arrangements for a birthday party. There are 16 white balloons and 24 red balloons. Each arrangement must be identical. What is the greatest number of arrangements you can make using every balloon?

MP YOU BE THE TEACHER **Your friend finds the GCF of the two numbers. Is your friend correct? Explain your reasoning.**

38.

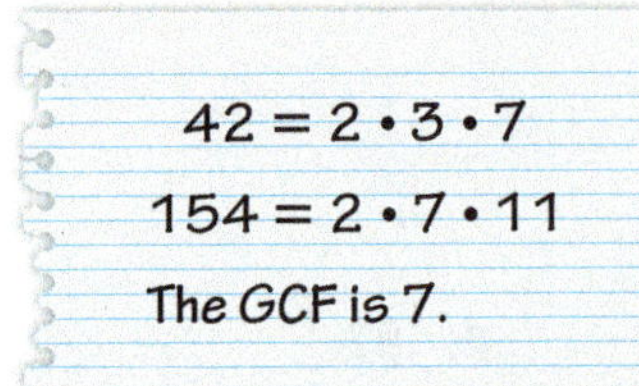

$42 = 2 \cdot 3 \cdot 7$

$154 = 2 \cdot 7 \cdot 11$

The GCF is 7.

39.

$36 = 2^2 \cdot 3^2$

$60 = 2^2 \cdot 3 \cdot 5$

The GCF is $2^2 \cdot 3 = 12$.

FINDING THE GCF **Find the GCF of the numbers.**

40. 35, 56, 63 **41.** 30, 60, 78 **42.** 42, 70, 84

43. 40, 55, 72 **44.** 18, 54, 90 **45.** 16, 48, 88

46. 52, 78, 104 **47.** 96, 120, 156 **48.** 280, 300, 380

49. **OPEN-ENDED** Write three numbers that have a GCF of 16. What method did you use to find your answer?

CRITICAL THINKING **Tell whether the statement is *always*, *sometimes*, or *never* true. Explain your reasoning.**

50. The GCF of two even numbers is 2. **51.** The GCF of two prime numbers is 1.

52. When one number is a multiple of another, the GCF of the numbers is the greater of the numbers.

53. **MP PROBLEM SOLVING** A science museum makes gift bags for students using 168 magnets, 48 robot figurines, and 24 packs of freeze-dried ice cream. What is the greatest number of gift bags that can be made using all of the items? How many of each item are in each gift bag?

54. **VENN DIAGRAM** Consider the numbers 252, 270, and 300.

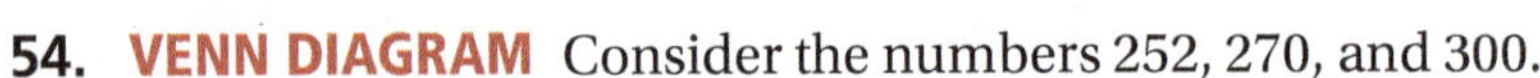

a. Create a Venn diagram using the prime factors of the numbers.

b. Use the Venn diagram to find the GCF of 252, 270, and 300.

c. What is the GCF of 252 and 270? 252 and 300? 270 and 300? Explain how you found your answers.

55. **MP REASONING** You are making fruit baskets using 54 apples, 36 oranges, and 73 bananas.

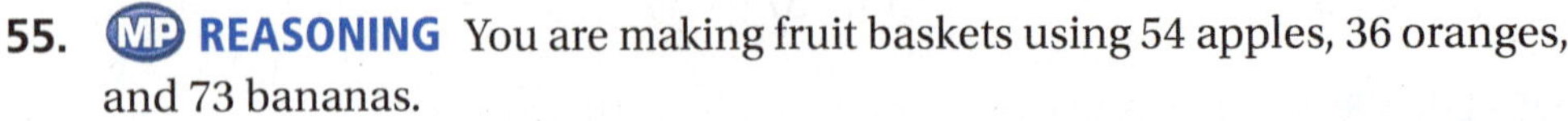

a. Explain why you cannot make identical fruit baskets without leftover fruit.

b. What is the greatest number of identical fruit baskets you can make with the least amount of fruit left over? Explain how you found your answer.

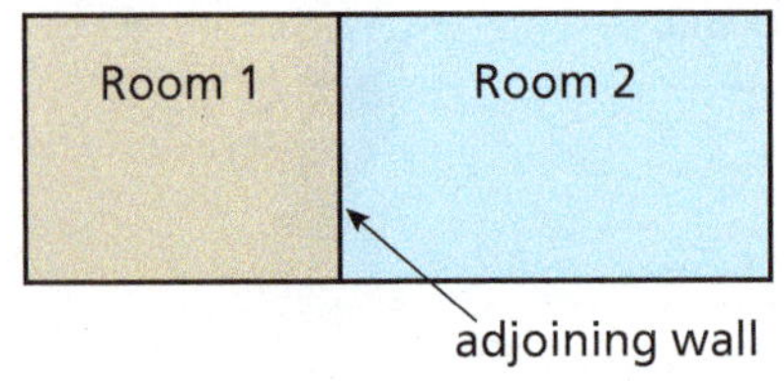

56. **DIG DEEPER!** Two rectangular, adjacent rooms share a wall. One-foot-by-one-foot tiles cover the floor of each room. Describe how the greatest possible length of the adjoining wall is related to the total number of tiles in each room. Draw a diagram that represents one possibility.

Common Errors

- **Exercises 40–48** Some students may struggle if they use a Venn diagram for a set of three numbers. Tell them that the same rules apply for a set of three as with a set of two.

Mini-Assessment

Find the GCF of the numbers.

1. 8, 20 4
2. 35, 56 7
3. 18, 45 9
4. You have 12 cans of lemonade, 54 bottles of water, and 84 cups of punch to put on refreshment tables. Each table must be identical. What is the greatest number of refreshment tables you can set up using every beverage? 6

Section Resources

Surface Level	Deep Level
Resources by Chapter • Extra Practice • Reteach • Puzzle Time Student Journal • Self-Assessment • Practice Differentiating the Lesson Tutorial Videos Skills Review Handbook Skills Trainer	Resources by Chapter • Enrichment and Extension Graphic Organizers Dynamic Assessment System • Section Practice

Concepts, Skills, & Problem Solving

38. no; The GCF is $2 \cdot 7 = 14$.

39. yes; The common prime factors are 2^2 and 3.

40. 7 **41.** 6

42. 14 **43.** 1

44. 18 **45.** 8

46. 26 **47.** 12

48. 20

49. *Sample answer:* 16, 32, and 48; Multiply 16 by 1, 2, and 3.

50. sometimes; 2 is the GCF of 4 and 6, but 6 is the GCF of 6 and 12.

51. always; A prime number has no factors besides 1 and itself.

52. never; The GCF is the lesser number.

53. 24; 7 magnets, 2 robot figurines, 1 freeze-dried ice cream

54. **a.** See Additional Answers.

b. 6

c. 18; 12; 30; *Sample answer:* Find the product of the factors in the overlap of the circles.

55. **a.** The GCF of the three numbers is 1.

b. 18; The GCF of 72, 54, and 36 is 18, leaving one banana left over.

56. See Additional Answers.

Laurie's Notes

Learning Target

Find the least common multiple of two numbers.

Success Criteria

- Explain the meaning of multiples of a number.
- Use lists of multiples to identify the least common multiple of numbers.
- Use prime factors to identify the least common multiple of numbers.

Warm Up

Cumulative, vocabulary, and prerequisite skills practice opportunities are available in the *Resources by Chapter* or at *BigIdeasMath.com.*

ELL Support

Tell students that as the word *greatest* means largest, the word *least* means smallest. Explain that the least common multiple is the smallest of the common multiples that are shared by two or more numbers.

Exploration 1

a–d. See Additional Answers.

e. It is the least of the common multiples; It is circled in each diagram for parts (a)–(d).

Exploration 2

a.

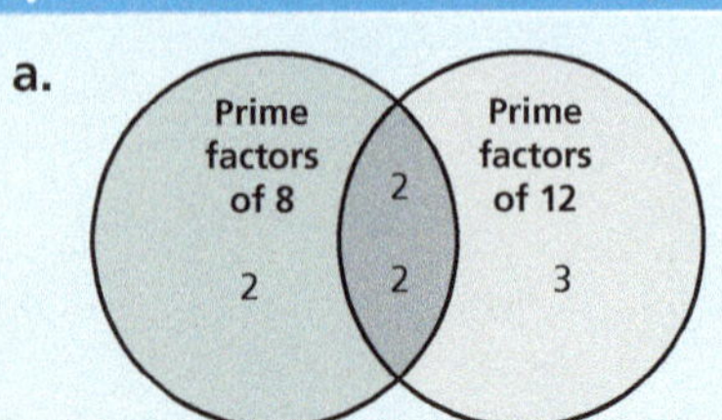

b. See Additional Answers.

c. The least common multiple is the product of the numbers.

d. 120 and 180; 60; 360

Preparing to Teach

- This lesson is similar to the last, in that students are presented with two methods for finding the **least common multiple** (LCM) of two numbers. You want students to be proficient with both methods, and be able to determine which method is more efficient for the given numbers.
- The least common denominator, when you add or subtract fractions with unlike denominators, is the least common multiple of the denominators. Because any common denominator can be used to add or subtract fractions, you want to make sure students see the real-life applications of multiples.

Motivate

- ? **Puzzle Time:** "A bell rings every 3 minutes, a dog barks every 4 minutes, and a person coughs every 5 minutes. If you just heard all three sounds, how long must you wait to hear the bell ring and the dog bark? the bell ring and the person cough? the dog bark and the person cough? all three sounds at the same time?" 12 minutes; 15 minutes; 20 minutes; 60 minutes
- Solicit information about how students found the answers. Using lists of multiples is likely one of the methods. Demonstrate this by drawing a Venn diagram for the first question.

Exploration 1

- If you have done the Motivate, students will not need an introduction to the exploration. If students ask how many multiples they need to list, tell them that there is no set number, but they may want to start by listing 5 or 6 multiples.
- Have each student work with his or her partner while you circulate around the room to see that they are recording the multiples correctly.
- ? "Do any of the number pairs have more than one multiple in common? Explain." Yes, 8 and 12 have 24 and 48 in common. If students answer "no," they may not have extended their lists enough to see other multiples.

Exploration 2

- Discuss the directions with students. They are using prime factorizations, so they should be comfortable with how to proceed.
- Listen to the students' explanations for part (c). The least common multiple of two numbers can be found by finding the product of the prime factors listed in the Venn diagram.
- **Big Idea:** The factors the two numbers have in common are written only once in the Venn diagram. This is an important connection for students to understand.
- ? "Think of two numbers that have no prime factors in common. What will the Venn diagram look like?" There will be no factors where the two circles intersect. "Does this method still work?" yes
- Part (d) summarizes finding the greatest common factor (GCF) and least common multiple (LCM). Students are often confused by the two concepts. When students have finished, ask a volunteer to share his or her work.

1.5 Least Common Multiple

Learning Target: Find the least common multiple of two numbers.

Success Criteria:
- I can explain the meaning of multiples of a number.
- I can use lists of multiples to identify the least common multiple of numbers.
- I can use prime factors to identify the least common multiple of numbers.

EXPLORATION 1 Identifying Common Multiples

Work with a partner. In parts (a)–(d), create a Venn diagram that represents the first several multiples of each number and identify any *common multiples*.

a. 8 and 12

b. 4 and 14

c. 10 and 15

d. 20 and 35

e. Look at the Venn diagrams in parts (a)–(d). Explain how to identify the *least common multiple* of each pair of numbers. Then circle it in each diagram.

EXPLORATION 2 Using Prime Factors

Work with a partner.

a. Create a Venn diagram that represents the prime factorizations of 8 and 12.

b. Repeat part (a) for the remaining number pairs in Exploration 1.

c. MP **STRUCTURE** Make a conjecture about the relationship between the least common multiples you found in Exploration 1 and the numbers in the Venn diagrams you just created.

d. The Venn diagram shows the prime factors of two numbers.

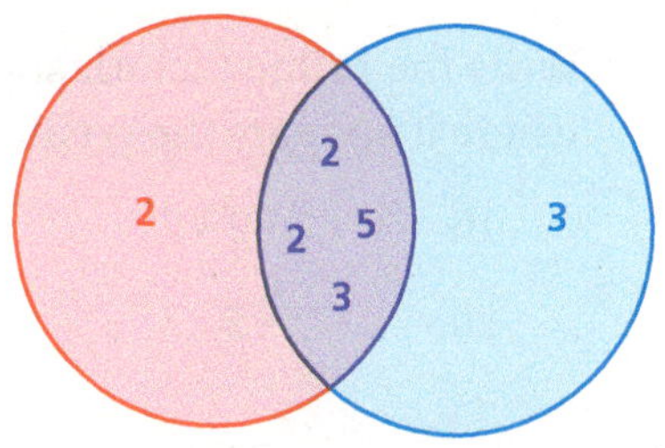

Use the diagram to complete the following tasks.

- Identify the two numbers.
- Find the greatest common factor.
- Find the least common multiple.

Math Practice

Analyze Conjectures

How can you test your conjecture in part (c)?

1.5 Lesson

Key Vocabulary

common multiples, *p. 28*

least common multiple, *p. 28*

Multiples that are shared by two or more numbers are called **common multiples**. The least of the common multiples is called the **least common multiple** (LCM). You can find the LCM of two or more numbers by listing multiples or using prime factors.

EXAMPLE 1 Finding the LCM Using Lists of Multiples

Find the LCM of 4 and 6.

List the multiples of each number.

Multiples of 4: 4, 8, (12), 16, 20, (24), 28, 32, (36), . . . Circle the common multiples.

Multiples of 6: 6, (12), 18, (24), 30, (36), . . .

Some common multiples of 4 and 6 are 12, 24, and 36. The least of these common multiples is 12.

So, the LCM of 4 and 6 is 12.

Try It **Find the LCM of the numbers using lists of multiples.**

1. 3, 8 **2.** 9, 12 **3.** 6, 10

EXAMPLE 2 Finding the LCM Using Prime Factorizations

Find the LCM of 16 and 20.

Make a factor tree for each number.

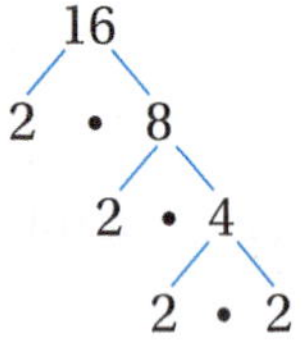

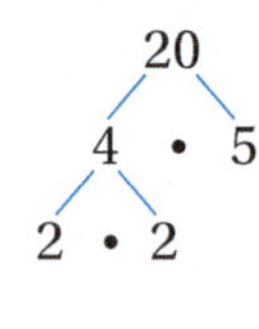

Write the prime factorization of each number. Circle each different factor where it appears the greater number of times.

16 = (2) • (2) • (2) • (2) 2 appears more often here, so circle all 2s.

20 = 2 • 2 • (5) 5 appears once. Do not circle the 2s again.

2 • 2 • 2 • 2 • 5 = 80 Find the product of the circled factors.

So, the LCM of 16 and 20 is 80.

Math Practice

Maintain Oversight

Explain why the method used in Example 2 works.

Try It **Find the LCM of the numbers using prime factorizations.**

4. 14, 18 **5.** 28, 36 **6.** 24, 90

Laurie's Notes

Scaffolding Instruction

- The explorations introduced the two methods for finding **common multiples**. Students may now start to confuse multiples and factors. You want them to focus on understanding, and not memorizing a procedure.
- **Emerging:** Students may not fully understand the difference between multiples and factors, and may make computation errors. In Example 1, students see that 4 and 6 have many common multiples, one of which is the least. Follow Example 1 by asking for the GCF of 4 and 6.
- **Proficient:** Students can explain what multiples are, and find the **least common multiple** of two numbers using at least one method. Proficient students can complete the Try It exercises, or begin with the Self-Assessment for Concepts & Skills exercises.

EXAMPLE 1

- **Turn and Talk:** "Explain the difference between factors and multiples of a number." Circulate and ask, "Is 8 a factor of 8? Is 8 a multiple of 8?"

? "What are the multiples of 4?" 4, 8, 12, 16, 20, 24, 26, 32, 36, . . .

? "What are the multiples of 6?" 6, 12, 18, 24, 30, 36, . . .

? "What multiples appear in both lists?" 12, 24, and 36 "What do you notice about all of the common multiples?" They are the multiples of 12.

- **FYI:** Students should not just say, "The least common multiple is 12." The complete answer is, "The least common multiple of 4 and 6 is 12."

Try It

- **Think-Pair-Share:** Students should read each exercise independently, and then work in pairs to solve the problems. These exercises are helping students make progress with the second success criterion.

ELL Support

Point out that the same tools used to find the GCF can be used to find the LCM. Have students work with a partner to complete Exercises 1–3. Each partner lists the multiples of one of the given numbers. Then partners compare their lists and circle the numbers that are common.

Beginner: Identify the LCM by stating the number.

Intermediate: Use a complete sentence to verbally identify the LCM.

Advanced: Explain the process and identify the LCM.

EXAMPLE 2

- Any factor that appears in either list is used in finding the LCM. This can be confusing. If needed, draw a Venn diagram to discuss this problem.
- The solution can be checked by using lists of multiples.

? "Does it matter which method you use? Explain." No, both methods will give you the correct answer. "How do you decide which method to use?" If the numbers are relatively small, use lists of multiples. If the numbers are relatively large, use prime factorizations.

Try It

- Ask volunteers to share their work at the board or document camera to check solutions.

Formative Assessment Tip

Turn and Talk

This technique allows all students in the class to have a voice. Using a three-foot voice, students turn and talk to their partners about a problem or discuss a question. There may be different roles that I ask partners to assume, so I refer to Partner A and Partner B. In discussing a procedure or explaining an answer, I might ask Partner A to talk uninterrupted for a fixed period of time. Then Partner B might be asked to repeat back what he or she heard, or to ask a question about what has been shared.

Example: "*Turn and Talk*, so that Partner A explains how lists of multiples can be used to find the LCM of two numbers."

It is important to establish norms: three-foot voices should be expected when students are doing partner work. Discuss with students the difference between *authentic listening* and being quiet while your partner is speaking.

Extra Example 1

Find the LCM of 4 and 9 using lists of multiples. 36

Try It

1. 24 **2.** 36

3. 30

Extra Example 2

Find the LCM of 16 and 24 using prime factorizations. 48

Try It

4. 126 **5.** 252

6. 360

Extra Example 3

Find the LCM of 3, 8, and 16. 48

Try It

7. 40
8. 60
9. *Sample answer:* 4, 10, 25

Self-Assessment
for Concepts & Skills

10. 18
11. 120
12. 55
13. *Sample answer:* 2, 3; $18 = 2 \cdot 9$, $18 = 3 \cdot 6$, $30 = 2 \cdot 15$, $30 = 3 \cdot 10$
14. *Sample answer:* Prime factorization because 13 and 14 do not have many prime factors.
15. GCF: Multiply the prime factors that appear in both rows of the table; $\text{GCF} = 2 \cdot 2 = 4$

    LCM: Multiply the factors that appear in at least one row of the table; $\text{LCM} = 2 \cdot 2 \cdot 2 \cdot 3 = 24$
16. Find the LCM of the denominators and rewrite the fractions as equivalent fractions having the LCM as a denominator.

Laurie's Notes

EXAMPLE 3

- ? "You want to find the LCM of three numbers. Which method do you think will be the most efficient and why?" Using prime factorizations, because listing the multiples of 18 is more challenging than listing the multiples of 4 and 15. Writing the prime factorizations of all three numbers is fairly quick.
- Work through the problem as shown.
- ? **Turn and Talk:** "Is it possible for the LCM of two numbers to be one of the numbers? Explain." Yes, the greater of the two numbers can be the LCM if the greater number is a multiple of the lesser number.
- **Big Idea:** The LCM of two numbers will always be greater than or equal to the greater of the two original numbers.

Try It

- Ask students to explain which method they used to find the LCM, and why they chose that method.
- **MP2 Reason Abstractly and Quantitatively & MP3 Construct Viable Arguments and Critique the Reasoning of Others:** In Exercise 9, students are given the LCM and they need to find the three original numbers. This is not a trivial problem, so ask students to describe their reasoning.

Self-Assessment for Concepts & Skills

- Students may be able to list multiples and write the prime factorizations of numbers. Can they explain what it means to find the least common multiple of two numbers? Can they extend this understanding to more than two numbers?
- Exercise 14 is key in helping students assess their understanding of which method to use, and why. Knowing that 13 is a prime number, students are more likely to choose prime factorization.
- Discuss student responses to Exercise 15. Are the responses procedural, or is there a conceptual understanding that relates to the GCF and the LCM?

ELL Support

Have students check comprehension by working in pairs. Remind them to use the methods they have learned. When they have completed Exercises 10–12, have them check their answers with another pair.

The Success Criteria Self-Assessment chart can be found in the *Student Journal* or online at *BigIdeasMath.com.*

EXAMPLE 3 Finding the LCM of Three Numbers

Find the LCM of 4, 15, and 18.

Write the prime factorization of each number. Circle each different factor where it appears the greatest number of times.

$4 = (2) \cdot (2)$ — 2 appears most often here, so circle both 2s.

$15 = 3 \cdot (5)$ — 5 appears here only, so circle 5.

$18 = 2 \cdot (3) \cdot (3)$ — 3 appears most often here, so circle both 3s.

$2 \cdot 2 \cdot 5 \cdot 3 \cdot 3 = 180$ — Find the product of the circled factors.

 So, the LCM of 4, 15, and 18 is 180.

Try It

Find the LCM of the numbers.

7. 2, 5, 8

8. 6, 10, 12

9. Write three numbers that have a least common multiple of 100.

Self-Assessment for Concepts & Skills

Solve each exercise. Then rate your understanding of the success criteria in your journal.

FINDING THE LCM **Find the LCM of the numbers.**

10. 6, 9

11. 30, 40

12. 5, 11

13. MP **REASONING** Write two numbers such that 18 and 30 are multiples of the numbers. Justify your answer.

14. MP **REASONING** You need to find the LCM of 13 and 14. Would you rather list their multiples or use their prime factorizations? Explain.

15. MP **CHOOSE TOOLS** A student writes the prime factorizations of 8 and 12 in a table as shown. She claims she can use the table to find the greatest common factor and the least common multiple of 8 and 12. How is this possible?

8 =	2	2	2	
12 =	2	2		3

16. **CRITICAL THINKING** How can you use least common multiples to add or subtract fractions with different denominators?

EXAMPLE 4 Modeling Real Life

One firefly flashes every 8 seconds. Another firefly flashes every 10 seconds. Both fireflies just flashed. After how many seconds will both fireflies flash at the same time again?

Understand the problem.

You are given the numbers of seconds between flashes for two different fireflies. You are asked when the fireflies will flash at the same time again.

Make a plan.

The LCM of the numbers of seconds between flashes represents the number of seconds it will take for both fireflies to flash at the same time again. So, find the LCM of 8 and 10 by listing the multiples of each number.

Solve and check.

Multiples of 8: 8, 16, 24, 32, 40, . . .

Multiples of 10: 10, 20, 30, 40, 50, . . .

The LCM of 8 and 10 is 40.

So, both fireflies will flash at the same time again after 40 seconds.

Another Method Find the LCM using prime factorizations.

$8 = 2 \cdot 2 \cdot 2$ $\qquad$ $10 = 2 \cdot 5$

So, the LCM is $2 \cdot 2 \cdot 2 \cdot 5 = 40$. ✓

Self-Assessment for Problem Solving

Solve each exercise. Then rate your understanding of the success criteria in your journal.

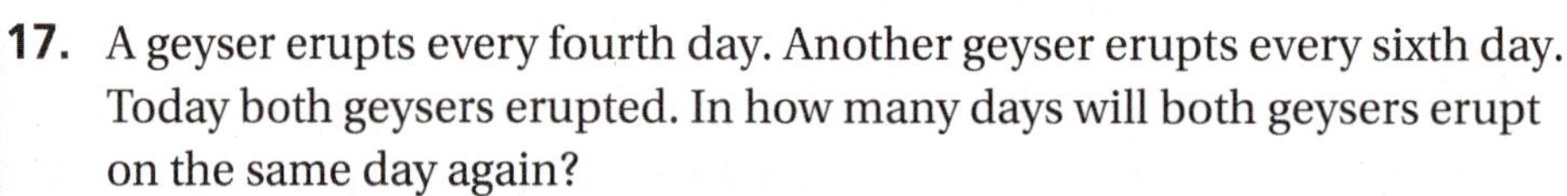

17. A geyser erupts every fourth day. Another geyser erupts every sixth day. Today both geysers erupted. In how many days will both geysers erupt on the same day again?

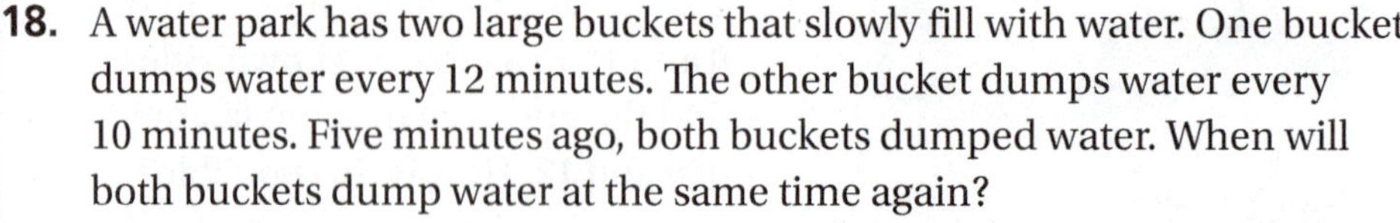

18. A water park has two large buckets that slowly fill with water. One bucket dumps water every 12 minutes. The other bucket dumps water every 10 minutes. Five minutes ago, both buckets dumped water. When will both buckets dump water at the same time again?

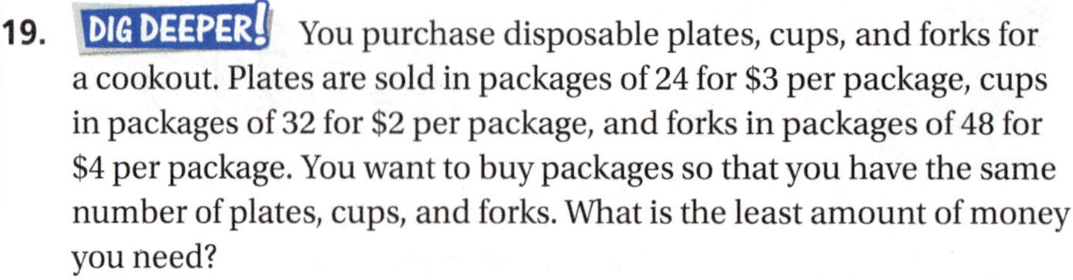

19. **DIG DEEPER!** You purchase disposable plates, cups, and forks for a cookout. Plates are sold in packages of 24 for $3 per package, cups in packages of 32 for $2 per package, and forks in packages of 48 for $4 per package. You want to buy packages so that you have the same number of plates, cups, and forks. What is the least amount of money you need?

Laurie's Notes

Discuss

- The problems on this page are similar to the Motivate puzzle. Spend time discussing application problems, such as comparison pricing (3 eight-ounce bottles versus 2 twelve-ounce bottles), scheduling (mow the lawn every 5 days and water the flowers every other day), and lighting displays (2 or 3 displays that cycle through a show).
- Students will understand that these problems involve finding the least common multiple. Having them interpret the results helps to build understanding of how and why multiples are used.

EXAMPLE 4

- **Turn and Talk:** "Read the problem. Tell your partner what the problem is asking and discuss a strategy for solving." Choose a group to share their response with the class.
- ? Refer to the strategy used in the example and ask, "What do the multiples represent in this problem?" how many seconds pass before the firefly flashes

Self-Assessment for Problem Solving

- Students may benefit from trying the exercises independently, and then working with peers to refine their work. It is important to provide time in class for problem solving, so that students become comfortable with the problem-solving plan.
- These exercises involve the concept of the least common multiple. The contexts should be familiar, or sound plausible, to students. Least common multiples are not just for adding and subtracting fractions.
- Students should work independently to assess their understanding of the second and third success criteria; the methods for finding the least common multiple.
- Have students share their approaches with a partner. In Exercise 18, they may think of the multiples of 12 in their heads, and realize when they get to 60 that it is divisible by 10. Students may forget that both buckets dumped five minutes ago. Remind them to read the problem carefully.
- In Exercise 19, they may reason that because 24 is a factor of 48, the solution to the problem is the LCM of 32 and 48.

The Success Criteria Self-Assessment chart can be found in the *Student Journal* or online at *BigIdeasMath.com*.

Closure

- **Exit Ticket:** Explain how to find the LCM of 8 and 15. *Sample answer:* Write the prime factorization of each number and circle each different factor where it appears the greatest number of times. Then find the product of the circled factors.

Extra Example 4

An advertising sign changes every 15 seconds. Another advertising sign changes every 25 seconds. Both signs just changed. After how many seconds will both signs change at the same time again? 75 seconds

Self-Assessment for Problem Solving

17. 12

18. 55 min

19. $26

Learning Target

Find the least common multiple of two numbers.

Success Criteria

- Explain the meaning of multiples of a number.
- Use lists of multiples to identify the least common multiple of numbers.
- Use prime factors to identify the least common multiple of numbers.

Review & Refresh

1. 6
2. 24
3. 38
4. 150
5. 216
6. 56
7. (2, 4)
8. (3, 1)
9. (4, 7)
10. (9, 6)

Concepts, Skills, & Problem Solving

11. 21
12. 24
13. 20
14. 5
15. 6
16. 6
17. 18
18. 12
19. 72
20. 40
21. 132
22. 36
23. 84
24. 45
25. 44
26. 90
27. 108
28. 90
29. 66
30. 180
31. 350
32. no; The LCM is 18.
33. 15

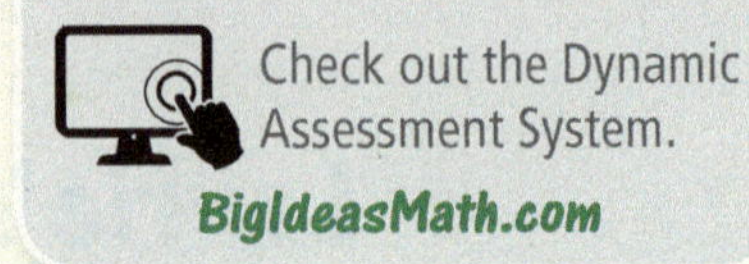

Assignment Guide and Concept Check

Scaffold assignments to support all students in their learning progression. The suggested assignments are a starting point. Continue to assign additional exercises and revisit with spaced practice to move every student toward proficiency.

Level	Assignment 1	Assignment 2
Emerging	3, 6, 9, 12, 15, 18, 23, 27, 32, 35	22, 30, 31, 33, 37, 41
Proficient	3, 6, 9, 12, 15, 16, 27, 30, 32, 37	22, 31, 33, 34, 39, 40, 41, 42, 44
Advanced	3, 6, 9, 12, 20, 22, 30, 31, 32, 40	34, 41, 42, 43, 44, 45, 46, 47

- Assignment 1 is for use after students complete the Self-Assessment for Concepts & Skills.
- Assignment 2 is for use after students complete the Self-Assessment for Problem Solving.
- The red exercises can be used as a concept check.

Review & Refresh Prior Skills

Exercises 1–3 Finding the GCF
Exercises 4–6 Dividing Whole Numbers
Exercises 7–10 Identifying Ordered Pairs

Common Errors

- **Exercises 11–13** Some students may struggle using a Venn diagram. Make sure they understand that the product of all prime factors in the circles is the LCM of the numbers represented by the circles.
- **Exercises 23–31** After writing the prime factorizations, students may struggle with which factors to use to find the LCM. If needed, students should draw a Venn diagram to clarify the problem.

1.5 Practice

Review & Refresh

Find the GCF of the numbers.

1. 18, 42 **2.** 72, 96 **3.** 38, 76, 114

Divide.

4. $900 \div 6$ **5.** $1944 \div 9$ **6.** $672 \div 12$

Write an ordered pair that corresponds to the point.

7. Point A

8. Point B

9. Point C

10. Point D

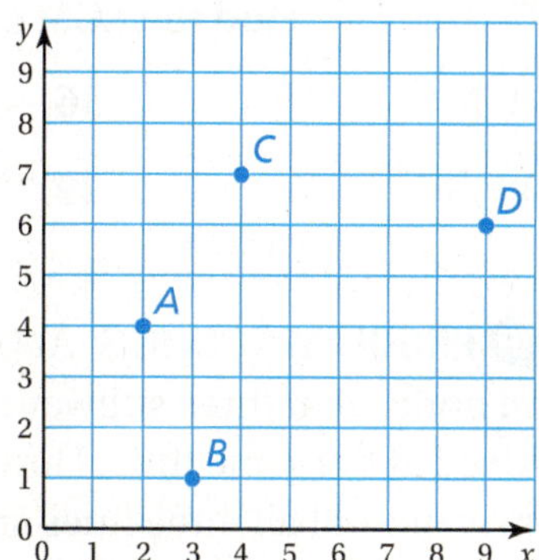

Concepts, Skills, & Problem Solving

USING A VENN DIAGRAM **Use a Venn diagram to find the least common multiple of the numbers.** (See Exploration 1, p. 27.)

11. 3, 7 **12.** 6, 8 **13.** 4, 5

FINDING THE LCM **Find the LCM of the numbers using lists of multiples.**

14. 1, 5 **15.** 2, 6 **16.** 2, 3

17. 2, 9 **18.** 3, 4 **19.** 8, 9

20. 5, 8 **21.** 11, 12 **22.** 12, 18

FINDING THE LCM **Find the LCM of the numbers using prime factorizations.**

23. 7, 12 **24.** 5, 9 **25.** 4, 11

26. 9, 10 **27.** 12, 27 **28.** 18, 45

29. 22, 33 **30.** 36, 60 **31.** 35, 50

32. MP **YOU BE THE TEACHER** Your friend finds the LCM of 6 and 9. Is your friend correct? Explain your reasoning.

$6 \times 9 = 54$

The LCM of 6 and 9 is 54.

33. **MODELING REAL LIFE** You have diving lessons every fifth day and swimming lessons every third day. Today you have both lessons. In how many days will you have both lessons on the same day again?

34. **MP REASONING** Which model represents an LCM that is different from the other three? Explain your reasoning.

A. 0 4 8 12 16 20 24

B.

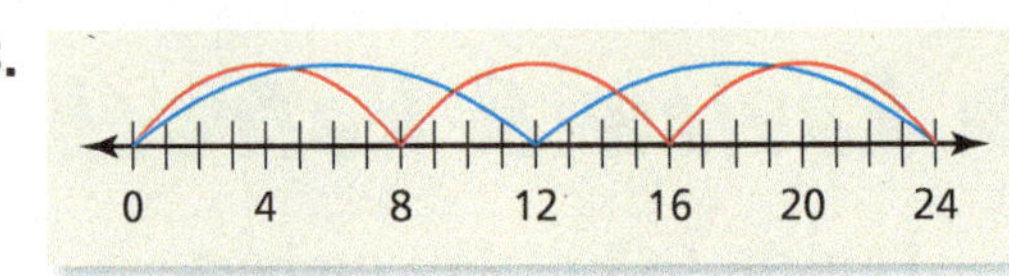

C. 0 4 8 12 16 20 24

D.

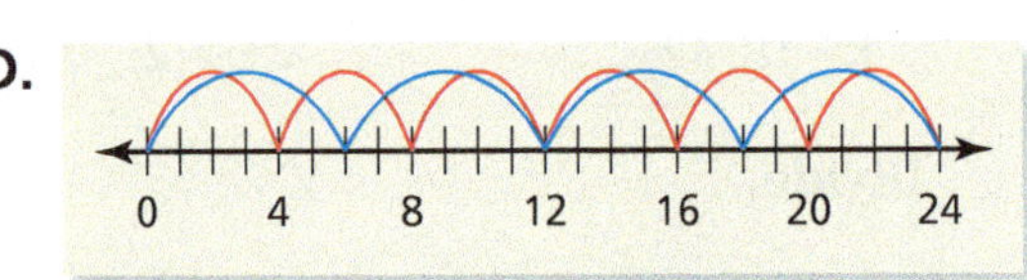

FINDING THE LCM **Find the LCM of the numbers.**

35. 2, 3, 7

36. 3, 5, 11

37. 4, 9, 12

38. 6, 8, 15

39. 7, 18, 21

40. 9, 10, 28

41. **MP PROBLEM SOLVING** At Union Station, you notice that three subway lines just arrived at the same time. How long must you wait until all three lines arrive at Union Station at the same time again?

Subway Line	Arrival Time
A	Every 10 min
B	Every 12 min
C	Every 15 min

42. **DIG DEEPER!** A radio station gives away \$15 to every 15th caller, \$25 to every 25th caller, and a free concert ticket to every 100th caller. When will the station first give away *all* three prizes to one caller? When this happens, how much money and how many tickets are given away?

43. **MP LOGIC** You and a friend are running on treadmills. You run 0.5 mile every 3 minutes, and your friend runs 2 miles every 14 minutes. You both start and stop running at the same time and run a whole number of miles. What are the least possible numbers of miles you and your friend can run?

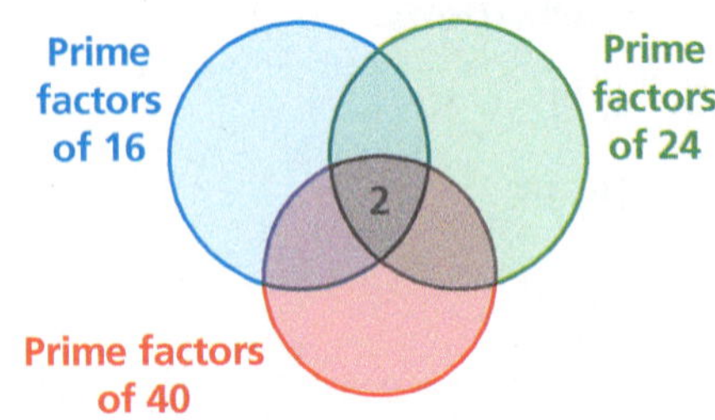

44. **VENN DIAGRAM** Refer to the Venn diagram.

   a. Copy and complete the Venn diagram.

   b. What is the LCM of 16, 24, and 40?

   c. What is the LCM of 16 and 40? 24 and 40? 16 and 24? Explain how you found your answers.

CRITICAL THINKING **Tell whether the statement is *always*, *sometimes*, or *never* true. Explain your reasoning.**

45. The LCM of two different prime numbers is their product.

46. The LCM of a set of numbers is equal to one of the numbers in the set.

47. The GCF of two different numbers is the LCM of the numbers.

Common Errors

- **Exercise 34** The number lines may confuse students. Explain to them that the loops of each number will intersect on common multiples.
- **Exercise 44** Some students may struggle if they use a Venn diagram for a set of three numbers. Tell them the same rules apply for a set of three as with a set of two.

Mini-Assessment

Find the LCM of the numbers.

1. 15, 18 90
2. 24, 32 96
3. 5, 8, 10 40
4. 6, 8, 12 24
5. Two model trains share a station but run on separate tracks. One train passes the station every 8 minutes. The other train passes the station every 14 minutes. Both trains just passed the station. After how many minutes will both trains pass the station at the same time again? 56 minutes

Section Resources

<table>
<tr><th>Surface Level</th><th>Deep Level</th></tr>
<tr><td>Resources by Chapter
• Extra Practice
• Reteach
• Puzzle Time
Student Journal
• Self-Assessment
• Practice
Differentiating the Lesson
Tutorial Videos
Skills Review Handbook
Skills Trainer</td><td>Resources by Chapter
• Enrichment and Extension
Graphic Organizers
Dynamic Assessment System
• Section Practice</td></tr>
<tr><th colspan="2">Transfer Level</th></tr>
<tr><td>Dynamic Assessment System
• End-of-Chapter Quiz</td><td>Assessment Book
• End-of-Chapter Quiz</td></tr>
</table>

Concepts, Skills, & Problem Solving

34. D; The LCM is 12, not 24.

35. 42 **36.** 165

37. 36 **38.** 120

39. 126 **40.** 1260

41. 60 min

42. 300th caller; $600, 3 tickets

43. you: 7 mi; your friend: 6 mi

44. a.

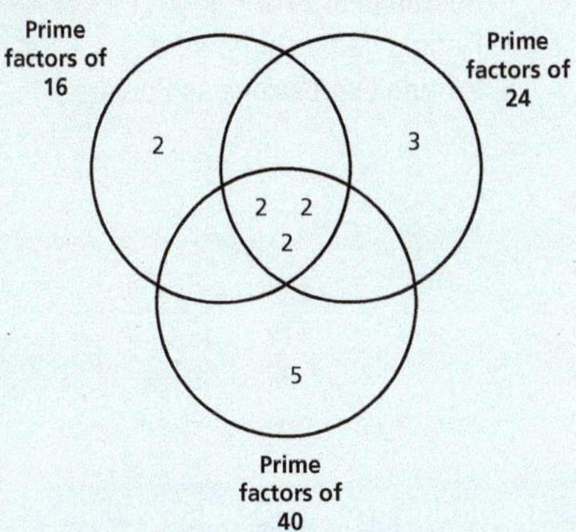

b. 240

c. 80; 120; 48; *Sample answer:* Find the product of the factors in each pair of circles.

45. always; The LCM is the product of the prime factors.

46. sometimes; *Sample answer:* The LCM of 4 and 6 is 12, the LCM of 5 and 10 is 10.

47. never; The GCF is at most the lesser number, and the LCM is at least the greater number.

Laurie's Notes

Skills Needed

Exercise 1

- Finding the GCF
- Multiplying Whole Numbers and Decimals
- Writing Numerical Expressions

Exercise 2

- Converting Measures within the Customary System
- Finding the Volume of a Rectangular Prism
- Finding Values of Powers
- Writing Expressions as Powers

Scaffolding Instruction

- The goal of this lesson is to help students become more comfortable with problem solving. These exercises combine numerical expressions and factors with prior skills from other courses. The solution for Exercise 1 is worked out below, to help you guide students through the problem-solving plan. Use the remaining class time to have students work on the other exercise.
- **Emerging:** The goal for these students is to feel comfortable with the problem-solving plan. Allow students to work in pairs to write the beginning steps of the problem-solving plan for Exercise 2. Keep in mind that some students may only be ready to do the first step.
- **Proficient:** Students may be able to work independently or in pairs to complete Exercise 2.
- Visit each pair to review their plan for the problem. Ask students to describe their plans.

ELL Support

Provide cultural support to ELLs as they work on Exercise 1. They may not be familiar with American sports teams. Explain that a team may promote itself by giving away T-shirts, bobblehead dolls, or other memorabilia. This is not unusual during professional sports events.

Using the Problem-Solving Plan

1. 12
2. 216 ft^3; 8 yd^3; $6\text{ ft} = 2\text{ yd}$

Performance Task

The *STEAM Video Performance Task* provides the opportunity for additional enrichment and greater depth of knowledge as students explore the mathematics of the chapter within a context tied to the chapter STEAM Video. The performance task and a detailed scoring rubric are provided at *BigIdeasMath.com*.

Using the Problem-Solving Plan

Exercise 1

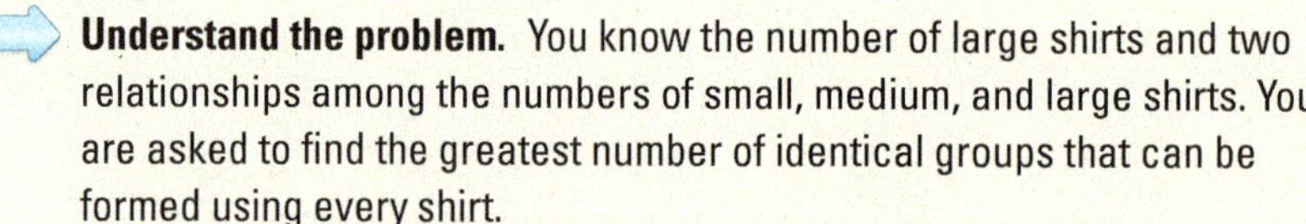

Understand the problem. You know the number of large shirts and two relationships among the numbers of small, medium, and large shirts. You are asked to find the greatest number of identical groups that can be formed using every shirt.

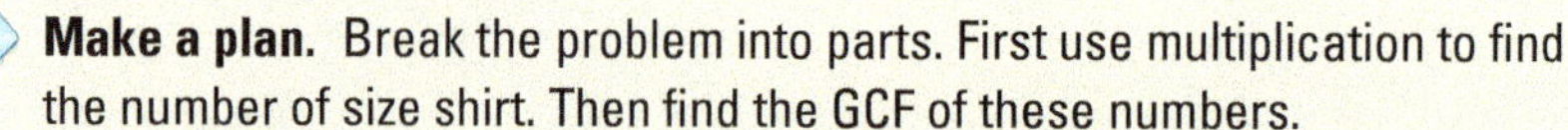

Make a plan. Break the problem into parts. First use multiplication to find the number of size shirt. Then find the GCF of these numbers.

Solve and check. Use the plan to solve the problem. Then check your solution.

- Find the number of each size shirt.

  There are 1.6 times as many small shirts as large shirts. There are 60 large shirts, so there are $1.6 \times 60 = 96$ small shirts.

  There are 1.5 times as many medium shirts as small shirts. There are 96 small shirts, so there are $1.5 \times 96 = 144$ medium shirts.

- Find the GCF of 60, 96, and 144 using a list of factors.

  Factors of 60: 1, 2, 3, 4, 5, 6, 10, 12, 15, 20, 30, 60

  Factors of 96: 1, 2, 3, 4, 6, 8, 12, 16, 24, 32, 48, 96

  Factors of 144: 1, 2, 3, 4, 6, 8, 9, 12, 16, 18, 24, 36, 48, 72, 144

  The common factors of 60, 96, and 144 are 1, 2, 3, 4, 6, and 12. The greatest of the common factors is 12. So, the greatest number of identical groups that can be formed using every shirt is 12.

- **Check:** Verify that the GCF of 60, 96, and 144 is 12 using the prime factorizations.

  $60 = 2 \cdot 2 \cdot 3 \cdot 5$

  $96 = 2 \cdot 2 \cdot 3 \cdot 2 \cdot 2 \cdot 2$ Circle the common prime factors.

  $144 = 2 \cdot 2 \cdot 3 \cdot 2 \cdot 2 \cdot 3$

  $2 \cdot 2 \cdot 3 = 12$ ✓ Find the product of the common prime factors.

1 Connecting Concepts

Problem-Solving Strategies

Using an appropriate strategy will help you make sense of problems as you study the mathematics in this course. You can use the following strategies to solve problems that you encounter.

- Use a verbal model.
- Draw a diagram.
- Write an equation.
- Solve a simpler problem.
- Sketch a graph or number line.
- Make a table.
- Make a list.
- Break the problem into parts.

Using the Problem-Solving Plan

1. A sports team gives away shirts at the stadium. There are 60 large shirts, 1.6 times as many small shirts as large shirts, and 1.5 times as many medium shirts as small shirts. The team wants to divide the shirts into identical groups to be distributed throughout the stadium. What is the greatest number of groups that can be formed using every shirt?

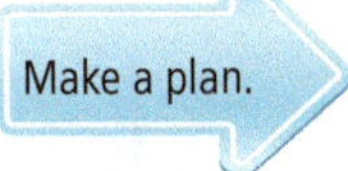

You know the number of large shirts and two relationships among the numbers of small, medium, and large shirts. You are asked to find the greatest number of identical groups that can be formed using every shirt.

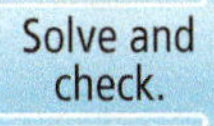

Break the problem into parts. First use multiplication to find the number of each size shirt. Then find the GCF of these numbers.

Solve and check.

Use the plan to solve the problem. Then check your solution.

2. An escape artist fills the tank shown with water. Find the number of cubic feet of water needed to fill the tank. Then find the number of cubic yards of water that are needed to fill the tank. Justify your answer.

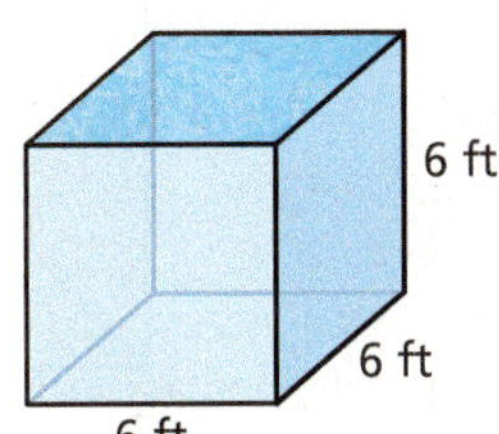

Performance Task

Setting the Table

At the beginning of this chapter, you watched a STEAM video called "Filling Piñatas." You are now ready to complete the performance task for this video, available at ***BigIdeasMath.com***. Be sure to use the problem-solving plan as you work through the performance task.

1 Chapter Review

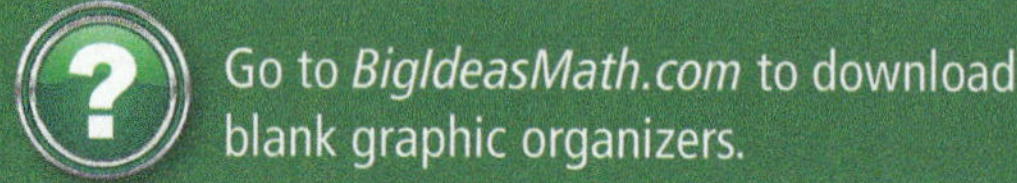

Review Vocabulary

Write the definition and give an example of each vocabulary term.

power, *p. 4*
base, *p. 4*
exponent, *p. 4*
perfect square, *p. 5*
numerical expression, *p. 10*
evaluate, *p. 10*
order of operations, *p. 10*
factor pair, *p. 16*
prime factorization, *p. 16*
factor tree, *p. 16*
Venn diagram, *p. 21*
common factors, *p. 22*
greatest common factor, *p. 22*
common mutliples, *p. 28*
least common multiple, *p. 28*

Graphic Organizers

You can use an **Information Frame** to organize and remember concepts. Here is an example of an Information Frame for the vocabulary term ***power***.

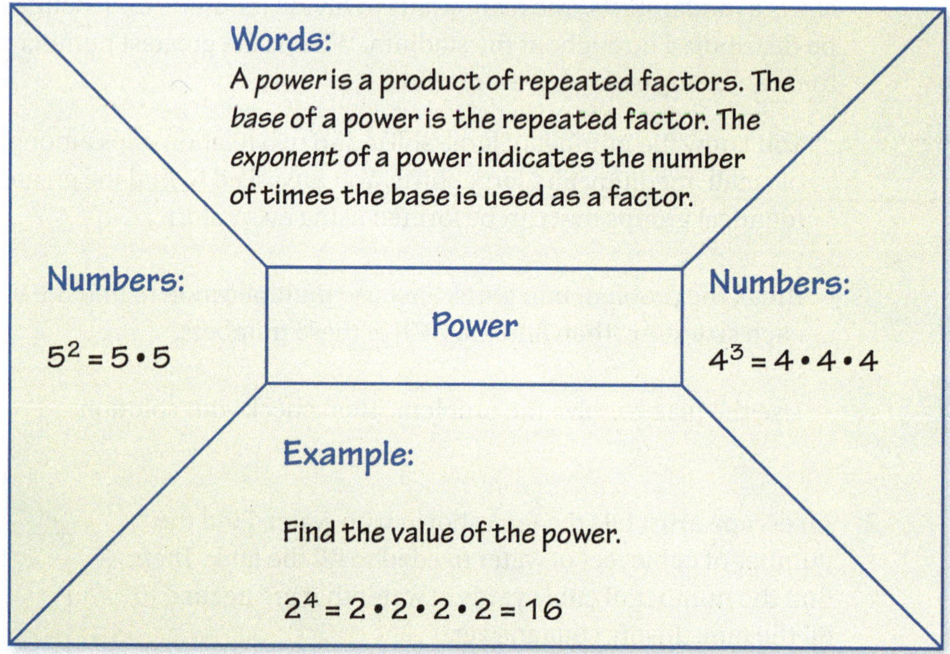

Choose and complete a graphic organizer to help you study the concept.

1. perfect square
2. numerical expression
3. order of operations
4. prime factorization
5. greatest common factor (GCF)
6. least common multiple (LCM)

"Dear Mom, I am sending you an Information Frame card for Mother's Day!"

Review Vocabulary

- As a review of the chapter vocabulary, have students revisit the vocabulary section in their *Student Journals* to fill in any missing definitions and record examples of each term.

Graphic Organizers

Sample answers

1.

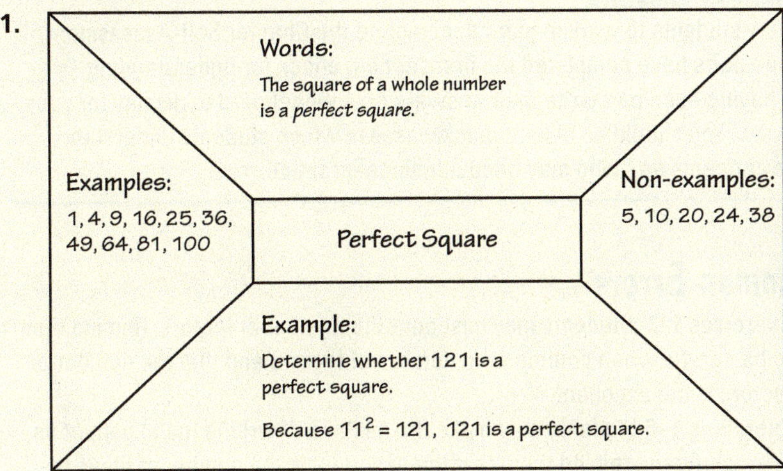

2.

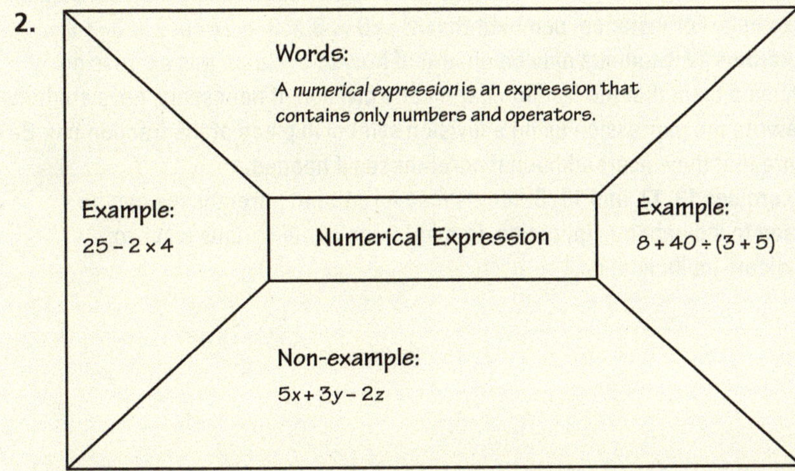

3.

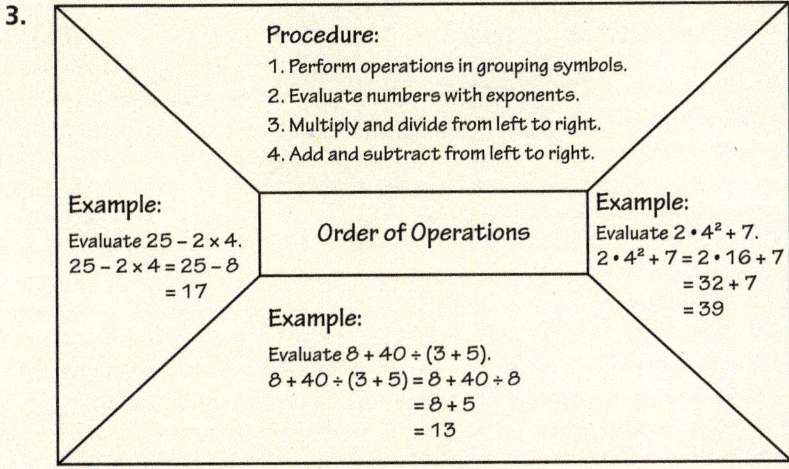

4–6. Answers at *BigIdeasMath.com*

List of Organizers

Available at *BigIdeasMath.com*

Definition and Example Chart
Example and Non-Example Chart
Four Square
Information Frame
Summary Triangle

About this Organizer

An **Information Frame** can be used to help students organize and remember concepts. Students write the concept in the middle rectangle. Then students write related categories in the spaces around the rectangle. Related categories may include: words, numbers, algebra, example, definition, non-example, visual, procedure, details, or vocabulary. Students can place their Information Frames on note cards to use as a quick study reference.

Chapter Self-Assessment

1. 3^6
2. 5^3
3. 17^5
4. 27
5. 64
6. 256
7. *Sample answer:* 4^2
8. 2^5; $4^2 = 2^4$
9. 225 in.^{2}
10. 16
11. 15
12. 15
13. 37
14. 2
15. 12
16. *Sample answer:* $2^3 \times (3^2 + 1)$

Chapter Self-Assessment

The Success Criteria Self-Assessment chart can be found in the *Student Journal* or online at *BigIdeasMath.com.*

ELL Support

Allow students to work in pairs to complete the Chapter Self-Assessment. Once pairs have completed the first section, check for understanding by having each pair write their answers on a whiteboard to display for your review. You should be able to quickly assess which students understand the concepts and who may need additional practice.

Common Errors

- **Exercises 1–3** Students may miscount the number of factors. Remind them to be careful when counting the number of factors and that the number of factors is the exponent.
- **Exercises 4–6** Students may make the mistake of writing the exponent as a factor. Again, remind them that the exponent is the number of times the base is used as a factor. You may want to demonstrate this point with a quick example. For instance, point out that $3^3 = 3 \times 3 \times 3 = 27$ but $3 \times 3 = 9$.
- **Exercise 12** Students may be unsure of how to evaluate this expression. Remind them that the fraction bar means division. If necessary, have students rewrite the expression using a division symbol in place of the fraction bar. Be sure that they insert additional parentheses if needed.
- **Exercises 12, 13, and 15** Students may forget that parentheses can be used to indicate multiplication. Remind them of the various ways to indicate multiplication.

Chapter Self-Assessment

As you complete the exercises, use the scale below to rate your understanding of the success criteria in your journal.

1	2	3	4
I do not understand.	I can do it with help.	I can do it on my own.	I can teach someone else.

1.1 Powers and Exponents (pp. 3–8)

Learning Target: Write and evaluate expressions involving exponents.

Write the product as a power.

1. $3 \times 3 \times 3 \times 3 \times 3 \times 3$
2. $5 \times 5 \times 5$
3. $17 \cdot 17 \cdot 17 \cdot 17 \cdot 17$

Find the value of the power.

4. 3^3
5. 2^6
6. 4^4
7. Write a power that has a value greater than 2^3 and less than 3^3.
8. Without evaluating, determine whether 2^5 or 4^2 is greater. Explain.
9. The bases on a softball field are square. What is the area of each base?

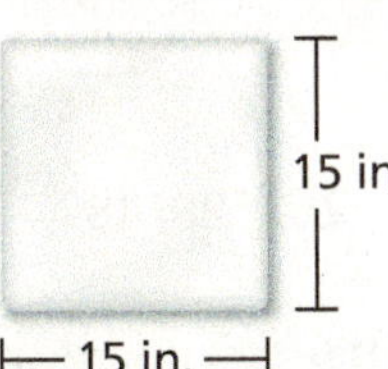

1.2 Order of Operations (pp. 9–14)

Learning Target: Write and evaluate numerical expressions using the order of operations.

Evaluate the expression.

10. $3 \times 6 - 12 \div 6$
11. $30 \div (14 - 2^2) \times 5$
12. $\dfrac{5(2.3 + 3.7)}{2}$
13. $4^3 - \dfrac{1}{2}(7^2 + 5)$
14. $20 \times (3^2 - 4) \div 50$
15. $5 + 3(4^2 - 2) \div 6$
16. Use grouping symbols and at least one exponent to write a numerical expression that has a value of 80.

1.3 Prime Factorization (pp. 15–20)

Learning Target: Write a number as a product of prime factors and represent the product using exponents.

List the factor pairs of the number.

17. 28 **18.** 44 **19.** 96

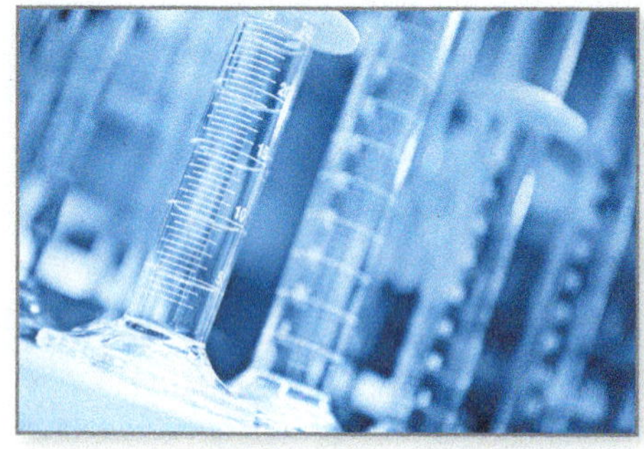

20. There are 36 graduated cylinders to put away on a shelf after science class. The shelf can fit a maximum of 20 cylinders across and 4 cylinders deep. The teacher wants each row to have the same number of cylinders. List the possible arrangements of the graduated cylinders on the shelf.

Write the prime factorization of the number.

21. 42 **22.** 50 **23.** 66

1.4 Greatest Common Factor (pp. 21–26)

Learning Target: Find the greatest common factor of two numbers.

Find the GCF of the numbers using lists of factors.

24. 27, 45 **25.** 30, 48 **26.** 28, 48

Find the GCF of the numbers using prime factorizations.

27. 24, 80 **28.** 52, 68 **29.** 32, 56

30. Write a pair of numbers that have a GCF of 20.

31. What is the greatest number of friends you can invite to an arcade using the coupon such that the tokens and slices of pizza are equally split between you and your friends with none left over? How many slices of pizza and tokens will each person receive?

Common Errors

- **Exercises 21–23** Students may think that smaller numbers have fewer factors. Remind students to keep finding factors until all factors are prime numbers.

Chapter Self-Assessment

17. 1, 28; 2, 14; 4, 7

18. 1, 44; 2, 22; 4, 11

19. 1, 96; 2, 48; 3, 32; 4, 24; 6, 16; 8, 12

20. 2 rows of 18, 3 rows of 12, 4 rows of 9

21. $2 \times 3 \times 7$

22. 2×5^2

23. $2 \times 3 \times 11$

24. 9

25. 6

26. 4

27. 8

28. 4

29. 8

30. *Sample answer:* 40, 60

31. 5 friends; 4 slices; 15 tokens

Chapter Self-Assessment

32. 28

33. 60

34. 84

35. 90

36. 60

37. 54

38. 72

39. *Sample answer:* 12, 14

40. *Sample answer:* 3, 9, 15

41. 30

42. 3 packs of hamburgers and 5 packs of buns

43. **a.** 350th

b. 10

Common Errors

- **Exercises 35–37** After writing the prime factorizations, students may struggle over which factors to use to find the LCM. If needed, students should draw a Venn diagram to clarify the problem.

Chapter Resources

Surface Level	Deep Level
Resources by Chapter • Extra Practice • Reteach • Puzzle Time Student Journal • Practice • Chapter Self-Assessment Differentiating the Lesson Tutorial Videos Skills Review Handbook Skills Trainer Game Library	Resources by Chapter • Enrichment and Extension Graphic Organizers Game Library

Transfer Level	
STEAM Video Dynamic Assessment System • Chapter Test	Assessment Book • Chapter Tests A and B • Alternative Assessment • STEAM Performance Task

1.5 Least Common Multiple (pp. 27–32)

Learning Target: Find the least common multiple of two numbers.

Find the LCM of the numbers using lists of multiples.

32. 4, 14 **33.** 6, 20 **34.** 12, 28

Find the LCM of the numbers using prime factorizations.

35. 6, 45 **36.** 10, 12 **37.** 18, 27

38. Find the LCM of 8, 12, and 18.

39. Write a pair of numbers that have an LCM of 84.

40. Write three numbers that have an LCM of 45.

41. You water your roses every sixth day and your hydrangeas every fifth day. Today you water both plants. In how many days will you water both plants on the same day again?

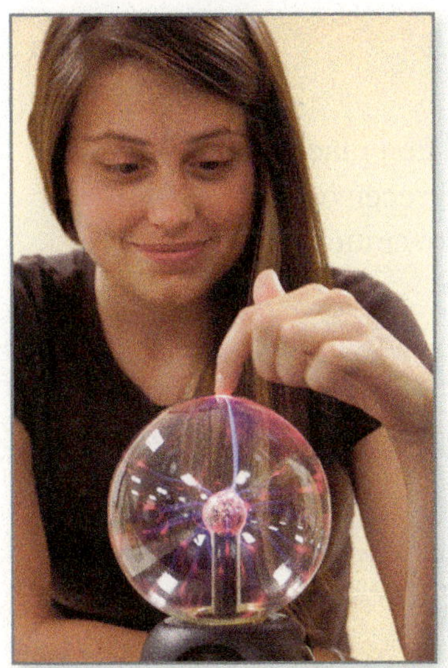

42. Hamburgers are sold in packages of 20, while buns are sold in packages of 12. What are the least numbers of packages you should buy in order to have the same number of hamburgers and buns?

43. A science museum is giving away a magnetic liquid kit to every 50th guest and a plasma ball to every 35th guest until someone receives both prizes.

a. Which numbered guest will receive both a magnetic liquid kit and a plasma ball?

b. How many people will receive a plasma ball?

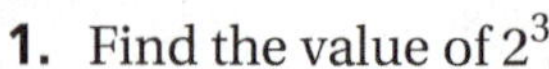

1 Practice Test

1. Find the value of 2^3.

2. Evaluate $\frac{5 + 4(12 - 2)}{3^2}$.

3. Write $264 \cdot 264 \cdot 264$ as a power.

4. List the factor pairs of 66.

5. Write the prime factorization of 56.

Find the GCF of the numbers.

6. 24, 54
7. 16, 32, 72
8. 52, 65

Find the LCM of the numbers.

9. 9, 24
10. 26, 39
11. 6, 12, 14

12. You have 16 yellow beads, 20 red beads, and 24 orange beads to make identical bracelets. What is the greatest number of bracelets that you can make using all of the beads?

13. A bag contains equal numbers of green marbles and blue marbles. You can divide all of the green marbles into groups of 12 and all the blue marbles into groups of 16. What is the least number of each color of marble that can be in the bag?

14. The ages of the members of a family are 65, 58, 27, 25, 5, and 2 years old. What is the total admission price for the family to visit the zoo?

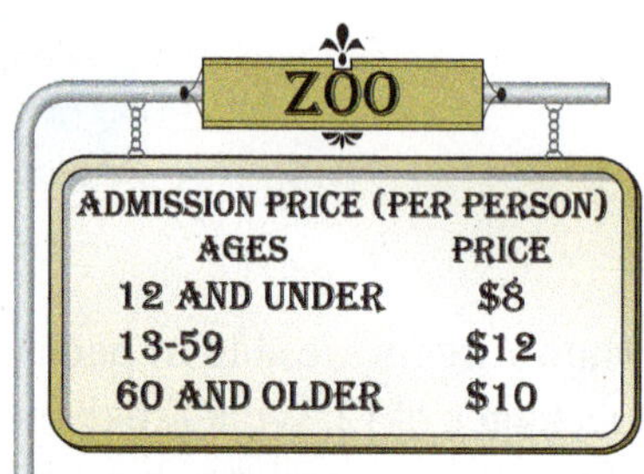

15. A competition awards prizes for fourth, third, second, and first place. The fourth place winner receives \$5. Each place above that receives a prize that is five times the amount of the previous prize. How much prize money is awarded?

16. You buy tealight candles and mints as party favors for a baby shower. The tealight candles come in packs of 12 for \$3.50. The mints come in packs of 50 for \$6.25. What is the least amount of money you can spend to buy the same number of candles and mints?

Practice Test Item References

Practice Test Questions	Section to Review
1, 3	1.1
2, 14, 15	1.2
4, 5	1.3
6–8, 12	1.4
9–11, 13, 16	1.5

Test-Taking Strategies

Remind students to quickly look over the entire test before they start so that they can budget their time. They should not spend too much time on any single problem. Urge students to try to work on a part of each problem, because partial credit is better than no credit. When they receive their tests, students should jot down simple examples of finding the greatest common factor and least common multiple on the back of the test. By doing this, they will not become confused when they are under pressure. Teach students to use the **Stop** and **Think** strategy before answering. **Stop** and carefully read the problem, and **Think** about what the answer should look like.

Common Errors

- **Exercise 1** Students may make the mistake of writing the exponent as a factor. Remind them that the exponent is the number of times the base is used as a factor. You may want to demonstrate this point with a quick example. For instance, point out that $2^3 = 2 \times 2 \times 2 = 8$ but $2 \times 3 = 6$.
- **Exercise 5** Students may think that smaller numbers have fewer factors. Remind students to keep finding factors until all factors are prime numbers.
- **Exercises 9–11** When using prime factorizations, students may struggle over which factors to use to find the LCM. If needed, students should draw a Venn diagram to clarify the problem.

Practice Test

1. 8
2. 5
3. 264^3
4. 1, 66; 2, 33; 3, 22; 6, 11
5. $2^3 \cdot 7$
6. 6
7. 8
8. 13
9. 72
10. 78
11. 84
12. 4
13. 48
14. $62
15. $780
16. $125

Test-Taking Strategies

Available at *BigIdeasMath.com*

After Answering Easy Questions, Relax

Answer Easy Questions First

Estimate the Answer

Read All Choices before Answering

Read Question before Answering

Solve Directly or Eliminate Choices

Solve Problem before Looking at Choices

Use Intelligent Guessing

Work Backwards

About this Strategy

When taking a multiple-choice test, be sure to read each question carefully and thoroughly. Before answering a question, determine exactly what is being asked, then eliminate the wrong answers and select the best choice.

Cumulative Practice

1. 1080
2. C
3. I
4. D

Item Analysis

1. **Gridded Response:** Correct answer: 1080

   Common error: The student does not properly carry the 2 to the hundreds place and gets 880.

2. **A.** The student does not follow the correct order of operations; subtracting 8 from 2^3 first.

   B. The student does not follow the correct order of operations; subtracting 8 from $3 \cdot 2^3$ instead of dividing 8 by 4.

   C. Correct answer

   D. The student does not follow the correct order of operations; calculating $(3 \cdot 2)^3$ instead of $3 \cdot 2^3$.

3. **F.** The student thinks the area is equal to the side length.

   G. The student doubles the side length instead of squaring the side length.

   H. The student calculates the perimeter instead of the area.

   I. Correct answer

4. **A.** The student does not find the *greatest* common factor.

   B. The student finds the product of only two of the common prime factors.

   C. The student does not find the *greatest* common factor.

   D. Correct answer

1 Cumulative Practice

Test-Taking Strategy
Solve Directly or Eliminate Choices

How many hyenas are 5−2²−1 hyenas?
(A) 0 (B) 2 (C) 8 (D) 10

Survival strategy: A

"Which strategy would you use on this one: solve directly or eliminate choices?"

1. What is the value of 8×135?

2. Which number is equivalent to the expression below?

$$3 \cdot 2^3 - 8 \div 4$$

A. 0 **B.** 4

C. 22 **D.** 214

3. The top of an end table is a square with a side length of 16 inches. What is the area of the tabletop?

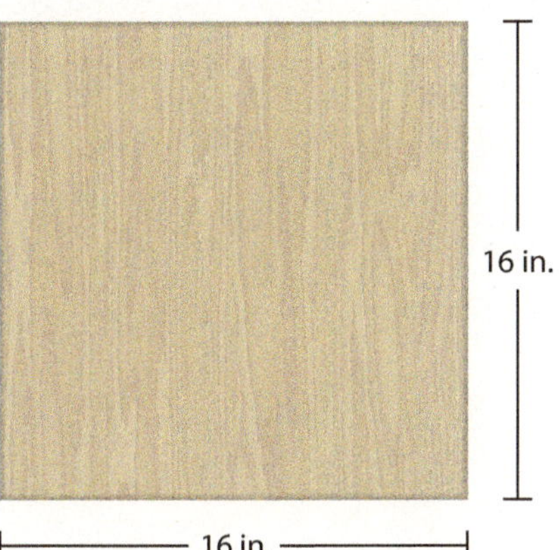

F. 16 in.^{2} **G.** 32 in.^{2}

H. 64 in.^{2} **I.** 256 in.^{2}

4. You are filling baskets using 18 green eggs, 36 red eggs, and 54 blue eggs. What is the greatest number of baskets that you can fill so that the baskets are identical and there are no eggs left over?

A. 3 **B.** 6

C. 9 **D.** 18

5. What is the value of $2^3 \cdot 3^2 \cdot 5$?

6. You hang the two strands of decorative lights shown below.

Strand 1: changes between red and blue every 15 seconds

Strand 2: changes between green and gold every 18 seconds

Both strands just changed color. After how many seconds will the strands change color at the same time again?

F. 3 seconds
G. 30 seconds
H. 90 seconds
I. 270 seconds

7. Point P is plotted in the coordinate plane below.

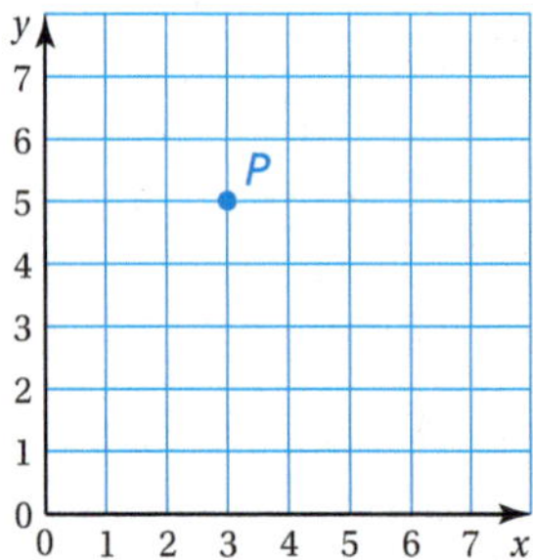

What are the coordinates of Point P?

A. (5, 3)
B. (4, 3)
C. (3, 5)
D. (3, 4)

8. What is the prime factorization of 1100?

F. $2 \times 5 \times 11$
G. $2^2 \times 5^2 \times 11$
H. $4 \times 5^2 \times 11$
I. $2^2 \times 5 \times 55$

Item Analysis (continued)

5. **Gridded Response:** Correct answer: 360

   Common error: The student multiplies the base and exponent for each power to get 180.

6. **F.** The student finds the GCF instead of the LCM.

   G. The student incorrectly multiplies 2, 3, and 5 to find the LCM.

   H. Correct answer

   I. The student incorrectly multiplies 15 and 18 to find the LCM.

7. **A.** The student switches the order of the *x*- and *y*-coordinates.

   B. The student switches the order of the *x*- and *y*-coordinates, and uses 4 instead of 5.

   C. Correct answer

   D. The student uses 4 instead of 5 for the *y*-coordinate.

8. **F.** The student lists the prime factors but does not include the correct exponent for each factor.

   G. Correct answer

   H. The student does not write 4 as 2×2.

   I. The student does not write 55 as 5×11.

Cumulative Practice

5. 360
6. H
7. C
8. G

Cumulative Practice

9. D

10. G

11. C

12. 5, 1, 3; The GCF is 1; 10 and 21 do not have common factors other than 1.

Item Analysis (continued)

9. **A.** The student finds the LCM of 3 and 8 only.

B. The student finds the LCM of 3 and 10 only.

C. The student finds the LCM of 8 and 10 only.

D. Correct answer

10. **F.** The student finds the area of the small square.

G. Correct answer

H. The student finds the area of the large square.

I. The student adds the areas of the small and large squares, rather than subtracting the area of the small square from the area of the large square.

11. **A.** The student does not recognize that 4 is composite.

B. The student does not recognize that 21 is composite.

C. Correct answer

D. The student does not recognize that 9 is composite.

12. **2 points** The student's explanation demonstrates a thorough understanding of finding the greatest common factor of three numbers. The student correctly finds the GCF of each pair of numbers and the GCF of 10, 15, and 21 is 1. The student may reason that the GCF of the three numbers must be 1, because two of the numbers, 10 and 21, have only 1 as a common factor.

1 point The student's explanation demonstrates a partial but limited understanding of finding the greatest common factor of three numbers. For instance, the student finds the GCF of each pair of numbers but does not find the GCF of all three numbers.

0 points The student provides no response, a completely incorrect or incomprehensible response, or a response that demonstrates insufficient understanding of finding the greatest common factor of three numbers.

9. What is the least common multiple of 3, 8, and 10?

A. 24 **B.** 30

C. 80 **D.** 120

10. What is the area of the shaded region of the figure below?

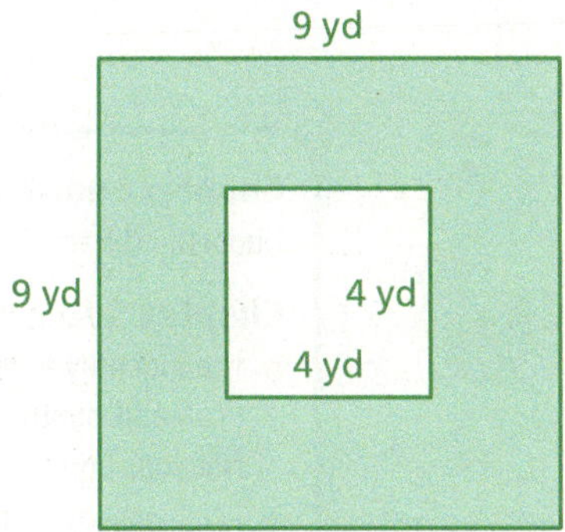

F. 16 yd^2 **G.** 65 yd^2

H. 81 yd^2 **I.** 97 yd^2

11. Which expression represents a prime factorization?

A. $4 \times 4 \times 7$ **B.** $2^2 \times 21 \times 23$

C. $3^4 \times 5 \times 7$ **D.** $5 \times 5 \times 9 \times 11$

12. Find the greatest common factor for each pair of numbers.

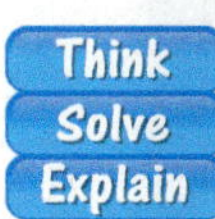

10 and 15 10 and 21 15 and 21

What can you conclude about the greatest common factor of 10, 15, and 21? Explain your reasoning.

2 Fractions and Decimals

2.1 Multiplying Fractions

2.2 Dividing Fractions

2.3 Dividing Mixed Numbers

2.4 Adding and Subtracting Decimals

2.5 Multiplying Decimals

2.6 Dividing Whole Numbers

2.7 Dividing Decimals

Chapter Learning Target:
Understand fractions and decimals.

Chapter Success Criteria:
- I can identify a fraction and a decimal.
- I can add, subtract, multiply, and divide fractions and decimals.
- I can evaluate expressions involving fractions and decimals using the order of operations.
- I can solve a problem using fractions and decimals.

Laurie's Notes

Chapter 2 Overview

By the end of this course, all students should be proficient in adding, subtracting, multiplying, and dividing fractions and decimals. Students were introduced to some of these concepts in prior courses, and now the remaining work will be completed in this course. This is the last opportunity that students will have to make sense of these computations. In future courses, the operations will be performed on rational numbers. For this reason, I urge you not to move quickly through this chapter. The explorations and visual models used throughout the chapter will enable students to develop the conceptual understanding necessary for making sense of the algorithms.

Students should understand that the meaning of each operation with fractions and decimals is the same as the meaning for whole numbers. Understanding this, and using visual representations, is essential to student success with these concepts.

Addition and subtraction with fractions and mixed numbers was completed in the prior course. Students should be able to represent fractions and mixed numbers using area models, tape diagrams, and number lines. All of these models will be used in the lessons on multiplication and division of fractions. Contextual problems are used to help students make sense of what it means to multiply and divide fractions.

Decimal operations were introduced in the prior course, but fluency is expected by the end of this course. Understanding place value, how to write decimals as fractions, and models that represent decimals are prerequisite skills. Throughout this chapter, and course, be sure to use precise language when reading decimals. Always say, "two and five-tenths" instead of "two point five." You want students to understand the fractional part in the number 2.5 and that will not be evident if point terminology is used.

The lesson on adding and subtracting decimals will reinforce the concept of working with like position values, just as you do with whole numbers. Multiplying two decimals will result in the same digits as multiplying with whole numbers, regardless of the position of the decimal points. The same is true for dividing two decimals. Students need to estimate and recognize patterns to understand where to place the decimal point in the answer. These ideas will be investigated prior to introducing an algorithm.

Suggested Pacing

Chapter Opener	1 Day
Section 1	1 Day
Section 2	3 Days
Section 3	2 Days
Section 4	1 Day
Section 5	1 Day
Section 6	1 Day
Section 7	2 Days
Connecting Concepts	1 Day
Chapter Review	1 Day
Chapter Test	1 Day
Total Chapter 2	15 Days
Year-to-Date	28 Days

Chapter Learning Target

Understand fractions and decimals.

Chapter Success Criteria

- Identify a fraction and a decimal.
- Add, subtract, multiply, and divide fractions and decimals.
- Evaluate expressions involving fractions and decimals using the order of operations.
- Solve a problem using fractions and decimals.

Chapter 2 Learning Targets and Success Criteria

Section	Learning Target	Success Criteria
2.1 Multiplying Fractions	Find products involving fractions and mixed numbers.	• Draw a model to explain fraction multiplication. • Multiply fractions. • Find products involving mixed numbers. • Interpret products involving fractions and mixed numbers to solve real-life problems.
2.2 Dividing Fractions	Compute quotients of fractions and solve problems involving division by fractions.	• Draw a model to explain division of fractions. • Find reciprocals of numbers. • Divide fractions by fractions. • Divide fractions and whole numbers.
2.3 Dividing Mixed Numbers	Compute quotients with mixed numbers and solve problems involving division with mixed numbers.	• Draw a model to explain division of mixed numbers. • Write a mixed number as an improper fraction. • Divide with mixed numbers. • Evaluate expressions involving mixed numbers using the order of operations.
2.4 Adding and Subtracting Decimals	Add and subtract decimals and solve problems involving addition and subtraction of decimals.	• Explain why it is necessary to line up the decimal points when adding and subtracting decimals. • Add decimals. • Subtract decimals. • Evaluate expressions involving addition and subtraction of decimals.
2.5 Multiplying Decimals	Multiply decimals and solve problems involving multiplication of decimals.	• Multiply decimals by whole numbers. • Multiply decimals by decimals. • Evaluate expressions involving multiplication of decimals.
2.6 Dividing Whole Numbers	Divide whole numbers and solve problems involving division of whole numbers.	• Use long division to divide whole numbers. • Write a remainder as a fraction. • Interpret quotients in real-life problems.
2.7 Dividing Decimals	Divide decimals and solve problems involving division of decimals.	• Divide decimals by whole numbers. • Divide decimals by decimals. • Divide whole numbers by decimals.

Progressions

Through the Grades		
Grade 5	**Grade 6**	**Grade 7**
• Add, subtract, multiply, and divide decimals to the hundredths place. • Interpret a fraction as division. Solve word problems involving division of whole numbers leading to answers in the form of a mixed number. • Multiply fractions or whole numbers by fractions.	• Divide fractions and mixed numbers. • Fluently add, subtract, multiply, and divide multi-digit decimals.	• Add, subtract, multiply, and divide rational numbers. • Apply properties of operations as strategies to perform operations with rational numbers.

Through the Chapter							
Standard	**2.1**	**2.2**	**2.3**	**2.4**	**2.5**	**2.6**	**2.7**
6.NS.A.1 Interpret and compute quotients of fractions, and solve word problems involving division of fractions by fractions, e.g., by using visual fraction models and equations to represent the problem.	▲	●	★				
6.NS.B.2 Fluently divide multi-digit numbers using the standard algorithm.						★	
6.NS.B.3 Fluently add, subtract, multiply, and divide multi-digit decimals using the standard algorithm for each operation.				●	●		★

Key

▲ = preparing ★ = complete

● = learning ■ = extending

STEAM Video

1. *Sample answer:* Add or subtract the distances.
2. *Sample answer:* Divide the distance by the distance to the Moon, then multiply by 3.

Performance Task

Sample answer: no; Using current technology, it would take decades to make a round trip to the farthest planets in our solar system.

Mathematical Practices

Students have opportunities to develop aspects of the mathematical practices throughout the chapter. Here are some examples.

1. **Make Sense of Problems and Persevere in Solving Them**
   2.7 Exercise 73, *p. 94*
2. **Reason Abstractly and Quantitatively**
   2.1 Exercise 69, *p. 52*
3. **Construct Viable Arguments and Critique the Reasoning of Others**
   2.3 Exercise 45, *p. 66*
4. **Model with Mathematics**
   2.4 Exercise 52, *p. 72*
5. **Use Appropriate Tools Strategically**
   2.4 Math Practice note, *p. 67*
6. **Attend to Precision**
   2.5 Exercise 55, *p. 79*
7. **Look for and Make Use of Structure**
   2.4 Exercise 58, *p. 72*
8. **Look for and Express Regularity in Repeated Reasoning**
   2.1 Math Practice note, *p. 45*

Laurie's Notes

STEAM Video

Before the Video

- To introduce the STEAM Video, read aloud the first paragraph of Space is Big and discuss the questions with your students.

? "Why do astronomers use astronomical units to measure distances in space?"

? "In what different ways can you compare the distances between objects and the locations of objects using the four mathematical operations?"

During the Video

- Pause the video at 2:13. The video shows a scale representation of the distances between Earth, the Moon, and the Sun.

? "What has happened in the video so far?" They have shown a scale representation of the distances between Earth, the Moon, and the Sun. Earth and the Moon would be about 8 inches apart if they were the size of beads.

? "What is the actual distance between the Moon and Earth?" 0.00256 AU
"How long would it take to travel to the Moon?" 3 days

- Watch the remainder of the video.

After the Video

? "How can you find the distance between two planets that are on the same side of the Sun?" Subtract their distances to the Sun from each other.

? "How can you find the distance between two planets that are on opposite sides of the Sun?" Add their distances to the Sun to each other.

- Have students work with a partner to answer Questions 1 and 2.
- As students discuss and answer the questions, listen for understanding and knowledge of operations with decimals.

Performance Task

- Use this information to spark students' interest and promote thinking about real-life problems.

? Ask "Is it realistic for a manned spacecraft to travel to each planet in our solar system? Explain why or why not."

- After completing the chapter, students will have gained the knowledge needed to complete "Space Explorers."

STEAM Video

Space is Big

An astronomical unit (AU) is the average distance between Earth and the Sun, about 93 million miles. Why do astronomers use astronomical units to measure distances in space? In what different ways can you compare the distances between objects and the locations of objects using the four mathematical operations?

Watch the STEAM Video "Space is Big." Then answer the following questions.

1. You know the distances between the Sun and each planet. How can you find the minimum and maximum distances between two planets as they rotate around the Sun?

2. The table shows the distances of three celestial bodies from Earth. It takes about three days to travel from Earth to the Moon. How can you estimate the amount of time it would take to travel from Earth to the Sun or to Venus?

Celestial body	Sun	Moon	Venus
Distance from Earth (AU)	1	0.00256	0.277

Performance Task

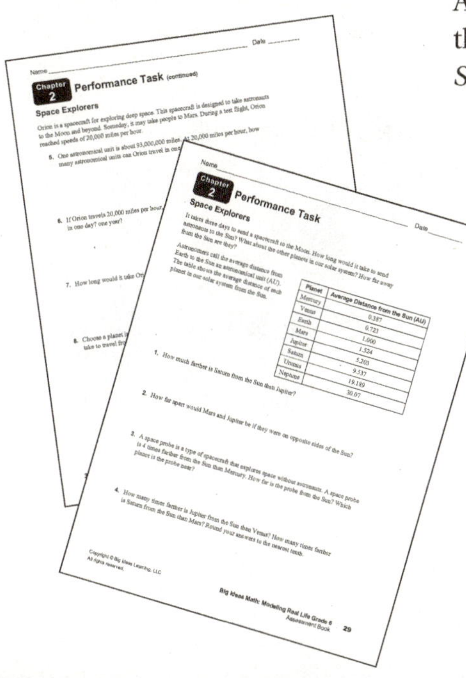

Name ________ Date ________

Chapter 2 Performance Task (continued)

Space Explorers

Orion is a spacecraft for exploring deep space. This spacecraft is designed to take astronauts to the Moon and beyond. Someday, it may take people to Mars. During a test flight, Orion reached speeds of 20,000 miles per hour.

5. One astronomical unit is about 93,000,000 miles. At 20,000 miles per hour, how many astronomical units can Orion travel in one

6. If Orion travels 20,000 miles per hour, in one day? one year?

7. How long would it take Ori

8. Choose a planet i take to travel fro

Name ________ Date ________

Chapter 2 Performance Task

Space Explorers

It takes three days to send a spacecraft to the Moon. How long would it take to send astronauts to the Sun? What about the other planets in our solar system? How far away from the Sun are they?

Astronomers call the average distance from Earth to the Sun an astronomical unit (AU). The table shows the average distance of each planet in our solar system from the Sun.

Planet	Average Distance from the Sun (AU)
Mercury	0.387
Venus	0.723
Earth	1.000
Mars	1.524
Jupiter	5.203
Saturn	9.537
Uranus	19.189
Neptune	30.07

1. How much farther is Saturn from the Sun than Jupiter?

2. How far apart would Mars and Jupiter be if they were on opposite sides of the Sun?

3. A space probe is a type of spacecraft that explores space without astronauts. A space probe is 4 times farther from the Sun than Mercury. How far is the probe from the Sun? Which planet is the probe near?

4. How many times farther is Jupiter from the Sun than Venus? How many times farther is Saturn from the Sun than Mars? Round your answers to the nearest tenth.

Copyright © Big Ideas Learning, LLC
All rights reserved.

Big Ideas Math: Modeling Real Life Grade 6
Assessment Book 29

Space Explorers

After completing this chapter, you will be able to use the concepts you learned to answer the questions in the *STEAM Video Performance Task*.

You will use a table that shows the average distances between the Sun and each planet in our solar system to find several distances in space. Then you will use the speed of the Orion spacecraft to answer questions about time and distance.

Is it realistic for a manned spacecraft to travel to each planet in our solar system? Explain why or why not.

Getting Ready for Chapter 2

Chapter Exploration

Work with a partner. The area model represents the multiplication of two fractions. Copy and complete the statement.

1. 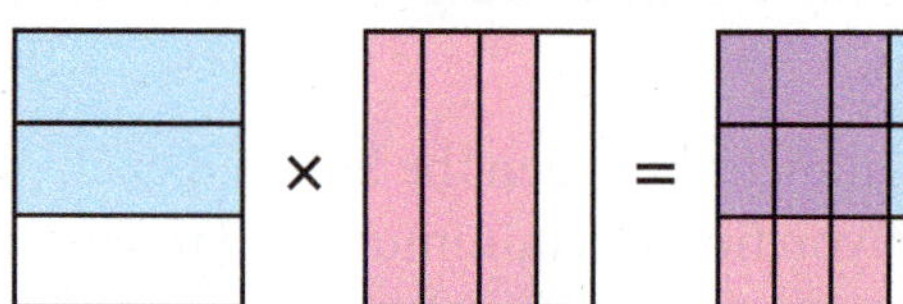

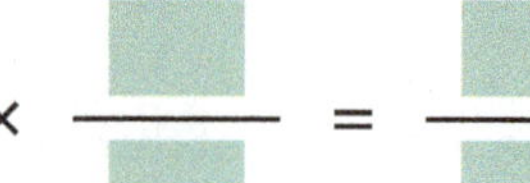

2. 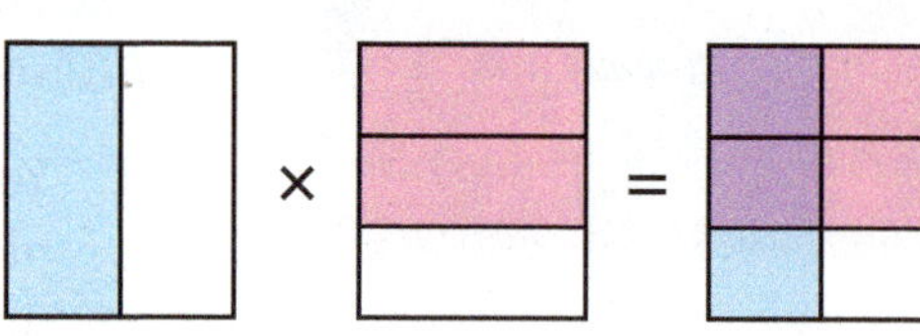

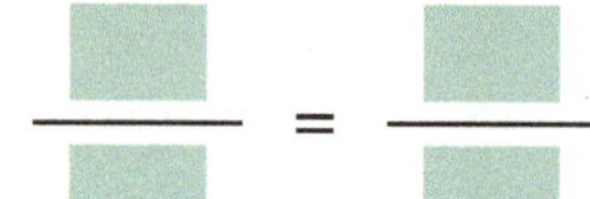

3. 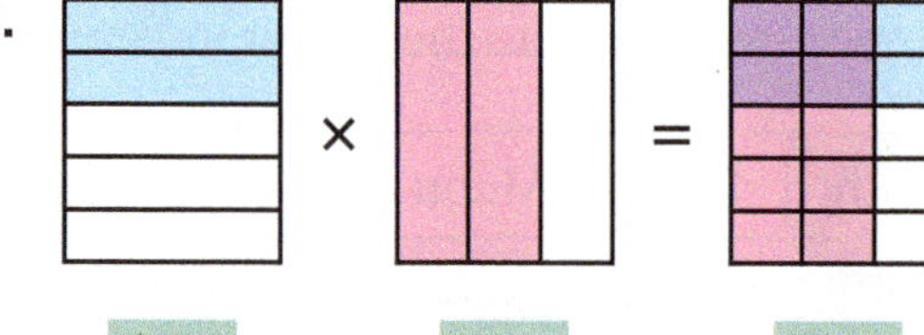

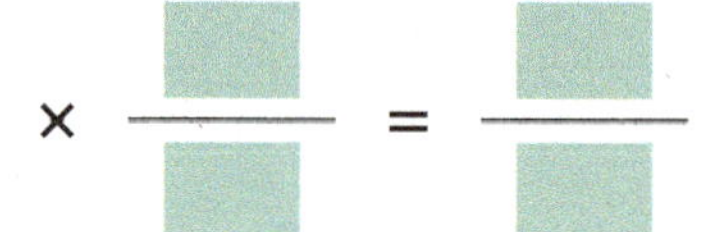

4. 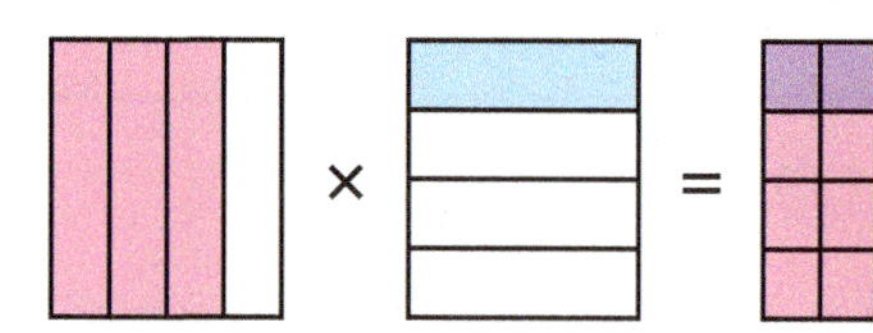

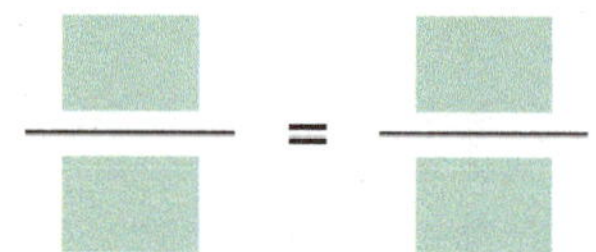

Work with a partner. Use an area model to find the product.

5. $\frac{1}{2} \times \frac{1}{3}$

6. $\frac{4}{5} \times \frac{1}{4}$

7. $\frac{1}{6} \times \frac{3}{4}$

8. $\frac{3}{5} \times \frac{1}{4}$

9. **MP MODELING REAL LIFE** You have a recipe that serves 6 people. The recipe uses three-fourths of a cup of milk.

   a. How can you use the recipe to serve *more* people? How much milk would you need? Give 2 examples.

   b. How can you use the recipe to serve *fewer* people? How much milk would you need? Give 2 examples.

Vocabulary

The following vocabulary terms are defined in this chapter. Think about what each term might mean and record your thoughts.

reciprocals

multiplicative inverses

Laurie's Notes

Chapter Exploration

- Students should be familiar with multiplying fractions by fractions and using area models to represent products.
- Reviewing fraction multiplication and area models will help ease the transition to performing the operations presented in the chapter.
- Fractions are used in everyday life in a variety of ways, including cooking and construction. In Exercise 9, emphasize the importance of using precise measurements when baking. For example, using too little milk can result in a dry, hard biscuit. Using too much milk can result in a moist, crumbly biscuit.

ELL Support

Be aware that students from foreign countries may use atypical phrases to express fractions, such as "two by three" for $\frac{2}{3}$. Explain that in American English "two by three" would signal multiplication, not division. In Exercise 9, students may not be familiar with U.S. customary measurements used for cooking. The metric system is used in most countries. Liters are used in place of cups, pints, quarts, and gallons. To give ELLs an idea of the size of a cup, explain that there are 2 cups in a pint, 2 pints in a quart, and about 1.06 quarts in a liter. So, there are approximately 4.24 cups in a liter.

Vocabulary

- These terms represent some of the vocabulary that students will encounter in Chapter 2. Discuss the terms as a class.
- Where have students heard the word *reciprocals* outside of a math classroom? In what contexts? Students may not be able to write the actual definition, but they may write phrases associated with reciprocals.
- Allowing students to discuss these terms now will prepare them for understanding the terms as they are presented in the chapter.
- When students encounter a new definition, encourage them to write in their *Student Journals.* They will revisit these definitions during the Chapter Review.

Topics for Review

- Decimal Place Value
- Estimating Whole Number Products and Quotients
- Factors of Whole Numbers
- Mixed Numbers and Improper Fractions
- Multiplying and Dividing Whole Numbers
- Simplifying Fractions

Chapter Exploration

1. $\frac{2}{3}; \frac{3}{4}; \frac{6}{12}$ or $\frac{1}{2}$

2. $\frac{1}{2}; \frac{2}{3}; \frac{2}{6}$ or $\frac{1}{3}$

3. $\frac{2}{5}; \frac{2}{3}; \frac{4}{15}$

4. $\frac{3}{4}; \frac{1}{4}; \frac{3}{16}$

5. $\frac{1}{6}$

6. $\frac{4}{20}$ or $\frac{1}{5}$

7. $\frac{3}{24}$ or $\frac{1}{8}$

8. $\frac{3}{20}$

9. **a.** *Sample answer:* Double the recipe, using $1\frac{1}{2}$ cups milk; triple the recipe, using $2\frac{1}{4}$ cups milk.

b. *Sample answer:* Halve the recipe, using $\frac{3}{8}$ cup milk; quarter the recipe, using $\frac{3}{16}$ cup milk.

Learning Target

Find products involving fractions and mixed numbers.

Success Criteria

- Draw a model to explain fraction multiplication.
- Multiply fractions.
- Find products involving mixed numbers.
- Interpret products involving fractions and mixed numbers to solve real-life problems.

Warm Up

Cumulative, vocabulary, and prerequisite skills practice opportunities are available in the *Resources by Chapter* or at *BigIdeasMath.com*.

ELL Support

Clarify the meaning of the word *model*. Students may be familiar with clothing models and supermodels. Remind them that math models were used throughout Chapter 1. Explain that a model is a representation or example of a system or structure. Models wear clothing to show others how it looks. In math, models show the process or structure used to solve a problem.

Exploration 1

See Additional Answers.

Exploration 2

a. $\frac{3}{5}$; *Sample answer:* Draw an area model with 5 rows and 4 columns. Shade 4 of the rows and 3 of the columns.

b. Multiply the numerators and the denominators of $\frac{3}{4}$ and $\frac{4}{5}$, and simplify the result.

Laurie's Notes

STATE STANDARDS
Preparing for 6.NS.A.1

Preparing to Teach

- In the previous course, students were introduced to multiplying fractions and mixed numbers. You want students to be able to explain the fraction multiplication algorithm, not just perform the computation. Models, particularly area models, will aid in mastery of the first success criterion. Simply finding products involving fractions and mixed numbers, without understanding, will hinder your students' ability to transfer their understanding.

Motivate

- Have students work with a partner to answer the questions.

What is $\frac{1}{2}$ of 20? 10 What is $\frac{1}{2}$ of 2? 1 What is $\frac{1}{2}$ of 1? $\frac{1}{2}$

What is $\frac{1}{2}$ of $\frac{1}{2}$? $\frac{1}{4}$ What is $\frac{1}{2}$ of $\frac{1}{4}$? $\frac{1}{8}$ What is $\frac{1}{2}$ of $\frac{3}{4}$? $\frac{3}{8}$

- You may need to provide models or hints for the last two questions. "What does $\frac{1}{2}$ of $\frac{1}{4}$ of a sandwich look like? What does $\frac{1}{2}$ of $\frac{3}{4}$ of a pizza look like?"

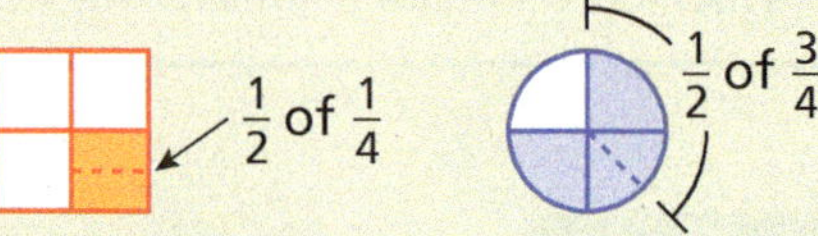

Exploration 1

- To demonstrate, fill a clear, plastic bottle with water until it is half full.
- ? "A bottle of water is $\frac{1}{2}$ full. You drink $\frac{2}{3}$ of the water. How can you find the portion of the bottle of water that you drink?" Before students look at the models, allow them to think about the problem independently, and then discuss with a partner.
- Regardless of the model, you want students to explain how the model is used to solve the problem. Solicit explanations for each model from different pairs.

Exploration 2

- ? **Turn and Talk:** Pose the problem. "What does $\frac{3}{4}$ of its width and $\frac{4}{5}$ of its length mean?" Listen to conversations. Is there an understanding that the size of the park is unknown, and doesn't need to be known?
- ? "Does the park need to be square?" no Ask a volunteer to explain.
- **MP4 Model with Mathematics:** Students will likely divide the rectangle into fourths in one direction and fifths in the other. Students can then use shading to represent the portion of the park that is covered by the playground.
- ? "What is the value of each small piece in the model?" $\frac{1}{20}$ "How many shaded pieces represent the area of the playground?" 12 pieces
- **MP8 Look for and Express Regularity in Repeated Reasoning:** Mathematically proficient students will look for a general method that can be used for multiplying fractions without using a model.

2.1 Multiplying Fractions

Learning Target: Find products involving fractions and mixed numbers.

Success Criteria:
- I can draw a model to explain fraction multiplication.
- I can multiply fractions.
- I can find products involving mixed numbers.
- I can interpret products involving fractions and mixed numbers to solve real-life problems.

EXPLORATION 1

Using Models to Solve a Problem

Work with a partner. A bottle of water is $\frac{1}{2}$ full. You drink $\frac{2}{3}$ of the water. Use one of the models to find the portion of the bottle of water that you drink. Explain your steps.

- number line

- area model

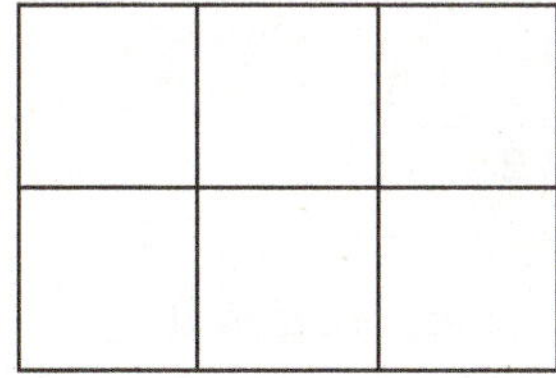

- tape diagram

EXPLORATION 2

Solving a Problem Involving Fractions

Work with a partner. A park has a playground that is $\frac{3}{4}$ of its width and $\frac{4}{5}$ of its length.

a. Use a model to find the portion of the park that is covered by the playground. Explain your steps.

b. How can you find the solution of part (a) without using a model?

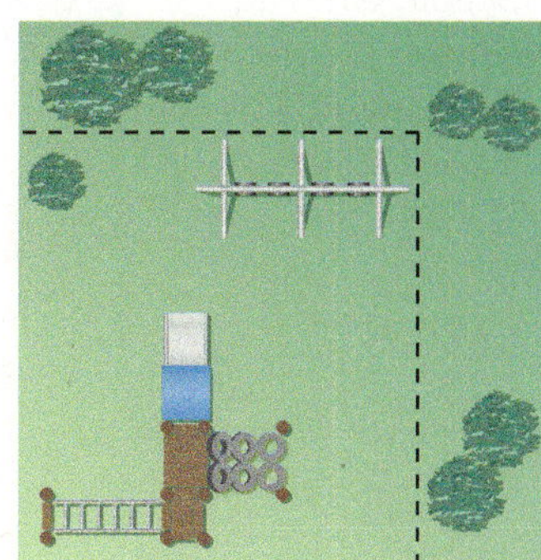

Math Practice

Find General Methods

How can you use your answer to find a method for multiplying fractions?

2.1 Lesson

EXAMPLE 1 Multiplying Fractions

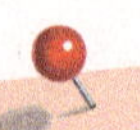

Think: What is one-fourth of one-half?

Find $\frac{1}{4} \times \frac{1}{2}$.

Use a model to find $\frac{1}{4}$ of $\frac{1}{2}$.

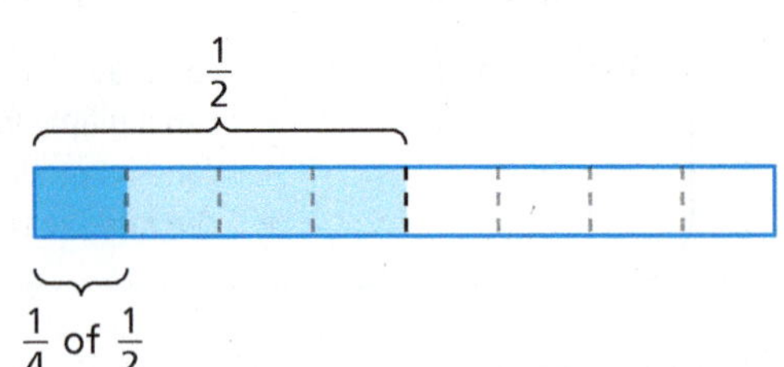

So, the product is $\frac{1}{8}$.

Try It Multiply.

1. $\frac{1}{3} \times \frac{1}{5}$ **2.** $\frac{2}{3} \times \frac{3}{4}$ **3.** $\frac{1}{2} \cdot \frac{5}{6}$

Key Idea

Multiplying Fractions

Words Multiply the numerators and multiply the denominators.

Numbers $\frac{3}{7} \times \frac{1}{2} = \frac{3 \times 1}{7 \times 2} = \frac{3}{14}$

Algebra $\frac{a}{b} \cdot \frac{c}{d} = \frac{a \cdot c}{b \cdot d}$, where $b, d \neq 0$

EXAMPLE 2 Multiplying Fractions

Remember

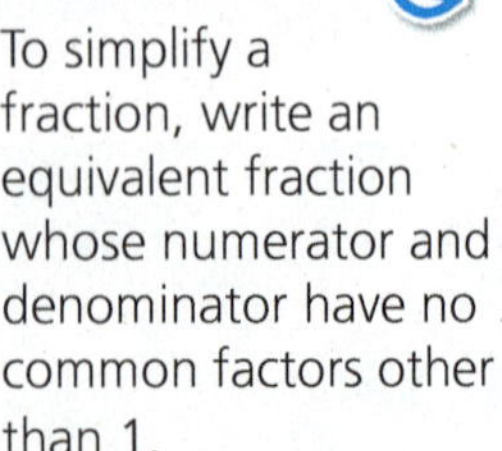

To simplify a fraction, write an equivalent fraction whose numerator and denominator have no common factors other than 1.

$\frac{24}{36} = \frac{24 \div 12}{36 \div 12} = \frac{2}{3}$

Find $\frac{8}{9} \cdot \frac{3}{4}$. **Estimate** $1 \cdot \frac{3}{4} = \frac{3}{4}$

$\frac{8}{9} \cdot \frac{3}{4} = \frac{8 \cdot 3}{9 \cdot 4}$ Multiply the numerators and the denominators.

$= \frac{24}{36}$, or $\frac{2}{3}$ Simplify.

The product is $\frac{2}{3}$. **Reasonable?** $\frac{2}{3} \approx \frac{3}{4}$ ✓

The symbol $\approx$ means *is approximately equal to*.

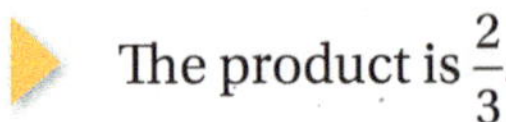

Try It Multiply. Write the answer in simplest form.

4. $\frac{3}{7} \times \frac{2}{3}$ **5.** $\frac{4}{9} \cdot \frac{3}{10}$ **6.** $\frac{6}{5} \cdot \frac{5}{8}$

Laurie's Notes

Scaffolding Instruction

- The explorations provide an opportunity for students to work with models to find the product of two fractions. Can students use the model to find the product of two fractions and to explain why the algorithm makes sense? Does their understanding extend to mixed numbers?
- **Emerging:** Students may be able to follow the algorithm but are not able to explain why it works. They may benefit from connecting visual models to the algorithms.
- **Proficient:** Students can use a model to explain why the fraction multiplication algorithm works, and are able to use estimation to check the reasonableness of their answers. Students can self-assess using Try It Exercises 1–6, and then draw a number line to represent and solve Example 3.
- Multiplying with mixed numbers is the focus of the second part of this lesson. All students need to understand how to find and model products of fractions and mixed numbers, which will lead to mastery of the third and fourth success criteria.

Key Idea

- **Connections:** Previously, when a fraction was multiplied by a whole number, the whole number was written as a fraction with a denominator of 1. This rule still works.

EXAMPLE 1

- **MP1 Make Sense of Problems and Persevere in Solving Them:** Mathematically proficient students continually ask themselves, "Does this make sense?" Models help them make sense of the answer and judge its reasonableness.
- Discuss the reasonableness of the answer: The product of $\frac{1}{4}$ and $\frac{1}{2}$ should be fairly small. Think of $\frac{1}{2}$ of the class. Now take $\frac{1}{4}$ of that group. It's not a lot.

Try It

- Note that multiplication is represented with • and × in these problems.

EXAMPLE 2

- The answer $\frac{24}{36}$ is correct but not simplified. Refer to the Remember note.
- This method for simplifying is used to show the multiplication of the fractions first, and then the simplification. An alternate method for simplification is dividing out common factors before multiplying, which is shown in the next course.

Try It

- Have students work independently, and then use *Thumbs Up* to indicate their understanding of multiplying fractions. Remember, simply performing the computation does not mean they can explain why the algorithm works.

Scaffold instruction to support all students in their learning. Learning is individualized and you may want to group students differently as they move in and out of these levels with each skill and concept. Student self-assessment and feedback help guide your instructional decisions about how and when to layer support for all students to become proficient learners.

Teaching Strategy

Use equivalent fractions to develop an understanding of fraction multiplication. In Exploration 1, you want to find $\frac{2}{3}$ of $\frac{1}{2}$, but it may not be obvious to students that $\frac{1}{2}$ can be split into thirds. Rename the quantity $\frac{1}{2}$ as $\frac{3}{6}$, so $\frac{2}{3} \times \frac{1}{2} = \frac{2}{3} \times \frac{3}{6}$. If $\frac{1}{3}$ of $\frac{3}{6}$ is $\frac{1}{6}$, then $\frac{2}{3}$ of $\frac{3}{6}$ is $\frac{2}{6}$ or $\frac{1}{3}$. By using number sense, students will begin to develop an understanding of how fractions are multiplied.

Extra Example 1

Find $\frac{1}{7} \times \frac{1}{5}$. $\frac{1}{35}$

Try It

1. $\frac{1}{15}$
2. $\frac{1}{2}$
3. $\frac{5}{12}$

Extra Example 2

Find $\frac{2}{25} \cdot \frac{5}{6}$. $\frac{1}{15}$

Try It

4. $\frac{2}{7}$
5. $\frac{2}{15}$
6. $\frac{3}{4}$

Extra Example 3

You have $\frac{5}{8}$ of a large bottle of shampoo. You pour $\frac{3}{10}$ of the shampoo into a smaller bottle. How much of the entire larger bottle do you pour into the smaller bottle? $\frac{3}{16}$

ELL Support

If Spanish-speaking students are in the class, have them describe *empanadas* before discussing Example 3. A comparable food is a sweet or savory turnover, which is made with pastry crust and filling. Point out the area model and talk through it. Allow students to work together on Try It Exercise 7. Tell them to follow the process from Example 3, but replace $\frac{3}{4}$ with $\frac{1}{4}$.

Beginner: Write the equation or draw a model to represent the product.

Intermediate: State the answer using a complete sentence. For example, "You use one-sixth of the entire bag."

Advanced: Explain each step.

Try It

7. $\frac{1}{6}$

Extra Example 4

Find $6\frac{1}{3} \times \frac{3}{4}$. $4\frac{3}{4}$

Try It

8. $\frac{7}{18}$
9. $1\frac{5}{9}$
10. $3\frac{1}{2}$

Laurie's Notes

EXAMPLE 3

- This problem is similar to Exploration 1. Can students read a contextual problem and recognize that fraction multiplication is needed?
- Pose the problem. "Tell a partner what you are asked to find and how you know." Listen for understanding that you are asked to find a part of a quantity, and that the product will tell you how much of the entire bag you use.
- Use the area model to demonstrate another method. Using the model, the product is $\frac{6}{12}$, or $\frac{1}{2}$ of the entire bag.

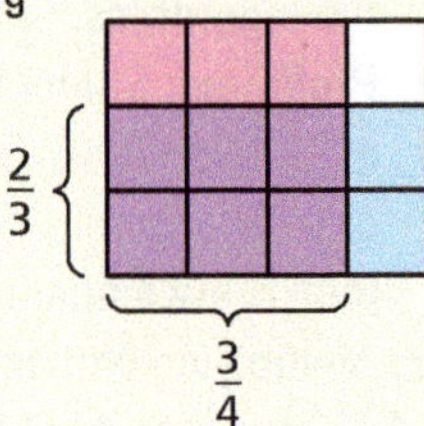

- Some students may be confused about using an area model to represent a context involving volume (the amount of flour). Solicit a volunteer to explain why the area model makes sense. Listen for understanding of the first success criterion: a model can be used to explain fraction multiplication.

Try It

- **Think-Pair-Share:** Students should read the question independently, and then work in pairs to answer the question.

Key Idea

- Before sharing the Key Idea, display the three models shown. Tell students to select one of the problems, and then use the model to find the product.

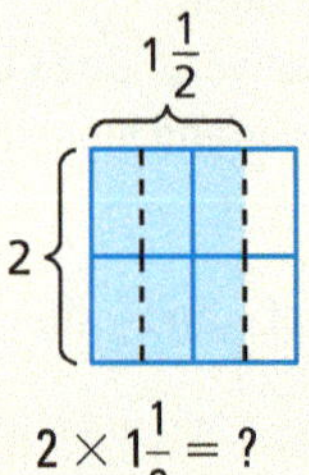

$2 \times 1\frac{1}{2} = ?$

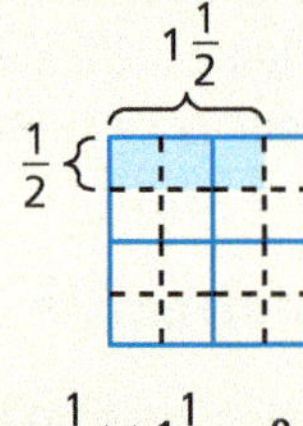

$\frac{1}{2} \times 1\frac{1}{2} = ?$

$1\frac{1}{2} \times 1\frac{1}{4} = ?$

- "How do you multiply with mixed numbers? Use your model to explain." Naming the parts of the model can be challenging. Students may find that if they label the dimensions as improper fractions, naming the parts makes sense.

EXAMPLE 4

- "Estimate $\frac{1}{2}$ of $2\frac{3}{4}$, and explain how you arrived at your estimate." $2\frac{3}{4}$ is close to 3, and $\frac{1}{2}$ of 3 is $1\frac{1}{2}$.
- "What is $2\frac{3}{4}$ as an improper fraction?" $\frac{11}{4}$
- Work through the problem as shown, and then discuss the Another Method note.

Try It

- Encourage students to estimate first, as it is really easy to make a computational error.

EXAMPLE 3 Solving a Problem Involving Fractions

You have $\frac{2}{3}$ of a bag of flour. You use $\frac{3}{4}$ of the flour to make empanada dough. How much of the entire bag do you use to make the dough?

FLOUR $\frac{3}{4}$ $\frac{2}{3}$

You use $\frac{3}{4}$ of $\frac{2}{3}$ of the bag. To find $\frac{3}{4}$ of $\frac{2}{3}$, multiply.

$$\frac{3}{4} \times \frac{2}{3} = \frac{3 \times 2}{4 \times 3}$$ Multiply the numerators and the denominators.

$$= \frac{6}{12}, \text{ or } \frac{1}{2}$$ Simplify.

So, you use $\frac{1}{2}$ of the entire bag.

Try It

7. **WHAT IF?** You use $\frac{1}{4}$ of the flour to make the dough. How much of the entire bag do you use to make the dough?

Key Idea

Multiplying Mixed Numbers

Write each mixed number as an improper fraction. Then multiply as you would with fractions.

EXAMPLE 4 Multiplying a Fraction and a Mixed Number

Another Method

Use a model.

2 $\quad \frac{3}{4}$

$\frac{1}{2}$ | $\frac{1}{2} \times 2 = 1$ | $\frac{1}{2} \times \frac{3}{4} = \frac{3}{8}$

So, $\frac{1}{2} \times 2\frac{3}{4} = 1 + \frac{3}{8} = 1\frac{3}{8}$. ✓

Find $\frac{1}{2} \times 2\frac{3}{4}$. **Estimate** $\frac{1}{2} \times 3 = 1\frac{1}{2}$

$$\frac{1}{2} \times 2\frac{3}{4} = \frac{1}{2} \times \frac{11}{4}$$ Write $2\frac{3}{4}$ as the improper fraction $\frac{11}{4}$.

$$= \frac{1 \times 11}{2 \times 4}$$ Multiply the numerators and the denominators.

$$= \frac{11}{8}, \text{ or } 1\frac{3}{8}$$ Simplify.

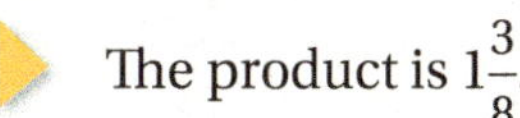

The product is $1\frac{3}{8}$. **Reasonable?** $1\frac{3}{8} \approx 1\frac{1}{2}$ ✓

Try It **Multiply. Write the answer in simplest form.**

8. $\frac{1}{3} \times 1\frac{1}{6}$

9. $3\frac{1}{2} \times \frac{4}{9}$

10. $4\frac{2}{3} \cdot \frac{3}{4}$

EXAMPLE 5 Multiplying Mixed Numbers

Find $1\frac{4}{5} \times 3\frac{2}{3}$.

Estimate $2 \times 4 = 8$

$1\frac{4}{5} \times 3\frac{2}{3} = \frac{9}{5} \times \frac{11}{3}$ — Write $1\frac{4}{5}$ and $3\frac{2}{3}$ as improper fractions.

$= \frac{9 \times 11}{5 \times 3}$ — Multiply the numerators and the denominators.

$= \frac{99}{15}$, or $6\frac{3}{5}$ — Simplify.

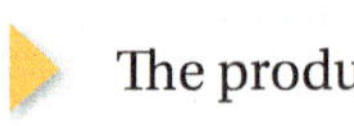

The product is $6\frac{3}{5}$.

Reasonable? $6\frac{3}{5} \approx 8$ ✓

Try It **Multiply. Write the answer in simplest form.**

11. $1\frac{7}{8} \bullet 2\frac{2}{5}$

12. $5\frac{5}{7} \times 2\frac{1}{10}$

13. $2\frac{1}{3} \bullet 7\frac{2}{3}$

Self-Assessment for Concepts & Skills

Solve each exercise. Then rate your understanding of the success criteria in your journal.

MULTIPLYING FRACTIONS AND MIXED NUMBERS **Multiply. Write the answer in simplest form.**

14. $\frac{1}{8} \times \frac{1}{6}$

15. $\frac{3}{8} \bullet \frac{2}{3}$

16. $2\frac{1}{6} \bullet 4\frac{2}{5}$

17. **MP REASONING** What is the missing denominator?

$$\frac{3}{7} \times \frac{1}{\square} = \frac{3}{28}$$

18. **MP USING TOOLS** Write a multiplication problem involving fractions that is represented by the model. Explain your reasoning.

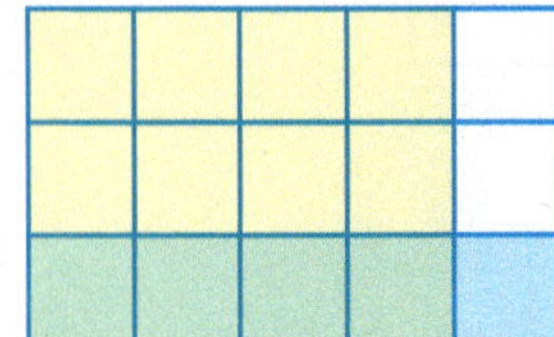

19. **MP USING TOOLS** Use the number line to find $\frac{3}{4} \times \frac{1}{2}$. Explain your reasoning.

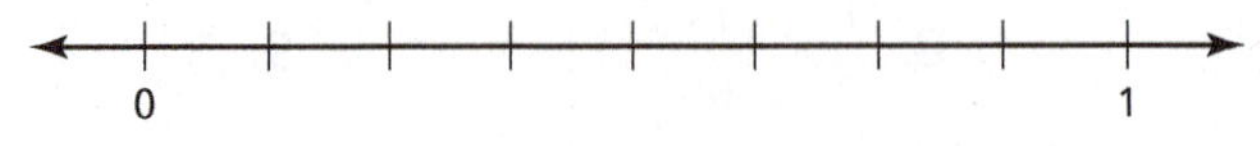

Laurie's Notes

EXAMPLE 5

- **Common Error:** Students may multiply the whole numbers, and then multiply the fractions as shown: $1\frac{4}{5} \times 3\frac{2}{3} \neq 3\frac{8}{15}$.
- Write the problem. Estimate the product.

? "What is the first step in multiplying mixed numbers?" Write the mixed numbers as improper fractions.

- As you work through this example, point out that by writing each of the mixed numbers as improper fractions, it ensures that all of the first number is multiplied by all of the second number.
- Finish working through the problem. Note that the answer is more reasonable than $3\frac{8}{15}$.
- You may want to show students one, or both, of the possible intermediate steps of simplifying. Writing $\frac{99}{15}$ as $6\frac{9}{15}$ before $6\frac{3}{5}$, or writing $\frac{99}{15}$ as $\frac{33}{5}$ before $6\frac{3}{5}$.

Try It

Have students use *Thumbs Up* to indicate their understanding of the third success criterion: finding products of mixed numbers.

Self-Assessment for Concepts & Skills

- Students may be able to multiply fractions and mixed numbers accurately. Students also need to recognize that drawing a model to explain the product is evidence of deeper understanding.
- Listening to how students estimate a product gives you insight into how they understand fractions and fraction multiplication.

ELL Support

Allow students to collaborate by working in groups to practice language as they complete the exercises. Remind students that for Exercises 14 and 15 they may use the same process as they did for Try It Exercise 7. Support groups as needed. Check comprehension by asking groups to present their answers, question-by-question, on their whiteboards. At a glance, you should be able to determine which groups have mastered the material. Reteach as needed.

The Success Criteria Self-Assessment chart can be found in the *Student Journal* or online at *BigIdeasMath.com*.

Extra Example 5

Find $2\frac{3}{5} \times 3\frac{1}{3}$. $8\frac{2}{3}$

Try It

11. $4\frac{1}{2}$
12. 12
13. $17\frac{8}{9}$

Self-Assessment for Concepts & Skills

14. $\frac{1}{48}$
15. $\frac{1}{4}$
16. $9\frac{8}{15}$
17. 4
18. $\frac{4}{5} \times \frac{1}{3}$; Four of five columns and one of three rows are shaded.
19. $\frac{3}{8}$; Three-fourths of the distance from 0 to $\frac{1}{2}$ is at $\frac{3}{8}$.

Extra Example 6

A grass practice field is $80\frac{1}{2}$ yards by $30\frac{3}{4}$ yards. Find the area of the practice field. $2475\frac{3}{8}$ square yards

Self-Assessment for Problem Solving

20. 4 h; *Sample answer:*

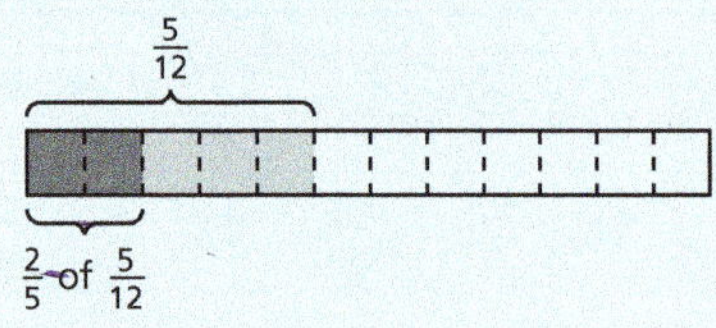

21. 1057 ft^2

22. $2\frac{1}{2}$ mi

Learning Target

Find products involving fractions and mixed numbers.

Success Criteria

- Draw a model to explain fraction multiplication.
- Multiply fractions.
- Find products involving mixed numbers.
- Interpret products involving fractions and mixed numbers to solve real-life problems.

Laurie's Notes

EXAMPLE 6

- Students have been using an area model in this lesson, so the formula is familiar.
- Pose the problem. "*Turn and Talk* to explain what the problem is asking, and then how to solve it." Have students begin solving the problem when they are confident in their strategies.

? "Why is the answer labeled with *square* meters?" Area is measured in square units.

- You may want to briefly explain the overestimates and underestimates in the Check Reasonableness note. To underestimate, estimate each number to the nearest whole number below the actual value. To overestimate, estimate each number to the nearest whole number above the actual value. Because the actual values are between the estimated values, the actual product is between the product of the underestimates and the product of the overestimates.

Self-Assessment for Problem Solving

- The goal for all students is to feel comfortable with the problem-solving plan. It is important for students to problem-solve in class, where they may receive support from you and their peers. Keep in mind that some students may only be ready to complete the first step.
- Students should work independently or with a partner on the exercises. Support students with probing questions and by providing feedback.
- Because this lesson is about multiplying fractions, students may simply calculate products without a deeper understanding of why they are multiplying. To make the connection to multiplication and ensure understanding, ask students which phrase in each exercise indicates multiplication.
- **MP4 Model with Mathematics:** Circulate while students are working and ask them to explain how a model helps them understand what the problem is asking.

The Success Criteria Self-Assessment chart can be found in the *Student Journal* or online at *BigIdeasMath.com*.

Closure

- **Exit Ticket:** "If you multiply two proper fractions, what do you know about the product? Explain." The product will be less than the greater fraction, because the product is a portion of the greater fraction. "If you multiply two mixed numbers, what do you know about the product? Explain." The product will be greater than the product of the whole number portions of the mixed numbers, because the mixed numbers are greater than their whole numbers.

EXAMPLE 6 Modeling Real Life

A city is resurfacing a basketball court. Find the area of the court.

Understand the problem.

You are given the dimensions of a basketball court. You are asked to find the area of the court.

Make a plan.

Use the formula for the area of a rectangle. Find the product of the length and the width of the court.

$21\frac{1}{3}$ m

$13\frac{1}{2}$ m

Solve and check.

$A = \ell w$ Write the formula.

$= 21\frac{1}{3} \cdot 13\frac{1}{2}$ Substitute for ℓ and w.

$= \frac{64}{3} \cdot \frac{27}{2}$ Write $21\frac{1}{3}$ and $13\frac{1}{2}$ as improper fractions.

$= \frac{64 \cdot 27}{3 \cdot 2}$ Multiply the numerators and the denominators.

$= \frac{1728}{6}$, or 288 Simplify.

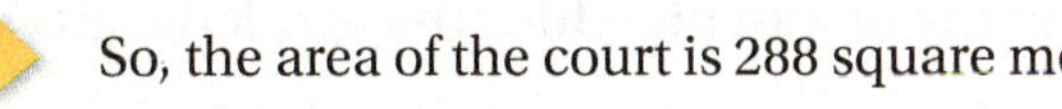

So, the area of the court is 288 square meters.

Check Reasonableness

Find an underestimate and an overestimate.

Underestimate:

$13 \cdot 21 = 273$

Overestimate:

$14 \cdot 22 = 308$

The answer is reasonable because $273 < 288 < 308$. ✓

Self-Assessment for Problem Solving

Solve each exercise. Then rate your understanding of the success criteria in your journal.

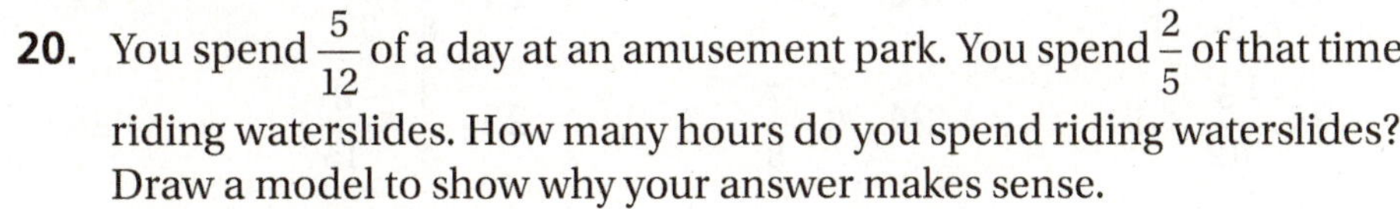

20. You spend $\frac{5}{12}$ of a day at an amusement park. You spend $\frac{2}{5}$ of that time riding waterslides. How many hours do you spend riding waterslides? Draw a model to show why your answer makes sense.

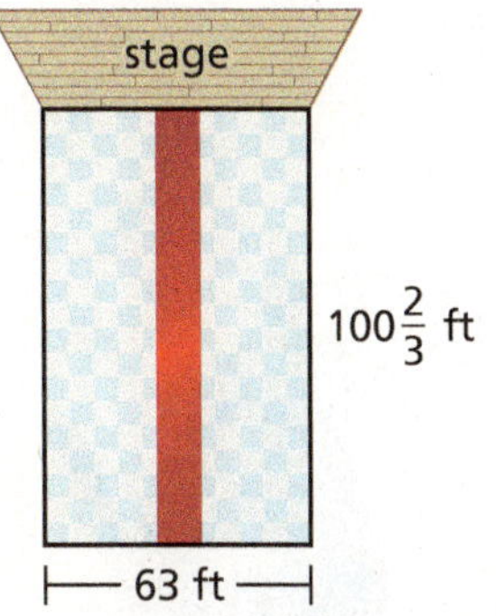

21. A venue is preparing for a concert on the floor shown. The width of the red carpet is $\frac{1}{6}$ of the width of the floor. What is the area of the red carpet?

22. You travel $9\frac{3}{8}$ miles from your house to a shopping mall. You travel $\frac{2}{3}$ of that distance on an interstate. The only road construction you encounter is on the first $\frac{2}{5}$ of the interstate. On how many miles of your trip do you encounter construction?

2.1 Practice

Review & Refresh

Find the LCM of the numbers.

1. 8, 10
2. 5, 7
3. 2, 5, 7
4. 6, 7, 10

Divide. Use a diagram to justify your answer.

5. $6 \div \frac{1}{2}$
6. $\frac{1}{4} \div 8$
7. $4 \div \frac{1}{3}$
8. $\frac{1}{5} \div 4$

Write the product as a power.

9. $10 \times 10 \times 10$
10. $5 \times 5 \times 5 \times 5$

11. How many inches are in $5\frac{1}{2}$ yards?

A. $15\frac{1}{2}$ **B.** $16\frac{1}{2}$ **C.** 66 **D.** 198

Concepts, Skills, & Problem Solving

MP **CHOOSE TOOLS** **A bottle of water is $\frac{2}{3}$ full. You drink the given portion of the water. Use a model to find the portion of the bottle of water that you drink.** (See Exploration 1, p. 45.)

12. $\frac{1}{2}$
13. $\frac{1}{4}$
14. $\frac{3}{4}$

MULTIPLYING FRACTIONS **Multiply. Write the answer in simplest form.**

15. $\frac{1}{7} \times \frac{2}{3}$
16. $\frac{5}{8} \cdot \frac{1}{2}$
17. $\frac{1}{4} \times \frac{2}{5}$
18. $\frac{3}{7} \times \frac{1}{4}$
19. $\frac{2}{3} \times \frac{4}{7}$
20. $\frac{5}{7} \times \frac{7}{8}$
21. $\frac{3}{8} \cdot \frac{1}{9}$
22. $\frac{5}{6} \cdot \frac{2}{5}$
23. $\frac{5}{12} \times 10$
24. $6 \cdot \frac{7}{8}$
25. $\frac{3}{4} \times \frac{8}{15}$
26. $\frac{4}{9} \times \frac{4}{5}$
27. $\frac{3}{7} \cdot \frac{3}{7}$
28. $\frac{5}{6} \times \frac{2}{9}$
29. $\frac{13}{18} \times \frac{6}{7}$
30. $\frac{7}{9} \cdot \frac{21}{10}$

31. MP **MODELING REAL LIFE** In an aquarium, $\frac{2}{5}$ of the fish are surgeonfish. Of these, $\frac{3}{4}$ are yellow tangs. What portion of all fish in the aquarium are yellow tangs?

32. MP **MODELING REAL LIFE** You exercise for $\frac{3}{4}$ of an hour. You jump rope for $\frac{1}{3}$ of that time. What portion of the hour do you spend jumping rope?

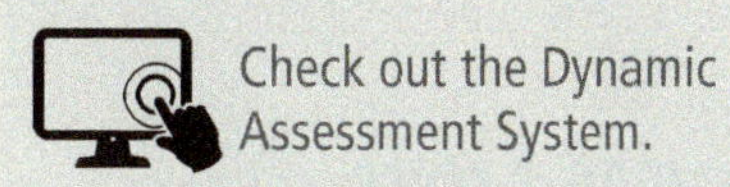

Assignment Guide and Concept Check

Scaffold assignments to support all students in their learning progression. The suggested assignments are a starting point. Continue to assign additional exercises and revisit with spaced practice to move every student toward proficiency.

Level	Assignment 1	Assignment 2
Emerging	4, 7, 10, 11, 14, 15, 23, 28, 36, 46, 48	31, 32, 33, 45, 52, 53, 54, 59, 63
Proficient	4, 7, 10, 11, 14, 19, 24, 28, 41, 46, 49, 60	31, 33, 52, 53, 54, 55, 62, 63, 65
Advanced	4, 7, 10, 11, 14, 24, 25, 27, 44, 47, 51, 61	34, 52, 53, 55, 64, 66, 67, 68, 69

- Assignment 1 is for use after students complete the Self-Assessment for Concepts & Skills.
- Assignment 2 is for use after students complete the Self-Assessment for Problem Solving.
- The red exercises can be used as a concept check.

Review & Refresh Prior Skills

Exercises 1–4 Finding the LCM
Exercises 5–8 Dividing Whole Numbers and Unit Fractions
Exercises 9 and 10 Writing Expressions as Powers
Exercise 11 Converting Measures within the Customary System

Common Errors

- **Exercises 15–30** Students may cross multiply instead of multiplying the numerators and multiplying the denominators.
- **Exercises 15–30** Students may try to get a common denominator, and then multiply the fractions. Tell them this is not needed when multiplying, but it is necessary for addition and subtraction. (Students will still end up with the same product, but the numbers will be greater before they simplify.)

Review & Refresh

1. 40
2. 35
3. 70
4. 210
5. 12; *Sample answer:*

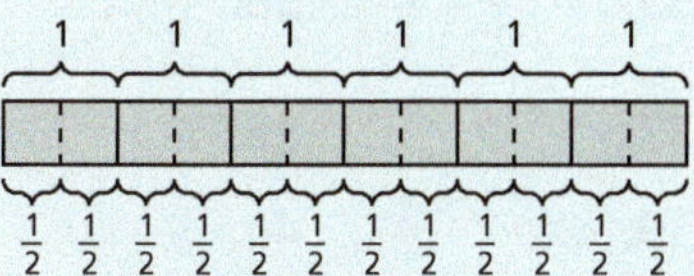

6. See Additional Answers.
7. 12; *Sample answer:*

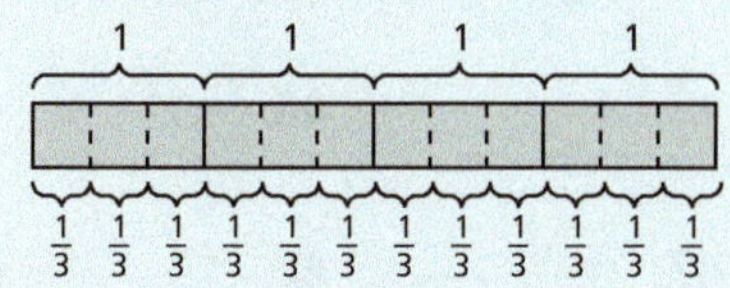

8. See Additional Answers.
9. 10^3
10. 5^4
11. D

Concepts, Skills, & Problem Solving

12. $\frac{1}{3}$
13. $\frac{1}{6}$
14. $\frac{1}{2}$
15. $\frac{2}{21}$
16. $\frac{5}{16}$
17. $\frac{1}{10}$
18. $\frac{3}{28}$
19. $\frac{8}{21}$
20. $\frac{5}{8}$
21. $\frac{1}{24}$
22. $\frac{1}{3}$
23. $4\frac{1}{6}$
24. $5\frac{1}{4}$
25. $\frac{2}{5}$
26. $\frac{16}{45}$
27. $\frac{9}{49}$
28. $\frac{5}{27}$
29. $\frac{13}{21}$
30. $1\frac{19}{30}$
31. $\frac{3}{10}$
32. $\frac{1}{4}$

Concepts, Skills, & Problem Solving

33. $>; \frac{9}{10} < 1$ **34.** $>; \frac{22}{15} > 1$

35. $=; \frac{7}{7} = 1$ **36.** $\frac{8}{9}$

37. 2 **38.** 2

39. 2 **40.** 5

41. 2 **42.** 1

43. $1\frac{1}{2}$ **44.** $3\frac{1}{2}$

45. $1\frac{3}{14}$ **46.** $23\frac{2}{5}$

47. $36\frac{2}{3}$ **48.** $7\frac{7}{8}$

49. $6\frac{4}{9}$ **50.** $17\frac{6}{7}$

51. $11\frac{3}{8}$

52. no; $4 \times 3\frac{7}{10} = 4 \times \frac{37}{10} = 14\frac{4}{5}$

53. no; $2\frac{1}{2} \times 7\frac{4}{5} = \frac{5}{2} \times \frac{39}{5} = 19\frac{1}{2}$

54. $\frac{3}{8}$ g

55. **a.** 7 ft^2

b. $10\frac{1}{3}$ ft^2

56. $\frac{2}{15}$ **57.** $2\frac{1}{12}$

58. $26\frac{2}{5}$ **59.** $\frac{27}{125}$

60. $\frac{9}{25}$ **61.** $\frac{121}{144}$

62. *Sample answer:* $\frac{1}{3}$

Common Errors

- **Exercises 36–51** Students may write $6\frac{2}{3}$ as $\frac{3 \times 6 \times 2}{3}$ instead of as $\frac{3 \times 6 + 2}{3}$. Make sure they have a good understanding of how to convert mixed numbers to improper fractions and vice versa.
- **Exercises 46 and 47** Students may forget how to write a whole number as an improper fraction. Remind them to express the whole number as an improper fraction by putting it over a denominator of 1.
- **Exercises 59–61** Students may not remember the definition of exponent and may multiply the fraction by the exponent. Remind them of the definition of exponent and that exponents are evaluated before multiplication in the order of operations.

REASONING Without finding the product, copy and complete the statement using <, >, or =. Explain your reasoning.

33. $\frac{4}{7}\ \square\ \frac{9}{10} \cdot \frac{4}{7}$

34. $\frac{5}{8} \times \frac{22}{15}\ \square\ \frac{5}{8}$

35. $\frac{5}{6}\ \square\ \frac{5}{6} \times \frac{7}{7}$

MULTIPLYING FRACTIONS AND MIXED NUMBERS Multiply. Write the answer in simplest form.

36. $1\frac{1}{3} \cdot \frac{2}{3}$

37. $6\frac{2}{3} \times \frac{3}{10}$

38. $2\frac{1}{2} \cdot \frac{4}{5}$

39. $\frac{3}{5} \cdot 3\frac{1}{3}$

40. $7\frac{1}{2} \times \frac{2}{3}$

41. $\frac{5}{9} \times 3\frac{3}{5}$

42. $\frac{3}{4} \cdot 1\frac{1}{3}$

43. $3\frac{3}{4} \times \frac{2}{5}$

44. $4\frac{3}{8} \cdot \frac{4}{5}$

45. $\frac{3}{7} \times 2\frac{5}{6}$

46. $1\frac{3}{10} \times 18$

47. $15 \cdot 2\frac{4}{9}$

48. $1\frac{1}{6} \times 6\frac{3}{4}$

49. $2\frac{5}{12} \cdot 2\frac{2}{3}$

50. $5\frac{5}{7} \cdot 3\frac{1}{8}$

51. $2\frac{4}{5} \times 4\frac{1}{16}$

YOU BE THE TEACHER Your friend finds the product. Is your friend correct? Explain your reasoning.

52.

$$4 \times 3\frac{7}{10} = 12\frac{7}{10}$$

53.

$$2\frac{1}{2} \times 7\frac{4}{5} = (2 \times 7) + \left(\frac{1}{2} \times \frac{4}{5}\right)$$
$$= 14 + \frac{2}{5}$$
$$= 14\frac{2}{5}$$

54. **MODELING REAL LIFE** A vitamin C tablet contains $\frac{1}{4}$ of a gram of vitamin C. You take $1\frac{1}{2}$ tablets every day. How many grams of vitamin C do you take every day?

55. **PROBLEM SOLVING** You make a banner for a football rally.

a. What is the area of the banner?

b. You add a $\frac{1}{4}$-foot border on each side. What is the area of the new banner?

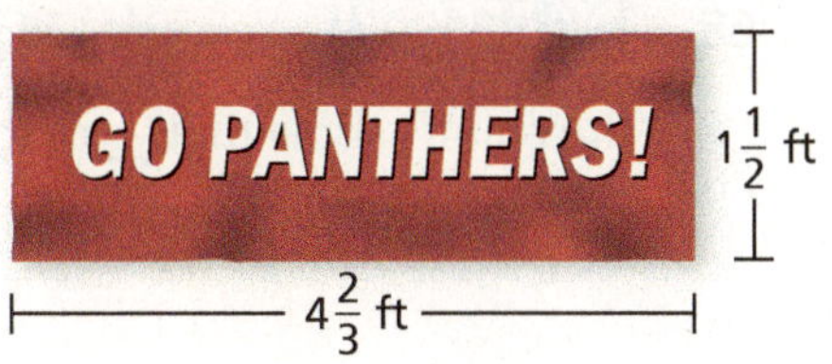

MULTIPLYING FRACTIONS AND MIXED NUMBERS Multiply. Write the answer in simplest form.

56. $\frac{1}{2} \times \frac{3}{5} \times \frac{4}{9}$

57. $\frac{4}{7} \cdot 4\frac{3}{8} \cdot \frac{5}{6}$

58. $1\frac{1}{15} \times 5\frac{2}{5} \times 4\frac{7}{12}$

59. $\left(\frac{3}{5}\right)^3$

60. $\left(\frac{4}{5}\right)^2 \times \left(\frac{3}{4}\right)^2$

61. $\left(\frac{5}{6}\right)^2 \cdot \left(1\frac{1}{10}\right)^2$

62. **OPEN-ENDED** Find a fraction that, when multiplied by $\frac{1}{2}$, is less than $\frac{1}{4}$.

63. MP **LOGIC** You are in a bike race. When you get to the first checkpoint, you are $\frac{2}{5}$ of the distance to the second checkpoint. When you get to the second checkpoint, you are $\frac{1}{4}$ of the distance to the finish. What is the distance from the start to the first checkpoint?

64. MP **NUMBER SENSE** Is the product of two positive mixed numbers ever less than 1? Explain.

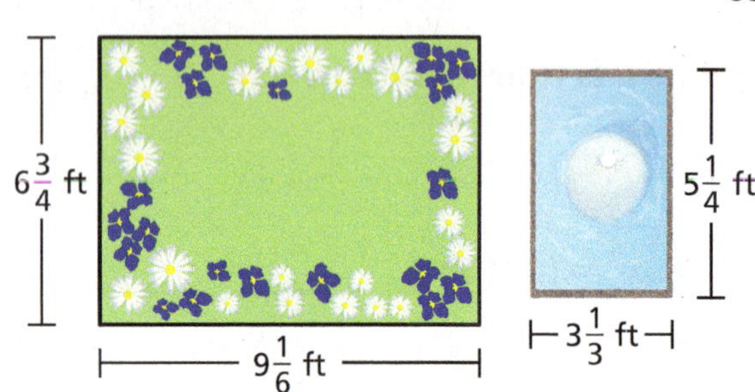

65. MP **REASONING** You plan to add a fountain to your garden.

a. Draw a diagram of the fountain in the garden. Label the dimensions.

b. Describe two methods for finding the area of the garden that surrounds the fountain.

c. Find the area. Which method did you use, and why?

66. MP **PROBLEM SOLVING** The cooking time for a ham is $\frac{2}{5}$ of an hour for each pound. What time should you start cooking a ham that weighs $12\frac{3}{4}$ pounds so that it is done at 4:45 P.M.?

67. MP **PRECISION** Complete the Four Square for $\frac{7}{8} \times \frac{1}{3}$.

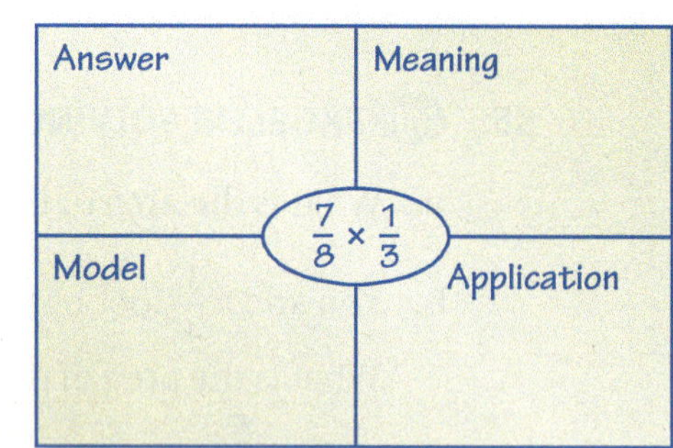

68. **DIG DEEPER!** You ask 150 people about their pets. The results show that $\frac{9}{25}$ of the people own a dog. Of the people who own a dog, $\frac{1}{6}$ of them also own a cat.

a. What portion of the people own a dog and a cat?

b. How many people own a dog but not a cat? Explain.

69. MP **NUMBER SENSE** Use each of the numbers from 1 to 9 exactly once to create three mixed numbers with the greatest possible product. Then use each of the numbers exactly once to create three mixed numbers with the least possible product. Find each product. Explain your reasoning. The fraction portion of each mixed number should be proper.

Mini-Assessment

Multiply. Write the answer in simplest form.

1. $\frac{1}{8} \times \frac{3}{5}$ $\frac{3}{40}$
2. $\frac{3}{8} \cdot \frac{2}{9}$ $\frac{1}{12}$
3. $\frac{1}{6} \times 4\frac{4}{5}$ $\frac{4}{5}$
4. $2\frac{1}{5} \cdot 3\frac{4}{7}$ $7\frac{6}{7}$
5. A rectangular dog kennel is $16\frac{1}{2}$ feet long by $12\frac{3}{4}$ feet wide. Find the area of the dog kennel. $210\frac{3}{8}$ square feet

Section Resources

Surface Level	Deep Level
Resources by Chapter • Extra Practice • Reteach • Puzzle Time Student Journal • Self-Assessment • Practice Differentiating the Lesson Tutorial Videos Skills Review Handbook Skills Trainer	Resources by Chapter • Enrichment and Extension Graphic Organizers Dynamic Assessment System • Section Practice

Concepts, Skills, & Problem Solving

63. 4 mi

64. no; Positive mixed numbers are greater than 1 and the product of two numbers greater than 1 is always greater than 1.

65. a. *Sample answer:*

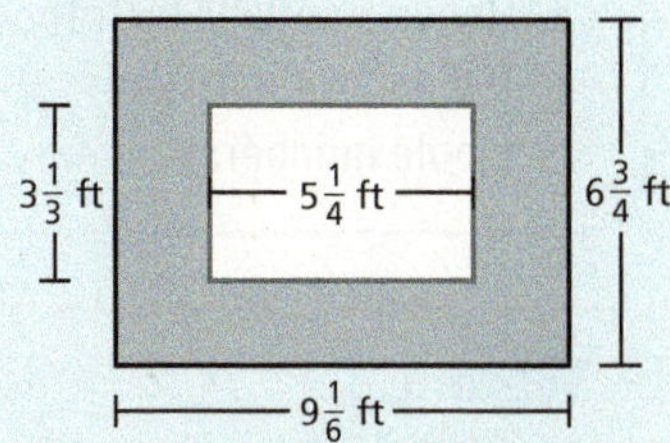

b. *Sample answer:* Subtract the area of the fountain from the total area of the garden; Use rectangles to find the area of each piece of the garden and add these areas.

c. $44\frac{3}{8}$ ft^2; *Sample answer:* subtract; fewer calculations

66. 11:39 A.M.

67. Answer: $\frac{7}{24}$; Meaning: $\frac{7}{8}$ of $\frac{1}{3}$;

Sample model:

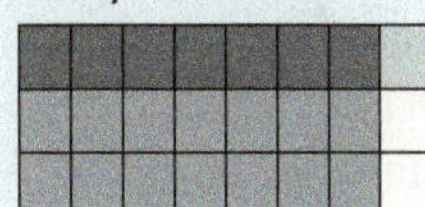

Sample application: The path around a park is $\frac{1}{3}$ mile long. You jog $\frac{7}{8}$ of the path. How far do you jog?

68. a. $\frac{3}{50}$

b. 45; $150 \times \left(\frac{9}{25} - \frac{3}{50}\right) = 45$

69. See Additional Answers.

Learning Target

Compute quotients of fractions and solve problems involving division by fractions.

Success Criteria

- Draw a model to explain division of fractions.
- Find reciprocals of numbers.
- Divide fractions by fractions.
- Divide fractions and whole numbers.

Warm Up

Cumulative, vocabulary, and prerequisite skills practice opportunities are available in the *Resources by Chapter* or at *BigIdeasMath.com*.

ELL Support

Discuss the meaning of the word *reciprocal*. In everyday language, a *reciprocal agreement* between two states is an exchange of privileges. For example, a Washington driver's license is honored in Pennsylvania as long as Washington honors a Pennsylvania driver's license. In math, a reciprocal of a fraction exchanges the numerator and the denominator.

Exploration 1

a. 6 **b.** 4

c. 2 **d.** $4\frac{1}{2}$

e. $2\frac{1}{2}$

Exploration 2

$\frac{3}{2}$; $\frac{4}{3}$; $\frac{5}{2}$; $\frac{3}{2}$; 3; To divide by a fraction, swap the numerator and denominator, then multiply.

Laurie's Notes

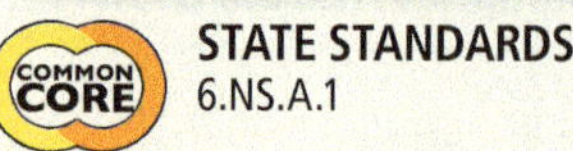

Preparing to Teach

- In the previous course, students divided unit fractions by whole numbers and vice versa. The first exploration contains fractions other than unit fractions, which is the next step in the progression of fraction division.
- Take time with the explorations. Modeling division and encouraging students to take ownership of the pattern will strengthen their understanding.

Motivate

- "How many pieces of licorice do I need to give each of you one-half of a piece?" Listen for one-half of the number of students in your class.
- **Model:** Show students six strips of paper. Say, "Imagine that these are pieces of licorice. How many halves are there in six pieces of licorice?" You may want to cut each piece of paper into halves. Then write: $6 \div \frac{1}{2} = 12$.
- "How many pieces of licorice do I need to give each of you one-third of a piece?" Listen for one-third of the number of students.
- **Model:** Use six new strips of paper to ask, "How many thirds are there in six pieces of licorice?" 18
- **MP3 Construct Viable Arguments and Critique the Reasoning of Others:** Creating and talking through a model is one way to construct a viable argument.

Exploration 1

- Give each student a strip of paper. Have them fold it to form four equal parts. Say, "This is a model of four. How many two-thirds are in four?" 6
- It may be helpful to provide a context, as suggested by the push-pin note.
- Have students use a pencil to divide each whole into thirds, and then count the two-thirds. From the model, students should count 6 two-thirds in four.

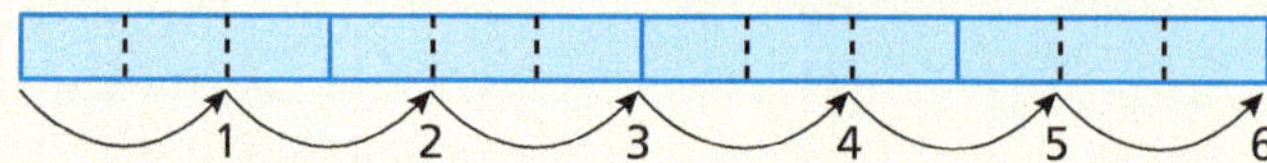

- Allow students to use strips of paper for the remaining parts and encourage them to create a context for each question.
- In part (d), the remaining piece is one-half the length of two-thirds.

Exploration 2

- Partners should say, "Four divided by two-thirds is six, so four times what number is six?" Pose the question, "Is the number *greater than 1* or *less than 1*?" greater than 1 Students may try a few numbers before finding $\frac{3}{2}$.
- "Is there a relationship between the divisor in the division expression and the second factor in the multiplication expression?" Listen for understanding of **reciprocals**.
- Ask several pairs to share their ideas and listen for the formation of the algorithm for dividing fractions.

2.2 Dividing Fractions

Learning Target: Compute quotients of fractions and solve problems involving division by fractions.

Success Criteria:
- I can draw a model to explain division of fractions.
- I can find reciprocals of numbers.
- I can divide fractions by fractions.
- I can divide fractions and whole numbers.

EXPLORATION 1 Dividing by Fractions

Math Practice

Apply Mathematics

Create a context for each question in Exploration 1. For example, in part (a), suppose you want to cut 4 yards of string into pieces that are $\frac{2}{3}$ of a yard. How many pieces can you cut?

Work with a partner. Answer each question using a model.

a. How many two-thirds are in four?

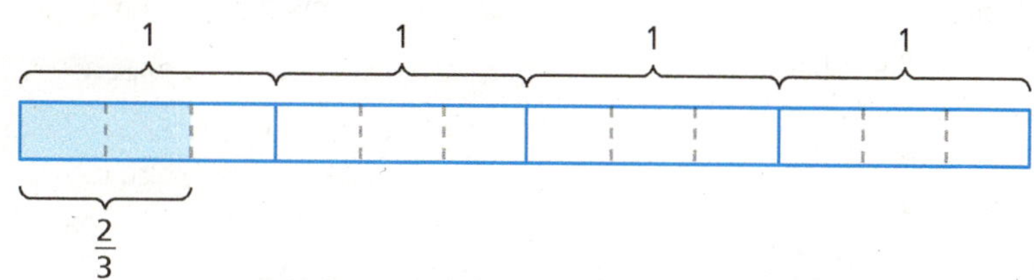

b. How many three-fourths are in three?

c. How many two-fifths are in four-fifths?

d. How many two-thirds are in three?

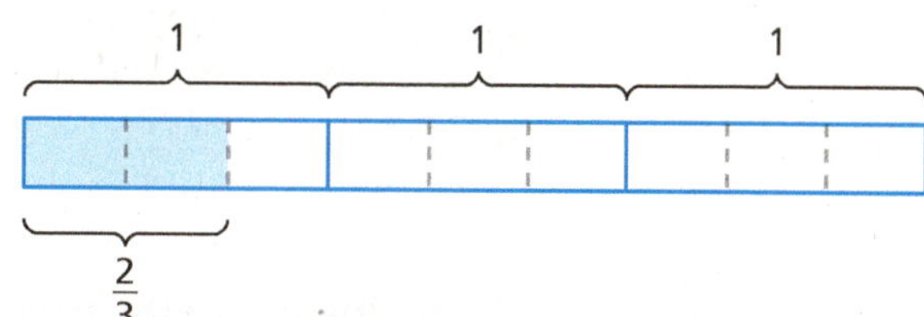

e. How many one-thirds are in five-sixths?

EXPLORATION 2 Finding a Pattern

Math Practice

Look for Structure

Can the pattern you found be applied to division by a whole number? Why or why not?

Work with a partner. The table shows the division expressions from Exploration 1. Complete each multiplication expression so that it has the same value as the division expression above it. What can you conclude about dividing by fractions?

Division Expression	$4 \div \frac{2}{3}$	$3 \div \frac{3}{4}$	$\frac{4}{5} \div \frac{2}{5}$	$3 \div \frac{2}{3}$	$\frac{5}{6} \div \frac{1}{3}$
Multiplication Expression	$4 \times ?$	$3 \times ?$	$\frac{4}{5} \times ?$	$3 \times ?$	$\frac{5}{6} \times ?$

2.2 Lesson

Key Vocabulary
reciprocals, *p. 54*
multiplicative inverses, *p. 54*

Two numbers whose product is 1 are **reciprocals**, or **multiplicative inverses**. To write the reciprocal of a number, first write the number as a fraction. Then invert the fraction. So, the reciprocal of a fraction $\frac{a}{b}$ is $\frac{b}{a}$, where $a \neq 0$ and $b \neq 0$.

The Meaning of a Word ▶ Invert

When you **invert** a glass, you turn it over.

EXAMPLE 1 **Writing Reciprocals**

	Original Number	*Fraction*	*Reciprocal*	*Check*
a.	$\frac{3}{5}$	$\frac{3}{5}$	$\frac{5}{3}$	$\frac{3}{5} \times \frac{5}{3} = 1$
b.	$\frac{9}{5}$	$\frac{9}{5}$	$\frac{5}{9}$	$\frac{9}{5} \times \frac{5}{9} = 1$
c.	2	$\frac{2}{1}$	$\frac{1}{2}$	$\frac{2}{1} \times \frac{1}{2} = 1$

Math Practice

Look for Structure

When any number is multiplied by 0, the product is 0. What does this tell you about the reciprocal of zero?

Try It **Write the reciprocal of the number.**

1. $\frac{3}{4}$ **2.** 5 **3.** $\frac{7}{2}$ **4.** $\frac{4}{9}$

Key Idea

Dividing Fractions

Words To divide a number by a fraction, multiply the number by the reciprocal of the fraction.

Numbers $\frac{1}{5} \div \frac{3}{4} = \frac{1}{5} \times \frac{4}{3} = \frac{1 \times 4}{5 \times 3}$

Algebra $\frac{a}{b} \div \frac{c}{d} = \frac{a}{b} \cdot \frac{d}{c} = \frac{a \cdot d}{b \cdot c}$, where b, c, and $d \neq 0$

Multi-Language Glossary at BigIdeasMath.com

Laurie's Notes

Scaffolding Instruction

- Visualizing a model will help students divide by a fraction. If the vocabulary is a stumbling block, have students look at the picture of the glass and talk about the meaning of *invert*.
- **Emerging:** Students may depend on a model and that's okay. Allow students to draw them instead of cutting strips of paper. They need practice visualizing the problem and using the rule of multiplying by the reciprocal. As problems become more complex, they will appreciate the efficiency of the algorithm.
- **Proficient:** Students understand the models and recognize the rule for dividing fractions. Do they understand the meaning of reciprocals, especially of whole numbers? They can self-assess using the Try It exercises and work cooperatively to find errors.

EXAMPLE 1

- To write the **reciprocal** of a whole number, you begin by representing the whole number over 1. Then switch the numerator and denominator.
- **Check:** The product of the reciprocals should equal 1.

Try It

- **Common Error:** When you ask students to write a number and its reciprocal, they may write: $\frac{3}{4} = \frac{4}{3}$. Reciprocals are not equal (except for 1). Students should write: $\frac{3}{4}, \frac{4}{3}$, or the reciprocal of $\frac{3}{4}$ is $\frac{4}{3}$.

◉ Check students' answers as they are working towards the second success criterion.

Key Idea

- Write the Key Idea on the board and leave it up for awhile.
- Note that the Words say, "To divide a number by a fraction, . . ." Students frequently ask which fraction to find the reciprocal of. Read this portion of the Words again. You are dividing a number (a whole number or a fraction) by a fraction. Remind students that a whole number can also be written as a fraction.
- **Connection:** Notice that this rule works for dividing whole numbers too. For example, $8 \div 2 = 8 \div \frac{2}{1} = 8 \times \frac{1}{2} = \frac{8}{1} \times \frac{1}{2} = \frac{8}{2} = 4$.
- Color-coding numbers may help all students, not just visual learners.

Scaffold instruction to support all students in their learning. Learning is individualized and you may want to group students differently as they move in and out of these levels with each skill and concept. Student self-assessment and feedback help guide your instructional decisions about how and when to layer support for all students to become proficient learners.

Extra Example 1

Write the reciprocal of each number.

a. $\frac{7}{8}$ $\frac{8}{7}$

b. $\frac{3}{2}$ $\frac{2}{3}$

c. 9 $\frac{1}{9}$

Try It

1. $\frac{4}{3}$ **2.** $\frac{1}{5}$

3. $\frac{2}{7}$ **4.** $\frac{9}{4}$

Extra Example 2

a. Find $\frac{5}{6} \div \frac{7}{12}$. $1\frac{3}{7}$

b. Find $\frac{1}{4} \div \frac{11}{20}$. $\frac{5}{11}$

Try It

5. 4

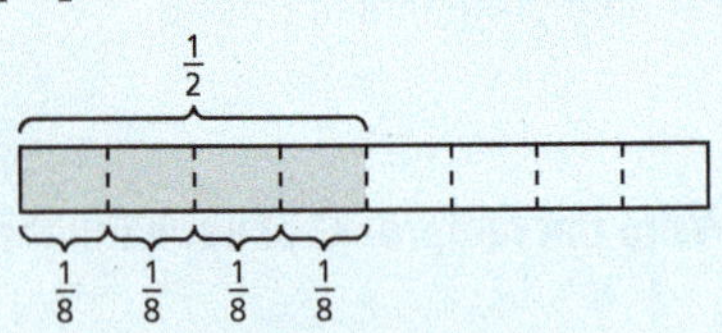

6. See Additional Answers.

7. $\frac{1}{2}$

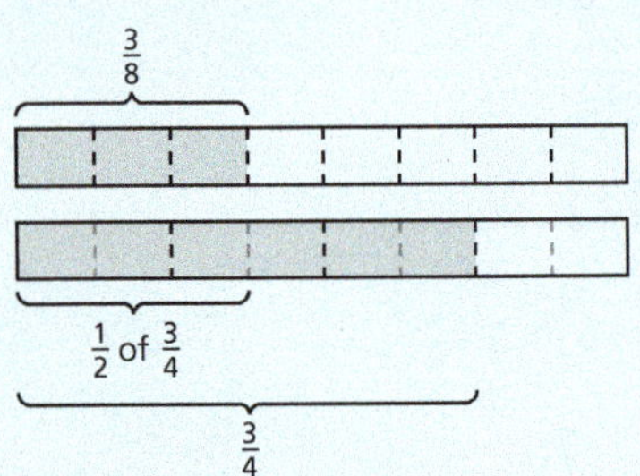

8. $\frac{4}{9}$

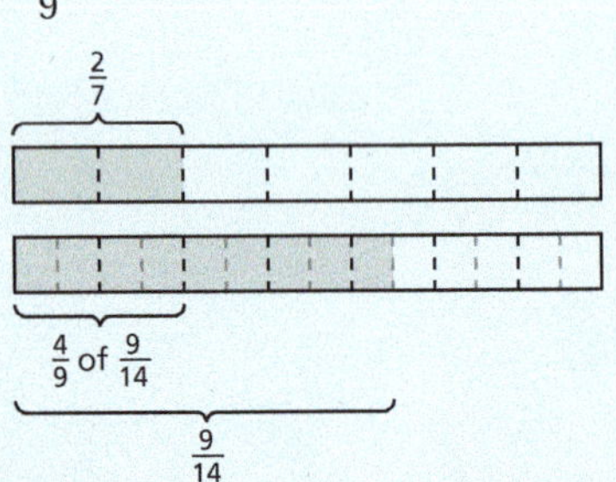

Laurie's Notes

EXAMPLE 2

- In part (a), students need to find how many five-twelfths are in three-fourths.
- Remind students that $\frac{3}{4} \div \frac{3}{4} = 1$. Because five-twelfths is less than three-fourths, there is at least 1 five-twelfths in three-fourths. Some students may realize that $\frac{3}{4} = \frac{9}{12}$, so the answer is less than 2.
- **Turn and Talk:** Have students explain how the model represents the answer. You may need to guide their thinking as you listen to conversations.
- Work through part (a) using the algorithm to verify the answer.
- In part (b), students need to find how many two-thirds are in one-sixth. Because one-sixth is much less than two-thirds, there aren't many. The answer must be very small.
- **Turn and Talk:** Again, have students describe how the model represents the answer. Listen for understanding that only $\frac{1}{4}$ of the $\frac{2}{3}$ piece will match the $\frac{1}{6}$ piece.
- Work through part (b) using the algorithm to verify the answer.
- **Common Error:** Some students may have the misconception that if you divide a fraction by a number greater than 1, the quotient is less than 1. Or, if you divide a fraction by a number less than 1, the quotient is greater than 1. This is not necessarily true. In parts (a) and (b), you divide a fraction by a number less than 1, but one quotient was greater than 1 and the other was less than 1.

  ? To clarify, ask, "Is a whole number divided by a smaller whole number *greater than 1* or *less than 1*?" greater than 1 "Is a whole number divided by a larger whole number *greater than 1* or *less than 1*?" less than 1 Tell students that the same holds true with fractions. The result depends upon the comparison of the divisor to the dividend.

Try It

- Ask students to predict whether the answer is *greater than 1*, *equal to 1*, or *less than 1*. This will give you an indication of their understanding of comparing fractions.

These exercises are instrumental to the first and third success criteria.

ELL Support

Have students work in pairs to complete the exercises. Remind students that they perform division of fractions by inverting the divisor, and then multiplying. Tell them to follow the process used in Example 2.

Beginner: Find the quotient using the algorithm or a model.

Intermediate: State the answer using a complete sentence. For example, "One-half divided by one-eighth is four."

Advanced: Explain each step.

EXAMPLE 2 Dividing a Fraction by a Fraction

a. **Find $\frac{3}{4} \div \frac{5}{12}$.**

$$\frac{3}{4} \div \frac{5}{12} = \frac{3}{4} \cdot \frac{12}{5}$$ Multiply by the reciprocal of $\frac{5}{12}$, which is $\frac{12}{5}$.

$$= \frac{3 \cdot 12}{4 \cdot 5}$$ Multiply fractions.

$$= \frac{36}{20}, \text{ or } 1\frac{4}{5}$$ Simplify.

Think: How many five-twelfths are in three-fourths?

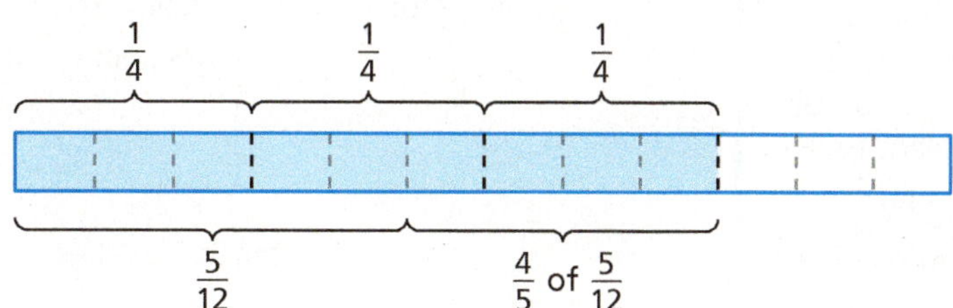

b. **Find $\frac{1}{6} \div \frac{2}{3}$.**

$$\frac{1}{6} \div \frac{2}{3} = \frac{1}{6} \times \frac{3}{2}$$ Multiply by the reciprocal of $\frac{2}{3}$, which is $\frac{3}{2}$.

$$= \frac{1 \times 3}{6 \times 2}$$ Multiply fractions.

$$= \frac{3}{12}, \text{ or } \frac{1}{4}$$ Simplify.

Example 2(b) is asking you to find how many $\frac{2}{3}$ are in $\frac{1}{6}$. Because the divisor is greater than the dividend, it can be helpful to model each number with a tape diagram.

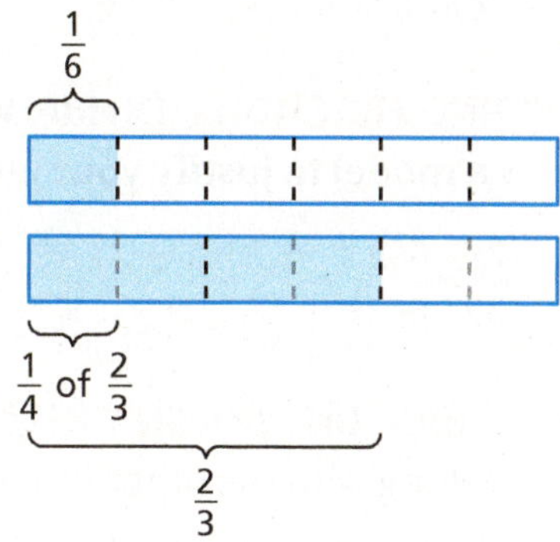

Try It **Divide. Write the answer in simplest form. Use a model to justify your answer.**

5. $\frac{1}{2} \div \frac{1}{8}$

6. $\frac{2}{5} \div \frac{3}{10}$

7. $\frac{3}{8} \div \frac{3}{4}$

8. $\frac{2}{7} \div \frac{9}{14}$

EXAMPLE 3 Dividing a Fraction by a Whole Number

Find $\frac{4}{5} \div 2$.

$$\frac{4}{5} \div 2 = \frac{4}{5} \div \frac{2}{1}$$ Write 2 as an improper fraction.

$$= \frac{4}{5} \times \frac{1}{2}$$ Multiply by the reciprocal of $\frac{2}{1}$, which is $\frac{1}{2}$.

$$= \frac{4 \times 1}{5 \times 2}$$ Multiply fractions.

$$= \frac{4}{10}, \text{ or } \frac{2}{5}$$ Simplify.

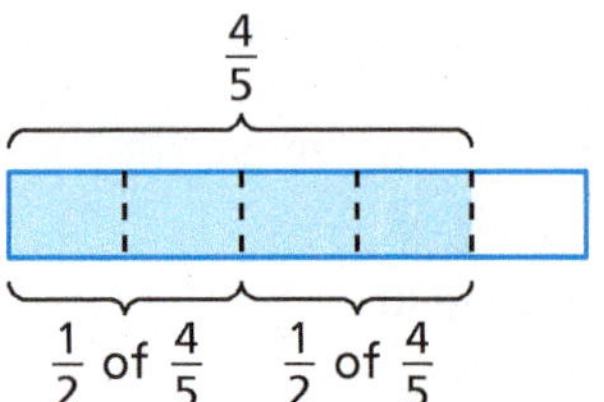

Remember

When dividing unit fractions by whole numbers, remember that dividing by a number n is equivalent to multiplying by $\frac{1}{n}$.

Try It **Divide. Write the answer in simplest form.**

9. $\frac{1}{3} \div 3$
10. $\frac{2}{3} \div 10$
11. $\frac{5}{8} \div 4$
12. $\frac{6}{7} \div 4$

Self-Assessment for Concepts & Skills

Solve each exercise. Then rate your understanding of the success criteria in your journal.

DIVIDING FRACTIONS **Divide. Write the answer in simplest form. Draw a model to justify your answer.**

13. $\frac{2}{3} \div \frac{5}{6}$
14. $\frac{6}{7} \div 3$

15. **WHICH ONE DOESN'T BELONG?** Which of the following does *not* belong with the other three? Explain your reasoning.

$\frac{2}{3} \div \frac{4}{5}$ $\frac{3}{2} \cdot \frac{4}{5}$ $\frac{5}{4} \times \frac{2}{3}$ $\frac{5}{4} \div \frac{3}{2}$

MATCHING **Match the expression with its value.**

16. $\frac{2}{5} \div \frac{8}{15}$
17. $\frac{8}{15} \div \frac{2}{5}$
18. $\frac{2}{15} \div \frac{8}{5}$
19. $\frac{8}{5} \div \frac{2}{15}$

A. $\frac{1}{12}$
B. $\frac{3}{4}$
C. 12
D. $1\frac{1}{3}$

Laurie's Notes

EXAMPLE 3

- This example represents the last success criterion.
- Students need to be able to interpret what the problem is asking. They should recognize that they are finding how many twos are in four-fifths.
- ? "What do you know about the quotient when you divide a proper fraction by a whole number?" The quotient will be less than 1.
- The model shows how to divide four-fifths into two equal parts. You can also model this division with a double tape diagram, as in Example 2(b), to find how many twos are in fourth-fifths.

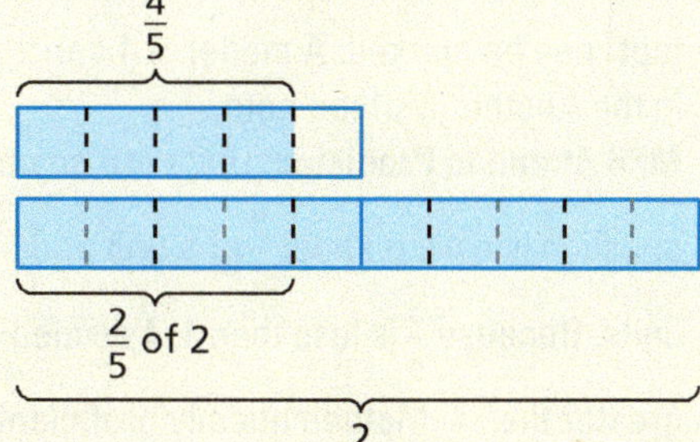

Try It

- Have pairs of students work on a whiteboard together. Remind them to estimate their answers before solving.
- ? Ask, "How can you check your answers?" Multiply the answer by the divisor and check that the product equals the dividend.

Formative Assessment Tip

Rating Scale

1	2	3	4
I do not understand.	I can do it with help.	I can do it on my own.	I can teach someone else.

At the end of the first day of instruction in Section 2.2, post a rating scale on the wall for each class. As students leave your room, give each student a sticker and tell them to place the stickers on their level of understanding. At the end of the last day of instruction in Section 2.3, display a new copy of the rating scale. Have students place stickers on the rating scale to rate their current understanding of the material. Compare the two rating scales to check for growth.

Self-Assessment for Concepts & Skills

- Students should complete the exercises independently. Look at students' models to gauge their understanding of dividing fractions.
- After completing Exercises 15–19, allow students to discuss their results in groups. There may be quite a bit of discussion surrounding the relationship between the four expressions in Exercise 15. Listen to the strategies that students use, which may include using the Commutative Property or writing all of the expressions with the same operation.
- As students share their answers with the class, highlight some of the strategies you noticed.
- Use the *Rating Scale* to assess students' understanding of dividing fractions. Repeat after Section 2.3 to check for growth.

The Success Criteria Self-Assessment chart can be found in the *Student Journal* or online at *BigIdeasMath.com*.

Extra Example 3

Find $\frac{2}{3} \div 6$. $\frac{1}{9}$

Try It

9. $\frac{1}{9}$
10. $\frac{1}{15}$
11. $\frac{5}{32}$
12. $\frac{3}{14}$

ELL Support

Have students work with a partner to complete the Self-Assessment for Concepts & Skills exercises. Then have each pair compare their answers with another pair and use a whiteboard to display the answers they agree upon. Review each group's answers and provide assistance as needed.

Self-Assessment for Concepts & Skills

13. $\frac{4}{5}$

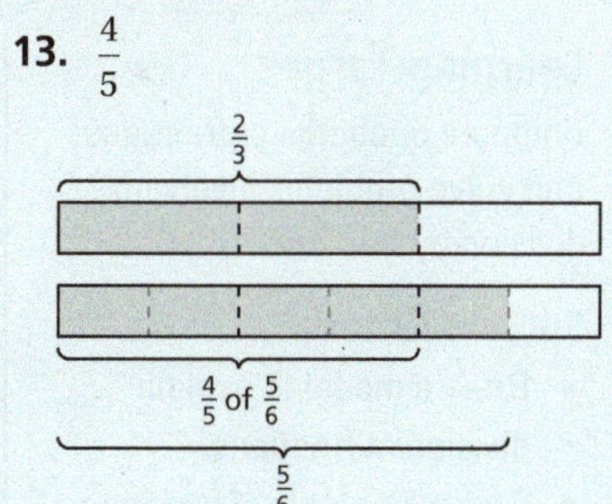

14. $\frac{2}{7}$

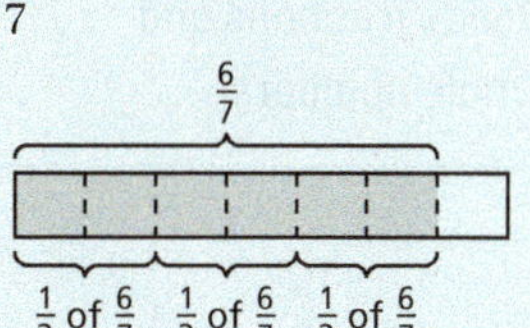

15. $\frac{3}{2} \cdot \frac{4}{5}$; The other expressions are equivalent to $\frac{2}{3} \cdot \frac{5}{4}$.
16. B
17. D
18. A
19. C

Extra Example 4

A length of rope is 8 meters long. How many $\frac{3}{5}$-meter pieces can be cut from the length of rope? How much rope is left over? 13; $\frac{1}{5}$ m

Self-Assessment for Problem Solving

20. 6; $\frac{1}{5}$ c

21. \$450

Learning Target

Compute quotients of fractions and solve problems involving division by fractions.

Success Criteria

- Draw a model to explain division of fractions.
- Find reciprocals of numbers.
- Divide fractions by fractions.
- Divide fractions and whole numbers.

Laurie's Notes

EXAMPLE 4

- Summarize with students what they have done so far: explained fraction division using a model, learned what a reciprocal is, divided two fractions, and divided a fraction by a whole number. Now they will look at dividing a whole number by a fraction, which completes the success criteria.
- A yardstick is a helpful physical model for this problem. Every 9 inches $\left(\frac{3}{4}\text{ of a foot}\right)$ can be marked. A model of 4 can also be drawn and marked, as shown in the Another Method note.
- **MP6 Attend to Precision:** Units are an important aspect of the problem. The question is asking about $\frac{3}{4}$ of a unit and how many of them are in 4 whole units. Because $\frac{3}{4}$ is less than 1, 4 divided by something less than 1 must be greater than 4. Mathematically proficient students continually consider the units involved in a problem.

Self-Assessment for Problem Solving

- Encourage students to use a Four Square to complete these exercises. Until students become comfortable with the problem-solving plan, they may only be ready to complete the first square.
- Have students complete the exercises independently. Circulate and ask probing questions.
- Because this entire section has been focused on division, students may automatically divide. Exercise 20 is similar to Example 4. Check to see that students are dividing the whole number by the fraction and listen for students' interpretation of the solution.

The Success Criteria Self-Assessment chart can be found in the *Student Journal* or online at *BigIdeasMath.com*.

Closure

- **Exit Ticket:** How many thirds are in two? In other words, what is $2 \div \frac{1}{3}$? Draw a model to explain your answer. 6

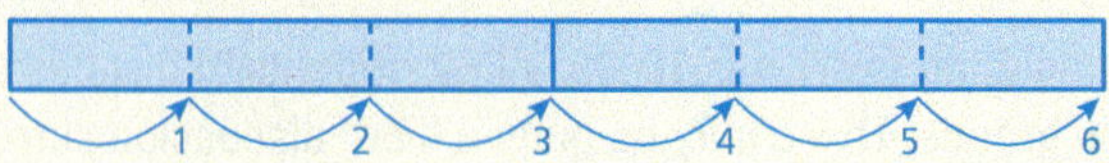

EXAMPLE 4 Modeling Real Life

A piece of wood is 4 feet long. How many $\frac{3}{4}$-foot pieces can you cut from the piece of wood? How much wood is left over?

Divide the length of the entire piece of wood by the length of a smaller piece. So, divide 4 by $\frac{3}{4}$. The quotient can be used to answer both questions.

$$4 \div \frac{3}{4} = 4 \times \frac{4}{3} \quad \text{Multiply by the reciprocal of } \frac{3}{4}\text{, which is } \frac{4}{3}.$$

$$= \frac{4 \times 4}{3} \quad \text{Multiply.}$$

$$= \frac{16}{3}\text{, or } 5\frac{1}{3} \quad \text{Simplify.}$$

You can cut five $\frac{3}{4}$-foot pieces from the piece of wood. The remaining piece is $\frac{1}{3}$ of a $\frac{3}{4}$-foot section. So, $\frac{1}{3} \bullet \frac{3}{4} = \frac{3}{12} = \frac{1}{4}$ foot of wood is left over.

Another Method Use a diagram.

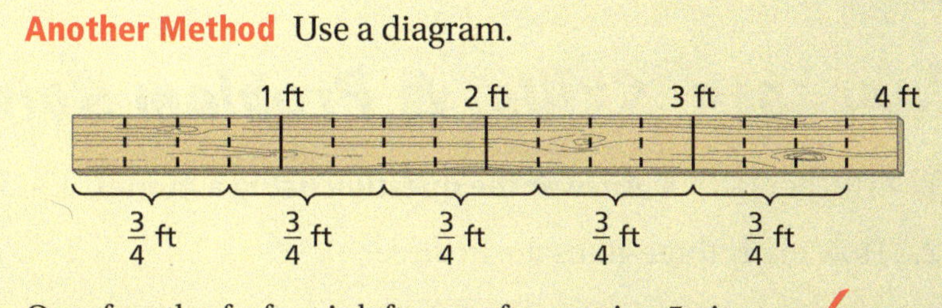

One-fourth of a foot is left over after cutting 5 pieces. ✓

Self-Assessment for Problem Solving

Solve each exercise. Then rate your understanding of the success criteria in your journal.

20. You have 5 cups of rice to make *bibimbap*, a popular Korean meal. The recipe calls for $\frac{4}{5}$ cup of rice per serving. How many full servings of bibimbap can you make? How much rice is left over?

21. A band earns $\frac{2}{3}$ of their profit from selling concert tickets and $\frac{1}{5}$ of their profit from selling merchandise. The band earns a profit of \$1500 from selling concert tickets. How much profit does the band earn from selling merchandise?

2.2 Practice

Go to *BigIdeasMath.com* to get HELP with solving the exercises.

Review & Refresh

Multiply. Write the answer in simplest form.

1. $\frac{7}{10} \cdot \frac{3}{4}$
2. $\frac{5}{6} \times 2\frac{1}{3}$
3. $\frac{4}{9} \times \frac{3}{8}$
4. $2\frac{2}{5} \cdot 6\frac{2}{3}$

Match the expression with its value.

5. $3 + 2 \times 4^2$
6. $(3 + 2) \times 4^2$
7. $2 + 3 \times 4^2$
8. $4^2 + 2 \times 3$

A. 22 **B.** 35 **C.** 50 **D.** 80

Find the area of the rectangle.

9. 
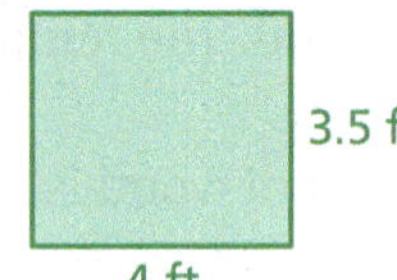

10. 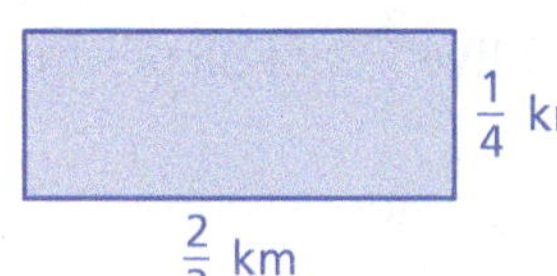

11. 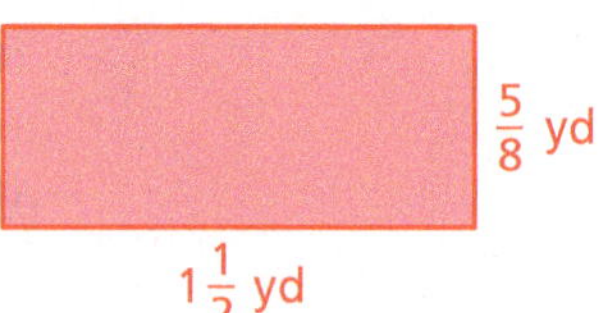

Concepts, Skills, & Problem Solving

MP **CHOOSE TOOLS** **Answer the question using a model.** (See Exploration 1, p. 53.)

12. How many three-fifths are in three?
13. How many two-ninths are in eight-ninths?
14. How many three-fourths are in seven-eighths?

WRITING RECIPROCALS **Write the reciprocal of the number.**

15. 8
16. $\frac{6}{7}$
17. $\frac{2}{5}$
18. $\frac{11}{8}$

DIVIDING FRACTIONS **Divide. Write the answer in simplest form.**

19. $\frac{1}{3} \div \frac{1}{2}$
20. $\frac{1}{8} \div \frac{1}{4}$
21. $\frac{2}{7} \div 2$
22. $\frac{6}{5} \div 3$
23. $\frac{2}{3} \div \frac{4}{9}$
24. $\frac{5}{6} \div \frac{2}{7}$
25. $12 \div \frac{3}{4}$
26. $8 \div \frac{2}{5}$
27. $\frac{3}{7} \div 6$
28. $\frac{12}{25} \div 4$
29. $\frac{2}{9} \div \frac{2}{3}$
30. $\frac{8}{15} \div \frac{4}{5}$
31. $\frac{1}{3} \div \frac{1}{9}$
32. $\frac{7}{10} \div \frac{3}{8}$
33. $\frac{14}{27} \div 7$
34. $\frac{5}{8} \div 15$
35. $\frac{27}{32} \div \frac{7}{8}$
36. $\frac{4}{15} \div \frac{10}{13}$
37. $9 \div \frac{4}{9}$
38. $10 \div \frac{5}{12}$

Assignment Guide and Concept Check

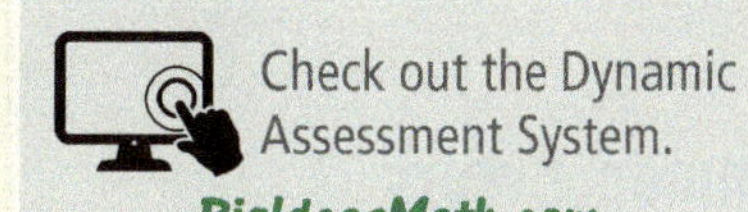

Scaffold assignments to support all students in their learning progression. The suggested assignments are a starting point. Continue to assign additional exercises and revisit with spaced practice to move every student toward proficiency.

Level	Assignment 1	Assignment 2
Emerging	4, 5, 6, 7, 8, 11, 13, 17, 19, 21, 26, 32, 55, 57	15, 22, 39, 40, 41, 42, 47, 60, 65
Proficient	4, 5, 6, 7, 8, 11, 13, 15, 17, 20, 22, 25, 32, 56, 58	39, 40, 41, 42, 43, 48, 60, 63, 64, 65
Advanced	4, 5, 6, 7, 8, 11, 14, 15, 23, 34, 37, 49, 56, 59, 62	39, 40, 44, 63, 64, 65, 66, 67, 68

- Assignment 1 is for use after students complete the Self-Assessment for Concepts & Skills.
- Assignment 2 is for use after students complete the Self-Assessment for Problem Solving.
- The red exercises can be used as a concept check.

Review & Refresh Prior Skills

Exercises 1–4 Multiplying Fractions and Mixed Numbers
Exercises 5–8 Using Order of Operations
Exercises 9–11 Finding the Area of a Rectangle

Common Errors

- **Exercise 15** Students may have difficulty rewriting a whole number as a fraction. Remind them that a whole number is a fraction with a denominator of 1.
- **Exercises 19–38** Students may find the reciprocal of the dividend instead of the divisor, or the reciprocal of both. Remind them that they only need to find the reciprocal of the divisor. Demonstrate this concept with a calculator. Enter the problem as a division problem, and then enter it as a multiplication problem with the reciprocal. Ask students to compare the answers. This comparison can also be made with the incorrect methods to demonstrate that they will not work.
- **Exercises 19–38** Students may find the reciprocal but forget to change the division to multiplication. Remind them that inverting the number is the *opposite*, so it requires the *opposite* operation.

Review & Refresh

1. $\frac{21}{40}$ **2.** $1\frac{17}{18}$
3. $\frac{1}{6}$ **4.** 16
5. B **6.** D
7. C **8.** A
9. 14 ft^2 **10.** $\frac{1}{6}\text{ km}^2$
11. $\frac{15}{16}\text{ yd}^2$

Concepts, Skills, & Problem Solving

12. 5 **13.** 4
14. $1\frac{1}{6}$ **15.** $\frac{1}{8}$
16. $\frac{7}{6}$ **17.** $\frac{5}{2}$
18. $\frac{8}{11}$ **19.** $\frac{2}{3}$
20. $\frac{1}{2}$ **21.** $\frac{1}{7}$
22. $\frac{2}{5}$ **23.** $1\frac{1}{2}$
24. $2\frac{11}{12}$ **25.** 16
26. 20 **27.** $\frac{1}{14}$
28. $\frac{3}{25}$ **29.** $\frac{1}{3}$
30. $\frac{2}{3}$ **31.** 3
32. $1\frac{13}{15}$ **33.** $\frac{2}{27}$
34. $\frac{1}{24}$ **35.** $\frac{27}{28}$
36. $\frac{26}{75}$ **37.** $20\frac{1}{4}$
38. 24

Concepts, Skills, & Problem Solving

39. yes; The division is correct.

40. no; $\frac{2}{5} \div \frac{8}{9} = \frac{2}{5} \times \frac{9}{8} = \frac{9}{20}$

41. $\frac{3}{25}$ **42.** $5\frac{5}{8}$

43. *Sample answer:* A pipe with a length of $\frac{5}{6}$ yard is cut into four equal pieces. How long is each piece? $\frac{5}{24}$ yd

44. *Sample answer:* The library is $\frac{2}{5}$ of a mile from the park and the school is $\frac{3}{8}$ of a mile from the park.

How many times greater is the distance to the library than the school? $1\frac{1}{15}$

45. *Sample answer:* You need $\frac{2}{3}$ pound of potting soil to repot 1 plant. How many plants can you repot with a 10-pound bag of potting soil? 15

46. *Sample answer:* A batch of trail mix weighs $\frac{4}{9}$ pound. There is $\frac{2}{7}$ pound of peanuts in the mix. What portion of the mix is peanuts? $\frac{9}{14}$

47. $\frac{12}{5}$ **48.** $\frac{1}{3}$

49. $\frac{1}{8}$

50. $<$; When you divide a fraction by a number greater than 1, the quotient is less than the fraction.

51. $=$; When you divide a fraction by 1, the quotient is the fraction.

52. $>$; When you divide a number by a fraction less than 1, the quotient is greater than the number.

53–63. See Additional Answers.

Common Errors

- **Exercise 49** Students may read the problem quickly and think that it is a multiplication problem instead of a division problem, and that the answer is 8. The answer is the reciprocal of 8. Tell them to think of the problem backwards. "56 multiplied by what number equals 7?" This should help them to see that the answer must be a fraction.
- **Exercises 54–62** Students may try to apply the Associative and Commutative Properties. Remind them that the Associative and Commutative Properties apply only to multiplication and addition. Also remind students to follow the order of operations for all the problems in this section.

YOU BE THE TEACHER Your friend finds the quotient. Is your friend correct? Explain your reasoning.

39.

$$\frac{4}{7} \div \frac{13}{28} = \frac{4}{7} \times \frac{28}{13}$$

$$= \frac{4 \times 28}{7 \times 13}$$

$$= \frac{112}{91}, \text{ or } 1\frac{3}{13}$$

40.

$$\frac{2}{5} \div \frac{8}{9} = \frac{5}{2} \times \frac{8}{9}$$

$$= \frac{5 \times 8}{2 \times 9}$$

$$= \frac{40}{18}, \text{ or } 2\frac{2}{9}$$

41. **REASONING** You have $\frac{3}{5}$ of an apple pie. You divide the remaining pie into 5 equal slices. What portion of the original pie is each slice?

42. **PROBLEM SOLVING** How many times longer is the baby alligator than the baby gecko?

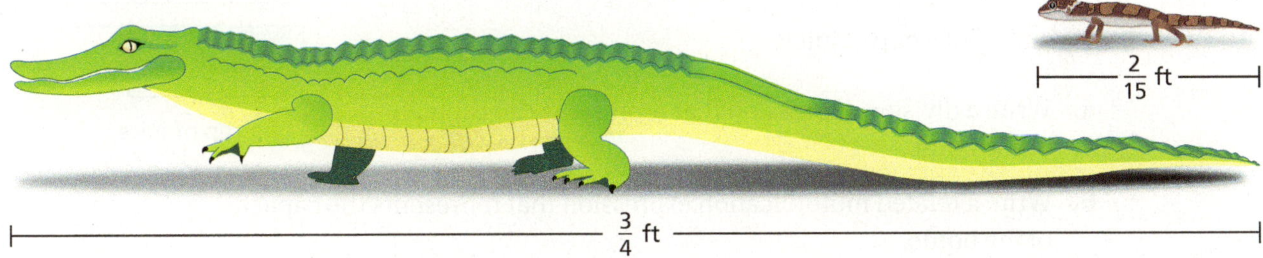

OPEN-ENDED Write a real-life problem for the expression. Then solve the problem.

43. $\frac{5}{6} \div 4$ **44.** $\frac{2}{5} \div \frac{3}{8}$ **45.** $10 \div \frac{2}{3}$ **46.** $\frac{2}{7} \div \frac{4}{9}$

NUMBER SENSE Copy and complete the statement.

47. $\frac{5}{12} \times \square = 1$ **48.** $3 \times \square = 1$ **49.** $7 \div \square = 56$

REASONING Without finding the quotient, copy and complete the statement using <, >, or =. Explain your reasoning.

50. $\frac{7}{9} \div 5 \ \square \ \frac{7}{9}$ **51.** $\frac{3}{7} \div 1 \ \square \ \frac{3}{7}$ **52.** $8 \div \frac{3}{4} \ \square \ 8$ **53.** $\frac{5}{6} \div \frac{7}{8} \ \square \ \frac{5}{6}$

ORDER OF OPERATIONS Evaluate the expression. Write the answer in simplest form.

54. $\frac{1}{6} \div 6 \div 6$ **55.** $\frac{7}{12} \div 14 \div 6$ **56.** $\frac{3}{5} \div \frac{4}{7} \div \frac{9}{10}$

57. $4 \div \frac{8}{9} - \frac{1}{2}$ **58.** $\frac{3}{4} + \frac{5}{6} \div \frac{2}{3}$ **59.** $\frac{7}{8} - \frac{3}{8} \div 9$

60. $\frac{9}{16} \div \frac{3}{4} \cdot \frac{2}{13}$ **61.** $\frac{3}{14} \cdot \frac{2}{5} \div \frac{6}{7}$ **62.** $\frac{10}{27} \cdot \left(\frac{3}{8} \div \frac{5}{24}\right)$

63. **NUMBER SENSE** When is the reciprocal of a fraction a whole number? Explain.

64. **MP MODELING REAL LIFE** You use $\frac{1}{8}$ of your battery for every $\frac{2}{5}$ of an hour that you video chat. You use $\frac{3}{4}$ of your battery video chatting. How long did you video chat?

65. **MP PROBLEM SOLVING** The table shows the portions of a family budget that are spent on several expenses.

Expense	Portion of Budget
Housing	$\frac{2}{5}$
Food	$\frac{4}{9}$
Automobiles	$\frac{1}{15}$
Recreation	$\frac{1}{40}$

a. How many times more is the expense for housing than for automobiles?

b. How many times more is the expense for food than for recreation?

c. The expense for automobile fuel is $\frac{1}{60}$ of the total expenses. What portion of the automobile expense is spent on fuel?

66. **CRITICAL THINKING** A bottle of juice is $\frac{2}{3}$ full. The bottle contains $\frac{4}{5}$ of a cup of juice.

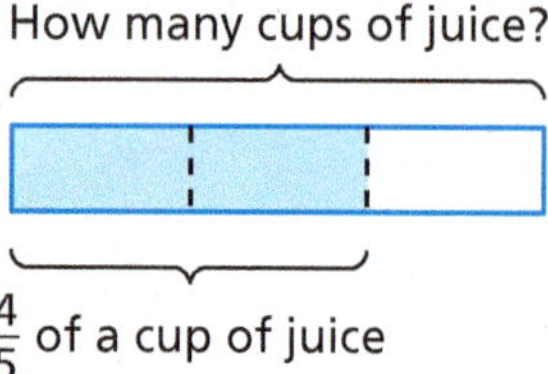

a. Write a division expression that represents the capacity of the bottle.

b. Write a related multiplication expression that represents the capacity of the bottle.

c. Explain how you can use the diagram to verify the expression in part (b).

d. Find the capacity of the bottle.

67. **DIG DEEPER!** You have 6 pints of glaze. It takes $\frac{7}{8}$ of a pint to glaze a bowl and $\frac{9}{16}$ of a pint to glaze a plate.

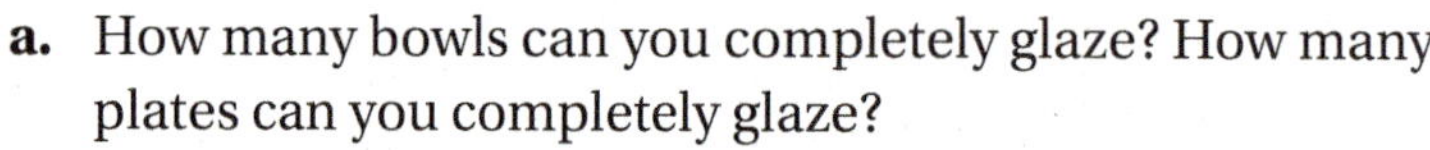

a. How many bowls can you completely glaze? How many plates can you completely glaze?

b. You want to glaze 5 bowls, and then use the rest for plates. How many plates can you completely glaze? How much glaze will be left over?

c. How many of each object can you completely glaze so that there is no glaze left over? Explain how you found your answer.

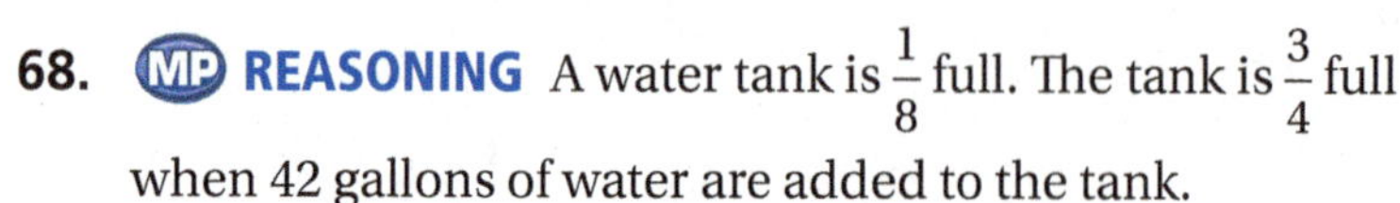

68. **MP REASONING** A water tank is $\frac{1}{8}$ full. The tank is $\frac{3}{4}$ full when 42 gallons of water are added to the tank.

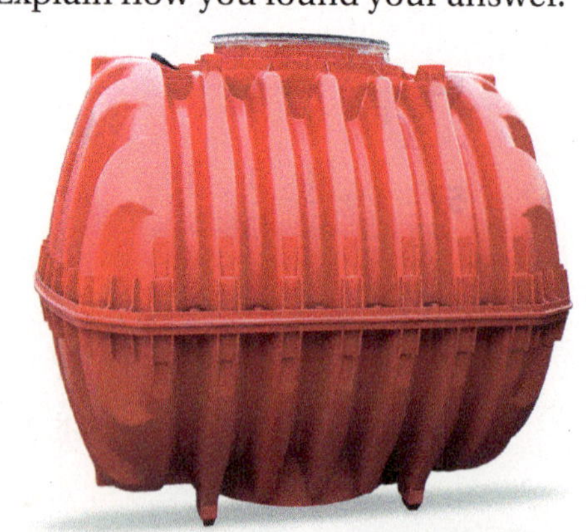

a. How much water can the tank hold?

b. How much water was originally in the tank?

c. How much water is in the tank when it is $\frac{1}{2}$ full?

Mini-Assessment

Divide. Write the answer in simplest form.

1. $\frac{1}{3} \div \frac{1}{6}$ 2
2. $\frac{4}{5} \div \frac{2}{3}$ $1\frac{1}{5}$
3. $\frac{3}{5} \div \frac{1}{2}$ $1\frac{1}{5}$
4. $\frac{4}{5} \div 6$ $\frac{2}{15}$
5. You have $\frac{3}{4}$ of a pumpkin pie. You divide the remaining pie into 6 equal slices. What fraction of the original pie is each slice? $\frac{1}{8}$

Surface Level	Deep Level
Resources by Chapter • Extra Practice • Reteach • Puzzle Time Student Journal • Self-Assessment • Practice Differentiating the Lesson Tutorial Videos Skills Review Handbook Skills Trainer	Resources by Chapter • Enrichment and Extension Graphic Organizers Dynamic Assessment System • Section Practice

Concepts, Skills, & Problem Solving

64. $2\frac{2}{5}$ h or 2 h 24 min

65. **a.** 6

b. $17\frac{7}{9}$

c. $\frac{1}{4}$

66. **a.** $\frac{4}{5} \div \frac{2}{3}$

b. $\frac{4}{5} \cdot \frac{3}{2}$

c. The diagram shows that the capacity of the bottle is $\frac{3}{2}$ times the amount of juice.

d. $1\frac{1}{5}$ c

67. **a.** 6 bowls; 10 plates

b. 2 plates; $\frac{1}{2}$ pt

c. 3 bowls and 6 plates; *Sample answer:* Used a table of values.

68. **a.** $67\frac{1}{5}$ gal

b. $8\frac{2}{5}$ gal

c. $33\frac{3}{5}$ gal

Learning Target

Compute quotients with mixed numbers and solve problems involving division with mixed numbers.

Success Criteria

- Draw a model to explain division of mixed numbers.
- Write a mixed number as an improper fraction.
- Divide with mixed numbers.
- Evaluate expressions involving mixed numbers using the order of operations.

Warm Up

Cumulative, vocabulary, and prerequisite skills practice opportunities are available in the *Resources by Chapter* or at *BigIdeasMath.com*.

ELL Support

A mixed number is a mixture of a whole number and a fraction, such as $1\frac{1}{2}$. In everyday language, the word *proper* means appropriate and *improper* means inappropriate. In math, however, the term *improper fraction* means a fraction in which the numerator is greater than the denominator, such as $\frac{3}{2}$. Like a mixed number, an improper fraction represents more than a whole.

Exploration 1

a. *Sample answer:* You make $\frac{3}{4}$ of a bracelet in 1 hour. How many bracelets do you make in $4\frac{1}{2}$ hours? 6

b–g. See Additional Answers.

Laurie's Notes

Preparing to Teach

- This is a different type of exploration, one in which students use their literacy skills as well as their math skills. The goal is for students to write a real-life problem that provides context for a division expression. Many students will find this challenging.
- After dividing fractions in the previous section, students will apply those skills to dividing with mixed numbers. Models are still an important connection.

Motivate

- Share a colorful story while holding a travel coffee mug. The essence of the story should result in the following facts: a coffee pot holds 12 cups and the mug holds $1\frac{1}{2}$ cups. How many times can the travel mug be filled?

? "What expression can you use to answer the question?" $12 \div 1\frac{1}{2}$ "What is the answer?" 8 times

Exploration 1

- Partners need to write a real-life problem that represents each division expression. Allow time for students to think about where these numbers may occur in real life. Students should contextualize the expressions faster as they progress through the parts.
- If students are struggling to create contexts, provide an example for part (a). Example: A city bus completes its route in $\frac{3}{4}$ of an hour. How many times does the bus complete its route in $4\frac{1}{2}$ hours?
- Visual models are drawn to represent division of mixed numbers. The labels above each diagram represent the quantity you have (the dividend). Below the diagram students should mark the size of the unit they want to fit into the quantity (the divisor). In part (a), they are counting the number of three-fourths in four and one-half.

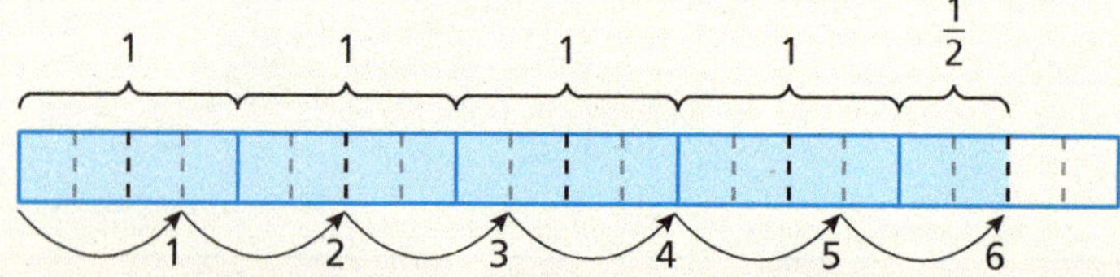

- In parts (d)–(g), students may have more difficulty because the quotient is not a whole number. Help students by asking them to think about what portion of the unit they are counting is represented by the amount that is left over. For example, in part (d), the remaining piece is $\frac{6}{7}$ of the $\frac{7}{6}$ unit they are counting.
- Ask volunteers to share their real-life problems.
- **MP3 Construct Viable Arguments and Critique the Reasoning of Others:** Take time to have a student talk through his or her approach to each problem in the exploration. Other students should listen carefully to the language used and the explanation given. You want students to be in the habit of communicating their thinking and having others critiquing their arguments.

2.3 Dividing Mixed Numbers

Learning Target: Compute quotients with mixed numbers and solve problems involving division with mixed numbers.

Success Criteria:
- I can draw a model to explain division of mixed numbers.
- I can write a mixed number as an improper fraction.
- I can divide with mixed numbers.
- I can evaluate expressions involving mixed numbers using the order of operations.

EXPLORATION 1 Dividing Mixed Numbers

Work with a partner. Write a real-life problem that represents each division expression described. Then solve each problem using a model. Check your answers.

Math Practice

Make Sense of Quantities

What values do the parts of the model represent?

a. How many three-fourths are in four and one-half?

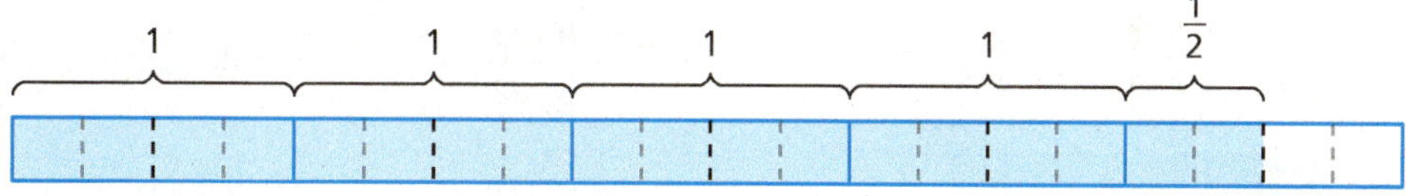

b. How many three-eighths are in two and one-fourth?

c. How many one and one-halves are in six?

d. How many seven-sixths are in three and one-third?

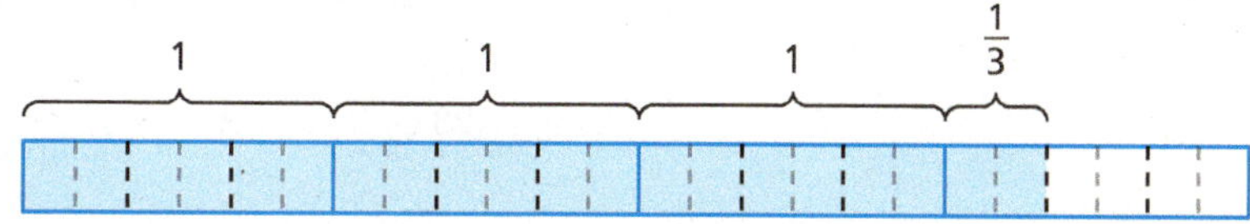

e. How many one and one-fifths are in five?

f. How many three and one-halves are in two and one-half?

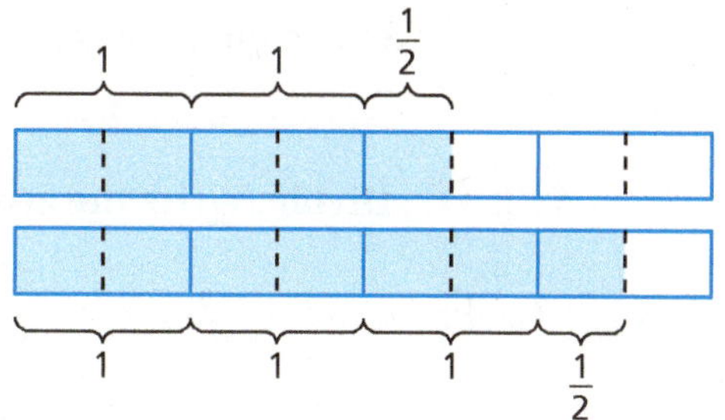

g. How many four and one-halves are in one and one-half?

2.3 Lesson

Key Idea

Dividing Mixed Numbers

Write each mixed number as an improper fraction. Then divide as you would with proper fractions.

EXAMPLE 1 Dividing with Mixed Numbers

a. **Find $2\frac{2}{3} \div \frac{2}{3}$.**

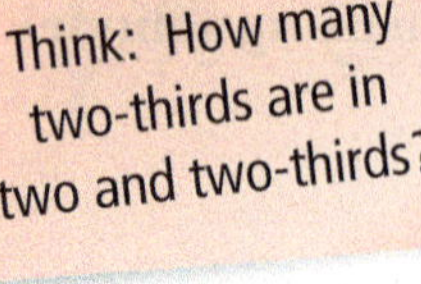

Think: How many two-thirds are in two and two-thirds?

$2\frac{2}{3} \div \frac{2}{3} = \frac{8}{3} \div \frac{2}{3}$ — Write $2\frac{2}{3}$ as the improper fraction $\frac{8}{3}$.

$= \frac{8}{3} \times \frac{3}{2}$ — Multiply by the reciprocal of $\frac{2}{3}$, which is $\frac{3}{2}$.

$= \frac{8 \times 3}{3 \times 2}$ — Multiply fractions.

$= \frac{24}{6}$, or 4 — Simplify.

So, the quotient is 4.

b. **Find $3\frac{5}{6} \div 1\frac{2}{3}$.**

Estimate $4 \div 2 = 2$

$3\frac{5}{6} \div 1\frac{2}{3} = \frac{23}{6} \div \frac{5}{3}$ — Write each mixed number as an improper fraction.

$= \frac{23}{6} \times \frac{3}{5}$ — Multiply by the reciprocal of $\frac{5}{3}$, which is $\frac{3}{5}$.

$= \frac{23 \times 3}{6 \times 5}$ — Multiply fractions.

$= \frac{69}{30}$, or $2\frac{3}{10}$ — Simplify.

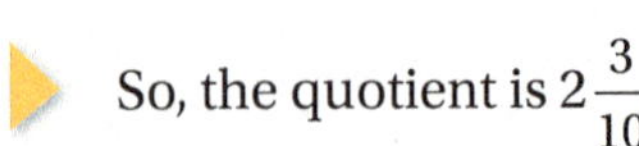

So, the quotient is $2\frac{3}{10}$.

Reasonable? $2\frac{3}{10} \approx 2$ ✓

Try It

Divide. Write the answer in simplest form.

1. $3\frac{2}{3} \div \frac{1}{3}$ **2.** $1\frac{3}{7} \div \frac{2}{3}$ **3.** $2\frac{1}{6} \div \frac{3}{4}$ **4.** $6\frac{1}{2} \div 2$

5. $10\frac{2}{3} \div 2\frac{2}{3}$ **6.** $8\frac{1}{4} \div 1\frac{1}{2}$ **7.** $3 \div 1\frac{3}{4}$ **8.** $\frac{3}{4} \div 2\frac{1}{2}$

Laurie's Notes

Scaffolding Instruction

- Continue to use models so that students get more practice visualizing fraction division. They should understand that the models can be used to represent all types of division.
- **Emerging:** Students understand that the algorithm for dividing fractions applies to mixed numbers as well. They may make computational errors or find the reciprocal of the dividend rather than the divisor. Students may also need practice estimating their answers to check for reasonableness. Guided instruction for Examples 1 and 2 will help students to master the success criteria.
- **Proficient:** Students comprehend the models and can apply the algorithm for dividing fractions to mixed numbers. If they are proficient with the order of operations, have students self-assess using the Try It exercises.
- Guide students in transferring the thinking they used in the exploration to the application in Example 3.

Key Idea

? "How do you write a mixed number as an improper fraction? Give an example." Multiply the denominator of the fraction by the whole number part, and then add the numerator. Put this quantity over the denominator of the fraction. *Sample answer:* $2\frac{3}{5} = \frac{5 \cdot 2 + 3}{5} = \frac{13}{5}$

? "How do you write a whole number as a fraction? Give an example." Write the whole number as the numerator of the fraction with a denominator of 1. *Sample answer:* $3 = \frac{3}{1}$

? "Why is dividing mixed numbers like dividing fractions?" You can write mixed numbers as fractions.

EXAMPLE 1

? In part (a), estimate the quotient first. Then ask, "What is the first step?" Write $2\frac{2}{3}$ as an improper fraction.

- **MP1 Make Sense of Problems and Persevere in Solving Them:** You want students to develop the habit of checking their work. In part (a), the model helps to connect the abstract problem with a visual of the solution.
- Ask a student to explain why the model verifies the quotient.
- In part (b), estimate the quotient and work through the problem as shown.
- Check the answer using a model.
- Help students interpret the answer. There are two groups of $1\frac{2}{3}$ in $3\frac{5}{6}$, with 3 left over out of the 10 needed for another group. So, the answer is $2\frac{3}{10}$.

Try It

- Before students begin, have them decide if the quotient is *greater than 1* or *less than 1*.
- Students should work with partners on these problems. Have pairs share their work at the board.

◉ Students are working on the second and third success criteria.

Scaffold instruction to support all students in their learning. Learning is individualized and you may want to group students differently as they move in and out of these levels with each skill and concept. Student self-assessment and feedback help guide your instructional decisions about how and when to layer support for all students to become proficient learners.

ELL Support

Remind students that when writing a mixed number as an improper fraction, the denominator stays the same. Have students complete Try It Exercises 1–8 in pairs.
Beginner: Find the quotient using the algorithm or a model.
Intermediate: State the answer using a complete sentence. For example, "Three and two-thirds divided by one-third is eleven."
Advanced: Explain each step.

Extra Example 1

a. Find $5\frac{1}{5} \div \frac{1}{2}$. $10\frac{2}{5}$

b. Find $7\frac{3}{4} \div 2\frac{2}{3}$. $2\frac{29}{32}$

Try It

1. 11
2. $2\frac{1}{7}$
3. $2\frac{8}{9}$
4. $3\frac{1}{4}$
5. 4
6. $5\frac{1}{2}$
7. $1\frac{5}{7}$
8. $\frac{3}{10}$

Extra Example 2

Evaluate $\frac{4}{5} - 3\frac{1}{2} \div 8\frac{1}{6}$. $\frac{13}{35}$

Try It

9. $8\frac{1}{8}$ **10.** $4\frac{8}{9}$

11. $1\frac{4}{5}$ **12.** $\frac{1}{3}$

Self-Assessment for Concepts & Skills

13. 8 **14.** $\frac{2}{21}$

15. $4\frac{3}{4}$

16. no; *Sample answer:*

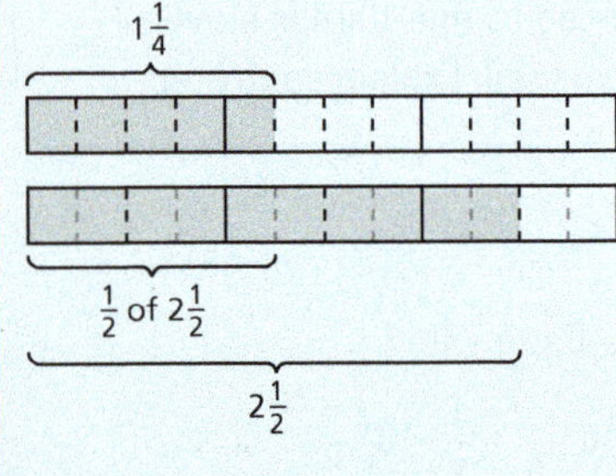

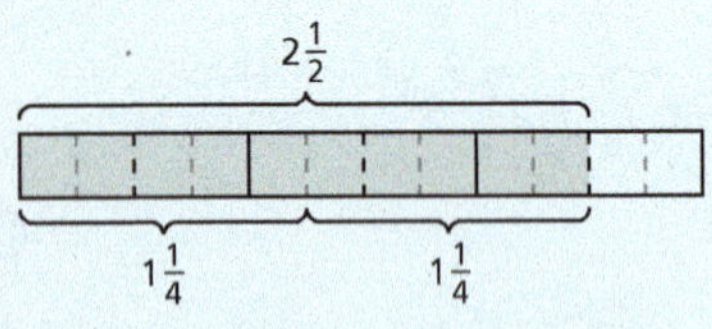

17. What is $\frac{1}{8}$ of $5\frac{1}{2}$?; $\frac{11}{16}$; 44

Laurie's Notes

EXAMPLE 2

- Write the problem on the board. Ask, "How many operations are involved in this problem?" 2 "Which operation is performed first?" division
- "What is your first step of evaluating this expression?" Change the mixed numbers to improper fractions.
- Have students use estimation to check that the answer is reasonable.

Try It

- These exercises require a bit more time and involve many skills. Have students work through the exercises independently, and then check their answers with a neighbor.
- All four problems involve the order of operations, however, Exercises 11 and 12 are not solved from left to right. Remind students that the order of operations does not change, no matter which types of numbers you use.

Self-Assessment for Concepts & Skills

- As students complete the exercises, check that they are changing mixed numbers to improper fractions, inverting the correct numbers, and simplifying the answers. Analyze their mistakes to determine if the mistakes are computational or misconceptions.
- Exercise 17 is an opportunity for students to examine different ways of saying the same thing, so they won't be fooled in the future.
- As students review the exercises and their answers, they should assess their progress with the success criteria.

ELL Support

Allow students to work in pairs to complete the exercises. Check comprehension by having each pair display their answers on a whiteboard for your review. Have pairs discuss Exercise 16 with another pair, and then share their ideas with the class.

The Success Criteria Self-Assessment chart can be found in the *Student Journal* or online at *BigIdeasMath.com.*

EXAMPLE 2 Using Order of Operations

Evaluate $5\frac{1}{4} \div 1\frac{1}{8} - \frac{2}{3}$.

$$5\frac{1}{4} \div 1\frac{1}{8} - \frac{2}{3} = \frac{21}{4} \div \frac{9}{8} - \frac{2}{3}$$ Write each mixed number as an improper fraction.

$$= \frac{21}{4} \times \frac{8}{9} - \frac{2}{3}$$ Multiply by the reciprocal of $\frac{9}{8}$, which is $\frac{8}{9}$.

$$= \frac{21 \times 8}{4 \times 9} - \frac{2}{3}$$ Multiply fractions.

$$= \frac{168}{36} - \frac{2}{3}$$ Multiply.

$$= \frac{14}{3} - \frac{2}{3}$$ Simplify.

$$= \frac{12}{3}, \text{ or } 4$$ Subtract.

Remember

Be sure to check your answers whenever possible. In Example 2, you can use estimation to check that your answer is reasonable.

$5\frac{1}{4} \div 1\frac{1}{8} - \frac{2}{3}$

$\approx 5 \div 1 - 1$

$= 5 - 1$

$= 4$ ✓

Try It

Evaluate the expression. Write the answer in simplest form.

9. $1\frac{1}{2} \div \frac{1}{6} - \frac{7}{8}$

10. $3\frac{1}{3} \div \frac{5}{6} + \frac{8}{9}$

11. $\frac{2}{5} + 2\frac{4}{5} \div 2$

12. $\frac{2}{3} - 1\frac{4}{7} \div 4\frac{5}{7}$

Self-Assessment for Concepts & Skills

Solve each exercise. Then rate your understanding of the success criteria in your journal.

EVALUATING EXPRESSIONS **Evaluate the expression. Write the answer in simplest form.**

13. $4\frac{4}{7} \div \frac{4}{7}$

14. $\frac{1}{2} \div 5\frac{1}{4}$

15. $\frac{3}{4} + 6\frac{2}{5} \div 1\frac{3}{5}$

16. MP **NUMBER SENSE** Is $2\frac{1}{2} \div 1\frac{1}{4}$ the same as $1\frac{1}{4} \div 2\frac{1}{2}$? Use models to justify your answer.

17. **DIFFERENT WORDS, SAME QUESTION** Which is different? Find "both" answers.

What is $5\frac{1}{2}$ divided by $\frac{1}{8}$?	What is the quotient of $5\frac{1}{2}$ and $\frac{1}{8}$?
What is $5\frac{1}{2}$ times 8?	What is $\frac{1}{8}$ of $5\frac{1}{2}$?

EXAMPLE 3 Modeling Real Life

One serving of tortilla soup is $1\frac{2}{3}$ cups. A restaurant cook makes 50 cups of soup. Is there enough to serve 35 people? Explain.

Math Practice

Make Sense of Quantities

Explain why the total amount divided by the amount per serving gives the number of servings.

Divide the total amount of soup by the amount per serving to find the number of available servings. So, divide 50 by $1\frac{2}{3}$.

$$50 \div 1\frac{2}{3} = 50 \div \frac{5}{3}$$ Write $1\frac{2}{3}$ as the improper fraction $\frac{5}{3}$.

$$= 50 \cdot \frac{3}{5}$$ Multiply by the reciprocal of $\frac{5}{3}$, which is $\frac{3}{5}$.

$$= \frac{50 \cdot 3}{5}$$ Multiply.

$$= \frac{150}{5}, \text{ or } 30$$ Simplify.

No. Because 30 is less than 35, there is not enough soup to serve 35 people.

Another Method Multiply the amount in one serving, $1\frac{2}{3}$ cups, by 35 to see how much soup is needed for 35 people.

$$1\frac{2}{3} \cdot 35 = \frac{5}{3} \cdot 35 = \frac{175}{3} = 58\frac{1}{3}$$

Because $58\frac{1}{3}$ is greater than 50, there is not enough soup to serve 35 people. ✓

Self-Assessment for Problem Solving

Solve each exercise. Then rate your understanding of the success criteria in your journal.

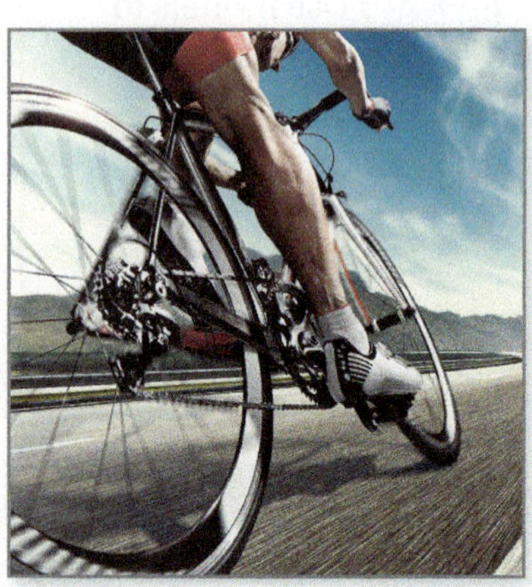

18. A watercooler contains 160 cups of water. During practice, each person on a team fills a water bottle with $3\frac{1}{3}$ cups of water from the cooler. Is there enough water for all 45 people on the team to fill their water bottles? Explain.

19. A cyclist is $7\frac{3}{4}$ kilometers from the finish line of a race. The cyclist rides at a rate of $25\frac{5}{6}$ kilometers per hour. How many minutes will it take the cyclist to finish the race?

Laurie's Notes

EXAMPLE 3

- Work through the problem as shown.
- ? "What does the quotient represent when you divide 50 by $1\frac{2}{3}$?" the number of servings from 50 cups of soup
- It is important that students know how to interpret answers.
- ? Refer to the Another Method note. "What does the product of $1\frac{2}{3}$ and 35 represent?" the amount of soup needed to serve 35 people
- ? "Will either approach $\left(50 \div 1\frac{2}{3} \text{ or } 1\frac{2}{3} \cdot 35\right)$ answer the question?" yes
- **MP2 Reason Abstractly and Quantitatively:** In thinking about this problem, mathematically proficient students have the ability to reason quantitatively from the context given.

Self-Assessment for Problem Solving

- Allow time in class for students to practice using the problem-solving plan. Remember, some students may only be ready to complete the first step.
- Allow time for students to complete the exercises independently.
- It is important that students can write a numerical expression to represent each situation.
- In Exercise 19, students need to recognize that the given units differ from the units in the question.
- Allow students to compare answers and share strategies. There may be different approaches.

The Success Criteria Self-Assessment chart can be found in the *Student Journal* or online at *BigIdeasMath.com.*

Formative Assessment Tip

Rating Scale

1	2	3	4
I do not understand.	I can do it with help.	I can do it on my own.	I can teach someone else.

At the end of the first day of instruction in Section 2.2, post a rating scale on the wall for each class. As students leave your room, give each student a sticker and tell them to place the stickers on their level of understanding. At the end of the last day of instruction in Section 2.3, display a new copy of the rating scale. Have students place stickers on the rating scale to rate their current understanding of the material. Compare the two rating scales to check for growth.

Closure

- **Connection:** How is division of mixed numbers like multiplication of mixed numbers? In each case, you must first rewrite the mixed numbers as improper fractions.
- As students leave your class, have them place a sticker on a new copy of the *Rating Scale* used in Section 2.2 to indicate their understanding of dividing fractions and mixed numbers. Compare the two rating scales to check for growth.

Extra Example 3

One serving of French onion soup is $1\frac{3}{4}$ cups. A restaurant cook makes 75 cups of soup. Is there enough to serve 40 people? Explain. Yes, because $42\frac{6}{7}$ is greater than 40, there is enough soup to serve 40 people.

Self-Assessment for Problem Solving

18. yes; They need 150 cups of water.

19. 18 min

Learning Target

Compute quotients with mixed numbers and solve problems involving division with mixed numbers.

Success Criteria

- Draw a model to explain division of mixed numbers.
- Write a mixed number as an improper fraction.
- Divide with mixed numbers.
- Evaluate expressions involving mixed numbers using the order of operations.

1. $\frac{7}{8}$
2. $\frac{7}{6}$
3. $\frac{1}{12}$
4. 32
5. 56
6. 396
7. 540
8. 96 m^3
9. 70 $in.^3$
10. 240 yd^3
11. B

Concepts, Skills, & Problem Solving

12. *Sample answer:* You need $\frac{2}{3}$ cup of yogurt to make 1 smoothie. How many smoothies can you make with $3\frac{1}{3}$ cups of yogurt? 5
13. *Sample answer:* A pepper plant is $1\frac{1}{6}$ feet tall and a cherry tomato plant is $5\frac{5}{6}$ feet tall. How many times taller is the cherry tomato plant than the pepper plant? 5
14. *Sample answer:* One bag of mulch covers $2\frac{1}{2}$ square meters of your garden. How many bags do you use to cover $8\frac{3}{4}$ square meters of your garden? $3\frac{1}{2}$
15. 3
16. $9\frac{1}{2}$
17. $9\frac{3}{4}$
18. $13\frac{2}{9}$
19. $3\frac{18}{19}$
20. $1\frac{4}{5}$
21. $\frac{9}{10}$
22. $\frac{4}{7}$
23. $12\frac{1}{2}$
24. 11
25. $1\frac{1}{5}$
26. $2\frac{1}{16}$
27. $\frac{2}{7}$
28. $\frac{10}{33}$
29. $1\frac{5}{18}$
30. $1\frac{1}{15}$

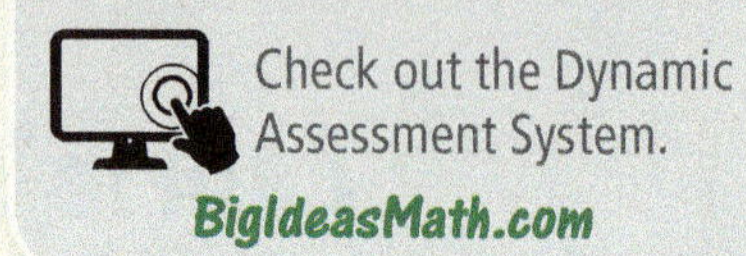

Assignment Guide and Concept Check

Scaffold assignments to support all students in their learning progression. The suggested assignments are a starting point. Continue to assign additional exercises and revisit with spaced practice to move every student toward proficiency.

Level	Assignment 1	Assignment 2
Emerging	4, 7, 8, 11, 13, 16, 22, 25, 35, 40	19, 27, 31, 32, 43, 46
Proficient	4, 7, 8, 11, 13, 16, 22, 25, 37, 41, 43	20, 28, 31, 32, 45, 46, 47
Advanced	4, 7, 8, 11, 13, 17, 21, 26, 39, 42, 44	28, 30, 31, 45, 46, 47, 48

- Assignment 1 is for use after students complete the Self-Assessment for Concepts & Skills.
- Assignment 2 is for use after students complete the Self-Assessment for Problem Solving.
- The red exercises can be used as a concept check.

Review & Refresh Prior Skills

Exercises 1–4 Dividing Fractions
Exercises 5–7 Finding the LCM
Exercises 8–10 Finding the Volume of a Rectangular Prism
Exercise 11 Using a Prime Factorization

Common Errors

- **Exercises 15–30** Students may try to divide the whole numbers and the fractions separately. Remind them to rewrite the mixed numbers as improper fractions and to think of each mixed number as one number.
- **Exercises 15–30** Students may find the reciprocal before writing the mixed number as an improper fraction. Remind them that the order of the steps in solving the problem does matter. Tell students to write out each step so they can keep track of the correct order.

2.3 Practice

Go to *BigIdeasMath.com* to get HELP with solving the exercises.

Review & Refresh

Divide. Write the answer in simplest form.

1. $\frac{1}{8} \div \frac{1}{7}$
2. $\frac{7}{9} \div \frac{2}{3}$
3. $\frac{5}{6} \div 10$
4. $12 \div \frac{3}{8}$

Find the LCM of the numbers.

5. 8, 14
6. 9, 11, 12
7. 12, 27, 30

Find the volume of the rectangular prism.

8. 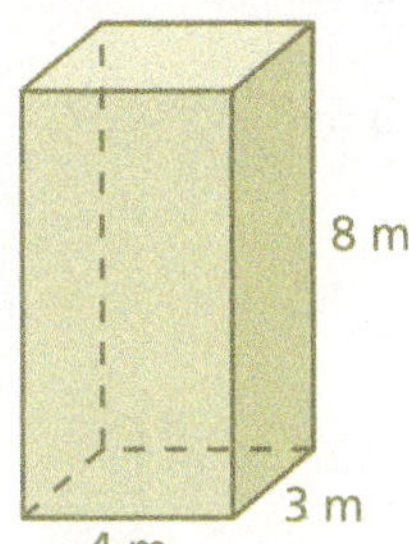

9. 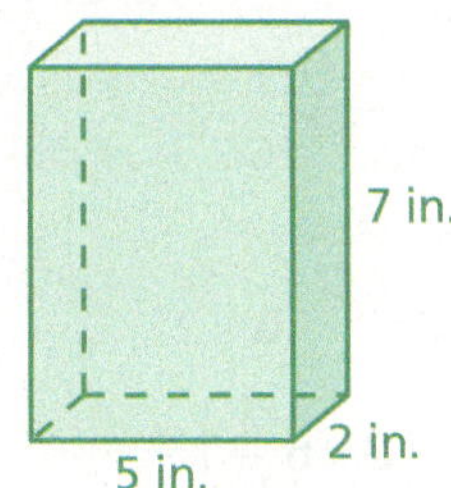

10. 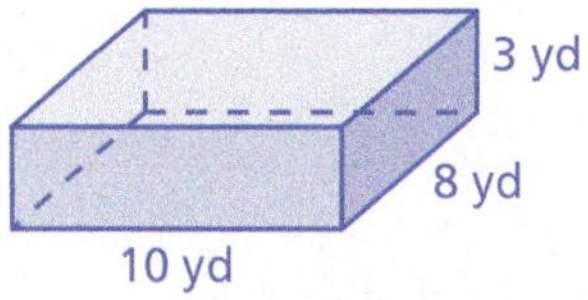

11. Which number is *not* a prime factor of 286?

   A. 2 **B.** 7 **C.** 11 **D.** 13

Concepts, Skills, & Problem Solving

MP **CHOOSE TOOLS** **Write a real-life problem that represents the division expression described. Then solve the problem using a model. Check your answer algebraically.** (See Exploration 1, p. 61.)

12. How many two-thirds are in three and one-third?
13. How many one and one-sixths are in five and five-sixths?
14. How many two and one-halves are in eight and three-fourths?

DIVIDING WITH MIXED NUMBERS **Divide. Write the answer in simplest form.**

15. $2\frac{1}{4} \div \frac{3}{4}$
16. $3\frac{4}{5} \div \frac{2}{5}$
17. $8\frac{1}{8} \div \frac{5}{6}$
18. $7\frac{5}{9} \div \frac{4}{7}$
19. $7\frac{1}{2} \div 1\frac{9}{10}$
20. $3\frac{3}{4} \div 2\frac{1}{12}$
21. $7\frac{1}{5} \div 8$
22. $8\frac{4}{7} \div 15$
23. $8\frac{1}{3} \div \frac{2}{3}$
24. $9\frac{1}{6} \div \frac{5}{6}$
25. $13 \div 10\frac{5}{6}$
26. $12 \div 5\frac{9}{11}$
27. $\frac{7}{8} \div 3\frac{1}{16}$
28. $\frac{4}{9} \div 1\frac{7}{15}$
29. $4\frac{5}{16} \div 3\frac{3}{8}$
30. $6\frac{2}{9} \div 5\frac{5}{6}$

31. **MP YOU BE THE TEACHER** Your friend finds the quotient of $3\frac{1}{2}$ and $1\frac{2}{3}$. Is your friend correct? Explain your reasoning.

$$3\frac{1}{2} \div 1\frac{2}{3} = 3\frac{1}{2} \times 1\frac{3}{2} = \frac{7}{2} \times \frac{5}{2} = \frac{7 \times 5}{2 \times 2} = \frac{35}{4}, \text{ or } 8\frac{3}{4}$$

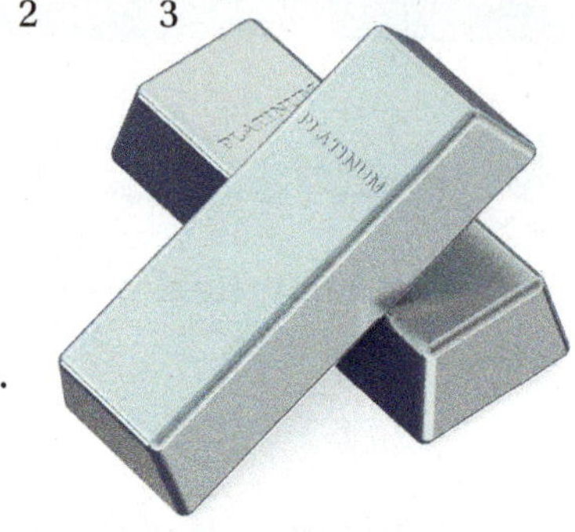

32. **MP PROBLEM SOLVING** A platinum nugget weighs $3\frac{1}{2}$ ounces. How many $\frac{1}{4}$-ounce pieces can be cut from the nugget?

ORDER OF OPERATIONS **Evaluate the expression. Write the answer in simplest form.**

33. $3 \div 1\frac{1}{5} + \frac{1}{2}$

34. $4\frac{2}{3} - 1\frac{1}{3} \div 2$

35. $\frac{2}{5} + 2\frac{1}{6} \div \frac{5}{6}$

36. $5\frac{5}{6} \div 3\frac{3}{4} - \frac{2}{9}$

37. $6\frac{1}{2} - \frac{7}{8} \div 5\frac{11}{16}$

38. $9\frac{1}{6} \div 5 + 3\frac{1}{3}$

39. $3\frac{3}{5} + 4\frac{4}{15} \div \frac{4}{9}$

40. $\frac{3}{5} \times \frac{7}{12} \div 2\frac{7}{10}$

41. $4\frac{3}{8} \div \frac{3}{4} \bullet \frac{4}{7}$

42. $1\frac{9}{11} \times 4\frac{7}{12} \div \frac{2}{3}$

43. $3\frac{4}{15} \div \left(8 \bullet 6\frac{3}{10}\right)$

44. $2\frac{5}{14} \div \left(2\frac{5}{8} \times 1\frac{3}{7}\right)$

45. **MP LOGIC** Your friend uses the model shown to state that $2\frac{1}{2} \div 1\frac{1}{6} = 2\frac{1}{6}$. Is your friend correct? Justify your answer using the model.

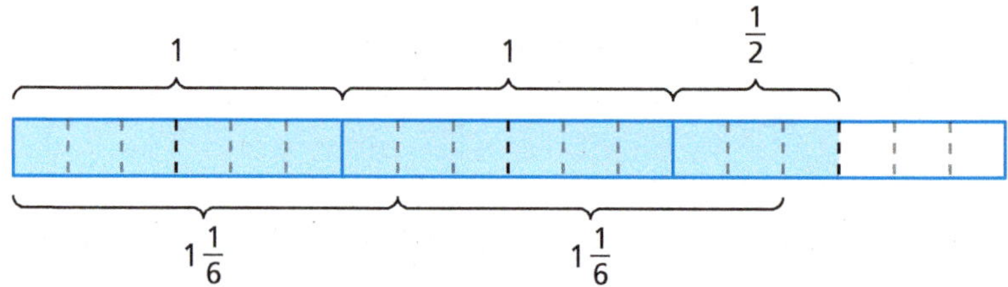

46. **MP MODELING REAL LIFE** A bag contains 42 cups of dog food. Your dog eats $2\frac{1}{3}$ cups of dog food each day. Is there enough food to last 3 weeks? Explain.

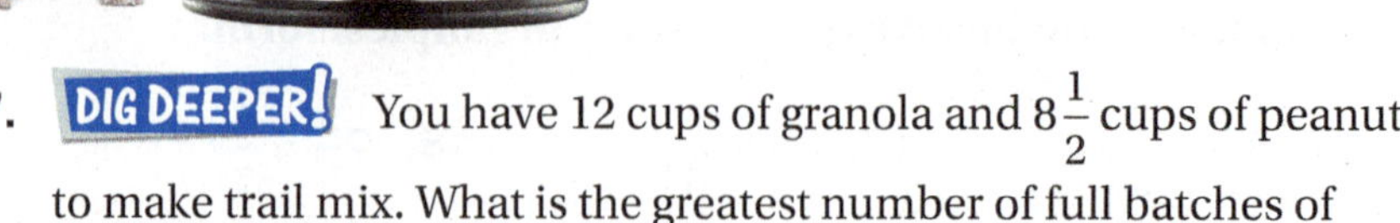

47. **DIG DEEPER!** You have 12 cups of granola and $8\frac{1}{2}$ cups of peanuts to make trail mix. What is the greatest number of full batches of trail mix you can make? Explain how you found your answer.

Trail Mix
$2\frac{3}{4}$ cups granola
$1\frac{1}{3}$ cups peanuts

48. **MP REASONING** At a track and field meet, the longest shot-put throw by a boy is 25 feet 8 inches. The longest shot-put throw by a girl is 19 feet 3 inches. How many times greater is the longest shot-put throw by the boy than by the girl?

Common Errors

- **Exercises 33–44** Students may forget to use the order of operations. Remind them about the order of operations. Have them use parentheses to help remember which parts to evaluate first.
- **Exercise 48** Students may incorrectly convert inches to feet. For example, writing 25 feet 8 inches as 25.8 feet. Remind students that they need to put the inches over 12 to convert inches to feet.

Mini-Assessment

Divide. Write the answer in simplest form.

1. $6\frac{1}{2} \div 2\frac{3}{4}$ $2\frac{4}{11}$
2. $4\frac{2}{3} \div 1\frac{1}{6}$ 4
3. $8\frac{4}{5} \div \frac{2}{5}$ 22
4. $6 \div 2\frac{3}{5}$ $2\frac{4}{13}$
5. A bag contains 13 cups of cat food. Your cats eat $1\frac{1}{2}$ cups of cat food each day. Is there enough food to last 2 weeks? Explain. No, because $8\frac{2}{3}$ is less than 14, there is not enough food to last two weeks.

Section Resources

Surface Level	Deep Level
Resources by Chapter • Extra Practice • Reteach • Puzzle Time Student Journal • Self-Assessment • Practice Differentiating the Lesson Tutorial Videos Skills Review Handbook Skills Trainer	Resources by Chapter • Enrichment and Extension Graphic Organizers Dynamic Assessment System • Section Practice
Transfer Level	
Dynamic Assessment System • Mid-Chapter Quiz	Assessment Book • Mid-Chapter Quiz

Concepts, Skills, & Problem Solving

31. no; $3\frac{1}{2} \div 1\frac{2}{3} = \frac{7}{2} \div \frac{5}{3} = 2\frac{1}{10}$
32. 14
33. 3
34. 4
35. 3
36. $1\frac{1}{3}$
37. $6\frac{9}{26}$
38. $5\frac{1}{6}$
39. $13\frac{1}{5}$
40. $\frac{7}{54}$
41. $3\frac{1}{3}$
42. $12\frac{1}{2}$
43. $\frac{7}{108}$
44. $\frac{22}{35}$
45. no; There are 2 full groups of $1\frac{1}{6}$ plus one piece remaining, which represents $\frac{1}{7}$ of $1\frac{1}{6}$.
46. no; $42 \div 2\frac{1}{3} = 18$
47. 4; *Sample answer:* $12 \div 2\frac{3}{4} = 4\frac{4}{11}$ and $8\frac{1}{2} \div 1\frac{1}{3} = 6\frac{3}{8}$, so you can make 4 full batches.
48. $1\frac{1}{3}$

Learning Target

Add and subtract decimals and solve problems involving addition and subtraction of decimals.

Success Criteria

- Explain why it is necessary to line up the decimal points when adding and subtracting decimals.
- Add decimals.
- Subtract decimals.
- Evaluate expressions involving addition and subtraction of decimals.

Warm Up

Cumulative, vocabulary, and prerequisite skills practice opportunities are available in the *Resources by Chapter* or at *BigIdeasMath.com*.

ELL Support

Explain that the word *decimal* is related to the number 10. Have students look at numbers to the left of the decimal point in the place value chart, beginning with the ones place. If they multiply 1 by 10, they get 10, which is one place value to the left. If they multiply 10 by 10, they get 100, and so on. Students can observe a similar progression to the right of the decimal point when dividing by 10. Other words related to the number 10 are decade (10 years) and deciliter (one-tenth of a liter).

Exploration 1

a–d. See Additional Answers.

Exploration 2

a–f. See Additional Answers.

Laurie's Notes

STATE STANDARDS
6.NS.B.3

Preparing to Teach

- In this lesson, students will extend decimal addition and subtraction from prior courses to include the reasoning for lining up the decimal point.
- **MP7 Look for and Make Use of Structure:** Decimals are another form of numbers. The rules governing operations with decimals are connected to operations with fractions. The goal is for students to see and make sense of these connections.

Motivate

$$\begin{array}{r} 317 \\ +\ 24 \\ \hline 557 \end{array}$$

- **Acting Time:** Write the addition problem as shown on the board before students arrive.
- When a student comments on the error, say, "It's easier this way. There's no regrouping." Use a similar example for subtraction.
- This should lead to a discussion about why whole numbers must be right-justified when adding or subtracting. Place value is the key.
- **MP3 Construct Viable Arguments and Critique the Reasoning of Others:** It is important to keep referring to place value and like units being added or subtracted. Students should provide reasoning beyond stating the rule of "line up the decimal point."
- ? "What do you do first when adding or subtracting fractions?" Find a common denominator. "How do you think this can help you when adding or subtracting decimals?" Write 0.23 and 0.47 as fractions to show that the numbers have a common denominator.
- Tell students that inserting a zero to the right of the decimal does not change the value, but it may be necessary to get common place values before adding or subtracting.

Exploration 1

- This exploration allows students to explore place values of decimals using addition and subtraction on a number line.
- ? In part (b), students may have difficulty identifying the increments. Ask, "What is $\frac{1}{10}$ divided by 10?" $\frac{1}{100}$
- Check that students are identifying the tick marks on the number lines accurately, and the points *A* and *B*.
- This is a good opportunity to display different methods for subtracting on a number line. Some students may identify the increments and count the tick marks, without using the algorithm. Others may find the values, and then use the algorithms.

Exploration 2

- This exploration begins to focus students' attention on the role of place value when adding or subtracting decimals. Check to see that students have correctly named the decimal places beyond hundredths.
- Each pair of numbers in parts (a)–(c) contain four digits. Check to see that students place the numbers in the chart correctly.
- Discuss the usefulness of the place value chart when adding or subtracting decimals. Students' comments should include keeping digits and decimal points aligned, and placing digits in the correct place-value position.

2.4 Adding and Subtracting Decimals

Learning Target: Add and subtract decimals and solve problems involving addition and subtraction of decimals.

Success Criteria:
- I can explain why it is necessary to line up the decimal points when adding and subtracting decimals.
- I can add decimals.
- I can subtract decimals.
- I can evaluate expressions involving addition and subtraction of decimals.

EXPLORATION 1

Using Number Lines

Work with a partner. Use each number line to find $A + B$ and $B - A$. Explain how you know you are correct.

a.

b.

c.

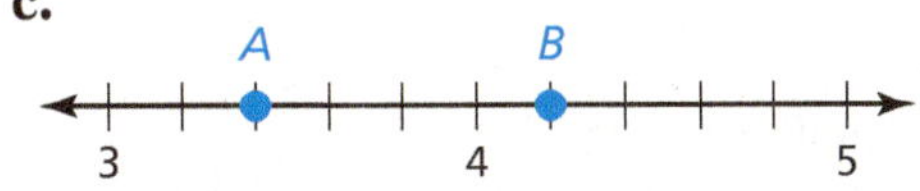

d.

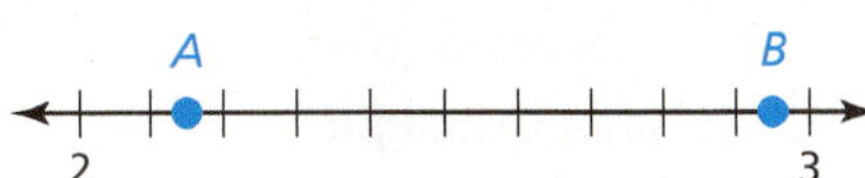

EXPLORATION 2

Extending the Place Value Chart

Work with a partner. Explain how you can use the place value chart below to add and subtract decimals beyond hundredths. Then find each sum or difference.

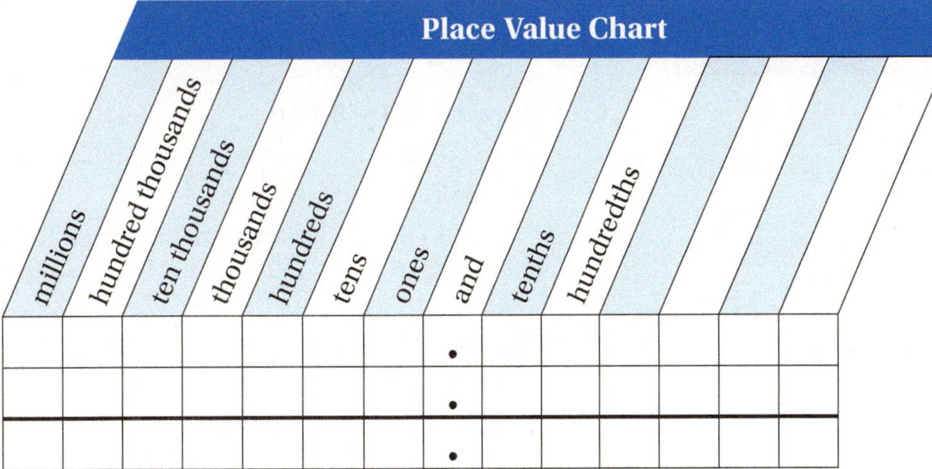

a. 16.05 + 2.945

b. 7.421 + 8.058

c. 38.72 − 8.618

d. 64.968 − 51.167

e. 225.1 + 85.0465

f. 1107.20592 − 102.3056

Math Practice

Recognize Usefulness of Tools

How does the place value chart help you perform the operations? How can you perform the operations without the chart?

2.4 Lesson

Adding and Subtracting Decimals

To add or subtract decimals, write the numbers vertically and line up the decimal points. Then bring down the decimal point and add or subtract as you would with whole numbers.

EXAMPLE 1 Adding Decimals

a. Add 8.13 + 2.76. **Estimate** $8 + 3 = 11$

Line up the decimal points.

$$\begin{array}{r} 8.13 \\ +\ 2.76 \\ \hline 10.89 \end{array}$$

Add as you would with whole numbers.

Reasonable? $10.89 \approx 11$ ✓

b. Add 1.459 + 23.7.

$$\begin{array}{r} \scriptstyle 1 \quad\;\; \\ 1.459 \\ +\ 23.700 \\ \hline 25.159 \end{array}$$

Insert zeros so that both numbers have the same number of decimal places.

Math Practice

Maintain Oversight

Why is it important to line up the decimal points when adding or subtracting decimals?

Try It **Add.**

1. 4.206 + 10.85 **2.** 15.5 + 8.229 **3.** 78.41 + 90.99

EXAMPLE 2 Subtracting Decimals

a. Subtract 5.508 − 3.174. **Estimate** $6 - 3 = 3$

Line up the decimal points.

$$\begin{array}{r} \scriptstyle 4\,10 \\ 5.\not{5}\not{0}8 \\ -\ 3.174 \\ \hline 2.334 \end{array}$$

Subtract as you would with whole numbers.

Reasonable? $2.334 \approx 3$ ✓

b. Subtract 21.9 − 1.605.

$$\begin{array}{r} \scriptstyle 9 \;\; \\ \scriptstyle 8\,\not{10}\,10 \\ 21.\not{9}\not{0}\not{0} \\ -\ 1.605 \\ \hline 20.295 \end{array}$$

Insert zeros so that both numbers have the same number of decimal places.

Try It **Subtract.**

4. 6.34 − 5.33 **5.** 27.9 − 0.905 **6.** 18.626 − 13.88

Laurie's Notes

Scaffolding Instruction

- Students explored adding and subtracting decimals using a place value chart. Can they extend that understanding to adding and subtracting decimals without a place value chart? Can they use estimation to check the reasonableness of their answers?
- **Emerging:** Students may depend on a place value chart and have difficulty explaining why the algorithm works. Allow them to use grid paper for Examples 1, 2, and the Try It exercises. Ask students to identify all the place values of each number, and make the connection that those values are lined up vertically.
- **Proficient:** Students can explain why lining up the decimal point is necessary, and no longer need the place value chart. Students can also estimate a sum or difference of decimals. Students can self-assess with the Try It exercises. Check their work for Exercises 1 and 5.
- In Example 3, students will evaluate expressions involving both addition and subtraction of decimals.

Key Idea

- **Connection:** To add or subtract fractions, you need a common denominator. To add or subtract decimals, you need common place values, adding tenths to tenths, hundredths to hundredths, and so on.

EXAMPLE 1

- Ask a volunteer to read the problems as you write them.
- As you work through the problem, ask about the value of the digits being added. For instance, the 3 and 6 are both hundredths.
- ? In part (b), ask, "What is a reasonable estimate? Explain." 25; $1 + 24$
- Discuss with students why $23.7 = 23.700$.
- Note the need to regroup from the tenths to the ones place. Check for student understanding of this process and notation.

Try It

- Circulate and check that students are lining up the decimal point, and inserting zeros if needed.

EXAMPLE 2

- **Common Error:** In part (b), students may want to subtract 21.9 from 1.605 because 21.9 has fewer digits. Students making this mistake have not understood the need to subtract like place values.
- Regrouping is necessary. Check for student understanding.

Try It

- Check Exercise 5, which requires inserting zeros and regrouping.
- Remind students that they should assess their understanding of the first three success criteria. Have students use *Fist of Five* to indicate their understanding of each success criterion.

Formative Assessment Tip

Fist of Five

This technique asks students to indicate the extent to which they understand a concept or procedure. Students hold 1 to 5 fingers in front of their chests, where 5 fingers represent mastery and 1 finger signifies uncertainty. This strategy can be a quick way for students to communicate where their learning is with respect to a specific success criterion.

Extra Example 1

a. Add $5.44 + 6.31$. 11.75

b. Add $2.8 + 5.547$. 8.347

Try It

1. 15.056 **2.** 23.729

3. 169.4

Extra Example 2

a. Subtract $6.124 - 2.409$. 3.715

b. Subtract $15.7 - 2.375$. 13.325

ELL Support

Remind students that they must align the decimal point when subtracting. Have students work in pairs to complete Try It Exercises 4–6.

Beginner: Write the numbers vertically and line up the decimal points to find the difference.

Intermediate/Advanced: State the answer using a complete sentence. For example, "Five and thirty-three hundredths subtracted from six and thirty-four hundredths is one and one-hundredth."

Try It

4. 1.01 **5.** 26.995

6. 4.746

Extra Example 3

You are installing a fence around a triangular garden with side lengths of 3.844 meters, 4.625 meters, and 5.156 meters. You already have 9.8 meters of fencing. The amount of fencing you need to purchase can be represented by $(3.844 + 4.625 + 5.156) - 9.8$. How much more fencing do you need to purchase? 3.825 meters

Try It

7. 15.133

Self-Assessment for Concepts & Skills

8. 11.172 **9.** 17.2003

10. Estimating allows you to check that your answer is reasonable.

11. Line up the decimal points and insert zeros if needed.

12. *Sample answer:* Add to find the total cost of two or more items; Subtract to find the change when paying for an item.

13. *Sample answer:* Move 0.001 from one number to the other so you have $3.840 + 30.000$; Mental math; It is less complicated.

14. *Sample answer:* 9.55, 10.6, 7.755

Laurie's Notes

EXAMPLE 3

- This example represents the last success criterion.
- Ask a volunteer to read the problem.
- Some students may need to write out each operation vertically.
- ? After students have worked through the problem, ask, "What is the highest score a gymnast can receive for this routine?" 16.9 "Does your answer make sense?" *Sample answer:* Yes, the total for deductions and penalties is about 2, so the estimated score is about 14.9.
- Have students *Turn and Talk* about how the order of operations played a part in this problem.

Self-Assessment for Concepts & Skills

- Exercises 8 and 9 give students information on their procedural understanding. If mistakes are made, have students determine if they made a computational error or lined up the place values incorrectly.
- Listen to students' explanations for Exercises 10, 11, and 13, to assess their understanding of number sense.
- For Exercise 12, look for student examples that go beyond the hundredths place to share with the class.

ELL Support

Have students complete Exercises 8 and 9 independently, and then practice language by comparing their answers with a partner. Then have students work in groups to discuss and complete Exercises 10–14. Have two groups compare their answers and come to consensuses on which are appropriate. If there is disagreement or uncertainty, provide support.

The Success Criteria Self-Assessment chart can be found in the *Student Journal* or online at *BigIdeasMath.com*.

EXAMPLE 3 Adding and Subtracting Decimals

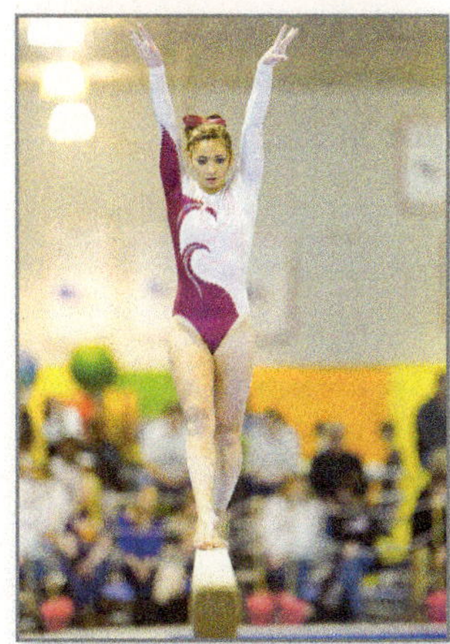

Difficulty score	6.9
Execution score deductions	1.534
Penalties	0.3

A gymnast's score for a routine is calculated by finding the sum of a difficulty score and an execution score, minus any penalties. The execution score starts at 10 and is reduced by deductions. The gymnast's score can be represented by

$$\mathbf{6.9 + (10 - 1.534) - 0.3.}$$

What is the gymnast's score?

Evaluate the expression to solve the problem.

$6.9 + (10 - 1.534) - 0.3$

$= 6.9 + 8.466 - 0.3$ Subtract inside parentheses.

$= 15.366 - 0.3$ Add.

$= 15.066$ Subtract.

So, the gymnast's score is 15.066.

Try It

7. **WHAT IF?** The execution score is adjusted and has 1.467 in deductions. What is the gymnast's score?

Self-Assessment for Concepts & Skills

Solve each exercise. Then rate your understanding of the success criteria in your journal.

ADDING AND SUBTRACTING DECIMALS Evaluate the expression.

8. 23.557 − 17.601 + 5.216

9. 16.5263 + 12.404 − 11.73

10. **MP CHOOSE TOOLS** Why is it helpful to estimate the answer before adding or subtracting decimals?

11. **WRITING** When adding or subtracting decimals, how can you be sure to add or subtract only digits that have the same place value?

12. **OPEN-ENDED** Describe two real-life examples of when you would need to add and subtract decimals.

13. **MP STRUCTURE** You add 3.841 + 29.999 as shown. Describe a method for adding the numbers using mental math. Which method do you prefer? Explain.

$$\begin{array}{r} {\scriptstyle 1\,1\,1\,1} \\ 3.841 \\ +\ 29.999 \\ \hline 33.840 \end{array}$$

14. **OPEN-ENDED** Write three decimals that have a sum of 27.905.

EXAMPLE 4 Modeling Real Life

The Lincoln Memorial Reflecting Pool is approximately rectangular. Its width is 50.9 meters, and its length is 618.44 meters. You walk the perimeter of the pool. About how many meters do you walk?

Understand the problem.

You are given the dimensions of a rectangular pool. You are asked to find the number of meters you walk around the perimeter of the pool.

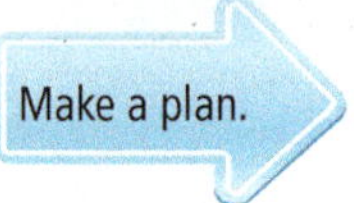

Draw a diagram and label the dimensions. Write the side lengths vertically and line up the decimal points to find the sum.

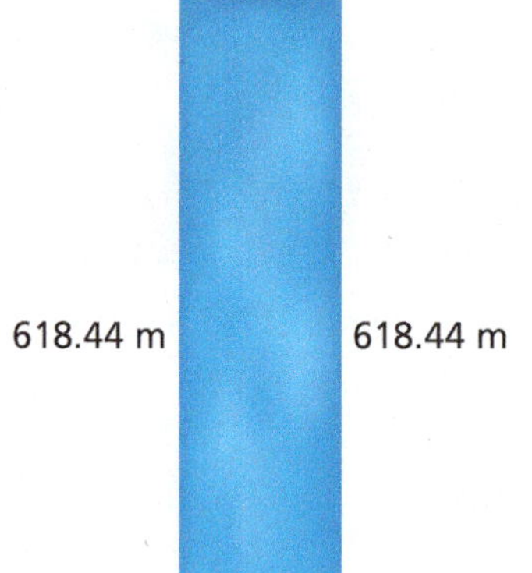

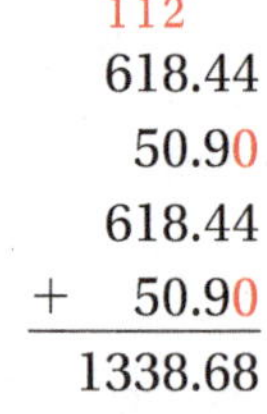

$$\begin{array}{r} {}^{112} \\ 618.44 \\ 50.90 \\ 618.44 \\ +\ \ 50.90 \\ \hline 1338.68 \end{array}$$

So, you walk about 1339 meters.

Check Reasonableness Estimate the distance by finding the sum of the side lengths rounded to the nearest ten.

$620 + 50 + 620 + 50 = 1340$ meters

The answer is reasonable because $1340 \approx 1338.68$. ✓

Self-Assessment for Problem Solving

Solve each exercise. Then rate your understanding of the success criteria in your journal.

15. A field hockey field is rectangular. Its width is 54.88 meters, and its perimeter is 289.76 meters. Find the length of the field.

16. DIG DEEPER! You mix 23.385 grams of sugar and 12.873 grams of baking soda in a glass container for an experiment. You place the container on a scale to find that the total mass is 104.2 grams. What is the mass of the container?

17. One molecule of water is made of two hydrogen atoms and one oxygen atom. The masses (in atomic mass units) for one atom of hydrogen and oxygen are shown. What is the mass (in atomic mass units) of one molecule of water?

Laurie's Notes

EXAMPLE 4

- **FYI:** The Lincoln Memorial Reflecting Pool was constructed in the 1920s. It has a depth of about 18 inches on the sides and 30 inches in the center, and holds approximately 6.75 million gallons of water. The pool was renovated in 2011–12 at a cost of over $30 million.
- Ask if any of your students have visited Washington, D.C., and this famous reflecting pool. If they have, they should have a sense of the size.
- Read the problem and ask what the phrase "walk the perimeter" means. It is a common phrase, but not all students will understand that it literally means to walk around the pool.
- Draw and label a sketch of the pool.
- Work through the problem as shown. Ask if there are other methods that can be used. Some students might suggest adding the length and width, and then doubling, meaning adding that sum to itself.
- **Extension:** Have students estimate the distance in feet. A meter is a bit longer than a yard, or 3 feet. If the perimeter is multiplied by 3, it would be approximately 4017 feet, or about $\frac{4}{5}$ mile.

Self-Assessment for Problem Solving

- The goal for all students is to feel comfortable with the problem-solving plan. It is important for students to problem-solve in class, where they may receive support from you and their peers. Keep in mind that some students may only be ready to complete the first step.
- Ask volunteers to give examples of how they use decimals in their everyday lives.
- These exercises each require multiple operations with decimals. Have students work on the exercises independently.
- Encourage students to make a diagram for Exercise 15.
- Extend Exercise 17 by asking students if they can solve the problem using mental math.
- Have students discuss their answers with a partner, and talk through any discrepancies.
- Have students use *Thumbs Up* to indicate their understanding of each success criterion.

The Success Criteria Self-Assessment chart can be found in the *Student Journal* or online at *BigIdeasMath.com.*

Closure

- **Writing Prompt:** Write a note to a friend that explains how to add and subtract decimals, and why lining up decimals points is necessary.

Extra Example 4

A parade route is in the shape of a trapezoid. It begins and ends at the same location. How many kilometers does a float travel in the parade?

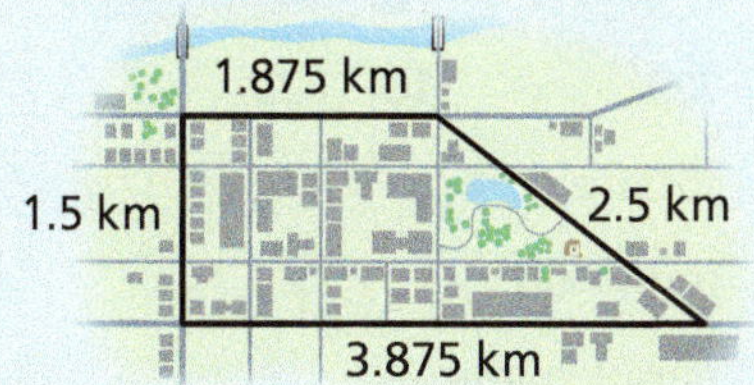

9.75 kilometers

Self-Assessment for Problem Solving

15. 90 m
16. 67.942 g
17. 18.0148 atomic mass units

Learning Target

Add and subtract decimals and solve problems involving addition and subtraction of decimals.

Success Criteria

- Explain why it is necessary to line up the decimal points when adding and subtracting decimals.
- Add decimals.
- Subtract decimals.
- Evaluate expressions involving addition and subtraction of decimals.

Review & Refresh

1. $4\frac{1}{3}$
2. $\frac{5}{6}$
3. $2\frac{1}{12}$
4. 4
5. 3
6. 12
7. 1
8. 16
9. 729
10. 625
11. square
12. trapezoid
13. parallelogram

Concepts, Skills, & Problem Solving

14. 13.177
15. 0.6457
16. 27.9192
17. 11.029
18. 6.474
19. 22.899
20. 34.098
21. 18.572
22. 17.005
23. 40
24. 9.998
25. 144
26. 142.009
27. 29.937
28. 34.313
29. 1.46
30. 3.32
31. 4.366
32. 3.561
33. 2.644
34. 2.884
35. 5.611
36. 13.061
37. 20.417
38. 43.937
39. 117.2583
40. 4.3058

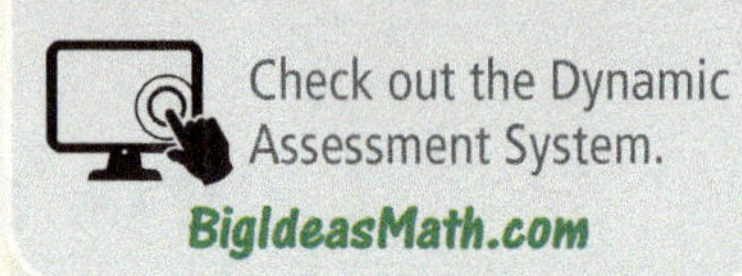

Assignment Guide and Concept Check

Scaffold assignments to support all students in their learning progression. The suggested assignments are a starting point. Continue to assign additional exercises and revisit with spaced practice to move every student toward proficiency.

Level	Assignment 1	Assignment 2
Emerging	3, 6, 9, 12, 13, 15, 17, 21, 23, 29, 31, 35, 47, 50	16, 28, 38, 41, 42, 43, 52, 56
Proficient	3, 6, 9, 12, 13, 15, 21, 22, 30, 31, 35, 39, 47, 50	16, 28, 40, 41, 42, 43, 52, 53, 54, 55, 56
Advanced	3, 6, 9, 12, 13, 15, 19, 22, 25, 33, 37, 40, 47, 51	41, 42, 52, 53, 54, 55, 56, 57, 58

- Assignment 1 is for use after students complete the Self-Assessment for Concepts & Skills.
- Assignment 2 is for use after students complete the Self-Assessment for Problem Solving.
- The red exercises can be used as a concept check.

Review & Refresh Prior Skills

Exercises 1–3 Dividing with Mixed Numbers
Exercises 4–6 Finding the GCF
Exercises 7–10 Finding Values of Powers
Exercises 11–13 Classifying Quadrilaterals

Common Errors

- **Exercises 17–40** Students may forget to insert zeros as placeholders. Remind them that each number added or subtracted needs to have the same number of decimal places to line up place values.

2.4 Practice

Go to *BigIdeasMath.com* to get HELP with solving the exercises.

Review & Refresh

Divide. Write the answer in simplest form.

1. $3\frac{1}{4} \div \frac{3}{4}$

2. $4\frac{1}{6} \div 5$

3. $6\frac{2}{3} \div 3\frac{1}{5}$

Find the GCF of the numbers.

4. 16, 28, 40

5. 39, 54, 63

6. 24, 72, 132

Find the value of the power.

7. 1^{12}

8. 2^4

9. 3^6

10. 5^4

Classify the quadrilateral.

11. 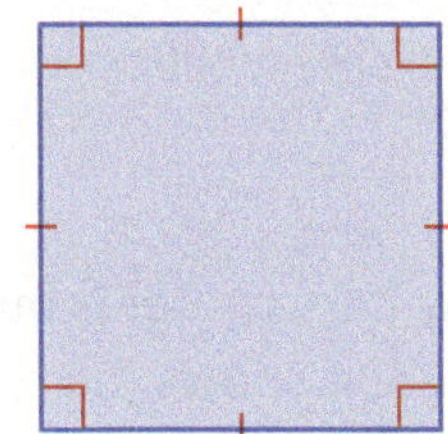

12. 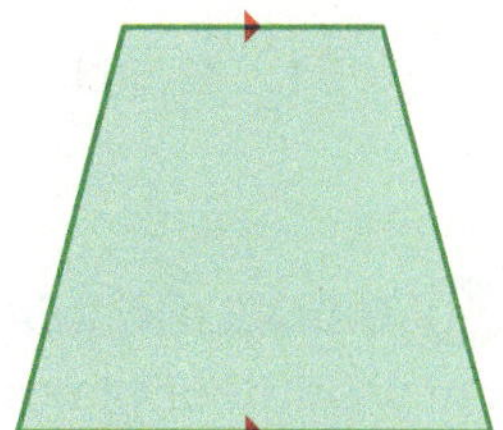

13. 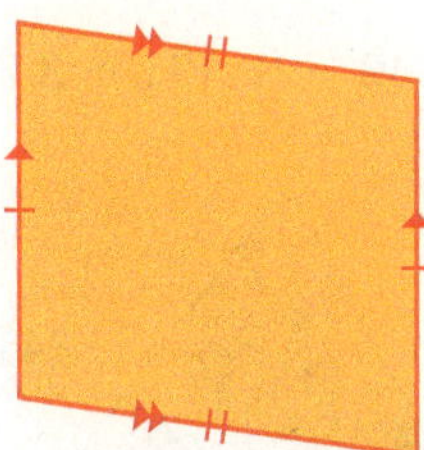

Concepts, Skills, & Problem Solving

MP USING TOOLS **Use a place value chart to find the sum or difference.** (See Exploration 2, p. 67.)

14. $4.63 + 8.547$

15. $3.6257 - 2.98$

16. $14.065 + 13.8542$

ADDING DECIMALS **Add.**

17. $7.82 + 3.209$

18. $3.7 + 2.774$

19. $12.829 + 10.07$

20. $20.35 + 13.748$

21. $11.212 + 7.36$

22. $14.91 + 2.095$

23. $31.994 + 8.006$

24. $3.946 + 6.052$

25. $41.226 + 102.774$

26. $122.781 + 19.228$

27. $17.440 + 12.497$

28. $15.255 + 19.058$

SUBTRACTING DECIMALS **Subtract.**

29. $4.58 - 3.12$

30. $8.629 - 5.309$

31. $6.98 - 2.614$

32. $15.131 - 11.57$

33. $13.5 - 10.856$

34. $25.82 - 22.936$

35. $17.651 - 12.04$

36. $19.255 - 6.194$

37. $56.217 - 35.8$

38. $62.486 - 18.549$

39. $152.883 - 35.6247$

40. $129.343 - 125.0372$

YOU BE THE TEACHER **Your friend finds the sum or difference. Is your friend correct? Explain your reasoning.**

41.

```
  6.058
+ 3.95
 10.008
```

42.

```
  9.5
- 7.18
  2.48
```

43. **PROBLEM SOLVING** Vehicles must weigh no more than 10.75 tons to cross a bridge. A truck weighs 11.638 tons. By how many tons does the truck exceed the weight limit?

ADDING AND SUBTRACTING DECIMALS **Evaluate the expression.**

44. $6.105 + 10.4 + 3.075$

45. $22.6 - 12.286 - 3.542$

46. $15.35 + 7.604 - 12.954$

47. $16.5 - 13.45 + 7.293$

48. $25.92 - 18.478 + 8.164$

49. $23.45 + 17.75 - 19.618$

50. $14.549 - (8.131 + 3.7024)$

51. $41.563 - (18.65 + 15.9214) + 9.6$

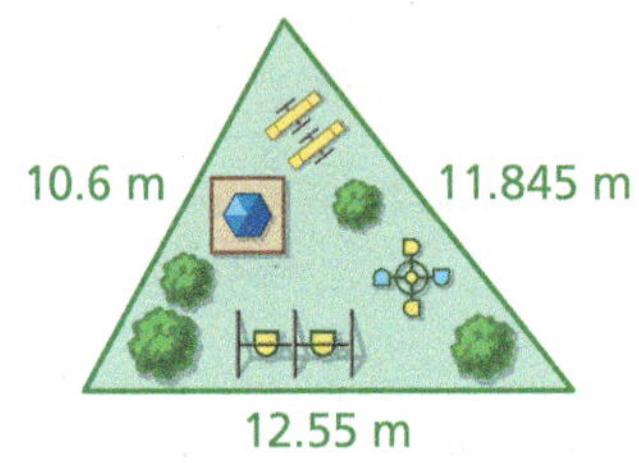

52. **MODELING REAL LIFE** A day-care center is building a new outdoor play area. The diagram shows the dimensions in meters. How much fencing is needed to enclose the play area?

53. **PROBLEM SOLVING** On a fantasy football team, a tight end scores 11.15 points and a running back scores 11.75 points. A wide receiver scores 1.05 points less than the running back. How many total points do the three players score?

MODELING REAL LIFE **An astronomical unit (AU) is the average distance between Earth and the Sun. In Exercises 54–57, use the table that shows the average distance of each planet in our solar system from the Sun.**

54. How much farther is Jupiter from the Sun than Mercury?

55. How much farther is Neptune from the Sun than Mars?

56. Estimate the greatest distance between Earth and Uranus.

57. Estimate the greatest distance between Venus and Saturn.

Planet	Average Distance from the Sun (AU)
Mercury	0.387
Venus	0.723
Earth	1.000
Mars	1.524
Jupiter	5.203
Saturn	9.537
Uranus	19.189
Neptune	30.07

58. **STRUCTURE** When is the sum of two decimals equal to a whole number? When is the difference of two decimals equal to a whole number? Explain.

Common Errors

- **Exercises 44–51** Students may get confused with the order of operations (they may want to use addition before subtraction). Remind them that when an expression has both addition and subtraction, they need to work left to right.

Mini-Assessment

Evaluate the expression.

1. 2.48 + 5.15 7.63
2. 4.197 + 5.82 10.017
3. 6.16 − 4.08 2.08
4. 5.8 − 2.382 3.418
5. At a home improvement store, you decide to purchase a hammer and a pack of nails. The hammer costs $8.53. The pack of nails costs $0.87. What is the total cost? How much change will you receive if you pay with a $10 bill? a $20 bill? $9.40; $0.60; $10.60

Section Resources

Surface Level	Deep Level
Resources by Chapter • Extra Practice • Reteach • Puzzle Time Student Journal • Self-Assessment • Practice Differentiating the Lesson Tutorial Videos Skills Review Handbook Skills Trainer	Resources by Chapter • Enrichment and Extension Graphic Organizers Dynamic Assessment System • Section Practice

Concepts, Skills, & Problem Solving

41. yes; The addition is correct.
42. no; $9.5 - 7.18 = 2.32$
43. 0.888 ton
44. 19.58
45. 6.772
46. 10
47. 10.343
48. 15.606
49. 21.582
50. 2.7156
51. 16.5916
52. 34.995 m
53. 33.6
54. 4.816 AU
55. 28.546 AU
56. 20.189 AU
57. 10.26 AU
58. The decimal parts in the sum total 1; The decimal parts in the difference are exactly the same.

Laurie's Notes

Learning Target

Multiply decimals and solve problems involving multiplication of decimals.

Success Criteria

- Multiply decimals by whole numbers.
- Multiply decimals by decimals.
- Evaluate expressions involving multiplication of decimals.

Warm Up

Cumulative, vocabulary, and prerequisite skills practice opportunities are available in the *Resources by Chapter* or at *BigIdeasMath.com*.

ELL Support

Point out that many different words can indicate multiplication, such as *times*, *multiply*, and *product*. Have students keep a record of the different phrases they read in word problems that indicate multiplication, so they will become familiar with them.

Exploration 1

a. i. 0.8×0.5; 0.4; *Sample answer:* 40 squares are shaded twice, and $\frac{40}{100} = 0.4$.

ii. 0.4×0.9; 0.36; *Sample answer:* 36 squares are shaded twice, and $\frac{36}{100} = 0.36$.

iii. 0.5×1.5; 0.75; *Sample answer:* 75 squares are shaded twice, and $\frac{75}{100} = 0.75$.

iv. 0.7×1.7; 1.19; *Sample answer:* 119 squares are shaded twice, and $\frac{119}{100} = 1.19$.

b–c. See Additional Answers.

Preparing to Teach

- Although students are required to multiply decimals using the standard algorithm, they can develop that procedural knowledge by building upon the area models used in prior grades.
- Beginning with decimals represented on a 10-by-10 grid, and then a 10-by-20 grid, gives all students an entry point to understanding decimal multiplication.
- **MP1 Make Sense of Problems and Persevere in Solving Them:** The area model for multiplication is a visual tool used to help students make sense of decimal multiplication. The factors are represented by the dimensions of the overlapping shaded rectangle and the area is the product. Making connections within mathematics is a habit you want all students to develop.

Motivate

- Show the class a quarter. Ask students to tell you the value of x quarters, where x is a multiple or power of 10. Record the value of the quarters.

? "What is the value of 10 quarters?" $10 \times \$0.25 = \$2.50$

? "What is the value of 20 quarters?" $20 \times \$0.25 = \$5.00$

? "What is the value of 100 quarters?" $100 \times \$0.25 = \$25.00$

- In today's lesson, students will extend their understanding of decimal multiplication beyond the context of money.

Exploration 1

? Discuss model (i) and say, "The large square is the unit square, representing the whole number 1. What does each small square represent?" 0.01 "When pink and blue are mixed together, what color is made?" purple It might be helpful to sketch the stages shown.

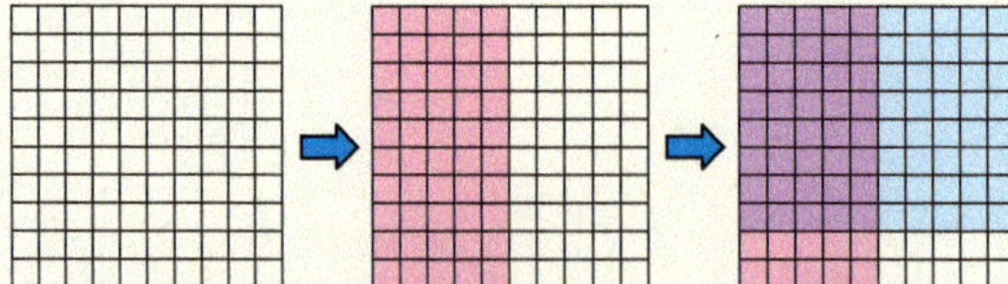

? "What number is represented by the pink shading? the blue shading?" 0.5; 0.8 "How is the product represented in the area model?" the purple shading

- Help students to understand that the area being considered is the rectangle with dimensions 0.5 by 0.8. Because the large square represents 1, the area must be less than 1.
- If available, offer each pair of students colored pencils and base-ten grid paper.

? Ask, "Why are the last two models larger than the first two models?" Because one factor is greater than 1.

? After completing part (a) for model (iv), ask, "Do you see a relationship to the problem 17×7?" The digits are the same, but the decimal point is in a different location.

- Have pairs discuss part (b). As you circulate, ask students to explain part (b) before starting part (c). Students should describe the process of multiplying decimals as the same as multiplying whole numbers, except that the decimal point will be placed differently.

2.5 Multiplying Decimals

Learning Target: Multiply decimals and solve problems involving multiplication of decimals.

Success Criteria:
- I can multiply decimals by whole numbers.
- I can multiply decimals by decimals.
- I can evaluate expressions involving multiplication of decimals.

EXPLORATION 1 Multiplying Decimals

Work with a partner.

a. Write the multiplication expression represented by each area model. Then find the product. Explain how you found your answer.

i.

ii.

iii.

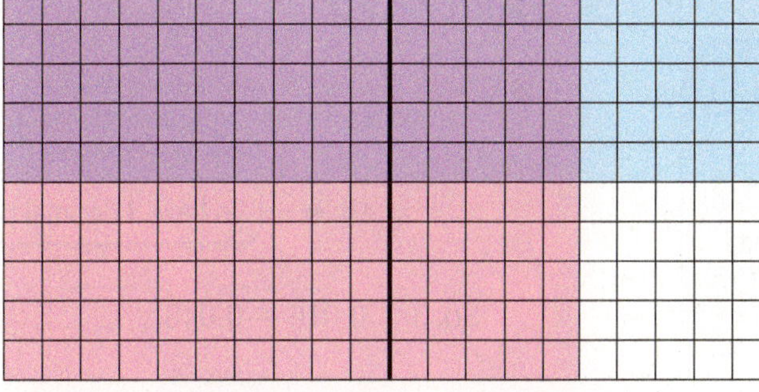

iv.

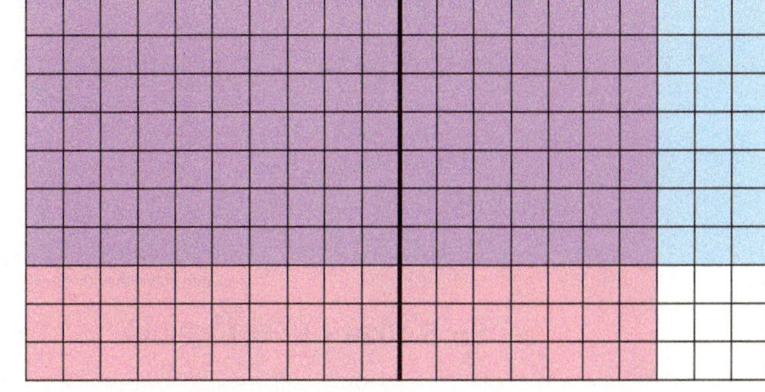

Math Practice

View as Components

How can you use an area model to find the product?

b. How can you find the products in part (a) without using a model? How do you know where to place the decimal points in the answers?

c. Find the product of 0.55 and 0.45. Explain how you found your answer.

2.5 Lesson

Key Idea

Multiplying Decimals by Whole Numbers

Words Multiply as you would with whole numbers. Then count the number of decimal places in the decimal factor. The product has the same number of decimal places.

Numbers

EXAMPLE 1 Multiplying Decimals and Whole Numbers

a. Find 6 × 3.91. **Estimate** $6 \times 4 = 24$

$$\begin{array}{r} \overset{5}{3.91} \\ \times \quad 6 \\ \hline 23.46 \end{array}$$

3.91 ← 2 decimal places

23.46 ← Count 2 decimal places from right to left.

So, $6 \times 3.91 = 23.46$. **Reasonable?** $23.46 \approx 24$ ✓

b. Find 3 × 0.016. **Estimate** $3 \times 0 = 0$

$$\begin{array}{r} \overset{1}{0.016} \\ \times \quad 3 \\ \hline 0.048 \end{array}$$

0.016 ← 3 decimal places

0.048 ← To have 3 decimal places, insert zeros to the left of 48.

So, $3 \times 0.016 = 0.048$. **Reasonable?** $0.048 \approx 0$ ✓

Math Practice

Look for Structure

Explain why you add the zero to the *left* of 48 in part (b).

c. Find 5.1024 • 12. **Estimate** $5 \cdot 12 = 60$

$$\begin{array}{r} 5.1024 \\ \times \quad 12 \\ \hline 102048 \\ 51024 \\ \hline 61.2288 \end{array}$$

5.1024 ← 4 decimal places

61.2288 ← Count 4 decimal places from right to left.

So, $5.1024 \cdot 12 = 61.2288$. **Reasonable?** $61.2288 \approx 60$ ✓

Try It **Multiply. Use estimation to check your answer.**

1. 12.3×8 **2.** 5×14.51 **3.** $20 \cdot 0.008$ **4.** $2.3275 \cdot 90$

Laurie's Notes

Scaffolding Instruction

- Students used concrete area models in the exploration, and will now connect area models to the standard algorithm for decimal multiplication. Can students verbalize the formal rule?
- **Emerging:** Additional practice for multiplying decimals is given in Examples 1 and 2. Students may want to continue using the area model, but the problems in the examples make that too tedious. They might be able to follow the algorithm for multiplying decimals but may not be confident in its origin.
- **Proficient:** If students are confident using the algorithm for multiplying decimals and explaining why it works, have them self-assess using Try It Exercises 1–8 before proceeding to Example 3.

Scaffold instruction to support all students in their learning. Learning is individualized and you may want to group students differently as they move in and out of these levels with each skill and concept. Student self-assessment and feedback help guide your instructional decisions about how and when to layer support for all students to become proficient learners.

Key Idea

- In each example shown, students should see that the product contains the same number of decimal places as the decimal factor. The whole number has no decimal places.

EXAMPLE 1

- Encourage students to estimate the product before beginning.
- Work through the three examples.
- **Common Error:** Students may count the number of decimal places from left to right when placing the decimal point in the product.
- **Connection:** When the decimal is very small, it may be helpful to have students write the number as a fraction, and then multiply.

$$3 \times \frac{16}{1000} = \frac{48}{1000} = 0.048$$

Remind students that this is another strategy they can use, like estimating, to check their answers when they multiply decimals.

Extra Example 1

a. Find 4.8×3. 14.4

b. Find 0.0045×5. 0.0225

c. Find $18 \cdot 7.039$. 126.702

Try It

- Students should use mental math to find an estimate in each exercise.
- **Neighbor Check:** Have students work independently, and then have their neighbors check their work. Have students discuss any discrepancies.

Try It

1. 98.4 **2.** 72.55

3. 0.16 **4.** 209.475

Laurie's Notes

Key Idea

- Students generally have little difficulty applying the rule for multiplying a decimal by a whole number. You want to be sure that students have an understanding of why the rule works, so they can extend that understanding to multiplying two decimals.
- Connect place value and fraction multiplication.
- **FYI:** If no multiplication error is made, locating the decimal point in the product is usually not difficult for students.
- The concepts students find most difficult are often related to trailing zeros in the product or inserting zeros in the product.

Extra Example 2

a. Multiply 1.3 × 3.5. 4.55

b. Multiply 5.8 × 0.02. 0.116

c. Multiply 2.65 • 0.74. 1.961

EXAMPLE 2

- Work through all parts of the example.
- Begin each problem by estimating the product. The last step should always be to judge the reasonableness of the solution compared to your estimate. This is especially important in part (b), where the product is much less than the first factor.
- In part (b), it is more difficult to estimate the size of the answer. You may want to remind students that they can also use fractions to estimate the answer.
- Ask students to record the number of decimal places in each factor. At this point, they should do this for all problems to verify the placement of the decimal in the product.

$$\begin{array}{rl} 3.1 & (1) \\ \times\ 0.005 & (3) \\ \hline 0.0155 & (4) \end{array}$$

Try It

5. 45.36 **6.** 24.408

7. 0.5688 **8.** 0.3570

Try It

- **Neighbor Check:** Have students work independently, and then have their neighbors check their work. Have students discuss any discrepancies.
- In Exercise 6, look for multiplication errors due to the 0 in 9.04.

ELL Support

Have students work in pairs to complete the exercises. Remind them to use the process they learned in Example 2. Point out that different symbols may be used to indicate multiplication (× or •).

Beginner: Write the numbers vertically and find the product.

Intermediate: State the answer using a complete sentence. For example, "Eight and one-tenth times five and six-tenths is forty-five and thirty-six hundredths."

Advanced: Explain each step of the process.

The rule for multiplying two decimals is similar to the rule for multiplying a decimal by a whole number.

Key Idea

Multiplying Decimals by Decimals

Words Multiply as you would with whole numbers. Then add the number of decimal places in the factors. The sum is the number of decimal places in the product.

Numbers

$$\begin{array}{r} 4.716 \\ \times \quad 0.2 \\ \hline 0.9432 \end{array} \quad \begin{array}{l} \leftarrow \text{3 decimal places} \\ \leftarrow \text{+ 1 decimal place} \\ \leftarrow \text{4 decimal places} \end{array}$$

EXAMPLE 2 Multiplying Decimals

a. Multiply 4.8 × 7.2. **Estimate** $5 \times 7 = 35$

$$\begin{array}{r} 4.8 \\ \times \quad 7.2 \\ \hline 96 \\ 336 \\ \hline 34.56 \end{array} \quad \begin{array}{l} \leftarrow \text{1 decimal place} \\ \leftarrow \text{+ 1 decimal place} \\ \\ \\ \leftarrow \text{2 decimal places} \end{array}$$

So, $4.8 \times 7.2 = 34.56$. **Reasonable?** $34.56 \approx 35$ ✓

b. Multiply 3.1 × 0.005. **Estimate** $3 \times 0 = 0$

$$\begin{array}{r} 3.1 \\ \times \quad 0.005 \\ \hline 0.0155 \end{array} \quad \begin{array}{l} \leftarrow \text{1 decimal place} \\ \leftarrow \text{+ 3 decimal places} \\ \leftarrow \text{4 decimal places} \end{array}$$

So, $3.1 \times 0.005 = 0.0155$. **Reasonable?** $0.0155 \approx 0$ ✓

c. Multiply 4.25 • 1.75. **Estimate** $4 \times 2 = 8$

$$\begin{array}{r} 4.25 \\ \times \quad 1.75 \\ \hline 2125 \\ 2975 \\ 425 \\ \hline 7.4375 \end{array} \quad \begin{array}{l} \leftarrow \text{2 decimal places} \\ \leftarrow \text{+ 2 decimal places} \\ \\ \\ \\ \leftarrow \text{4 decimal places} \end{array}$$

So, $4.25 \cdot 1.75 = 7.4375$. **Reasonable?** $7.4375 \approx 8$ ✓

Try It **Multiply. Use estimation to check your answer.**

5. 8.1×5.6

6. 2.7×9.04

7. 6.32×0.09

8. 1.785×0.2

EXAMPLE 3 Evaluating an Expression

What is the value of 2.44(4.5 − 3.175)?

A. 3.233 **B.** 3.599 **C.** 7.805 **D.** 32.33

Step 1: Evaluate the expression in parentheses first.

$$\begin{array}{r} 4.5\,0\,0 \\ -\;3.1\,7\,5 \\ \hline 1.3\,2\,5 \end{array}$$

So, 2.44(4.5 − 3.175) = 2.44(1.325).

Step 2: Multiply the result from Step 1 by 2.44.

$$\begin{array}{r} 1.3\,2\,5 \\ \times\quad 2.4\,4 \\ \hline 5\,3\,0\,0 \\ 5\,3\,0\,0 \\ 2\,6\,5\,0 \\ \hline 3.2\,3\,3\,0\,0 \end{array}$$

1.325 ← 3 decimal places
× 2.44 ← + 2 decimal places
3.23300 ← 5 decimal places

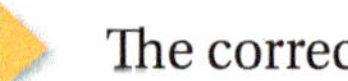

The correct answer is **A**.

> **Math Practice**
>
> **Look for Structure**
>
> In Step 2, why is multiplying 1.325 × 2.44 the same as multiplying 2.44 × 1.325?

Try It **Evaluate the expression.**

9. 12.67 + 8.2 • 1.9

10. 6.4(1.8 • 7.5)

Self-Assessment for Concepts & Skills

Solve each exercise. Then rate your understanding of the success criteria in your journal.

EVALUATING AN EXPRESSION **Evaluate the expression.**

11. 8 × 11.215

12. 9.42 • 6.83

13. 0.15(4.3 − 2.417)

14. MP **NUMBER SENSE** If you know 12 × 24 = 288, how can you find 0.12 × 0.24?

15. MP **NUMBER SENSE** Is the product 1.23 × 8 greater than or less than 8? Explain.

16. MP **REASONING** Copy the problem and place the decimal point in the product.

$$\begin{array}{r} 1.78 \\ \times\quad 4.9 \\ \hline 8722 \end{array}$$

Laurie's Notes

EXAMPLE 3

- This example represents the third success criterion.
- ? "What operations are involved in this problem?" multiplication and subtraction
- You may need to remind students that a number written next to the parenthesis implies multiplication.
- ? "Which operation should you perform first and why?" subtraction; Using order of operations, the operation inside the parentheses is performed first.
- **Common Error:** Students may write 4.5 below 3.175 because 4.5 has fewer digits. Regardless of the number of digits, 3.175 is being subtracted from 4.5.
- ? In Step 2, ask, "How many decimal places are in the first factor?" 3 "How many decimal places are in the second factor?" 2 "How many decimal places are in the product?" 5
- Remind students that when counting the 5 decimal places, they must count from right to left.
- **MP6 Attend to Precision:** Once the decimal point is located, trailing zeros are generally not written. Mathematically proficient students understand that the zeros are necessary for determining the location of the decimal point but not in representing the decimal product.

Try It

- Remind students to use the order of operations for Exercise 9.

Self-Assessment for Concepts & Skills

- Have students complete the exercises, and then rate their understanding using the Success Criteria Self-Assessment chart.
- Encourage students to estimate their answers to check for reasonableness.
- Students' explanations in Exercises 14 and 15 will give you a glimpse into their understanding of the success criteria.

ELL Support

Allow students to complete the exercises in pairs for additional practice with mathematical language. Remind them to think of the process they used for the Try It exercises. Check for understanding of Exercises 11–13 and 16 by having each pair display their answers on a whiteboard for your review. Ask students to find the products in Exercises 14 and 15. At a glance, you should be able to determine which groups have mastered the material. Reteach as needed.

The Success Criteria Self-Assessment chart can be found in the *Student Journal* or online at *BigIdeasMath.com*.

Extra Example 3

What is the value of $5.7(5.1 + 4.86)$?

A. 1.368 **B.** 15.66

C. 33.93 **D.** 56.772

D

Try It

9. 28.25 **10.** 86.4

Self-Assessment for Concepts & Skills

11. 89.72 **12.** 64.3386

13. 0.28245

14. Place the decimal point and insert a 0 so that there are four decimal places.

15. greater than; 1.23 is greater than 1.

16. 8.722

Laurie's Notes

EXAMPLE 4

- Have students read and discuss the problem in groups. As you circulate, ask probing questions to each group. "What is the problem asking? How can you solve it? Can you estimate the answer? What unit will the answer have?"
- Because the problem involves multiplying 2 three-digit numbers, students may want to check their work with another group member to validate their products.
- "The exact product is 7.8325, so why is it rounded to $7.83 before finishing the problem?" Money is rounded to the nearest cent (or hundredths place).
- Examples 3 and 4 both contain multiplication and subtraction of decimals. Discuss with students why the operations are performed in different orders in the two problems.

Self-Assessment for Problem Solving

- Encourage students to use a Four Square to complete these exercises. Until students become comfortable with the problem-solving plan, they may only be ready to complete the first square.
- **MP1 Make Sense of Problems and Persevere in Solving Them:** Students will analyze the given information and make a plan for solving the problem using decimal operations. Encourage students to begin by verbalizing their thinking or drawing a diagram. Support students with probing questions and by providing feedback.
- These exercises require more than one operation. Some students may benefit from using a verbal model to organize their thoughts before solving.
- After students solve the problems independently, have them share their work and explanations. Then have students use *Fist of Five* to indicate their understanding of decimal multiplication in real-life problems.

The Success Criteria Self-Assessment chart can be found in the *Student Journal* or online at *BigIdeasMath.com.*

Closure

- **Sentence Summary:** Give each student an index card. Ask students to write about what they have learned about decimal multiplication. Allow time for students to reflect and discourage responses like, "I learned how to multiply decimals." Use these responses to plan your instruction for the next day.

Extra Example 4

You buy 4.5 pounds of bananas at $0.49 per pound. You pay with a $20 bill. How much change do you receive? $17.79

Self-Assessment for Problem Solving

17. yes; $1.77

18. $1378.125\ ft^2$

19. $2.25

Formative Assessment Tip

Sentence Summary
This technique asks students to write a single sentence to describe what they have learned about a topic. You may ask students to summarize new information, make a comparison, or describe a problem and solution. Give students time to reflect before writing. Discourage responses like, "I learned how to subtract." *Sentence Summary* gives you a quick glimpse into each student's level of understanding of the material.

Learning Target

Multiply decimals and solve problems involving multiplication of decimals.

Success Criteria

- Multiply decimals by whole numbers.
- Multiply decimals by decimals.
- Evaluate expressions involving multiplication of decimals.

EXAMPLE 4 Modeling Real Life

Zinc: $2.41 per ounce

A science teacher buys 3.25 ounces of zinc for an experiment. The teacher pays with a $10 bill. How much change does the teacher receive?

Find the cost of 3.25 ounces of zinc at $2.41 per ounce. Then subtract that amount from $10.

Step 1: Multiply 2.41 by 3.25 to find the cost of the zinc.

$$\begin{array}{r l}
2.41 & \leftarrow \text{2 decimal places} \\
\times\ 3.25 & \leftarrow +\ \text{2 decimal places} \\
\hline
1205 & \\
482 & \\
723 & \\
\hline
7.8325 & \leftarrow \text{4 decimal places}
\end{array}$$

The cost of 3.25 ounces of zinc is $7.83.

Step 2: Subtract the cost of the zinc from the amount of money the teacher uses to buy the zinc.

$10.00 - 7.83 = 2.17$

So, the teacher receives $2.17 in change.

Self-Assessment for Problem Solving

Solve each exercise. Then rate your understanding of the success criteria in your journal.

17. You earn $9.15 per hour painting a fence. It takes 6.75 hours to paint the fence. Did you earn enough money to buy the jersey shown? If so, how much money do you have left? If not, how much money do you need to earn?

18. A sand volleyball court is a rectangle that has a length of 52.5 feet and a width that is half of the length. In case of rain, the court is covered with a tarp. How many square feet of tarp are needed to cover the court?

19. **DIG DEEPER!** You buy 4 cases of bottled water and 5 bottles of fruit punch for a birthday party. Each case of bottled water costs $2.75, and each bottle of fruit punch costs $1.35. You hand the cashier a $20 bill. How much change will you receive?

2.5 Practice

Review & Refresh

Add or subtract.

1. $12.29 - 6.15$
2. $4.6 + 11.81$
3. $9.34 + 17.009$
4. $18.247 - 16.262$

Divide.

5. $78 \div 3$
6. $65 \div 13$
7. $57 \div 19$
8. $84 \div 12$

9. What is $4\frac{1}{3} \times \frac{4}{5}$?

   A. $2\frac{1}{8}$ **B.** $3\frac{7}{15}$ **C.** $4\frac{4}{15}$ **D.** $5\frac{5}{12}$

Evaluate the expression.

10. $4 + 6^2 \div 2$
11. $(35 + 9) \div 4 - 3^2$
12. $8^2 \div [(14 - 12) \times 2^3]$

Concepts, Skills, & Problem Solving

MP USING TOOLS **Use an area model to find the product.** (See Exploration 1, p. 73.)

13. 2.1×1.5
14. 0.6×0.4
15. 0.7×0.3
16. 2.7×2.3

MULTIPLYING DECIMALS AND WHOLE NUMBERS **Multiply. Use estimation to check your answer.**

17. 4.8×7
18. 6.3×5
19. 7.19×16
20. 0.87×21
21. 1.95×11
22. 5.89×5
23. 3.472×4
24. 8.188×12
25. 100×0.024
26. 19×0.004
27. 3.27×14
28. $46 \cdot 5.448$
29. 50×12.21
30. $104 \cdot 4.786$
31. 0.0038×9
32. 10×0.0093

MP YOU BE THE TEACHER **Your friend finds the product. Is your friend correct? Explain your reasoning.**

33.

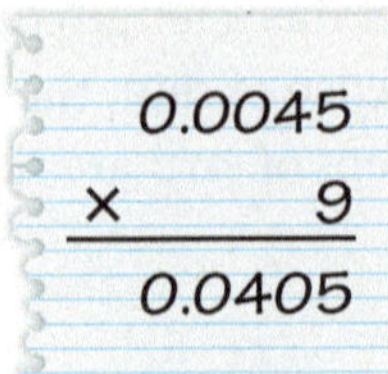

34.

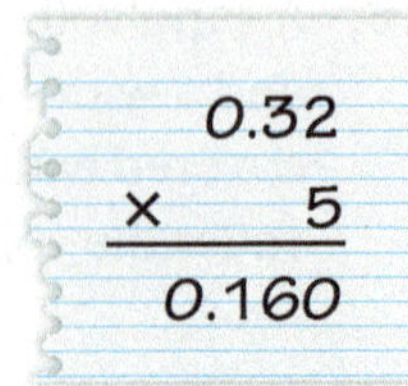

35. **MP MODELING REAL LIFE** The weight of an object on the Moon is about 0.167 of its weight on Earth. How much does a 180-pound astronaut weigh on the Moon?

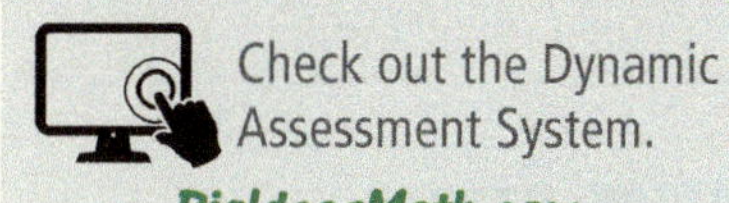

Assignment Guide and Concept Check

Scaffold assignments to support all students in their learning progression. The suggested assignments are a starting point. Continue to assign additional exercises and revisit with spaced practice to move every student toward proficiency.

Level	Assignment 1	Assignment 2
Emerging	4, 8, 9, 12, 14, 17, 28, 33, 36, 45, 60, 64	34, 35, 52, 53, 54, 55, 72
Proficient	4, 8, 9, 12, 13, 17, 29, 33, 37, 45, 59, 64	34, 35, 52, 53, 54, 66, 67, 68, 72
Advanced	4, 8, 9, 12, 13, 22, 30, 33, 37, 46, 59, 61, 68	34, 52, 54, 56, 67, 72, 73, 74

- Assignment 1 is for use after students complete the Self-Assessment for Concepts & Skills.
- Assignment 2 is for use after students complete the Self-Assessment for Problem Solving.
- The red exercises can be used as a concept check.

Review & Refresh Prior Skills

Exercises 1–4 Adding and Subtracting Decimals
Exercises 5–8 Dividing Whole Numbers
Exercise 9 Multiplying Fractions and Mixed Numbers
Exercises 10–12 Using Order of Operations

Common Errors

- **Exercises 17–32** Students might count the decimal places to the left of the decimal point instead of the right. Remind them that they are looking to the right of the decimal point. Stress that estimating the product first will help.
- **Exercises 17–32** When determining where to place the decimal point, students might count left to right instead of right to left. Tell students to count from the least to greatest place value, so that means they must start counting decimal places from the right.
- **Exercises 25, 26, 31, and 32** Students might ignore the zeros when counting the number of decimal places, or forget to add them when finding the product. Remind them that zeros are placeholders and are important for determining the correct answer. For example, 0.024 is not the same number as 0.24.

Review & Refresh

1. 6.14 **2.** 16.41
3. 26.349 **4.** 1.985
5. 26 **6.** 5
7. 3 **8.** 7
9. B **10.** 22
11. 2 **12.** 4

Concepts, Skills, & Problem Solving

13. 3.15
14. 0.24
15. 0.21
16. 6.21
17. 33.6
18. 31.5
19. 115.04
20. 18.27
21. 21.45
22. 29.45
23. 13.888
24. 98.256
25. 2.4
26. 0.076
27. 45.78
28. 250.608
29. 610.5
30. 497.744
31. 0.0342
32. 0.093
33. yes; $9 \times 45 = 405$ and the factors have 4 decimal places.
34. no; $0.32 \times 5 = 1.60$
35. 30.06 lb

Concepts, Skills, & Problem Solving

36. 0.14
37. 0.024
38. 0.00021
39. 0.000072
40. 0.0036
41. 0.03
42. 0.0000032
43. 0.000012
44. 2.48
45. 109.74
46. 5.6952
47. 3.886
48. 117.96438
49. 13.7104
50. 0.03822
51. 51.3156
52. no; $4.9 \times 3.8 = 18.62$
53. \$3.24
54. \$1085.52
55. Carlton Centre: 731.44 ft; Burj Khalifa: 2715.84 ft; Q1: 1059.44 ft; Federation Tower: 1226.72 ft; One World Trade Center: 1774.48 ft; Gran Torre Santiago: 984 ft
56. $(7.12 \times 8.22) \times 100$
    $= 7.12 \times (8.22 \times 100)$
    $= 7.12 \times 822 = 5852.64$
57. 45.4
58. 137
59. 4.355
60. 23.112
61. 2.016
62. 71.984
63. 150.183
64. 36.225
65. 1.887

Common Errors

- **Exercises 36–51** Students may only count the number of decimal places in one number instead of two. Remind them that they need to count the number of decimal places in both numbers.

MULTIPLYING DECIMALS Multiply.

36. $\begin{array}{r} 0.7 \\ \times\ 0.2 \\ \hline \end{array}$

37. $\begin{array}{r} 0.08 \\ \times\ 0.3 \\ \hline \end{array}$

38. $\begin{array}{r} 0.007 \\ \times\ 0.03 \\ \hline \end{array}$

39. $\begin{array}{r} 0.0008 \\ \times\ 0.09 \\ \hline \end{array}$

40. $\begin{array}{r} 0.004 \\ \times\ 0.9 \\ \hline \end{array}$

41. $\begin{array}{r} 0.06 \\ \times\ 0.5 \\ \hline \end{array}$

42. $\begin{array}{r} 0.0008 \\ \times\ 0.004 \\ \hline \end{array}$

43. $\begin{array}{r} 0.0002 \\ \times\ 0.06 \\ \hline \end{array}$

44. 12.4×0.2

45. $18.6 \cdot 5.9$

46. 7.91×0.72

47. 1.16×3.35

48. 6.478×18.21

49. 1.9×7.216

50. 0.0021×18.2

51. $6.109 \cdot 8.4$

52. **MP YOU BE THE TEACHER** Your friend finds the product of 4.9 and 3.8. Is your friend correct? Explain your reasoning.

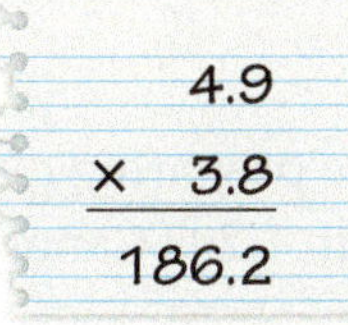

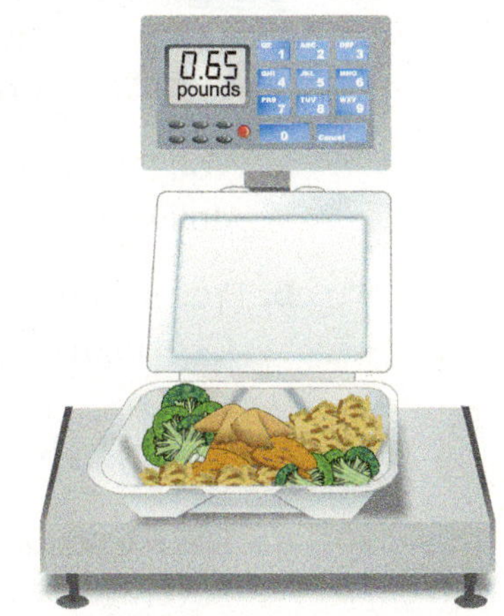

53. **MP PROBLEM SOLVING** A Chinese restaurant offers buffet takeout for \$4.99 per pound. How much does your takeout meal cost?

54. **MP PROBLEM SOLVING** On a tour of an old gold mine, you find a nugget containing 0.82 ounce of gold. Gold is worth \$1323.80 per ounce. How much is your nugget worth?

55. **MP PRECISION** One meter is approximately 3.28 feet. Find the height of each building in feet.

Continent	Tallest Building	Height (meters)
Africa	Carlton Centre	223
Asia	Burj Khalifa	828
Australia	Q1	323
Europe	Federation Tower	374
North America	One World Trade Center	541
South America	Gran Torre Santiago	300

56. **MP REASONING** Show how to evaluate $(7.12 \times 8.22) \times 100$ without multiplying two decimals.

EVALUATING AN EXPRESSION Evaluate the expression.

57. $2.4 \times 16 + 7$

58. $6.85 \times 2 \times 10$

59. $1.047 \times 5 - 0.88$

60. $4.32(3.7 + 1.65)$

61. $23.98 - 1.7^2 \cdot 7.6$

62. $12 \cdot 5.16 + 10.064$

63. $0.9(8.2 \cdot 20.35)$

64. $7.5^2(6.084 - 5.44)$

65. $0.629[81 \div (10 \times 2.7)]$

66. **MP REASONING** Without multiplying, how many decimal places does 3.4^2 have? 3.4^3? 3.4^4? Explain your reasoning.

67. **MP MODELING REAL LIFE** You buy 2.6 pounds of apples and 1.475 pounds of peaches. You hand the cashier a $20 bill. How much change will you receive?

MP PATTERNS **Describe the pattern. Find the next three numbers.**

68. 1, 0.6, 0.36, 0.216, . . .

69. 15, 1.5, 0.15, 0.015, . . .

70. 0.04, 0.02, 0.01, 0.005, . . .

71. 5, 7.5, 11.25, 16.875, . . .

72. **DIG DEEPER!** You are preparing for a trip to Canada. At the time of your trip, each U.S. dollar is worth 1.293 Canadian dollars and each Canadian dollar is worth 0.773 U.S. dollar.

a. You exchange 150 U.S. dollars for Canadian dollars. How many Canadian dollars do you receive?

b. You spend 120 Canadian dollars on the trip. Then you exchange the remaining Canadian dollars for U.S. dollars. How many U.S. dollars do you receive?

73. **OPEN-ENDED** You and four friends have dinner at a restaurant.

a. Draw a restaurant menu that has main items, desserts, and beverages, with their prices.

b. Write a guest check that shows what each of you ate. Find the subtotal.

c. Multiply by 0.07 to find the tax. Then find the total.

d. Round the total to the nearest whole number. Multiply by 0.20 to estimate a tip. Including the tip, how much did the dinner cost?

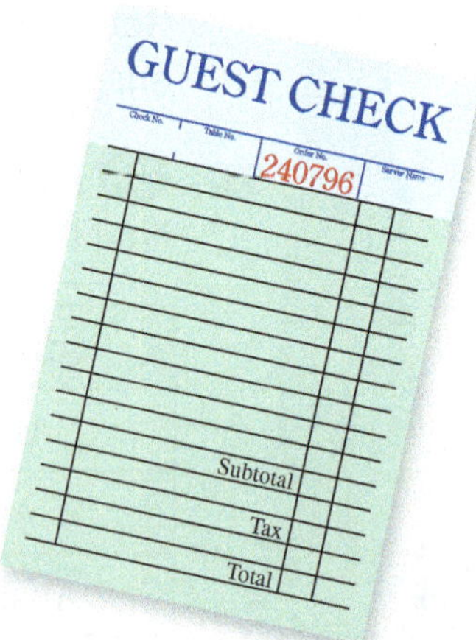

74. **GEOMETRY** A rectangular painting has an area of 9.52 square feet.

a. Draw three different ways in which this can happen.

b. The cost of a frame depends on the perimeter of the painting. Which of your drawings from part (a) is the least expensive to frame? Explain your reasoning.

c. The thin, black framing costs $1 per foot. The fancy framing costs $5 per foot. Will the fancy framing cost five times as much as the black framing? Explain why or why not.

d. Suppose the cost of a frame depends on the outside perimeter of the frame. Does this change your answer to part (c)? Explain why or why not.

Common Errors

- **Exercise 73** Students may find the estimated tip amount but not the entire dinner cost in part (d). Remind them to read the question carefully.

Mini-Assessment

Multiply.

1. 9.6 × 5 48
2. 4.321 × 2 8.642
3. 20.25 × 0.6 12.15
4. 2.18 • 3.24 7.0632
5. Apples are on sale for $1.29 per pound. You buy 4.25 pounds of apples. How much will it cost to buy the apples? $5.48

Section Resources

Surface Level	Deep Level
Resources by Chapter • Extra Practice • Reteach • Puzzle Time Student Journal • Self-Assessment • Practice Differentiating the Lesson Tutorial Videos Skills Review Handbook Skills Trainer	Resources by Chapter • Enrichment and Extension Graphic Organizers Dynamic Assessment System • Section Practice

Concepts, Skills, & Problem Solving

66. 2; 3; 4; There is one decimal place in each factor.
67. $14.03
68. Each number is 0.6 times the previous number; 0.1296, 0.07776, 0.046656
69. Each number is 0.1 times the previous number; 0.0015, 0.00015, 0.000015
70. Each number is 0.5 times the previous number; 0.0025, 0.00125, 0.000625
71. Each number is 1.5 times the previous number; 25.3125, 37.96875, 56.953125
72. a. $193.95
    b. $57.16
73. *Answers should include, but are not limited to:*
    a. menu with main items, desserts, beverages, and prices
    b. guest check for 5 people showing items, prices, and subtotal
    c. tax and total with tax are shown
    d. amount rounded to nearest dollar, 20% tip, and total cost including tip are shown
74. a. See Additional Answers.
    b. the 3.4 ft-by-2.8 ft frame; It has the least perimeter.
    c. yes; The perimeter is the same, the cost is found by multiplying by $1 or $5.
    d. yes; The fancy framing will have a greater perimeter.

Learning Target

Divide whole numbers and solve problems involving division of whole numbers.

Success Criteria

- Use long division to divide whole numbers.
- Write a remainder as a fraction.
- Interpret quotients in real-life problems.

Warm Up

Cumulative, vocabulary, and prerequisite skills practice opportunities are available in the *Resources by Chapter* or at *BigIdeasMath.com*.

ELL Support

Explain that students will divide whole numbers. Point out that the word *whole* has the homophone *hole*, which has a very different meaning. A hole is an empty space. A whole number is a number that is not negative and does not have a fraction or decimal part. For example, 0, 1, and 24 are whole numbers. It is important to listen to everything that is said to determine which word is being used.

Exploration 1

a–b. See Additional Answers.

c. 5007.5 lb

d. *Sample answer:* There will be about 19,000 pounds of trash collected during City Cleanup Day 2020.

Laurie's Notes

Preparing to Teach

- As students continue multi-digit division from prior courses, they will extend the standard algorithm beyond two-digit divisors and four-digit dividends. This is an important step in preparing students for decimal division. Students need to be confident with these problems to make the transition to dividing decimals.
- **MP1 Make Sense of Problems and Persevere in Solving Them:** Students can analyze information and look for entry points to begin a solution path. They can consider a problem with numbers such as 841 and 23 and ask themselves if they could solve the problem with smaller numbers, such as 80 and 2.

Motivate

- Ask 12 volunteers to go to the front of the room and arrange themselves into six groups of two.
- ? "What division equation can you write to describe what these students just did?" $12 \div 6 = 2$, or $12 \div 2 = 6$
- Write the equation $12 \div 4 = 3$ on the board, and ask a volunteer to describe what the 12 students should do now. Make 3 groups of 4, or make 4 groups of 3. Without a context stated, either description is correct.

Exploration 1

- Take time to discuss the importance of recycling. Do students recycle at home? Is there a recycling program at your school? How does recycling help the environment?
- In part (a), encourage students to make mathematical connections. Students decide which operations are needed for their conclusions, if any. For example, "The trash collected increases each year" doesn't require an operation. Whereas, "1420 more pounds of trash were collected in 2017 than in 2016" requires subtraction. Discuss the conclusions as a class.
- ? In part (b), guide students to see relationships involving multiplication or division. Ask, "How many times more recyclables were collected in 2016 than 2014?" 4 times more
- **Common Error:** The word *times* does not immediately imply that multiplication is to be done. In the previous sample conclusion, *times* is used, and it is a division problem. Point out that the problem can be rephrased as a multiplication problem. Then students can use fact families to find the quotient.
- In part (c), ask a volunteer to explain how to find an average.
- Part (d) can have several answers, so it is important that students explain their reasoning. Analyzing a bar graph and predicting an outcome are a review of statistical skills from prior courses.

2.6 Dividing Whole Numbers

Learning Target: Divide whole numbers and solve problems involving division of whole numbers.

Success Criteria:
- I can use long division to divide whole numbers.
- I can write a remainder as a fraction.
- I can interpret quotients in real-life problems.

EXPLORATION 1 Using a Double Bar Graph

Work with a partner. The double bar graph shows the history of a citywide cleanup day.

a. Make five conclusions from the graph.

b. Compare the results of the city cleanup day in 2016 to the results in 2014.

c. What is the average combined amount of trash and recyclables collected each year over the four-year period?

d. Make a prediction about the amount of trash collected in a future year.

Math Practice

Calculate Accurately

How can you extend what you know about long division to divide any pair of multi-digit whole numbers accurately?

2.6 Lesson

You have used long division to divide whole numbers. When the *divisor* divides evenly into the *dividend*, the *quotient* is a whole number.

$$\overset{20}{15\overline{)300}}$$

Divisor → 15; 20 ← Quotient; 300 ← Dividend

When the divisor does not divide evenly into the dividend, you obtain a remainder. When this occurs, you can write the quotient as a mixed number.

EXAMPLE 1 Dividing Whole Numbers

a. Find 672 ÷ 8.

$$\begin{array}{r} 84 \\ 8\overline{)672} \\ -64\downarrow \\ \hline 32 \\ -32 \\ \hline 0 \end{array}$$

There are eight groups of 8 in 67.

There are four groups of 8 in 32.

There is no remainder.

So, 672 ÷ 8 = 84.

Check Find the product of the quotient and the divisor.

84	quotient
× 8	divisor
672	dividend ✓

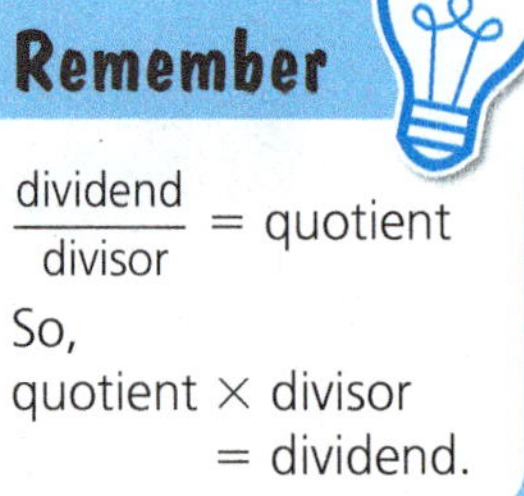

$\frac{\text{dividend}}{\text{divisor}} = \text{quotient}$

So,

quotient × divisor = dividend.

b. Find the quotient of 9216 and 150.

$$\begin{array}{r} 61\text{ R}66 \\ 150\overline{)9216} \\ -900\downarrow \\ \hline 216 \\ -150 \\ \hline 66 \end{array}$$

There are six groups of 150 in 921.

There is one group of 150 in 216.

The remainder is 66.

The quotient is $61\frac{66}{150}$, or $61\frac{11}{25}$.

Try It **Divide. Use estimation to check your answer.**

1. 234 ÷ 9

2. $\frac{6096}{30}$

3. 45,691 ÷ 28

4. Find the quotient of 9920 and 320.

Laurie's Notes

Scaffolding Instruction

- Students have used long division to divide whole numbers with up to two-digit divisors and four-digit dividends. Now they will extend that understanding to all whole numbers, with no limitations.
- Writing a quotient as a mixed number is likely to be a new procedure for all students.
- **Emerging:** Students can set up a division problem but may struggle with place value or estimating the answer. They will benefit from guided instruction for Examples 1 and 2. Some students may have difficulty lining up the columns when they perform long division. Have them use grid paper as an aid.
- **Proficient:** Students can fluently divide using the standard algorithm with multi-digit numbers, check their answers using estimation, and explain why division is used to solve some real-life problems. Explain the procedure of changing a whole-number remainder into a fraction so that the quotient is written as a mixed number. Students can self-assess using the Try It exercises.

EXAMPLE 1

- **Common Error:** Students may want to put the first digit of the quotient above the first digit in the dividend, and that is not always correct.
- ? **Teaching Tip:** When you write the problem $8\overline{)672}$ on the board, use one hand to cover the 72 in the dividend and ask, "Can 8 be divided into 6?" no Now move your hand to reveal 67 in the dividend and ask, "Can 8 be divided into 67?" yes This technique helps students to focus on the process.
- Ask students about each step in the division process. Note the downward arrow, which students may find helpful in working through the steps.
- ? "How do you check an answer to a division problem?" Multiply the answer (the quotient) by the divisor and you should get the dividend.
- Tell students to write the quotient as a mixed number if there is a remainder. Although it is acceptable to identify only the whole-number part as the quotient, this course will always refer to the entire answer as the quotient.

Try It

- Note the different ways of indicating division.
- Remind students to estimate their answers to check for reasonableness.
- **Chalkboard Splash:** Have students work in groups. Ask each group to send one person to the board and assign Exercise 2, 3, or 4.
- ◉ Ask students to read the first two success criteria and use *Thumbs Up* to indicate their understanding.

ELL Support

Remind students to follow the process used in Example 1 and to simplify fractions if necessary.
Beginner: Write the numbers in long-division form and find the quotient.
Intermediate: State the answer using a complete sentence. For example, "Six hundred seventy-two divided by eight is eighty-four."
Advanced: Explain each step of the process.

Scaffold instruction to support all students in their learning. Learning is individualized and you may want to group students differently as they move in and out of these levels with each skill and concept. Student self-assessment and feedback help guide your instructional decisions about how and when to layer support for all students to become proficient learners.

Formative Assessment Tip

Chalkboard Splash
This technique allows students to solve a problem, while others critique their reasoning. Several students respond to a prompt at the same time on the board. *Chalkboard Splash* is a good way to show multiple representations of the same problem. To be informative, students must show all steps. Once complete, allow the rest of the class to ask questions. The students at the board will need to be able to defend and explain their reasoning. *Chalkboard Splash* allows you to check students' conceptual knowledge and ability to construct a viable argument.

Extra Example 1

a. Find $816 \div 6$. 136

b. Find the quotient of 8485 and 250. $33\frac{47}{50}$

Try It

1. 26 **2.** $203\frac{1}{5}$

3. $1631\frac{23}{28}$ **4.** 31

Extra Example 2

You make 18 equal payments for a video game system with games. You pay a total of $468. How much is each payment? $26

Try It

5. $46

Self-Assessment for Concepts & Skills

6. 73

7. 432

8. $47\frac{9}{22}$

9. a. dividend

   b. quotient

   c. divisor

10. 3999 ÷ 129; *Sample answer:* 3999 ÷ 129 has a greater dividend and a lesser divisor than 3834 ÷ 142.

11. no; If the remainder is greater than the divisor, then the quotient should be increased until the remainder is less than the divisor.

Laurie's Notes

EXAMPLE 2

- This example extends the computational skill of dividing whole numbers to a contextual problem. The context of money may help students make sense of division.
- **Turn and Talk:** Ask students to explain what the problem is asking and make a plan for solving it. Set a timer for 1–2 minutes for each person to share his or her ideas.
- ? "Should the answer be *greater than $1380* or *less than $1380*?" less than $1380 "How do you know?" Listen for student understanding that dividing a whole-number quantity by a whole number greater than 1 will result in a lesser amount.
- ? "Which operation will be used to solve the problem and why?" division; Because making 12 equal payments means to make 12 equal groups of money, so you need to divide the total by 12.
- Be sure to check that students correctly place the first 1 in the quotient above the 3 in the dividend.
- ? Refer students to the Check note.
- Have students explain what the solution means in the context of the problem. Is the answer reasonable for the context?

Self-Assessment for Concepts & Skills

- Exercises 6–8 give you information about the students' procedural understanding of the standard division algorithm.
- Exercises 10 and 11 give you a peek into students' conceptual understanding.
- The skills represented in these exercises are important to dividing with decimals in the next section.

ELL Support

Have students complete the exercises in groups. They may assume roles according to their language abilities, as described in the leveled practice ELL Support on page T-82. Remind students to think of the process they used for the Try It exercises. When they have finished, have two groups come together to review their answers. If there is disagreement, have students reach a consensus. Provide support as needed.

The Success Criteria Self-Assessment chart can be found in the *Student Journal* or online at *BigIdeasMath.com*.

EXAMPLE 2 Solving a Problem Using Division

You make 12 equal payments for a go-kart. You pay a total of $1380. How much is each payment?

You want to find the number of groups of 12 in $1380. So, find the quotient of 1380 and 12 using long division.

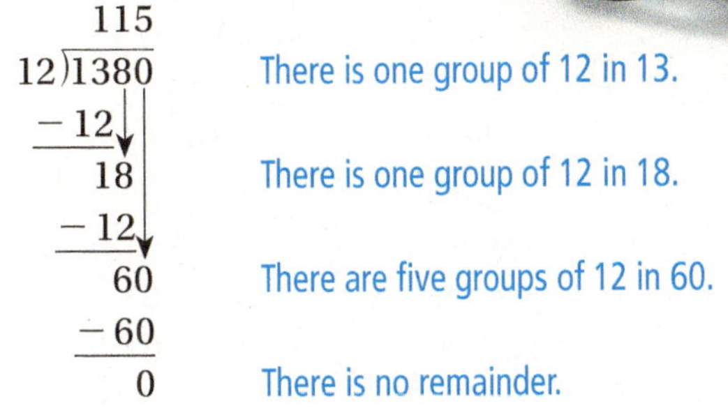

$$\begin{array}{r} 115 \\ 12\overline{)1380} \\ -12\downarrow \\ 18 \\ -12\downarrow \\ 60 \\ -60 \\ 0 \end{array}$$

There is one group of 12 in 13.

There is one group of 12 in 18.

There are five groups of 12 in 60.

There is no remainder.

Check Find the product of the quotient and the divisor.

$$\begin{array}{r} 115 \\ \times\ 12 \\ \hline 230 \\ 115 \\ \hline 1380 \end{array}$$

115 quotient

12 divisor

1380 dividend 

The quotient of 1380 and 12 is 115.

So, each payment is $115.

Try It

5. **WHAT IF?** You make 30 equal payments for the go-kart. How much is each payment?

Self-Assessment for Concepts & Skills

Solve each exercise. Then rate your understanding of the success criteria in your journal.

DIVIDING WHOLE NUMBERS Divide. Use estimation to check your answer.

6. 876 ÷ 12
7. 3024 ÷ 7
8. 1043 ÷ 22

$$\begin{array}{r} 26 \\ 34\overline{)884} \end{array}$$

9. **VOCABULARY** Use the division problem shown to tell whether the number is the divisor, dividend, or quotient.

   a. 884 **b.** 26 **c.** 34

10. **MP NUMBER SENSE** Without calculating, decide which is greater: 3999 ÷ 129 or 3834 ÷ 142. Explain.

11. **MP REASONING** In a division problem, can the remainder be greater than the divisor? Explain.

EXAMPLE 3 Modeling Real Life

A 301-foot-high swing at an amusement park can take 64 people on each ride. A total of 10,250 people ride the swing today. All the rides are full except for the last ride. How many rides are given? How many people are on the last ride?

To find the number of rides given, first you need to find the number of groups of 64 people in 10,250 people. So, find the quotient of 10,250 and 64.

160 R10	
64)10,250	There is one group of 64 in 102.
− 64	
385	There are six groups of 64 in 385.
− 384	
10	There are no groups of 64 in 10.
− 0	
10	The remainder is 10.

Do not stop here. You must write a 0 in the ones place of the quotient.

The quotient is $160\frac{10}{64}$. This means there are 160 full rides, with 10 people remaining.

So, 161 rides are given, with 10 people on the last ride.

Check Find the product of the quotient and the divisor.

$$64 \cdot 160\frac{10}{64} = 64\left(160 + \frac{10}{64}\right) = 64(160) + 64\left(\frac{10}{64}\right) = 10{,}240 + 10 = 10{,}250 \checkmark$$

Self-Assessment for Problem Solving

Solve each exercise. Then rate your understanding of the success criteria in your journal.

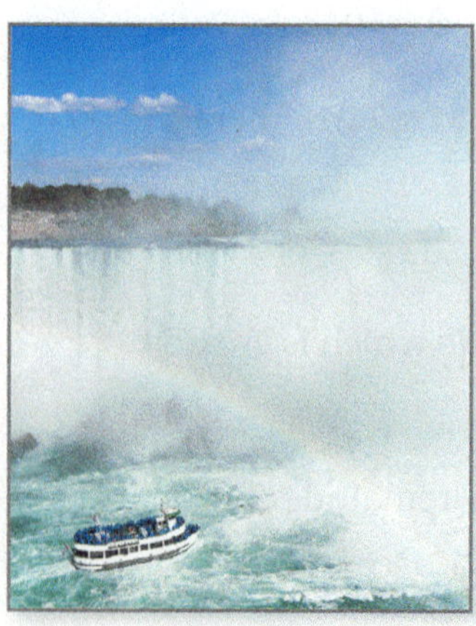

12. In a movie's opening weekend, 879,575 tickets are sold in 755 theaters. The average cost of a ticket is $9.50. What is the average amount of money earned by each theater?

13. A boat can carry 582 passengers to the base of a waterfall. A total of 13,105 people ride the boat today. All the rides are full except for the first ride. How many rides are given? How many people are on the first ride?

14. **DIG DEEPER!** A new year begins at 12:00 A.M. on January 1. What is the date and time 12,345 minutes after the start of a new year?

Laurie's Notes

Discuss

- ? "Who likes roller coasters?"
- Search the Internet for a video of a roller coaster ride. If possible, show a video of Skyrush at Hershey Park, PA because it is referenced in the Closure.
- Explain that there is a lot of math used at an amusement park.

EXAMPLE 3

- Review how to write a quotient with a remainder as a mixed number. Use a simple problem, such as $14 \div 4 = 3 + \frac{2}{4} = 3\frac{1}{2}$.
- Ask a volunteer to read the problem.
- Probe student understanding by asking how they could solve the problem if there were a few times when the line was empty, and rides occurred that were partially full. Can they find the total number of rides? Students need to realize that long division will not help answer this type of question.
- ? "How can you find the number of rides given?" Divide the total number of riders by 64 because there are 64 riders on each ride.
- **Common Error:** In this problem, simplifying the remainder is unnecessary and may cause students to say 5 people are on the last ride.
- **MP6 Attend to Precision:** Be sure to discuss the 0 needed in the ones place of the quotient. If students have made an estimate to begin with, they will recognize that 160 makes more sense than 16.
- ? "10 is less than a whole group of 64. What does the remainder mean and how can you write the remainder?" The remainder of 10 is the number of people on the last ride. Write 10 out of 64, which is $\frac{10}{64}$.
- Have students read the Check note with a partner and discuss why it is mathematically sound. Listen for understanding that a mixed number is the sum of a whole number and a fraction, so the Distributive Property can be used to find the product.

Self-Assessment for Problem Solving

- Students may benefit from trying the exercises independently and then working with peers to refine their work. It is important to provide time in class for problem solving, so that students become comfortable with the problem-solving plan.
- These exercises evaluate students' understanding of real-life situations and how division can be used to solve them. Students may assume they should divide rather than read each problem carefully.
- Exercises 13 and 14 exemplify why the remainder is important.
- Have students assess their understanding of the third success criterion after discussing these exercises.

The Success Criteria Self-Assessment chart can be found in the *Student Journal* or online at *BigIdeasMath.com*.

Closure

- The theoretical ride capacity for Skyrush (at Hershey Park, PA) is 1350 riders per hour. There are 2 trains with 32 riders each. About how many rides is this per train per hour? about 21 rides per train per hour

Extra Example 3

A record-breaking roller coaster at an amusement park can take 28 people on each ride. A total of 24,539 people ride the roller coaster today. All the rides are full except for the last ride. How many rides are given? How many people are on the last ride? 877 rides; 11 people

Self-Assessment for Problem Solving

12. \$11,067.50

13. 23 rides; 301 people

14. January 9, 1:45 P.M.

Learning Target

Divide whole numbers and solve problems involving division of whole numbers.

Success Criteria

- Use long division to divide whole numbers.
- Write a remainder as a fraction.
- Interpret quotients in real-life problems.

Review & Refresh

1. 30.32
2. 29.282
3. 1.8004
4. 62.96686
5. 1, 26; 2, 13
6. 1, 72; 2, 36; 3, 24; 4, 18; 6, 12; 8, 9
7. 1, 50; 2, 25; 5, 10
8. 1, 98; 2, 49; 7, 14
9. B
10. C
11. D
12. A

Concepts, Skills, & Problem Solving

13. 16,648 people
14. 3
15. 4162 people
16. 9570 people
17. 31
18. 32
19. $12\frac{13}{24}$
20. $105\frac{4}{61}$
21. 73
22. $38\frac{6}{163}$
23. $53\frac{1}{118}$
24. 7
25. 60
26. 66
27. $47\frac{110}{173}$
28. $209\frac{13}{32}$

Check out the Dynamic Assessment System.
BigIdeasMath.com

Assignment Guide and Concept Check

Scaffold assignments to support all students in their learning progression. The suggested assignments are a starting point. Continue to assign additional exercises and revisit with spaced practice to move every student toward proficiency.

Level	Assignment 1	Assignment 2
Emerging	4, 8, 9, 10, 11, 12, 13, 14, 15, 16, 20, 21, 23, 27	29, 30, 31, 32, 35
Proficient	4, 8, 9, 10, 11, 12, 13, 14, 15, 16, 20, 21, 22, 27	28, 29, 30, 31, 34, 35
Advanced	4, 8, 9, 10, 11, 12, 13, 14, 15, 16, 18, 22, 28, 37	29, 30, 31, 33, 35, 36

- Assignment 1 is for use after students complete the Self-Assessment for Concepts & Skills.
- Assignment 2 is for use after students complete the Self-Assessment for Problem Solving.
- The red exercises can be used as a concept check.

Review & Refresh Prior Skills

Exercises 1–4 Multiplying Decimals
Exercises 5–8 Finding Factor Pairs
Exercises 9–12 Dividing Fractions

Common Errors

- **Exercises 20, 25, and 28** Students may forget to use 0 as a place holder in the quotient. Remind them to estimate the answers to check their results.

2.6 Practice

Review & Refresh

Multiply.

1. 8×3.79
2. 12.1×2.42
3. 6.43×0.28
4. $9.526 \cdot 6.61$

List the factor pairs of the number.

5. 26
6. 72
7. 50
8. 98

Match the expression with its value.

9. $\frac{6}{7} \div \frac{3}{5}$
10. $\frac{3}{7} \div \frac{6}{5}$
11. $\frac{6}{5} \div \frac{3}{7}$
12. $\frac{3}{5} \div \frac{6}{7}$

A. $\frac{7}{10}$ B. $1\frac{3}{7}$ C. $\frac{5}{14}$ D. $2\frac{4}{5}$

Concepts, Skills, & Problem Solving

OPERATIONS WITH WHOLE NUMBERS **The bar graph shows the attendance at a food festival. Use the graph to answer the question.** (See Exploration 1, p. 81.)

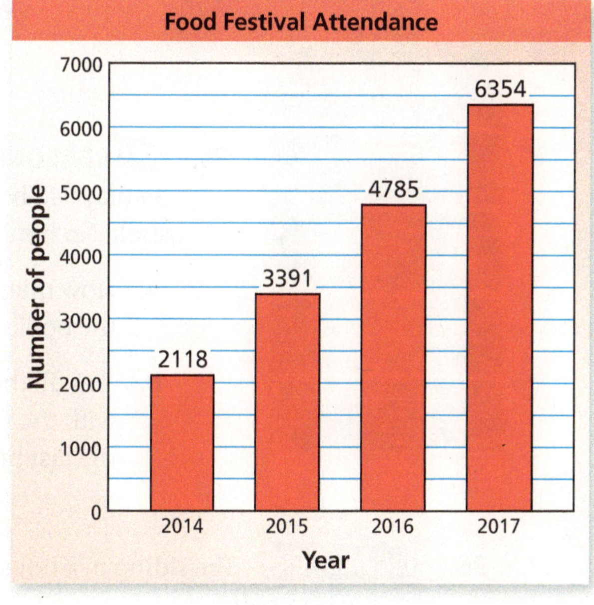

13. What is the total attendance at the food festival from 2014 to 2017?
14. How many times more people attended the food festival in 2017 than in 2014?
15. What is the average attendance at the festival each year over the four-year period?
16. The festival projects that the attendance for 2018 will be twice the attendance in 2016. What is the projected attendance for 2018?

DIVIDING WHOLE NUMBERS **Divide. Use estimation to check your answer.**

17. $837 \div 27$
18. $1088 \div 34$
19. $903 \div 72$
20. $6409 \div 61$
21. $\frac{5986}{82}$
22. $6200 \div 163$
23. $6255 \div 118$
24. $\frac{588}{84}$
25. $7440 \div 124$
26. $26{,}862 \div 407$
27. $8241 \div 173$
28. $\frac{33{,}505}{160}$

29. MP **MODELING REAL LIFE** A pharmacist divides 364 pills into prescription bottles. Each bottle contains 28 pills. How many bottles does the pharmacist fill?

MP **YOU BE THE TEACHER** **Your friend finds the quotient. Is your friend correct? Explain your reasoning.**

30.

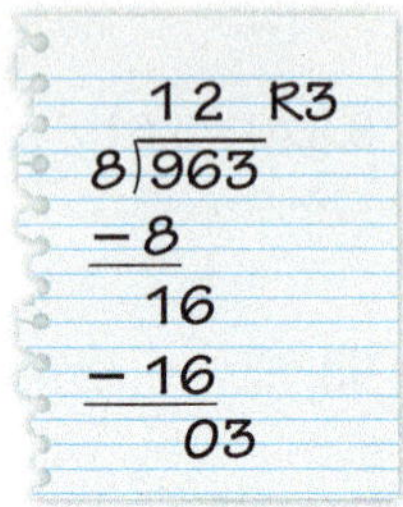

31.

19
12)1308
−12
108
−108
0

GEOMETRY **Find the perimeter of the rectangle.**

32.

Area = 35 in.^{2}

7 in.

33.

12 ft

34.

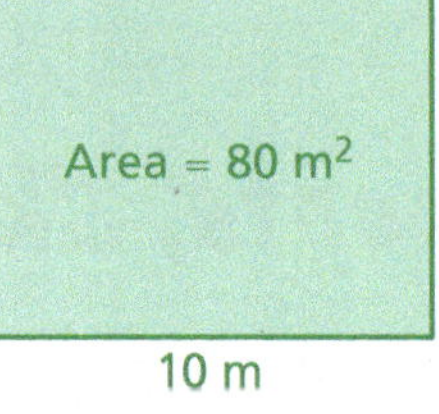

10 m

35. MP **REASONING** You borrow bookcases like the one shown to display 943 books at a book sale. You plan to put 22 books on each shelf. No books will be on top of the bookcases.

a. How many bookcases must you borrow to display all the books?

b. You fill the shelves of each bookcase in order, starting with the top shelf. How many books are on each shelf of the last bookcase?

36. **DIG DEEPER!** The siding of a house is 2250 square feet. The siding needs two coats of paint.

a. What is the minimum cost of the paint needed to complete the job?

b. How much paint is left over when you spend the minimum amount?

Can Size	Cost	Coverage
1 quart	$18	80 square feet
1 gallon	$29	320 square feet

37. **CRITICAL THINKING** Use the digits 3, 4, 6, and 9 to complete the division problem. Use each digit once.

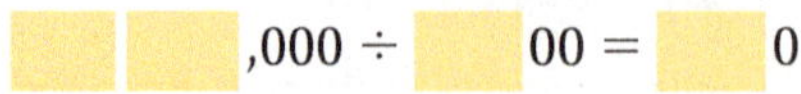

Common Errors

- **Exercises 32–34** Students may not give a complete answer. Remind them the units of measure should be included with the numerical answer.

Mini-Assessment

Find the value of the expression.

1. $495 \div 15$ 33
2. $374 \div 17$ 22
3. Find the quotient of 807 and 12. $67\frac{1}{4}$
4. $7590 \div 125$ $60\frac{18}{25}$
5. There are 240 students and 16 rooms. How many students will be in each class if there is an equal number of students in each class? 15

Section Resources

Surface Level	Deep Level
Resources by Chapter • Extra Practice • Reteach • Puzzle Time Student Journal • Self-Assessment • Practice Differentiating the Lesson Tutorial Videos Skills Review Handbook Skills Trainer	Resources by Chapter • Enrichment and Extension Graphic Organizers Dynamic Assessment System • Section Practice

Concepts, Skills, & Problem Solving

29. 13

30. no; The answer should be 120 R3.

31. no; The answer should be 109.

32. 24 in.

33. 42 ft

34. 36 m

35. **a.** 9

b. from top shelf down: 22, 22, 19, 0, 0

36. **a.** $424

b. $\frac{3}{4}$ qt, or $\frac{3}{16}$ gal

37. *Sample answer:* $36{,}000 \div 900 = 40$

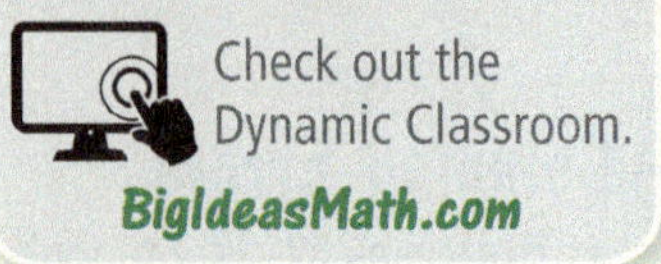

Learning Target

Divide decimals and solve problems involving division of decimals.

Success Criteria

- Divide decimals by whole numbers.
- Divide decimals by decimals.
- Divide whole numbers by decimals.

Warm Up

Cumulative, vocabulary, and prerequisite skills practice opportunities are available in the *Resources by Chapter* or at *BigIdeasMath.com.*

ELL Support

Point out that different phrases can indicate division, such as *divided by, divided into, goes into,* and *quotient.* Have students keep a record of the different phrases they read in word problems that indicate division, so they can become familiar with them. Make sure students understand how each phrase signals which number is the dividend, and which is the divisor.

Exploration 1

a. See Additional Answers.

b. 7; 7; 7; 7; The quotients are the same; *Sample answer:* Multiply both numbers by the same power of 10, then divide whole numbers.

Laurie's Notes

COMMON CORE STATE STANDARDS 6.NS.B.3

Preparing to Teach

- Students understand the importance of place value and zeros in various operations with numbers. Students' understanding of division will now extend to decimals.
- Estimating reasonable answers will continue to be an important practice.
- **MP5 Use Appropriate Tools Strategically:** Area models and calculators are suitable tools for this exploration and help students make sense of the problems. Exploring division within a concrete model will lay the foundation for the procedure.

Motivate

- Give students some contexts for dividing a dollar amount into three or four parts. Have students estimate the quotient using compatible numbers.
- ? "Three siblings purchase a gift for their parents that costs $22.98. About how much does each sibling pay?" Round $22.98 to $24; $24 ÷ 3 = $8
- ? "Four friends share the cost of a pizza and drinks that total $18.75. About how much does each friend owe?" Round $18.75 to $20; $20 ÷ 4 = $5
- ? "You pay $4.32 for three pens. Does each pen cost more than $2?" No, the cost for each pen is about $4.50 ÷ 3 = $1.50.

Exploration 1

- Because area models were used in the exploration in Section 2.5, these area models should look familiar. Have students *Think-Pair-Share* about what the area models represent. Then have pairs state the multiplication fact that is represented and give two related division expressions for each model.
- Check that pairs are finding the correct quotients for each expression in part (a).
- "Look at model (i). One division equation is 0.4 ÷ 0.5 = 0.8. Why does a quotient less than 1 makes sense?" 0.4 is less than 0.5, so the quotient must be less than 1. "This is similar to saying that I have 40 squares and I want to put them into groups of 50 squares. So, the number of groups is less than 1."
- ? If students are having difficulty recognizing the relationship in part (b), write 119 ÷ 17 = 7 horizontally on the board and the other three equations underneath. Ask, "Why do you think all of the quotients equal 7?" *Sample answer:* Each expression has the same number of decimal places in the dividend as the divisor. When they have the same number of places, you get the same quotient as if they were whole numbers.
- Use equivalent fractions to show why the expressions are equivalent. For example, $1.19 \div 0.17 = \frac{1.19}{0.17} = \frac{1.19 \times 100}{0.17 \times 100} = \frac{119}{17}$.
- **Note:** When the dividend and the divisor are multiplied by the same number, the quotient's value stays the same.
- **MP2 Reason Abstractly and Quantitatively:** Mathematically proficient students are able to create equivalent representations of a problem. This will aid in students' understanding of the success criteria.

2.7 Dividing Decimals

Learning Target: Divide decimals and solve problems involving division of decimals.

Success Criteria:
- I can divide decimals by whole numbers.
- I can divide decimals by decimals.
- I can divide whole numbers by decimals.

EXPLORATION 1 Dividing Decimals

Work with a partner.

a. Write two division expressions represented by each area model. Then find the quotients. Explain how you found your answer.

i.

ii.

iii.

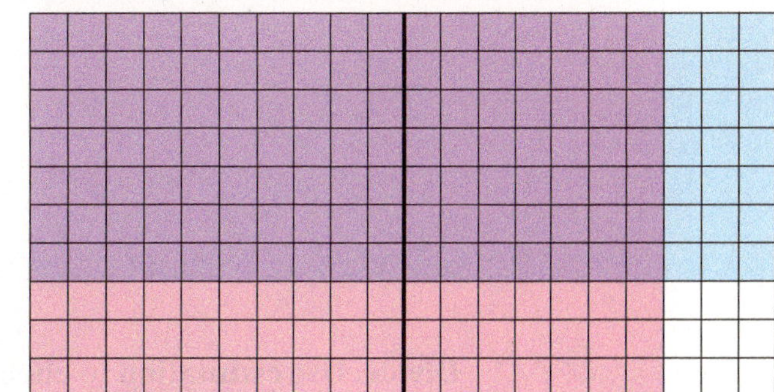

b. Use a calculator to find 119 ÷ 17, 11.9 ÷ 1.7, 1.19 ÷ 0.17, and 0.119 ÷ 0.017. What do you notice? Explain how you can use long division to divide any pair of multi-digit decimals.

Math Practice

Construct Arguments

Why do the quotients in part (b) have the relationship you observed?

2.7 Lesson

Key Idea

Dividing Decimals by Whole Numbers

Words Place the decimal point in the quotient above the decimal point in the dividend. Then divide as you would with whole numbers. Continue until there is no remainder.

Numbers

$$\begin{array}{r} 1.83 \\ 4\overline{)7.32} \end{array}$$

Place the decimal point in the quotient above the decimal point in the dividend.

EXAMPLE 1 Dividing Decimals by Whole Numbers

a. Find 7.6 ÷ 4. **Estimate** $8 \div 4 = 2$

$$\begin{array}{r} 1.9 \\ 4\overline{)7.6} \\ -4 \\ \hline 3\,6 \\ -3\,6 \\ \hline 0 \end{array}$$

Place the decimal point in the quotient above the decimal point in the dividend.

So, 7.6 ÷ 4 = 1.9. **Reasonable?** $1.9 \approx 2$ ✓

b. Find 4.374 ÷ 12.

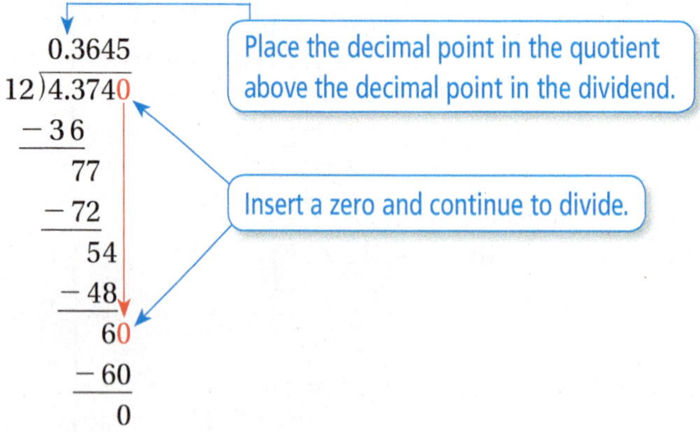

So, 4.374 ÷ 12 = 0.3645. **Check** $0.3645 \times 12 = 4.374$ ✓

Try It **Divide. Use estimation to check your answer.**

1. 36.4 ÷ 2 **2.** 22.2 ÷ 6 **3.** 59.64 ÷ 7

4. 3.12 ÷ 16 **5.** 6.224 ÷ 4 **6.** 43.407 ÷ 14

Laurie's Notes

Scaffolding Instruction

- In a previous course, students divided decimals to the hundredths place. In this course, students will become fluent with division and multiply by powers of 10 when dividing by decimals. In the next course, students will convert a fraction or mixed number to a decimal using long division.
- **Emerging:** Students may understand that decimals can be divided by whole numbers and decimals but struggle with the procedure. Guided instruction with the examples will help students understand the success criteria.
- **Proficient:** Students understand the need for making the divisor a whole number, and can insert zeros in the dividend when necessary. They can estimate their answers to check for reasonableness. After reviewing the Key Ideas, have students self-assess using Try It Exercises 1–10.

Key Idea

- Placing the decimal point in the quotient above the decimal point in the dividend makes sense to the students.
- **FYI:** Some students may have difficulty lining up the columns when they perform long division. Have them use grid paper as an aid.

EXAMPLE 1

- Work through both parts of the example. Begin by estimating the quotient and end with judging the reasonableness of your answer.
- Students often ask where the decimal point is written in the work below the dividend. "Why don't you bring down the decimal point?" In theory, you can bring the decimal point down. But, once the decimal point is placed in the quotient, you treat the problem as if you were dividing whole numbers.
- ? "If the divisor is greater than the dividend, what do you know about the quotient?" It will be less than 1.
- You may want to share whole number examples to illustrate the above question. For example, use $8 \div 4$ and $4 \div 8$.
- ? In part (b), place the decimal point in the quotient. Then ask, "Does 12 go into 4?" no "Does 12 go into 43?" yes
- ? In this problem, a zero must be inserted at the end of the dividend to continue dividing. Ask, "Is 4.374 equivalent to 4.3740? 4.37400?" yes; yes
- Students may want to know how many zeros to insert. Tell students to continue to insert zeros until the division ends with a zero remainder.

Scaffold instruction to support all students in their learning. Learning is individualized and you may want to group students differently as they move in and out of these levels with each skill and concept. Student self-assessment and feedback help guide your instructional decisions about how and when to layer support for all students to become proficient learners.

Extra Example 1

a. Find $3.5 \div 7$. 0.5

b. Find $16.92 \div 8$. 2.115

Try It

1. 18.2 **2.** 3.7

3. 8.52 **4.** 0.195

5. 1.556 **6.** 3.1005

Laurie's Notes

Key Idea

- **MP2 Reason Abstractly and Quantitatively & MP3 Construct Viable Arguments and Critique the Reasoning of Others:** Throughout the examples, students should be encouraged to explain their thinking about the process. Multiplying the dividend and divisor by the same power of 10 is equivalent to multiplying the numerator and denominator of a fraction by the same number. Make sure students make this connection.
- Discuss why the rule works. When you multiply both the dividend and the divisor by the same power of 10, the quotient is not changed. You may want to remind students of the exploration.
- Remind students that they need to multiply by a large enough power of 10 to make the divisor a whole number. Only when you divide by a whole number can you place the decimal point in the quotient.

Extra Example 2

a. Find $68.4 \div 5.7$. 12

b. Find $0.336 \div 0.42$. 0.8

EXAMPLE 2

- Work through parts (a) and (b). The original expression in part (a) can be read as "182 tenths $\div$ 14 tenths." Multiply the divisor and the dividend by 10 to get the equivalent expression $182 \div 14$.
- Complete the check as part of each example to model this good habit for students.
- Refer to the push-pin note. Show students that multiplying the divisor and the dividend by the same power of 10 does not change the quotient because it is the same as multiplying the quotient by 1. For example,

$$18.2 \div 1.4 = \frac{18.2}{1.4} = \frac{18.2}{1.4} \times 1 = \frac{18.2}{1.4} \times \frac{10}{10} = \frac{182}{14}.$$

Try It

7. 8 **8.** 17

9. 9.41 **10.** 0.9

Try It

- Note the two representations of division in these exercises.
- Ask students to estimate the answer before they begin. If students can identify a reasonable estimate, it will help them check the placement of the decimal point. Discuss this as a class.

ELL Support

Remind students to multiply by a large enough power of 10 to make the divisor a whole number and to follow the process used in Example 2.
Beginner: Write the numbers in long-division form and find the quotient.
Intermediate: State the answer using a complete sentence. For example, "Nine and six-tenths divided by one and two-tenths is eight."
Advanced: Explain each step of the process.

Key Idea

Dividing Decimals by Decimals

Words Multiply the divisor *and* the dividend by a power of 10 to make the divisor a whole number. Then place the decimal point in the quotient above the decimal point in the dividend and divide as you would with whole numbers. Continue until there is no remainder.

Numbers $1.2\overline{)4.56}$ $\qquad$ $\begin{array}{r} 3.8 \\ 12\overline{)45.6} \end{array}$

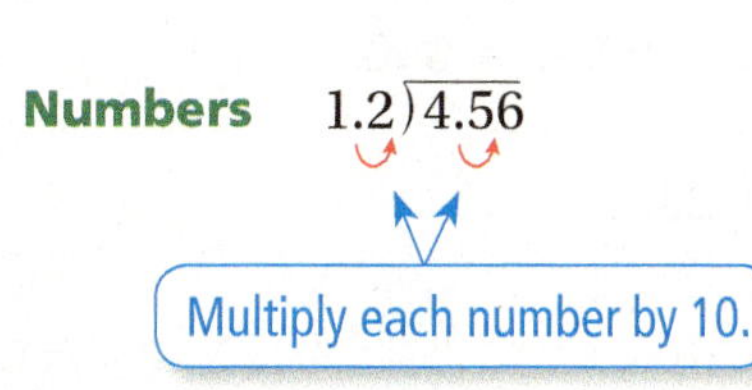

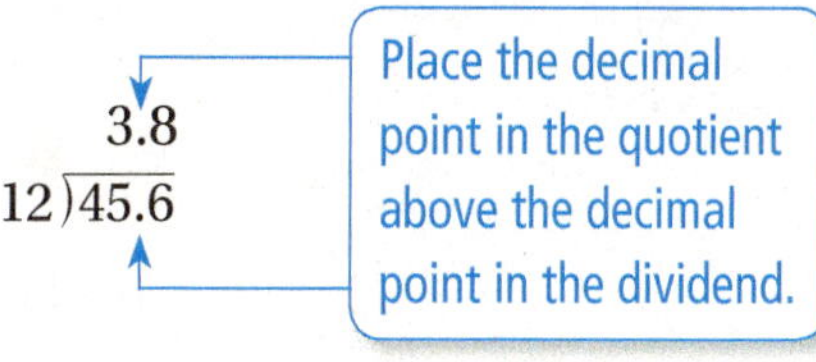

EXAMPLE 2 Dividing Decimals

Multiplying the divisor and the dividend by a power of 10 does not change the quotient.

For example:

$18.2 \div 1.4 = 13$

$182 \div 14 = 13$

$1820 \div 140 = 13$

a. Find 18.2 ÷ 1.4.

$1.4\overline{)18.2}$ → $\begin{array}{r} 13. \\ 14\overline{)182.} \\ -\underline{14} \\ 42 \\ -\underline{42} \\ 0 \end{array}$

Multiply each number by 10.

Place the decimal point in the quotient above the decimal point in the dividend.

So, $18.2 \div 1.4 = 13$.

Check $13 \times 1.4 = 18.2$ ✓

b. Find 0.273 ÷ 0.39.

$0.39\overline{)0.273}$ → $\begin{array}{r} 0.7 \\ 39\overline{)27.3} \\ -\underline{273} \\ 0 \end{array}$

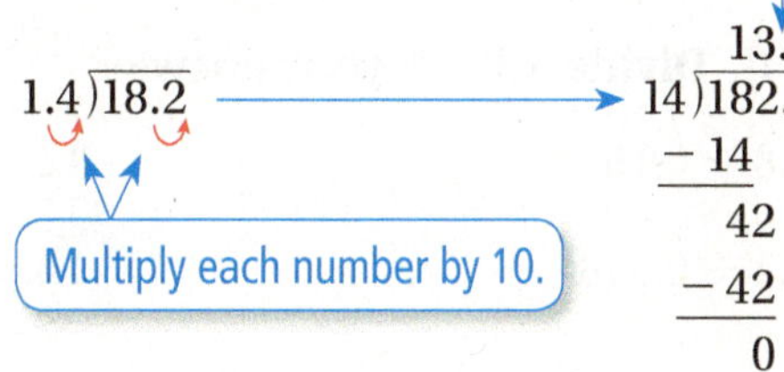

So, $0.273 \div 0.39 = 0.7$.

Check $0.7 \times 0.39 = 0.273$ ✓

Try It **Divide. Check your answer.**

7. $1.2\overline{)9.6}$

8. $3.4\overline{)57.8}$

9. $21.643 \div 2.3$

10. $0.459 \div 0.51$

EXAMPLE 3 Inserting Zeros in the Dividend and the Quotient

Remember to check your answer by multiplying the quotient by the divisor.

a. Find 2.45 ÷ 0.007.

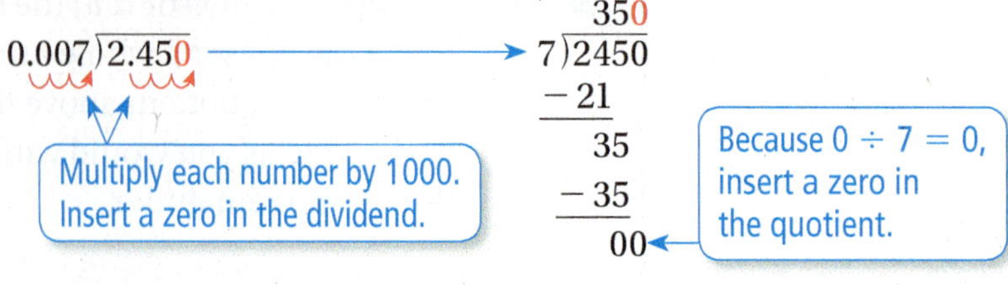

So, 2.45 ÷ 0.007 = 350.

b. Find 32 ÷ 1.25.

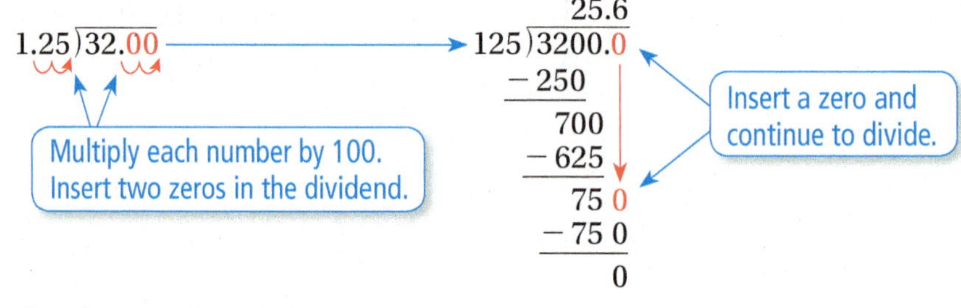

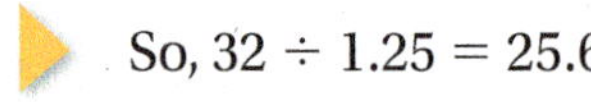
So, 32 ÷ 1.25 = 25.6.

Try It Divide. Check your answer.

11. 3.8 ÷ 0.16

12. 15.6 ÷ 0.78

13. 7.2 ÷ 0.048

14. 42 ÷ 3.75

Self-Assessment for Concepts & Skills

Solve each exercise. Then rate your understanding of the success criteria in your journal.

DIVIDING DECIMALS **Divide. Check your answer.**

15. 37.7 ÷ 13

16. 33 ÷ 4.4

17. 2.16 ÷ 0.009

18. MP **NUMBER SENSE** Fix the one that is not correct.

6.1 4)24.4	61 4)244	6.1 4)2.44

19. MP **NUMBER SENSE** Rewrite 2.16)18.5 so that the divisor is a whole number.

20. MP **STRUCTURE** Write 1.8 ÷ 6 as a multiplication problem with a missing factor. Explain your reasoning.

Laurie's Notes

EXAMPLE 3

- "How can you estimate the answer to $2.45 \div 0.007$?" Listen for students to explain that the quotient has to be greater than 2.45.
- Sometimes students focus on the process and forget about the mathematics behind the process. For example, they may talk about moving decimal points but lose sight of why doing so doesn't change the problem.
- In part (a), ask "What number do you need to multiply by to make the divisor a whole number?" 1000 Show students the mathematics by writing 2.45×1000 and 0.007×1000 off to the side.
- Remind them that $2.45 \div 0.007$ and $2450 \div 7$ will have the same answers.
- In part (b), ask, "Will dividing 32 by a number slightly greater than 1 result in an answer *greater than 32* or *less than 32*?" less than 32 "What number do you need to multiply by to make the divisor a whole number?" 100 "How will that affect the dividend?" $32 \times 100 = 3200$
- Students need to understand that the number 3200 is equivalent to 3200.0.

Try It

- After completing Exercises 11–13, ask students to *Pass the Problem* for Exercise 14. Listen to students' discussions to assess their level of understanding.

Self-Assessment for Concepts & Skills

- Check that students are using zeros appropriately.
- Remind students that Exercises 19 and 20 do not ask them to actually divide. The goal of these exercises is to create an equivalent expression or equation. This is important for mastery of the first two success criteria.

ELL Support

Have students work in pairs to complete the exercises. Remind them to think of the process they used for the Try It exercises. When they have finished, have two pairs come together to review their answers. If there is disagreement, have students reach a consensus. Check comprehension by having each group display their answers on a whiteboard for your review. Reteach as needed.

The Success Criteria Self-Assessment chart can be found in the *Student Journal* or online at *BigIdeasMath.com*.

Extra Example 3

a. Find $1.76 \div 0.004$. 440

b. Find $68 \div 0.08$. 850

Try It

11. 23.75 **12.** 20

13. 150 **14.** 11.2

Formative Assessment Tip

Pass the Problem

This technique provides students the opportunity to work with others to solve a problem that requires more than a few steps. One way to use *Pass the Problem* is to begin by placing students in groups. Pose a problem that one student from each group begins to work on. After the completion of the first step, the problem is passed to the student seated to the right. The recipient completes the next step, or makes corrections to the problem. If changes are made, they must explain why there was an error. This continues until all steps are complete. *Pass the Problem* gives all students the opportunity to participate in the lesson and receive feedback on their work. When students have finished the problem, they will confer with one another to discuss the problem and offer additional feedback. One thing you hope to hear is positive feedback on the clarity of thinking that was recorded, allowing students to make sense of the work.

Self-Assessment for Concepts & Skills

15. 2.9 **16.** 7.5

17. 240

18. $4\overline{)2.44}$ = 0.61 **19.** $216\overline{)1850}$

20. $6 \times \square = 1.8$; Use the dividend as the product and the divisor as a factor.

Extra Example 4

In 2015, there were 6.7 thousand commercial FM radio stations. In 1990, there were 4.4 thousand. How many times more commercial FM radio stations were there in 2015 than in 1990? Round your answer to the nearest tenth. 1.5

Self-Assessment for Problem Solving

21. $15.24 for 6 issues; $0.05

22. 33 mi/h

23. Year 1 to Year 2; 2.1

Learning Target

Divide decimals and solve problems involving division of decimals.

Success Criteria

- Divide decimals by whole numbers.
- Divide decimals by decimals.
- Divide whole numbers by decimals.

Laurie's Notes

EXAMPLE 4

? "How many cell phone subscribers were there in 1995?" 33.79 million
"In what year were there about 208 million cell phone subscribers?" 2005
"Describe the general trend of the graph." The graph is increasing.

- **Common Error:** Students often read this type of question as, "How many more?" versus, "How many *times* more?" Relate this to a question about themselves that they might understand, such as, "How much older is your aunt than you?" versus, "How many times older is your aunt than you?"

? "If you want to round to the nearest whole number, what place value do you need to look at?" the tenths

- Rounding to the nearest whole number may be difficult for students due to the decimal point. Remind students that rounding to the nearest whole number is still done in the same way as any other place value.
- You may want to briefly explain the underestimate and overestimate in the Check Reasonableness note. To underestimate, round the dividend down and the divisor up to the nearest whole number. To overestimate, round the dividend up and the divisor down to the nearest whole number.
- **Extension:** Suggest extending the example by having students continue to divide and see what happens. In this case, it does not terminate. This is a concept students will study in the next course.

Self-Assessment for Problem Solving

- Allow time in class for students to practice using the problem-solving plan. Remember, some students may only be ready to complete the first step.
- Remind students that decimals are a part of their everyday lives and are very important. Ask them if they would rather pay $1.25 or $125? Is a reasonable tax rate 0.08 or 0.8? Misplacing a decimal point, even by one place value, makes a huge difference!
- Students may expect to divide but look for their choices of dividend. This should give you an indication of their understanding. Students may need to be reminded that the greater number is not always the dividend.
- Students may benefit from using grid paper to line up columns.
- **MP1 Making Sense of Problems and Persevere in Solving Them:** Students need to analyze the problems to decide how division provides a pathway to a solution. They also need to check the reasonableness of their answers within the context of the problem. Can students see the connection between the division equation and its multiplication family?

The Success Criteria Self-Assessment chart can be found in the *Student Journal* or online at *BigIdeasMath.com*.

Closure

- Use 8.4 and 0.42 to write an example whose quotient is greater than 1 and an example whose quotient is less than 1. Solve each problem.
$8.4 \div 0.42 = 20$; $0.42 \div 8.4 = 0.05$

EXAMPLE 4 Modeling Real Life

How many times more cell phone subscribers were there in 2015 than in 1990? Round to the nearest whole number.

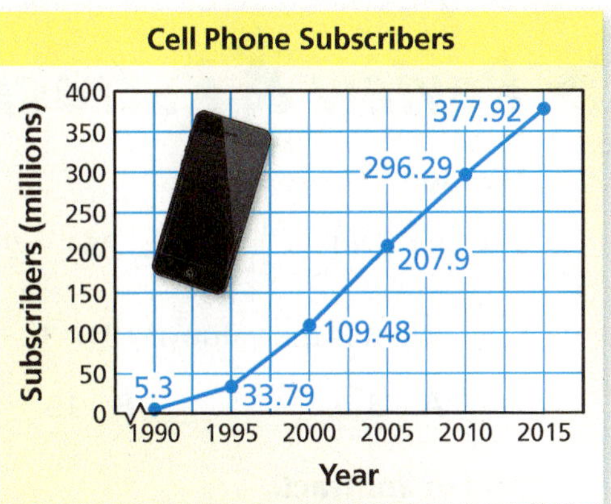

Divide the number of subscribers in 2015 by the number of subscribers in 1990.

From the graph, there were 377.92 million subscribers in 2015 and 5.3 million in 1990. So, divide 377.92 by 5.3.

Check Reasonableness

Find an underestimate and an overestimate.

Underestimate:

$$370 \div 6 = 61\frac{2}{3}$$

Overestimate:

$$380 \div 5 = 76$$

The answer is reasonable because

$61\frac{2}{3} < 71 < 76.$ ✓

$5.3\overline{)377.92}$ → $53\overline{)3779.2}$

```
     71.3  ← Rounds to 71.
53)3779.2
  -371
     69
    -53
     16 2
    -15 9
        3
```

So, there were about 71 times more subscribers in 2015 than in 1990.

Self-Assessment for Problem Solving

Solve each exercise. Then rate your understanding of the success criteria in your journal.

21. A magazine subscription costs \$29.88 for 12 issues or \$15.24 for 6 issues. Which subscription costs more per issue? How much more?

22. The track of a roller coaster is 1.265 miles long. The ride lasts for 2.3 minutes. What is the average speed of the roller coaster in miles per hour?

23. DIG DEEPER! The table shows the number of visitors to a website each year for 4 years. Does the number of visitors increase more from Year 1 to Year 2 or from Year 3 to Year 4? How many times greater is the increase?

Year	Visitors (millions)
1	2.4
2	32.22
3	88.4
4	102.6

2.7 Practice

Review & Refresh

Divide.

1. $84 \div 14$ **2.** $391 \div 23$ **3.** $1458 \div 54$ **4.** $\frac{68,134}{163}$

5. What is the value of $18 + 3^2 \div [3 \times (8 - 5)]$?

A. 3 **B.** 19 **C.** 27 **D.** 49

Add or subtract.

6. $7.635 - 5.046$ **7.** $12.177 + 3.09$ **8.** $14.008 - 9.433$

Concepts, Skills, & Problem Solving

DIVIDING DECIMALS **Write two division expressions represented by the area model. Then find the quotients. Explain how you found your answer.** (See Exploration 1, p. 87.)

9.

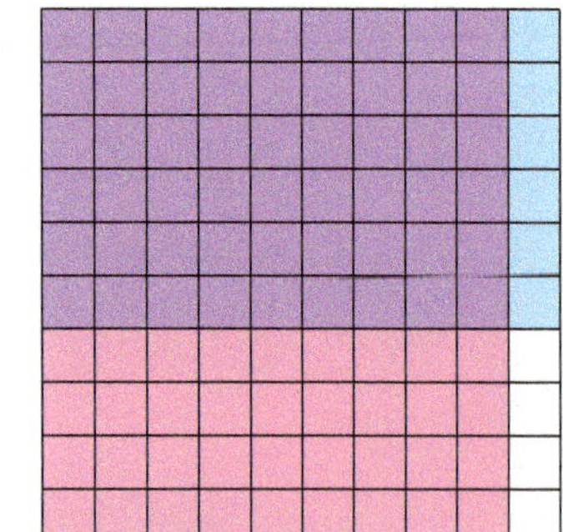

10.

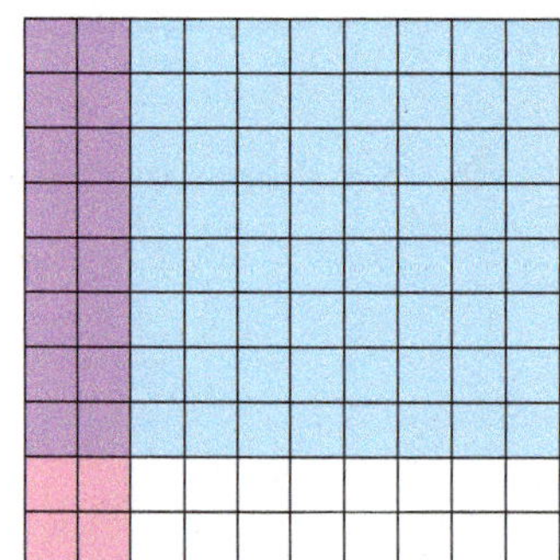

DIVIDING DECIMALS BY WHOLE NUMBERS **Divide. Use estimation to check your answer.**

11. $6\overline{)25.2}$ **12.** $5\overline{)33.5}$ **13.** $7\overline{)3.5}$ **14.** $8\overline{)10.4}$

15. $38.79 \div 9$ **16.** $37.72 \div 4$ **17.** $43.4 \div 7$ **18.** $22.505 \div 7$

19. $44.64 \div 8$ **20.** $0.294 \div 3$ **21.** $3.6 \div 24$ **22.** $52.014 \div 20$

MP YOU BE THE TEACHER **Your friend finds the quotient. Is your friend correct? Explain your reasoning.**

23.

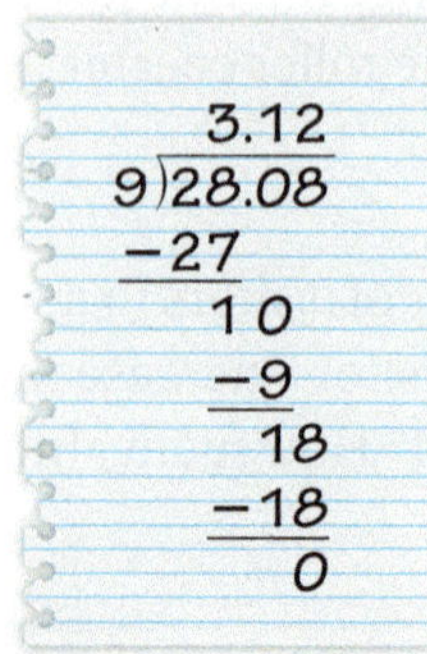

24.

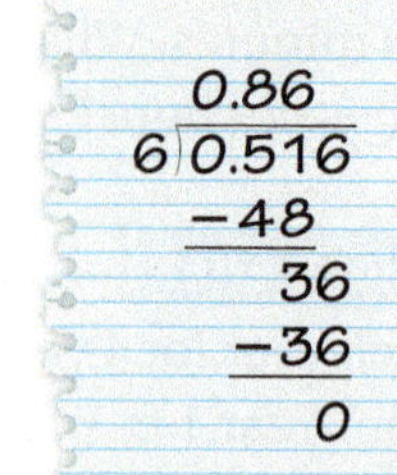

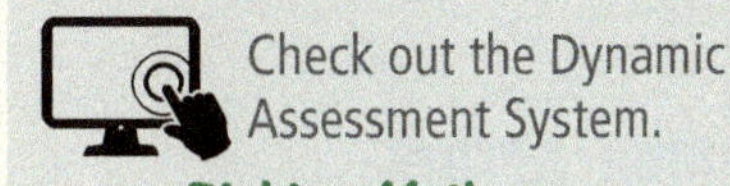

Assignment Guide and Concept Check

Scaffold assignments to support all students in their learning progression. The suggested assignments are a starting point. Continue to assign additional exercises and revisit with spaced practice to move every student toward proficiency.

Level	Assignment 1	Assignment 2
Emerging	4, 5, 8, 10, 13, 21, 27, 40, 48, 56, 61	23, 24, 25, 26, 36, 51, 55, 63, 65, 71
Proficient	4, 5, 8, 10, 13, 21, 22, 23, 28, 38, 40, 49, 56, 63	24, 26, 51, 55, 66, 67, 71, 72, 74
Advanced	4, 5, 8, 10, 14, 22, 23, 28, 38, 41, 50, 56, 64, 68	24, 52, 55, 66, 71, 72, 73, 74, 75

- Assignment 1 is for use after students complete the Self-Assessment for Concepts & Skills.
- Assignment 2 is for use after students complete the Self-Assessment for Problem Solving.
- The red exercises can be used as a concept check.

Review & Refresh Prior Skills

Exercises 1–4 Dividing Whole Numbers
Exercise 5 Using Order of Operations
Exercises 6–8 Adding and Subtracting Decimals

- **Exercises 11–22** Students may divide without placing the decimal point in the quotient. Tell them to place the decimal point immediately after they put the numbers in long-division form. Remind students to use estimation to check the reasonableness of their answers.
- **Exercises 11–22** Students may have difficulty keeping their columns organized and forget to include placeholder zeros or put in extra placeholders. Have them use grid paper as an organizational tool to help line up the numbers.

Review & Refresh

1. 6
2. 17
3. 27
4. 418
5. B
6. 2.589
7. 15.267
8. 4.575

& Problem Solving

9. $0.54 \div 0.6 = 0.9$, $0.54 \div 0.9 = 0.6$; Rewrote $0.6 \times 0.9 = 0.54$.
10. $0.16 \div 0.8 = 0.2$, $0.16 \div 0.2 = 0.8$; Rewrote $0.8 \times 0.2 = 0.16$.
11. 4.2
12. 6.7
13. 0.5
14. 1.3
15. 4.31
16. 9.43
17. 6.2
18. 3.215
19. 5.58
20. 0.098
21. 0.15
22. 2.6007
23. yes; The long division is correct.
24. no; The quotient should be 0.086.

Concepts, Skills, & Problem Solving

25. $29.95

26. the 12-pack; One box costs $0.74 in the 4-pack, $0.72 in the 12-pack, and $0.73 in the 24-pack.

27. 12
28. 9
29. 52.1
30. 0.08
31. 0.8
32. 6.2
33. 11.7
34. 2.23
35. 8.3
36. 2.7
37. 0.23
38. 12.25
39. 352.5
40. 400
41. 7200
42. 460
43. 40
44. 13.6
45. 12.5
46. 31,250
47. 180
48. 66.8
49. 48
50. 272
51. 9.60
52. 1.33
53. 6.04
54. 12.21

55. no; $0.32\overline{)146.4} \longrightarrow 32\overline{)14{,}640}$

56. 7.945
57. 1.62
58. 25.2
59. 10.12
60. 2.35
61. 8.046
62. 4.96
63. 7.1
64. 47.376
65. 4.8 ft
66. 850

67. =; Both quotients can be written as $666 \div 74$.

68. >; The first quotient has a greater dividend and lesser divisor.

69. <; The second quotient has a lesser divisor.

70. <; The second quotient can be written as $756 \div 63$, which has a greater dividend than the first quotient.

Common Errors

- **Exercises 27–54** Students may try to multiply by a power of 10 to make the dividend a whole number, instead of the divisor. While this method will still provide the same answer, it is easier for students to divide when the divisor is the smallest whole number possible. Remind them to multiply by whatever power of 10 will make the divisor a whole number.
- **Exercises 27–54** Some students may forget to multiply the dividend by the same multiple of 10 that they used to multiply the divisor. Remind them that they must multiply both numbers in the problem by the same multiple of 10.
- **Exercises 27–54** Remind students that they should check their answers by multiplying the quotient by the divisor and confirm that the product is equal to the dividend.

25. MP **PROBLEM SOLVING** You buy the same pair of pants in 3 different colors for \$89.85. How much does each pair of pants cost?

26. MP **REASONING** Which pack of fruit punch is the best buy? Explain.

DIVIDING DECIMALS **Divide. Check your answer.**

27. $2.1\overline{)25.2}$
28. $3.8\overline{)34.2}$
29. $36.47 \div 0.7$
30. $0.984 \div 12.3$
31. $6.64 \div 8.3$
32. $83.266 \div 13.43$
33. $0.09\overline{)1.053}$
34. $35.903 \div 16.1$
35. $0.996 \div 0.12$
36. $4.63\overline{)12.501}$
37. $0.005\overline{)0.00115}$
38. $56.7175 \div 4.63$
39. $4.23 \div 0.012$
40. $0.52 \div 0.0013$
41. $95.04 \div 0.0132$
42. $32.2 \div 0.07$
43. $1.37\overline{)54.8}$
44. $44.2 \div 3.25$
45. $4.04\overline{)50.5}$
46. $250 \div 0.008$
47. $11.16 \div 0.062$
48. $12.5\overline{)835}$
49. $597.6 \div 12.45$
50. $0.435\overline{)118.32}$

DIVIDING DECIMALS **Divide. Round to the nearest hundredth.**

51. $80.89 \div 8.425$
52. $0.8 \div 0.6$
53. $38.9 \div 6.44$
54. $11.6 \div 0.95$

55. MP **YOU BE THE TEACHER** Your friend rewrites the problem. Is your friend correct? Explain your reasoning.

ORDER OF OPERATIONS **Evaluate the expression.**

56. $7.68 + 3.18 \div 12$
57. $10.56 \div 3 - 1.9$
58. $19.6 \div 7 \times 9$
59. $5.5 \times 16.56 \div 9$
60. $35.25 \div 5 \div 3$
61. $13.41 \times (5.4 \div 9)$
62. $6.2 \cdot (5.16 \div 6.45)$
63. $132.06 \div (4^2 + 2.6)$
64. $4.8[23.9841 \div (1.16 + 1.27)]$

65. MP **MODELING REAL LIFE** A person's running stride is about 1.14 times the person's height. Your friend's stride is 5.472 feet. How tall is your friend?

66. MP **PROBLEM SOLVING** You have 3.4 gigabytes available on your tablet. A song is about 0.004 gigabyte. How many songs can you download onto your tablet?

MP **REASONING** **Without finding the quotient, copy and complete the statement using <, >, or =. Explain your reasoning.**

67. $6.66 \div 0.74$ ☐ $66.6 \div 7.4$
68. $32.2 \div 0.7$ ☐ $3.22 \div 7$
69. $160.72 \div 16.4$ ☐ $160.72 \div 1.64$
70. $75.6 \div 63$ ☐ $7.56 \div 0.63$

71. **DIG DEEPER!** The table shows the top three times in a swimming event at the Summer Olympics. The event consists of a team of four women swimming 100 meters each.

Women's 4 × 100 Freestyle Relay		
Medal	**Country**	**Time (seconds)**
Gold	Australia	210.65
Silver	United States	211.89
Bronze	Canada	212.89

a. Suppose the times of all four swimmers on each team were the same. For each team, how much time does it take a swimmer to swim 100 meters?

b. Suppose each U.S. swimmer completed 100 meters a quarter second faster. Would the U.S. team have won the gold medal? Explain your reasoning.

72. **MP PROBLEM SOLVING** To approximate the number of bees in a hive, multiply the number of bees that leave the hive in one minute by 3 and divide by 0.014. You count 25 bees leaving a hive in one minute. How many bees are in the hive?

73. **MP PROBLEM SOLVING** You are saving money to buy a new bicycle that costs \$155.75. You have \$30 and plan to save \$5 each week. Your aunt decides to give you an additional \$10 each week.

a. How many weeks will you have to save until you have enough money to buy the bicycle?

b. How many more weeks would you have to save to buy a new bicycle that costs \$203.89? Explain how you found your answer.

Applesauce	
3.9-ounce bowl	\$0.52
24-ounce jar	\$2.63

74. **MP PRECISION** A store sells applesauce in two sizes.

a. How many bowls of applesauce fit in a jar? Round your answer to the nearest hundredth.

b. Explain two ways to find the better buy.

c. Which is the better buy?

75. **GEOMETRY** The large rectangle's dimensions are three times the dimensions of the small rectangle.

23.1 ft
49.2 ft

a. How many times greater is the perimeter of the large rectangle than the perimeter of the small rectangle?

b. How many times greater is the area of the large rectangle than the area of the small rectangle?

c. Are the answers to parts (a) and (b) the same? Explain why or why not.

d. What happens in parts (a) and (b) if the dimensions of the large rectangle are two times the dimensions of the small rectangle?

Mini-Assessment

Divide.

1. 6.8 ÷ 2 3.4
2. 0.963 ÷ 3 0.321
3. 7.6 ÷ 3.2 2.375
4. 15.47 ÷ 2.6 5.95
5. Each box of gourmet popcorn for a school fundraiser costs $6.75. The total amount received from the popcorn sale is $4893.75. How many boxes of popcorn were sold? 725

Section Resources

Surface Level	Deep Level
Resources by Chapter • Extra Practice • Reteach • Puzzle Time Student Journal • Self-Assessment • Practice Differentiating the Lesson Tutorial Videos Skills Review Handbook Skills Trainer	Resources by Chapter • Enrichment and Extension Graphic Organizers Dynamic Assessment System • Section Practice
Transfer Level	
Dynamic Assessment System • End-of-Chapter Quiz	Assessment Book • End-of-Chapter Quiz

Concepts, Skills, & Problem Solving

71. **a.** Australia: 52.6625 sec
United States: 52.9725 sec
Canada: 53.2225 sec

b. no; The team total would have been 210.89 seconds.

72. about 5357

73. **a.** 9

b. 3; *Sample answer:* Use the same method as part (a) to find the total number of weeks needed, then subtract the number of weeks in part (a).

74. **a.** about 6.15

b. *Sample answer:* Compare the cost of 6.15 bowls to the cost of 1 jar; Find the cost per ounce for each container.

c. the jar

75. **a.** 3

b. 9

c. no; The perimeter is measured in feet and the area is measured in square feet.

d. perimeter: 2 times greater; area: 4 times greater

Skills Needed

Exercise 1

- Converting Measures within the Customary System
- Dividing Whole Numbers
- Multiplying Whole Numbers

Exercise 2

- Finding the LCM
- Multiplying Decimals and Whole Numbers

Exercise 3

- Multiplying Fractions and Mixed Numbers
- Writing Expressions

ELL Support

Remind students that a gallon is a part of the U.S. customary system for liquid measurement, and not the metric system. A gallon is approximately 3.79 liters. Explain that there are 4 quarts, 8 pints, 16 cups, or 128 fluid ounces in a gallon.

Using the Problem-Solving Plan

1. 64 glasses
2. 3.6 h
3. $132\frac{31}{32}$ ft^2;

$$10 \times 14 - 2\left(\frac{15}{8}\right)^2 = 140 - 7\frac{1}{31}$$
$$= 132\frac{31}{32}$$

Performance Task

The *STEAM Video Performance Task* provides the opportunity for additional enrichment and greater depth of knowledge as students explore the mathematics of the chapter within a context tied to the chapter STEAM Video. The performance task and a detailed scoring rubric are provided at *BigIdeasMath.com.*

Laurie's Notes

Scaffolding Instruction

- The goal of this lesson is to help students become more comfortable with problem solving. These exercises combine operations with fractions and decimals with prior skills from the previous chapter and other courses. The solution for Exercise 1 is worked out below to help you guide students through the problem-solving plan. Use the remaining class time to have students work on the other exercises.
- **Emerging:** The goal for these students is to feel comfortable with the problem-solving plan. Allow students to work in pairs to write the beginning steps of the problem-solving plan for Exercise 2. Keep in mind that some students may only be ready to do the first step.
- **Proficient:** Students may be able to work independently or in pairs to complete Exercises 2 and 3.
- Visit each pair to review their plan for each problem. Ask students to describe their plans.

Using the Problem-Solving Plan

Exercise 1

 **Understand the problem.** You know the capacities of the water jug and the glass. You are asked to determine how many glasses the water jug can fill.

 **Make a plan.** First, use what you know about converting measures to find the number of fluid ounces in 5 gallons. Then divide this amount by the capacity of the glass to find the number of glasses that can be filled.

 **Solve and check.** Use the plan to solve the problem. Then check your solution.

- Convert 5 gallons to fluid ounces.
  5 gallons = 5×1 gallon and there are 4 quarts in a gallon, so
  5×4 quarts = 20 quarts.
  20 quarts = 20×1 quart and there are 2 pints in a quart, so
  20×2 pints = 40 pints.
  40 pints = 40×1 pint and there are 2 cups in a pint, so
  40×2 cups = 80 cups.
  80 cups = 80×1 cup and there are 8 fluid ounces in a cup, so
  80×8 fluid ounces = 640 fluid ounces.
- Find the number of glasses that can be filled.
  Each glass holds 10 fluid ounces, so the number of glasses that can be filled is 640 fluid ounces $\div$ 10 fluid ounces = 64.
  So, 64 glasses can be completely filled before you need to change the water jug again.
- **Check:** Verify the operations performed using the inverse relationship between multiplication and division.
  $640 \div 10 = 64$ because $64 \times 10 = 640$. ✓
  $80 \times 8 = 640$ because $640 \div 8 = 80$. ✓
  $40 \times 2 = 80$ because $80 \div 2 = 40$. ✓
  $20 \times 2 = 40$ because $40 \div 2 = 20$. ✓
  $5 \times 4 = 20$ because $20 \div 4 = 5$. ✓

Connecting Concepts

Using the Problem-Solving Plan

1. You change the water jug on the watercooler. How many glasses can be completely filled before you need to change the water jug again?

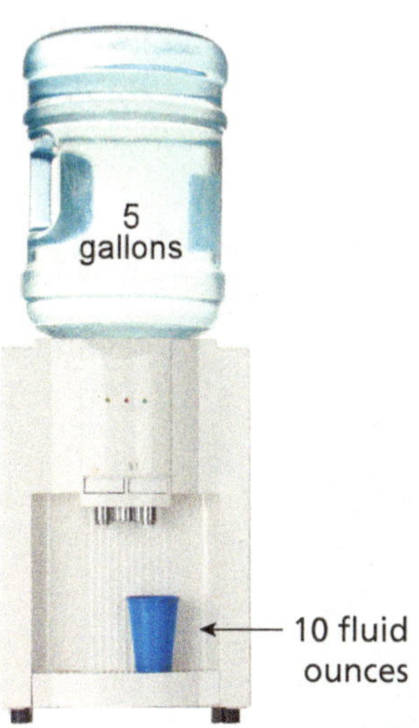

Understand the problem. You know the capacities of the water jug and the glass. You are asked to determine how many glasses the water jug can fill.

Make a plan. First, use what you know about converting measures to find the number of fluid ounces in 5 gallons. Then divide this amount by the capacity of the glass to find the number of glasses that can be filled.

Solve and check. Use the plan to solve the problem. Then check your solution.

2. Two ferries just departed from their docks at the same time. Ferry A departs from its dock every 1.2 hours. Ferry B departs from its dock every 1.8 hours. How long will it be until both ferries depart from their docks at the same time again?

3. You want to paint the ceiling of your bedroom. The ceiling has two square skylights as shown. Each skylight has a side length of $1\frac{7}{8}$ feet. How many square feet will you paint? Justify your answer.

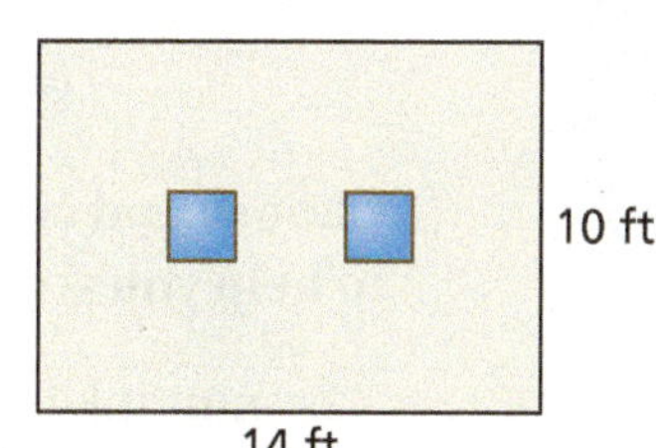

Performance Task

Space Explorers

At the beginning of this chapter, you watched a STEAM video called "Space is Big." You are now ready to complete the performance task for this video, available at ***BigIdeasMath.com***. Be sure to use the problem-solving plan as you work through the performance task.

2 Chapter Review

Go to *BigIdeasMath.com* to download blank graphic organizers.

Review Vocabulary

Write the definition and give an example of each vocabulary term.

reciprocals, *p. 54* multiplicative inverses, *p. 54*

Graphic Organizers

You can use a **Summary Triangle** to explain a concept. Here is an example of a Summary Triangle for ***dividing fractions***.

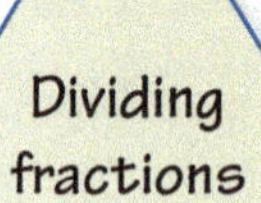

Dividing fractions

Procedure: To divide a number by a fraction, multiply the number by the reciprocal of the fraction.

Algebra: $\frac{a}{b} \div \frac{c}{d} = \frac{a}{b} \cdot \frac{d}{c} = \frac{a \cdot d}{b \cdot c}$, where b, c, and $d \neq 0$

Example: $\frac{1}{5} \div \frac{3}{4} = \frac{1}{5} \times \frac{4}{3} = \frac{1 \times 4}{5 \times 3} = \frac{4}{15}$

Choose and complete a graphic organizer to help you study the concept.

1. multiplying fractions
2. multiplying mixed numbers
3. reciprocals
4. dividing mixed numbers
5. adding and subtracting decimals
6. multiplying decimals by decimals
7. dividing whole numbers
8. dividing decimals by decimals

"I finished my Summary Triangle about characteristics of igloos. I built one to use as my dog house. I'm calling it a dog-gloo."

Review Vocabulary

- As a review of the chapter vocabulary, have students revisit the vocabulary section in their *Student Journals* to fill in any missing definitions and record examples of each term.

Graphic Organizers

Sample answers:

1.

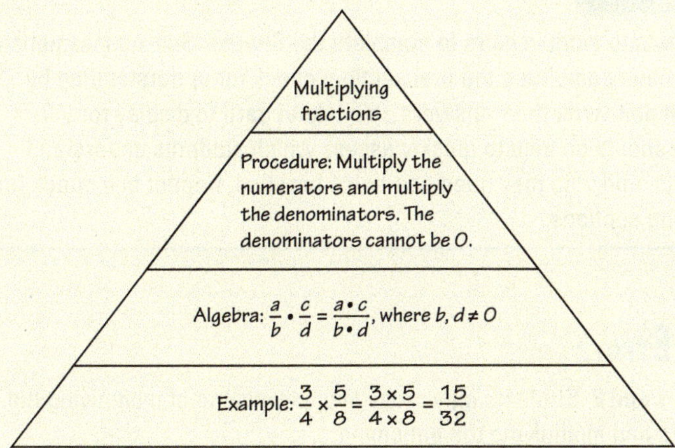

2.

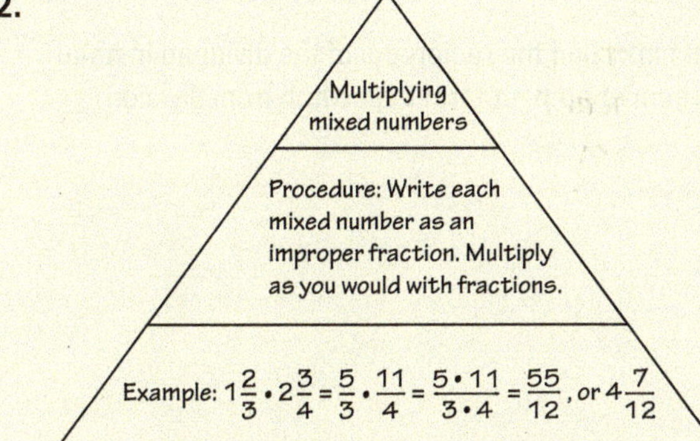

3.

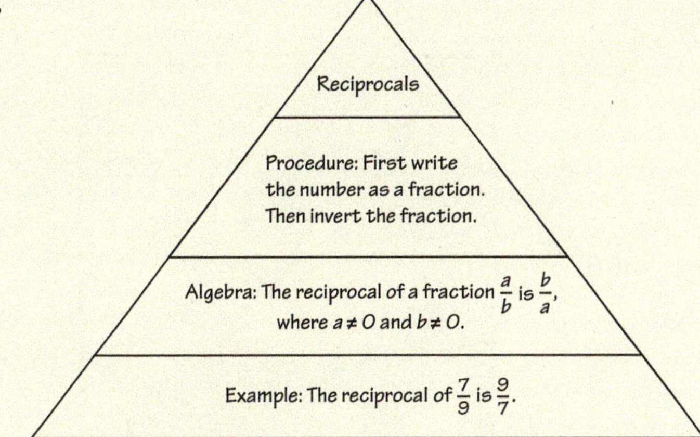

4–8. Answers at *BigIdeasMath.com*

List of Organizers

Available at *BigIdeasMath.com*

Definition and Example Chart

Example and Non-Example Chart

Four Square

Information Frame

Summary Triangle

About this Organizer

A **Summary Triangle** can be used to explain a concept. Typically, the Summary Triangle is divided into 3 or 4 parts. Students write the concept in the top part. Then students write related categories in the middle part(s). Related categories may include: procedure, explanation, description, definition, theorem, or formula. In the bottom part, students write an example to illustrate the concept. A Summary Triangle can be used as an assessment tool, in which students complete the missing parts. Students may also place their Summary Triangles on note cards to use as a quick study reference.

Chapter Self-Assessment

1. $\frac{16}{99}$
2. $\frac{6}{25}$
3. $12\frac{4}{15}$
4. $1\frac{17}{63}$
5. *Sample answer:* $\frac{7}{8}, \frac{3}{4}$
6. 32 yd
7. 24 min
8. $\frac{9}{10}$
9. $\frac{1}{20}$
10. 15
11. $2\frac{26}{27}$
12. 15
13. *Sample answer:* $\frac{2}{5}, \frac{9}{14}$

Chapter Self-Assessment

The Success Criteria Self-Assessment chart can be found in the *Student Journal* or online at *BigIdeasMath.com*.

ELL Support

Allow students to work in pairs to complete the Chapter Self-Assessment. Once pairs have completed the first section, check for understanding by having each pair write their answers on a whiteboard to display for your review. You should be able to quickly assess which students understand the concepts, and who may need additional practice. Repeat this check for the remaining sections.

Common Errors

- **Exercises 1 and 2** Students may cross multiply instead of multiplying the numerators and multiplying the denominators.
- **Exercises 3 and 4** Students may not change the mixed numbers into improper fractions.
- **Exercises 8–11** Students may find the reciprocal of the dividend instead of the divisor, the reciprocal of both, or forget to switch from division to multiplication.

Chapter Self-Assessment

As you complete the exercises, use the scale below to rate your understanding of the success criteria in your journal.

1	2	3	4
I do not understand.	I can do it with help.	I can do it on my own.	I can teach someone else.

2.1 Multiplying Fractions (pp. 45–52)

Learning Target: Find products involving fractions and mixed numbers.

Multiply. Write the answer in simplest form.

1. $\frac{2}{9} \times \frac{8}{11}$

2. $\frac{3}{10} \cdot \frac{4}{5}$

3. $2\frac{3}{10} \times 5\frac{1}{3}$

4. $\frac{2}{7} \times 4\frac{4}{9}$

5. Write two fractions whose product is $\frac{21}{32}$.

6. A costume designer needs to make 12 costumes for the school play. Each costume requires $2\frac{2}{3}$ yards of fabric. How many yards of fabric does the costume designer need to make all the costumes?

7. You spend $\frac{4}{5}$ of an hour on your homework. You spend $\frac{1}{2}$ of that time working on your science homework. How many minutes do you spend working on science homework?

2.2 Dividing Fractions (pp. 53–60)

Learning Target: Compute quotients of fractions and solve problems involving division by fractions.

Divide. Write the answer in simplest form.

8. $\frac{3}{4} \div \frac{5}{6}$

9. $\frac{2}{5} \div 8$

10. $5 \div \frac{1}{3}$

11. $\frac{8}{9} \div \frac{3}{10}$

12. A box contains 10 cups of pancake mix. You use $\frac{2}{3}$ cup each time you make pancakes. How many times can you make pancakes?

13. Write two fractions whose quotient is $\frac{28}{45}$.

2.3 Dividing Mixed Numbers (pp. 61–66)

Learning Target: Compute quotients with mixed numbers and solve problems involving division with mixed numbers.

Divide. Write the answer in simplest form.

14. $1\frac{2}{5} \div \frac{4}{7}$

15. $5\frac{5}{8} \div 3$

16. $5 \div 2\frac{6}{7}$

17. $4\frac{1}{8} \div 2\frac{1}{4}$

18. Evaluate $5\frac{5}{7} \div 1\frac{3}{5} \cdot 4\frac{2}{3}$. Write the answer in simplest form.

19. You have $23\frac{1}{2}$ pounds of blueberries to store in freezer bags. Each bag holds $3\frac{3}{4}$ pounds of blueberries. What is the minimum number of freezer bags needed to store all the blueberries?

20. A squirrel feeder holds $4\frac{1}{2}$ cups of seeds. Another squirrel feeder holds $6\frac{7}{8}$ cups of seeds. One scoop of seeds is $1\frac{5}{8}$ cups. How many scoops of seeds do you need to fill both squirrel feeders?

2.4 Adding and Subtracting Decimals (pp. 67–72)

Learning Target: Add and subtract decimals and solve problems involving addition and subtraction of decimals.

Add.

21. $3.78 + 8.94$

22. $19.89 + 4.372$

23. $24.916 + 17.385$

Subtract.

24. $7.638 - 2.365$

25. $14.21 - 4.103$

26. $5.467 - 2.736$

27. Write three decimals that have a sum of 10.806.

28. To make fuel for the main engines of a space shuttle, 102,619.377 kilograms of liquid hydrogen and 616,496.4409 kilograms of liquid oxygen are mixed together in the external tank. How much fuel is stored in the external tank?

Common Errors

- **Exercises 14–20** Students may not change the mixed numbers into improper fractions.
- **Exercise 18** Students may evaluate the multiplication before the division. Remind them that multiplication and division are performed from left to right.
- **Exercises 22, 25, and 28** Students may forget to insert zeros as placeholders. Remind them that each number added or subtracted needs to have the same number of decimal places to line up place values.

Chapter Self-Assessment

14. $2\frac{9}{20}$

15. $1\frac{7}{8}$

16. $1\frac{3}{4}$

17. $1\frac{5}{6}$

18. $16\frac{2}{3}$

19. 7

20. 7

21. 12.72

22. 24.262

23. 42.301

24. 5.273

25. 10.107

26. 2.731

27. *Sample answer:* 2.2, 4.4, 4.206

28. 719,115.8179 kg

Chapter Self-Assessment

29. 2067.746

30. 76.08425

31. 0.012444

32. 45.9848

33. 5.08 cm

34. 192

35. $25\frac{6}{203}$

36. $134\frac{7}{8}$

37. 6; 48

38. 15

39. 0.083

40. 25

41. 5.75

42. 12.3

43. 7

Common Errors

- **Exercises 30 and 31** Students may not count the decimal places of both decimal factors.
- **Exercises 39–41** Students may divide without placing the decimal point in the quotient.

Chapter Resources

Surface Level	Deep Level
Resources by Chapter • Extra Practice • Reteach • Puzzle Time Student Journal • Practice • Chapter Self-Assessment Differentiating the Lesson Tutorial Videos Skills Review Handbook Skills Trainer Game Library	Resources by Chapter • Enrichment and Extension Graphic Organizers Game Library
Transfer Level	
STEAM Video Dynamic Assessment System • Chapter Test	Assessment Book • Chapter Tests A and B • Alternative Assessment • STEAM Performance Task

2.5 Multiplying Decimals (pp. 73–80)

Learning Target: Multiply decimals and solve problems involving multiplication of decimals.

Multiply. Use estimation to check your answer.

29. 26.174×79

30. 9.475×8.03

31. 0.051×0.244

32. Evaluate $3.76(2.43 + 9.8)$.

33. Hair grows about 1.27 centimeters each month. How much does hair grow in 4 months?

2.6 Dividing Whole Numbers (pp. 81–86)

Learning Target: Divide whole numbers and solve problems involving division of whole numbers.

Divide. Use estimation to check your answer.

34. $7296 \div 38$

35. $5081 \div 203$

36. $\frac{17{,}264}{128}$

37. Your local varsity basketball team offers bus transportation for a playoff game. Each bus holds 56 people. A total of 328 people sign up. All buses are full except for the last bus. How many buses are used? How many people are in the last bus?

38. You have 600 elastic bands to make railroad bracelets. How many complete bracelets can you make?

Railroad Bracelet Supplies
- loom
- hook
- clip
- 28 elastic bands for outer rails
- 10 elastic bands for inner track

2.7 Dividing Decimals (pp. 87–94)

Learning Target: Divide decimals and solve problems involving division of decimals.

Divide. Check your answer.

39. $0.498 \div 6$

40. $8.9 \div 0.356$

41. $21.85 \div 3.8$

42. Evaluate $\frac{14.075 + 24.67}{3.15}$.

43. Your beginning balance on your lunch account is \$42. You buy lunch for \$1.80 every day and sometimes buy a snack for \$0.85. After 20 days, you have a balance of \$0.05. How many snacks did you buy?

Practice Test

Evaluate the expression. Write the answer in simplest form.

1. $5.138 + 2.624$
2. $\frac{5}{6} \div \frac{10}{21}$
3. $0.25\overline{)5.46}$
4. $\frac{9}{16} \times \frac{2}{3}$
5. $8\frac{3}{4} \div 2\frac{7}{8}$
6. 4.87×7.23
7. $1875 \div 125$
8. $10 \div \frac{2}{5}$
9. $57.82 \div 0.784$
10. $5.316 - 1.942$
11. 6.729×8.3
12. $\frac{13{,}376}{248}$

13. On a road trip, you notice that the gas tank is $\frac{1}{4}$ full. The gas tank can hold 18 gallons, and the vehicle averages 22 miles per gallon. Will you make it to your destination 110 miles away before you run out of gas? Explain.

14. For a diving event, the highest and the lowest of seven scores are discarded. Next, the total of the remaining scores is multiplied by the degree of difficulty of the dive. That value is then multiplied by 0.6 to determine the final score. Find the final score for the dive.

15. You are cutting as many $20\frac{1}{2}$-inch pieces from the board to make ladder steps for a tree fort. How many steps can you make? How much wood is left over?

120 in.

$20\frac{1}{2}$ in.

16. You spend $2\frac{1}{2}$ hours online. You spend $\frac{1}{5}$ of that time writing a blog. How long do you spend writing your blog?

17. You and a friend take pictures at a motocross event. Your camera can take 24 pictures in 3.75 seconds. Your friend's camera can take 36 pictures in 4.5 seconds. Evaluate the expression $(36 \div 4.5) \div (24 \div 3.75)$ to find how many times faster your friend's camera is than your camera.

Practice Test Item References

Practice Test Questions	Section to Review
4, 13, 16	2.1
2, 8	2.2
5, 15	2.3
1, 10	2.4
6, 11, 14	2.5
7, 12	2.6
3, 9, 17	2.7

Test-Taking Strategies

Remind students to quickly look over the entire test before they start so that they can budget their time. When students hurry, they may make unintentional mistakes, such as writing a mixed number as an improper fraction incorrectly or inverting the wrong fraction in a division problem. Have them use the **Stop** and **Think** strategy before they write their answers.

Common Errors

- **Exercises 2, 5, and 8** Students might find the reciprocal of the dividend instead of the divisor.
- **Exercises 3 and 9** Students may place the decimal point in the wrong place. Encourage them to use grid paper to keep their work organized. Remind students to check their answers by multiplying.
- **Exercises 3 and 9** Students may forget to multiply the dividend by the same multiple of 10 that they used to multiply the divisor. Remind them that they must multiply *both* numbers by the same multiple of 10.
- **Exercise 5** Students might forget to change the mixed numbers to improper fractions.
- **Exercises 6 and 11** Students may only count the number of decimal places in one number instead of two. Remind them that they need to count *both* sets of decimal places. Stress estimation as a check for reasonableness.

Practice Test

1. 7.762
2. $1\frac{3}{4}$
3. 21.84
4. $\frac{3}{8}$
5. $3\frac{1}{23}$
6. 35.2101
7. 15
8. 25
9. 73.75
10. 3.374
11. 55.8507
12. $53\frac{29}{31}$
13. no; You can travel: $\frac{1}{4} \times 18 \times 22 = 99$ miles.
14. 73.47
15. 5; $17\frac{1}{2}$ in.
16. $\frac{1}{2}$ h
17. 1.25

Test-Taking Strategies

Available at *BigIdeasMath.com*

After Answering Easy Questions, Relax

Answer Easy Questions First

Estimate the Answer

Read All Choices before Answering

Read Question before Answering

Solve Directly or Eliminate Choices

Solve Problem before Looking at Choices

Use Intelligent Guessing

Work Backwards

About this Strategy

When taking a multiple-choice test, be sure to read each question carefully and thoroughly. After reading the question, estimate the answer before trying to solve it.

Cumulative Practice

1. B
2. 24
3. F
4. B
5. I

Item Analysis

1. **A.** The student does not follow the correct order of operations; multiplying 3 and 2 before evaluating the power.

   B. Correct answer

   C. The student does not follow the correct order of operations; subtracting before multiplying.

   D. The student does not follow the correct order of operations; performing the operations from left to right.

2. **Gridded Response:** Correct answer: 24

   Common error: The student finds the LCM of 48 and 120 is 240, instead of finding the GCF of 48 and 120.

3. **F.** Correct answer

   G. The student does not subtract correctly in the tenths place.

   H. The student subtracts the 3 from the 4 in the hundredths place, instead of subtracting 4 from 13, and does not borrow from the ones place.

   I. The student does not subtract correctly in the tenths place and ones place.

4. **A.** The student incorrectly calculates the expression by multiplying the numerators and multiplying the denominators.

   B. Correct answer

   C. The student incorrectly calculates the expression by inverting the dividend instead of the divisor.

   D. The student incorrectly calculates the expression by inverting both the divisor and the dividend.

5. **F.** The student finds the total length of each streamer, instead of the numbers of streamers needed.

   G. The student finds a common multiple but not the *least* common multiple.

   H. The student switches the number of black streamers with the number of orange streamers.

   I. Correct answer

2 Cumulative Practice

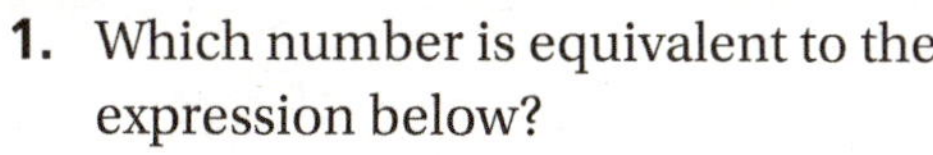

Test-Taking Strategy
Estimate the Answer

$5\frac{1}{2}$ treats are divided evenly between you and Fluffy. How many do you get?
(A) $1\frac{1}{2}$ (B) $2\frac{3}{4}$ (C) $5\frac{1}{2}$ (D) 11

Fluffy: 1/2
Me: Five

"Using estimation you can see that the answer is about 3. So, you should choose B."

1. Which number is equivalent to the expression below?

$$6 \times 8 - 2 \times 3^2$$

A. 12 **B.** 30

C. 324 **D.** 414

2. What is the greatest common factor of 48 and 120?

3. Which number is equivalent to $5.139 - 2.64$?

F. 2.499 **G.** 2.599

H. 3.519 **I.** 3.599

4. Which number is equivalent to $\frac{4}{9} \div \frac{5}{7}$?

A. $\frac{20}{63}$ **B.** $\frac{28}{45}$

C. $\frac{45}{28}$ **D.** $\frac{63}{20}$

5. You buy orange and black streamers for a party. The orange streamers are 9 feet long, and the black streamers are 12 feet long. What are the least numbers of streamers you should buy in order for the total length of the orange streamers to be the same as the total length of the black streamers?

F. 36 orange streamers and 36 black streamers

G. 12 orange streamers and 9 black streamers

H. 3 orange streamers and 4 black streamers

I. 4 orange streamers and 3 black streamers

6. Which number is a prime factor of 572?

A. 4 B. 7

C. 13 D. 22

7. Which number is equivalent to $7059 \div 301$?

F. 23 G. $23\frac{136}{7059}$

H. $23\frac{136}{301}$ I. 136

8. A square wall tile has side lengths of 4 inches. You use 360 of the tiles. What is the area of the wall covered by the tiles?

A. 16 in.^{2} B. 360 in.^{2}

C. 1440 in.^{2} D. 5760 in.^{2}

9. Which expression is equivalent to a perfect square?

F. $3 + 2^2 \times 7$ G. $34 + 18 \div 3^2$

H. $(80 + 4) \div 4$ I. $3^2 + 6 \times 5 \div 3$

10. What is the missing denominator in the expression below?

$$\frac{4}{8} \div \frac{2}{\square} = \frac{3}{4}$$

A. 1 B. 2

C. 3 D. 8

11. What is 4.56×0.7?

Item Analysis (continued)

6. **A.** The student finds a factor of 572 but not a *prime* factor.

   B. The student identifies 7 as a prime number, but it is not a factor of 572.

   C. Correct answer

   D. The student finds a factor of 572 but not a *prime* factor.

7. **F.** The student does not include the fractional part of the answer.

   G. The student incorrectly uses the dividend when writing the fractional part of the answer.

   H. Correct answer

   I. The student confuses the remainder with the quotient.

8. **A.** The student finds the area of one tile, instead of the area of the wall.

   B. The student finds the number of tiles.

   C. The student multiplies the side length of one tile by the number of tiles, instead of multiplying the area of one tile by the number of tiles.

   D. Correct answer

9. **F.** The student does not follow the correct order of operations; performing the addition before the multiplication to get 49 instead of 31.

   G. Correct answer

   H. The student does not follow the correct order of operations; performing the division before calculating the expression inside the parentheses to get 81 instead of 21.

   I. The student does not follow the correct order of operations; performing the addition before the multiplication to get 25 instead of 19.

10. **A.** The student incorrectly inverts the dividend, and then reasons that 4 times 1 equals 4.

    B. The student ignores the fractions, and then reasons that 8 divided by 2 is 4.

    C. Correct answer

    D. The student uses the same denominator for the divisor as the dividend.

11. **Gridded Response:** Correct answer: 3.192

    Common error: The student only counts the number of decimal places in the first number and gets 31.92.

Cumulative Practice

6. C
7. H
8. D
9. G
10. C
11. 3.192

Cumulative Practice

12. F

13. C

14. *Part A* $112\frac{3}{4}$ in.

Part B $5\frac{5}{9}$

15. G

Item Analysis (continued)

12. **F.** Correct answer

G. The student finds the differences between the dimensions of the rectangles, and then multiplies those differences.

H. The student subtracts the area of the small rectangle from the area of the large rectangle.

I. The student multiplies the areas of the small and large rectangles.

13. **A.** The student incorrectly interprets 5 as a factor 4 times to be the product of 5 and 4.

B. The student switches the base and the exponent.

C. Correct answer

D. The student incorrectly counts five factors of 5 instead of four.

14. **4 points** The student's work and explanations demonstrate a thorough understanding of multiplying and dividing mixed numbers and whole numbers. The student calculates the length and width of the walkway correctly to get $112\frac{3}{4}$ inches for Part A and $5\frac{5}{9}$ times as long for Part B. The student shows accurate, complete work for both parts and provides clear and complete explanations.

3 points The student's work and explanations demonstrate an essential but less than thorough understanding of multiplying and dividing mixed numbers and whole numbers.

2 points The student's work and explanations demonstrate a partial but limited understanding of multiplying and dividing mixed numbers and whole numbers.

1 point The student's work and explanations demonstrate a very limited understanding of multiplying and dividing mixed numbers and whole numbers.

0 points The student provides no response, a completely incorrect or incomprehensible response, or a response that demonstrates insufficient understanding of multiplying and dividing mixed numbers and whole numbers.

15. **F.** The student incorrectly writes the mixed number $6\frac{7}{8}$ as $\frac{48}{8}$.

G. Correct answer

H. The student divides $6\frac{7}{8}$ by 3 instead of dividing by 30.

I. The student multiplies $6\frac{7}{8}$ by 30 instead of dividing.

12. The area of the large rectangle is how many times the area of the small rectangle?

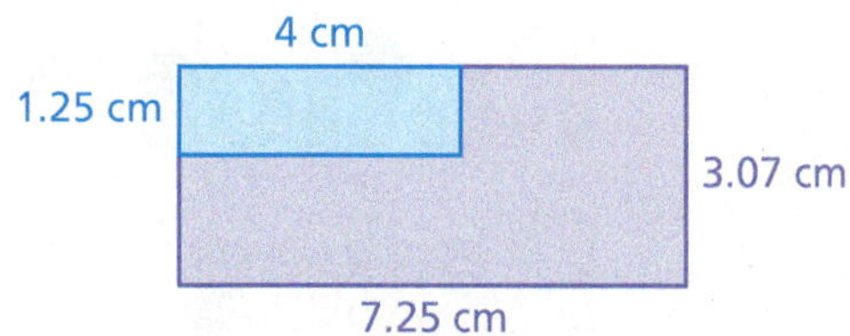

F. 4.4515 **G.** 5.915

H. 17.2575 **I.** 111.2875

13. Which expression is equivalent to $5 \times 5 \times 5 \times 5$?

A. 5×4 **B.** 4^5

C. 5^4 **D.** 5^5

14. A walkway is built using identical concrete blocks.

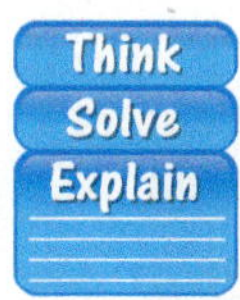

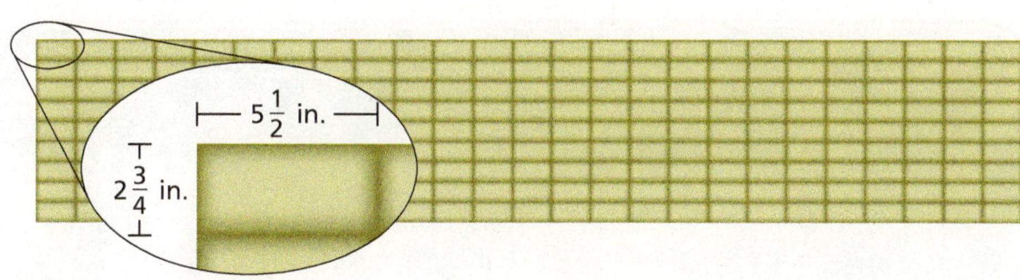

Part A How much longer, in inches, is the length of the walkway than the width of the walkway? Show your work and explain your reasoning.

Part B How many times longer is the length of the walkway than the width of the walkway? Show your work and explain your reasoning.

15. A meteoroid moving at a constant speed travels $6\frac{7}{8}$ miles in 30 seconds. How far does the meteoroid travel in 1 second?

F. $\frac{1}{5}$ mile **G.** $\frac{11}{48}$ mile

H. $2\frac{7}{24}$ miles **I.** $206\frac{1}{4}$ miles

3 Ratios and Rates

Chapter Learning Target:
Understand ratios.

Chapter Success Criteria:

- I can write and interpret ratios.
- I can name ratios equivalent to a given ratio.
- I can solve a problem using ratios.
- I can convert units of measure using ratio reasoning.

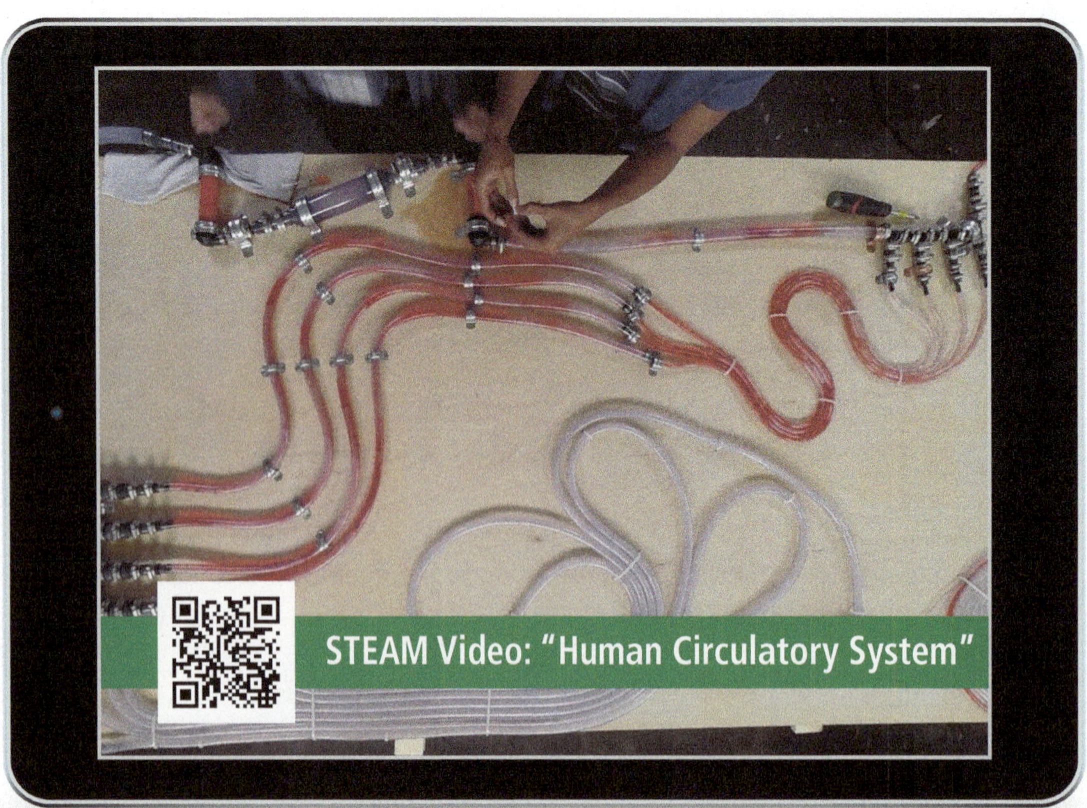

Laurie's Notes

Chapter 3 Overview

Students need time to think and discuss with their peers in a supportive learning environment. Be sure to model the expectation that all students engage in their learning, that errors lead to learning, and explanations help students to assess their understanding of the concepts.

A major focus of this course is the study of ratios and rates. In studying these topics, it is natural to make connections to whole-number multiplication and division. In this chapter, students have the opportunity to review and become more confident with these operations.

This chapter begins with introductory skills associated with writing and representing ratios. Fractional notation is purposely avoided. Instead, the number $\frac{a}{b}$ is referred to as the value of the ratio $a : b$. Once the concept of a ratio has been introduced, equivalent ratios can be used to solve a wide variety of problems.

Students used tape diagrams in prior grades to show the relationship between numbers. For example, 13 can be decomposed into the two numbers 5 and 8. When the visual model is drawn to scale, it is called a tape diagram and can be used to find equivalent ratios. Another visual model that can be used is a double number line.

Students will also use the structure of a ratio table to find equivalent ratios, which in turn are used to solve real-life applications. In the third lesson, various operations are used to create ratio tables. Students will come to understand that in most cases a ratio table is the result of extending pairs of rows (or columns) of a multiplication table.

Once students have a good understanding of ratios, and can solve a variety of ratio problems using a tape diagram or a ratio table, rates are introduced. Students begin by graphing ratios in the first quadrant and recognizing that there is a constant rate at which the line is increasing. The connection to slope will be made in subsequent grades.

Rates, unit rates, and converting measures complete the chapter. Common applications of rates, such as miles per hour and cost per ounce, are familiar to students. Converting rates, or simply converting a measurement to a different unit, integrates prior computational skills and ratio work.

Suggested Pacing

Chapter Opener	1 Day
Section 1	3 Days
Section 2	3 Days
Section 3	3 Days
Section 4	3 Days
Section 5	3 Days
Section 6	3 Days
Connecting Concepts	1 Day
Chapter Review	1 Day
Chapter Test	1 Day
Total Chapter 3	22 Days
Year-to-Date	50 Days

Chapter Learning Target

Understand ratios.

Chapter Success Criteria

- Write and interpret ratios.
- Name ratios equivalent to a given ratio.
- Solve a problem using ratios.
- Convert units of measure using ratio reasoning.

Chapter 3 Learning Targets and Success Criteria

Section	Learning Target	Success Criteria
3.1 Ratios	Understand the concepts of ratios and equivalent ratios.	• Write and interpret ratios using appropriate notation and language. • Recognize multiplicative relationships in ratios. • Describe how to determine whether ratios are equivalent. • Name ratios equivalent to a given ratio.
3.2 Using Tape Diagrams	Use tape diagrams to model and solve ratio problems.	• Interpret tape diagrams that represent ratio relationships. • Draw tape diagrams to model ratio relationships. • Find the value of one part of a tape diagram. • Use tape diagrams to solve ratio problems.
3.3 Using Ratio Tables	Use ratio tables to represent equivalent ratios and solve ratio problems.	• Use various operations to create tables of equivalent ratios. • Use ratio tables to solve ratio problems. • Use ratio tables to compare ratios.
3.4 Graphing Ratio Relationships	Represent ratio relationships in a coordinate plane.	• Create and plot ordered pairs from a ratio relationship. • Create graphs to solve ratio problems. • Create graphs to compare ratios.
3.5 Rates and Unit Rates	Understand the concept of a unit rate and solve rate problems.	• Find unit rates. • Use unit rates to solve rate problems. • Use unit rates to compare rates.
3.6 Converting Measures	Use ratio reasoning to convert units of measure.	• Write conversion facts as unit rates. • Convert units of measure using ratio tables. • Convert units of measure using conversion factors. • Convert rates using conversion factors.

Progressions

Through the Grades		
Grade 5	**Grade 6**	**Grade 7**
• Multiply and divide decimals. • Convert standard measurement units within a measurement system.	• Understand ratios and describe ratio relationships. • Understand unit rates and rates. • Use ratio and rate reasoning to solve real-world and mathematical problems. • Compare ratios using tables. • Solve unit rate problems. • Use ratio reasoning to convert measurement units.	• Find unit rates associated with ratios of fractions, areas, and other quantities in like or different units. • Decide whether two quantities are proportional using ratio tables and graphs. • Represent proportional relationships with equations.

Through the Chapter						
Standard	**3.1**	**3.2**	**3.3**	**3.4**	**3.5**	**3.6**
6.RP.A.1 Understand the concept of a ratio and use ratio language to describe a ratio relationship between two quantities.	●	●	●	★		
6.RP.A.2 Understand the concept of a unit rate $\frac{a}{b}$ associated with a ratio $a : b$ with $b \neq 0$, and use rate language in the context of a ratio relationship.					★	
6.RP.A.3 Use ratio and rate reasoning to solve real-world and mathematical problems, e.g., by reasoning about tables of equivalent ratios, tape diagrams, double number line diagrams, or equations.	●	●	●	●	●	●
6.RP.A.3a Make tables of equivalent ratios relating quantities with whole-number measurements, find missing values in the tables, and plot the pairs of values on the coordinate plane. Use tables to compare ratios.			●	●	★	
6.RP.A.3b Solve unit rate problems including those involving unit pricing and constant speed.					★	
6.RP.A.3d Use ratio reasoning to convert measurement units; manipulate and transform units appropriately when multiplying or dividing quantities.						★

Key

▲ = preparing ★ = complete

● = learning ■ = extending

STEAM video

1. Multiply the number of minutes by 5.
2. *Sample answer:* Divide 5 by the number of times your heart beats in 1 minute.
3. *Sample answer:* Compare the amounts in the small and large veins by writing both amounts in quarts or both amounts in gallons.

Performance Task

Sample answer: The accuracy needed depends on the situation. For instance, converting units to estimate mileage of a cross-country trip does not require a great deal of accuracy. However, conversions of quantities of medications must be very accurate, and mistakes could be life-threatening.

Mathematical Practices

Students have opportunities to develop aspects of the mathematical practices throughout the chapter. Here are some examples.

1. **Make Sense of Problems and Persevere in Solving Them**
   3.2 Exercise 27, *p. 120*
2. **Reason Abstractly and Quantitatively**
   3.3 Exercise 38, *p. 128*
3. **Construct Viable Arguments and Critique the Reasoning of Others**
   3.1 Exercise 40, *p. 113*
4. **Model with Mathematics**
   3.6 Exercise 35, *p. 147*
5. **Use Appropriate Tools Strategically**
   3.6 Math Practice note, *p. 141*
6. **Attend to Precision**
   3.5 Math Practice note, *p. 135*
7. **Look for and Make Use of Structure**
   3.4 Exercise 26, *p. 134*
8. **Look for and Express Regularity in Repeated Reasoning**
   3.3 Math Practice note, *p. 124*

Laurie's Notes

STEAM Video

Before the Video

- This video discusses the human circulatory system and uses a model to demonstrate how blood is pumped through the body. It incorporates the concept of converting measures by calculating the length of tubing needed for the model.
- ? "What units of measure for length, area, and volume are you familiar with?"
- ? "Can you represent a measurement using more than one unit of measure?"

During the Video

- ? Pause the video at 1:13. The video states various measurements and a conversion factor. Ask, "What has happened in the video so far?" *Sample answer:* They have built a model of the human circulatory system. They stated that it takes the heart 1 minute to pump all 5 liters of blood through the body.
- Tell students to pay close attention to the information in the next part of the video.
- Continue to play the video until 2:30 and then pause to discuss the following questions as a class.
- ? "What are they trying to find?" The length of the tubing (in centimeters) needed for the model.
- ? "What information do they know?" They know the area of the cross section is about 0.31 square inch and the volume is about 300 cubic centimeters for the tubing representing the large arteries. They also know the formula for volume of a tube is the area of its cross section times its length.
- ? "Before calculating the length of large tubing that is needed for the model, what did they have to do with area of the cross section that was given in square inches?" They had to convert square inches to square centimeters.
- Watch the remainder of the video.

After the Video

- Have students work with a partner to answer Questions 1–3.
- As students discuss the questions, listen for an understanding of converting measures.
- If students struggle with the questions, prompt them to think about using conversion facts.
- ? "What key piece of information was needed to convert from square inches to square centimeters?" 6.45 square centimeters is approximately 1 square inch.

Performance Task

- Use this information to spark student' interest and promote thinking about real-life problems.
- ? Ask, "How accurate must conversions be in real-life situations?"
- After completing the chapter, students will have gained the knowledge needed to complete "Oops! Unit Conversion Mistakes."

STEAM Video

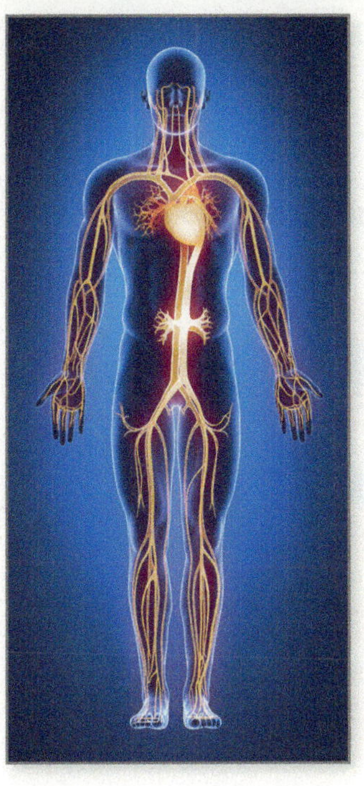

Human Circulatory System

Watch the STEAM Video "Human Circulatory System." Then answer the following questions.

1. Enid says the heart pumps about 5 liters of blood each minute. How can you find the amount of blood the heart pumps for any given number of minutes?
2. Explain how you can estimate the amount of blood your heart pumps in one heart beat.
3. The table shows the amounts of blood contained in several different types of blood vessels. How can you make meaningful comparisons of the amounts?

Vessel	Volume
Aorta and large arteries	300 mL
Small arteries	0.4 L
Small veins	2.43 qt
Large veins	0.24 gal

Performance Task

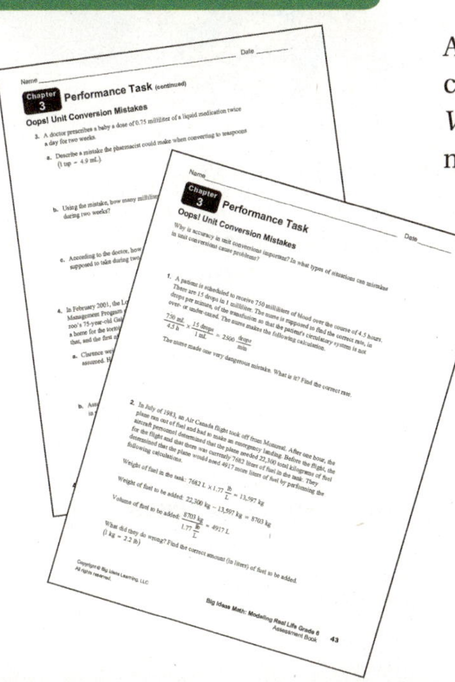

Name ______ Date ______

Chapter 3 Performance Task (continued)

Oops! Unit Conversion Mistakes

3. A doctor prescribes a baby a dose of 0.75 milliliter of a liquid medication twice a day for two weeks.

a. Describe a mistake the pharmacist could make when converting to teaspoons (1 tsp ≈ 4.9 mL).

Name ______ Date ______

Chapter 3 Performance Task

Oops! Unit Conversion Mistakes

Why is accuracy in unit conversions important? In what types of situations can mistakes in unit conversions cause problems?

1. A patient is scheduled to receive 750 milliliters of blood over the course of 4.5 hours. There are 15 drops in 1 milliliter. The nurse is supposed to find the correct rate, in drops per minute, of the transfusion so that the patient's circulatory system is not over- or under-taxed. The nurse makes the following calculation.

$\frac{750 \text{ mL}}{4.5 \text{ h}} \times \frac{15 \text{ drops}}{1 \text{ mL}} = 2500 \frac{\text{drops}}{\text{min}}$

The nurse made one very dangerous mistake. What is it? Find the correct rate.

2. In July of 1983, an Air Canada flight took off from Montreal. After one hour, the plane ran out of fuel and had to make an emergency landing. Before the flight, the aircraft personnel determined that the plane needed 22,300 total kilograms of fuel for the flight and that there was currently 7682 liters of fuel in the tank. They determined that the plane would need 4917 more liters of fuel by performing the following calculations.

Weight of fuel in the tank: $7682 \text{ L} \times 1.77 \frac{\text{lb}}{\text{L}} = 13{,}597 \text{ kg}$

Weight of fuel to be added: $22{,}300 \text{ kg} - 13{,}597 \text{ kg} = 8703 \text{ kg}$

Volume of fuel to be added: $\frac{8703 \text{ kg}}{1.77 \frac{\text{lb}}{\text{L}}} = 4917 \text{ L}$

What did they do wrong? Find the correct amount (in liters) of fuel to be added. (1 kg = 2.2 lb)

Big Ideas Math: Modeling Real Life Grade 6 Assessment Book 43

Oops! Unit Conversion Mistakes

After completing this chapter, you will be able to use the concepts you learned to answer the questions in the *STEAM Video Performance Task*. You will be shown unit conversion mistakes in the following real-life situations.

Blood transfusion

Airplane fuel

Baby medication

Zoo enclosure

In each situation, you will analyze and correct the mistake in the unit conversion. How accurate must conversions be in real-life situations?

Getting Ready for Chapter 3

Chapter Exploration

Work with a partner. What portion of the rectangle is red? How did you write your answer?

1.

2. 

3. 

4. 

5. 

6. 

7. 

8. 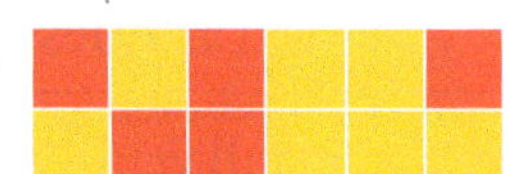

9. 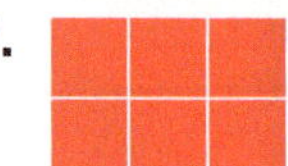

10. Work with a partner. In Exercises 1–9, which of the rectangles have the same portion of red tiles? Explain your reasoning.

Work with a partner. Use square color tiles to build two different-sized rectangles that represent the description.

11. Five-sixths of the tiles are blue.
12. Three-fourths of the tiles are yellow.
13. Four-fifths of the tiles are green.
14. Five-sevenths of the tiles are red.

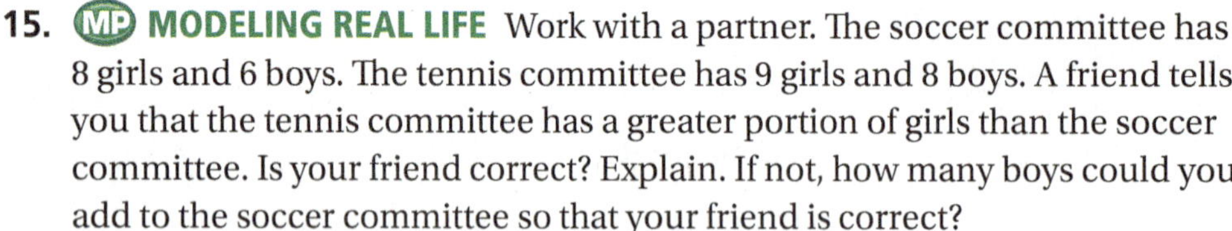

15. **MP MODELING REAL LIFE** Work with a partner. The soccer committee has 8 girls and 6 boys. The tennis committee has 9 girls and 8 boys. A friend tells you that the tennis committee has a greater portion of girls than the soccer committee. Is your friend correct? Explain. If not, how many boys could you add to the soccer committee so that your friend is correct?

Vocabulary

The following vocabulary terms are defined in this chapter. Think about what each term might mean and record your thoughts.

ratio	rate	equivalent rates
equivalent ratios	unit rate	

Laurie's Notes

Check out the digital flash cards.
BigIdeasMath.com

Chapter Exploration

- Students should be familiar with representing fractions using area models.
- Lead in to the upcoming terminology by using words and phrases associated with ratios, such as *relationship*, *out of*, *for every*, and *equivalent*.
- In Exercises 11–14, note that students are representing equivalent ratios without using precise language. In representing these relationships, students can be creative with the tiles. For example, a student may use more than two colors in a rectangle. Be sure to share students' representations with the rest of the class and make comparisons between them.

ELL Support

- For Exercise 15, students may not realize that in the United States sports are often connected to schools. A school may have many types of sports teams, such as baseball, football, basketball, track, gymnastics, or swimming. In northern climates, some schools even have ski teams. Many ELLs are familiar with the sport Americans call *soccer*, however, they may know it as *football*. Explain how American football is different from what the rest of the world considers to be football.

Vocabulary

- These terms represent some of the vocabulary students will encounter in Chapter 3. Have students discuss these terms as a class.
- Where have students heard the word *ratio* outside of a math classroom? In what contexts? Students may not be able to write the actual definition, but they may write phrases associated with ratios.
- Allowing students to discuss these terms now will prepare them for understanding the terms as they are presented in the chapter.
- When students encounter a new definition, encourage them to write in their *Student Journals*. They will revisit these definitions during the Chapter Review.

Topics for Review

- Converting Measures within the Customary or Metric System
- Equivalent Fractions
- Identifying Patterns
- Multiplying and Dividing Decimals
- Multiplying and Dividing by Fractions

Chapter Exploration

1. *Sample answer:* $\frac{4}{12}$; as a fraction

2. *Sample answer:* $\frac{12}{18}$; as a fraction

3. *Sample answer:* $\frac{5}{9}$; as a fraction

4. *Sample answer:* $\frac{4}{9}$; as a fraction

5. *Sample answer:* $\frac{6}{9}$; as a fraction

6. *Sample answer:* $\frac{16}{24}$; as a fraction

7. *Sample answer:* $\frac{4}{12}$; as a fraction

8. *Sample answer:* $\frac{5}{12}$; as a fraction

9. *Sample answer:* $\frac{6}{6}$; as a fraction

10. 1 and 7; 2, 5, and 6;

Sample answer: $\frac{12}{18} = \frac{6}{9} = \frac{16}{24}$

11. *Sample answers:*

R	B	B	B	B	B	B

R	B	B	B
B	R	B	B
B	B	B	B

12. *Sample answers:*

Y	Y	Y	G

G	G	G	Y
Y	Y	Y	Y
Y	Y	Y	Y

13. *Sample answers:*

G	G	B	G	G

G	B	G	G	G
G	G	G	B	G

14–15. See Additional Answers.

Learning Target

Understand the concepts of ratios and equivalent ratios.

Success Criteria

- Write and interpret ratios using appropriate notation and language.
- Recognize multiplicative relationships in ratios.
- Describe how to determine whether ratios are equivalent.
- Name ratios equivalent to a given ratio.

Warm Up

Cumulative, vocabulary, and prerequisite skills practice opportunities are available in the *Resources by Chapter* or at *BigIdeasMath.com*.

ELL Support

Clarify the meaning of the word *relationship*. Explain that the mother of Sam's mother is Sam's grandmother. The word *grandmother* describes Sam's relationship to his mother's mother. If necessary, draw a family tree on the board to clarify and describe other relationships within a family. Explain that ratios describe relationships between quantities, which are the amounts of different items. Tell students that they will be creating tables to show ratio relationships. In a mathematical context, a *table* is a type of chart, not a type of furniture.

Exploration 1

a–c. See Additional Answers.

Exploration 2

a. yes

b. Add 3 parts of iced tea for every 1 part of lemonade added.

Laurie's Notes

Preparing to Teach

- Students are familiar with comparing measurable attributes using language such as *longer than*, *less than*, *heavier than*, and so on.
- A **ratio** is a comparison of two quantities, and there is language and notation associated with ratios.
- Represent the **value of the ratio** $a : b$ as the number $\frac{a}{b}$. Meaning, the quantity a is $\frac{a}{b}$ times b (also the quantity b is $\frac{b}{a}$ times a). For example, the ratio $1 : 3$ means 1 is $\frac{1}{3}$ times 3 (or 3 is $\frac{3}{1}$ times 1). This sounds like awkward language and unnecessarily complicated, however, when interpreting ratios and using ratios to solve problems, this is the type of reasoning students often have to use.

Motivate

- Ask for two volunteers. Hand 3 blocks to Student A and 1 to Student B.
- Ask the other students to describe the relationship between the numbers of blocks. Student A has 2 more blocks (additive relationship) or 3 times as many blocks (multiplicative relationship).
- Hand each student 1 more block. "Describe the relationship now." The additive relationship is still the same but the multiplicative relationship changed.
- Continue to add 1 block and ask about the relationships. You want students to realize that the relationship is never 3 to 1 again.
- You will revisit this scenario in the Closure.

Exploration 1

- State the learning target and success criteria for this section, and then relate these to the Motivate activity.
- Although the language and notation of ratios will likely be revealed in the Motivate, remind students that they should always read introductory text and directions. The definition of a ratio is provided before Exploration 1.
- **MP4 Model with Mathematics:** Remind students that they can use a table to organize the possible numbers of girls and boys in the science class.
- Part (b) is not asking students to compare actual numbers, just relative quantities. Can students make a valid statement?
- **MP3 Construct Viable Arguments and Critique the Reasoning of Others:** When discussing part (b), focus on student reasoning. Solicit several comments. Ask other students if they agree with explanations offered. "Student B, do you agree with what Student A said? Why?"

Exploration 2

- Expect students to read the problem and work with a partner or group. You are listening to conversations, not teaching the problem.
- **Common Misconception:** Students may believe that if you add or subtract the same quantity to each number in a ratio, it is still the same relationship.
- Students may not have the language of **equivalent ratios**, yet it seems logical to double or triple the recipe. Record student answers so that you may reference these answers when discussing equivalent ratios.

3.1 Ratios

Learning Target: Understand the concepts of ratios and equivalent ratios.

Success Criteria:
- I can write and interpret ratios using appropriate notation and language.
- I can recognize multiplicative relationships in ratios.
- I can describe how to determine whether ratios are equivalent.
- I can name ratios equivalent to a given ratio.

A **ratio** is a comparison of two quantities. Consider two quantities a and b. The ratio $a : b$ indicates that there are a units of the first quantity for every b units of the second quantity.

EXPLORATION 1 Writing Ratios

Work with a partner. A science class has two times as many girls as it has boys.

a. Discuss possible numbers of boys and girls in the science class.

b. What comparisons can you make between your class and the science class? Can you determine which class has more girls? more boys? Explain your reasoning.

c. Write three ratios that you observe in your classroom. Describe what each ratio represents.

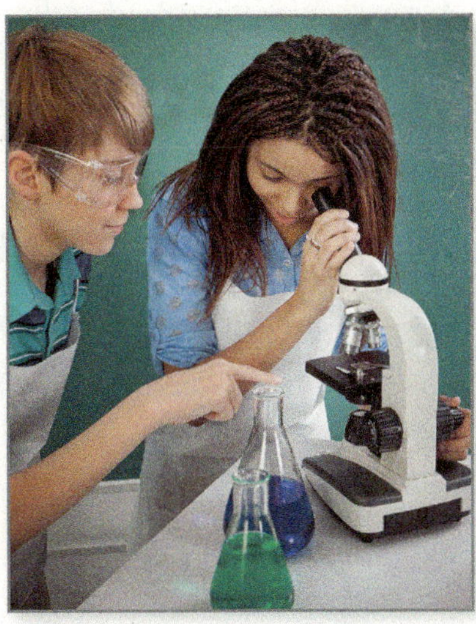

Math Practice

Use a Table
How can you use a table to represent the relationship between the numbers of girls and boys?

EXPLORATION 2 Using Ratios in a Recipe

Work with a partner. The ratio of iced tea to lemonade in a recipe is 3 : 1. You begin by combining 3 cups of iced tea with 1 cup of lemonade.

a. You add 1 cup of iced tea and 1 cup of lemonade to the mixture. Does this change the taste of the mixture?

b. Describe how you can make larger amounts without changing the taste.

3.1 Lesson

Key Vocabulary
ratio, *p. 108*
value of a ratio, *p. 109*
equivalent ratios, *p. 109*

Key Idea

Ratio

Words A **ratio** is a comparison of two quantities. Ratios can be part-to-part, part-to-whole, or whole-to-part comparisons. Ratios may or may not include units.

Examples 2 cats *to* 6 dogs

1 cat *for every* 3 dogs

3 dogs *per* 1 cat

3 dogs *for each* cat

3 dogs *out of every* 4 pets

2 cats *out of* 8 pets

Algebra The ratio of a to b can be written as $a : b$.

Reading
Phrases that indicate ratios include *for each*, *for every*, and *per*.

EXAMPLE 1 Writing Ratios

You have the coins shown.

a. Write the ratio of pennies to quarters.

6 pennies → 6 to 7 ← 7 quarters

So, the ratio of pennies to quarters is 6 to 7, or 6 : 7.

b. Write the ratio of quarters to dimes.

7 quarters → 7 to 3 ← 3 dimes

So, the ratio of quarters to dimes is 7 to 3, or 7 : 3.

c. Write the ratio of dimes to the total number of coins.

3 dimes → 3 to 16 ← 16 coins

So, the ratio of dimes to the total number of coins is 3 to 16, or 3 : 16.

Try It **Write the indicated ratio using the coins in Example 1.**

1. dimes to pennies
2. quarters to the total number of coins

Multi-Language Glossary at *BigIdeasMath.com*

Laurie's Notes

Scaffolding Instruction

- Students explored how to use a ratio to describe the relationship between two quantities. They were also introduced to the concept of **equivalent ratios**.
- **Emerging:** Additional practice for writing and interpreting ratios is given in Examples 1 and 2. Students should recognize that ratio relationships can be part-to-part, part-to-whole, or whole-to-part. Help students make sense of the definition for **value of a ratio**.
- **Proficient:** If students are confident in writing and interpreting ratios that are part-to-part, part-to-whole, and whole-to-part, they can self-assess with Try It Exercises 1–3 and continue independently with Example 3.
- In Example 4, guided instruction may be needed for all students.

Key Idea

- In discussing the Key Idea, solicit examples of part-to-part, part-to-whole, and whole-to-part comparisons.
- Explain that phrases *for each*, *for every*, and *per* indicate that you are comparing two quantities. This is ratio language.
- When discussing the second and third examples, be sure to note that the **ratio** $a : b$ is not the same as the ratio $b : a$. In comparing two unequal quantities, there are two ways of writing the ratio.
- Note that although fractional representation is not introduced at this time, students may see the connection.

EXAMPLE 1

- Work through each part of the example.
- Ask students to identify each of the ratios as being part-to-part, part-to-whole, or whole-to-part comparisons.

? Extension: "What is the ratio of the value of the dimes to the value of the quarters?" Three dimes equal $0.30. Seven quarters equal $1.75. So, the ratio is $0.30 to $1.75.

Try It

- **Note:** Remind students that the Try It exercises throughout the lesson provide an opportunity to check and build understanding. The goal is deep learning of the skill or concept so that students are able to apply and transfer this knowledge to solve problems. The ability to write a ratio to describe a relationship between two quantities is the beginning step.
- Have students use *Thumbs Up* to indicate their understanding of writing ratios.

Scaffold instruction to support all students in their learning. Learning is individualized and you may want to group students differently as they move in and out of these levels with each skill and concept. Student self-assessment and feedback help guide your instructional decisions about how and when to layer support for all students to become proficient learners.

Extra Example 1

You have the marbles shown.

a. Write the ratio of green marbles to red marbles. 4 to 7, or 4 : 7

b. Write the ratio of blue marbles to green marbles. 9 to 4, or 9 : 4

c. Write the ratio of red marbles to the total number of marbles. 7 to 20, or 7 : 20

Try It

1. 3 to 6, or 3 : 6
2. 7 to 16, or 7 : 16

Teaching Strategy

Manipulatives help students develop a visual understanding of various mathematical concepts. You can use different colors of linking cubes, counters, or square tiles to represent quantities. A visual representation is helpful for students when making comparisons or drawing conclusions about quantities. In most cases, the order in which the objects are referenced matters.

For example, if the ratio of apples to blueberries is 1 : 3, you can use 1 red and 3 blue tiles to represent the ratio.

From the same model, students will see the ratio of blueberries to apples is 3 : 1.

Extra Example 2

a. The ratio of rock songs to pop songs in your music collection is 1 : 7. Find and interpret the value of the ratio. $\frac{1}{7}$; The number of rock songs is $\frac{1}{7}$ times the number of pop songs.

b. In your friend's music collection, the number of rock songs is 3 times the number of pop songs. Write the ratio of rock songs to pop songs. 3 : 1

Try It

3. 5; The number of adult elephants is 5 times the number of baby elephants.

Laurie's Notes

Discuss

- Discuss the definition of the **value of the ratio**.
- To help students develop an understanding of ratio language and notation, use the following example to discuss the value of the ratio.
  Example: The kitchen staff said that for every 5 students who like tuna sandwiches, 3 students do not. The ratio of students who like tuna sandwiches to students who do not is 5 : 3, so the value of the ratio is $\frac{5}{3}$.

EXAMPLE 2

- Interpreting the ratio means that students can make a comparative statement about the two quantities in the ratio.
- **Teaching Strategy:** Have students use 1 red tile and 2 blue tiles to represent the ratio of rubies to diamonds. Looking at the tiles, students can see that there are $\frac{1}{2}$ as many rubies as diamonds and twice as many diamonds as rubies.

Try It

- Students may find but not interpret the value of the ratio. Encourage them to read the problem carefully.

ELL Support

Explain that a sanctuary is a place where animals are helped and protected. They can live freely there, without harm from hunters. Have ELLs work in pairs to visually model the ratio by drawing squares to represent adult elephants and circles to represent baby elephants.

Beginner: Draw 5 squares and 1 circle. They will then state the value of the ratio as 5.

Intermediate: State the value of the ratio and verbally explain that the number of adult elephants is 5 times the number of baby elephants.

Advanced: State the value of the ratio and provide a written explanation that the number of adult elephants is 5 times the number of baby elephants.

Key Idea

- Define **equivalent ratios**. Students may say that finding equivalent ratios is similar to finding equivalent fractions. The value of the ratio is a fractional representation of the ratio.
- **Big Idea:** To find an equivalent ratio, each quantity in the ratio is multiplied by the same value.
- Variables have not been defined, however, students used letters to represent numbers in prior grades. It may be helpful to write the algebraic representation as $\frac{a}{b} = \frac{a \times n}{b \times n} = \frac{c}{d}$.
- Use the recorded answers from Exploration 2 to help students make the connection to equivalent ratios.
- **Teaching Strategy:** Use colored tiles to demonstrate two ratios that are equivalent. Then ask students to add more tiles but keep the ratio the same.

The number $\frac{a}{b}$ associated with the ratio $a : b$ is called the **value of the ratio**. It describes the multiplicative relationship between the quantities in a ratio.

EXAMPLE 2 Writing and Interpreting Ratios

a. The ratio of rubies to diamonds on a ring is 1 : 2. Find and interpret the value of the ratio.

The value of the ratio 1 : 2 is $\frac{1}{2}$. So, the multiplicative relationship is $\frac{1}{2}$.

 The number of rubies is $\frac{1}{2}$ times the number of diamonds.

b. On another ring, the number of rubies is 4 times the number of diamonds. Write the ratio of rubies to diamonds.

Because the number of rubies is 4 times the number of diamonds, there are 4 rubies per diamond.

 So, the ratio of rubies to diamonds is 4 : 1.

Try It

3. An elephant sanctuary contains adult and baby elephants. The ratio of adult elephants to baby elephants is 5 : 1. Find and interpret the value of the ratio.

Key Idea

Equivalent Ratios

Words Two ratios that describe the same relationship are **equivalent ratios**. Two ratios are equivalent when you can multiply each quantity in one ratio by the same positive number to obtain the other ratio. The values of equivalent ratios are equivalent.

Example 1 : 3 and 2 : 6 are equivalent.

1 : 3 (×2, ×2) → 2 : 6

$$\frac{1}{3} = \frac{1 \times 2}{3 \times 2} = \frac{2}{6}$$

Algebra Two ratios $a : b$ and $c : d$ are equivalent when there exists a positive number n such that $a \times n = c$ and $b \times n = d$.

EXAMPLE 3 Determining Whether Ratios Are Equivalent

Determine whether the ratios are equivalent.

a. 4 : 3 and 20 : 15

You can multiply each number in the first ratio by 5 to obtain the numbers in the second ratio.

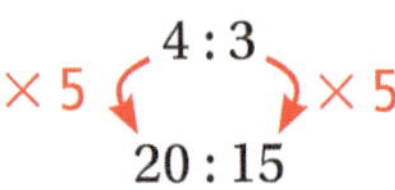

Also, the values of the ratios are equivalent.

$$\frac{4}{3} = \frac{4 \times 5}{3 \times 5} = \frac{20}{15}$$

So, the ratios are equivalent.

b. 5 : 7 and 10 : 21

You need to multiply each number in the ratio by different amounts to obtain the numbers in the second ratio.

Also, the values of the ratios are not equivalent.

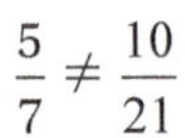

$$\frac{5}{7} \neq \frac{10}{21}$$

So, the ratios are not equivalent.

Try It **Determine whether the ratios are equivalent.**

4. 1 : 1 and 6 : 6 **5.** 1 : 2 and 3 : 4 **6.** 8 : 3 and 6 : 16

Self-Assessment for Concepts & Skills

Solve each exercise. Then rate your understanding of the success criteria in your journal.

WRITING AND INTERPRETING RATIOS **Write the ratio. Then find and interpret the value of the ratio.**

7. sharks to dolphins **8.** dolphins : animals

IDENTIFYING EQUIVALENT RATIOS **Determine whether the ratios are equivalent. Explain your reasoning.**

9. 2 : 3 and 24 : 36 **10.** 5 : 7 and 20 : 28 **11.** 3 : 10 and 9 : 25

12. DIFFERENT WORDS, SAME QUESTION Which is different? Find "both" answers.

What kind of relationship is 2 peaches to 5 pears?	What kind of relationship is 2 pears out of every 5 fruit?
What kind of relationship is 2 pears per 5 peaches?	What kind of relationship is 2 peaches for every 5 pears?

Laurie's Notes

EXAMPLE 3

- Work through parts (a) and (b) as shown.
- Students may use number sense in deciding if the two ratios in part (b) are equivalent. They may say that the value of the ratio 5 : 7 is $\frac{5}{7}$, which is greater than $\frac{1}{2}$. The value of the ratio 10 : 21 is $\frac{10}{21}$, which is less than $\frac{1}{2}$. Therefore, the two ratios cannot be equivalent.

Try It

- Circulate as students are completing the exercises. Note the reasoning used by students.
- Ask several students to share their thinking about the exercises, and then ask other students to discuss what they've heard.

Self-Assessment for Concepts & Skills

- At this point, students should be very familiar with the learning target, and the success criteria for meeting the learning target. Can students now apply this knowledge to solve a contextual problem?
- Have students use *Thumbs Up* to indicate their understanding of each success criterion.

ELL Support

Check comprehension by having students work in pairs to complete the exercises. Remind them that the process they used for Try It Exercise 3 may also be used for Exercises 7, 8, and 12. After students complete the exercises, have two pairs present their answers to each other, and revise them if there is any disagreement. Provide support as needed.

The Success Criteria Self-Assessment chart can be found in the *Student Journal* or online at *BigIdeasMath.com*.

Extra Example 3

Determine whether the ratios are equivalent.

a. 5 : 7 and 25 : 28 not equivalent

b. 7 : 8 and 21 : 24 equivalent

Try It

4. equivalent

5. not equivalent

6. not equivalent

Self-Assessment for Concepts & Skills

7. 4 : 5; $\frac{4}{5}$; The number of sharks is $\frac{4}{5}$ times the number of dolphins.

8. 5 : 9; $\frac{5}{9}$; The number of dolphins is $\frac{5}{9}$ times the number of animals.

9. equivalent; $\frac{2}{3} = \frac{24}{36}$

10. equivalent; $\frac{5}{7} = \frac{20}{28}$

11. not equivalent; $\frac{3}{10} \neq \frac{9}{25}$

12. What kind of relationship is 2 pears out of every 5 fruit?; part-to-whole; part-to-part

Laurie's Notes

Extra Example 4

Noah is biking at a pace of 10 yards every 2 seconds. Beth's pace is 20 yards every 3 seconds. Are they biking at the same pace? If not, who is faster?
no; Beth

Self-Assessment for Problem Solving

13. $\frac{5}{3}$; The number of wolves is $\frac{5}{3}$ times the number of cougars.

14. no; your friend

15. $\frac{3}{7}$

Learning Target

Understand the concepts of ratios and equivalent ratios.

Success Criteria

- Write and interpret ratios using appropriate notation and language.
- Recognize multiplicative relationships in ratios.
- Describe how to determine whether ratios are equivalent.
- Name ratios equivalent to a given ratio.

EXAMPLE 4

- Students can use a ratio to describe the relationship between two quantities and determine if two ratios are equivalent. They will now connect those concepts to solving contextual problems.
- It is important that you allow students to do the thinking. Pose the problem and give students time to think about it before they talk with a partner. Allow time for different strategies to emerge.
- "Tell a partner what you know about the two speedwalkers from reading this problem."
- You want students to hear and understand the thinking of others. There may be different strategies, or reasoning, that students use in solving this problem.
- ? After the first student has shared his or her thinking, ask, "Did anyone think to solve this problem differently?" If you have a document camera, encourage students to display their work to the class.

Self-Assessment for Problem Solving

- The goal for all students is to feel comfortable with the problem-solving plan. It is important for students to problem-solve in class, where they may receive support from you and their peers. Keep in mind that some students may only be ready to complete the first step.
- Students should work independently or with a partner on the exercises. Support students with probing questions and by providing feedback.
- Coach students not to solve the problem for their partners. Model what guided questions sound like.
- As students are working through the exercises, encourage them to assess their understanding of the learning target and success criteria, keeping the focus on the learning target. Tell students to rate their understanding of each success criterion.

The Success Criteria Self-Assessment chart can be found in the *Student Journal* or online at *BigIdeasMath.com*.

Closure

- Reflect on the Motivate scenario in which 3 blocks were given to Student A and 1 block was given to Student B. Demonstrate your proficiency of the learning target by explaining the scenario and how additional blocks could be given to the two students so that the ratio of blocks is still equivalent to 3 : 1.
  Sample answer: Give 3 more blocks to Student A and 1 more block to Student B to get the ratio 6 : 2. You can multiply both of the quantities in 3 : 1 by 2 to obtain the ratio 6 : 2, so the ratios are equivalent.

EXAMPLE 4 Modeling Real Life

Meg is speedwalking at a pace of 5 meters every 2 seconds. Sean's pace is 10 meters every 5 seconds. Are they speedwalking at the same pace? If not, who is faster?

Write a ratio to represent each person's pace.

Meg's pace: 5 : 2

Sean's pace: 10 : 5

To decide whether Meg and Sean are speedwalking at the same pace, determine whether the ratios are equivalent.

$$5:2 \xrightarrow{\times 2 \;\; \times 2.5} 10:5$$

Not equivalent

So, they are not speedwalking at the same pace. To decide who is faster, use an equivalent ratio to compare Meg's pace to Sean's pace.

Meg's pace: $$5:2 \xrightarrow{\times 2 \;\; \times 2} 10:4$$

Meg walks 10 meters every 4 seconds. It takes Sean 5 seconds to walk the same distance.

So, Meg is speedwalking faster than Sean.

Math Practice

Construct Arguments

A classmate uses a multiplier of 2.5 for Meg's pace to find 12.5 : 5. Can you use this ratio to decide who is faster? Explain.

Self-Assessment for Problem Solving

Solve each exercise. Then rate your understanding of the success criteria in your journal.

13. The ratio of wolves to cougars in a forest is 5 : 3. Find and interpret the value of the ratio.

14. You are kayaking at a pace of 63 feet every 12 seconds. Your friend's pace is 21 feet every 3 seconds. Are you and your friend kayaking at the same pace? If not, who is faster?

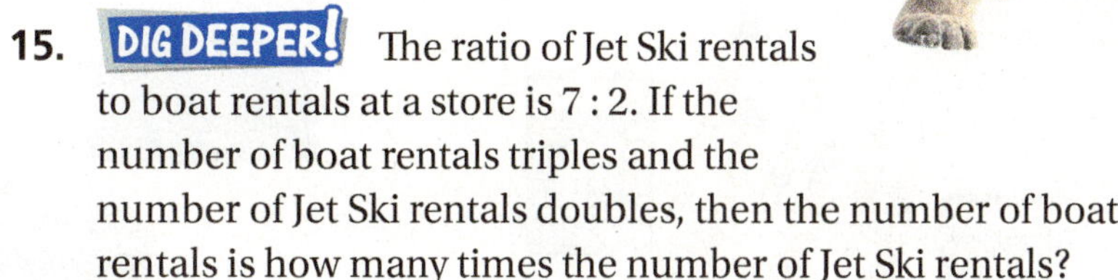

15. **DIG DEEPER!** The ratio of Jet Ski rentals to boat rentals at a store is 7 : 2. If the number of boat rentals triples and the number of Jet Ski rentals doubles, then the number of boat rentals is how many times the number of Jet Ski rentals?

3.1 Practice

Review & Refresh

Divide. Check your answer.

1. $15.4 \div 2.2$
2. $56.07 \div 8.9$
3. $8.43\overline{)12.645}$
4. $11.6\overline{)51.62}$

Find the value of the power.

5. 8^2
6. 1^6
7. 3^4
8. 2^6

The Venn diagram shows the prime factors of two numbers. Identify the numbers. Then find the GCF and the LCM of the two numbers.

9.

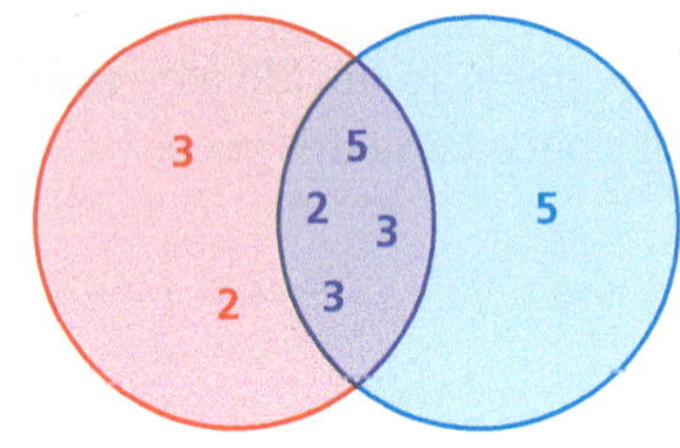

10.

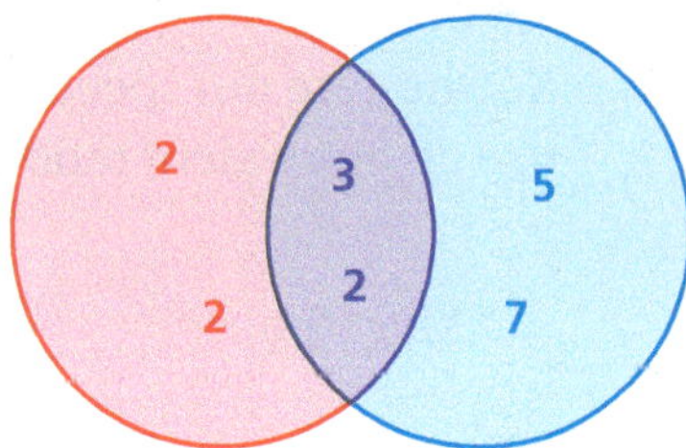

Concepts, Skills, & Problem Solving

USING RATIOS **You mix the amounts of iced tea and lemonade shown. Describe how you can make larger amounts without changing the taste.** (See Exploration 2, p. 107.)

11.

12.

WRITING RATIOS **Write the ratio.**

13. frogs to turtles

14. basketballs to soccer balls

15. calculators : pencils

16. shirts : pants

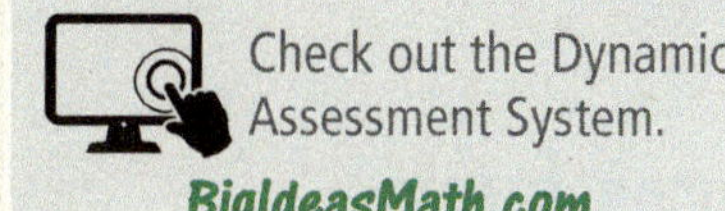

Assignment Guide and Concept Check

Scaffold assignments to support all students in their learning progression. The suggested assignments are a starting point. Continue to assign additional exercises and revisit with spaced practice to move every student toward proficiency.

Level	Assignment 1	Assignment 2
Emerging	3, 7, 10, 12, 13, 14, 25, 26, 33, 38, 40	17, 18, 21, 23, 29, 31, 41, 42, 45
Proficient	3, 7, 10, 12, 14, 15, 25, 29, 34, 38, 40	21, 41, 42, 43, 44, 45, 47, 48
Advanced	3, 7, 10, 12, 15, 16, 31, 32, 34, 39, 40	20, 41, 46, 47, 48, 49, 50, 51

- Assignment 1 is for use after students complete the Self-Assessment for Concepts & Skills.
- Assignment 2 is for use after students complete the Self-Assessment for Problem Solving.
- The red exercises can be used as a concept check.

Review & Refresh Prior Skills

Exercises 1–4 Dividing Decimals
Exercises 5–8 Finding Values of Powers
Exercises 9 and 10 Finding the GCF and LCM

Review & Refresh

1. 7
2. 6.3
3. 1.5
4. 4.45
5. 64
6. 1
7. 81
8. 64
9. 540, 450; GCF: 90; LCM: 2700
10. 24, 210; GCF: 6; LCM: 840

Concepts, Skills, & Problem Solving

11. Add 2 parts of iced tea for every 1 part of lemonade added.
12. Add 2 parts of iced tea for every 3 parts of lemonade added
13. 2 to 5, or 2 : 5
14. 6 to 4, or 6 : 4
15. 2 to 6, or 2 : 6
16. 3 to 7, or 3 : 7

Concepts, Skills, & Problem Solving

17. 12 : 16

18. *Sample answer:* chairs to tables; Five chairs can be placed around one table.

19. *Sample answer:* 1 out of every 7 contestants wins a prize.

20. *Sample answer:* 5 daisies out of 26 flowers in a vase

21. *Sample answer:* 2 days in a weekend per 5 weekdays

22. *Sample answer:* jogging 7 miles per 1 hour

23. **a.** 4; The number of sunny days is 4 times the number of rainy days.

    b. 5 : 1

24. not equivalent

25. equivalent

26. not equivalent

27. not equivalent

28. equivalent

29. not equivalent

30. equivalent

31. equivalent

32. not equivalent

33. *Sample answer:* 9 : 3; $\frac{9}{3} = \frac{3}{1}$

34. *Sample answer:* 28 : 8; $\frac{28}{8} = \frac{7}{2}$

35. *Sample answer:* 12 : 12; $\frac{12}{12} = \frac{6}{6}$

36. *Sample answer:* 0 : 40; $\frac{0}{40} = \frac{0}{8}$

37. 18

38. 24

39. 21

40. no; $\frac{4}{8} \neq \frac{8}{12}$, so the ratios are not equivalent.

41. *Sample answer:* 2 cups of water and 4 cups of cornstarch, 3 cups of water and 6 cups of cornstarch; $\frac{1}{2} = \frac{2}{4} = \frac{3}{6}$

42. 32

Common Errors

- **Exercises 33–39** Students may add or subtract the same amount to each number in the ratio, saying, for example, that 2 : 3 and 4 : 5 are equivalent. Make it very clear that the numbers you add or subtract must be in the same ratio. You cannot add or subtract the same number, as when multiplying or dividing.
- **Exercise 42** Remind students to read the problem carefully to determine what is being asked.

17. **MP MODELING REAL LIFE** Twelve of the 28 students in a class own a dog. What is the ratio of students who own a dog to students who do not?

18. **MP LOGIC** Name two things that you would like to have in a ratio of 5 : 1 but not in a ratio of 1 : 5. Explain your reasoning.

OPEN-ENDED **Describe a real-life relationship that can be represented by the ratio.**

19. 1 out of every 7

20. 5 to 26

21. 2 per 5

22. 7 : 1

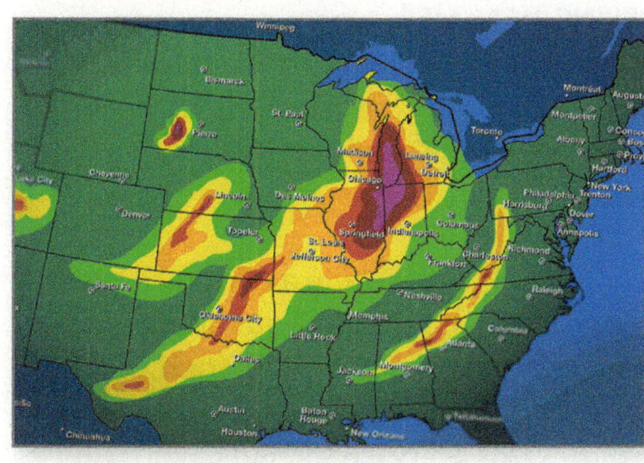

23. **MP MODELING REAL LIFE** During a given month, the ratio of sunny days to rainy days is 4 : 1.

 a. Find and interpret the value of the ratio.

 b. In another month, the number of sunny days is 5 times the number of rainy days. Write the ratio of sunny days to rainy days.

IDENTIFYING EQUIVALENT RATIOS **Determine whether the ratios are equivalent.**

24. 2 : 3 and 4 : 9

25. 3 : 8 and 9 : 24

26. 1 : 4 and 2 : 6

27. 5 : 3 and 15 : 12

28. 6 : 10 and 12 : 20

29. 2 : 3 and 4 : 5

30. 28 : 32 and 7 : 8

31. 24 : 100 and 6 : 25

32. 85 : 210 and 340 : 735

WRITING EQUIVALENT RATIOS **Write a ratio that is equivalent to the given ratio. Justify your answer.**

33. 3 : 1

34. 7 : 2

35. 6 : 6

36. 0 : 8

WRITING EQUIVALENT RATIOS **Fill in the blank so that the ratios are equivalent.**

37. 3 : 9 and 6 : ___

38. 2 : 6 and 8 : ___

39. ___ : 6 and 7 : 2

40. **MP YOU BE THE TEACHER** Your friend says that the two ratios are equivalent. Is your friend correct? Explain your reasoning.

> 4 : 8
> +4 ↓ ↓ +4
> 8 : 12
>
> Because you can add 4 to each number in the first ratio to obtain the numbers in the second ratio, the ratios are equivalent.

41. **OPEN-ENDED** A *non-Newtonian* liquid demonstrates properties of both a solid and a liquid. A recipe for a non-Newtonian liquid calls for 1 cup of water and 2 cups of cornstarch. Find two possible combinations of water and cornstarch that you can use to make a larger batch. Justify your answer.

42. **MP PROBLEM SOLVING** You are downloading songs to your tablet. The ratio of pop songs to rock songs is 5 : 4. You download 40 pop songs. How many rock songs do you download?

43. **MP PROBLEM SOLVING** In the contiguous United States, the ratio of states that border an ocean to states that do not border an ocean is 7 : 9. How many of the states border an ocean?

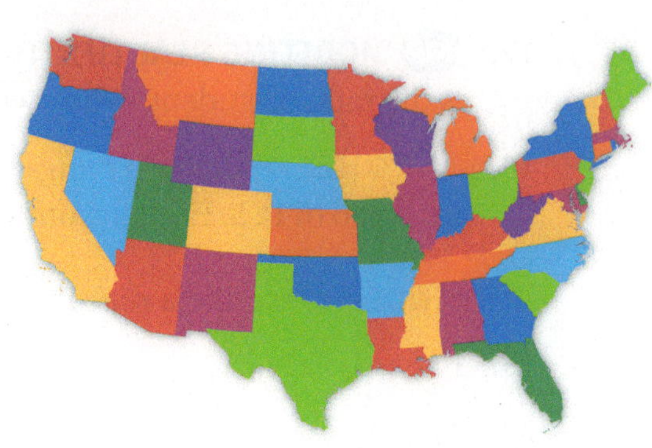

44. **MP REASONING** The value of a ratio is $\frac{4}{3}$. The second quantity in the ratio is how many times the first quantity in the ratio? Explain your reasoning.

45. **MP MODELING REAL LIFE** A train moving at a constant speed travels 3 miles every 5 minutes. A car moving at a constant speed travels 12 miles every 20 minutes. Are the vehicles traveling at the same speed? If not, which is faster?

46. **CRITICAL THINKING** To win a relay race, you must swim 200 yards before your opponent swims 190 yards. You swim at a pace of 50 yards every 40 seconds. Your opponent swims at a pace of 10 yards every 8.5 seconds. Who wins the race? Justify your answer.

47. **DIG DEEPER!** There are 3 boys for every 2 girls in a dance competition. Does it make sense for there to be a total of 9 people in the competition? Explain.

48. **GEOMETRY** Use the blue and green rectangles.

   a. Find the ratio of the length of the blue rectangle to the length of the green rectangle. Repeat this for width, perimeter, and area.

   b. Compare your ratios in part (a).

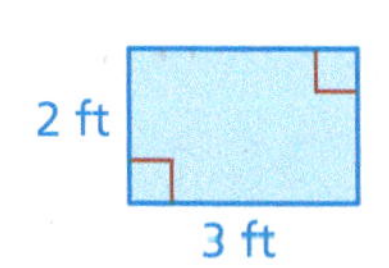

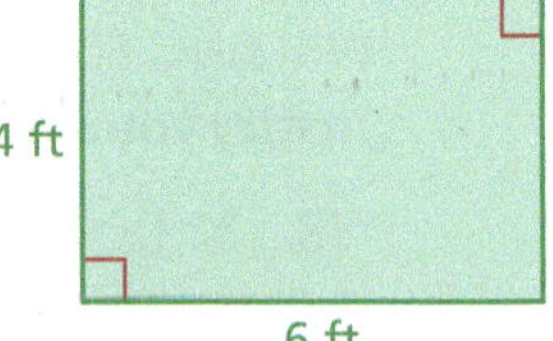

49. **MP STRUCTURE** The ratio of the side lengths of a triangle is 2 : 3 : 4. The shortest side is 15 inches. What is the perimeter of the triangle? Explain.

TOKENS	
1 Token	$0.50
10 Tokens	$5.00
25 Tokens	$10.00
50 Tokens	$25.00
90 Tokens	$40.00

50. **MP PROBLEM SOLVING** A restaurant sells tokens that customers use to play games while waiting for their orders.

   a. Which option is the best deal? Justify your answer.

   b. What suggestions, if any, would you give to the restaurant about how it could modify the prices of tokens?

51. **DIG DEEPER!** There are 12 boys and 10 girls in your gym class. If 6 boys joined the class, how many girls would need to join for the ratio of boys to girls to remain the same? Justify your answer.

Common Errors

- **Exercise 48** Students may need reminded how to find the perimeter and area of a rectangle. They may see that the green rectangle's dimensions are twice the blue rectangle's dimensions and then assume that all of the ratios will be 1 : 2. Show students why the ratio of the area of the blue rectangle to the area of the green rectangle is 1 : 4.

Mini-Assessment

In a pet shop, there are 12 dogs, 9 cats, and 17 fish. Write the ratio.

1. cats to dogs 9 to 12, or 9 : 12
2. fish : dogs 17 to 12, or 17 : 12

Determine whether the ratios are equivalent.

3. 4 : 7 and 8 : 16 not equivalent
4. 12 : 48 and 2 : 8 equivalent
5. A car moving at a constant speed travels 16 miles every 20 minutes. A truck moving at a constant speed travels 4 miles every 5 minutes. Are the vehicles traveling at the same speed? If not, which is faster? yes

Section Resources

Surface Level	Deep Level
Resources by Chapter • Extra Practice • Reteach • Puzzle Time Student Journal • Self-Assessment • Practice Differentiating the Lesson Tutorial Videos Skills Review Handbook Skills Trainer	Resources by Chapter • Enrichment and Extension Graphic Organizers Dynamic Assessment System • Section Practice

Concepts, Skills, & Problem Solving

43. 21

44. $\frac{3}{4}$; The ratio of the first quantity to the second quantity is 4 : 3. The ratio of the second quantity to first quantity is 3 : 4. So, the second quantity is $\frac{3}{4}$ times the first quantity.

45. yes

46. you; You swim 200 yards in 160 seconds and your opponent swims 190 yards in 161.5 seconds.

47. no; The ratio of boys to people in the competition is 3 : 5, and there is no ratio of a whole number to 9 that is equivalent to the ratio 3 : 5.

48. **a.** 3 : 6, 2 : 4, 10 : 20, 6 : 24

b. The ratios for length, width, and perimeter are all equivalent to 1 : 2, but the ratio for area is different (1 : 4).

49. 67.5 in.; *Sample answer:* 2 : 3 : 4 is equivalent to 15 : 22.5 : 30, and $15 + 22.5 + 30 = 67.5$.

50. **a.** 25 Tokens for \$10.00; *Sample answer:* $\frac{25}{10}$ is greater than $\frac{1}{0.5}$, $\frac{10}{5}$, $\frac{50}{25}$, and $\frac{90}{40}$.

b. *Sample answer:* Increase the price of 25 tokens to \$12.50, or decrease the price per token as the number of tokens purchased increases.

51. 5 girls; *Sample answer:* $\frac{12}{10} = \frac{18}{15}$

Learning Target

Use tape diagrams to model and solve ratio problems.

Success Criteria

- Interpret tape diagrams that represent ratio relationships.
- Draw tape diagrams to model ratio relationships.
- Find the value of one part of a tape diagram.
- Use tape diagrams to solve ratio problems.

Warm Up

Cumulative, vocabulary, and prerequisite skills practice opportunities are available in the *Resources by Chapter* or at *BigIdeasMath.com*.

ELL Support

Students may already know the word *tape*. Explain that the word *tape* has different meanings. It may mean an object that joins paper together or the action of joining the paper together. Explain that another type of tape, a tape measure, helps to measure length. If possible, demonstrate the use of some tape and a tape measure. Tell students that a tape diagram is similar to a tape measure. It allows you to compare quantities.

Exploration 1

a. The expert trail is 4 times as long as the beginner trail.

b. *Sample answers:* beginner trail: 1000 feet; Each part of the tape diagram represents a length of 1000 feet, and the length of the expert trail is 4000 feet; $4 \times 1000 = 4000$

c. See Additional Answers.

Laurie's Notes

Preparing to Teach

- Students have drawn tape diagrams (or bar models) in earlier grades.
- In this lesson, tape diagrams are used to solve ratio problems.
- It is important for students to understand that each rectangular part (or bar) in the tape diagram represents the same quantity.
- The tape diagram shown represents a part-to-part ratio of 2 : 3. The part-to-whole ratio is 2 : 5 (or 3 : 5) and the whole-to-part ratio is 5 : 2 (or 5 : 3).

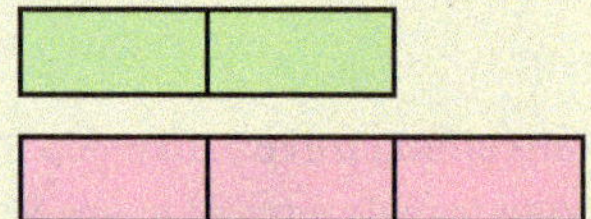

Motivate

- Ask for two volunteers. Hand 4 linking cubes to Student A and 1 linking cube to Student B. Ask a series of questions about the relationship between their linking cubes.
- ? "If the linking cube Student B is holding represents 3 movie tickets, how many movie tickets does Student A have? Explain." 12 movie tickets; Each cube represents 3 tickets, so $3 \times 4 = 12$ tickets.
- ? "If the linking cubes Student A is holding represent 8 movie tickets, how many movie tickets does Student B have? Explain." 2 movie tickets; Each cube represents 2 tickets, so $2 \times 1 = 2$ tickets.
- ? "Together you know they have 30 movie tickets. How many movie tickets does each cube represent? Explain." 6 movie tickets; There are 5 cubes representing 30 total tickets, so each cube represents $30 \div 5 = 6$ tickets.
- When using linking cubes, it's natural for students to put them together so they see a length of 5 cubes. Students are able to reason that each cube must represent 6 movie tickets.

Exploration 1

- A tape diagram is purposely shown without numbers. You want students to use quantitative reasoning and see the model as a 1 : 4 ratio.
- In part (a), students are asked to interpret what the model means. You want to hear a multiplicative relationship. The expert trail is 4 times the length of the beginner trail, or the beginner trail is only $\frac{1}{4}$ as long as the expert trail. It is important for students to realize that they don't know the actual length of either trail, only the multiplicative relationship between the trails.
- **MP2 Reason Abstractly and Quantitatively:** Students should connect the Motivate to the tape diagram. Each linking cube is a rectangular part (or bar) in the diagram.
- ? If students are stuck on part (c), ask, "How many total linking cubes were used in the Motivate?" 5 linking cubes "How does the total relate to the linking cubes each student was holding?" The linking cubes each student held were the parts, and together they were the total. Now have students work with a partner to finish the exploration.
- Have a summary discussion. Ask students to share their explanations.

3.2 Using Tape Diagrams

Learning Target: Use tape diagrams to model and solve ratio problems.

Success Criteria:
- I can interpret tape diagrams that represent ratio relationships.
- I can draw tape diagrams to model ratio relationships.
- I can find the value of one part of a tape diagram.
- I can use tape diagrams to solve ratio problems.

You can use a visual model, called a *tape diagram*, to represent the relationship between two quantities in a ratio.

EXPLORATION 1

Using a Tape Diagram

Work with a partner. The tape diagram models the lengths of two snowboarding trails.

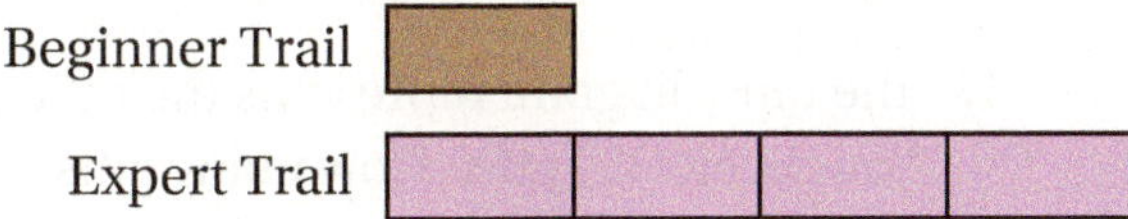

Math Practice

Make Sense of Quantities
How does the tape diagram help you make sense of the quantities and the relationship between the quantities?

a. What can you determine from the tape diagram?

b. Choose a length for one of the trails. What conclusions can you make from the tape diagram? Explain your reasoning.

c. Suppose you know the combined length of the trails or the difference in the lengths of the trails. Explain how you can use that information to find the lengths of the two trails. Provide an example with your explanation.

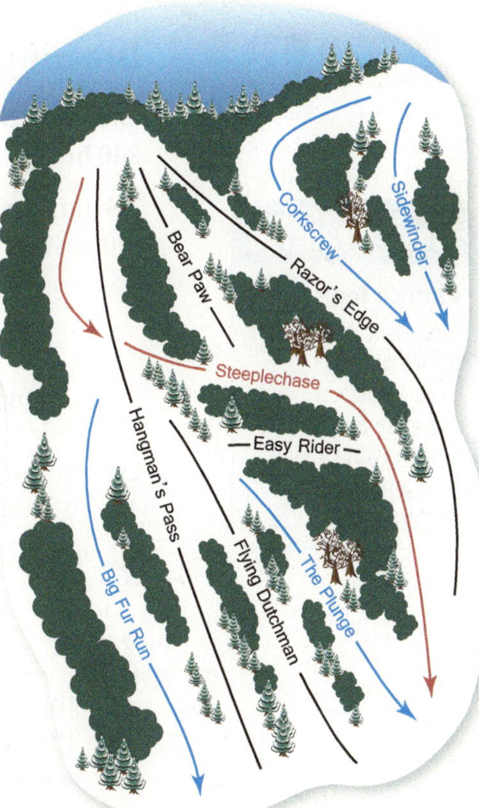

3.2 Lesson

You can use tape diagrams to represent ratios and solve ratio problems.

EXAMPLE 1 Interpreting a Tape Diagram

The tape diagram represents the ratio of blue monsters to green monsters you caught in a game. You caught 10 green monsters. How many blue monsters did you catch?

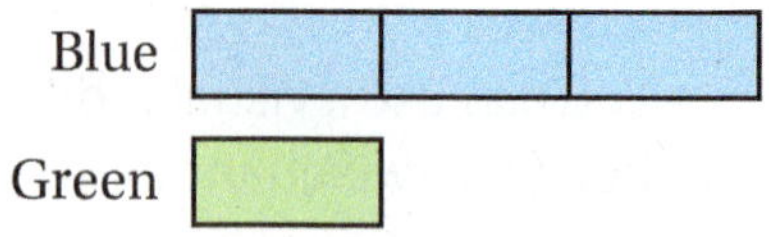

The 1 part for green represents 10 monsters. So, the 3 parts for blue represents $3 \times 10 = 30$ monsters.

▶ You caught 30 blue monsters.

Reading

The tape diagram shows that the ratio of blue monsters to green monsters is 3 : 1.

Try It

1. The tape diagram represents the ratio of gifts received to gifts given. You received 4 gifts. How many gifts did you give?

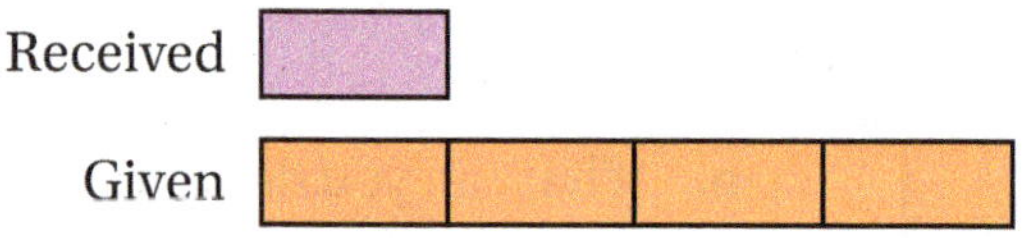

EXAMPLE 2 Drawing a Tape Diagram

There are 3 bones in a cat for every 4 bones in a dog. The cat has 240 bones. How many bones does the dog have?

The ratio of bones in the cat to bones in the dog is 3 : 4. Represent the ratio using a tape diagram.

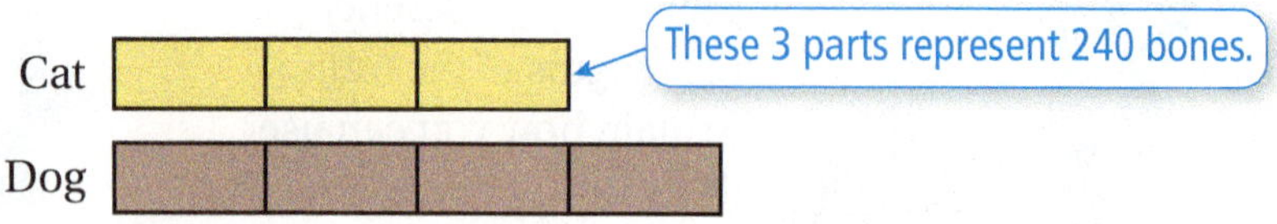

One part represents $240 \div 3 = 80$ bones. So, 4 parts represent $4 \times 80 = 320$ bones.

▶ The dog has 320 bones.

Math Practice

Choose Tools

Represent the ratio using counters or other objects. Compare this method with drawing a tape diagram. Which do you prefer?

Try It

2. There are 8 bones in a large snake for every 3 bones in a small snake. The small snake has 150 bones. How many bones does the large snake have?

Laurie's Notes

Scaffolding Instruction

- Students explored using a tape diagram to model the relationship between the lengths of two ski trails. You should have a sense as to how students interpreted each rectangular part in the model. Did they see the tape diagram as a model of multiple equivalent ratios, or did they see it as one fixed length for each trail that was in the ratio of 1 : 4? Probe as needed so that students are able to assess their own understanding.
- **Emerging**: Students might have followed the reasoning used for each part of the exploration, yet may not be ready to work independently. Going through Examples 1 and 2, either independently or with guided instruction, will help students become proficient with the first three success criteria.
- **Proficient**: Students may feel confident. Are they ready to be independent? The Try It exercises will help students assess their understanding. Interpreting the language of the problem and finding the missing quantity can be challenging.
- Be sure that any guided instruction for this lesson expects students to do the thinking. Labeling what is known about each part of the tape diagram is helpful for students.

EXAMPLE 1

- ? Draw the tape diagram and ask, "How can you represent the information given about the green monsters?" You can write 10 in the green rectangle.
- **Extension:** "Tell your neighbor any other statements you can make about how many monsters you caught." *Sample answers:* You caught a total of 40 monsters. You caught 20 more blue monsters than green monsters. You caught 20 less green monsters than blue monsters.
- Having students recognize these comparative relationships now will be helpful in understanding Example 3.

Try It

- Ask a volunteer to share his or her work and thinking.
- **Extension**: State the value of the ratio. $\frac{1}{4}$

EXAMPLE 2

- ? "There are 3 bones in a cat for every 4 bones in a dog." Pause. "How can you draw a tape diagram to show this relationship?" Listen for 3 parts and 4 parts in a tape diagram.
- ? "Do you know how many bones either animal has?" no
- ? "Does a cat have only 3 bones? Explain." No, a cat has 3 bones for every 4 bones a dog has.
- Share the rest of the information and have students work with a partner to solve the problem.
- Circulate and look at student work. Ask a volunteer to share his or her work under a document camera, or by drawing a quick sketch on the board.
- ? **Extension:** "How many total bones are in both animals?" 560 bones

Try It

- **Whiteboards:** Have students solve the problem. Ask two volunteers to share by displaying their whiteboards. Discuss any differences in their work.

Scaffold instruction to support all students in their learning. Learning is individualized and you may want to group students differently as they move in and out of these levels with each skill and concept. Student self-assessment and feedback help guide your instructional decisions about how and when to layer support for all students to become proficient learners.

Extra Example 1

The tape diagram represents the ratio of bell peppers to jalapeño peppers in a garden. There are 4 jalapeño peppers. How many bell peppers are in the garden?

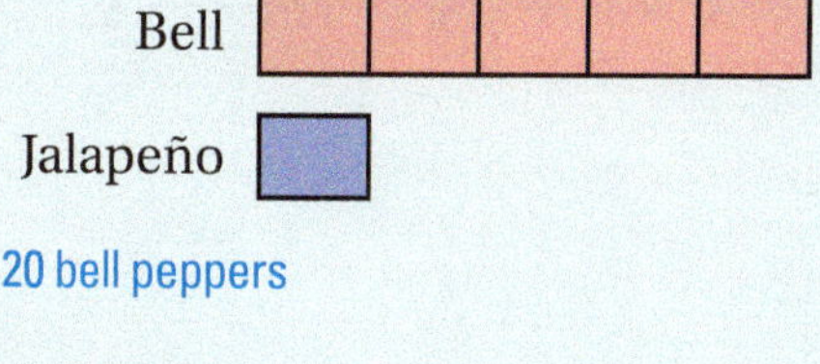

20 bell peppers

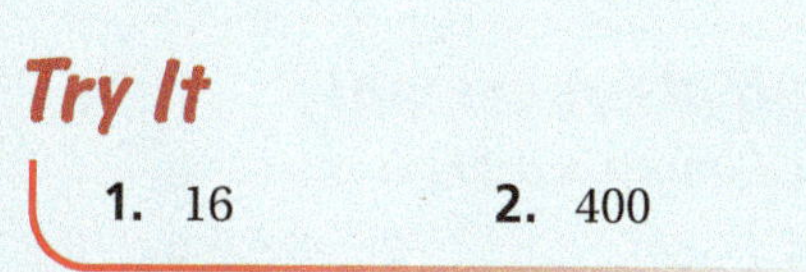

Try It

1. 16 **2.** 400

Extra Example 2

There are 7 fiction books for every 5 nonfiction books on a shelf. There are 15 nonfiction books. How many fiction books are on the shelf? 21 fiction books

ELL Support

In Try It Exercise 2, explain that they need to draw a tape diagram to represent the ratio 8 : 3. Guide them to write the number of bones in each rectangular part. Have them work in groups to solve the problem.
Beginner: Draw and label a tape diagram, writing the number 50 in each part and the total numbers at the ends.
Intermediate: Use a tape diagram to solve the problem and show their work.
Advanced: Use a tape diagram to solve the problem and explain their answers.

Extra Example 3

The ratio of time a student spends on science homework to time the student spends on math homework is 2 : 5. The total amount of time the student spends on homework for these subjects is 63 minutes. How much time does the student spend on homework for each subject? science: 18 minutes; math: 45 minutes

Try It

3. yours: $16; your friend's: $24

Self-Assessment
for Concepts & Skills

4. 2 : 3; yes; no; $\frac{2}{3} = \frac{6}{9}$ but $\frac{2}{3} \neq \frac{8}{16}$
5. Divide the total value by the number of parts.
6. *Sample answer:* a tape with 3 parts and a tape with 1 part; a tape with 6 parts and a tape with 2 parts
7. 7 winning tickets, 28 losing tickets
8. 16 winning tickets, 64 losing tickets

Laurie's Notes

EXAMPLE 3

- Pose the problem and give students time to start thinking about a plan for solving. If you have been asking students about totals in previous problems, they should have an entry point for this problem.
- Point to the model and say, "Tell your neighbor how the $40 is represented in the tape diagram." Listen for an understanding that both parts combined represent the $40.

? "How many total parts are there?" 8 parts

? "What helped you to solve the problem?" Listen for students finding the value of one part of the tape diagram to use in solving the problem.

Try It

Neighbor Check: Discuss with students that this exercise is helping them make progress with all of the success criteria. Where is their learning with respect to creating a tape diagram? Can students determine the value of each part of the diagram? Do they understand how to use the value of each part to solve a ratio problem?

Self-Assessment for Concepts & Skills

If students completed Try It Exercise 3 without guidance, have them complete the self-assessment in their *Student Journals*. Otherwise, review the meaning of each success criterion, have students complete the exercises, and then rate their understanding using the self-assessment chart.

- Ask several students to share their reasoning for Exercise 4. Discuss any differences.

? **MP3 Critique the Reasoning of Others and Construct Viable Arguments:** Ask several students to share their thinking for Exercise 5. Discuss the language and clarity of explanations. Then ask, "If you were unclear before, did any of the explanations help you make sense of this question?"

ELL Support

Check comprehension by having students complete the exercises. Have them work in groups and remind them of the processes they used in previous problems, including drawing tape diagrams. After students complete the exercises, have two groups present their answers to each other, and revise them if there is any disagreement. Provide support as needed.

The Success Criteria Self-Assessment chart can be found in the *Student Journal* or online at *BigIdeasMath.com*.

EXAMPLE 3 Using a Tape Diagram to Solve a Ratio Problem

The ratio of your monthly allowance to your friend's monthly allowance is 5 : 3. The monthly allowances total $40. How much is each allowance?

Represent the ratio 5 : 3 using a tape diagram.

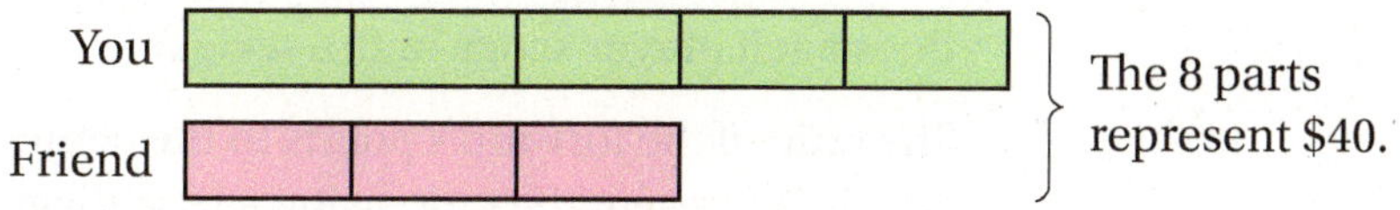

1 part represents $\$40 \div 8 = \$5$.

5 parts represent $5 \times \$5 = \$25$.

3 parts represent $3 \times \$5 = \$15$.

So, your allowance is $25, and your friend's allowance is $15.

Check Verify that the ratio of allowances is 5 : 3.

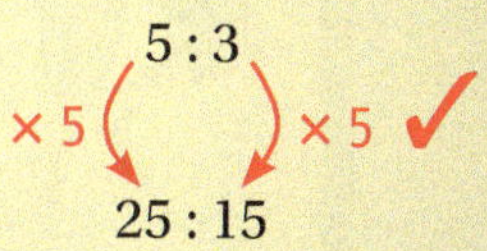

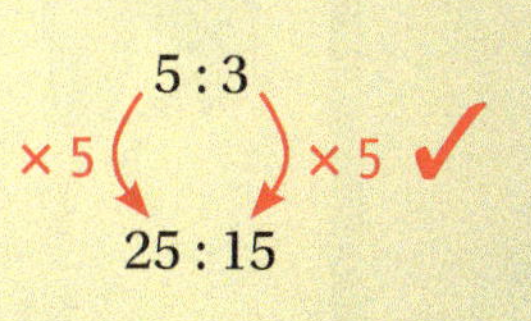

Try It

3. **WHAT IF?** Repeat Example 3 when the ratio of your monthly allowance to your friend's monthly allowance is 2 to 3.

Self-Assessment for Concepts & Skills

Solve each exercise. Then rate your understanding of the success criteria in your journal.

4. **MP STRUCTURE** What ratio is represented by the tape diagram? Can you use the tape diagram to model the ratio 6 : 9? Can you use the tape diagram to model the ratio 8 : 16? Explain your reasoning.

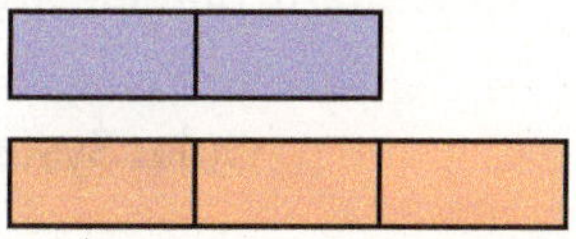

5. **MP REASONING** You are given a tape diagram and the total value of the parts. How can you find the value of 1 part?

6. **DRAWING A TAPE DIAGRAM** Describe two ways that you can represent the ratio 12 : 4 using a tape diagram.

USING A TAPE DIAGRAM You are given the number of tickets in a bag and the ratio of winning tickets to losing tickets. How many of each kind of ticket are in the bag?

7. 35 tickets; 1 to 4

8. 80 tickets; 2 : 8

EXAMPLE 4 Modeling Real Life

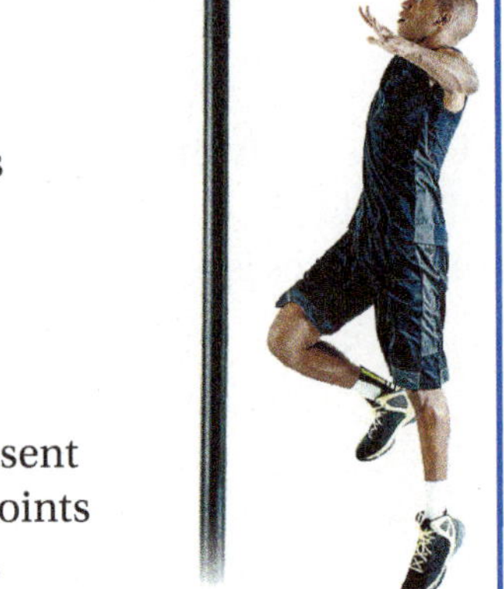

In a seven-game basketball series, a team's power forward scores 8 points for every 5 points the center scores. The forward scores 60 more points than the center in the series. How many points does each player score in the series?

The ratio of the forward's points to the center's points is 8 : 5. Represent the ratio using a tape diagram.

Forward | | | | | | | | |

Center | | | | | |

These 3 parts represent the additional 60 points the forward scores.

Math Practice

Justify Conclusions

How can you use the value of a ratio to verify that 8 : 5 and 160 : 100 are equivalent?

1 part represents $60 \div 3 = 20$ points.

8 parts represent $8 \times 20 = 160$ points.

5 parts represent $5 \times 20 = 100$ points.

So, the forward scores 160 points in the series and the center scores 100 points in the series.

Self-Assessment for Problem Solving

Solve each exercise. Then rate your understanding of the success criteria in your journal.

9. The tape diagram represents the ratio of the numbers of planets in two different solar systems. There are 8 planets in Solar System B. How many planets are in Solar System A?

Solar System A | | | |

Solar System B | | | | |

10. You and your friend play an arcade game. You score 5 points for every 9 points that your friend scores. You score 320 points less than your friend. How many points do you each score?

11. **DIG DEEPER!** Your team wins 18 medals at a track meet that are either gold, silver, or bronze. The ratio of silver medals to total medals is 2 : 9 and the ratio of gold medals to silver medals is 1 : 1. How many of each medal were won by your team?

Laurie's Notes

EXAMPLE 4

- Read the first sentence and ask, "What is being compared?" scoring by the power forward and center "How do you know?" Because of the phrase "8 points for every 5 points."
- "Does the number of games in the series matter?" no
- "Can you draw a diagram to model the quantities being compared?" Be patient and give wait time for students to think about a visual model.
- "How many parts represent the total points scored by both players?" 13 parts
- "How many parts represent the difference between the players?" 3 parts
- "What additional information do you know in the problem?" The forward scores 60 more points than the center.
- Now have students work independently or with a partner to finish the problem.
- Stop and ask students, "What was the *Muddiest Point* in this lesson and what helped you clarify your thinking?"

Self-Assessment for Problem Solving

- Students may benefit from trying the exercises independently, and then working with peers to refine their work. It is important to provide time in class for problem solving, so that students become comfortable with the problem-solving plan.
- Remind students to label their tape diagrams with the given information and continue to label as they work through the problem.
- There have been several opportunities for students to make connections between the examples and the success criteria. Now have students record their understanding of the success criteria in their journals.

The Success Criteria Self-Assessment chart can be found in the *Student Journal* or online at *BigIdeasMath.com.*

Closure

- **Exit Ticket:** You make 18 batches of muffins and zucchini bread for a bake sale. The ratio of the number of batches of muffins you make to the number of batches of zucchini bread you make is 4 : 5. If each batch of muffins makes 12 muffins, how many total muffins do you make? 96 muffins

Formative Assessment Tip

Muddiest Point

This technique is the opposite of *Point of Most Significance*. Students are asked to reflect on the most difficult or confusing point in the lesson. Their reflections are often collected at the end of the lesson so that the following day's instruction can address any confusion, however, this technique may be used at any time. It is important to know whether there was a point in the lesson that was confusing for students so that the lesson can be modified. Share with students what you learn from their reflections. Students will take reflections more seriously if they see that you value and use them.

Extra Example 4

You donate clothing to a charity. You donate 2 pairs of pants for every 3 shirts you donate. You donate 4 more shirts than pairs of pants. How many of each type of clothing do you donate to the charity? 8 pairs of pants and 12 shirts

Self-Assessment for Problem Solving

9. 6

10. you: 400, your friend: 720

11. 4 gold, 4 silver, 10 bronze

Learning Target

Use tape diagrams to model and solve ratio problems.

Success Criteria

- Interpret tape diagrams that represent ratio relationships.
- Draw tape diagrams to model ratio relationships.
- Find the value of one part of a tape diagram.
- Use tape diagrams to solve ratio problems.

Review & Refresh

1. equivalent
2. equivalent
3. not equivalent
4. not equivalent
5. $\frac{1}{2}$
6. $1\frac{3}{4}$
7. $13\frac{7}{16}$
8. B

Concepts, Skills, & Problem Solving

9. 800 m
10. 300 m
11. beginner trail: 400 m, expert trail: 1600 m
12. beginner trail: 250 m, expert trail: 1000 m
13. 6 h
14. 15 h
15. 2
16. 7
17. 9
18. 15
19. 27
20. 16

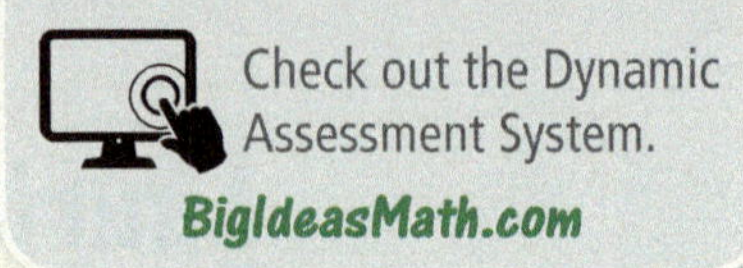

Assignment Guide and Concept Check

Scaffold assignments to support all students in their learning progression. The suggested assignments are a starting point. Continue to assign additional exercises and revisit with spaced practice to move every student toward proficiency.

Level	Assignment 1	Assignment 2
Emerging	3, 7, 8, 10, 11, 13, 15, 17, 23	14, 18, 22, 27, 28, 30
Proficient	3, 7, 8, 10, 11, 14, 16, 18, 22	19, 26, 27, 28, 31
Advanced	3, 7, 8, 10, 11, 14, 18, 19, 26	28, 29, 30, 31, 32

- Assignment 1 is for use after students complete the Self-Assessment for Concepts & Skills.
- Assignment 2 is for use after students complete the Self-Assessment for Problem Solving.
- The red exercises can be used as a concept check.

Review & Refresh Prior Skills

Exercises 1–4 Identifying Equivalent Ratios
Exercises 5–7 Multiplying Fractions and Mixed Numbers
Exercise 8 Multiplying Decimals

3.2 Practice

Review & Refresh

Determine whether the ratios are equivalent.

1. 11 : 4 and 22 : 8
2. 12 : 18 and 2 : 3
3. 56 : 81 and 7 : 9
4. 2 : 12 and 6 : 24

Multiply. Write the answer in simplest form.

5. $\frac{7}{10} \cdot \frac{5}{7}$
6. $2\frac{1}{3} \cdot \frac{3}{4}$
7. $5\frac{3}{8} \cdot 2\frac{1}{2}$

8. Melissa earns $7.40 per hour working at a grocery store. She works 14.25 hours this week. How much does she earn?

   A. $83.13 **B.** $105.45 **C.** $156.75 **D.** $1054.50

Concepts, Skills, & Problem Solving

USING A TAPE DIAGRAM **Use the tape diagram in Exploration 1 to answer the question.** (See Exploration 1, p. 115.)

9. The beginner trail is 200 meters long. How long is the expert trail?
10. The expert trail is 1200 meters long. How long is the beginner trail?
11. The combined length of the trails is 2000 meters. How long is each trail?
12. The expert trail is 750 meters longer than the beginner trail. How long is each trail?

INTERPRETING A TAPE DIAGRAM **The tape diagram represents the ratio of the time you spend tutoring to the time your friend spends tutoring. You tutor for 3 hours. How many hours does your friend spend tutoring?**

13.

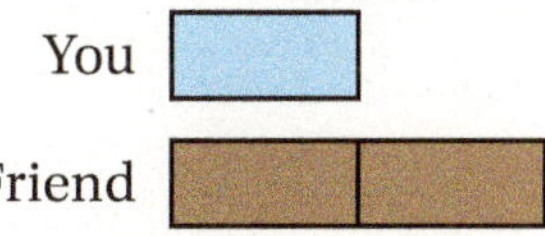

14.

DRAWING A TAPE DIAGRAM **A bag contains red marbles and blue marbles. You are given the number of red marbles in the bag and the ratio of red marbles to blue marbles. Find the number of blue marbles in the bag.**

15. 10 red marbles; 5 to 1
16. 3 red marbles; 3 : 7
17. 12 red marbles; 4 : 3
18. 6 red marbles; 2 for every 5
19. 18 red marbles; 6 to 9
20. 12 red marbles; 3 : 4

USING A TAPE DIAGRAM **A bowl contains blueberries and strawberries. You are given the total number of berries in the bowl and the ratio of blueberries to strawberries. How many of each berry are in the bowl?**

21. 16 berries; 3 : 1

22. 10 berries; 2 for every 3

23. 12 berries; 1 to 2

24. 20 berries; 4 : 1

25. 48 berries; 9 to 3

26. 46 berries; 11 for every 12

27. **MP PROBLEM SOLVING** You separate bulbs of garlic into two groups: one for planting and one for cooking. The tape diagram represents the ratio of bulbs for planting to bulbs for cooking. You use 6 bulbs for cooking. Each bulb has 8 cloves. How many cloves of garlic will you plant?

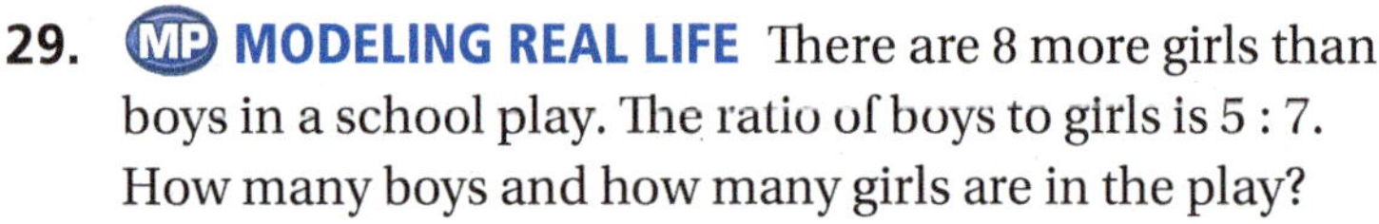

28. **MP MODELING REAL LIFE** Methane gas contains carbon atoms and hydrogen atoms in the ratio of 1 : 4. A sample of methane gas contains 92 hydrogen atoms. How many carbon atoms are in the sample? How many total atoms are in the sample?

CH_4 Methane

29. **MP MODELING REAL LIFE** There are 8 more girls than boys in a school play. The ratio of boys to girls is 5 : 7. How many boys and how many girls are in the play?

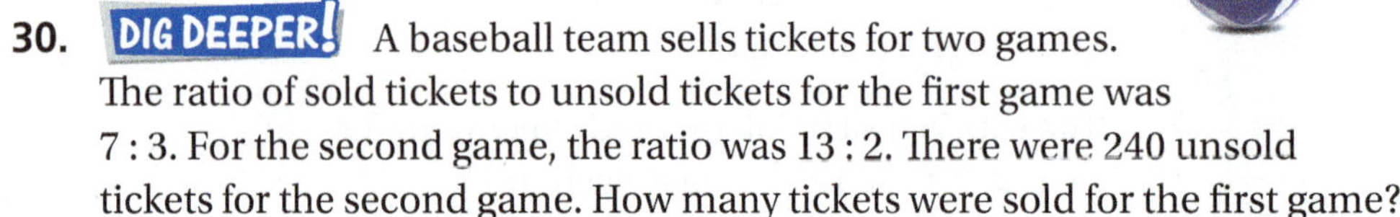

30. **DIG DEEPER!** A baseball team sells tickets for two games. The ratio of sold tickets to unsold tickets for the first game was 7 : 3. For the second game, the ratio was 13 : 2. There were 240 unsold tickets for the second game. How many tickets were sold for the first game?

31. **MP PROBLEM SOLVING** You have $150 in a savings account and you have some cash. The tape diagram represents the ratio of the amounts of money. You want to have twice the amount of money in your savings account as you have in cash. How much of your cash should you deposit into your savings account?

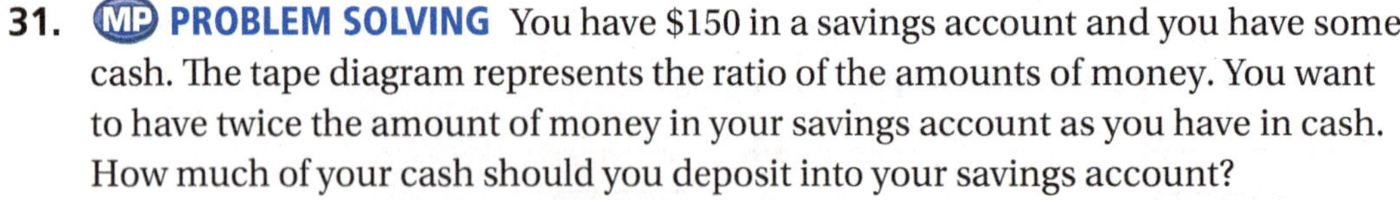

32. **DIG DEEPER!** A fish tank contains tetras, guppies, and minnows. The ratio of tetras to guppies is 4 : 2. The ratio of minnows to guppies is 1 : 3. There are 60 fish in the tank. How many more tetras are there than minnows? Justify your answer.

Common Errors

- **Exercise 32** Students may stop solving the problem after finding the number of tetras in the fish tank. Remind students to read the problem carefully to determine what is being asked.

Mini-Assessment

A bag contains pennies and nickels. You are given the number of pennies in the bag and the ratio of pennies to nickels. Find the number of nickels in the bag.

1. 18 pennies; 6 to 1 3 nickels
2. 8 pennies; 2 : 7 28 nickels
3. You have $40 for a video game and your parents will contribute some money. The tape diagram represents the amounts of money. How much money will your parents contribute?

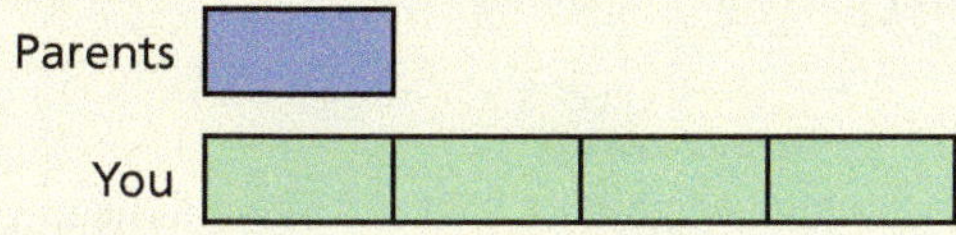

$10

4. There are 12 more girls than boys in a drama club. The ratio of girls to boys is 9 : 5. How many girls and how many boys are in the drama club?

27 girls and 15 boys

Section Resources

Surface Level	Deep Level
Resources by Chapter • Extra Practice • Reteach • Puzzle Time Student Journal • Self-Assessment • Practice Differentiating the Lesson Tutorial Videos Skills Review Handbook Skills Trainer	Resources by Chapter • Enrichment and Extension Graphic Organizers Dynamic Assessment System • Section Practice

Concepts, Skills, & Problem Solving

21. 12 blueberries, 4 strawberries
22. 4 blueberries, 6 strawberries
23. 4 blueberries, 8 strawberries
24. 16 blueberries, 4 strawberries
25. 36 blueberries, 12 strawberries
26. 22 blueberries, 24 strawberries
27. 288
28. 23 carbon atoms, 115 total atoms
29. 20 boys, 28 girls
30. 1260
31. $200
32. 30; 4 : 2 and 6 : 3 are equivalent, so the ratio tetras to guppies to minnows is 6 : 3 : 1. This is equivalent to 36 : 18 : 6, and $36 - 6 = 30$.

Learning Target

Use ratio tables to represent equivalent ratios and solve ratio problems.

Success Criteria

- Use various operations to create tables of equivalent ratios.
- Use ratio tables to solve ratio problems.
- Use ratio tables to compare ratios.

Warm Up

Cumulative, vocabulary, and prerequisite skills practice opportunities are available in the *Resources by Chapter* or at *BigIdeasMath.com*.

ELL Support

Explain that the word *double* means two times or twice. A number line is a line with numbers. A double number line is two number lines put together that show values for two things that are being compared.

Exploration 1

a. See Additional Answers.

b. *Sample answers:* As cups of milk increase by 2, calories increase by 180; The number of calories is 90 times the number of cups of milk.

c. *Sample answers:* Multiply or divide each quantity in one ratio by the same number; Add the numbers in the given ratio to the respective quantities in one ratio.

Exploration 2

a–b. See Additional Answers.

Laurie's Notes

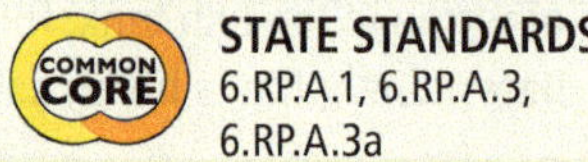

STATE STANDARDS
6.RP.A.1, 6.RP.A.3, 6.RP.A.3a

Preparing to Teach

- You can find and organize equivalent ratios in a **ratio table**. In this lesson, various operations are used to create ratio tables.
- Another way to organize equivalent ratios is to make a double number line. Help students see the connection between the double number line and the ratio table.
- **Common Misconception:** Students sometimes think there is only one correct ratio table when solving a problem. Address this misconception when two students have the same answer but different tables.

Motivate

- **Story Time:** Tell students that you took a five-mile float trip down a river. For each mile, the drop in elevation was the same.
- Draw the table as shown and ask students to fill in the missing values.

Number of Miles	1	2	3	5
Drop in Elevation (feet)		80		

40, 120, 200

- Ask students to explain how they found the missing values.

Exploration 1

- Students should not have difficulty with the context of this problem, though they may skip over the direction line.
- When asked to think about any relationships in part (b), students may use ratio language.
- **MP3 Construct Viable Arguments and Critique the Reasoning of Others:** There are many different ways to find equivalent ratios. Having students share their thinking will likely preview several of the strategies used in this lesson. If students think a ratio is a fraction, it won't make sense to them that you can add the values from the two columns. You want students to explain their thinking. Expect others to ask questions if the explanation is unclear.

Exploration 2

- Students may label the increments on the double number line with the same values as the ratio table. Others may think that the increments must be multiples of 10 or 100. This is a good class discussion.
- **Connection:** The double number line can help students realize there are infinitely many ratios equivalent to a given ratio. Before part (b), ask, "How many calories are in 8 cups?" 720 calories "How many cups of milk contain 1800 calories?" 20 cups
- "Can the ratio table be used to find the number of calories in 3 cups of milk? 3.5 cups of milk?" Students may find it easier to think about these questions on a double number line because they know there are other numbers between 2 and 4, such as 3 and 3.5. If students haven't recognized that the columns in a ratio table represent equivalent ratios, it will not make sense to them that the columns can be in any order.

3.3 Using Ratio Tables

Learning Target: Use ratio tables to represent equivalent ratios and solve ratio problems.

Success Criteria:
- I can use various operations to create tables of equivalent ratios.
- I can use ratio tables to solve ratio problems.
- I can use ratio tables to compare ratios.

EXPLORATION 1 Making a Table of Equivalent Ratios

Work with a partner. You buy milk that contains 180 calories per 2 cups.

a. You measure 2 cups of the milk for a recipe and pour it into a pitcher. You repeat this four more times. Make a table to show the numbers of calories and cups in the pitcher as you add the milk.

b. Describe any relationships you see in your table.

c. Describe ways that you can find equivalent ratios using different operations.

Math Practice

Compare Arguments

Compare your explanations in part (c) with another group. If they are different, are they both correct?

EXPLORATION 2 Creating a Double Number Line

Work with a partner.

a. Represent the ratio in Exploration 1 by labeling the increments on the *double number line* below. Can you label the increments in more than one way?

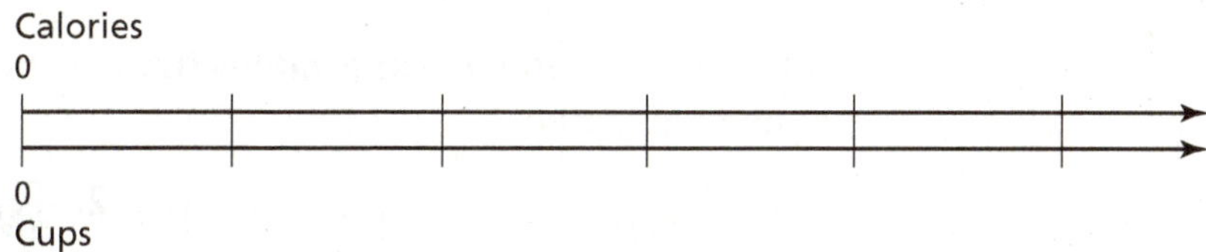

b. How can you use the double number line to find the number of calories in 3 cups of milk? 3.5 cups of milk?

3.3 Lesson

Key Vocabulary
ratio table, *p. 122*

You can find and organize equivalent ratios in a **ratio table**. You can generate a ratio table by using repeated addition or multiplication.

EXAMPLE 1 Completing Ratio Tables

Find the missing values in each ratio table. Then write the equivalent ratios.

a.

Triangles	1	2		4
Sides	3		9	

b.

Frogs	4	20		
Toads	6		90	180

a. Because the original ratio is 1 triangle to 3 sides, you can repeatedly add 1 to the first row and repeatedly add 3 to the second row.

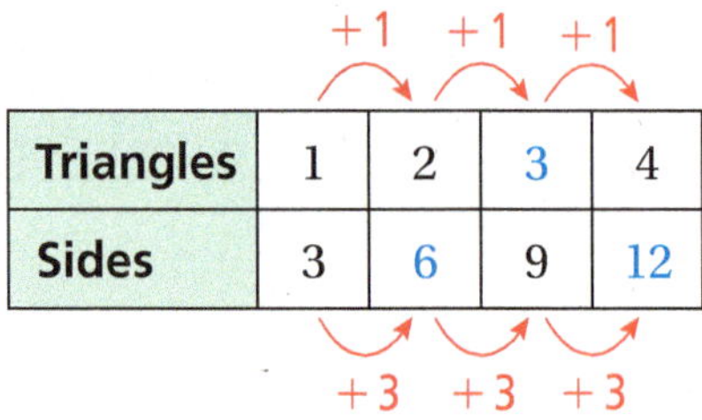

Triangles	1	2	3	4
Sides	3	6	9	12

The equivalent ratios are 1 : 3, 2 : 6, 3 : 9, and 4 : 12.

b. You can use multiplication to find the missing values.

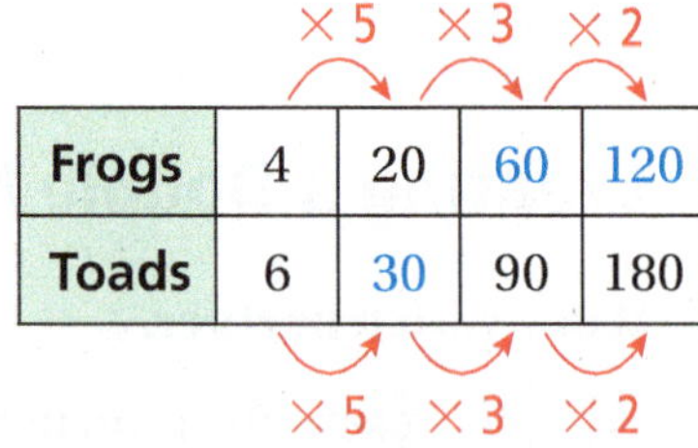

Frogs	4	20	60	120
Toads	6	30	90	180

The equivalent ratios are 4 : 6, 20 : 30, 60 : 90, and 120 : 180.

Math Practice

Find Entry Points

How can you help a classmate understand where to begin when finding missing values in a ratio table?

Try It **Find the missing values in the ratio table. Then write the equivalent ratios.**

1.

Hands	4		12	16
People	2	4		

2.

Miles	4		24	96
Hours	3	6		

Multi-Language Glossary at *BigIdeasMath.com*

Laurie's Notes

Scaffolding Instruction

- The explorations introduced two models that can be used to represent equivalent ratios: a ratio table and a double number line. Students may not recognize the equivalent ratios in one or both of these models. Another factor to consider in planning instruction is the underlying number sense involved when finding values in either model.
- **Emerging**: Students might have followed the reasoning used for each exploration, yet may not be ready to work independently. Going through Examples 1 and 2, either independently or with guided instruction, will help students understand how various operations can be used to complete a ratio table.
- **Proficient**: Students may be confident in identifying equivalent ratios and recognizing how different operations can be used to write equivalent ratios in a ratio table. These students should work with a partner to read through Examples 1 and 2, and then complete the Try It exercises.
- Whether students are provided guided instruction or work independently, they should use arrows to indicate which operations are being performed.

Discuss

- Begin the lesson by connecting the columns in a **ratio table** to equivalent ratios. Use a context, such as number of weeks and number of days for the two rows. All of the columns will be equivalent to 1 : 7.

EXAMPLE 1

- **MP7 Look for and Make Use of Structure:** Students will use the structure of a ratio table to find equivalent ratios.
- Draw the table shown in part (a).

? **Think-Pair-Share:** "How can you find the missing values in the table?"

- **MP1 Make Sense of Problems and Persevere in Solving Them:** Some students may have difficulty getting started. Encourage students to analyze the ratio table and explain the meaning of equivalent ratios.
- Students may believe that they are just counting by ones and threes. You want them to connect this counting to an operation.
- **Common Misconception:** In part (b), students may reason that because 20 is 16 more than 4, you need to add 16 to 6 to get 22. Ask them if the ratio 20 : 22 is equivalent to the original ratio of 4 : 6. The disconnect is that they've forgotten you add the ratio to itself (4 : 6 → 8 : 12), not the same number (i.e. 16) to each part of the ratio. This can be highlighted in the first step of part (a). Instead of multiplying by 2, you can add the ratio to itself.
- **Note**: These examples guide students into thinking about various operations because the tables are partially completed. In the application problems, students need to think about the operation path that leads to a target number.

Try It

? **Connection:** "In Exercise 1, what is the relationship between the first and third columns? first and fourth columns?" *Sample answers:* The third column is 3 times the first column; The fourth column is 4 times the first column.

- It is important for students to share their work and thinking, as different operations can be used. In Exercise 2, some students may have thought to multiply by 2 to find the first missing value, while others thought to add 4 to the value for miles and add 3 to the value for hours.

Formative Assessment Tip

Think-Pair-Share

This technique allows students to share their thinking about a problem with their partners after they have had time to consider the problem alone. Once partners have discussed the problem, small groups or the whole class should discuss the problem.

The initial time working alone is important for students to develop their own understanding of the mathematics. "Private think time" is what I call it. Once students have engaged in the problem, sharing with partners helps confirm their understanding or perhaps the need to modify their thinking. Sharing their thinking with the whole class is more comfortable for students when they have had the chance to discuss their thinking with partners.

Extra Example 1

Find the missing values in each ratio table. Then write the equivalent ratios.

a.

Cars	2		6
Trucks	5	10	

4, 15; 2 : 5, 4 : 10, 6 : 15

b.

Markers	3	9	
Crayons	4		48

36, 12; 3 : 4, 9 : 12, 36 : 48

Try It

1. 8, 6, 8; 4 : 2, 8 : 4, 12 : 6, 16 : 8
2. 8, 18, 72; 4 : 3, 8 : 6, 24 : 18, 96 : 72

Extra Example 2

Find the missing values in each ratio table. Then write the equivalent ratios.

a.

Feet	5	25		
Seconds	2		14	28

35, 70, 10; 5 : 2, 25 : 10, 35 : 14, 70 : 28

b.

Miles	4		5	
Gallons	1	5		$\frac{9}{4}$

20, 9, $\frac{5}{4}$; 4 : 1, 20 : 5, 5 : $\frac{5}{4}$, 9 : $\frac{9}{4}$

Try It

3. 3, 10, 20; 1 : 5, 2 : 10, 4 : 20, 3 : 15

4. 48, 1, 3; 24 : 2, 12 : 1, 48 : 4, 36 : 3

Laurie's Notes

Discuss

- Students have seen addition and multiplication used to complete ratio tables. Pose questions to see if other operations also make sense.
- ? "Do you think the operations of subtraction and division can be used to complete a ratio table?"

EXAMPLE 2

- These two problems help students understand that more than one operation can be used in a ratio table. They need to think about what combination of operations will get them to the target number. Students with good number sense will have less difficulty with this.
- ? "In part (a), is there another way to find the number of cents in 8 dollars? Explain." Yes, you can multiply each of the values in the first column by 8.

Try It

- Remind students of the success criteria. They are working towards being able to create a ratio table using various operations to solve a ratio problem, and there is more than one correct route. Exposure to multiple solution paths in the previous problems is important.
- Solicit solutions that represent different approaches.

ELL Support

In Exercise 3, explain that the numbers in the bottom row of the ratio table identify the total number of flower petals. Each flower has five petals. Ask, "If there are two flowers, how many petals are there?" It may be helpful to have students draw the flowers. Have students work in groups to complete the table.

Beginner: Draw flowers to represent each column of the ratio table. Each flower should have 5 petals. They will use the drawings to complete the table.

Intermediate: Complete the ratio table and write the equivalent ratios.

Advanced: Explain what each ratio means. For example, "One flower has five petals."

You can also generate a ratio table by using subtraction or division. In summary, you can find equivalent ratios by:

- adding or subtracting quantities in equivalent ratios.
- multiplying or dividing each quantity in a ratio by the same number.

EXAMPLE 2 Completing Ratio Tables

Find the missing values in each ratio table. Then write the equivalent ratios.

a.

Dollars	1			8
Cents	100	300	900	

b.

Meters	3		2	
Minutes	1	2		$\frac{5}{3}$

> In Example 2(a), notice that you obtain the fourth column by subtracting the values in the first column from the values in the third column.
> $9 - 1 = 8$
> $900 - 100 = 800$

a. You can use a combination of operations to find the missing values.

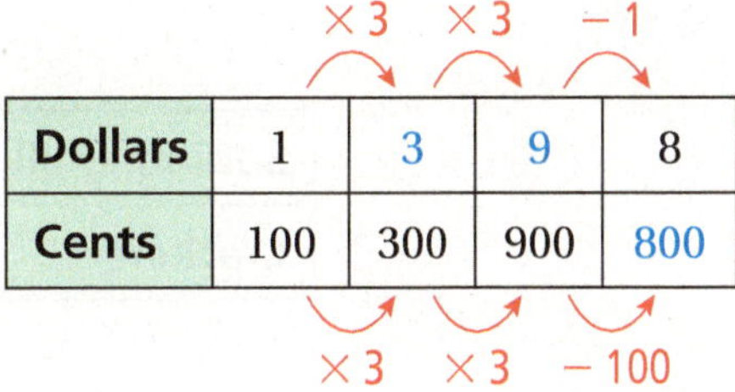

×3 ×3 −1

Dollars	1	3	9	8
Cents	100	300	900	800

×3 ×3 −100

The equivalent ratios are 1 : 100, 3 : 300, 9 : 900, and 8 : 800.

b. You can use a combination of operations to find the missing values.

×2 ÷3 +3

Meters	3	6	2	5
Minutes	1	2	$\frac{2}{3}$	$\frac{5}{3}$

×2 ÷3 +1

The equivalent ratios are $3 : 1$, $6 : 2$, $2 : \frac{2}{3}$, and $5 : \frac{5}{3}$.

Try It **Find the missing values in the ratio table. Then write the equivalent ratios.**

3.

Flowers	1	2	4	
Petals	5			15

4.

Students	24	12		36
Teachers	2		4	

EXAMPLE 3 Solving a Ratio Problem

A nutrition label shows that there are 75 milligrams of sodium in every 12 crackers. You eat 30 crackers. How much sodium do you consume?

Method 1: Use a double number line. Increment the number lines using the original ratio of 75 to 12.

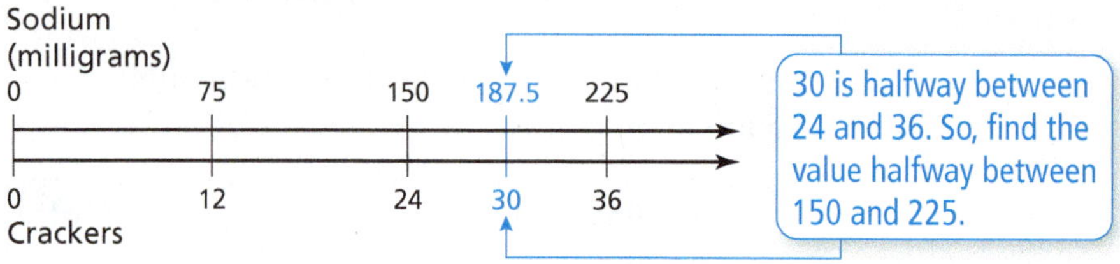

So, you consume 187.5 milligrams of sodium in 30 crackers.

Method 2: Use a ratio table. The ratio of milligrams of sodium to crackers is 75 to 12. Find an equivalent ratio with 30 crackers.

	÷ 2 →	× 5 →	
Sodium (milligrams)	75	37.5	187.5
Crackers	12	6	30
	÷ 2 →	× 5 →	

So, you consume 187.5 milligrams of sodium in 30 crackers.

Math Practice

Repeat Calculations

How can you obtain the third column in the table from the first column using one operation?

Try It

5. **WHAT IF?** You eat 21 crackers. How much sodium do you consume?

Self-Assessment for Concepts & Skills

Solve each exercise. Then rate your understanding of the success criteria in your journal.

COMPLETING A RATIO TABLE Find the missing values in the ratio table. Then write the equivalent ratios.

6.

Fruit	2		6
Vegetables	6	12	

7.

Gnats	2	14		5
Flies	8		28	

8. **WRITING** Explain how creating a ratio table using repeated addition is similar to creating a ratio table using multiplication.

Laurie's Notes

EXAMPLE 3

- Ask a volunteer to read the problem.
- ? "Should you make a double number line or a ratio table?" either
- ? **MP2 Reason Abstractly and Quantitatively:** "Can you estimate the amount of sodium in 30 crackers?" Listen for something similar to: "I know that $75:12 = 150:24$ by doubling; $75:12 = 225:36$ by tripling; 30 is halfway between 24 and 36, so the answer is halfway between 150 and 225, or about 190. There are approximately 190 milligrams of sodium in 30 crackers."
- ? **Think-Pair-Share:** "How do you label the increments on the double number line?" Listen to students' reasoning.
- A common question students may ask about making a ratio table is, "How many columns are needed?" I tell my students to begin by making 4 or 5 columns, and add more if you still need to find the solution.
- Having students show their work at the board or under a document camera leads to rich discussion about the various strategies that can be used.
- Have students work with a partner to solve the problem using a ratio table.
- Be sure to solicit a variety of approaches.
- **MP8 Look for and Express Regularity in Repeated Reasoning:** Dividing by 2 is the same as multiplying by $\frac{1}{2}$. So, the two operations used in Method 2 are equivalent to multiplying by $\frac{5}{2}$, or 2.5. Some students will be able to recognize and use this type of shortcut, while others will need to use multiple operations.

Try It

- If students have difficulty getting started, ask them to talk about the previous example.
- ? "Is it easier to think about a double number line or a ratio table?"

Self-Assessment for Concepts & Skills

- Review the success criteria with students and have them complete the exercises. The first two exercises can also be solved using a double number line.
- As students work through the exercises, they should be thinking: How am I doing with my learning? Am I making progress with each of the success criteria? If not, where is my understanding not complete?

ELL Support

Allow students to work with a partner to check understanding of what they learned. For Exercises 6 and 7, have students take turns asking and answering questions about the missing values in the ratio tables. For example, Student A may ask, "How many pieces of fruit are there when there are 12 vegetables?" Student B should respond, "4 pieces of fruit for 12 vegetables." Partners reverse roles for Exercise 7.

The Success Criteria Self-Assessment chart can be found in the *Student Journal* or online at *BigIdeasMath.com*.

Extra Example 3

A nutrition label shows that there are 370 calories in every 100 grams of cereal. You eat 40 grams of the cereal. How many calories do you consume? 148 calories

Try It

5. 131.25 mg

Self-Assessment for Concepts & Skills

6. 4, 18; $2:6$, $4:12$, $6:18$
7. 7, 56, 20; $2:8$, $14:56$, $7:28$, $5:20$
8. Multiplying the quantities of a ratio by k gives the same result as adding the quantities of the ratio together k times.

Extra Example 4

You and your friend make tea. You add 1.5 teaspoons of sugar for every 8 fluid ounces of tea. Your friend adds 1.75 teaspoons of sugar for every 10 fluid ounces of the same tea. Whose tea is sweeter? your tea

Self-Assessment *for Problem Solving*

9. $26\frac{1}{4}$ tbsp

10. your friend's

Learning Target

Use ratio tables to represent equivalent ratios and solve ratio problems.

Success Criteria

- Use various operations to create tables of equivalent ratios.
- Use ratio tables to solve ratio problems.
- Use ratio tables to compare ratios.

Laurie's Notes

EXAMPLE 4

- There are different approaches rather than one correct approach for solving ratio problems using a ratio table or a double number line.
- **Teaching Tip:** You can model this problem by using red and blue food coloring. Fill two clear glasses with the same amount of water. Add 3 drops of red and 1 drop of blue into one glass. Stir. It will appear to be a shade of purple. Then add 5 drops of red and 3 drops of blue into the other glass. Stir.
- ? "Are the shades of purple the same? Which is redder? Which is bluer?" Have students share their thinking as a class. Without a ratio table, many students will rely on their eyesight.
- Give time for students to work with a partner on this example.
- ? "How will you know that the frosting is redder?" Listen for understanding of the need to compare equal amounts of something—drops of red, drops of blue, or total amount of drops.

Self-Assessment for Problem Solving

- Allow time in class for students to practice using the problem-solving plan. Remember, some students may only be ready to complete the first step.
- Students should work independently or with a partner on the exercises. Expect students to move to different locations in the classroom to offer or solicit help.
- ? Remind students to look back at previous problems and lessons. "Have you solved a problem similar to this before?"
- As students are working through the exercises, encourage them to assess their understanding of the learning target and success criteria, keeping the focus on the learning target. Tell students to rate their understanding of each success criterion.

The Success Criteria Self-Assessment chart can be found in the *Student Journal* or online at *BigIdeasMath.com*.

Closure

- **Exit Ticket:** A recipe takes 900 soy beans to make a gallon of soy milk. How many soy beans are needed to make 2.5 gallons of soy milk? 2250 soy beans

EXAMPLE 4 Modeling Real Life

You and your teacher make colored frosting. You add 3 drops of red food coloring for every 1 drop of blue food coloring. Your teacher adds 5 drops of red for every 3 drops of blue. Whose frosting is redder?

Understand the problem.

You are given the numbers of drops of food coloring that you and your teacher use to make frosting. You are asked to determine whose frosting is redder.

Make a plan.

Use ratio tables to compare the frostings. Find ratios in which the number of drops of red, the number of drops of blue, or the total number of drops is the same. Then compare the quantities to determine which is redder.

Solve and check.

Create ratio tables for 3 : 1 and 5 : 3 using repeated addition. Include a column for the total number of drops in each frosting.

Your Frosting		
Drops of Red	Drops of Blue	Total Drops
3	1	4
6	2	8
9	3	12
12	4	16
15	5	20

Your Teacher's Frosting		
Drops of Red	Drops of Blue	Total Drops
5	3	8
10	6	16
15	9	24
20	12	32
25	15	40

Look Back
The tables show that when both frostings have a total of 16 drops, your frosting has 2 more drops of red and 2 fewer drops of blue. So, your frosting is redder. 

When both frostings have 3 drops of blue, your frosting has $9 - 5 = 4$ more drops of red than your teacher's frosting.

So, your frosting is redder than your teacher's frosting.

Self-Assessment for Problem Solving

Solve each exercise. Then rate your understanding of the success criteria in your journal.

9. You mix 7 tablespoons of vinegar for every 4 tablespoons of baking soda to produce a chemical reaction. You use 15 tablespoons of baking soda. How much vinegar do you use?

10. You make a carbonated beverage by adding 7 ounces of soda water for every 3 ounces of regular water. Your friend uses 11 ounces of soda water for every 4 ounces of regular water. Whose beverage is more carbonated?

3.3 Practice

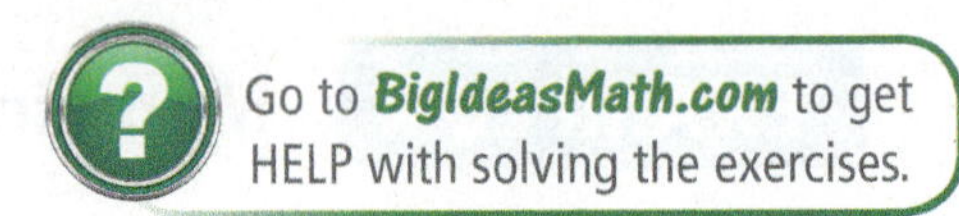

Review & Refresh

A bag contains green tokens and black tokens. You are given the number of green tokens in the bag and the ratio of green tokens to black tokens. Find the number of black tokens in the bag.

1. 8 green tokens; 4 for every 1

2. 6 green tokens; 2 : 7

3. 24 green tokens; 8 to 5

4. 36 green tokens; 3 for every 4

Find the GCF of the numbers.

5. 8, 16

6. 48, 80

7. 15, 45, 100

Evaluate the expression.

8. $35 - 2 \times 4^2$

9. $12 \div (1 + 3^3 - 2^4)$

10. $8^2 \div [(11 - 3) \cdot 2]$

Find the perimeter of the rectangle.

11.

Area = 48 yd^2

8 yd

12.

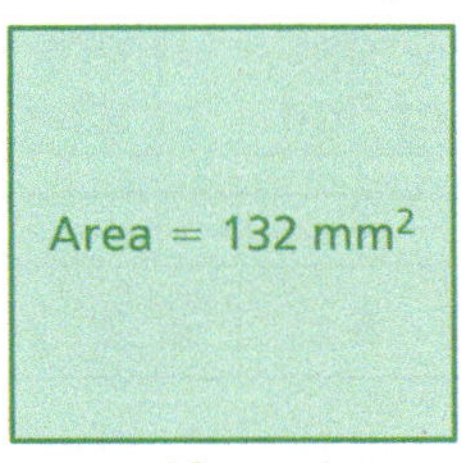

Concepts, Skills, & Problem Solving

USING A RATIO TABLE **Use a ratio table to find the number of calories in the indicated number of cups of milk from Exploration 1. Explain your method.** (See Exploration 1, p. 121.)

13. 16 cups

14. 18 cups

15. 5.5 cups

COMPLETING RATIO TABLES **Find the missing value(s) in the ratio table. Then write the equivalent ratios.**

16.

Boys	1	
Girls	5	10

17.

Burgers	3		9
Hot Dogs	5	10	

18.

People	6		18
Benches	3	12	

19.

Adults	2	1		18
Children	14		21	

20.

Pies	5		$\frac{10}{3}$	
Cakes	3	12		5

21.

Plums	14	42		
Grapes	7		3	24

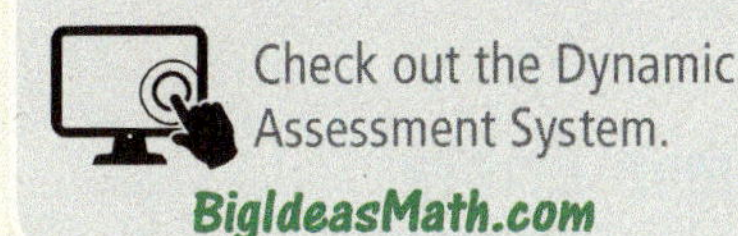

Assignment Guide and Concept Check

Scaffold assignments to support all students in their learning progression. The suggested assignments are a starting point. Continue to assign additional exercises and revisit with spaced practice to move every student toward proficiency.

Level	Assignment 1	Assignment 2
Emerging	4, 7, 10, 12, 14, 17, 19, 22, 23, 27	20, 24, 25, 28, 29, 30, 31, 37
Proficient	4, 7, 10, 12, 14, 19, 20, 22, 24, 27	29, 30, 31, 32, 33, 35, 37, 40
Advanced	4, 7, 10, 12, 15, 20, 21, 22, 26, 28	30, 32, 34, 36, 38, 39, 41, 42

- Assignment 1 is for use after students complete the Self-Assessment for Concepts & Skills.
- Assignment 2 is for use after students complete the Self-Assessment for Problem Solving.
- The red exercises can be used as a concept check.

Review & Refresh Prior Skills

Exercises 1–4 Using a Tape Diagram
Exercises 5–7 Finding the GCF
Exercises 8–10 Using Order of Operations
Exercises 11 and 12 Find the Perimeter of a Rectangle and Dividing Whole Numbers

Common Errors

- **Exercises 16–21** Students may add or subtract the same amount to each number in the ratio, saying, for example, that 2 : 3 and 4 : 5 are equivalent. Make it very clear that the numbers you add or subtract must be in the same ratio. You cannot add or subtract the same number, as when multiplying or dividing.

Review & Refresh

1. 2 **2.** 21
3. 15 **4.** 48
5. 8 **6.** 16
7. 5 **8.** 3
9. 1 **10.** 4
11. 28 yd **12.** 46 mm

Concepts, Skills, & Problem Solving

13. 1440; *Sample answer:* $2 \times 8 = 16$ and $180 \times 8 = 1440$

14. 1620; *Sample answer:* $2 \times 9 = 18$ and $180 \times 9 = 1620$

15. 495; *Sample answer:* $(2 \div 2) \times 5.5 = 5.5$ and $(180 \div 2) \times 5.5 = 495$

16.

Boys	1	2
Girls	5	10

1 : 5, 2 : 10

17.

Burgers	3	6	9
Hot dogs	5	10	15

3 : 5, 6 : 10, 9 : 15

18.

People	6	24	18
Benches	3	12	9

6 : 3, 24 : 12, 18 : 9

19.

Adults	2	1	3	18
Children	14	7	21	126

2 : 14, 1 : 7, 3 : 21, 18 : 126

20.

Pies	5	20	$\frac{10}{3}$	$\frac{25}{3}$
Cakes	3	12	2	5

$5:3, 20:12, \frac{10}{3}:2, \frac{25}{3}:5$

21.

Plums	14	42	6	48
Grapes	7	21	3	24

14 : 7, 42 : 21, 6 : 3, 48 : 24

Concepts, Skills, & Problem Solving

22. no; *Sample answer:*
$\frac{5}{3} \neq \frac{25}{9} \neq \frac{125}{27}$

23. 16

24. 16

25. $60

26. 18

27. 1840

28. 1050

29. **a.** 392; no; *Sample answer:* $392 < 400$

b. $16,400; no; *Sample answer:* $\$16{,}400 < \$16{,}800$

30. 180 mg

Common Errors

- **Exercises 23–26** There are many ways that students can use a ratio table to solve the problem. Emphasize to students that the tables shown are just templates that are similar to the examples.

22. **MP YOU BE THE TEACHER** Your friend creates a ratio table for the ratio 5 : 3. Is your friend correct? Explain your reasoning.

A	5	25	125
B	3	9	27

COMPLETING RATIO TABLES Complete the ratio table to solve the problem.

23. For every 3 tickets you sell, your friend sells 4 tickets. You sell a total of 12 tickets. How many tickets does your friend sell?

You	3			12
Friend	4			

24. A store sells 2 printers for every 5 computers. The store sells 40 computers. How many printers does the store sell?

Printers	2		8	
Computers	5	10		40

25. First and second place in a contest use a ratio to share a cash prize. When first place pays \$100, second place pays \$60. How much does first place pay when second place pays \$36?

First	100		
Second	60		36

26. A grade has 81 girls and 72 boys. The grade is split into groups that have the same ratio of girls to boys as the whole grade. How many girls are in a group that has 16 boys?

Girls	81		
Boys	72		16

USING A DOUBLE NUMBER LINE Find the missing quantity in the double number line.

27. Pounds: 0, 460, ?

Pallets: 0, 4, 16

28.

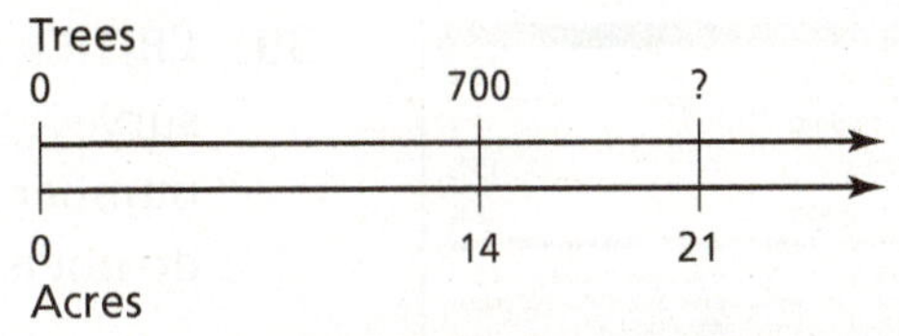

29. **MP PROBLEM SOLVING** A company sets sales goals for employees each month.

a. At her current pace, how many items will Kristina sell in 28 days? Is she on track to meet the goal? Explain.

b. At his current pace, how many dollars worth of product will Jim sell in 28 days? Is he on track to meet the goal? Explain.

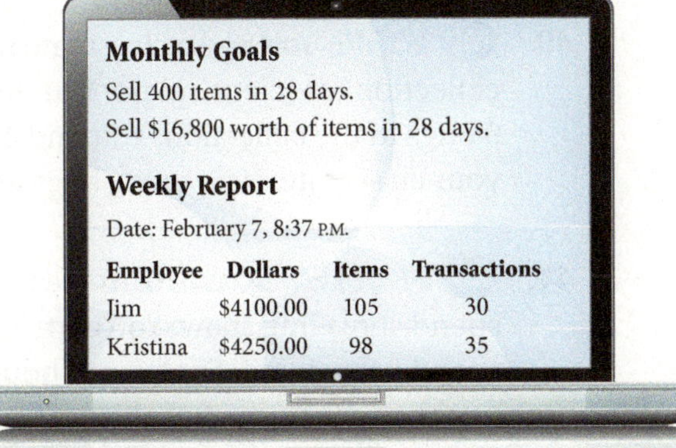

30. **MP MODELING REAL LIFE** A gold alloy contains 15 milligrams of gold for every 4 milligrams of copper. A jeweler uses 48 milligrams of copper to make the alloy. How much gold does the jeweler use to make the alloy?

31. **MP MODELING REAL LIFE** You make candles by adding 2 fluid ounces of scented oil for every 22 fluid ounces of wax. Your friend makes candles by adding 3 fluid ounces of the same scented oil for every 37 fluid ounces of wax. Whose candles are more fragrant? Explain your reasoning.

32. **MP MODELING REAL LIFE** A mint milk shake contains 1.25 fluid ounces of milk for every 4 ounces of ice cream. A strawberry milk shake contains 1.75 fluid ounces of milk for every 5 ounces of ice cream. Which milk shake is thicker? Explain.

CRITICAL THINKING **Two whole numbers *A* and *B* satisfy the following conditions. Find *A* and *B*.**

33. $A + B = 30$

$A : B$ is equivalent to $2 : 3$.

34. $A + B = 44$

$A : B$ is equivalent to $4 : 7$.

35. $A - B = 18$

$A : B$ is equivalent to $11 : 5$.

36. $A - B = 25$

$A : B$ is equivalent to $13 : 8$.

Nutrition Facts

8 servings per container

Serving size	**1 ounce (28g)**
Amount per serving	
Calories	**161**
	% Daily Value*
Total Fat 13g	**20%**
Saturated Fat 3g	**13%**
Trans Fat 0g	
Cholesterol 0mg	**0%**
Sodium 4mg	**0%**
Total Carbohydrate 9g	**3%**
Dietary Fiber 1g	**3%**
Total Sugars 1g	
Includes 0g Added Sugars	**0%**
Protein 4g	
Vitamin D 0mcg	0%
Calcium 14.8mg	1%
Iron 2.67mg	15%
Potassium 264mg	8%

* The % Daily Value (DV) tells you how much a nutrient in a serving of food contributes to a daily diet. 2,000 calories a day is used for general nutrition advice.

37. **MP MODELING REAL LIFE** A nutrition label shows that there are 161 calories in 28 grams of dry roasted cashews. You eat 9 cashews totaling 12 grams.

a. Do you think it is possible to find the number of calories you consume? Explain your reasoning.

b. How many cashews are in one serving?

38. **MP REASONING** The ratio of three numbers is $4 : 5 : 3$. The sum of the numbers is 54. What are the three numbers?

39. **CRITICAL THINKING** Seven out of every 8 students surveyed own a bike. The difference between the number of students who own a bike and those who do not is 72. How many students were surveyed?

40. **MP LOGIC** You and a classmate have a bug collection for science class. You find 5 out of every 9 bugs in the collection. You find 4 more bugs than your classmate. How many bugs are in the collection?

41. **MP PROBLEM SOLVING** You earn \$72 for every 8 hours you spend shoveling snow. You earn \$60 for every 5 hours you spend babysitting. For every 3 hours you spend babysitting, you spend 2 hours shoveling snow. You babysit for 15 hours in January. How much money do you earn in January?

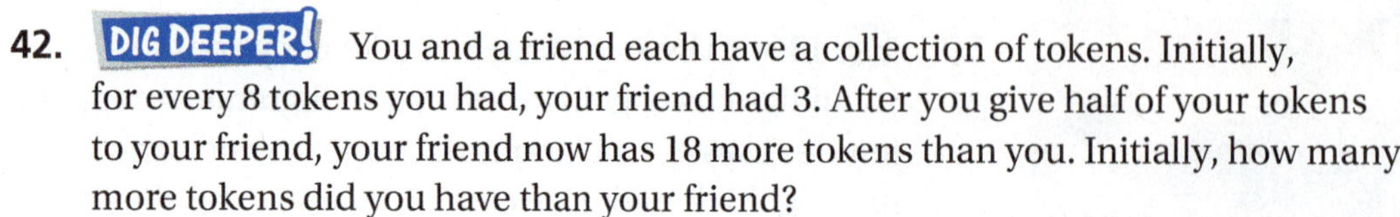

42. **DIG DEEPER!** You and a friend each have a collection of tokens. Initially, for every 8 tokens you had, your friend had 3. After you give half of your tokens to your friend, your friend now has 18 more tokens than you. Initially, how many more tokens did you have than your friend?

Common Errors

- **Exercise 38** Students may have trouble with compound ratios. Let them know that a ratio with 3 parts compares 3 quantities instead of 2 quantities.
- **Exercise 42** Students may have difficulty solving this problem. The key to solving this problem is recognizing that the ratio changes from 8 : 3 to 4 : 7 after giving away half of the tokens in the first quantity.

Mini-Assessment

Find the missing values in the ratio table. Then write the equivalent ratios.

1.

Shirts	3		15
Shorts	5	15	

9, 25; 3 : 5, 9 : 15, 15 : 25

2.

Calories	400	100	
Servings	3		$\frac{15}{4}$

500, $\frac{3}{4}$; 400 : 3, 100 : $\frac{3}{4}$, 500 : $\frac{15}{4}$

3. To make trail mix, Factory A combines 2 pounds of nuts for every 3 pounds of dried fruit. Factory B combines 5 pounds of nuts for every 8 pounds of dried fruit. Which factory has a fruitier trail mix? Explain. Factory B; *Sample answer:* When both trail mixes have 10 pounds of nuts, Factory B has $16 - 15 = 1$ more pound of dried fruit than Factory A.

4. A soccer team has 12 girls and 18 boys. The team is split into groups that have the same ratio of girls to boys as that of the whole team. How many girls are in a group that has 9 boys? 6 girls

Section Resources

Surface Level	Deep Level
Resources by Chapter • Extra Practice • Reteach • Puzzle Time Student Journal • Self-Assessment • Practice Differentiating the Lesson Tutorial Videos Skills Review Handbook Skills Trainer	Resources by Chapter • Enrichment and Extension Graphic Organizers Dynamic Assessment System • Section Practice

Transfer Level	
Dynamic Assessment System • Mid-Chapter Quiz	Assessment Book • Mid-Chapter Quiz

Concepts, Skills, & Problem Solving

31. yours; $\frac{2}{22} > \frac{3}{37}$
32. mint; $\frac{1.75}{5} = \frac{7}{20} > \frac{5}{16} = \frac{1.25}{4}$
33. $A = 12, B = 18$
34. $A = 16, B = 28$
35. $A = 33, B = 15$
36. $A = 65, B = 40$
37. **a.** yes; *Sample answer:* Find a ratio equivalent to 161 : 28 that has 12 on the right.
    b. 21
38. 18, 22.5, 13.5
39. 96
40. 36
41. $270
42. 30

Learning Target

Represent ratio relationships in a coordiante plane.

Success Criteria

- Create and plot ordered parirs from a ratio relationship.
- Create graphs to solve ratio problems.
- Create graphs to compare ratios.

Warm Up

Cumulative, vocabulary, and prerequisite skills practice opportunities are available in the *Resources by Chapter* or at *BigIdeasMath.com*.

ELL Support

The words *coordinate* and *plane* may be familiar to students from other contexts. Explain that when you match clothing colors, you coordinate clothes. A point on a graph coordinates two values. Demonstrate the two pronunciations of *coordinate* and have students repeat. Explain that students may know a plane as a vehicle that flies, but in math the word has a different meaning. Discuss the meaning of the term *coordinate plane*. A coordinate plane is a two-dimensional surface in which points are plotted.

Exploration 1

a. See Additional Answers.

b. *Sample answer:* How far does the airplane travel in 4 hours? (Answer: 1200 miles)

Exploration 2

See Additional Answers.

Laurie's Notes

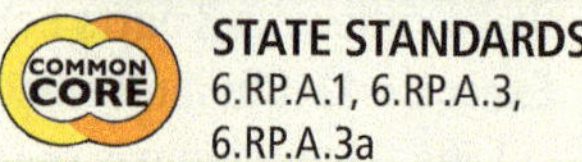

Preparing to Teach

- In the previous course, students plotted ordered pairs generated from a rule. Plotting was restricted to Quadrant I. The Motivate in this lesson will be helpful in reminding students about graphing.
- Plotting rational numbers in the coordinate plane is part of analyzing proportional relationships which students will continue in the next course. Later, this skill will be important for studying linear equations and graphs of functions.
- The examples throughout this lesson do not distinguish between discrete and continuous data graphically, but you can ask students what numbers make sense. In drawing a line through the data, students observe the linear relationship through the origin.

Motivate

- **Story Time:** Tell students that you have been so busy doing schoolwork that you had to hire a teenager to do some yard work on weekends, or whatever job seems plausible.
- Show students the graph and say, "Tell a neighbor how much I'm paying the worker per hour, and how you know."
- Discuss what students know about the graph, reviewing language that will be helpful in the explorations.

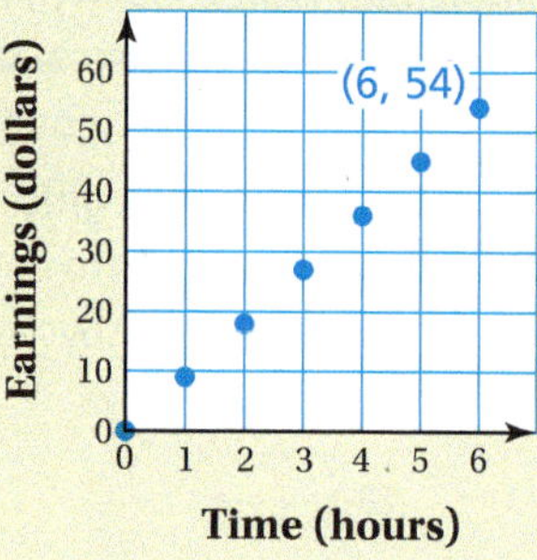

Exploration 1

? Some students may make a ratio table of times and distances for the airplane that represent ordered pairs in the graph. If you notice that a group is stuck, have them look at the graph from the Motivate and ask, "How can you use that graph to help you think about this problem?"

? While discussing the problem, ask, "Does it make sense to connect the ordered pairs? Explain." Yes, it is possible for an airplane to travel 1.5 hours.

Exploration 2

- The first graph models the additive process that students will use to make a ratio table.
- In the second graph, make sure that students realize both blue arrows start at the origin.

? "How are the paired values in your table related?" They represent equivalent ratios.

? "How are the green arrows related to the structure within the ratio table?" The ratio 5 : 2 is equivalent to the ratio 15 : 6 because both parts of the original ratio are multiplied by 3.

? **Turn and Talk:** "Why does it make sense to connect the ordered pairs in this problem? Does the ordered pair (0, 0) make sense?"

3.4 Graphing Ratio Relationships

Learning Target: Represent ratio relationships in a coordinate plane.

Success Criteria:
- I can create and plot ordered pairs from a ratio relationship.
- I can create graphs to solve ratio problems.
- I can create graphs to compare ratios.

EXPLORATION 1 Using a Coordinate Plane

Math Practice

Label Axes

Could you have placed each quantity on the other axis? Explain why or why not.

Work with a partner. An airplane travels 300 miles per hour.

a. Represent the relationship between distance and time in a coordinate plane. Explain your choice for labeling and scaling the axes.

b. Write a question that can be answered using the graph. Exchange your question with another group. Answer their question and discuss the solution with the other group.

EXPLORATION 2 Identifying Relationships in Graphs

Work with a partner. Use the graphs to make a ratio table. Explain how the blue, red, and green arrows correspond to the ratio table.

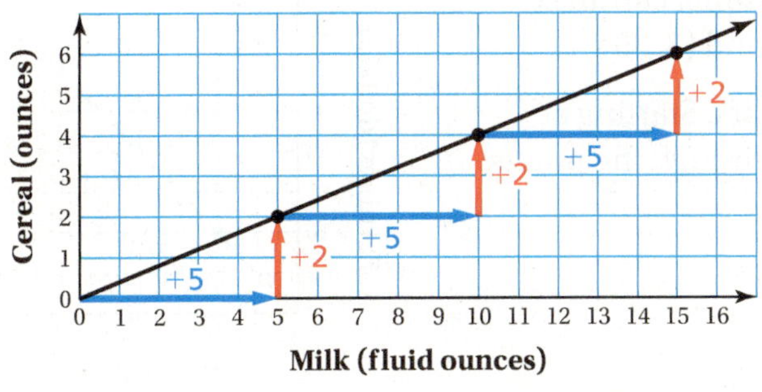

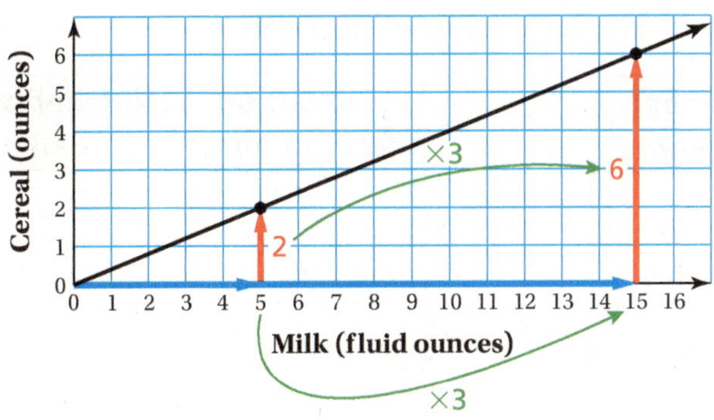

3.4 Lesson

For a ratio of two quantities, you can use equivalent ratios to create ordered pairs of the form (first quantity, second quantity). You can plot these ordered pairs in a coordinate plane and draw a line, starting at (0, 0), through the points.

EXAMPLE 1 Graphing Ratio Relationships

Represent each ratio relationship using a graph.

Remember

When plotting an ordered pair (x, y), the number x corresponds to the horizontal axis and the number y corresponds to the vertical axis.

a.

Flour (cups)	4	8	12
Water (cups)	2	4	6

The ordered pairs (flour, water) are (4, 2), (8, 4), and (12, 6).

Plot the ordered pairs. Starting at (0, 0), draw a line through the points.

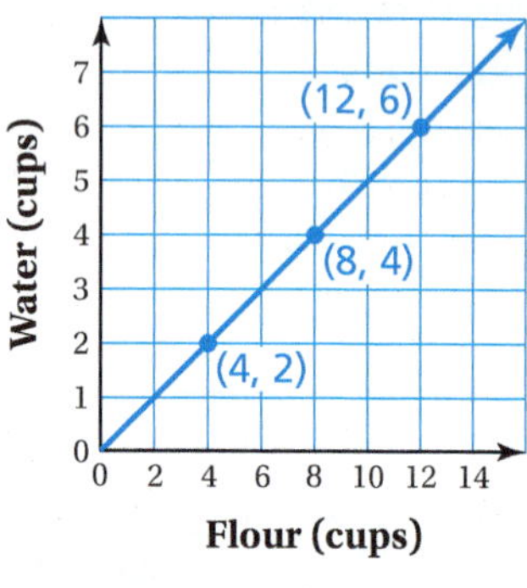

Relationships involving time are often graphed with time on the horizontal axis.

b.

Time (hours)	1	2	3
Earnings (dollars)	10	20	30

The ordered pairs (time, earnings) are (1, 10), (2, 20), and (3, 30).

Plot the ordered pairs. Starting at (0, 0), draw a line through the points.

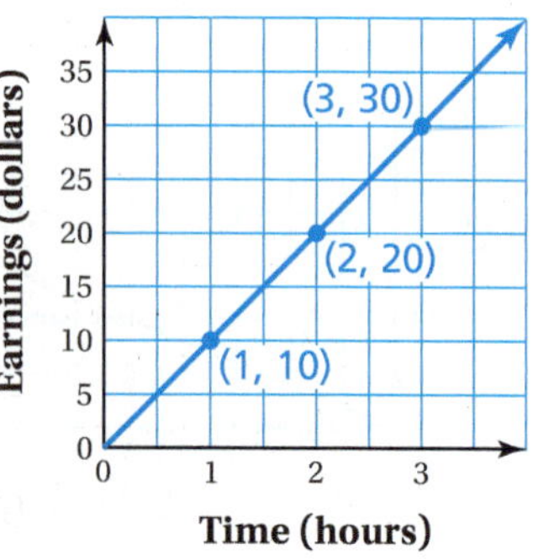

Try It **Represent the ratio relationship using a graph.**

1.

Time (minutes)	Number of Words
1	50
2	100
3	150

2.

Number of 6th Graders	Number of 7th Graders
5	4
10	8
15	12

Laurie's Notes

Scaffolding Instruction

- The explorations involved analyzing equivalent ratios, relating quantities, and graphing the paired values in the coordinate plane to solve real-world application problems. In Exploration 1, the context was familiar and involved different units on each axis.
- **Emerging:** Students may not be confident in plotting ordered pairs correctly, perhaps reversing x and y. The Remember note addresses this. Going through Example 1, either independently or with guided instruction, will help students become proficient with the first success criterion.
- **Proficient:** If students are confident in graphing ratio relationships from a ratio table, have them self-assess using Try It Exercises 1 and 2 before beginning Example 2. In Example 2, students need to be able to interpret the graph.
- Check to see that students are labeling the axes of their graphs properly.

EXAMPLE 1

- The graphs in this example use addition and multiplication in the ratio tables, just like in the explorations.

? "In part (a), what does the data in the ratio table represent?" equivalent ratios for cups of flour and cups of water

- Part (a) is an example where the order is arbitrary. The flour and water values in the table could have been reversed.

? "In part (a), why do you start the graph at (0, 0)?" You can have small amounts of flour and water, and if there were 0 cups of flour there will be 0 cups of water.

? "In part (b), how do you interpret the data in the ratio table?" The data represents how much money you earn if you are paid \$10 per hour.

- **Big Idea:** The scale on each axis does not need to be the same. In plotting part (b), the increments on the vertical axis can be 5, 10, or any other convenient number.

Try It

- Have students work independently on the exercises and then compare their work with a neighbor. If a student uses a different scale than his or her neighbor, the graph may appear more or less steep.
- Discuss as a class how the scale affects the steepness of the graph.

ELL Support

Have students work in groups to complete Exercise 1.
Beginner: Create and label the graph, and plot points with the help of peers.
Intermediate: Interpret the meaning of each point. For example, "At one minute there are fifty words."
Advanced: Explain what each graph represents.

Extra Example 1

Represent each ratio relationship using a graph.

a.

Time (minutes)	1	2	3
Number of Pages	4	8	12

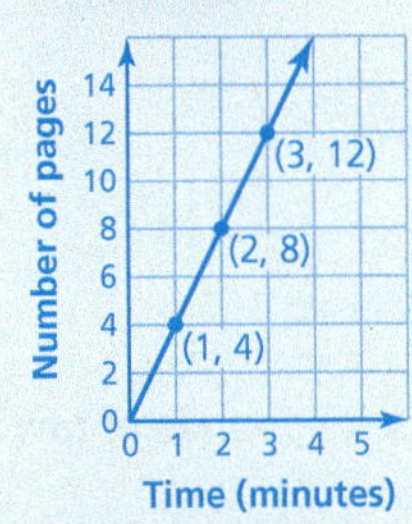

b.

Olive Oil (fluid ounces)	6	12	18
Vinegar (fluid ounces)	4	8	12

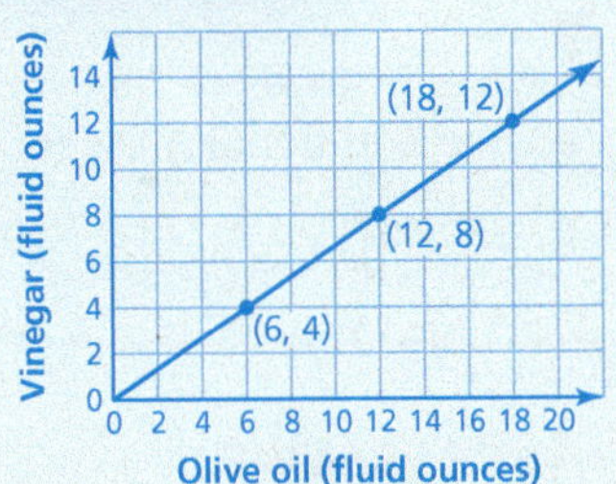

Try It

1.

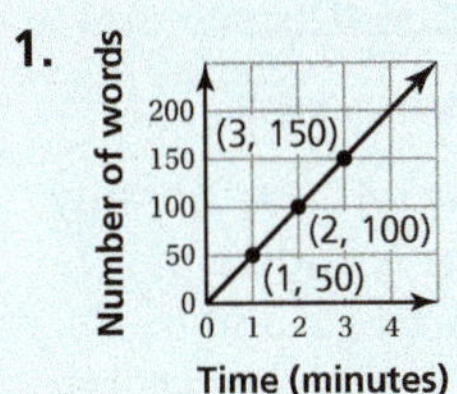

2.

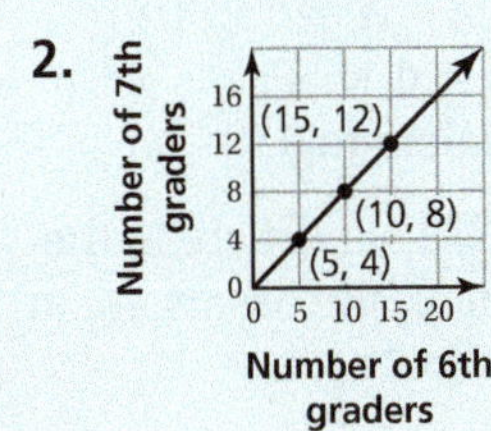

Extra Example 2

You buy raw pecans for $8.50 per pound.

a. Represent the ratio relationship using a graph.

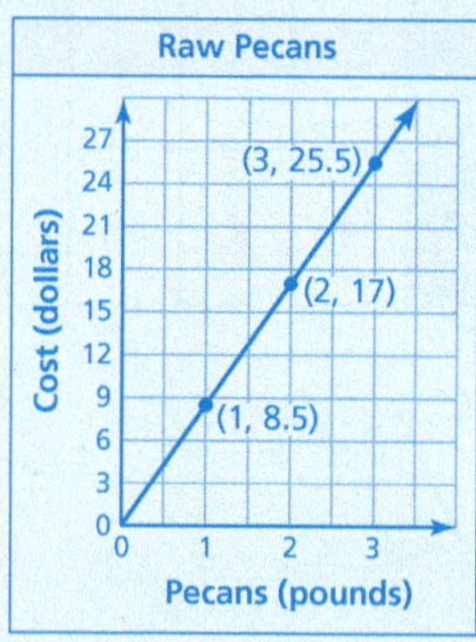

b. How much does 1.5 pounds of raw pecans cost? $12.75

Try It

3. **a.** See Additional Answers.
   b. $37.50

Self-Assessment for Concepts & Skills

4.

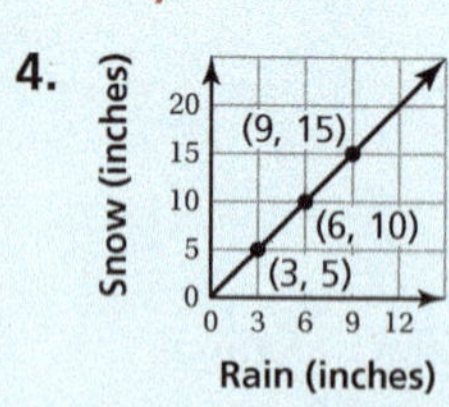

5. *Sample answer:* For any ratio $a : b$, adding or subtracting a and b generates an equivalent ratio. $a - a = 0$ and $b - b = 0$, so $a : b$ is equivalent to $0 : 0$.

6. (24, 4); 24 and 4 are in the ratio 6 : 1, the others are in the ratio 4 : 1.

Laurie's Notes

Formative Assessment Tip

Writing Prompt

This technique asks students to give feedback at the end of the lesson, activity, or learning experience. The *Writing Prompt* allows you to collect feedback in a short period of time (two minutes) on student learning.

Used at the end of the class, a *Writing Prompt* is similar to an *Exit Ticket*. The written responses give students time to reflect on their learning, how well they believe they understand the concept or skill, and where they are still uncertain. It is important to share responses with students on the following day and let them know how you have adjusted the lesson based on their responses. Students need to know that you value their feedback and that instruction will be modified accordingly. Students will take the *Writing Prompt* more seriously if it is valued and used.

EXAMPLE 2

- Pose the problem and have students discuss what quantities will be represented in the ratio table.
- Ask questions about the graph to see if students are able to read information from the graph, meaning, how much does 2 pounds of dark chocolate cashews cost?
- Explain that the graph continues as implied with the arrow and that fractional parts of a pound can be purchased.
- **Extension:** Have students use a double number line to solve the problem.

Try It

- This exercise uses an easier rate than Example 2. Students should be independent in working this problem.

Self-Assessment for Concepts & Skills

- The first two success criteria involve students making a graph from a ratio table and using the graph to solve problems. As students reflect on their understanding of graphing ratio relationships, can they explain any difficulty or confusion they may have at this point?
- **Common Misconception:** Students may not be sure why the graph of a ratio relationship begins at (0, 0). Some students believe it should begin at (1, 1). When ratios are equivalent, it does not mean that the two quantities being compared are the same, which a ratio of 1 : 1 implies.

ELL Support

Have students complete the exercises in pairs. Remind them to think about the process they used for Try It Exercises 1 and 2. After students complete the exercises, have two pairs present their answers to each other and revise them if there is any disagreement. Provide support as needed.

The Success Criteria Self-Assessment chart can be found in the *Student Journal* or online at *BigIdeasMath.com*.

EXAMPLE 2 Using a Graph to Solve a Ratio Problem

You buy dark chocolate cashews for $12.50 per pound.

Relationships involving cost are often graphed with cost on the vertical axis.

a. Represent the ratio relationship using a graph.

Create a ratio table.

Cashews (pounds)	1	2	3
Cost (dollars)	12.5	25	37.5

The ordered pairs (cashews, cost) are (1, 12.5), (2, 25), and (3, 37.5). Plot the ordered pairs and draw a line, starting at (0, 0), through the points.

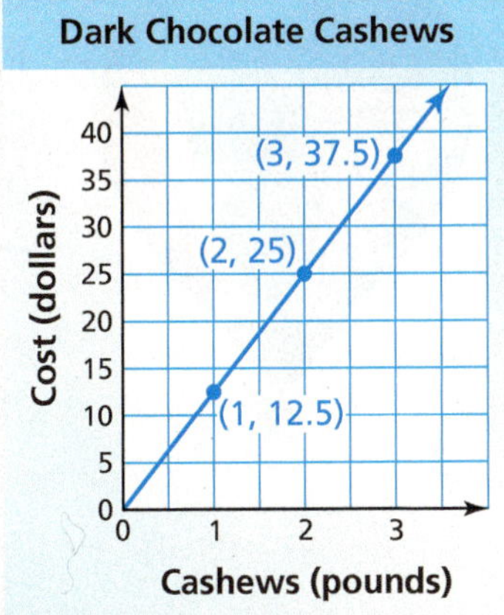

b. How much does 2.5 pounds of dark chocolate cashews cost?

Using the graph, you can see that the cost of 2.5 pounds is halfway between $25 and $37.50.

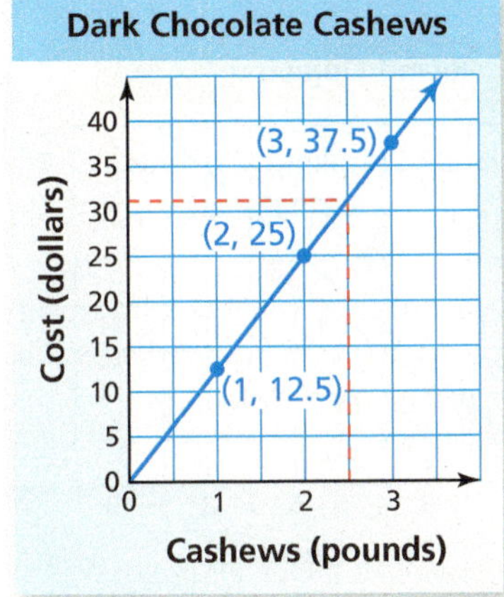

So, 2.5 pounds of dark chocolate cashews cost $31.25.

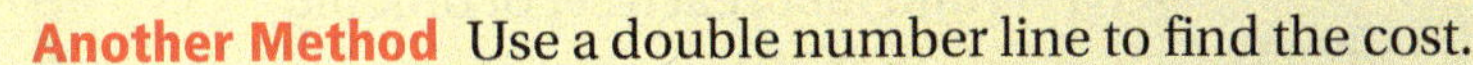

Another Method Use a double number line to find the cost.

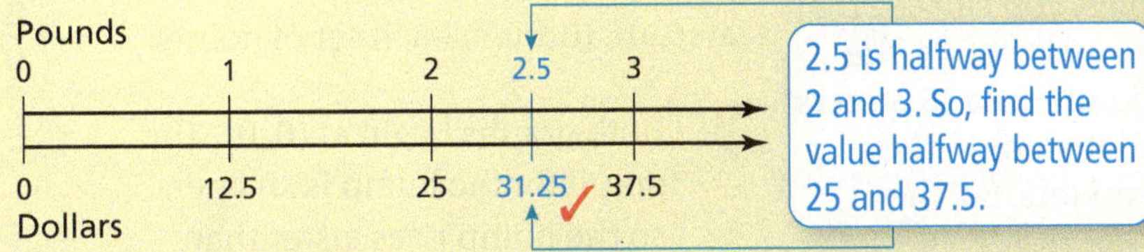

Try It

3. **WHAT IF?** Repeat Example 2 when the cost of the dark chocolate cashews is $15 per pound.

Self-Assessment for Concepts & Skills

Solve each exercise. Then rate your understanding of the success criteria in your journal.

4. **GRAPHING A RATIO RELATIONSHIP** Represent the ratio relationship using a graph.

Rain (inches)	Snow (inches)
3	5
6	10
9	15

5. **CRITICAL THINKING** Use what you know about equivalent ratios to explain why the graph of a ratio relationship passes through (0, 0).

6. **WHICH ONE DOESN'T BELONG?** Which ordered pair does *not* belong with the other three? Explain your reasoning.

(4, 1) (8, 2) (12, 3) (24, 4)

EXAMPLE 3 Modeling Real Life

A hot-air balloon rises 9 meters every 3 seconds. A blimp rises 7 meters every 2 seconds. Graph each ratio relationship in the same coordinate plane. Which rises faster?

Create ratio tables for each rising object. Then plot the ordered pairs (time, height) from the table and use the graph to determine which rises faster.

Balloon	
Time (seconds)	Height (meters)
3	9
6	18
9	27

Blimp	
Time (seconds)	Height (meters)
2	7
4	14
6	21

Balloon: (3, 9), (6, 18), (9, 27)

Blimp: (2, 7), (4, 14), (6, 21)

Plot and label each set of ordered pairs. Then draw a line, starting at (0, 0), through each set of points.

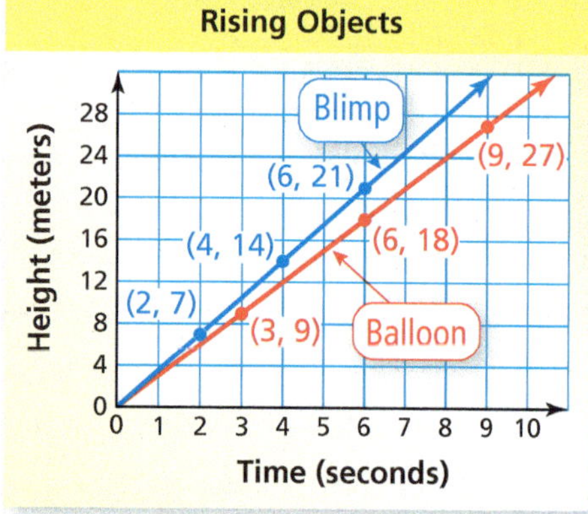

Both graphs begin at (0, 0). The graph for the blimp is steeper, so the blimp rises faster than the hot-air balloon.

Check From the ratio tables, you can see that every 6 seconds, the balloon rises 18 meters and the blimp rises 21 meters. So, the blimp rises faster. ✓

Self-Assessment for Problem Solving

Solve each exercise. Then rate your understanding of the success criteria in your journal.

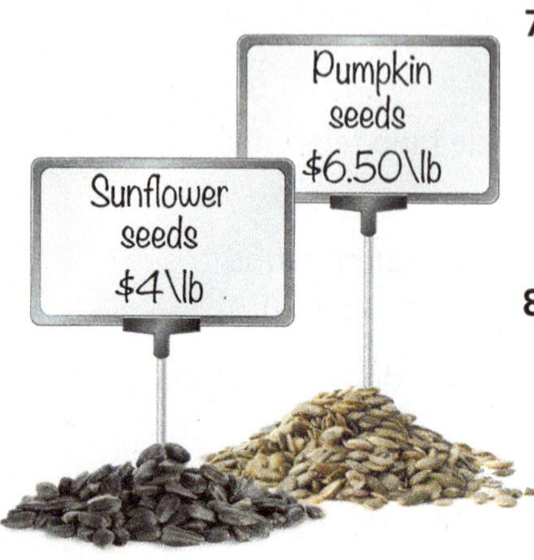

7. You are skateboarding at a pace of 30 meters every 5 seconds. Your friend is in-line skating at a pace of 9 meters every 2 seconds. Graph each ratio relationship in the same coordinate plane. Who is faster?

8. You buy 2.5 pounds of pumpkin seeds and 2.5 pounds of sunflower seeds. Use a graph to find your total cost. Then use the graph to determine how much more you pay for pumpkin seeds than for sunflower seeds.

Laurie's Notes

EXAMPLE 3

- Students solved comparison problems in previous lessons. Can they apply their understanding of solving comparison problems and constructing graphs of ratio relationships to help them compare two ratios?
- Students need to recognize that in extending their ratio tables they are looking for values in the two tables that include the same quantity. In this problem, it occurs at time equal to 6 seconds.
- Through this example, students will get their first informal sense of slope. In the next course, students will understand slope in terms of steepness and make the connection with the unit rate.
- ? **Turn and Talk:** "What do you notice about the two graphs that helps answer the question?"
- Have different groups share their thinking about this problem.

Self-Assessment for Problem Solving

- The goal for all students is to feel comfortable with the problem-solving plan. It is important for students to problem-solve in class, where they may receive support from you and their peers. Keep in mind that some students may only be ready to complete the first step.
- **Think-Pair-Share:** Students should have time to think quietly before sharing their thinking with a partner. You might have groups of four that work together, first allowing each student time to think independently. Expect students to move to different locations in the classroom to offer or solicit help.
- ? Remind students to look back at previous problems and lessons. "Have you solved a problem similar to this before?"
- As students are working through the exercises, encourage them to assess their understanding of the learning target and success criteria, keeping the focus on the learning target. Tell students to rate their understanding of each success criterion.

The Success Criteria Self-Assessment chart can be found in the *Student Journal* or online at *BigIdeasMath.com*.

Closure

- **Writing Prompt:** When equivalent ratios are graphed in a coordinate plane, I know . . .

Extra Example 3

You swim 20 meters every 20 seconds. Your friend swims 35 meters every 30 seconds. Graph each ratio relationship in the same coordinate plane. Who swims faster?

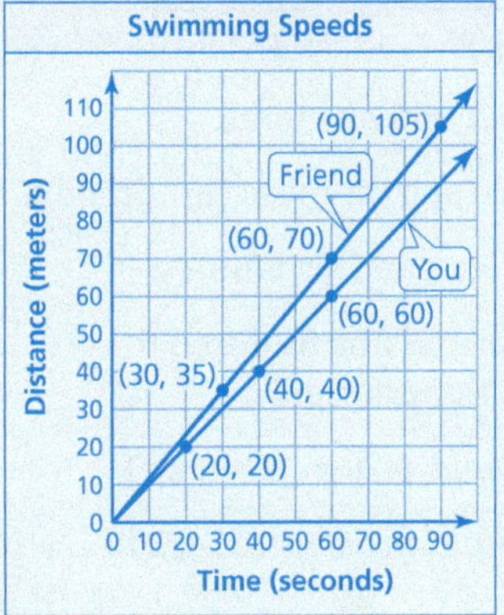

your friend

Self-Assessment for Problem Solving

7.

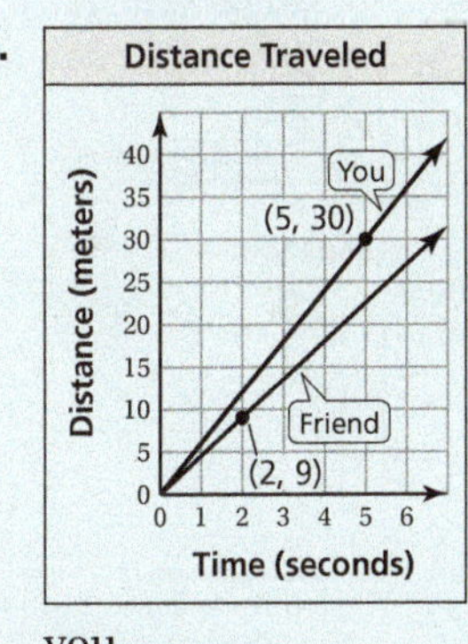

you

8. \$26.25; \$6.25

Learning Target

Represent ratio relationships in a coordinate plane.

Success Criteria

- Create and plot ordered pairs from a ratio relationship.
- Create graphs to solve ratio problems.
- Create graphs to compare ratios.

Review & Refresh

1.

Chickens	8	16	24
Eggs	6	12	18

8 : 6, 16 : 12, 24 : 18

2.

Fish	6	3	12	15
Snails	2	1	4	5

6 : 2, 3 : 1, 12 : 4, 15 : 5

3. seven and one tenth
4. three and fifty-four hundredths
5. thirteen and six tenths
6. eight and one hundred thirty-two thousandths
7. *Sample answer:* 8 : 4, 2 : 1
8. *Sample answer:* 12 : 4, 3 : 1

Concepts, Skills, & Problem Solving

9.

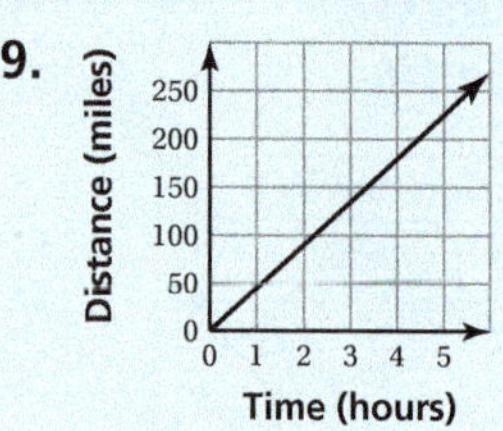

10.

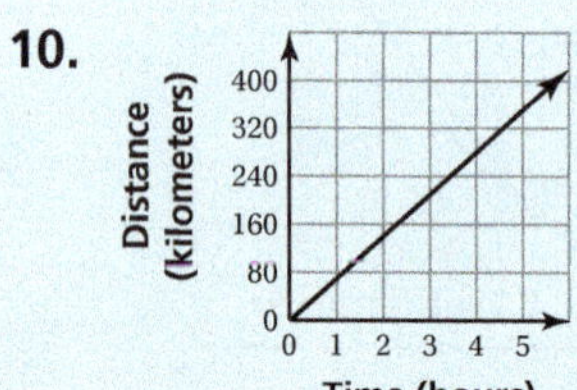

11.

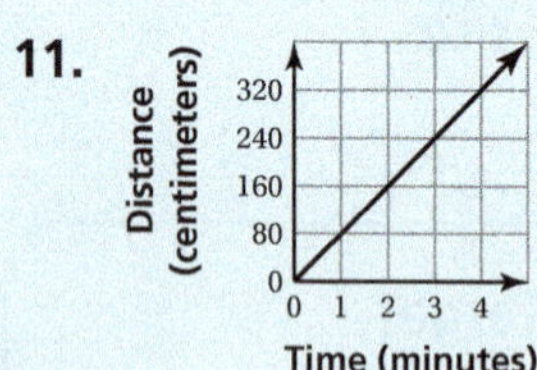

12.

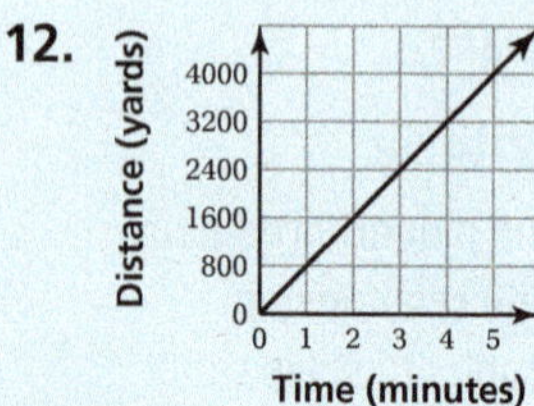

13–18. See Additional Answers.

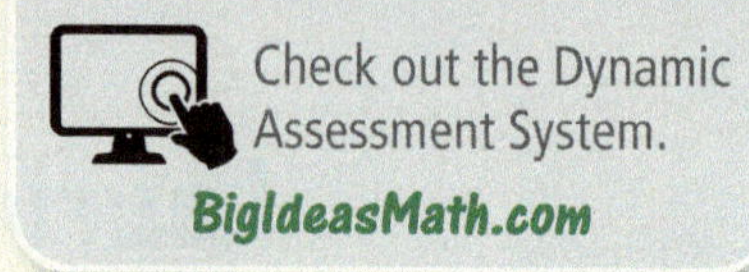

Assignment Guide and Concept Check

Scaffold assignments to support all students in their learning progression. The suggested assignments are a starting point. Continue to assign additional exercises and revisit with spaced practice to move every student toward proficiency.

Level	Assignment 1	Assignment 2
Emerging	2, 6, 8, 9, 13, 15	16, 19, 20, 21, 23, 25
Proficient	2, 6, 8, 11, 14, 16	18, 19, 20, 21, 22, 23, 24, 25
Advanced	2, 6, 8, 12, 14, 18	20, 21, 22, 23, 24, 25, 26

- Assignment 1 is for use after students complete the Self-Assessment for Concepts & Skills.
- Assignment 2 is for use after students complete the Self-Assessment for Problem Solving.
- The red exercises can be used as a concept check.

Review & Refresh Prior Skills

Exercises 1 and 2 Completing Ratio Tables
Exercises 3–6 Identifying Decimal Place Value
Exercises 7 and 8 Writing Equivalent Ratios

3.4 Practice

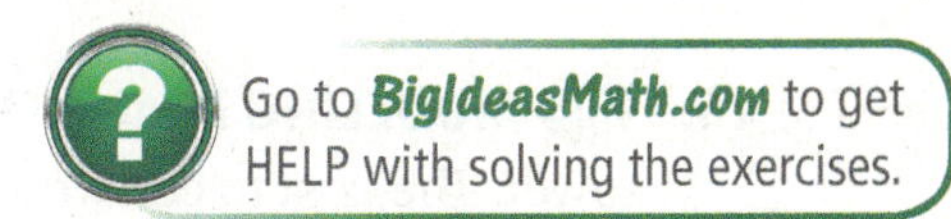

Review & Refresh

Find the missing values in the ratio table. Then write the equivalent ratios.

1.

Chickens	8		24
Eggs	6	12	

2.

Fish	6	3		15
Snails	2		4	

Write the name of the decimal number.

3. 7.1

4. 3.54

5. 13.6

6. 8.132

Write two equivalent ratios that describe the relationship.

7. baseballs to gloves

8. ladybugs to bees

Concepts, Skills, & Problem Solving

USING A COORDINATE PLANE **Represent the relationship between distance and time in a coordinate plane.** (See Exploration 1, p. 129.)

9. A train travels 45 miles per hour.

10. A motorcycle travels 70 kilometers per hour.

11. A snail travels 80 centimeters per minute.

12. A whale travels 800 yards per minute.

GRAPHING RATIO RELATIONSHIPS **Represent the ratio relationship using a graph.**

13.

Height (inches)	20	40	60
Weight (pounds)	30	60	90

14.

Students	9	18	27
Computers	4	8	12

15.

Ribbon (inches)	1	2	3
String (inches)	3	6	9

16.

Water (gallons)	30	60	90
Soda (gallons)	5	10	15

17.

Cherries	5	10	15
Limes	8	16	24

18.

Jog (miles)	2	4	6
Sprint (meters)	400	800	1200

19. **MP MODELING REAL LIFE** A radio station collects donations for a new broadcast tower. The cost to construct the tower is $25.50 per inch.

   a. Represent the ratio relationship using a graph.

   b. How much does it cost to fund 4.5 inches of the construction?

20. **MP MODELING REAL LIFE** Your school organizes a clothing drive as a fundraiser for a class trip. The school earns $100 for every 400 pounds of donated clothing.

   a. Represent the ratio relationship using a graph.

   b. How much money does your school earn for donating 2200 pounds of clothing?

21. **MP NUMBER SENSE** Just by looking at the graph, determine who earns a greater hourly wage. Explain.

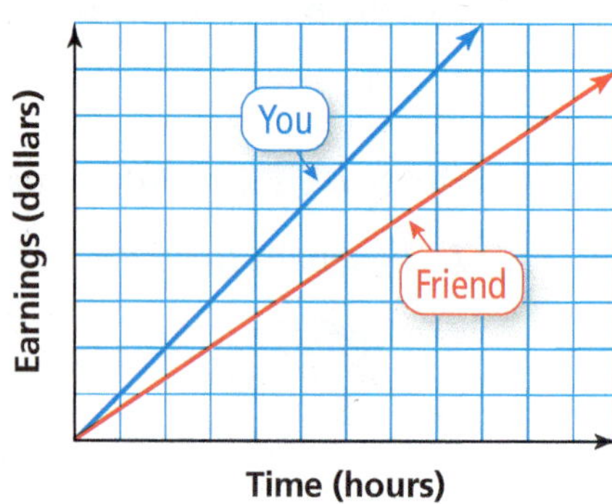

22. **MP MODELING REAL LIFE** An airplane traveling from Chicago to Los Angeles travels 15 miles every 2 minutes. On the return trip, the plane travels 25 miles every 3 minutes. Graph each ratio relationship in the same coordinate plane. Does the plane fly faster when traveling to Los Angeles or to Chicago?

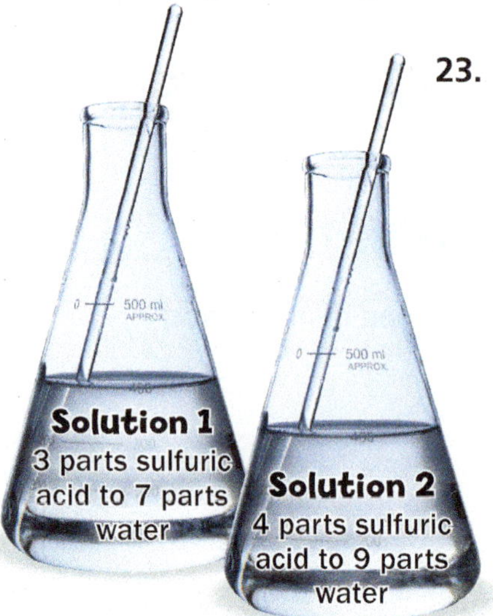

23. **MP MODELING REAL LIFE** Your freezer produces 8 ice cubes every 2 hours. Your friend's freezer produces 24 ice cubes every 5 hours. Graph each ratio relationship in the same coordinate plane. Whose freezer produces ice faster?

24. **MP CHOOSE TOOLS** A chemist prepares two acid solutions.

   a. Use a ratio table to determine which solution is more acidic.

   b. Use a graph to determine which solution is more acidic.

   c. Which method do you prefer? Explain.

25. **DIG DEEPER!** A company offers a nut mixture with 7 peanuts for every 3 almonds. The company changes the mixture to have 9 peanuts for every 5 almonds, but the number of nuts per container does not change.

   a. How many nuts are in the smallest possible container?

   b. Almonds cost more than peanuts. Use a graph to determine whether the company should change the price of the mixture. Explain.

26. **MP STRUCTURE** The point (p, q) is on the graph of values from a ratio table. What are two additional points on the graph?

Common Errors

- **Exercise 26** Students may not realize that they can find another point on the graph of values from a ratio table by multiplying both coordinates by the same number k. So, in general, another point on the graph is (kp, kq). Lead students to this conclusion without giving away the answer.

Mini-Assessment

1. Represent the ratio relationship using a graph.

Time (minutes)	10	20	30
Liters Added	5	10	15

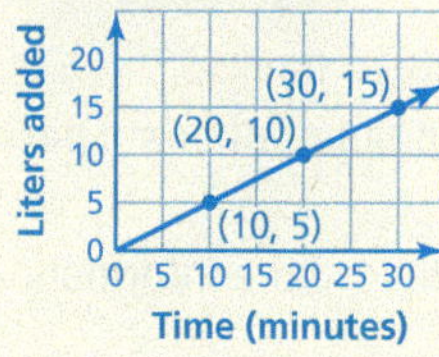

2. Using the graph from Exercise 1, how many liters are added after 40 minutes? 20 liters
3. Fourth-grade students are selling candles as a fundraiser for a class trip. The class earns $1.50 for every $5 worth of candles sold. Represent the ratio relationship using a graph.

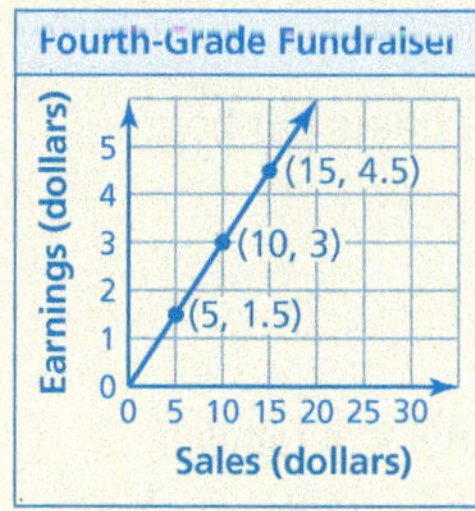

4. Using the graph from Exercise 3, how much money does the fourth-grade class earn for selling $25 worth of candles? $7.50

Section Resources

Surface Level	Deep Level
Resources by Chapter • Extra Practice • Reteach • Puzzle Time Student Journal • Self-Assessment • Practice Differentiating the Lesson Tutorial Videos Skills Review Handbook Skills Trainer	Resources by Chapter • Enrichment and Extension Graphic Organizers Dynamic Assessment System • Section Practice

Concepts, Skills, & Problem Solving

19. a.

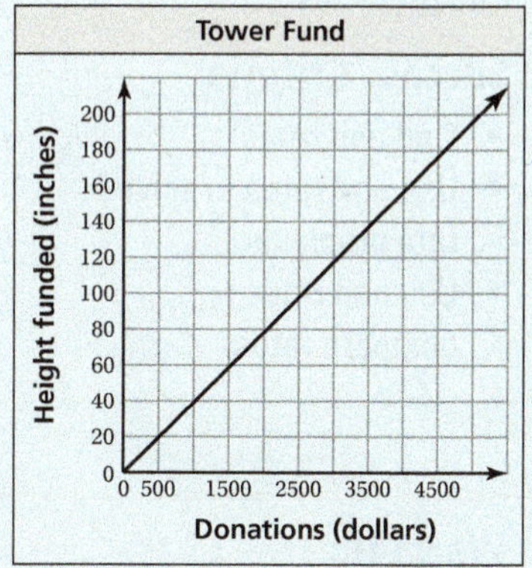

b. $114.75

20. a.

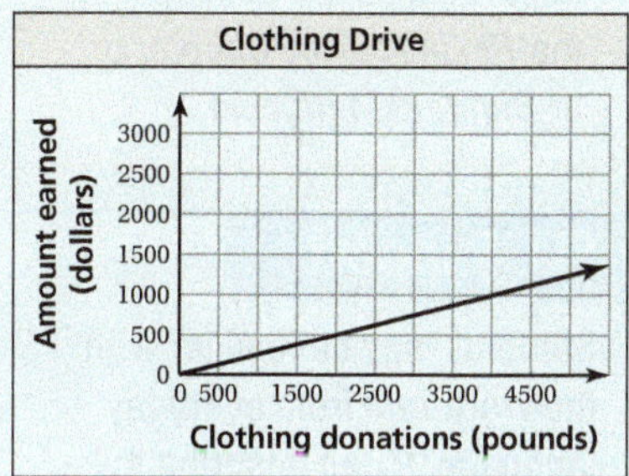

b. $550

21. you; The graph that represents your earnings is steeper.

22. Flight Speeds

Chicago

23. See Additional Answers.

24. a. solution 2

b. solution 2

c. *Sample answer:* graph; The rates are visible more quickly.

25. See Additional Answers.

26. *Sample answer:* $(2p, 2q)$, $(3p, 3q)$

Learning Target

Understand the concept of a unit rate and solve rate problems.

Success Criteria

- Find unit rates.
- Use unit rates to solve rate problems.
- Use unit rates to compare rates.

Warm Up

Cumulative, vocabulary, and prerequisite skills practice opportunities are available in the *Resources by Chapter* or at *BigIdeasMath.com*.

ELL Support

Students may be familiar with the word *rate* from everyday language. It can describe the ranking or value of something. For example, grade AA eggs are rated at the highest quality. Rate can also mean a measure of one thing against another. For example, your heart rate may be 65 beats per minute. This second meaning matches the mathematical definition.

Exploration 1

a. *Sample answer:* The car traveled 80 miles in 2 hours.

b. 130 mi; *Sample answer:* Use a ratio table.

c. See Additional Answers.

Exploration 2

a. Answers will vary. Look for the ratio of each number of hand claps to 12 seconds.

b. See Additional Answers.

Laurie's Notes

STATE STANDARDS
6.RP.A.2, 6 RP.A.3,
6 RP.A.3a, 6.RP.A.3b

Preparing to Teach

- In working with rates, it is very important to specify the units. You may notice that when students write an answer, they are more likely to forget the units than when they say the answer aloud.
- Given the **rate** a units : b units, students will find the **unit rate** $\frac{a}{b}$ units : 1 unit and the related unit rate $\frac{b}{a}$ units : 1 unit.

Motivate

- Have students practice finding a pulse using their wrists or necks.
- Help students calculate their heart rates, which is the number of beats per unit of time.
- Count the number of beats in a 6 second time period. Record the information as a rate. For example, $\frac{7 \text{ beats}}{6 \text{ seconds}}$.
- Ask students to predict their heart rates for one minute. For example, they should recognize that by multiplying both the beats and seconds by 10, the rate is $\frac{70 \text{ beats}}{60 \text{ seconds}}$, which is the same as 70 beats per minute.

? "If you know the number of beats in 10 seconds, how can you find the number of beats per minute?" Multiply by a factor of 6.

- Discuss the idea that they can find their heart rates in beats per hour; however, this is not a common rate.

Exploration 1

- Students may not know a formal definition for *rate*, but it is a familiar concept. They just found their heart rates and have heard rates, such as 65 miles per hour, 32 miles per gallon, \$7.50 per hour, and \$1.99 per pound.
- In part (a), most students will write a rate of distance per unit of time, though some may write a rate of time per unit of distance. Both are correct observations from the diagram. Note that the units of time might be 2 hours or 120 minutes.
- Probe to determine if there are different solution methods in part (b).
- In part (c), students are asked to draw a speedometer, which displays a unit rate. Listen for this understanding. Students may not know the definition for *unit rate*, but they might say the car travels 40 miles in 1 hour.

Exploration 2

- **Teaching Tip:** It is helpful for you to be the timer. The counter will quickly realize the need for a strategy to keep track of the number of claps, like using their fingers or making a tally mark for each group of ten.

? "Why is 12 seconds a convenient unit of time?" You can multiply by 5 to find the number of claps per minute.

- In discussing part (b), some students may argue that it would be difficult to keep a constant rate for 2 minutes. If this comment is made, ask partners to discuss how accurate they think their answers for the number of claps in two minutes really is. Students generally believe that the rate of claps will slow down as time is extended.

3.5 Rates and Unit Rates

Learning Target: Understand the concept of a unit rate and solve rate problems.

Success Criteria:
- I can find unit rates.
- I can use unit rates to solve rate problems.
- I can use unit rates to compare rates.

EXPLORATION 1 Using a Diagram

Work with a partner. The diagram shows a story problem.

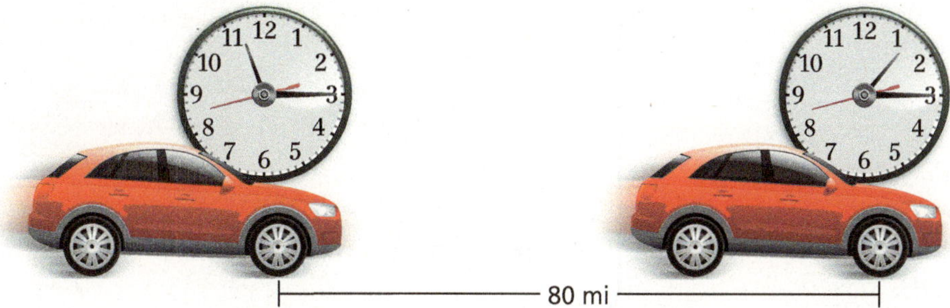

Math Practice

Specify Units
What are the units for the speed in part (c)? Why is it important to keep track of units in ratio problems?

a. What information can you obtain from the diagram?

b. Assuming that the car travels at a constant speed, how far does the car travel in 3.25 hours? Explain your method.

c. Draw a speedometer that shows the speed of the car. How can you use the speedometer to answer part (b)?

EXPLORATION 2 Using Equivalent Ratios

Work with a partner. Count the number of times you can clap your hands in 12 seconds. Have your partner record your results. Then switch roles with your partner and repeat the process.

a. Using your results and your partner's results, write ratios that represent the numbers of claps for every 12 seconds.

b. Explain how you can use the ratios in part (a) to find the numbers of times you and your partner can clap your hands in 2 minutes, in 2.5 minutes, and in 3 minutes.

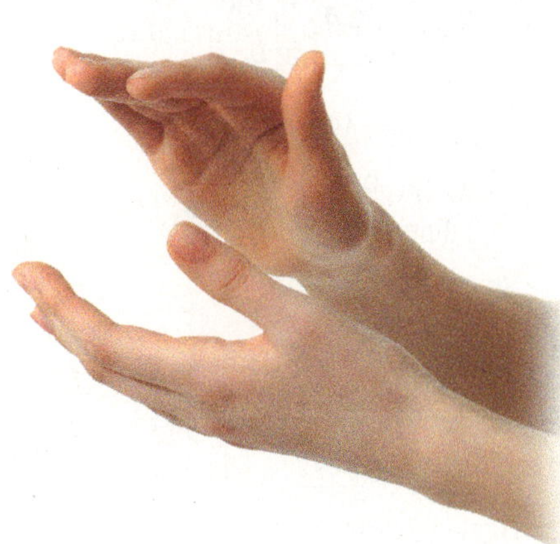

3.5 Lesson

Key Vocabulary
rate, *p. 136*
unit rate, *p. 136*
equivalent rates, *p. 136*

A **rate** is a ratio of two quantities using different units. You solved various ratio problems in the previous sections that involved rates. Now you will use *unit rates* to solve rate problems.

Key Idea

Unit Rate

Words A **unit rate** compares a quantity to one unit of another quantity. **Equivalent rates** have the same unit rate.

Numbers You pay \$27 for 3 pizzas.

Rate: \$27 : 3 pizzas

Unit rate: \$9 : 1 pizza

Algebra Rate: a units : b units Unit rate: $\frac{a}{b}$ units : 1 unit

EXAMPLE 1 Finding Unit Rates

You make fruit juice by adding 4 pints of water for every 2 cups of concentrate.

a. Find the unit rate.

The ratio of pints of water to cups of concentrate is 4 : 2. Divide each quantity by 2 to find the unit rate.

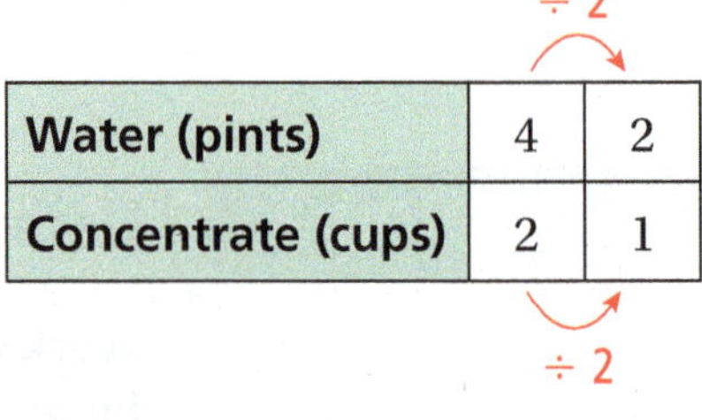

Water (pints)	4	2
Concentrate (cups)	2	1

The unit rate is 2 pints of water per cup of concentrate.

b. Write the ratio of cups of concentrate to pints of water. Then find the unit rate.

The ratio of cups of concentrate to pints of water is 2 : 4. Divide each quantity by 4 to find the unit rate.

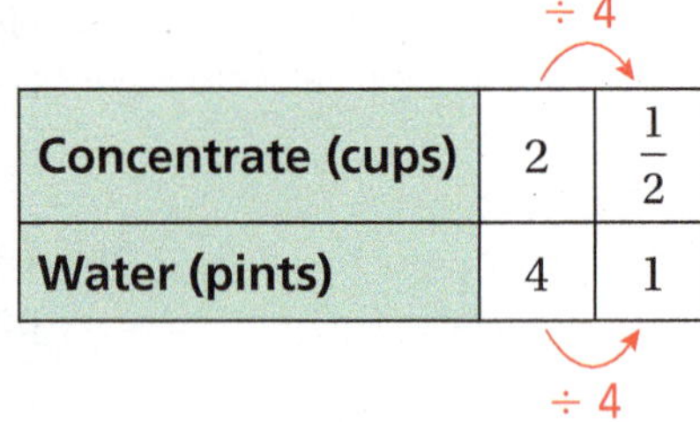

Concentrate (cups)	2	$\frac{1}{2}$
Water (pints)	4	1

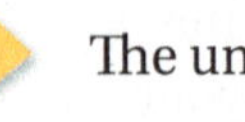

The unit rate is $\frac{1}{2}$ cup of concentrate per pint of water.

For a rate $a : b$, the associated rate $b : a$ has a unit rate of $\frac{b}{a} : 1$. This can be useful when solving rate problems.

Try It

1. **WHAT IF?** Repeat Example 1 when you add 4 pints of water for every 3 cups of concentrate.

Laurie's Notes

Scaffolding Instruction

- Using ratio reasoning, students explored rates and unit rates within several contexts.
- **Emerging:** Although students can write the initial rate, they may require support in finding the unit rate. Going through Example 1, either independently or with guided instruction, will help prepare students for using unit rates to solve problems.
- **Proficient:** Students confident in finding a unit rate can self-assess using Try It Exercise 1, and then work with a partner to complete Example 2.
- Guided instruction may be needed for all students with Example 3.

Key Idea

- Write the Key Idea.
- When students write a **rate**, it is very important to include the related units. The units identify the context of the rate. Without the units, $\frac{27}{3} = 9$ doesn't convey the context of $9 per pizza. Note that the word "per" is often used in reading unit rates.
- Discuss the algebraic connection involved in writing a rate as a **unit rate**. In Exploration 1, students wrote 80 miles per 2 hours as 40 miles per 1 hour. In Exploration 2, students wrote the number of claps per 12 seconds as the equivalent number of claps per 1 minute.

EXAMPLE 1

- In part (a), the ratio table helps students see a representation of the mental math they may use when finding the unit rate.
- Ask students to compare and contrast 2 pints of water per 1 cup of concentrate with 1 cup of concentrate per 2 pints of water. They are both rates, a pints : b cups and b cups : a pints. The first is a unit rate because 2 pints of water are compared to 1 cup of concentrate.

? **Turn and Talk:** "How can you write 1 cup of concentrate per 2 pints of water as a unit rate?" Divide each quantity by 2.

- **Big Idea:** Each ratio table shows why the ratio $a : b$ is equivalent to $\frac{a}{b} : 1$. This may not be obvious to students, particularly when $a < b$, which is the case in part (b).

Try It

- This problem may seem more difficult to students because writing the unit rates for 4 pints : 3 cups and 3 cups : 4 pints, involve fractions.
- Students should note the importance of units in this problem. Because there are 2 cups in a pint, the rate 4 pints : 3 cups is the same as the ratio 8 cups : 3 cups. Labeling answers with units is important.

ELL Support

Have students work in pairs to complete Exercise 1.
Beginner: Write out the unit rates.
Intermediate: Read aloud the answers as sentences. For example, "The unit rate is four-thirds pints of water per cup of concentrate."
Advanced: Describe the process used to complete the exercise.

Formative Assessment Tip

Whiteboards
Whiteboards can be used to provide individual responses, or used with small groups to encourage student collaboration and consensus on a problem or solution method. Whiteboards can be used at the beginning of class for the Warm Up or throughout the lesson to elicit student responses.

Unlike writing on scrap paper (individual response) or chart paper (group response), responses can be erased and modified easily. As understanding progresses, responses can reflect this growth.

Use whiteboards for more than quick responses. Sizable whiteboards can be used to communicate thinking, providing evidence of how a problem was solved. When students display their whiteboards in the front of the room, classmates can critique their reasoning or methods of solution.

Extra Example 1

You make green paint by adding 6 quarts of blue paint for every 2 pints of yellow paint.

a. Find the unit rate. 3 quarts of blue paint per pint of yellow paint

b. Express the ratio as pints of yellow paint to quarts of blue paint. Then find the unit rate. 2 : 6; $\frac{1}{3}$ pint of yellow paint per quart of blue paint

Try It

1. a. $\frac{4}{3}$ pints of water per cup of concentrate

   b. 3 : 4; $\frac{3}{4}$ cup of concentrate per pint of water

Extra Example 2

At mid-latitudes, Earth spins 3 miles every 10 seconds.

a. How far does Earth spin in 45 seconds at mid-latitudes? $13\frac{1}{2}$ miles

b. How many seconds does it take Earth to spin 25 miles at mid-latitudes? $83\frac{1}{3}$ seconds

Try It

2. **a.** 18 mi

   b. $\frac{10}{3} = 3\frac{1}{3}$ sec

Self-Assessment for Concepts & Skills

3. $\frac{1}{10}$ revolution/sec
4. 350 words/page
5. 20 pounds per 4 feet; It has a unit rate of 5 pounds per foot, the others have a unit rate of 4 pounds per foot.

Laurie's Notes

EXAMPLE 2

- When a spacecraft or parts of spacecraft no longer work, they are left to float around space indefinitely. It is usually too expensive to retrieve these objects, so they are left to orbit Earth until they fall back down or collide with other space junk.
- A ratio table models the situation.
- ? In part (a), ask, "How can you find the unit rate?" Divide distance and time by 6.
- Relate the unit rate back to the algebraic representation in the Key Idea.
- **Extension:** Ask students to work with a partner using whiteboards. Demonstrate how to find the unit rate when comparing time to distance. Circulate. Ask students to display their boards. Did all groups write a unit rate of $\frac{6}{5}$ seconds per mile? Did any group write 1.2 seconds per mile? Discuss the answers displayed on their whiteboards.
- Pose the question in part (b). Again ask students to work on a whiteboard. Look for different approaches. Students may use a double number line, a ratio table, or a calculation without a visual model.
- Check that answers have the correct labels.

Try It

- **Whiteboards:** Have students complete parts (a) and (b). Students should recognize that the unit rate of miles per second, is a speed. Finding the unit rate of seconds per mile is not as common. However, seconds per mile is useful in answering the question: How long will it take to reach a certain distance?
- **Neighbor Check:** Have students work independently, and then have their neighbors check their work. Have students discuss any discrepancies.

Self-Assessment for Concepts & Skills

- Students have worked through problems where they needed to find a unit rate. The unit rate was then used to solve rate problems.
- These exercises provide students the opportunity to assess their own understanding of rates and unit rates at this point.
- **Extension:** Ask students what type of problems they can solve using the unit rates in Exercises 3 and 4.

ELL Support

Have students complete the exercises in groups. Remind them to think about the process they used with Try It Exercise 1. After students complete the exercises, have two groups present their answers to each other, and revise them if there is any disagreement. Provide support as needed.

The Success Criteria Self-Assessment chart can be found in the *Student Journal* or online at *BigIdeasMath.com*.

EXAMPLE 2 Using a Unit Rate to Solve a Rate Problem

A piece of space junk travels 5 miles every 6 seconds.

a. How far does the space junk travel in 30 seconds?

The ratio of miles to seconds is 5 : 6. Divide by 6 to find the unit rate in miles per second. Then multiply each quantity by 30 to find the distance traveled in 30 seconds.

(÷ 6, × 30)

Distance (miles)	5	$\frac{5}{6}$	25
Time (seconds)	6	1	30

(÷ 6, × 30)

▶ The space junk travels 25 miles in 30 seconds.

b. How many seconds does it take the space junk to travel 2 miles?

The ratio of seconds to miles is 6 : 5. Divide by 5 to find the unit rate in seconds per mile. Then multiply each quantity by 2 to find the time to travel 2 miles.

(÷ 5, × 2)

Time (seconds)	6	$\frac{6}{5}$	$\frac{12}{5}$
Distance (miles)	5	1	2

(÷ 5, × 2)

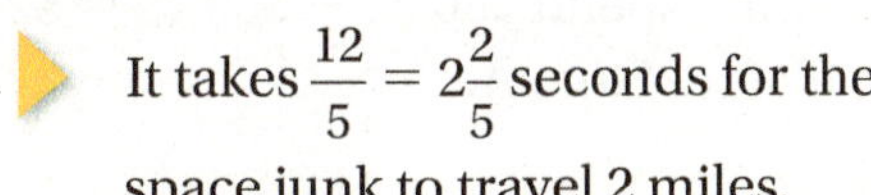

▶ It takes $\frac{12}{5} = 2\frac{2}{5}$ seconds for the space junk to travel 2 miles.

In Example 2, notice that you can use one step in each ratio table. Multiply by $\frac{1}{6} \times 30 = 5$ in part (a) and $\frac{1}{5} \times 2 = \frac{2}{5}$ in part (b).

Try It

2. **WHAT IF?** Repeat Example 2 when the space junk travels 3 miles every 5 seconds.

Self-Assessment for Concepts & Skills

Solve each exercise. Then rate your understanding of the success criteria in your journal.

FINDING UNIT RATES **Write a unit rate for the situation.**

3. 5 revolutions in 50 seconds

4. 1400 words for every 4 pages

5. **WHICH ONE DOESN'T BELONG?** Which rate does *not* belong with the other three? Explain your reasoning.

8 pounds for every 2 feet

12 pounds per 3 feet

20 pounds per 4 feet

24 pounds for every 6 feet

EXAMPLE 3 Modeling Real Life

You buy 2 pounds of salmon filets at Store A for \$21.50. Your friend buys 3 pounds of salmon filets at Store B for \$33.75. How much less would you spend for 5 pounds of salmon filets at the store with the better deal?

Use ratio tables to find the cost of 5 pounds of salmon filets at each store.

Store A	
Cost (dollars)	Salmon (pounds)
21.50	2
10.75	1
53.75	5

Store B	
Cost (dollars)	Salmon (pounds)
33.75	3
11.25	1
56.25	5

Find the unit rate at each store.

Find the cost of 5 pounds at each store.

So, you would spend $\$56.25 - \$53.75 = \$2.50$ less for 5 pounds of salmon filets at Store A.

Check The cost at Store A is $\$11.25 - \$10.75 = \$0.50$ cheaper per pound than the cost at Store B. Because you are buying 5 pounds, you will pay $5 \times \$0.50 = \$2.50$ less at Store A. ✓

Self-Assessment for Problem Solving

Solve each exercise. Then rate your understanding of the success criteria in your journal.

6. You buy 10 pounds of bird seed at Store A for \$11.50. Your friend buys 15 pounds of bird seed at Store B for \$19.50. How much less would you spend by buying 20 pounds of bird seed at the store with the better deal?

7. A person hikes 4 miles in 2.5 hours. Find the unit rate in miles per hour. Then find the unit rate in hours per mile. How is each unit rate useful in a real-life situation?

8. **DIG DEEPER!** How many bagels can you buy with a \$20 bill? Can you buy at most n times this many bagels with n \$20 bills? Explain your reasoning.

Laurie's Notes

EXAMPLE 3

- Ask a volunteer to read the problem.
- Do students have an understanding of what the question is asking?
- ? **Turn and Talk:** "What is the problem asking you to do? What information is given? Do your have a strategy for starting the problem?"
- ? "What does having the 'better deal' mean in this problem?" Listen for a complete answer referencing a lower price per pound. Students may only say, "lower price." The "better deal" refers to a rate so units are necessary.
- There are different approaches rather than one correct approach when solving rate problems using a ratio table or a double number line.
- **Whiteboards:** Having a record of student work on a whiteboard enables the work to be shared efficiently.

Self-Assessment for Problem Solving

- Encourage students to use a Four Square to complete the exercises. Until students become comfortable with the problem-solving plan, they may only be ready to complete the first step.
- Students should recognize that several of these exercises use the ratio $a : b$ and $b : a$. Although *miles per hour* is a very common rate, *hours per mile* is useful as well.
- ? Remind students to look back at previous problems and lessons. "Have you solved a problem similar to this before?"
- Remember, students need the opportunity to review the success criteria. "I know I have met the learning target because I am confident with all of the success criteria."

The Success Criteria Self-Assessment chart can be found in the *Student Journal* or online at *BigIdeasMath.com*.

Closure

- **Exit Ticket:** You walk 5 kilometers in 45 minutes. Find the unit rate and interpret what it means. $\frac{1}{9}$ kilometer per minute; You walk $\frac{1}{9}$ kilometer in 1 minute.

Extra Example 3

You buy 3 pounds of chicken at Store A for $11.97. Your friend buys 4 pounds of chicken at Store B for $13.16. How much less would you spend for 7 pounds of chicken at the store with the better deal? $4.90 less for 7 pounds at Store B

Self-Assessment for Problem Solving

6. $3
7. 1.6 mi/h; 0.625 h/mi; *Sample answer:* Use the first rate to find how far you can hike in a given time. Use the second rate to find how long it will take to hike a given distance.
8. $13; no; 13 bagels cost $19.50, and one bagel costs $1.50, so with 3 $20 bills you can buy another bagel.

Learning Target

Understand the concept of a unit rate and solve rate problems.

Success Criteria

- Find unit rates.
- Use unit rates to solve rate problems.
- Use unit rates to compare rates.

Review & Refresh

1. 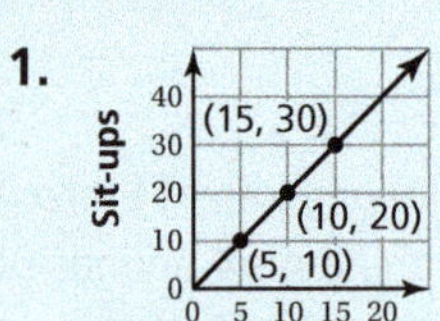

2. 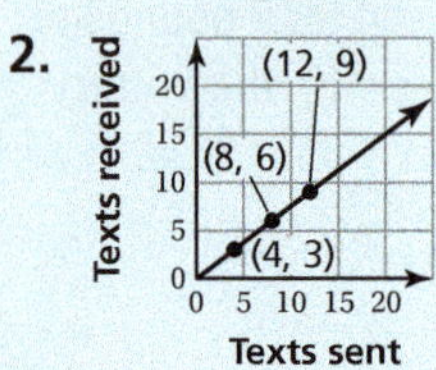

3. See Additional Answers.

4. 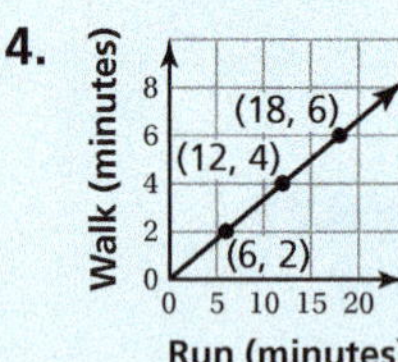

5. $\frac{2}{3}$

6. $\frac{1}{16}$

7. $1\frac{7}{12}$

8. 2

9. 19.241

10. 1.043

11. 7.919

12. C

Concepts, Skills, & Problem Solving

13. Answers will vary. Multiply the hand clap rate in Exploration 2(a) by 2.5.

14. Answers will vary. Multiply the hand clap rate in Exploration 2(a) by 8.75.

15. Answers will vary. Multiply the hand clap rate in Exploration 2(a) by 11.25.

16. 12 animals/mi^2

17. \$20/guest

18. \$7/week

19. 6 necklaces/h

20. 45 mi/h

21. 19 students/class

22. 140 kB/sec

23. 110 calories/serving

24. 72 mi/gal

25. \$2.5/oz

26. $\frac{2}{3}, \frac{16}{3}$

27. $\frac{1}{6}, \frac{17}{6}$

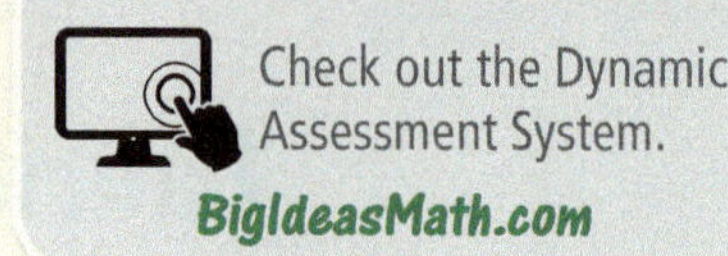

Assignment Guide and Concept Check

Scaffold assignments to support all students in their learning progression. The suggested assignments are a starting point. Continue to assign additional exercises and revisit with spaced practice to move every student toward proficiency.

Level	Assignment 1	Assignment 2
Emerging	3, 8, 11, 12, 15, 16, 17, 26, 30	23, 25, 27, 28, 29, 33, 37
Proficient	3, 8, 11, 12, 15, 18, 20, 27, 31	28, 29, 33, 34, 35, 36, 37
Advanced	3, 8, 11, 12, 15, 23, 25, 27, 33	34, 35, 36, 37, 38, 39

- Assignment 1 is for use after students complete the Self-Assessment for Concepts & Skills.
- Assignment 2 is for use after students complete the Self-Assessment for Problem Solving.
- The red exercises can be used as a concept check.

Review & Refresh Prior Skills

Exercises 1–4 Graphing Ratio Relationships
Exercises 5 and 6 Dividing Fractions
Exercises 7 and 8 Dividing with Mixed Numbers
Exercises 9–11 Adding and Subtracting Decimals
Exercise 12 Multiplying Whole Numbers and Fractions

3.5 Practice

Go to *BigIdeasMath.com* to get HELP with solving the exercises.

Review & Refresh

Represent the ratio relationship using a graph.

1.

Push-Ups	5	10	15
Sit-Ups	10	20	30

2.

Texts Sent	4	8	12
Texts Received	3	6	9

3.

Seeds	15	30	45
Plants	12	24	36

4.

Run (minutes)	6	12	18
Walk (minutes)	2	4	6

Divide. Write the answer in simplest form.

5. $\frac{1}{5} \div \frac{3}{10}$

6. $\frac{3}{8} \div 6$

7. $3\frac{1}{6} \div 2$

8. $5\frac{1}{3} \div 2\frac{2}{3}$

Add or subtract.

9. $6.94 + 12.301$

10. $8.753 - 7.71$

11. $14.532 - 6.613$

12. The winner in an election for class president received $\frac{3}{4}$ of the 240 votes. How many votes did the winner receive?

A. 60 **B.** 150 **C.** 180 **D.** 320

Concepts, Skills, & Problem Solving

USING EQUIVALENT RATIOS **Use the ratio in Exploration 2 to estimate the number of times you can clap your hands in the given amount of time.** (See Exploration 2, p. 135.)

13. 0.5 minute

14. 1.75 minutes

15. 2.25 minutes

FINDING UNIT RATES **Write a unit rate for the situation.**

16. 24 animals in 2 square miles

17. $100 for every 5 guests

18. $28 saved in 4 weeks

19. 18 necklaces made in 3 hours

20. 270 miles in 6 hours

21. 228 students in 12 classes

22. 2520 kilobytes in 18 seconds

23. 880 calories in 8 servings

24. 1080 miles on 15 gallons

25. $12.50 for 5 ounces

USING UNIT RATES **Find the missing values in the ratio table.**

26.

Inches	2		
Years	3	1	8

27.

Gallons	30	1	17
Seconds	5		

28. MP **MODELING REAL LIFE** Lightning strikes Earth 1000 times in 10 seconds.

   a. How many times does lightning strike in 12 seconds?

   b. How many seconds does it take for lightning to strike 7250 times?

29. MP **MODELING REAL LIFE** You earn \$35 for washing 7 cars.

   a. How much do you earn for washing 4 cars?

   b. You earn \$45. How many cars did you wash?

COMPARING RATES **Decide whether the rates are equivalent.**

30. 24 laps in 6 minutes
    72 laps in 18 minutes

31. 126 points for every 3 games
    210 points for every 5 games

32. 15 breaths for every 36 seconds
    90 breaths for every 3 minutes

33. \$16 for 4 pounds
    \$1 for 4 ounces

34. MP **MODELING REAL LIFE** An office printer prints 25 photos in 12.5 minutes. A home printer prints 15 photos in 6 minutes. Which printer is faster? How many more photos can you print in 12 minutes using the faster printer?

35. MP **MODELING REAL LIFE** You jog 2 kilometers in 12 minutes. Your friend jogs 3 kilometers in 16.5 minutes. Who jogs faster? How much sooner will the faster jogger finish a five-kilometer race?

36. MP **PROBLEM SOLVING** A softball team has a budget of \$200 for visors. The athletic director pays \$90 for 12 sun visors. Is there enough money in the budget to purchase 15 more sun visors? Explain your reasoning.

37. **DIG DEEPER!** The table shows the amounts of food collected by two homerooms. Homeroom A collects 21 additional items of food. How many more items does Homeroom B need to collect to have more items per student?

	Homeroom A	Homeroom B
Students	24	16
Canned Food	30	22
Dry Food	42	24

38. MP **REASONING** A runner completed a 26.2-mile marathon in 210 minutes.

   a. Estimate the unit rate, in miles per minute.

   b. Estimate the unit rate, in minutes per mile.

   c. Another runner says, "I averaged 10-minute miles in the marathon." Is this runner talking about the unit rate described in part (a) or in part (b)? Explain your reasoning.

39. **DIG DEEPER!** You can complete one-half of a job in an hour. Your friend can complete one-third of the same job in an hour. How long will it take to complete the job if you work together?

Common Errors

- **Exercise 39** Students may struggle with this exercise. Encourage them to use the first two sentences to write individual work rates. Then ask how they can find the combined work rate (by adding the individual work rates). Using the combined work rate $\frac{5}{6}$ of the job per hour, they will have to realize that they need to turn $\frac{5}{6}$ into 1 in the "Portion Completed" row of the ratio table, and the corresponding time will be the answer.

Mini-Assessment

Write a unit rate for the situation.

1. $54 for every 3 guests $18 per guest
2. 354 miles in 6 hours 59 miles per hour
3. Find the missing values in the ratio table.

Feet	50		
Seconds	6	1	9

$\frac{50}{6}$, 75

4. Decide whether the rates are equivalent.

$8 for 2 pounds

$2 for 0.25 pound

not equivalent

Section Resources

Surface Level	Deep Level
Resources by Chapter • Extra Practice • Reteach • Puzzle Time Student Journal • Self-Assessment • Practice Differentiating the Lesson Tutorial Videos Skills Review Handbook Skills Trainer	Resources by Chapter • Enrichment and Extension Graphic Organizers Dynamic Assessment System • Section Practice

Concepts, Skills, & Problem Solving

28. **a.** 1200

b. 72.5 sec

29. **a.** $20

b. 9

30. equivalent

31. equivalent

32. not equivalent

33. equivalent

34. home; 6

35. your friend; 2.5 min

36. no; 15 visors cost $112.50 > $110.

37. 17

38. **a.** about 0.12 mi/min

b. about 8.0 min/mi

c. b; "10-minute miles" is 10 minutes per mile.

39. 1.2 h

Laurie's Notes

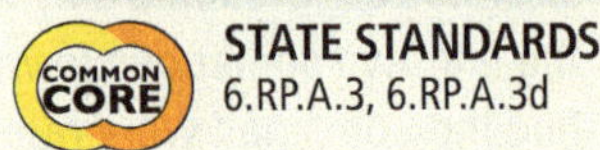

Learning Target

Use ratio reasoning to convert units of measure.

Success Criteria

- Write conversion facts as unit rates.
- Convert units of measure using ratio tables.
- Convert units of measure using conversion factors.
- Convert rates using conversion factors.

Warm Up

Cumulative, vocabulary, and prerequisite skills practice opportunities are available in the *Resources by Chapter* or at *BigIdeasMath.com*.

ELL Support

Students may be more familiar with the metric system. Explain that different measurements are used in the United States. To compare quantities from the metric system to quantities used here, one must convert units of measure. *To convert* means *to change*. When you convert a unit of measure, you describe the exact same amount but using a different unit.

Exploration 1

a. $3\frac{3}{4}$ L/gal

b. $\frac{1}{4}$ gal/L

c. See Additional Answers.

Exploration 2

Sample answer: Divide by 60 to find the rate in inches per second, then find the length on the centimeter ruler corresponding to the number of inches.

Preparing to Teach

- Converting one measurement or rate to another can be confusing to students. Students are not always confident about which operation to use and will often ask if they should multiply or divide, even if they know the conversion fact. While going through this lesson, be sure to emphasize to students that they should keep track of the units by always labeling quantities and using ratio reasoning when thinking about the problem.

Motivate

- Mark the beginning and end of a 10-foot distance in your classroom. Ask a volunteer to walk at a normal pace from start to finish. Record his or her time in seconds and rate in feet per seconds. For example, 10 feet per 3.8 seconds.
- ? "Can this rate be written as a unit rate? Can you write the rate as feet per minute, meters per second, or centimeters per minute?"
- Explain to the students that in this lesson, they will rewrite a rate by using conversion facts, such as 60 seconds = 1 minute or 1 inch = 2.54 centimeters.

Exploration 1

- **Big Idea:** In this exploration, students will write the unit rate relationship between two quantities, in both directions. For example, \$5 per pound is the same as $\frac{1}{5}$ pound per \$1.
- **Teaching Tip:** If possible, have one-gallon milk jugs, one-liter bottles, a bucket of water, and paper towels to demonstrate this exploration to the class.
- The mix of customary and metric units is intentional. Students should know that there are 4 quarts in 1 gallon. A liter has slightly more liquid volume than a quart, so 1 gallon won't completely fill the 4 liters.
- **MP6 Attend to Precision:** This is an appropriate time to talk about estimation. The purpose of the measurement will influence how precise the estimate should be.

Exploration 2

- Have calculators available. This exploration is about students making sense of rewriting rates using different units of measure. You want students to focus on making sense of the conversions, not on worrying about messy computations. Again, estimation plays a role.
- Some students may find it easier to think about the question if they know the caterpillar's rate. You can make one up. The rate could be 1 inch per minute, 2 inches per minute, or perhaps *x* inches per minute.
- **MP5 Use Appropriate Tools Strategically:** Students should recognize the usefulness of a ruler that contains both centimeters and inches.
- Ask several volunteers to share their work and thinking.

3.6 Converting Measures

Learning Target: Use ratio reasoning to convert units of measure.

Success Criteria:
- I can write conversion facts as unit rates.
- I can convert units of measure using ratio tables.
- I can convert units of measure using conversion factors.
- I can convert rates using conversion factors.

EXPLORATION 1 Estimating Unit Conversions

Work with a partner. You are given 4 one-liter containers and a one-gallon container.

a. A full one-gallon container can be used to fill the one-liter containers, as shown below. Write a unit rate that estimates the number of liters per gallon.

b. A full one-liter container can be used to partially fill the one-gallon container, as shown below. Write a unit rate that estimates the number of gallons per liter.

c. Estimate the number of liters in 5.5 gallons and the number of gallons in 12 liters. What method(s) did you use? What other methods could you have used?

EXPLORATION 2 Converting Units in a Rate

Math Practice

Recognize Usefulness of Tools

When would rulers be a useful tool for converting between centimeters and inches? When would they not be useful?

Work with a partner. The rate that a caterpillar moves is given in inches per minute. Using the rulers below, how can you convert the rate to centimeters per second? Justify your answer.

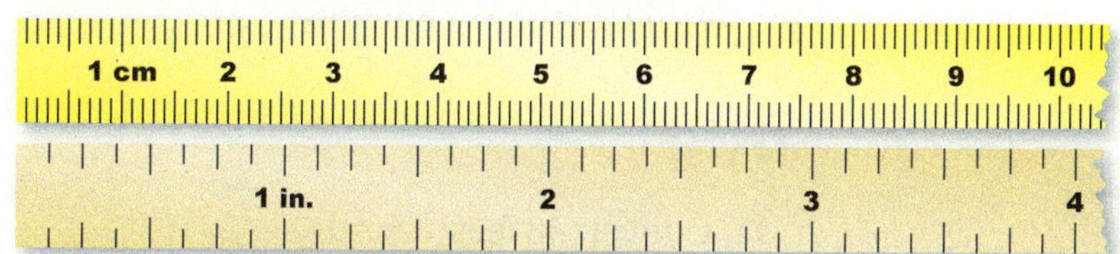

3.6 Lesson

Key Vocabulary
U.S. customary system, p. 142
metric system, p. 142
conversion factor, p. 143
unit analysis, p. 143

The **U.S. customary system** is a system of measurement that contains units for length, capacity, and weight. The **metric system** is a decimal system of measurement, based on powers of 10, that contains units for length, capacity, and mass.

You can use unit rates and ratio tables to convert measures within the same system and between systems.

EXAMPLE 1 Converting Measures within the Same System

For a list of conversion facts, see the Mathematics Reference Sheet in the back of this book.

Convert 36 quarts to gallons.

Because 1 gallon = 4 quarts, there are 4 quarts per gallon, and $\frac{1}{4}$ gallon per quart. You can use either of these unit rates to find an equivalent rate with 36 quarts.

Method 1: Create a ratio table using the unit rate 4 quarts per gallon. Multiply each quantity by 9 to find the number of gallons in 36 quarts.

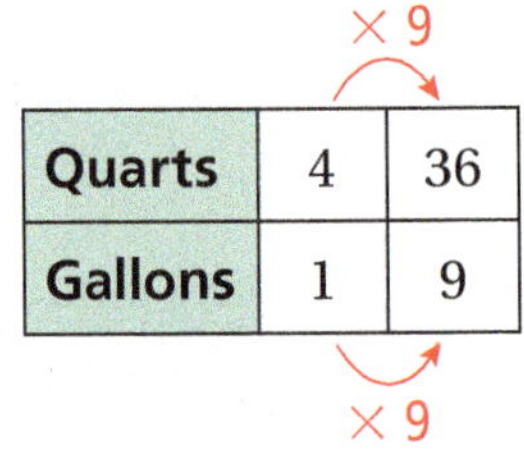

Quarts	4	36
Gallons	1	9

So, 36 quarts is 9 gallons.

Method 2: Create a ratio table using the unit rate $\frac{1}{4}$ gallon per quart. Multiply each quantity by 36 to find the number of gallons in 36 quarts.

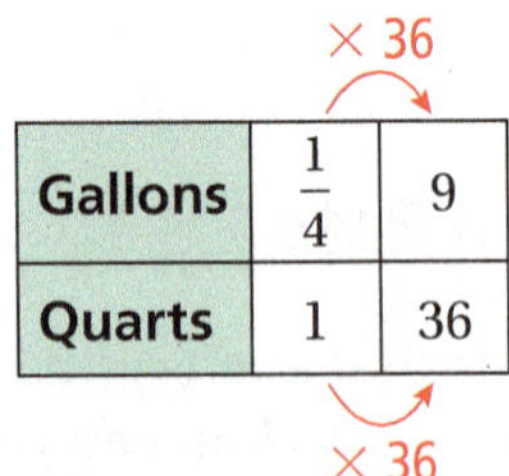

Gallons	$\frac{1}{4}$	9
Quarts	1	36

So, 36 quarts is 9 gallons.

Another Method Use a graph.

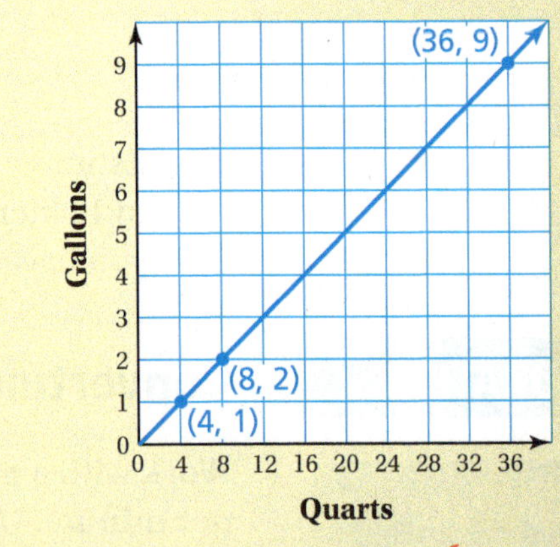

So, 36 quarts is 9 gallons. ✓

Try It

1. Convert 48 feet to yards.

Laurie's Notes

Scaffolding Instruction

- The explorations provide a good introduction to converting units of measure. In prior grades, students converted measures within the same system. Now students will also convert measures between systems using ratio reasoning. This is generally a challenging lesson for many students. Lack of familiarity with measurement conversions may create additional challenges.
- **Emerging:** Students will need support in representing the computations and thinking about what information is needed to solve the problem. Guided instruction with the examples will help students gain confidence and understanding.
- **Proficient:** Students may be confident in converting units of measure and converting units within a rate. They may be independent with the beginning Try It exercises.
- Guided instruction may be needed for all students with problems that require more than one conversion.

EXAMPLE 1

- **MP6 Attend to Precision:** Some students may ask, "Why not just divide by 4 because there are 4 quarts in a gallon?" That is indeed what happens, however paying attention to the units is a good habit to develop.
- Method 1 uses the unit rate 4 quarts per gallon.
- ? Method 2 shows students another way of thinking about the conversion. "How many gallons are in a quart?" $\frac{1}{4}$ gallon "How can you use this relationship to solve the problem?" You can create a ratio table using the unit rate $\frac{1}{4}$ gallon per quart.
- Discuss using a graph as another method for solving this problem. Notice that for every increase of 4 quarts, the gallons increase by 1.

Try It

- In addition to solving the problem, have students show a representation of their work. Students need to keep track of the units.

ELL Support

Students unfamiliar with feet and yards need to know that there are 3 feet in 1 yard. Display a yardstick and point out where 1, 2, and 3 feet are located. Then have them work in groups to solve the problem. Remind them to follow one of the methods they practiced in Example 1. They can use the other method to check their answers.

Beginner: Create a ratio table, using arrows and multiplication.

Intermediate: Describe the ratio table using a sentence. For example, "There are three feet in every one yard."

Advanced: Explain how they found their answers.

Scaffold instruction to support all students in their learning. Learning is individualized and you may want to group students differently as they move in and out of these levels with each skill and concept. Student self-assessment and feedback help guide your instructional decisions about how and when to layer support for all students to become proficient learners.

Extra Example 1

Convert 72 inches to feet. 6 feet

Try It

1. 16 yd

Laurie's Notes

EXAMPLE 2

- Students should estimate a reasonable answer before they begin solving. Hold up a meter stick. "About how many feet is this?" a little more than 3 feet "So, about how many feet would 10 meters be?" a little more than 30 feet
- Students may ask if the problem can be solved by either method shown. Yes, and the focus should be on ratio reasoning. Does the method make sense and why?
- The second method in this example demonstrates that either unit rate can be used. A person familiar with customary measurements may know that there are approximately 3.28 feet in a meter. A person familiar with metric measurements, may know that there is approximately 0.3 meter in a foot. Either knowledge will allow you to convert meters to feet.
- It is important for students to understand that the conversion fact they use may result in a slightly different answer and that is acceptable. Encourage students to determine which method is more convenient to use when converting.

Try It

- Students who have competed in a 3K, 5K, or 10K race may be familiar with the conversion fact for miles and kilometers. If not, students can look up a conversion fact in the Mathematics Reference Sheet in the back of their books.
- **Popsicle Sticks:** Solicit a solution to this problem.

Key Idea

- Write the Key Idea.
- When students are writing a **conversion factor** it is very important to include the related units.
- Students will need to use **unit analysis** to decide which conversion factor will produce the appropriate units.
- Multiplying by a conversion factor does not change the value of the quantity. Using the correct conversion factor will result in a "cross out" of a unit appearing in both a numerator and a denominator.

Formative Assessment Tip

Popsicle Sticks

This technique ensures that any student can be called on during questioning time in class. Write the name of each student on a Popsicle stick. Place the sticks in a cup (or can). When questions are posed in class during *No-Hands Questioning*, each student should think and be prepared to answer. If you only call on students who raise their hands, students can then opt out of being engaged. All students think they have an equal chance of being called on when a stick is pulled randomly, so they engage more in the lesson.

If there are certain students that you want to hear from, the cup can have an inner cylinder where select sticks are placed. It will appear that the process is still random, and the voices you have not heard much from will still have the opportunity to prepare and formulate their answers.

Extra Example 2

Convert 5 kilometers to miles.
about 3.1 miles, or about 3.11 miles

Try It

2. 11.27 km or 11.29 km

EXAMPLE 2 Converting Measures Between Systems

In Example 2, it is more efficient to use the unit rate in Method 1 because there is 1 unit of the quantity you are converting. The answers are slightly different due to differences in the rounding used with conversion facts, but both answers are acceptable.

Convert 10 meters to feet.

Because 1 meter ≈ 3.28 feet, there are about 3.28 feet per meter. Because 1 foot ≈ 0.3 meter, there is about 0.3 meter per foot. You can use either of these unit rates to find an equivalent rate with 10 meters.

Method 1: Create a ratio table using the unit rate 3.28 feet per meter.

× 10

Feet	3.28	32.8
Meters	1	10

× 10

So, 10 meters is about 32.8 feet.

Method 2: Create a ratio table using the unit rate 0.3 meter per foot.

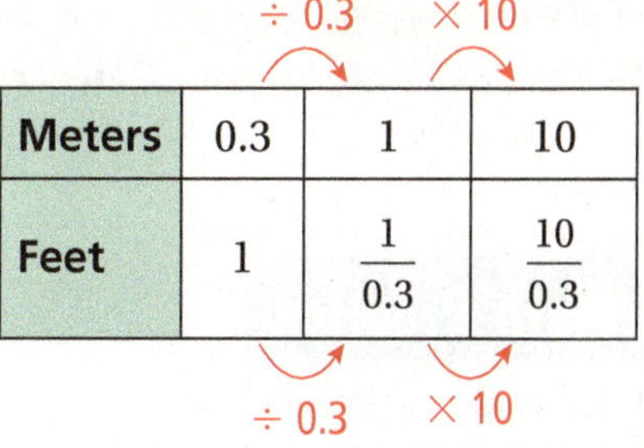

÷ 0.3 × 10

Meters	0.3	1	10
Feet	1	$\frac{1}{0.3}$	$\frac{10}{0.3}$

÷ 0.3 × 10

So, 10 meters is about $\frac{10}{0.3} \approx 33.33$ feet.

Try It

2. Convert 7 miles to kilometers. Round to the nearest hundredth if necessary.

Another way to convert units of measure is to multiply by one or more *conversion factors*.

Key Idea

Because the quantities in a conversion factor are equal, conversion factors are equal to 1. So, you can multiply a quantity by a conversion factor and not change its value.

Conversion Factor

A **conversion factor** is a rate in which the two quantities are equal. When using conversion factors, write rates using fraction notation.

	Relationship	***Conversion Factors***
Example	1 ft = 12 in.	1 ft per 12 in., or $\frac{1 \text{ ft}}{12 \text{ in.}}$
		12 in. per 1 ft, or $\frac{12 \text{ in.}}{1 \text{ ft}}$

You can use **unit analysis** to decide which conversion factor will produce the appropriate units. You can "cross out" a unit that appears in both a numerator and a denominator of a product.

EXAMPLE 3 Using Conversion Factors

Another Method Use a double number line.

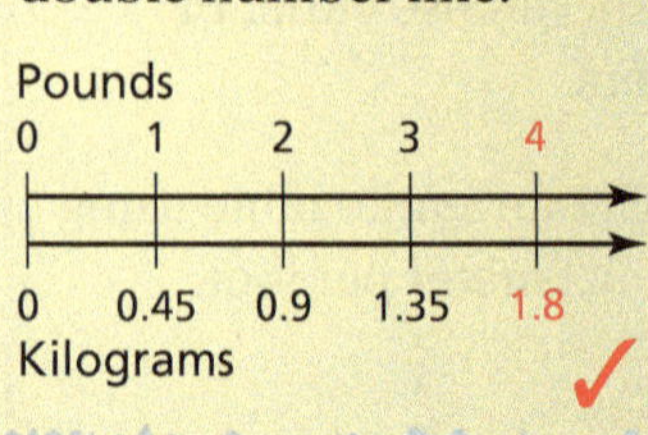

a. Convert 4 pounds to kilograms.

Use a conversion factor.

1 lb ≈ 0.45 kg

$$4 \text{ lb} \approx 4 \text{ lb} \times \frac{0.45 \text{ kg}}{1 \text{ lb}} = 1.8 \text{ kg}$$

So, 4 pounds is about 1.8 kilograms.

b. Convert 5 yards per second to yards per minute.

Write 5 yards per second as a fraction. Then use a conversion factor.

1 min = 60 sec

$$5 \text{ yards per second} = \frac{5 \text{ yd}}{1 \text{ sec}} \times \frac{60 \text{ sec}}{1 \text{ min}} = \frac{300 \text{ yd}}{1 \text{ min}}$$

So, 5 yards per second is 300 yards per minute.

Math Practice

Analyze Relationships

In part (b), explain how you know to use a conversion factor of $\frac{60 \text{ sec}}{1 \text{ min}}$ rather than $\frac{1 \text{ min}}{60 \text{ sec}}$.

Try It

3. Convert 20 quarts to liters. Round to the nearest hundredth if necessary.

4. Convert 60 kilometers per hour to miles per hour. Round to the nearest hundredth if necessary.

Self-Assessment for Concepts & Skills

Solve each exercise. Then rate your understanding of the success criteria in your journal.

5. **DIFFERENT WORDS, SAME QUESTION** Which is different? Find "both" answers.

Convert 5 inches to centimeters.	Find the number of inches in 5 centimeters.
How many centimeters are in 5 inches?	Five inches equals how many centimeters?

CONVERTING MEASURES **Copy and complete the statement. Round to the nearest hundredth if necessary.**

6. $\frac{12 \text{ m}}{\text{min}} \approx \frac{\square \text{ ft}}{\text{min}}$

7. $\frac{12 \text{ ft}}{\text{sec}} = \frac{\square \text{ yd}}{\text{min}}$

Laurie's Notes

EXAMPLE 3

- Ask students what they know about pounds and kilograms. Which is heavier, a pound of chocolate or a kilogram of chocolate? Tell students that 1 pound ≈ 0.45 kilogram and 1 kilogram ≈ 2.2 pounds.
- **Turn and Talk:** "How can you convert 4 pounds to kilograms?" Once students have had a chance to discuss, draw a *Popsicle Stick* to solicit a response. Ask the chosen student to share his or her work at the board or document camera.
- **MP2 Reason Abstractly and Quantitatively:** Did the student use a coherent representation of the quantities? Students should be paying attention to how units and labels are used.
- In part (b), students may guess that they need to multiply by 60. Can they verify this by representing the work with units?

Try It

- Students may need to refer to the Mathematics Reference Sheet in the back of their books.
- **Feedback:** Circulate and observe students' work. It is not uncommon for two neighbors to use different processes, and perhaps only one solution is correct. Without suggesting which work is correct, draw attention to the different answers and tell them to explain their thinking to one another.

Self-Assessment for Concepts & Skills

- Do students view conversions within one system differently than conversions between systems? For instance, is converting 8 yards to feet the same type of process as converting 8 yards to meters? Ask students to reflect on this as they consider the success criteria.
- Exercise 6 involves converting meters to feet within a rate. Do students view this differently than just converting meters to feet?

ELL Support

Remind students that are struggling with customary measurements to use the Mathematics Reference Sheet in the back of the book. Allow students to work in pairs to complete the exercises. For Exercise 5, have students take turns reading and interpreting each question. This is a good opportunity for ELLs to practice language while they check understanding of what they learned.

The Success Criteria Self-Assessment chart can be found in the *Student Journal* or online at *BigIdeasMath.com*.

Extra Example 3

a. Convert 13 inches to centimeters. about 33.02 centimeters, or about 33.33 centimeters

b. Convert 70 miles per hour to miles per day. 1680 miles per day

Try It

3. 19 L or 18.87 L
4. 37.2 mi/h or 37.27 mi/h

Self-Assessment for Concepts & Skills

5. Find the number of inches in 5 centimeters; 1.95 in. or 1.97 in.; 12.7 cm or 12.82 cm
6. 39.36 or 40
7. 240

Extra Example 4

A biker's goal is to complete a mile in 3 minutes or less. The biker's speed is 28 feet per second. Does the biker meet the goal? If not, how much faster (in feet per second) must the biker be to meet the goal? no; $1\frac{1}{3}$ feet per second faster

Self-Assessment for Problem Solving

8. no; $2\text{ L} > 2\text{ qt}$

9. $8\frac{1}{3}$

10. yes

Learning Target

Use ratio reasoning to convert units of measure.

Success Criteria

- Write conversion facts as unit rates.
- Convert units of measure using ratio tables.
- Convert units of measure using conversion factors.
- Convert rates using conversion factors.

Laurie's Notes

Discuss

- Solving a conversion problem may require a conversion fact that students are not familiar with, regardless of whether the conversion is within the same system or between systems.
- Remind students that when using a conversion factor, where they place each quantity is very important.

EXAMPLE 4

- If there are runners in your class, ask them to share information about rates of runners. For instance, a long distance runner may run a six-minute mile, meaning 6 minutes per mile. How fast is this in seconds per mile, or minutes per foot? Each of these examples is a rate that compares time to distance.
- Work though the example, noting how labeling units is important to keeping track of the quantities.

Self-Assessment for Problem Solving

- Allow time in class for students to practice using the problem-solving plan. Remember, some students may only be able to complete the first step.
- Have students work with a partner or in a group to solve the exercises. Work should be recorded so that it can be shared with others under a document camera or at the board.
- In Exercise 8, some students may not complete any computations. They may reason that a liter is more liquid volume than a quart, so two liters of water will not fit into a two-quart pitcher.
- Exercises 9 and 10 will provide evidence of students' progress towards the learning target.
- As students are working through these exercises, encourage them to assess their understanding of the learning target and success criteria, keeping the focus on the learning target. Tell students to rate their understanding of each success criterion.

The Success Criteria Self-Assessment chart can be found in the *Student Journal* or online at *BigIdeasMath.com*.

Closure

- A major league pitcher throws a 90-mile-per-hour fastball. Convert this speed to feet per second. 132 feet per second

EXAMPLE 4 Modeling Real Life

A runner's goal is to complete a mile in 4 minutes or less. The runner's speed is 20 feet per second. Does the runner meet the goal? If not, how much faster (in feet per second) must the runner be to meet the goal?

To meet the goal, the runner must complete 1 mile in 4 minutes or less. The minimum speed required is 1 mile per 4 minutes.

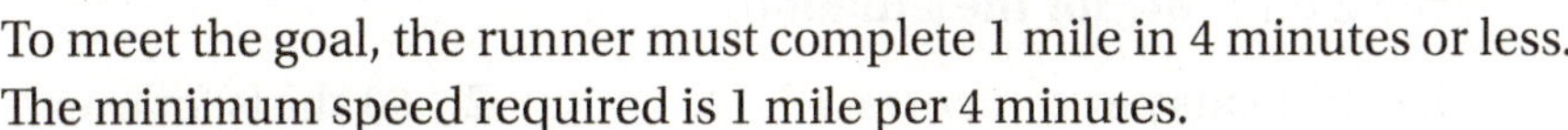

To compare this speed to the runner's speed of 20 feet per second, convert the minimum speed of 1 mile per 4 minutes to feet per second.

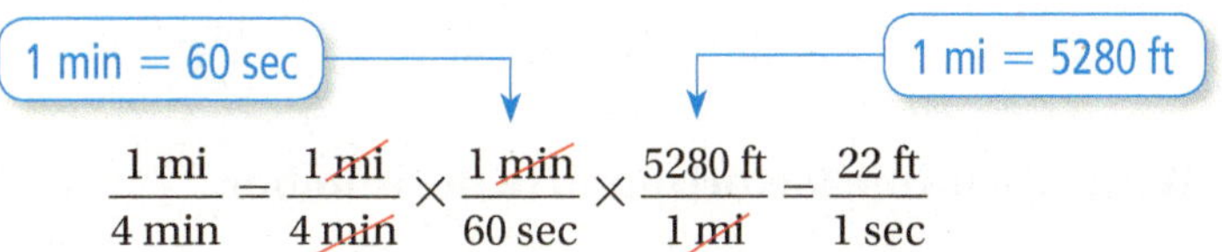

$$\frac{1 \text{ mi}}{4 \text{ min}} = \frac{1 \text{ mi}}{4 \text{ min}} \times \frac{1 \text{ min}}{60 \text{ sec}} \times \frac{5280 \text{ ft}}{1 \text{ mi}} = \frac{22 \text{ ft}}{1 \text{ sec}}$$

So, the runner did not meet the goal because a speed of 20 feet per second is below the minimum speed of 22 feet per second. The runner must be $22 - 20 = 2$ feet per second faster to meet the goal.

Check Verify that the distances traveled in 4 minutes at the runner's speed and in 4 minutes at the additional speed have a sum of 1 mile.

At runner's speed

$$4 \text{ min} \times \frac{60 \text{ sec}}{1 \text{ min}} \times \frac{20 \text{ ft}}{1 \text{ sec}} = 4800 \text{ ft}$$

At additional speed

$$4 \text{ min} \times \frac{60 \text{ sec}}{1 \text{ min}} \times \frac{2 \text{ ft}}{1 \text{ sec}} = 480 \text{ ft}$$

The sum of the distances is $4800 + 480 = 5280$ feet, or 1 mile. ✓

Self-Assessment for Problem Solving

Solve each exercise. Then rate your understanding of the success criteria in your journal.

8. Will all of the water from a full two-liter bottle fit into a two-quart pitcher? Explain.

9. DIG DEEPER! The speed of light is about 300,000 kilometers per second. The Sun is about 93 million miles from Earth. How many minutes does it take for sunlight to reach Earth?

10. A race car driver's goal is to complete a 1000-kilometer auto race in 4 hours or less. The driver's average speed is 4200 meters per minute. Does the driver meet the goal? If not, how much faster (in meters per minute) must the driver be to meet the goal?

3.6 Practice

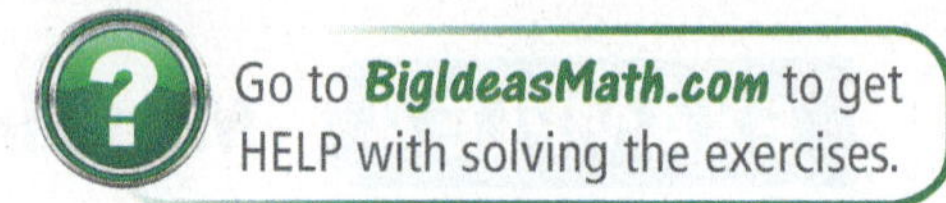

Review & Refresh

Write a unit rate for the situation.

1. 102 beats per 2 minutes
2. 60 shirts for every 5 clothing racks
3. $100 donated for every 5 volunteers
4. 30 milliliters every 4 hours
5. What is the LCM of 6, 12, and 18?

   A. 6 **B.** 18 **C.** 36 **D.** 72

Write the prime factorization of the number.

6. 56
7. 74
8. 63
9. 132

Write the product as a power.

10. 6×6
11. $18 \times 18 \times 18 \times 18$
12. $12 \times 12 \times 12 \times 12 \times 12$

Concepts, Skills, & Problem Solving

COMPARING MEASURES **Answer the question. Explain your answer.** (See Explorations 1 & 2, p. 141.)

13. Which juice container is larger: 2 L or 1 gal?
14. Which is longer: 1 in. or 2 cm?

CONVERTING MEASURES **Copy and complete the statement.**

15. 3 pt = ___ c
16. 1500 mL = ___ L
17. 40 oz = ___ lb
18. 5 ft = ___ in.
19. 6 gal = ___ qt
20. 48 cm = ___ mm
21. 500 cm = ___ m
22. 6000 g = ___ kg
23. 32 fl oz = ___ c

CONVERTING MEASURES **Copy and complete the statement. Round to the nearest hundredth if necessary.**

24. 12 L ≈ ___ qt
25. 14 m ≈ ___ ft
26. 4 ft ≈ ___ m
27. 64 lb ≈ ___ kg
28. 0.3 km ≈ ___ mi
29. 75.2 in. ≈ ___ cm
30. 17 kg ≈ ___ lb
31. 15 cm ≈ ___ in.
32. 9 mi ≈ ___ km

33. **GRAPHING RELATIONSHIPS** Represent the relationship between each pair of units in a coordinate plane.

    a. feet and yards **b.** pounds and kilograms

34. **MP MODELING REAL LIFE** Earth travels 30 kilometers each second as it revolves around the Sun. How many miles does Earth travel in 1 second?

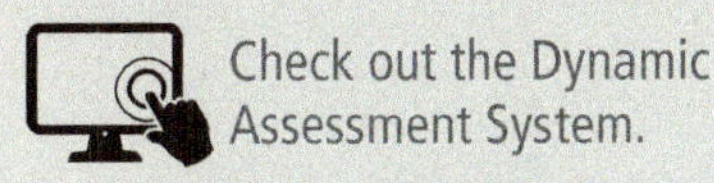

Assignment Guide and Concept Check

Scaffold assignments to support all students in their learning progression. The suggested assignments are a starting point. Continue to assign additional exercises and revisit with spaced practice to move every student toward proficiency.

Level	Assignment 1	Assignment 2
Emerging	4, 5, 9, 12, 13, 15, 18, 21, 24, 25, 38, 47	31, 34, 35, 39, 42, 48, 49, 52, 54, 55, 57
Proficient	4, 5, 9, 12, 13, 16, 19, 22, 26, 31, 39, 45	33, 41, 42, 43, 44, 49, 52, 54, 55, 57
Advanced	4, 5, 9, 12, 13, 17, 20, 23, 29, 32, 41, 50	33, 42, 53, 56, 57, 58, 59, 60

- Assignment 1 is for use after students complete the Self-Assessment for Concepts & Skills.
- Assignment 2 is for use after students complete the Self-Assessment for Problem Solving.
- The red exercises can be used as a concept check.

Review & Refresh Prior Skills

Exercises 1–4 Finding Unit Rates
Exercise 5 Finding the LCM
Exercises 6–9 Writing a Prime Factorization
Exercises 10–12 Writing Expressions as Powers

Common Errors

- **Exercises 13 and 14** Students may try to compare the measurements without converting the units. Remind them that they cannot compare quantities unless the units are the same.
- **Exercises 24–32** Students may disagree about which unit rate they should use from the Mathematics Reference Sheet. Remind students that either unit rate will work, but they may have slightly different answers due to differences in the rounding used with conversion facts. Assure students that both answers are acceptable.

Review & Refresh

1. 51 beats/min
2. 12 shirts/clothing rack
3. \$20/volunteer
4. 7.5 mL/h
5. C
6. $2 \times 2 \times 2 \times 7$, or $2^3 \times 7$
7. 2×37
8. $3 \times 3 \times 7$, or $3^2 \times 7$
9. $2 \times 2 \times 3 \times 11$, or $2^2 \times 3 \times 11$
10. 6^2
11. 18^4
12. 12^5

Concepts, Skills, & Problem Solving

13. 1 gal; 1 gal = 4 qt, 2 L ≈ 2.1 qt, and 4 qt > 2.1 qt
14. 1 in.; 1 in. = 2.54 cm > 2 cm
15. 6
16. 1.5
17. 2.5
18. 60
19. 24
20. 480
21. 5
22. 6
23. 4
24. 12.63 or 12.72
25. 45.92 or 46.67
26. 1.2 or 1.22
27. 28.8 or 29.09
28. 0.19
29. 191.01 or 192.82
30. 37.4 or 37.78
31. 5.91 or 5.85
32. 14.49 or 14.52
33. See Additional Answers.
34. about 18.6 mi or about 18.63 mi

Concepts, Skills, & Problem Solving

35. **a.** about 60.67 m or about 59.7 m

b. about 8.04 km or about 7.91 km

36. 90

37. 5.66 or 5.7

38. 1.3 or 1.32

39. 8.07 or 8.06

40. 1320

41. 0.0175

42. yes; 1.06 qt $\approx$ 1 L

43. **a.** 300 qt/h

b. 4.75 L/min or 4.72 L/min

44. 6 gal

45. $<$

46. $<$

47. $>$

48. $>$

49. $>$

50. $>$

Common Errors

- **Exercise 39** Students may change the wrong units. For example, a student may change from hours to minutes instead of kilometers to miles. Remind them to read the units carefully.

35. **MP MODELING REAL LIFE** The Mackinac Bridge in Michigan is the third-longest suspension bridge in the United States.

a. How high above the water is the roadway in meters?

b. The bridge has a length of 26,372 feet. What is the length in kilometers?

USING CONVERSION FACTORS **Copy and complete the statement. Round to the nearest hundredth if necessary.**

36. 12 cu ft ≈ ___ gal

37. 6 qt ≈ ___ L

38. 5 L ≈ ___ gal

39. $\frac{13 \text{ km}}{\text{h}} \approx \frac{\square \text{ mi}}{\text{h}}$

40. $\frac{22 \text{ L}}{\text{min}} = \frac{\square \text{ L}}{\text{h}}$

41. $\frac{63 \text{ mi}}{\text{h}} = \frac{\square \text{ mi}}{\text{sec}}$

42. **MP YOU BE THE TEACHER** Your friend converts 8 liters to quarts. Is your friend correct? Explain your reasoning.

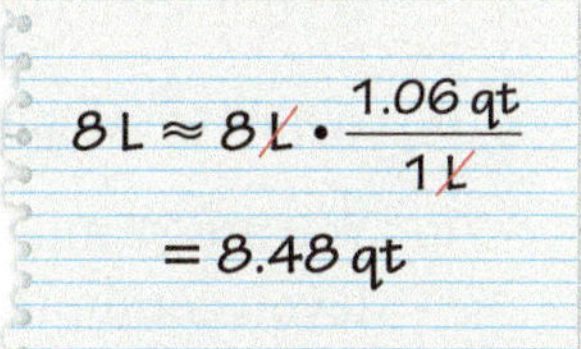

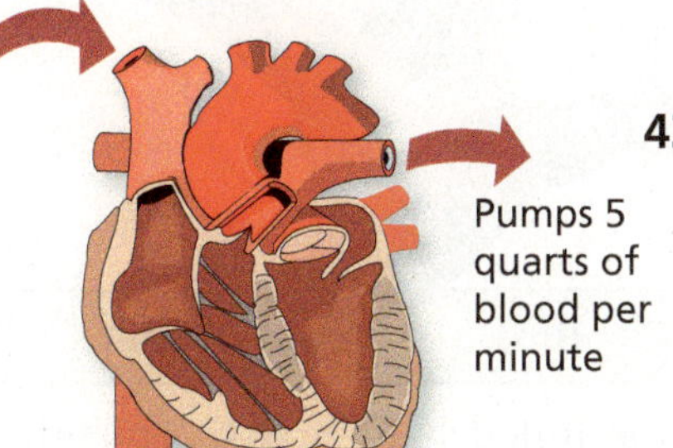

43. **MP MODELING REAL LIFE** The diagram shows the number of quarts of blood the human heart pumps per minute.

a. How many quarts of blood does the human heart pump per hour?

b. How many liters of blood does the human heart pump per minute?

44. **MP PROBLEM SOLVING** After washing dishes, water drips from the faucet. The graph shows the number of cups of water that drip from the faucet over time. How many gallons of water drip from the faucet in 24 hours?

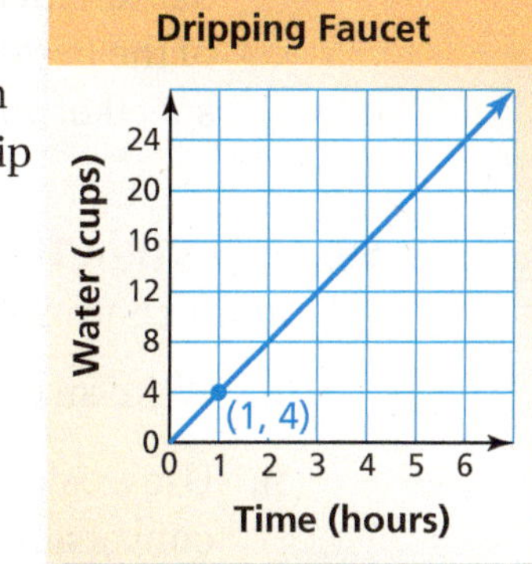

COMPARING MEASURES **Copy and complete the statement using < or >.**

45. 30 oz ___ 8 kg

46. 6 ft ___ 300 cm

47. 3 gal ___ 6 L

48. 10 in. ___ 200 mm

49. 5 lb ___ 1200 g

50. 1500 m ___ 3000 ft

USING DERIVED UNITS **Copy and complete the statement. Round to the nearest hundredth if necessary.**

51. $\dfrac{3\text{ km}}{\text{min}} \approx \dfrac{\square\text{ mi}}{\text{h}}$

52. $\dfrac{17\text{ gal}}{\text{h}} = \dfrac{\square\text{ qt}}{\text{min}}$

53. $\dfrac{600\text{ cm}}{\text{min}} \approx \dfrac{\square\text{ in.}}{\text{sec}}$

54. MP **MODELING REAL LIFE** You are riding on a zip line. Your speed is 15 miles per hour. What is your speed in feet per second?

55. MP **PROBLEM SOLVING** Thunder is the sound caused by lightning. You hear thunder 5 seconds after a lightning strike. The speed of sound is about 1225 kilometers per hour. About how many miles away was the lightning?

56. MP **PROBLEM SOLVING** Boston, Massachusetts, and Buffalo, New York, are hit by snowstorms that last 3 days. Boston accumulates snow at a rate of 1.5 feet every 36 hours. Buffalo accumulates snow at a rate of 0.01 inch every minute. Which city accumulates more snow in 3 days? How much more snow?

57. **DIG DEEPER!** You travel 4000 feet every minute on a snowmobile.

a. The evening speed limit for snowmobiles in your state is 55 miles per hour. Is your speed less than or equal to the speed limit? Justify your answer.

b. What is your pace in minutes per mile?

c. You are 22 miles from your house at 6:00 P.M. If you continue to travel at this speed, do you reach your house in time for dinner at 6:30 P.M.?

58. MP **REASONING** The table shows the flying speeds of several birds.

a. Which bird is the fastest? Which is the slowest?

b. The peregrine falcon has a dive speed of 322 kilometers per hour. Is the dive speed of the peregrine falcon faster than the flying speed of any of the birds? Explain.

Bird	Speed
Spine-tailed swift	2843.2 m/min
Spur-winged goose	129.1 ft/sec
Eider duck	31.3 m/sec
Mallard	65 mi/h

59. MP **STRUCTURE** Consider the conversion facts 1 inch = 2.54 centimeters and 1 centimeter ≈ 0.39 inch.

a. Write an expression for the exact number of inches in 1 centimeter.

b. Use a calculator to evaluate your expression in part (a). Explain why measurement conversions may be slightly different when converting between metric units and U.S. customary units using the conversion facts in the back of the book.

60. **DIG DEEPER!** One liter of paint covers 100 square feet. How many gallons of paint does it take to cover a room whose walls have an area of 800 square meters?

- **Exercises 51–53** Students may write the units they are trying to remove in the numerator for both conversion factors. Remind students to use unit analysis and make sure that the appropriate units will "cross out." Some students may need to convert one unit, and then convert the other unit as a separate problem.

Mini-Assessment

1. 7 pt = ____ c 14
2. 16 qt ≈ ____ L 15.2, or 15.09
3. 3 in. ≈ ____ cm 7.62, or 7.69
4. $\frac{30 \text{ gal}}{\text{h}} \approx \frac{\_\_\_\_ \text{ qt}}{\text{min}}$ 2
5. A newborn baby weighs 8 pounds. About how many kilograms does the baby weigh? about 3.6 kilograms, or about 3.64 kilograms

Section Resources

<table>
<tr><th>Surface Level</th><th>Deep Level</th></tr>
<tr><td>Resources by Chapter
• Extra Practice
• Reteach
• Puzzle Time
Student Journal
• Self-Assessment
• Practice
Differentiating the Lesson
Tutorial Videos
Skills Review Handbook
Skills Trainer</td><td>Resources by Chapter
• Enrichment and Extension
Graphic Organizers
Dynamic Assessment System
• Section Practice</td></tr>
<tr><th colspan="2">Transfer Level</th></tr>
<tr><td>Dynamic Assessment System
• End-of-Chapter Quiz</td><td>Assessment Book
• End-of-Chapter Quiz</td></tr>
</table>

51. 111.6 or 111.80

52. 1.13

53. 3.9 or 3.94

54. 22 ft/sec

55. about 1.05 mi or about 1.06 mi

56. Buffalo; 0.6 ft = 7.2 in.

57. **a.** less than; Your speed is about 45.45 miles per hour.

b. 1.32 min/mi

c. yes

58. **a.** spine-tailed swift; mallard

b. yes, 322 km/h ≈ 5367 m/min

59. **a.** $1 \text{ cm} = \frac{1}{2.54} \text{ in.}$

b. about 0.3937007874; Some conversion facts are rounded.

60. about 22 gal or about 23 gal

Skills Needed

Exercise 1
- Dividing Decimals by Whole Numbers
- Interpreting Ratios
- Multiplying Decimals
- Using a Tape Diagram

Exercise 2
- Finding the LCM
- Interpreting Ratios

Exercise 3
- Finding the GCF
- Interpreting Ratios

Using the Problem-Solving Plan

1. 0.375 gal water, 0.125 gal glue, 0.25 gal borax
2. 2 packages yogurt cups, 3 packages frozen fruit bars
3. 54 and 45; $\frac{6}{5} = \frac{54}{45}$

Performance Task

The *STEAM Video Performance Task* provides the opportunity for additional enrichment and greater depth of knowledge as students explore the mathematics of the chapter within a context tied to the chapter STEAM Video. The performance task and a detailed scoring rubric are provided at *BigIdeasMath.com.*

Laurie's Notes

Scaffolding Instruction

- The goal of this lesson is to help students become more comfortable with problem solving. These exercises combine ratio concepts with prior skills from other chapters. The solution for Exercise 1 is worked out below, to help you guide students through the problem-solving plan. Use the remaining class time to have students work on the other exercises.
- **Emerging:** The goal for these students is to feel comfortable with the problem-solving plan. Allow students to work in pairs to write the beginning steps of the problem-solving plan for Exercises 2 and 3. Keep in mind that some students may only be ready to do the first step.
- **Proficient:** Students may be able to work independently or in pairs to complete Exercises 2 and 3.
- Visit each pair to review their plan for each problem. Ask students to describe their plans.

ELL Support

Many ELLs will only be familiar with metric measurements. As they work through Exercise 1, explain that 0.75 gallon is about 3 liters. Have them work in groups to practice language as they use the problem-solving plan.

Using the Problem-Solving Plan

Exercise 1

Understand the problem. You know the ratio of the ingredients in the slime and that you are making 0.75 gallon of slime. You are asked to find the number of gallons of each ingredient needed to make 0.75 gallon of slime.

Make a plan. Represent the ratio 3 : 1 : 2 using a tape diagram. Because there are 6 parts that represent 0.75 gallon, divide 0.75 by 6 to find the value of one part of the tape diagram. Then use the value of one part to find the number of gallons of each ingredient you should use.

Solve and check. Use the plan to solve the problem. Then check your solution.

- Use the following tape diagram:

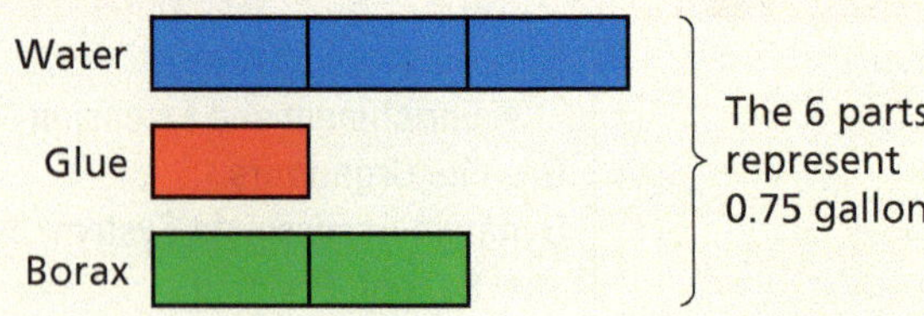

- Because there are 6 parts, you know that 1 part represents 0.75 gallon $\div$ 6 = 0.125 gallon.

  3 parts represent 3 $\times$ 0.125 gallon = 0.375 gallon.
  1 part represents 1 $\times$ 0.125 gallon = 0.125 gallon.
  2 parts represent 2 $\times$ 0.125 gallon = 0.25 gallon.

  So, you need 0.375 gallon of water, 0.125 gallon of glue, and 0.25 gallon of borax.
- **Check:** Verify that the total of water, glue, and borax is 0.75 gallon.

  $0.375 + 0.125 + 0.25 = 0.75$ ✓

Connecting Concepts

Using the Problem-Solving Plan

1. You mix water, glue, and borax in the ratio of 3 : 1 : 2 to make slime. How many gallons of each ingredient should you use to make 0.75 gallon of slime?

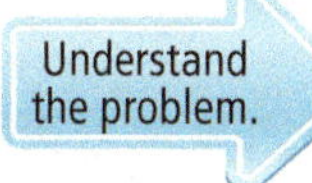

You know the ratio of the ingredients in the slime and that you are making 0.75 gallon of slime. You are asked to find the number of gallons of each ingredient needed to make 0.75 gallon of slime.

Represent the ratio 3 : 1 : 2 using a tape diagram. Because there are 6 parts that represent 0.75 gallon, divide 0.75 by 6 to find the value of one part of the tape diagram. Then use the value of one part to find the number of gallons of each ingredient you should use.

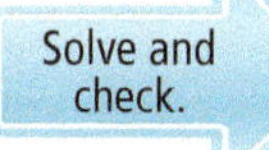

Use the plan to solve the problem. Then check your solution.

2. You buy yogurt cups and frozen fruit bars for a party. Yogurt cups are sold in packages of six. The ratio of the number of yogurt cups in a package to the number of frozen fruit bars in a package is 3 : 2. What are the least numbers of packages you should buy in order to have the same numbers of yogurt cups and frozen fruit bars?

3. The greatest common factor of two whole numbers is 9. The ratio of the greater number to the lesser number is 6 : 5. What are the two numbers? Justify your answer.

Performance Task

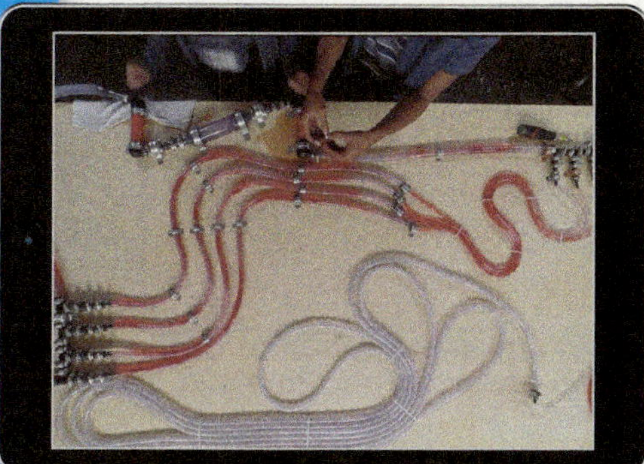

Oops! Unit Conversion Mistakes

At the beginning of this chapter, you watched a STEAM Video called "Human Circulatory System." You are now ready to complete the performance task related to this video, available at ***BigIdeasMath.com***. Be sure to use the problem-solving plan as you work through the performance task.

3 Chapter Review

Review Vocabulary

Write the definition and give an example of each vocabulary term.

ratio, *p. 108*
value of a ratio, *p. 109*
equivalent ratios, *p. 109*
ratio table, *p. 122*
rate, *p. 136*
unit rate, *p. 136*
equivalent rates, *p. 136*
U.S. customary system, *p. 142*
metric system, *p. 142*
conversion factor, *p. 143*
unit analysis, *p. 143*

Graphic Organizers

You can use a **Definition and Example Chart** to organize information about a concept. Here is an example of a Definition and Example Chart for the vocabulary term ***ratio***.

Ratio: a comparison of two quantities. Ratios can be part-to-part, part-to-whole, or whole-to-part comparisons.

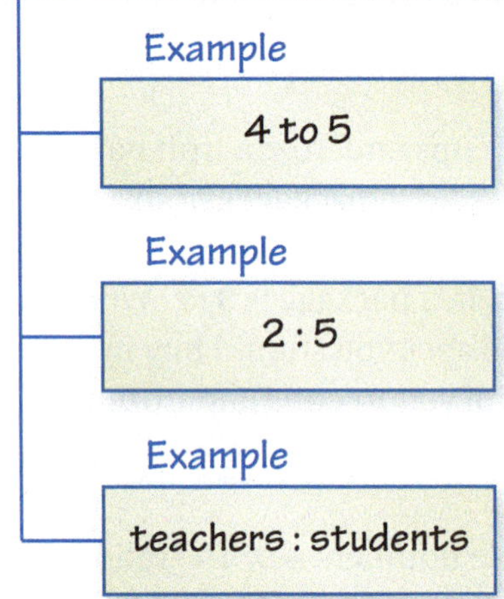

Choose and complete a graphic organizer to help you study the concept.

1. value of a ratio
2. equivalent ratios
3. tape diagram
4. ratio table
5. rate
6. unit rate
7. conversion factor

"My math teacher taught us how to make a Definition and Example Chart."

Review Vocabulary

As a review of the chapter vocabulary, have students revisit the vocabulary section in their *Student Journals* to fill in any missing definitions and record examples of each term.

Graphic Organizers

Sample answers:

1.

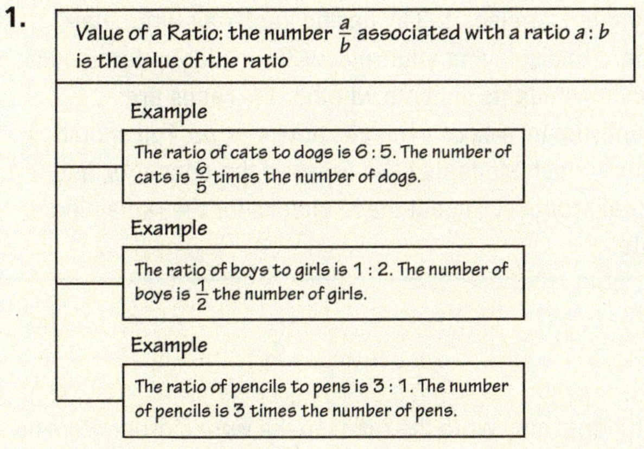

2.

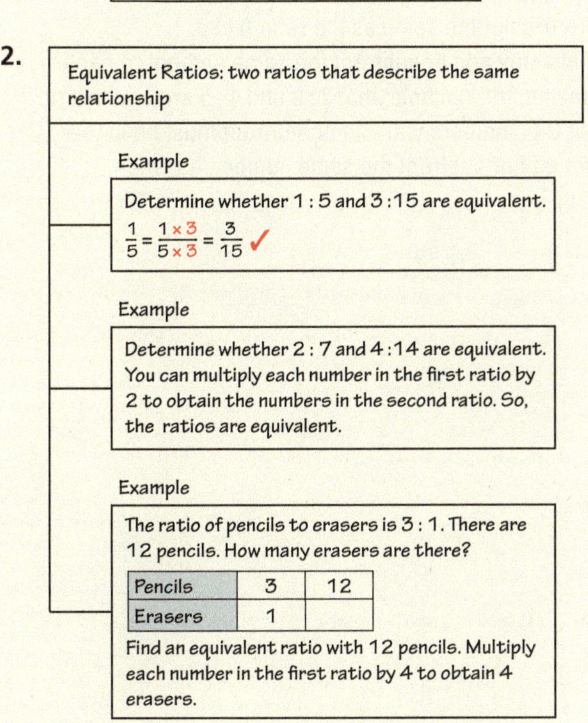

3–7. Answers at *BigIdeasMath.com*

List of Organizers

Available at *BigIdeasMath.com*

Definition and Example Chart

Example and Non-Example Chart

Four Square

Information Frame

Summary Triangle

About this Organizer

A **Definition and Example Chart** can be used to organize information about a concept. Students fill in the top rectangle with a term and its definition or description. Students fill in the rectangles that follow with examples to illustrate the term. Each sample answer shows three examples, but students can show more or fewer examples. Definition and Example Charts are useful for concepts that can be illustrated with more than one type of example.

Chapter Self-Assessment

1. 3 : 2, or 3 to 2
2. 6 : 3, or 6 to 3
3. a. $\frac{2}{3}$; The number of hydrogen atoms is $\frac{2}{3}$ times the number of nitrogen atoms.

   b. 3 : 1
4. equivalent
5. not equivalent
6. not equivalent
7. equivalent
8. *Sample answer:* 10 : 14, 15 : 21
9. 8
10. no; your friend

Chapter Self-Assessment

The Success Criteria Self-Assessment chart can be found in the *Student Journal* or online at *BigIdeasMath.com.*

ELL Support

Allow students to work in pairs to complete the Chapter Self-Assessment. Check for understanding of Exercises 1–3 by having each pair write their answers on a whiteboard to display for your review. Check for understanding of Exercises 4–7 by having students indicate whether the ratios are equivalent using a thumbs up for *yes* or a thumbs down for *no.* You should be able to quickly assess which students have grasped the concepts, and who may need additional practice. Repeat these checks for the remaining sections as appropriate.

Common Errors

- **Exercises 1 and 2** Students may write the ratios in the wrong order. Remind them that the ratio *a* to *b* is not the same as the ratio *b* to *a.*
- **Exercises 4–7** Students may add or subtract the same amount to each number in the ratio, saying, for example, that 2 : 3 and 4 : 5 are equivalent. Make it very clear that the numbers you add or subtract must be in the same ratio. You cannot add or subtract the same number, as when multiplying and dividing.

Chapter Self-Assessment

As you complete the exercises, use the scale below to rate your understanding of the success criteria in your journal.

1	2	3	4
I do not understand.	I can do it with help.	I can do it on my own.	I can teach someone else.

3.1 Ratios *(pp. 107–114)*

Learning Target: Understand the concepts of ratios and equivalent ratios.

Write the ratio.

1. butterflies : caterpillars

2. saxophones : trumpets

3. The ratio of hydrogen atoms to nitrogen atoms in a container is 2 : 3.

   a. Find and interpret the value of the ratio.

   b. In another container, the number of hydrogen atoms is 3 times the number of nitrogen atoms. Write the ratio of hydrogen atoms to nitrogen atoms.

Determine whether the ratios are equivalent.

4. 5 : 2 and 30 : 12

5. 4 : 3 and 8 : 7

6. 6 : 4 and 18 : 6

7. 18 : 12 and 3 : 2

8. Write two equivalent ratios that have values of $\frac{5}{7}$.

9. During a chess match, there are 12 pieces left on the board. The ratio of white pieces to black pieces is 2 : 1. How many white pieces are on the board?

10. You run at a pace of 2 miles every 17 minutes. Your friend runs at a pace of 3 miles every 24 minutes. Are you and your friend running at the same pace? If not, who is running faster?

3.2 Using Tape Diagrams *(pp. 115–120)*

Learning Target: Use tape diagrams to model and solve ratio problems.

The tape diagram represents the ratio of the time you spend reading to the time your friend spends reading. You read for 8 hours. How many hours does your friend spend reading?

11. You

Friend

12. You

Friend

13. The tape diagram represents the ratio of customers to guides on a mountain climbing trip. There are 6 guides on the trip. How many customers are on the trip?

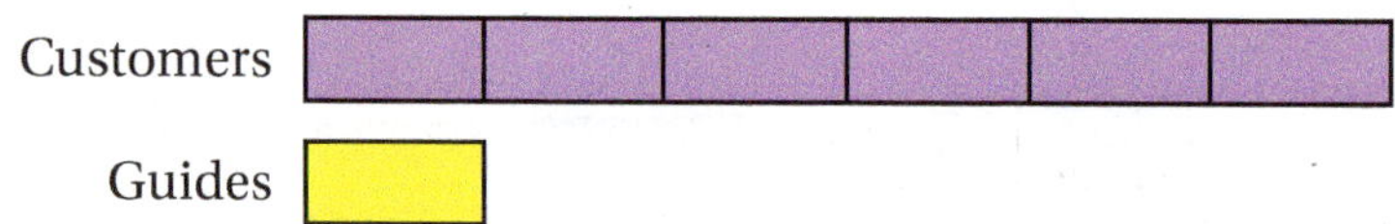

A container has peppermint gum and spearmint gum. You are given the number of pieces of peppermint gum in the container and the ratio of peppermint gum to spearmint gum. Find the number of pieces of spearmint gum in the container.

14. 24 peppermint; 8 to 5

15. 18 peppermint; 2 : 3

16. 32 peppermint; 8 to 7

17. 40 peppermint; 5 : 2

A theater sells adult tickets and student tickets. You are given the total number of tickets sold and the ratio of adult tickets sold to student tickets sold. How many of each type of ticket are sold?

18. 120 tickets; 6 to 4

19. 165 tickets; 8 to 7

20. 210 tickets; 16 : 5

21. 248 tickets; 5 : 3

22. You perform 7 sit-ups for every 2 pull-ups as part of an exercise routine. You perform 25 more sit-ups than pull-ups. How many sit-ups and how many pull-ups do you perform?

Chapter Self-Assessment

11. 4 h

12. 32 h

13. 36

14. 15

15. 27

16. 28

17. 16

18. 72 adult tickets, 48 student tickets

19. 88 adult tickets, 77 student tickets

20. 160 adult tickets, 50 student tickets

21. 155 adult tickets, 93 student tickets

22. 35 sit-ups, 10 pull-ups

Chapter Self-Assessment

23.

Levers	6	12	18
Pulleys	3	6	9

6 : 3, 12 : 6, 18 : 9

24.

Nails	5	10	15
Screws	2	4	6

5 : 2, 10 : 4, 15 : 6

25.

Cars	3	6	18
Trucks	4	8	24

3 : 4, 6 : 8, 18 : 24

26.

Customers	8	4	20
Servings	12	6	30

8 : 12, 4 : 6, 20 : 30

27. 600

28. 112.5

29. *Sample answer:*

×2 ÷8 +4 −2

Pumpkins Grown	4	8	1	5	3
Seeds Planted	12	24	3	15	9

×2 ÷8 +12 −6

30. 72

31. 60 sec

32. welder A

33. your friend's

3.3 Using Ratio Tables (pp. 121–128)

Learning Target: Use ratio tables to represent equivalent ratios and solve ratio problems.

Find the missing values in the ratio table. Then write the equivalent ratios.

23.

Levers	6		18
Pulleys	3	6	

24.

Nails	5	10	
Screws	2		6

25.

Cars	3	6	
Trucks	4		24

26.

Customers	8	4	
Servings	12		30

Find the missing quantity in the double number line.

27.

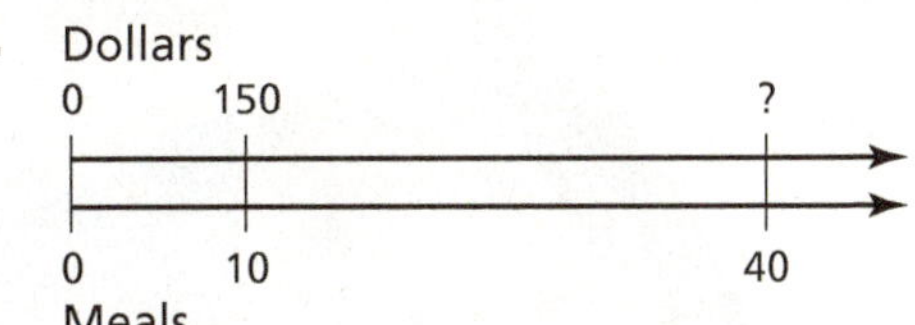

28.

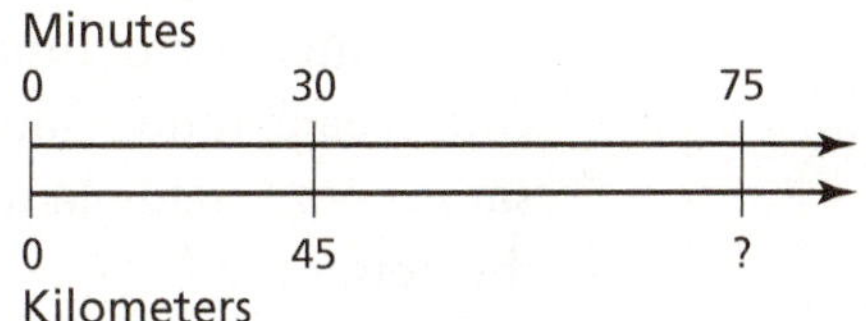

29. Use all four operations to complete the ratio table. Justify your answer.

Pumpkins Grown	4				
Seeds Planted	12				

30. A song has 12 beats every 5 seconds. How many beats are there in 30 seconds?

31. On New Year's Eve, the Times Square ball is lowered 47 feet every 20 seconds. How long does it take for the ball to be lowered 141 feet?

32. Welder A charges \$300 for every 4 hours of labor. Welder B charges \$240 for every 3 hours of labor. Which welder offers a better deal?

33. You make lemonade by adding 11 cups of water for every 3 cups of lemon juice. Your friend makes lemonade by adding 9 cups of water for every 2 cups of lemon juice. Whose lemonade is more watered down?

3.4 Graphing Ratio Relationships (pp. 129–134)

Learning Target: Represent ratio relationships in a coordinate plane.

Represent the ratio relationship using a graph.

34.

Time (years)	1	2	3
Penguins	6	12	18

35.

Televisions	12	24	36
Houses	4	8	12

36. You buy magnesium sulfate for $1.50 per pound.

  a. Represent the ratio relationship using a graph.

  b. How much does 3.5 pounds of magnesium sulfate cost?

37. A 5-ounce can of tuna costs $0.90. A 12-ounce can of tuna costs $2.40. Graph each ratio relationship in the same coordinate plane. Which is the better buy?

3.5 Rates and Unit Rates (pp. 135–140)

Learning Target: Understand the concept of a unit rate and solve rate problems.

Write a unit rate for the situation.

38. 12 stunts in 4 movies

39. 3600 stitches in 3 minutes

40. $18 for 6 pounds

41. 240 people in 5 buses

42. A train travels 120 miles in 3 hours. Write two unit rates that describe the relationship between the number of miles and the number of hours the train travels.

43. Mercury orbits the Sun 3 times in 264 days.

  a. How many times does Mercury orbit the Sun in 440 days?

  b. How many days does it take Mercury to orbit the Sun 8 times?

- **Exercise 36** Make sure students plot the ordered pairs correctly.
- **Exercises 38–41** Students may not write the units on the rates. Compare rates to ratios but with different units. Illustrate the importance of the units with an examination of the speed of a car. In the United States, speed is measured in miles per hour, but in most of Europe, speed is measured in kilometers per hour. If you say that the speed of a car is 35, you do not know if it is miles or kilometers per hour.

Chapter Self-Assessment

34.

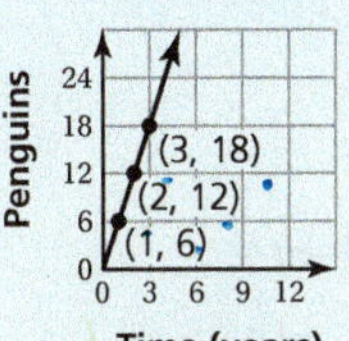

35.

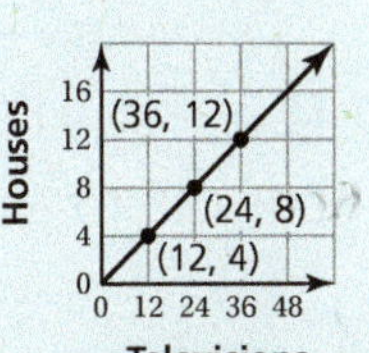

36. a.

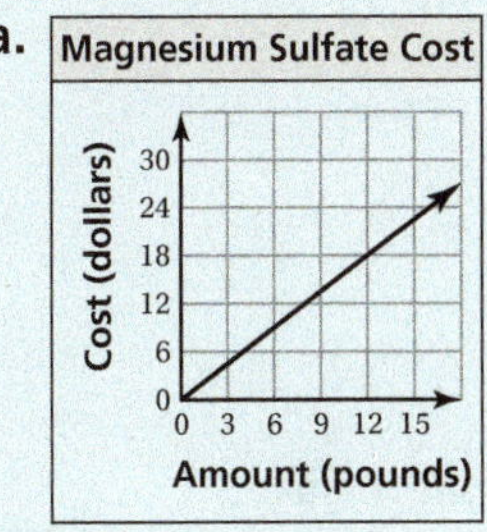

b. $5.25

37.

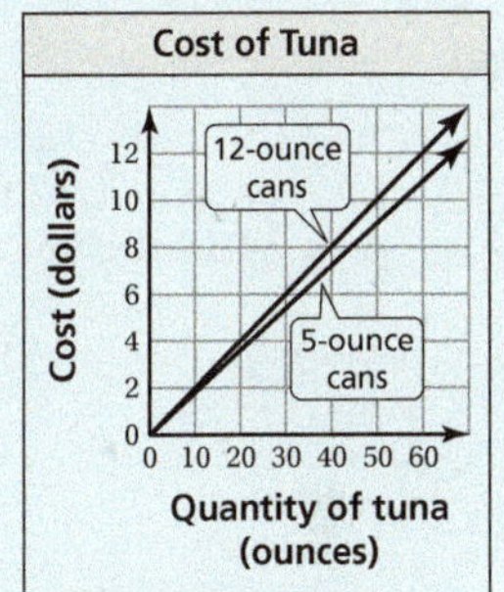

5-ounce can

38. 3 stunts/movie

39. 1200 stitches/min

40. $3/lb

41. 48 people/bus

42. 40 mi/h, 0.025 h/mi

43. a. 5

b. 704

Chapter Self-Assessment

44. 6 mi

45. not equivalent

46. not equivalent

47. you; 14 min

48. 20

49. 4

50. 3.5

51. 3.16 or 3.18

52. 23.37 or 23.59

53. 6.75 or 6.82

54. 120

55. 52

56. 0.04

57. *Sample answer:* 1 qt = 2 pt = 4 c = 32 fl oz, so multiply by 32.

58. 600 gal

59. yes

60. 14.04 in./yr or 14.17 in./yr

Common Errors

- **Exercises 48–53** Students may place the original unit in the numerator of the conversion factor. Visually demonstrate to students that the original units will not "cross out."

Chapter Resources

Surface Level	Deep Level
Resources by Chapter • Extra Practice • Reteach • Puzzle Time Student Journal • Practice • Chapter Self-Assessment Differentiating the Lesson Tutorial Videos Skills Review Handbook Skills Trainer Game Library	Resources by Chapter • Enrichment and Extension Graphic Organizers Game Library
Transfer Level	
STEAM Video Dynamic Assessment System • Chapter Test	Assessment Book • Chapter Tests A and B • Alternative Assessment • STEAM Performance Task

44. A cyclist travels 4 miles in 20 minutes. At this rate, how many miles does the cyclist travel in 30 minutes?

Decide whether the rates are equivalent.

45. 18 keystrokes in 3 seconds
48 keystrokes in 16 seconds

46. 210 miles in 3 hours
780 miles in 12 hours

47. You and a friend are picking up trash on a beach. You fill 2 bags with trash in 28 minutes. Your friend fills 3 bags with trash in 48 minutes. Who fills bags with trash faster? How much sooner will the faster person fill 7 bags with trash?

3.6 Converting Measures *(pp. 141–148)*

Learning Target: Use ratio reasoning to convert units of measure.

Copy and complete the statement. Round to the nearest hundredth if necessary.

48. 2.5 c = ___ fl oz

49. 12 ft = ___ yd

50. 3500 mg = ___ g

51. 3 L ≈ ___ qt

52. 9.2 in. ≈ ___ cm

53. 15 lb ≈ ___ kg

54. $\frac{\$2}{\text{min}} = \frac{\$\_\_\_}{\text{h}}$

55. $\frac{13 \text{ gal}}{\text{h}} = \frac{\_\_\_ \text{ qt}}{\text{h}}$

56. $\frac{8 \text{ ft}}{\text{h}} \approx \frac{\_\_\_ \text{ m}}{\text{min}}$

57. Explain how to use conversion factors to find the number of fluid ounces in any given number of quarts of a liquid.

58. Water flows through a pipe at a rate of 10 gallons per minute. How many gallons of water flow through the pipe in an hour?

59. Germany suggests a speed limit of 130 kilometers per hour on highways. Is the speed shown greater than the suggested limit?

60. The distance between two stars increases at a rate of 3 centimeters per month. What is the rate in inches per year?

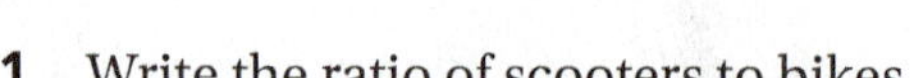

3 Practice Test

1. Write the ratio of scooters to bikes.

2. Determine whether the ratios 8 : 7 and 15 : 14 are equivalent.

Find the missing values in the ratio table. Then write the equivalent ratios.

3.

Lemons	4		36
Limes	2	6	

4.

Rabbits	2	12	
Hamsters	9		45

5. Represent the ratio relationship using a graph.

Cranberry Juice (cups)	2	4	6
Grape Juice (cups)	3	6	9

6. You travel 224 miles in 4 hours. Find the unit rate.

Copy and complete the statement. Round to the nearest hundredth if necessary.

7. 6 cm ≈ ▭ in.

8. 30 L ≈ ▭ gal

9. $\frac{10 \text{ gal}}{\text{h}} = \frac{\square \text{ gal}}{\text{wk}}$

10. $\frac{4 \text{ ft}}{\text{sec}} \approx \frac{\square \text{ m}}{\text{sec}}$

11. During a baseball season, Team A scores 9 runs for every 7 runs that Team B scores. The total number of runs scored by both teams is 1440. How many runs does each team score?

12. At a movie theater, the ratio of filled seats to empty seats is 6 : 5. There are 120 empty seats. How many seats are filled?

13. You and your friend mix water and citric acid. You add 3 cups of citric acid for every 16 cups of water. Your friend adds 2 cups of citric acid for every 12 cups of water. Whose mixture is more acidic?

14. Determine which windsurfer is faster. Explain your reasoning.

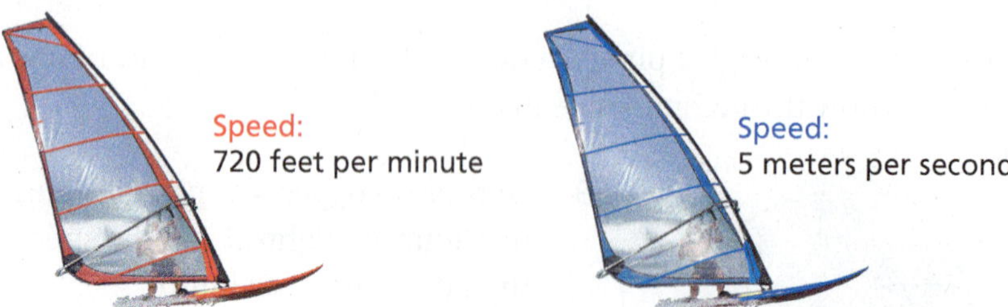

15. In a rectangle, the ratio of the length to the width is 5 : 2. The length of the rectangle is 13.875 feet greater than the width. What are the perimeter and the area of the rectangle?

Practice Test Item References

Practice Test Questions	Section to Review
1, 2	3.1
11, 15	3.2
3, 4, 12, 13	3.3
5	3.4
6	3.5
7–10, 14	3.6

Test-Taking Strategies

Remind students to quickly look over the entire test before they start so that they can budget their time. Remind them that the test is on ratios, rates, ratio relationships, and converting measures, and that they need to read the problems carefully. Remind students to **Stop** and **Think** before they write their answers.

Common Errors

- **Exercises 7–10** When converting units, students may use a conversion factor that is the reciprocal of what it should be. Remind students that the conversion factor should be such that the original units divide out and the new units remain.

Practice Test

1. 3 : 3, or 3 to 3
2. not equivalent
3.

Lemons	4	12	36
Limes	2	6	18

4 : 2, 12 : 6, 36 : 18

4.

Rabbits	2	12	10
Hamsters	9	54	45

2 : 9, 12 : 54, 10 : 45

5.

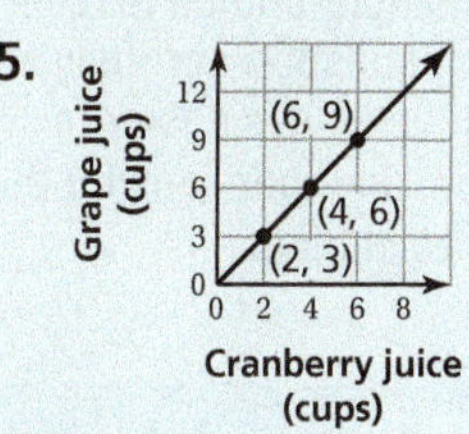

6. 56 mi/h
7. 2.34 or 2.36
8. 7.8 or 7.92
9. 1680
10. 1.2 or 1.22
11. Team A scores 810 runs, Team B scores 630 runs
12. 144
13. yours
14. blue; 5 m/sec $\approx$ 984 ft/min
15. 64.75 ft; 213.90625 ft^2

Test-Taking Strategies

Available at *BigIdeasMath.com*

After Answering Easy Questions, Relax
Answer Easy Questions First
Estimate the Answer
Read All Choices before Answering
Read Question before Answering
Solve Directly or Eliminate Choices
Solve Problem before Looking at Choices
Use Intelligent Guessing
Work Backwards

About this Strategy

When taking a multiple-choice test, be sure to read each question carefully and thoroughly. Sometimes it is easier to solve the problem, and then look for the answer among the choices.

Cumulative Practice

1. B
2. 35.42 or 35.48
3. G
4. B
5. I

Item Analysis

1. **A.** The student multiplies the fractions.

   B. Correct answer

   C. The student finds the reciprocal of the second number, but then adds the numerators and adds the denominators.

   D. The student finds the reciprocal of the first number, and then multiplies the fractions.

2. **Gridded Response:** Correct answer: 35.42 or 35.48

   Common error: The student multiplies by $\frac{1 \text{ mi}}{1.61 \text{ km}}$ rather than multiplying by $\frac{1.61 \text{ km}}{1 \text{ mi}}$ and gets 13.66.

3. **F.** The student does not follow the correct order of operations; uses division as the last step rather than addition.

   G. Correct answer

   H. The student does not follow the correct order of operations; calculates $(2 \cdot 4)^2$ instead of $2 \cdot 4^2$.

   I. The student does not follow the correct order of operations; adds the 3 before division and multiplication are completed.

4. **A.** The student finds the value of one part of the tape diagram but does not multiply by 2 to find the number of green beads.

   B. Correct answer

   C. The student finds the number of red beads.

   D. The student finds the total number of beads.

5. **F.** The student finds the LCM of 8 and 12.

   G. The student finds the LCM of 8 and 20.

   H. The student finds the LCM of 12 and 20.

   I. Correct answer

3 Cumulative Practice

1. Which number is equivalent to $\frac{2}{9} \div \frac{4}{5}$?

A. $\frac{8}{45}$

B. $\frac{5}{18}$

C. $\frac{7}{13}$

D. $3\frac{3}{5}$

2. Your speed while waterskiing is 22 miles per hour. How fast are you traveling in kilometers per hour? Round your answer to the nearest hundredth.

3. Which number is equivalent to the expression below?

$$2 \cdot 4^2 + 3(6 \div 2)$$

F. 25

G. 41

H. 73

I. 105

4. The tape diagram models the ratio of red beads to green beads in a bracelet. The bracelet uses 12 red beads. How many green beads are in the bracelet?

A. 4 green beads

B. 8 green beads

C. 12 green beads

D. 20 green beads

5. What is the least common multiple of 8, 12, and 20?

F. 24

G. 40

H. 60

I. 120

6. Which number is equivalent to $2.34 \times 1.08 \times 5.6$?

A. 12.787632 B. 14.15232

C. 23.5872 D. 14,152.32

7. The school store sells 4 pencils for \$0.50. At this rate, what is the cost (in dollars) of 10 pencils?

8. A factor tree for 14,700 is shown. Which factor of 14,700 is *not* a perfect square?

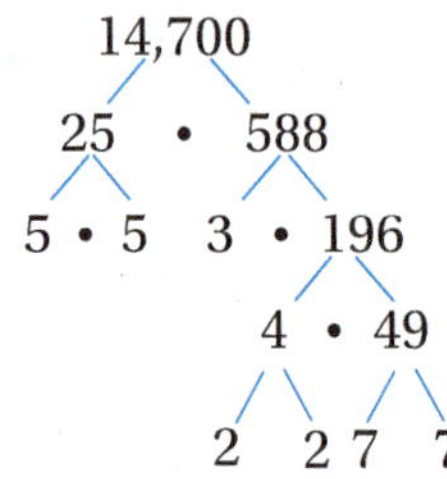

F. 25 G. 49

H. 196 I. 588

9. Which of the following is a ratio of frogs to snakes?

A. 4 : 8 B. 8 : 12

C. 8 : 4 D. 4 : 12

Item Analysis (continued)

6. **A.** The student multiplies by 5.06 instead of 5.6.
   B. Correct answer
   C. The student multiplies by 1.8 instead of 1.08.
   D. The student places the decimal point in the wrong location.

7. **Gridded Response:** Correct answer: 1.25
   Common error: The student multiplies 10 times $0.50 to get $5.00.

8. **F.** The student does not recognize that 25 is the perfect square of 5.
   G. The student does not recognize that 49 is the perfect square of 7.
   H. The student does not recognize that 196 is the perfect square of 14.
   I. Correct answer

9. **A.** The student reverses the order and finds the ratio of snakes to frogs.
   B. The student finds the ratio of frogs to total animals.
   C. Correct answer
   D. The student finds the ratio of snakes to total animals.

Cumulative Practice

6. B
7. 1.25
8. I
9. C

Cumulative Practice

10. F

11. D

12. *Part A: Sample answer:*

Scrambled Eggs	6	9	18
Hard-boiled Eggs	2	3	6

Part B:

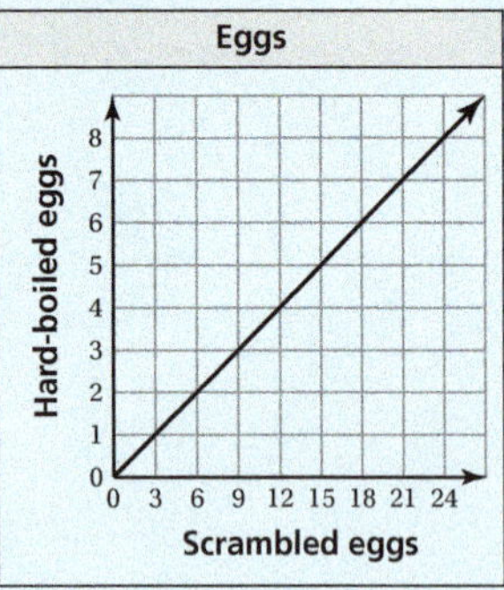

Part C: 5

Item Analysis (continued)

10. F. Correct answer

G. The student multiplies the base and exponent.

H. The student writes an expression for 5^3 rather than 3^5.

I. The student adds the base five times, rather than multiplying the base five times.

11. A. The student performs the operations from left to right, rather than using order of operations.

B. The student performs multiplication before evaluating the exponent.

C. The student performs addition before multiplication.

D. Correct answer

12. 4 points The student's work and explanations demonstrate a thorough understanding of ratios and equivalent ratios. The student finds three appropriate equivalent ratios and represents them on the graph accurately. The student correctly calculates that the restaurant serves 5 hard-boiled eggs when it serves 15 scrambled eggs.

3 points The student's work and explanations demonstrate an essential but less than thorough understanding of ratios and equivalent ratios.

2 points The student's work and explanations demonstrate a partial but limited understanding of ratios and equivalent ratios.

1 point The student's work and explanations demonstrate a very limited understanding of ratios and equivalent ratios.

0 points The student provides no response, a completely incorrect or incomprehensible response, or a response that demonstrates insufficient understanding of ratios and equivalent ratios.

10. Which expression is equivalent to 3^5?

F. $3 \times 3 \times 3 \times 3 \times 3$ **G.** 3×5

H. $5 \times 5 \times 5$ **I.** $3 + 3 + 3 + 3 + 3$

11. Which is the correct order of operations when evaluating $5 + 4 \times 2^3$?

k. Add 5 and 4. **l.** Add 5 and 32.

m. Evaluate 2^3. **n.** Multiply 4 and 2.

p. Multiply 4 and 8. **q.** Add 5 and 512.

r. Multiply 9 and 8. **s.** Evaluate 8^3.

t. Multiply 9 and 2. **u.** Evaluate 18^3.

A. k, t, u **B.** n, s, q

C. m, k, r **D.** m, p, l

12. The ratio of scrambled eggs to hard-boiled eggs served at a restaurant is 6 : 2.

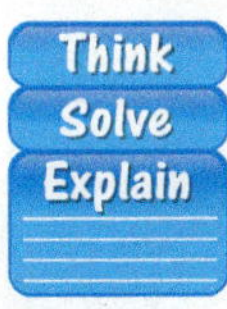

Part A Make a ratio table showing three possible combinations of scrambled eggs and hard-boiled eggs.

Part B Represent the ratio relationship using a graph.

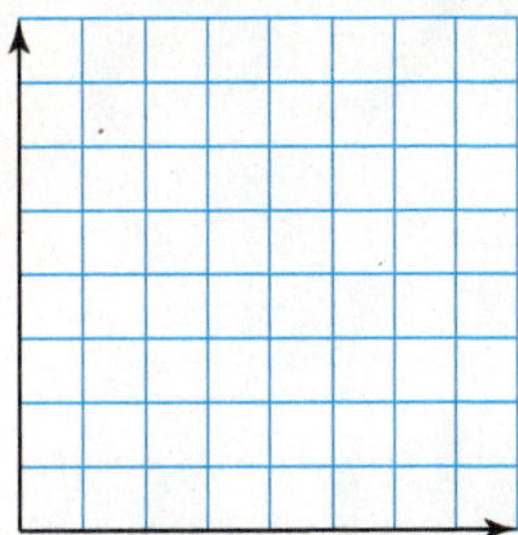

Part C Use the graph to find the number of hard-boiled eggs served when the restaurant serves 15 scrambled eggs.

Percents

4.1 Percents and Fractions

4.2 Percents and Decimals

4.3 Comparing and Ordering Fractions, Decimals, and Percents

4.4 Solving Percent Problems

Chapter Learning Target:
Understand percents.

Chapter Success Criteria:
- I can write fractions and decimals as percents.
- I can write percents as fractions and as decimals.
- I can order fractions, decimals, and percents.
- I can solve percent problems.

Laurie's Notes

Chapter 4 Overview

This chapter is your students' first formal introduction to percents, though it is hard to imagine that they have not heard percents referenced in school, the news, or advertisements. Asking students what percents are and what they mean is an interesting way to begin the chapter.

A major goal of this chapter is to describe percents as another way of representing fractions and decimals. More specifically, because the term *percent* means *per one hundred*, you can write percents as fractions or decimals. The terminology and notation may be new to students but the concept is not.

The first two lessons examine the relationship between fractions and percents, and then decimals and percents. Mathematical language and models will be used to make these connections. For example, $\frac{1}{2}$ is equivalent to $\frac{50}{100}$, or fifty-hundredths. If you replace *hundredths* with *percent*, then $\frac{1}{2}$ is equivalent to fifty percent. Further, when you find $\frac{1}{2}$ of a quantity, or $\frac{50}{100}$ of the quantity, that is the same as finding 50% of the quantity.

The chapter continues with a lesson on comparing and ordering the three representations of numbers. Again, be sure to use precise language when reading fractions and decimals. Help students further develop their number sense by working with number line representations of fractions and decimals. There are many online tools that may aid in this understanding.

The last lesson of the chapter is on solving percent problems. Tape diagrams are used to model the whole, the part, and the percent. Help students understand how the model is labeled, and how to use and interpret the model. Students will continue working with percents in the next course.

Suggested Pacing

Chapter Opener	1 Day
Section 1	2 Days
Section 2	2 Days
Section 3	2 Days
Section 4	3 Days
Connecting Concepts	1 Day
Chapter Review	1 Day
Chapter Test	1 Day
Total Chapter 4	13 Days
Year-to-Date	63 Days

Chapter Learning Target

Understand percents.

Chapter Success Criteria

- Write fractions and decimals as percents.
- Write percents as fractions and as decimals.
- Order fractions, decimals, and percents.
- Solve percent problems.

Chapter 4 Learning Targets and Success Criteria

Section	Learning Target	Success Criteria
4.1 Percents and Fractions	Write percents as fractions and fractions as percents.	• Draw models to represent fractions and percents. • Write percents as fractions. • Write equivalent fractions with denominators of 100. • Write fractions as percents.
4.2 Percents and Decimals	Write percents as decimals and decimals as percents.	• Draw models to represent decimals. • Explain why the decimal point moves when multiplying and dividing by 100. • Write percents as decimals. • Write decimals as percents.
4.3 Comparing and Ordering Fractions, Decimals, and Percents	Compare and order fractions, decimals, and percents.	• Rewrite a group of fractions, decimals, and percents using the same representation. • Explain how to compare fractions, decimals, and percents. • Order fractions, decimals, and percents from least to greatest.
4.4 Solving Percent Problems	Find a percent of a quantity and solve percent problems.	• Represent percents of numbers using an equation, a ratio table, or a model. • Find percents of numbers. • Find the whole given a part and the percent.

Progressions

Through the Grades		
Grade 5	**Grade 6**	**Grade 7**
• Multiply and divide by powers of 10 and explain the placement of the decimal point. • Compare decimals to the thousandths place. • Find equivalent fractions.	• Use ratio and rate reasoning to solve real-world and mathematical problems. • Find percent as a rate per 100; solve problems involving finding the whole, given a part and the percent. • Understand ordering of rational numbers.	• Use proportionality to solve multistep percent problems. Solve percent problems involving percents of increase and decrease, and simple interest. • Compare fractions, decimals, and percents.

Through the Chapter				
Standard	**4.1**	**4.2**	**4.3**	**4.4**
6.RP.A.3 Use ratio and rate reasoning to solve real-world and mathematical problems, e.g., by reasoning about tables of equivalent ratios, tape diagrams, double number line diagrams, or equations.				★
6.RP.A.3c Find a percent of a quantity as a rate per 100 (e.g., 30% of a quantity means $\frac{30}{100}$ times the quantity); solve problems involving finding the whole, given a part and the percent.	▲	▲		★
6.NS.C.7a Interpret statements of inequality as statements about the relative position of two numbers on a number line diagram.	▲	▲	●	
6.NS.C.7b Write, interpret, and explain statements of order for rational numbers in real-world contexts.	▲	▲	●	

Key

▲ = preparing ★ = complete

● = learning ■ = extending

STEAM Video

1. *Sample answer:* Out of every 100 nucleotides in a DNA sample, 60 are either A or T and 40 are either C or G.
2. Sample 2; *Sample answer:* Sample 2 shows 61 A and T nucleotides out of 100 total nucleotides, which is closest to 60 percent, and 39 C and G nucleotides out of 100 total nucleotides, which is closest to 40 percent.

Performance Task

Convert all of the portions to fractions or decimals and compare them.

Mathematical Practices

Students have opportunities to develop aspects of the mathematical practices throughout the chapter. Here are some examples.

1. **Make Sense of Problems and Persevere in Solving Them**
   4.4 Exercise 51, *p. 187*
2. **Reason Abstractly and Quantitatively**
   4.3 Exercise 44, *p. 180*
3. **Construct Viable Arguments and Critique the Reasoning of Others**
   4.4 Exercise 49, *p. 187*
4. **Model with Mathematics**
   4.4 Exercise 36, *p. 186*
5. **Use Appropriate Tools Strategically**
   4.1 Exercise 19, *p. 167*
6. **Attend to Precision**
   4.3 Exercise 36, *p. 180*
7. **Look for and Make Use of Structure**
   4.2 Math Practice note, *p. 169*
8. **Look for and Express Regularity in Repeated Reasoning**
   4.4 Exercise 63, *p. 188*

Laurie's Notes

STEAM Video

Before the Video

- To introduce the STEAM Video, read aloud the first paragraph of Chargaff's Rules and discuss the question with your students.

? "What can you learn about an organism from its DNA?"

During the Video

- The video shows two detectives discussing a crime scene and the remains of a sandwich.
- Pause the video at 2:14 and explain Chargaff's Rules.
  - DNA from any cell of any organism should have a 1 : 1 ratio of pyrimidine (thymine and cytosine) and purine (adenine and guanine) bases.
  - The amount of guanine is equal to the amount of cytosine, and the amount of adenine is equal to the amount of thymine.

? Continue to play the video until 3:14 and then pause to ask, "How can Veronica find out what kind of animal salivated on the sandwich?" by comparing the proportions of nucleotides

- Watch the remainder of the video.

After the Video

- Have students work with a partner to answer Questions 1 and 2.
- As students discuss and answer the questions, listen for a basic understanding of percents.

Performance Task

- Use this information to spark students' interest and promote thinking about real-life problems.

? Ask, "How can you order the portions of your friend's ancestry from least to greatest?"

- After completing the chapter, students will have gained the knowledge needed to complete "Genetic Ancestry."

STEAM Video

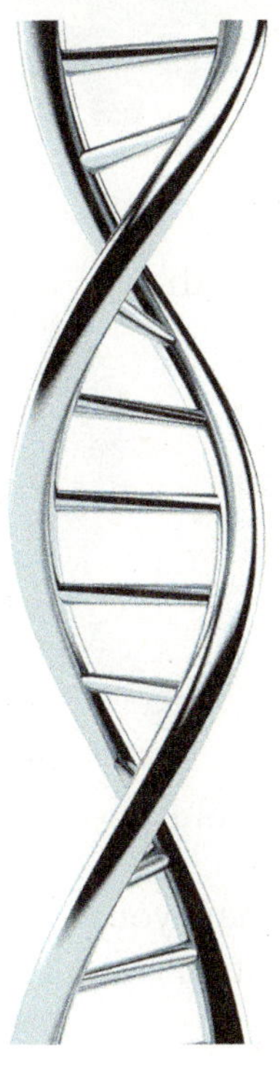

Chargaff's Rules

DNA is a molecule made up of four *nucleotide bases* called adenine (A), thymine (T), cytosine (C), and guanine (G). DNA contains the genetic information for a living organism. What can you learn about an organism from its DNA?

Watch the STEAM Video "Chargaff's Rules." Then answer the following questions.

1. Veronica says that the DNA of most mammals contains about 60 percent A and T nucleotides and 40 percent C and G nucleotides. What do you think this means?
2. Use your answer in Question 1 to determine which of the following DNA samples is most likely to belong to a mammal. Explain your reasoning.

	Sample 1	Sample 2	Sample 3
A and T Nucleotides	38	61	60
C and G Nucleotides	62	39	100

Performance Task

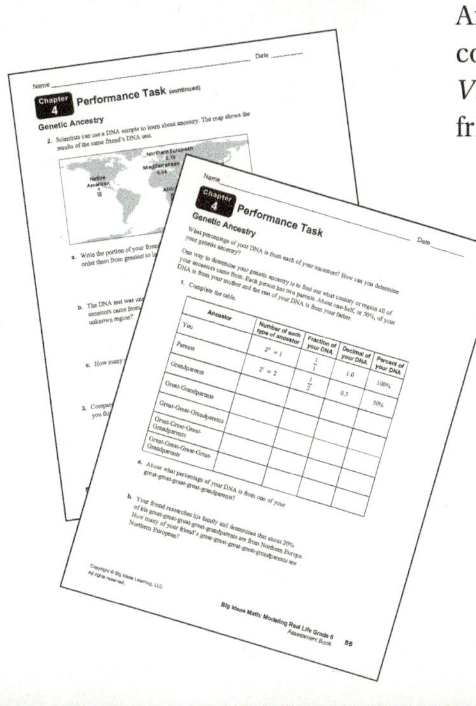

Name ______ Date ______

Chapter 4 Performance Task (continued)

Genetic Ancestry

2. Scientists can use a DNA sample to learn about ancestry. The map shows the results of the same friend's DNA test.

Name ______ Date ______

Chapter 4 Performance Task

Genetic Ancestry

What percentage of your DNA is from each of your ancestors? How can you determine your genetic ancestry?

One way to determine your genetic ancestry is to find out what country or region all of your ancestors came from. Each person has two parents. About one-half, or 50%, of your DNA is from your mother and the rest of your DNA is from your father.

1. Complete the table.

Ancestor	Number of each type of ancestor	Fraction of your DNA	Decimal of your DNA	Percent of your DNA
You	$2^0 = 1$	$\frac{1}{1}$	1.0	100%
Parents	$2^1 = 2$	$\frac{1}{2}$	0.5	50%
Grandparents				
Great-Grandparents				
Great-Great-Grandparents				
Great-Great-Great-Grandparents				
Great-Great-Great-Great-Grandparents				

a. About what percentage of your DNA is from one of your great-great-great-great-grandparents?

b. Your friend researches his family and determines that about 20% of his great-great-great-great-grandparents are from Northern Europe. How many of your friend's great-great-great-great-grandparents are Northern European?

Copyright © Big Ideas Learning, LLC All rights reserved.

Big Ideas Math: Modeling Real Life Grade 6 Assessment Book 55

Genetic Ancestry

After completing this chapter, you will be able to use the concepts you learned to answer the questions in the *STEAM Video Performance Task*. You will be given the results of your friend's ancestry test.

Native American: $\frac{1}{50}$

African: $\frac{30}{40}$

Northern European: 0.10

Southwest Asian: $\frac{3}{75}$

Mediterranean: 0.06

You will be asked to compare the portions of your friend's ancestry from different regions of the world. How can you order the portions of your friend's ancestry from least to greatest.

Getting Ready for Chapter 4

Chapter Exploration

1. **THE MEANING OF A WORD** Work with a partner. Match the "cent" word with its definition.

a. centipede	**b.** centimeter	**c.** centennial	**d.** centiliter
e. centuple	**f.** century	**g.** centenarian	**h.** centigram

J. 100-year anniversary	**K.** one-hundredth of a gram
L. multiply by 100	**M.** bug with many legs
N. one-hundredth of a liter	**O.** one-hundredth of a meter
P. 100 years	**Q.** person who is at least 100 years old

2. **THE MEANING OF A WORD** Work with a partner. Describe a situation where you have seen the word *per* used and explain its use. In your own words, what do you think the word percent means? Use the word *percent* in a sentence.

Work with a partner. Represent the shaded portion of the square as (a) a fraction whose denominator is 100, (b) a fraction in simplest form, (c) a decimal, and (d) a percent.

3. 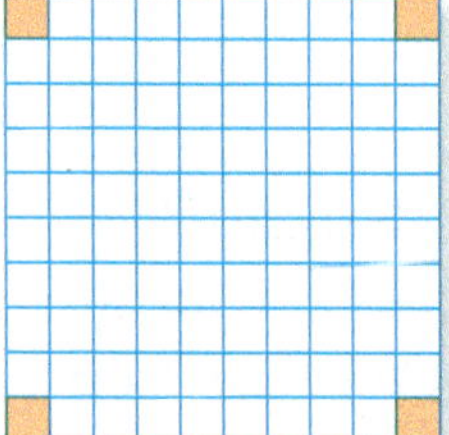

4. 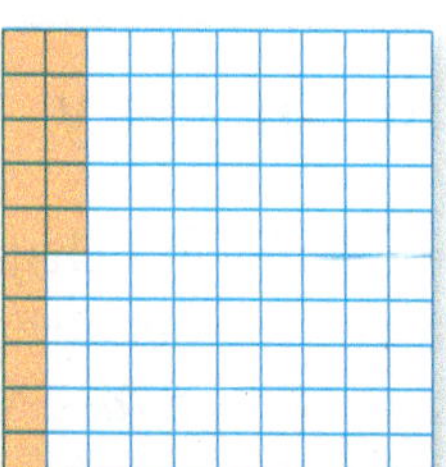

5. 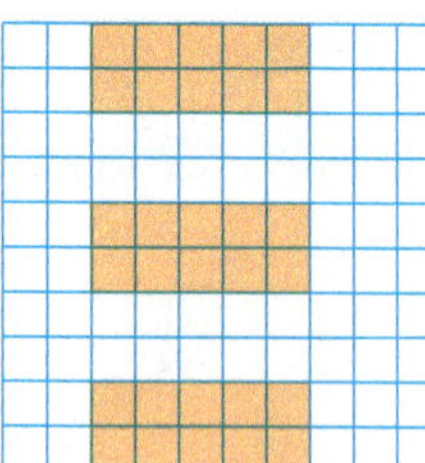

6. 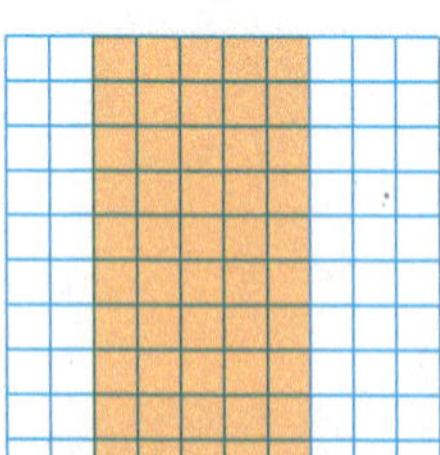

7. 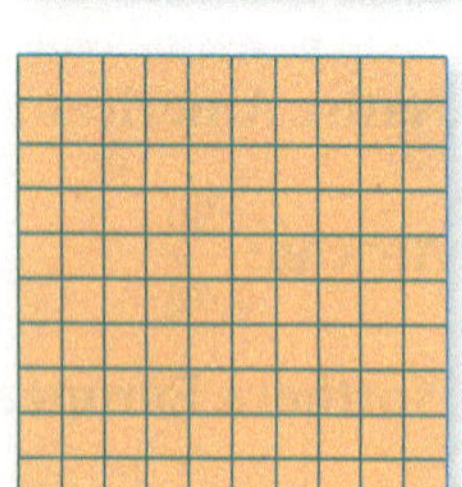

8. 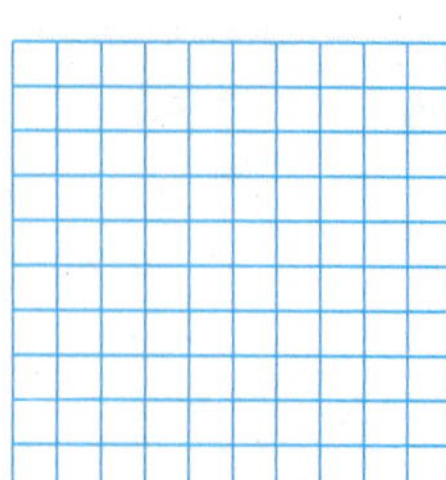

Vocabulary

The following terms are used in this chapter. Think about what each term might mean and record your thoughts.

percent	fraction	decimal

Laurie's Notes

Chapter Exploration

- Students are familiar with the word *cent*, but they may struggle with the words in Exercise 1. Encourage students to read each definition carefully and match it to the correct "cent" word.
- In Exercises 3–8, each 10-by-10 grid has 100 small squares which makes it a convenient model when representing fractions, decimals, or percents.
- Be sure students understand that any square(s) can be shaded in a 10-by-10 grid.
- Representing a percent as a fraction and as a decimal is essential to solving percent problems later in the chapter.

ELL Support

Before starting Exercise 1, make sure ELLs are familiar with the word *penny*. Display a penny and ask, "What is a penny worth?" 1 cent Explain that the root word *cent* refers to one hundred. Ask, "How many pennies equal one dollar?" 100 pennies Explain that a penny is one-hundredth of one dollar, or one percent of one dollar.

Vocabulary

- These terms represent some of the vocabulary that students will encounter in Chapter 4. Discuss the terms as a class.
- Where have students heard the word *percent* outside of a math classroom? In what contexts? Students may not be able to write the actual definition, but they may write phrases associated with percents.
- Allowing students to discuss these terms now will prepare them for understanding the terms as they are presented in the chapter.
- When students encounter a new definition, encourage them to write in their *Student Journals*. They will revisit these definitions during the Chapter Review.

Topics for Review

- Equivalent Fractions
- Multiply and Divide Decimals
- Multiply and Divide by Fractions
- Ratios

Chapter Exploration

1. **a.** M **b.** O
   c. J **d.** N
   e. L **f.** P
   g. Q **h.** K
2. *Sample answer:* miles per hour, used as a rate of speed; rate per hundred; Sixty percent of the students ride the bus.
3. **a.** $\frac{4}{100}$ **b.** $\frac{1}{25}$
   c. 0.04 **d.** 4%
4. **a.** $\frac{15}{100}$ **b.** $\frac{3}{20}$
   c. 0.15 **d.** 15%
5. **a.** $\frac{30}{100}$ **b.** $\frac{3}{10}$
   c. 0.3 **d.** 30%
6. **a.** $\frac{50}{100}$ **b.** $\frac{1}{2}$
   c. 0.5 **d.** 50%
7. **a.** $\frac{100}{100}$ **b.** 1
   c. 1 **d.** 100%
8. **a.** $\frac{0}{100}$ **b.** 0
   c. 0 **d.** 0%

Learning Target

Write percents as fractions and fractions as percents.

Success Criteria

- Draw models to represent fractions and percents.
- Write percents as fractions.
- Write equivalent fractions with denominators of 100.
- Write fractions as percents.

Warm Up

Cumulative, vocabulary, and prerequisite skills practice opportunities are available in the *Resources by Chapter* or at *BigIdeasMath.com.*

ELL Support

Reinforce the connection of *one hundred* to the root word *cent*. Explain that the word *percent* means "per one hundred" and the value of a percent can be described in hundredths. For example, $25\% = \frac{25}{100}$, or twenty-five hundredths. Explain that 25% is related to the value of a quarter, twenty-five hundredths of a dollar. Many ELLs may be unfamiliar with the names of U.S. coins. Display a penny, a nickel, a dime, and a quarter to review their names. Ask what each coin is worth and write each value as a percent of a dollar.

Exploration 1

a–d. See Additional Answers.

Laurie's Notes

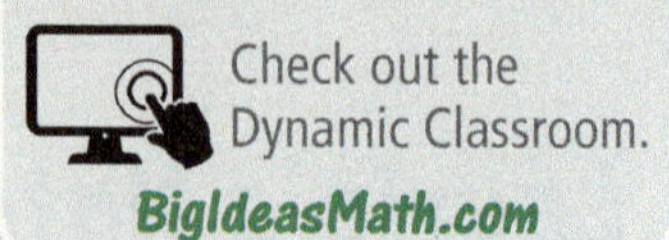

STATE STANDARDS
Preparing for 6.RP.A.3c, 6.NS.C.7a, 6.NS.C.7b

Preparing to Teach

- After working with fractions, decimals, and ratios in previous chapters, students will now extend their understanding to percents. Students will connect percent models to fraction and decimal models.
- Percent models, drawn on 10-by-10 grids, offer access to all students and provide a strategy for explanation at a conceptual level.
- **MP5 Use Appropriate Tools Strategically:** Mathematically proficient students who use models to describe foundational concepts will eventually visualize these models to analyze more complex problems. Modeling helps students make sense of answers.

Motivate

- Shake a few real coins in your hand to draw attention to the money. Be sure to include a dollar coin.
- Tell students to write each U.S. coin as a fractional amount of $1.00.
  penny: $\frac{1}{100}$; nickel: $\frac{5}{100}$; dime: $\frac{10}{100}$; quarter: $\frac{25}{100}$; half-dollar: $\frac{50}{100}$; dollar: $\frac{100}{100}$
- The word **percent** is used in common language. Discuss applications and contexts.

? "Where have you heard the word percent used?" *Sample answers:* 80% on a test; 50% chance of rain; 25% discount on a sale item; 6% interest rate

- Discuss the examples in the Meaning of a Word (century, cent, and centavo) and the notation.
- **FYI:** In French, the word *cent* (pronounced sont) means 100.

Exploration 1

- Make sure students understand the model. Ten rows and ten columns make one hundred parts.

? "Where have you used a 10-by-10 grid before?" modeling fractions and decimals Some students may say it looks like base-ten blocks for whole numbers (flats, rods, units).

- Caution students to read the directions carefully. They should read the directions once to themselves, and then have a partner read them out loud.

? "Does it matter where the squares are shaded?" no

- Ratios can be written as *a* to *b* or *a* : *b*. It is not necessary for students to simplify.
- Some students may need prompting to consider part-to-whole comparisons. Listen to their discussions for the last question.

4.1 Percents and Fractions

Learning Target: Write percents as fractions and fractions as percents.

Success Criteria:
- I can draw models to represent fractions and percents.
- I can write percents as fractions.
- I can write equivalent fractions with denominators of 100.
- I can write fractions as percents.

The Meaning of a Word ▶ Percent

A century is 100 years.

A cent is one hundredth of a dollar.

In Mexico, a centavo is one hundredth of a peso.

Cent means *one hundred*, so **percent** means *per one hundred*. The symbol for percent is %.

EXPLORATION 1 Interpreting Models

Work with a partner. Write a percent, a fraction, and a ratio shown by each model. How are percents, fractions, and ratios related?

a. 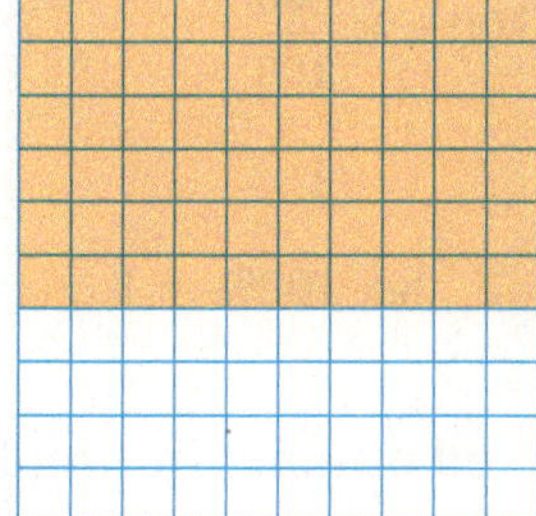

b. 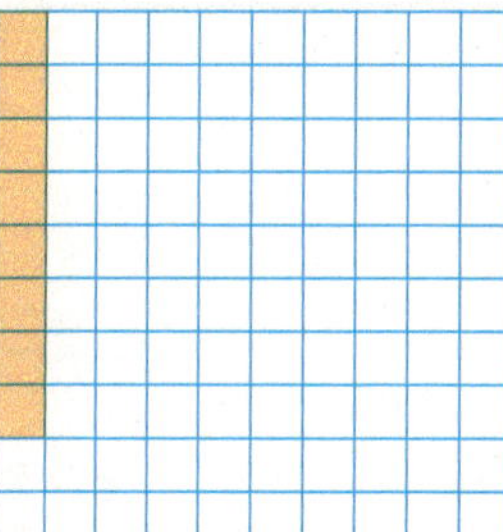

c. 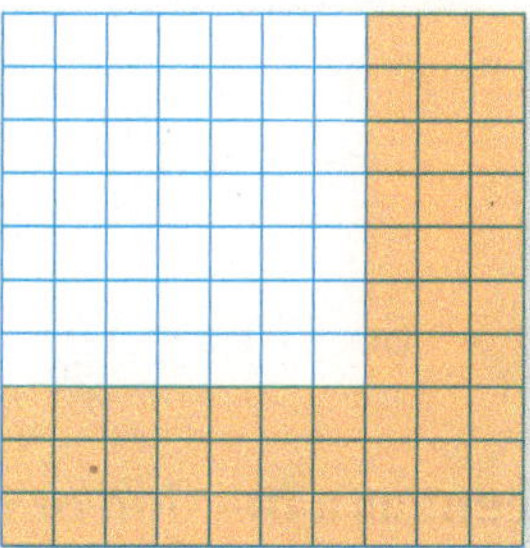

d. 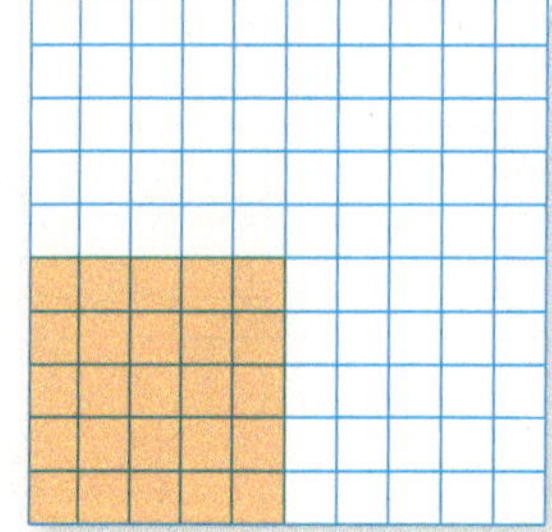

Math Practice

Use Definitions

How does the meaning of *percent* help you determine how to write the percent of each diagram that is shaded?

4.1 Lesson

Key Vocabulary
percent, *p. 164*

Key Idea

Writing Percents as Fractions

Words A **percent** is the value of a part-to-whole ratio where the whole is 100. So, you can write a percent as a fraction with a denominator of 100. The symbol % is used to denote a percent.

Numbers $60\% = 60 \text{ out of } 100 = \frac{60}{100}$

(part; per one hundred (whole); part; per; one hundred (whole))

Algebra $n\% = \frac{n}{100}$

EXAMPLE 1 Writing Percents as Fractions

Fractions and percents that are equivalent represent the same number using different notations.

a. Write 35% as a fraction in simplest form.

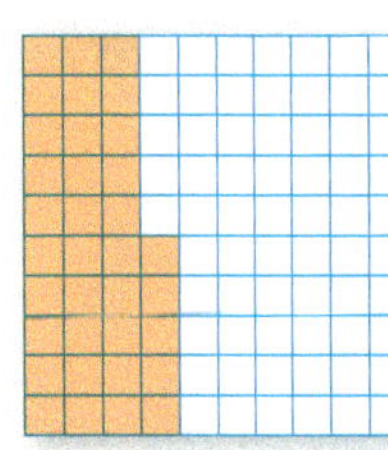

$35\% = \frac{35}{100}$ Write as a fraction with a denominator of 100.

$= \frac{7}{20}$ Simplify.

So, $35\% = \frac{7}{20}$.

b. Write 100% as a fraction in simplest form.

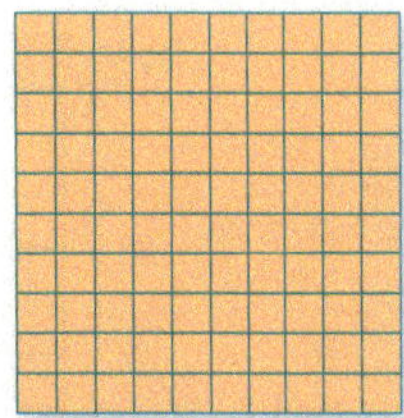

$100\% = \frac{100}{100}$ Write as a fraction with a denominator of 100.

$= 1$ Simplify.

So, $100\% = 1$.

c. Write 174% as a mixed number in simplest form.

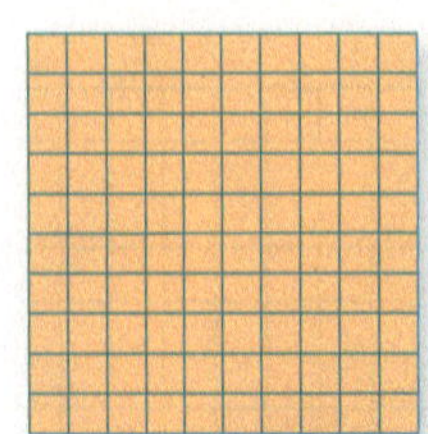

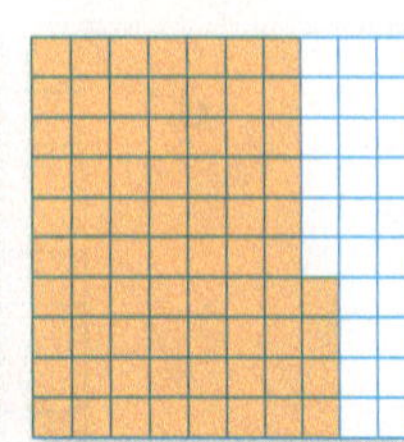

$174\% = \frac{174}{100}$ Write as a fraction with a denominator of 100.

$= \frac{87}{50}$, or $1\frac{37}{50}$ Simplify.

So, $174\% = 1\frac{37}{50}$.

Try It **Write the percent as a fraction or mixed number in simplest form.**

1. 5% **2.** 168% **3.** 36% **4.** 83%

Multi-Language Glossary at *BigIdeasMath.com*

Laurie's Notes

Scaffolding Instruction

- Students explored the origin of the word *percent* and percent models. Can students make the connection between fractions and ratios that are part-to-whole and their equivalent percents?
- **Emerging:** Students may see the fractional part of a model but struggle to explain its meaning. These students need more practice relating a fraction with a denominator of 100 to a percent model. Some students may still depend on a 10-by-10 grid. Examples 1 and 2 will transition students from the model to the numerical representation.
- **Proficient:** Students can explain percent models and write percents as fractions, and vice versa. After reviewing the Key Ideas, have students self-assess using the Try It exercises.

Key Idea

- Write the Key Idea and read the definition of **percent** out loud.
- Discuss the Numbers and explain that *per one hundred* means *for each one hundred.*
- Discuss the Algebra.

EXAMPLE 1

- Work through all parts of the example.
- ? "What is 100% as a fraction?" 1
- ? "If the percent is greater than 100%, what do you know about the equivalent fraction?" The fraction will be greater than 1.
- ? "Can you think of a context where the percent is greater than 100%?" *Sample answer:* When you earn 110% on a 10-point quiz, it means that you earned at least 1 bonus point.
- Discuss the push-pin note. Students need to understand that equivalent fractions and percents are different representations but have the same value. For example, 30% and $\frac{3}{10}$ represent the same value. This concept is important throughout future mathematics.

Try It

- Have students work in pairs to complete the exercises. Then have each pair compare their answers with another pair and discuss any discrepancies.

ELL Support

Explain that a strategy for simplifying fractions is to determine if both the numerator and denominator can be divided by 2, 3, 4, 5, and so on. When the numerator and denominator no longer have a common factor other than 1, the fraction is in simplest form. Have students work in pairs.
Beginner: Write the percent as a fraction, and then simplify if possible.
Intermediate: State the answer using a complete sentence. For example, "Five percent equals one-twentieth."
Advanced: Explain each step of the process.

Scaffold instruction to support all students in their learning. Learning is individualized and you may want to group students differently as they move in and out of these levels with each skill and concept. Student self-assessment and feedback help guide your instructional decisions about how and when to layer support for all students to become proficient learners.

Extra Example 1

a. Write 76% as a fraction in simplest form. $\frac{19}{25}$

b. Write 200% as a fraction in simplest form. 2

c. Write 118% as a mixed number in simplest form. $1\frac{9}{50}$

Try It

1. $\frac{1}{20}$
2. $1\frac{17}{25}$
3. $\frac{9}{25}$
4. $\frac{83}{100}$

Extra Example 2

a. Write $\frac{13}{20}$ as a percent. 65%

b. Write $\frac{3}{500}$ as a percent. 0.6%

Try It

5. 62% **6.** 95%

7. 0.5% **8.** 150%

ELL Support

Allow students to check their comprehension by working in groups to complete the Self-Assessment for Concepts & Skills exercises. Provide support as needed. For Exercise 9, have students begin by drawing models on whiteboards to share with the class. Have each group display their answers on a whiteboard for your review. Point out that it is easier to compare numbers when they are written in the same form.

Self-Assessment for Concepts & Skills

9. See Additional Answers.

10. 45%

11. 0.01; 0.01 = 1%, the others are equal to 10%.

12–13. See Additional Answers.

Formative Assessment Tip

Entry Ticket

This technique is similar to *Exit Ticket*. You pose a short problem, or ask a question, at the end of class. Students write their responses on tickets as part of their homework. Students give you their *Entry Tickets* as they enter your class the next day. Because they are short responses, you can read them quickly to decide if you need to answer any questions or clear up any misconceptions.

Laurie's Notes

Key Idea

? "What are equivalent fractions?" two fractions that represent the same amount

? "How do you write equivalent fractions with a denominator of 100?" Find a number you can multiply the denominator by to make it 100, and then multiply the numerator by the same number.

- Students may ask about fractions that cannot be written as equivalent fractions with denominators of 100. Assure students that they will learn other techniques for writing such fractions as percents.

EXAMPLE 2

- In part (a), you multiply the numerator and denominator by 2 to make the denominator 100.

? Ask, "What can you do in part (b) to make the denominator 100?" Divide the numerator and denominator by 10.

- **Connection:** In part (a), the models for $\frac{3}{50}$ and $\frac{6}{100}$ would be equivalent. Demonstrate this equivalence using simpler fractions, such as $\frac{1}{4} = \frac{4}{16}$.

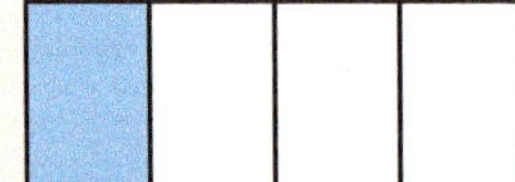 = 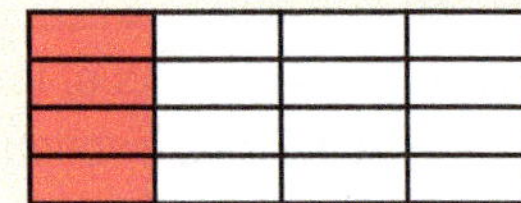

? "How many hundredths are in $\frac{1}{4}$?" 25

Try It

Neighbor Check: Have students work independently on these exercises, which are related to the fourth success criterion. Then have their neighbors check their work.

Self-Assessment for Concepts & Skills

- Exercises 9 and 10 inform students about their ability to convert percents to fractions and vice versa.
- If time permits, ask students to write one of their answers to Exercise 12 on a sticky note. Draw a long number line on the board with endpoints labeled 0 and 1. Ask a volunteer to mark the location of 40%. Have students place their sticky notes where they believe the values lie on the number line. Discuss the placement of the notes as a class.

The Success Criteria Self-Assessment chart can be found in the *Student Journal* or online at *BigIdeasMath.com*.

- **Entry Ticket:** If you have completed Examples 1 and 2 by the end of the first day, write this list on the board and ask students to put the numbers in order from least to greatest.

$\frac{1}{2}$, 60%, $\frac{2}{5}$, 75%, $\frac{3}{10}$, 90%, $\frac{3}{20}$, 25% $\frac{3}{20}$, 25%, $\frac{3}{10}$, $\frac{2}{5}$, $\frac{1}{2}$, 60%, 75%, 90%

For students who forget their *Entry Tickets* the next day, have extra tickets available with the list of numbers. Those students can complete their *Entry Tickets* at the back of the room before going to their seats.

Key Idea

Writing Fractions as Percents

Words Write an equivalent fraction with a denominator of 100. Then write the numerator with the percent symbol.

Numbers $\frac{1}{4} = \frac{1 \times 25}{4 \times 25} = \frac{25}{100} = 25\%$

EXAMPLE 2 Writing Fractions as Percents

a. Write $\frac{3}{50}$ as a percent.

$\frac{3}{50} = \frac{3 \times 2}{50 \times 2} = \frac{6}{100} = 6\%$

Because $50 \times 2 = 100$, multiply the numerator and denominator by 2. Write the numerator with a percent symbol.

b. Write $\frac{9}{1000}$ as a percent.

$\frac{9}{1000} = \frac{9 \div 10}{1000 \div 10} = \frac{0.9}{100} = 0.9\%$

Because $1000 \div 10 = 100$, divide the numerator and denominator by 10. Write the numerator with a percent symbol.

Try It **Write the fraction or mixed number as a percent.**

5. $\frac{31}{50}$ **6.** $\frac{19}{20}$ **7.** $\frac{1}{200}$ **8.** $1\frac{1}{2}$

Self-Assessment for Concepts & Skills

Solve each exercise. Then rate your understanding of the success criteria in your journal.

9. WRITING A FRACTION Write 40% as a fraction in simplest form. Draw a model that represents this fraction.

10. WRITING A PERCENT Write $\frac{9}{20}$ as a percent.

11. WHICH ONE DOESN'T BELONG? Which number does *not* belong with the other three? Explain your reasoning.

$\frac{10}{100}$ 10% $\frac{1}{10}$ 0.01

12. OPEN-ENDED Write three different fractions that are less than 40%.

13. 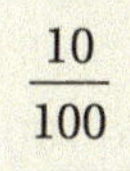 **NUMBER SENSE** Can $1\frac{1}{4}$ be written as a percent? Explain.

EXAMPLE 3 Modeling Real Life

Midwestern United States

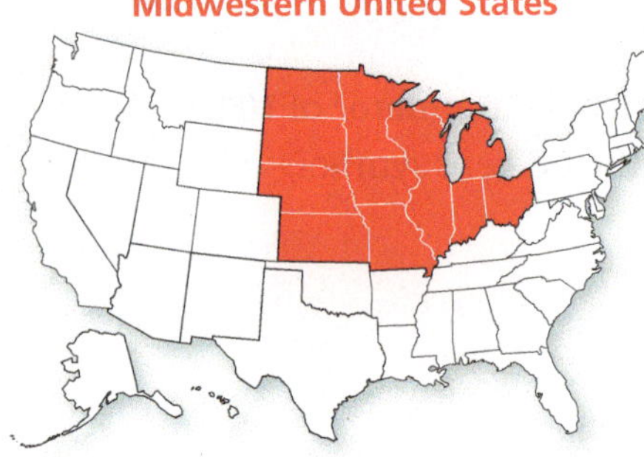

A drought affects 9 out of 12 midwestern states. What percent of the midwestern states are affected by the drought?

Write a fraction that represents the portion of midwestern states affected by the drought. Then convert the fraction to a percent.

$$\frac{\text{number of states affected}}{\text{total number of midwestern states}} = \frac{9}{12}$$

The denominator of 12 is not a factor of 100. But 4 is a factor of both 12 and 100. So, first write an equivalent fraction whose denominator is 4. Then convert that fraction to a percent.

$\frac{9}{12} = \frac{3}{4}$ — Divide the numerator and denominator by 3.

$= \frac{75}{100}$ — Multiply the numerator and denominator by 25.

$= 75\%$ — Write the numerator with a percent symbol.

So, 75% of the midwestern states are affected by the drought.

Check Reasonableness Notice that $\frac{9}{12} = \frac{9 \times 8}{12 \times 8} = \frac{72}{96}$. Because $\frac{72}{96} > \frac{72}{100}$, you know that $\frac{9}{12} > 72\%$. The answer is reasonable because $75\% > 72\%$. ✓

Self-Assessment for Problem Solving

Solve each exercise. Then rate your understanding of the success criteria in your journal.

14. You and a friend fill balloons with water. Two out of every 25 balloons pop while they are being filled. What percent of the balloons do *not* pop while they are being filled?

15. During the month of April, it rains 2 days for every 3 days that it does not rain. What percent of the days in April does it rain?

16. DIG DEEPER! There are 100 students in a band. Ninety percent of the students are either 12 or 13 years old. The number of 13-year-olds is 125% of the number of 12-year-olds. The rest of the students are 14 years old. Write the portion of the band for each age as a fraction and a percent.

Laurie's Notes

EXAMPLE 3

- ? "Can you name the midwestern states?"
- ? "Is 9 out of 12 a part-to-part comparison or part-to-whole comparison? Explain." part-to-whole; The whole is all 12 midwestern states and the part is the 9 states affected by the drought.
- ? "Is 12 a factor of 100?" no
- Explain that by simplifying $\frac{9}{12}$, you obtain a new denominator that is a factor of 100.
- Continue to solve the problem as shown. Point out that they are answering the question, "9 is what percent of 12?"
- ? **Extension:** "What if it rains in 4 midwestern states? Can you tell what percent of the midwestern states affected by the drought receive rain? Explain." No, you know that it rains in 4 midwestern states, but you don't know if it rains in 4 midwestern states affected by the drought. So, at least 1 midwestern state affected by the drought will receive rain, but as many as 4 of the states affected by the drought can receive rain.

Self-Assessment for Problem Solving

- The goal for all students is to feel comfortable with the problem-solving plan. It is important for students to problem-solve in class, where they may receive support from you and their peers. Keep in mind that some students may only be ready to complete the first step.
- If students have trouble getting started, encourage them to draw a picture or a model to represent the situation. Ask how their pictures are similar to the picture of the midwestern states in Example 3.
- In Exercise 14, make sure that students notice the word *not*.
- Have students use *Fist of Five* to indicate their understanding of the third and fourth success criteria.

The Success Criteria Self-Assessment chart can be found in the *Student Journal* or online at *BigIdeasMath.com*.

Closure

- **Writing Prompt:**
  To write a percent as a fraction, . . .
  To write a fraction as a percent, . . .

Extra Example 3

You delete 12 out of 20 pictures on your digital camera. What percent of the pictures do you delete? 60%

Self-Assessment for Problem Solving

14. 92% **15.** 40%

16. 12-year-olds: $\frac{2}{5}$, 40%;

13-year-olds: $\frac{1}{2}$, 50%;

14-year-olds: $\frac{1}{10}$, 10%

Learning Target

Write percents as fractions and fractions as percents.

Success Criteria

- Draw models to represent fractions and percents.
- Write percents as fractions.
- Write equivalent fractions with denominators of 100.
- Write fractions as percents.

Review & Refresh

1. 3000
2. 112
3. 1.5
4. 6.44 or 6.45
5. 1.69 or 1.72
6. 20.25 or 20.45
7. 10
8. 52
9. 13
10. 42
11. 52
12. $36\frac{7}{8}$
13. 3 : 1
14. 8 : 4
15. 4 : 1
16. 3 : 8

Concepts, Skills, & Problem Solving

17–19. See Additional Answers.

20. $\frac{9}{20}$
21. $\frac{9}{10}$
22. $\frac{3}{20}$
23. $\frac{7}{100}$
24. $\frac{17}{50}$
25. $\frac{79}{100}$
26. $\frac{31}{40}$
27. $1\frac{22}{25}$
28. $\frac{2}{25}$
29. $2\frac{6}{25}$
30. $\frac{1}{400}$
31. $\frac{1}{250}$
32. yes; $n\% = \frac{n}{100}$
33. 10%
34. 20%
35. 55%
36. 0.25%
37. 8%
38. 54%
39. 1.2%
40. 72%
41. 185%
42. 282%
43. 300.5%
44. 401.4%
45. no; $\frac{56}{100} = 56\%$

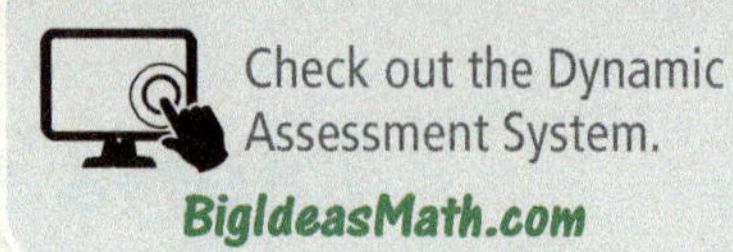

Assignment Guide and Concept Check

Scaffold assignments to support all students in their learning progression. The suggested assignments are a starting point. Continue to assign additional exercises and revisit with spaced practice to move every student toward proficiency.

Level	Assignment 1	Assignment 2
Emerging	3, 5, 11, 14, 19, 21, 28, 29, 31, 34, 37, 41	26, 32, 42, 45, 46, 47, 48, 54
Proficient	3, 5, 11, 14, 19, 21, 28, 29, 30, 37, 39, 41	26, 32, 44, 45, 46, 48, 49, 52, 54, 57
Advanced	3, 5, 11, 14, 19, 26, 28, 29, 30, 35, 39, 44	32, 43, 45, 49, 50, 54, 55, 56, 57, 58

- Assignment 1 is for use after students complete the Self-Assessment for Concepts & Skills.
- Assignment 2 is for use after students complete the Self-Assessment for Problem Solving.
- The red exercises can be used as a concept check.

Review & Refresh Prior Skills

Exercises 1–6 Converting Measures
Exercises 7–12 Dividing Whole Numbers
Exercises 13–16 Writing Ratios

Common Errors

- **Exercises 17–19** Students may not shade the correct number of squares in the 10-by-10 grid. Remind them to check their work.
- **Exercises 20–31** Students may write the percent as a fraction using the wrong denominator, or try to remove the decimal point when writing it over 100. For example, a student may write $\frac{775}{100}$ instead of $\frac{77.5}{100}$. Remind students that the denominator represents the whole and the denominator will always be 100. Tell students that the number to the left of the percent symbol will be the numerator.
- **Exercises 33–44** Students may not know when it is appropriate to use an equivalent fraction to write a fraction as a percent. Brainstorm some denominators that are easily rewritten as denominators of 100, such as 4, 5, 10, 20, and 25.

4.1 Practice

Review & Refresh

Copy and complete the statement. Round to the nearest hundredth if necessary.

1. 3 km = ___ m
2. 7 gal = ___ c
3. 54 in. = ___ yd
4. 4 mi ≈ ___ km
5. 6.5 L ≈ ___ gal
6. 45 lb ≈ ___ kg

Divide.

7. 120 ÷ 12
8. 208 ÷ 4
9. 195 ÷ 15
10. 1428 ÷ 34
11. 8528 ÷ 164
12. 295 ÷ 8

Use the table to write the ratio.

13. birch to willow
14. trees : oak
15. oak : willow
16. birch to trees

Tree	Oak	Birch	Willow
Number	4	3	1

Concepts, Skills, & Problem Solving

MP **USING TOOLS** **Use a 10-by-10 grid to model the percent.** (See Exploration 1, p. 163.)

17. 10%
18. 55%
19. 45%

WRITING PERCENTS AS FRACTIONS **Write the percent as a fraction or mixed number in simplest form.**

20. 45%
21. 90%
22. 15%
23. 7%
24. 34%
25. 79%
26. 77.5%
27. 188%
28. 8%
29. 224%
30. 0.25%
31. 0.4%

32. MP **YOU BE THE TEACHER** Your friend writes 225% as a fraction. Is your friend correct? Explain your reasoning.

$$225\% = \frac{225}{100} = \frac{9}{4}$$

WRITING FRACTIONS AS PERCENTS **Write the fraction or mixed number as a percent.**

33. $\frac{1}{10}$
34. $\frac{1}{5}$
35. $\frac{11}{20}$
36. $\frac{1}{400}$
37. $\frac{2}{25}$
38. $\frac{27}{50}$
39. $\frac{3}{250}$
40. $\frac{18}{25}$
41. $1\frac{17}{20}$
42. $2\frac{41}{50}$
43. $3\frac{1}{200}$
44. $4\frac{7}{500}$

45. MP **YOU BE THE TEACHER** Your friend writes $\frac{14}{25}$ as a percent. Is your friend correct? Explain your reasoning.

$$\frac{14}{25} = \frac{14 \times 4}{25 \times 4} = \frac{56}{100} = 0.56\%$$

46. **MP MODELING REAL LIFE** During a 10-year period, 6 out of 30 Major League Baseball teams won the World Series. What percent of Major League Baseball teams won the World Series during the 10-year period?

47. **MP MODELING REAL LIFE** A doctor conducts an experiment to test new treatments for a medical condition. Of the 16 volunteers in the experiment, 4 do not receive any treatment. What percent of the volunteers do not receive any treatment?

48. **MP LOGIC** Of the students in your class, 12% are left-handed and the rest are right-handed. What fraction of the students are left-handed? Are there more right-handed or left-handed students? Explain.

49. **MP NUMBER SENSE** You have 125% of the tickets required for a prize. What fraction of the required tickets do you have? Do you need more tickets for the prize? Explain.

FINDING PERCENTS **Find the percent.**

50. 3 is what percent of 8?

51. 13 is what percent of 16?

52. 9 is what percent of 16?

53. 33 is what percent of 40?

54. **MP MODELING REAL LIFE** A survey asked students to choose their favorite social media website.

Social Media Website	Number of Students
Website A	35
Website B	13
Website C	22
Website D	10

a. What fraction of the students chose Website A?

b. What percent of the students chose Website C?

55. **DIG DEEPER!** The percent of the total area of the United States that is in each of four states is shown.

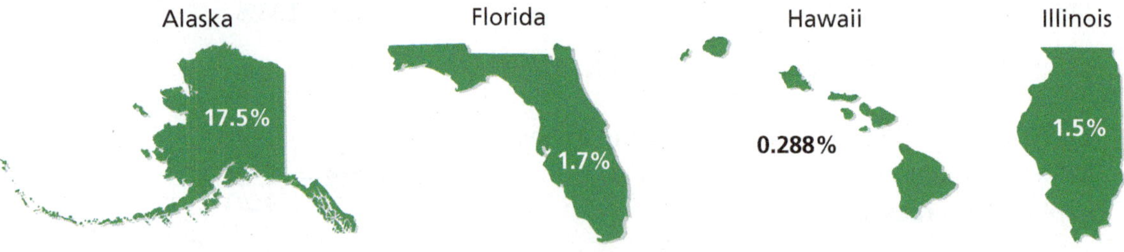

a. Write the percents as fractions in simplest form.

b. Compared to the map of Florida, is the map of Alaska the correct size? Explain your reasoning.

c. **RESEARCH** Which of the 50 states are larger than Illinois?

56. **CRITICAL THINKING** A school fundraiser raised 120% of last year's goal and 25% of this year's goal. Did the fundraiser raise more money this year? Explain your reasoning.

57. **CRITICAL THINKING** How can you use a 10-by-10 grid to model $\frac{1}{2}$%?

58. **MP REASONING** Write $\frac{1}{12}$ as a percent. Explain how you found your answer.

Mini-Assessment

1. Use a 10-by-10 grid to model 38%.

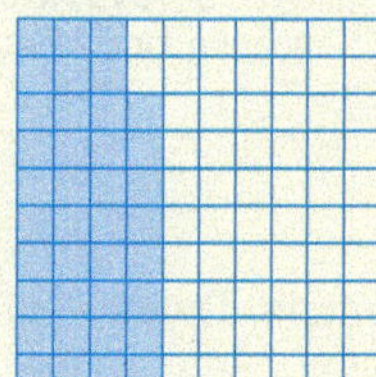

2. Write 54% as a fraction in simplest form. $\frac{27}{50}$
3. Write 142% as a mixed number in simplest form. $1\frac{21}{50}$
4. Write $\frac{3}{25}$ as a percent. 12%
5. You eat 4 out of 5 slices of a loaf of bread. What percent of the bread do you eat? 80%

Section Resources

Surface Level	Deep Level
Resources by Chapter • Extra Practice • Reteach • Puzzle Time Student Journal • Self-Assessment • Practice Differentiating the Lesson Tutorial Videos Skills Review Handbook Skills Trainer	Resources by Chapter • Enrichment and Extension Graphic Organizers Dynamic Assessment System • Section Practice

Concepts, Skills, & Problem Solving

46. 20% **47.** 25%

48. $\frac{3}{25}$; right-handed students; $\frac{22}{25}$ of the students must be right-handed and $\frac{22}{25} > \frac{3}{25}$.

49. $1\frac{1}{4}$; No, you have more than you need.

50. 37.5% **51.** 81.25%

52. 56.25% **53.** 82.5%

54. **a.** $\frac{7}{16}$ **b.** 27.5%

55. **a.** $\frac{7}{40}, \frac{17}{1000}, \frac{9}{3125}, \frac{3}{200}$

b. no; Alaska's area is more than 10 times as great as Florida's.

c. AK, TX, CA, MT, NM, AZ, NV, CO, OR, WY, MI, MN, UT, ID, KS, NE, SD, WA, ND, OK, MO, FL, WI, GA

56. It depends on the goals; The fundraiser earned more this year only if $\frac{1}{4}$ of this year's goal is greater than $1\frac{1}{5}$ of last year's goal.

57. Shade half of one of the squares.

58. $8\frac{1}{3}$%; *Sample answer:* Multiply the numerator and the denominator by $\frac{25}{3}$. Then write the result as a mixed number.

Learning Target

Write percents as decimals and decimals as percents.

Success Criteria

- Draw models to represent decimals.
- Explain why the decimal point moves when multiplying and dividing by 100.
- Write percents as decimals.
- Write decimals as percents.

Warm Up

Cumulative, vocabulary, and prerequisite skills practice opportunities are available in the *Resources by Chapter* or at *BigIdeasMath.com.*

ELL Support

Remind students that just as the word *percent* is related to 100, the word *decimal* is related to the number 10. Review other words related to the number 10, such as *decade* (10 years). Review words with the prefix *deci-*, such as *deciliter* (one-tenth of a liter). Point out that when you multiply a whole number by 10, you insert a zero at the end of the number.

Exploration 1

a. 100%; 1 **b.** 33%; 0.33

c. 37%; 0.37 **d.** 64%; 0.64

e. 50%; 0.5 **f.** 60%; 0.6

g. 130%; 1.3

A percent is written as a decimal by removing the percent symbol and dividing by 100.

Laurie's Notes

STATE STANDARDS
Preparing for 6.RP.A.3c, 6.NS.C.7a, 6.NS.C.7b

Preparing to Teach

- Students are familiar with a 10-by-10 grid from the last section. They will now extend its use to decimals.
- From the previous course, students should remember how the placement of the decimal point is affected when multiplying and dividing by powers of 10.
- Relating percents to money (part of a dollar) is often a helpful technique.
- **MP5 Use Appropriate Tools Strategically:** Mathematically proficient students use models to help make sense of different representations of numbers. All students will benefit from using models to build their understanding using visual representations before transitioning to an algorithm.

Motivate

- Share a fictional story about collecting student homework on a USB drive and the need to purchase a new drive with greater capacity. Work the following nonfictional facts into the story.
  - Most common USB drives hold 8 GB (gigabytes) or 16 GB.
  - A 32 GB USB drive holds 4 times or 400% as much data as the 8 GB. A 32 GB USB drive holds 2 times or 200% as much data as the 16 GB.

Exploration 1

- The shaded squares on a 10-by-10 grid do not have to be adjacent or consecutive.
- Ask students what strategies they can use to find the total shaded squares.
- Check in with students as they work through parts (a) and (b). There are three steps in each part: write a percent, write a decimal, and describe the relationship between the two representations.
- **Common Error:** In part (a), students may write 100% = 100 instead of 100% = 1.
- In part (e), a common question from students is whether they can leave the answer as 0.50 versus 0.5. The two decimals are equivalent. Explain that you generally write the simplified version 0.5 for the same reason you simplify fractions.
- If time allows, divide the class into four groups. Give each group a different rule to follow.

  Group A: Multiply by 100. Group B: Multiply by 0.01.
  Group C: Divide by 100. Group D: Divide by 0.01.
  - Use whiteboards, an electronic polling system, or scrap paper for groups to record their answers. Have students apply the rule to the numbers 60 and 2.5. Check the results from each group after each problem.
  - Students should recognize the pattern. Groups A and D have the same answers, as do Groups B and C. Discuss the results.
- **MP7 Look for and Make Use of Structure:** "What value represents a whole for decimals? for percents? How does the relationship between the wholes relate to the pattern?"

4.2 Percents and Decimals

Learning Target: Write percents as decimals and decimals as percents.

Success Criteria:
- I can draw models to represent decimals.
- I can explain why the decimal point moves when multiplying and dividing by 100.
- I can write percents as decimals.
- I can write decimals as percents.

EXPLORATION 1 Interpreting Models

Work with a partner. Write a percent and a decimal shown by each model. How are percents and decimals related?

a. 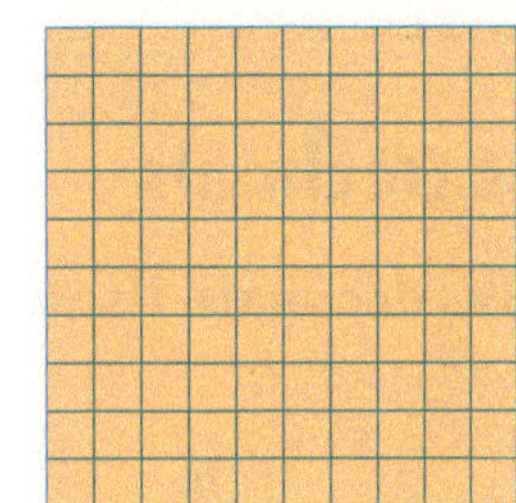

b. 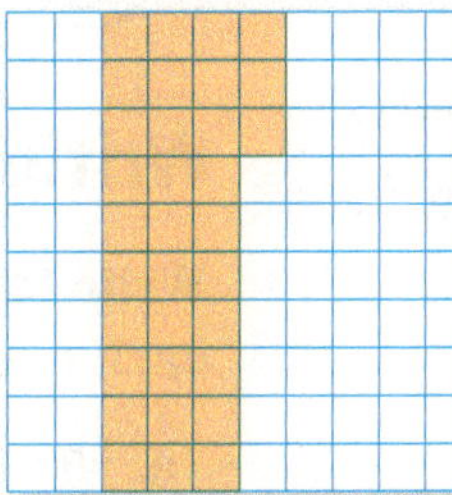

c. 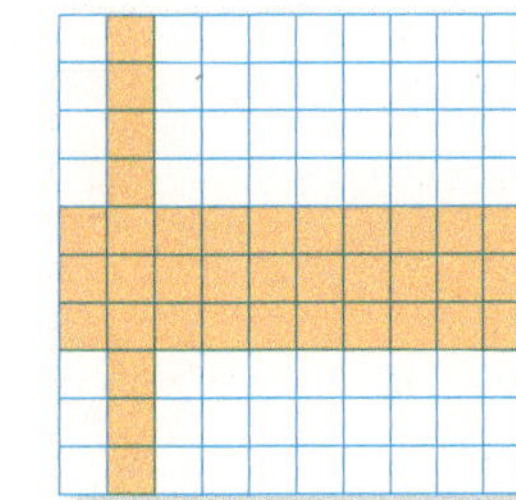

d. 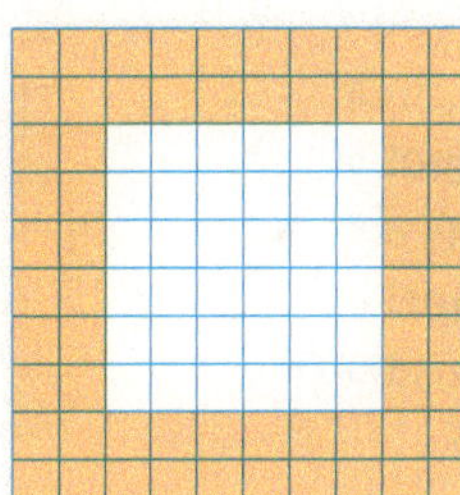

e. 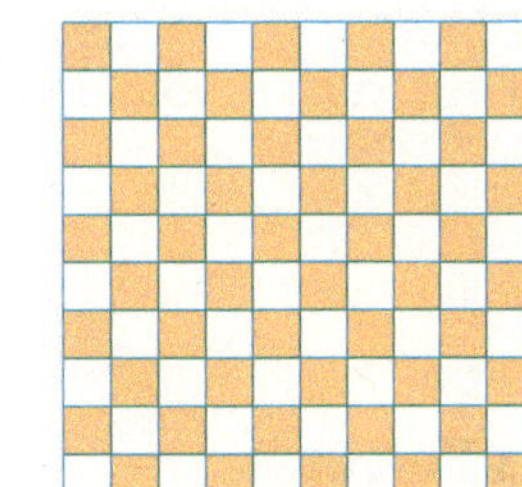

f. 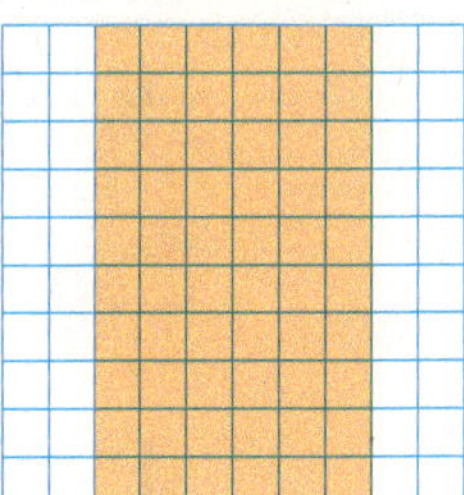

g. 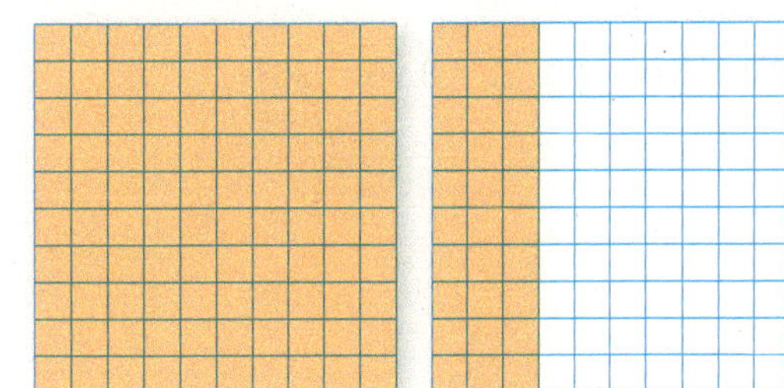

Math Practice

Look for Patterns

How does the decimal point move when you rewrite a percent as a decimal and a decimal as a percent? Explain why this occurs.

4.2 Lesson

Key Idea

Math Practice

Justify Conclusions

Use place value to explain why dividing by 100 moves the decimal point two places to the left.

Writing Percents as Decimals

Words Remove the percent symbol. Then divide by 100, which moves the decimal point two places to the left.

Numbers 23% = 23.% = 0.23

Model

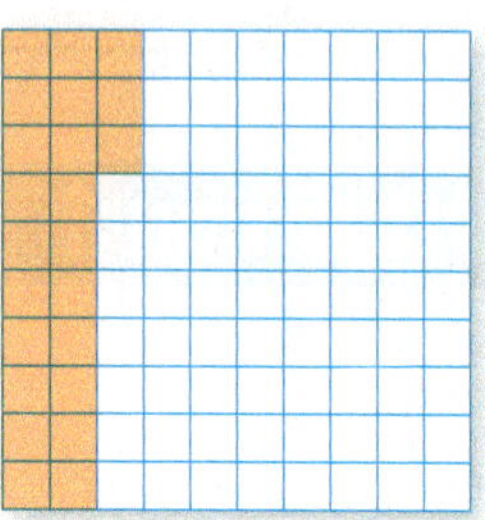

EXAMPLE 1 Writing Percents as Decimals

Write (a) 52% and (b) 7% as decimals. Use a model to represent each decimal.

a. 52% = 52.% = 0.52

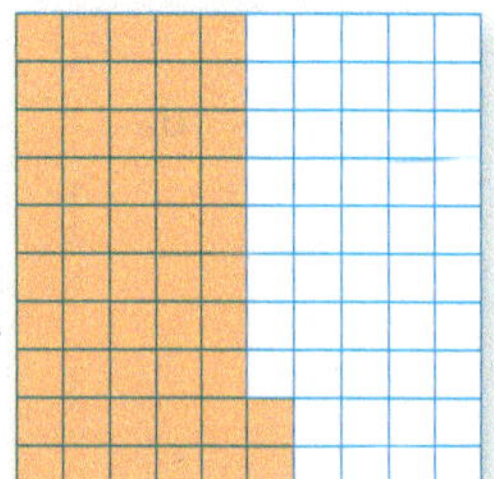

b. 7% = 07.% = 0.07

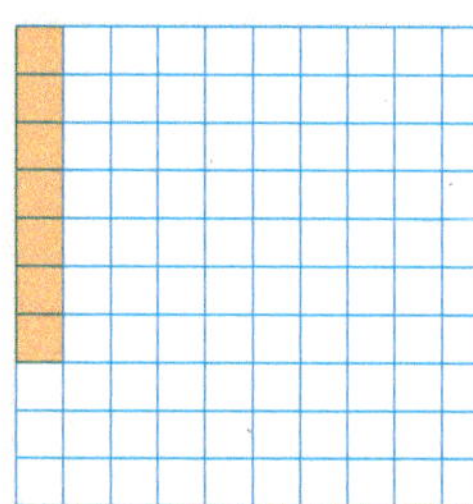

When writing a percent as a decimal, you may need to include one or more zeros so that the digits are in the correct place-value positions.

Try It **Write the percent as a decimal. Use a model to represent the decimal.**

1. 24% **2.** 3% **3.** 107% **4.** 92.5%

Key Idea

Writing Decimals as Percents

Words Multiply by 100, which moves the decimal point two places to the right. Then add a percent symbol.

Numbers 0.36 = 0.36 = 36%

Model

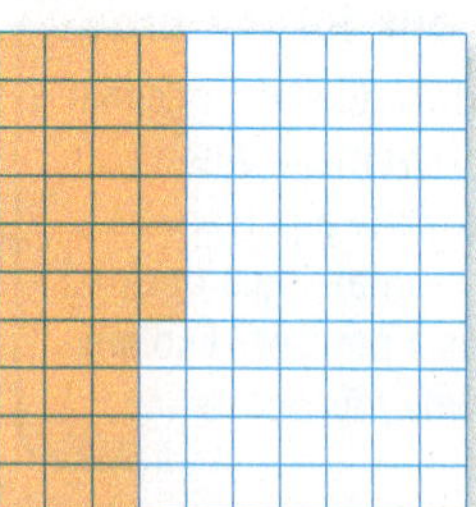

Laurie's Notes

Scaffolding Instruction

- The exploration introduced students to describing models as decimals. Throughout this lesson, listen to their conversations about the meaning of the models, as they progress from models to numerical representations.
- **Emerging:** Students may still depend on a model. Examples 1 and 2 provide practice writing percents as decimals and vice versa. Students need to know when to multiply by 100 and when to divide by 100.
- **Proficient:** Students move from models to percents and decimals with ease. They understand why the decimal point moves to the left or to the right when multiplying or dividing by 100. Have students self-assess using the Try It exercises to measure their achievement of the third and fourth success criteria.

Scaffold instruction to support all students in their learning. Learning is individualized and you may want to group students differently as they move in and out of these levels with each skill and concept. Student self-assessment and feedback help guide your instructional decisions about how and when to layer support for all students to become proficient learners.

Key Idea

- To reinforce the meaning behind moving the decimal point, say "23 percent, 23 per one hundred, or 23 hundredths."

EXAMPLE 1

- Work through both parts of the example.
- ? "52% is close to which benchmark fraction?" $\frac{1}{2}$
- The model shows an amount that is just more than 50%, or just more than $\frac{1}{2}$.
- Point out the push-pin note. In part (b), 7% means 7 per one hundred, or seven-hundredths. To write that, you have to insert a zero to the left of the seven, 0.07.
- Students generally do well with two-digit problems, as in part (a).
- Students may have difficulty with percents greater than 100% or less than 1%.
- Reinforce the meaning behind moving the decimal point.
  - 25% is 25 per one hundred or 0.25.
  - 250% is 250 per one hundred or 2.5.
  - 0.25% is 25 hundredths per one hundred or 0.0025.
  - 0.025% is 25 thousandths per one hundred or 0.00025.

Extra Example 1

Write (a) 66% and (b) 2% as decimals. Use a model to represent each decimal.

a. 0.66

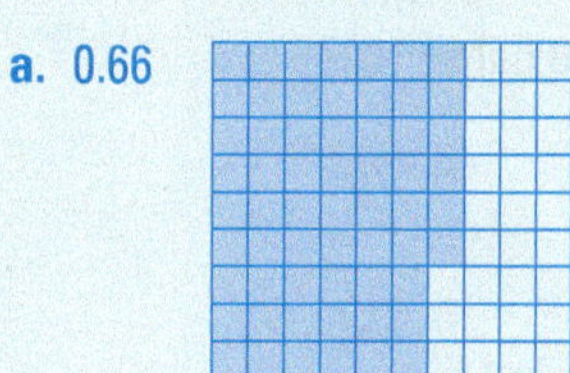

b. 0.02

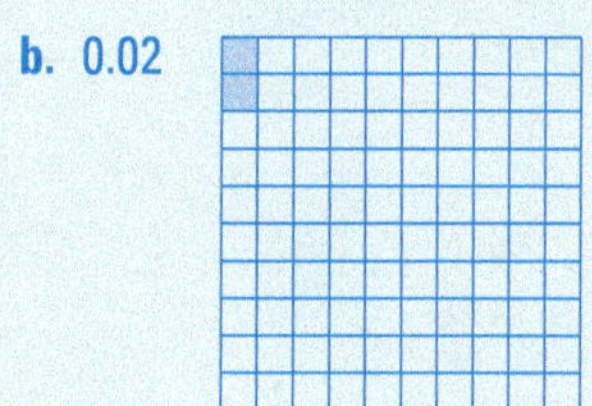

Try It

- Students should read each exercise independently, and then work in pairs to answer them. Have pairs discuss their results with another pair.

ELL Support

Have students work in pairs to complete Try It Exercises 1–4. Remind them that when writing a percent as a decimal, they need to move the decimal point two places to the left.
Beginner: Write the answer and show work.
Intermediate: State the answer using a complete sentence. For example, "Twenty-four percent is twenty-four hundredths."
Advanced: Explain the process.

Try It

1. 0.24

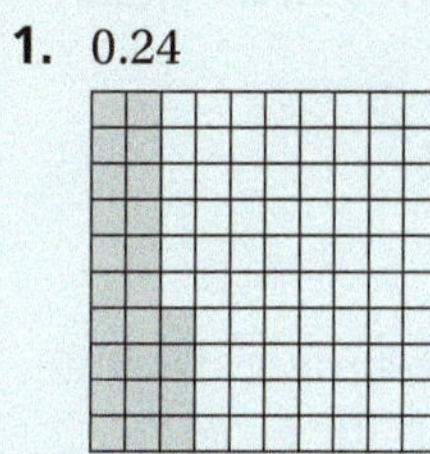

2–4. See Additional Answers.

Key Idea

- **Connection:** Dividing by 100 is equivalent to multiplying by 0.01. The decimal point moves two places to the left. Multiplying by 100 is equivalent to dividing by 0.01. The decimal point moves two places to the right.

Extra Example 2

a. Write 0.29 as a percent. 29%

b. Write 0.775 as a percent. 77.5%

c. Write 2.5 as a percent. 250%

d. Write 0.0075 as a percent. 0.75%

Try It

5. 94% **6.** 120%

7. 31.6% **8.** 0.5%

Extra Example 3

On a science test, you earn 76 out of a possible 100 points. Which of the following is *not* another way of expressing 76 out of 100?

A. $\frac{4}{5}$ **B.** 76%

C. $\frac{19}{25}$ **D.** 0.76

A

Try It

9. $\frac{9}{10}$, 0.9, 90%

Self-Assessment for Concepts & Skills

10–12. See Additional Answers.

13. 71%

14. 5.2%

15. 966%

16. *Sample answer:* Dividing by 100 is the same as multiplying by 0.01.

Laurie's Notes

EXAMPLE 2

- Work through each part as shown.

Try It

- Remind students that they are working on the fourth success criterion.
- Have students work in pairs to complete the exercises. Then have each pair compare their answers with another pair and discuss any discrepancies.

EXAMPLE 3

- Note the test-taking strategy of eliminating choices.
- Ask students to explain their reasoning as they eliminate some choices.

Try It

- Unlike Example 3, students do not have answers to choose from. They should write the three forms of "90 out of 100."

Self-Assessment for Concepts & Skills

- **Common Error:** Students may move the decimal point in the wrong direction. Look for students' understanding of moving the decimal point.

ELL Support

Have students complete Exercises 10–15 independently. Then have students check their work with a partner. If their work differs, partners need to come to agreement on the answers. Provide assistance as needed. Have each pair write their final answers on a whiteboard to display for your review.

The Success Criteria Self-Assessment chart can be found in the *Student Journal* or online at *BigIdeasMath.com*.

EXAMPLE 2 Writing Decimals as Percents

a. **Write 0.47 as a percent.**

$0.47 = 0.47 = 47\%$

b. **Write 0.663 as a percent.**

$0.663 = 0.663 = 66.3\%$

c. **Write 1.8 as a percent.**

$1.8 = 1.80 = 180\%$

d. **Write 0.009 as a percent.**

$0.009 = 0.009 = 0.9\%$

Try It **Write the decimal as a percent.**

5. 0.94 **6.** 1.2 **7.** 0.316 **8.** 0.005

EXAMPLE 3 Writing a Fraction as a Percent and a Decimal

On a math test, you earn 92 out of a possible 100 points. Which of the following is *not* another way of expressing 92 out of 100?

A. $\frac{23}{25}$ **B.** 92% **C.** $\frac{17}{20}$ **D.** 0.92

Write "92 out of 100" as a fraction, a decimal, and a percent.

$92 \text{ out of } 100 = \frac{92}{100}$ $= 92\%$ Eliminate Choice B.

$= \frac{23}{25}$ Eliminate Choice A.

$= 0.92$ Eliminate Choice D.

So, the correct answer is **C**.

Try It

9. **WHAT IF?** You earn 90 out of a possible 100 points on the test. Write "90 out of 100" as a fraction, a decimal, and a percent.

Self-Assessment for Concepts & Skills

Solve each exercise. Then rate your understanding of the success criteria in your journal.

WRITING PERCENTS AS DECIMALS **Write the percent as a decimal. Use a model to represent the decimal.**

10. 32% **11.** 54.5% **12.** 108%

WRITING DECIMALS AS PERCENTS **Write the decimal as a percent.**

13. 0.71 **14.** 0.052 **15.** 9.66

16. **WRITING** Explain why the decimal point moves left when dividing a number by 100.

EXAMPLE 4 Modeling Real Life

The figure shows the portions of ultraviolet (UV) rays reflected by four different surfaces. How many times more UV rays are reflected by water than by sea foam?

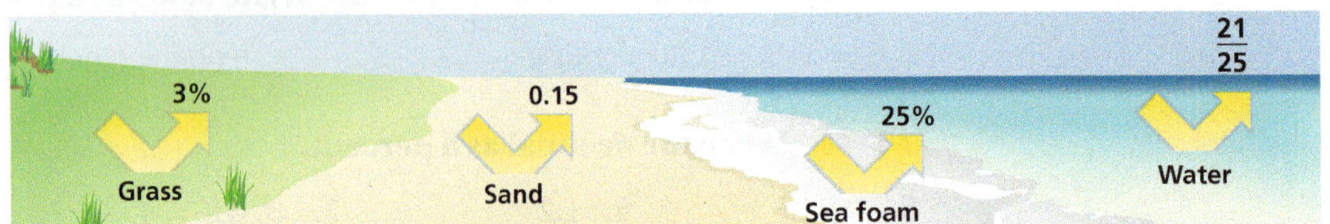

The diagram shows that sea foam reflects 25% of UV rays and water reflects $\frac{21}{25}$ of UV rays. First, write 25% and $\frac{21}{25}$ as decimals.

Sea foam: $25\% = 25.\% = 0.25$ **Water:** $\frac{21}{25} = \frac{84}{100} = 0.84$

Next, divide 0.84 by 0.25.

$$0.25\overline{)0.84} \longrightarrow \begin{array}{r} 3.36 \\ 25\overline{)84.00} \\ -75 \\ \hline 9\,0 \\ -7\,5 \\ \hline 1\,50 \\ -1\,50 \\ \hline 0 \end{array}$$

So, water reflects 3.36 times more UV rays than sea foam.

Another Method First, write 25% as a fraction:

$25\% = \frac{25}{100} = \frac{1}{4}.$

Then divide $\frac{21}{25}$ by $\frac{1}{4}$.

$$\begin{aligned} \frac{21}{25} \div \frac{1}{4} &= \frac{21}{25} \cdot 4 \\ &= \frac{84}{25} \\ &= 3\frac{9}{25}, \text{ or } 3.36 \ \checkmark \end{aligned}$$

Self-Assessment for Problem Solving

Solve each exercise. Then rate your understanding of the success criteria in your journal.

17. Write the amount of occupied space on the computer as a percent.

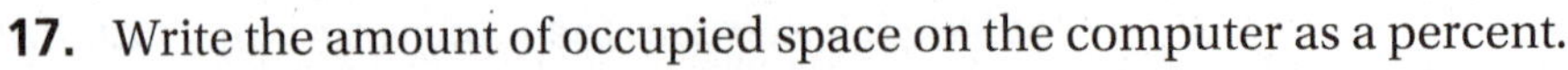

Volume	Capacity	Free Space
(C:)	150 GB	132 GB

18. *Salinity* is a measure of the salt content of a body of water. One researcher measures the salinity of the Indian Ocean as 3.2%. Another researcher measures the salinity of the Dead Sea as 34%. A bucket of water from the Indian Ocean contains 56 grams of salt. How much salt is contained in the same amount of water from the Dead Sea? Justify your answer.

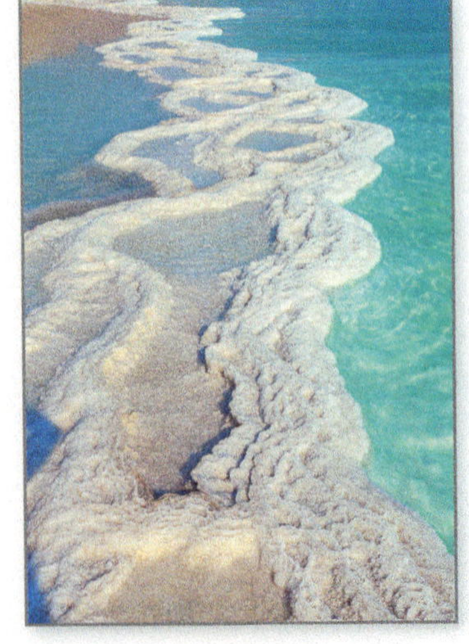

Laurie's Notes

EXAMPLE 4

- **FYI:** UV rays are necessary for our bodies to produce vitamin D, a substance that helps strengthen bones. The downside of UV rays is that when reflected off snow or sand, they can cause photokeratitis, sunburn of the cornea.
- This example reviews all three forms: percents, decimals, and fractions, as well as division of decimals.
- Review the Another Method note, in which fraction division is used. Have students compare both methods to decide which one they prefer.

? "What fundamental question is this problem asking?" How many times more? This is a language connection.

Self-Assessment for Problem Solving

- Students may benefit from trying the exercises independently, and then working with peers to refine their work. It is important to provide time in class for problem solving, so that students become comfortable with the problem-solving plan.
- Students may be comfortable moving from decimals to percents, and vice versa. Applying these skills to real-life problems is important.
- Students should complete Exercise 18 independently, and then compare strategies with a neighbor.
- **MP1 Make Sense of Problems and Persevere in Solving Them:** Students can analyze problems and restate what they need to find. While considering a solution pathway, they need to ask, "Does this make sense?"

The Success Criteria Self-Assessment chart can be found in the *Student Journal* or online at *BigIdeasMath.com.*

Closure

- **Quick Write:** Write the prompts on the board.

To write a percent as a decimal, . . .
To write a decimal as a percent, . . .

Remind students to write their main ideas first, and then elaborate if they have time. When reviewing their responses, look for students reversing the movement of the decimal point.

Extra Example 4

In Example 4, how many times more UV rays are reflected by water than by grass? 28

Self-Assessment for Problem Solving

17. 12%

18. 595 g; *Sample answer:* $56 \div 0.032 = 1750$, 34% of 1750 is 595.

Formative Assessment Tip

Quick Write
This technique allows students to write about a process or concept in their own words. Give students 2–4 minutes to respond to a short writing prompt, or sentence stem, relating to the lesson. Then collect the responses and review the information. *Quick Write* not only provides you a quick assessment of your students' level of understanding, but it also helps students become more aware of their own learning.

Learning Target

Write percents as decimals and decimals as percents.

Success Criteria

- Draw models to represent decimals.
- Explain why the decimal point moves when multiplying and dividing by 100.
- Write percents as decimals.
- Write decimals as percents.

Review & Refresh

1. 14%
2. 40%
3. 0.4%
4. 508%
5.

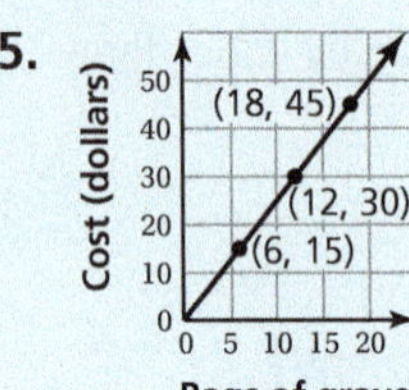

6.

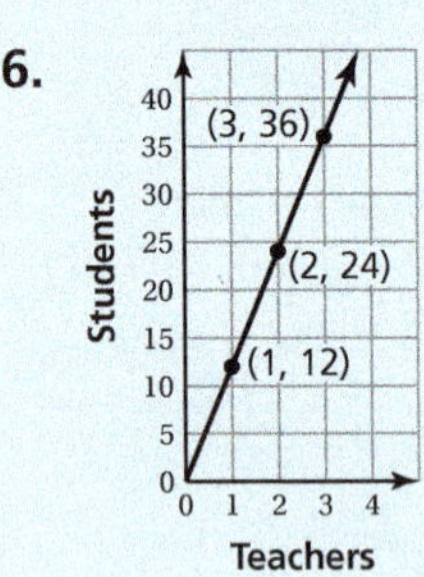

7. $\frac{2}{21}$
8. $\frac{1}{12}$
9. $4\frac{1}{5}$
10. $7\frac{7}{12}$

Concepts, Skills, & Problem Solving

11. 51%, 0.51
12. 144%, 1.44
13. 0.78
14. 0.55
15. 0.185
16. 0.574
17. 0.33
18. 0.09
19. 0.4763
20. 0.9125
21. 1.66
22. 2.17
23. 0.0006
24. 0.00034
25. 74%
26. 52%
27. 89%
28. 76.8%
29. 99%
30. 49%
31. 48.7%
32. 12.8%
33. 368%
34. 512%
35. 3.71%
36. 0.46%
37. no; 0.86 = 0.86 = 86%

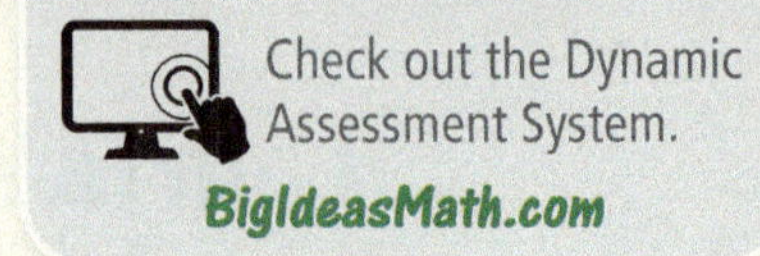

Assignment Guide and Concept Check

Scaffold assignments to support all students in their learning progression. The suggested assignments are a starting point. Continue to assign additional exercises and revisit with spaced practice to move every student toward proficiency.

Level	Assignment 1	Assignment 2
Emerging	4, 5, 9, 12, 14, 15, 18, 21, 23, 30, 31, 34, 35	20, 37, 38, 39, 40, 41, 42, 43, 45, 48
Proficient	4, 5, 9, 12, 14, 15, 18, 21, 23, 30, 31, 34, 35	20, 37, 38, 39, 40, 41, 42, 43, 44, 45, 46, 48, 49
Advanced	4, 5, 9, 12, 14, 15, 18, 22, 24, 30, 31, 34, 36	37, 44, 46, 47, 48, 49, 50

- Assignment 1 is for use after students complete the Self-Assessment for Concepts & Skills.
- Assignment 2 is for use after students complete the Self-Assessment for Problem Solving.
- The red exercises can be used as a concept check.

Review & Refresh Prior Skills

Exercises 1–4 Writing Fractions as Percents
Exercises 5 and 6 Graphing Ratio Relationships
Exercises 7–10 Multiplying Fractions and Mixed Numbers

Common Errors

- **Exercises 13–36** Students may move the decimal point the wrong way, forget to insert zeros as placeholders, or move the decimal point too many places (especially when the percent is greater than 100).

4.2 Practice

Go to **BigIdeasMath.com** to get HELP with solving the exercises.

Review & Refresh

Write the fraction or mixed number as a percent.

1. $\frac{7}{50}$ **2.** $\frac{2}{5}$ **3.** $\frac{1}{250}$ **4.** $5\frac{2}{25}$

Represent the ratio relationship using a graph.

5.

Bags of Gravel	6	12	18
Cost (dollars)	15	30	45

6.

Teachers	1	2	3
Students	12	24	36

Multiply. Write the answer in simplest form.

7. $\frac{3}{7} \times \frac{2}{9}$ **8.** $\frac{5}{12} \times \frac{1}{5}$ **9.** $4\frac{2}{3} \times \frac{9}{10}$ **10.** $2\frac{1}{6} \times 3\frac{1}{2}$

Concepts, Skills, & Problem Solving

INTERPRETING MODELS **Write the percent and the decimal shown by the model.** (See Exploration 1, p. 169.)

11.

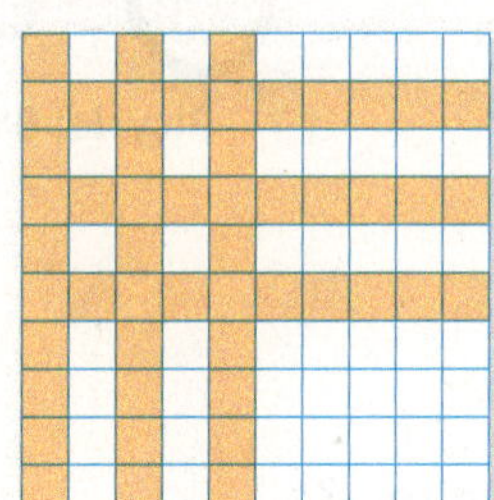

12.

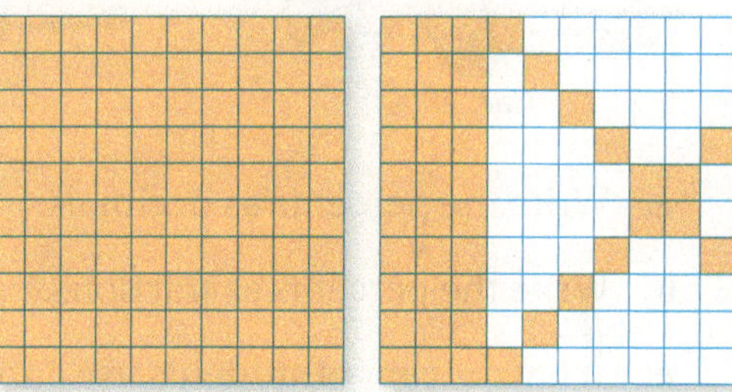

WRITING PERCENTS AS DECIMALS **Write the percent as a decimal.**

13. 78% **14.** 55% **15.** 18.5%

16. 57.4% **17.** 33% **18.** 9%

19. 47.63% **20.** 91.25% **21.** 166%

22. 217% **23.** 0.06% **24.** 0.034%

WRITING DECIMALS AS PERCENTS **Write the decimal as a percent.**

25. 0.74 **26.** 0.52 **27.** 0.89

28. 0.768 **29.** 0.99 **30.** 0.49

31. 0.487 **32.** 0.128 **33.** 3.68

34. 5.12 **35.** 0.0371 **36.** 0.0046

37. MP **YOU BE THE TEACHER** Your friend writes 0.86 as a percent. Is your friend correct? Explain your reasoning.

0.86 = 00.86 = 0.0086%

MATCHING **Match the decimal with its equivalent percent.**

38. 0.42 **39.** 4.02 **40.** 0.042 **41.** 0.0402

A. 4.02% **B.** 42% **C.** 4.2% **D.** 402%

42. **MP MODELING REAL LIFE** About 80% of the precipitation that enters Crater Lake falls directly on the surface of the lake. Write this percent as a decimal.

43. **MP MODELING REAL LIFE** About 0.34 of the length of a cat is its tail. Write this decimal as a percent.

44. **OPEN-ENDED** Write three different decimals that are between 10% and 20%.

WRITING PERCENTS AS FRACTIONS AND DECIMALS **Write the percent as a fraction in simplest form and as a decimal.**

45. 36% **46.** 23.5% **47.** 16.24%

48. **DIG DEEPER!** The percents of students who travel to school by car, bus, and bicycle are shown for a school of 825 students.

Car: 20%

School bus: 48%

Bicycle: 8%

a. Write the percents as decimals.

b. Write the percents as fractions.

c. What percent of students use another method to travel to school?

d. **RESEARCH** Make a bar graph that represents how the students in your class travel to school.

49. **MP LOGIC** A running back was the MVP (most valuable player) in 0.14 of the first 50 Super Bowls.

a. What percent of the MVPs were running backs?

b. What fraction of the MVPs were *not* running backs?

50. **CHOOSING A METHOD** Students in a class were asked to tell their favorite color.

a. What percent said red, blue, or yellow?

b. How many times more students said red than yellow?

c. Use two methods to find the percent of students who said green. Which method do you prefer? Explain.

Favorite Color

PURPLE 14%
GREEN ?
YELLOW 0.04
RED 0.26
BLUE 40%

Mini-Assessment

Write the percent as a decimal.

1. 13% 0.13 **2.** 130% 1.3

Write the decimal as a percent.

3. 0.0098 0.98% **4.** 2.25 225%

5. Forty-three percent of your cell phone ringtones are pop songs. Write this percent as a decimal. 0.43

Section Resources

Surface Level	Deep Level
Resources by Chapter • Extra Practice • Reteach • Puzzle Time Student Journal • Self-Assessment • Practice Differentiating the Lesson Tutorial Videos Skills Review Handbook Skills Trainer	Resources by Chapter • Enrichment and Extension Graphic Organizers Dynamic Assessment System • Section Practice
Transfer Level	
Dynamic Assessment System • Mid-Chapter Quiz	Assessment Book • Mid-Chapter Quiz

Concepts, Skills, & Problem Solving

38. B **39.** D

40. C **41.** A

42. 0.8 **43.** 34%

44. *Sample answer:* 0.11, 0.13, 0.19

45. $\frac{9}{25}$, 0.36 **46.** $\frac{47}{200}$, 0.235

47. $\frac{203}{1250}$, 0.1624

48. **a.** car: 0.2, school bus: 0.48, bicycle: 0.08

b. car: $\frac{1}{5}$, school bus: $\frac{12}{25}$, bicycle: $\frac{2}{25}$

c. 24%

d. *Answer should include, but is not limited to:* A bar graph showing either the *number* of students or the *portion* of students in the class that get to school in various ways.

49. **a.** 14%

b. $\frac{43}{50}$

50. **a.** 70%

b. 6.5

c. 16%; *Sample answer:* subtracting percents; It gives whole number calculations.

Learning Target

Compare and order fractions, decimals, and percents.

Success Criteria

- Rewrite a group of fractions, decimals, and percents using the same representation.
- Explain how to compare fractions, decimals, and percents.
- Order fractions, decimals, and percents from least to greatest.

Warm Up

Cumulative, vocabulary, and prerequisite skills practice opportunities are available in the *Resources by Chapter* or at *BigIdeasMath.com.*

ELL Support

Tell students that fractions, decimals, and percents all represent parts of wholes. Explain that students will now compare and order them. Point out that the word *order* has different meanings. Students may order food at a restaurant or order clothing online. Order also means to arrange things in a specific way. In this lesson, students will order different types of numbers from least to greatest.

Exploration 1

a–f. See Additional Answers

Laurie's Notes

STATE STANDARDS
6.NS.C.7a, 6.NS.C.7b

Preparing to Teach

- Being able to write a number as a fraction, a decimal, and a percent paves the way for students to compare and order different forms of numbers.
- **MP2 Reason Abstractly and Quantitatively:** In the lesson, students will compare numbers by converting between different representations.

  Mathematically proficient students should reason that $\frac{6}{11} > 0.48$ because $\frac{6}{11} > \frac{1}{2}$ and $\frac{1}{2} > 0.48$.

Motivate

- Write each number on an index card: $\frac{1}{10}$, $\frac{13}{20}$, $\frac{4}{5}$, 0.18, 0.45, 0.5, 35%, 60%, 85%.

  Write them on the board, so that all students can see them.
- **Popsicle Sticks:** Distribute the 9 cards.
- Ask the 3 students holding fraction cards to stand in order from least to greatest. Then ask the 3 students holding decimal cards and the 3 students holding percent cards to do the same.
- Have each group of students describe the strategies for ordering themselves.
- ? Ask the students holding $\frac{1}{10}$, 0.18, and 35% to stand. "Is it possible to order them?" yes "How do you know their positions compared to each other?" Listen for students to mention number lines and converting to the same type of number.

Exploration 1

- If possible, mark a number line with masking tape on the floor near each group that will represent the numbers zero to two. (Physically being a number on the line cements students' understanding of conversion and order.) Another possibility is to position 3–4 desks in single file and place masking tape across them to use as a number line and have sticky notes available for the numbers.
- The focus is to complete every exercise with each of the four students becoming the "dot" to represent each number in the appropriate position.
- ? As you visit each group, ask them to explain their method for number placement. Then ask probing questions, "Will your method work every time? Which exercise was the most difficult and why?"
- **Common Error:** Students might say that 0.9% is equal to 0.09 or that 4% is equal to 0.4. Watch for students' placement of zeros in their conversions.
- **MP5 Use Appropriate Tools Strategically:** Visual and concrete models help students analyze mathematical problems. Practicing with different tools gives all students access to beginning a solution method.
- ◎ This exploration provides students with an investigation of all the success criteria.

4.3 Comparing and Ordering Fractions, Decimals, and Percents

Learning Target: Compare and order fractions, decimals, and percents.

Success Criteria:
- I can rewrite a group of fractions, decimals, and percents using the same representation.
- I can explain how to compare fractions, decimals, and percents.
- I can order fractions, decimals, and percents from least to greatest.

EXPLORATION 1 Using a Number Line to Order Numbers

Work with three partners. Create a number line on the floor. Have your group stand on the number line to represent the four numbers in each list. Use the results to order each list of numbers from least to greatest. How did you know where to stand?

Math Practice

Find Entry Points

What strategies can you use to determine where to stand?

a.

0.25	0.9%	40%	0.5

b.

0%	$\frac{3}{4}$	30%	$\frac{1}{20}$

c.

100%	0.125	75%	$\frac{3}{10}$

d.

12.5%	1.02	$\frac{1}{100}$	25%

e.

0.3	$\frac{1}{8}$	4%	0.75

f.

$\frac{51}{50}$	105%	1.5	$\frac{9}{10}$

4.3 Lesson

When comparing and ordering fractions, decimals, and percents, write the numbers as all fractions, all decimals, or all percents.

EXAMPLE 1 Comparing Fractions, Decimals, and Percents

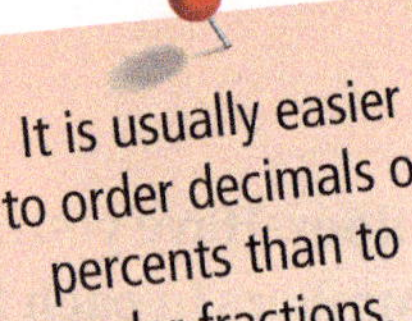

a. Which is greater, $\frac{3}{20}$ or 16%?

Write $\frac{3}{20}$ as a percent: $\frac{3}{20} = \frac{3 \times 5}{20 \times 5} = \frac{15}{100} = 15\%$.

15% is less than 16%. So, 16% is the greater number.

b. Which is greater, 79% or 0.08?

Write 79% as a decimal: 79% = 79.% = 0.79.

0.79 is greater than 0.08. So, 79% is the greater number.

Try It **Tell which number is greater.**

1. 25%, $\frac{7}{25}$

2. 0.49, 94%

EXAMPLE 2 Ordering Fractions, Decimals, and Percents

Order 3%, $\frac{1}{50}$, 0.005, 0.8%, and 0.025 from least to greatest.

Remember

To order numbers from least to greatest, write them as they appear on a number line from left to right.

One way to order the numbers is to first write each number as a percent.

$\frac{1}{50} = \frac{1 \times 2}{50 \times 2} = \frac{2}{100} = 2\%$ 0.005 = 0.005 = 0.5% 0.025 = 0.025 = 2.5%

Graph the percents on a number line.

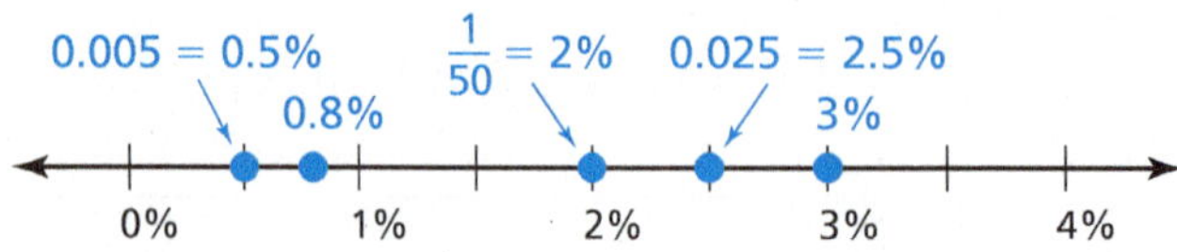

So, the order from least to greatest is 0.005, 0.8%, $\frac{1}{50}$, 0.025, and 3%.

Try It **Order the numbers from least to greatest.**

3. $\frac{3}{10}$, 15%, 0.2, $\frac{3}{8}$, 0.09

4. 100%, 0.95, 1.2, $\frac{5}{4}$, 110%

Laurie's Notes

Scaffolding Instruction

- Earlier in the chapter, students wrote percents as fractions, fractions as percents, percents as decimals, and decimals as percents. The exploration was a natural extension of comparing the three forms of numbers.
- **Emerging:** Students may lack confidence in moving between the three equivalent forms of numbers and will benefit from guided instruction for Examples 1–3.
- **Proficient:** Students can accurately move between percents and decimals, change decimals to fractions, and graph them on a number line. After completing the Try It exercises, have students proceed to the Self-Assessment exercises.

EXAMPLE 1

? Refer to the push-pin note and ask, "Why is this true?" Listen for understanding that ordering decimals by place values is easier than ordering fractions with unlike denominators.

? "To compare $\frac{3}{20}$ and 16%, should you write $\frac{3}{20}$ as a percent or 16% as a fraction? Explain." Either answer is correct, but students should be able to explain their choices. If time permits, discuss and work through both options.

? "Can you compare $\frac{3}{20}$ and 16% by writing each as a decimal?" yes Show students that $\frac{3}{20} = \frac{15}{100} = 0.15$ and $16\% = 0.16$.

? Work through part (b) as shown. Then ask, "What is 0.08 as a percent?" 8%

- **Common Error:** Students may say 80% because they are comparing it to 79%.
- **MP2 Reason Abstractly and Quantitatively:** Take time to review and analyze the efficiency of the different strategies.

Try It

These exercises provide feedback on students' understanding of the first success criterion.

EXAMPLE 2

- Rewrite all the numbers as percents.
- The number line allows students to order the percents from least to greatest using a visual representation. Guide students in choosing the length and increments of the number line effectively.

ELL Support

Explain that it is easier to convert all numbers to the same form when comparing numbers. Review the steps of converting fractions and decimals to percents. Have students work in groups to complete Try It Exercises 3 and 4.
Beginner: Write the ordered list of numbers and show work.
Intermediate: Read the ordered list of numbers out loud.
Advanced: Explain each step.

Scaffold instruction to support all students in their learning. Learning is individualized and you may want to group students differently as they move in and out of these levels with each skill and concept. Student self-assessment and feedback help guide your instructional decisions about how and when to layer support for all students to become proficient learners.

Extra Example 1

a. Which is greater, $\frac{17}{20}$ or 80%? $\frac{17}{20}$

b. Which is greater, 28% or 0.29? 0.29

Try It

1. $\frac{7}{25}$ **2.** 94%

Extra Example 2

Order $\frac{1}{25}$, 1.4%, 0.029, 1.7%, and 0.009 from least to greatest.

0.009, 1.4%, 1.7%, 0.029, $\frac{1}{25}$

Try It

3. 0.09, 15%, 0.2, $\frac{3}{10}$, $\frac{3}{8}$

4. 0.95, 100%, 110%, 1.2, $\frac{5}{4}$

Extra Example 3

You, your sister, and a friend each take the same number of shots at a hockey goal. You make 0.67 of your shots, your sister makes 68% of her shots, and your friend makes $\frac{17}{20}$ of her shots. Who made the fewest shots? you

Try It

5. yes; no

Self-Assessment
for Concepts & Skills

6.

$\frac{18}{25}$	0.72	72%
$\frac{17}{20}$	0.85	85%
$\frac{13}{50}$	0.26	26%
$\frac{31}{50}$	0.62	62%
$\frac{9}{20}$	0.45	45%

7. *Sample answer:* Write $\frac{3}{5}$ as a percent and compare to 59%.

8. 0.34

9. 0.85

10. $\frac{9}{50}$

11. 0.1, 12%, $\frac{4}{25}$

12. $\frac{6}{5}$, 125%, 130%, 1.35, 1.5

Laurie's Notes

Discuss

- Ask students where they encounter fractions, decimals, or percents in their everyday lives. You may need to prompt ideas by providing a few examples, such as using a $\frac{5}{8}$-inch wrench, having a 0.324 batting average, or having 24% battery life.
- Tell students that when comparing, there may be situations where numbers are represented in different forms.

EXAMPLE 3

- Note the scale on the number line. A common misconception is that the scale must be in increments of 1, 5, or 10.

? "Why are increments of 0.02 helpful in this problem? Increments of 0.02 allow you to graph these three decimals precisely. "Can increments of 0.10 be used?" You can use increments of 0.10, but it will be more difficult to find each decimal's location precisely.

Try It

- **Think-Pair-Share:** Have students read the question independently, and then work in pairs to answer the question. Have each pair compare their answer with another pair and discuss any discrepancies.
- Have students graph the three numbers on a number line.

Self-Assessment for Concepts & Skills

- Exercise 6 provides a view of students' foundational understanding of comparing fractions, decimals, and percents. Are students confident with all three forms?
- Exercise 7 provides insight into students' conceptual understanding.
- In Exercises 11 and 12, check students' equivalent forms of the numbers to ensure that they don't just accidentally choose the correct order.
- Ask students to share which methods they prefer and why.
- **MP3 Construct Viable Arguments and Critique the Reasoning of Others:** There are several ways in which students may justify their answers. Take time to hear a variety of approaches.

ELL Support

Have students work in groups to discuss and complete the exercises. Have two groups compare their answers. If there is disagreement or uncertainty, provide support. Check answers by having each combined group display the answers they agree upon on a whiteboard.

The Success Criteria Self-Assessment chart can be found in the *Student Journal* or online at *BigIdeasMath.com*.

EXAMPLE 3 Comparing Numbers to Solve a Real-Life Problem

You, your sister, and a friend each take the same number of shots at a soccer goal. You make 72% of your shots, your sister makes $\frac{19}{25}$ of her shots, and your friend makes 0.67 of his shots. Who made the fewest shots?

To determine who made the fewest shots, find who made the least portion of their shots. One way to do this is to first write each number as a decimal.

You: $72\% = 72.\% = 0.72$ **Sister:** $\frac{19}{25} = \frac{19 \times 4}{25 \times 4} = \frac{76}{100} = 0.76$

Graph the decimals on a number line.

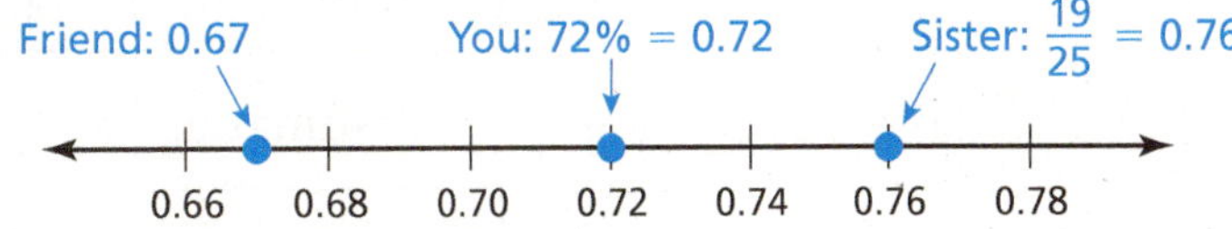

0.67 is the least number. So, your friend made the fewest shots.

Try It

5. **WHAT IF?** Your friend makes $\frac{3}{4}$ of his shots. Did your friend make more shots than you? your sister?

Self-Assessment for Concepts & Skills

Solve each exercise. Then rate your understanding of the success criteria in your journal.

Fraction	Decimal	Percent
$\frac{18}{25}$	0.72	
$\frac{17}{20}$		85%
$\frac{13}{50}$		
	0.62	
		45%

6. **MP NUMBER SENSE** Copy and complete the table.

7. **MP NUMBER SENSE** How would you decide whether $\frac{3}{5}$ or 59% is greater? Explain.

COMPARING NUMBERS Tell which number is greater.

8. 33%, 0.34

9. 0.85, $\frac{4}{5}$

10. $\frac{9}{50}$, 17%

ORDERING NUMBERS Order the numbers from least to greatest.

11. 12%, 0.1, $\frac{4}{25}$

12. 1.35, 125%, $\frac{6}{5}$, 1.5, 130%

EXAMPLE 4 Modeling Real Life

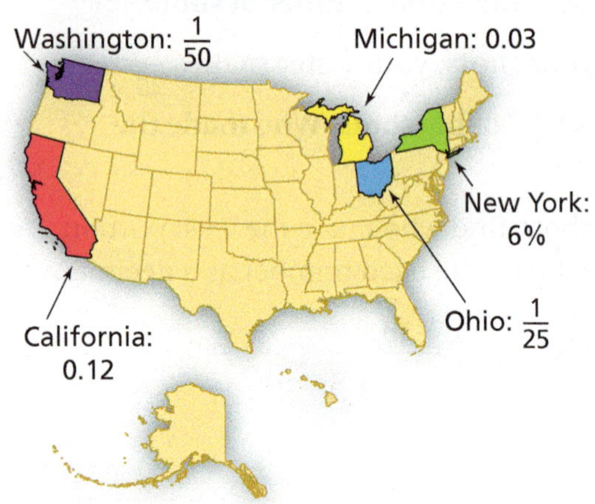

The map shows the portions of the U.S. population that live in five states. List the five states in order by population from least to greatest.

Begin by writing each portion as a fraction, a decimal, and a percent.

State	Fraction	Decimal	Percent
Michigan	$\frac{3}{100}$	0.03	3%
New York	$\frac{6}{100}$	0.06	6%
Washington	$\frac{1}{50}$	0.02	2%
California	$\frac{12}{100}$	0.12	12%
Ohio	$\frac{1}{25}$	0.04	4%

Graph the percent for each state on a number line.

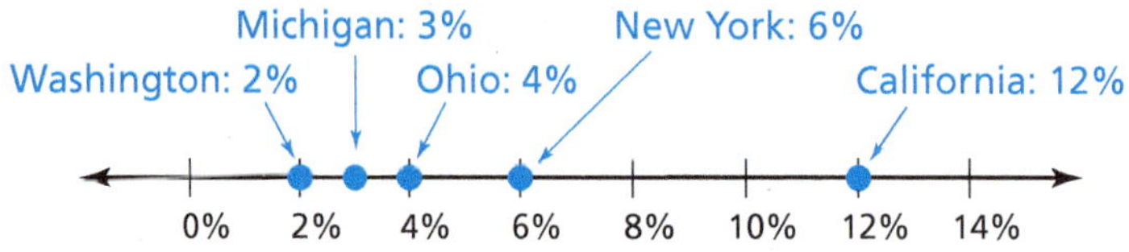

The states in order by population from least to greatest are Washington, Michigan, Ohio, New York, and California.

Self-Assessment for Problem Solving

Solve each exercise. Then rate your understanding of the success criteria in your journal.

Ring	Portion that is Copper
Red gold	25%
Pink gold	0.2
Rose gold	$\frac{9}{40}$

13. The table shows the portions of copper in three rings. Which ring has the highest portion of copper?

14. **DIG DEEPER!** The table shows the results of five teams competing in a scavenger hunt. List the five teams in order by the portion of items collected from least to greatest. What is the minimum number of items in the scavenger hunt? Explain.

Team	1	2	3	4	5
Portion Collected	$\frac{3}{4}$	0.8	77.5%	0.825	$\frac{13}{20}$

Laurie's Notes

EXAMPLE 4

- Give students time to read the information in the problem.
- "Interpret what it means for $\frac{1}{50}$ of the U.S. population to live in Washington."

  One in every fifty U.S. residents lives in Washington.

MP8 Look for and Express Regularity in Repeated Reasoning: "If there are 100 U.S. residents, how many live in Washington?" 2 "If there are 1000 U.S. residents, how many live in Washington?" 20

- Discuss the columns of the table. Note that the decimals and percents are easier to compare than the fractions.

Self-Assessment for Problem Solving

- Allow time in class for students to practice using the problem-solving plan. Remember, some students may only be able to complete the first step.

Circulate as students work and ask, "What did you do first? Why did you choose that method?"

- In Exercise 13, if students choose to write all numbers as percents, do they understand that $0.2 = 20\%$? If they write all numbers as decimals, do they see that $0.2 = 0.200$?
- **Turn and Talk:** After completing the exercises, have students compare strategies and answers with a partner.

The Success Criteria Self-Assessment chart can be found in the *Student Journal* or online at *BigIdeasMath.com*.

Formative Assessment Tip

Flashcards

This technique allows students to compare solutions or ways of thinking about different problems. Each student writes a problem on the front of an index card and then solves the problem on the back. Students must show their work. Students exchange cards but do not look at the backs of the cards they receive. Students then solve the problems on the fronts of the cards they received. After answering, each student checks his or her answer with the answer on the back. Students return the cards to the original owners and work together to correct any errors.

Closure

- **Flashcards:** Divide students into groups. Ask students to write a percent between 25% and 40% on the fronts of their cards. Tell students to write their percents as a decimal and a fraction on the backs of the cards. There should be no talking during this time. Have students exchange cards with the person across from them. If there is an odd number of students in the group, they can all pass to the left.
- **Extension:** When all of the students in the group are finished, ask them to use the backs of their cards (the decimal and fraction representations) to order the cards from least to greatest. Circulate and check each group's order.

Extra Example 4

The table shows the portions of the population of Rhode Island that live in each county. List the counties in order by population from least to greatest.

Counties	Portion of Rhode Island Population
Bristol	4%
Kent	0.16
Newport	0.08
Providence	$\frac{3}{5}$
Washington	$\frac{3}{25}$

Bristol, Newport, Washington, Kent, Providence

Self-Assessment for Problem Solving

13. red gold

14. 5, 1, 3, 2, 4; 40; *Sample answer:* 40 is the LCD of the numbers written as fractions.

Learning Target

Compare and order fractions, decimals, and percents.

Success Criteria

- Rewrite a group of fractions, decimals, and percents using the same representation.
- Explain how to compare fractions, decimals, and percents.
- Order fractions, decimals, and percents from least to greatest.

Review & Refresh

1. 0.12
2. 0.9837
3. 0.00046
4.

Cashews	5	45
Almonds	4	36

5 : 4, 45 : 36

5.

Cost (dollars)	2	3	13.5
Time (minutes)	50	75	337.5

2 : 50, 3 : 75, 13.5 : 337.5

6. 31.8
7. 162.9
8. 18.7693
9. 5.7084
10. 3
11. 17
12. 8

Concepts, Skills, & Problem Solving

13. $\frac{3}{10}$, 40%, 0.65, 80%
14. $\frac{1}{25}$, 9%, 20%, 0.27
15. $\frac{1}{8}$, 15%, 0.25, $\frac{27}{100}$
16. 95%
17. 20%
18. $\frac{37}{50}$
19. $\frac{13}{25}$
20. 86%
21. 76%
22. $\frac{5}{8}$
23. 0.12
24. 17%
25. 140%
26. $\frac{3}{8}$
27. 80%
28. $\frac{8}{25}$, 38%, 0.41
29. 0.63, $\frac{13}{20}$, 68%
30. 84%, $\frac{43}{50}$, $\frac{7}{8}$, 0.91
31. 0.15%, 0.015, $\frac{3}{20}$

32–34. See Additional Answers.

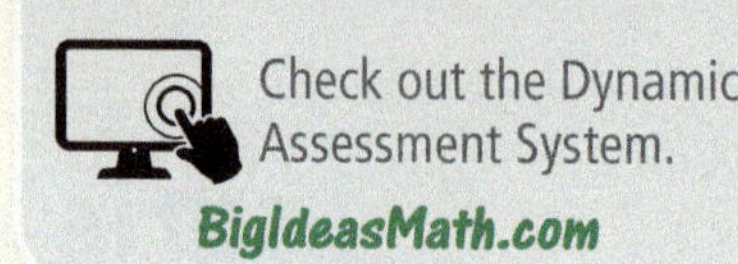

Assignment Guide and Concept Check

Scaffold assignments to support all students in their learning progression. The suggested assignments are a starting point. Continue to assign additional exercises and revisit with spaced practice to move every student toward proficiency.

Level	Assignment 1	Assignment 2
Emerging	3, 5, 9, 12, 14, 16, 25, 27, 28, 31	19, 33, 34, 35, 38, 39, 40, 41, 43
Proficient	3, 5, 9, 12, 14, 16, 19, 25, 28, 30	32, 35, 37, 38, 39, 40, 41, 42, 43
Advanced	3, 5, 9, 12, 14, 20, 22, 25, 32, 33	36, 38, 39, 40, 41, 42, 43, 44

- Assignment 1 is for use after students complete the Self-Assessment for Concepts & Skills.
- Assignment 2 is for use after students complete the Self-Assessment for Problem Solving.
- The red exercises can be used as a concept check.

Review & Refresh Prior Skills

Exercises 1–3 Writing Percents as Decimals
Exercises 4 and 5 Completing Ratio Tables
Exercises 6 and 7 Multiplying Decimals and Whole Numbers
Exercises 8 and 9 Multiplying Decimals
Exercises 10–12 Finding the GCF

Common Errors

- **Exercises 16–27** Students may try to order the numbers without converting them, or convert them mentally and make a mistake. Remind students that they must first convert all the numbers to one form and they should show their work to ensure accurate conversions.

4.3 Practice

Go to **BigIdeasMath.com** to get HELP with solving the exercises.

Review & Refresh

Write the percent as a decimal.

1. 12% **2.** 98.37% **3.** 0.046%

Find the missing value(s) in the ratio table. Then write the equivalent ratios.

4.

Cashews	5	
Almonds	4	36

5.

Cost (dollars)	2		13.5
Time (minutes)	50	75	

Multiply.

6. $\begin{array}{r} 5.3 \\ \times\ 6 \\ \hline \end{array}$ **7.** $\begin{array}{r} 18.1 \\ \times\ \ 9 \\ \hline \end{array}$ **8.** 12.43×1.51 **9.** 0.852×6.7

Find the GCF of the numbers.

10. 15, 36 **11.** 51, 85 **12.** 88, 112

Concepts, Skills, & Problem Solving

USING A NUMBER LINE **Use a number line to order the numbers from least to greatest.** (See Exploration 1, p. 175.)

13. 80%, 0.65, $\frac{3}{10}$, 40% **14.** 0.27, 20%, $\frac{1}{25}$, 9% **15.** $\frac{1}{8}$, 0.25, 15%, $\frac{27}{100}$

COMPARING NUMBERS **Tell which number is greater.**

16. 0.9, 95% **17.** 20%, 0.02 **18.** $\frac{37}{50}$, 37% **19.** 50%, $\frac{13}{25}$

20. 0.086, 86% **21.** 76%, 0.67 **22.** 60%, $\frac{5}{8}$ **23.** 0.12, 1.2%

24. 17%, $\frac{4}{25}$ **25.** 140%, 0.14 **26.** $\frac{3}{8}$, 30% **27.** 80%, $\frac{7}{10}$

ORDERING NUMBERS **Order the numbers from least to greatest.**

28. 38%, $\frac{8}{25}$, 0.41 **29.** 68%, 0.63, $\frac{13}{20}$

30. $\frac{43}{50}$, 0.91, $\frac{7}{8}$, 84% **31.** 0.15%, $\frac{3}{20}$, 0.015

32. 2.62, $2\frac{2}{5}$, 26.8%, 2.26, 271% **33.** $\frac{87}{200}$, 0.44, 43.7%, $\frac{21}{50}$

34. MP **NUMBER SENSE** You answer 21 out of 25 questions correctly on a test. Do you reach your goal of answering at least 80% of the questions correctly?

35. MP **MODELING REAL LIFE** The table shows the approximate portions of the world population that live in four countries. Order the countries by population from least to greatest.

Country	Brazil	India	Russia	United States
Portion of World Population	2.8%	$\frac{7}{40}$	$\frac{1}{50}$	0.044

MP **PRECISION** **Order the numbers from least to greatest.**

36. 66.1%, 0.66, $\frac{133}{200}$, 0.667

37. $\frac{111}{500}$, 21%, 0.211, $\frac{11}{50}$

MATCHING **Tell which letter shows the graph of the number.**

38. $\frac{2}{5}$

39. 45.2%

40. 0.435

41. $\frac{89}{200}$

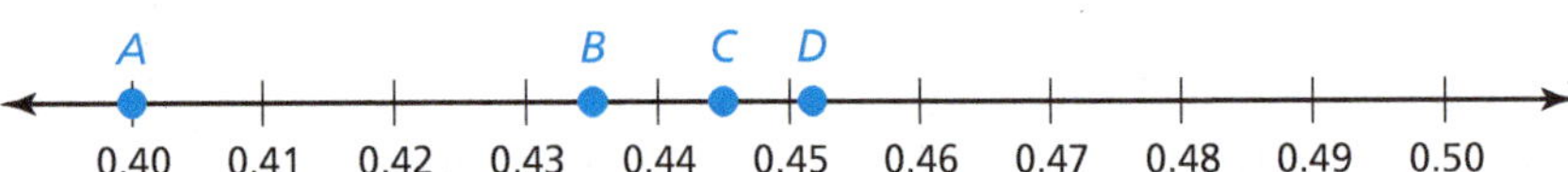

42. MP **PRECISION** The Tour de France is a bicycle road race. The whole race is made up of 21 small races called *stages*. The table shows how several stages compare to the whole Tour de France in a recent year. Order the stages by distance from shortest to longest.

Stage	1	7	8	17	21
Portion of Total Distance	$\frac{11}{200}$	0.044	$\frac{6}{125}$	0.06	4%

43. MP **PRECISION** The table shows the portions of the day that several animals sleep.

a. Order the animals by sleep time from least to greatest.

b. Estimate the portion of the day that you sleep.

c. Where do you fit on the ordered list?

Animal	Portion of Day Sleeping
Dolphin	0.433
Lion	56.3%
Rabbit	$\frac{19}{40}$
Squirrel	$\frac{31}{50}$
Tiger	65.8%

44. MP **NUMBER SENSE** Tell what whole number you can substitute for a in each list so the numbers are ordered from least to greatest. If there is none, explain why.

a. $\frac{1}{a}$, $\frac{a}{20}$, 28%

b. $\frac{3}{a}$, $\frac{a}{5}$, 75%

Mini-Assessment

Tell which number is greater.

1. 27%, 0.48 0.48

2. $\frac{3}{4}$, 76% 76%

Order the numbers from least to greatest.

3. $\frac{5}{8}$, 60%, 0.65 60%, $\frac{5}{8}$, 0.65

4. 1.15, $\frac{1}{5}$, 15%, 151% 15%, $\frac{1}{5}$, 1.15, 151%

5. You, your aunt, and a friend each take the same online trivia quiz. You answer 74% of the questions correctly, your aunt answers 0.82 of the questions correctly, and your friend answers $\frac{20}{25}$ of the questions correctly. Who answered the fewest questions correctly? you

Section Resources

Surface Level	Deep Level
Resources by Chapter • Extra Practice • Reteach • Puzzle Time Student Journal • Self-Assessment • Practice Differentiating the Lesson Tutorial Videos Skills Review Handbook Skills Trainer	Resources by Chapter • Enrichment and Extension Graphic Organizers Dynamic Assessment System • Section Practice

Concepts, Skills, & Problem Solving

35. Russia, Brazil, United States, India

36. 0.66, 66.1%, $\frac{133}{200}$, 0.667

37. 21%, 0.211, $\frac{11}{50}$, $\frac{111}{500}$

38. *A*

39. *D*

40. *B*

41. *C*

42. 21, 7, 8, 1, 17

43. **a.** dolphin, rabbit, lion, squirrel, tiger

b. *Sample answer:* 33%

c. first

44. **a.** 5

b. There is none; $\frac{3}{a}$ is less than 75% when a is greater than 4, but when a is greater than 4, $\frac{a}{5}$ is greater than 75%.

Learning Target

Find a percent of a quantity and solve percent problems.

Success Criteria

- Represent percents of numbers using an equation, a ratio table, or a model.
- Find percents of numbers.
- Find the whole given a part and the percent.

Warm Up

Cumulative, vocabulary, and prerequisite skills practice opportunities are available in the *Resources by Chapter* or at *BigIdeasMath.com.*

ELL Support

Explain that a percent, similar to a fraction, represents the value of a part-to-whole ratio where the whole is 100. Remind students that the word *whole* has the homophone *hole*, which has a very different meaning. *Whole* means an entire quantity, while a *hole* is an empty space. It is important to listen to everything that is said to determine which word is being used.

Exploration 1

a–b. See Additional Answers.

Exploration 2

a. *Sample answer:* Multiply or divide by 0.75.

b. *Sample answer:* Write 80 under 100%, divide the model into four parts.

Laurie's Notes

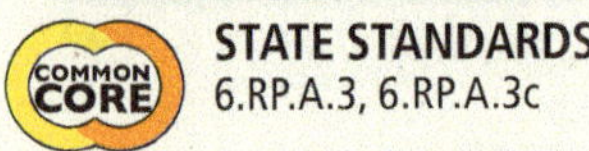

Preparing to Teach

- After comparing percents, fractions, and decimals in the previous section, students will now extend their understanding to solving percent problems. The goal for students is to use models and ratio tables to make sense of percent problems and determine the reasonableness of their answers.
- **MP1 Make Sense of Problems and Persevere in Solving Them:** All students will benefit from using the percent bar model as a visual means to think about percents. Modeling helps students conceptualize the problem and take the next step.

Motivate

? Draw a 24-tower showing different ways 24 can be divided into groups of equal size. Then ask:

- "What is $\frac{1}{2}$ of 24?" 12
- "What is $\frac{3}{4}$ of 24?" 18
- "What is $\frac{5}{6}$ of 24?" 20

12			12		
8		8		8	
6		6	6		6
4	4	4	4	4	4

Exploration 1

- This exploration uses percent bar models that may remind students of tape diagrams and double number lines. The labels on the bottom and top represent a quantity and its associated percent. Notice in part (a) that 100% corresponds to 60 and 0% corresponds to 0.

? "What is 50% of 60?" 30 "How do you know?" 30 corresponds to the 50% mark and half of 60 is 30. "What percent corresponds to 15? Explain." 25%; 15 is half of 30 and 25% is half of 50%. Continue this type of questioning as students find the missing values.

- You will find that most students have an intuitive understanding of many of the numbers on the models. Take advantage of this understanding to build an awareness that it is not only about halves and halves of halves (quarters).

  Discuss the position of $33\frac{1}{3}\%$, which is $\frac{1}{3}$ of the way from 0% to 100%.
- Part (b) allows students the freedom to choose their own percents and corresponding numbers. Listen to their explanations. If they are using the same percents as in part (a), ask them to challenge themselves by finding percents such as 5% or 10%.

Exploration 2

- This exploration adds context to the percent bar model. In part (a), students should discuss that 75% represents the discounted price and 100% represents the full price. Listen for understanding that you know one of the prices and you need to find the other.
- In part (b), listen for understanding that writing $80 below 100% on the percent bar model leads to finding the dollar amount that corresponds to 75%.

4.4 Solving Percent Problems

Learning Target: Find a percent of a quantity and solve percent problems.

Success Criteria:
- I can represent percents of numbers using an equation, a ratio table, or a model.
- I can find percents of numbers.
- I can find the whole given a part and the percent.

EXPLORATION 1 Using Percent Models

Work with a partner.

a. Find the missing values. What does the model represent?

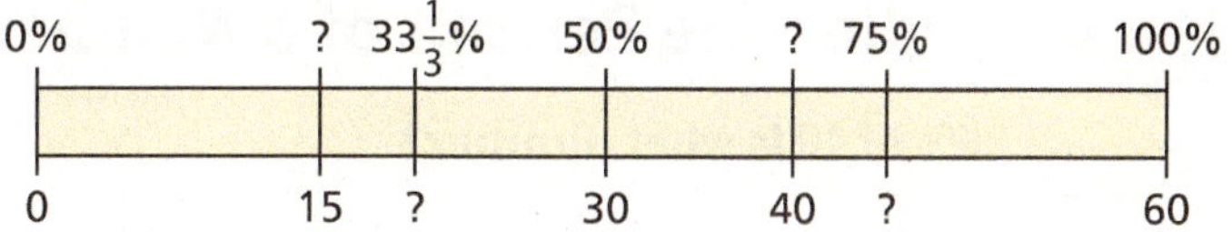

b. Label at least three percents and their corresponding numbers on the model below. How do you know you are correct?

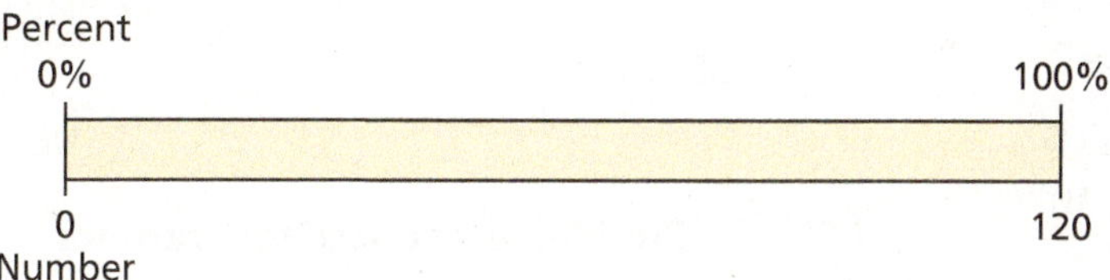

EXPLORATION 2 Solving a Percent Problem

Work with a partner. You purchase a national parks annual pass for 75% of the full price of the pass.

a. Suppose you know the full price or the discounted price. How can you find the other price? Compare your answers with other students in your class.

b. Suppose the full price of the pass is \$80. How can you use a percent model to find the purchase price?

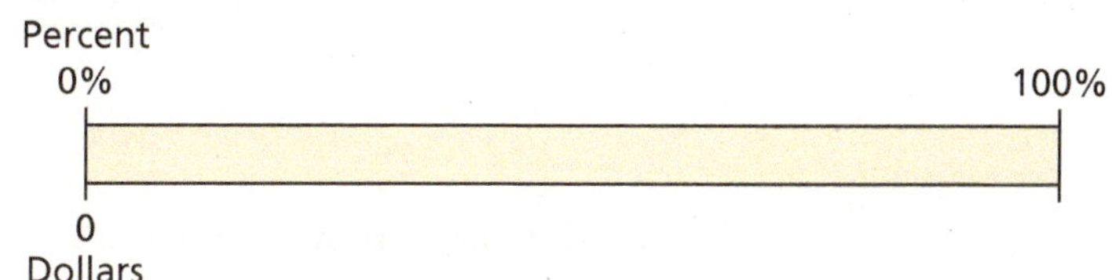

Math Practice

Consider Simpler Forms

Suppose you know 1% and 10% of the full price. How can you use these values to find the purchase price?

4.4 Lesson

Key Idea

Finding the Percent of a Number

Words Write the percent as a fraction or decimal. Then multiply by the whole. The percent times the whole equals the part.

Numbers 20% of 60 is 12.

$0.2 \times 60 = 12$

$\frac{1}{5} \times 60 = 12$

Model

Percent: 0% 20% 40% 60% 80% 100%

Number: 0 12 24 36 48 60

EXAMPLE 1 Finding the Percent of a Number

25% of 40 is what number?

$25\% \text{ of } 40 = \frac{1}{4} \times 40$ Write the percent as a fraction and multiply.

$= \frac{40}{4} = 10$ Simplify.

Percent: 0% 25% 50% 75% 100%

Number: 0 10 20 30 40

So, 25% of 40 is 10.

You can use mental math to check your answer in Example 1.
10% of 40 = 4
5% of 40 = 2
So, 25% of 40 is
4 + 4 + 2 = 10.

Try It Find the percent of the number.

1. 90% of 20

2. 75% of 32

Because $n\%$ means n per 100, you can also solve percent problems using part-to-whole ratios.

EXAMPLE 2 Finding the Percent of a Number Using a Ratio Table

60% of 150 is what number?

Use a ratio table to find the part. Let one row be the *part*, and let the other row be the *whole*. Find an equivalent ratio with 150 as the whole.

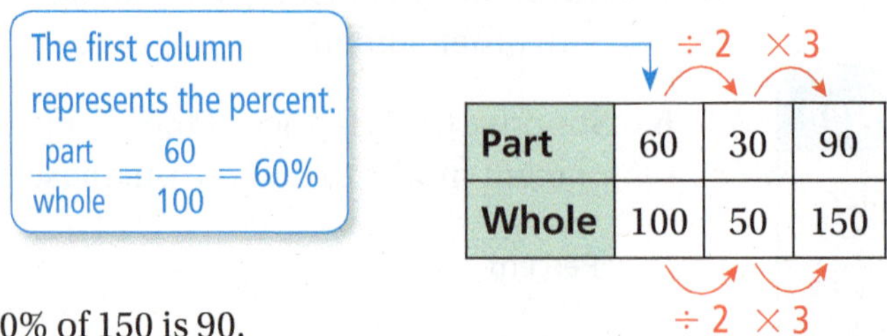

Part	60	30	90
Whole	100	50	150

So, 60% of 150 is 90.

Try It Find the percent of the number.

3. 10% of 110

4. 30% of 75

Laurie's Notes

Scaffolding Instruction

- In the exploration, students developed their number sense by using percent models to find percents of wholes and missing percents.
- **Emerging:** Students may still be developing confidence in converting between fractions, decimals, and percents. Visual representations of percent problems support their understanding of the problem. Going through each example and making sense of the model is necessary.
- **Proficient:** Students may be confident using a percent bar model to represent a percent problem. Can they use an equation to represent the problem? After reviewing the Key Ideas, have students self-assess using the Try It exercises.
- Guided instruction may be needed to solve percent problems in which the whole is unknown. This is a long lesson, so avoid rushing through the content.

Key Idea

- In previous sections, students wrote percents as fractions and decimals. This section shows percents written as decimals or simplified fractions in one step. Spend time showing the simplification if necessary.
- Be sure to emphasize "the *percent* times the *whole* equals the *part*."
- **Connection:** Connect this idea to multiplying a fraction by a whole number.

EXAMPLE 1

? "What is 25% as a fraction?" $\frac{1}{4}$ "How can you find $\frac{1}{4}$ of 40?" Multiply $\frac{1}{4}$ and 40.

- Discuss the percent bar model. Each part, $\frac{1}{4}$ or 25%, represents 10.
- Discuss the push-pin note. Percent benchmarks help students recognize reasonable answers. Similarly, if students know that 10% of a number is 8, then 30% of the number is 8 + 8 + 8, or 24.

EXAMPLE 2

- This example helps students apply and connect the skill of working with ratio tables to finding the percent of a number.
- Draw the ratio table and identify the first column as 60% (60 is the part and 100 is the whole). The goal is to make the last column have a whole of 150.
- Point out that because the columns of the tables show equivalent ratios, the top number in each column is 60% of the bottom number.
- **MP5 Use Appropriate Tools Strategically:** Have students check Example 1 using a ratio table and check Example 2 using a fraction.

Try It

Think-Pair-Share: Have students read each exercise independently, and then work in pairs to model and solve them. After completing the exercises, the pair should compare their answers with another pair and discuss any discrepancies. Listen for understanding of the first two success criteria.

Scaffold instruction to support all students in their learning. Learning is individualized and you may want to group students differently as they move in and out of these levels with each skill and concept. Student self-assessment and feedback help guide your instructional decisions about how and when to layer support for all students to become proficient learners.

Extra Example 1

80% of 75 is what number? 60

Try It

1. 18
2. 24

Extra Example 2

40% of 200 is what number? 80

Try It

3. 11
4. $22\frac{1}{2}$

Extra Example 3

60% of what number is 42? 70

ELL Support

Have ELLs work in a group to complete Try It Exercises 5 and 6. Demonstrate the intermediate steps that are not shown in Example 3, such as $15\% = \frac{15}{100} = \frac{3}{20}$. To divide by a fraction, you multiply by its reciprocal. For example, $9 \div \frac{3}{20} = 9 \times \frac{20}{3}$. Provide support as needed.

Beginner: Write the answer and show work.

Intermediate: State the answer using a complete sentence. For example, "Fifteen percent of sixty is nine."

Advanced: Explain the steps.

Try It

5. 60 **6.** 200

Extra Example 4

140% of what number is 126? 90

Try It

7. 50 **8.** 40

Laurie's Notes

Key Idea

? "What are the related division equations for $3 \times 12 = 36$?" $36 \div 3 = 12$ and $36 \div 12 = 3$

- Say, "In Examples 1 and 2, you found the percent of a number using *percent* × *whole* = *part*. Now, you will find the whole using the related division equation, *part* ÷ *percent* = *whole*."
- Write the Key Idea. Emphasize the original multiplication equation and the related division equation.
- Students should recognize that the percent can be represented as a fraction or a decimal.

EXAMPLE 3

? "Will the answer be *greater than 48* or *less than 48*? Explain." greater than 48; If 50% of a number is 48, then the number must be greater than 48.

"How do you write 50% as a fraction in simplest form?" $\frac{1}{2}$

- Write the word equation: *part* ÷ *percent* = *whole*. Then work through the example as shown.
- **MP5 Use Appropriate Tools Strategically:** Draw the percent bar model. Each part (25%) represents 24, so two parts (50%) represent 48. The whole (100%) is 96. So, the answer is reasonable.

Try It

- Encourage students to make a model before writing a numerical expression. Can they estimate the answer?

EXAMPLE 4

- This example helps students apply and connect the skill of working with ratio tables to finding the whole given the part and the percent.

? "Will the answer be *greater than 72* or *less than 72*? Explain." less than 72; If 120% of a number is 72, then the number must be less than 72 because 120% is greater than 100%.

- Draw the ratio table and identify the first column as 120% (120 is the part and 100 is the whole). The goal is to make the last column have a part of 72.
- Work through the problem as shown, or have students suggest ways to create the ratio table.
- Point out that because the columns of the tables show equivalent ratios, the top number in each column is 120% of the bottom number.
- **MP5 Use Appropriate Tools Strategically:** Have students check Example 3 using a ratio table and check Example 4 using a fraction.

Try It

- **Chalkboard Splash:** Have students work in groups. Ask each group to send one person to the board and assign Exercise 8.

◉ Listen to students' conversations and check for understanding of the third success criterion.

You can use a related division equation to find the whole given the part and the percent.

Key Idea

Finding the Whole

Write the percent as a fraction or decimal. Then divide the part by the fraction or decimal.

Words The part divided by the percent equals the whole.

Numbers 20% of 60 is 12.

$$\frac{1}{5} \times 60 = 12 \longrightarrow 12 \div \frac{1}{5} = 60$$

Multiplication equation — Related division equation

EXAMPLE 3 Finding the Whole

50% of what number is 48?

The question can be represented by the multiplication equation $50\% \times \square = 48$. By definition, $\square = 48 \div 50\%$.

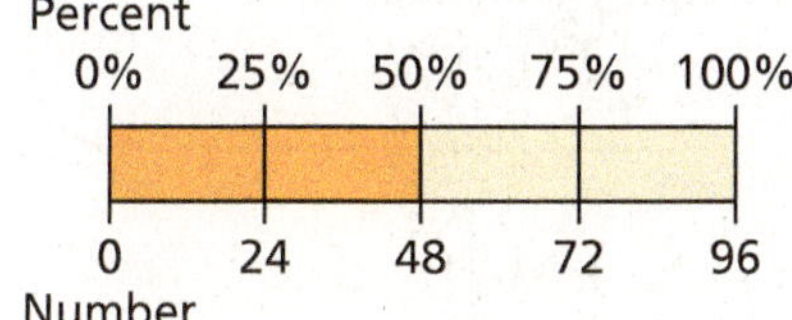

$$48 \div 50\% = 48 \div \frac{1}{2}$$ Write the percent as a fraction.

$$= 96$$ Multiply 48 by the reciprocal of $\frac{1}{2}$, which is 2.

So, 50% of 96 is 48.

Try It **Find the whole.**

5. 15% of what number is 9?

6. 5% of what number is 10?

EXAMPLE 4 Finding the Whole Using a Ratio Table

120% of what number is 72?

Use a ratio table to find the whole. Find an equivalent ratio with 72 as the part.

The first column represents the percent. $\frac{\text{part}}{\text{whole}} = \frac{120}{100} = 120\%$

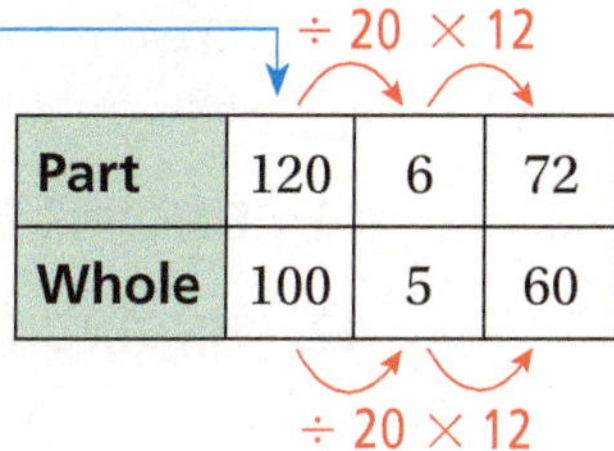

Part	120	6	72
Whole	100	5	60

So, 120% of 60 is 72.

Try It **Find the whole.**

7. 62% of what number is 31?

8. 125% of what number is 50?

EXAMPLE 5 Solving a Percent Problem

The width of a rectangular room is 80% of its length. What is the area of the room?

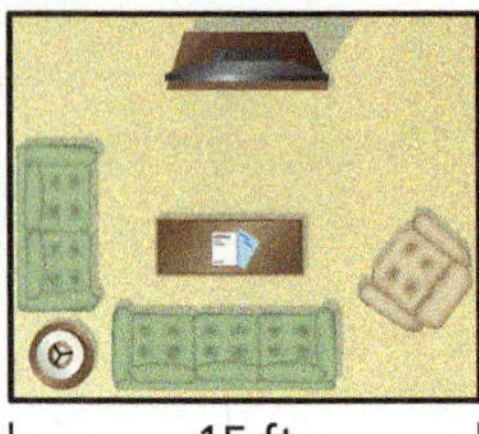

Find 80% of 15 feet to determine the width of the room.

80% of $15 = 0.8 \times 15$

$= 12$

The width is 12 feet.

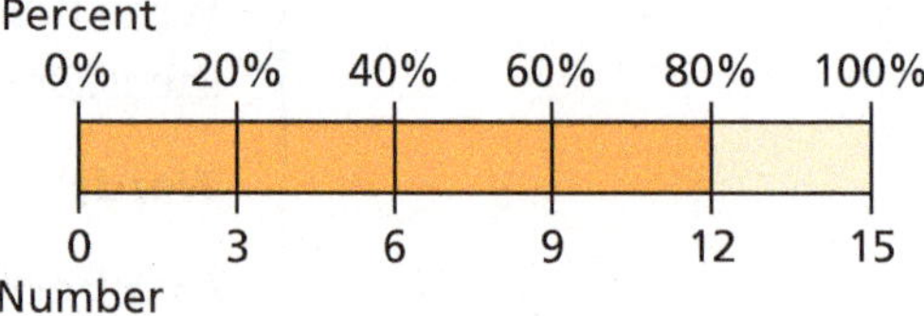

Use the formula for the area of a rectangle.

$\text{Area} = \ell w$

$= 15(12)$

$= 180$

So, the area of the room is 180 square feet.

Try It

9. The width of a rectangular stage is 55% of its length. The stage is 120 feet long. What is the area of the stage?

Self-Assessment for Concepts & Skills

Solve each exercise. Then rate your understanding of the success criteria in your journal.

10. **DIFFERENT WORDS, SAME QUESTION** Which is different? Find "both" answers.

What is twenty percent of 30?	What is one-fifth of 30?
Twenty percent of what number is 30?	What is two-tenths of 30?

11. **FINDING THE PERCENT OF A NUMBER** Find 12% of 75.

12. **FINDING THE WHOLE** 35% of what number is 21?

13. MP **NUMBER SENSE** If 52 is 130% of a number, is the number greater than or less than 52? Explain.

14. MP **STRUCTURE** How can you find 10% of any number without multiplying or dividing? Explain your reasoning.

Laurie's Notes

EXAMPLE 5

- ? "What information is given?" The length of the room is 15 feet and the width is 80% of the length.
- Write "80% of 15 = ?" and ask students what method(s) can be used to answer the question.
- **MP1 Make Sense of Problems and Persevere in Solving Them:** Students should know a variety of ways to find 80% of 15. It is important that students find an approach to solving a problem that makes sense.
- Students need a basic understanding that if the width is 80% of the length, the width is shorter than the length. This may not be obvious to all students.
- The percent bar model visually shows the 5 equal parts of 15. Students can use this model to find 20%, 40%, 60%, or 80% of 15.
- **MP6 Attend to Precision:** Be sure that students label the answer with the correct units. Note that the question asks for the area.

Try It

- **Turn and Talk:** Tell students to answer the question using a percent bar model and a decimal.
- You may need to remind students to find the area, not just the width. Read the question out loud to pairs who stop too soon.

Self-Assessment for Concepts & Skills

- Some of these exercises differ from the examples. Probe students' understanding of the concept of percents and the ways in which problems can be presented.
- In Exercise 10, do students comprehend the different ways in which a percent problem can be written? There are many ways of saying the same thing.
- Consider students' explanations in Exercise 13. Well-developed number sense allows students to quickly decide if the answer is greater than or less than the original number. Allow students who have mastered this understanding to explain to others who are struggling.
- ? Distribute *Response Cards* with A, B, and C to students. "Which percent representation do you find most helpful? Hold up A for *equation*, B for *ratio table*, or C for *bar model*." Student responses will provide insight into your students' stage of thinking.

ELL Support

Have students complete Exercises 11 and 12 with a partner. Have each pair display their answers on a whiteboard for your review. Then have two pairs form a group to discuss and complete Exercises 13 and 14. Have two groups compare their answers. If there is disagreement, provide support.

The Success Criteria Self-Assessment chart can be found in the *Student Journal* or online at *BigIdeasMath.com*.

Extra Example 5

The length of a rectangular garden is 225% of its width. The width of the garden is 4 meters. What is the area of the garden? 36 square meters

Try It

9. 7920 ft^2

Formative Assessment Tip

Response Cards

This technique is used as a quick check to see whether students' knowledge of a skill, technique, or procedure is correct. Students are given cards at the beginning of class that are held up in front of them in response to a question. The cards can be prepared in advance with particular responses, such as A, B, C, and D; or 1, 2, and 3; or True and False. The cards can also be left blank for students to write their responses on. If you plan to use the cards multiple times, consider laminating them. *Response Cards* give all students the opportunity to participate in the lesson, because you are soliciting information from everyone and not just those who raise their hands. Because the cards are held facing the teacher, it is a private way to gather quick information about students' understanding.

Self-Assessment for Concepts & Skills

10. Twenty percent of what number is 30?; 150; 6

11. 9 **12.** 60

13. less than 52; 52 is more than 100% of the number.

14. Move the decimal point of the number one place to the left; *Sample answer:* Multiplying by 10% is the same as dividing by 10.

Extra Example 6

Using coupons, you spend $135 grocery shopping. This is 75% of the total retail price of the groceries. How much more would you have spent if you had not used the coupons?

A. $45.00 **B.** $75.00

C. $101.25 **D.** $180.00

A

Self-Assessment *for Problem Solving*

15. $70

16. $70

17. $18

Learning Target

Find a percent of a quantity and solve percent problems.

Success Criteria

- Represent percents of numbers using an equation, a ratio table, or a model.
- Find percents of numbers.
- Find the whole given a part and the percent.

Laurie's Notes

EXAMPLE 6

- It helps to know a little about online auctions. Bidders enter secret maximum bids. Through automated bidding, the winning bid is greater than the second greatest maximum bid but often less than the winner's maximum bid. This may help students understand that the winning bid is the part and the maximum bid is the whole.
- Read the problem and guide students through the problem-solving plan.
- Say, "$120 is the part and your maximum bid is the whole."
- **MP4 Model with Mathematics:** Students should know a variety of ways to find a number such that 120 is 60% of that number. It is important that students find an approach to solving a problem that makes sense.

? "Is $200 the answer to the question? Explain." No, the question asks how much *more* you were willing to pay for the tickets than you actually paid.

Self-Assessment for Problem Solving

- Encourage students to use a Four Square to complete these exercises. Until students become comfortable with the problem-solving plan, they may only be ready to complete the first square.
- Have students work in pairs or groups.
- Percents are very common in consumer applications. The context may not be understood by all students. This is often true with problems about sale items. Be sure students understand the context for each exercise before they make a plan.
- Remind students that the first answer they need to find may not be the answer to the actual question.
- Some students may use the guess-and-check method. Although this is not an efficient method, if they can find the answer and explain the process, it does show some measure of understanding.
- **MP2 Reason Abstractly and Quantitatively:** Students can use reasoning skills to make sense of contextual problems, and then use computational skills to solve them. The quantities and operations have meanings that are evident in the students' work.

The Success Criteria Self-Assessment chart can be found in the *Student Journal* or online at *BigIdeasMath.com*.

Closure

- Use mental math to find the following percents of 120: 10%, 15%, and 20%. 12, 18, 24

EXAMPLE 6 Modeling Real Life

You win an online auction for concert tickets. Your winning bid is 60% of your maximum bid. How much more were you willing to pay for the tickets than you actually paid?

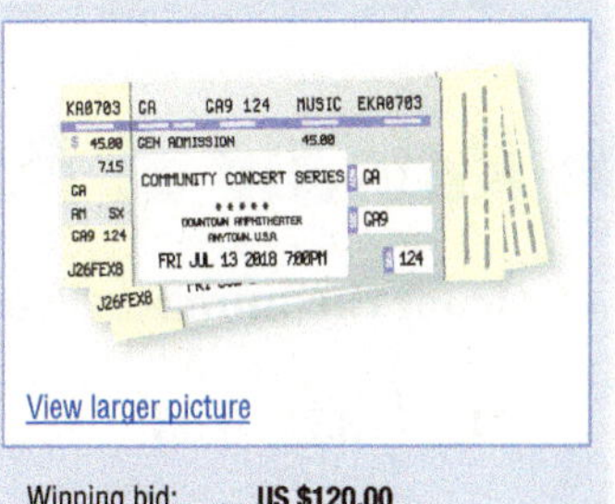

A. \$72 **B.** \$80

C. \$120 **D.** \$200

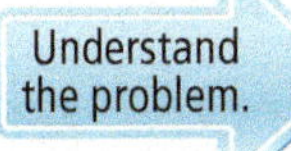

You are given the winning bid and the percent of your maximum bid represented by the winning bid. You are asked to find how much more you were willing to pay for the tickets than you actually paid.

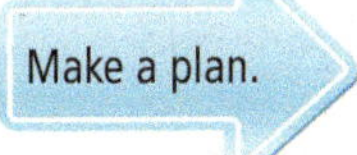

Your maximum bid is the whole and your winning bid is the part. Create a model using the fact that 60% of the whole is \$120 to find the maximum bid. Then subtract the winning bid from the maximum bid to determine how much more you were willing to pay.

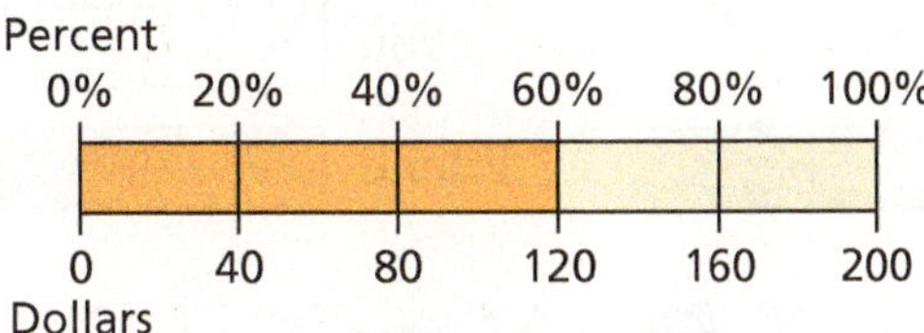

Your maximum bid is \$200, and your winning bid is \$120. So, you were willing to pay $\$200 - \$120 = \$80$ more for the tickets.

 The correct answer is **B**.

> **Look Back**
> Verify that the additional \$80 you were willing to pay is $100\% - 60\% = 40\%$ of the maximum bid.
>
> The model shows that 40% of the maximum bid is \$80. ✓

Self-Assessment for Problem Solving

Solve each exercise. Then rate your understanding of the success criteria in your journal.

15. You raise \$420 during a fundraising event. The amount of money that you raise is 120% of your goal. How much more did you raise than your goal?

16. A shirt is on sale for 60% of the original price. The original price is \$28 more than the sale price. What was the original price?

17. You have a meal at a restaurant. The sales tax is 8%. You leave a tip for the waitress that is 20% of the pretax price. You spend a total of \$23.04. What is the pretax price of the meal?

4.4 Practice

Review & Refresh

Order the numbers from least to greatest.

1. $\frac{1}{8}$, 35%, 0.33
2. 0.3, $\frac{9}{25}$, 0.35, 33%
3. $\frac{13}{50}$, 22%, 0.28, $\frac{1}{5}$, 0.41

Write the percent as a fraction or mixed number in simplest form.

4. 65%
5. 0.45%
6. 110%

Divide.

7. $19.2 \div 1.6$
8. $0.61\overline{)0.244}$
9. $0.9\overline{)0.558}$
10. $4.65 \div 0.003$

The tape diagram represents the ratio of the time you spend online to the time your friend spends online. You are online for 30 minutes. How many minutes does your friend spend online?

11. 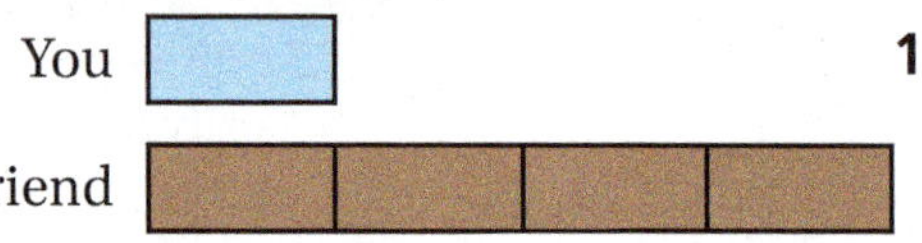 You [1 part]
    Friend [4 parts]

12. 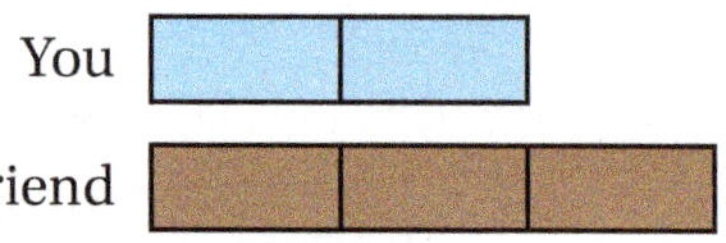 You [2 parts]
    Friend [3 parts]

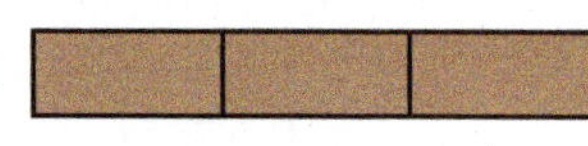

Concepts, Skills, & Problem Solving

MP USING TOOLS **An annual pass to a park costs \$120. Use a percent model to find the given percent of the full price of the annual pass.** (See Exploration 2, p. 181.)

13. 25%
14. 50%
15. 200%

FINDING THE PERCENT OF A NUMBER **Find the percent of the number. Explain your method.**

16. 20% of 60
17. 10% of 40
18. 50% of 70
19. 30% of 30
20. 10% of 90
21. 15% of 20
22. 25% of 50
23. 5% of 60
24. 30% of 70
25. 75% of 48
26. 45% of 45
27. 92% of 19
28. 40% of 60
29. 38% of 22
30. 70% of 20
31. 87% of 55
32. 140% of 60
33. 120% of 33
34. 175% of 54
35. 250% of 146

36. **MP MODELING REAL LIFE** The tail of the spider monkey is 64% of the length shown. What is the length of the tail?

37. **MP PROBLEM SOLVING** A family pays \$45 each month for cable television. The cost increases 7%.
    a. How many dollars is the increase?
    b. What is the new monthly cost?

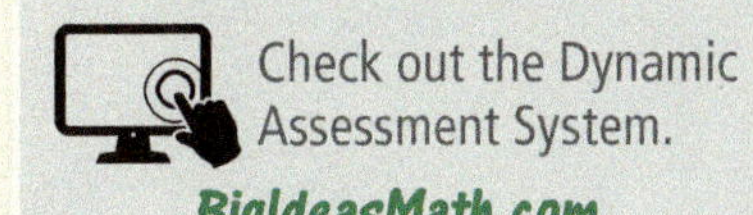

Assignment Guide and Concept Check

Scaffold assignments to support all students in their learning progression. The suggested assignments are a starting point. Continue to assign additional exercises and revisit with spaced practice to move every student toward proficiency.

Level	Assignment 1	Assignment 2
Emerging	3, 6, 10, 12, 13, 17, 18, 32, 39, 40, 46	15, 36, 37, 38, 42, 49, 50, 55, 61
Proficient	3, 6, 10, 12, 13, 21, 23, 33, 40, 42, 48	15, 38, 49, 50, 53, 58, 59, 61, 62, 64
Advanced	3, 6, 10, 12, 13, 21, 23, 35, 40, 44, 48	38, 49, 53, 57, 60, 62, 63, 64, 65, 66, 67

- Assignment 1 is for use after students complete the Self-Assessment for Concepts & Skills.
- Assignment 2 is for use after students complete the Self-Assessment for Problem Solving.
- The red exercises can be used as a concept check.

Review & Refresh Prior Skills

Exercises 1–3 Ordering Numbers
Exercises 4–6 Writing Percents as Fractions
Exercises 7–10 Dividing Decimals
Exercises 11 and 12 Interpreting a Tape Diagram

Common Errors

- **Exercises 32–35** Students often struggle with percents greater than 100%. They may find an answer significantly greater than or less than what they should. Encourage students to estimate their answers first and remind them that percents greater than 100% will have answers that are greater than the original number.

Review & Refresh

1. $\frac{1}{8}$, 0.33, 35%

2. 0.3, 33%, 0.35, $\frac{9}{25}$

3. $\frac{1}{5}$, 22%, $\frac{13}{50}$, 0.28, 0.41

4. $\frac{13}{20}$ **5.** $\frac{9}{2000}$

6. $1\frac{1}{10}$ **7.** 12

8. 0.4 **9.** 0.62

10. 1550 **11.** 120

12. 45

Concepts, Skills, & Problem Solving

13. \$30 **14.** \$60

15. \$240 **16.** 12

17. 4 **18.** 35

19. 9 **20.** 9

21. 3 **22.** 12.5

23. 3 **24.** 21

25. 36 **26.** 20.25

27. 17.48 **28.** 24

29. 8.36 **30.** 14

31. 47.85 **32.** 84

33. 39.6 **34.** 94.5

35. 365 **36.** 35.2 in.

37. a. \$3.15

b. \$48.15

Concepts, Skills, & Problem Solving

38. yes; $40\% = \frac{2}{5}$

39. 140

40. 90

41. 84

42. 36

43. 80

44. 20

45. 25

46. 20

47. 20

48. 24

49. no; $5 \div 20\% = 5 \div \frac{1}{5} = 25$

50. $12

51. 18

52. 75 pounds

53. 125,000

54. 20-fl oz bottle; It costs $0.29 per fluid ounce, and the other bottle costs $0.32 per fluid ounce.

38. **YOU BE THE TEACHER** Your friend finds 40% of 75. Is your friend correct? Explain your reasoning.

$$40\% \text{ of } 75 = \frac{2}{5} \times 75 = 30$$

FINDING THE WHOLE **Find the whole. Explain your method.**

39. 10% of what number is 14?
40. 20% of what number is 18?
41. 25% of what number is 21?
42. 75% of what number is 27?
43. 15% of what number is 12?
44. 85% of what number is 17?
45. 140% of what number is 35?
46. 160% of what number is 32?
47. 125% of what number is 25?
48. 175% of what number is 42?

49. **YOU BE THE TEACHER** Your friend answers the question "20% of what number is 5?" Is your friend correct? Explain your reasoning.

$$5 \div 20\% = \frac{5}{20} = \frac{1}{4}$$

THE PASTA BOWL
dine-in, takeout, or delivery
Grand Opening SPECIAL
25% OFF

50. **PROBLEM SOLVING** You have a coupon for a restaurant. You save $3 on a meal. What was the original cost of the meal?

51. **PROBLEM SOLVING** The results of a survey are shown at the right. In the survey, 12 students said that they would like to learn French. How many of the students surveyed would like to learn Spanish?

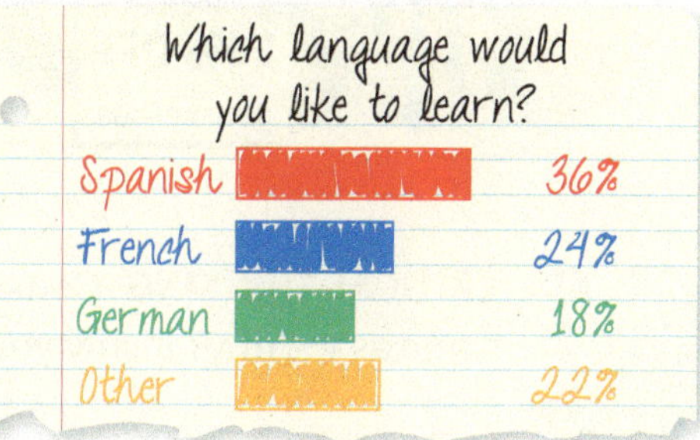

52. **MODELING REAL LIFE** A sixth grader weighs 90 pounds, which is 120% of what he weighed in fourth grade. How much did he weigh in fourth grade?

53. **LOGIC** In an asteroid field, 75% of the asteroids are *carbonaceous* asteroids. There are 375,000 carbonaceous asteroids in the asteroid field. How many asteroids are *not* carbonaceous?

54. **DIG DEEPER!** A bottle contains 20 fluid ounces of lotion and sells for $5.80. The 20-fluid-ounce bottle contains 125% of the lotion in the next smallest size, which sells for $5.12. Which is the better buy? Explain.

COMPARING PERCENTS **Copy and complete the statement using <, >, or = .**

55. 80% of 60 ☐ 60% of 80

56. 20% of 30 ☐ 30% of 40

57. 120% of 5 ☐ 0.8% of 250

58. 85% of 40 ☐ 25% of 136

59. **TIME** How many minutes is 40% of 2 hours?

60. **LENGTH** How many inches is 78% of 3 feet?

61. **GEOMETRY** The width of the rectangle is 75% of its length.

a. What is the area of the rectangle?

b. The length of the rectangle is doubled. What percent of the length is the width now? Explain your reasoning.

62. **MP PRECISION** To pass inspection, a new basketball should bounce between 68% and 75% of the starting height. A new ball is dropped from 6 feet and bounces back 4 feet 1 inch. Does the ball pass inspection? Explain.

63. **MP REPEATED REASONING** You know that 15% of a number n is 12. How can you use this to find 30% of n? 45% of n? Explain.

64. **MP REASONING** You have a coupon for 10% off the sale price of a surfboard. Which is the better buy? Explain your reasoning.

- 40% off the regular price
- 30% off the regular price and then 10% off the sale price

65. **CRITICAL THINKING** Consider two different numbers x and y. Is x% of y the same as y% of x? Justify your answer.

66. **GEOMETRY** Square $ABCD$ and Square $EFGH$ both have side lengths of 8 inches. The squares overlap and form Rectangle $ABGH$, which has a length of 10 inches. What percent of Rectangle $ABGH$ is shaded purple?

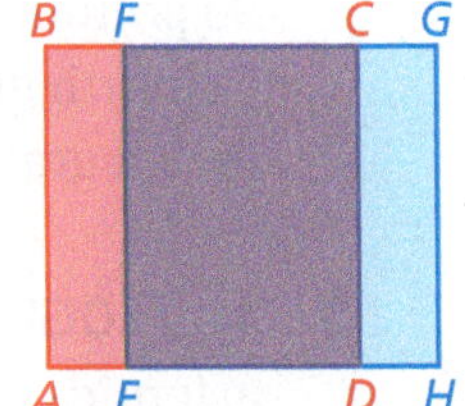

67. **DIG DEEPER!** On three 150-point geography tests, you earned grades of 88%, 94%, and 90%. The final test is worth 250 points. What *percent* do you need on the final to earn 93% of the total points on all tests?

Common Errors

- **Exercises 59 and 60** Students may forget to convert the units after they find the percent. Remind them to read the question carefully.

Mini-Assessment

Find the percent of the number.

1. 15% of 70 10.5
2. 65% of 80 52
3. 150% of 88 132
4. 120% of what number is 60? 50
5. How many inches is 110% of 6 feet? 79.2

Section Resources

Surface Level	Deep Level
Resources by Chapter • Extra Practice • Reteach • Puzzle Time Student Journal • Self-Assessment • Practice Differentiating the Lesson Tutorial Videos Skills Review Handbook Skills Trainer	Resources by Chapter • Enrichment and Extension Graphic Organizers Dynamic Assessment System • Section Practice
Transfer Level	
Dynamic Assessment System • End-of-Chapter Quiz	Assessment Book • End-of-Chapter Quiz

Concepts, Skills, & Problem Solving

55. $=$
56. $<$
57. $>$
58. $=$
59. 48
60. 28.08
61. a. 432 in.^{2}
    b. 37.5%; The width is 18 inches, and $\frac{18}{48} = 37.5\%$.
62. yes; The ball must bounce back to between $4\frac{2}{25}$ feet and $4\frac{1}{2}$ feet. It bounced back to $4\frac{1}{12}$ feet, so it passes.
63. *Sample answer:* Because $30\% = 2 \times 15\%$, 30% of $n = 2 \times 12 = 24$; Because $45\% = 3 \times 15\%$, 45% of $n = 3 \times 12 = 36$.
64. 40% off the regular price; The price with 40% off the regular price is \$90. The price with 30% off the regular price and then 10% off the sale price is \$94.50.
65. yes; $\frac{x}{100} \cdot y = \frac{y}{100} \cdot x$
66. 60%
67. 97.2%

Skills Needed

Exercise 1

- Using a Tape Diagram
- Writing Percents as Fractions

Exercise 2

- Finding Percents
- Interpreting Ratios
- Writing Fractions as Percents

Exercise 3

- Dividing Whole Numbers
- Finding the Whole
- Multiplying Whole Numbers

Exercise 4

- Adding Decimals
- Finding the Percent of a Number
- Multiplying Whole Numbers and Decimals
- Using Tape Diagrams

ELL Support

In Exercise 4, review the names of U.S. coins. Some students may not know that there is a dollar coin as well as a paper dollar. Tell students that they are worth the same amount.

Using the Problem-Solving Plan

1. Team A: 28 points, Team B: 35 points
2. 30%; *Sample answer:* 3 out of 10 guinea pigs are male, which is 30%.
3. 16; $21 \div 0.0625 = 336$ and $336 \div 21 = 16$.
4. $9.94

Performance Task

The *STEAM Video Performance Task* provides the opportunity for additional enrichment and greater depth of knowledge as students explore the mathematics of the chapter within a context tied to the chapter STEAM Video. The performance task and a detailed scoring rubric are provided at *BigIdeasMath.com.*

Laurie's Notes

Scaffolding Instruction

- The goal of this lesson is to help students become more comfortable with problem solving. The exercises on this page combine concepts of percents with prior skills from other chapters and courses. The solution for Exercise 1 is worked out below, to help you guide students through the problem-solving plan. Use the remaining class time to have students work on the other exercises.
- **Emerging:** The goal for these students is to feel comfortable with the problem-solving plan. Allow students to work in pairs to write the beginning steps of the problem-solving plan for Exercise 2. Keep in mind that some students may only be ready to do the first step.
- **Proficient:** Students may be able to work independently or in pairs to complete Exercises 2–4.
- Visit each pair to review their plan for each problem. Ask students to describe their plans.

Using the Problem-Solving Plan

Exercise 1

 **Understand the problem.** You know that Team A's score is 80% of Team B's score, and the total points scored is 63. You are asked to find the final score of the football game.

 **Make a plan.** Because 80% means 80 per 100, write the relationship between the scores of the teams as a ratio. Then represent the situation using a tape diagram. Use the total points to find the value of each part of the tape diagram and the final score of the game.

 **Solve and check.** Use the plan to solve the problem. Then check your solution.

- The ratio of the score of Team A (the part) to the score of Team B (the whole) is $\frac{80}{100}$, which simplifies to $\frac{4}{5}$.
- Using the simplified ratio, create a tape diagram.

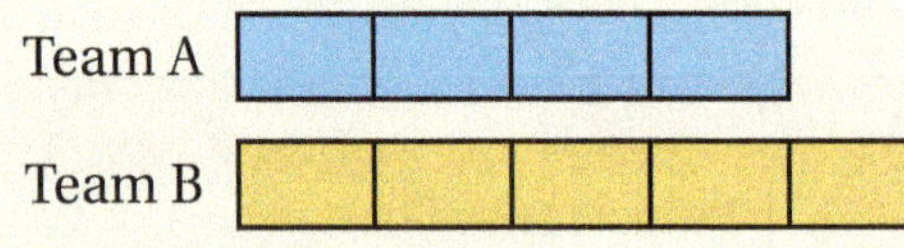

- Because there are 9 parts, you know that 1 part represents $63 \text{ points} \div 9 = 7 \text{ points}$.

  4 parts represent 4×7 points $=$ 28 points.

  5 parts represent 5×7 points $=$ 35 points.

  So, the final score of the game is Team A with 28 points and Team B with 35 points.

  Check: 80% of $35 = \frac{4}{5} \times 35 = \frac{140}{5} = 28$ ✓

  28 points + 35 points = 63 total points ✓

Connecting Concepts

Using the Problem-Solving Plan

1. During a football game, a total of 63 points are scored by the two teams. Team A scores 80% of the number of points that Team B scores. What is the final score of the game?

Understand the problem. You know that Team A's score is 80% of Team B's score, and the total points scored is 63. You are asked to find the final score of the football game.

Make a plan. Because 80% means 80 per 100, write the relationship between the scores of the teams as a ratio. Then represent the situation using a tape diagram. Use the total points to find the value of each part of the tape diagram and the final score of the game.

Solve and check. Use the plan to solve the problem. Then check your solution.

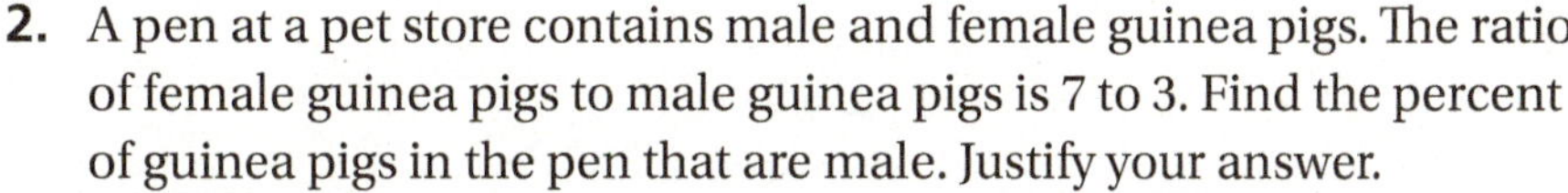

2. A pen at a pet store contains male and female guinea pigs. The ratio of female guinea pigs to male guinea pigs is 7 to 3. Find the percent of guinea pigs in the pen that are male. Justify your answer.

3. You multiply two numbers. The first number, 21, is 6.25% of the product. What is the second number? Justify your answer.

4. You have a bag containing dollar coins, dimes, and pennies. The bag contains 40 coins. The number of dollar coins is 20% of the total number of coins. The number of pennies is $\frac{7}{9}$ of the number of dimes. How much money is in the bag?

Performance Task

Genetic Ancestry

At the beginning of this chapter, you watched a STEAM video called "Chargaff's Rules." You are now ready to complete the performance task for this video, available at ***BigIdeasMath.com***. Be sure to use the problem-solving plan as you work through the performance task.

4 Chapter Review

Go to *BigIdeasMath.com* to download blank graphic organizers.

Review Vocabulary

Write the definition and give an example of the vocabulary term.

percent, *p. 164*

Graphic Organizers

You can use a **Four Square** to organize information about a concept. Each of the four squares can be a category, such as definition, vocabulary, example, non-example, words, algebra, table, numbers, visual, graph, or equation. Here is an example of a Four Square for ***finding the percent of a number***.

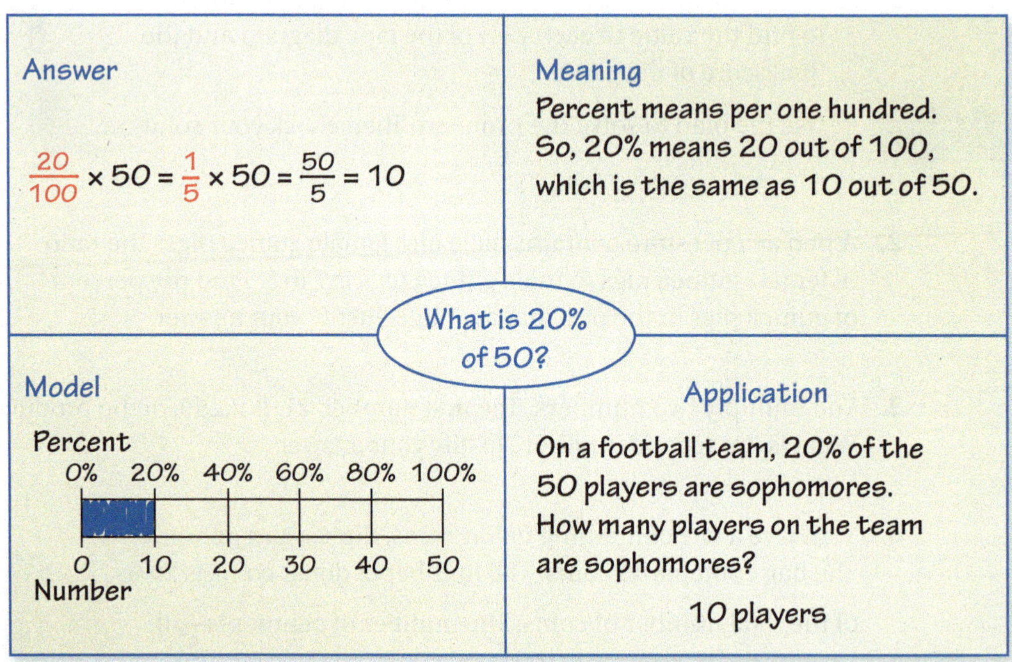

Choose and complete a graphic organizer to help you study the concept.

1. percent
2. writing percents as fractions
3. writing fractions as percents
4. writing percents as decimals
5. writing decimals as percents
6. finding the whole

"Sorry, but I have limited space in my Four Square. I needed pet names with only three letters."

Review Vocabulary

- As a review of the chapter vocabulary, have students revisit the vocabulary section in their *Student Journals* to fill in any missing definitions and record examples of each term.

Graphic Organizers

Sample answers:

1.

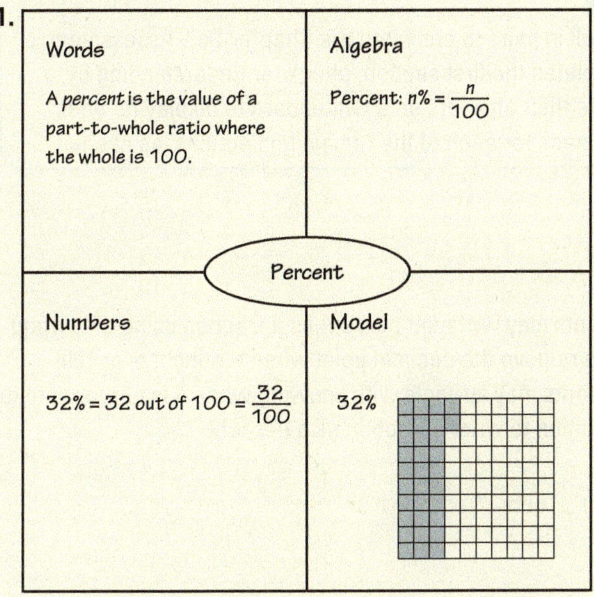

2.

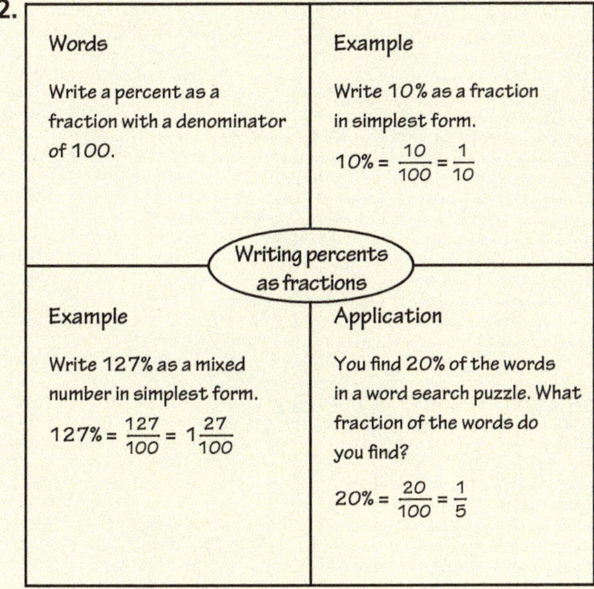

3–6. Available at *BigIdeasMath.com*.

List of Organizers

Available at *BigIdeasMath.com*
Definition and Example Chart
Example and Non-Example Chart
Four Square
Information Frame
Summary Triangle

About this Organizer

A **Four Square** can be used to organize information about a concept. Students write the concept in the oval. Then students use each of the four squares surrounding the oval to represent a related category. Related categories may include: definition, vocabulary, example, non-example, words, algebra, table, numbers, visual, graph, or equation. Encourage students to use categories that will help them study the concept. Students can place their Four Squares on note cards to use as a quick study reference.

The Four Square shown for *finding the percent of a number* is different from the sample answers because it focuses on a specific problem instead of a general concept.

Chapter Self-Assessment

1. $\frac{3}{25}$
2. $\frac{22}{25}$
3. $\frac{1}{125}$
4. $1\frac{27}{100}$
5. $\frac{1}{40}$
6. $\frac{9}{50}$
7. 60%
8. 172%
9. 142%
10. 40%
11. 528%
12. 1.75%
13. *Sample answer:* $\frac{11}{25}$
14. *Sample answer:* 378%
15. $\frac{23}{50}$
16. $\frac{2}{5}$
17. 35%

Chapter Self-Assessment

The Success Criteria Self-Assessment chart can be found in the *Student Journal* or online at *BigIdeasMath.com.*

ELL Support

Allow students to work in pairs to complete the Chapter Self-Assessment. Once they have completed the first section, check for understanding by having each pair write their answers on a whiteboard to display for your review. Repeat this check for each of the remaining sections, as needed.

Common Errors

- **Exercises 1–6** Students may write the percent as a fraction using the wrong denominator, or try to remove the decimal point when writing it over 100.
- **Exercises 7–12** Students may struggle with knowing when it is appropriate to use an equivalent fraction to write a fraction as a percent.

Chapter Self-Assessment

As you complete the exercises, use the scale below to rate your understanding of the success criteria in your journal.

1	2	3	4
I do not understand.	I can do it with help.	I can do it on my own.	I can teach someone else.

4.1 Percents and Fractions (pp. 163–168)

Learning Target: Write percents as fractions and fractions as percents.

Write the percent as a fraction or mixed number in simplest form.

1. 12% **2.** 88% **3.** 0.8%

4. 127% **5.** 2.5% **6.** 18%

Write the fraction or mixed number as a percent.

7. $\frac{3}{5}$ **8.** $1\frac{18}{25}$ **9.** $1\frac{21}{50}$

10. $\frac{14}{35}$ **11.** $5\frac{7}{25}$ **12.** $\frac{7}{400}$

13. Write a fraction in simplest form that is greater than 43% and less than 47%.

14. Write a percent that is greater than $3\frac{3}{4}$ and less than $3\frac{4}{5}$.

15. Your computer displays the progress of a downloading video. What fraction of the video is downloaded?

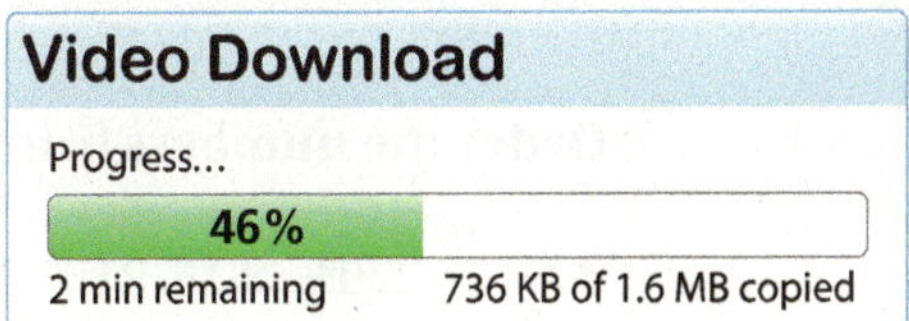

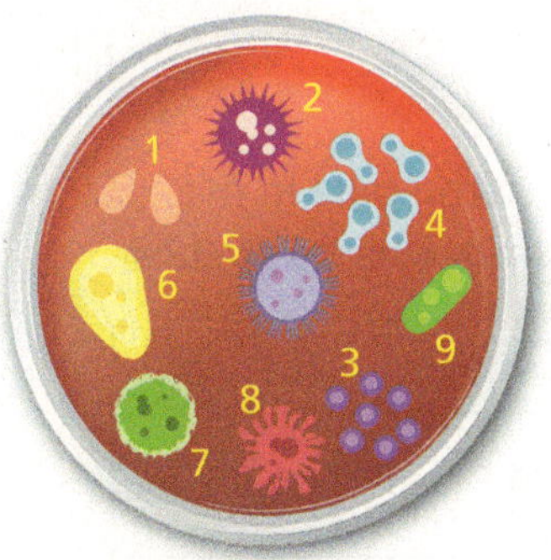

16. You complete 40% of your homework problems before dinner. What fraction of the problems did you complete before dinner?

17. There are nine different colonies of bacteria on the Petri dish. What percent of the bacteria on the Petri dish is from Colony 3?

4.2 Percent and Decimals (pp. 169–174)

Learning Target: Write percents as decimals and decimals as percents.

Write the percent as a decimal.

18. 76% **19.** 6% **20.** 17%

21. 0.8% **22.** 0.016% **23.** 334%

Write the decimal as a percent.

24. 0.15 **25.** 0.77 **26.** 0.56

27. 1.06 **28.** 1.24 **29.** 0.097

30. Write a decimal that is greater than 0.62% and less than 0.64%.

31. Write a percent that is greater than 0.026 and less than 0.028.

32. On a fishing trip, 38% of the fish that you catch are perch. Write this percent as a decimal.

4.3 Comparing and Ordering Fractions, Decimals, and Percents (pp. 175–180)

Learning Target: Compare and order fractions, decimals, and percents.

Tell which number is greater.

33. $\frac{1}{2}$, 52% **34.** $\frac{12}{5}$, 245% **35.** 0.46, 43% **36.** 0.023, 22%

Order the numbers from least to greatest.

37. $\frac{9}{4}$, 220%, 2.15, 218% **38.** 0.88, $\frac{7}{8}$, 92%, $\frac{9}{10}$, 0.89

39. Write a percent that is greater than $\frac{13}{25}$ and less than 0.54.

40. The table shows the portions of students in your grade who participate in five activities. List the activities in order by number of students from least to greatest.

Activity	Band	Chorus	Debate	Gymnastics	Theater
Portion of Students	0.14	$\frac{3}{25}$	$\frac{1}{20}$	11%	0.08

Common Errors

- **Exercises 18–29** Students may move the decimal point the wrong way, forget to insert zeros as placeholders, or move the decimal too many places (especially when the percent is greater than 100).
- **Exercises 33–38** Students may try to order the numbers without converting them, or convert them mentally and make a mistake.

Chapter Self-Assessment

18. 0.76

19. 0.06

20. 0.17

21. 0.008

22. 0.00016

23. 3.34

24. 15%

25. 77%

26. 56%

27. 106%

28. 124%

29. 9.7%

30. *Sample answer:* 0.0063

31. *Sample answer:* 2.7%

32. 0.38

33. 52%

34. 245%

35. 0.46

36. 22%

37. 2.15, 218%, 220%, $\frac{9}{4}$

38. $\frac{7}{8}$, 0.88, 0.89, $\frac{9}{10}$, 92%

39. *Sample answer:* 53%

40. debate, theater, gymnastics, chorus, band

Chapter Self-Assessment

41. 48; *Sample answer:* $\frac{3}{5} \times 80 = 48$

42. 44; *Sample answer:* $\frac{4}{5} \times 55 = 44$

43. 72; *Sample answer:* $\frac{3}{2} \times 48 = 72$

44. 63; *Sample answer:*
42% of 150 $= \frac{21}{50} \times 150 = 63$

45. 84; *Sample answer:* $\frac{28}{25} \times 75 = 84$

46. 18.9; *Sample answer:*
$\frac{9}{20} \times 42 = 18\frac{9}{10}$

47. 50; *Sample answer:* $35 \div \frac{7}{10} = 50$

48. 75; *Sample answer:* $21 \div \frac{7}{25} = 75$

49. 150; *Sample answer:*
$84 \div \frac{14}{25} = 150$

50. 480; *Sample answer:*
$96 \div \frac{1}{5} = 480$

51. 40; *Sample answer:* $56 \div \frac{7}{5} = 40$

52. 64; *Sample answer:* $112 \div \frac{7}{4} = 64$

53. 39

54. \$39

55. 2

56. **a.** 25; 4

b. 19

Common Errors

- **Exercises 41–46** If the number ends with a zero and students multiply by a decimal, they may forget about the zero and their answers will be off by one place value. Encourage students to estimate their answers first.

Chapter Resources

Surface Level	Deep Level
Resources by Chapter • Extra Practice • Reteach • Puzzle Time Student Journal • Practice • Chapter Self-Assessment Differentiating the Lesson Tutorial Videos Skills Review Handbook Skills Trainer Game Library	Resources by Chapter • Enrichment and Extension Graphic Organizers Game Library
Transfer Level	
STEAM Video Dynamic Assessment System • Chapter Test	Assessment Book • Chapter Tests A and B • Alternative Assessment • STEAM Performance Task

4.4 Solving Percent Problems (pp. 181–188)

Learning Target: Find a percent of a quantity and solve percent problems.

Find the percent of the number. Explain your method.

41. 60% of 80

42. 80% of 55

43. 150% of 48

44. 42% of 150

45. 112% of 75

46. 45% of 42

Find the whole. Explain your method.

47. 70% of what number is 35?

48. 28% of what number is 21?

49. 56% of what number is 84?

50. 20% of what number is 96?

51. 140% of what number is 56?

52. 175% of what number is 112?

53. Each cell of a dog contains 78 chromosomes. Exactly 50% of the chromosomes are inherited from the father. How many chromosomes in each cell of the dog are inherited from the father?

54. You went to the mall with $80. You spent 25% of your money on a pair of shorts and 65% of the remainder on sandals. How much did you spend on the sandals?

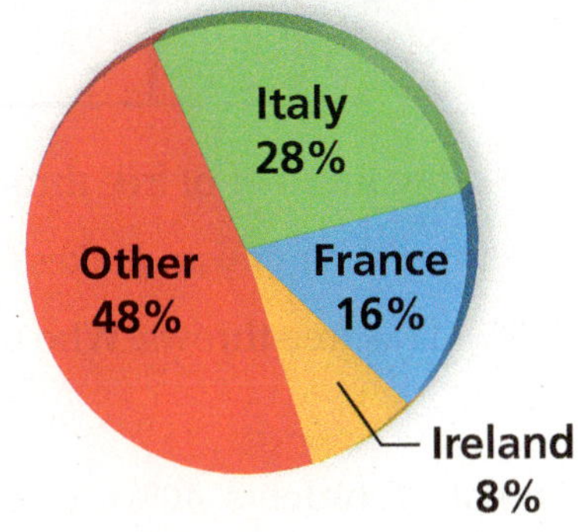

55. The results of a survey are shown at the left. In the survey, 7 students said that they would most like to visit Italy. How many of the students surveyed would most like to visit Ireland?

56. You answer 24 questions on a 100-point test correctly and earn a 96%.

a. All of the questions are worth the same number of points. How many questions are on the test? How many points is each question worth?

b. Your friend earns a grade of 76% on the same test. How many questions did your friend answer correctly?

4 Practice Test

Write the fraction or mixed number as a percent.

1. $\frac{21}{25}$

2. $\frac{17}{20}$

3. $1\frac{2}{5}$

Write the decimal as a percent.

4. 0.42

5. 7.88

6. 0.5854

Write the percent as a fraction in simplest form and as a decimal.

7. 0.96%

8. 65%

9. 25.7%

Tell which number is greater.

10. $\frac{16}{25}$, 65%

11. 56%, 5.6

Order the numbers from least to greatest.

12. 85%, $\frac{7}{10}$, 0.74, $\frac{4}{5}$

13. 130%, 1.32, $\frac{6}{5}$, $\frac{5}{4}$, 1.28

14. 80% of 90 is what number?

15. 120% of 75 is what number?

16. 40% of what number is 34?

17. 130% of what number is 52?

18. A goalie's saves (•) and goals scored against (×) are shown. What percent of shots did the goalie save? Explain.

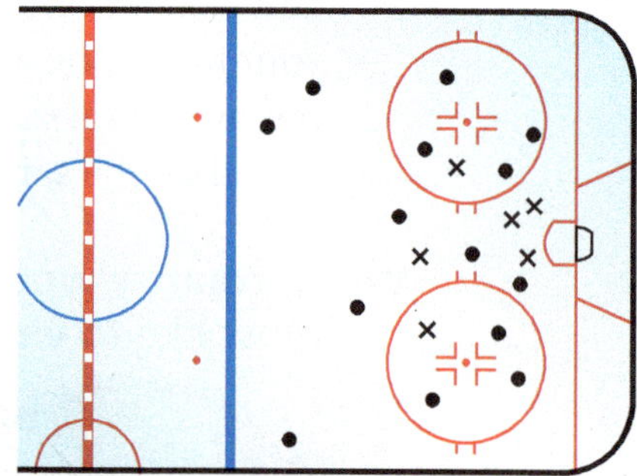

19. About 62% of the human body is composed of water. Write this percent as a fraction in simplest form.

20. You, your cousin, and a friend each take the same number of free throws at a basketball hoop. You make $\frac{17}{20}$ of your free throws, your cousin makes 0.8 of her free throws, and your friend makes 87.5% of his free throws. Who made the most free throws?

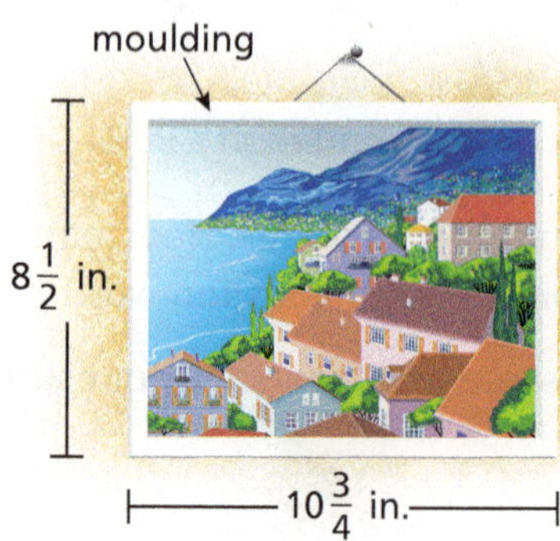

21. In a class of 20 students, 40% are boys. Twenty-five percent of the boys and 50% of the girls wear glasses. How many students in the class wear glasses?

22. Eighty percent of the picture frame is glass. What is the area of the moulding?

Practice Test Item References

Practice Test Questions	Section to Review
1–3, 7–9, 18, 19	4.1
4–9	4.2
10–13, 20	4.3
14–17, 21, 22	4.4

Test-Taking Strategies

Remind students to quickly look over the entire test before they start so that they can budget their time. Remind them that the test is on percents, and that they need to read the problems carefully. Students need to think of the different representations of each number as they work through the test, such as 0.5, $\frac{1}{2}$, and 50%. Remind students to **Stop** and **Think** before they write their answers.

Common Errors

- **Exercises 10–13** Students may try to order the numbers without converting them, or convert them mentally and make a mistake. Remind students that it is necessary to convert all the numbers to one form.
- **Exercises 14 and 15** Students might find a number that is significantly greater or less than the correct answer. Encourage students to estimate their answers first and remind them that percents greater than 100% will have answers that are greater than the original number.

Practice Test

1. 84%
2. 85%
3. 140%
4. 42%
5. 788%
6. 58.54%
7. $\frac{6}{625}$; 0.0096
8. $\frac{13}{20}$; 0.65
9. $\frac{257}{1000}$; 0.257
10. 65%
11. 5.6
12. $\frac{7}{10}$, 0.74, $\frac{4}{5}$, 85%
13. $\frac{6}{5}$, $\frac{5}{4}$, 1.28, 130%, 1.32
14. 72
15. 90
16. 85
17. 40
18. 70%; There are 14 saves and 20 shots.
19. $\frac{31}{50}$
20. your friend
21. 8
22. $18\frac{11}{40}$ in.^{2}

Test-Taking Strategies

Available at *BigIdeasMath.com*

After Answering Easy Questions, Relax

Answer Easy Questions First

Estimate the Answer

Read All Choices before Answering

Read Question before Answering

Solve Directly or Eliminate Choices

Solve Problem before Looking at Choices

Use Intelligent Guessing

Work Backwards

About this Strategy

When taking a timed test, it is often best to skim the test and answer the easy questions first. Read each question carefully and thoroughly. Be careful that you record your answer in the correct position on the answer sheet.

Cumulative Practice

1. C
2. G
3. 28
4. D
5. H

Item Analysis

1. **A.** The student finds the number of pints in 1 quart.
   B. The student divides 8 by 2 instead of multiplying 8 by 2.
   C. Correct answer
   D. The student multiplies 8 by 4 instead of multiplying 8 by 2.
2. **F.** The student does not recognize that $\frac{1}{4} = \frac{25}{100} = 25\%$.
   G. Correct answer
   H. The student does not recognize that $\frac{5}{20} = \frac{25}{100} = 25\%$.
   I. The student does not recognize that $\frac{25}{100} = 25\%$.
3. **Gridded Response:** Correct answer: 28

   Common error: The student adds 6 to each value to get 13, rather than multiplying by 4.
4. **A.** The student incorrectly chooses to divide 24 by 100 times the percent.
   B. The student switches the order of division instead of choosing to multiply.
   C. The student incorrectly chooses to multiply by 100 times the percent.
   D. Correct answer
5. **F.** The student multiplies the numerator and denominator.
   G. The student uses the digits from the numerator and denominator.
   H. Correct answer
   I. The student divides 5 by 4 and writes the quotient as a percent.

4 Cumulative Practice

1. How many pints are in 8 quarts?

   A. 2 pints **B.** 4 pints

   C. 16 pints **D.** 32 pints

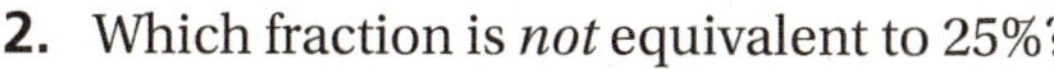
2. Which fraction is *not* equivalent to 25%?

   F. $\frac{1}{4}$ **G.** $\frac{2}{5}$

   H. $\frac{5}{20}$ **I.** $\frac{25}{100}$

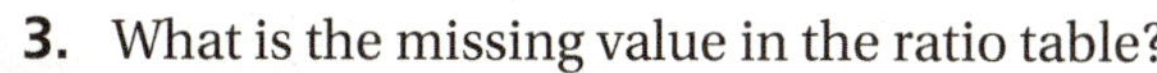
3. What is the missing value in the ratio table?

Pairs of Shoes	7		56
Pairs of Boots	2	8	16

4. Your friend was finding the percent of a number in the box below.

> 25% of 24 is what number?
>
> $25\% \text{ of } 24 = 24 \div \frac{1}{4}$
>
> $= 96$

What should your friend do to correct the error?

   A. Divide 24 by 25. **B.** Divide $\frac{1}{4}$ by 24.

   C. Multiply 24 by 25. **D.** Multiply 24 by $\frac{1}{4}$.

5. Which percent is equivalent to $\frac{4}{5}$?

   F. 20% **G.** 45%

   H. 80% **I.** 125%

Test-Taking Strategy
Answer Easy Questions First

One dog and one cat fall off a log into the water. What percent of them know how to dog paddle?
Ⓐ 0% Ⓑ 25% Ⓒ 50% Ⓓ 100%
I'm going to start writing the questions.

"Answer the easy questions first. Then try the hard ones."

6. Which pair of numbers does *not* have a least common multiple less than 100?

A. 10, 15
B. 12, 16
C. 16, 18
D. 18, 24

7. You are comparing the costs of buying bottles of water at the supermarket. Which of the following has the least cost per liter?

F. 6 one-liter bottles for $1.80

G. 1 two-liter bottle for $0.65

H. 8 half-liter bottles for $1.50

I. 12 half-liter bottles for $1.98

8. What is 75% of 36?

9. Which number is equivalent to $\frac{5}{12} \times \frac{4}{9}$?

A. $\frac{5}{27}$
B. $\frac{3}{7}$
C. $\frac{15}{16}$
D. $\frac{5}{3}$

10. Which list of numbers is in order from least to greatest?

F. $0.8, \frac{5}{8}, 70\%, 0.09$
G. $\frac{5}{8}, 70\%, 0.8, 0.09$
H. $0.09, \frac{5}{8}, 0.8, 70\%$
I. $0.09, \frac{5}{8}, 70\%, 0.8$

Item Analysis (continued)

6. **A.** The student does not find the LCM correctly; the LCM of 10 and 15 is 30, which is less than 100.

   B. The student does not find the LCM correctly; the LCM of 12 and 16 is 48, which is less than 100.

   C. Correct answer

   D. The student does not find the LCM correctly; the LCM of 18 and 24 is 72, which is less than 100.

7. **F.** Correct answer

   G. The student does not correctly compare this unit cost ($0.325 per liter) to the unit cost in answer choice F ($0.30 per liter).

   H. The student does not correctly compare this unit cost ($0.375 per liter) to the unit cost in answer choice F ($0.30 per liter).

   I. The student does not correctly compare this unit cost ($0.33 per liter) to the unit cost in answer choice F ($0.30 per liter).

8. **Gridded Response:** Correct answer: 27

   Common error: The student finds 25% of 36 is 9, rather than finding 75% of 36.

9. **A.** Correct answer

   B. The student adds the numerators and adds the denominators instead of multiplying them.

   C. The student divides instead of multiplying.

   D. The student multiplies the numerators and uses the greatest of the two denominators.

10. **F.** The student thinks that 0.8 is less than 0.09 and does not know how to compare decimal numbers with fractions or percents.

    G. The student orders the numbers using the numerator or the leading digit.

    H. The student orders the decimal numbers and fractions correctly but thinks that 70% is equal to 70.

    I. Correct answer

Cumulative Practice

6. C
7. F
8. 27
9. A
10. I

Cumulative Practice

11. C

12. G

13. *Part A:* $\frac{3}{25}$; $\frac{1}{5}$ is cherry and $\frac{1}{5} \times \frac{3}{5} = \frac{3}{25}$.

Part B: 12%; $\frac{3}{25} = \frac{12}{100}$

Item Analysis (continued)

11. **A.** The student divides 1.32 by 0.6.

B. The student divides 1.32 by 0.06.

C. Correct answer

D. The student divides 1.32 by 0.0006.

12. **F.** The student subtracts 2 from each value in the ratio.

G. Correct answer

H. The student adds 14 to each value in the ratio.

I. The student adds 4 to each value in the ratio.

13. **2 points** The student's explanation demonstrates a thorough understanding of multiplying fractions and writing fractions as percents. The student correctly determines that the amount of the cherry gelatin eaten as a fraction of the total dessert is $\frac{3}{25}$ and as a percent is 12%.

1 point The student's explanation demonstrates a partial but limited understanding of multiplying fractions and writing fractions as percents. For instance, the student finds the correct fraction but incorrect percent, or vice versa.

0 points The student provides no response, a completely incorrect or incomprehensible response, or a response that demonstrates insufficient understanding of multiplying fractions and writing percents as fractions.

11. Which number is equivalent to $1.32 \div 0.006$?

A. 2.2 **B.** 22

C. 220 **D.** 2200

12. Which ratio is equivalent to $4:14$?

F. $2:12$ **G.** $10:35$

H. $18:28$ **I.** $8:18$

13. For a party, you make a gelatin dessert in a rectangular pan and cut the dessert into equal-sized pieces, as shown below.

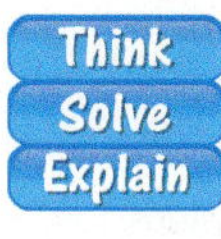

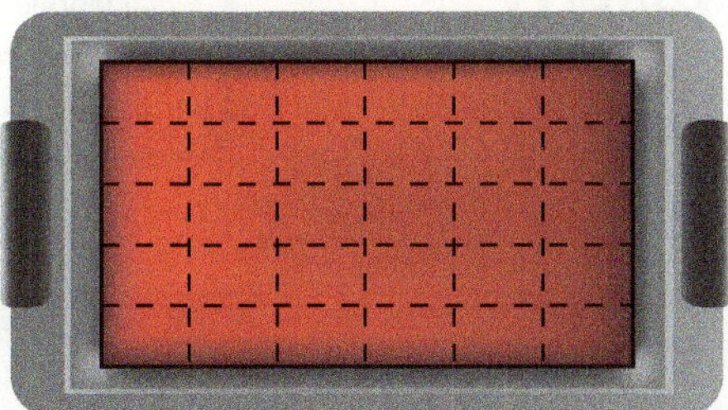

The dessert consists of 5 layers of equal height. Each layer is a different flavor, as shown below by a side view of the pan.

Your guests eat $\frac{3}{5}$ of the pieces of the dessert.

Part A Write the amount of cherry gelatin that your guests eat as a fraction of the total dessert. Justify your answer.

Part B Write the amount of cherry gelatin that your guests eat as a percent of the total dessert. Justify your answer.

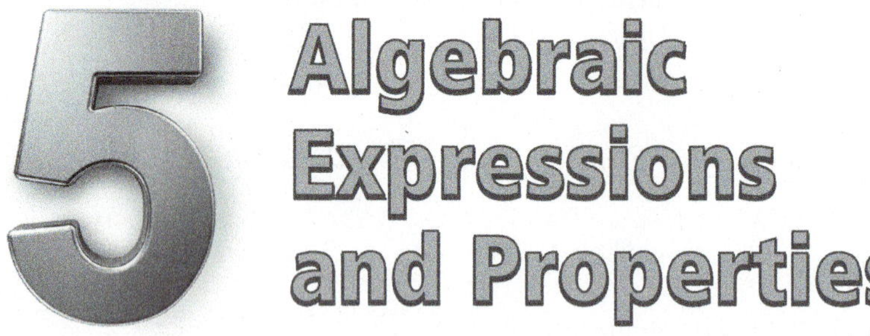

5 Algebraic Expressions and Properties

Chapter Learning Target:
Understand algebraic expressions.

Chapter Success Criteria:

- I can identify parts of an algebraic expression.
- I can write algebraic expressions.
- I can solve a problem using algebraic expressions.
- I can interpret algebraic expressions in real-life problems.

Laurie's Notes

Chapter 5 Overview

This chapter is a continuation of the algebra strand that students explored in prior courses. Students will now extend this understanding to include: writing and evaluating algebraic expressions, using properties with algebraic expressions, and factoring expressions.

Students used variables in prior courses, often in the context of finding the area or the perimeter of a geometric figure. Formulas were written as verbal models and then variables were introduced. For example:

Area of rectangle = length times width
Area of rectangle = length $\times$ width
$$A = \ell \times w$$

Keep in mind that the different notations used to represent operations, particularly multiplication and division, are not understood by all students. In the first lesson, where algebraic expressions are introduced, take time to review the different representations. For example, in prior courses 3__ or 3 ▢ meant thirty-something. In algebra, $3x$ means 3 times a quantity called x.

A major goal for this chapter is that students become confident in writing and evaluating algebraic expressions. The order of operations, including exponents and grouping symbols, is extended to algebraic expressions.

In prior courses, students were introduced to the Commutative and Associative Properties. They may forget, or mix up, the names of these two properties, but students generally have a good sense of how the properties apply to numbers. Students should also be able to provide examples of why the Commutative and Associative Properties do not apply to subtraction and division. The Addition Property of Zero and the Multiplication Properties of Zero and One are also presented in this chapter. All the properties are shown with words, numbers, and variables.

Students have some experience using the Distributive Property with numerical expressions. A common misconception students often have is that the Distributive Property is *only* about multiplying. They see the equal sign as an arrow. For example, $3(x + 7) \rightarrow 3x + 21$. Students may not recognize that factoring is represented in the Distributive Property as well. For example, $3x + 21 = 3(x + 7)$. The last two lessons of the chapter clarify and connect these ideas. In Section 5.4, when students are working on the exploration, probe their understanding of what the equal sign implies. For example, $3(x + 4) = 3x + 12$ and $3x + 12 = 3(x + 4)$.

Suggested Pacing

Chapter Opener	1 Day
Section 1	2 Days
Section 2	2 Days
Section 3	2 Days
Section 4	2 Days
Section 5	3 Days
Connecting Concepts	1 Day
Chapter Review	1 Day
Chapter Test	1 Day
Total Chapter 5	15 Days
Year-to-Date	78 Days

Chapter Learning Target

Understand algebraic expressions.

Chapter Success Criteria

- Identify parts of an algebraic expression.
- Write algebraic expressions.
- Solve a problem using algebraic expressions.
- Interpret algebraic expressions in real-life problems.

Chapter 5 Learning Targets and Success Criteria

Section	Learning Target	Success Criteria
5.1 Algebraic Expressions	Evaluate algebraic expressions given values of their variables.	• Identify parts of an algebraic expression. • Evaluate algebraic expressions with one or more variables. • Evaluate algebraic expressions with one or more operations.
5.2 Writing Expressions	Write algebraic expressions and solve problems involving algebraic expressions.	• Write numerical expressions. • Write algebraic expressions. • Write and evaluate algebraic expressions that represent real-life problems.
5.3 Properties of Addition and Multiplication	Identify equivalent expressions and apply properties to generate equivalent expressions.	• Explain the meaning of equivalent expressions. • Use properties of addition to generate equivalent expressions. • Use properties of multiplication to generate equivalent expressions.
5.4 The Distributive Property	Apply the Distributive Property to generate equivalent expressions.	• Explain how to apply the Distributive Property. • Use the Distributive Property to simplify algebraic expressions. • Use the Distributive Property to combine like terms.
5.5 Factoring Expressions	Factor numerical and algebraic expressions.	• Use the Distributive Property to factor numerical expressions. • Identify the greatest common factor of terms including variables. • Use the Distributive Property to factor algebraic expressions. • Interpret factored expressions in real-life problems.

Progressions

Through the Grades		
Grade 5	**Grade 6**	**Grade 7**
• Use parentheses, brackets, or braces in numerical expressions. • Write and interpret numerical expressions.	• Use the distributive property to factor algebraic expressions. • Write and evaluate algebraic expressions. • Apply the properties of operations to show expressions are equivalent.	• Add, subtract, factor, and expand linear expressions with rational coefficients. • Understand that rewriting expressions in different forms can show how the quantities are related.

Through the Chapter					
Standard	**5.1**	**5.2**	**5.3**	**5.4**	**5.5**
6.NS.B.4 Find the greatest common factor of two whole numbers less than or equal to 100 and the least common multiple of two whole numbers less than or equal to 12. Use the distributive property to express a sum of two whole numbers 1-100 with a common factor as a multiple of a sum of two whole numbers with no common factor.					★
6.EE.A.2a Write expressions that record operations with numbers and with letters standing for numbers.		★			
6.EE.A.2b Identify parts of an expression using mathematical terms (sum, term, product, factor, quotient, coefficient); view one or more parts of an expression as a single entity.	●			●	★
6.EE.A.2c Evaluate expressions at specific values of their variables. Include expressions that arise from formulas used in real-world problems. Perform arithmetic operations, including those involving whole-number exponents, in the conventional order when there are no parentheses to specify a particular order (Order of Operations).	●				
6.EE.A.3 Apply the properties of operations to generate equivalent expressions.			●	●	★
6.EE.A.4 Identify when two expressions are equivalent (i.e., when the two expressions name the same number regardless of which value is substituted into them).			●	●	★

Key

▲ = preparing ★ = complete

● = learning ■ = extending

STEAM Video

1. *Sample answer:* so that the Sun is at the same angle and the time between measurements is the same
2. *Sample answer:* 10.5 in.; 10.5 is halfway between 7 and 14.
3. *Sample answer:* 30 in.; 38 in.; 47 in.

Performance Task

Sample answer: no; The pattern may not continue long-term.

Mathematical Practices

Students have opportunities to develop aspects of the mathematical practices throughout the chapter. Here are some examples.

1. **Make Sense of Problems and Persevere in Solving Them**
   5.4 Math Practice note, *p. 221*
2. **Reason Abstractly and Quantitatively**
   5.2 Exercise 43, *p. 214*
3. **Construct Viable Arguments and Critique the Reasoning of Others**
   5.5 Exercise 56, *p. 232*
4. **Model with Mathematics**
   5.1 Exercise 50, *p. 208*
5. **Use Appropriate Tools Strategically**
   5.1 Self-Assessment 21, *p. 204*
6. **Attend to Precision**
   5.2 Math Practice note, *p. 210*
7. **Look for and Make Use of Structure**
   5.4 Exercise 34, *p. 225*
8. **Look for and Express Regularity in Repeated Reasoning**
   5.2 Exploration 1b, *p. 209*

Laurie's Notes

STEAM Video

Before the Video

- To introduce the STEAM Video, read aloud the first paragraph of Shadow Drawings and discuss the question with your students.

? "Can you think of any other real-life situations in which you would want to use an expression to represent a changing quantity?"

During the Video

- The video shows shadow drawings of a plant after 1, 2, and 3 weeks of growth.

? Pause the video at 1:25 and ask, "What has happened in the video so far?" Tory is making a shadow drawing of a plant she got three weeks before. Each week she made a shadow drawing on the same day at the same time. Robert suggests measuring the drawings to predict the growth rate of the plant.

? "How can measuring the drawings help predict the growth rate of the plant?" *Sample answer:* Measuring the height each week may show a pattern in the amount of growth in one week.

- Watch the remainder of the video.

After the Video

- Have students work with a partner to answer Questions 1–3.
- As students discuss and answer the questions, listen for understanding and knowledge of writing and evaluating algebraic expressions.

Performance Task

- Use this information to spark students' interest and promote thinking about real-life problems.

? Ask, "Do the expressions provide accurate predictions far into the future?"

- After completing the chapter, students will have gained the knowledge needed to complete "Describing Change."

STEAM Video

Shadow Drawings

Expressions can be used to represent the growth of living things over time. Can you think of any other real-life situations in which you would want to use an expression to represent a changing quantity?

Watch the STEAM Video "Shadow Drawings." Then answer the following questions.

1. Tory traces the shadow of a plant each week on the same day of the week and at the same time of day. Why does she need to be so careful about the timing of the drawing?

2. The table shows the height of the plant each week for the first three weeks. About how tall was the plant after 1.5 weeks? Explain your reasoning.

Week	1	2	3
Height (inches)	7	14	22

3. Predict the height of the plant when Tory makes her next three weekly drawings.

Performance Task

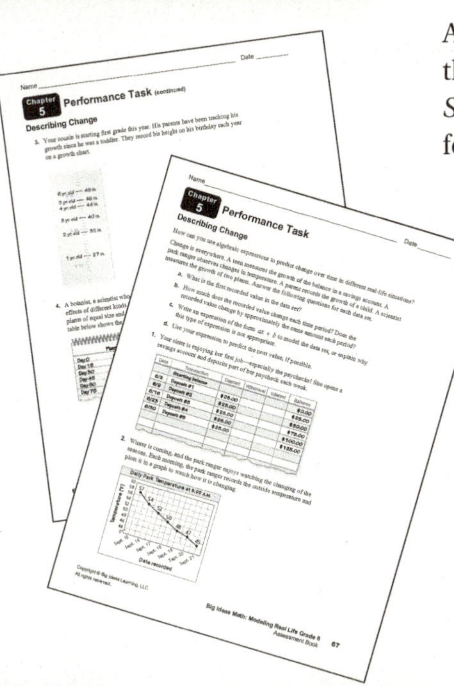

Name _______ Date _______

Chapter 5 **Performance Task** (continued)

Describing Change

3. Your cousin is starting first grade this year. His parents have been tracking his growth since he was a toddler. They record his height on his birthday each year on a growth chart.

6 yr. old — 48 in.
5 yr. old — 46 in.
4 yr. old — 44 in.
3 yr. old — 40 in.
2 yr. old — 35 in.
1 yr. old — 27 in.

4. A botanist, a scientist who ... effects of different kinds ... plants of equal size and ... table below shows the ...

Day 0
Day 15
Day 30
Day 45
Day 60
Day 70

Name _______ Date _______

Chapter 5 **Performance Task**

Describing Change

How can you use algebraic expressions to predict change over time in different real-life situations?

Change is everywhere. A teen measures the growth of the balance in a savings account. A park ranger observes changes in temperature. A parent records the growth of a child. A scientist measures the growth of two plants. Answer the following questions for each data set.

a. What is the first recorded value in the data set?
b. How much does the recorded value change each time period? Does the recorded value change by approximately the same amount each period?
c. Write an expression of the form $ax + b$ to model the data set, or explain why this type of expression is not appropriate.
d. Use your expression to predict the next value, if possible.

1. Your sister is enjoying her first job—especially the paychecks! She opens a savings account and deposits part of her paycheck each week.

Date	Transaction	Deposit	Withdrawal	Interest	Balance
	Starting balance				$0.00
6/2	Deposit #1	$25.00			$25.00
6/9	Deposit #2	$25.00			$50.00
6/16	Deposit #3	$25.00			$75.00
6/23	Deposit #4	$25.00			$100.00
6/30	Deposit #5	$25.00			$125.00

2. Winter is coming, and the park ranger enjoys watching the changing of the seasons. Each morning, the park ranger records the outside temperature and plots it in a graph to watch how it is changing.

Big Ideas Math: Modeling Real Life Grade 6
Assessment Book 67

Describing Change

After completing this chapter, you will be able to use the concepts you learned to answer the questions in the *STEAM Video Performance Task*. You will be given data sets for the following real-life situations.

Savings account

Temperature

Human growth

Plant growth

You will be asked to use given data to write expressions and make predictions. Do the expressions provide accurate predictions far into the future?

Getting Ready for Chapter 

Chapter Exploration

1. Work with a partner.

   a. You babysit for 3 hours. You receive $24. What is your hourly wage?

   - Write the problem. Underline the important numbers and units you need to solve the problem.
   - Read the problem carefully a second time. Circle the key phrase for the question.

   You babysit for 3 hours. You receive $24.
   What is your hourly wage?

   - Write each important number or phrase, with its units, on a piece of paper. Write $+$, $-$, $\times$, $\div$, and $=$ on five other pieces of paper.

   hourly wage ($ per hour)

   - Arrange the pieces of paper to answer the question, "What is your hourly wage?"
   - Evaluate the expression that represents the hourly wage.

   hourly wage = ☐ ÷ ☐   Write.

   = ☐   Evaluate.

   ▶ So, your hourly wage is $ ☐ per hour.

   b. How can you use your hourly wage to find how much you will receive for any number of hours worked?

Vocabulary

The following vocabulary terms are defined in this chapter. Think about what each term might mean and record your thoughts.

algebraic expression
variable
constant
equivalent expressions
factoring an expression

Laurie's Notes

Chapter Exploration

- Ask students to name jobs they have had where they earned money. Students may say babysitting, delivering newspapers, odd jobs for neighbors, grocery shopping for an elderly person, or dog walking.
- ? Discuss the difference between being paid by the hour and being paid for completing a job. "What are the advantages and disadvantages of each method of payment?" Listen for responses that include *hours worked* compared to *hours paid*.
- Manipulating the pieces of paper allows students to make sense of writing a mathematical model.
- **Common Question:** Students may ask, "Why go through all this work when I already knew the answer?" Tell them that you are modeling a process: read and re-read, underline important numbers and units, circle what you are trying to solve for, and then write an expression.
- **Another Method:** You can also set up the problem as: $24 = hourly wage ($ per hour) × 3 hours. Although this is a true statement, it is helpful to have all of the computations on one side of the equation. Let students know that they will learn how to solve equations similar to this at a later time, when the answer may not be so obvious.

ELL Support

Explain that it is not uncommon for American teenagers to earn money by taking care of younger children. An adult may ask a teenager to care for their children so they can go out for an evening. This is known as *babysitting*. ELLs may come from cultures in which childcare is a communal activity that does not involve financial compensation. Explain that the phrase *hourly wage* describes the amount of money a person is paid for every hour worked. In this situation, the hourly wage describes the amount of money you will be paid for every hour you care for children.

Vocabulary

- These terms represent some of the vocabulary that students will encounter in Chapter 5. Discuss the terms as a class.
- Where have students heard the word *constant* outside of a math classroom? In what contexts? Students may not be able to write the actual definition, but they may write phrases associated with constant.
- Allowing students to discuss these terms now will prepare them for understanding the terms as they are presented in the chapter.
- When students encounter a new definition, encourage them to write in their *Student Journals*. They will revisit these definitions during the Chapter Review.

Topics for Review

- Factors of Whole Numbers
- Greatest Common Factor
- Interpreting Numerical Expressions
- Multiples of Whole Numbers
- Using Order of Operations

Chapter Exploration

1. a. Check that students have underlined 3 hours and $12, circled hourly wage, written those values and the operations on pieces of paper, formed the correct equation and arrived at an answer of $8.

   b. Multiply $8 by the number of hours worked.

Learning Target

Evaluate algebraic expressions given values of their variables.

Success Criteria

- Identify parts of an algebraic expression.
- Evaluate algebraic expressions with one or more variables.
- Evaluate algebraic expressions with one or more operations.

Warm Up

Cumulative, vocabulary, and prerequisite skills practice opportunities are available in the *Resources by Chapter* or at *BigIdeasMath.com.*

ELL Support

Clarify the meaning of the word *variable.* Explain that *to vary* is *to change*, so a variable is something that can change. For example, weather is variable. There may be variable cloudiness from day to day. In the context of math, a variable is a symbol that represents one or more numbers, such as *x* or *y*. When the value of a variable in an expression changes, the value of the expression may change as well.

Exploration 1

a. number of hours worked; *Sample answer:* 4; $24 ÷ 4 = $6

b. price of each baking mold; *Sample answer:* $4; 5 × $4 = $20

c. total race distance; *Sample answer:* 5000 ft; 5000 ft − 2000 ft = 3000 ft

d. number of months; *Sample answer:* 5; 25 cm + 1.6 × 5 = 33 cm

Laurie's Notes

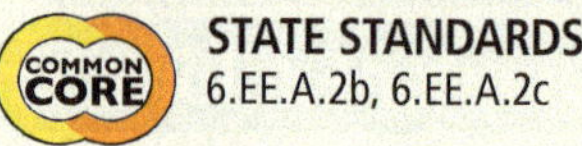

STATE STANDARDS
6.EE.A.2b, 6.EE.A.2c

Preparing to Teach

- In prior chapters, students performed operations with different representations of numbers and compared their magnitudes. As students continue to problem-solve, they will need to consider both numerical and algebraic expressions.
- Many students struggle with solving word problems, but not because the mathematics is too difficult. They struggle because they do not know how to approach word problems. Help students hone their reading skills so that they can become better problem solvers.
- Several new vocabulary terms are introduced in this lesson. Consistently using precise mathematical language will help students master the first success criterion.

Motivate

- Ask six students to stand at the front of the room. Give each student an index card with a number written on the card (possible numbers: 1, 3, 4, 5, 8, 9). Write simple expressions on the board, drawing boxes where the **variables** would be. Tell the six students holding cards to place their cards in the boxes and announce the values of each expression for their numbers. Examples:

$$\square + 14 \qquad 27 - \square \qquad \square^2 \qquad 6 \cdot \square$$

- You can vary the expressions and numbers to fit the level of your class. The goal is for students to recognize that the value of the expression changes (or varies) for each number substituted.
- ? After several examples, erase the boxes and replace them with variables. Then ask, "What do the letters mean?" The letters (or variables) have the same meanings as the boxes. They are unknown values that represent numbers. "Does anyone know what these expressions are called?" **algebraic expressions**

Exploration 1

- This exploration requires a variety of different skills. First, students must ask, "What do I need to know?" This is a literacy skill. Do they understand what they need to know to answer the question in each part? Secondly, students must choose a reasonable value for the missing amount. Using that value, can they find a numerical solution?
- Work through part (a) as a class. Begin by asking what they need to know and then discuss a reasonable number of hours. Listen for suggestions of "easy" numbers (factors of 24).
- After students complete parts (b)–(d), ask pairs to share their solutions on the board. Point out the different values chosen to complete each expression. This is a preview of evaluating algebraic expressions.
- **MP6 Attend to Precision:** Students need opportunities to communicate using precise mathematical language. In the exploration, their language is something you want to pay attention to. Listen to how students refer to the quantities, particularly their references to units for each of the parts.

5.1 Algebraic Expressions

Learning Target: Evaluate algebraic expressions given values of their variables.

Success Criteria:
- I can identify parts of an algebraic expression.
- I can evaluate algebraic expressions with one or more variables.
- I can evaluate algebraic expressions with one or more operations.

EXPLORATION 1 Evaluating Expressions

Math Practice

Make Sense of Quantities

What are the units in the problem? How does this help you write an expression?

Work with a partner. Identify any missing information that is needed to answer each question. Then choose a reasonable quantity and write an expression for each problem. After you have written the expression, evaluate it using mental math or some other method.

a. You receive $24 for washing cars. How much do you earn per hour?

b. You buy 5 silicone baking molds at a craft store. How much do you spend?

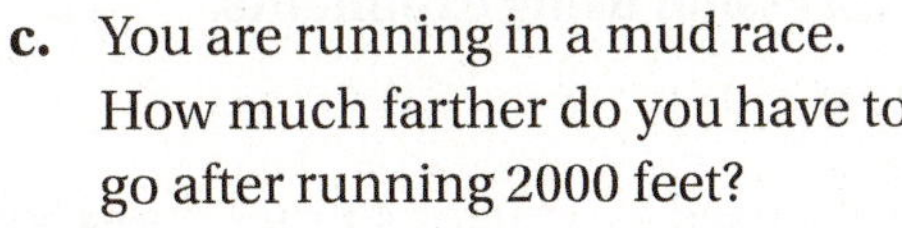

c. You are running in a mud race. How much farther do you have to go after running 2000 feet?

d. A rattlesnake is 25 centimeters long when it hatches. The snake grows at a rate of about 1.6 centimeters per month for several months. What is the length of the rattlesnake?

5.1 Lesson

Key Vocabulary
algebraic expression, *p. 202*
variable, *p. 202*
term, *p. 202*
coefficient, *p. 202*
constant, *p. 202*

An **algebraic expression** is an expression that may contain numbers, operations, and one or more *variables.* A **variable** is a symbol that represents one or more numbers. Each number or variable by itself, or product of numbers and variables in an algebraic expression, is called a **term**.

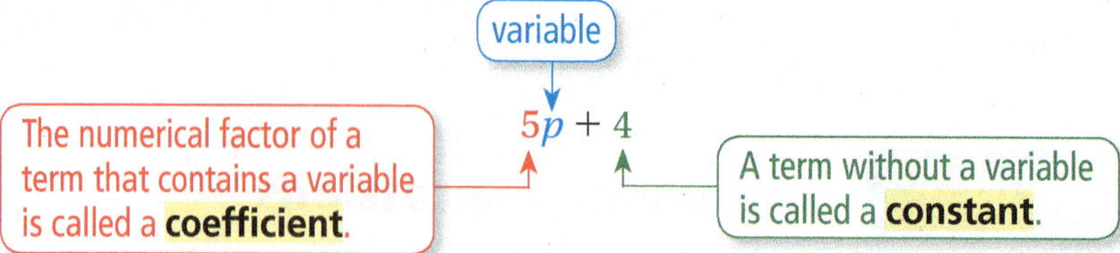

EXAMPLE 1 Identifying Parts of an Algebraic Expression

Identify the terms, coefficients, and constants in each expression.

a. $5x + 13$

$5x + 13$

Terms: $5x$, 13

Coefficient: 5

Constant: 13

b. $2z^2 + y + 3$

$2z^2 + y + 3$

Terms: $2z^2$, $1y$, 3

Coefficients: 2, 1

Constant: 3

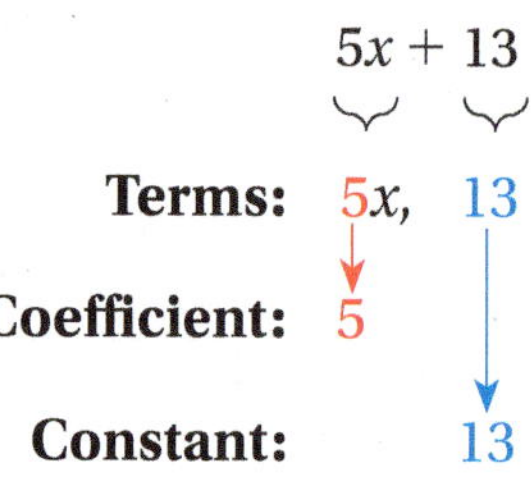

A variable by itself has a coefficient of 1. So, the term *y* in Example 1(b) has a coefficient of 1.

Try It **Identify the terms, coefficients, and constants in the expression.**

1. $12 + 10c$ **2.** $15 + 3w + \frac{1}{2}$ **3.** $z^2 + 9z$

EXAMPLE 2 Writing Algebraic Expressions Using Exponents

Write each expression using exponents.

a. $d \cdot d \cdot d \cdot d$

Because d is used as a factor 4 times, its exponent is 4.

So, $d \cdot d \cdot d \cdot d = d^4$.

b. $1.5 \cdot h \cdot h \cdot h$

Because h is used as a factor 3 times, its exponent is 3.

So, $1.5 \cdot h \cdot h \cdot h = 1.5h^3$.

Try It **Write the expression using exponents.**

4. $j \cdot j \cdot j \cdot j \cdot j \cdot j$ **5.** $9 \cdot k \cdot k \cdot k \cdot k \cdot k$

Multi-Language Glossary at BigIdeasMath.com

Laurie's Notes

Scaffolding Instruction

- Going from words and sentences to numbers, variables, and operations emphasizes the efficiency of **algebraic expressions**.
- **Emerging:** Students may be able to identify the information in a real-life problem but struggle to interpret its meaning in relation to evaluating algebraic expressions. Examples 1–5 provide additional practice evaluating algebraic expressions before using them in real-life problems.
- **Proficient:** Students use precise mathematical language and evaluate algebraic expressions with ease. Have them self-assess using Try It Exercises 1–3 and 9–16.

EXAMPLE 1

- Write $5x + 13$. Discuss the words: **term**, **variable**, **coefficient**, and **constant**. Reassure students that these words will become familiar with use.
- ? "How many terms are there in $5x + 13$?" 2 "Name the terms." $5x$ and 13 Be sure students understand that in this expression 5 is not a term, however, $5x$ is a term.
- In working through part (b), ask students to identify the variables first.
- ? "What is the coefficient of the z^2 term?" 2 "What is the coefficient of y term?" 1 It's common for students to say that there isn't a coefficient of y, or mistakenly identify the coefficient as 0.
- Explain that $1y = y$. Tell students that the coefficient 1 is not usually written in front of the term.

Try It

Have students work in pairs to complete the exercises. Then have students share their answers verbally or on the board. Use *Fist of Five* to check their understanding of the first success criterion.

EXAMPLE 2

- ? Write 3^2 and ask, "How do you read this?" 3 squared or 3 raised to the second power "What does the exponent mean?" how many times 3 is a factor
- This example connects to a prior lesson on powers and exponents, that is now extending to variables.
- In part (b), tell students that only the variable h is being raised to the power.

Try It

- **Neighbor Check:** Have students work independently, and then have their neighbors check their work. Have students discuss any discrepancies.

Scaffold instruction to support all students in their learning. Learning is individualized and you may want to group students differently as they move in and out of these levels with each skill and concept. Student self-assessment and feedback help guide your instructional decisions about how and when to layer support for all students to become proficient learners.

Extra Example 1

Identify the terms, coefficients, and constants in each expression.

a. $3a + 17$
Terms: $3a$, 17
Coefficient: 3
Constant: 17

b. $4x^2 + 5x + 7$
Terms: $4x^2$, $5x$, 7
Coefficients: 4, 5
Constant: 7

Try It

1. Terms: 12, $10c$
   Coefficient: 10
   Constant: 12
2. Terms: 15, $3w$, $\frac{1}{2}$
   Coefficient: 3
   Constants: 15, $\frac{1}{2}$
3. Terms: z^2, $9z$
   Coefficients: 1, 9
   Constant: none

Extra Example 2

Write each expression using exponents.

a. $x \cdot x \cdot x \cdot x \cdot x$ x^5

b. $7 \cdot d \cdot d \cdot d$ $7d^3$

Try It

4. j^6
5. $9k^5$

Extra Example 3

a. Evaluate $15 - y$ when $y = 3$. 12

b. Evaluate $24 \div w$ when $w = 4$. 6

Try It

6. 33

7. 13

8. 36

Extra Example 4

a. Evaluate $f + g$ when $f = 11$ and $g = 7$. 18

b. Evaluate $j \cdot k$ when $j = 12$ and $k = \frac{3}{4}$. 9

ELL Support

Allow students to work in groups to complete Try It Exercises 9–12. Circulate and listen to discussions. Expect students to perform according to their different language levels.

Beginner: Write the expression using the values of the variables and evaluate.

Intermediate: State the answer using a complete sentence. For example, "When p is twenty-four and q is eight, p divided by q is three."

Advanced: Explain the process.

Try It

9. 3

10. 32

11. 16

12. 192

Laurie's Notes

EXAMPLE 3

- Work through the example as a class. Use color-coding to help students recognize that substitution has occurred.
- There is only one operation in each part, so the order of operations is not necessary.
- Discuss the push-pin note. Students should be comfortable seeing multiplication represented in each of the three forms.

? "Can you use all three forms to represent multiplication of two numbers? Explain." No, if the numbers are 3 and 4, $3 \cdot 4$ and 3(4) are okay, but writing 34 is not.

- **Note:** Now that variables have been introduced, multiplication will not be represented with × when variables are present. This is to avoid confusion with the variable x.

Try It

- Have students work independently on the exercises and then compare their answers with a neighbor.
- Listen to their answers for Exercise 8. When dividing by $\frac{1}{2}$, did they multiply by the reciprocal or use a different strategy?

EXAMPLE 4

- Encourage students to use color-coding to differentiate between the two values being substituted.
- Check that students replace each variable with the correct value. Tell them to be careful when the values of the variables are not written in the same order as the variables in the expression.

? In part (b), "How do you divide a whole number by a fraction?" Multiply by the reciprocal of the fraction.

? "What strategies can you use to multiply 16 by $\frac{3}{2}$?" Listen for a variety of strategies. For example, students may say, "Multiply 16 by 3 to get 48 and then divide 48 by 2," or "$\frac{3}{2}$ is $1\frac{1}{2}$ and half of 16 is 8, so add 8 to 16."

- **MP2 Reason Abstractly and Quantitatively:** Allowing students to share different strategies of performing a computation helps them to develop computational fluency and the ability to reason quantitatively.

Try It

- Have students work in pairs to complete the exercises. Then have students share their answers verbally or on the board. Check students' work.

? "In Exercise 12, what other ways can you write $p \cdot q$?" pq or $(p)(q)$

◎ Students are continuing to work on the second success criterion.

To evaluate an algebraic expression, substitute a number for each variable. Then use the order of operations to find the value of the numerical expression.

EXAMPLE 3 Evaluating Algebraic Expressions

a. Evaluate $k + 10$ when $k = 25$.

$k + 10 = 25 + 10$ Substitute 25 for k.

$= 35$ Add 25 and 10.

b. Evaluate $4 \cdot n$ when $n = 12$.

$4 \cdot n = 4 \cdot 12$ Substitute 12 for n.

$= 48$ Multiply 4 and 12.

You can write the product of 4 and n in several ways.

$4 \cdot n$

$4n$

$4(n)$

Try It

6. Evaluate $24 + c$ when $c = 9$.
7. Evaluate $d - 17$ when $d = 30$.
8. Evaluate $18 \div q$ when $q = \frac{1}{2}$.

EXAMPLE 4 Evaluating an Expression with Two Variables

a. Evaluate $n - m$ when $m = 12$ and $n = 30$.

$n - m = 30 - 12$ Substitute 30 for n and 12 for m.

$= 18$ Subtract 12 from 30.

b. Evaluate $a \div b$ when $a = 16$ and $b = \frac{2}{3}$.

$a \div b = 16 \div \frac{2}{3}$ Substitute 16 for a and $\frac{2}{3}$ for b.

$= 16 \cdot \frac{3}{2}$ Multiply by the reciprocal of $\frac{2}{3}$, which is $\frac{3}{2}$.

$= 24$ Multiply.

Try It **Evaluate the expression when $p = 24$ and $q = 8$.**

9. $p \div q$
10. $q + p$
11. $p - q$
12. $p \cdot q$

EXAMPLE 5 Evaluating Expressions with Two Operations

a. Evaluate $3x - 14$ when $x = 5$.

$$3x - 14 = 3(5) - 14$$ Substitute 5 for x.

$$= 15 - 14$$ Using order of operations, multiply 3 and 5.

$$= 1$$ Subtract 14 from 15.

b. Evaluate $n^2 + 8.5$ when $n = 2$.

$$n^2 + 8.5 = 2^2 + 8.5$$ Substitute 2 for n.

$$= 4 + 8.5$$ Using order of operations, evaluate 2^2.

$$= 12.5$$ Add 4 and 8.5.

Try It **Evaluate the expression when $y = 6$.**

13. $5y + 1$
14. $30 - 24 \div y$
15. $y^2 - 7$
16. $1.5 + y^2$

Self-Assessment for Concepts & Skills

Solve each exercise. Then rate your understanding of the success criteria in your journal.

17. **WHICH ONE DOESN'T BELONG?** Which expression does *not* belong with the other three? Explain your reasoning.

$2x + 1$	$5w \cdot c$	$3(4) + 5$	$2y \cdot z$

18. **ALGEBRAIC EXPRESSIONS** Identify the terms, coefficients, and constants in the expression $9h + 1$.

EVALUATING EXPRESSIONS **Evaluate the expression when $m = 8$.**

19. $m - 7$
20. $5m + 4$

21. MP **USING TOOLS** Does the value of the expression $20 - x$ *increase*, *decrease*, or *stay the same* as x increases? Use technology to justify your answer.

22. **OPEN-ENDED** Write an algebraic expression using more than one operation. When you evaluate the expression, how do you know which operation to perform first?

23. MP **STRUCTURE** Is the expression $8.2 \div m \cdot m \cdot m \cdot m$ the same as the expression $8.2 \div m^4$? Explain your reasoning.

Laurie's Notes

EXAMPLE 5

- Students are asked to evaluate expressions involving more than one operation. They need to remember the order of operations.
- ? Write the expressions and ask, "How many operations will be performed in part (a)? in part (b)?" 2; 2
- ? "In part (a), which operation should you perform first?" multiplication "In part (b), which operation should you perform first?" evaluate the exponent
- These questions usually elicit a comment about the order of operations, at which time you can probe for understanding.
- Make students aware that they are working on the third success criterion, so that they can assess their understanding in the Self-Assessment for Concepts & Skills.

Try It

- Have students complete the exercises independently and then display their answers on whiteboards. Check students' work and look for errors involving the order of operations.

Self-Assessment for Concepts & Skills

- **MP6 Attend to Precision:** Have students work in groups to complete Exercise 17. This exercise should lead to a rich discussion that includes vocabulary, such as *terms, constants, coefficients, variables, expressions*, and *operations*. Students should share their reasoning using precise mathematical language.
- Have students complete Exercises 18–23 independently.
- **MP5 Use Appropriate Tools Strategically:** In Exercise 21, encourage students to use a calculator to substitute larger values for x in the expression $20 - x$.
- In Exercises 22 and 23, check their level of understanding of the second and third success criteria.

ELL Support

Allow students to practice language by working in pairs. Have two pairs compare their answers. If there is a disagreement, pairs should work together to reach a consensus. Check comprehension of Exercises 17–19 by having each group write their final answers on a whiteboard. Discuss Exercises 21–23 with students to check for understanding.

The Success Criteria Self-Assessment chart can be found in the *Student Journal* or online at *BigIdeasMath.com*.

Extra Example 5

a. Evaluate $\frac{t}{5} + 6$ when $t = 45$. 15

b. Evaluate $v^2 - 4$ when $v = 9$. 77

Try It

13. 31

14. 26

15. 29

16. 37.5

Self-Assessment for Concepts & Skills

17. $3(4) + 5$; the other three are algebraic expressions.

18. Terms: $9h$, 1
Coefficient: 9
Constant: 1

19. 1

20. 44

21. decrease; When you subtract greater and greater values from 20, you will have less and less left.

22. *Sample answer:* $5x + 4$; Use the order of operations.

23. no; $8.2 \div m \cdot m \cdot m \cdot m = \left(\frac{8.2}{m}\right) \cdot m^3$ and $8.2 \div m^4 = \frac{8.2}{m^4}$

Extra Example 6

You are saving money to buy a video game that costs \$50. Your uncle gives you \$20 and you save \$4 each week. The expression $20 + 4w$ gives the amount of money you save after w weeks. Can you buy the video game after 8 weeks? yes

Self-Assessment for Problem Solving

24. yes

25. yes; You need \$63 to buy the jacket and have \$66.

Formative Assessment Tip

Misconception Check

This technique gives students the opportunity to think about their own understanding of a concept or process. Write a worked-out problem on the board that demonstrates a common misconception, a mistake that students often make about a concept or process. Ask students if they agree or disagree with the solution and to explain why. Allow time for students to think about the problem independently and write an explanation. Then ask volunteers to share their explanations with the class. Listening to the thinking of others may solidify or modify their own beliefs.

Learning Target

Evaluate algebraic expressions given values of their variables.

Success Criteria

- Identify parts of an algebraic expression.
- Evaluate algebraic expressions with one or more variables.
- Evaluate algebraic expressions with one or more operations.

Laurie's Notes

EXAMPLE 6

- You may want to begin by displaying the first two sentences only. Then ask students to write an expression that represents the situation.
- **Think-Pair-Share:** Allow time for students to read the problem independently and consider the next step. Then have students work in pairs to discuss the problem, make a plan, use the plan to solve, and check their solutions. Have each pair compare their answer with another pair, and then explain their method. Ask volunteers to share their methods with the class.
- Discuss the Another Method note. Encourage students to think about how this strategy is similar to their own and why the strategy makes sense. You want students to see and appreciate different methods of solving a problem. Do not be surprised if some students substitute values for the variable until they get to, or exceed, \$125. The guess-and-check method is valid but not always efficient.

Self-Assessment for Problem Solving

- The goal for all students is to feel comfortable with the problem-solving plan. It is important for students to problem-solve in class, where they may receive support from you and their peers. Keep in mind that some students may only be ready to complete the first step.
- Have students work on the exercises independently. Each exercise requires students to read the problem, comprehend the situation, and determine what is being asked.
- Ask volunteers to share their strategies and allow others to ask questions for clarification.

The Success Criteria Self-Assessment chart can be found in the *Student Journal* or online at *BigIdeasMath.com.*

Closure

Misconception Check: "Do you agree or disagree with this solution? Explain."

Evaluate $5n - 3m$ when $m = 4$ and $n = 6$.

$$\begin{aligned} 5n - 3m &= 5(4) - 3(6) \\ &= 20 - 18 \\ &= 2 \end{aligned}$$

Sample answer: disagree; The wrong values were substituted for the variables.

EXAMPLE 6 Modeling Real Life

You are saving to buy a meteorite fragment for \$125. You begin with \$45 and you save \$3 each week. The expression $45 + 3w$ gives the amount of money you save after w weeks. Can you buy the meteorite after 20 weeks?

Understand the problem.

You are given an expression that represents your savings after w weeks. You are asked whether you have enough money to buy a \$125 meteorite after 20 weeks.

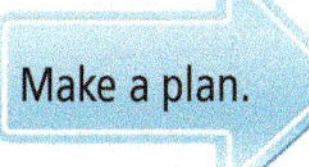

To find the amount of money you save after 20 weeks, evaluate the expression when $w = 20$. Then compare the value of the expression to the price of the meteorite.

$45 + 3w = 45 + 3(20)$	Substitute 20 for w.
$= 45 + 60$	Multiply 3 and 20.
$= 105$	Add 45 and 60.

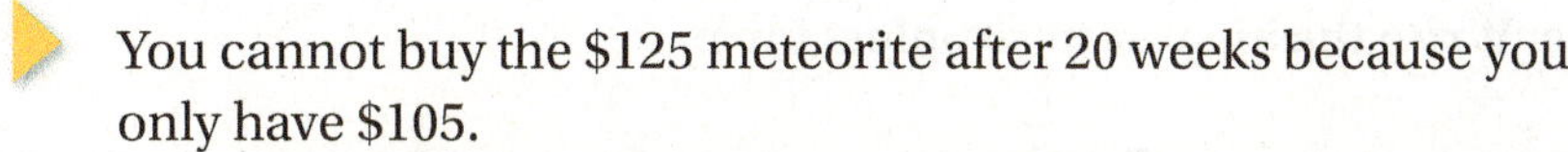

You cannot buy the \$125 meteorite after 20 weeks because you only have \$105.

Another Method You start with \$45, so you need to save another $125 - 45 = \$80$. At \$3 per week, it will take you $\frac{80}{3} \approx 27$ weeks of saving.

$$45 + 3(27) = 45 + 81 = \$126 \checkmark$$

Self-Assessment for Problem Solving

Solve each exercise. Then rate your understanding of the success criteria in your journal.

24. The expression $12.25m + 29.99$ gives the cost (in dollars) of a gym membership for m months. You have \$180 to spend on a membership. Can you buy a one-year membership?

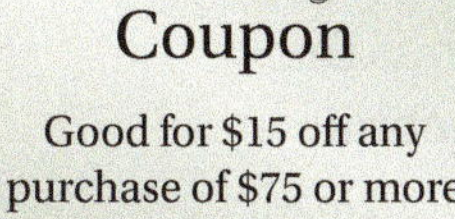

25. DIG DEEPER! The expression $p - 15$ gives the amount (in dollars) you pay after using the coupon when the original amount of a purchase is p dollars. The expression $30 + 6n$ gives the amount of money (in dollars) you save after n weeks. A jacket costs \$78. Can you buy the jacket after 6 weeks? Explain.

5.1 Practice

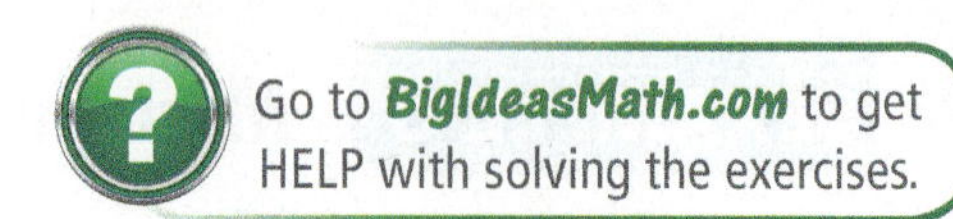

Review & Refresh

You ask 40 students which of three items from the cafeteria they like the best. You record the results on the piece of paper shown.

What is your favorite cafeteria food?
Pizza: 30%
Pasta: 18 students
Salad: 10 students

1. What percent of students answered salad?
2. How many students answered pizza?
3. What percent of students answered pasta?

Find the missing quantity in the double number line.

4. 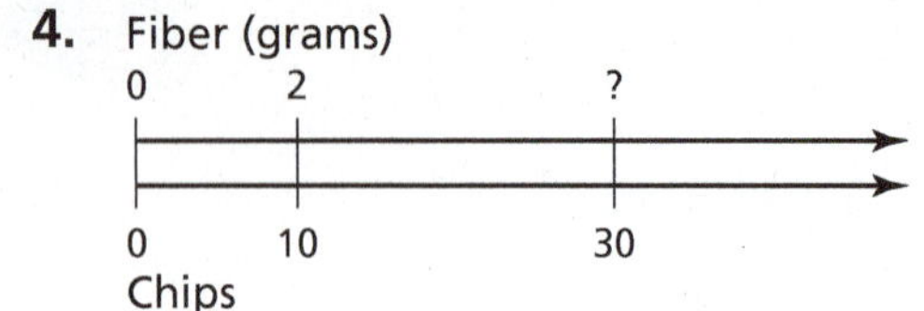

5. 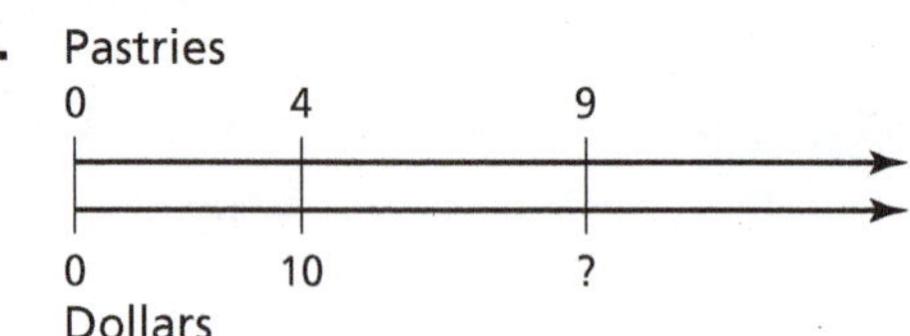

Divide. Write the answer in simplest form.

6. $1\frac{3}{8} \div \frac{3}{4}$

7. $2\frac{7}{9} \div 2$

8. $4 \div 4\frac{2}{5}$

9. $3\frac{2}{3} \div 1\frac{2}{7}$

Concepts, Skills, & Problem Solving

EVALUATING EXPRESSIONS **Write and evaluate an expression for the problem.** (See Exploration 1, p. 201.)

10. The scores on your first two history tests are 82 and 95. By how many points did you improve on your second test?
11. You buy a hat for \$12 and give the cashier a \$20 bill. How much change do you receive?
12. You receive \$8 for raking leaves for 2 hours. What is your hourly wage?
13. Music lessons cost \$20 per week. How much do 6 weeks of lessons cost?

ALGEBRAIC EXPRESSIONS **Identify the terms, coefficients, and constants in the expression.**

14. $7h + 3$

15. $g + 12 + 9g$

16. $5c^2 + 7d$

17. $2m^2 + 15 + 2p^2$

18. $6 + n^2 + \frac{1}{2}d$

19. $8x + \frac{x^2}{3}$

Terms: $2, x^2, y$
Coefficient: 2
Constant: none

20. MP YOU BE THE TEACHER Your friend finds the terms, coefficients, and constants in the algebraic expression $2x^2y$. Is your friend correct? Explain your reasoning.

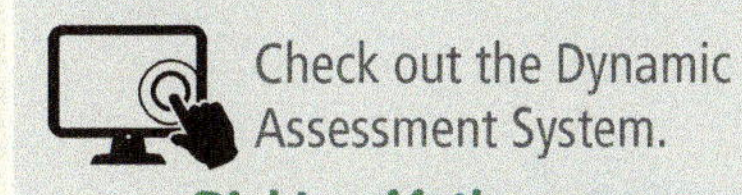

Assignment Guide and Concept Check

Scaffold assignments to support all students in their learning progression. The suggested assignments are a starting point. Continue to assign additional exercises and revisit with spaced practice to move every student toward proficiency.

Level	Assignment 1	Assignment 2
Emerging	2, 3, 5, 9, 12, 14, 15, 22, 25, 26, 31, 33, 37, 38, 51	16, 18, 20, 27, 28, 47, 48, 50, 55, 57, 60, 61
Proficient	2, 3, 5, 9, 12, 15, 17, 23, 24, 26, 33, 37, 39, 44, 51	19, 20, 27, 28, 29, 49, 50, 53, 56, 58, 60, 61, 62
Advanced	2, 3, 5, 9, 12, 18, 19, 27, 35, 39, 44, 45, 55	20, 28, 30, 49, 50, 53, 58, 60, 61, 62, 64, 65

- Assignment 1 is for use after students complete the Self-Assessment for Concepts & Skills.
- Assignment 2 is for use after students complete the Self-Assessment for Problem Solving.
- The red exercises can be used as a concept check.

Review & Refresh Prior Skills

Exercises 1 and 3 Finding Percents
Exercise 2 Finding the Percent of a Number
Exercises 4 and 5 Using a Double Number Line
Exercises 6–9 Dividing with Mixed Numbers

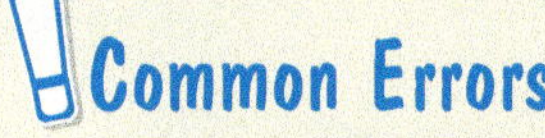

Common Errors

- **Exercises 14–19** Students may not list all of the coefficients of the variable terms. Remind them that a variable term such as *g* has a coefficient of 1, and that coefficients may also be fractions as in Exercises 18 and 19.

Review & Refresh

1. 25%
2. 12
3. 45%
4. 6
5. 22.5
6. $1\frac{5}{6}$
7. $1\frac{7}{18}$
8. $\frac{10}{11}$
9. $2\frac{23}{27}$

Concepts, Skills, & Problem Solving

10. $95 - 82$; 13
11. $20 - 12$; \$8
12. $8 \div 2$; \$4
13. 20×6; \$120
14. Terms: $7h$, 3
Coefficient: 7
Constant: 3
15. Terms: g, 12, $9g$
Coefficients: 1, 9
Constant: 12
16. Terms: $5c^2$, $7d$
Coefficients: 5, 7
Constant: none
17. Terms: $2m^2$, 15, $2p^2$
Coefficients: 2, 2
Constant: 15
18. Terms: 6, n^2, $\frac{1}{2}d$
Coefficients: 1, $\frac{1}{2}$
Constant: 6
19. Terms: $8x$, $\frac{x^2}{3}$
Coefficients: 8, $\frac{1}{3}$
Constant: none
20. no; The only term is $2x^2y$.

Concepts, Skills, & Problem Solving

21. a. Terms: $2\ell, 2w$
Coefficients: 2, 2
Constant: none

b. The coefficient 2 of ℓ represents that there are 2 lengths on the rectangle. The coefficient 2 of w represents that there are 2 widths on the rectangle.

22. b^3 **23.** g^5

24. $8w^4$ **25.** $5.2y^3$

26. a^2c^2 **27.** $2.1xz^4$

28. yes; There are 4 factors of n.

29. $(5d)^2$

30. $x^4 + x^3 + x^2 + x$

31. 9 **32.** 10

33. 11 **34.** 9

35. 10 **36.** 17

37. 6 **38.** 2

39. 5 **40.** 15

41. 9 **42.** 1

43. 4 **44.** 6

45. 24 **46.** 36

47. \$15; \$105

48. 24; 48; 72

49. 32; 16; 8

Common Errors

- **Exercises 24–27** Students may raise all the factors to the same power. Discuss the difference between $8w^4 = 8 \cdot w \cdot w \cdot w \cdot w$ and $(8w)^4 = 8w \cdot 8w \cdot 8w \cdot 8w$.
- **Exercises 31–46** Students may substitute the wrong value(s) for the variable(s). Tell students to write out the expression and then write the value(s) of the variable(s) underneath the variable(s) before substituting the value(s).

21. **PERIMETER** You can use the expression $2\ell + 2w$ to find the perimeter of a rectangle, where ℓ is the length and w is the width.

  a. Identify the terms, coefficients, and constants in the expression.

  b. Interpret the coefficients of the terms.

USING EXPONENTS **Write the expression using exponents.**

22. $b \cdot b \cdot b$
23. $g \cdot g \cdot g \cdot g \cdot g$
24. $8 \cdot w \cdot w \cdot w \cdot w$
25. $5.2 \cdot y \cdot y \cdot y$
26. $a \cdot a \cdot c \cdot c$
27. $2.1 \cdot x \cdot z \cdot z \cdot z \cdot z \cdot z$

28. **YOU BE THE TEACHER** Your friend writes the product using exponents. Is your friend correct? Explain your reasoning.

29. **AREA** Write an expression using exponents that represents the area of the square.

As I was going to St. Ives
I met a man with seven wives
Each wife had seven sacks
Each sack had seven cats
Each cat had seven kits
Kits, cats, sacks, wives
How many were going to St. Ives?

30. **REASONING** Suppose the man in the St. Ives poem has x wives, each wife has x sacks, each sack has x cats, and each cat has x kits. Write an expression using exponents that represents the total number of kits, cats, sacks, and wives.

EVALUATING EXPRESSIONS **Evaluate the expression when $a = 3$, $b = 2$, and $c = 12$.**

31. $6 + a$
32. $b \cdot 5$
33. $c - 1$
34. $27 \div a$
35. $12 - b$
36. $c + 5$
37. $2a$
38. $c \div 6$
39. $a + b$
40. $c + a$
41. $c - a$
42. $a - b$
43. $\frac{c}{a}$
44. $\frac{c}{b}$
45. $b \cdot c$
46. $c(a)$

47. **PROBLEM SOLVING** You earn $15n$ dollars for mowing n lawns. How much do you earn for mowing 1 lawn? 7 lawns?

EVALUATING EXPRESSIONS **Copy and complete the table.**

48.

x	3	6	9
$x \cdot 8$			

49.

x	2	4	8
$64 \div x$			

50. **MP MODELING REAL LIFE** Due to gravity, an object falls $16t^2$ feet in t seconds. You drop a rock from a bridge that is 75 feet above the water. Will the rock hit the water in 2 seconds? Explain.

EVALUATING EXPRESSIONS **Evaluate the expression when $a = 10$, $b = 9$, and $c = 4$.**

51. $2a + 3$

52. $4c - 7.8$

53. $\frac{a}{4} + \frac{1}{3}$

54. $\frac{24}{b} + 8$

55. $c^2 + 6$

56. $a^2 - 18$

57. $a + 9c$

58. $bc + 12.3$

59. $3a + 2b - 6c$

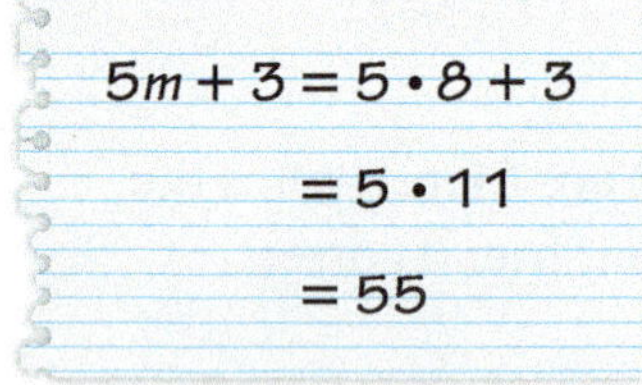

60. **MP YOU BE THE TEACHER** Your friend evaluates the expression when $m = 8$. Is your friend correct? Explain your reasoning.

61. **MP PROBLEM SOLVING** After m months, the height of a plant is $(10 + 3m)$ millimeters. How tall is the plant after 8 months? 3 years?

62. **MP STRUCTURE** You use a video streaming service to rent x new releases and y standard rentals. Which expression tells you how much money you will need?

$3x + 4y$ $\quad$ $4x + 3y$ $\quad$ $7(x + y)$

Standard Rentals
$3

New Releases
$4

63. **OPEN-ENDED** You float 2000 feet along a lazy river water ride. The ride takes less than 10 minutes. Give two examples of possible times and speeds.

64. **DIG DEEPER!** The expression $20a + 13c$ is the cost (in dollars) for a adults and c students to enter a science center.

    a. How much does it cost for an adult? a student? Explain your reasoning.

    b. Find the total cost for 4 adults and 24 students.

    c. You find the cost for a group. Then the numbers of adults and students in the group both double. Does the cost double? Explain your answer using an example.

    d. In part (b), the number of adults is cut in half, but the number of students doubles. Is the cost the same? Explain your answer.

65. **MP REASONING** The volume of the cube (in cubic inches) is equal to four times the area of one of its faces (in square inches). What is the volume of the cube?

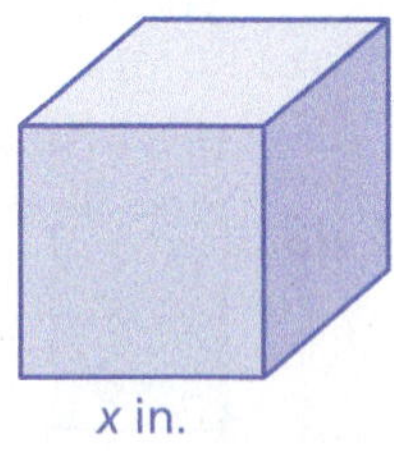

Common Errors

- **Exercises 51–59** Students may forget about the order of operations, or they may substitute the wrong value(s) for the variable(s). Review the order of operations. Before substituting, have students write or identify which operations are involved in the problem and which should be evaluated first.
- **Exercise 62** Students may rush through the problem and choose the first expression. Remind them to read the problem carefully.

Mini-Assessment

Evaluate the expression when $x = 2$, $y = 5$, and $z = 10$.

1. $5 + x$ 7
2. $3y$ 15
3. $z - y$ 5
4. $x \cdot y$ 10
5. Your friend earns $7x$ dollars for working x hours. How much does your friend earn for working 16 hours? 40 hours? $112; $280

Section Resources

Surface Level	Deep Level
Resources by Chapter • Extra Practice • Reteach • Puzzle Time Student Journal • Self-Assessment • Practice Differentiating the Lesson Tutorial Videos Skills Review Handbook Skills Trainer	Resources by Chapter • Enrichment and Extension Graphic Organizers Dynamic Assessment System • Section Practice

Concepts, Skills, & Problem Solving

50. no; In 2 seconds, the rock has only fallen 64 feet.

51. 23 **52.** 8.2

53. $2\frac{5}{6}$ **54.** $10\frac{2}{3}$

55. 22 **56.** 82

57. 46 **58.** 48.3

59. 24

60. no; $5m + 3 = 40 + 3 = 43$

61. 34 mm; 118 mm

62. $4x + 3y$

63. *Sample answer:* 8 min at 250 ft/min; 9 min at $222\frac{2}{9}$ ft/min

64. **a.** $20; $13; The coefficients represent the ticket prices.

b. $392

c. yes; *Sample answer:* $20(3) + 13(10) = 190$, $20(6) + 13(20) = 380$

d. no; *Sample answer:* $20(2) + 13(48) = 664$

65. 64 in.^{3}

Learning Target

Write algebraic expressions and solve problems involving algebraic expressions.

Success Criteria

- Write numerical expressions.
- Write algebraic expressions.
- Write and evaluate algebraic expressions that represent real-life problems.

Warm Up

Cumulative, vocabulary, and prerequisite skills practice opportunities are available in the *Resources by Chapter* or at *BigIdeasMath.com.*

ELL Support

Discuss the meaning of the word *expression*. In everyday language, an expression is used to describe something using descriptive language rather than the literal meaning. For example, when describing heavy rain, someone may use the expression, "It's raining cats and dogs!" In mathematics, an expression is used to represent a mathematical phrase containing numbers, operations, and/or variables.

Exploration 1

a. See Additional Answers.

b. *Sample answer:* $20 - p$

c. 20: customer has \$20; $4.65s$: total cost; 4.65: price per sandwich; s: number of sandwiches; no; Egg salad and grilled cheese both cost \$4.65, and the number of sandwiches is unknown.

Laurie's Notes

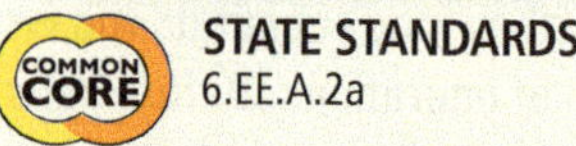

Preparing to Teach

- Students evaluated algebraic expressions in the last section and now they will build on that knowledge to write algebraic expressions that represent real-life problems.
- It is important for students to know that a variable can represent any value in an algebraic expression, but some values may not be reasonable. Writing an algebraic expression to represent a context provides an efficient method for testing multiple values.
- **MP8 Look for and Express Regularity in Repeated Reasoning:** When students write and then evaluate algebraic expressions for different values, they develop a general method, or shortcut. This occurs as a result of the calculations being repeated. Look for this understanding as students work through the exploration.

Motivate

- A synonym is one of two or more words or phrases that have the same meaning. For example, *loud* and *noisy* both can mean producing much noise.
- On the board, write the expression $3 \cdot n$. Ask multiple volunteers to read the expression aloud. Listen for various phrases, such as "3 times n," "3 multiplied by n," and "the product of 3 and n."
- **Discuss:** In math class, you often hear words or phrases that suggest a particular operation. In fact, there are several words that may imply the same operation. Today's lesson provides practice reading a situation and translating it into an algebraic expression.

Exploration 1

- **MP8 Look for and Express Regularity in Repeated Reasoning:** This exploration encourages students to see the differences between numerical and algebraic expressions. When writing an algebraic expression, students should recognize that the operations can be performed repeatedly by substituting different numbers for the variable(s).
- Introduce the exploration by asking about students' favorite sandwiches and which sandwich they would order from those recommended by the chef.
- In part (a), check to see that students are writing a numerical expression versus writing the result of the numerical expression. You want students to see the repetition in the last column, so that they can visualize the algebraic expression.
- In part (b), students can choose any variable for their algebraic expressions. Have them discuss what the variable represents in the situation. Ask students to share and explain their algebraic expressions.
- **MP3 Construct Viable Arguments and Critique the Reasoning of Others:** In part (c), ask a volunteer to give his or her explanation of the expression $20 - 4.65s$ and then ask if there are any other interpretations. Students should feel comfortable justifying their statements and discussing other explanations.

5.2 Writing Expressions

Learning Target: Write algebraic expressions and solve problems involving algebraic expressions.

Success Criteria:
- I can write numerical expressions.
- I can write algebraic expressions.
- I can write and evaluate algebraic expressions that represent real-life problems.

EXPLORATION 1 Writing Expressions

Work with a partner. You use a $20 bill to buy lunch at a café. You order a sandwich from the menu board shown.

Math Practice

Use Expressions
How do the numerical expressions help you generalize the situation and write an algebraic expression?

a. Complete the table. In the last column, write a numerical expression for the amount of change you receive.

Sandwich	Price (dollars)	Change Received (dollars)
Reuben		
BLT		
Egg salad		
Roast beef		

b. MP **REPEATED REASONING** Write an algebraic expression that represents the amount of change you receive when you order any sandwich from the menu board.

c. The expression $20 - 4.65s$ represents the amount of change one customer receives after ordering from the menu board. Explain what each part of the expression represents. Do you know what the customer ordered? Explain your reasoning.

5.2 Lesson

Some words can imply math operations.

Operation	Addition	Subtraction	Multiplication	Division
Key Words and Phrases	added to plus sum of more than increased by total of and	subtracted from minus difference of less than decreased by fewer than take away	multiplied by times product of twice	divided by quotient of

EXAMPLE 1 Writing Numerical Expressions

Write each phrase as an expression.

a. 8 fewer than 21

$21 - 8$ — The phrase *fewer than* means *subtraction*.

b. the product of 30 and 9

30×9, or $30 \cdot 9$ — The phrase *product of* means *multiplication*.

Math Practice

Communicate Precisely

What other phrases can you use to describe the operations in Example 1?

Try It **Write the phrase as an expression.**

1. the sum of 18 and 35

2. 6 times 50

EXAMPLE 2 Writing Algebraic Expressions

Write each phrase as an expression.

a. 14 more than a number x

$x + 14$ — The phrase *more than* means *addition*.

b. a number y minus 75

$y - 75$ — The word *minus* means *subtraction*.

c. the quotient of 3 and a number z

$3 \div z$, or $\frac{3}{z}$ — The phrase *quotient of* means *division*.

Common Error

When writing expressions involving subtraction or division, order is important. For example, the quotient of a number x and 2 means

$x \div 2$, not $2 \div x$.

Try It **Write the phrase as an expression.**

3. 25 less than a number b

4. a number x divided by 4

5. the total of a number t and 11

6. 100 decreased by a number k

Laurie's Notes

Scaffolding Instruction

- In the exploration, students extended their knowledge of writing numerical expressions to writing algebraic expressions. They used numerical expressions to explore writing an algebraic expression to represent a situation.
- **Emerging:** Students may struggle to choose a variable to represent an unknown value, or need practice writing the variable with an operation to indicate the meaning of a phrase. Students will benefit from guided instruction for the examples.
- **Proficient:** Students can translate phrases into algebraic expressions. They have strong literacy skills and can justify their expressions. Have students self-assess using the Try It exercises.

Discuss

- Review the table of words that can imply math operations. Ask students to add to the list.
- Remind students that these words and phrases must *always* be read in context. They cannot just pick out a word or phrase and assume that it will represent the same operation every time.
  - Clarify this misconception using the two scenarios. First, Ann buys a pen for \$2.50 and a notebook for \$3.25. What is the total of her purchases? Second, Ann buys 5 pens for \$2.50 each. What is the total of her purchases? Although "total of" is used in both situations, the expressions require two different operations (addition and multiplication, respectively).

EXAMPLE 1

- In part (a), remind students that for subtraction phrases they should always look for the key words *from* and *than* to know that the order of the numbers must be switched from the way the phrase is written.

EXAMPLE 2

? Refer students to the Common Error note and ask, "Is order important for addition and multiplication? Explain." No, addition and multiplication are commutative.

- Work through the example. Remind students that subtraction and division are not commutative. In part (b), the expression is *not* $75 - y$. In part (c), the expression is *not* $z \div 3$.

Try It

- **Neighbor Check:** Have students work independently, and then have their neighbors check their work. Have students discuss any discrepancies.
- **MP6 Attend to Precision:** Students communicate precisely to their peers by translating phrases into algebraic expressions and referring to the parts of the expressions using the correct vocabulary.

Scaffold instruction to support all students in their learning. Learning is individualized and you may want to group students differently as they move in and out of these levels with each skill and concept. Student self-assessment and feedback help guide your instructional decisions about how and when to layer support for all students to become proficient learners.

Extra Example 1

Write each phrase as an expression.

a. 34 divided by 2 $34 \div 2$

b. 35 increased by 43 $35 + 43$

Try It

1. $18 + 35$
2. $6 \cdot 50$

Extra Example 2

Write each phrase as an expression.

a. the difference of a number t and 95 $t - 95$

b. 2 times a number w $2w$

c. the total of a number x and 8 $x + 8$

Try It

3. $b - 25$
4. $x \div 4$
5. $t + 11$
6. $100 - k$

ELL Support

Have students work in pairs to discuss and complete Try It Exercises 3–6. Write each phrase on the board and underline *less than*, *divided by*, *total*, and *decreased by*. Explain that these phrases imply mathematical operations.
Beginner: Write the expression.
Intermediate: State the expression. For example, "*b* minus twenty-five."
Advanced: Explain why their expression is correct.

Extra Example 3

The number of students in the science club is 4 more than twice the number of students in the math club. Let m be the number of students in the math club. Which expression can you use to represent the number of students in the science club?

A. $4m + 2$ **B.** $2m + 4$

C. $2m - 4$ **D.** $4 - 2m$

B

Try It

7. $2t + 5$

Self-Assessment for Concepts & Skills

8. $7 + 11$

9. $9 - 5$

10. x take away 12; $x - 12$; $x + 12$

11. no; The first means $x - 12$, and the second means $12 - x$.

Laurie's Notes

EXAMPLE 3

- **MP1 Make Sense of Problems and Persevere in Solving Them:** Ask a volunteer to read the problem. Given the amount of words, some students may have difficulty getting started. Encourage students to re-read the problem and underline key words.
- Some students may be unfamiliar with interstates. Ask if anyone has been on these interstates. Are they close to home or in your state? If not, which interstates are close? What purpose do interstates serve?
- **Common Error:** Choice C is a very common *wrong* answer. Ask students to think about the value of the expression when $m = 100$. "Something negative" is a common response.
- Refer students to the push-pin note. Remind them that they have seen capital letters as variables before. A variable is just a symbol that represents a value and it can be lowercase or uppercase, as long as you are consistent. Just avoid any letter that may be confused with a number (e.g., O, I).

Try It

- In Exercise 7, some students may write $5 + 2t$ and others may write $2t + 5$. Addition is commutative, so this is fine. Caution students that subtraction is *not* commutative, so there is only one way to correctly write "five less than twice as many tokens."

Self-Assessment for Concepts & Skills

- These exercises encompass many of the words and phrases that students have been translating into operations.
- Students should work on the exercises independently. Then have them compare their answers with another student and discuss any differences.
- In Exercises 9 and 11, listen for students confusing the order of the terms. Ask volunteers to explain why only one expression is correct.

ELL Support

Allowing students to work in pairs provides extra support from peers and the opportunity to practice language. Check comprehension of Exercises 8–10 by having pairs write their answers on whiteboards. Discuss explanations for Exercise 11 to check for understanding.

The Success Criteria Self-Assessment chart can be found in the *Student Journal* or online at *BigIdeasMath.com*.

EXAMPLE 3 Writing an Algebraic Expression

Variables can be lowercase or uppercase. Make sure you consistently use the same case for a variable when solving a problem.

The length of Interstate 90 from the West Coast to the East Coast is 153.5 miles more than 2 times the length of Interstate 15 from southern California to northern Montana. Let *m* be the length of Interstate 15. Which expression can you use to represent the length of Interstate 90?

A. $2m + 153.5$ **B.** $2m - 153.5$

C. $153.5 - 2m$ **D.** $153.5m + 2$

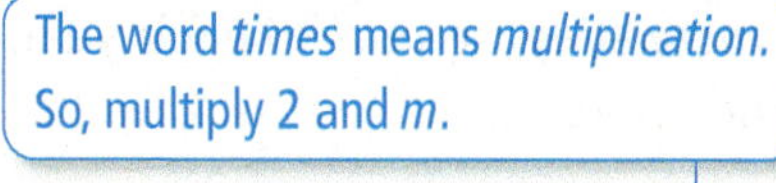

The phrase *more than* means *addition*.
So, add $2m$ and 153.5.

$2m + 153.5$

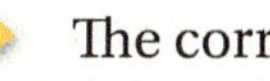

The correct answer is **A.**

Try It

7. Your friend has 5 more than twice as many game tokens as you. Let *t* be the number of game tokens you have. Write an expression for the number of game tokens your friend has.

Self-Assessment for Concepts & Skills

Solve each exercise. Then rate your understanding of the success criteria in your journal.

WRITING EXPRESSIONS **Write the phrase as an expression.**

8. the sum of 7 and 11

9. 5 subtracted from 9

10. **DIFFERENT WORDS, SAME QUESTION** Which is different? Write "both" expressions.

12 more than *x*	*x* increased by 12
x take away 12	the sum of *x* and 12

11. **MP PRECISION** Your friend says that the phrases below have the same meaning. Is your friend correct? Explain your reasoning.

the difference of a number *x* and 12

the difference of 12 and a number *x*

EXAMPLE 4 Modeling Real Life

You plant a cypress tree that is 10 inches tall. Each year, its height increases by 15 inches. Write an expression that represents the height (in inches) after *t* years. What is the height after 9 years?

10 in.

Make a table showing the height of the tree each year for the first several years. Use the results to write an expression and evaluate the expression when $t = 9$.

The height is *increasing*, so *add* 15 each year, as shown in the table.

Year, t	Height (inches)
0	10
1	$10 + 15(1) = 25$
2	$10 + 15(2) = 40$
3	$10 + 15(3) = 55$
4	$10 + 15(4) = 70$

When t is 0, the height is 10 inches.

You can see that an expression is $10 + 15t$.

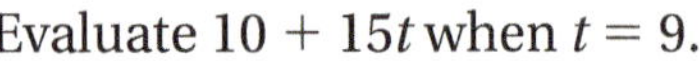

Sometimes, as in Example 3, a variable represents a single value. Other times, as in Example 4, a variable can represent more than one value.

Evaluate $10 + 15t$ when $t = 9$.

$$10 + 15t = 10 + 15(9) = 145$$

So, the height (in inches) after t years is $10 + 15t$. After 9 years, the height of the tree is 145 inches.

Self-Assessment for Problem Solving

Solve each exercise. Then rate your understanding of the success criteria in your journal.

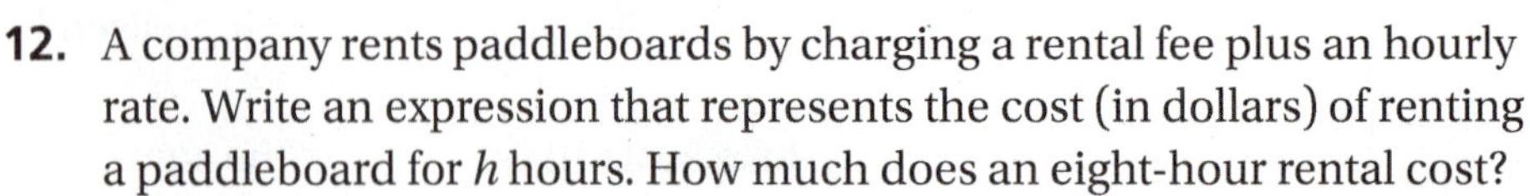

12. A company rents paddleboards by charging a rental fee plus an hourly rate. Write an expression that represents the cost (in dollars) of renting a paddleboard for h hours. How much does an eight-hour rental cost?

13. DIG DEEPER! A county fair charges an entry fee of \$7 and \$0.75 for each ride token. You have \$15. Write an expression that represents the amount (in dollars) you have left after entering the fair and purchasing n tokens. How many tokens can you purchase? How much money do you have left after purchasing 6 tokens?

Laurie's Notes

EXAMPLE 4

- Say, "You want to organize some information about this problem, so set up a table to keep track of the height each year."
- Make a table with two columns (year, height). It is not natural to start with the year 0, so be sure to discuss this. Each year students should add 15 to the last number.
- ? "How can you find the height after 9 years without computing all the years between 4 and 9?" Write an expression and evaluate it for 9 years.
- Work with students to develop the general expression $10 + 15t$ and verify that it works for years 0 through 4.
- ? "Check your answer. Does it make sense?" Students may not be able to visualize 145 inches, so tell them to convert to feet to see if it is reasonable.
- This example addresses the third success criterion.

Self-Assessment for Problem Solving

- Allow time in class for students to practice using the problem-solving plan. Remember, some students may only be able to complete the first step.
- Have students work independently, and then discuss the exercises as a class. Select two volunteers to display their work on the board.
- Exercise 12 is very similar to Example 4. As you circulate, remind students who are struggling to refer back to the example to jumpstart their thinking.
- Are students showing progress in relating words to numbers, variables, and symbols?

The Success Criteria Self-Assessment chart can be found in the *Student Journal* or online at *BigIdeasMath.com*.

Closure

- **Four Corners:** Designate each of four corners in your classroom as one of the four operations: addition, subtraction, multiplication, and division. Give each student an index card with a word or a phrase that represents one of the four operations (some phrases may be repeated). Tell students to move to the corners of the room that represent their cards.
- This is an informal, whole-class assessment of the first two success criteria.

Extra Example 4

A bamboo shoot is 4 inches tall. During its growing season, it grows 3 inches a day. Write an expression that represents the height (in inches) after d days. What is the height after 14 days?

$4 + 3d$; 46 inches

Self-Assessment for Problem Solving

12. $15 + 12h$; \$111

13. $8 - 0.75n$; 10; \$3.50

Formative Assessment Tip

Four Corners

This technique allows students to place a problem into one of four categories or answer choices. Designate each of four corners in your classroom as a different category or answer. Give each student an index card with a problem written on it and ask them to move to the corners of the room that correspond to their cards. Have students discuss with others in their corner and determine if they are all in the appropriate corner. Allow students to change corners if necessary. Have each group read their cards to the class, so that everyone hears which problems are related to each category or answer. Discuss any discrepancies as a class.

Learning Target

Write algebraic expressions and solve problems involving algebraic expressions.

Success Criteria

- Write numerical expressions.
- Write algebraic expressions.
- Write and evaluate algebraic expressions that represent real-life problems.

Review & Refresh

1. Terms: $4f$, 8
   Coefficient: 4
   Constant: 8
2. Terms: $\frac{4}{5}$, $3s$, 2
   Coefficient: 3
   Constants: $\frac{4}{5}$, 2
3. Terms: $9h^2$, $\frac{8}{9}p$, 1
   Coefficients: 9, $\frac{8}{9}$
   Constant: 1
4. 7.5
5. 2361.6 or 2400
6. 4860 or 4909.09
7. $\frac{4}{5}$
8. $\frac{4}{9}$
9. $\frac{2}{15}$
10. $3\frac{1}{2}$

Concepts, Skills, & Problem Solving

11. 10: you have \$10; $5.25n$: total cost; 5.25: price per sandwich; n: number of sandwiches
12. 20: you have \$20; $4.95n$: total cost; 4.95: price per sandwich; n: number of sandwiches
13. 100: you have \$100; $6.75n$: total cost; 6.75: price per sandwich; n: number of sandwiches
14. $8 - 5$
15. $3 \cdot 12$
16. $28 \div 7$
17. $6 + 10$
18. $18 - 3$
19. $15 + 17$
20. $x - 13$
21. $5 \cdot d$
22. $18 \div a$
23. $s - 6$
24. $7 + w$
25. t^3
26. no; The expression is $\frac{8}{y}$.
27. yes; The expression is correct.
28. a. $x \div 5$
    b. *Sample answer:* If the total cost is \$30, then the cost per person is $x \div 5 = 30 \div 5 = \$6$.
29. a.

Days	1	2	3	4	5
Samples	15	30	45	60	75

    b. $15n$

Assignment Guide and Concept Check

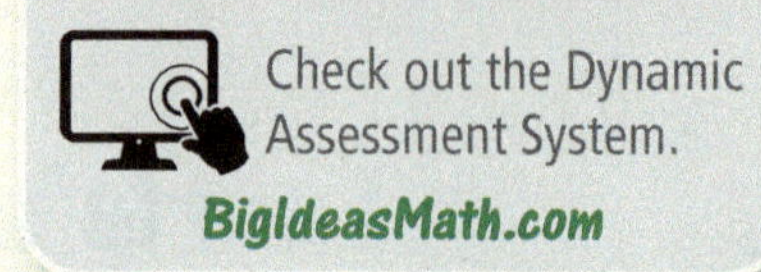

Scaffold assignments to support all students in their learning progression. The suggested assignments are a starting point. Continue to assign additional exercises and revisit with spaced practice to move every student toward proficiency.

Level	Assignment 1	Assignment 2
Emerging	3, 6, 9, 13, 14, 16, 17, 21, 22, 26	24, 25, 27, 28, 29, 30, 31, 37, 39, 41
Proficient	3, 6, 9, 13, 14, 17, 21, 22, 23, 26	24, 25, 27, 29, 30, 33, 37, 39, 40, 41
Advanced	3, 6, 9, 13, 14, 21, 22, 24, 25, 26	27, 33, 34, 38, 40, 41, 42, 43

- Assignment 1 is for use after students complete the Self-Assessment for Concepts & Skills.
- Assignment 2 is for use after students complete the Self-Assessment for Problem Solving.
- The red exercises can be used as a concept check.

Review & Refresh Prior Skills

Exercises 1–3 Identifying Parts of Algebraic Expressions
Exercises 4–6 Using Conversion Factors
Exercises 7–10 Dividing Fractions

Common Errors

- **Exercises 14–25** Students may write subtraction problems in the wrong order. Have students look for the key words *from* and *than* to know that the order of the numbers must be switched from the way the phrase is written. For example, "5 less *than* 8" means $8 - 5$, not $5 - 8$.
- **Exercises 14–25** Students may write division problems in the wrong order. For example, they may write "28 divided by 7" as $7 \div 28$ instead of $28 \div 7$.

5.2 Practice

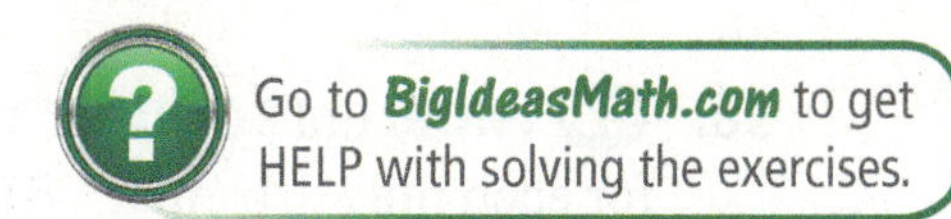

Review & Refresh

Identify the terms, coefficients, and constants in the expression.

1. $4f + 8$
2. $\frac{4}{5} + 3s + 2$
3. $9h^2 + \frac{8}{9}p + 1$

Copy and complete the statement.

4. $\frac{2\text{ c}}{\text{min}} = \frac{\square\text{ gal}}{\text{h}}$
5. $\frac{12\text{ m}}{\text{sec}} \approx \frac{\square\text{ ft}}{\text{min}}$
6. $\frac{3\text{ lb}}{\text{sec}} \approx \frac{\square\text{ kg}}{\text{h}}$

Divide. Write the answer in simplest form.

7. $\frac{1}{2} \div \frac{5}{8}$
8. $\frac{1}{3} \div \frac{3}{4}$
9. $\frac{2}{5} \div 3$
10. $3 \div \frac{6}{7}$

Concepts, Skills, & Problem Solving

MP STRUCTURE **The expression represents the amount of change you receive after buying *n* sandwiches. Explain what each part of the expression represents.** (See Exploration 1, p. 209.)

11. $10 - 5.25n$
12. $20 - 4.95n$
13. $100 - 6.75n$

WRITING EXPRESSIONS **Write the phrase as an expression.**

14. 5 less than 8
15. the product of 3 and 12
16. 28 divided by 7
17. the total of 6 and 10
18. 3 fewer than 18
19. 17 added to 15
20. 13 subtracted from a number x
21. 5 times a number d
22. the quotient of 18 and a number a
23. the difference of a number s and 6
24. 7 increased by a number w
25. a number t cubed

MP YOU BE THE TEACHER **Your friend writes the phrase as an expression. Is your friend correct? Explain your reasoning.**

26. The quotient of 8 and a number y is $\frac{y}{8}$.

27. 16 decreased by a number x is $16 - x$.

28. **MP NUMBER SENSE** Five friends share the cost of a dinner equally.
    a. Write an expression that represents the cost (in dollars) per person.
    b. Make up a reasonable total cost and test your expression.

29. **MP MODELING REAL LIFE** A biologist analyzes 15 bacteria samples each day.
    a. Copy and complete the table.
    b. Write an expression that represents the total number of samples analyzed after n days.

Days	1	2	3	4	5
Total Samples					

30. MP **PROBLEM SOLVING** To rent a moving truck for the day, it costs \$33 plus \$1 for each mile driven.

a. Write an expression that represents the cost (in dollars) to rent the truck.

b. You drive the truck 300 miles. How much do you pay?

WRITING PHRASES **Give two ways to write the expression as a phrase.**

31. $n + 6$ **32.** $4w$ **33.** $15 - b$ **34.** $14 - 3z$

EVALUATING EXPRESSIONS **Write the phrase as an expression. Then evaluate the expression when $x = 5$ and $y = 20$.**

35. 3 less than the quotient of a number y and 4

36. the sum of a number x and 4, all divided by 3

37. 6 more than the product of 8 and a number x

38. the quotient of 40 and the difference of a number y and 16

39. MP **MODELING REAL LIFE** It costs \$3 to bowl a game and \$2 for shoe rental.

a. Write an expression that represents the total cost (in dollars) of g games.

b. Use your expression to find the total cost of 8 games.

40. MP **MODELING REAL LIFE** Florida has 8 less than 5 times the number of counties in Arizona. Georgia has 25 more than twice the number of counties in Florida.

a. Write an expression that represents the number of counties in Florida.

b. Write an expression that represents the number of counties in Georgia.

c. Arizona has 15 counties. How many do Florida and Georgia have?

41. MP **PATTERNS** There are 140 people in a singing competition. The graph shows the results for the first five rounds.

a. Write an expression that represents the number of people after each round.

b. Assuming this pattern continues, how many people compete in the ninth round? Explain your reasoning.

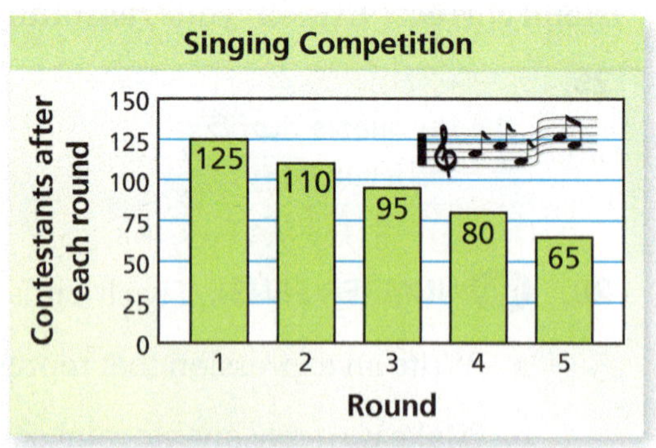

42. MP **NUMBER SENSE** The difference between two numbers is 8. The lesser number is a. Write an expression that represents the greater number.

43. MP **NUMBER SENSE** One number is four times another. The greater number is x. Write an expression that represents the lesser number.

Common Errors

- **Exercises 35–38** Students may write the problem in the wrong order, such as $\frac{y-3}{4}$ instead of $\frac{y}{4} - 3$. Tell students to write out the phrase and put parentheses around the different parts of the expression before writing an algebraic expression. Then evaluate the expression using the order of operations. For example, "3 less than (the quotient of a number y and 4)."

Mini-Assessment

Write the phrase as an expression.

1. the product of 5 and 7 $5 \cdot 7$
2. the sum of a number b and 3 $b + 3$
3. the quotient of 9 and a number y $\frac{9}{y}$
4. 8 less than a number x $x - 8$
5. It costs $15 for one surfing lesson and $25 per day to rent a surfboard. Write an expression for the total cost of one lesson and renting a surfboard for y days. $15 + 25y$

Section Resources

Surface Level	Deep Level
Resources by Chapter • Extra Practice • Reteach • Puzzle Time Student Journal • Self-Assessment • Practice Differentiating the Lesson Tutorial Videos Skills Review Handbook Skills Trainer	Resources by Chapter • Enrichment and Extension Graphic Organizers Dynamic Assessment System • Section Practice

Transfer Level	
Dynamic Assessment System • Mid-Chapter Quiz	Assessment Book • Mid-Chapter Quiz

Concepts, Skills, & Problem Solving

30. **a.** $33 + m$

b. $333

31–34. Sample answers given.

31. the sum of n and 6; 6 more than a number n

32. 4 times a number w; the product of 4 and a number w

33. a number b less than 15; 15 take away a number b

34. the difference of 14 and the product of 3 and a number z; 14 minus the product of 3 and a number z

35. $\frac{y}{4} - 3$; 2

36. $\frac{x+4}{3}$; 3

37. $8x + 6$; 46

38. $\frac{40}{y-16}$; 10

39. **a.** $2 + 3g$

b. $26

40. **a.** $5a - 8$

b. $2f + 25$

c. Florida has 67 counties. Georgia has 159 counties.

41. **a.** $140 - 15n$

b. 20; There are $140 - 15(8) = 20$ people left after the eighth round.

42. $a + 8$

43. $\frac{x}{4}$

Learning Target

Identify equivalent expressions and apply properties to generate equivalent expressions.

Success Criteria

- Explain the meaning of equivalent expressions.
- Use properties of addition to generate equivalent expressions.
- Use properties of multiplication to generate equivalent expressions.

Warm Up

Cumulative, vocabulary, and prerequisite skills practice opportunities are available in the *Resources by Chapter* or at *BigIdeasMath.com*.

ELL Support

Discuss the meaning of the word *property*. In everyday language, property refers to things that people own. For example, your clothing and toys are your property. A house or land is also commonly referred to as property. In mathematics, a property is a rule.

Exploration 1

a–b. See Additional Answers.

Laurie's Notes

Preparing to Teach

- Students will identify expressions that are equivalent and then review the properties of addition and multiplication with numbers before applying them to algebraic expressions.
- **MP3 Construct Viable Arguments and Critique the Reasoning of Others:** Mathematically proficient students justify their conclusions, communicate them to others, and respond to the arguments of others. In this lesson, students will make conjectures about which operations are commutative and associative. Expect clear communication of their thinking.

Motivate

- **Acting Time:** If there is a bit of an actor in you, start the class by pretending that you're brushing your teeth (about 10 seconds). Then take a tube of toothpaste out and apply some to the toothbrush. This will clearly evoke a few comments about the order in which you performed the two tasks.
- ? As students begin to comment, say, "Oh, does the order matter? Hmmm…"
- If brushing your teeth doesn't work for you, put a sock over a shoe or anything obviously in the wrong order. Do something that students will remember. Catch their attention!
- Have students think of other examples where order matters and ask volunteers to share.
- ? Then have students think of examples where order does *not* matter and ask volunteers to share. If students are struggling to think of ideas, say, "When you make a ham and cheese sandwich, does it matter if you put the ham on the bread and then the cheese?"

Exploration 1

- **Turn and Talk:** Ask students to discuss the meaning of the word *equivalent*. Students may say, "the same" or "equal." Refer to a balance, a visual that students used in prior courses. A balance shows that although each side looks different, they have the same "weight" when the sides are raised to the same height. Tell students to keep this in mind as they explore possible **equivalent expressions**.
- ? In part (a), tell students to read the directions carefully and skim the tables. Ask, "What kind of numbers do you want to choose as your four values for x?" They will probably mention "easy" numbers. Discuss what makes a number easy to compute with. Remind students that the four values they choose for the first table will be used for the other tables as well.
- After completing the tables, partners should discuss whether any expressions are equivalent and explain their reasoning.
- ? "What helps you remember the meaning of the Commutative and Associative Properties?" Listen for the root words *commute* and *associate*. "In part (b), how do you know the expressions in each example are equivalent?" The values of the expressions are the same on both sides of the equal sign.
- ? Discuss where the properties apply in part (a). "How do you know whether the algebraic expressions are equivalent?" The operations are the same in both expressions and the values of the expressions are the same for any value of x.

5.3 Properties of Addition and Multiplication

Learning Target: Identify equivalent expressions and apply properties to generate equivalent expressions.

Success Criteria:
- I can explain the meaning of equivalent expressions.
- I can use properties of addition to generate equivalent expressions.
- I can use properties of multiplication to generate equivalent expressions.

EXPLORATION 1 Identifying Equivalent Expressions

Work with a partner.

a. Choose four values for a variable x. Then evaluate each expression for each value of x. Are any of the expressions *equivalent*? Explain your reasoning.

x				
$4 + x + 4$				

x				
$16x$				

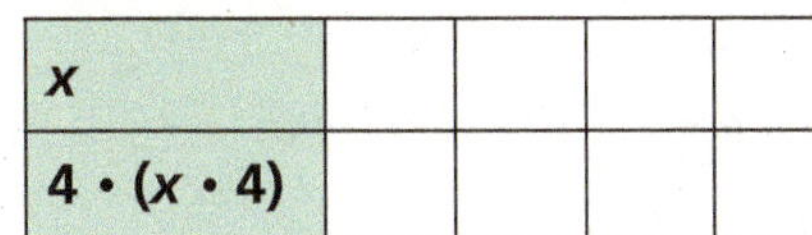

x				
$4 \cdot (x \cdot 4)$				

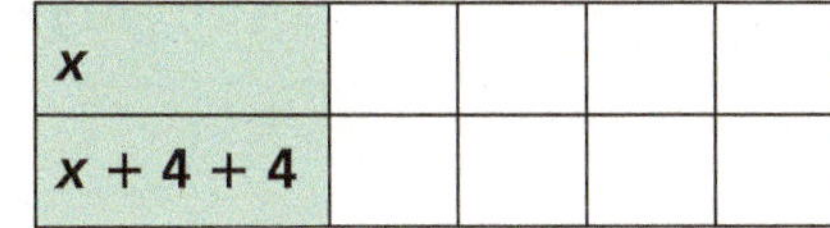

x				
$x + 4 + 4$				

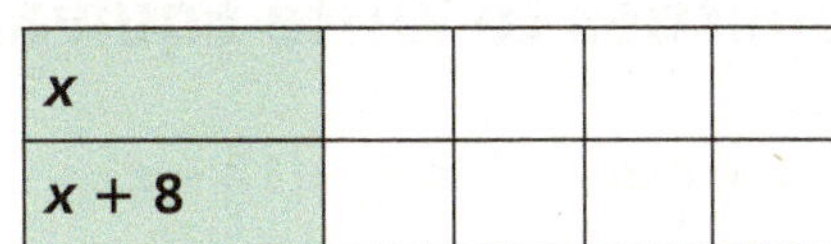

x				
$x + 8$				

x				
$(4 \cdot x) \cdot 4$				

b. You have used the following properties in a previous course. Use the examples to explain the meaning of each property.

Commutative Property of Addition: $3 + 5 = 5 + 3$

Commutative Property of Multiplication: $9 \cdot 3 = 3 \cdot 9$

Associative Property of Addition: $8 + (3 + 1) = (8 + 3) + 1$

Associative Property of Multiplication: $12 \cdot (6 \cdot 2) = (12 \cdot 6) \cdot 2$

Are these properties true for algebraic expressions? Explain your reasoning.

Math Practice

Use Counterexamples

Use a counterexample to show that the Commutative Property is not true for division.

5.3 Lesson

Key Vocabulary
equivalent expressions, *p. 216*

Expressions that result in the same number for any value of each variable are **equivalent expressions**. You can use the Commutative and Associative Properties to write equivalent expressions.

Key Ideas

Commutative Properties

Words Changing the order of addends or factors does not change the sum or product.

Numbers $5 + 8 = 8 + 5$
$5 \cdot 8 = 8 \cdot 5$

Algebra $a + b = b + a$
$a \cdot b = b \cdot a$

Associative Properties

Words Changing the grouping of addends or factors does not change the sum or product.

Numbers $(7 + 4) + 2 = 7 + (4 + 2)$
$(7 \cdot 4) \cdot 2 = 7 \cdot (4 \cdot 2)$

Algebra $(a + b) + c = a + (b + c)$
$(a \cdot b) \cdot c = a \cdot (b \cdot c)$

EXAMPLE 1 Using Properties to Write Equivalent Expressions

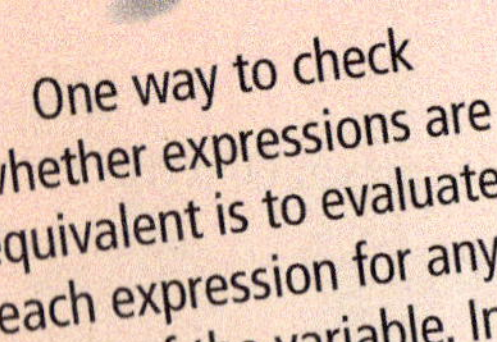

One way to check whether expressions are equivalent is to evaluate each expression for any value of the variable. In Example 1(a), use $x = 2$.

$7 + (12 + x) \stackrel{?}{=} 19 + x$

$7 + (12 + 2) \stackrel{?}{=} 19 + 2$

$21 = 21$ ✓

a. Simplify the expression $7 + (12 + x)$.

$7 + (12 + x) = (7 + 12) + x$ Associative Property of Addition

$= 19 + x$ Add 7 and 12.

b. Simplify the expression $(6.1 + x) + 8.4$.

$(6.1 + x) + 8.4 = (x + 6.1) + 8.4$ Commutative Property of Addition

$= x + (6.1 + 8.4)$ Associative Property of Addition

$= x + 14.5$ Add 6.1 and 8.4.

c. Simplify the expression $5(11y)$.

$5(11y) = (5 \cdot 11)y$ Associative Property of Multiplication

$= 55y$ Multiply 5 and 11.

Try It **Simplify the expression. Explain each step.**

1. $10 + (a + 9)$
2. $\left(c + \frac{2}{3}\right) + \frac{1}{2}$
3. $5(4n)$

Laurie's Notes

Scaffolding Instruction

- Students have applied properties to numerical expressions and explored substituting values for variables in algebraic expressions. They will now use the Commutative and Associative Properties, as well as the Properties of Zero and One, to show that expressions are equivalent.
- Review the meanings of *simplify*, *evaluate*, and *solve* with all students.
- **Emerging:** Students can evaluate expressions for given values but need practice applying the properties of addition and multiplication to find equivalent algebraic expressions.
- **Proficient:** Students understand **equivalent expressions** and are confident in using all the properties, even when variables are present. After reviewing the Key Ideas, students can proceed to Self-Assessment Exercises 7–13.

Key Ideas

- Write the Commutative and Associative Properties. The key word for the Commutative Property is *order*. The key word for the Associative Property is *grouping*.
- For the Commutative Property, multiplication can be represented in different ways: $ab = ba$ or $a \cdot b = b \cdot a$. This is also true for the Associative Property: $(ab)c = a(bc)$ versus $(a \cdot b) \cdot c = a \cdot (b \cdot c)$.
- Discuss that the variables can represent all the types of numbers students have studied: whole numbers, fractions, and decimals. Tell students that as they encounter other types of numbers (integers), they will need to verify that the properties still apply.

EXAMPLE 1

- Students have used these properties to simplify numerical expressions, now they will apply them to algebraic expressions.
- **MP6 Attend to Precision:** The challenges students have with these problems are that the answers seem obvious. Students often say, "Just combine the numbers and then tag on the variable." Remind students that this is only true for addition and multiplication.
- Note how the expression in part (c) does not contain multiplication dots.

Try It

- **Neighbor Check:** Have students work independently, and then have their neighbors check their work. Have students discuss any discrepancies.

ELL Support

Have students work in pairs to discuss and complete the exercises.
Beginner: Write the simplified expression.
Intermediate: State the simplified expression. For example, "Nineteen plus *a*."
Advanced: Relate the original expression to the simplified expression using a complete sentence. For example, "Ten plus the quantity *a* plus nine equals nineteen plus *a*."

Scaffold instruction to support all students in their learning. Learning is individualized and you may want to group students differently as they move in and out of these levels with each skill and concept. Student self-assessment and feedback help guide your instructional decisions about how and when to layer support for all students to become proficient learners.

Extra Example 1

a. Simplify the expression $(r + 3.2) + 6.7$. $r + 9.9$

b. Simplify the expression $4(3p)$. $12p$

c. Simplify the expression $(6 \cdot b) \cdot 7$. $42b$

Try It

1. $10 + (a + 9) = 10 + (9 + a)$ Comm. Prop. of Add.
$= (10 + 9) + a$ Assoc. Prop. of Add.
$= 19 + a$ Add 10 and 9.

2. $\left(c + \frac{2}{3}\right) + \frac{1}{2} = c + \left(\frac{2}{3} + \frac{1}{2}\right)$ Assoc. Prop. of Add.
$= c + 1\frac{1}{6}$ Add $\frac{2}{3}$ and $\frac{1}{2}$.

3. $5(4n) = (5 \cdot 4)n$ Assoc. Prop. of Mult.
$= 20n$ Multiply 5 and 4.

Extra Example 2

a. Simplify the expression $0 + (s + 4)$.
$s + 4$

b. Simplify the expression $(h \cdot 1) \cdot 8$.
$8h$

Try It

4. $12 \cdot b \cdot 0 = 12 \cdot (b \cdot 0)$
Assoc. Prop. of Mult.
$= 12 \cdot 0$
Mult. Prop. of Zero
$= 0$
Mult. Prop. of Zero

5. $1 \cdot m \cdot 24 = (1 \cdot m) \cdot 24$
Assoc. Prop. of Mult.
$= m \cdot 24$
Mult. Prop. of One
$= 24m$
Comm. Prop. of Mult.

6. $(t + 15) + 0 = t + (15 + 0)$
Assoc. Prop. of Add.
$= t + 15$
Add. Prop. of Zero

ELL Support

Have students work independently on Self-Assessment for Concepts & Skills Exercises 7–9. Then have students compare their answers with a partner to check understanding and practice language. Discuss Exercises 10 and 11 with students to verify understanding.

Self-Assessment for Concepts & Skills

7–9. See Additional Answers.

10. Expressions are equivalent when they result in the same number for any values of their variables; *Sample answer:* $(4 + 3)x$, $7x$

11. *Sample answer:* $(5 \cdot x) \cdot 1$

Laurie's Notes

Key Ideas

- Write and discuss the three new properties. Students may say (or at least think) that these properties are obvious.
- Adding zero, in any form, does not change the value of the quantity.
- Multiplying by zero, in any form, produces a product of 0.
- Multiplying by 1, in any form, does not change the value of the quantity.

  Remind students that 1 can be represented in different ways: 1, $\left(\frac{1}{2} + \frac{1}{2}\right)$, or $\frac{3}{3}$.
- The Addition Property of Zero is also known as the Identity Property of Addition (or the Additive Identity Property). The Multiplication Property of One is also know as the Identity Property of Multiplication (or the Multiplicative Identity Property). Meaning you end up with the same value you started with, so the values are *identical*.

EXAMPLE 2

- Work through both parts and point out the properties as they are used. Mention to students that the first steps in both parts involve the Associative Property of Multiplication. In part (a), you get the same result if you group $(0 \cdot p)$ first.
- In part (b), students may apply the Commutative Property of Multiplication first: writing $r \cdot 1$ as $1 \cdot r$ to group $(4.5 \cdot 1)$ and then apply the Multiplication Property of One. Encourage students to share different methods with the class.

Try It

Think-Pair-Share: Students should read each exercise independently and then work in pairs to simplify the expressions. After completing the exercises, have each pair compare their answers with another pair and discuss any discrepancies. As students are working on the last two success criteria, listen to their conversations to identify any common errors or misconceptions.

Self-Assessment for Concepts & Skills

- Have students work independently.
- Exercises 7–9 are accessible to all students because they are similar to Examples 1 and 2.
- Exercises 10 and 11 provide an indication of students' understanding of the success criteria. Do students understand what *equivalent* means in terms of algebraic expressions? Can they write an expression that can be simplified?
- Allow time for students to test their expressions in Exercise 11 to ensure they meet the requirements.
- **MP3 Construct Viable Arguments and Critique the Reasoning of Others:** Ask volunteers to write their expressions on the board for Exercise 11. Then ask the class if they agree or disagree with each expression.

The Success Criteria Self-Assessment chart can be found in the *Student Journal* or online at *BigIdeasMath.com*.

Key Ideas

Addition Property of Zero

Words The sum of any number and 0 is that number.

Numbers $7 + 0 = 7$ **Algebra** $a + 0 = a$

Multiplication Properties of Zero and One

Words The product of any number and 0 is 0.

The product of any number and 1 is that number.

Numbers $9 \cdot 0 = 0$ **Algebra** $a \cdot 0 = 0$

$4 \cdot 1 = 4$ $a \cdot 1 = a$

EXAMPLE 2 Using Properties to Write Equivalent Expressions

a. Simplify the expression $9 \cdot 0 \cdot p$.

$9 \cdot 0 \cdot p = (9 \cdot 0) \cdot p$ Associative Property of Multiplication

$= 0 \cdot p$ Multiplication Property of Zero

$= 0$ Multiplication Property of Zero

b. Simplify the expression $4.5 \cdot r \cdot 1$.

$4.5 \cdot r \cdot 1 = 4.5 \cdot (r \cdot 1)$ Associative Property of Multiplication

$= 4.5 \cdot r$ Multiplication Property of One

$= 4.5r$ Rewrite.

Try It **Simplify the expression. Explain each step.**

4. $12 \cdot b \cdot 0$ **5.** $1 \cdot m \cdot 24$ **6.** $(t + 15) + 0$

Self-Assessment for Concepts & Skills

Solve each exercise. Then rate your understanding of the success criteria in your journal.

USING PROPERTIES **Simplify the expression. Explain each step.**

7. $(7 + c) + 4$ **8.** $4(b \cdot 6)$ **9.** $0 \cdot b \cdot 9$

10. **WRITING** Explain what it means for expressions to be equivalent. Then give an example of equivalent expressions.

11. **OPEN-ENDED** Write an algebraic expression that can be simplified using the Associative Property of Multiplication and the Multiplication Property of One.

EXAMPLE 3 Modeling Real Life

You and six friends play on a basketball team. A sponsor paid \$100 for the league fee, x dollars for each player's T-shirt, and \$68.25 for basketballs. Write an expression that represents the total amount (in dollars) the sponsor paid. Then find the total amount paid when each T-shirt costs \$14.50.

Use a verbal model to write an expression that represents the sum of the league fee, the cost of the T-shirts, and the cost of the basketballs. Then evaluate the expression when $x = 14.5$.

Common Error

You **and** six friends are on the team, so use 7, not 6, to represent the number of T-shirts.

League fee (dollars)	+	Number of T-shirts	•	Cost per T-shirt (dollars)	+	Cost of basketballs (dollars)
\$100		7		x		\$68.25

$100 + 7x + 68.25 = 7x + 100 + 68.25$ — Commutative Property of Addition

$= 7x + (100 + 68.25)$ — Associative Property of Addition

$= 7x + 168.25$ — Add 100 and 68.25.

Evaluate $7x + 168.25$ when $x = 14.5$.

$$7x + 168.25 = 7(14.5) + 168.25 = 101.5 + 168.25 = 269.75$$

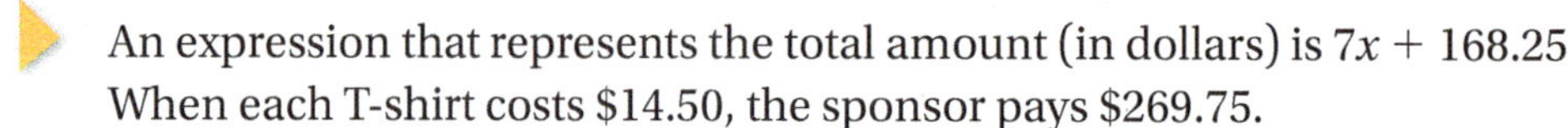

An expression that represents the total amount (in dollars) is $7x + 168.25$. When each T-shirt costs \$14.50, the sponsor pays \$269.75.

Self-Assessment for Problem Solving

Solve each exercise. Then rate your understanding of the success criteria in your journal.

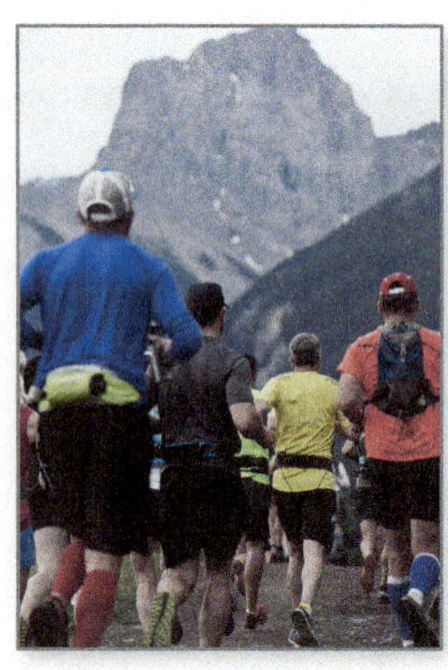

12. You and five friends form a team for an outdoor adventure race. Your team needs to raise money to pay for \$130 of travel fees, x dollars for each team member's entry fee, and \$85.50 for food. Use an algebraic expression to find the total amount your team needs to raise when the entry fee is \$25.50 per person.

13. You have \$50 and a \$15 gift card to spend online. You purchase a pair of headphones for \$34.99 and 8 songs for x dollars each. Use an algebraic expression to find the amount you have left when each song costs \$1.10.

Laurie's Notes

EXAMPLE 3

- Ask a student to read the problem aloud. Ask how many T-shirts were purchased and refer students to the Common Error note.
- Ask what information is needed to find the total amount and write a verbal model. Then use the verbal model to write an expression.
- "Can the expression be simplified using properties?"
- Ask students to explain why $7x + 168.25$ is an equivalent expression and how the properties of addition helped solve this problem. Listen for students' understanding of the success criteria.
- **Extension:** "If the sponsor decides to purchase different T-shirts that cost $17.30 each, then what will the new total be?" $289.35 "How much more will the sponsor pay?" $19.60

Self-Assessment for Problem Solving

- Allow time in class for students to practice using the problem-solving plan. Students should work independently. Support students with probing questions and feedback. Encourage students who are struggling to begin by using a verbal model. Remember, some students may only be able to complete the first step.
- Remind students to think back to similar problems they have solved and ask, "How did I approach that problem? Will the same approach work for this problem?"
- As students complete the exercises, ask, "Do your answers seem reasonable? Is there a way to check your answers?"
- Writing an expression to represent a context is an essential skill for writing and solving equations.

The Success Criteria Self-Assessment chart can be found in the *Student Journal* or online at *BigIdeasMath.com*.

Closure

- **Four Square:** Have students place $3.5 + (y + 1.1)$ in the ovals of their *Four Squares*. Then have students label each square as one of the four categories: writing an equivalent expression, identifying properties, evaluating the expression, and application. Students may choose a reasonable value for evaluating the expression and create a context for the application. *Sample answer:*

Writing an Equivalent Expression	Identifying Properties
$3.5 + (y + 1.1) = 3.5 + (1.1 + y)$ $= (3.5 + 1.1) + y$ $= 4.6 + y$	Commutative Property of Addition; Associative Property of Addition; Add 3.5 and 1.1.
Evaluating the Expression	**Application**
Evaluate $3.5 + (y + 1.1)$ when $y = 4.4$. $3.5 + (y + 1.1) = 3.5 + (4.4 + 1.1)$ $= 3.5 + 5.5$ $= 9$	You purchase a stapler for $3.50, a binder for *y* dollars, and a pen for $1.10. Use an algebraic expression to find the total amount you paid when the binder costs $4.40. $9

Center oval: $3.5 + (y + 1.1)$

Extra Example 3

You hand out 425 programs on the first night of your school's variety show, *p* programs on the second night, and 520 programs on the third night. Write an expression that represents the total number of programs you handed out. Then find the total number of programs that you handed out if you handed out 515 programs on the second night.

$p + 945$; 1460 programs

Self-Assessment for Problem Solving

12. $368.50 **13.** $21.21

Formative Assessment Tip

Four Square

A *Four Square* is often used as a study reference, however, it can be used to assess students' understanding of a concept. One way to use a *Four Square* is to write a problem in the oval and label each of the four squares surrounding the oval as a related category. Related categories may include: answer, meaning, application, algebra, numbers, model, graph, or equation. You can also ask students to illustrate each of the four depth of knowledge levels in the squares surrounding the problem. Consider hanging students' *Four Squares* around the classroom so they see a variety of ways to display information about a particular problem.

Learning Target

Identify equivalent expressions and apply properties to generate equivalent expressions.

Success Criteria

- Explain the meaning of equivalent expressions.
- Use properties of addition to generate equivalent expressions.
- Use properties of multiplication to generate equivalent expressions.

Review & Refresh

1. $10 + p$ 2. $6m$
3. $b \div 15$ 4. $s - 7$
5. $2^2 \times 3^2$ 6. $2^4 \times 3^2$
7. 3×7^2 8. 5×41
9. 11.592 10. 4.543
11. 13.641 12. 6.412

Concepts, Skills, & Problem Solving

13. 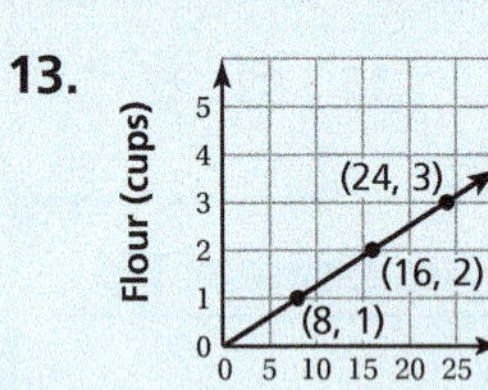

14. 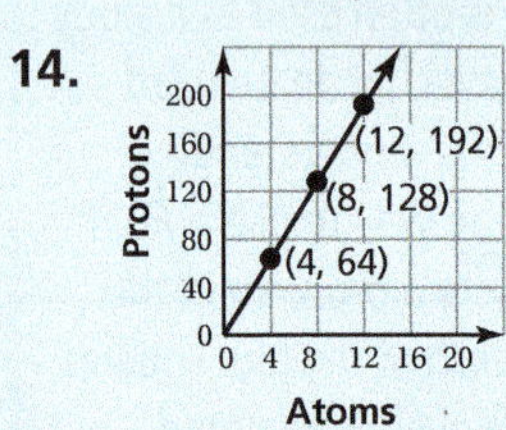

15. B 16. C
17. A 18. D
19. Comm. Prop. of Mult.
20. Assoc. Prop. of Add.
21. Assoc. Prop. of Mult.
22. Comm. Prop. of Add.
23. Add. Prop. of Zero
24. Mult. Prop. of One
25. no; The statement illustrates the Commutative Property of Addition.
26. $6 + (5 + x) = (6 + 5) + x$
Assoc. Prop. of Add.
$= 11 + x$
Add 6 and 5.
27. $(14 + y) + 3 = (y + 14) + 3$
Comm. Prop. of Add.
$= y + (14 + 3)$
Assoc. Prop. of Add.
$= y + 17$
Add 14 and 3

28–37. See Additional Answers.

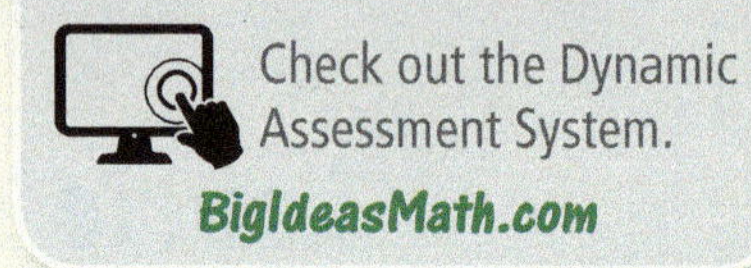

Assignment Guide and Concept Check

Scaffold assignments to support all students in their learning progression. The suggested assignments are a starting point. Continue to assign additional exercises and revisit with spaced practice to move every student toward proficiency.

Level	Assignment 1	Assignment 2
Emerging	4, 6, 12, 14, 15, 16, 17, 18, 19, 20, 21, 22, 23, 24	25, 26, 28, 31, 33, 38, 39, 41, 47, 48
Proficient	4, 6, 12, 14, 15, 16, 17, 18, 19, 20, 21, 22, 23, 24, 43, 46	25, 27, 28, 31, 33, 39, 40, 41, 44, 48
Advanced	4, 6, 12, 14, 15, 16, 17, 18, 19, 20, 21, 22, 23, 24, 44, 46	25, 31, 32, 33, 34, 40, 42, 48, 49

- Assignment 1 is for use after students complete the Self-Assessment for Concepts & Skills.
- Assignment 2 is for use after students complete the Self-Assessment for Problem Solving.
- The red exercises can be used as a concept check.

Review & Refresh Prior Skills

Exercises 1–4 Writing Expressions
Exercises 5–8 Writing a Prime Factorization
Exercises 9–12 Adding and Subtracting Decimals
Exercises 13 and 14 Graphing Ratio Relationships

Common Errors

- **Exercises 26–37** Students are often confused by the differences between the Commutative and Associative Properties and may incorrectly label steps. Show students that the Associative Property moves the parentheses but does not change the position of the terms. The Commutative Property changes the positions of the terms.

5.3 Practice

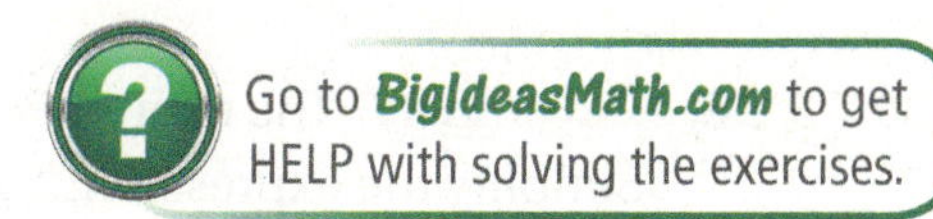

Review & Refresh

Write the phrase as an expression.

1. 10 added to a number p

2. the product of 6 and a number m

3. the quotient of a number b and 15

4. 7 fewer than a number s

Write the prime factorization of the number.

5. 36 **6.** 144 **7.** 147 **8.** 205

Evaluate the expression.

9. $8.092 + 3.5$

10. $16.78 - 12.237$

11. $9.17 + 1.83 + 2.641$

12. $8.43 - 6.218 + 4.2$

Represent the ratio relationship using a graph.

13.

Oil (teaspoons)	8	16	24
Flour (cups)	1	2	3

14.

Atoms	4	8	12
Protons	64	128	192

Concepts, Skills, & Problem Solving

MATCHING **Match the expression with an equivalent expression.**
(See Exploration 1, p. 215.)

15. $3 + 3 + y$ **16.** $(y \cdot y) \cdot 3$ **17.** $3 \cdot 1 \cdot y$ **18.** $(3 + 0) + (y + y)$

A. $y \cdot 3$ **B.** $y + 3 + 3$ **C.** $y(3 \cdot y)$ **D.** $(3 + y) + y$

IDENTIFYING PROPERTIES **Tell which property the statement illustrates.**

19. $5 \cdot p = p \cdot 5$

20. $2 + (12 + r) = (2 + 12) + r$

21. $4 \cdot (x \cdot 10) = (4 \cdot x) \cdot 10$

22. $x + 7.5 = 7.5 + x$

23. $(c + 2) + 0 = c + 2$

24. $a \cdot 1 = a$

25. MP **YOU BE THE TEACHER** Your friend states the property that the statement illustrates. Is your friend correct? Explain your reasoning.

$(7 + x) + 3 = (x + 7) + 3$
Associative Property of Addition

USING PROPERTIES **Simplify the expression. Explain each step.**

26. $6 + (5 + x)$

27. $(14 + y) + 3$

28. $6(2b)$

29. $7(9w)$

30. $3.2 + (x + 5.1)$

31. $(0 + a) + 8$

32. $9 \cdot c \cdot 4$

33. $(18.6 \cdot d) \cdot 1$

34. $\left(3k + 4\frac{1}{5}\right) + 8\frac{3}{5}$

35. $(2.4 + 4n) + 9$

36. $(3s) \cdot 8$

37. $z \cdot 0 \cdot 12$

38. **GEOMETRY** The expression $12 + x + 4$ represents the perimeter of a triangle. Simplify the expression.

39. **MP PRECISION** A case of scout cookies has 10 cartons. A carton has 12 boxes. The amount you earn on a whole case is $10(12x)$ dollars.

a. What does x represent?

b. Simplify the expression.

40. **MP MODELING REAL LIFE** A government estimates the cost to design new radar technology over a period of m months. The government estimates \$840,000 for equipment, \$15,000 for software, and \$40,000 per month for wages. Use an algebraic expression to find the total cost the government estimates when the project takes 16 months to complete.

WRITING EXPRESSIONS **Write the phrase as an expression. Then simplify the expression.**

41. 7 plus the sum of a number x and 5

42. the product of 8 and a number y, multiplied by 9

USING PROPERTIES **Copy and complete the statement using the specified property.**

	Property	Statement
43.	Associative Property of Multiplication	$7(2y) =$
44.	Commutative Property of Multiplication	$13.2 \cdot (x \cdot 1) =$
45.	Associative Property of Addition	$17 + (6 + 2x) =$
46.	Addition Property of Zero	$2 + (c + 0) =$
47.	Multiplication Property of One	$1 \cdot w \cdot 16 =$

48. **GEOMETRY** Five identical triangles form the trapezoid shown.

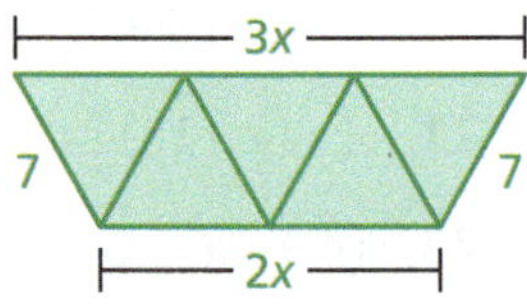

a. What is the perimeter of the trapezoid?

b. How can you use some or all of the triangles to form a new trapezoid with a perimeter of $3x + 14$? Explain your reasoning.

49. **DIG DEEPER!** You and a friend sell hats at a fair booth. You sell 16 hats on the first shift and 21 hats on the third shift. Your friend sells x hats on the second shift.

a. The expression $37(14) + 10x$ represents the amount (in dollars) that you both earn. How can you tell that your friend is selling the hats for a lower price?

b. You earn more money than your friend. What can you say about the value of x?

Common Errors

- **Exercises 43–47** If students are struggling to identify properties, ask them to think about how they can complete the statement without looking at the property. Once they know how to simplify the expression, tell them to look at the definitions of the properties and identify which property they used.

Mini-Assessment

Simplify the expression. Explain each step.

1. $7 + (3 + y)$

   $(7 + 3) + y$ Associative Property of Addition
   $10 + y$ Add 7 and 3.

2. $4(8x)$

   $(4 \cdot 8)x$ Associative Property of Multiplication
   $32x$ Multiply 4 and 8.

3. $6 + (b + 4)$

   $6 + (4 + b)$ Commutative Property of Addition
   $(6 + 4) + b$ Associative Property of Addition
   $10 + b$ Add 6 and 4.

4. $(7 \cdot d) \cdot 1$

   $7 \cdot (d \cdot 1)$ Associative Property of Multiplication
   $7 \cdot d$ Multiplication Property of One
   $7d$ Rewrite.

5. The expression $5 + x + 7$ represents the perimeter of a triangle. Simplify the expression. $12 + x$

Section Resources

Surface Level	Deep Level
Resources by Chapter • Extra Practice • Reteach • Puzzle Time Student Journal • Self-Assessment • Practice Differentiating the Lesson Tutorial Videos Skills Review Handbook Skills Trainer	Resources by Chapter • Enrichment and Extension Graphic Organizers Dynamic Assessment System • Section Practice

Concepts, Skills, & Problem Solving

38. $x + 16$

39. **a.** the amount per box
b. $120x$

40. $1,495,000

41. $7 + (x + 5); x + 12$

42. $8 \cdot (y \cdot 9); 72y$

43. $(7 \cdot 2) \cdot y$

44. $13.2 \cdot (1 \cdot x)$

45. $(17 + 6) + 2x$

46. $2 + c$

47. $w \cdot 16$

48. **a.** $5x + 14$
b. *Sample answer:* Remove the two triangles at the right so the side lengths are x, 7, $2x$, and 7.

49. **a.** *Sample answer:* From the expression, the 37 hats you sold cost $14 each and the x hats your friend sold cost $10 each.
b. x is at most 51.

Laurie's Notes

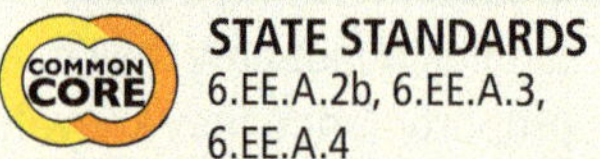

STATE STANDARDS
6.EE.A.2b, 6.EE.A.3, 6.EE.A.4

Learning Target

Apply the Distributive Property to generate equivalent expressions.

Success Criteria

- Explain how to apply the Distributive Property.
- Use the Distributive Property to simplify algebraic expressions.
- Use the Distributive Property to combine like terms.

Warm Up

Cumulative, vocabulary, and prerequisite skills practice opportunities are available in the *Resources by Chapter* or at *BigIdeasMath.com.*

ELL Support

Explain that the word *distributive* is related to the word *distribute*. When you distribute flyers to a class, you give a flyer to each person in the class. When using the Distributive Property to simplify an expression, you multiply each term in the parentheses by the number outside the parentheses before finding the sum or difference.

Exploration 1

a. $3x + 12$; $48 + 8y$; $9n$; n; Rewrite the area of the large rectangle as the sum of the areas of the smaller rectangles; There is a total of 9 parts and a difference of 1 part.

b. Answers will vary. Students should evaluate each expression for several values to show they are equivalent.

c. See Additional Answers.

Preparing to Teach

- In prior courses, students used the Distributive Property for numerical expressions. Now they will apply the Distributive Property to algebraic expressions. This property is very important to algebraic work in future courses. Allow students the time they need to be successful.
- In the exploration, students will use models and basic computation facts to find and verify equivalent algebraic expressions.
- **MP2 Reason Abstractly and Quantitatively:** Mathematically proficient students can identify quantities in a model and interpret the relationship. A model provides a foundation for the Distributive Property that is accessible to all students.

Motivate

- Draw two rectangles on the board that have the same width but different lengths. Label the dimensions.
- Have students write an expression for the total area of the rectangles: (_______ • _______) + (_______ • _______).
- Rearrange the rectangles by aligning the shortest sides to form one rectangle. Label the dimensions. Have students write an expression for the area: _______ • (_______ + _______).

? "Can the expressions be set equal to each other? Explain." Yes, both expressions represent the same area.

Exploration 1

? For the first two models, point out that there is one label for the width but two labels for the length. "Are the lengths represented by these two labels equal?" yes "If you consider the entire model as one large rectangle and then consider it as two smaller rectangles next to each other, are the total areas different? Explain." No, the two smaller rectangles together will have the same area as the larger rectangle because they represent the same area but in a different arrangement.

- Use the two different ways of identifying the length of each rectangle to create two different equivalent expressions to represent the area.

? Students will be able to count the boxes in the third model to find their sum and difference. This is similar to what students did with pictures models in prior courses. They should see $5n + 4n$ is $9n$. "What happens when the 4 n boxes are next to the 5 n boxes?" It forms a rectangle that is n wide and $(5 + 4)$ long. So the area is $n(5 + 4)$ square units. The Commutative Property allows students to write the expression as $9n$. Have students explain $5n - 4n$.

- In part (c), listen for understanding that the numerical expressions are equivalent because they have the same value. Students should also realize that the operations will be the same in both algebraic expressions and the values of the algebraic expressions will be the same for any value of x.
- **MP7 Look for and Make Use of Structure:** As students practice using both models, they will realize that the resulting expressions are equivalent and provide a structure for simplifying. Later in the lesson, this structure helps students reverse the Distributive Property to combine **like terms**.

5.4 The Distributive Property

Learning Target: Apply the Distributive Property to generate equivalent expressions.

Success Criteria:
- I can explain how to apply the Distributive Property.
- I can use the Distributive Property to simplify algebraic expressions.
- I can use the Distributive Property to combine like terms.

EXPLORATION 1 Using Models to Simplify Expressions

Work with a partner.

a. Use the models to simplify the expressions. Explain your reasoning.

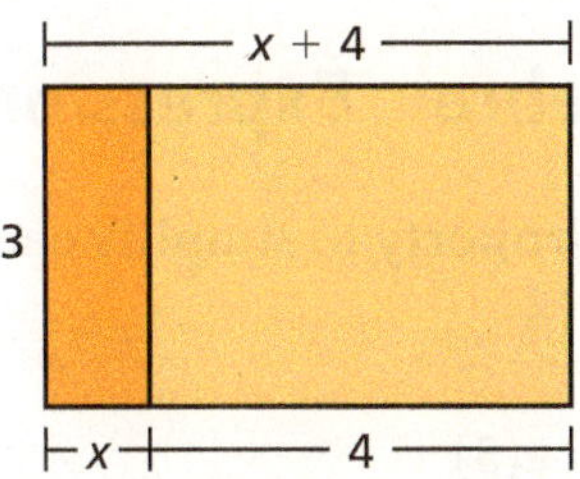

$3(x + 4) =$ 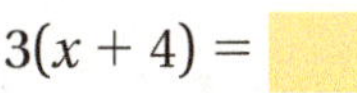

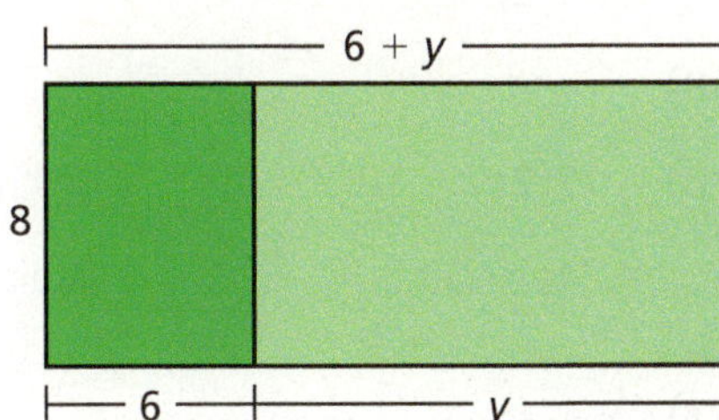

$8(6 + y) =$ 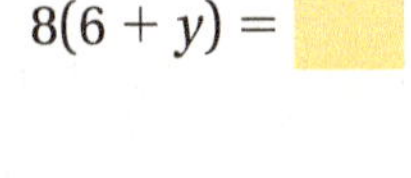

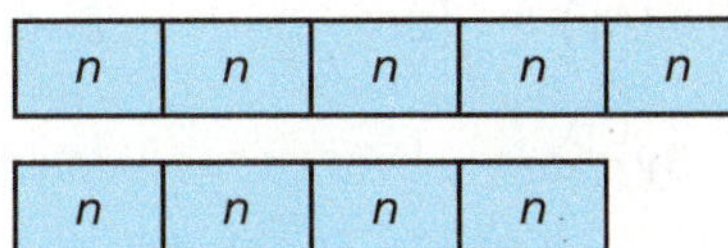

$5n + 4n =$

$5n - 4n =$

b. In part (a), check that the original expressions are equivalent to the simplified expressions.

c. You used the Distributive Property in a previous course. Use the example to explain the meaning of the property.

Distributive Property: $6(20 + 3) = 6(20) + 6(3)$

Is this property true for algebraic expressions? Explain your reasoning.

Math Practice

Find Entry Points

How can the Distributive Property be used to find the product of 9 and 32?

5.4 Lesson

Key Vocabulary
like terms, *p. 223*

Key Idea

Distributive Property

Words To multiply a sum or difference by a number, multiply each term in the sum or difference by the number outside the parentheses. Then simplify.

Numbers $3(7 + 2) = 3 \times 7 + 3 \times 2$ **Algebra** $a(b + c) = ab + ac$

$3(7 - 2) = 3 \times 7 - 3 \times 2$ $a(b - c) = ab - ac$

EXAMPLE 1 Simplifying Algebraic Expressions

Use the Distributive Property to simplify each expression.

a. $4(n + 5)$

$4(n + 5) = 4(n) + 4(5)$ Distributive Property

$= 4n + 20$ Multiply.

b. $12(2y - 3)$

$12(2y - 3) = 12(2y) - 12(3)$ Distributive Property

$= 24y - 36$ Multiply.

c. $\frac{1}{2}(6y - 2z)$

$\frac{1}{2}(6y - 2z) = \frac{1}{2}(6y) - \frac{1}{2}(2z)$ Distributive Property

$= 3y - z$ Multiply.

d. $9(6 + x + 2)$

$9(6 + x + 2) = 9(6) + 9(x) + 9(2)$ Distributive Property

$= 54 + 9x + 18$ Multiply.

$= 9x + 54 + 18$ Commutative Property of Addition

$= 9x + (54 + 18)$ Associative Property of Addition

$= 9x + 72$ Add 54 and 18.

You can use the Distributive Property when there are more than two terms in the sum or difference.

Try It **Use the Distributive Property to simplify the expression.**

1. $7(a + 2)$

2. $3(d - 11)$

3. $12\left(a + \frac{2}{3}b\right)$

4. $7(2 + 6 - 4d)$

Multi-Language Glossary at *BigIdeasMath.com*

Laurie's Notes

Scaffolding Instruction

- In the exploration, students built upon experiences with the Distributive Property from prior courses and now have a sense of the usefulness of the Distributive Property.
- **Emerging:** Students understand that there is an order for distributing over the parentheses but make computational errors or neglect to multiply all the parts in the parentheses. They will benefit from guided instruction for the examples.
- **Proficient:** Students understand the models and are confident in applying the Distributive Property. Have students self-assess using the Try It exercises.

Key Idea

- Draw attention to how the multiplication is shown.
- Students may ask why you would want to write 3×9 as $3(7 + 2)$ and 3×5 as $3(7 - 2)$. The answer is that you wouldn't! Simple values are being used to demonstrate the property instead of using a problem such as 8×67.
- Spend more time discussing the algebraic representation. In the problem $a(b + c)$, ask what *operations* students see. Not all students will see two. Some may only see addition.
- Explain that the blue arrows are used to remind you to distribute 3 to all parts of the expression in the parentheses. The arrows can also be written above the expression.

? "Do you know where the arrows go in the other three examples?"

EXAMPLE 1

- Slowly work through each part. Introducing a variable expression is *not* a small change!
- Using the order of operations, you should complete the operation inside the parentheses first, however, n and 5 are not **like terms** so they cannot be combined. The next operation to be performed is multiplication, so distribute 4 to n and 5. Use arrows to show that 4 is being distributed to both n and 5.
- **Common Error:** Students may only multiply the first term in the parentheses when simplifying instead of all the terms. It is important to watch each student simplify at least one expression and offer guidance as needed. Guided practice now will prevent repeated mistakes later.

Try It

- **Think-Pair-Share:** Have students read each exercise independently and then work in pairs to simplify the expressions. After completing the exercises, the pair should compare their answers with another pair and discuss any discrepancies. Listen for understanding of using the Distributive Property to simplify algebraic expressions.
- Look for students avoiding Exercise 3. Encourage students by asking probing questions that involve fractions.
- In Exercise 4, some students may recognize that $7(2 + 6 - 4d)$ is equivalent to $7(8 - 4d)$.

Scaffold instruction to support all students in their learning. Learning is individualized and you may want to group students differently as they move in and out of these levels with each skill and concept. Student self-assessment and feedback help guide your instructional decisions about how and when to layer support for all students to become proficient learners.

Extra Example 1

Use the Distributive Property to simplify each expression.

a. $11(x + 7)$ $11x + 77$

b. $8(c - 4)$ $8c - 32$

c. $\frac{1}{3}(9x - 3y)$ $3x - y$

d. $3(4 + r + 3)$ $3r + 21$

ELL Support

Have students work in pairs to complete Try It Exercises 1–4.
Beginner: Use the Distributive Property to simplify the expression and write out each step.
Intermediate: Verbally explain each step using complete sentences.
Advanced: Explain how the Distributive Property is used to simplify the expression.

Try It

1. $7a + 14$
2. $3d - 33$
3. $12a + 8b$
4. $56 - 28d$

Extra Example 2

Simplify each expression.

a. $7w + 11 + 3w - 4$ $10w + 7$

b. $b + b + b + b$ $4b$

c. $2c + 3(f + 5c)$ $17c + 3f$

Try It

5. $8 + 2z$
6. $4b + 17$

ELL Support

Provide support for Self-Assessment for Concepts & Skills Exercise 7 by reading the ELL Support on page T-221 to students. Allow students to work in pairs for Exercises 8–10. Have pairs display their answers on whiteboards for your review.

Self-Assessment
for Concepts & Skills

7. *Sample answer:* You must distribute or give the number outside the parentheses to the terms inside the parentheses.
8. $3x + 30$
9. $60n - 30$
10. $15w + 5$

Laurie's Notes

Discuss

? Write $5x + 2x + 2 + 19$ on the board. Ask, "How many terms are in the expression?" 4 "Why are 2 and 19 **like terms**?" They are both constants. "Why are $5x$ and $2x$ like terms?" They both have the same variable raised to the same exponent.

EXAMPLE 2

- Refer students to the push-pin note. The Distributive Property works in reverse. Remind them that this is similar to what they did with the n boxes in the exploration.
- Work through parts (a) and (b) as shown. These problems should make sense to students.
- In part (a), you may want to show combining like terms that contain variables using the visual shown.

$$3x + 2x = \underbrace{\overbrace{x + x + x}^{3x} + \overbrace{x + x}^{2x}}_{5x} = 5x$$

? Part (c) is more involved. Write part (c) and ask, "How many operations do you see?" 5 operations "What are they?" multiply, add, multiply, subtract, multiply

- **MP7 Look for and Make Use of Structure:** Help students recognize the structure of this expression. I like to read it as, "7 times the variable z plus 2 times the quantity z minus $5y$." Before working with the $7z$, the Distributive Property must be used.
- Use arrows to help students see 2 is distributed to both z and $5y$.

Try It

- **Neighbor Check:** Have students work independently, and then have their neighbors check their work. Have students discuss any discrepancies.
- **Thumbs Up:** Ask students to assess their understanding of using the Distributive Property to combine like terms.

Self-Assessment for Concepts & Skills

- Exercise 7 asks students to explain their interpretations of the Distributive Property before applying the skill in Exercises 8–10. This will help you analyze your students' level of understanding.
- Identify the reasons for incorrect answers for Exercises 8–10. Are the errors computational? Can students complete Exercises 8 and 9 successfully but not 10, or vice versa? Make sure students are aware of the reasons for any mistakes.

The Success Criteria Self-Assessment chart can be found in the *Student Journal* or online at *BigIdeasMath.com*.

In an algebraic expression, **like terms** are terms that have the same variables raised to the same exponents. Constant terms are also like terms.

like terms → $5x + 2x$; like terms → $2 + 19$

$$5x + 2x + 2 + 19$$

You can use the Distributive Property to *combine* like terms.

EXAMPLE 2 Combining Like Terms

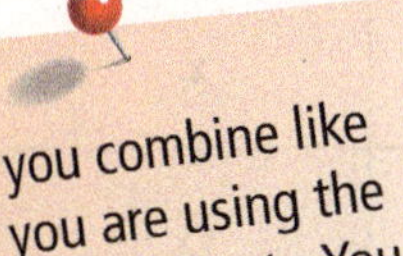

When you combine like terms, you are using the Distributive Property. You are applying the rules

$ab + ac = a(b + c)$

and

$ab - ac = a(b - c)$.

Simplify each expression.

a. $3x + 9 + 2x - 5$

$3x + 9 + 2x - 5 = 3x + 2x + 9 - 5$	Commutative Property of Addition
$= (3 + 2)x + 9 - 5$	Distributive Property
$= 5x + 4$	Simplify.

b. $y + y + y$

$y + y + y = 1y + 1y + 1y$	Multiplication Property of One
$= (1 + 1 + 1)y$	Distributive Property
$= 3y$	Add coefficients.

c. $7z + 2(z - 5y)$

$7z + 2(z - 5y) = 7z + 2(z) - 2(5y)$	Distributive Property
$= 7z + 2z - 10y$	Multiply.
$= (7 + 2)z - 10y$	Distributive Property
$= 9z - 10y$	Add coefficients.

Try It **Simplify the expression.**

5. $8 + 3z - z$

6. $3(b + 5) + b + 2$

Self-Assessment for Concepts & Skills

Solve each exercise. Then rate your understanding of the success criteria in your journal.

7. WRITING One meaning of the word *distribute* is *to give something to each member of a group*. How can this help you remember the Distributive Property?

SIMPLIFYING EXPRESSIONS **Use the Distributive Property to simplify the expression.**

8. $3(x + 10)$

9. $15(4n - 2)$

10. $2w + 4 + 13w + 1$

EXAMPLE 3 Modeling Real Life

José is x years old. His brother, Felipe, is 2 years older than José. Their aunt, Maria, is three times as old as Felipe. Write and simplify an expression that represents Maria's age in years.

Use a table to organize the given information and write an expression that represents each person's age in years.

Name	Description	Expression
José	He is x years old.	x
Felipe	He is 2 years *older* than José. So, *add* 2 to x.	$x + 2$
Maria	She is three *times* as old as Felipe. So, *multiply* 3 and $(x + 2)$.	$3(x + 2)$

Look Back
If José is 10 years old, then Felipe is $10 + 2 = 12$ years old and Maria is $3(12) = 36$ years old. So, you should obtain 36 when you evaluate $3x + 6$ for $x = 10$.

$3x + 6 = 3(10) + 6$
$= 36$ ✓

Simplify the expression that represents Maria's age.

$3(x + 2) = 3(x) + 3(2)$ Distributive Property

$= 3x + 6$ Multiply.

 Maria's age in years is represented by the expression $3x + 6$.

Self-Assessment for Problem Solving

Solve each exercise. Then rate your understanding of the success criteria in your journal.

11. You purchase a remote-controlled drone for d dollars. Your friend purchases a drone that costs \$35 more than your drone. Your brother purchases a drone that costs three times as much as your friend's drone. Write and simplify an expression that represents the cost (in dollars) of your brother's drone.

12. Write and simplify an expression that represents the total cost (in dollars) of buying the items shown for each member of a baseball team.

13. **DIG DEEPER!** One molecule of caffeine contains x oxygen atoms, twice as many nitrogen atoms as oxygen atoms, 4 more carbon atoms than nitrogen atoms, and 1.25 times as many hydrogen atoms as carbon atoms. Write and simplify an expression that represents the difference of the number of hydrogen atoms and the number of oxygen atoms in 1 molecule of caffeine. Justify your answer..

Laurie's Notes

EXAMPLE 3

- Write the table representing each person's age in words and algebraically. Connect this problem to writing expressions in Section 5.2.
- ? "Is there a way to check your expression?" Choose an age for José and use it to find Felipe's and Maria's ages. Substitute the age of José in the simplified expression to check that it is the same age you calculated for Maria. Refer students to the Look Back note.
- **Extension:** "If José is 12, find each person's age." Felipe: 14; Maria: 42

Self-Assessment for Problem Solving

- The goal for all students is to feel comfortable with the problem-solving plan. It is important for students to problem-solve in class, where they may receive support from you and their peers. Keep in mind that some students may only be ready to complete the first step.
- Each problem has an application of the Distributive Property. Remind students that making tables may help them organize their thoughts.
- Have students complete Exercises 11 and 12 independently, and then prepare to explain their methods.
- **Turn and Talk:** Have students review their methods and answers. Allow time for discussion and to ask questions that they are unable to resolve themselves.
- Have pairs work together on Exercise 13 to write equivalent expressions for the number of hydrogen atoms. Encourage pairs to substitute values to verify their expressions. Ask volunteers to explain their methods.
- Have students use *Fist of Five* to indicate their understanding of the success criteria.

The Success Criteria Self-Assessment chart can be found in the *Student Journal* or online at *BigIdeasMath.com*.

Formative Assessment Tip

One-Minute Card

This technique provides a quick assessment of students' understanding of a concept. Write a short prompt on the board and allow 1 minute for students to consider the prompt. Give each student an index card and allow 1 minute for students to write their responses. When time is up, collect the cards and review the responses. The next day, spend a few minutes discussing any misconceptions or exceptional responses.

Closure

- **One-Minute Card:** Explain how to simplify the expression $5(n + 8)$ using the Distributive Property.

Extra Example 3

You are x years old. Your father is 25 years older than you. Your grandfather is two times older than your father. Write and simplify an expression that represents your grandfather's age in years. $2(x + 25)$; $2x + 50$

Self-Assessment for Problem Solving

11. $3(d + 35) = 3d + 105$
12. $(10 + x)y = 10y + xy$
13. $1.25(2x + 4) - x = 2.5x + 5 - x = 1.5x + 5$; There are x oxygen atoms, $2x$ nitrogen atoms, $2x + 4$ carbon atoms, and $1.25(2x + 4)$ hydrogen atoms in one molecule of caffeine. So, the difference of the number of hydrogen atoms and the number of oxygen atoms is $1.25(2x + 4) - x = 1.5x + 5$.

Learning Target

Apply the Distributive Property to generate equivalent expressions.

Success Criteria

- Explain how to apply the Distributive Property.
- Use the Distributive Property to simplify algebraic expressions.
- Use the Distributive Property to combine like terms.

Review & Refresh

1. $(s + 4) + 8 = s + (4 + 8)$
   Assoc. Prop. of Add.
   $= s + 12$
   Add 4 and 8.

2. $(12 + x) + 2 = (x + 12) + 2$
   Comm. Prop. of Add.
   $= x + (12 + 2)$
   Assoc. Prop. of Add.
   $= x + 14$
   Add 12 and 2.

3. $3(4n) = (3 \cdot 4)n$
   Assoc. Prop. of Mult.
   $= 12n$
   Multiply 3 and 4.

4. 15 boys, 12 girls
5. 12 boys, 20 girls
6. 9 boys, 13 girls
7. 14 boys, 8 girls
8. 43
9. 123
10. $52\frac{5}{12}$
11. $260\frac{8}{31}$

Concepts, Skills, & Problem Solving

12. $5z + 30$; Rewrite area of the large rectangle as the sum of the areas of the smaller rectangles.
13. $6s$; The sum of 4 parts and 2 parts is 6 parts.
14. $3x + 12$
15. $10b - 60$
16. $6s - 54$
17. $56 + 7y$
18. $96 + 8a$
19. $18n + 9$
20. $72 - 12k$
21. $90 - 54w$
22. $63 + 9c$
23. $3 + \frac{1}{4}x$
24. $40g + 24$
25. $78 + 6z$
26. $4x + 4y$
27. $25x - 25y$
28. $7p + 7q + 63$
29. $n + 2 + 3m$
30. C
31. A
32. D
33. B
34. $5(r + 15), 5r + 5 \cdot 15$; $5(r + 15) = 5r + 5 \cdot 15$

Check out the Dynamic Assessment System.
BigIdeasMath.com

Assignment Guide and Concept Check

Scaffold assignments to support all students in their learning progression. The suggested assignments are a starting point. Continue to assign additional exercises and revisit with spaced practice to move every student toward proficiency.

Level	Assignment 1	Assignment 2
Emerging	3, 7, 11, 12, 13, 14, 16, 19, 25, 36, 37, 38	29, 30, 31, 32, 33, 34, 35, 40, 41, 42, 49, 52
Proficient	3, 7, 11, 12, 13, 16, 18, 19, 25, 36, 38, 43	29, 30, 31, 32, 33, 35, 42, 44, 48, 49, 50, 51, 52
Advanced	3, 7, 11, 12, 13, 21, 23, 24, 29, 43, 45, 48	42, 46, 49, 50, 51, 52, 53

- Assignment 1 is for use after students complete the Self-Assessment for Concepts & Skills.
- Assignment 2 is for use after students complete the Self-Assessment for Problem Solving.
- The red exercises can be used as a concept check.

Review & Refresh Prior Skills

Exercises 1–3 Using Properties
Exercises 4–7 Using a Tape Diagram
Exercises 8–11 Dividing Whole Numbers

Common Errors

- **Exercises 14–29** Students may forget to distribute to each term in the parentheses, especially when there are more than two terms. Tell students to write the expression in the parentheses on their papers and draw arrows from the number being distributed to each term.

5.4 Practice

Go to **BigIdeasMath.com** to get HELP with solving the exercises.

Review & Refresh

Simplify the expression. Explain each step.

1. $(s + 4) + 8$
2. $(12 + x) + 2$
3. $3(4n)$

You are given the difference of the numbers of boys and girls in a class and the ratio of boys to girls. How many boys and how many girls are in the class?

4. 3 more boys; 5 for every 4
5. 8 more girls; 3 for every 5
6. 4 more girls; 9 for every 13
7. 6 more boys; 7 for every 4

Divide.

8. $301 \div 7$
9. $1722 \div 14$
10. $629 \div 12$
11. $8068 \div 31$

Concepts, Skills, & Problem Solving

USING MODELS **Use the model to simplify the expression. Explain your reasoning.** (See Exploration 1, p. 221.)

12. $5(z + 6) =$ ▭

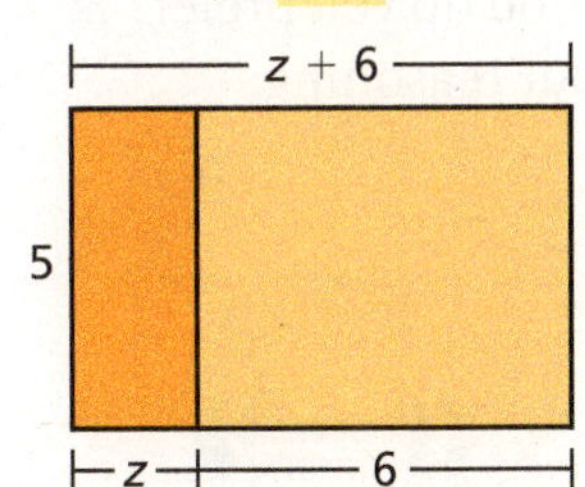

13. $4s + 2s =$ ▭

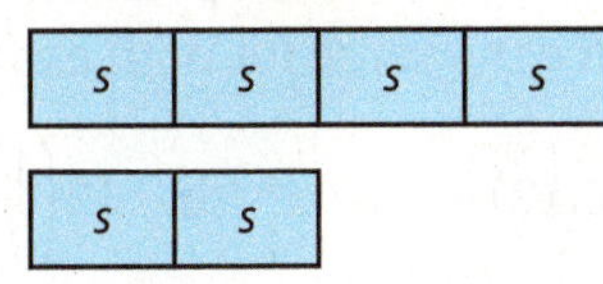

SIMPLIFYING EXPRESSIONS **Use the Distributive Property to simplify the expression.**

14. $3(x + 4)$
15. $10(b - 6)$
16. $6(s - 9)$
17. $7(8 + y)$
18. $8(12 + a)$
19. $9(2n + 1)$
20. $12(6 - k)$
21. $18(5 - 3w)$
22. $9(3 + c + 4)$
23. $\frac{1}{4}(8 + x + 4)$
24. $8(5g + 5 - 2)$
25. $6(10 + z + 3)$
26. $4(x + y)$
27. $25(x - y)$
28. $7(p + q + 9)$
29. $\frac{1}{2}(2n + 4 + 6m)$

MATCHING **Match the expression with an equivalent expression.**

30. $6(n + 4)$
31. $2(3n + 9)$
32. $6(n + 2)$
33. $3(2n + 3)$

A. $3(2n + 6)$
B. $6n + 9$
C. $3(2n + 8)$
D. $6n + 12$

34. MP STRUCTURE Each day, you run on a treadmill for r minutes and lift weights for 15 minutes. Which expressions can you use to find how many minutes of exercise you do in 5 days? Explain your reasoning.

$5(r + 15)$ | $5r + 5 \cdot 15$ | $5r + 15$ | $r(5 + 15)$

35. MP **MODELING REAL LIFE** A cheetah can run 103 feet per second. A zebra can run x feet per second. Write and simplify an expression that represents how many feet farther the cheetah can run in 10 seconds.

COMBINING LIKE TERMS **Simplify the expression.**

36. $6(x + 4) + 1$

37. $5 + 8(3 + x)$

38. $x + 3 + 5x$

39. $7y + 6 - 1 + 12y$

40. $4d + 9 - d - 8$

41. $n + 3(n - 1)$

42. $2v + 8v - 5v$

43. $5(z + 4) + 5(2 - z)$

44. $2.7(w - 5.2)$

45. $\frac{2}{3}y + \frac{1}{6}y + y$

46. $\frac{3}{4}\left(z + \frac{2}{5}\right) + 2z$

47. $7(x + y) - 7x$

48. $4x + 9y + 3(x + y)$

49. MP **YOU BE THE TEACHER** Your friend simplifies the expression. Is your friend correct? Explain your reasoning.

$$\begin{aligned} 8x - 2x + 5x &= 8x - 7x \\ &= (8 - 7)x \\ &= x \end{aligned}$$

50. MP **REASONING** Evaluate each expression by (1) using the Distributive Property and (2) evaluating inside the parentheses first. Which method do you prefer? Is your preference the same for both expressions? Explain your reasoning.

a. $2(3.22 - 0.12)$

b. $12\left(\frac{1}{2} + \frac{2}{3}\right)$

51. **DIG DEEPER!** An art club sells 42 large candles and 56 small candles.

a. Write and simplify an expression that represents the profit.

b. A large candle costs \$5, and a small candle costs \$3. What is the club's profit?

52. MP **REASONING** Find the difference between the perimeters of the rectangle and the hexagon. Interpret your answer.

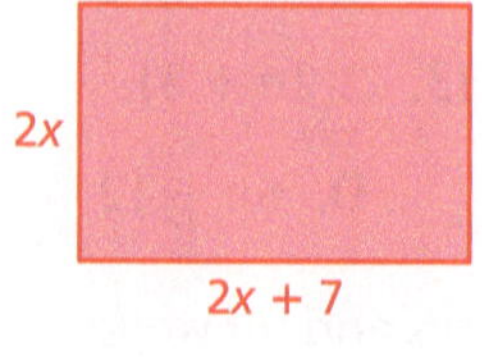

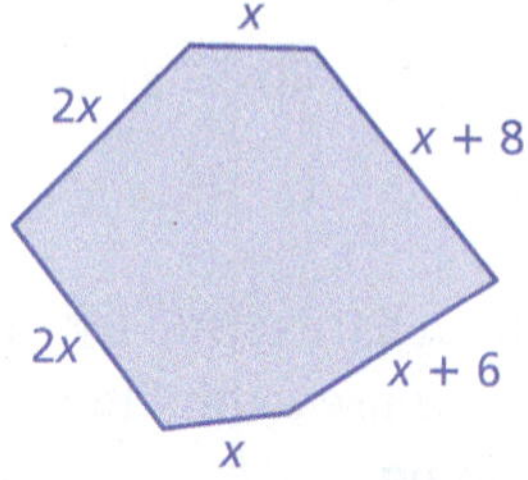

53. **PUZZLE** Add one set of parentheses to the expression $7 \cdot x + 3 + 8 \cdot x + 3 \cdot x + 8 - 9$ so that it is equivalent to $2(9x + 10)$.

Common Errors

- **Exercises 36–48** Students may struggle to combine like terms when using the Distributive Property. Remind them to bring the common factor outside the parentheses and place the terms that will be added or subtracted inside the parentheses.

Mini-Assessment

Use the Distributive Property to simplify the expression.

1. $6(x + 4)$ $6x + 24$
2. $14(g - 2)$ $14g - 28$
3. $3(a + 12)$ $3a + 36$
4. $8(n + 3 + 4)$ $8n + 56$
5. You are y years old. Your cousin is 3 years older than you. Your friend is two times as old as your cousin. Write and simplify an expression that represents your friend's age in years. $2(y + 3)$; $2y + 6$

Section Resources

Surface Level	Deep Level
Resources by Chapter • Extra Practice • Reteach • Puzzle Time Student Journal • Self-Assessment • Practice Differentiating the Lesson Tutorial Videos Skills Review Handbook Skills Trainer	Resources by Chapter • Enrichment and Extension Graphic Organizers Dynamic Assessment System • Section Practice

Concepts, Skills, & Problem Solving

35. $10(103 - x) = 1030 - 10x$

36. $6x + 25$ **37.** $29 + 8x$

38. $6x + 3$ **39.** $19y + 5$

40. $3d + 1$ **41.** $4n - 3$

42. $5v$ **43.** 30

44. $2.7w - 14.04$

45. $1\frac{5}{6}y$ **46.** $2\frac{3}{4}z + \frac{3}{10}$

47. $7y$ **48.** $7x + 12y$

49. no; $8x - 2x + 5x = 11x$

50. **a.** 6.2

b. 14

Sample answer: The preferred method is not the same for both expressions. For part (a), evaluating inside the parentheses first makes for easier and fewer calculations. For part (b), using the Distributive Property will eliminate the fractions.

51. **a.** $42(10 - x) + 56(5 - y) = 700 - 42x - 56y$

b. $322

52. 0; The perimeters are equal.

53. $7(x + 3) + 8 \cdot x + 3 \cdot x + 8 - 9 = 2(9x + 10)$

Learning Target

Factor numerical and algebraic expressions.

Success Criteria

- Use the Distributive Property to factor numerical expressions.
- Identify the greatest common factor of terms including variables.
- Use the Distributive Property to factor algebraic expressions.
- Interpret factored expressions in real-life problems.

Warm Up

Cumulative, vocabulary, and prerequisite skills practice opportunities are available in the *Resources by Chapter* or at *BigIdeasMath.com.*

ELL Support

Remind students that the word *factor* has a special meaning in math. In everyday life, a factor is a circumstance that influences an outcome. In math, a factor is a number or quantity that when multiplied with another produces a given number or expression. Remind students that when finding the greatest common factor of two numbers, it will be the greatest of the factors that are shared by both numbers.

Exploration 1

a–c. See Additional Answers.

Laurie's Notes

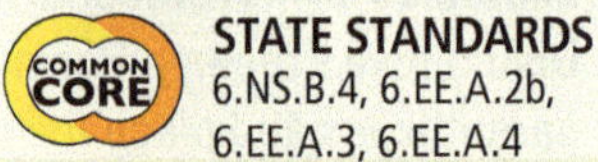

STATE STANDARDS
6.NS.B.4, 6.EE.A.2b, 6.EE.A.3, 6.EE.A.4

Preparing to Teach

- In this lesson, students will extend their understanding of the greatest common factor and the Distributive Property to factoring expressions. Recognizing common factors will allow students to represent expressions in different forms.
- The models in the exploration are similar to the models that were used to explore the Distributive Property in the previous section.
- This section links students' understanding of the number system to expressions and equations. Students should make connections between arithmetic and algebra. Common factors are important to both and provide flexibility in representing quantitative relationships.

Motivate

- Write this problem on the board: $\frac{2}{3} \cdot \frac{4}{5} \cdot \frac{5}{8} = ?$
- When simplifying the product, students should quickly see that there are many common factors. Tell students that they should look for the *greatest* common factor between the numerator and denominator to simplify.

Exploration 1

- Begin working through the first model as a class.
- ? Ask, "Which number can represent the width of the larger rectangle?" 1, 2, 4, or 8 "Is the width a factor of both 8 and 24?" yes
- **Note:** Tell students that when factoring, they should not use 1 as a common factor because it will not change the expression in the parentheses. Although 1 is a possible width of the larger rectangle, students should choose a number greater than 1 to use in their expressions.
- Once students choose the width, have them fill in the other question marks in the model. Do students know where to place the numbers in the expression?
- **MP8 Look for and Express Regularity in Repeated Reasoning:** Discuss the Math Practice note with students and have pairs check their answers.
- The first model has three possible factors greater than one, so you can ask each pair to find and check another expression. Have students share their answers with the class to see if all possible widths have been used.
- Have students work with their partners to finish part (a) and then share their answers.
- ? "Why is there only one expression for the $3x$ and 18 rectangle?" 3 and x are the only factors of $3x$ and x is not a factor of 18.
- Listen to conversations as they complete parts (b) and (c). Ask volunteers to share their strategies with the class.

5.5 Factoring Expressions

Learning Target: Factor numerical and algebraic expressions.

Success Criteria:
- I can use the Distributive Property to factor numerical expressions.
- I can identify the greatest common factor of terms including variables.
- I can use the Distributive Property to factor algebraic expressions.
- I can interpret factored expressions in real-life problems.

EXPLORATION 1 Finding Dimensions

Work with a partner.

a. The models show the area (in square units) of each part of a rectangle. Use the models to find missing values that complete the expressions. Explain your reasoning.

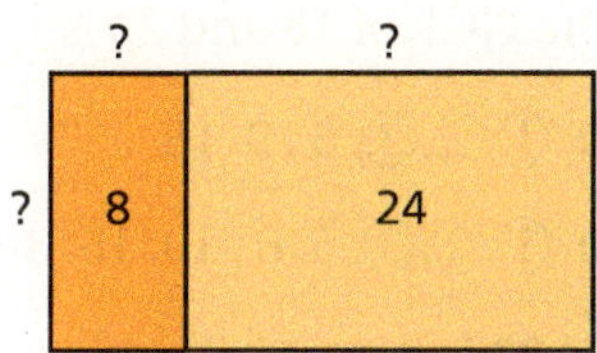

$8 + 24 = \square(\square + \square)$

Math Practice

Check Progress
Do your answers in the first two models seem reasonable? How can you check your answers?

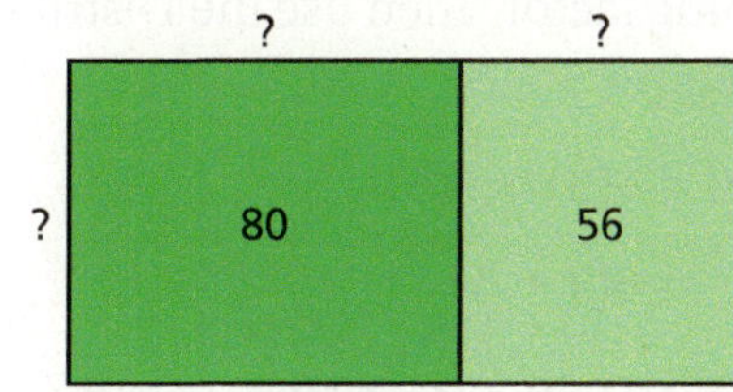

$80 + 56 = \square(\square + \square)$

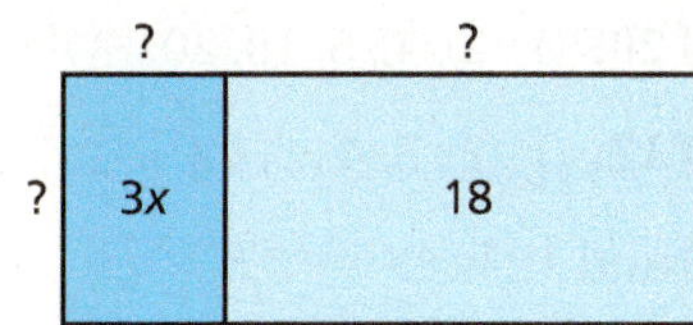

$3x + 18 = \square(\square + \square)$

b. In part (a), check that the original expressions are equivalent to the expressions you wrote. Explain your reasoning.

c. Explain how you can use the Distributive Property to rewrite a sum of two whole numbers with a common factor.

5.5 Lesson

Key Vocabulary
factoring an expression, p. 228

Key Idea

Factoring an Expression

Words Writing a numerical expression or algebraic expression as a product of factors is called **factoring the expression**. You can use the Distributive Property to factor expressions.

Numbers $3 \cdot 7 + 3 \cdot 2 = 3(7 + 2)$

$3 \cdot 7 - 3 \cdot 2 = 3(7 - 2)$

Algebra $ab + ac = a(b + c)$

$ab - ac = a(b - c)$

EXAMPLE 1 Factoring Numerical Expressions

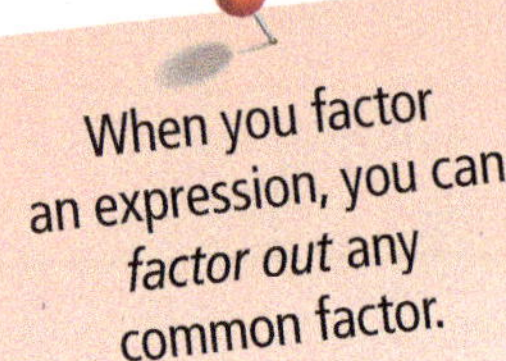

When you factor an expression, you can *factor out* any common factor.

a. Factor 18 + 30 using the GCF.

One way to find the GCF of 18 and 30 is to list their factors.

Factors of 18: (1), (2), (3), (6), 9, 18

Factors of 30: (1), (2), (3), 5, (6), 10, 15, 30

Circle the common factors.

The GCF of 18 and 30 is 6.

Write each term of the expression as a product of the GCF and the remaining factor. Then use the Distributive Property to factor the expression.

$18 + 30 = 6(3) + 6(5)$ Rewrite using GCF.

$= 6(3 + 5)$ Distributive Property

b. Factor 20 − 12 using the GCF.

One way to find the GCF of 20 and 12 is to list their factors.

Factors of 20: (1), (2), (4), 5, 10, 20

Factors of 12: (1), (2), 3, (4), 6, 12

Circle the common factors.

The GCF of 20 and 12 is 4.

Write each term of the expression as a product of the GCF and the remaining factor. Then use the Distributive Property to factor the expression.

$20 - 12 = 4(5) - 4(3)$ Rewrite using GCF.

$= 4(5 - 3)$ Distributive Property

Try It **Factor the expression using the GCF.**

1. $9 + 15$ **2.** $60 + 45$ **3.** $30 - 20$

Multi-Language Glossary at *BigIdeasMath.com*

Laurie's Notes

Scaffolding Instruction

- Students can use the Distributive Property to simplify numerical and algebraic expressions. They will now connect the greatest common factor to factoring expressions.
- **Emerging:** Students may be able to find common factors but struggle to identify the GCF of numerical and algebraic expressions. Students will benefit from guided instruction for the examples.
- **Proficient:** Students can successfully apply the Distributive Property and find the GCF of two numbers. They can apply these skills to factor both numerical and algebraic expressions. Review the Key Idea and have students self-assess using the Try It exercises.

Key Idea

? "What does the Distributive Property state?" $a(b + c) = ab + ac$

- **MP7 Look for and Make Use of Structure:** Discuss equality. Students often view the equal sign as computation on the left side that results in the answer on the right. Equality means that the quantities on each side of the equal sign have the same value. The Distributive Property can be written as (the numerical or algebraic expression) = (the factored form of the expression).
- Students may think of factoring out the GCF as the reverse of the Distributive Property.
- **MP6 Attend to Precision:** Use precise language. When an expression is rewritten as the product of factors, it is called **factoring the expression**.
- Explain that when students combined like terms in the last section, they were essentially factoring out the variable.

EXAMPLE 1

? "How can you find the GCF of 18 and 30?" *Sample answer:* List the factors of each number and identify the greatest number that is common to both lists.

- In part (a), discuss that you can factor 2 out of the expression. The resulting factors are 2 and a sum of 9 and 15. Then you can factor 3 out of the sum, so the GCF is still 6.
- **MP7 Look for and Make Use of Structure:** While $18 + 30 = 48$ is a true statement, it does not answer the question. The GCF of 18 and 30 is 6, so there will be a factor of 6 in the expression. Students will apply this structure in part (b).

Try It

Have students work independently on the exercises, which are related to the first success criterion. Then have their neighbors check their work.

Scaffold instruction to support all students in their learning. Learning is individualized and you may want to group students differently as they move in and out of these levels with each skill and concept. Student self-assessment and feedback help guide your instructional decisions about how and when to layer support for all students to become proficient learners.

Extra Example 1

a. Factor $20 + 8$ using the GCF. $4(5 + 2)$

b. Factor $32 - 20$ using the GCF. $4(8 - 5)$

ELL Support

Have students work in pairs to complete Try It Exercises 1–3. Remind students that to find factors, they can use the strategy of starting with 1 and working their way up the whole numbers. "Can the number be divided by 1? 2? 3? 4? 5? and so on." Each partner should write the list of factors for one of the given numbers. Then partners should compare their lists, circle the GCF, and use the Distributive Property to factor the expression.

Beginner: Factor the expression using the GCF and show work.

Intermediate: Verbally describe each step of factoring the expression.

Advanced: Explain the process.

Try It

1. $3(3 + 5)$
2. $15(4 + 3)$
3. $10(3 - 2)$

Extra Example 2

a. Factor $33 - 121x$ using the GCF.
$11(3 - 11x)$

b. Factor $18a + 42b$ using the GCF.
$6(3a + 7b)$

Try It

4. $7(x + 7)$
5. $4(2y - 11)$
6. $5(5a + 2b)$

Self-Assessment for Concepts & Skills

7. $8(2 + 3)$
8. $7(7 - 4)$
9. $2(4y + 7)$
10. $6(4n + 3)$; $6(4n + 3) = 24n + 18$, the other expressions are equivalent to $24n + 36$.
11. The GCF of 18, 30, and 9 is 3, so factor out a 3; $3(6x + 10y + 3z)$
12. x; Both terms have x as a factor; $x(x + 4)$

Laurie's Notes

EXAMPLE 2

- Students often have less difficulty factoring algebraic expressions.
- Factor the GCF out of each term in the expression and then use the Distributive Property.

? "How can you check your answers?" Use the Distributive Property to multiply the factors and verify that the product is the same as the original expression.

- Tell students that they are following the same procedure as in Example 1. Example 1 is factoring *numerical* expressions, while Example 2 is factoring *algebraic* expressions. In both examples, students need to factor out the GCF and use the Distributive Property to write the expression as a product of its factors. Help students realize that the methods are the same and both examples result in factored forms of the expressions.

Try It

Have students factor the expressions independently and then share with a partner. Discuss any discrepancies and correct any errors. Students are working on the second and third success criteria.

Self-Assessment for Concepts & Skills

- Have students complete the exercises independently and then compare their answers with a partner.

? Ask, "Did anyone answer Exercise 10 correctly without distributing?" Ask students who did not distribute to share their methods.

- Solicit volunteers to write their work for Exercises 11 and 12 on the board and explain their reasoning.
- **MP6 Attend to Precision:** There are several mathematical terms in these exercises that students are expected to know and understand. There are opportunities for students to communicate precisely and mathematically when explaining their reasoning.

ELL Support

Allow students extra support and the opportunity to practice language by working in pairs. For all exercises that require factoring, have partners each factor a different term and compare factors to find the GCF. Have pairs write their answers on whiteboards for your review. Discuss Exercises 10–12 with students to check for understanding.

The Success Criteria Self-Assessment chart can be found in the *Student Journal* or online at *BigIdeasMath.com.*

EXAMPLE 2 Factoring Algebraic Expressions

a. Factor $3x + 42$ using the GCF.

You can find the GCF of $3x$ and 42 by writing their prime factorizations.

$3x = 3 \cdot x$

$42 = 2 \cdot 3 \cdot 7$

Circle the common prime factor.

The GCF of $3x$ and 42 is 3. Use the GCF to factor the expression.

$3x + 42 = 3(x) + 3(14)$ — Rewrite using GCF.

$= 3(x + 14)$ — Distributive Property

b. Factor $63z - 27y$ using the GCF.

You can find the GCF of $63z$ and $27y$ by writing their prime factorizations.

$63z = 3 \cdot 3 \cdot 7 \cdot z$

$27y = 3 \cdot 3 \cdot 3 \cdot y$

Circle the common prime factors.

The GCF of $63z$ and $27y$ is $3 \cdot 3 = 9$. Use the GCF to factor the expression.

$63z - 27y = 9(7z) - 9(3y)$ — Rewrite using GCF.

$= 9(7z - 3y)$ — Distributive Property

Try It **Factor the expression using the GCF.**

4. $7x + 49$ **5.** $8y - 44$ **6.** $25a + 10b$

Self-Assessment for Concepts & Skills

Solve each exercise. Then rate your understanding of the success criteria in your journal.

FACTORING EXPRESSIONS **Factor the expression using the GCF.**

7. $16 + 24$ **8.** $49 - 28$ **9.** $8y + 14$

10. WHICH ONE DOESN'T BELONG? Which expression does *not* belong with the other three? Explain your reasoning.

$3(8n + 12)$ $4(6n + 9)$ $6(4n + 3)$ $12(2n + 3)$

11. MP **REASONING** Use what you know about factoring to explain how you can factor the expression $18x + 30y + 9z$. Then factor the expression.

12. CRITICAL THINKING Identify the GCF of the terms $(x \cdot x)$ and $(4 \cdot x)$. Explain your reasoning. Then use the GCF to factor the expression $x^2 + 4x$.

EXAMPLE 3 Modeling Real Life

You receive a discount on each book you buy for your electronic reader. The original price of each book is x dollars. You buy 5 books for a total of $(5x - 15)$ dollars. Factor the expression. What can you conclude about the discount?

To factor $5x - 15$, you can find the GCF of $5x$ and 15 by writing their prime factorizations.

$5x = 5 \cdot x$

$15 = 5 \cdot 3$

Circle the common prime factor.

So, the GCF of $5x$ and 15 is 5. Use the GCF to factor the expression.

$5x - 15 = 5(x) - 5(3)$ Rewrite using GCF.

$= 5(x - 3)$ Distributive Property

Check Suppose that the original price of each book is \$6. Verify that each expression has the same value when $x = 6$.

$5x - 15 = 5(6) - 15 = 15$

$5(x - 3) = 5(6 - 3) = 15$ ✓

The factor 5 represents the number of books purchased. The factor $(x - 3)$ represents the discounted price of each book. This factor is a difference of two terms, showing that the original price, \$$x$, of each book is decreased by \$3.

So, the factored expression shows a \$3 discount for every book you buy. The original expression shows a total savings of \$15.

Self-Assessment for Problem Solving

Solve each exercise. Then rate your understanding of the success criteria in your journal.

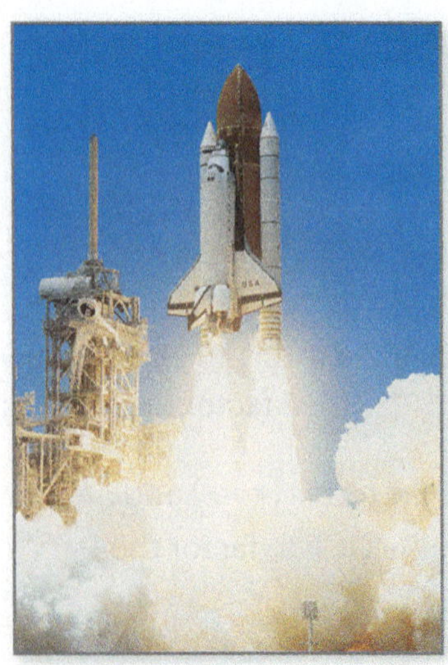

13. A youth club receives a discount on each pizza purchased for a party. The original price of each pizza is x dollars. The club leader purchases 8 pizzas for a total of $(8x - 32)$ dollars. Factor the expression. What can you conclude about the discount?

14. Three crates of food are packed on a shuttle departing for the Moon. Each crate weighs x pounds. On the Moon, the combined weight of the crates is $(3x - 81)$ pounds. What can you conclude about the weight of each crate on the Moon?

Laurie's Notes

EXAMPLE 3

- Ask a volunteer to read the problem.
- ❓ "How many books do you buy and what is the cost of each book?" You buy 5 books and each book costs x dollars.
- ❓ "Do $5x$ and 15 have any common factors other than 1?" yes "What are they?" 5 Write the expression $5x - 15$ in factored form by factoring out the common factor of 5.
- **MP1 Make Sense of Problems and Persevere in Solving Them:** Looking at the factored form (the answer) and asking what it would be equivalent to if they distribute the 5, helps students make sense of the problem. In other words, they are checking that the answer is correct.
- ❓ "Because $5x - 15 = 5(x - 3)$, what does the factored form mean in the context of the problem?" There is a $3 discount on each book you buy. "What is the total savings?" $15
- Have students read the Check note and verify the expression using another value for the original price of the book.

✓ *Self-Assessment* for Problem Solving

- Encourage students to use a Four Square to complete the exercises. Until students become comfortable with the problem-solving plan, they may only be ready to complete the first square.
- These problems have a lot of information for students to digest. Allow plenty of time for students to read and re-read the problems.
- **MP4 Model with Mathematics:** In both exercises, students need to see how factoring the expression helps to answer the question and what the factored form means in the context of the problem. If students are struggling to find an entry point, ask probing questions or refer back to Example 3.
- Have students share answers and discuss the information that the factored form provides.

The Success Criteria Self-Assessment chart can be found in the *Student Journal* or online at *BigIdeasMath.com*.

Closure

- **Example and Non-Example Chart:** Have students work in pairs to create an Example and Non-Example Chart for algebraic expressions with two terms that can be factored. Then have pairs compare their charts with another pair and discuss any discrepancies. Solicit volunteers to share their charts and reasoning. *Sample answer:*

Algebraic Expressions that Can Be Factored

Examples	Non-Examples
$3x + 12$	$4x + 3$
$22y - 11$	$91 - 37y$
$48y + 24z$	$32 + 17c$

Extra Example 3

You receive a discount on each song you purchase for your MP3 player. The original price of each song is x dollars. You purchase 3 songs for a total of $(3x - 6)$ dollars. Factor the expression. What can you conclude about the discount?

$3(x - 2)$; The discount is $2 per song.

Self-Assessment for Problem Solving

13. $8(x - 4)$; The discount is $4 per pizza.
14. Each crate weighs 27 pounds less on the Moon than on Earth.

Formative Assessment Tip

Example and Non-Example Chart
This technique allows students to demonstrate their understanding of a concept by comparing examples and non-examples. Students write examples of the concept in the left column and non-examples in the right column. Students should be able to explain their choices and reasoning. Allow time for students to receive feedback from you and their peers.

Learning Target

Factor numerical and algebraic expressions.

Success Criteria

- Use the Distributive Property to factor numerical expressions.
- Identify the greatest common factor of terms including variables.
- Use the Distributive Property to factor algebraic expressions.
- Interpret factored expressions in real-life problems.

Review & Refresh

1. $2n + 16$
2. $12 + 3m$
3. $7b - 21$
4. $40 - 10w$
5. $5 + p$
6. $r - 18$
7. $11d$
8. $c \div 25$
9. equivalent
10. equivalent
11. C
12. B
13. A
14. D

Concepts, Skills, & Problem Solving

15. *Sample answer:* $4(3 + 4)$; Use a common factor as the height and find the lengths.
16. *Sample answer:* $8(6 + 4)$; Use a common factor as the height and find the lengths.
17. $7(1 + 2)$
18. $6(2 + 7)$
19. $11(2 + 1)$
20. $5(14 + 19)$
21. $12(5 - 3)$
22. $20(5 - 4)$
23. $28(3 + 1)$
24. $16(3 + 5)$
25. $19(1 + 5)$
26. $11(4 - 1)$
27. $6(3 - 2)$
28. $16(3 + 1)$
29. $14(7 - 5)$
30. $2(29 + 14)$
31. $3(24 - 13)$
32. $3(23 + 28)$
33. yes; yes; you can factor c out of each expression.
34. D

Assignment Guide and Concept Check

Scaffold assignments to support all students in their learning progression. The suggested assignments are a starting point. Continue to assign additional exercises and revisit with spaced practice to move every student toward proficiency.

Level	Assignment 1	Assignment 2
Emerging	4, 6, 10, 11, 12, 13, 14, 16, 17, 21, 35, 37	26, 30, 34, 42, 49, 51, 52, 53, 54, 55, 56, 57, 59
Proficient	4, 6, 10, 11, 12, 13, 14, 16, 19, 21, 36, 37	32, 34, 49, 50, 51, 52, 53, 54, 55, 56, 57, 58, 59
Advanced	4, 6, 10, 11, 12, 13, 14, 16, 26, 32, 42, 49	33, 46, 50, 51, 56, 57, 58, 59, 60

- Assignment 1 is for use after students complete the Self-Assessment for Concepts & Skills.
- Assignment 2 is for use after students complete the Self-Assessment for Problem Solving.
- The red exercises can be used as a concept check.

Review & Refresh Prior Skills

Exercises 1–4 Simplifying Expressions
Exercises 5–8 Writing Expressions
Exercises 9 and 10 Comparing Rates
Exercises 11–14 Writing Decimals as Percents

Common Errors

- **Exercises 17–32** Students may factor out a common factor but not the *greatest* common factor. For example, students might say that $12 + 42 = 2(6 + 21)$. While this is a true statement, it does not use the GCF. Students should realize that 6 and 21 still have the common factor of 3.

5.5 Practice

Review & Refresh

Use the Distributive Property to simplify the expression.

1. $2(n + 8)$ **2.** $3(4 + m)$ **3.** $7(b - 3)$ **4.** $10(4 - w)$

Write the phrase as an expression.

5. 5 plus a number p

6. 18 less than a number r

7. 11 times a number d

8. a number c divided by 25

Decide whether the rates are equivalent.

9. 84 feet in 12 seconds
217 feet in 31 seconds

10. 12 cups of soda for every 54 cups of juice
8 cups of soda for every 36 cups of juice

Match the decimal with its equivalent percent.

11. 0.36 **12.** 3.6 **13.** 0.0036 **14.** 0.036

A. 0.36% **B.** 360% **C.** 36% **D.** 3.6%

Concepts, Skills, & Problem Solving

FINDING DIMENSIONS **The model shows the area (in square units) of each part of a rectangle. Use the model to find missing values that complete the expression. Explain your reasoning.** (See Exploration 1, p. 227.)

15. $12 + 16 = \square(\square + \square)$

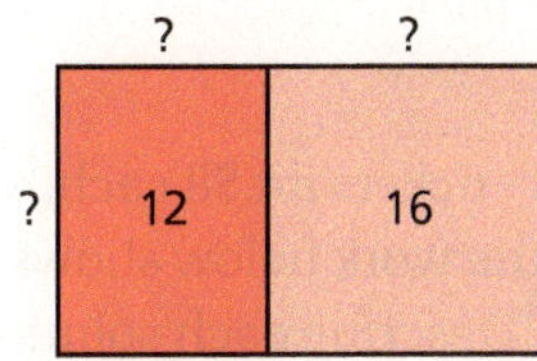

16. $48 + 32 = \square(\square + \square)$

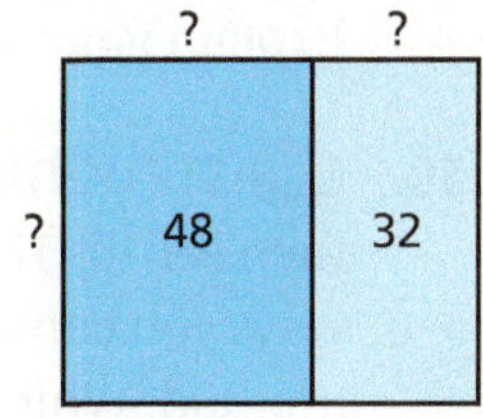

FACTORING NUMERICAL EXPRESSIONS **Factor the expression using the GCF.**

17. $7 + 14$ **18.** $12 + 42$ **19.** $22 + 11$ **20.** $70 + 95$

21. $60 - 36$ **22.** $100 - 80$ **23.** $84 + 28$ **24.** $48 + 80$

25. $19 + 95$ **26.** $44 - 11$ **27.** $18 - 12$ **28.** $48 + 16$

29. $98 - 70$ **30.** $58 + 28$ **31.** $72 - 39$ **32.** $69 + 84$

33. MP REASONING The whole numbers a and b are divisible by c, where b is greater than a. Is $a + b$ divisible by c? Is $b - a$ divisible by c? Explain your reasoning.

34. MULTIPLE CHOICE Which expression is *not* equivalent to $81x + 54$?

A. $27(3x + 2)$ **B.** $3(27x + 18)$ **C.** $9(9x + 6)$ **D.** $6(13x + 9)$

FACTORING ALGEBRAIC EXPRESSIONS **Factor the expression using the GCF.**

35. $2x + 10$	**36.** $15x + 6$	**37.** $26x - 13$	**38.** $50x - 60$
39. $36x + 9$	**40.** $14x - 98$	**41.** $18p + 26$	**42.** $16m + 40$
43. $24 + 72n$	**44.** $50 + 65h$	**45.** $76d - 24$	**46.** $27 - 45c$
47. $18t + 38x$	**48.** $90y + 65z$	**49.** $10x - 25y$	**50.** $24y + 88x$

51. **OPEN-ENDED** Use the Distributive Property to write two expressions that are equivalent to $8x + 16$.

MATCHING **Match the expression with an equivalent expression.**

52. $8x + 16y$	**53.** $4x + 8y$	**54.** $16x + 8y$	**55.** $8x + 4y$
A. $4(2x + y)$	**B.** $2(4y + 2x)$	**C.** $4(2x + 4y)$	**D.** $8(y + 2x)$

56. MP **YOU BE THE TEACHER** Your friend factors the expression $24x + 56$. Is your friend correct? Explain your reasoning.

$$24x + 56 = 8(3x) + 8(7)$$
$$= (8 + 8) \cdot (3x + 7)$$
$$= 16(3x + 7)$$

57. MP **MODELING REAL LIFE** You sell soup mixes for a fundraiser. For each soup mix you sell, the company that makes the soup receives x dollars, and you receive the remaining amount. You sell 16 soup mixes for a total of $(16x + 96)$ dollars. How much money do you receive for each soup mix that you sell?

58. MP **PROBLEM SOLVING** A clothing store is having a sale on holiday socks. Each pair of socks costs x dollars. You leave the store with 6 pairs of socks and spend a total of $(6x - 14)$ dollars. You pay with \$40. How much change do you receive? Explain your reasoning.

59. MP **STRUCTURE** You buy 37 concert tickets for \$8 each, and then sell all 37 tickets for \$11 each. The work below shows two ways you can determine your profit. Describe each solution method. Which do you prefer? Explain your reasoning.

$$\text{Profit} = 37(11) - 37(8)$$
$$= 407 - 296$$
$$= \$111$$

$$\text{Profit} = 37(11) - 37(8)$$
$$= 37(11 - 8)$$
$$= 37(3)$$
$$= \$111$$

60. **DIG DEEPER!** The prime factorizations of two numbers are shown, where a and b represent prime numbers. Write the sum of the two numbers as an expression of the form $14(\square + \square)$. Explain your reasoning.

Number 1: $2 \cdot 11 \cdot 5 \cdot a$ **Number 2:** $7 \cdot b \cdot 3 \cdot 3$

Common Errors

- **Exercises 35–50** As students factor out the GCF, they may forget to include the variables in their answers. Remind students they can check their answers by using the Distributive Property to simplify the expressions.

Mini-Assessment

Factor the expression using the GCF.

1. $24 - 18$ $6(4 - 3)$
2. $32 + 16$ $16(2 + 1)$
3. $6x + 42$ $6(x + 7)$
4. $36m - 54n$ $18(2m - 3n)$
5. You sell T-shirts for a fundraiser. For each T-shirt you sell, the company that makes the shirts receives x dollars, and you receive the remaining amount. You sell 12 T-shirts for a total of $(12x + 72)$ dollars. How much money do you receive for each T-shirt that you sell? $6

Section Resources

Surface Level	Deep Level
Resources by Chapter • Extra Practice • Reteach • Puzzle Time Student Journal • Self-Assessment • Practice Differentiating the Lesson Tutorial Videos Skills Review Handbook Skills Trainer	Resources by Chapter • Enrichment and Extension Graphic Organizers Dynamic Assessment System • Section Practice
Transfer Level	
Dynamic Assessment System • End-of-Chapter Quiz	Assessment Book • End-of-Chapter Quiz

Concepts, Skills, & Problem Solving

35. $2(x + 5)$ **36.** $3(5x + 2)$

37. $13(2x - 1)$ **38.** $10(5x - 6)$

39. $9(4x + 1)$ **40.** $14(x - 7)$

41. $2(9p + 13)$ **42.** $8(2m + 5)$

43. $24(1 + 3n)$ **44.** $5(10 + 13h)$

45. $4(19d - 6)$ **46.** $9(3 - 5c)$

47. $2(9t + 19x)$ **48.** $5(18y + 13z)$

49. $5(2x - 5y)$ **50.** $8(3y + 11x)$

51. *Sample answer:* $8(x + 2)$, $4(2x + 4)$

52. C **53.** B

54. D **55.** A

56. no; $24x + 56 = 8(3x + 7)$

57. $6

58. $12; You save $14 by getting two pairs free, so each pair costs $7 and $40 - (6 \cdot 7 - 14) = 12$.

59. The first solution calculates the total spent and the total earned, then subtracts. The second solution uses the Distributive Property first. *Sample answer:* second; There are fewer calculations.

60. $14(55 + 9)$; *Sample answer:* For each number to have a factor of 14, the missing primes must be $a = 7$ and $b = 2$.

Skills Needed

Exercise 1

- Factoring Algebraic Expressions
- Finding the Whole
- Writing Expressions

Exercise 2

- Converting Measures
- Evaluating Expressions
- Multiplying Decimals
- Writing Expressions

Exercise 3

- Evaluating Expressions
- Writing Equivalent Ratios
- Writing Expressions

ELL Support

Remind students that pounds are used to measure weight and the U.S. customary system is considerably different than the metric system. A pound is approximately 0.45 kilogram. Ounces are often used to measure lighter quantities and tons are used to measure heavier quantities. A pound is equivalent to 16 ounces and 2000 pounds equal one ton.

Using the Problem-Solving Plan

1. \$140
2. $2.2z$ or $z \div 0.45$; 44.88 lb or $45\frac{1}{3}$ lb
3. a. $\frac{7}{2}n$; *Sample answer:* 2 : 7 is equivalent to $1 : \frac{7}{2}$.

   b. 42

Performance Task

The *STEAM Video Performance Task* provides the opportunity for additional enrichment and greater depth of knowledge as students explore the mathematics of the chapter within a context tied to the chapter STEAM Video. The performance task and a detailed scoring rubric are provided at *BigIdeasMath.com.*

Laurie's Notes

Scaffolding Instruction

- The goal of this lesson is to help students become more comfortable with problem solving. These exercises combine numerical and algebraic expressions with prior skills from other chapters. The solution for Exercise 1 is worked out below, to help you guide students through the problem-solving plan. Use the remaining class time to have students work on the other exercises.
- **Emerging:** The goal for these students is to feel comfortable with the problem-solving plan. Allow students to work in pairs to write the beginning steps of the problem-solving plan for Exercise 2. Keep in mind that some students may only be ready to do the first step.
- **Proficient:** Students may be able to work independently or in pairs to complete Exercises 2 and 3.
- Visit each pair to review their plan for each problem. Ask students to describe their plans.

Using the Problem-Solving Plan

Exercise 1

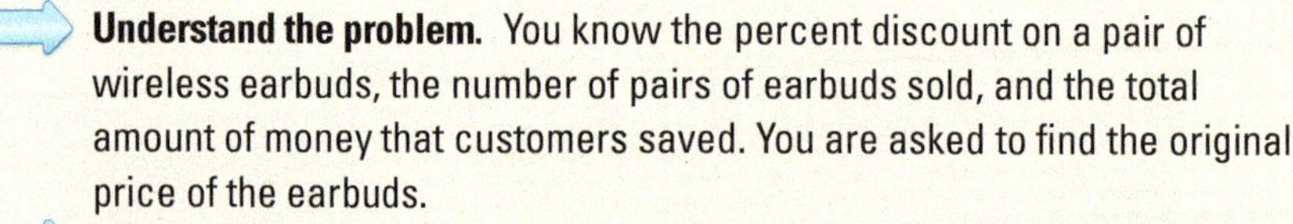

Understand the problem. You know the percent discount on a pair of wireless earbuds, the number of pairs of earbuds sold, and the total amount of money that customers saved. You are asked to find the original price of the earbuds.

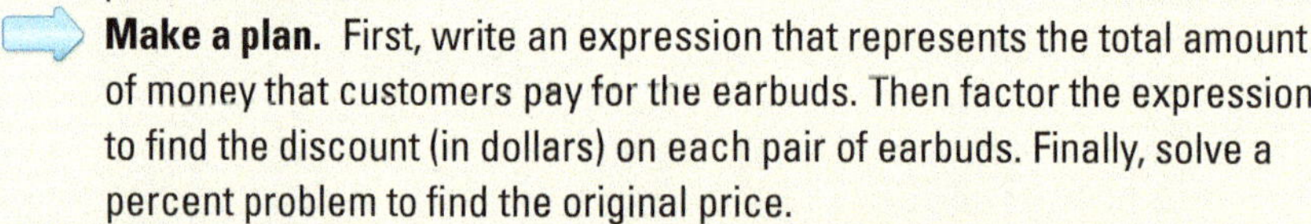

Make a plan. First, write an expression that represents the total amount of money that customers pay for the earbuds. Then factor the expression to find the discount (in dollars) on each pair of earbuds. Finally, solve a percent problem to find the original price.

Solve and check. Use the plan to solve the problem. Then check your solution.

- The store sells 18 pairs of earbuds for an original price of $\$x$ each. Customers saved a total of \$882. The expression that represents the total amount of money that customers pay for the earbuds is $18x - 882$.
- Write the prime factorizations of $18x$ and 882 to find the GCF.

  $18x = 2 \cdot 3 \cdot 3 \cdot x$ — Circle the common prime factors.

  $882 = 2 \cdot 3 \cdot 3 \cdot 7 \cdot 7$

  The GCF of $18x$ and 882 is $2 \cdot 3 \cdot 3 = 18$.
- Use the GCF to factor the expression.

  $18x - 882 = 18(x) - 18(49)$ — Rewrite using GCF.

  $= 18(x - 49)$ — Distributive Property

  The factor $(x - 49)$ represents the discounted price of each pair of earbuds. Showing the original price, $\$x$, of each pair of earbuds is decreased by \$49.
- Solve the percent problem: 35% of what number is \$49?

  $49 \div 35\% = 49 \div \frac{7}{20}$ — Write the percent as a fraction.

  $= 140$ — Multiply 49 by the reciprocal of $\frac{7}{20}$.

  So, the original price of the earbuds is \$140.

  Check: Verify the total amount of money that customers saved. The total amount of money that customers would have spent is $18 \cdot \$140 = \$2520$. So, 35% of $\$2520 = \frac{7}{20} \cdot \$2520 = \frac{\$17{,}640}{20} = \$882$, which is the total amount of money that customers saved. ✓

Connecting Concepts

Using the Problem-Solving Plan

1. A store sells 18 pairs of the wireless earbuds shown. Customers saved a total of $882 on the earbuds. Find the original price of the earbuds.

Understand the problem. You know the percent discount on a pair of wireless earbuds, the number of pairs of earbuds sold, and the total amount of money that customers saved. You are asked to find the original price of the earbuds.

Make a plan. First, write an expression that represents the total amount of money that customers pay for the earbuds. Then factor the expression to find the discount (in dollars) on each pair of earbuds. Finally, solve a percent problem to find the original price.

Solve and check. Use the plan to solve the problem. Then check your solution.

2. All of the weight plates in a gym are labeled in kilograms. You want to convert the weights to pounds. Write an expression to find the number of pounds in z kilograms. Then find the weight in pounds of a plate that weighs 20.4 kilograms.

3. You buy apple chips and banana chips in the ratio of 2 : 7.

   a. How many ounces of banana chips do you buy when you buy n ounces of apple chips? Explain.

   b. You buy 12 ounces of apple chips. How many ounces of banana chips do you buy?

Performance Task

Describing Change

At the beginning of this chapter, you watched a STEAM video called "Shadow Drawings." You are now ready to complete the performance task related to this video, available at ***BigIdeasMath.com***. Be sure to use the problem-solving plan as you work through the performance task.

5 Chapter Review

Review Vocabulary

Write the definition and give an example of each vocabulary term.

algebraic expression, *p. 202*
variable, *p. 202*
term, *p. 202*
coefficient, *p. 202*
constant, *p. 202*
equivalent expressions, *p. 216*
like terms, *p. 223*
factoring an expression, *p. 228*

Graphic Organizers

You can use an **Example and Non-Example Chart** to list examples and non-examples of a concept. Here is an Example and Non-Example Chart for the ***Commutative Property of Addition***.

Commutative Property of Addition

Examples	Non-Examples
$a + b = b + a$	$a \cdot b = b \cdot a$
$2.1 + 9 = 9 + 2.1$	$(7 + 4) + 2 = 7 + (4 + 2)$
$17 + 34 = 34 + 17$	$b \cdot 0 = 0$
$(6 + x) + 8 = (x + 6) + 8$	$46 \cdot 1 = 46$
$(3 + y) + 1 = 1 + (3 + y)$	$2(12 + x) = 2(12) + 2(x)$

Choose and complete a graphic organizer to help you study the concept.

1. algebraic expressions
2. variable
3. Commutative Property of Multiplication
4. Associative Property of Addition
5. Associative Property of Multiplication
6. Addition Property of Zero
7. Multiplication Property of Zero
8. Multiplication Property of One
9. Distributive Property

"I finished my Example and Non-Example Chart about things we need on the moon."

Review Vocabulary

- As a review of the chapter vocabulary, have students revisit the vocabulary section in their *Student Journals* to fill in any missing definitions and record examples of each term.

Graphic Organizers

Sample answers:

1. Algebraic Expressions

Examples	Non-Examples
$4x + 3$	9 fewer than 28
$2y$	$91 - 37$
$5z^2 + w + 1$	$x + 13 = 15$
$\frac{m}{10} - 6$	75%

2. Variable

Examples	Non-Examples
m	2
x	%
y	+
z	78.5

3. Commutative Property of Multiplication

Examples	Non-Examples
$a \cdot b = b \cdot a$	$a + b = b + a$
$7 \cdot 5 = 5 \cdot 7$	$a(b + c) = ab + ac$
$2 \cdot x \cdot 4 = 2 \cdot 4 \cdot x$	$21 + 0 = 21$
$x(4 + 5) = (4 + 5)x$	$78 \cdot 1 = 78$

4. Associative Property of Addition

Examples	Non-Examples
$a + (b + c) = (a + b) + c$	$x + y = y + x$
$3 + (5 + m) = (3 + 5) + m$	$a(b + c) = ab + ac$
$6 + (4 + 11) = (6 + 4) + 11$	$m \cdot n = n \cdot m$
$x + (y + 5) = (x + y) + 5$	$a \cdot (b \cdot c) = (a \cdot b) \cdot c$

5–9. Available at *BigIdeasMath.com*.

List of Organizers

Available at *BigIdeasMath.com*

Definition and Example Chart

Example and Non-Example Chart

Four Square

Information Frame

Summary Triangle

About this Organizer

An **Example and Non-Example Chart** can be used to list examples and non-examples of a concept. Students write examples of the concept in the left column and non-examples in the right column. Blank Example and Non-Example Charts can be included on tests or quizzes for this purpose.

Chapter Self-Assessment

1. Terms: $9x$, 2, $8y$
   Coefficients: 9, 8
   Constant: 2
2. Terms: $3x^2$, x, 7
   Coefficients: 3, 1
   Constant: 7
3. Terms: 1, $\frac{q}{4}$, $7q$
   Coefficients: $\frac{1}{4}$, 7
   Constant: 1
4. 4
5. 5
6. 16
7. 24
8. 140
9. 16
10. 29
11. 12
12. 100
13. \$56
14. 305 points
15. \$70
16. $2(x^2 + 4) - 5$

Chapter Self-Assessment

The Success Criteria Self-Assessment chart can be found in the *Student Journal* or online at *BigIdeasMath.com.*

ELL Support

Allow students to work in pairs to complete the Chapter Self-Assessment. After students complete the first section, check for understanding of Exercises 1–3 by having students indicate whether each term is a constant using a thumbs up for *yes* or a thumbs down for *no*. Check for understanding of Exercises 13–16 by having each pair write their answers on a whiteboard to display for your review. You should be able to quickly assess which students understand the concepts and who may need additional practice. Use these techniques for the remaining sections.

Common Errors

- **Exercises 4–12** Students may substitute the wrong value(s) for the variable(s). Tell students to write out the expression and then write the value(s) of the variable(s) underneath the variable(s) before substituting the value(s).

Chapter Self-Assessment

As you complete the exercises, use the scale below to rate your understanding of the success criteria in your journal.

1	2	3	4
I do not understand.	I can do it with help.	I can do it on my own.	I can teach someone else.

5.1 Algebraic Expressions (pp. 201–208)

Learning Target: Evaluate algebraic expressions given values of their variables.

Identify the terms, coefficients, and constants in the expression.

1. $9x + 2 + 8y$

2. $3x^2 + x + 7$

3. $1 + \frac{q}{4} + 7q$

Evaluate the expression when $x = 20$, $y = 4$, and $z = 7$.

4. $x \div 5$

5. $12 - z$

6. $4y$

7. $y + x$

8. $x \cdot z$

9. $x - y$

10. $3z + 8$

11. $8y - x$

12. $\frac{x^2}{y}$

13. The amount earned (in dollars) for recycling p pounds of copper is $2p$. How much do you earn for recycling 28 pounds of copper?

14. While playing a video game, you score p game points and b triple bonus points. An expression for your score is $p + 3b$. What is your score when you earn 245 game points and 20 triple bonus points?

15. Tickets for a baseball game cost a dollars for adults and c dollars for children. The expression $2a + 3c$ represents the cost (in dollars) for a family to go to the game. What is the cost for the family when an adult ticket is \$17 and a child ticket is \$12?

16. Add one set of parentheses to the expression $2x^2 + 4 - 5$ so that the value of the expression is 75 when $x = 6$.

5.2 Writing Expressions (pp. 209–214)

Learning Target: Write algebraic expressions and solve problems involving algebraic expressions.

Write the phrase as an expression.

17. 9 fewer than 23

18. 6 more than the quotient of 15 and 3

19. the product of a number d and 32

20. a number t decreased by 17

21. Your basketball team scored 4 fewer than twice as many points as the other team.

a. Write an expression that represents the number of points your team scored.

b. The other team scored 24 points. How many points did your team score?

22. The boiling temperature (in degrees Celsius) of platinum is 199 more than four times the boiling temperature (in degrees Celsius) of zinc.

a. Write an expression that represents the boiling temperature (in degrees Celsius) of platinum.

b. The boiling temperature of zinc is 907 degrees Celsius. What is the boiling temperature of platinum?

23. Write an algebraic expression with two variables, x and y, that has a value of 50 when $x = 3$ and $y = 5$.

5.3 Properties of Addition and Multiplication (pp. 215–220)

Learning Target: Identify equivalent expressions and apply properties to generate equivalent expressions.

Simplify the expression. Explain each step.

24. $10 + (2 + y)$

25. $(21 + b) + 1$

26. $3(7x)$

27. $1(3.2w)$

28. $5.3 + (w + 1.2)$

29. $(0 + t) + 9$

30. The expression $7 + 3x + 4$ represents the perimeter of the triangle. Simplify the expression.

7

3x

4

31. Write an algebraic expression that can be simplified using the Associative Property of Addition.

Common Errors

- **Exercises 17–20** Students may write the subtraction or division problems in the wrong order. For subtraction problems, have students look for the key words *from* and *than* to know that the order of the numbers must be switched from the way the phrase is written.
- **Exercises 24–29** Students are often confused by the differences between the Commutative and Associative Properties and may incorrectly label steps. Show students that the Associative Property moves the parentheses but does not change the positions of the terms. The Commutative Property changes the positions of the terms.

Chapter Self-Assessment

17. $23 - 9$ **18.** $15 \div 3 + 6$

19. $32d$ **20.** $t - 17$

21. **a.** $2p - 4$

b. 44

22. **a.** $4z + 199$

b. 3827°C

23. *Sample answer:* $10x + 4y$

24. $10 + (2 + y) = (10 + 2) + y$
Assoc. Prop. of Add.
$= 12 + y$
Add 10 and 2.

25. $(21 + b) + 1 = (b + 21) + 1$
Comm. Prop. of Add.
$= b + (21 + 1)$
Assoc. Prop. of Add.
$= b + 22$
Add 21 and 1.

26. $3(7x) = (3 \cdot 7)x$
Assoc. Prop. of Mult.
$= 21x$
Multiply 3 and 7.

27. $1(3.2w) = (1 \cdot 3.2)w$
Assoc. Prop. of Mult.
$= 3.2\,w$
Mult. Prop. of One

28. $5.3 + (w + 1.2)$
$= 5.3 + (1.2 + w)$
Comm. Prop. of Add.
$= (5.3 + 1.2) + w$
Assoc. Prop. of Add.
$= 6.5 + w$
Add 5.3 and 1.2.

29. $(0 + t) + 9 = t + 9$
Add. Prop. of Zero

30. $3x + 11$

31. *Sample answer:* $5 + (3 + x)$

Chapter Self-Assessment

32. $2x + 24$

33. $44b - 33$

34. $8s - 8$

35. $36 + 6y$

36. $9n + 15$

37. $7t + 2$

38. $8z + 5$

39. $3(15 + x) = 45 + 3x$

40. $4(v + 30) = 4v + 120$

41. $6(7 - 2)$

42. $5(3 + 7)$

43. $4(9x - 7)$

44. $8(3 + 8x)$

45. $30(2 - 5x)$

46. $8(2x + 7y)$

47. The discount is $2 per jersey.

48. $3

Common Errors

- **Exercises 32–35** Students may forget to distribute to each term in the parentheses. Tell students to write the expression on their papers and draw arrows from the number being distributed to each term.
- **Exercises 36–38** Students may try to add a constant to a term with a variable. For example, they may try to add $4n$ to 15 instead of adding $4n$ to $5n$. Students may not be confident with *like terms*. Remind them that because $4n$ has a variable and you do not know the value of that variable, you cannot add $4n$ to 15.

Chapter Resources

Surface Level	Deep Level
Resources by Chapter • Extra Practice • Reteach • Puzzle Time Student Journal • Practice • Chapter Self-Assessment Differentiating the Lesson Tutorial Videos Skills Review Handbook Skills Trainer Game Library	Resources by Chapter • Enrichment and Extension Graphic Organizers Game Library
Transfer Level	
STEAM Video Dynamic Assessment System • Chapter Test	Assessment Book • Chapter Tests A and B • Alternative Assessment • STEAM Performance Task

5.4 The Distributive Property (pp. 221–226)

Learning Target: Apply the Distributive Property to generate equivalent expressions.

Use the Distributive Property to simplify the expression.

32. $2(x + 12)$ **33.** $11(4b - 3)$ **34.** $8(s - 1)$ **35.** $6(6 + y)$

Simplify the expression.

36. $5(n + 3) + 4n$ **37.** $t + 2 + 6t$ **38.** $3z + 14 + 5z - 9$

39. A family of three goes to a salon. Each person gets a haircut and highlights. The cost of each haircut is \$15, and the cost per person for highlights is x dollars. Write and simplify an expression that represents the total cost (in dollars) for the family at the salon.

40. Each day, you take vocal lessons for v minutes and trumpet lessons for 30 minutes. Write and simplify an expression to find how many minutes of lessons you take in 4 days.

5.5 Factoring Expressions (pp. 227–232)

Learning Target: Factor numerical and algebraic expressions.

Factor the expression using the GCF.

41. $42 - 12$ **42.** $15 + 35$ **43.** $36x - 28$

44. $24 + 64x$ **45.** $60 - 150x$ **46.** $16x + 56y$

47. A soccer team receives a discount on each jersey purchased. The original price of each jersey is x dollars. The team buys 18 jerseys for a total of $(18x - 36)$ dollars. What can you conclude about the discount?

48. You sell apple cider for a fundraiser. For each gallon of cider you sell, the company that makes the cider receives x dollars, and you receive the remaining amount. You sell 15 gallons of cider for $(15x + 45)$ dollars. How much money do you receive for each gallon of cider that you sell?

5 Practice Test

1. Identify the terms, coefficients, and constants of $\frac{q}{3} + 6 + 9q$.

2. Evaluate $4b - a$ when $a = 12$ and $b = 7$.

Write the phrase as an expression.

3. 25 more than 50

4. 6 less than the quotient of 32 and a number y

Simplify the expression. Explain each step.

5. $3.1 + (8.6 + m)$

6. $\left(\frac{2}{3} \cdot t\right) \cdot 1\frac{1}{2}$

7. $4(x + 8)$

8. $4t + 7 + 2t - 2$

Factor the expression using the GCF.

9. $18 + 24$

10. $15x + 20$

11. $32x - 40y$

12. Playing time is added at the end of a soccer game to make up for stoppages. An expression for the length (in minutes) of a 90-minute soccer game with x minutes of stoppage time is $90 + x$. How long is a game with 4 minutes of stoppage time?

13. The expression $15 \cdot x \cdot 6$ represents the volume of a rectangular prism with a length of 15, a width of x, and a height of 6. Simplify the expression.

14. The Coiling Dragon Cliff Skywalk in China is 128 feet longer than the length x (in feet) of the Tianmen Skywalk in China. The world's longest glass-bottom bridge, located in China's Zhangjiajie National Park, is about 4.3 times longer than the Coiling Dragon Cliff Skywalk. Write and simplify an expression that represents the length (in feet) of the world's longest glass-bottom bridge.

15. A youth group is making and selling sandwiches to raise money. The cost to make each sandwich is h dollars. The group sells 150 sandwiches for a total of $(150h + 450)$ dollars. How much profit does the group earn for each sandwich sold?

16. You make party favors for an event. You tie 9 inches of ribbon around each party favor. Write an expression for the number of inches of ribbon needed for n party favors. The ribbon costs \$3 for each *yard*. Write an expression for the total cost (in dollars) of the ribbon.

Practice Test Item References

Practice Test Questions	Section to Review
1, 2, 12	5.1
3, 4, 16	5.2
5, 6, 13	5.3
7, 8, 14	5.4
9–11, 15	5.5

Test-Taking Strategies

Remind students to quickly look over the entire test before they start so that they can budget their time. When writing expressions, students need to pay attention to the order of the terms. Remind students to **Stop** and **Think** before they write their answers.

Common Errors

- **Exercise 2** Students may not replace the variables correctly. Tell students to rewrite the expression with parentheses in place of the variables and then place the values of the variables in the parentheses.

Practice Test

1. Terms: $\frac{q}{3}$, 6, $9q$
   Coefficients: $\frac{1}{3}$, 9
   Constant: 6
2. 16
3. $50 + 25$
4. $32 \div y - 6$
5. $3.1 + (8.6 + m)$
   $= (3.1 + 8.6) + m$
   Assoc. Prop. of Add.
   $= 11.7 + m$
   Add 3.1 and 8.6.
6. $\left(\frac{2}{3} \cdot t\right) \cdot 1\frac{1}{2} = \left(t \cdot \frac{2}{3}\right) \cdot 1\frac{1}{2}$
   Comm. Prop. of Mult.
   $= t \cdot \left(\frac{2}{3} \cdot 1\frac{1}{2}\right)$
   Assoc. Prop. of Mult.
   $= t$
   Multiply $\frac{2}{3}$ and $1\frac{1}{2}$.
7. $4(x + 8) = 4(x) + 4(8)$
   Distributive Property
   $= 4x + 32$
   Multiply.
8. $4t + 7 + 2t - 2$
   $= 4t + 2t + 7 - 2$
   Comm. Prop. of Add.
   $= (4 + 2)t + 7 - 2$
   Distributive Property
   $= 6t + 5$
   Simplify.
9. $6(3 + 4)$
10. $5(3x + 4)$
11. $8(4x - 5y)$
12. 94 min
13. $90x$
14. $4.3(x + 128) = 4.3x + 550.4$
15. $3
16. $9n$; $3\left(\frac{1}{4}n\right)$

Test-Taking Strategies

Available at *BigIdeasMath.com*

After Answering Easy Questions, Relax

Answer Easy Questions First

Estimate the Answer

Read All Choices before Answering

Read Question before Answering

Solve Directly or Eliminate Choices

Solve Problem before Looking at Choices

Use Intelligent Guessing

Work Backwards

About this Strategy

When taking a multiple-choice test, be sure to read each question carefully and thoroughly. After skimming the test and answering the easy questions, stop for a few seconds, take a deep breath, and relax. Work through the remaining questions carefully, using your knowledge and test-taking strategies. Remember, you already completed many of the questions on the test!

Cumulative Practice

1. C
2. G
3. 26

Item Analysis

1. **A.** The student does not consider that there is a cost for *each* game. The student finds the sum of the admission price and the price per game, and does not use a variable to represent the number of games.

   B. The student multiplies the number of games by the sum of the admission price and the price per game. This expression multiplies the admission price by the number of games, not just the price per game.

   C. Correct answer

   D. The student uses x to represent the number of admissions, not the number of games.

2. **F.** The student does not identify the correct ratio of flour to sugar.

   G. Correct answer

   H. The student does not identify the correct ratio of flour to sugar.

   I. The student reverses the order of the numbers in the ratio.

3. **Gridded Response:** Correct answer: 26

   Common error: The student multiplies the cost of a hardcover book by the number of paperback books and the cost of a paperback book by the number of hardcover books to get an answer of $24.

5 Cumulative Practice

1. The student council is organizing a school fair. Council members are making signs to show the prices for admission and for each game a person can play.

SCHOOL FAIR	
Admission	\$2.00
Price per game	\$0.25

Let x represent the number of games. Which expression can you use to determine the total amount (in dollars) a person pays for admission and playing x games?

A. 2.25 **B.** $2.25x$

C. $2 + 0.25x$ **D.** $2x + 0.25$

2. Which ratio relationship is represented in the graph?

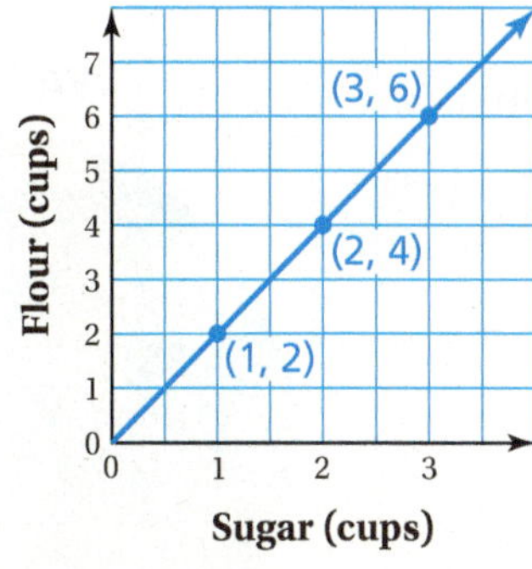

F. 2 cups of flour for every $\frac{1}{2}$ cup of sugar

G. 6 cups of flour for every 3 cups of sugar

H. 1 cup of flour for every 4 cups of sugar

I. $\frac{1}{2}$ cup of flour for every 1 cup of sugar

3. At a used bookstore, you can purchase two types of books.

You can use the expression $3h + 2p$ to find the total cost (in dollars) for h hardcover books and p paperback books. What is the total cost (in dollars) for 6 hardcover books and 4 paperback books?

4. Your friend divided two decimal numbers. Her work is shown in the box below. What should your friend change in order to divide the two decimal numbers correctly?

$$0.07\overline{)14.56} \rightarrow 7\overline{)14.56}^{\;2.08}$$

A. Rewrite the problem as $0.07\overline{)0.1456}$.

B. Rewrite the problem as $0.07\overline{)1456}$.

C. Rewrite the problem as $7\overline{)0.1456}$.

D. Rewrite the problem as $7\overline{)1456}$.

5. What is the value of $4.391 + 5.954$?

F. 9.12145

G. 9.245

H. 9.345

I. 10.345

6. The circle graph shows the eye color of students in a sixth-grade class. Nine students in the class have brown eyes. How many students are in the class?

A. 4 students

B. 18 students

C. 20 students

D. 405 students

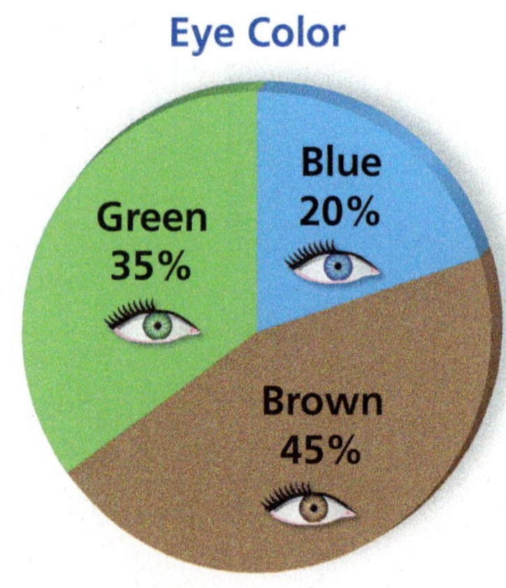

7. Properties of Addition and Multiplication are used to simplify an expression.

$$\begin{aligned} 36 \cdot 23 + 33 \cdot 64 &= 36 \cdot 23 + 64 \cdot 33 \\ &= 36 \cdot 23 + 64 \cdot (23 + 10) \\ &= 36 \cdot 23 + 64 \cdot 23 + 64 \cdot 10 \\ &= x \cdot 23 + 64 \cdot 10 \end{aligned}$$

What number belongs in place of the x?

Item Analysis (continued)

4. **A.** The student moves the decimal point in the dividend two places but in the wrong direction and does not move the decimal point in the divisor.

   B. The student moves the decimal point in the dividend correctly but does not move the decimal point in the divisor.

   C. The student moves the decimal point in the divisor correctly but moves the decimal point in the dividend two places in the wrong direction.

   D. Correct answer

5. **F.** The student adds each place value and inserts the 1s instead of carrying them.

   G. The student does not carry any of the 1s.

   H. The student does not carry the 1 from the tenths place to the ones place.

   I. Correct answer

6. **A.** The student multiplies 9 by 45% instead of dividing 9 by 45%.

   B. The student uses a benchmark of 50%.

   C. Correct answer

   D. The student multiplies 9 by 45 instead of dividing 9 by 45%.

7. **Gridded Response:** Correct answer: 100

   Common error: The student does not recognize the application of the Distributive Property and instead tries to work backwards from 2300. The student makes a place value error while dividing 2300 by 23 to get 1000.

Cumulative Practice

4. D

5. I

6. C

7. 100

Cumulative Practice

8. I

9. B

10. G

11. C

12. F

13. 1800

14. C

Item Analysis (continued)

8. F. The student identifies a factor pair of 1350 instead of the prime factorization of 1350.

G. The student lists the prime factors but does not include the correct exponent for each factor.

H. The student identifies a factor pair of 1350 instead of the prime factorization of 1350.

I. Correct answer

9. A. The student finds the value of miles per minute instead of miles per hour.

B. Correct answer

C. The student reverses the conversions; identifying 3600 hours as 1 second and 5280 miles as 1 foot, instead of 1 hour as 3600 seconds and 1 mile as 5280 feet.

D. The student finds the value of feet per hour instead of miles per hour.

10. F. The student does not distribute a to c.

G. Correct answer

H. The student incorrectly distributes the addition of a.

I. The student incorrectly distributes the addition of a and then multiplies the resulting sums.

11. A. The student divides by $1\frac{2}{7}$ instead of multiplying by $1\frac{2}{7}$.

B. The student finds the product of the whole numbers and then adds it to the product of the fractional parts of the mixed numbers.

C. Correct answer

D. The student adds the mixed numbers instead of multiplying.

12. F. Correct answer

G. The student does not find the LCM correctly; the LCM of 3 and 8 is 24.

H. The student does not find the LCM correctly; the LCM of 6 and 8 is 24.

I. The student does not find the LCM correctly; the LCM of 12 and 24 is 24.

13. 2 points The students' explanation demonstrates a thorough understanding of the Associative and Commutative Properties of Multiplication. For instance, the student explains that the Commutative Property can be used to rewrite the expression as $(18 \times 25) \times 4$ and then the Associative Property can be used to rewrite the expression as $18 \times (25 \times 4)$. Then the student uses compatible numbers to get 18×100 and a final answer of 1800.

1 point The student's explanation demonstrates a partial but limited understanding of the Associative and Commutative Properties of Multiplication. For instance, the student shows correct, efficient steps but provides no explanation.

0 points The student provides no response, a completely incorrect or incomprehensible response, or a response that demonstrates insufficient understanding of the Associative and Commutative Properties of Multiplication.

14. A. The student does not recognize that 64 is the perfect square of 8.

B. The student does not recognize that 81 is the perfect square of 9.

C. Correct answer

D. The student does not recognize that 100 is the perfect square of 10.

8. What is the prime factorization of 1350?

F. $10 \cdot 135$ G. $2 \cdot 3 \cdot 5$

H. $6 \cdot 225$ I. $2 \cdot 3^3 \cdot 5^2$

9. A horse gallops at a speed of 44 feet per second. What is the speed of the horse in miles per hour?

A. $\frac{1}{2}$ mile per hour B. 30 miles per hour

C. $64\frac{8}{15}$ miles per hour D. 158,400 miles per hour

10. Which equation correctly demonstrates the Distributive Property?

F. $a(b + c) = ab + c$

G. $a(b + c) = ab + ac$

H. $a + (b + c) = (a + b) + (a + c)$

I. $a + (b + c) = (a + b) \cdot (a + c)$

11. Which number is equivalent to $2\frac{4}{5} \cdot 1\frac{2}{7}$?

A. $2\frac{8}{45}$ B. $2\frac{8}{35}$

C. $3\frac{3}{5}$ D. $4\frac{3}{35}$

12. Which pair of numbers does *not* have a least common multiple of 24?

F. 2, 12 G. 3, 8

H. 6, 8 I. 12, 24

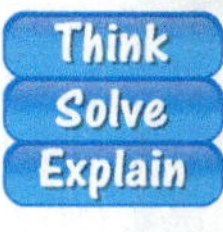

13. Use the Properties of Multiplication to simplify the expression in an efficient way. Show your work and explain how you used the Properties of Multiplication.

$$(25 \times 18) \times 4$$

14. Which number is *not* a perfect square?

A. 64 B. 81

C. 96 D. 100

6 Equations

6.1 Writing Equations in One Variable

6.2 Solving Equations Using Addition or Subtraction

6.3 Solving Equations Using Multiplication or Division

6.4 Writing Equations in Two Variables

Chapter Learning Target:
Understand equations.

Chapter Success Criteria:
- I can identify key words and phrases.
- I can write word sentences as equations.
- I can solve equations using properties of equality.
- I can model different types of equations to solve real-life problems.

Laurie's Notes

Chapter 6 Overview

The algebra strand continues in this course as students learn to write and solve equations in one variable with nonnegative rational-number solutions. Students will also analyze the quantitative relationship between independent and dependent variables.

Solving equations is a process for deciding which values from a set of numbers make an equation true. Over time, the process will gradually increase in complexity. At this stage, students are working with single-step equations and can often solve the problems using mental math.

Students will ask, "Why do I need to write the step when I know the answer? I can do it in my head." Acknowledge that they are correct in their thinking and also in their solutions. Thinking, "What can I add to 2 to get 6?" is correct. In fact, the same thinking can be used to solve any of the equations shown.

$$x + 2 = 6 \qquad 24 + x = 97 \qquad 43.6 = x + 3.8 \qquad 12\frac{5}{8} = 3\frac{2}{3} + x$$

You want students to understand that performing the inverse operation allows them to solve the equation. Recording the step is part of the equation-solving process.

The equations shown are equivalent, but students often think of them differently.

(a) $x + 7 = 12$ **(b)** $12 = x + 7$ **(c)** $7 + x = 12$ **(d)** $12 = 7 + x$

In this chapter, equations in the same forms as (a) and (b) are the most common, because students are learning to record the equation-solving process.

Addition, subtraction, multiplication, and division are used to solve equations in this chapter. You don't want students to think they *must* use an inverse operation to solve equations. In particular, multiplying by the reciprocal is a more efficient method for solving an equation with a fractional coefficient.

In the last lesson, students will write and graph equations in two variables. Students will graph the equation by first creating a table of solutions to the equation and then plotting the ordered pairs.

Suggested Pacing

Chapter Opener	1 Day
Section 1	3 Days
Section 2	2 Days
Section 3	2 Days
Section 4	3 Days
Connecting Concepts	1 Day
Chapter Review	1 Day
Chapter Test	1 Day
Total Chapter 6	14 Days
Year-to-Date	92 Days

Chapter Learning Target

Understand equations.

Chapter Success Criteria

- Identify key words and phrases.
- Write word sentences as equations.
- Solve equations using properties of equality.
- Model different types of equations to solve real-life problems.

Chapter 6 Learning Targets and Success Criteria

Section	Learning Target	Success Criteria
6.1 Writing Equations in One Variable	Write equations in one variable and write equations that represent real-life problems.	• Identify key words and phrases that indicate equality. • Write word sentences as equations. • Create equations to represent real-life problems.
6.2 Solving Equations Using Addition or Subtraction	Write and solve equations using addition or subtraction.	• Determine whether a value is a solution of an equation. • Apply the Addition and Subtraction Properties of Equality to generate equivalent equations. • Solve equations using addition or subtraction. • Create equations involving addition or subtraction to solve real-life problems.
6.3 Solving Equations Using Multiplication or Division	Write and solve equations using multiplication or division.	• Apply the Multiplication and Division Properties of Equality to generate equivalent equations. • Solve equations using multiplication or division. • Create equations involving multiplication or division to solve real-life problems.
6.4 Writing Equations in Two Variables	Write equations in two variables and analyze the relationship between the two quantities.	• Determine whether an ordered pair is a solution of an equation in two variables. • Distinguish between independent and dependent variables. • Write and graph an equation in two variables. • Create equations in two variables to solve real-life problems.

Progressions

Through the Grades		
Grade 5	**Grade 6**	**Grade 7**
• Generate numerical patterns, identify the relationship, and form ordered pairs.	• Determine if a value is a solution. • Write and solve one-step equations. • Write equations in two variables.	• Write, graph, and solve one-step equations (includes negative numbers). • Solve two-step equations. Compare algebraic solutions to arithmetic solutions.

Through the Chapter				
Standard	**6.1**	**6.2**	**6.3**	**6.4**
6.EE.B.5 Understand solving an equation or inequality as a process of answering a question: which values from a specified set, if any, make the equation or inequality true? Use substitution to determine whether a given number in a specified set makes an equation or inequality true.	●	●	●	
6.EE.B.6 Use variables to represent numbers and write expressions when solving a real-world or mathematical problem; understand that a variable can represent an unknown number, or, depending on the purpose at hand, any number in a specified set.	●	●	●	●
6.EE.B.7 Solve real-world and mathematical problems by writing and solving equations of the form $x + p = q$ and $px = q$ for cases in which p, q, and x are all nonnegative rational numbers.	●	●	★	
6.EE.B.9 Use variables to represent two quantities in a real-world problem that change in relationship to one another; write an equation to express one quantity, thought of as the dependent variable, in terms of the other quantity, thought of as the independent variable. Analyze the relationship between the dependent and independent variables using graphs and tables, and relate these to the equation.				★

Key

▲ = preparing ★ = complete

● = learning ■ = extending

STEAM Video

1. *Sample answer:* Estimate the number of pitches needed to climb the wall and multiply by the time it takes to climb one pitch.
2. *Sample answer:* yes; Divide the height of the wall by the average climbing rate in feet per minute.
3. *Sample answer:* speed $\times$ time = height, so substitute the known values and find the missing value that makes the equation true.

Performance Task

Sample answer: no; Many factors affect climbers on different routes.

Mathematical Practices

Students have opportunities to develop aspects of the mathematical practices throughout the chapter. Here are some examples.

1. **Make Sense of Problems and Persevere in Solving Them**
   6.1 Math Practice note, *p. 245*
2. **Reason Abstractly and Quantitatively**
   6.3 Exercise 43, *p. 264*
3. **Construct Viable Arguments and Critique the Reasoning of Others**
   6.2 Exercise 35, *p. 257*
4. **Model with Mathematics**
   6.1 Exercise 25, *p. 250*
5. **Use Appropriate Tools Strategically**
   6.2 Exercise 14, *p. 256*
6. **Attend to Precision**
   6.4 Exercise 59, *p. 272*
7. **Look for and Make Use of Structure**
   6.4 Math Practice note, *p. 265*
8. **Look for and Express Regularity in Repeated Reasoning**
   6.3 Math Practice note, *p. 259*

Laurie's Notes

STEAM Video

Before the Video

- To introduce the STEAM Video, read aloud the first paragraph of Rock Climbing and discuss the question with your students.
- ? "Can you think of any other real-life situations where equations are useful?"

During the Video

- Pause the video at 1:50 and ask, "What has happened in the video so far?" Alex and Tory discussed a style of rock climbing called *sport climbing*.
- ? "What are they trying to find?" how long it will take to climb a cliff wall
  "What will they use to make this prediction?" an equation
- Watch the remainder of the video.

After the Video

- ? "Why might the actual climb time vary from the estimation?" *Sample answer:* You might slow down due to a difficult pitch.
- Have students work with a partner to answer Questions 1–3.
- As students discuss and answer the questions, listen for understanding of writing and solving equations.

Performance Task

- Use this information to spark students' interest and promote thinking about real-life problems.
- ? Ask, "Will the average speed of the climbers on Route 1 provide accurate predictions for the amount of time it takes to climb other routes? Explain why or why not."
- After completing the chapter, students will have gained the knowledge needed to complete "Planning the Climb."

STEAM Video

Rock Climbing

Equations can be used to solve many different kinds of problems in real life, such as estimating the amount of time it will take to climb a rock wall. Can you think of any other real-life situations where equations are useful?

In rock climbing, a *pitch* is a section of a climbing route between two anchor points. Watch the STEAM Video "Rock Climbing." Then answer the following questions.

1. How can you use pitches to estimate the amount of time it will take to climb a rock wall?
2. Are there any other methods you could use to estimate the amount of time it will take to climb a rock wall? Explain.
3. You know two of the three pieces of information below. Explain how you can find the missing piece of information.

   Average climbing speed

   Height of rock wall

   Time to complete climb

Performance Task

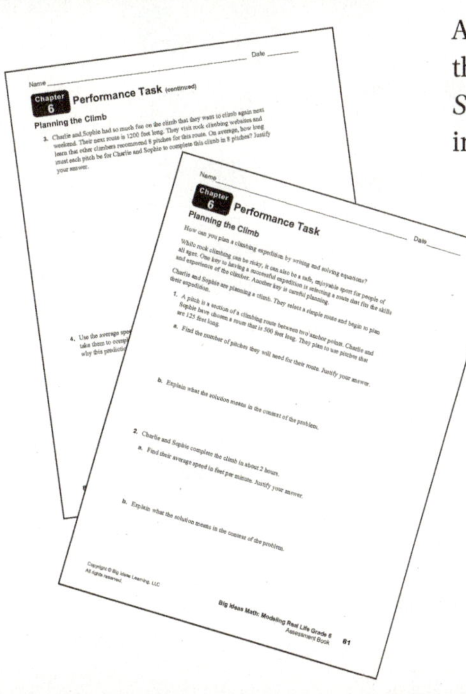

Name ______ Date ______

Chapter 6 **Performance Task**

Planning the Climb

How can you plan a climbing expedition by writing and solving equations?

While rock climbing can be risky, it can also be a safe, enjoyable sport for people of all ages. One key to having a successful expedition is selecting a route that fits the skills and experience of the climber. Another key is careful planning.

Charlie and Sophie are planning a climb. They select a simple route and begin to plan their expedition.

1. A pitch is a section of a climbing route between two anchor points. Charlie and Sophie have chosen a route that is 500 feet long. They plan to use pitches that are 125 feet long.
   a. Find the number of pitches they will need for their route. Justify your answer.
   b. Explain what the solution means in the context of the problem.
2. Charlie and Sophie complete the climb in about 2 hours.
   a. Find their average speed in feet per minute. Justify your answer.
   b. Explain what the solution means in the context of the problem.

Copyright © Big Ideas Learning, LLC All rights reserved.

Big Ideas Math: Modeling Real Life Grade 6 Assessment Book 81

Name ______ Date ______

Chapter 6 **Performance Task** (continued)

Planning the Climb

3. Charlie and Sophie had so much fun on the climb that they want to climb again next weekend. Their next route is 1200 feet long. They visit rock climbing websites and learn that other climbers recommend 8 pitches for this route. On average, how long must each pitch be for Charlie and Sophie to complete this climb in 8 pitches? Justify your answer.

Planning the Climb

After completing this chapter, you will be able to use the concepts you learned to answer the questions in the *STEAM Video Performance Task*. You will be given information about two rock-climbing routes.

Route 1: 500 feet, 125 feet per pitch

Route 2: 1200 feet, 8 pitches

You will find the average speed of the climbers on Route 1 and the amount of time it takes to complete Route 2. Will the average speed of the climbers on Route 1 provide accurate predictions for the amount of time it takes to climb other routes? Explain why or why not.

Getting Ready for Chapter 6

Chapter Exploration

Work with a partner. Every equation that has an unknown variable can be written as a question. Write a question that represents the equation. Then answer the question.

	Equation	Question	Answer to Question
1.	$x + 3 = 7$		
2.	$5 - x = 2$		
3.	$3x = 12$		
4.	$x \div 5 = 3$		
5.	$20 \div x = 4$		

Work with a partner. Write an equation that represents the question. Then answer the question.

	Question	Equation	Answer to Question
6.	What number can be added to 7 to get 12?		
7.	What number can be subtracted from 11 to get 3?		
8.	What number can be multiplied by 10 to get 30?		
9.	What number can be divided by 7 to get 3?		
10.	MP **MODELING REAL LIFE** Your friend says that he will be 21 years old in 7 years. How old is he now?		

Vocabulary

The following vocabulary terms are defined in this chapter. Think about what each term might mean and record your thoughts.

equation
inverse operations
equation in two variables
independent variable
dependent variable

Laurie's Notes

Chapter Exploration

- In the exploration, students will extend their understanding of algebraic expressions to representing and solving equations. At this point, students are relying on their mental math skills. Do not expect them to state inverse operations when answering the questions.
- ? Work through Exercise 1 as a class. Ask, "What number can be added to 3 to get 7?" 4 "Is there another question that represents this equation?" *Sample answer:* What number increased by 3 equals 7? Help students realize that there is more than one way to phrase each question.
- ? After students complete Exercises 1–5, ask, "Can you represent Exercise 2 with the question: *What number can you subtract 5 from to get 2?* Explain." No, subtracting a number from 5 is not the same as subtracting 5 from a number; subtraction is not commutative.
- Exercises 6–10 extend writing expressions to writing equations.

Vocabulary

- These terms represent some of the vocabulary that students will encounter in Chapter 6. Discuss the terms as a class.
- Where have students heard the term *independent variable* outside of a math classroom? In what contexts? Students may not be able to write the actual definition, but they may write phrases associated with *independent variable*.
- Allowing students to discuss these terms now will prepare them for understanding the terms as they are presented in the chapter.
- When students encounter a new definition, encourage them to write in their *Student Journals*. They will revisit these definitions during the Chapter Review.

ELL Support

Explain the terms *independent variable* and *dependent variable*. Write "independent" on the board with a slash after the prefix *in-* (in/dependent). Say, "The prefix *in-* comes from the Latin language. When *in-* is at the beginning of a word, it often means "not". Being dependent means you rely on something or someone. Being independent means you do *not* rely on something or someone. The prefix makes the word the opposite of dependent. In math, the dependent variable relies on the independent variable. The value of the dependent variable *depends* on the value of the independent variable, but the independent variable can change freely."

Topics for Review

- Evaluating Expressions
- Order of Operations
- Writing Expressions

Chapter Exploration

1. What number can be added to 3 to get 7?; 4
2. What number can be subtracted from 5 to get 2?; 3
3. What number can be multiplied by 3 to get 12?; 4
4. What number can be divided by 5 to get 3?; 15
5. What number can 20 be divided by to get 4?; 5
6. $x + 7 = 12$; 5
7. $11 - x = 3$; 8
8. $10x = 30$; 3
9. $x \div 7 = 3$; 21
10. $x + 7 = 21$; 14 years old

Learning Target

Write equations in one variable and write equations that represent real-life problems.

Success Criteria

- Identify key words and phrases that indicate equality.
- Write word sentences as equations.
- Create equations to represent real-life problems.

Warm Up

Cumulative, vocabulary, and prerequisite skills practice opportunities are available in the *Resources by Chapter* or at *BigIdeasMath.com.*

ELL Support

Students may not be familiar with Reuben or BLT sandwiches. Explain that a Reuben sandwich is made with rye bread, corned beef, Swiss cheese, sauerkraut, and Thousand Island dressing. You may want to describe each ingredient. Explain that BLT stands for bacon, lettuce, and tomato.

Exploration 1

a. *Sample answer:* The total is \$20.25 for 3 roast beef sandwiches at \$6.75 each; the amount used for payment or the change received

b. Customer A: $6.45a = 19.35$; 3 sandwiches; $6.45 \times 3 = 19.35$
Customer B: $4.95b = 9.90$; 2 sandwiches; $4.95 \times 2 = 9.90$
Customer C: $5.25c = 21.00$; 4 sandwiches; $5.25 \times 4 = 21.00$
Customer D: $4.65d = 23.25$; 5 sandwiches; $4.65 \times 5 = 23.25$

Laurie's Notes

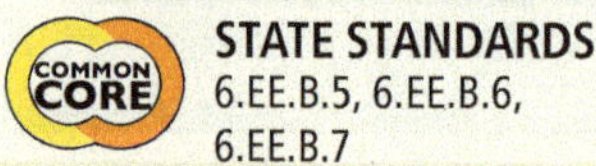

STATE STANDARDS
6.EE.B.5, 6.EE.B.6, 6.EE.B.7

Preparing to Teach

- In the previous chapter, students translated phrases into expressions. Now they will extend this understanding to translating sentences into equations.
- Equivalent means to have the same value. Because each expression in an equation represents the same quantity, the expressions can be written on either side of the equal sign. In other words, the Symmetric Property holds true for equality: if $a = b$, then $b = a$.
- **MP1 Make Sense of Problems and Persevere in Solving Them:** The first step in solving a problem is to understand the language and what the problem is about. Students need to explain the meaning of a problem to find an entry point for the solution. In the exploration, students will read through the information multiple times and interpret the situation.

Motivate

- Ask four students to volunteer. Give two volunteers cards with word phrases and give two volunteers cards with word sentences. Don't tell them the difference. Simply tell them that two of the cards are similar in some way and the other two are similar in another way. Have them sort themselves and explain their grouping.
  Example word phrases: ORANGE JUICE FOR HEALTHY LIVING
  THE LONG COLD WINTER
  Example word sentences: I LIKE ORANGE JUICE.
  WINTER IS HERE.
- Discuss the difference between expressions (word phrases) and **equations** (word sentences). Note that variables can be used in each. A *phrase* is a group of words that has meaning but is not a full sentence. A *sentence* is a group of words that must include a subject and a verb. In an equation, the equal sign is the verb.

Exploration 1

- Students may be intimidated by problems that have a lot of words. This menu board was used in Section 5.2, so students should have a sense of understanding and confidence.
- In part (a), the equation is provided. Tell students to discuss the questions with their partners and then share with the class. This provides an entry point.
- For part (b), ask four students to role-play the situation by designating them as Customers A, B, C, and D. Give each customer the appropriate amount of play money, and then assign each customer to a different corner of the room. Divide the remaining students among the four corners.
- Tell students to analyze the problem as a group, write an equation, and determine how many sandwiches that customer buys.
- Have the customers go to the front of the room and explain their group's work.
- Look for similarities in problem solving. Ask students how their equations represent the same situation.

$$\text{Amount used for payment} - \left(\text{Number of sandwiches} \cdot \text{Price per sandwich}\right) = \text{Change received}$$

6.1 Writing Equations in One Variable

Learning Target: Write equations in one variable and write equations that represent real-life problems.

Success Criteria:
- I can identify key words and phrases that indicate equality.
- I can write word sentences as equations.
- I can create equations to represent real-life problems.

EXPLORATION 1 Writing Equations

Work with a partner. Customers order sandwiches at a café from the menu board shown.

a. The equation $6.75x = 20.25$ represents the purchase of one customer from the menu board. What does the equation tell you about the purchase? What cannot be determined from the equation?

b. The four customers in the table buy multiple sandwiches of the same type. For each customer, write an equation that represents the situation. Then determine how many sandwiches each customer buys. Explain your reasoning.

	Sandwich	Amount Used for Payment	Change Received
Customer A	Reuben	$20	$0.65
Customer B	Chicken salad	$10	$0.10
Customer C	BLT	$30	$9.00
Customer D	Egg salad	$50	$26.75

Math Practice

Analyze Givens
What information do you need to solve the problem?

6.1 Lesson

Key Vocabulary
equation, *p. 246*

An **equation** is a mathematical sentence that uses an equal sign, =, to show that two expressions are equal.

Expressions	***Equations***
$4 + 8$	$4 + 8 = 12$
$x + 8$	$x + 8 = 12$

To write a word sentence as an equation, look for key words or phrases such as *is*, *the same as*, or *equals* to determine where to place the equal sign.

EXAMPLE 1 Writing Equations

Write each word sentence as an equation.

a. The sum of a number n and 7 is 15.

The sum of a number n and 7 is 15.

$n + 7 \quad = 15$ *Sum of* means *addition*.

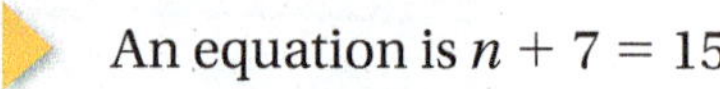

An equation is $n + 7 = 15$.

b. A number y decreased by 4 is 3.

A number y decreased by 4 is 3.

$y - 4 \quad = 3$ *Decreased by* means *subtraction*.

An equation is $y - 4 = 3$.

c. 48 equals 12 times a number p.

48 equals 12 times a number p.

$48 \quad = \quad 12p$ *Times* means *multiplication*.

An equation is $48 = 12p$.

Try It **Write the word sentence as an equation.**

1. 9 less than a number b equals 2.
2. The product of a number g and 5 is 30.
3. A number k increased by 10 is the same as 24.
4. The quotient of a number q and 4 is 12.
5. $2\frac{1}{2}$ is the same as the sum of a number w and $\frac{1}{2}$.

Multi-Language Glossary at *BigIdeasMath.com*

Laurie's Notes

Scaffolding Instruction

- Students need to be able to translate words into mathematical symbols. The more they practice with you, with peers, and independently, the more confident they will become.
- **Emerging:** Students attempt word problems but struggle to verbalize the problems in their own words and rewrite the information as **equations**. Some students may need additional time to read and understand the situations. The examples provide opportunities for students to practice writing word sentences as equations.
- **Proficient:** Students are comfortable writing equations and explaining the meanings of equations. The Self-Assessment exercises will provide feedback about students' understanding of writing equations.

Scaffold instruction to support all students in their learning. Learning is individualized and you may want to group students differently as they move in and out of these levels with each skill and concept. Student self-assessment and feedback help guide your instructional decisions about how and when to layer support for all students to become proficient learners.

EXAMPLE 1

- Note the use of color to connect the words and the operation. If possible, change colors when writing the examples on the board.
- **Common Error:** Subtraction is not commutative, so the order in which the terms are written does matter. In part (b), *a number y decreased by 4* is not the same as *4 decreased by a number y*.
- ? **Representation:** The notation $12p$ is still somewhat new to students. Be sure to ask, "What does $12p$ mean?" Multiply 12 by the value of p.
- ? Ask a few questions about parts (a) and (c):
  - "Is $7 + n = 15$ correct for part (a)? Explain." Yes, addition is commutative.
  - "Is $48 = p(12)$ correct for part (c)? Explain." Yes, multiplication is commutative. It is standard notation, however, to write the number (the coefficient) before the variable.

Try It

- **Think-Pair-Share:** Students should read the exercises independently and then work in pairs to write the equations. After completing the exercises, have each pair compare their answers with another pair and discuss any discrepancies.
- **Common Error:** In Exercise 4, *the quotient of a number q and 4* ($q \div 4$) is not the same as *the quotient of 4 and a number q* ($4 \div q$). Division is not commutative.

ELL Support

Have students practice language by working in pairs to complete the exercises. Monitor their discussions. Expect students at different language levels to perform as described.
Beginner: Write the equation.
Intermediate: State the equation. For example, "*b* minus nine equals two."
Advanced: Explain the process used to write the equation.

Extra Example 1

Write each word sentence as an equation.

a. A number m added to 3 equals 15. $3 + m = 15$

b. The difference of a number w and 6 is the same as 12. $w - 6 = 12$

c. 22 is twice a number h. $22 = 2h$

Try It

1. $b - 9 = 2$
2. $5g = 30$
3. $k + 10 = 24$
4. $q \div 4 = 12$
5. $2\frac{1}{2} = w + \frac{1}{2}$

Extra Example 2

You make 20 balloon bouquets for a party. Each bouquet has 4 red balloons and 3 blue balloons. Let b be the total number of red and blue balloons. Which equation can be used to find b?

A. $b = 20(4 + 3)$

B. $b = 20 + (4 + 3)$

C. $b = 7(20 + 4 + 3)$

D. $b = 7(4 + 3)$

A

Try It

6. D

Self-Assessment
for Concepts & Skills

7. An equation has an equal sign and an expression does not.
8. A number n is 4 less than 8; $n = 8 - 4$; $n - 4 = 8$
9. *Sample answer:* A number n subtracted from 28 is 5.
10. The variable represents the number of items in both cases; The variable can be any whole number in $4x$ but not in $4x = 20$.

Laurie's Notes

EXAMPLE 2

- Students may need to read the problem more than once. A verbal model can help students organize their thoughts and analyze the information.

? After completing the example, ask, "Is $25(4 + 6) = c$ also correct?" yes

- **MP6 Attend to Precision:** Be mindful of the examples you demonstrate in class. You do not want to mislead students into thinking that all of the arithmetic occurs on the left side of the equation and the answer is always on the right side of the equation. This is often referred to as the "rightward arrow." You do not want students to view the equal sign as an arrow ($3 + 4 \rightarrow 7$ or $3 + x \rightarrow 7$). Mathematically proficient students understand the symbols they use, including the equal sign.

? **Extension:** "How many of each color of candle is needed?" 100 yellow and 150 purple

Try It

? Have students work in pairs on Exercise 6. Ask guiding questions such as, "How can you adjust the equation you wrote in Example 2 to write this equation?"

Self-Assessment for Concepts & Skills

- These exercises assess the first two success criteria in several ways. Students have opportunities to demonstrate their understanding of the differences between expressions and equations, as well as their ability to write word sentences as equations.
- Vocabulary is important throughout this chapter. Students should not only recognize and understand the mathematical terms, but they will need to read problems with context and make decisions about their solutions.

ELL Support

Have students practice language by working in pairs to complete the exercises. Then have two pairs compare answers and revise if there is disagreement. Check comprehension by asking one group of four to explain an answer to another group, as you monitor the explanation.

The Success Criteria Self-Assessment chart can be found in the *Student Journal* or online at *BigIdeasMath.com*.

EXAMPLE 2 Writing an Equation

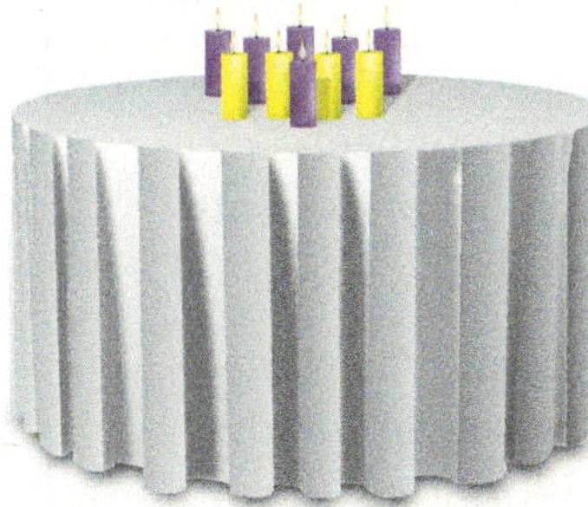

Ten servers decorate 25 tables for a wedding. Each table is decorated as shown. Let c be the total number of yellow and purple candles. Which equation can you use to find c?

A. $c = 25 + (4 \times 6)$ **B.** $c = 25(4 + 6)$

C. $c = 10(25 + 4 + 6)$ **D.** $c = 10(4 + 6)$

Use a verbal model to write an equation.

Verbal Model Total number of candles = Number of tables • Number of candles on each table

Variable Let c be the total number of candles.

Equation $c \quad = \quad 25 \quad \cdot \quad (4 + 6)$

 The correct answer is **B**.

Try It

6. **WHAT IF?** Each server decorates one table. Which equation can you use to find c?

Self-Assessment for Concepts & Skills

Solve each exercise. Then rate your understanding of the success criteria in your journal.

7. **VOCABULARY** How are expressions and equations different?

8. **DIFFERENT WORDS, SAME QUESTION** Which is different? Write "both" equations.

4 less than a number n is 8.

A number n is 4 less than 8.

A number n minus 4 equals 8.

4 subtracted from a number n is 8.

9. **OPEN-ENDED** Write a word sentence for the equation $28 - n = 5$.

10. **WRITING** You purchase x items for \$4 each. Explain how the variable in the expression $4x$ and the variable in the equation $4x = 20$ are similar. Explain how they are different.

EXAMPLE 3 Modeling Real Life

After two rounds, 24 students are eliminated from a spelling bee. There are 96 students remaining. Find the number of students who started the spelling bee.

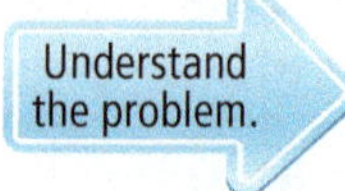

You are given the numbers of students who have and have not been eliminated from a spelling bee. You are asked for the number of students who started the spelling bee.

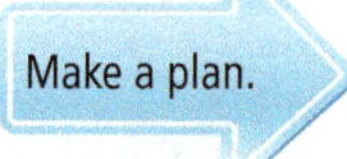

Write and solve an equation relating the number of students who started, the number eliminated, and the number remaining. Use a verbal model.

Verbal Model Number of students who started − Number of students eliminated = Number of students remaining

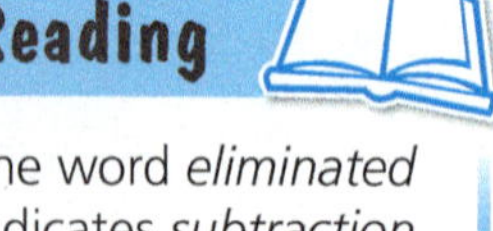

The word *eliminated* indicates *subtraction*.

Variable Let s be the number of students who started.

Equation $s \quad - \quad 24 \quad = \quad 96$

An equation is $s - 24 = 96$. Because you can think of the equation as saying, "*What number minus 24 is 96?*," you know that s is 24 more than 96.

So, $96 + 24 = 120$ students started the spelling bee.

Check Verify that $120 - 24 = 96$.

$$120 - 24 = 120 - 20 - 4$$
$$= 100 - 4$$
$$= 96 \checkmark$$

Self-Assessment for Problem Solving

Solve each exercise. Then rate your understanding of the success criteria in your journal.

11. After four rounds, 74 teams are eliminated from a robotics competition. There are 18 teams remaining. Write and solve an equation to find the number of teams that started the competition.

30 grams

12. The mass of the blue copper sulfate crystal is two-thirds the mass of the red fluorite crystal. Write an equation you can use to find the mass (in grams) of the blue copper sulfate crystal.

m grams

13. **DIG DEEPER!** A customer receives \$20 in change after using \$200 to purchase several sessions at Rock Crawlers Climbing Gym. Each session cost is \$15. There is a special for \$3 off per session if you purchase 10 or more sessions. How many sessions did the customer purchase?

Laurie's Notes

EXAMPLE 3

- Ask a volunteer to read the problem. Refer students to the Reading note.
- **Common Error:** Students may subtract 24 from 96.
- **MP4 Model with Mathematics:** The verbal model says in words how the problem can be solved. As I say to my students, "If you can't say in words how to solve the problem, don't try to write an equation. You need to understand the problem first." Once the problem is understood, an equation is one way to model the situation.
- **MP6 Attend to Precision:** The variable is defined to be *the number of students who started*, not just *students*. Often students are too brief in describing what the variable represents. You want students to develop the habit of being precise when defining their variables.

Self-Assessment for Problem Solving

- Allow time in class for students to practice using the problem-solving plan. Encourage students to begin each problem by writing a verbal model. This not only gives students an intermediate step for writing an equation, but also provides insight into their reading comprehension.
- Some students may see real-life problems as too complicated and want to go back to simpler problems like Example 1. Build their confidence by explaining that those problems are the building blocks. Reassure them that they are capable of learning the next step. Problems in real life will be in context. Encourage them to be math detectives!
- Have groups share their work and discuss the reasonableness of their answers. It is important to maintain a classroom culture in which mistakes are viewed as opportunities for learning.

The Success Criteria Self-Assessment chart can be found in the *Student Journal* or online at *BigIdeasMath.com*.

Formative Assessment Tip

Creating Context
Students create their own contexts to represent a particular problem. Students should solve the problems on the backs of their papers and check their answers for reasonableness. Then students trade papers and identify any revisions that should be made. Collect and review each real-life problem. Identify problems that work well, problems that need more information, and problems that may be misleading.
Another way to provide feedback is to have a class discussion about ways to revise or improve each real-life problem. The process of writing and revising real-life problems enhances students' ability to problem-solve.

Closure

- **Creating Context:** Have students work in pairs to write a real-life problem that can be modeled by $\frac{x}{5} = 12$. Remind them to identify what x represents.

Extra Example 3

After three rounds, 15 contestants are eliminated from a singing competition. There are 55 contestants remaining. Find the number of contestants who started the competition.
$c - 15 = 55$; 70 contestants

Self-Assessment for Problem Solving

11. $t - 74 = 18; 92$

12. $m = \frac{2}{3}(30)$

13. 15

Learning Target

Write equations in one variable and write equations that represent real-life problems.

Success Criteria

- Identify key words and phrases that indicate equality.
- Write word sentences as equations.
- Create equations to represent real-life problems.

Review & Refresh

1. $3(2 + 9)$
2. $9(w + 8)$
3. $6(7 + 4n)$
4. $6(3h + 5k)$
5. C
6. 13
7. 3
8. 28
9. 5
10. 26 ft
11. 34 cm
12. 60 mi

Concepts, Skills, & Problem Solving

13. $6.75x = 33.75$; 5
14. $6.75x = 60.75$; 9
15. $y - 9 = 8$
16. $x + 4 = 12$
17. $9b = 36$
18. $w \div 5 = 6$
19. $54 = t + 9$
20. $5 = \frac{1}{4}c$
21. $n - 9.5 = 27$
22. $11\frac{3}{4} = y \div 6\frac{1}{4}$
23. yes; "5 less than a number n" means "$n - 5$" and "is 12" means "$= 12$".
24. $6042 = 1780 + a$

Assignment Guide and Concept Check

Scaffold assignments to support all students in their learning progression. The suggested assignments are a starting point. Continue to assign additional exercises and revisit with spaced practice to move every student toward proficiency.

Level	Assignment 1	Assignment 2
Emerging	4, 5, 9, 12, 14, 16, 17, 18, 21	23, 24, 25, 26, 27, 30
Proficient	4, 5, 9, 12, 14, 16, 18, 20, 21	23, 24, 25, 26, 27, 28, 29, 30
Advanced	4, 5, 9, 12, 14, 19, 20, 21, 22	23, 27, 28, 29, 30, 31, 32

- Assignment 1 is for use after students complete the Self-Assessment for Concepts & Skills.
- Assignment 2 is for use after students complete the Self-Assessment for Problem Solving.
- The red exercises can be used as a concept check.

Review & Refresh Prior Skills

Exercise 1 Factoring Numerical Expressions
Exercises 2–4 Factoring Algebraic Expressions
Exercise 5 Writing Percents as Fractions
Exercises 6–9 Evaluating Expressions
Exercises 10–12 Finding the Perimeter of a Rectangle

Common Errors

- **Exercises 15–22** Students may write the equations in the wrong order or forget parts of the equation. Remind them of the guidelines for writing expressions. Remind students that these are equations, so there will be equal signs in the answers and numbers and/or variables on each side.

6.1 Practice

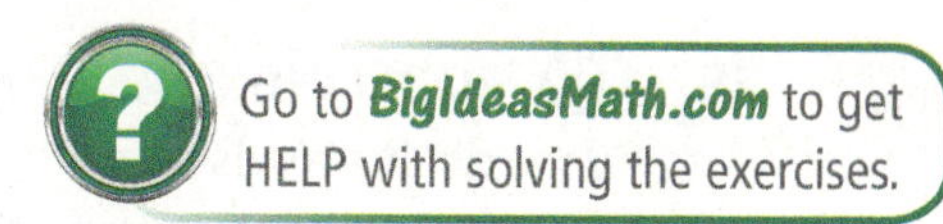

Review & Refresh

Factor the expression using the GCF.

1. $6 + 27$ **2.** $9w + 72$ **3.** $42 + 24n$ **4.** $18h + 30k$

5. Which number is *not* equal to 225%?

A. $2\frac{1}{4}$ **B.** $\frac{9}{4}$ **C.** $\frac{50}{40}$ **D.** $\frac{45}{20}$

Evaluate the expression when $a = 7$.

6. $6 + a$ **7.** $a - 4$ **8.** $4a$ **9.** $\frac{35}{a}$

Find the perimeter of the rectangle.

10.

11.

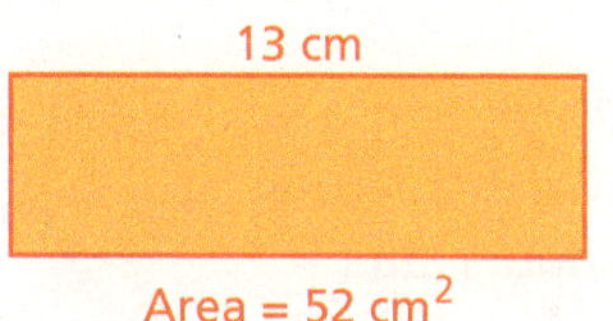

12.

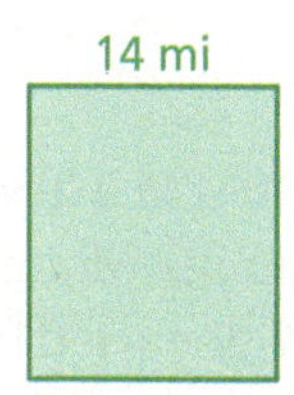

Concepts, Skills, & Problem Solving

WRITING EQUATIONS **A roast beef sandwich costs \$6.75. A customer buys multiple roast beef sandwiches. Write an equation that represents the situation. Then determine how many sandwiches the customer buys.** (See Exploration 1, p. 245.)

13.

Amount Used for Payment	\$50
Change Received	\$16.25

14.

Amount Used for Payment	\$80
Change Received	\$19.25

WRITING EQUATIONS **Write the word sentence as an equation.**

15. A number y decreased by 9 is 8.

16. The sum of a number x and 4 equals 12.

17. 9 times a number b is 36.

18. A number w divided by 5 equals 6.

19. 54 equals 9 more than a number t.

20. 5 is one-fourth of a number c.

21. 9.5 less than a number n equals 27.

22. $11\frac{3}{4}$ is the quotient of a number y and $6\frac{1}{4}$.

23. MP **YOU BE THE TEACHER** Your friend writes the word sentence as an equation. Is your friend correct? Explain your reasoning.

5 less than a number n is 12.
$n - 5 = 12$

24. MP **MODELING REAL LIFE** Students and faculty raise \$6042 for band uniforms. The faculty raised \$1780. Write an equation you can use to find the amount a (in dollars) the students raised.

25. MP **MODELING REAL LIFE** You hit a golf ball 90 yards. It travels three-fourths of the distance to the hole. Write an equation you can use to find the distance d (in yards) from the tee to the hole.

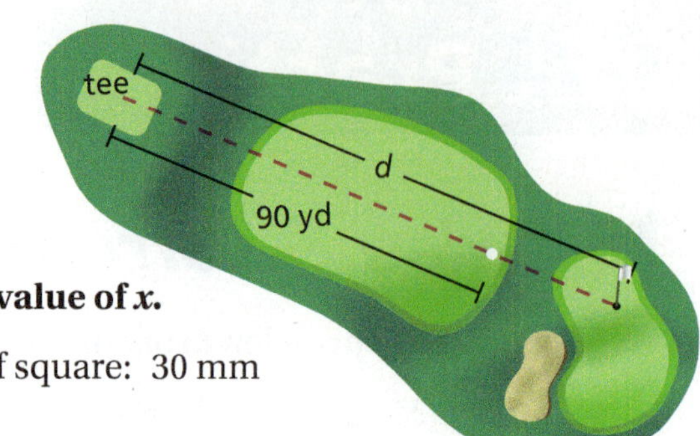

GEOMETRY Write an equation you can use to find the value of x.

26. Perimeter of triangle: 16 in.

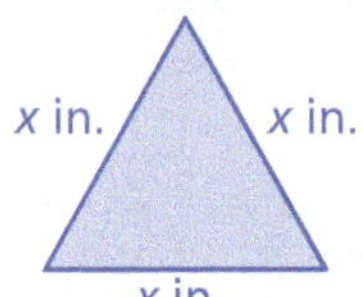

27. Perimeter of square: 30 mm

28. MP **MODELING REAL LIFE** You sell instruments at a Caribbean music festival. You earn \$326 by selling 12 sets of maracas, 6 sets of claves, and x djembe drums. Find the number of djembe drums you sold.

29. MP **PROBLEM SOLVING** Neil Armstrong set foot on the Moon 109.4 hours after *Apollo 11* departed from the Kennedy Space Center. *Apollo 11* landed on the Moon about 6.6 hours before Armstrong's first step. How many hours did it take for *Apollo 11* to reach the Moon?

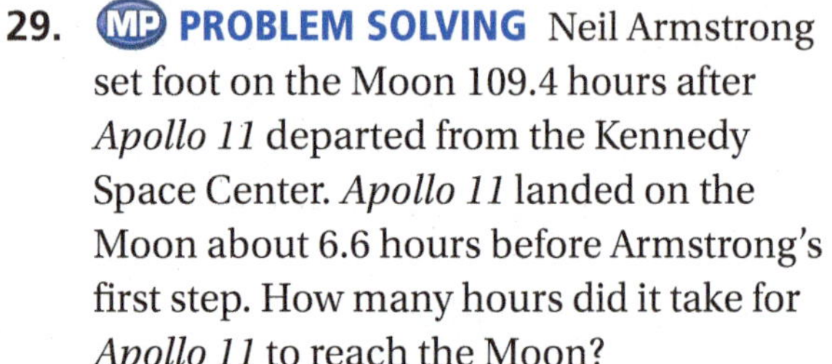

30. MP **LOGIC** You buy a basket of 24 strawberries. You eat them as you walk to the beach. It takes the same amount of time to walk each block. When you are halfway there, half of the berries are gone. After walking 3 more blocks, you still have 5 blocks to go. You reach the beach 28 minutes after you began. One-sixth of your strawberries are left.

   a. Is there enough information to find the time it takes to walk each block? Explain.

   b. Is there enough information to find how many strawberries you ate while walking the last block? Explain.

31. **DIG DEEPER!** Find a sales receipt from a store that shows the total price of the items and the total amount paid including sales tax.

   a. Write an equation you can use to find the sales tax rate r.

   b. Can you use r to find the *percent* for the sales tax? Explain.

32. **GEOMETRY** A square is cut from a rectangle. The side length of the square is half of the unknown width w. The area of the shaded region is 84 square inches. Write an equation you can use to find the width (in inches).

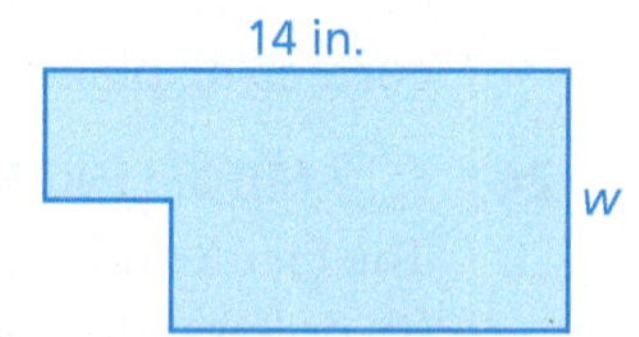

Common Errors

- **Exercise 31** Students may forget that the sales tax rate r is the decimal form of the percent of sales tax. Remind them that they are using the decimal form of the percent in part (a).

Mini-Assessment

Write the word sentence as an equation.

1. The sum of a number x and 5 equals 20. $x + 5 = 20$
2. 64 equals 33 more than a number y. $64 = y + 33$
3. A number c decreased by 12 is 4. $c - 12 = 4$
4. 10 is the quotient of a number s and 8. $10 = \frac{s}{8}$
5. You went grocery shopping with \$40.65. You left the store with \$5.10. Write an equation you can use to find the cost c of the groceries. *Sample answer:* $5.10 + c = 40.65$

Section Resources

Surface Level	Deep Level
Resources by Chapter • Extra Practice • Reteach • Puzzle Time Student Journal • Self-Assessment • Practice Differentiating the Lesson Tutorial Videos Skills Review Handbook Skills Trainer	Resources by Chapter • Enrichment and Extension Graphic Organizers Dynamic Assessment System • Section Practice

Concepts, Skills, & Problem Solving

25. $90 = \frac{3}{4}d$
26. $16 = 3x$
27. $30 = 4x$
28. 8
29. 102.8
30. a. yes; You can find the total length and divide by the time.
    b. no; You did not eat the strawberries at a constant rate.
31. a. *Answer should include, but is not limited to:* The equation should have the form total amount paid = total price + (total price × rate).
    b. yes; Multiplying r by 100 gives the percent for the sales tax.
32. $14w - \frac{w^2}{4} = 84$

Laurie's Notes

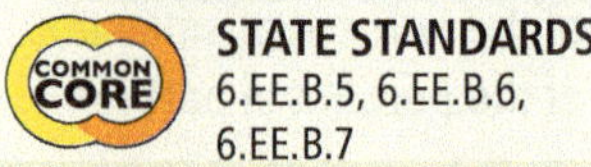

STATE STANDARDS
6.EE.B.5, 6.EE.B.6, 6.EE.B.7

Preparing to Teach

- In the previous section, students wrote equations in one variable. Now they will use the properties of equality to solve equations.
- The explorations are accessible to all students because the familiar models support their confidence.
- Students begin solving equations by using mental math to estimate and then check their answers to see if they make sense. Using mental math to estimate an answer is a tool that students should utilize.

Motivate

- Ask six volunteers to go to the front of the room. Designate three students as Team A and the other three as Team B.
- After they are grouped, say, "I change my mind. I want [name a seventh student] to join Team A." Team B will immediately want someone else to join their team so it will be fair (or balanced).
- Change your mind again and have two students from Team A sit down. Team A will say that the teams are unfair because they have one less person.
- Students have a sense about fairness and want everyone to be treated the same. This idea can be transferred to equations. You want to treat both sides of an equation the same way.

Exploration 1

- ? "What does the tape diagram in Step 1 represent?" Listen for understanding that because the lengths of tape are the same, they are equivalent.
- Ask students to share their answers with the class.
- ? In part (a), some students may have written $x + 4 = 12$, while others may have written $12 = x + 4$, $4 + x = 12$, or $12 = 4 + x$. Ask, "Are they all correct? Explain." Listen for understanding that the equations are all correct because addition is commutative and equality is symmetric.
- **MP2 Reason Abstractly and Quantitatively:** As students investigate the lengths of tape and analyze their relationships, they will begin to make sense of the quantities represented in the models and use reasoning to draw conclusions between the models and the mathematics.

Exploration 2

- Discuss the balanced scale. If any quantity is added to one side, then the same amount must be added to the other. The same is true for subtraction.
- **Note:** If a real scale is available, use it to model equality. Seeing physical objects balance a scale will make more sense to students than looking at pictures of scales with variables and numbers. Help students connect the two balanced sides of the scale to the two sides of an equation.
- Encourage discussion as students work on parts (a) and (b). Listen for students relating their physical actions to solving an equation.
- In part (c), refer students to the Math Practice note and solicit volunteers to share their descriptions.

Learning Target

Write and solve equations using addition or subtraction.

Success Criteria

- Determine whether a value is a solution of an equation.
- Apply the Addition and Subtraction Properties of Equality to generate equivalent equations.
- Solve equations using addition or subtraction.
- Create equations involving addition or subtraction to solve real-life problems.

Warm Up

Cumulative, vocabulary, and prerequisite skills practice opportunities are available in the *Resources by Chapter* or at *BigIdeasMath.com.*

ELL Support

Remind students that the word *tape* has different meanings. It may mean an object that joins things together or the action of joining things together. A tape measure helps to measure length. If possible, demonstrate the use of some tape and a tape measure. Remind students that a tape diagram is similar to a tape measure. It allows you to compare quantities.

Exploration 1

a. $12 = x + 4; x = 8$

b. See Additional Answers

Exploration 2

a–b. See Additional Answers.

c. $x = 5$; Subtract 2 from each side of the equation.

6.2 Solving Equations Using Addition or Subtraction

Learning Target: Write and solve equations using addition or subtraction.

Success Criteria:
- I can determine whether a value is a solution of an equation.
- I can apply the Addition and Subtraction Properties of Equality to generate equivalent equations.
- I can solve equations using addition or subtraction.
- I can create equations involving addition or subtraction to solve real-life problems.

EXPLORATION 1 Solving an Equation Using a Tape Diagram

Work with a partner. A student solves an equation using the tape diagrams below.

Step 1:

12	
x	4

Step 2:

8	4
x	4

Step 3:

8
x

a. What equation did the student solve? What is the solution?

b. Explain how the tape diagrams in Steps 2 and 3 relate to the equation and its solution.

EXPLORATION 2 Solving an Equation Using a Model

Work with a partner.

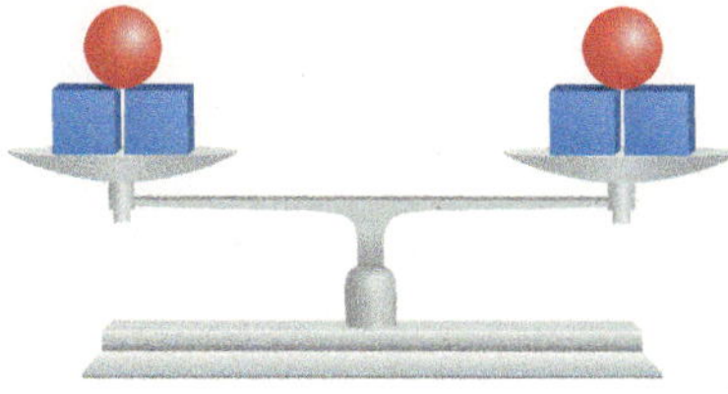

When two sides of a scale weigh the same, the scale will balance.

a. How are the two sides of an equation similar to a balanced scale?

b. When you add weight to one side of a balanced scale, what can you do to balance the scale? What if you subtract weight from one side of a balanced scale? How does this relate to solving an equation?

c. MP **CHOOSE TOOLS** Choose a model to represent and solve the equation $x + 2 = 7$. Then describe how you can solve the equation algebraically.

Math Practice

Analyze Relationships

How can you use the relationship between addition and subtraction to solve $x + 2 = 7$?

6.2 Lesson

Key Vocabulary
solution, *p. 252*
inverse operations, *p. 253*

Reading
The symbol $\neq$ means *is not equal to.*

Equations may be true for some values and false for others. A **solution** of an equation is a value that makes the equation true.

Value of x	$x + 3 = 7$	Are both sides equal?
3	$3 + 3 \stackrel{?}{=} 7$ $6 \neq 7$ ✗	no
4	$4 + 3 \stackrel{?}{=} 7$ $7 = 7$ ✓	yes
5	$5 + 3 \stackrel{?}{=} 7$ $8 \neq 7$ ✗	no

So, the value $x = 4$ is a solution of the equation $x + 3 = 7$.

EXAMPLE 1 Checking Solutions

Tell whether the given value is a solution of the equation.

a. $p + 10 = 38;\ p = 18$

$18 + 10 \stackrel{?}{=} 38$ — Substitute 18 for p.

$28 \neq 38$ ✗ — Sides are *not* equal.

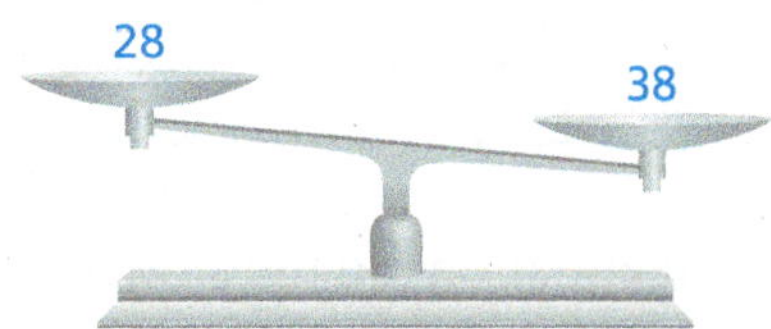

So, $p = 18$ is *not* a solution.

b. $4y = 56;\ y = 14$

$4(14) \stackrel{?}{=} 56$ — Substitute 14 for y.

$56 = 56$ ✓ — Sides are equal.

 So, $y = 14$ is a solution.

Try It **Tell whether the given value is a solution of the equation.**

1. $a + 6 = 17;\ a = 9$

2. $9 - g = 5;\ g = 3$

3. $35 = 7n;\ n = 5$

4. $\frac{q}{2} = 28;\ q = 14$

Multi-Language Glossary at *BigIdeasMath.com*

Laurie's Notes

Scaffolding Instruction

- In the previous section, students wrote equations and intuitively solved them using mental math. Now they will formalize the solving process and use the Addition and Subtraction Properties of Equality. Understanding **inverse operations** provides a pathway for using the properties.
- **Emerging:** Students may have followed the modeling in the explorations but lack confidence in solving equations algebraically. These students will benefit from guided instruction for the examples. Take time to explain each step.
- **Proficient:** Students are aware that they must "undo" the operations to solve equations but may not formally name them. Have students review the Key Ideas before they proceed to the Self-Assessment exercises.

Discuss

- The table at the top of the page reminds students that substitution can be used to tell whether a value is a **solution** of an equation. In other words, is the equation balanced?
- Tell students that when an equation is not balanced, the sides are not equal ($\neq$). When the value produces the same result on both sides, then the value is a solution of the equation.

EXAMPLE 1

- Work through each part.
- **MP6 Attend to Precision:** Be careful to use precise language. You *substitute* for the value of the variable. You do not *plug it in*!

? "What does $4y$ mean, forty-something?" No, it means 4 times the value of y.

Try It

- **Neighbor Check:** Have students work independently, and then have their neighbors check their work. Have students discuss any discrepancies.
- **Common Error:** In Exercise 4, students may quickly look at the numbers 2, 14, and 28 and say 14 is a solution without thinking about the operation. Caution students to work slowly and actually substitute the value for the variable.

Scaffold instruction to support all students in their learning. Learning is individualized and you may want to group students differently as they move in and out of these levels with each skill and concept. Student self-assessment and feedback help guide your instructional decisions about how and when to layer support for all students to become proficient learners.

Extra Example 1

Tell whether the given value is a solution of the equation.

a. $t - 5 = 17; t = 12$ no

b. $b \div 6 = 8; b = 48$ yes

Try It

1. no
2. no
3. yes
4. no

Laurie's Notes

Key Ideas

- Discuss real-life **inverse operations** such as: putting your shoes on and taking them off; going to school and coming home from school; an airplane taking off and landing; or turning a light switch on and off.
- Write the Key Ideas and discuss the Words, Numbers, and Algebra.
- How you record what is being done mathematically to each side of the equation is very important. You should not be sloppy. Encourage students to acquire good habits from the start.
- ? Refer students to the push-pin note. "Why is $x + 4 = 5$ equivalent to $x + 2 = 3$?" Because they have the same solution. This is an important skill to develop. Students will continue to use equivalent equations throughout their future mathematics courses.
- **MP6 Attend to Precision:** To communicate precisely, students need to understand symbols and mathematical terms and use them correctly. Symbols and words intertwine as the language of mathematics and the language of problem solving. Students need to practice using both symbols and words to explain mathematical thinking.

Discuss

- Explain to students that although they can probably solve many of these problems using mental math, another equally important part of solving equations is the *process*.
- ? "How can you solve a problem when you cannot find the answer using mental math?"

  Write a few examples on the board.

  (a) $x - 5 = 13$ **(b)** $19.49 = x - 8.7$ **(c)** $x - 4\frac{3}{5} = 6\frac{2}{3}$

  "You can use mental math for (a), but for (b) and (c), you probably want to use paper and pencil. What is the process now?"

EXAMPLE 2

- Note that the variable is not always on the left side of the equation. You want students to be just as comfortable solving $x - 7 = 18$ as $18 = x - 7$.
- Discuss with students how to determine if their answers are correct by substituting the solution for the variable in the original equation or by using a visual model, such as a number line.
- **Big Idea:** Whatever number is added to one side of the equation is also added to the other. Using an alternate color to show this will help the many students who are visual learners. Notice in the examples that the *process* is annotated along the right side of the equation.

Try It

- Ask volunteers to share their work at the board and answer questions.
- **Thumbs Up:** Ask students to assess their understanding of using the Addition Property of Equality.

Extra Example 2

a. Solve $p - 8 = 14$. $p = 22$

b. Solve $11 = y - 4$. $y = 15$

ELL Support

Have students practice language by working in groups to complete Try It Exercises 5–7. Expect students to perform as follows.

Beginner: Write the solution.

Intermediate: State the solution. For example, "*k* equals four."

Advanced: Explain the process used to find the solution.

Try It

5. $k = 4$
6. $n = 14$
7. $r = 21$

You can use *inverse operations* to solve equations. **Inverse operations** "undo" each other. Addition and subtraction are inverse operations.

Key Ideas

Addition Property of Equality

Words When you add the same number to each side of an equation, the two sides remain equal.

Numbers
$$\begin{aligned} 8 &= 8 \\ +5 &\quad +5 \\ 13 &= 13 \end{aligned}$$

Algebra
$$\begin{aligned} x - 4 &= 5 \\ +4 &\quad +4 \\ x &= 9 \end{aligned}$$

Subtraction Property of Equality

Words When you subtract the same number from each side of an equation, the two sides remain equal.

Numbers
$$\begin{aligned} 8 &= 8 \\ -5 &\quad -5 \\ 3 &= 3 \end{aligned}$$

Algebra
$$\begin{aligned} x + 4 &= 5 \\ -4 &\quad -4 \\ x &= 1 \end{aligned}$$

You can add or subtract any number on each side of an equation to generate an equivalent equation. For example, $x + 4 = 5$ and $x + 2 = 3$ are equivalent equations.

$$\begin{aligned} x + 4 &= 5 \\ -2 &= -2 \\ x + 2 &= 3 \end{aligned}$$

EXAMPLE 2 Solving Equations Using Addition

a. Solve $x - 2 = 6$.

$x - 2 = 6$	Write the equation.
$+2 \quad +2$	Addition Property of Equality
$x = 8$	Simplify.

Undo the subtraction.

The solution is $x = 8$.

Check
$x - 2 = 6$
$8 - 2 \stackrel{?}{=} 6$
$6 = 6$ ✓

b. Solve $18 = x - 7$.

$18 = x - 7$	Write the equation.
$+7 \quad +7$	Addition Property of Equality
$25 = x$	Simplify.

The solution is $x = 25$.

Check Verify that $25 - 7 = 18$.

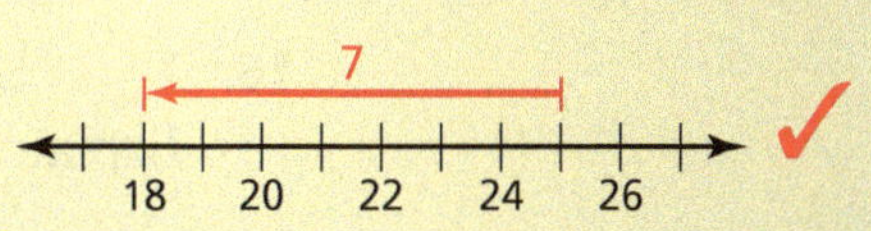

Try It Solve the equation. Check your solution.

5. $k - 3 = 1$ **6.** $n - 10 = 4$ **7.** $15 = r - 6$

EXAMPLE 3 Solving Equations Using Subtraction

a. Solve $x + 2 = 9$.

Undo the addition.

$x + 2 = \quad 9$	Write the equation.
$\underline{-2} \quad \underline{-2}$	Subtraction Property of Equality
$x = \quad 7$	Simplify.

 The solution is $x = 7$.

Check

$x + 2 = 9$

$7 + 2 \stackrel{?}{=} 9$

$9 = 9$ ✓

b. Solve $26 = 11 + x$.

$26 = \quad 11 + x$	Write the equation.
$\underline{-11} \quad \underline{-11}$	Subtraction Property of Equality
$15 = x$	Simplify.

 The solution is $x = 15$.

Another Method

26	
11	x
11	15 ✓

Try It **Solve the equation. Check your solution.**

8. $s + 8 = 17$ **9.** $9 = y + 6$ **10.** $13 + m = 20$

Self-Assessment *for Concepts & Skills*

Solve each exercise. Then rate your understanding of the success criteria in your journal.

CHECKING SOLUTIONS Tell whether the given value is a solution of the equation.

11. $n + 8 = 42;\ n = 36$ **12.** $g - 9 = 24;\ g = 35$

SOLVING EQUATIONS Solve the equation. Check your solution.

13. $x - 8 = 12$ **14.** $b + 14 = 33$

15. **WRITING** When solving $x + 5 = 16$, why do you subtract 5 from the left side of the equation? Why do you subtract 5 from the right side of the equation?

16. **MP REASONING** Do the equations have the same solution? Explain your reasoning.

$$x - 8 = 6$$
$$x - 6 = 8$$

17. **MP STRUCTURE** Just by looking at the equation $x + 6 + 2x = 2x + 6 + 4$, find the value of x. Explain your reasoning.

Laurie's Notes

EXAMPLE 3

- "How do you undo the operation of addition?" subtraction
- Work through the parts as shown.
- "Why isn't 9 subtracted from each side of the equation in part (a)?" It wouldn't achieve the goal of getting the variable by itself on one side of the equation. You need to subtract 2 from each side of the equation.
- **Big Idea:** Whatever is subtracted from one side of the equation is also subtracted from the other. Using an alternate color to show this will help visual learners. Notice that the *process* is annotated along the right side of the equation.
- Refer students to the Another Method note in which a tape diagram is used.

Try It

- Ask volunteers to share their work at the board. Have them explain, algebraically or using a model, how they used the Subtraction Property of Equality.

Self-Assessment for Concepts & Skills

- Have students complete the exercises independently. Make sure they show all their work so that they can analyze any mistakes.
- **Turn and Talk:** Have students compare answers with their partners and review each other's work to find reasons for any disagreements. Error analysis allows students to defend their answers, view various strategies, and deepen their learning experience.
- **MP3 Construct Viable Arguments and Critique the Reasoning of Others:** Reading others' work, listening to explanations, asking clarifying questions, rewording thoughts to make better sense, and identifying flaws in reasoning all contribute to mathematical proficiency.

These exercises are assessing the first three success criteria.

ELL Support

Allow students to work in pairs. Check comprehension of Exercises 11–14, 16, and 17. Ask *yes* or *no* questions that allow students to answer with a thumbs up or down, or ask for the value of the unknown variable. Have students display their answers on whiteboards for your review.

The Success Criteria Self-Assessment chart can be found in the *Student Journal* or online at *BigIdeasMath.com*.

Extra Example 3

a. Solve $z + 5 = 14$. $z = 9$

b. Solve $18 = r + 6$. $r = 12$

Try It

8. $s = 9$

9. $y = 3$

10. $m = 7$

Self-Assessment for Concepts & Skills

11. no

12. no

13. $x = 20$

14. $b = 19$

15. so that x is by itself; so that the two sides remain equal

16. yes; Each solution is $x = 14$.

17. 4; $x = 4$ makes the two sides equal.

Extra Example 4

You climb 12 feet on a rock climbing wall that is 25 feet high. What is the remaining distance to the top?

$12 + d = 25$; $d = 13$ feet

Self-Assessment for Problem Solving

18. $45 = h + 24$; 21 in.; yes; *Sample answer:* The rockhopper penguin looks like it is about half the height of the emperor penguin.

19. 14th, 8th

Learning Target

Write and solve equations using addition or subtraction.

Success Criteria

- Determine whether a value is a solution of an equation.
- Apply the Addition and Subtraction Properties of Equality to generate equivalent equations.
- Solve equations using addition or subtraction.
- Create equations involving addition or subtraction to solve real-life problems.

Formative Assessment Tip

3-2-1

This technique provides a structured way for students to reflect on their learning, typically at the conclusion of a lesson or chapter. Students are asked to respond to three writing prompts: giving 3 responses to the first prompt, 2 responses to the second prompt, and 1 response to the third prompt. All 6 responses relate to what students have learned during the lesson or chapter. Collect and review student responses to help you plan instruction for the next day.

Laurie's Notes

EXAMPLE 4

- This example uses skills that students developed in the last section.
- Information for writing the verbal model may be on the picture itself.
- Students may want to skip writing the equation and simply jump to $25.50 + 275.95 - 50.00$ to arrive at the answer. Remind them that the equation helps to explain why subtraction is needed to solve the problem.
- Students should check their answers in the original equation and within the context of the problem. Does the answer make sense? Refer students to the push-pin note and remind them to include units.
- **Note:** Tell students to be careful when using s as a variable because it may resemble a handwritten 5.

Self-Assessment for Problem Solving

- Allow time in class for students to practice using the problem-solving plan. Remember, some students may only be able to complete the first step.
- As students begin these exercises independently, many may say that they don't know how to begin. Encourage them to write a verbal model first. They may have to explain the problem to you to hear the words they need to use. They should write them down and then consider their relationship before writing an equation.
- In Exercise 18, students are specifically asked to write and solve an equation to represent the situation. Exercise 19 does not specify a method for solving, but students may use an equation.
- As you circulate, remind students to check their answers. Are they reasonable? Do they make sense?
- **Chalkboard Splash:** For each problem, choose two students to put their equations and work on the board. Look for different approaches. Encourage other students to ask questions.
- Students are assessing their understanding of the last two success criteria.

The Success Criteria Self-Assessment chart can be found in the *Student Journal* or online at *BigIdeasMath.com.*

Closure

- **3-2-1:** Ask students to write 3 ideas or concepts that they learned, 2 examples or uses of those ideas, and 1 unanswered question or misunderstanding that they want clarified.
- The next day, begin class by sharing positive responses and clarifying any questions or misunderstandings.

EXAMPLE 4 Modeling Real Life

Your aunt gives you $50 to help buy the reflector telescope shown. After you buy the telescope, you have $25.50 left. How much money did you have before your aunt gave you $50?

Use a verbal model to write an equation that represents the situation. Then solve the equation.

Verbal Model Starting amount (dollars) + Aunt's money (dollars) − Telescope price (dollars) = Amount left (dollars)

Variable Let s be the starting amount.

Equation

$s + 50 - 275.95 = 25.50$	Write the equation.
$s + 50 - 275.95 + 275.95 = 25.50 + 275.95$	Addition Property of Equality
$s + 50 = 301.45$	Simplify.
$s + 50 - 50 = 301.45 - 50$	Subtraction Property of Equality
$s = 251.45$	Simplify.

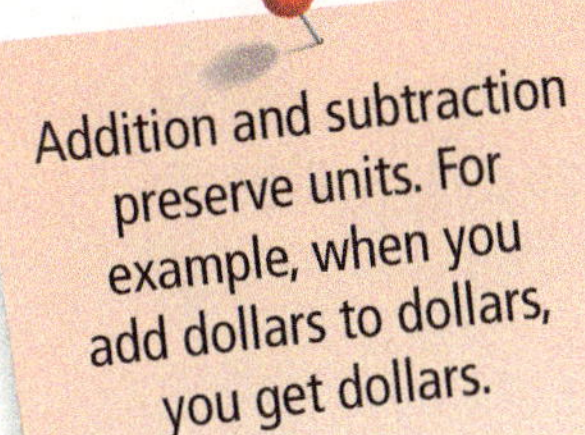

You had $251.45 before your aunt gave you money.

Another Method Solve the problem arithmetically by working backwards from $25.50.

$25.50 + 275.95 - 50 = \$251.45$ ✓

Self-Assessment for Problem Solving

Solve each exercise. Then rate your understanding of the success criteria in your journal.

18. An emperor penguin is 45 inches tall. It is 24 inches taller than a rockhopper penguin. Write and solve an equation to find the height (in inches) of a rockhopper penguin. Is your answer reasonable? Explain.

19. **DIG DEEPER!** You get in an elevator and go up 2 floors and down 8 floors before exiting. Then you get back in the elevator and go up 4 floors before exiting on the 12th floor. On what floors did you enter the elevator?

6.2 Practice

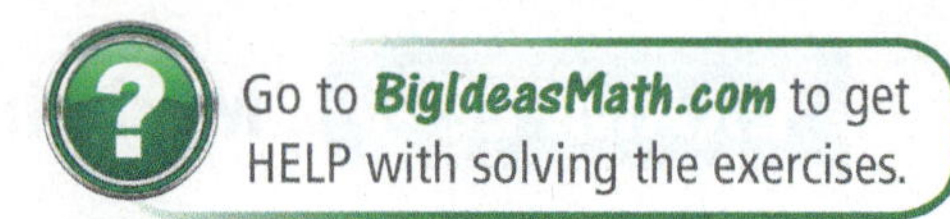

Review & Refresh

Write the word sentence as an equation.

1. The sum of a number x and 9 is 15.
2. 12 less than a number m equals 20.
3. The product of a number d and 7 is 63.
4. 18 divided by a number s equals 3.

Divide. Write the answer in simplest form.

5. $\frac{1}{2} \div \frac{1}{4}$
6. $12 \div \frac{3}{8}$
7. $8 \div \frac{4}{5}$
8. $\frac{7}{9} \div \frac{3}{2}$

9. Which ratio is *not* equivalent to 72 : 18?

   A. 36 : 9 **B.** 18 : 6 **C.** 4 : 1 **D.** 288 : 72

Evaluate the expression.

10. $(2 + 5^2) \div 3$
11. $6 + 2^3 \cdot 3 - 5$
12. $4 \cdot [3 + 3(20 - 4^2 - 2)]$

13. Find the missing values in the ratio table. Then write the equivalent ratios.

Snakes	2		24
Mice	5	20	

Concepts, Skills, & Problem Solving

MP **CHOOSE TOOLS** **Use a model to solve the equation.** (See Explorations 1 and 2, p. 251.)

14. $n + 7 = 9$
15. $t + 4 = 5$
16. $c + 2 = 8$

CHECKING SOLUTIONS **Tell whether the given value is a solution of the equation.**

17. $x + 42 = 85; x = 43$
18. $8b = 48; b = 6$
19. $19 - g = 7; g = 15$
20. $\frac{m}{4} = 16; m = 4$
21. $w + 23 = 41; w = 28$
22. $s - 68 = 11; s = 79$

SOLVING EQUATIONS **Solve the equation. Check your solution.**

23. $y - 7 = 3$
24. $z - 3 = 13$
25. $8 = r - 14$
26. $p + 5 = 8$
27. $k + 6 = 18$
28. $64 = h + 30$
29. $f - 27 = 19$
30. $25 = q + 14$
31. $\frac{3}{4} = j - \frac{1}{2}$
32. $x + \frac{2}{3} = \frac{9}{10}$
33. $1.2 = m - 2.5$
34. $a + 5.5 = 17.3$

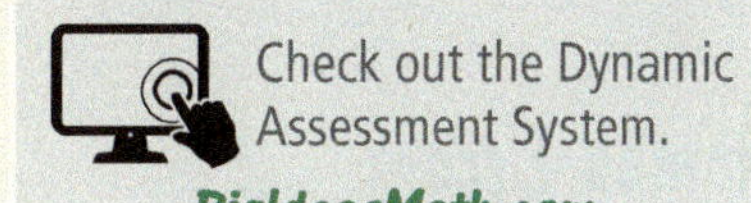

Assignment Guide and Concept Check

Scaffold assignments to support all students in their learning progression. The suggested assignments are a starting point. Continue to assign additional exercises and revisit with spaced practice to move every student toward proficiency.

Level	Assignment 1	Assignment 2
Emerging	2, 6, 9, 12, 13, 16, 18, 19, 25, 27, 49	31, 35, 36, 37, 38, 45, 46, 54, 55, 60
Proficient	2, 6, 9, 12, 13, 16, 19, 20, 28, 29, 31, 49, 50	33, 35, 36, 38, 39, 47, 48, 54, 56, 57, 58, 60
Advanced	2, 6, 9, 12, 13, 16, 20, 22, 32, 33, 51, 54	35, 36, 39, 40, 48, 57, 58, 59, 60, 61, 62

- Assignment 1 is for use after students complete the Self-Assessment for Concepts & Skills.
- Assignment 2 is for use after students complete the Self-Assessment for Problem Solving.
- The red exercises can be used as a concept check.

Review & Refresh Prior Skills

Exercises 1–4 Writing Equations in One Variable
Exercises 5–8 Dividing Fractions
Exercise 9 Identifying Equivalent Ratios
Exercises 10–12 Using Order of Operations
Exercise 13 Using a Ratio Table

Common Errors

- **Exercises 17–22** Students may use the same operation instead of the inverse operation to solve. Remind them that they are checking to see if the value of the variable makes the equation true, so they should focus on simplifying one side of the equation and then compare the answer to the other side.
- **Exercises 23–34** Students may use the same operation instead of the inverse operation to solve. Simplify the equation on the board to demonstrate that this will not work. Students may have ignored the side with the variable when they made this mistake. Remind them to check their answers in the original equation.
- **Exercises 23–34** Students may add or subtract the number on the side without the variable. For example, they might write $14 - 14 = k + 6 - 14$ instead of $14 - 6 = k + 6 - 6$. Remind students that they are trying to get the variable by itself, so they should start on the side with the variable and use the inverse of that operation.

Review & Refresh

1. $x + 9 = 15$
2. $m - 12 = 20$
3. $d \cdot 7 = 63$
4. $18 \div s = 3$
5. 2
6. 32
7. 10
8. $\frac{14}{27}$
9. B
10. 9
11. 25
12. 36
13.

Snakes	2	8	24
Mice	5	20	60

2:5, 8:20, 24:60

Concepts, Skills, & Problem Solving

14. $n = 2$
15. $t = 1$
16. $c = 6$
17. yes
18. yes
19. no
20. no
21. no
22. yes
23. $y = 10$
24. $z = 16$
25. $r = 22$
26. $p = 3$
27. $k = 12$
28. $h = 34$
29. $f = 46$
30. $q = 11$
31. $j = 1\frac{1}{4}$
32. $x = \frac{7}{30}$
33. $m = 3.7$
34. $a = 11.8$

Concepts, Skills, & Problem Solving

35. no; Subtract 7 to get $x = 6$.

36. no; Add to both sides to get $46 = y$.

37. $366 = x - 30$; 396 m

38. $22 - x = 13$; 9

39. 10,641 mi^2

40. Subtract 3 from each side. (Subtraction Property of Equality); Subtract 3 from 3 and 3 from 12; Add x and 0. (Addition Property of Zero)

41. $w - 13 = 15$; $w = 28$

42. $k + 7 = 34$; $k = 27$

43. $9 = n - 7$; $n = 16$

44. $93 = g + 58$; $g = 35$

45. $k + 11 = 29$; $k = 18$

46. $p - 19 = 6$; $p = 25$

47. $46 = 18 + d$; $d = 28$

48. $84 = c - 99$; $c = 183$

Common Errors

- **Exercises 37–39** Students may struggle to determine what information is important in the word problem. Encourage them to simplify the word problem as they did in the previous section.
- **Exercises 41–48** Students may write the wrong equation and create a subtraction problem that they do not know how to complete because the answer is negative. Remind them to read the word sentence carefully. Refer them to the previous section for help writing the equation.

MP YOU BE THE TEACHER **Your friend solves the equation. Is your friend correct? Explain your reasoning.**

35.

$$\begin{aligned} x + 7 &= 13 \\ +7 \quad & \quad +7 \\ x &= 20 \end{aligned}$$

36.

$$\begin{aligned} 34 &= y - 12 \\ -12 \quad & \quad +12 \\ 22 &= y \end{aligned}$$

37. **MP MODELING REAL LIFE** The main span of the Sunshine Skyway Bridge is 366 meters long. The bridge's main span is 30 meters shorter than the main span of the Dames Point Bridge. Write and solve an equation to find the length (in meters) of the main span of the Dames Point Bridge.

38. **MP PROBLEM SOLVING** A park has 22 elm trees. Elm leaf beetles have been attacking the trees. After removing several of the diseased trees, there are 13 healthy elm trees left. Write and solve an equation to find the number of elm trees that were removed.

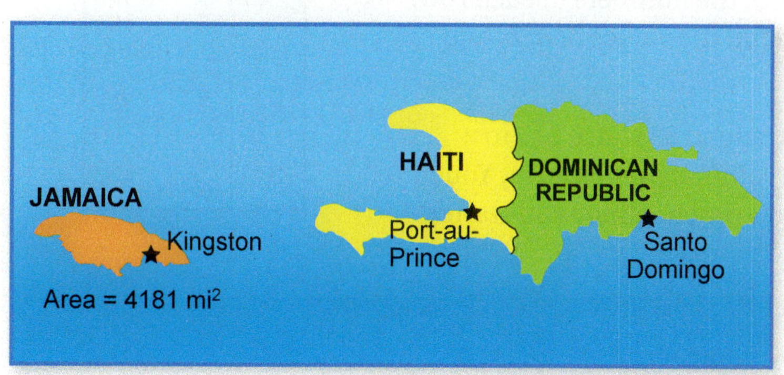

39. **MP PROBLEM SOLVING** The area of Jamaica is 6460 square miles less than the area of Haiti. Find the area (in square miles) of Haiti.

40. **MP REASONING** The solution of the equation $x + 3 = 12$ is shown. Explain each step. Use a property, if possible.

	Write the equation.
$x + 3 = 12$	
$x + 3 - 3 = 12 - 3$	
$x + 0 = 9$	
$x = 9$	

WRITING EQUATIONS **Write the word sentence as an equation. Then solve the equation.**

41. 13 subtracted from a number w is 15.

42. A number k increased by 7 is 34.

43. 9 is the difference of a number n and 7.

44. 93 is the sum of a number g and 58.

45. 11 more than a number k equals 29.

46. A number p decreased by 19 is 6.

47. 46 is the total of 18 and a number d.

48. 84 is 99 fewer than a number c.

SOLVING EQUATIONS **Solve the equation. Check your solution.**

49. $b + 7 + 12 = 30$

50. $y + 4 - 1 = 18$

51. $m + 18 + 23 = 71$

52. $v - 7 = 9 + 12$

53. $5 + 44 = 2 + r$

54. $22 + 15 = d - 17$

GEOMETRY **Solve for x.**

55. Perimeter = 48 ft

x
20 ft
12 ft

56. Perimeter = 132 in.

57. Perimeter = 93 ft

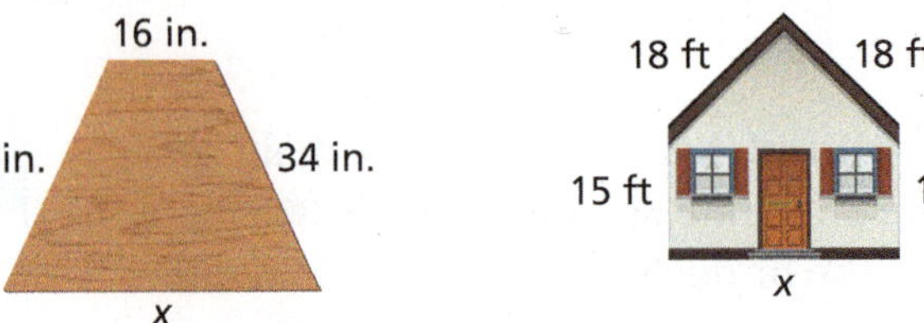

58. **SIMPLIFYING AND SOLVING** Compare and contrast the two problems.

Simplify the expression $2(x + 3) - 4$.

$$2(x + 3) - 4 = 2x + 6 - 4$$
$$= 2x + 2$$

Solve the equation $x + 3 = 4$.

$$x + 3 = 4$$
$$\underline{-3} \quad \underline{-3}$$
$$x = 1$$

59. **PUZZLE** In a *magic square*, the sum of the numbers in each row, column, and diagonal is the same. Find the values of a, b, and c. Justify your answers.

a	37	16
19	25	b
34	c	28

60. **MP REASONING** On Saturday, you spend \$33, give \$15 to a friend, and receive \$20 for mowing your neighbor's lawn. You have \$21 left. Use two methods to find how much money you started with that day.

61. **DIG DEEPER!** You have \$15.

Bumper Cars:	\$1.75
Super Pendulum:	\$1.25 more than Ferris Wheel
Giant Slide:	\$0.50 less than Bumper Cars
Ferris Wheel:	\$1.50 more than Giant Slide

a. How much money do you have left if you ride each ride once?

b. Do you have enough money to ride each ride twice? Explain.

62. **CRITICAL THINKING** Consider the equation $15 - y = 8$. Explain how you can solve the equation using the Addition and Subtraction Properties of Equality.

Common Errors

- **Exercises 49–54** Students may lose one of the numbers when solving for the variable. For example: $b + 7 + 12 = 30$

$$\begin{aligned} b + 7 + 12 &= 30 \\ -7 \quad &\;\; -7 \\ b &= 23 \end{aligned}$$

Remind them to be very careful when solving for the variable. Encourage them to simplify and combine like terms before solving. Developing this skill will be valuable in future courses. Students should check their answers in the original equation. This will help them to catch their mistakes.

Mini-Assessment

Solve the equation.

1. $y - 10 = 4$ $y = 14$
2. $25 = f + 13$ $f = 12$
3. $q - 67 = 3$ $q = 70$
4. $s + 24 = 35$ $s = 11$
5. You get in an elevator and go up 4 floors. You exit on the 12th floor. Write and solve an equation to find what floor you got on the elevator. $x + 4 = 12$; You got on the elevator on the 8th floor.

Section Resources

Surface Level	Deep Level
Resources by Chapter • Extra Practice • Reteach • Puzzle Time Student Journal • Self-Assessment • Practice Differentiating the Lesson Tutorial Videos Skills Review Handbook Skills Trainer	Resources by Chapter • Enrichment and Extension Graphic Organizers Dynamic Assessment System • Section Practice
Transfer Level	
Dynamic Assessment System • Mid-Chapter Quiz	Assessment Book • Mid-Chapter Quiz

Concepts, Skills, & Problem Solving

49. $b = 11$
50. $y = 15$
51. $m = 30$
52. $v = 28$
53. $r = 47$
54. $d = 54$
55. 16 ft
56. 48 in.
57. 27 ft
58. *Sample answer:* Both are finding something equivalent to the given problem. The left problem uses the Distributive Property and the right problem uses the Subtraction Property of Equality.
59. $a = 22$; $b = 31$; $c = 13$; The constant sum is 75, and $a + 53 = 75$, $b + 44 = 75$, and $c + 62 = 75$.
60. $49
61. **a.** $5.25

    b. no; It costs $9.75 to ride each ride once.
62. Add y to each side, then subtract 8 from each side.

Learning Target

Write and solve equations using multiplication or division.

Success Criteria

- Apply the Multiplication and Division Properties of Equality to generate equivalent equations.
- Solve equations using multiplication or division.
- Create equations involving multiplication or division to solve real-life problems.

Warm Up

Cumulative, vocabulary, and prerequisite skills practice opportunities are available in the *Resources by Chapter* or at *BigIdeasMath.com*.

ELL Support

In Exploration 2, point out the use of the word *bill* and explain that another word for bill is *check*. A restaurant bill lists the food and drinks that a person orders, the price of each item, and the total cost. The word *bill* can also be used to mean other things, such as a bird's beak or a dollar bill.

Exploration 1

a. $20 = 4x$; $x = 5$

b. Step 2 divides both 20 and $4x$ into four equal parts, Step 3 uses one part to show the value of x.

Exploration 2

a. $4

b. See Additional Answers.

c. $x = 3$; Divide each side of the equation by 5.

Laurie's Notes

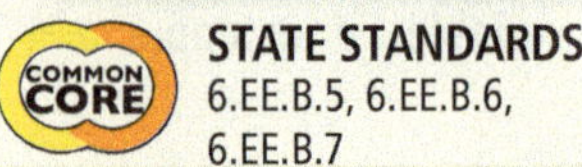

Preparing to Teach

- The properties of equality will now extend to include multiplication and division.
- Using tape diagrams to manipulate visual pieces of one-step equations will build students' confidence. Students' sense of fairness allows them to appreciate that the equal pieces relate to equal values.
- **MP1 Make Sense of Problems and Persevere in Solving Them:** In the beginning, solving equations may be difficult for students because of the notation, representations, or symbols. Solving equations is a simple skill for teachers, and in time it will be simple for students as well. It is important to be clear in your language and notation so that students do not develop misconceptions about how equations are solved.

Motivate

- Write the following on the board. Have students fill in all ten squares using each of the digits 0 to 9. Read the first equation as "12 times a single-digit number equals a two-digit number that ends in 0."

$12 \times \boxed{5} = \boxed{6}0$ $\qquad \boxed{4}\boxed{8} \div 4 = 12$

$\boxed{7} = \boxed{3}5 \div 5$ $\qquad \boxed{1} \times 0 = \boxed{0}$

$7\boxed{2} = \boxed{9} \times 8$

- This helps students to think of multiplication and division as inverse operations.

Exploration 1

- Allow time for partners to explore the three steps in the visual model.
- For part (a), remind students to find the equation represented by the model and its solution.
- Listen to explanations for part (b). Ask volunteers to explain their thinking.
- Ask, "How can you check your answer?" *Sample answer:* By substituting the solution for the variable in the equation and checking for reasonableness.

Exploration 2

- Ask a volunteer to read the problem aloud.
- Make sure that students notice the balanced scale. "Which side of the scale represents the robots?" the left side "What does the other side represent?" the $12 bill
- As partners work on part (a), remind them to show their processes.
- Did any students say, "take 1 red ball off the left side and 1 blue block off the right side," and assume that the scale was still balanced? If so, ask them to make a tape diagram to represent the problem.
- Listen to the strategies used in parts (b) and (c). Ask volunteers to share their strategies with the class. Do students see the multiplicative nature of *for every red ball there are 4 blue blocks*?
- **Extension:** "If the lunch bill is $11.01, how much does each robot pay?" $3.67

6.3 Solving Equations Using Multiplication or Division

Learning Target: Write and solve equations using multiplication or division.

Success Criteria:
- I can apply the Multiplication and Division Properties of Equality to generate equivalent equations.
- I can solve equations using multiplication or division.
- I can create equations involving multiplication or division to solve real-life problems.

EXPLORATION 1 Solving an Equation Using a Tape Diagram

Work with a partner. A student solves an equation using the tape diagrams below.

Step 1:

20
$4x$

Step 2:

5	5	5	5
x	x	x	x

Step 3:

5
x

Math Practice

Maintain Oversight

How do these explorations help you solve equations of the form $ax = b$?

a. What equation did the student solve? What is the solution?

b. Explain how the tape diagrams in Steps 2 and 3 relate to the equation and its solution.

EXPLORATION 2 Solving an Equation Using a Model

Work with a partner. Three robots go out to lunch. They decide to split the $12 bill evenly. The scale represents the number of robots and the price of the meal.

a. How much does each robot pay?

b. When you triple the weight on one side of a balanced scale, what can you do to balance the scale? What if you divide the weight on one side of a balanced scale in half? How does this relate to solving an equation?

c. **MP CHOOSE TOOLS** Choose a model to represent and solve the equation $5x = 15$. Then describe how you can solve the equation algebraically.

6.3 Lesson

Key Ideas

Remember

Inverse operations "undo" each other. Multiplication and division are inverse operations.

Multiplication Property of Equality

Words When you multiply each side of an equation by the same nonzero number, the two sides remain equal.

Numbers

$$\frac{8}{4} = 2$$

$$\frac{8}{4} \cdot 4 = 2 \cdot 4$$

$$8 = 8$$

Algebra

$$\frac{x}{4} = 2$$

$$\frac{x}{4} \cdot 4 = 2 \cdot 4$$

$$x = 8$$

Multiplicative Inverse Property

Words The product of a nonzero number n and its reciprocal, $\frac{1}{n}$, is 1.

Numbers $5 \cdot \frac{1}{5} = 1$

Algebra $n \cdot \frac{1}{n} = \frac{1}{n} \cdot n = 1, n \neq 0$

EXAMPLE 1 Solving Equations Using Multiplication

a. Solve $\frac{w}{4} = 12$.

$\frac{w}{4} = 12$ Write the equation.

Undo the division. → $\frac{w}{4} \cdot 4 = 12 \cdot 4$ Multiplication Property of Equality

$w = 48$ Simplify.

The solution is $w = 48$.

Check

$$\frac{w}{4} = 12$$

$$\frac{48}{4} \stackrel{?}{=} 12$$

$$12 = 12 \checkmark$$

b. Solve $\frac{2}{7}x = 6$.

$\frac{2}{7}x = 6$ Write the equation.

Use the Multiplicative Inverse Property. → $\frac{7}{2} \cdot \left(\frac{2}{7}x\right) = \frac{7}{2} \cdot 6$ Multiplication Property of Equality

$x = 21$ Simplify.

The solution is $x = 21$.

Try It **Solve the equation. Check your solution.**

1. $\frac{a}{8} = 6$

2. $14 = \frac{2y}{5}$

3. $3z \div 2 = 9$

Laurie's Notes

Scaffolding Instruction

- In this lesson, students will use the inverse operations of multiplication and division to solve equations.
- **Emerging:** Students may depend on models and will benefit from guided instruction for the examples.
- **Proficient:** Students are comfortable with inverse operations and understand how to use them to solve equations. Review the Key Ideas, and then have students self-assess using the Self-Assessment exercises.
- The process of solving equations is the foundation for all algebraic work. It will take time for students to become proficient.

Key Ideas

- Discuss the Words, Numbers, and Algebra.
- **Representation:** Point out that division is often represented in the fraction format. Tell students to rewrite equations like $x \div 4 = 2$ as $x/4 = 2$.
- **Connection:** When multiplying a fraction and a whole number, students may benefit from writing the whole number over a denominator of 1.

  Numbers: $\frac{8}{4} \cdot \frac{4}{1} = \frac{32}{4} = 8$ Algebra: $\frac{x}{4} \cdot \frac{4}{1} = \frac{4x}{4} = x$

- Remind students to use the multiplication dot instead of $\times$ when working with variables.
- Students may have used the Multiplicative Inverse Property to check reciprocals in Section 2.2, but it is now formally defined. Remind students that 5 and $\frac{1}{5}$ are multiplicative inverses (or reciprocals).

EXAMPLE 1

? "In part (b), what can you multiply each side by to solve for x?" $\frac{7}{2}$

- Another way to solve this equation is to multiply by 7 and then divide by 2.
- Discuss how to check that the answers are correct.
- **Big Idea:** Multiply each side of the equation by the same factor. Using an alternate color to show this will help visual learners.

Try It

- **MP5 Use Appropriate Tools Strategically:** Students can choose to use a model to solve the equations.
- In Exercise 2, it may be helpful for students to rewrite $\frac{2y}{5}$ as $\frac{2}{5}y$.
- In Exercise 3, writing division as a fraction is not obvious to many students. Use a simple problem like $12 \div 4 = \frac{12}{4} = 3$ to point out that in $3z \div 2$ the numerator is $3z$ and the denominator is 2.
- **Chalkboard Splash:** For each exercise, choose two students to put their work on the board. Look for different approaches. Encourage other students to ask questions.

Scaffold instruction to support all students in their learning. Learning is individualized and you may want to group students differently as they move in and out of these levels with each skill and concept. Student self-assessment and feedback help guide your instructional decisions about how and when to layer support for all students to become proficient learners.

Extra Example 1

a. Solve $\frac{t}{6} = 9$. $t = 54$

b. Solve $2y \div 8 = 7$. $y = 28$

ELL Support

Have students work in pairs to discuss and complete Try It Exercises 1–3.
Beginner: Write the solution.
Intermediate: State the solution. For example, "*a* equals forty-eight."
Advanced: Explain the process used to find the solution.

Try It

1. $a = 48$
2. $y = 35$
3. $z = 6$

Extra Example 2

Solve $7c = 35$. $c = 5$

Try It

4. $p = 6$
5. $q = 5$
6. $r = 9$

ELL Support

Have all students proceed as described in Laurie's Notes for the Self-Assessment for Concepts & Skills. Have pairs of native speakers check answers with pairs of ELLs. To check answers, have each group display their solutions on a whiteboard for your review.

Self-Assessment for Concepts & Skills

7. $y = 9$
8. $s = 7$
9. $\frac{1}{4}x = 27$; The others are equivalent to $x = 12$.
10. $6; 3 \cdot 6 = 18$
11. $12; 12 \div 2 = 6$

Laurie's Notes

Key Idea

- Write the Key Idea and discuss the Words, Numbers, and Algebra.
- **Representation:** Remind students that $4x$ is how multiplication is represented.
- **Common Misconception:** Students sometimes think that when $\frac{4x}{4}$ is simplified to x, the 4s have just been "crossed out" because they are the same. Explain that the numerator and denominator have a common factor of 4 that can be *divided out*, in the same way that a common factor of 4 is divided out when simplifying $\frac{12}{16}$.
- Discuss the push-pin note with students.

EXAMPLE 2

? "How do you undo the operation of multiplication?" division

- **MP1 Make Sense of Problems and Persevere in Solving Them:** Work through the problem. Being clear about notation and symbols will help students make sense of the mathematics and how to work towards the solution.
- Discuss the last step in the solution. This can be confusing for students because of the 5 on each side of the equation. On the left, 5 is the ones digit in a two-digit number. On the right, $5b$ means 5 times the value of b. If the equation had been written as $65 = b(5)$, it would have been even more confusing. Remember that students may not yet be comfortable with multiplication represented as $5b$. It's not uncommon to see a wrong answer of $b = 6$. The 5s were "crossed out" on both sides! It might be helpful to write $\frac{5 \cdot 13}{5} = \frac{5 \cdot b}{5}$ as an intermediate step.

Try It

- Note that variables can appear on either side of the equal sign.
- Ask volunteers to share their work at the board.

Self-Assessment for Concepts & Skills

- Students should work independently on the exercises. Remind them to show their work and check their solutions. Look at their reasoning for Exercises 9–11.
- **Turn and Talk:** Have pairs compare their answers and reasoning. If they differ, they should analyze their work to find and correct any errors. Then have each pair check their answers with another pair.
- Ask students to indicate their understanding of the first two success criteria using *Fist of Five.*

The Success Criteria Self-Assessment chart can be found in the *Student Journal* or online at *BigIdeasMath.com.*

You can multiply or divide each side of an equation by any number to generate an equivalent equation. For example, $4x = 32$ and $2x = 16$ are equivalent equations.

$$4x = 32$$
$$\frac{4x}{2} = \frac{32}{2}$$
$$2x = 16$$

Key Idea

Division Property of Equality

Words When you divide each side of an equation by the same nonzero number, the two sides remain equal.

Numbers

$$8 \cdot 4 = 32$$
$$8 \cdot 4 \div 4 = 32 \div 4$$
$$8 = 8$$

Algebra

$$4x = 32$$
$$\frac{4x}{4} = \frac{32}{4}$$
$$x = 8$$

EXAMPLE 2 Solving an Equation Using Division

Solve $65 = 5b$.

$65 = 5b$ Write the equation.

Undo the multiplication.  $\frac{65}{5} = \frac{5b}{5}$ Division Property of Equality

$13 = b$ Simplify.

The solution is $b = 13$.

Check

$65 = 5b$

$65 \stackrel{?}{=} 5(13)$

$65 = 65$ ✓

Try It **Solve the equation. Check your solution.**

4. $p \cdot 3 = 18$

5. $12q = 60$

6. $81 = 9r$

Self-Assessment for Concepts & Skills

Solve each exercise. Then rate your understanding of the success criteria in your journal.

SOLVING EQUATIONS **Solve the equation. Check your solution.**

7. $6 = \frac{2y}{3}$

8. $8s = 56$

9. **WHICH ONE DOESN'T BELONG?** Which equation does *not* belong with the other three? Explain your reasoning.

$\frac{1}{4}x = 27$ $3x = 36$ $\frac{3}{4}x = 9$ $4x = 48$

MP STRUCTURE **Just by looking at the equation, find the value of x. Explain your reasoning.**

10. $5x + 3x = 5x + 18$

11. $8x + \frac{x}{2} = 8x + 6$

EXAMPLE 3 Modeling Real Life

The area of a rectangular LED "sky screen" in Beijing, China, is 7500 square meters. The width of the sky screen is 30 meters. What is the length of the sky screen?

Use the given information to draw a diagram. Then substitute for the area A and the width w in the formula for the area of a rectangle, $A = \ell w$. Solve for the length ℓ.

$A = 7500\ \text{m}^2$ | 30 m

$A = \ell w$ — Use the formula for area of a rectangle.

$7500 = 30\ell$ — Substitute 7500 for A and 30 for w.

$\frac{7500}{30} = \frac{30\ell}{30}$ — Division Property of Equality

$250 = \ell$ — Simplify.

So, the sky screen is 250 meters long.

Self-Assessment for Problem Solving

Solve each exercise. Then rate your understanding of the success criteria in your journal.

Area = $1625\ \text{mm}^2$

12. The area of the screen of the smart watch is shown. What are possible dimensions for the length and the width of the screen? Justify your answer.

13. A rock climber climbs at a rate of 720 feet per hour. Write and solve an equation to find the number of minutes it takes for the rock climber to climb 288 feet.

14. DIG DEEPER! A gift card stores data using a black, magnetic stripe on the back of the card. Find the width w of the stripe.

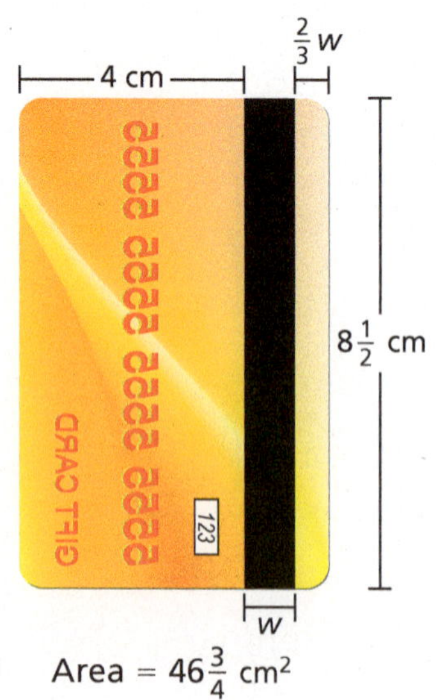

Area = $46\frac{3}{4}\ \text{cm}^2$

Laurie's Notes

EXAMPLE 3

- Ask a volunteer to read the problem aloud.
- ? "The width of the sky screen is 30 meters. Can you think of something that is 30 meters tall?" *Sample answer:* a very tall building
- You can help students visualize a square meter by using 4 meter sticks to make a square. Then ask students to estimate the area (in square meters) of a board in your classroom. Answers will vary. Ask students if their thoughts about the size of the sky screen have changed and why.
- ? "What additional information do you need to know to solve the problem?" the formula for the area of a rectangle "What is the formula?" $A = \ell w$ "What do you need to find?" the length
- Substitute the known information and continue to solve as shown. Remind students that variables can appear on either side of an equals sign.
- Remind students to include units in their answers. The sky screen is 250 meters long, not just 250.

Self-Assessment for Problem Solving

- Encourage students to use a Four Square to complete these exercises. Until students become comfortable with the problem-solving plan, they may only be ready to complete the first square.
- Have students work independently on Exercises 12 and 13 and then in pairs for Exercise 14. Remind them that they know how to combine like terms and use the Distributive Property to simplify an expression.
- Allow time for students to check their work and discuss their answers with a partner. Address any questions.
- Students need to realize that many real-life problems do not have "pretty" numbers for answers. The world is full of fractions and decimals!

The Success Criteria Self-Assessment chart can be found in the *Student Journal* or online at *BigIdeasMath.com*.

Closure

- **Write Your Own:** Write an equation that can be solved by (a) multiplying both sides by $\frac{2}{3}$ and (b) dividing both sides by 8. *Sample answers:* $\frac{3}{2}p = 9$; $8y = 24$

Extra Example 3

A driver travels 2500 miles at a rate of 500 miles per day. How many days does it take to complete the trip?
$500d = 2500$; 5 days

Self-Assessment for Problem Solving

12. *Sample answer:* 25 mm by 65 mm; The width is about $\frac{1}{3}$ of the length.
13. $12m = 288$; 24 min
14. $\frac{9}{10}$ cm

Formative Assessment Tip

Write Your Own
This technique allows students to practice writing and evaluating their own problems. You provide a description of the type of problem students are to create. Descriptions may be broad or specific. Students write and solve their own problems that satisfy the conditions you describe. Then have students trade problems to check that the conditions are met and the problems are solved correctly.

Learning Target

Write and solve equations using multiplication or division.

Success Criteria

- Apply the Multiplication and Division Properties of Equality to generate equivalent equations.
- Solve equations using multiplication or division.
- Create equations involving multiplication or division to solve real-life problems.

Review & Refresh

1. $y = 11$
2. $m = 1$
3. $p = \frac{5}{8}$
4. C
5. $\frac{2}{45}$
6. $\frac{5}{21}$
7. $\frac{7}{10}$
8. $4\frac{2}{3}$
9. 0.36
10. 0.39
11. 11.3353
12. 3.6572

Concepts, Skills, & Problem Solving

13. $x = 1$
14. $y = 3$
15. $z = 7$
16. $s = 70$
17. $t = 30$
18. $x = 24$
19. $r = 32$
20. $a = 4$
21. $z = 7$
22. $y = 10$
23. $k = 6$
24. $x = 15$
25. $w = 12.5$
26. $d = 78$
27. $v = 45$
28. $d = 18$
29. $m = \frac{3}{20}$
30. $b = 8$
31. $k = 2\frac{2}{3}$
32. $c = 66$
33. $b = 7.2$
34. $n = 2.56$
35. $m = 6$
36. no; Multiply by 4 to get $x = 112$.
37. $$3x = 9$$
$$3x \cdot \frac{1}{3} = 9 \cdot \frac{1}{3}$$
$$x = 3$$

Check out the Dynamic Assessment System.
BigIdeasMath.com

Assignment Guide and Concept Check

Scaffold assignments to support all students in their learning progression. The suggested assignments are a starting point. Continue to assign additional exercises and revisit with spaced practice to move every student toward proficiency.

Level	Assignment 1	Assignment 2
Emerging	3, 4, 8, 12, 15, 16, 18, 21, 23	26, 29, 31, 36, 38, 39, 40, 44
Proficient	3, 4, 8, 12, 15, 18, 23, 25, 28	32, 35, 36, 37, 38, 39, 41, 42, 43, 44
Advanced	3, 4, 8, 12, 15, 28, 30, 32, 35	36, 37, 39, 41, 42, 43, 44, 45

- Assignment 1 is for use after students complete the Self-Assessment for Concepts & Skills.
- Assignment 2 is for use after students complete the Self-Assessment for Problem Solving.
- The red exercises can be used as a concept check.

Review & Refresh Prior Skills

Exercises 1–3 Solving Equations
Exercise 4 Evaluating Expressions
Exercises 5 and 6 Multiplying Fractions
Exercises 7 and 8 Multiplying Fractions and Mixed Numbers
Exercises 9–12 Multiplying Decimals

Common Errors

- **Exercises 16–35** Students may do the same operation on both sides instead of the opposite operation. This is most common with problems like Exercise 18, where the equation is written in division format instead of fraction format. Remind students that to get the variable alone, they must use the inverse operation.

6.3 Practice

Review & Refresh

Solve the equation. Check your solution.

1. $y - 5 = 6$
2. $m + 7 = 8$
3. $\frac{7}{8} = \frac{1}{4} + p$
4. What is the value of a^3 when $a = 4$?

   A. 12 **B.** 43 **C.** 64 **D.** 81

Multiply. Write the answer in simplest form.

5. $\frac{1}{5} \cdot \frac{2}{9}$
6. $\frac{5}{12} \times \frac{4}{7}$
7. $2\frac{1}{3} \cdot \frac{3}{10}$
8. $1\frac{3}{4} \times 2\frac{2}{3}$

Multiply.

9. 0.4×0.9
10. 0.78×0.5
11. 2.63×4.31
12. 1.115×3.28

Concepts, Skills, & Problem Solving

MP CHOOSE TOOLS **Use a model to solve the equation.** (See Explorations 1 and 2, p. 259.)

13. $8x = 8$
14. $9 = 3y$
15. $2z = 14$

SOLVING EQUATIONS **Solve the equation. Check your solution.**

16. $\frac{s}{10} = 7$
17. $6 = \frac{t}{5}$
18. $5x \div 6 = 20$
19. $24 = \frac{3}{4}r$
20. $3a = 12$
21. $5 \cdot z = 35$
22. $40 = 4y$
23. $42 = 7k$
24. $7x = 105$
25. $75 = 6 \cdot w$
26. $13 = d \div 6$
27. $9 = v \div 5$
28. $\frac{5d}{9} = 10$
29. $\frac{3}{5} = 4m$
30. $136 = 17b$
31. $\frac{2}{3} = \frac{1}{4}k$
32. $\frac{2c}{15} = 8.8$
33. $7b \div 12 = 4.2$
34. $12.5 \cdot n = 32$
35. $3.4m = 20.4$

36. **MP YOU BE THE TEACHER** Your friend solves the equation $x \div 4 = 28$. Is your friend correct? Explain your reasoning.

$$x \div 4 = 28$$
$$\frac{x \div 4}{4} = \frac{28}{4}$$
$$x = 7$$

37. **ANOTHER WAY** Show how you can solve the equation $3x = 9$ by multiplying each side by the reciprocal of 3.

38. **MP MODELING REAL LIFE** Forty-five basketball players participate in a three-on-three tournament. Write and solve an equation to find the number of three-person teams in the tournament.

39. **MP MODELING REAL LIFE** A theater has 1200 seats. Each row has 20 seats. Write and solve an equation to find the number of rows in the theater.

GEOMETRY Solve for x. Check your answer.

40. Area = 45 square units

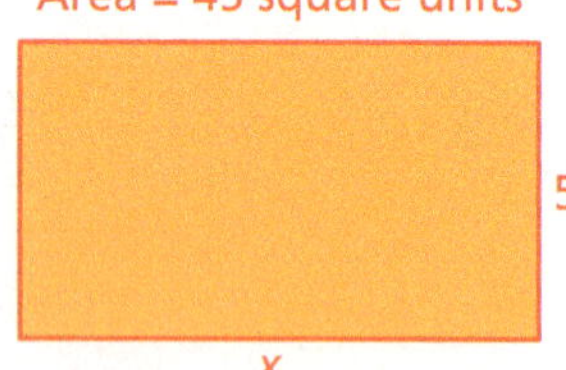

41. Area = 176 square units

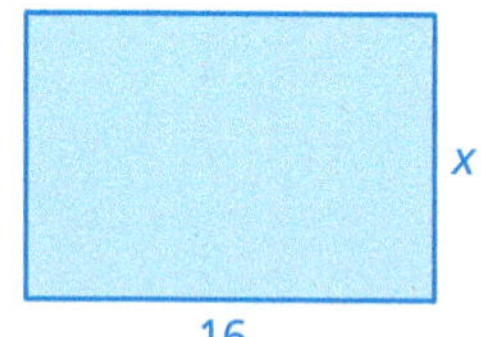

42. **MP LOGIC** On a test, you earn 92% of the possible points by correctly answering 6 five-point questions and 8 two-point questions. How many points p is the test worth?

43. **MP MODELING REAL LIFE** You use index cards to play a homemade game. The object is to be the first to get rid of all your cards. How many cards are in your friend's stack?

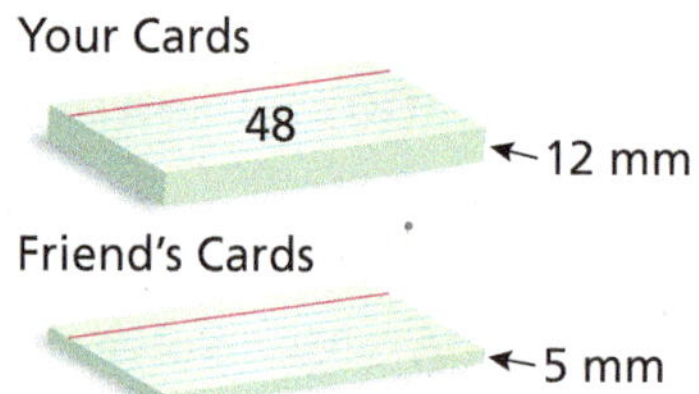

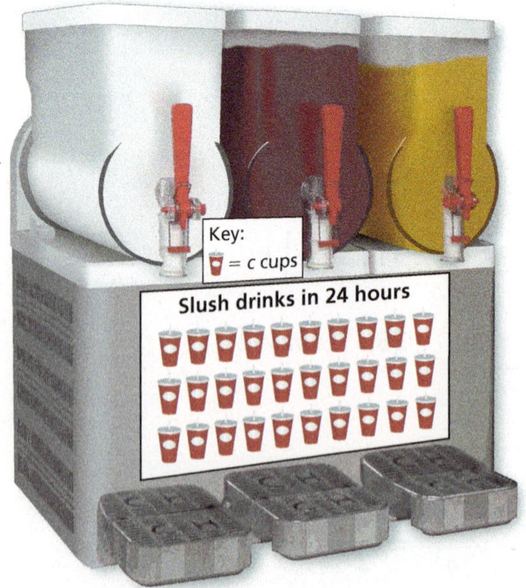

44. **DIG DEEPER!** A slush drink machine fills 1440 cups in 24 hours.

   a. Find the number c of cups each symbol represents.

   b. To lower costs, you replace the cups with paper cones that hold 20% less. Find the number n of paper cones that the machine can fill in 24 hours.

45. **MP NUMBER SENSE** The area of the picture is 100 square inches. The length is 4 times the width. Find the length and width of the picture.

Mini-Assessment

Solve the equation.

1. $\frac{t}{5} = 7$ $t = 35$
2. $12d = 60$ $d = 5$
3. $16 = \frac{s}{2}$ $s = 32$
4. $35 = g \div 5$ $g = 175$
5. You pay $1.56 for 4 pounds of bananas. Write and solve an equation to find how much it costs for one pound of bananas. $4x = 1.56$; It costs $0.39 for one pound of bananas.

Section Resources

Surface Level	Deep Level
Resources by Chapter • Extra Practice • Reteach • Puzzle Time Student Journal • Self-Assessment • Practice Differentiating the Lesson Tutorial Videos Skills Review Handbook Skills Trainer	Resources by Chapter • Enrichment and Extension Graphic Organizers Dynamic Assessment System • Section Practice

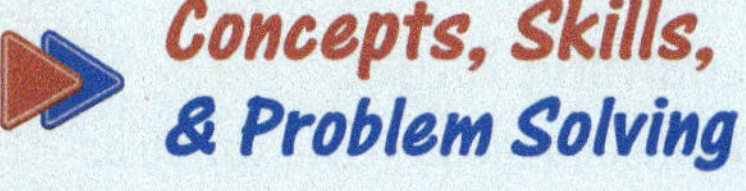

Concepts, Skills, & Problem Solving

38. $3x = 45$; 15
39. $20x = 1200$; 60
40. 9
41. 11
42. 50
43. 20
44. a. 48

    b. 1800
45. length: 20 in.; width: 5 in.

Learning Target

Write equations in two variables and analyze the relationship between the two quantities.

Success Criteria

- Determine whether an ordered pair is a solution of an equation in two variables.
- Distinguish between independent and dependent variables.
- Write and graph an equation in two variables.
- Create equations in two variables to solve real-life problems.

Warm Up

Cumulative, vocabulary, and prerequisite skills practice opportunities are available in the *Resources by Chapter* or at *BigIdeasMath.com*.

ELL Support

Explain that students will analyze the relationships between quantities. Remind them of the meaning of the word *relationship*. Draw a family tree on the board and describe the relationships within a family. Explain that a graph is a visual way to show the relationship between two quantities (or variables).

Exploration 1

a. *Sample answer:* The distance is 300 times the time; distance

b. $y = 300x$; *Sample answer:* Find the distance for a given time; In 6 hours, the airplane flies $y = 300(6) = 1800$ miles.

c. $y = 1500 - 300x$; *Sample answer:* Find the coordinates of two ordered pairs, then draw a line through the points.

Laurie's Notes

COMMON CORE STATE STANDARDS 6.EE.B.6, 6.EE.C.9

Preparing to Teach

- Students will extend their understanding of writing and solving equations in one variable to writing and graphing **equations in two variables**.
- As students model situations mathematically, they will look for relationships among multiple representations.
- **MP8 Look for and Express Regularity in Repeated Reasoning:** Students will create equations, tables, and graphs in two variables. They will recognize patterns in the table of values and the same pattern will be apparent in the graph as they are plotting points in the coordinate plane.
- Mastery of these skills shows evidence of reaching the learning target.

Motivate

- Hold up a gallon jug partially filled with water. The jug should not be transparent. Don't tell students the amount of water that is in the jug. Tell them that you have been drinking water out of the jug for a few days.
- "How much water is left in the jug?" Listen for understanding that it depends on how much water you already drank. Stress this importance.
- "What are the two quantities that are related in this problem?" amount of water you drank and amount of water remaining
- Tell students to keep this in mind as they begin the exploration.

Exploration 1

- **FYI:** This exploration may require more time than others. The work in this section is the foundation for work with functions in future courses.
- This exploration connects two prior skills: making a table of values and graphing ordered pairs. Although the data in the table are not written as ordered pairs, you may refer to them as such.
- ? "What does the ordered pair (3, 900) mean?" After 3 hours, the plane will have traveled 900 miles.
- **Think-Pair-Share:** Have students review the directions, table, and graph independently. Then allow time for pairs to discuss part (a). Ask students to share their thoughts with the class before completing parts (b) and (c).
- **Note:** In part (b), most students will use x and y as their variables. It is equally correct to write $d = 300t$ where d is the distance the plane travels and t is the time (in hours). Be sure that students realize that they may choose any variables. Logical choices help in understanding the context of the problem.
- ? **Extension:** To help students consider portions of an hour, ask, "In part (b), can the airplane fly for 3.5 hours?" yes "How far will it travel in 3.5 hours?" 1050 miles "Is that verified by the graph? Explain." Yes, (3.5, 1050) is a coordinate in the graph.
- Have students share their equations and graphs for part (c). Select one of each to display using a document camera or on the board. Have the student explain his or her work.

6.4 Writing Equations in Two Variables

Learning Target: Write equations in two variables and analyze the relationship between the two quantities.

Success Criteria:
- I can determine whether an ordered pair is a solution of an equation in two variables.
- I can distinguish between independent and dependent variables.
- I can write and graph an equation in two variables.
- I can create equations in two variables to solve real-life problems.

EXPLORATION 1 Writing Equations in Two Variables

Work with a partner. In Section 3.4 Exploration 1, you used a ratio table to create a graph for an airplane traveling 300 miles per hour. Below is one possible ratio table and graph.

Time (hours)	1	2	3	4
Distance (miles)	300	600	900	1200

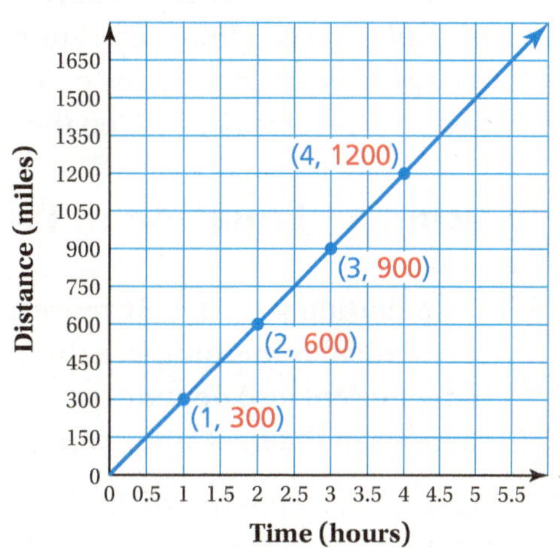

Math Practice

Look for Patterns
How can you use the patterns in the table to help you write an equation?

a. Describe the relationship between the two quantities. Which quantity *depends* on the other quantity?

b. Use variables to write an equation that represents the relationship between the time and the distance. What can you do with this equation? Provide an example.

c. Suppose the airplane is 1500 miles away from its destination. Write an equation that represents the relationship between time and distance from the destination. How can you represent this relationship using a graph?

6.4 Lesson

An **equation in two variables** represents two quantities that change in relationship to one another. A **solution of an equation in two variables** is an ordered pair that makes the equation true.

Key Vocabulary

equation in two variables, *p. 266*

solution of an equation in two variables, *p. 266*

independent variable, *p. 266*

dependent variable, *p. 266*

EXAMPLE 1 Identifying Solutions of Equations in Two Variables

Tell whether the ordered pair is a solution of the equation.

a. $y = 2x$; $(3, 6)$

$6 \stackrel{?}{=} 2(3)$ Substitute.

$6 = 6$ ✓ Compare.

So, (3, 6) is a solution.

b. $y = 4x - 3$; $(4, 12)$

$12 \stackrel{?}{=} 4(4) - 3$

$12 \neq 13$ ✗

So, (4, 12) is *not* a solution.

Try It

Tell whether the ordered pair is a solution of the equation.

1. $y = 7x$; $(2, 21)$

2. $y = 5x + 1$; $(3, 16)$

Equations in two variables have an *independent variable* and a *dependent variable*. The variable representing the quantity that can change freely is the **independent variable**. The other variable is called the **dependent variable** because its value *depends* on the independent variable.

EXAMPLE 2 Using an Equation in Two Variables

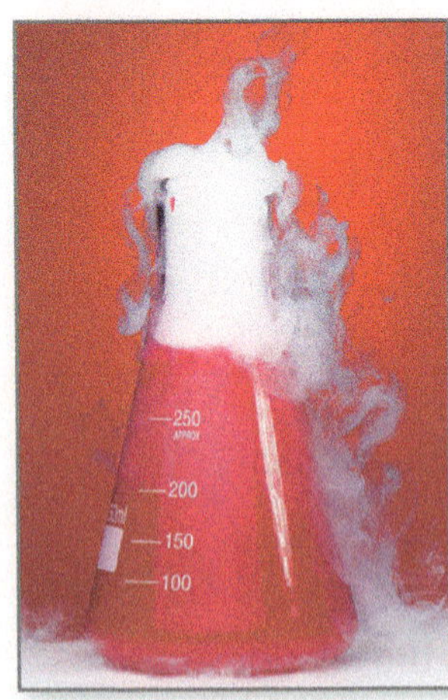

The equation $y = 64 - 8x$ represents the amount y (in fluid ounces) of chemical remaining in a flask after you pour x cups. Identify the independent and dependent variables. How much of the chemical remains in the flask after you pour 5 cups?

Because the amount y of fluid ounces remaining depends on the number x of cups you pour, y is the dependent variable and x is the independent variable.

Use the equation to find the value of y when $x = 5$.

$y = 64 - 8x$ Write the equation.

$= 64 - 8(5)$ Substitute 5 for x.

$= 24$ Simplify.

There are 24 fluid ounces remaining.

Try It

3. The equation $y = 10x + 25$ represents the amount y (in dollars) in your savings account after x weeks. Identify the independent and dependent variables. How much is in your savings account after 8 weeks?

Multi-Language Glossary at BigIdeasMath.com

Laurie's Notes

Scaffolding Instruction

- Students' prior knowledge is essential to mastering the success criteria in this lesson. Their work with ratios and proportional relationships is now combined with representing quantitative relationships between dependent and independent variables.
- **Emerging:** Students need guided instruction for each of the examples.
- **Proficient:** Students can solve and graph equations in two variables. After reviewing the vocabulary, they may proceed to Example 4.

EXAMPLE 1

- ? "How do you know if (3, 6) is a solution of the equation in part (a)?" Substitute 3 for x and 6 for y and see if the equation is true.
- ◉ To determine whether an ordered pair is a solution of an equation, students need to simplify the expressions on both sides of the equal sign to see if the expressions are equivalent.
- Write the equation in part (b). Students should notice two operations on the right side of the equation. Perform the multiplication before the subtraction.
- Mention using parentheses to represent multiplication when you substitute 4 for x. The dot and $\times$ symbol are not commonly used in this context.

Discuss

- In contextual problems, it is often understood which variable "can change freely." This is typically called x. Describe the terms **independent variable** and **dependent variable**. Provide examples of how one variable can depend on another.
- The language in this lesson will help students understand functions and function language in future courses.

EXAMPLE 2

- **MP1 Make Sense of Problems and Persevere in Solving Them:** The similarity to the Motivate should help students understand the context and make sense of the variables used in the equation.
- **MP6 Attend to Precision:** Students need to pay attention to the units in this problem: x is measured in cups and y is measured in fluid ounces.
- ? "Which is the independent variable? Explain." x; Because the amount of y fluid ounces depends on the number of x cups you pour.
- ? "How many fluid ounces are in a half-gallon? a cup?" 64 ounces; 8 ounces
- Discuss the equation and why it makes sense. I find it helpful to make a table of values, with $x = 0$ through 3. "How can you find the amount of chemical remaining after pouring 5 cups?" Substitute 5 for x and simplify.

Try It

? "What do 10 and 25 represent?" 10 represents the amount of money (in dollars) that you deposit into your savings account each week, 25 represents the original balance of your savings account (in dollars)

Scaffold instruction to support all students in their learning. Learning is individualized and you may want to group students differently as they move in and out of these levels with each skill and concept. Student self-assessment and feedback help guide your instructional decisions about how and when to layer support for all students to become proficient learners.

Extra Example 1

Tell whether the ordered pair is a solution of the equation.

a. $y = 3x$; (3, 6) no

b. $y = 2x + 1$; (2, 5) yes

Try It

1. no
2. yes

Extra Example 2

The equation $y = 16 - 2x$ represents the amount y (in ounces) of trail mix remaining after you eat x servings. Identify the independent and dependent variables. How much of the trail mix remains after you eat 6 servings? x is the independent variable and y is the dependent variable; 4 ounces

Try It

3. independent variable: x, dependent variable: y; $105

Extra Example 3

Graph $y = 3x + 1$.

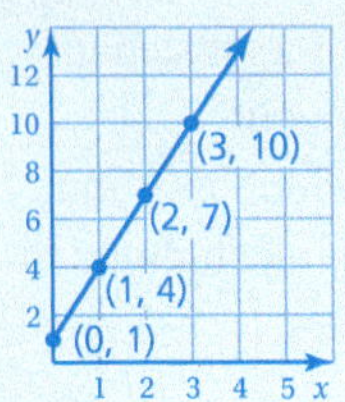

ELL Support

Have students practice language by working in groups to complete Try It Exercises 4–6. Expect students to perform as follows.
Beginner: Graph the equation.
Intermediate: Describe the points on the graph. For example, "When x is one, y is three."
Advanced: Explain how to graph the equation.

Try It

4. 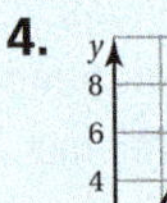 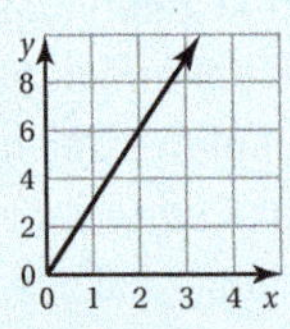

5. 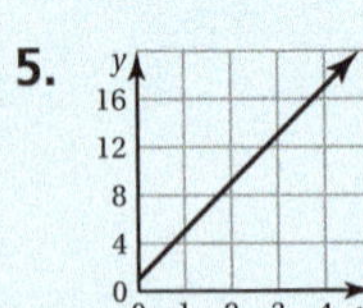

6. 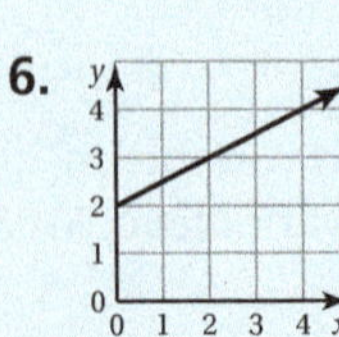

Laurie's Notes

Key Idea

- Write the Key Idea and example as shown. The goal is for students to see the connection between the different representations: equations (symbols), tables, and graphs. As students become more comfortable with these representations, they will recognize patterns such as the constant rate of change.
- Discuss the push-pin note.
- **Extension:** "Do you think the graph of every equation will be a line?" Answers will vary. You do not need to tell the whole story of different types of functions, but make sure students realize that there are equations whose graphs are not lines. Graphing equations will become important for studying linear equations and graphs of functions in future courses.

EXAMPLE 3

- Earlier, students used ratio tables to find ordered pairs to plot in a coordinate plane. Now they will use an equation to make a table of values by substituting values for the independent variable to find values for the dependent variable.
- Students can use a table to find ordered pairs by writing the independent variable first and then its corresponding dependent variable (x, y) or whichever variables they choose. The table provides organization so that students don't mix up the x- and y-values when writing the ordered pairs. It also ensures that they keep using the correct equation when substituting.
- Have students plot a few points and use a straightedge to connect them. "Do the points lie in the same line? They should. If one or two look 'off', check your table to see if you made any errors when substituting." Remind students that they are working on the third success criterion.
- "How many points should you plot and why?" *Sample answer:* At least three, so if one is not on the line I can catch my mistake.
- Notice the Remember note. It is important to use precise language when referring to parts of a graph.

Try It

- Have graph paper available for students.
- **Popsicle Sticks:** Select three students to show each of the three graphs using a document camera or on the board.
- Discuss any questions. Can students find their own mistakes?

Key Idea

Tables, Graphs, and Equations

You can use tables and graphs to represent equations in two variables. The independent variable is graphed on the horizontal axis, and the dependent variable is graphed on the vertical axis. The table and graph below represent the equation $y = x + 2$.

Independent Variable, *x*	Dependent Variable, *y*	Ordered Pair, (*x*, *y*)
1	3	(1, 3)
2	4	(2, 4)
3	5	(3, 5)

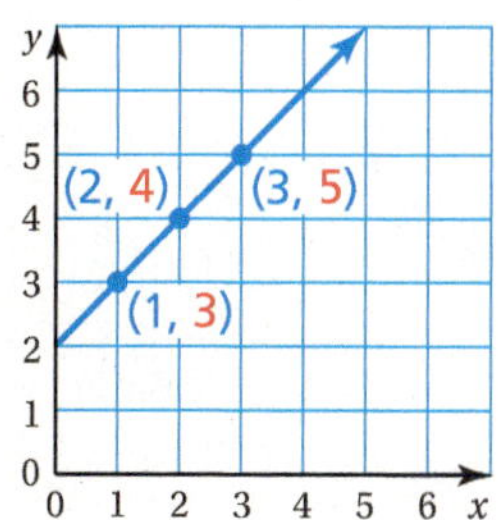

When you draw a line through the points, you graph *all* the solutions of the equation.

EXAMPLE 3 Graphing an Equation in Two Variables

Graph $y = 2x + 1$.

To graph the equation, first make a table.

Independent Variable, *x*	$y = 2x + 1$	Dependent Variable, *y*	Ordered Pair, (*x*, *y*)
0	$y = 2(0) + 1$	1	(0, 1)
1	$y = 2(1) + 1$	3	(1, 3)
2	$y = 2(2) + 1$	5	(2, 5)
3	$y = 2(3) + 1$	7	(3, 7)

Then plot the ordered pairs and draw a line through the points.

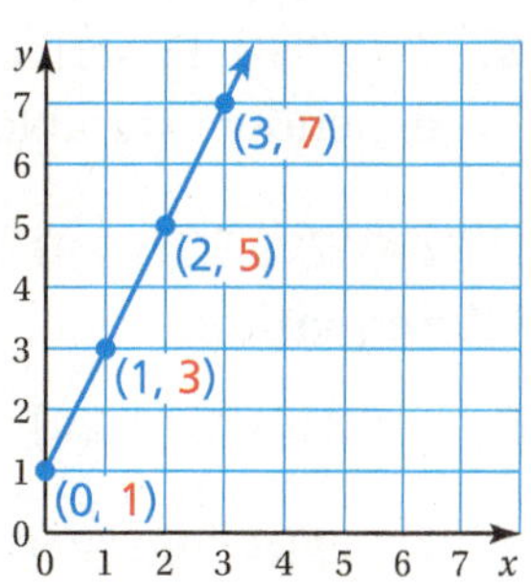

Remember

In a coordinate plane, the horizontal axis is often called the *x-axis*. The vertical axis is often called the *y-axis*. In real-life problems, other variables can be used.

Try It **Graph the equation.**

4. $y = 3x$

5. $y = 4x + 1$

6. $y = \frac{1}{2}x + 2$

EXAMPLE 4 Writing and Graphing an Equation in Two Variables

An athlete burns 200 calories weight lifting. The athlete then works out on an elliptical trainer and burns 10 calories for every minute. Write and graph an equation that represents the total number of calories burned during the workout.

Use a verbal model to write an equation.

Verbal Model Total number of calories burned = Calories burned weight lifting + Calories burned per minute • Number of minutes

Variables Let c be the total number of calories burned, and let m be the number of minutes on the elliptical trainer.

Equation $c = 200 + 10 \cdot m$

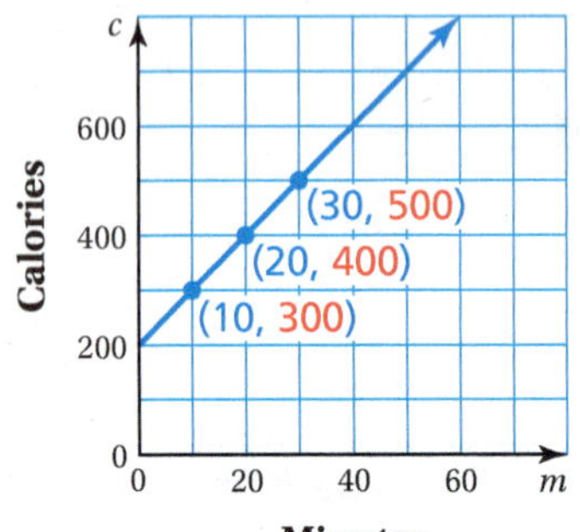

To graph the equation, first notice that the total number of calories burned depends on the number of minutes. So, create a table and plot the ordered pairs with minutes m on the horizontal axis and calories c on the vertical axis. Then draw a line through the points.

Minutes, m	Calories, c
10	300
20	400
30	500

Try It

7. It costs $25 to rent a kayak plus $8 for each hour. Write and graph an equation that represents the total cost (in dollars) of renting the kayak.

Self-Assessment for Concepts & Skills

Solve each exercise. Then rate your understanding of the success criteria in your journal.

8. **WRITING** Describe the difference between independent variables and dependent variables.

IDENTIFYING SOLUTIONS Tell whether the ordered pair is a solution of the equation.

9. $y = 3x + 8$; (4, 20)

10. $y = 6x - 14$; (7, 29)

11. **MP PRECISION** Explain how to graph an equation in two variables.

12. **WHICH ONE DOESN'T BELONG?** Which one does *not* belong with the other three? Explain your reasoning.

$y = 12x + 25$ $c = 10t - 5$ $a = 7b + 11$ $n = 4n - 6$

Laurie's Notes

EXAMPLE 4

- Ask a volunteer to read the problem. Explain any vocabulary that is unfamiliar.
- **MP1 Make Sense of Problems and Persevere in Solving Them:** Write the verbal model. The words act as a road map for how to solve the problem. You write the equation by translating the words into symbols. This is a practice that you want to develop in your students. Encourage students to say in words how they are going to solve the problem before writing an equation.
- ? Ask, "What are the variables in this problem?" the total calories burned, the minutes spent on the elliptical trainer
- Write the equation. Students may ask whether $200 + 10m = c$ is also correct. Explain that it is correct, but the form dependent variable = expression is more convenient for graphing.
- ? Ask, "What do you know about the workout when $m = 0$?" The athlete has not spent any time on the elliptical trainer.
- Ask volunteers to help complete the table.
- Discuss the scale on the graph. Because there are 10 calories for every minute, it makes sense to scale the vertical axis differently than the horizontal axis.

Try It

- Students should write a verbal model for the problems, define the variables, and then write an equation by translating the words into symbols. Finding a few ordered pairs, graphing them, and drawing a line through the points completes the representation of the cost of renting a kayak.

Self-Assessment for Concepts & Skills

- Students are assessing their understanding of the first three success criteria. These are important skills to develop before moving on to creating and solving an equation in two variables to model a real-life situation.
- Students should work independently and share answers only when you ask them to. Listening to their conversations for Exercises 8, 11, and 12 may be eye-opening. Students should use correct vocabulary and encourage others to be specific in their explanations. Select some interesting explanations to share with the whole class.

The Success Criteria Self-Assessment chart can be found in the *Student Journal* or online at *BigIdeasMath.com*.

Extra Example 4

A teenager burns 100 calories in a yoga class. The teen then walks on an inclined treadmill and burns 5 calories for every minute. Write and graph an equation that represents the total number of calories burned.

Let c = calories burned and m = number of minutes on the inclined treadmill; $c = 100 + 5m$

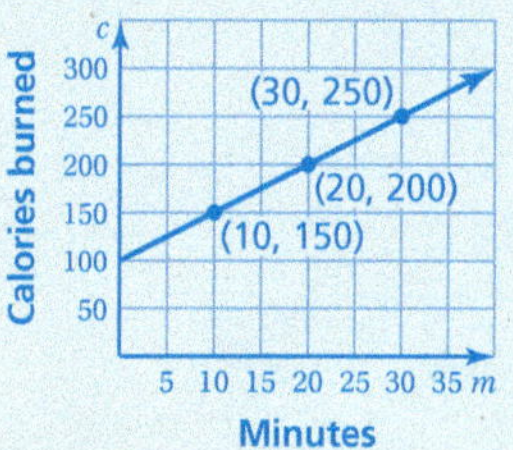

Try It

7. See Additional Answers.

ELL Support

Allow students extra support and language practice by working in pairs to complete the Self-Assessment for Concepts & Skills. Check understanding of Exercises 9 and 10 by having each pair display their answers on a whiteboard for your review. Discuss Exercises 8, 11, and 12 as a class.

Self-Assessment for Concepts & Skills

8. *Sample answer:* An independent variable can change freely. A dependent variable depends on the independent variable.
9. yes
10. no
11. Create a table. Plot the ordered pairs from the table. Draw a line through the points.
12. $n = 4n - 6$; This one is not an equation in two variables.

Extra Example 5

A bus averages 60 miles per hour between two cities. Write and graph an equation that represents the relationship between the time and the distance traveled. How long does it take the bus to travel 210 miles? $d = 60t$, 3.5 hours

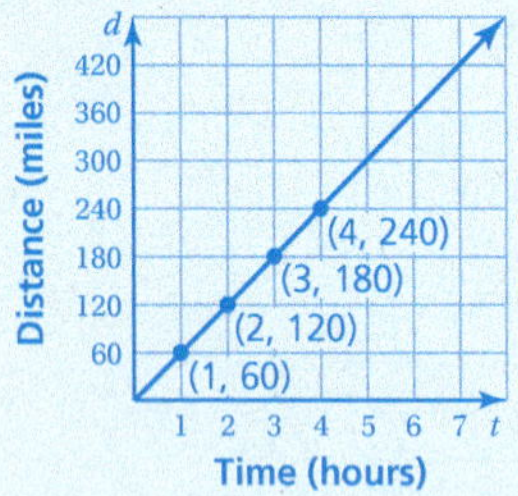

Self-Assessment for Problem Solving

13. $y = 8x$

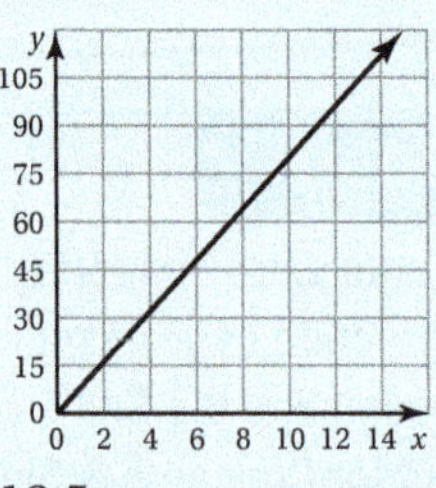

12.5 sec

14. about 4.09 mi

Learning Target

Write equations in two variables and analyze the relationship between the two quantities.

Success Criteria

- Determine whether an ordered pair is a solution of an equation in two variables.
- Distinguish between independent and dependent variables.
- Write and graph an equation in two variables.
- Create equations in two variables to solve real-life problems.

Laurie's Notes

Discuss

- Write and discuss the distance formula at the top of the page. Relate this formula to work done with rates in Section 3.5. Speed is an example of a rate.
- Remind students that the unit of time in the rate must match the unit of time in the formula. For example, if a car travels 60 miles per hour for 10 minutes, then you cannot just multiply 60 by 10 to find the distance.

EXAMPLE 5

- Ask a volunteer to read the problem aloud.
- ? "Why is time the independent variable?" Because the distance traveled depends on the amount of time the train travels.
- Be sure that students label the axes with both words and variables.
- Demonstrate how to interpret the graph from left to right. As the amount of time increases, the distance traveled increases.
- ? "Using the distance formula, what equation represents this situation?" $d = 40t$
  "How can you use this to find the answer?" Substitute 220 for d and solve for t.
  "How can you use the graph to check the reasonableness of your answer?" Compare your answer to the t-coordinate that corresponds to $d = 220$.
- If time permits, make a ratio table to find the time it takes to travel 220 miles, as shown in the Another Method note.
- **MP7 Look for and Make Use of Structure:** The structure of a ratio table may help students understand another way to solve the problem.

Self-Assessment for Problem Solving

- Allow time in class for students to practice using the problem-solving plan. Remember, some students may only be able to complete the first step.
- Have students work on Exercise 13 independently and then work in a group to discuss their representations and reach a consensus.
- Allow students to work in pairs to complete Exercise 14. Tell students that drawing a diagram to represent the situation may provide an entry point.

The Success Criteria Self-Assessment chart can be found in the *Student Journal* or online at *BigIdeasMath.com*.

Formative Assessment Tip

Parking Lot

Give each student two sticky notes. Ask them to write something they learned on one note and something they still have a question about on the other. Write "Parking Lot" at the top of a large sheet of paper and draw a line down the middle of the paper. On one side write "Something I Learned" and on the other side write "Something I Have a Question About." Hang the paper near the door so students can place their sticky notes as they leave. Replace the paper for each class and review the notes to help direct your instruction for the next day.

Closure

- Use *Parking Lot* to assess your students' understanding of the section.

You can model many rate problems by using the *distance formula*, $d = rt$, where d is the distance traveled, r is the speed, and t is the time.

EXAMPLE 5 Modeling Real Life

A train averages 40 miles per hour between two cities. Write and graph an equation that represents the relationship between the time and the distance traveled. How long does it take the train to travel 220 miles?

The rate r is 40 miles per hour. Using the distance formula, an equation that represents the relationship between time and distance traveled is $d = 40t$.

Make a table and graph the equation.

Time (hours), t	1	2	3	4
Distance (miles), d	40	80	120	160

d
240
160
80
0
0 2 4 6 t
(1, 40) (2, 80) (3, 120) (4, 160)
Distance (miles)
Time (hours)

Use the equation to find the value of t when $d = 220$.

$d = 40t$ Write the equation.

$220 = 40t$ Substitute 220 for d.

$5.5 = t$ Divide each side by 40.

The train travels 220 miles in 5.5 hours.

Another Method Use a ratio table.

Time (hours), t	1	0.5	5.5
Distance (miles), d	40	20	220

(÷2, then ×11 applied to both rows)

Math Practice

Use a Graph
Use the graph to show that your answer is reasonable.

Self-Assessment for Problem Solving

Solve each exercise. Then rate your understanding of the success criteria in your journal.

13. A sky lantern rises at an average speed of 8 feet per second. Write and graph an equation that represents the relationship between the time and the distance risen. How long does it take the lantern to rise 100 feet?

14. You and a friend start biking in opposite directions from the same point. You travel 108 feet every 8 seconds. Your friend travels 63 feet every 6 seconds. How far apart are you and your friend after 15 minutes?

6.4 Practice

Review & Refresh

Solve the equation.

1. $4x = 36$ **2.** $\frac{x}{8} = 5$ **3.** $\frac{4x}{3} = 8$ **4.** $\frac{2}{5}x = 6$

Divide. Write the answer in simplest form.

5. $3\frac{1}{2} \div \frac{4}{5}$ **6.** $7 \div 5\frac{1}{4}$ **7.** $\frac{3}{11} \div 1\frac{1}{8}$ **8.** $7\frac{1}{2} \div 1\frac{1}{3}$

9. Find the area of the carpet tile. Then find the area covered by 120 carpet tiles.

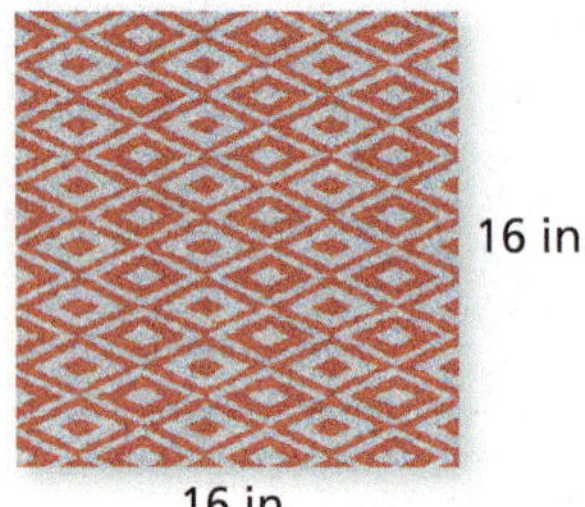

Copy and complete the statement. Round to the nearest hundredth if necessary.

10. 8 m = ▢ cm **11.** 88 oz = ▢ lb

12. 3 c ≈ ▢ mL **13.** 15 km ≈ ▢ mi

Divide.

14. $6\overline{)34.8}$ **15.** $4\overline{)12.8}$ **16.** $45.92 \div 2.8$ **17.** $39.525 \div 4.25$

Concepts, Skills, & Problem Solving

WRITING EQUATIONS **Use variables to write an equation that represents the relationship between the time and the distance.** (See Exploration 1, p. 265.)

18. An eagle flies 40 miles per hour.

19. A person runs 175 yards per minute.

IDENTIFYING SOLUTIONS **Tell whether the ordered pair is a solution of the equation.**

20. $y = 4x; (0, 4)$ **21.** $y = 3x; (2, 6)$ **22.** $y = 5x - 10; (3, 5)$

23. $y = x + 7; (1, 6)$ **24.** $y = x + 4; (2, 4)$ **25.** $y = x - 5; (6, 11)$

26. $y = 6x + 1; (2, 13)$ **27.** $y = 7x + 2; (2, 0)$ **28.** $y = 2x - 3; (4, 5)$

29. $y = 3x - 3; (1, 0)$ **30.** $7 = y - 5x; (4, 28)$ **31.** $y + 3 = 6x; (3, 15)$

32. **MP YOU BE THE TEACHER** Your friend determines whether (5, 1) is a solution of $y = 3x + 2$. Is your friend correct? Explain your reasoning.

$y = 3x + 2; (5, 1)$

$1 \stackrel{?}{=} 3(5) + 2$

$1 \neq 17$

So, (5, 1) is not a solution.

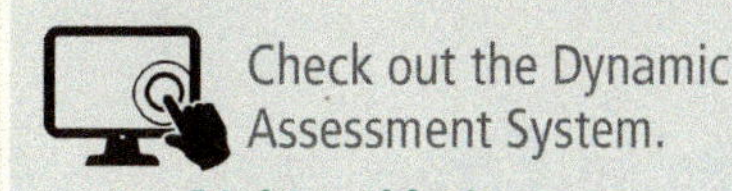

Assignment Guide and Concept Check

Scaffold assignments to support all students in their learning progression. The suggested assignments are a starting point. Continue to assign additional exercises and revisit with spaced practice to move every student toward proficiency.

Level	Assignment 1	Assignment 2
Emerging	3, 8, 9, 12, 17, 18, 21, 23, 25, 32, 33, 41, 44, 48	26, 37, 38, 39, 40, 53, 54, 55, 57, 61, 66
Proficient	3, 8, 9, 12, 17, 19, 25, 26, 32, 34, 42, 44, 45, 51	37, 38, 39, 40, 54, 55, 56, 58, 62, 66
Advanced	3, 8, 9, 12, 17, 19, 26, 30, 32, 36, 43, 45, 50, 52	56, 60, 63, 64, 65, 66, 67, 68, 69

- Assignment 1 is for use after students complete the Self-Assessment for Concepts & Skills.
- Assignment 2 is for use after students complete the Self-Assessment for Problem Solving.
- The red exercises can be used as a concept check.

Review & Refresh Prior Skills

Exercises 1–4 Solving Equations
Exercises 5–8 Dividing Fractions and Mixed Numbers
Exercise 9 Powers and Exponents
Exercises 10–13 Converting Units
Exercises 14–17 Dividing Decimals

- **Exercises 20–31** Students may substitute incorrectly for *x* and *y*. Remind them that the first coordinate of the ordered pair is always the *x*-value and the second coordinate is always the *y*-value.

Review & Refresh

1. $x = 9$
2. $x = 40$
3. $x = 6$
4. $x = 15$
5. $4\frac{3}{8}$
6. $1\frac{1}{3}$
7. $\frac{8}{33}$
8. $5\frac{5}{8}$
9. 256 in.^{2}; 30,720 in.^{2}
10. 800
11. 5.5
12. 711
13. 9.3 or 9.32
14. 5.8
15. 3.2
16. 16.4
17. 9.3

Concepts, Skills, & Problem Solving

18. $y = 40x$
19. $y = 175x$
20. no
21. yes
22. yes
23. no
24. no
25. no
26. yes
27. no
28. yes
29. yes
30. no
31. yes
32. yes; The steps are correct.

Concepts, Skills, & Problem Solving

33. independent variable: w, dependent variable: A

34. independent variable: s, dependent variable: c

35. independent variable: p, dependent variable: t

36. independent variable: m, dependent variable: h

37. *Sample answer:* your test score

38. *Sample answer:* the time it takes to stop your bike

39. *Sample answer:* the amount of data you use

40. *Sample answer:* the number of hours you work

41.
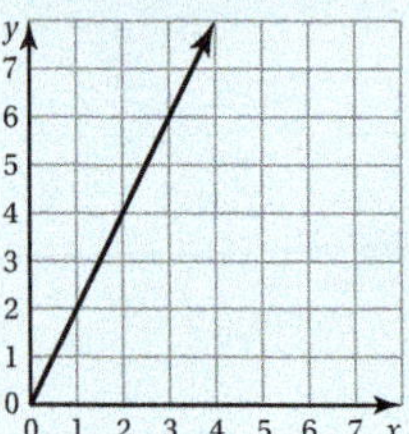

42.
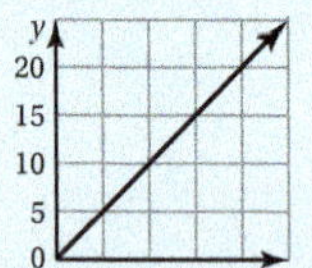

43.
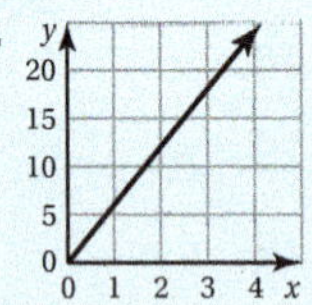

44.
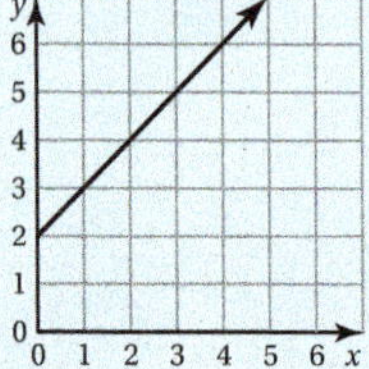

45.
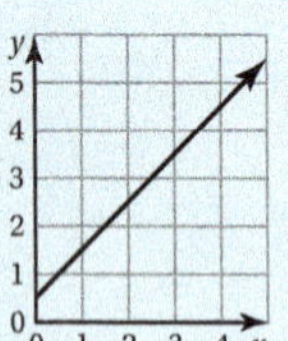

46.
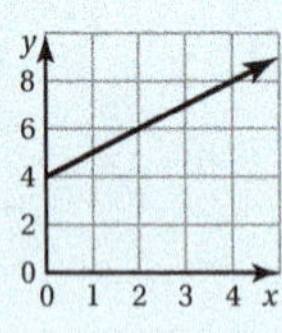

47.
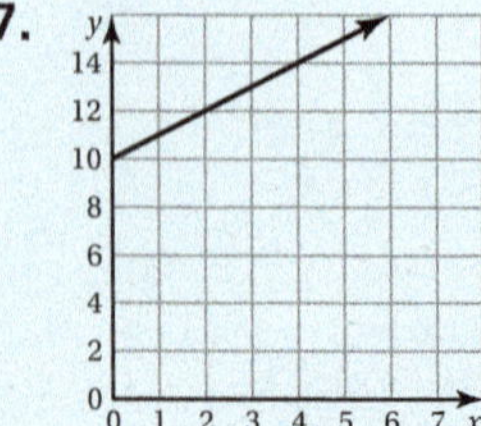

48–55. See Additional Answers.

Common Errors

- **Exercises 33–36** Students may have trouble identifying the independent variable. Remind them that the independent variable represents the quantity that "can change freely."

IDENTIFYING VARIABLES **Identify the independent and dependent variables.**

33. The equation $A = 25w$ represents the area A (in square feet) of a rectangular dance floor with a width of w feet.

34. The equation $c = 0.09s$ represents the amount c (in dollars) of commission a salesperson receives for making a sale of s dollars.

35. The equation $t = 12p + 12$ represents the total cost t (in dollars) of a meal with a tip of p percent (in decimal form).

36. The equation $h = 60 - 4m$ represents the height h (in inches) of the water in a tank m minutes after it starts to drain.

OPEN-ENDED **Complete the table by describing possible independent or dependent variables.**

	Independent Variable	Dependent Variable
37.	The number of hours you study for a test	
38.	The speed you are pedaling a bike	
39.		Your monthly cell phone bill
40.		The amount of money you earn

GRAPHING EQUATIONS **Graph the equation.**

41. $y = 2x$

42. $y = 5x$

43. $y = 6x$

44. $y = x + 2$

45. $y = x + 0.5$

46. $y = x + 4$

47. $y = x + 10$

48. $y = 3x + 2$

49. $y = 2x + 4$

50. $y = \frac{2}{3}x + 8$

51. $y = \frac{1}{4}x + 6$

52. $y = 2.5x + 12$

53. **MP MODELING REAL LIFE** A cheese pizza costs $5. Additional toppings cost $1.50 each. Write and graph an equation that represents the total cost (in dollars) of a pizza.

54. **MP MODELING REAL LIFE** It costs $35 for a membership at a wholesale store. The monthly fee is $15. Write and graph an equation that represents the total cost (in dollars) of a membership.

55. **MP PROBLEM SOLVING** The maximum size of a text message is 160 characters. A space counts as one character.

a. Write an equation that represents the number of remaining (unused) characters in a text message as you type.

b. Identify the independent and dependent variables.

c. How many characters remain in the message shown?

56. **MP CHOOSE TOOLS** A car averages 60 miles per hour on a road trip. Use a graph to represent the relationship between the time and the distance traveled.

MP PRECISION Write and graph an equation that represents the relationship between the time and the distance traveled.

57. 

Moves 2 meters every 3 hours

58. 

59. 

Moves 660 feet every 10 seconds

60. 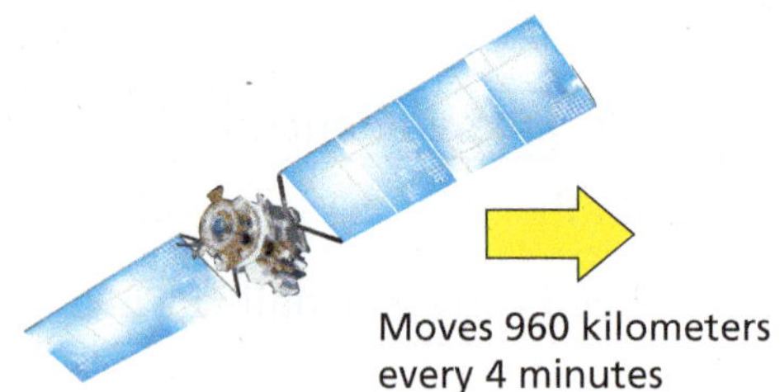

IDENTIFYING SOLUTIONS Fill in the blank so that the ordered pair is a solution of the equation.

61. $y = 8x + 3$; (1, ___)

62. $y = 12x + 2$; (___ , 14)

63. $y = 9x + 4$; (___ , 22)

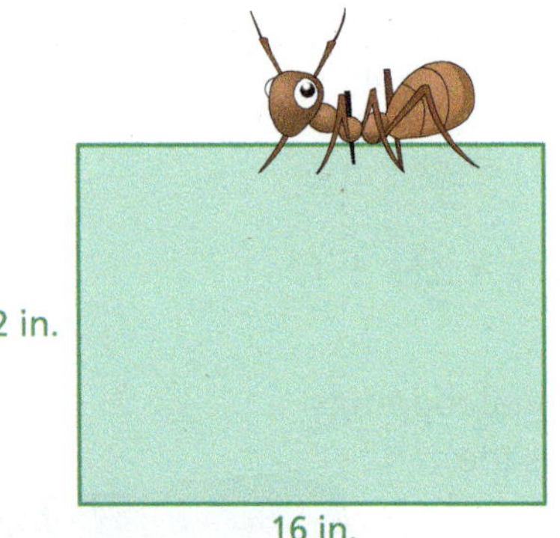

64. **DIG DEEPER!** Can the dependent variable cause a change in the independent variable? Explain.

65. **OPEN-ENDED** Write an equation that has (3, 4) as a solution.

66. **MP MODELING REAL LIFE** You walk 5 city blocks in 12 minutes. How many city blocks can you walk in 2 hours?

67. **GEOMETRY** How fast should the ant walk to go around the rectangle in 4 minutes?

68. **MP MODELING REAL LIFE** To estimate how far you are from lightning (in miles), count the number of seconds between a lightning flash and the thunder that follows. Then divide the number of seconds by 5. Use two different methods to find the number of seconds between a lightning flash and the thunder that follows when a storm is 2.4 miles away.

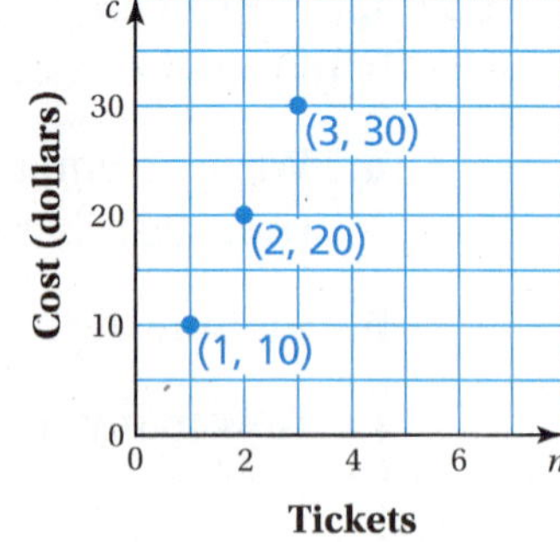

69. **MP REASONING** The graph represents the cost c (in dollars) of buying n tickets to a baseball game.

a. Should the points be connected with a line to show all the solutions? Explain your reasoning.

b. Write an equation that represents the graph.

Common Errors

- **Exercises 57–60** Students may not realize that the rate is given. Remind them that they need to convert this rate into a unit rate before using the distance formula $d = rt$.
- **Exercise 69** When discussing part (a), tell students that it does not make sense to draw a line between the points because you can't sell part of a ticket. This exercise illustrates the difference between discrete and continuous domains of functions, which they will study in future courses.

Mini-Assessment

Tell whether the ordered pair is a solution of the equation.

1. $y = x + 11$; (2, 13) yes
2. $y = 5x$; (3, 8) no
3. $y = 3x - 7$; (4, 5) yes
4. Graph $y = 2x + 3$.

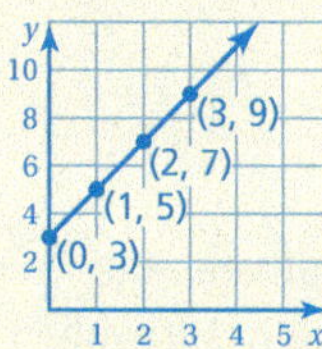

5. You walk 2 city blocks in 10 minutes. How many city blocks can you walk in 1 hour? 12 city blocks

Section Resources

Surface Level	Deep Level
Resources by Chapter • Extra Practice • Reteach • Puzzle Time Student Journal • Self-Assessment • Practice Differentiating the Lesson Tutorial Videos Skills Review Handbook Skills Trainer	Resources by Chapter • Enrichment and Extension Graphic Organizers Dynamic Assessment System • Section Practice
Transfer Level	
Dynamic Assessment System • End-of-Chapter Quiz	Assessment Book • End-of-Chapter Quiz

Concepts, Skills, & Problem Solving

56.

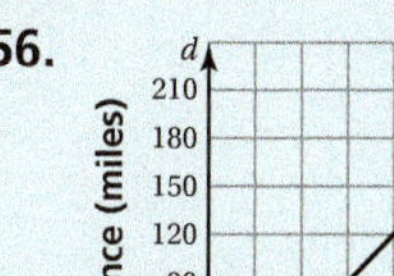

57. $d = \frac{2}{3}t$

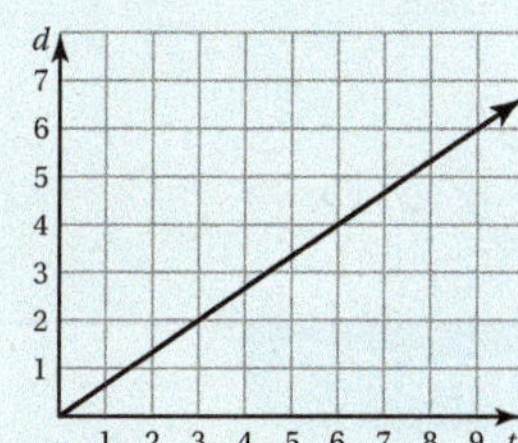

58. $d = \frac{5}{6}t$

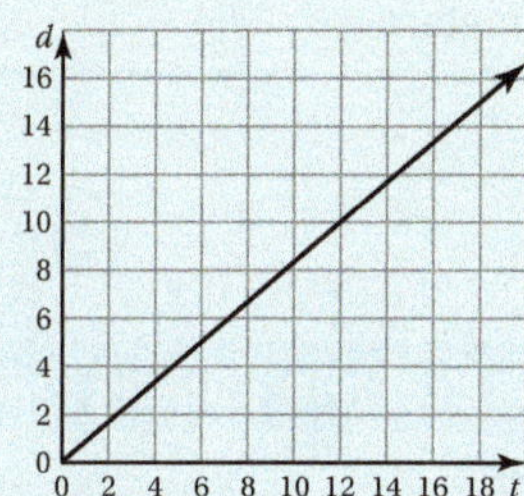

59. $d = 66t$

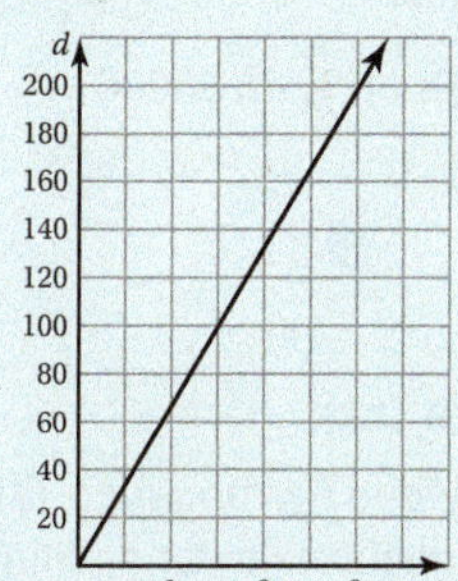

60. See Additional Answers.

61. 11

62. 1

63. 2

64. no; By definition, the independent variable can change freely.

65. *Sample answer:* $y = 2x - 2$

66. 50

67. 14 in./min

68. 12 sec

69. **a.** no; You can only buy whole numbers of tickets.

b. $c = 10n$

Skills Needed

Exercise 1

- Converting Measures
- Writing Equations in Two Variables

Exercise 2

- Factoring Expressions
- Writing Equations in Two Variables

Exercise 3

- Interpreting Ratios
- Writing Equations in Two Variables

ELL Support

Remind students that a mile is 1760 yards or approximately 1609.34 meters.

Using the Problem-Solving Plan

1. 19.75 mi
2. \$5; \$75.20
3. $T = 8000 + 1.4d$; \$5000

Performance Task

The *STEAM Video Performance Task* provides the opportunity for additional enrichment and greater depth of knowledge as students explore the mathematics of the chapter within a context tied to the chapter STEAM Video. The performance task and a detailed scoring rubric are provided at *BigIdeasMath.com*.

Laurie's Notes

Scaffolding Instruction

- The goal of this lesson is to help students become more comfortable with problem solving. These exercises combine writing and solving equations with prior skills from other chapters. The solution for Exercise 1 is worked out below, to help you guide students through the problem-solving plan. Use the remaining class time to have students work on the other exercises.
- **Emerging:** The goal for these students is to feel comfortable with the problem-solving plan. Allow students to work in pairs to write the beginning steps of the problem-solving plan for Exercise 2. Keep in mind that some students may only be ready to do the first step.
- **Proficient:** Students may be able to work independently or in pairs to complete Exercises 2 and 3.
- Visit each pair to review their plan for each problem. Ask students to describe their plans.

Using the Problem-Solving Plan

Exercise 1

Understand the problem. You know the initial distance between the tornado and the station, and the average speed the tornado is traveling away from the station. You are asked to determine how far the tornado is from the station after 30 minutes.

Make a plan. First, convert the average speed to miles per minute. Then write an equation that represents the distance d (in miles) between the tornado and the station after t minutes. Use the equation to find the value of d when $t = 30$.

Solve and check. Use the plan to solve the problem. Then check your solution.

- Convert 440 yards per minute to miles per minute.

  $$\frac{440 \text{ yd}}{1 \text{ min}} \cdot \frac{1 \text{ mi}}{1760 \text{ yd}} = \frac{0.25 \text{ mi}}{1 \text{ min}}$$

  So, 440 yards per minute can be written as 0.25 mile per minute.
- Write an equation that represents the distance d (in miles) between the tornado and the station after t minutes: $d = 0.25t + 12.25$.
- Find the value of d when $t = 30$.

  $d = 0.25(30) + 12.25$ Substitute 30 for t.

  $d = 7.5 + 12.25$ Multiply 0.25 and 30.

  $d = 19.75$ Add 7.5 and 12.25.

  So, the tornado is 19.75 miles from the station after 30 minutes.
- **Check:** Verify the answer by representing the distance d in yards.

  Convert 12.25 miles to yards: $12.25 \text{ mi} \cdot \frac{1760 \text{ yd}}{1 \text{ mi}} = 21{,}560 \text{ yd}$.

  Write an equation: $d = 440t + 21{,}560$.

  Evaluate the equation: $d = 440(30) + 21{,}560 = 13{,}200 + 21{,}560 = 34{,}760$.

  Convert 34,760 yards to miles: $34{,}760 \text{ yd} \cdot \frac{1 \text{ mi}}{1760 \text{ yd}} = 19.75 \text{ mi}$. ✓

Connecting Concepts

Using the Problem-Solving Plan

1. A tornado forms 12.25 miles from a weather station. It travels away from the station at an average speed of 440 yards per minute. How far from the station is the tornado after 30 minutes?

Understand the problem. You know the initial distance between the tornado and the station, and the average speed the tornado is traveling away from the station. You are asked to determine how far the tornado is from the station after 30 minutes.

Make a plan. First, convert the average speed to miles per minute. Then write an equation that represents the distance d (in miles) between the tornado and the station after t minutes. Use the equation to find the value of d when $t = 30$.

Solve and check. Use the plan to solve the problem. Then check your solution.

2. You buy 96 cans of soup to donate to a food bank. The store manager discounts the cost of each case for a total discount of \$40. Use an equation in two variables to find the discount for each case of soup. What is the total cost when each can of soup originally costs \$1.20?

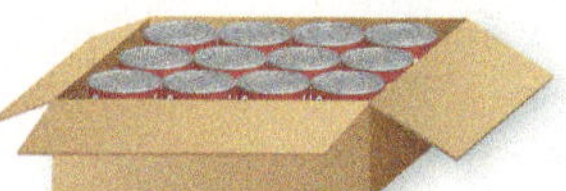

1 case = 12 cans

3. The diagram shows the initial amount raised by an organization for cancer research. A business agrees to donate \$2 for every \$5 donated by the community during an additional fundraising event. Write an equation that represents the total amount raised (in dollars). How much money does the community need to donate for the organization to reach its fundraising goal?

Performance Task

Planning the Climb

At the beginning of this chapter, you watched a STEAM video called "Rock Climbing." You are now ready to complete the performance task related to this video, available at **BigIdeasMath.com**. Be sure to use the problem-solving plan as you work through the performance task.

6 Chapter Review

Go to *BigIdeasMath.com* to download blank graphic organizers.

Review Vocabulary

Write the definition and give an example of each vocabulary term.

equation, *p. 246*
solution, *p. 252*
inverse operations, *p. 253*
equation in two variables, *p. 266*
solution of an equation in two variables, *p. 266*
independent variable, *p. 266*
dependent variable, *p. 266*

Graphic Organizers

You can use an **Example and Non-Example Chart** to list examples and non-examples of a concept. Here is an Example and Non-Example Chart for the vocabulary term ***equation***.

Equation

Examples	Non-Examples
$x = 5$	5
$2a = 16$	$2a$
$x + 4 = 19$	$x + 4$
$5 = x + 3$	$x + 3$
$12 - 7 = 5$	$12 - 7$
$\frac{3}{4}y = 6$	$\frac{3}{4}$

Choose and complete a graphic organizer to help you study the concept.

1. inverse operations
2. solving equations using addition or subtraction
3. solving equations using multiplication or division
4. equations in two variables
5. independent variables
6. dependent variables

"I need a good non-example of a cool animal for my Example and Non-Example Chart."

Review Vocabulary

- As a review of the chapter vocabulary, have students revisit the vocabulary section in their *Student Journals* to fill in any missing definitions and record examples of each term.

Graphic Organizers

Sample answers:

1. Inverse Operations

Examples	Non-Examples
addition and subtraction multiplication and division	addition and multiplication addition and division subtraction and multiplication subtraction and division

2. Solving Equations Using Addition or Subtraction

Examples	Non-Examples
$y + 9 = 12$	$2a = 16$
$a - 11 = 3$	$0.4b = 4$
$10 = x - 19$	$\frac{3}{4}y = 6$
$25 = r + 14$	$\frac{y}{6} = 0$

3. Solving Equations Using Multiplication or Division

Examples	Non-Examples
$2a = 16$	$x - 1 = 5$
$\frac{y}{4} = 6$	$y + 9 = 12$
$0.4b = 4$	$a - 11 = 3$
$\frac{6}{7} = \frac{x}{14}$	$10 = x - 19$

4–6. Answers at *BigIdeasMath.com.*

List of Organizers

Available at *BigIdeasMath.com*

Definition and Example Chart

Example and Non-Example Chart

Four Square

Information Frame

Summary Triangle

About this Organizer

An **Example and Non-Example Chart** can be used to list examples and non-examples of a concept. Students write examples of the concept in the left column and non-examples in the right column. Blank Example and Non-Example Charts can be included on tests or quizzes for this purpose.

Chapter Self-Assessment

1. $m \cdot 2 = 8$
2. $t - 6 = 7$
3. $m + 5 = 7$
4. $8 = g \div 3$
5. $\frac{1}{3}h = 6$
6. $t + 12 = 16$; 4
7. *Sample answer:* $x + 5 = 13$
8. *Sample answer:* A number y increased by 3 is 5.

Chapter Self-Assessment

The Success Criteria Self-Assessment chart can be found in the *Student Journal* or online at *BigIdeasMath.com*.

ELL Support

Allow students to work in pairs to complete the Chapter Self-Assessment. After students complete the first section, check for understanding by having each pair display their answers on a whiteboard for your review. You should be able to quickly assess whether the majority of the class understands the concepts. You will also be able to quickly determine who may need additional help. Use this technique for the remaining sections.

Common Errors

- **Exercises 1–4** Students may write the equations in the wrong order or forget parts of the equation. Remind them of the guidelines they used for writing expressions. Remind students that these are equations, so there will be an equal sign in each answer and number(s) and/or variable(s) on each side.

Chapter Self-Assessment

As you complete the exercises, use the scale below to rate your understanding of the success criteria in your journal.

1	2	3	4
I do not understand.	I can do it with help.	I can do it on my own.	I can teach someone else.

6.1 Writing Equations in One Variable *(pp. 245–250)*

Learning Target: Write equations in one variable and write equations that represent real-life problems.

Write the word sentence as an equation.

1. The product of a number m and 2 is 8.

2. 6 less than a number t is 7.

3. A number m increased by 5 is 7.

4. 8 is the quotient of a number g and 3.

5. The height of the 50-milliliter beaker is one-third the height of the 2000-milliliter beaker. Write an equation you can use to find the height (in centimeters) of the 2000-milliliter beaker.

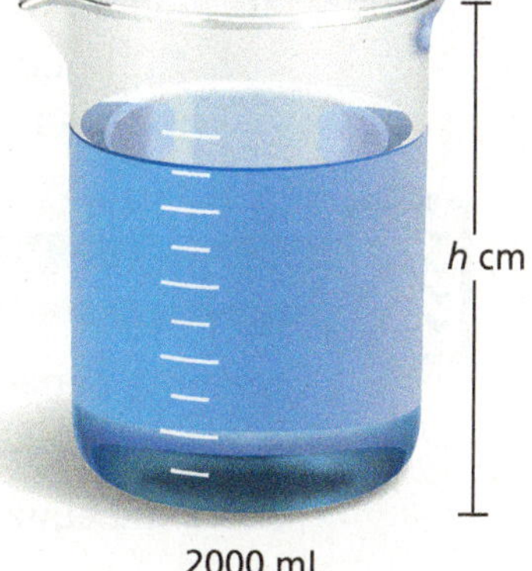

6. There are 16 teams in a basketball tournament. After two rounds, 12 teams are eliminated. Write and solve an equation to find the number of teams remaining after two rounds.

7. Write an equation that has a solution of $x = 8$.

8. Write a word sentence for the equation $y + 3 = 5$.

6.2 Solving Equations Using Addition or Subtraction (pp. 251–258)

Learning Target: Write and solve equations using addition or subtraction.

9. Tell whether $x = 7$ is a solution of $x + 9 = 16$.

Solve the equation. Check your solution.

10. $x - 1 = 8$

11. $m + 7 = 11$

12. $21 = p - 12$

Write the word sentence as an equation. Then solve the equation.

13. 5 more than a number x is 9.

14. 82 is the difference of a number b and 24.

15. A stuntman is running on the roof of a train. His combined speed is the sum of the speed of the train and his running speed. The combined speed is 73 miles per hour, and his running speed is 15 miles per hour. Find the speed of the train.

16. Before swallowing a large rodent, a python weighs 152 pounds. After swallowing the rodent, the python weighs 164 pounds. Find the weight of the rodent.

6.3 Solving Equations Using Multiplication or Division (pp. 259–264)

Learning Target: Write and solve equations using multiplication or division.

Solve the equation. Check your solution.

17. $6 \cdot q = 54$

18. $k \div 3 = 21$

19. $\frac{5}{7}a = 25$

20. The weight of an object on the Moon is about 16.5% of its weight on Earth. The weight of an astronaut on the Moon is 24.75 pounds. How much does the astronaut weigh on Earth?

21. Write an equation that can be solved using multiplication and has a solution of $x = 12$.

22. At a farmers' market, you buy 4 pounds of tomatoes and 2 pounds of sweet potatoes. You spend 80% of the money in your wallet. How much money is in your wallet before you pay?

Common Errors

- **Exercises 10–12** Students may add or subtract the number on the side without the variable. For example, they might write $14 - 14 = k + 6 - 14$ instead of $14 - 6 = k + 6 - 6$. Remind students that they are trying to get the variable by itself, so they should start on the side with the variable and use the inverse of that operation.
- **Exercises 17–19** Students may do the same operation on both sides instead of the opposite operation. This is most common with problems like Exercise 18, where the equation is written in division format instead of fraction format. Remind them that to get the variable alone, they need to use the inverse operation.

Chapter Self-Assessment

9. yes

10. $x = 9$

11. $m = 4$

12. $p = 33$

13. $x + 5 = 9; x = 4$

14. $82 = b - 24; b = 106$

15. 58 mi/h

16. 12 lb

17. $q = 9$

18. $k = 63$

19. $a = 35$

20. 150 lb

21. *Sample answer:* $x \div 4 = 3$

22. $20

Chapter Self-Assessment

23. yes **24.** no

25. independent variable: m, dependent variable: E

26.

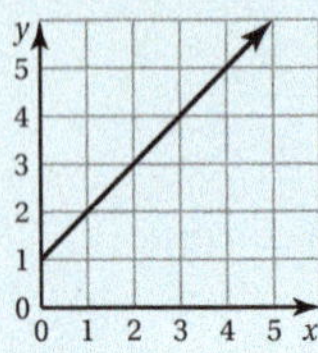

27.

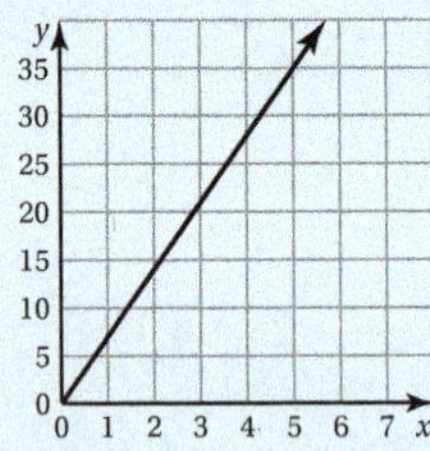

28.

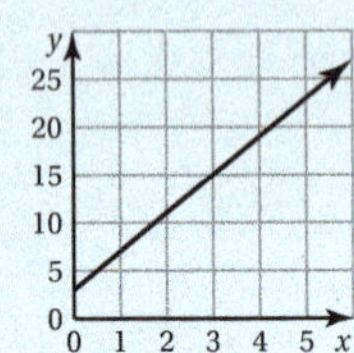

29.

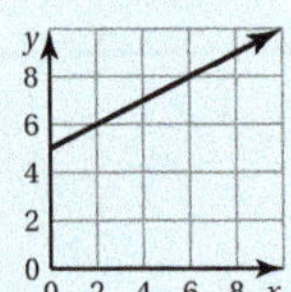

30. $c = 3 + 2.50m$

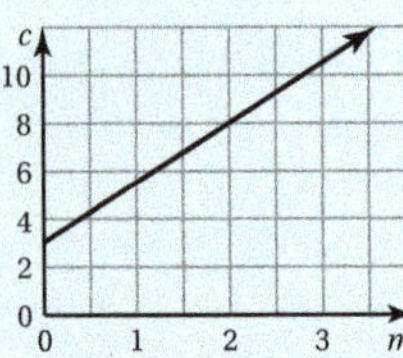

$15.50

31. $c = 25h + 100$

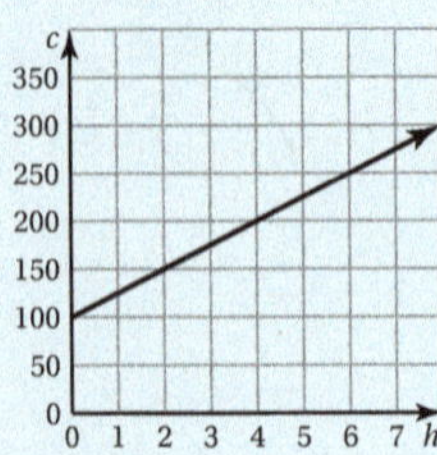

$250

32. See Additional Answers.

Common Errors

- **Exercises 23 and 24** Students may substitute for x and y incorrectly. Remind them that the first coordinate of the ordered pair is always the x-value and the second coordinate is always the y-value.

Chapter Resources

Surface Level	Deep Level
Resources by Chapter • Extra Practice • Reteach • Puzzle Time Student Journal • Practice • Chapter Self-Assessment Differentiating the Lesson Tutorial Videos Skills Review Handbook Skills Trainer Game Library	Resources by Chapter • Enrichment and Extension Graphic Organizers Game Library
Transfer Level	
STEAM Video Dynamic Assessment System • Chapter Test	Assessment Book • Chapter Tests A and B • Alternative Assessment • STEAM Performance Task

6.4 Writing Equations in Two Variables (pp. 265–272)

Learning Target: Write equations in two variables and analyze the relationship between the two quantities.

Tell whether the ordered pair is a solution of the equation.

23. $y = 3x + 1$; (2, 7)

24. $y = 7x - 4$; (4, 22)

25. The equation $E = 360m$ represents the kinetic energy E (in joules) of a roller-coaster car with a mass of m kilograms. Identify the independent and dependent variables.

Graph the equation.

26. $y = x + 1$

27. $y = 7x$

28. $y = 4x + 3$

29. $y = \frac{1}{2}x + 5$

30. A taxi ride costs \$3 plus \$2.50 per mile. Write and graph an equation that represents the total cost (in dollars) of a taxi ride. What is the total cost of a five-mile taxi ride?

31. Write and graph an equation that represents the total cost (in dollars) of renting the bounce house. How much does it cost to rent the bounce house for 6 hours?

32. A car averages 50 miles per hour on a trip. Write and graph an equation that represents the relationship between the time and the distance traveled. How long does it take the car to travel 525 miles?

Practice Test

1. Write "7 times a number s is 84" as an equation.

Solve the equation. Check your solution.

2. $15 = 7 + b$

3. $v - 6 = 16$

4. $5x = 70$

5. $\frac{6m}{7} = 30$

6. Tell whether (3, 27) is a solution of $y = 9x$.

7. Tell whether (8, 36) is a solution of $y = 4x + 2$.

8. The drawbridge shown consists of two identical sections that open to allow boats to pass. Write an equation you can use to find the length s (in feet) of each section of the drawbridge.

9. Each ticket to a school dance is \$4. The total amount collected in ticket sales is \$332. Find the number of students attending the dance.

10. A soccer team sells T-shirts for a fundraiser. The company that makes the T-shirts charges \$10 per shirt plus a \$20 shipping fee per order.

    a. Write and graph an equation that represents the total cost (in dollars) of ordering the shirts.

    b. Choose an ordered pair that lies on your graph in part (a). Interpret it in the context of the problem.

11. You hand in 2 homework pages to your teacher. Your teacher now has 32 homework pages to grade. Find the number of homework pages that your teacher originally had to grade.

GUEST CHECK

240796

1	Cheeseburger	7	49
2	Onion rings	7	00
1	Chx finger basket	9	50
1	12" Combo sub	6	50
2	Sodas	3	00
	Tax	2	51
	Total	36	00

12. Write an equation that represents the total cost (in dollars) of the meal shown with a tip that is a percent of the check total. What is the total cost of the meal when the tip is 15%?

Practice Test Item References

Practice Test Questions	Section to Review
1, 8, 9, 11	6.1
2, 3, 11	6.2
4, 5, 8, 9	6.3
6, 7, 10, 12	6.4

Test-Taking Strategies

Remind students to quickly look over the entire test before they start so that they can budget their time. When working with equations, they need to write all numbers and variables clearly. Some numbers and variables are easy to confuse. Have them pay attention to 6, *s*, 4, 9, 7, and *x*. Remind students to line up terms in each step and to not crowd their work. Have them use the **Stop** and **Think** strategy before they write their answers.

Common Errors

- **Exercises 2 and 3** Students may add or subtract the number on the side without the variable. For example, they might write $14 - 14 = k + 6 - 14$ instead of $14 - 6 = k + 6 - 6$. Remind students that they are trying to get the variable by itself, so they should start on the side with the variable and use the inverse of that operation.

Practice Test

1. $7s = 84$
2. $b = 8$
3. $v = 22$
4. $x = 14$
5. $m = 35$
6. yes
7. no
8. $2s = 366$
9. 83
10. **a.** $c = 20 + 10t$

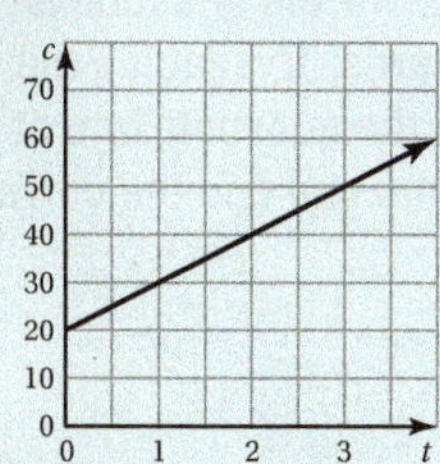

b. *Sample answer:* The ordered pair (3, 50) represents 3 shirts being ordered for \$50.

11. 30
12. $c = 36 + 36p$; \$41.40

Test-Taking Strategies

Available at *BigIdeasMath.com*

After Answering Easy Questions, Relax
Answer Easy Questions First
Estimate the Answer
Read All Choices before Answering
Read Question before Answering
Solve Directly or Eliminate Choices
Solve Problem before Looking at Choices
Use Intelligent Guessing
Work Backwards

About this Strategy

One way to answer the question is to work backwards. Try placing the responses into the question, one at a time, to see if you can find the correct solution.

Cumulative Practice

1. A
2. H
3. C
4. H
5. 53

Item Analysis

1. **A.** Correct answer
   B. The student rounds 27 to 30 and divides by 3.
   C. The student subtracts 3 from 27.
   D. The student multiplies 3 and 27.

2. **F.** The student finds a common factor of the three numbers but not the *greatest* common factor.
   G. The student finds a common factor of the three numbers but not the *greatest* common factor.
   H. Correct answer
   I. The student finds the greatest common factor of 16 and 32 but does not include 24.

3. **A.** The student writes an expression that represents the difference of 18 and 5 instead of the sum. The student misinterprets *less than* and writes the expression on the right side of the equation in the wrong order.
   B. The student misinterprets *less than* and writes the expression on the right side of the equation in the wrong order.
   C. Correct answer
   D. The student writes an expression that represents the difference of 18 and 5 instead of the sum.

4. **F.** The student finds the value of one part of the tape diagram.
   G. The student finds the number of tickets that the friend sold.
   H. Correct answer
   I. The student finds the number of tickets that the student sold.

5. **Gridded Response:** Correct answer: 53
   Common error: The student adds 112 and 59 to get 171.

6 Cumulative Practice

Test-Taking Strategy
Work Backwards

You like taking x catnaps each day, where $3x=24$. How many is that?
Ⓐ 6 Ⓑ 7 Ⓒ 8 Ⓓ 9

ZZZZZZZ

"Work backwards by trying 6, 7, 8, and 9. You will see that 3(8)=24. So, C is correct."

1. You buy roses at a flower shop for \$3 each. How many roses can you buy with \$27?

A. 9 **B.** 10
C. 24 **D.** 81

2. You are making identical fruit baskets using 16 apples, 24 pears, and 32 bananas. What is the greatest number of baskets you can make using all of the fruit?

F. 2 **G.** 4
H. 8 **I.** 16

3. Which equation represents the word sentence?

The sum of 18 and 5 is equal to 9 less than a number y.

A. $18 - 5 = 9 - y$ **B.** $18 + 5 = 9 - y$
C. $18 + 5 = y - 9$ **D.** $18 - 5 = y - 9$

4. The tape diagram shows the ratio of tickets sold by you and your friend. How many more tickets did you sell than your friend?

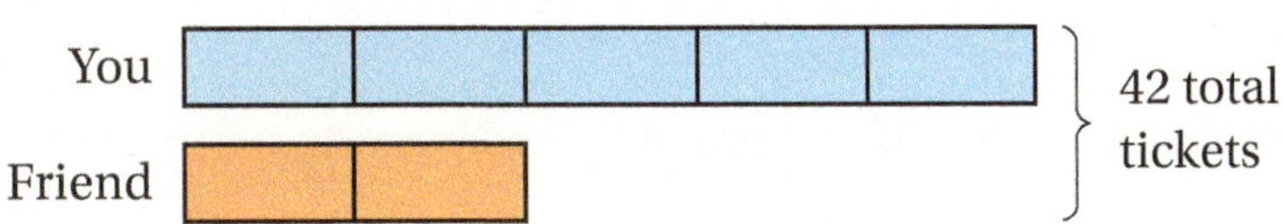

F. 6 **G.** 12
H. 18 **I.** 30

5. What is the value of x that makes the equation true?

$$59 + x = 112$$

6. The steps your friend took to divide two mixed numbers are shown.

$$3\frac{3}{5} \div 1\frac{1}{2} = \frac{18}{5} \times \frac{3}{2}$$
$$= \frac{27}{5}$$
$$= 5\frac{2}{5}$$

What should your friend change in order to divide the two mixed numbers correctly?

A. Find a common denominator of 5 and 2.

B. Multiply by the reciprocal of $\frac{18}{5}$.

C. Multiply by the reciprocal of $\frac{3}{2}$.

D. Rename $3\frac{3}{5}$ as $2\frac{8}{5}$.

7. A company ordering parts receives a charge of \$25 for shipping and handling plus \$20 per part. Which equation represents the cost c (in dollars) of ordering p parts?

F. $c = 25 + 20p$

G. $c = 20 + 25p$

H. $p = 25 + 20c$

I. $p = 20 + 25c$

8. Which property is illustrated by the statement?

$$5(a + 6) = 5(a) + 5(6)$$

A. Associative Property of Multiplication

B. Commutative Property of Multiplication

C. Commutative Property of Addition

D. Distributive Property

9. What is the value of the expression?

$$46.8 \div 0.156$$

Item Analysis (continued)

6. **A.** The student confuses the intended division algorithm with an addition/subtraction algorithm.
   B. The student multiplies by the reciprocal of the dividend rather than multiplying by the reciprocal of the divisor.
   C. Correct answer
   D. The student renames the first number in the expression, as if the student is going to follow a subtraction algorithm.

7. **F.** Correct answer
   G. The student multiplies the variable by 25 instead of 20.
   H. The student switches *p* and *c*.
   I. The student switches *p* and *c*, and multiplies the variable by 25 instead of 20.

8. **A.** The student confuses the Associative Property of Multiplication with the Distributive Property.
   B The student confuses the Commutative Property of Multiplication with the Distributive Property.
   C. The student confuses the Commutative Property of Addition with the Distributive Property.
   D. Correct answer

9. **Gridded Response:** Correct answer: 300

   Common error: The student incorrectly places the decimal point in the product.

Cumulative Practice

6. C

7. F

8. D

9. 300

Cumulative Practice

10. F

11. A

12. G

13. *Part A* $850 + 150w = 4000$; 21 weeks

Part B $\frac{3}{4}(20a) = 150$

Part C $10

Item Analysis (continued)

10. **F.** Correct answer

G. The student chooses a benchmark percent that visually approximates the percent of the mural that is painted red.

H. The student thinks that the quantity of 48 squares is the same as 48%.

I. The student chooses a benchmark percent that approximates the quantity of squares painted red.

11. **A.** Correct answer

B. The student incorrectly uses the Distributive Property; switching the coefficient with the constant in the parentheses.

C. The student incorrectly uses the Distributive Property; switching the factor outside the parentheses with the coefficient inside the parentheses.

D. The student incorrectly adds $2x$ and 5 to get $7x$.

12. **F.** The student does not follow the correct order of operations; multiplies before evaluating the expression inside the parentheses.

G. Correct answer

H. The student does not follow the correct order of operations; incorrectly applies the exponent before evaluating the expression inside the parentheses.

I. The student does not follow the correct order of operations; incorrectly applies the exponent before evaluating the expression inside the parentheses.

13. **4 points** The student's work and explanations demonstrate a thorough understanding of writing and solving equations. In Part A, the student writes and solves $850 + 150w = 4000$, or an equivalent equation, to find that Jeff can afford the car in 21 weeks. In Part B, the student writes $\frac{3}{4}(20a) = 150$, or an equivalent equation, to find the amount a per hour needed. In Part C, the student solves the equation correctly to find that Jeff needs to earn $10 per hour. The student provides accurate work with clear and complete explanations.

3 points The student's work and explanations demonstrate an essential but less than thorough understanding of writing and solving equations.

2 points The student's work and explanations demonstrate a partial but limited understanding of writing and solving equations.

1 point The student's work and explanations demonstrate a very limited understanding of writing and solving equations.

0 points The student provides no response, a completely incorrect or incomprehensible response, or a response that demonstrates insufficient understanding of writing and solving equations.

10. In the mural below, the squares that are painted red are marked with the letter R.

R	R	R															R	R	R
R	R	R															R	R	R
R	R	R															R	R	R
							R	R	R	R	R	R							
							R	R	R	R	R	R							
R	R	R															R	R	R
R	R	R															R	R	R
R	R	R															R	R	R

What percent of the mural is painted red?

F. 24% **G.** 25%

H. 48% **I.** 50%

11. Which expression is equivalent to $28x + 70$?

A. $14(2x + 5)$ **B.** $14(5x + 2)$

C. $2(14x + 5)$ **D.** $14(7x)$

12. What is the first step in evaluating the expression?

$$3 \cdot (5 + 2)^2 \div 7$$

F. Multiply 3 and 5. **G.** Add 5 and 2.

H. Evaluate 5^2. **I.** Evaluate 2^2.

13. Jeff wants to save \$4000 to buy a used car. He has already saved \$850. He plans to save an additional \$150 each week.

Part A Write and solve an equation to represent the number of weeks remaining until he can afford the car.

Jeff saves \$150 per week by saving $\frac{3}{4}$ of what he earns at his job each week. He works 20 hours per week.

Part B Write an equation to represent the amount per hour that Jeff must earn to save \$150 per week. Explain your reasoning.

Part C What is the amount per hour that Jeff must earn? Show your work and explain your reasoning.

7 Area, Surface Area, and Volume

Chapter Learning Target:
Understand measurement.

Chapter Success Criteria:

- I can explain how to find areas of figures.
- I can explain how to find surface areas and volumes of solids.
- I can describe and draw three-dimensional figures.
- I can apply units of measurement to solve real-life problems.

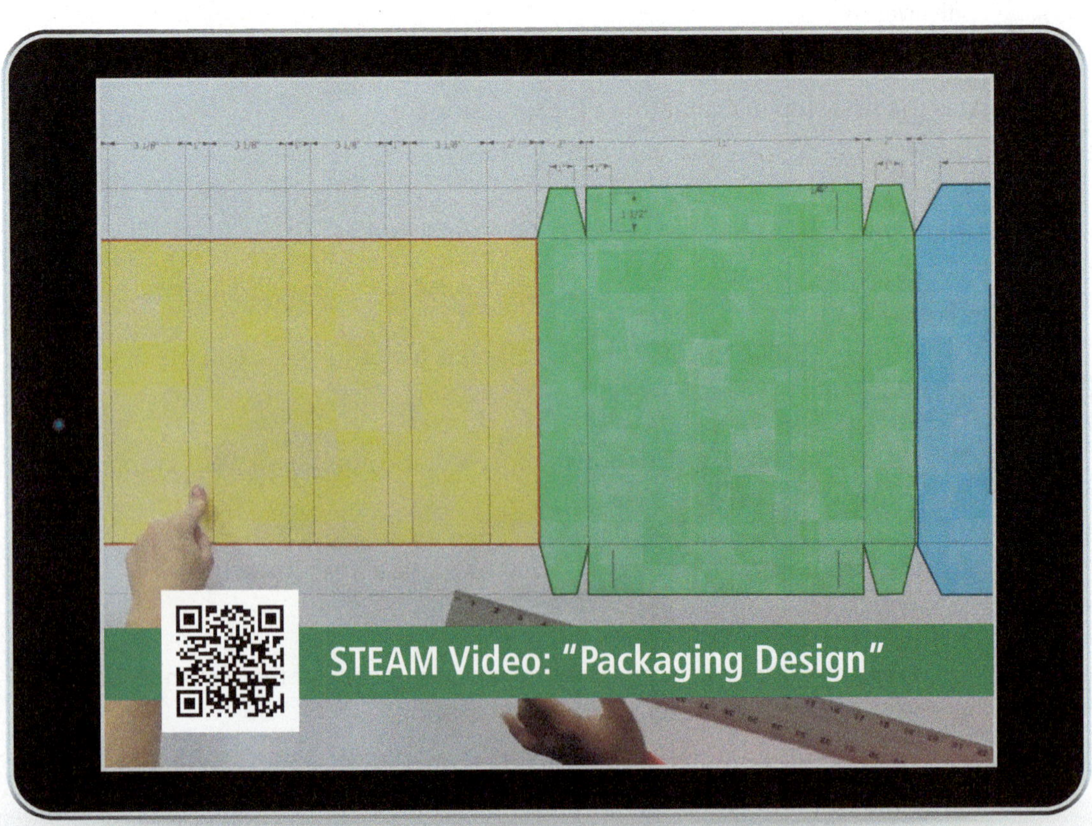

Laurie's Notes

Chapter 7 Overview

This chapter on geometric measurement is a strand in mathematics that connects numbers and the computational work students have learned to the study of geometry. In previous courses, students explored two- and three-dimensional shapes. Now they will extend measurement concepts by deriving various area, surface area, and volume formulas.

The three types of measurement associated with two- and three-dimensional figures each have particular units associated with them. Students may know they need to write linear units (cm, ft) for perimeter and edge lengths, square units (cm^2, sq ft) for area, and cubic units (cm^3, cu ft) for volume, but they do not understand why! As you work through the chapter, be intentional in mentioning the units and ask what a square centimeter looks like or a cubic foot. What do students visualize when they hear these words?

Distance	Area	Volume
linear units	square units	cubic units
cm	cm^2	cm^3
ft	sq ft	cu ft

The chapter begins with investigating the areas of triangles and several quadrilaterals. Students should know the definitions of these figures; however, you might begin the chapter by having students draw the different polygons they know and tell a partner what they know about each. A general discussion will help refresh students' memories.

Each of the area formulas can be derived from the formula for the area of a rectangle. The explorations in each section are similar, with students investigating different approaches to make sense of how the dimensions are used to find the area of the figure, and how the formulas relate to one another. You want students to make sense of the formulas, not just memorize them.

Students apply their understanding of area when they find the surface area of prisms and pyramids. The approach used to develop an understanding of surface area is to recognize the two-dimensional net that can be folded to form the prism or the pyramid. All of the faces will be polygons. It is very important that students have the tactile experience of drawing, cutting, and folding nets.

The final lesson is finding the volume of a rectangular prism, a concept students learned in the previous course. Their learning is now extended to include dimensions that are fractional lengths and conversions between different cubic units, such as a cubic yard to a cubic foot.

Having many physical models available in the classroom will enhance all of the learning in this chapter. Save packaging from retail products so that students can see and hold models. Two-dimensional pictures of three-dimensional objects do not provide the same learning experience.

Suggested Pacing

Chapter Opener	1 Day
Section 1	1 Day
Section 2	1 Day
Section 3	2 Days
Section 4	2 Days
Section 5	2 Days
Section 6	2 Days
Section 7	2 Days
Connecting Concepts	1 Day
Chapter Review	1 Day
Chapter Test	1 Day
Total Chapter 7	16 Days
Year-to-Date	108 Days

Chapter Learning Target

Understand measurement.

Chapter Success Criteria

- Explain how to find areas of figures.
- Explain how to find surface areas and volumes of solids.
- Describe and draw three-dimensional figures.
- Apply units of measurement to solve real-life problems.

Chapter 7 Learning Targets and Success Criteria

Section	Learning Target	Success Criteria
7.1 Areas of Parallelograms	Find areas and missing dimensions of parallelograms.	• Explain how the area of a rectangle is used to find the area of a parallelogram. • Use the base and the height of a parallelogram to find its area. • Use the area of a parallelogram and one of its dimensions to find the other dimension.
7.2 Areas of Triangles	Find areas and missing dimensions of triangles, and find areas of composite figures.	• Explain how the area of a parallelogram is used to find the area of a triangle. • Use the base and the height of a triangle to find its area. • Use the area of a triangle and one of its dimensions to find the other dimension. • Use decomposition to find the area of a figure.
7.3 Areas of Trapezoids and Kites	Find areas of trapezoids, kites, and composite figures.	• Explain how the area of a parallelogram is used to find the area of a trapezoid. • Decompose trapezoids and kites into smaller shapes. • Use decomposition to find the area of a figure. • Use the bases and the height of a trapezoid to find its area.
7.4 Three-Dimensional Figures	Describe and draw three-dimensional figures.	• Find the numbers of faces, edges, and vertices of a three-dimensional figure. • Draw prisms and pyramids. • Draw the front, side, and top views of a three-dimensional figure.
7.5 Surface Areas of Prisms	Represent prisms using nets and use nets to find surface areas of prisms.	• Draw nets to represent prisms. • Use nets to find surface areas of prisms. • Use a formula to find the surface area of a cube. • Apply surface areas of prisms to solve real-life problems.
7.6 Surface Areas of Pyramids	Represent pyramids using nets and use nets to find surface areas of pyramids.	• Draw nets to represent pyramids. • Use nets to find surface areas of pyramids. • Apply surface areas of pyramids to solve real-life problems.
7.7 Volumes of Rectangular Prisms	Find volumes and missing dimensions of rectangular prisms.	• Use a formula to find the volume of a rectangular prism. • Use a formula to find the volume of a cube. • Use the volume of a rectangular prism and two of its dimensions to find the other dimension. • Apply volumes of rectangular prisms to solve real-life problems.

Progressions

Through the Grades		
Grade 5	**Grade 6**	**Grade 7**
• Find the area of a rectangle with fractional side lengths. • Understand volume, and measure it by counting unit cubes. • Find the volumes of rectangular prisms using a formula. • Classify two-dimensional figures based on properties.	• Write and evaluate algebraic expressions. • Find the areas of triangles, special quadrilaterals, and polygons. • Find the volumes of prisms with fractional edge lengths. • Use nets made up of rectangles and triangles to find surface areas.	• Describe the cross sections that result from slicing three-dimensional figures. • Solve real-world and mathematical problems involving area, volume, and surface area of two- and three-dimensional objects.

Through the Chapter							
Standard	**7.1**	**7.2**	**7.3**	**7.4**	**7.5**	**7.6**	**7.7**
6.EE.A.2c Evaluate expressions at specific values of their variables. Include expressions that arise from formulas used in real-world problems. Perform arithmetic operations, including those involving whole-number exponents, in the conventional order when there are no parentheses to specify a particular order (Order of Operations).	●	●	★				
6.G.A.1 Find the area of right triangles, other triangles, special quadrilaterals, and polygons by composing into rectangles or decomposing into triangles and other shapes; apply these techniques in the context of solving real-world and mathematical problems.	●	●	★				
6.G.A.2 Find the volume of a right rectangular prism with fractional edge lengths by packing it with unit cubes of the appropriate unit fraction edge lengths, and show that the volume is the same as would be found by multiplying the edge lengths of the prism. Apply the formulas $V = lwh$ and $V = bh$ to find volumes of right rectangular prisms with fractional edge lengths in the context of solving real-world and mathematical problems.							★
6.G.A.4 Represent three-dimensional figures using nets made up of rectangles and triangles, and use the nets to find the surface area of these figures. Apply these techniques in the context of solving real-world and mathematical problems.				▲	●	★	

Key

▲ = preparing ★ = complete

● = learning ■ = extending

STEAM Video

1. *Sample answer:*

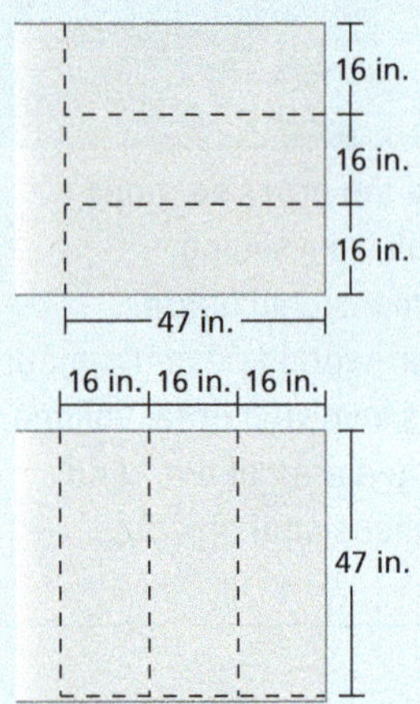

2. 399 in.^{2}

Performance Task

Sample answer: The surface area is the least amount of material needed to make the packaging.

Mathematical Practices

Students have opportunities to develop aspects of the mathematical practices throughout the chapter. Here are some examples.

1. **Make Sense of Problems and Persevere in Solving Them**
   7.3 Math Practice note, *p. 297*
2. **Reason Abstractly and Quantitatively**
   7.2 Exercise 28, *p. 296*
3. **Construct Viable Arguments and Critique the Reasoning of Others**
   7.5 Exercise 36, *p. 317*
4. **Model with Mathematics**
   7.7 Exercise 19, *p. 330*
5. **Use Appropriate Tools Strategically**
   7.6 Exercise 12, *p. 323*
6. **Attend to Precision**
   7.2 Math Practice note, *p. 291*
7. **Look for and Make Use of Structure**
   7.3 Exercise 35, *p. 304*
8. **Look for and Express Regularity in Repeated Reasoning**
   7.5 Math Practice note, *p. 311*

Laurie's Notes

STEAM Video

Before the Video

- To introduce the STEAM Video, read aloud the first paragraph of Packaging Design and discuss the prompt with your students.
- "Describe another situation in which you need to find the surface area of an object."

During the Video

- ? Pause the video at 0:52 and ask, "What has happened in the video so far?" Alex and Tory are discussing the design Alex made for a box to hold cookies.
- ? "What is Tory trying to find?" The amount of waste there will be. "What information does Tory need to find the amount of waste?" *Sample answer:* The area of the paper and the surface area of the box.
- Watch the remainder of the video.

After the Video

- ? "Why does Alex suggest placing the design along the length?" So there is less waste.
- ? "How does Tory find the amount of waste?" Tory finds the surface area of the design and takes it away from the area of the rectangle that contains it.
- Have students work with a partner to answer Questions 1 and 2.
- As students discuss and answer the questions, listen for understanding of surface area.

Performance Task

- Use this information to spark students' interest and promote thinking about real-life problems.
- ? Ask, "When a company is deciding on packaging for a product, why should the surface area of the packaging also be considered?"
- After completing the chapter, students will have gained the knowledge needed to complete "Maximizing the Volumes of Boxes."

STEAM Video

Packaging Design

Surface area can be used to determine amounts of materials needed to create objects. Describe another situation in which you need to find the surface area of an object.

Watch the STEAM Video "Packaging Design." Then answer the following questions. Alex is cutting a design out of paper and folding it to form a box.

1. Tory says that the length of the design is 47 inches and the width is 16 inches. Show several ways that you can arrange three of the designs on a roll of paper that is 48 inches wide. You can make the length of the paper as long as is needed.

2. Tory says that the cut-out design has an area of 619 square inches. What is the least possible amount of paper that is wasted when you cut out three of the designs?

48 in.

Performance Task

Maximizing the Volumes of Boxes

After completing this chapter, you will be able to use the concepts you learned to answer the questions in the *STEAM Video Performance Task*. You will be given the dimensions of a small box and two larger boxes.

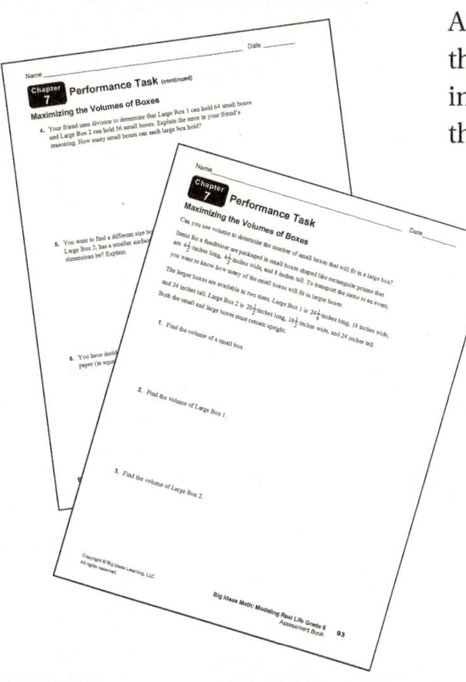

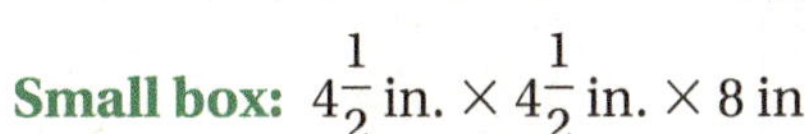
Small box: $4\frac{1}{2}$ in. × $4\frac{1}{2}$ in. × 8 in.

Large box 1: $24\frac{1}{4}$ in. × 18 in. × 24 in.

Large box 2: $20\frac{1}{2}$ in. × $18\frac{1}{2}$ in. × 24 in.

You will be asked to determine how many small boxes can be placed in each larger box. When a company is deciding on packaging for a product, why should the surface area of the packaging also be considered?

Getting Ready for Chapter 

Chapter Exploration

The formulas for the areas of polygons can be derived from one area formula, the area of a rectangle.

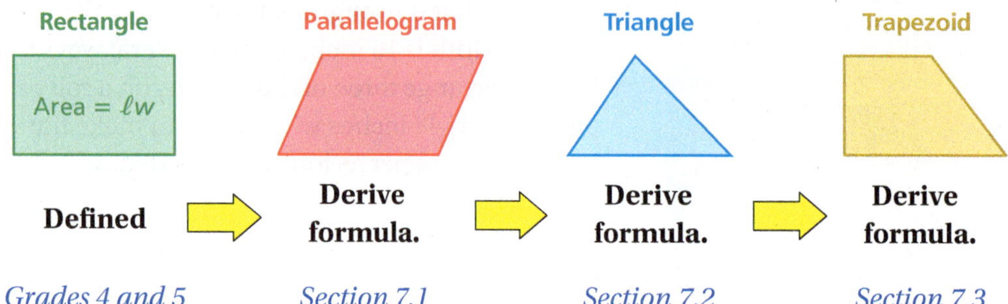

Work with a partner. Find (a) the dimensions of the figures and (b) the areas of the figures. What do you notice?

1. 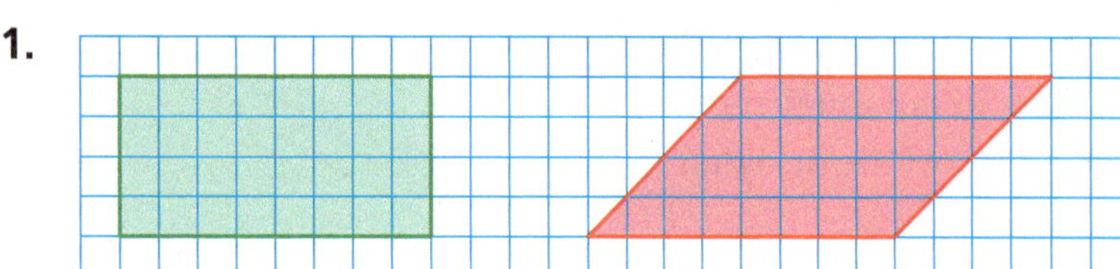

2. 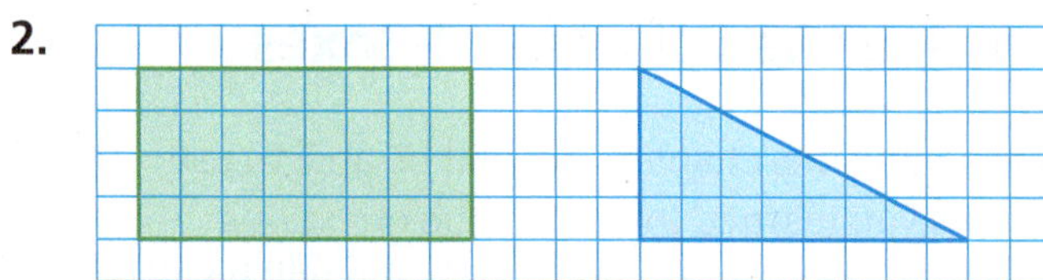

3. 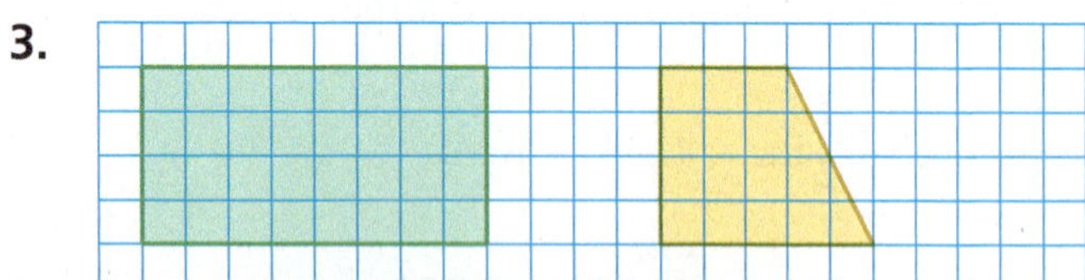

Vocabulary

The following vocabulary terms are defined in this chapter. Think about what each term might mean and record your thoughts.

prism

pyramid

surface area

volume

Laurie's Notes

Chapter Exploration

- Students should be familiar with formulas for the area of a square and the area of a rectangle.
- Students may have memorized the formulas but have little understanding of why the formulas make sense. In the exploration, students will connect the area of a rectangle to the areas of parallelograms, triangles, and trapezoids.
- Remind students to include units when describing dimensions and areas.
- ? Ask, "What type of units do you use to measure area?" square units
- ? "Why is area measured using square units?" There are two dimensions with multiplication in the formula (unit $\times$ unit $=$ unit^2).
- Work through Exercise 1 as a class.
- ? "What do you notice about the dimensions of the figures?" *Sample answer:* The length of the rectangle is the same as the base of the parallelogram and the width of the rectangle is the same as the height of the parallelogram.
- ? "What do you notice about the areas of the figures?" *Sample answer:* The areas are the same.
- Allow students to work in pairs to complete Exercises 2 and 3.

Vocabulary

- These terms represent some of the vocabulary that students will encounter in Chapter 7. Discuss the terms as a class.
- Where have students heard the term *pyramid* outside of a math classroom? In what contexts? Students may not be able to write the actual definition, but they may write phrases associated with a *pyramid*.
- Allowing students to discuss these terms now will prepare them for understanding the terms as they are presented in the chapter.
- When students encounter a new definition, encourage them to write in their *Student Journals*. They will revisit these definitions during the Chapter Review.

ELL Support

Point out that the terms *area* and *volume* may be familiar from everyday language. An area is a given space or region. In math, surface area is the sum of the areas of all of the faces of a solid. The word *volume* may be familiar from a button on a radio or television. It describes the degree of loudness or the intensity of a sound. Volume is also used to refer to one item in a series, such as the first volume in a series of books or the first album in a music collection. In math, however, volume is a measure of the amount of space occupied by a three-dimensional figure.

Topics for Review

- Areas of Squares, Rectangles, and Triangles
- Classifying Two-Dimensional Figures
- Operations with Decimals
- Operations with Fractions
- Parallel and Perpendicular Lines
- Solving Equations
- Volumes of Rectangular Prisms

Chapter Exploration

1. a. rectangle: length = 8 units, width = 4 units; parallelogram: base = 8 units, height = 4 units
   b. rectangle: 32 units^2; parallelogram: 32 units^2

   The areas are the same.
2. a. rectangle: length = 8 units, width = 4 units; triangle: base = 8 units, height = 4 units
   b. rectangle: 32 units^2; triangle: 16 units^2

   The area of the triangle is one-half the area of the rectangle.
3. a. rectangle: length = 8 units, width = 4 units; trapezoid: bases are 3 units and 5 units, height = 4 units
   b. rectangle: 32 units^2; trapezoid: 16 units^2

   The area of the trapezoid is one-half the area of the rectangle.

Learning Target

Find areas and missing dimensions of parallelograms.

Success Criteria

- Explain how the area of a rectangle is used to find the area of a parallelogram.
- Use the base and the height of a parallelogram to find its area.
- Use the area of a parallelogram and one of its dimensions to find the other dimension.

Warm Up

Cumulative, vocabulary, and prerequisite skills practice opportunities are available in the *Resources by Chapter* or at *BigIdeasMath.com.*

ELL Support

Explain that understanding word parts helps you determine the meaning of words. Write the words *parallel/o/gram* and *poly/gon*, with the separations shown. Point out that *parallel* means beside each other and give the example of parallel bars in gymnastics. Ask students for other examples. The suffix *–gram* is derived from *to write or draw*. A parallelogram is a drawing with two sets of parallel lines. The prefix *poly-* means *many* and *–gon* refers to angles. A polygon is a figure with three or more angles.

Exploration 1

a. They are the same.

b. 18 cm^2

c. no; *Sample answer:* The area is not changed by how it is calculated.

d. $A = bh$

Laurie's Notes

Preparing to Teach

- In prior courses, students used rectangular area models to represent one- and two-digit multiplication. In this course, they used area models to represent the Distributive Property. Now, students will use the definition of the area of a rectangle to derive the formula for the area of a parallelogram.
- Students will use the equation-solving skills they developed in the previous chapter to manipulate area formulas to find a dimension, such as base or height. They are not yet ready to find diagonal lengths.
- **MP7 Look for and Make Use of Structure:** It is important that students see the progression of the formulas in this chapter. They will use the formula for the area of a rectangle and deductive reasoning to derive the other formulas. You are seeking conceptual understanding, so that if students cannot remember a specific formula, they will be able to derive it visually because they have done it before. They have ownership of the formula!

Motivate

- **Story Time:** Tell students you worked as a short-order cook at a diner while in college. Combining your love of math with cooking, you cut a piece of toast on a diagonal. Then you arranged the pieces so they were no longer square.
- Distribute two right triangle pieces or a square piece of paper that students can fold on a diagonal and tear apart.
- ? Ask, "How many different shapes can you make using the toast?" 3 "Did the amount of toast change?" no "What did change?" the shape Have students share their shapes with the class.
- Explain that in the next few lessons, students will cut and rearrange a shape to make a shape for which they already know the area formula.

Discuss

- **Think-Pair-Share:** Have students draw a parallelogram and make a list of its characteristics. Have pairs compare their drawings and lists. Then have students write the definition of a parallelogram and have a class discussion.

Exploration 1

- **Teaching Strategy:** Have 1-centimeter grid paper available for students.
- In part (a), tell students to draw rectangles large enough to manipulate. Look for students cutting their rectangles into two rectangles and forming other rectangles. Applaud them for being clever, but ask them to cut their rectangles so that they create parallelograms that are *not* rectangles (cut at an angle).
- Ask students to explain how the process in part (a) helps them in part (b).
- In decomposing to find an area, students need to see that the length and width of a rectangle becomes the base and height of the corresponding parallelogram and vice versa. Redirect students who prefer to just count squares. They need the experience of decomposing a parallelogram into rectangles to justify the formula for the area of a parallelogram.
- Now, students have the formula for the area of a parallelogram. Throughout the lesson, remind students of how they used deductive reasoning to find it!

7.1 Areas of Parallelograms

Learning Target: Find areas and missing dimensions of parallelograms.

Success Criteria:
- I can explain how the area of a rectangle is used to find the area of a parallelogram.
- I can use the base and the height of a parallelogram to find its area.
- I can use the area of a parallelogram and one of its dimensions to find the other dimension.

A **polygon** is a closed figure in a plane that is made up of three or more line segments that intersect only at their endpoints. Several examples of polygons are parallelograms, rhombuses, triangles, trapezoids, and kites.

The formula for the area of a parallelogram can be derived from the definition of the area of a rectangle. Recall that the area of a rectangle is the product of its length ℓ and its width w. The process you use to derive this and other area formulas in this chapter is called *deductive reasoning*.

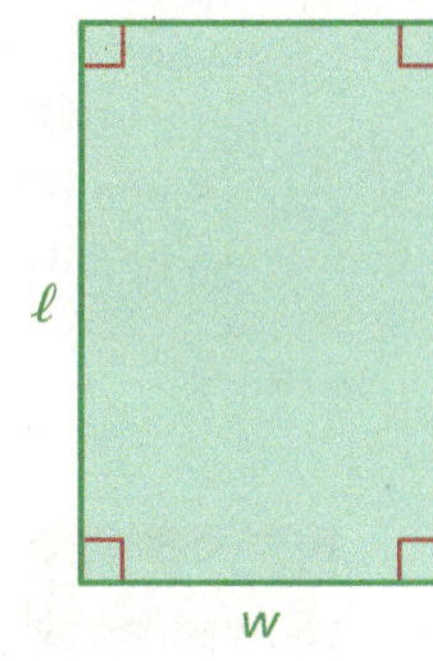

EXPLORATION 1 Deriving the Area Formula of a Parallelogram

Work with a partner.

a. Draw *any* rectangle on a piece of centimeter grid paper. Cut the rectangle into two pieces that can be arranged to form a parallelogram. What do you notice about the areas of the rectangle and the parallelogram?

b. Copy the parallelogram below on a piece of centimeter grid paper. Cut the parallelogram and rearrange the pieces to find its area.

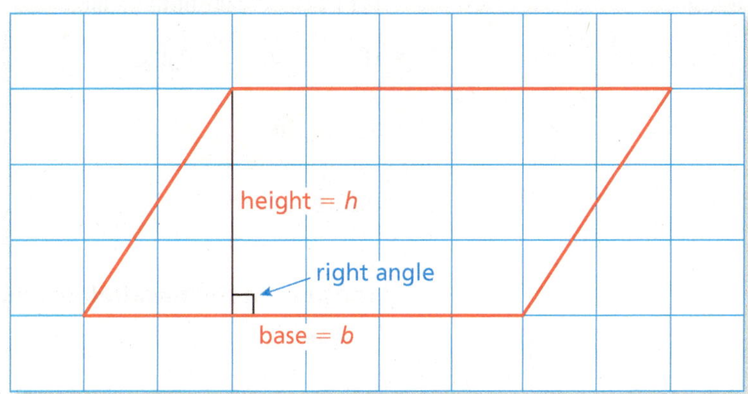

c. Draw *any* parallelogram on a piece of centimeter grid paper and find its area. Does the area change when you use a different side as the base? Explain your reasoning.

d. Use your results to write a formula for the area A of a parallelogram.

Math Practice

Justify Conclusions

How does decomposing the parallelogram into other figures help you justify your formula?

7.1 Lesson

Key Vocabulary
polygon, *p. 285*

The *area* of a polygon is the amount of surface it covers. You can find the area of a parallelogram in much the same way as you can find the area of a rectangle.

Key Idea

Area of a Parallelogram

Words The area A of a parallelogram is the product of its base b and its height h.

Algebra $A = bh$

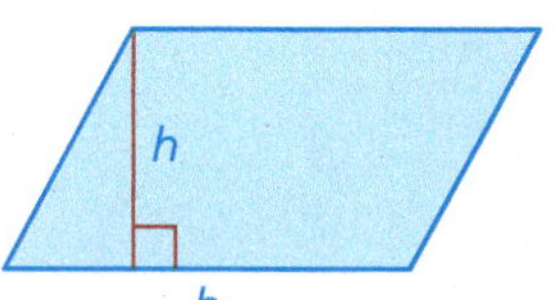

The base of a parallelogram does not have to be horizontal. Any side of a parallelogram can be the base.

EXAMPLE 1 Finding Areas of Parallelograms

Find the area of each parallelogram.

a.

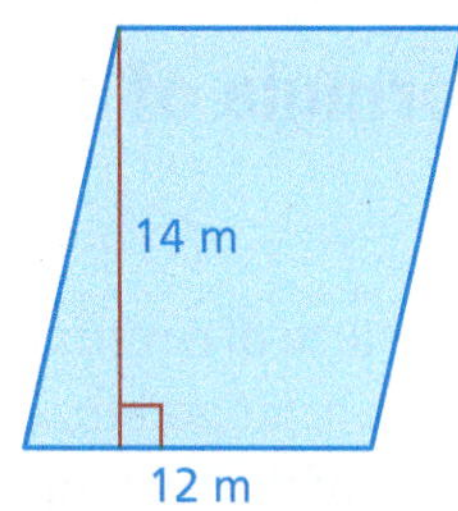

$A = bh$ Write formula.

$= 12(14)$ Substitute values.

$= 168$ Multiply.

The area of the parallelogram is 168 square meters.

b.

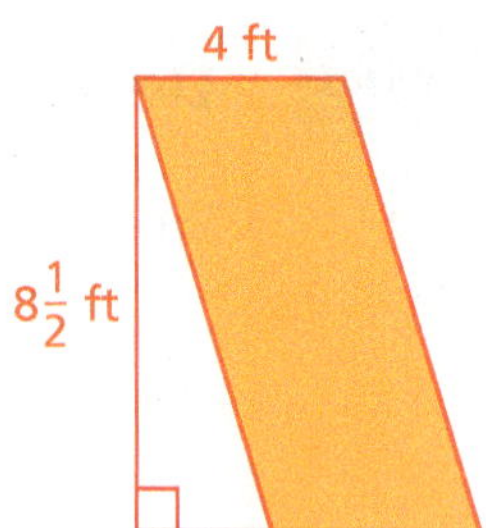

$A = bh$

$= 4\left(8\frac{1}{2}\right)$

$= 34$

The area of the parallelogram is 34 square feet.

Remember

Area is measured in square units.

Try It **Find the area of the parallelogram.**

1.

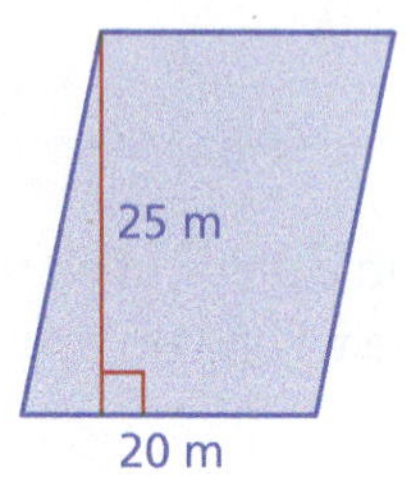

2.

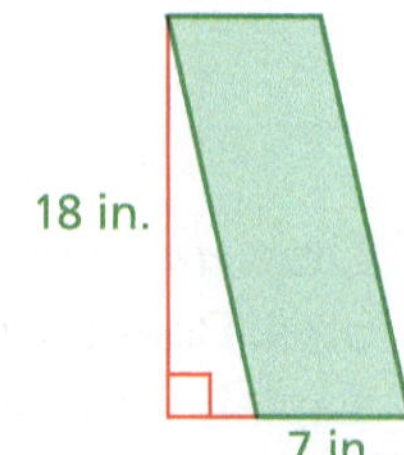

3.

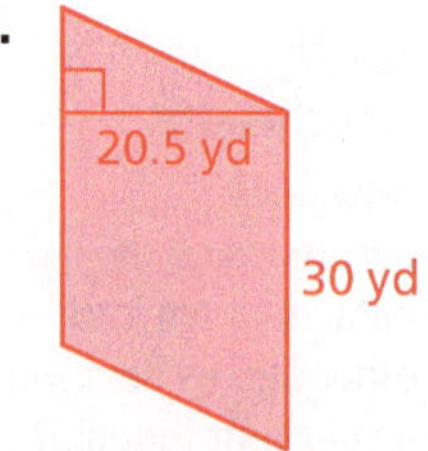

Multi-Language Glossary at *BigIdeasMath.com*

Laurie's Notes

Scaffolding Instruction

- Students will see how the equation-solving skills they developed in the previous chapter can assist in solving problems that depend on the formula for the area of a parallelogram.
- **Emerging:** Students may lack confidence and prefer to draw on grid paper to create rectangles or use the formula without understanding. Provide guided instruction for the examples. Relate the examples to how students derived the formula for the area of a parallelogram in the exploration.
- **Proficient:** Students understand the development of the formula for the area of a parallelogram and can concentrate on solving problems. Students may proceed to the Self-Assessment for Concepts & Skills exercises.

Key Idea

- The *height* of a parallelogram is the perpendicular distance from a base to the opposite side.
- It is very important that students recognize that the height of a parallelogram is *not* a side of the parallelogram, unless the figure is a rectangle or a square.
- Try to connect the concept of the height of a parallelogram to the height (or altitude) of a kite. The length of the string is *not* the height of a kite.
- Ask students to think about b and h in the formula as variables. Ask them what value(s) they may stand for and guide them to realize that they are ranges of values (> 0).
- **Teaching Strategy:** Have students discuss why any side of a parallelogram can be the base. Demonstrate by physically turning a parallelogram drawn on grid paper and identify the new base and height.

string

h

EXAMPLE 1

- ? "What type of units do you use to measure area?" square units "Why is area measured using square units?" There are two dimensions with multiplication in the formula ($m \times m = m^2$).
- Review how square units are written: m^2, sq m, or square meters.
- Ask students if they can solve these without the formula. Students can check their answers by decomposing the parallelogram into a rectangle, as they did in the exploration.

Try It

- Students should note that in Exercise 2, the height is shown outside of the parallelogram. The same could have been done for the other two exercises.

ELL Support

Allow students to work in groups to practice language as they complete Try It Exercises 1–3. Expect students at different language levels to perform as described.

Beginner: Write the steps.

Intermediate: State the formula with the substituted values and the area.

Advanced: Describe the process.

Scaffold instruction to support all students in their learning. Learning is individualized and you may want to group students differently as they move in and out of these levels with each skill and concept. Student self-assessment and feedback help guide your instructional decisions about how and when to layer support for all students to become proficient learners.

Teaching Strategy

Grid paper is a tool that lends itself to both algebraic and geometric concepts. It can be used to create a visual model to help students "see" a problem. Students can draw a shape on grid paper and approximate the area by counting squares. They can decompose a shape by cutting the paper and rearranging the pieces to form another shape. A parallelogram, drawn on grid paper, can be rotated to show that a base can be any side.

Extra Example 1

Find the area of each parallelogram.

a.

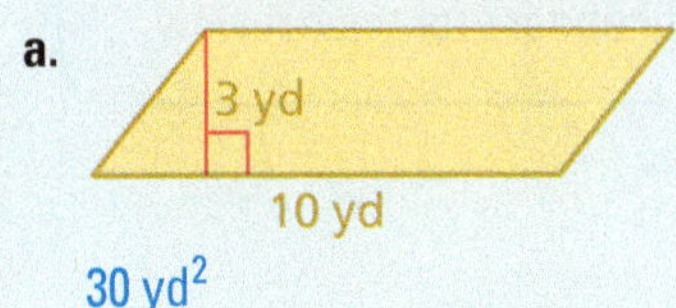

30 yd^2

b.

$7\frac{1}{2}$ cm

3 cm

$22\frac{1}{2} \text{ cm}^2$

Try It

1. 500 m^2
2. 126 in.^2
3. 615 yd^2

Extra Example 2

Find the area of the parallelogram in square feet.

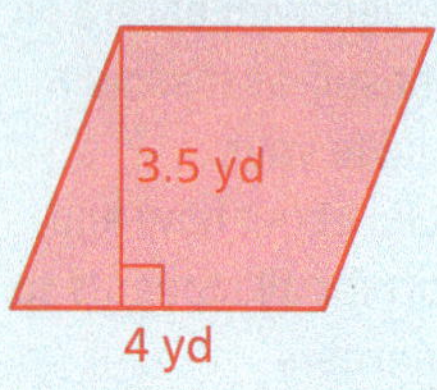

126 ft^2

Try It

4. $400{,}000 \text{ cm}^2$

ELL Support

Allow students to work in pairs to complete the Self-Assessment for Concepts & Skills exercises. Then have two pairs check understanding by comparing answers and resolving differences. You may want to check Exercises 6 and 7 by having each group display their answers on a whiteboard for your review.

Self-Assessment for Concepts & Skills

5. *Sample answer:* Reform a parallelogram with base b and height h as a rectangle with length b and width h.
6. 80 ft^2
7. 14.4 km^2
8. *Sample answer:*

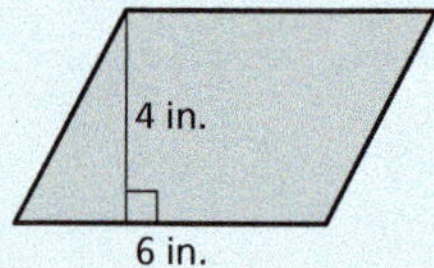

Laurie's Notes

Discuss

- Students may struggle to convert square units. Have them read and discuss the information at the top of the page.
- Another Method: $\left(\frac{3 \text{ feet}}{\text{yard}}\right)^2 = \frac{3^2 \text{ feet}^2}{\text{yard}^2} = \frac{9 \text{ feet}^2}{\text{yard}^2}$.
- Students may benefit from additional practice converting square units. Examples:
  (a) $1 \text{ m}^2 =$ ____ cm^2 10,000 (b) $1 \text{ ft}^2 =$ ___ in.^2 144

EXAMPLE 2

- The parallelogram in this example is a rhombus. A rhombus is a parallelogram with four congruent sides. So, you can find the area of a rhombus using the formula $A = bh$.
- At first glance, this example looks similar to Example 1. Have students analyze the problem. Then discuss how it differs from the previous Try It exercises. Students may say that it differs because the horizontal segment is the height; however, Try It Exercise 3 is labeled in the same way.
- Tell them to read the problem carefully. You want them to see that the dimensions are given in feet, but the answer must be in square inches.
- Students may ask why they cannot just multiply the 5 square feet by 12. There are 12 inches in 1 foot, so there are 144 square inches in 1 square foot. Dimensional analysis is a strategy that students will use throughout mathematics and science.
- ? Have students check their answers using another method. Ask, "Instead of multiplying 2.5 and 2, is there another way to start this problem?" Continue to ask probing questions until students realize they can find the area by first converting both dimensions from feet to inches, and then multiplying 24 and 30 to get 720 square inches.

Try It

- **Neighbor Check:** After completing Exercise 4, have neighbors pair up to share strategies and answers. Students are working on the second success criterion.

Self-Assessment for Concepts & Skills

- Have students work independently on these exercises.
- Look at students' explanations in Exercise 5 to check their understanding of the first success criterion.
- Exercises 6–8 provide insight into students' use of the formula for the area of a parallelogram. In Exercise 8, students are asked to demonstrate a higher level of thinking by working backwards.

The Success Criteria Self-Assessment chart can be found in the *Student Journal* or online at *BigIdeasMath.com*.

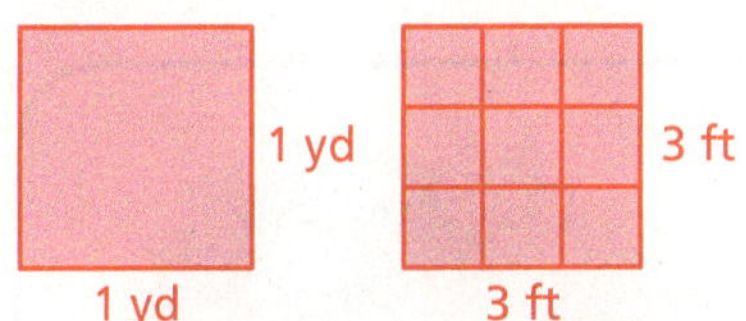

When finding areas, you may need to convert square units. The diagrams at the left show that there are 9 square feet per square yard.

$$1 \text{ yd}^2 = (1 \text{ yd})(1 \text{ yd}) = (3 \text{ ft})(3 \text{ ft}) = 9 \text{ ft}^2$$

You can use a similar procedure to convert other square units.

EXAMPLE 2 Finding the Area of a Parallelogram

Find the area of the parallelogram in square inches.

$A = bh$	Write formula.
$= 2.5(2)$	Substitute values.
$= 5$	Multiply.

The area of the parallelogram is 5 square feet.
To convert the area to square inches, use a conversion factor.
Notice that $1 \text{ ft}^2 = (1 \text{ ft})(1 \text{ ft}) = (12 \text{ in.})(12 \text{ in.}) = 144 \text{ in.}^2$.

$$5 \text{ ft}^2 = 5 \cancel{\text{ft}^2} \times \frac{144 \text{ in.}^2}{1 \cancel{\text{ft}^2}} = 720 \text{ in.}^2$$

The area of the parallelogram is 5 square feet, or 720 square inches.

Try It

4. Find the area of the parallelogram in square centimeters.

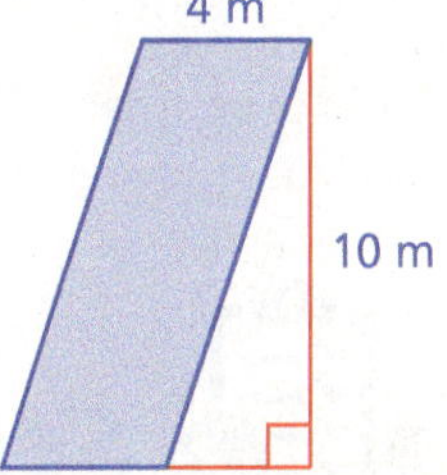

Self-Assessment for Concepts & Skills

Solve each exercise. Then rate your understanding of the success criteria in your journal.

5. **WRITING** Explain how to use the area of a rectangle to find the area of a parallelogram.

FINDING AREA **Find the area of the parallelogram.**

6.

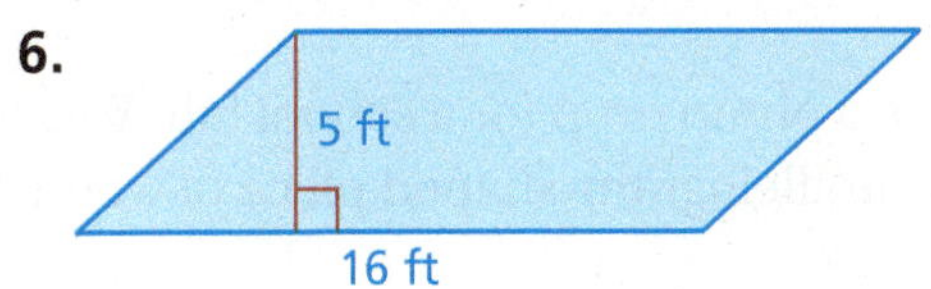

7.

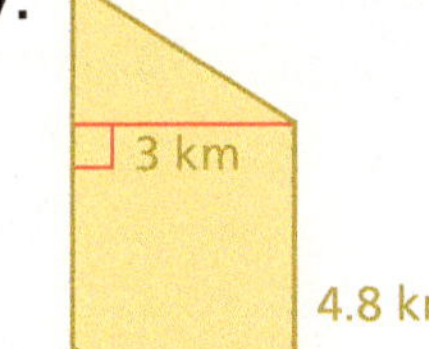

8. **MP REASONING** Draw a parallelogram that has an area of 24 square inches.

EXAMPLE 3 Modeling Real Life

The area of the parallelogram-shaped forest bordered by roads is 99,000 square yards. What is the length of the deer trail?

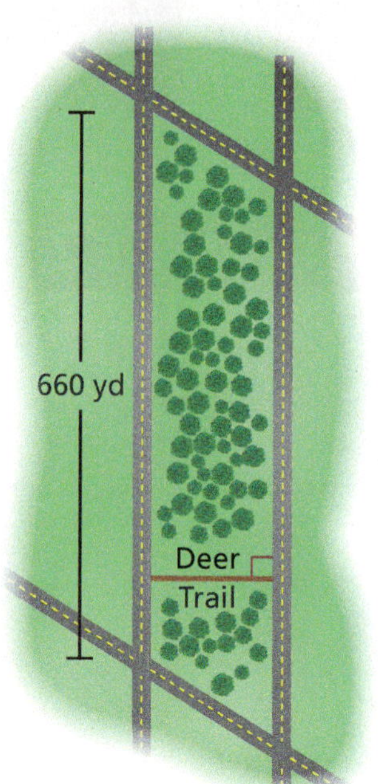

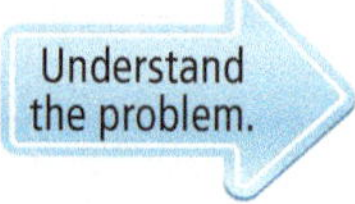

You are given the area of a parallelogram-shaped forest, and the map shows the length of one of its bases. You are asked to find the length of the deer trail, which represents the height of the parallelogram.

Use the formula for the area of a parallelogram. Substitute for the area and the base, then solve for the height.

$A = bh$ — Write formula for area of a parallelogram.

$99{,}000 = 660h$ — Substitute 99,000 for A and 660 for b.

$\frac{99{,}000}{660} = \frac{660h}{660}$ — Division Property of Equality

$150 = h$ — Simplify.

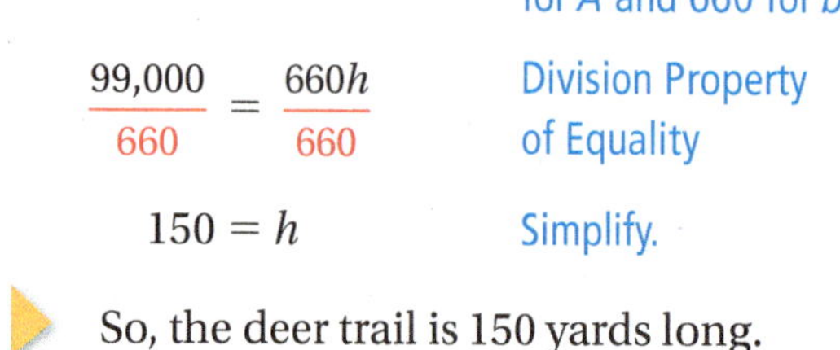

Check $A = bh$

$99{,}000 \stackrel{?}{=} 660(150)$

$99{,}000 = 99{,}000$ ✓

So, the deer trail is 150 yards long.

Self-Assessment for Problem Solving

Solve each exercise. Then rate your understanding of the success criteria in your journal.

9. The side of an office building in Hamburg, Germany, is in the shape of a parallelogram. The area of the side of the building is about 2150 square meters. What is the length x of the portion of the building that extends over the river?

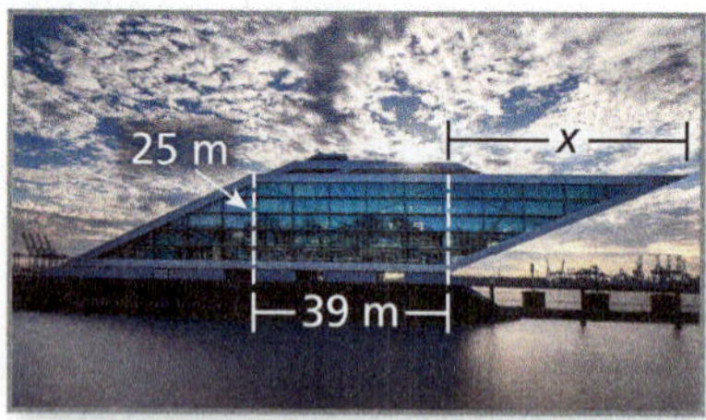

10. You make a photo prop for a school fair. You cut a 10-inch square out of a parallelogram-shaped piece of wood. What is the area of the photo prop?

11. A galaxy contains a parallelogram-shaped dust field. The dust field has a base of 150 miles. The height is 14% of the base. What is the area of the dust field?

Laurie's Notes

EXAMPLE 3

- Have a volunteer read the problem aloud.
- You want students to identify what is known and what they need to find. The problem-solving plan should guide their thinking. It takes time and practice to develop good problem-solving habits.
- ❓ "What are you asked to find?" the length of the deer trail "What does the length of the deer trail represent in the figure?" the height of the parallelogram "How do you know?" Because it is the perpendicular distance from a base to the opposite side.
- ◉ This problem has an unknown that is *not* the area. Students will need to write the formula, substitute the known values, and then solve for the unknown. They can find the quotient using long division.
- Have students work in pairs to finish solving the problem. Then have pairs compare their work and solutions with others.
- **MP1 Make Sense of Problems and Persevere in Solving Them:** Mathematically proficient students analyze the given information, determine what they are trying to find, and make a plan. They listen to the viewpoints of others and ask, "Does this answer make sense?"

Self-Assessment for Problem Solving

- Allow time in class for students to work independently on these exercises. Remember, some students may only be able to complete the first step of the problem-solving plan.
- ◉ The goal of these exercises is for students to problem-solve using the area of a parallelogram.
- In Exercise 10, students need to realize that different units are used within the problems.
- For each exercise, look for students who used different methods and have them write their work on the board. Then ask volunteers to explain how to check the work. Help students see the value in different methods.

The Success Criteria Self-Assessment chart can be found in the *Student Journal* or online at *BigIdeasMath.com.*

Closure

- Determine the area and the perimeter of each parallelogram. Then order the parallelograms from least to greatest area and least to greatest perimeter.

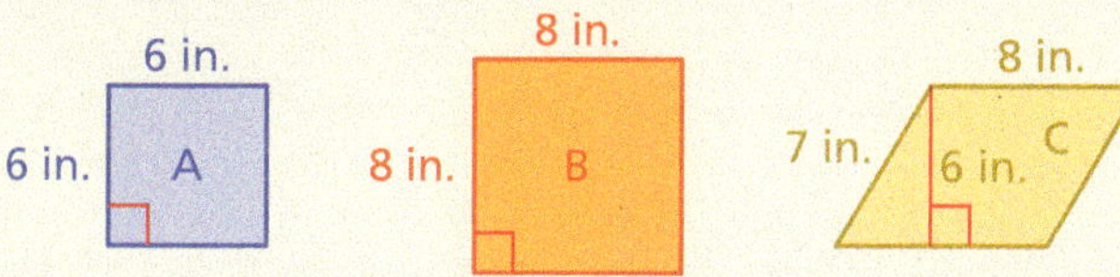

A: 36 in.^{2}, 24 in.; B: 64 in.^{2}, 32 in.; C: 48 in.^{2}, 30 in.; A, C, B; A, C, B

Extra Example 3

The area of a parallelogram-shaped pond bordered by a stone path is 1800 square feet. What is the length of the bridge?

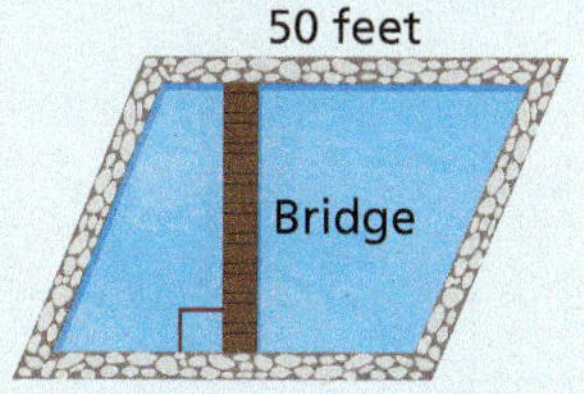

36 feet

Self-Assessment for Problem Solving

9. 47 m
10. 4508 in.^{2}
11. 3150 mi^2

Learning Target

Find areas and missing dimensions of parallelograms.

Success Criteria

- Explain how the area of a rectangle is used to find the area of a parallelogram.
- Use the base and the height of a parallelogram to find its area.
- Use the area of a parallelogram and one of its dimensions to find the other dimension.

Review & Refresh

1. 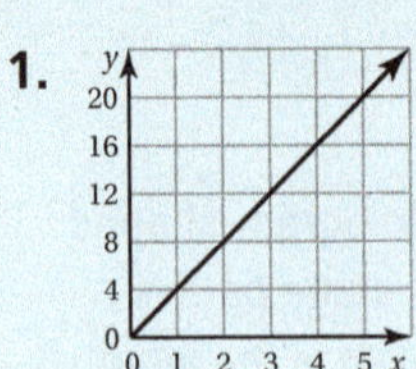

2. 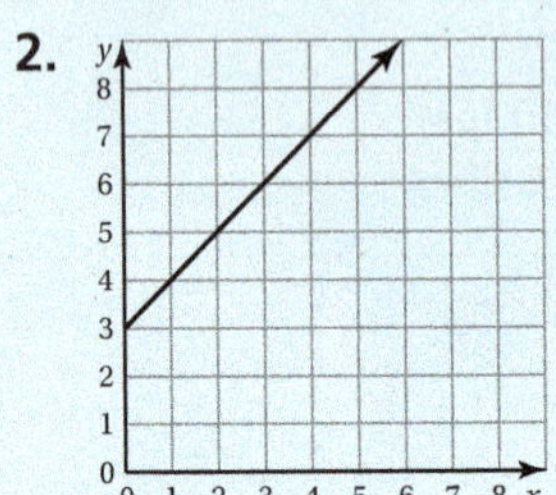

3. 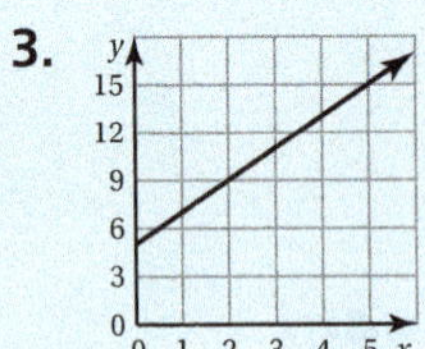

4. 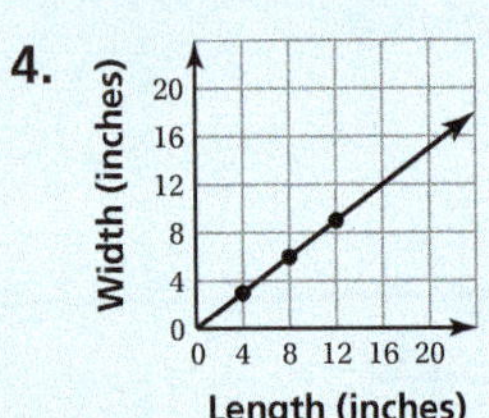

5. 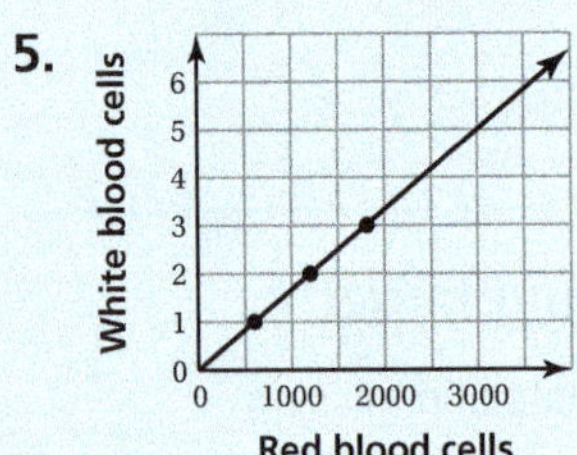

6. $5 \cdot 11$
7. $2^2 \cdot 3 \cdot 5$
8. $2 \cdot 3 \cdot 5^2$
9. $2 \cdot 3^2 \cdot 7$
10. 18.07
11. 2.891
12. 8.9992

Concepts, Skills, & Problem Solving

13. 12 units^2
14. 9 units^2
15. 24 units^2
16. 18 ft^2
17. 840 mm^2
18. 187 km^2
19. 3750 cm^2
20. 243 in.^{2}
21. 894 mi^2

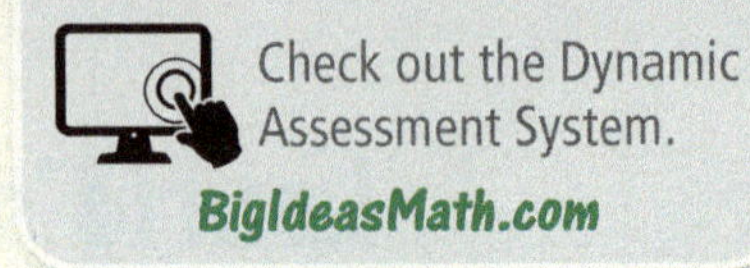

Assignment Guide and Concept Check

Scaffold assignments to support all students in their learning progression. The suggested assignments are a starting point. Continue to assign additional exercises and revisit with spaced practice to move every student toward proficiency.

Level	Assignment 1	Assignment 2
Emerging	3, 5, 9, 12, 13, 16, 17, 19	14, 22, 23, 24, 27, 29, 33
Proficient	3, 5, 9, 12, 14, 18, 19, 20	22, 25, 27, 28, 30, 33
Advanced	3, 5, 9, 12, 15, 20, 21, 22	26, 28, 31, 32, 33, 34

- Assignment 1 is for use after students complete the Self-Assessment for Concepts & Skills.
- Assignment 2 is for use after students complete the Self-Assessment for Problem Solving.
- The red exercises can be used as a concept check.

Review & Refresh Prior Skills

Exercises 1–3 Graphing Equations
Exercises 4 and 5 Graphing Ratio Relationships
Exercises 6–9 Writing a Prime Factorization
Exercises 10–12 Adding and Subtracting Decimals

Common Errors

- **Exercises 20 and 21** Students may incorrectly identify a side of the parallelogram as the height. Remind them that the *height* is the perpendicular distance from a base to the opposite side.

7.1 Practice

Graph the equation.

1. $y = 4x$
2. $y = x + 3$
3. $y = 2x + 5$

Represent the ratio relationship using a graph.

4.

Length (inches)	4	8	12
Width (inches)	3	6	9

5.

Red Blood Cells	600	1200	1800
White Blood Cells	1	2	3

Write the prime factorization of the number.

6. 55
7. 60
8. 150
9. 126

Add or subtract.

10. $2.36 + 15.71$
11. $9.035 - 6.144$
12. $28.351 - 19.3518$

Concepts, Skills, & Problem Solving

USING TOOLS **Rearrange the parallelogram as a rectangle. Then find the area.** (See Exploration 1, p. 285.)

13.

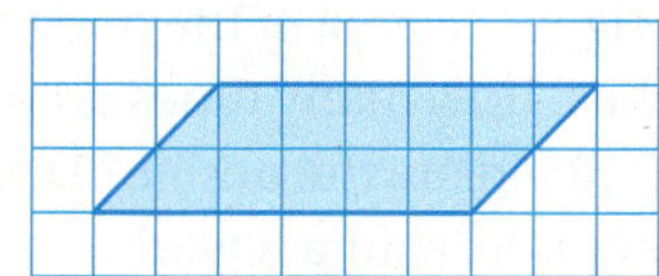

14.

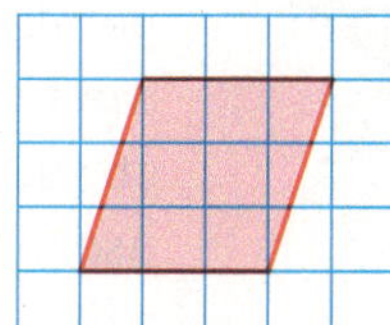

15.

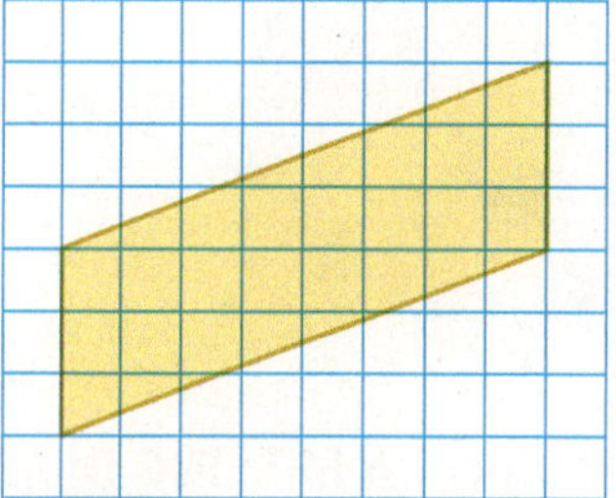

FINDING AREA **Find the area of the parallelogram.**

16.

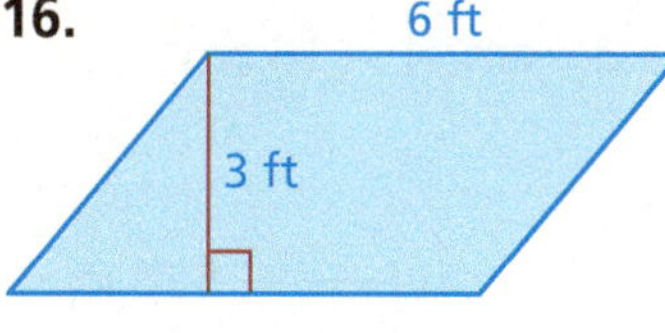

17.

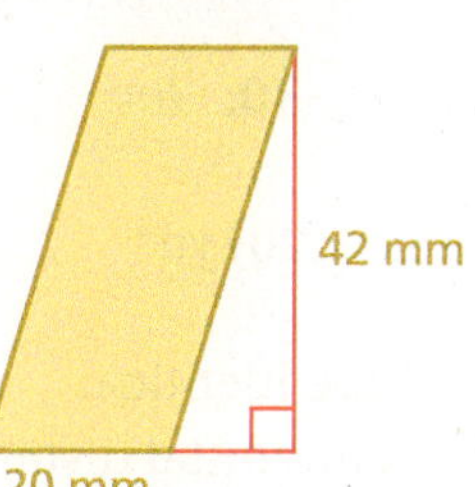

18.

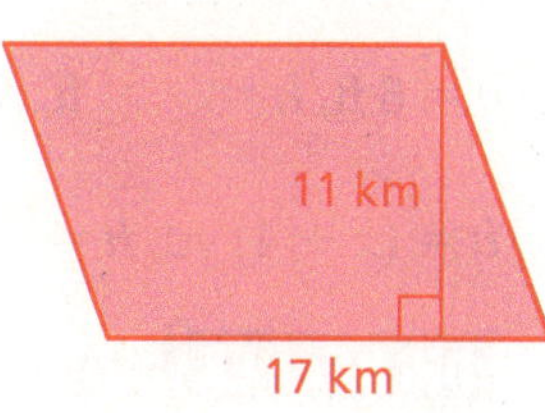

19.

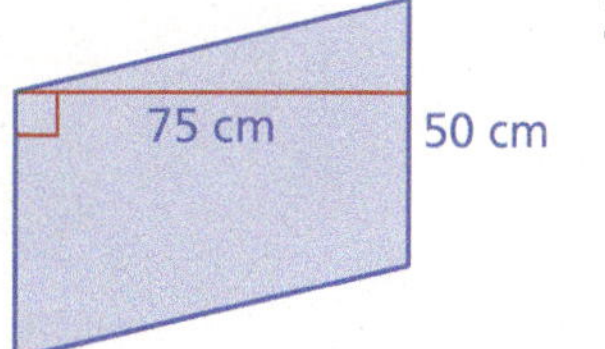

20.

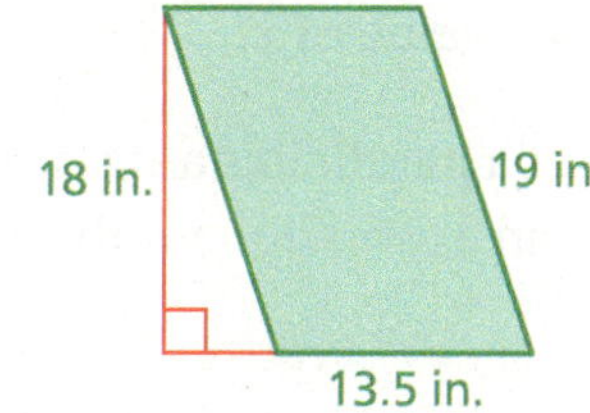

21.

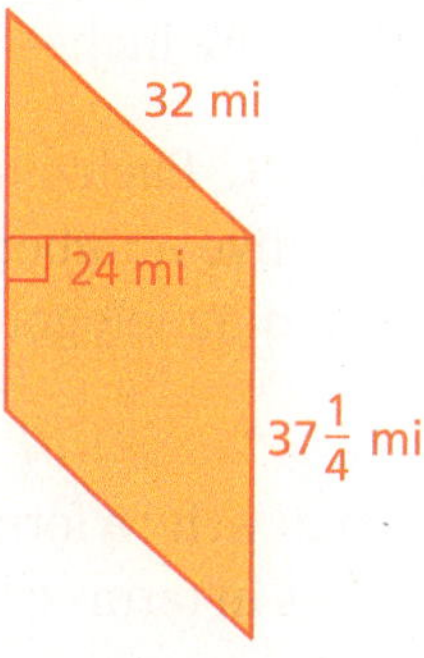

22. **YOU BE THE TEACHER** Your friend finds the area of the parallelogram. Is your friend correct? Explain your reasoning.

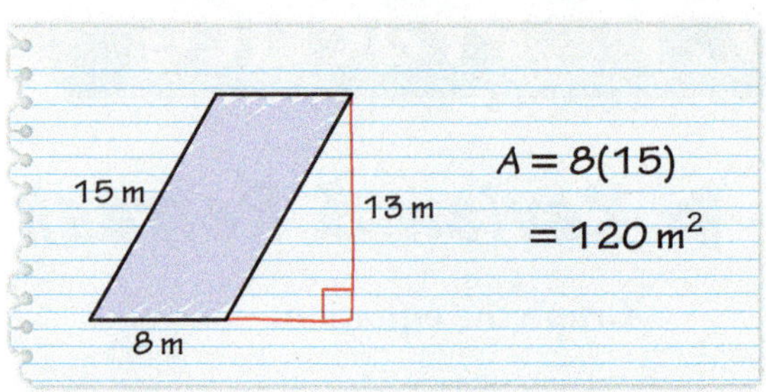

23. **MODELING REAL LIFE** A ceramic tile in the shape of a parallelogram has a base of 4 inches and a height of 1.5 inches. What is the area of the tile?

FINDING AREA **Find the area of the parallelogram. Round to the nearest hundredth if necessary.**

24. Area = ☐ cm^2

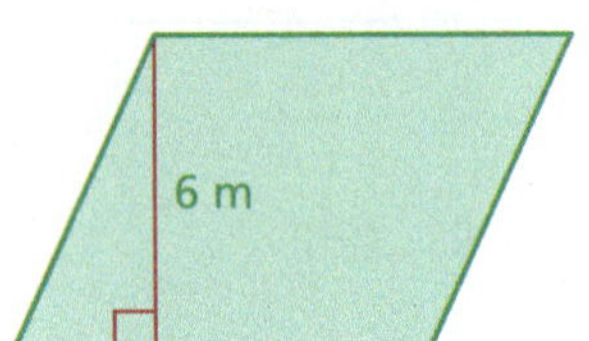

25. Area ≈ ☐ mi^2

1320 yd
1496 yd

26. Area ≈ ☐ ft^2

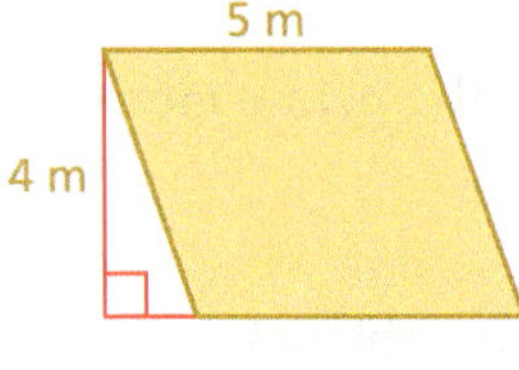

27. **OPEN-ENDED** Your deck has an area of 128 square feet. After adding a section, the area will be $(s^2 + 128)$ square feet. Draw a diagram of how this can happen.

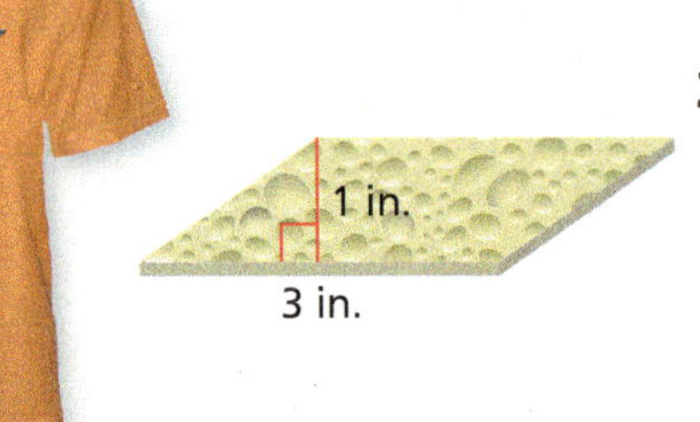

28. **MODELING REAL LIFE** You use the parallelogram-shaped sponge to create the T-shirt design. The area of the design is 66 square inches. How many times do you use the sponge to create the design? Draw a diagram to support your answer.

FINDING A MISSING DIMENSION **Find the missing dimension of the parallelogram described.**

29. $b = 6$ ft, $h =$ ☐ ft, $A = 54\text{ ft}^2$

30. $b =$ ☐ cm, $h = 2.5$ cm, $A = 16\text{ cm}^2$

31. $b = (x + 4)$ yd, $h =$ ☐ yd, $A = (5x + 20)\text{ yd}^2$

32. **DIG DEEPER!** The staircase has three identical parallelogram-shaped panels. The horizontal distance between each panel is 4.25 inches. The area of each panel is 287 square inches. What is the value of x?

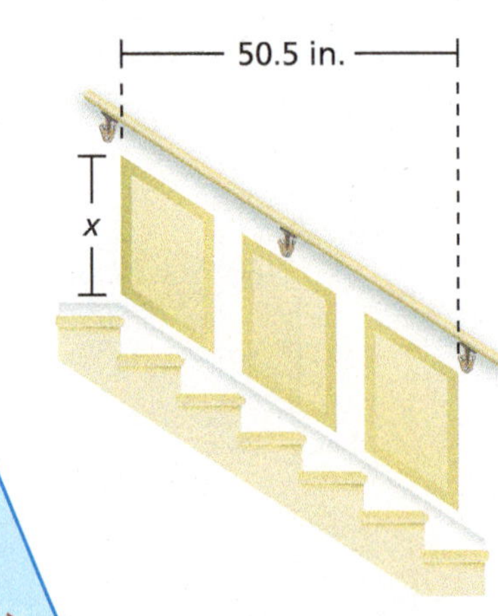

33. **LOGIC** Each dimension of a parallelogram is multiplied by a positive number n. Write an expression for the area of the new parallelogram.

34. **CRITICAL THINKING** Rearrange the rhombus shown to write a formula for the area of a rhombus in terms of its diagonals.

Common Errors

- **Exercises 24–26** Students may find the area using the given units instead of converting to the specified units. Remind students to read the problem carefully to determine what is being asked.

Mini-Assessment

Find the area of the parallelogram.

1. 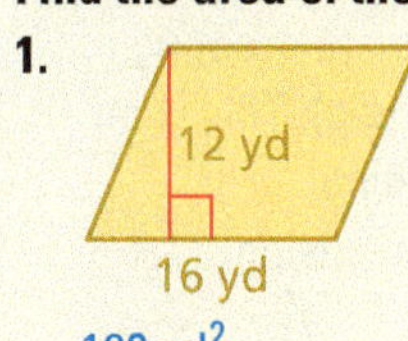

192 yd^2

2. 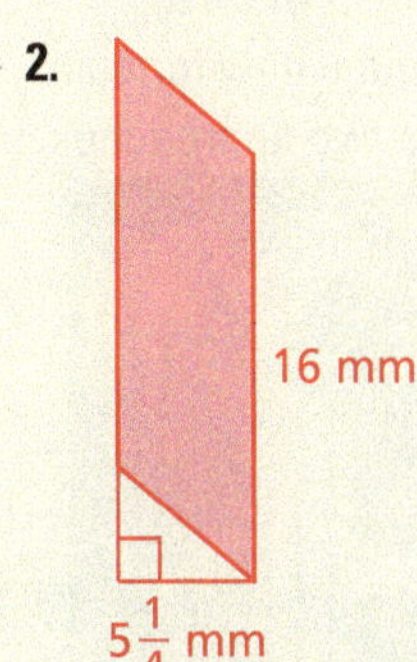

84 mm^2

3. Find the height of the parallelogram.
Area = 300 $in.^2$

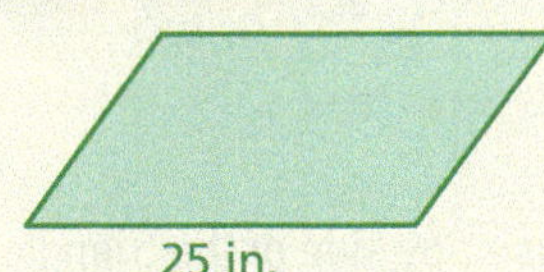

12 in.

4. A window in the shape of a parallelogram has a base of 4.5 feet and a height of 3 feet. What is the area of the window? 13.5 ft^2

Section Resources

Surface Level	Deep Level
Resources by Chapter • Extra Practice • Reteach • Puzzle Time Student Journal • Self-Assessment • Practice Differentiating the Lesson Tutorial Videos Skills Review Handbook Skills Trainer	Resources by Chapter • Enrichment and Extension Graphic Organizers Dynamic Assessment System • Section Practice

Concepts, Skills, & Problem Solving

22. no; $A = 8(13) = 104$ m^2
23. 6 $in.^2$
24. 480,000
25. 0.64
26. 215.17 or 222.22
27. *Sample answer:*

8 ft	128 sq ft	s^2
	16 ft	8 ft

28. 22

29. 9
30. 6.4
31. 5
32. 20.5 in.
33. n^2bh or n^2A
34. $A = \frac{1}{2}ab$, where a and b are the diagonal lengths

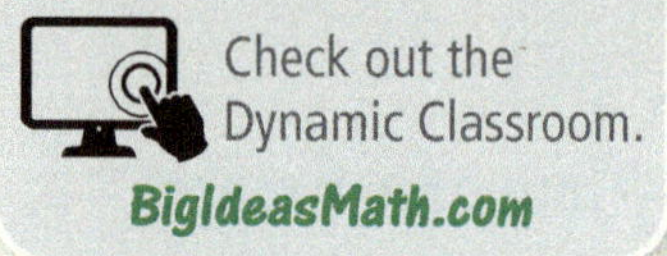

Laurie's Notes

STATE STANDARDS
6.EE.A.2c, 6.G.A.1

Learning Target

Find areas and missing dimensions of triangles, and find areas of composite figures.

Success Criteria

- Explain how the area of a parallelogram is used to find the area of a triangle.
- Use the base and the height of a triangle to find its area.
- Use the area of a triangle and one of its dimensions to find the other dimension.
- Use decomposition to find the area of a figure.

Warm Up

Cumulative, vocabulary, and prerequisite skills practice opportunities are available in the *Resources by Chapter* or at *BigIdeasMath.com.*

ELL Support

Build on the study of word parts by discussing the words *composition* and *decomposition*. Students may be familiar with *composition* from a language arts class. Explain that a *composition* is a creation that does not only include writing. It may also refer to a piece of music. Its parts, *com–* and *–position*, mean "to put together" and come from the Latin language. The prefix *de–* reverses the action, so *decomposition* means "to take apart." In this lesson, students will "take apart" a figure to find its area.

Exploration 1

a. Divide the area of the parallelogram by 2.

b. 20 cm^2; $\frac{1}{2}bh$

c. Check students' work.

d–e. See Additional Answers.

Preparing to Teach

- Grid paper, parallelograms, and rectangles provide the foundation for this exploration: deriving the area formula of a triangle. Students are creating a mental file of formulas, based on the same polygon (rectangle). This is an important building block of achieving conceptual understanding.
- Students' equation-solving skills will continue to be useful in solving area problems.
- **MP3 Construct Viable Arguments and Critique the Reasoning of Others:** Deductive reasoning is again used to make a conjecture about a new formula, the area of a triangle. Students should be able to analyze the two approaches used to derive the formula for the area of a triangle.

Motivate

- The Flatiron (or Fuller) Building in New York City was built in 1902 on a triangular block formed by Fifth Avenue, Broadway, and East 22nd Street.
- ? "Why do you think it is called the Flatiron Building?" *Sample answer:* Its shape is similar to a flatiron (for pressing clothes).
- ? "If you had an office in this building, where would you want it to be and why?" *Sample answer:* At the most acute angle of the top floor, because it has the best view.

Exploration 1

- Using 1-centimeter grid paper allows students to use any side of the triangle as a base and find its length in centimeters.
- In part (a), students should reason that the area of each triangle is one-half the area of the parallelogram.
- ? In part (b), students may just count the centimeter squares. Although this will result in a valid approximation, you want them to be more precise. Ask, "How can you use what you did in part (a) to find the area?" Students should work backwards to make another copy of the triangle and then put them together to make a parallelogram. Use similar questioning to help guide them in part (c).
- **Common Error:** In parts (b) and (c), students may arrange their triangles with the bases together. The labels for the base and height have no meaning for this quadrilateral. Students need to arrange the triangles so that the base of the triangle is also the base of the quadrilateral. Suggest that students color-code each side of the triangle before cutting to avoid the wrong arrangement.

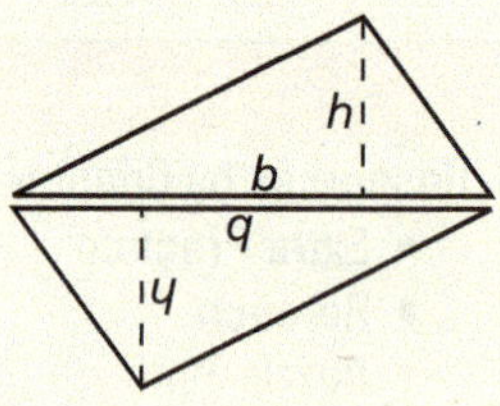

- In parts (c)–(e), you want students to see that the base and height of the triangle are the base and height of the parallelogram, regardless of which side they call the base. Small differences in areas may be due to measuring.
- In part (e), draw dashed segments to represent the parallelogram that the triangle comes from. This helps solidify the deductive reasoning.
- ◉ Achieving success with the first success criterion is dependent on this exploration.

7.2 Areas of Triangles

Learning Target: Find areas and missing dimensions of triangles, and find areas of composite figures.

Success Criteria:
- I can explain how the area of a parallelogram is used to find the area of a triangle.
- I can use the base and the height of a triangle to find its area.
- I can use the area of a triangle and one of its dimensions to find the other dimension.
- I can use decomposition to find the area of a figure.

EXPLORATION 1 Deriving the Area Formula of a Triangle

Work with a partner.

a. Draw *any* parallelogram on a piece of centimeter grid paper. Cut the parallelogram into two identical triangles. How can you use the area of the parallelogram to find the area of each triangle?

b. Copy the triangle below on a piece of centimeter grid paper. Find the area of the triangle. Explain how you found the area.

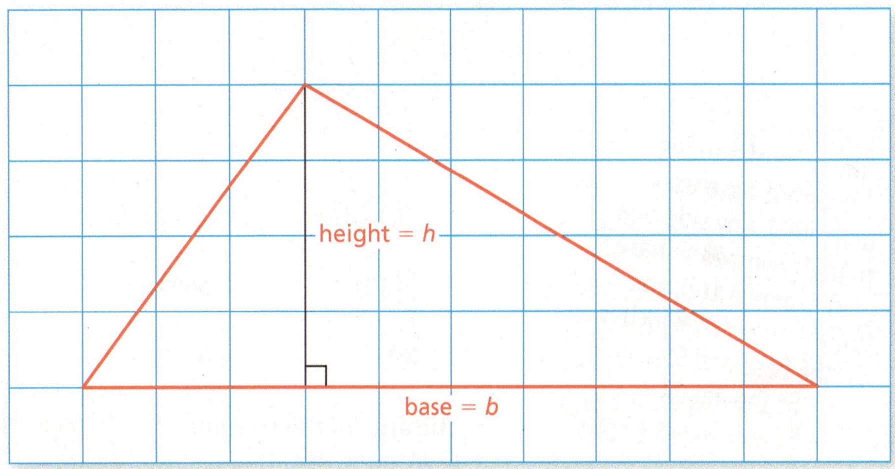

c. Draw *any* acute triangle on a piece of centimeter grid paper and find its area. Repeat this process for a right triangle and an obtuse triangle.

d. Do the areas change in part (c) when you use different sides as the base? Explain your reasoning.

e. Use your results to write a formula for the area A of a triangle. Use the formula to find the area of the triangle shown.

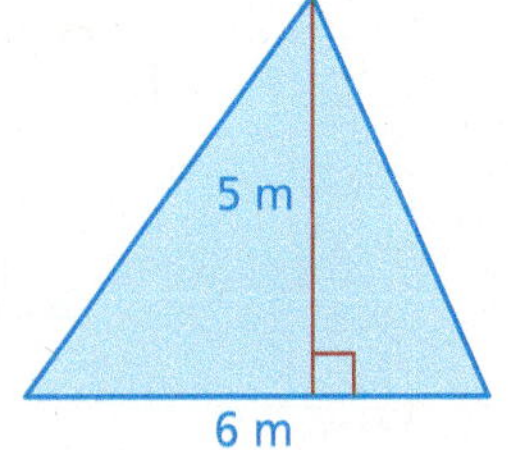

Math Practice

Calculate Accurately

If you use the base and the height to calculate the area in part (d), how can you estimate the dimensions so that your calculations are accurate?

7.2 Lesson

Key Vocabulary
composite figure, *p. 294*

Key Idea

Area of a Triangle

Words The area A of a triangle is one-half the product of its base b and its height h.

Algebra $A = \frac{1}{2}bh$

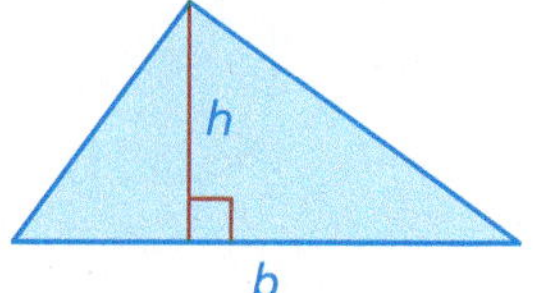

EXAMPLE 1 Finding Areas of Triangles

Find the area of each triangle.

a.

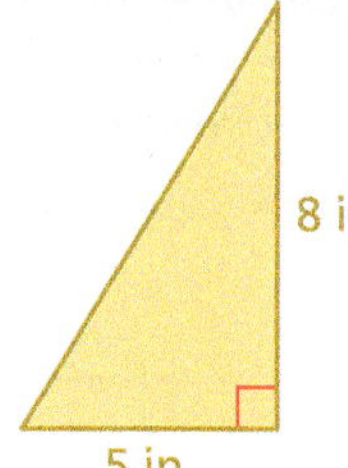

$A = \frac{1}{2}bh$ Write formula.

$= \frac{1}{2}(5)(8)$ Substitute values.

$= \frac{1}{2}(40)$ Multiply.

$= 20$ Multiply.

The area of the triangle is 20 square inches.

b.

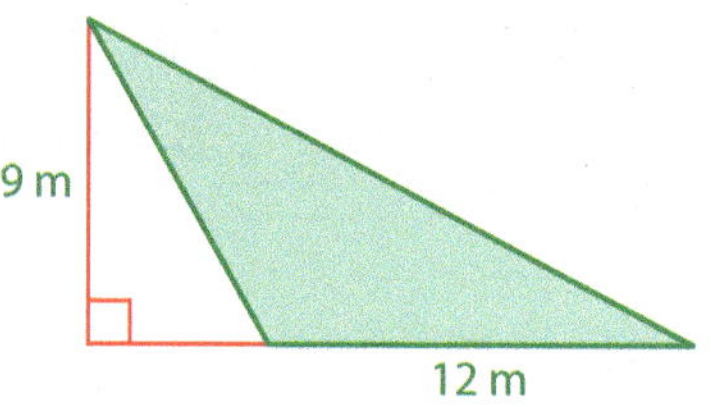

$A = \frac{1}{2}bh$

$= \frac{1}{2}(12)(9)$

$= 6(9)$

$= 54$

The area of the triangle is 54 square meters.

The base of a triangle does not have to be horizontal. Any side of a triangle can be the base. In Example 1(a), you could have used 8 inches as the base and 5 inches as the height.

Try It Find the area of the triangle.

1.

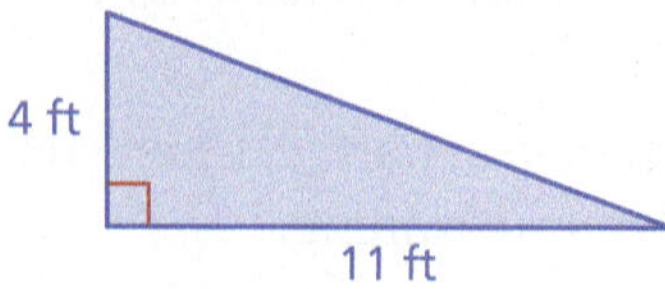

2.

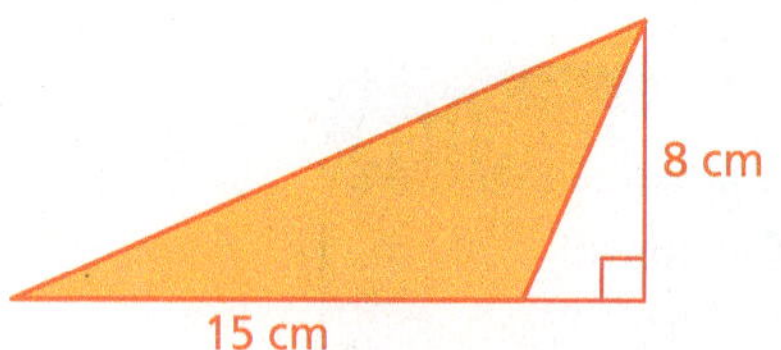

3.

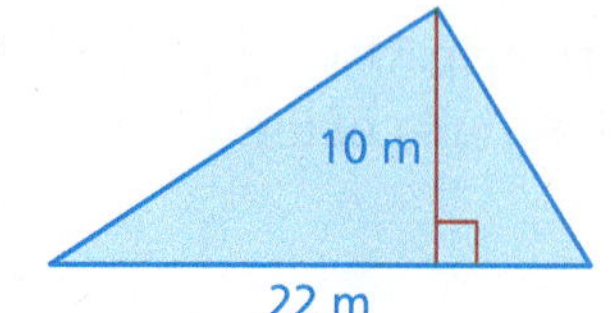

4.

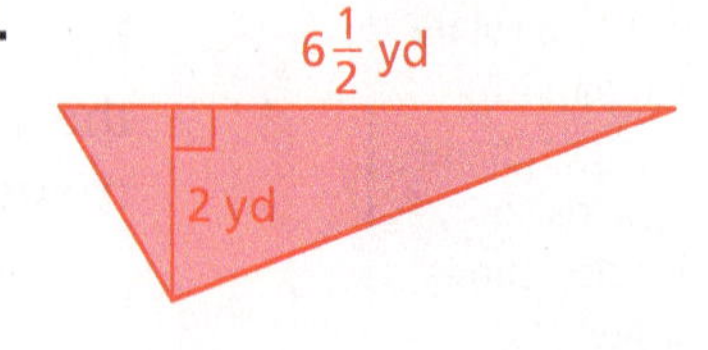

Multi-Language Glossary at BigIdeasMath.com

Laurie's Notes

Scaffolding Instruction

- Although the focus of this section is finding the area of a triangle, algebraic properties are essential to solving the problems. Students will not only use properties of equality, but also the Commutative and Associative Properties.
- **Emerging:** Students still depend on cutting out the triangle or drawing the missing piece of the parallelogram. They may also lack confidence in setting up an equation to solve for an unknown. Students will benefit from guided instruction for Examples 1 and 2.
- **Proficient:** Students understand the derivation of the formula for the area of a triangle and can use the formula to find unknown dimensions. After reviewing the Key Idea, students may proceed to the Self-Assessment for Concepts & Skills exercises.

Key Idea

- The *base* of a triangle can be any of its sides.
- The *height* of a triangle is the perpendicular distance from a base to the opposite vertex.
- **FYI:** The formula $A = \frac{1}{2}bh$ is sometimes written as $A = \frac{bh}{2}$. Students may make computational mistakes due to the fraction in the formula.

EXAMPLE 1

- The idea of dividing by 2 as another way of taking $\frac{1}{2}$ of a number makes sense to students. For example: $\frac{1}{2}$ of 10 is the same as $10 \div 2$.
- **Common Error:** In part (a), students may want to take $\frac{1}{2}$ of 5 and $\frac{1}{2}$ of 8, because they think it is the Distributive Property.
- Note the different strategies shown in the third steps. In part (a), the product of 5 and 8 was found (Associative Property), and then $\frac{1}{2}$ of that product was computed. In part (b), the product of $\frac{1}{2}$ and 12 was found, and then that product was multiplied by 9.
- **Check:** For each part, you can draw dashed segments to represent the parallelogram that the triangle comes from, find its area, and verify that one-half the parallelogram's area is the same as the triangle's area.

◉ Students are working on the second success criterion.

Try It

- Exercise 2 is similar to Example 1(b). Remind students that the red segment is *not* a side of the triangle, just information to understand the height.
- In Exercise 4, remind students that the height is drawn perpendicular to the base of the triangle. Upside down is okay!

Scaffold instruction to support all students in their learning. Learning is individualized and you may want to group students differently as they move in and out of these levels with each skill and concept. Student self-assessment and feedback help guide your instructional decisions about how and when to layer support for all students to become proficient learners.

Extra Example 1

Find the area of each triangle.

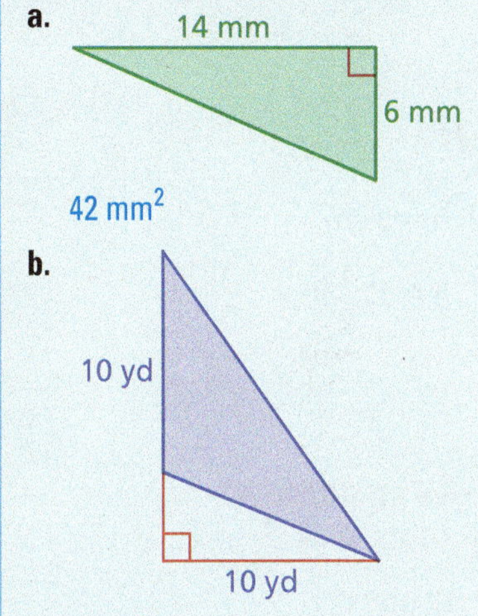

a. 42 mm^2

b. 50 yd^2

ELL Support

Have students practice language by working in groups to complete Try It Exercises 1–4. Expect students to perform as follows.

Beginner: Write the steps.

Intermediate: State the formula with the substituted values and the area. For example, "One-half times eleven times four equals twenty-two. The area is twenty-two square feet."

Advanced: Describe the process.

Try It

1. 22 ft^2
2. 60 cm^2
3. 110 m^2
4. $6\frac{1}{2} \text{ yd}^2$

Extra Example 2

Find the height of the triangle.

Area = 24 in.^{2}

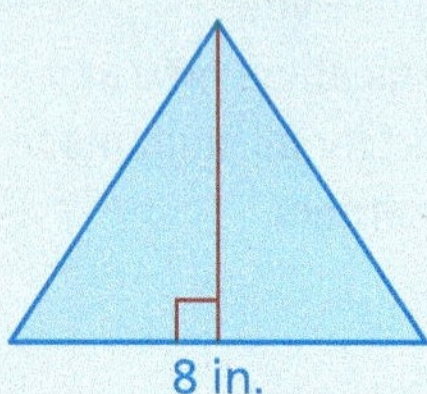

6 in.

Try It

5. $b = 8$ cm
6. $h = 17\frac{1}{2}$ ft

Self-Assessment for Concepts & Skills

7. 12 units^2
8. *Sample answer:* A triangle has one-half the area of a parallelogram with the same base b and height h.
9. $b = 10$ mm
10. $h = 3$ mi

Laurie's Notes

EXAMPLE 2

- In this example, students will use the area of a triangle to find an unknown dimension of the triangle.
- Solving for a variable that is not alone on one side of the formula is the next step in the gradual development of solving any triangle area problem.
- This is an opportunity to solidify lessons from Chapters 5 and 6 by using algebraic properties to simplify and solve an equation.
- After substituting 56 and 12, ask "Why can $\frac{1}{2}b(12)$ be written as $6b$?" The Commutative Property of Multiplication allows you to multiply $\frac{1}{2}$ and 12.
- Encourage students to justify their work.
- **MP7 Look for and Make Use of Structure:** In working with area formulas, mathematically proficient students will apply algebraic properties to solve problems.

Try It

- Have students work on the exercises independently and then share with a partner. They should explain their methods, listen to questions or comments, and revise their work if needed.

Self-Assessment for Concepts & Skills

- These exercises assess the first three success criteria.
- In Exercise 7, students need to distinguish the base from the other sides of the triangle. They should understand that any side can be a base as long as the height is drawn to it.
- Listen to students' explanations for Exercise 8. You want students to "see" a triangle as one-half of a parallelogram, so they understand that the area of a triangle is one-half the product of its base and its height. Their conceptual understanding is evident if they are composing a parallelogram and then decomposing it to consider the triangle.

ELL Support

Allow students to work in pairs. Monitor discussion of Exercise 8. Check comprehension by having each pair display their answers for Exercises 7, 9, and 10 on a whiteboard for your review.

The Success Criteria Self-Assessment chart can be found in the *Student Journal* or online at *BigIdeasMath.com.*

EXAMPLE 2 Finding a Missing Dimension

Find the base of the triangle.

Use the formula for the area of a triangle. Substitute for the area and the height, then solve for the base.

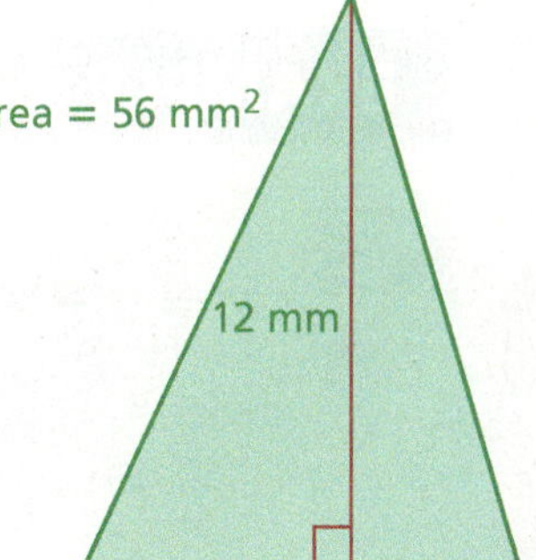

$A = \frac{1}{2}bh$	Write formula for area of a triangle.
$56 = \frac{1}{2}b(12)$	Substitute 56 for A and 12 for h.
$56 = 6b$	Simplify.
$\frac{56}{6} = \frac{6b}{6}$	Division Property of Equality
$9\frac{1}{3} = b$	Simplify.

So, the base is $9\frac{1}{3}$ millimeters.

Math Practice

Construct Arguments

Write an argument that explains why $\frac{1}{2}b(12)$ and $6b$ are equivalent expressions.

Try It **Find the missing dimension of the triangle.**

5. 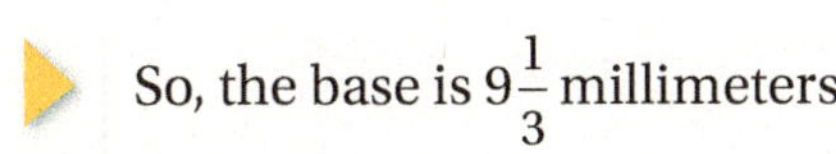
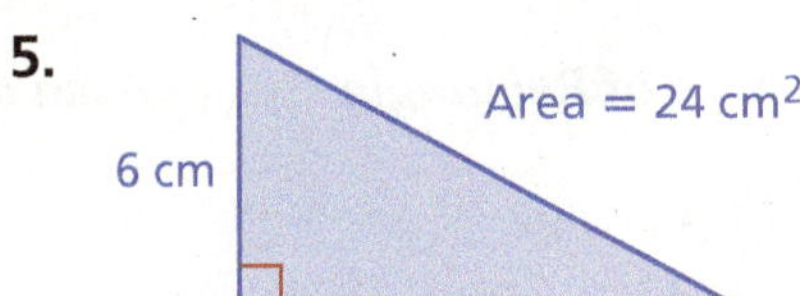

6. 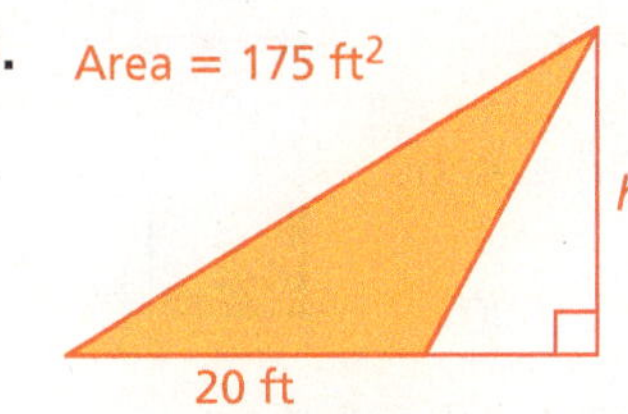

Self-Assessment for Concepts & Skills

Solve each exercise. Then rate your understanding of the success criteria in your journal.

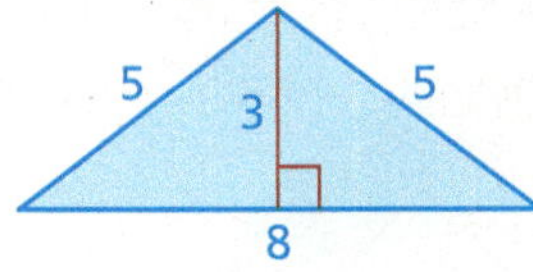

7. **FINDING AREA** Find the area of the triangle at the left.

8. **WRITING** Explain how to use the area of a parallelogram to find the area of a triangle.

FINDING A MISSING DIMENSION **Find the missing dimension of the triangle.**

9. 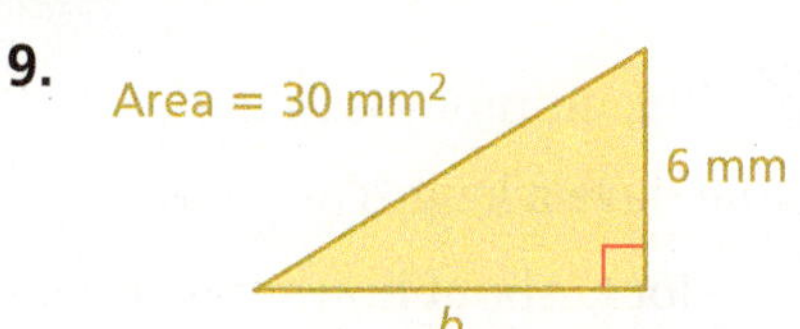

10. 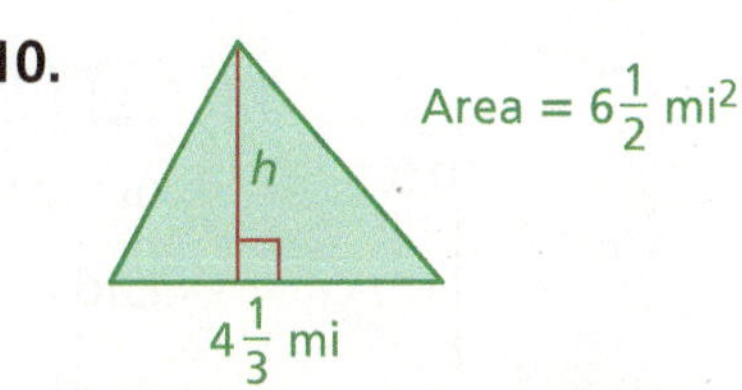

A **composite figure** is made up of triangles, squares, rectangles, and other two-dimensional figures. To find the area of a composite figure, separate it into figures with areas you know how to find. This is called *decomposition.*

EXAMPLE 3 Modeling Real Life

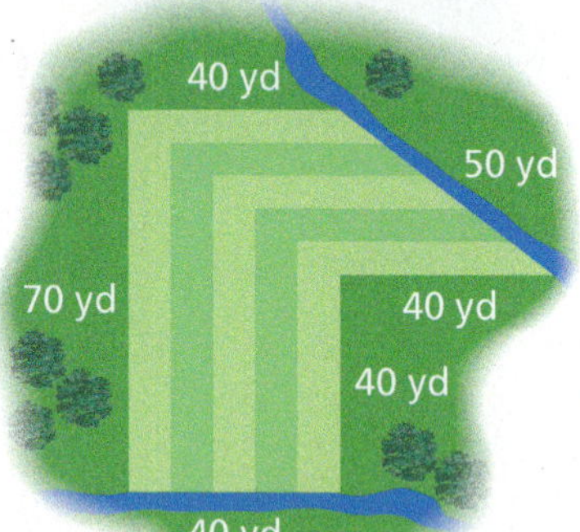

Find the area of the fairway between two streams on a golf course.

There are several ways to separate the fairway into figures with areas you can find using formulas. It appears that one way is to separate the fairway into a rectangle and a right triangle.

Identify each shape and find any missing dimensions. Then find the area of each shape.

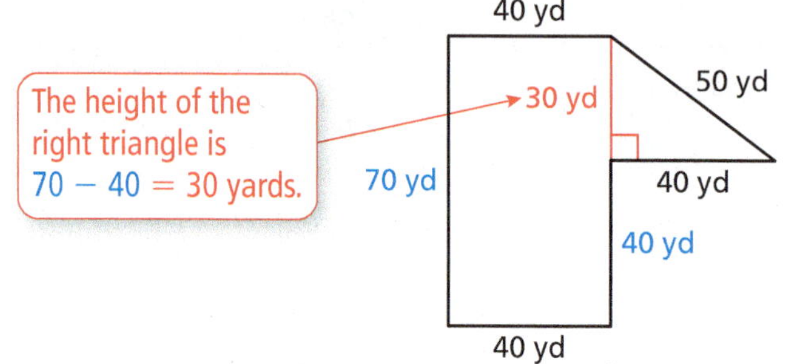

Another Method It appears that you can separate the fairway into a parallelogram, a triangle, and a square.

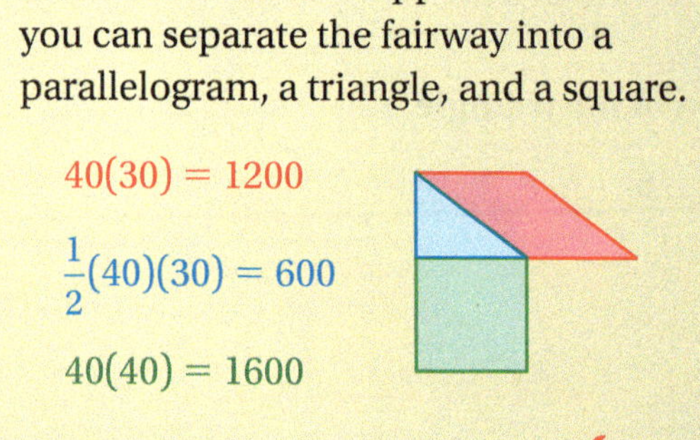

$40(30) = 1200$

$\frac{1}{2}(40)(30) = 600$

$40(40) = 1600$

$1200 + 600 + 1600 = 3400 \text{ yd}^2$ ✓

Area of Rectangle

$$A = \ell w$$
$$= 70(40)$$
$$= 2800$$

Area of Right Triangle

$$A = \frac{1}{2}bh$$
$$= \frac{1}{2}(40)(30)$$
$$= 600$$

So, the area of the fairway is $2800 + 600 = 3400$ square yards.

Self-Assessment for Problem Solving

Solve each exercise. Then rate your understanding of the success criteria in your journal.

11. A wildlife conservation group buys the 9 square miles of land shown. What is the distance from Point A to Point B?

C
3 mi
B
A

12. DIG DEEPER! The chimney is made using bricks that have a length of $\frac{2}{3}$ foot and a width of $\frac{1}{3}$ foot. About how many bricks are used to form the side of the chimney shown? Explain.

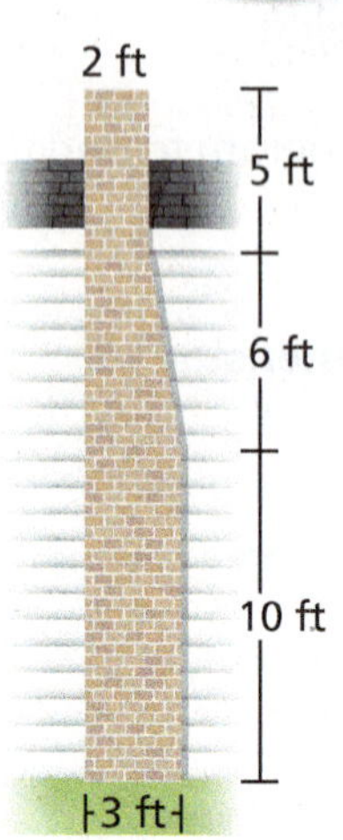

Laurie's Notes

Discuss

- Draw a couple of composite figures on the board and say, "These are examples of composite figures. What do you think a composite figure is?" Listen for a figure that is made up of triangles, squares, rectangles, and other two-dimensional figures. Composite figures do not have to be composed of only polygons.
- Have students read the definition of a **composite figure**.

EXAMPLE 3

- Draw the composite figure shown (the fairway) and label all of the given dimensions.
- Ask students to talk with a partner about different ways the figure can be decomposed. Suggest that their methods need to result in figures in which the dimensions are known or can be found. If a student needs to know the measurement of the side of the triangle, ask how it can be found.
- **MP1 Make Sense of Problems and Persevere in Solving Them:** Instead of modeling the problem for them, have students work through the problem with their partners. Students should have a pathway into the problem so that they can be successful.
- Give students a few minutes to discuss with their partners. Then have students share in groups.
- **Teaching Strategy:** Select students to present their solutions and look for a variety of methods. Then have them evaluate each method and decide which one(s) are most efficient. Refer students to the Another Method note if that strategy does not surface.

Self-Assessment for Problem Solving

- Allow time in class for problem solving, so that students become comfortable with the problem-solving plan. Have students work independently and then compare answers and methods with a group.
- Make sure they use correct units in their answers. Exercise 11 is a linear measurement, but Exercise 12 is an area measurement.
- These exercises address the third and fourth success criteria.

The Success Criteria Self-Assessment chart can be found in the *Student Journal* or *online at BigIdeasMath.com.*

Closure

- Draw a sketch of the Bermuda Triangle and ask students to find the area of this triangular region. about 450,000 mi^2

Teaching Strategy

When students are working alone or with partners on a problem, circulate to view different approaches. Make notes about the order in which you want to call on students, so you can control the sequence of responses. You do not want the first response to be the most polished or efficient. Look for work that clearly demonstrates the outcome(s).

Extra Example 3

Find the area of the swimming pool.

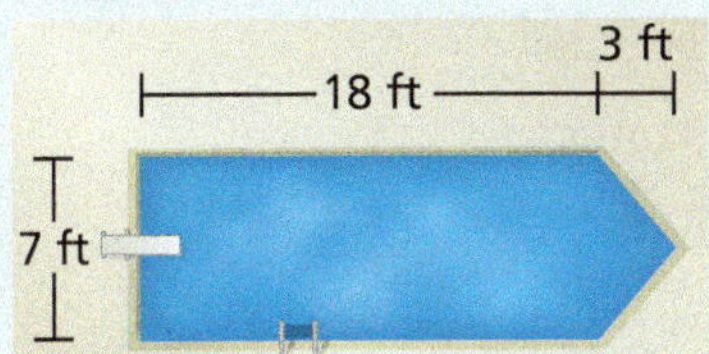

136.5 ft^2

Self-Assessment for Problem Solving

11. 6 mi

12. 247.5; *Sample answer:*

$$2(5+6+10)+1(10)+\frac{1}{2}(6)(1)=55\text{ ft}^2,$$

$$55 \div \left[\left(\frac{2}{3}\right)\left(\frac{1}{3}\right)\right]=247.5$$

Learning Target

Find areas and missing dimensions of triangles, and find areas of composite figures.

Success Criteria

- Explain how the area of a parallelogram is used to find the area of a triangle.
- Use the base and the height of a triangle to find its area.
- Use the area of a triangle and one of its dimensions to find the other dimension.
- Use decomposition to find the area of a figure.

Review & Refresh

1. 72 in.^2
2. 10.5 km^2
3. 255 mi^2
4. Mult. Prop. of One
5. Comm. Prop. of Mult.
6. Assoc. Prop. of Add.
7. C

Concepts, Skills, & Problem Solving

8. $17\frac{1}{2} \text{ units}^2$
9. 14 units^2
10. 9 units^2
11. 6 cm^2
12. 90 mi^2
13. 1620 in.^2
14. 189 mm^2
15. 1125 cm^2
16. 132 m^2

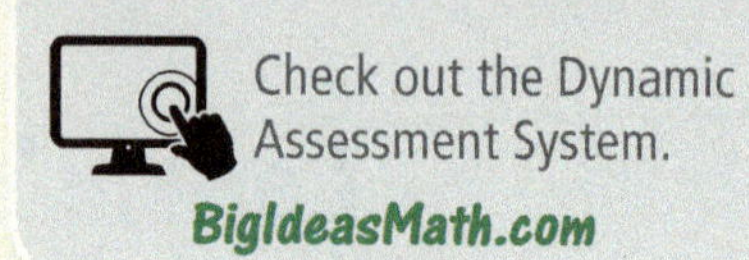

Assignment Guide and Concept Check

Scaffold assignments to support all students in their learning progression. The suggested assignments are a starting point. Continue to assign additional exercises and revisit with spaced practice to move every student toward proficiency.

Level	Assignment 1	Assignment 2
Emerging	3, 6, 7, 8, 11, 12, 13, 20	10, 15, 17, 18, 19, 23, 24, 29
Proficient	3, 6, 7, 9, 11, 14, 15, 21	10, 17, 18, 19, 24, 26, 27, 29
Advanced	3, 6, 7, 10, 14, 15, 16, 22	17, 19, 24, 26, 27, 28, 29

- Assignment 1 is for use after students complete the Self-Assessment for Concepts & Skills.
- Assignment 2 is for use after students complete the Self-Assessment for Problem Solving.
- The red exercises can be used as a concept check.

Review & Refresh Prior Skills

Exercises 1–3 Finding the Area of a Parallelogram
Exercises 4–6 Identifying Properties
Exercise 7 Using Order of Operations

Common Errors

- **Exercises 11–16** Students may multiply the base and the height and forget to multiply by $\frac{1}{2}$. Tell students to write the formula and then identify the value of each variable before substituting.
- **Exercises 11–16** Students may mentally find the area by multiplying one-half the base and one-half the height. The answer will be one-half the value of the correct answer. Remind students that the area is one-half the product of the base and the height.
- **Exercises 12 and 14** Students may be confused by the drawing and labeling of obtuse triangles. Remind students that the height of the triangle is the perpendicular distance from the base to the opposite vertex. For obtuse triangles, the height may be labeled outside of the triangle.

7.2 Practice

Review & Refresh

Find the area of the parallelogram.

1. 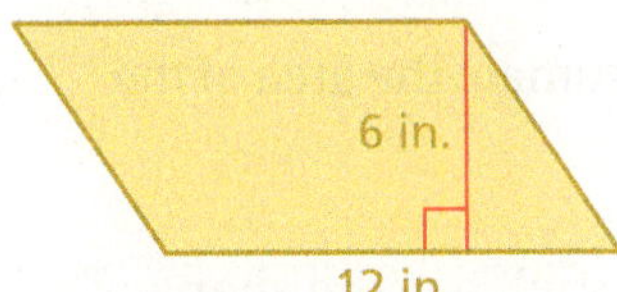

2. 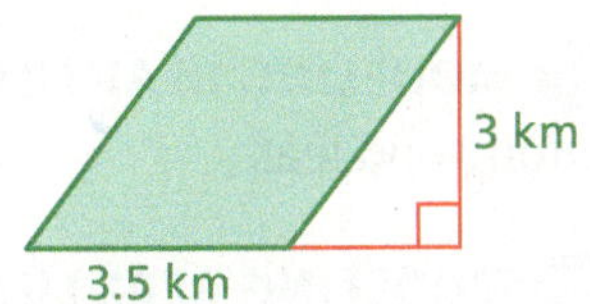

3. 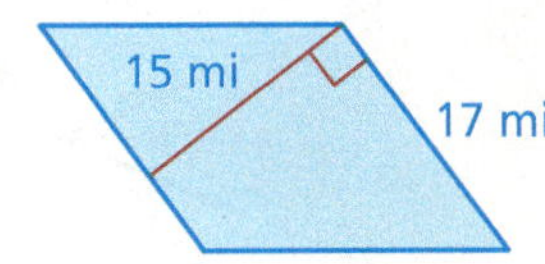

Tell which property the statement illustrates.

4. $n \cdot 1 = n$

5. $4 \cdot m = m \cdot 4$

6. $(x + 2) + 5 = x + (2 + 5)$

7. What is the first step when using order of operations?

A. Multiply and divide from left to right.

B. Add and subtract from left to right.

C. Perform operations in grouping symbols.

D. Evaluate numbers with exponents.

Concepts, Skills, & Problem Solving

MP USING TOOLS **Find the area of the triangle by forming a parallelogram.** (See Exploration 1, p. 291.)

8. 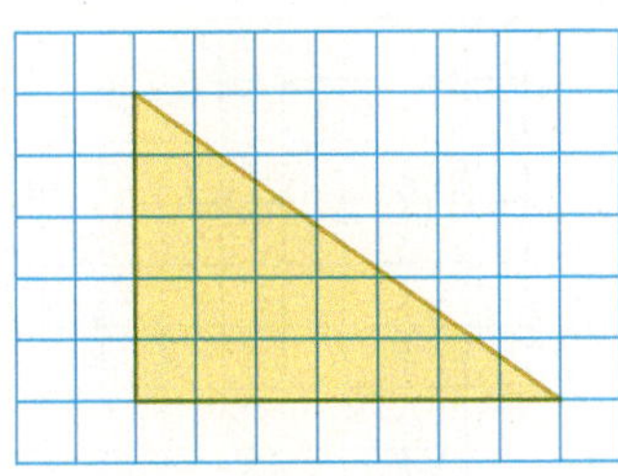

9. 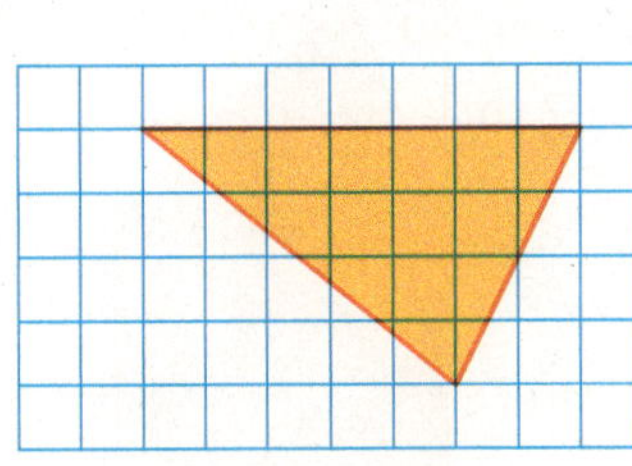

10. 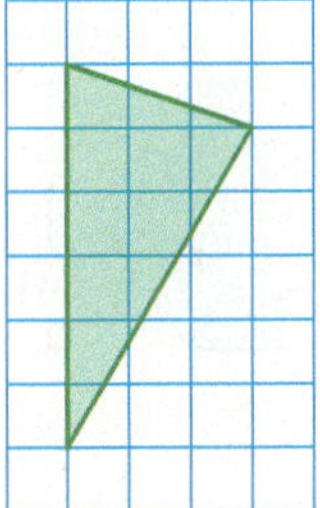

FINDING AREA **Find the area of the triangle.**

11. 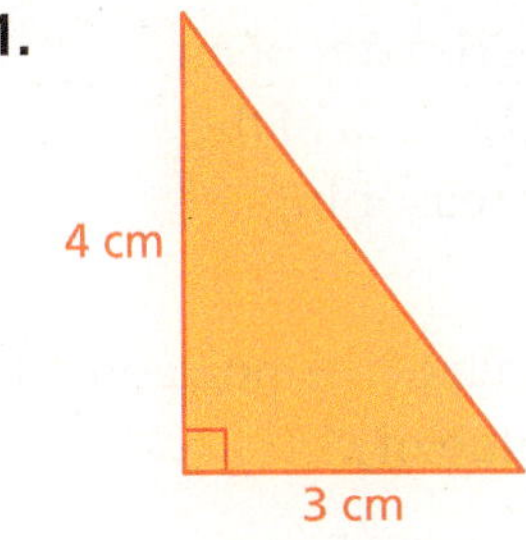

12. 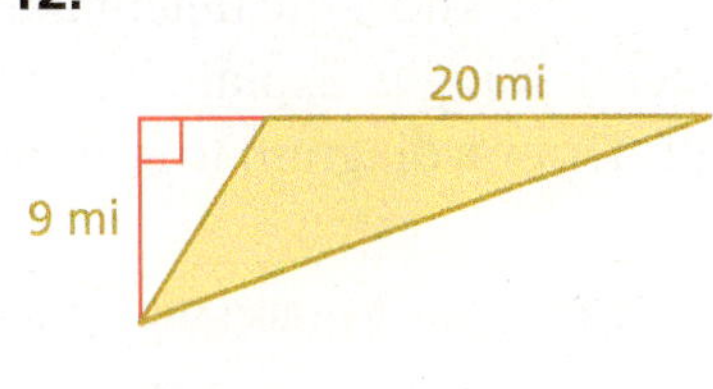

13. 

14. 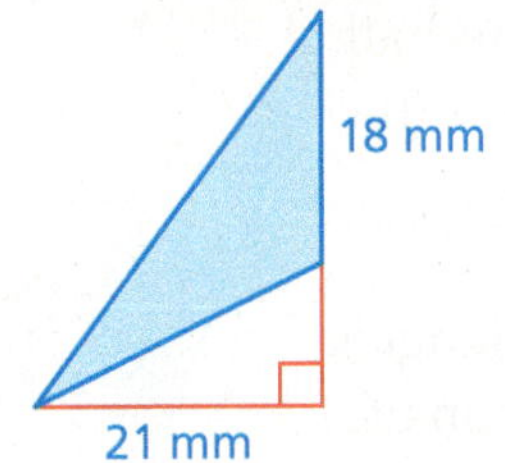

15. 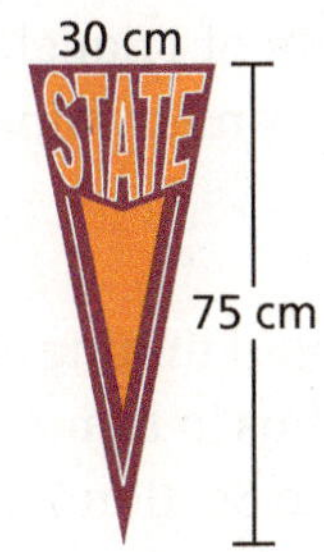

16. 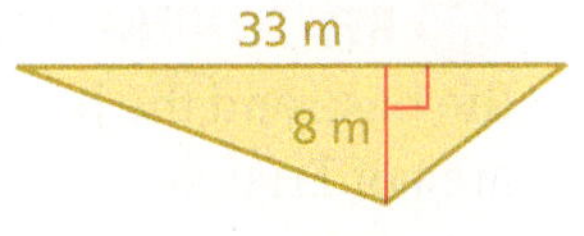

17. **MP YOU BE THE TEACHER** Your friend finds the area of the triangle. Is your friend correct? Explain your reasoning.

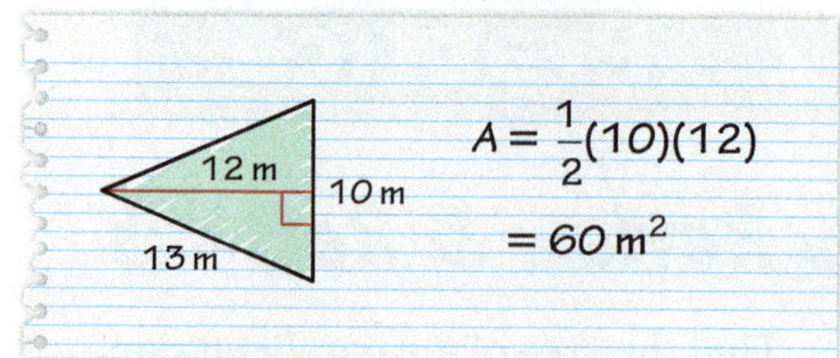

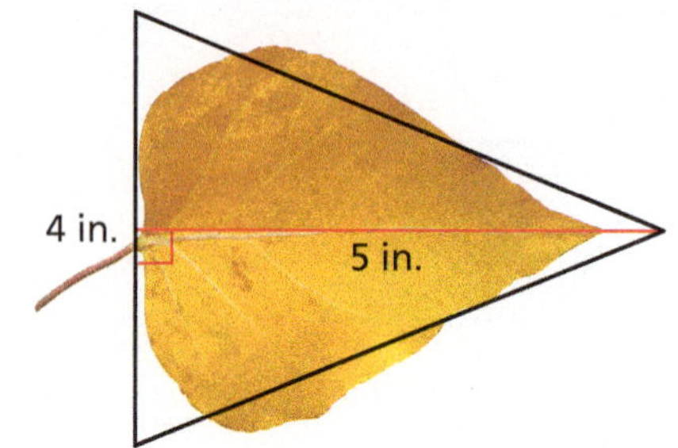

18. **MP MODELING REAL LIFE** Estimate the area of the cottonwood leaf.

19. **MP MODELING REAL LIFE** A shelf has the shape of a triangle. The base of the shelf is 36 centimeters, and the height is 18 centimeters. Find the area of the shelf in square inches.

FINDING A MISSING DIMENSION **Find the missing dimension of the triangle.**

20. 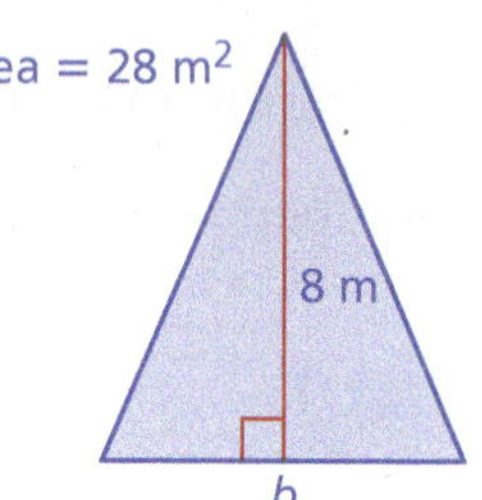

21. 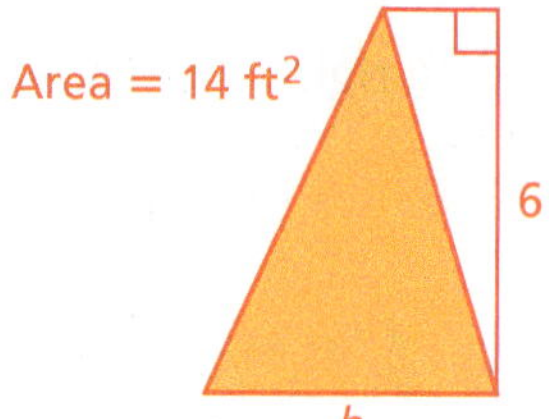

22. 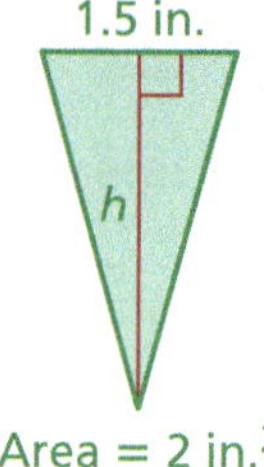

COMPOSITE FIGURES **Find the area of the figure.**

23. 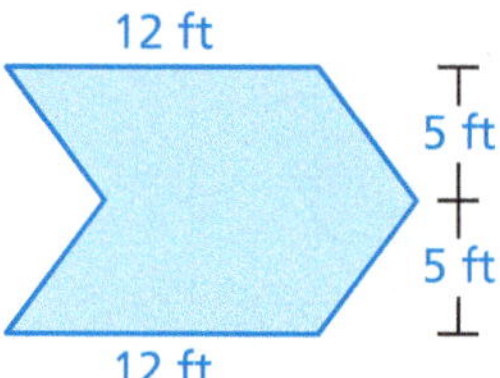

24. 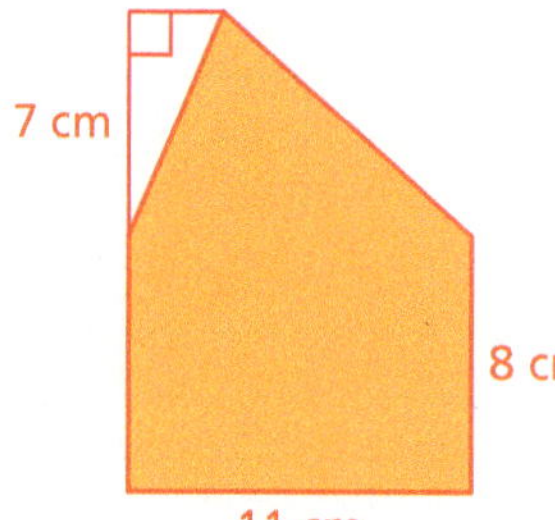

25. 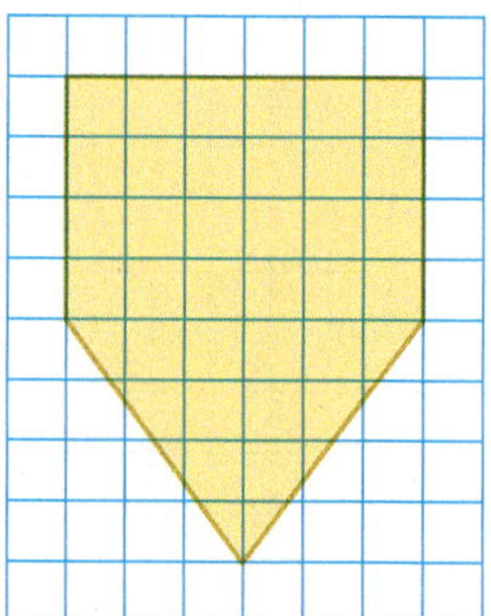

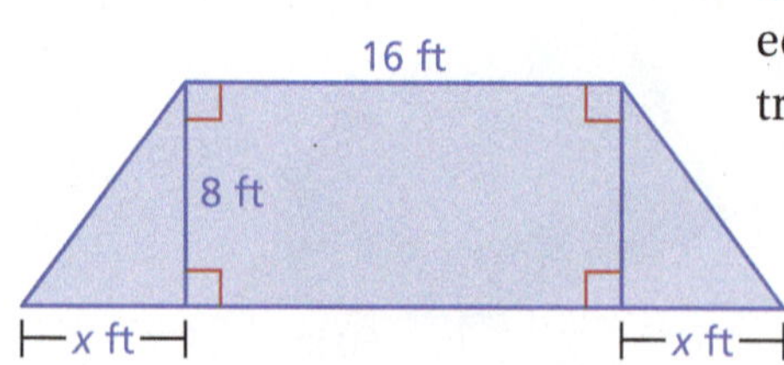

26. **WRITING** You know the height and the perimeter of an equilateral triangle. Explain how to find the area of the triangle. Draw a diagram to support your reasoning.

27. **CRITICAL THINKING** The total area of the polygon is 176 square feet. What is the value of x?

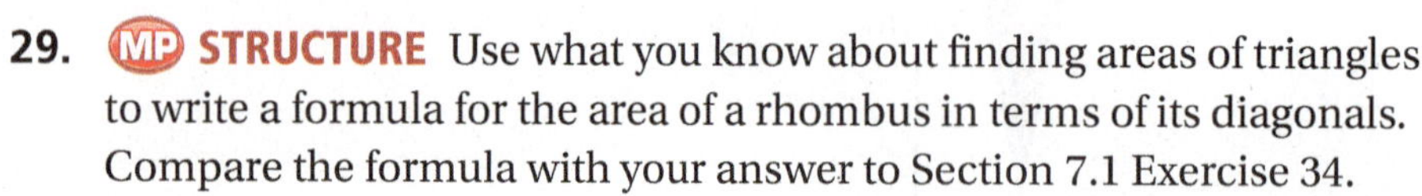

28. **MP REASONING** The base and the height of Triangle A are one-half the base and the height of Triangle B. How many times greater is the area of Triangle B?

29. **MP STRUCTURE** Use what you know about finding areas of triangles to write a formula for the area of a rhombus in terms of its diagonals. Compare the formula with your answer to Section 7.1 Exercise 34.

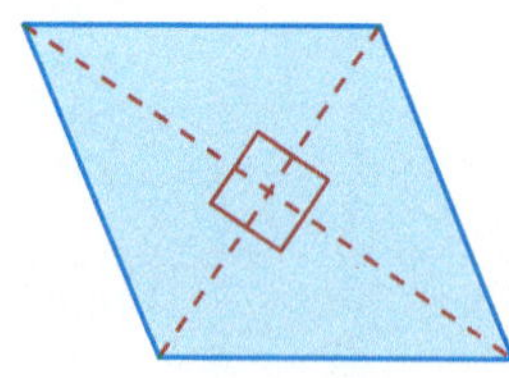

- **Exercises 23–25** Students may forget to include one or more parts of the composite figure or may include a part more than once. Tell them to draw and label each part, find the area of each part, and then add the areas of the parts to find the area of the composite figure.

Mini-Assessment

Find the area of the triangle.

1.

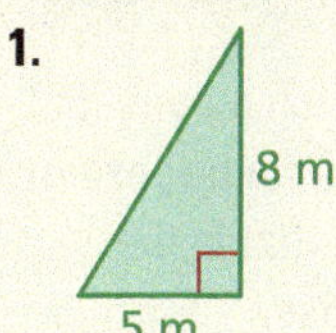

$20 m^2$

2.

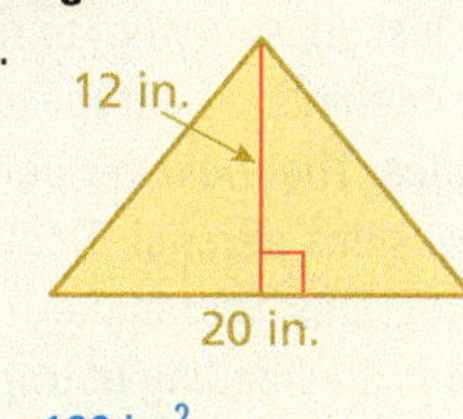

$120 in.^2$

3.

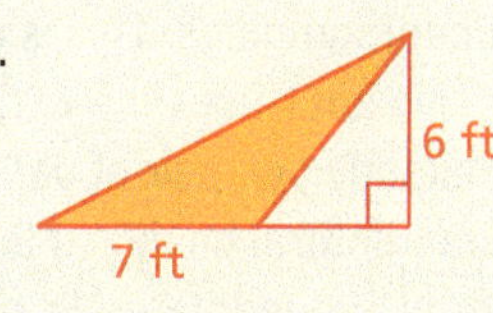

$21 ft^2$

4. Find the missing dimension of the triangle.

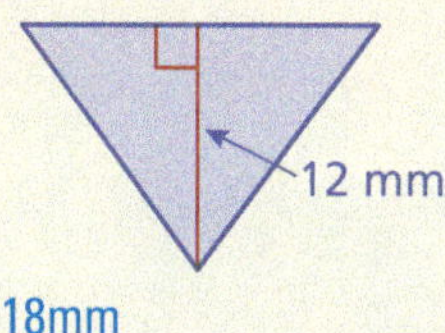

18mm

5. Find the area of the softball field.

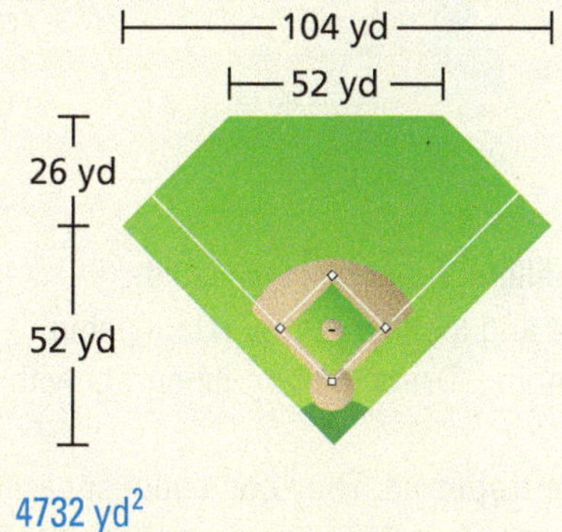

$4732 yd^2$

Section Resources

Surface Level	Deep Level
Resources by Chapter • Extra Practice • Reteach • Puzzle Time Student Journal • Self-Assessment • Practice Differentiating the Lesson Tutorial Videos Skills Review Handbook Skills Trainer	Resources by Chapter • Enrichment and Extension Graphic Organizers Dynamic Assessment System • Section Practice

17. yes; $A = \frac{1}{2}bh$

18. about $10 in.^2$

19. about $50.2 in.^2$

20. $b = 7$ m

21. $b = 4\frac{2}{3}$ ft

22. $h = 2\frac{2}{3}$ in.

23. $120 ft^2$

24. $126\frac{1}{2} cm^2$

25. $36 units^2$

26. Find the length of the base by dividing the perimeter by 3. Then multiply one-half of the base by the height.

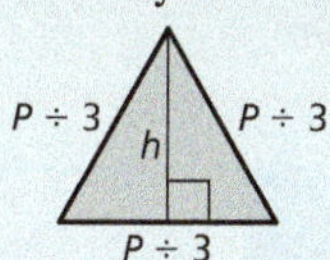

27. 6

28. 4

29. $A = \frac{1}{2}ab$, where a and b are the diagonal lengths; *Sample answer:* The formula is the same.

Learning Target

Find areas of trapezoids, kites, and composite figures.

Success Criteria

- Explain how the area of a parallelogram is used to find the area of a trapezoid.
- Decompose trapezoids and kites into smaller shapes.
- Use decomposition to find the area of a figure.
- Use the bases and the height of a trapezoid to find its area.

Warm Up

Cumulative, vocabulary, and prerequisite skills practice opportunities are available in the *Resources by Chapter* or at *BigIdeasMath.com.*

ELL Support

Write *tra/pez/oid* with the separations shown and display a trapezoid. Explain the meaning of each part: *tra–* means "four," *–pez–* means "foot," and *–oid* means "shaped." In math, a trapezoid is a shape with four vertices (feet) with exactly one pair of parallel sides. In English, the word part *ped* (from *pez*) means "foot" in words like *pedicure* and *centipede.* Point out that the traditional shape of a kite is the shape described by the word *kite* in math.

Exploration 1

a. Divide the area of the parallelogram by 2.

b. 26 cm^2; *Sample answer:* Find one-half the area of the parallelogram with a base of 10 units and a height of 4 units.

c. Check students' work.

d. $A = \frac{1}{2}h(b_1 + b_2)$; 20 m^2

Laurie's Notes

COMMON CORE **STATE STANDARDS**
6.EE.A.2c, 6.G.A.1

Preparing to Teach

- In this lesson, students will use prior learning about quadrilaterals and their attributes. They will once again use 1-centimeter grid paper as a tool to form new understandings. This is a long lesson, so try not to rush.
- **Note:** This book uses the *exclusive* definition of a trapezoid, which means that it has exactly one pair of parallel sides. The *inclusive* definition of a trapezoid is a quadrilateral having at least two sides parallel. This means that in the hierarchy of quadrilaterals, parallelograms, rectangles, rhombuses (or rhombi), and squares all fall under the heading of trapezoids.
- Deductive reasoning is used to make a conjecture about a new formula, the area of a trapezoid. Students will build an argument for deriving the formula.

Motivate

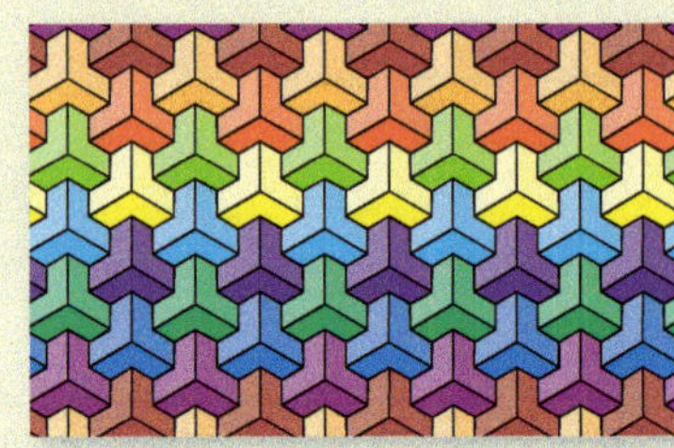

- Display this common optical design. Identify the concave hexagons that fit together to make this tessellation.
- ? "Can you draw a segment to decompose each hexagon into two congruent quadrilaterals?" yes "What type of quadrilateral will you have?" trapezoid

- Explain that students will explore the area of a trapezoid.

Exploration 1

- Part (a) makes a connection between parallelograms and trapezoids. Students will begin with a known concept and look for a new relationship. Have students share their work and reasoning. Draw the parallelogram with dashed lines that the trapezoid is half of.
- ? In part (b), all students start with the same trapezoid. They can count squares to approximate the area, but you want them to find the exact area. Ask, "How can you use what you learned in part (a) to find the area?"
- **Teaching Strategy:** Now that students see the connection to a parallelogram, they are asked to make their own trapezoids in part (c) and find its exact area.
- ? "Will the method you used in part (b) work for all trapezoids?" Have students share their trapezoids and methods for finding the areas from part (c). There are several ways to find the area, so some students may have been creative.
- In part (d), have students label the height with h and the bases with b_1 and b_2. Are they able to articulate a formula that works for all trapezoids?
- After students write a formula, they should apply it to the trapezoid shown.
- Refer to the Math Practice note for another way to decompose a trapezoid.
- Students can also decompose a trapezoid by cutting it from the midpoint of a nonparallel side to the midpoint of the opposite nonparallel side. Rotate one part 180° about a shared vertex, to form a parallelogram in which the base is the sum of the two trapezoid bases and the height is half the trapezoid height.

7.3 Areas of Trapezoids and Kites

Learning Target: Find areas of trapezoids, kites, and composite figures.

Success Criteria:
- I can explain how the area of a parallelogram is used to find the area of a trapezoid.
- I can decompose trapezoids and kites into smaller shapes.
- I can use decomposition to find the area of a figure.
- I can use the bases and the height of a trapezoid to find its area.

EXPLORATION 1 Deriving the Area Formula of a Trapezoid

Work with a partner.

a. Draw *any* parallelogram on a piece of centimeter grid paper. Cut the parallelogram into two identical trapezoids. How can you use the area of the parallelogram to find the area of each trapezoid?

b. Copy the trapezoid below on a piece of centimeter grid paper. Find the area of the trapezoid. Explain how you found the area.

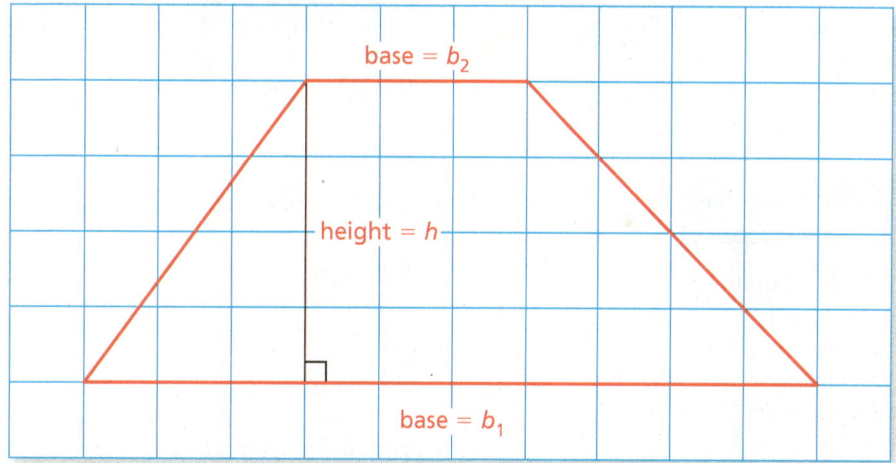

c. Draw *any* trapezoid on a piece of centimeter grid paper and find its area.

d. Use your results to write a formula for the area A of a trapezoid. Use the formula to find the area of the trapezoid shown.

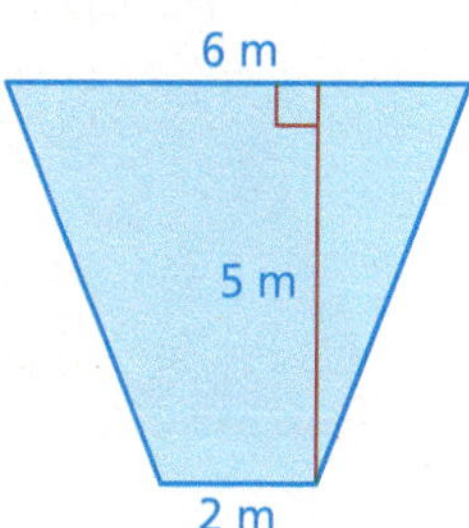

Math Practice

Make a Plan

How can you use the diagram below to justify the formula you wrote in part (d)?

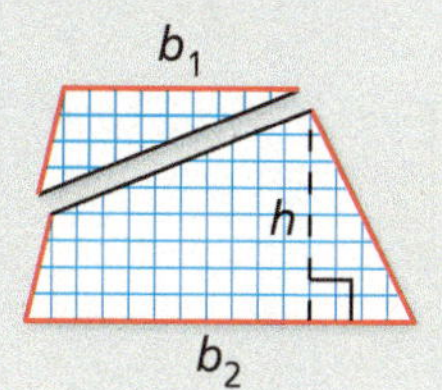

7.3 Lesson

Key Vocabulary
kite, *p. 298*

You can use decomposition to find areas of trapezoids and *kites*. A **kite** is a quadrilateral that has two pairs of adjacent sides with the same length and opposite sides with different lengths.

EXAMPLE 1 Finding Areas of Trapezoids and Kites

Find the area of each figure.

a.

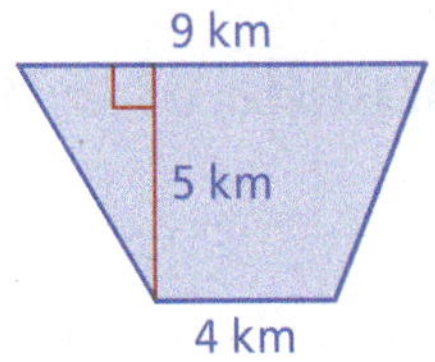

Decompose the trapezoid into a triangle and a rectangle. Find the sum of the areas of the figures.

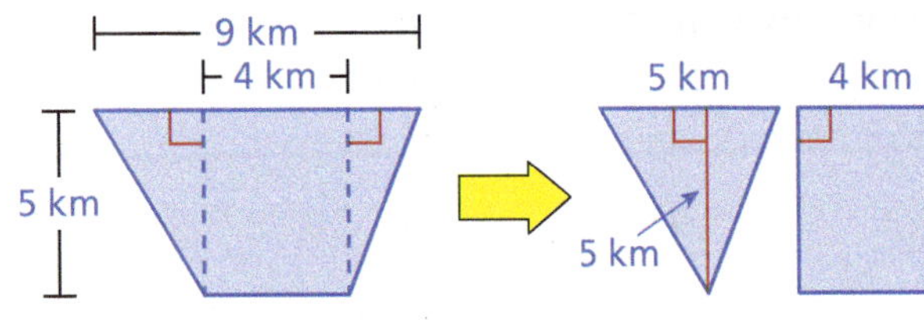

$$A = \frac{1}{2}(5)(5) + 5(4)$$

$$= 12\frac{1}{2} + 20$$

$$= 32\frac{1}{2}$$

The area of the trapezoid is $32\frac{1}{2}$ square kilometers.

b.

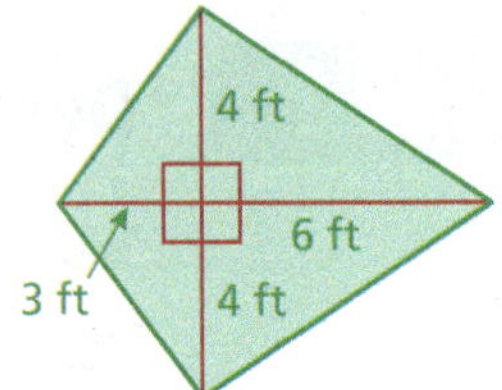

Decompose the kite into two triangles. Find the sum of the areas of the triangles.

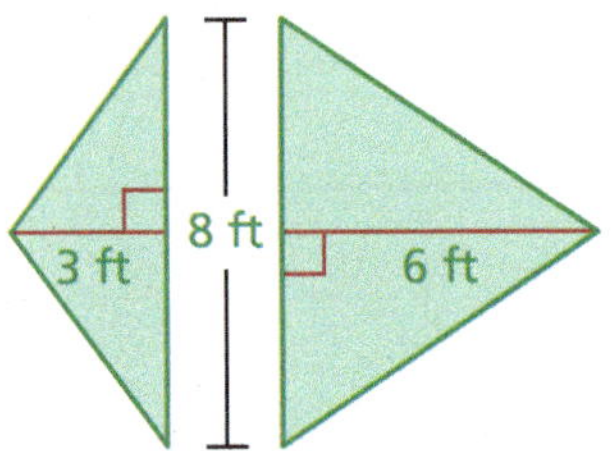

$$A = \frac{1}{2}(8)(3) + \frac{1}{2}(8)(6)$$

$$= 12 + 24$$

$$= 36$$

The area of the kite is 36 square feet.

Math Practice

Look for Structure
Can you find the area of the trapezoid in part (a) using only two triangles? Explain.

Try It **Find the area of the figure.**

1.

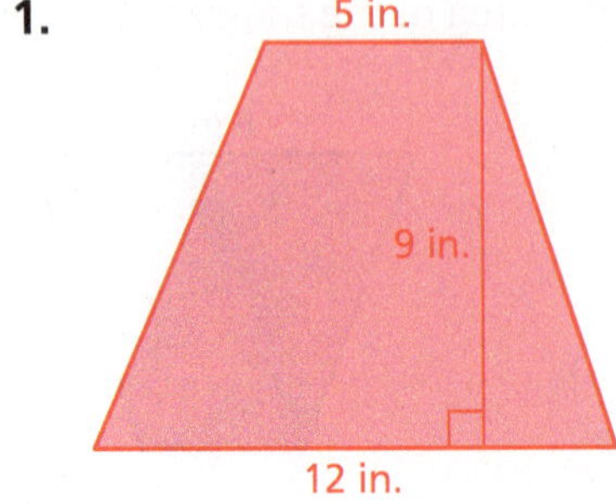

2.

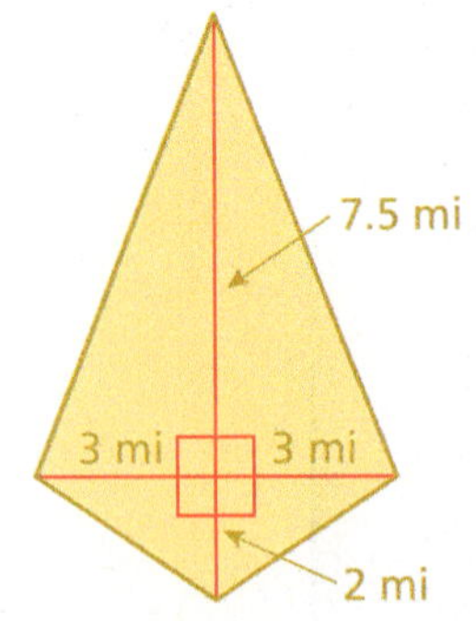

Laurie's Notes

Scaffolding Instruction

- Students will continue finding areas of special quadrilaterals using known shapes. The exploration introduced trapezoids and the lesson will include kites.
- **Note:** This book uses the *exclusive* definition of a kite, which means that it has *exactly* two pairs of adjacent sides with the same length. The *inclusive* definition of a kite is a quadrilateral that has *at least* two pairs of adjacent sides with the same length. The inclusive definition places rhombuses and squares under the heading of kites in the hierarchy of quadrilaterals.
- Prior skills are important. Decomposition provides a pathway for finding area. Simplifying expressions and solving equations using known algebraic properties are essential skills for solving area problems.
- **Emerging:** Students may depend on grid paper for a visual model. They may have difficulty finding dimensions when decomposing figures and need practice using the formulas.
- **Proficient:** Students have shown competency in applying formulas. They successfully analyze composite figures and solve equations in one variable. They may proceed to the Self-Assessment for Concepts & Skills exercises.

Discuss

- Remind students that a *trapezoid* is a quadrilateral with exactly one pair of parallel sides.
- Discuss the definition of a **kite**.
- **Teaching Strategy:** You can use a flowchart to discuss the relationship between kites and other quadrilaterals.

EXAMPLE 1

- Say, "Do you remember decomposing figures in Section 7.2? You will do that again by separating these figures into more familiar shapes."
- For part (a), draw the trapezoid on the board and ask students to imagine which shapes they can cut it into (without using any trapezoids). After discussing, have students draw the shapes and label the dimensions. Remind them to add the areas of the parts to find the area of the trapezoid.
- As you circulate, look for different ways to decompose the figure. Ask students to share their strategies with the class.
- "Can you separate a trapezoid into two triangles and one rectangle? one parallelogram and one triangle?" yes; yes "Will the area be the same?" yes
- For part (b), draw the kite on the board and ask students to decompose it.
- Students may separate the kite into two or four triangles. Did all students make the same two triangles? There are two ways of decomposing a kite into a set of two triangles. Did all students find the same area?
- Pay attention to the units in the answers.
- This example addresses both the second and third success criteria.

Try It

- Allow students to work in pairs, but have each student make a drawing. Then have partners compare drawings before finding the area.

Scaffold instruction to support all students in their learning. Learning is individualized and you may want to group students differently as they move in and out of these levels with each skill and concept. Student self-assessment and feedback help guide your instructional decisions about how and when to layer support for all students to become proficient learners.

Teaching Strategy

One way to show the hierarchical relationships of quadrilaterals is to draw a flowchart. Because rectangles, rhombuses, and squares are special parallelograms, they have all of the properties of parallelograms. You can discuss the attributes of each quadrilateral in the flowchart.

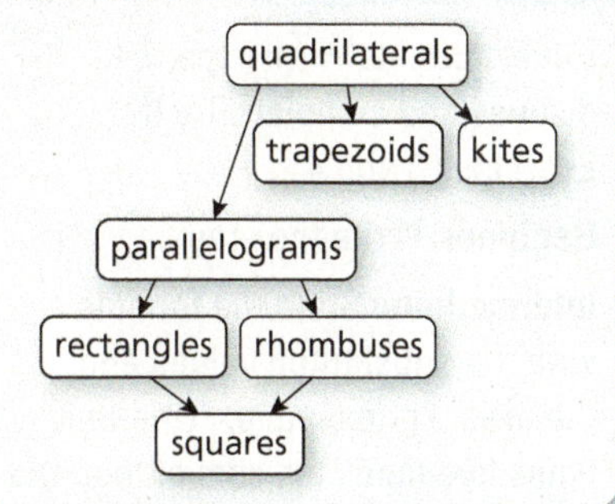

Extra Example 1

Find the area of each figure.

a.

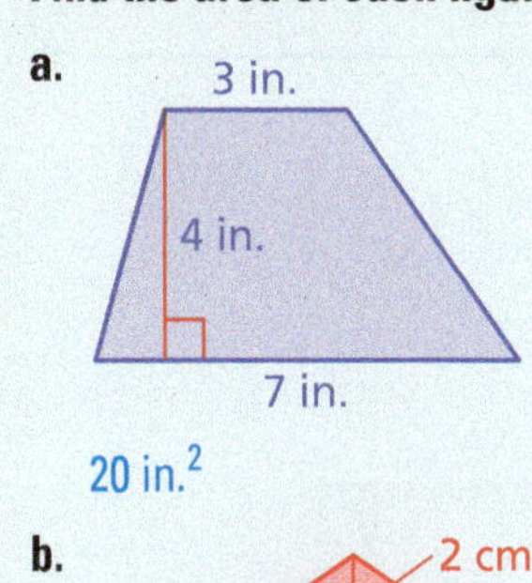

20 in.^2

b.

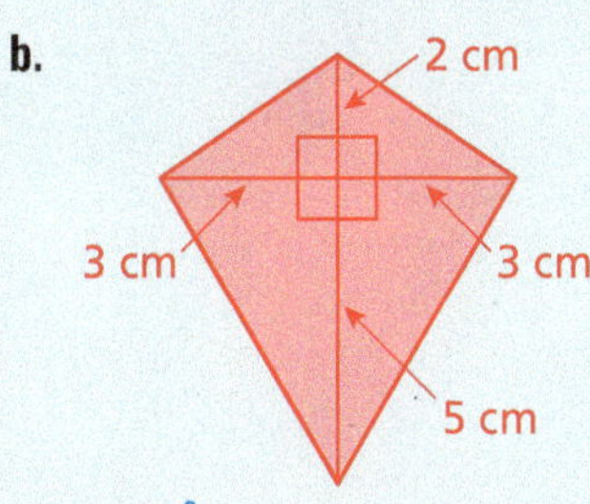

21 cm^2

Try It

1. 76.5 in.^2
2. 28.5 mi^2

Extra Example 2

Find the area of each trapezoid.

a.

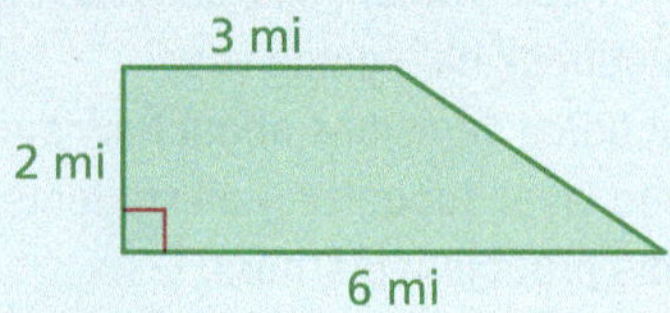

9 mi²

b.

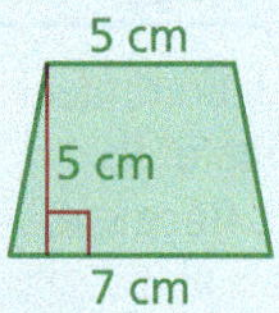

30 cm²

ELL Support

Have students work in pairs to discuss and complete Try It Exercises 3 and 4.

Beginner: Write the steps.

Intermediate: State the formula with the substituted values and the area. For example, "One-half times five times the sum of four and eight equals thirty. The area is thirty square millimeters."

Advanced: Explain the process.

Try It

3. 30 mm²

4. 30 in.²

Laurie's Notes

Key Idea

- The *height* of a trapezoid is the perpendicular distance between the parallel bases.
- Write and discuss the Algebra. Students derived this formula in the exploration.
- Again, remind students that to find $\frac{1}{2}$ of a number they can divide the number by 2.
- Show a diagram of a trapezoid as $\frac{1}{2}$ of its corresponding parallelogram.

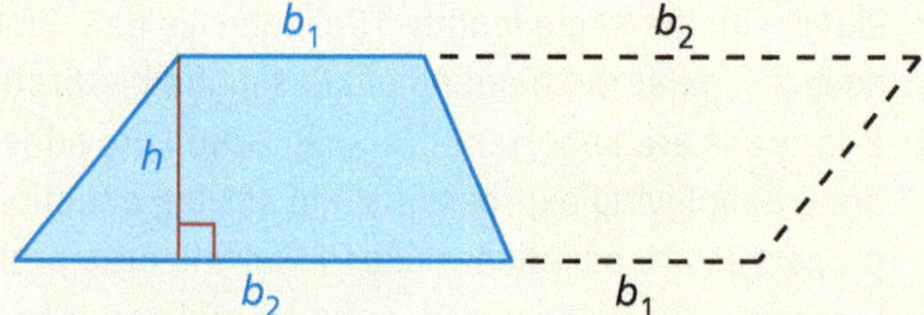

EXAMPLE 2

- Work through both parts as shown.
- Write the formula first. Show how the values are substituted for the variables. In performing the operations, find the sum first. Then find the product of the sum and the height of the trapezoid. Finally, multiply the product by $\frac{1}{2}$.
- Discuss the factors and terms involved in the formula: $\frac{1}{2}$, h, and $(b_1 + b_2)$. Then discuss the order of operations.

? "In what other way can the computations be completed in part (a)?" *Sample answer:* First, multiply $\frac{1}{2}$ and 6. Then use the Distributive Property to multiply 3 by both 5 and 9. Finally, add 15 and 27.

- **MP7 Look for and Make Use of Structure:** You want students to recognize that while there are three variables, $(b_1 + b_2)$ is one factor in the formula. There are different ways in which the factors can be multiplied. If the height is an odd number, you might not want to take $\frac{1}{2}$ of the height as the first step.
- Pay attention to the units in the answers.

Try It

- In Exercise 3, note that the height is a side of the trapezoid and that it is not a vertical segment. Remind students that the height is the perpendicular distance between the parallel bases.

Students are working on the fourth success criterion.

In Example 1(a), you could have used a copy of the trapezoid to form a parallelogram. As you may have discovered in the exploration, this leads to the following formula for the area of a trapezoid.

Area of a Trapezoid

Words The area A of a trapezoid is one-half the product of its height h and the sum of its bases b_1 and b_2.

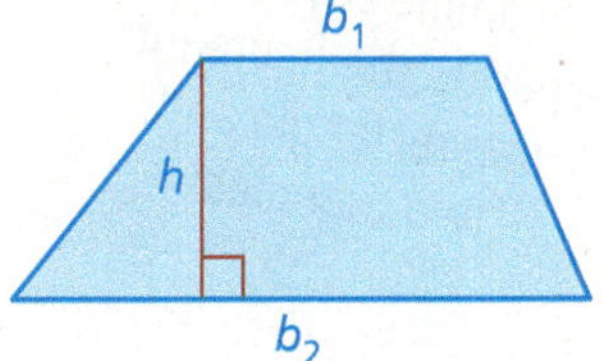

Algebra $A = \frac{1}{2}h(b_1 + b_2)$

EXAMPLE 2 Finding Areas of Trapezoids

Find the area of each trapezoid.

a.

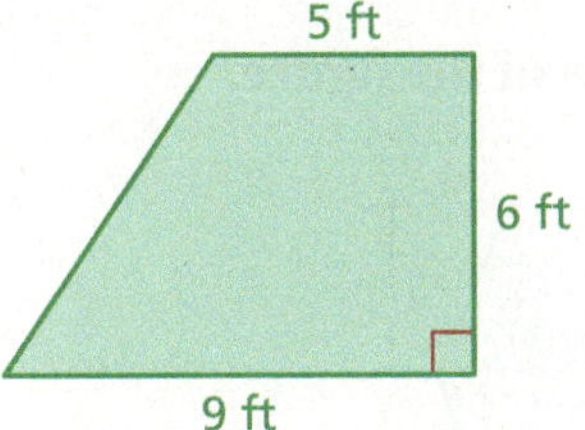

b.

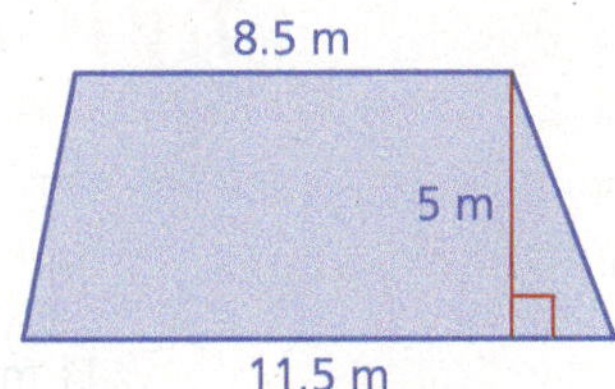

a.

$A = \frac{1}{2}h(b_1 + b_2)$ Write formula.

$= \frac{1}{2}(6)(5 + 9)$ Substitute.

$= \frac{1}{2}(6)(14)$ Add.

$= 42$ Multiply.

The area of the trapezoid is 42 square feet.

b.

$A = \frac{1}{2}h(b_1 + b_2)$

$= \frac{1}{2}(5)(8.5 + 11.5)$

$= \frac{1}{2}(5)(20)$

$= 50$

The area of the trapezoid is 50 square meters.

Try It **Find the area of the trapezoid.**

3.

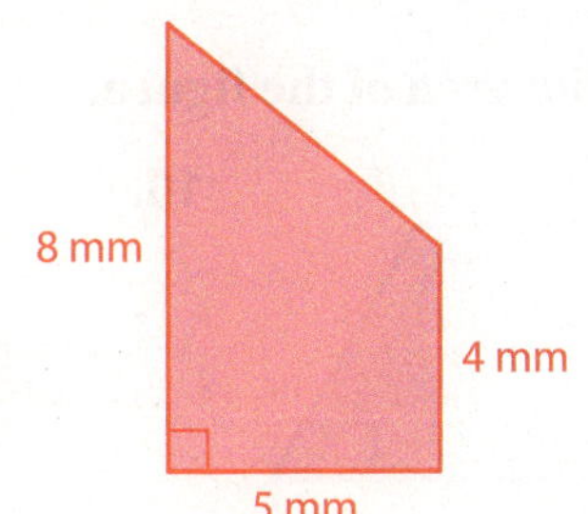

4.

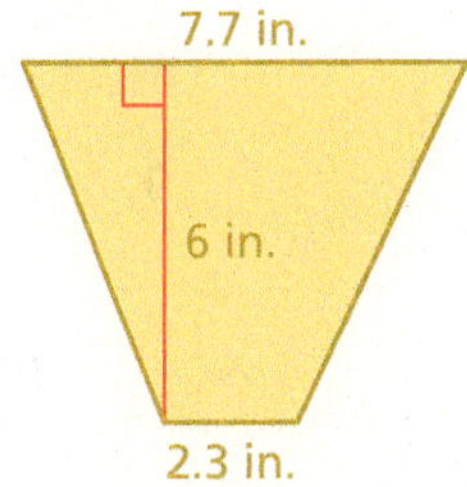

EXAMPLE 3 Finding the Area of a Composite Figure

There is often more than one way to separate composite figures. In Example 3, you can separate the figure into one rectangle and two triangles.

Find the area of the figure.

You can separate the figure into a rectangle and a trapezoid. Identify the height of the trapezoid. Then find the area of each shape.

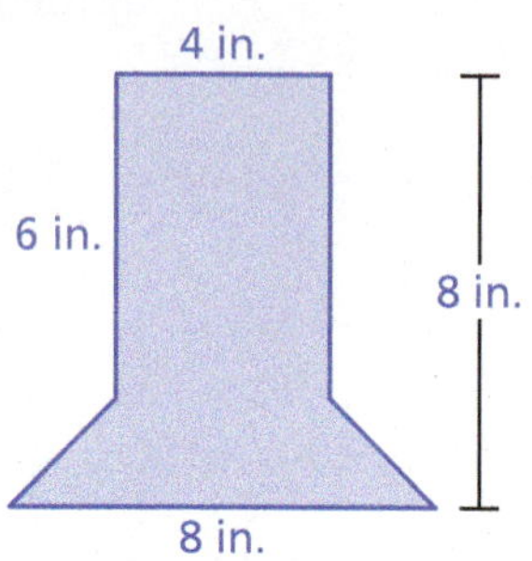

4 in.
6 in. rectangle
trapezoid
2 in.
8 in.

Area of Rectangle

$$A = \ell w$$
$$= 6(4)$$
$$= 24$$

Area of Trapezoid

$$A = \frac{1}{2}h(b_1 + b_2)$$
$$= \frac{1}{2}(2)(4 + 8)$$
$$= 12$$

So, the area of the figure is $24 + 12 = 36$ square inches.

Try It Find the area of the figure.

5. 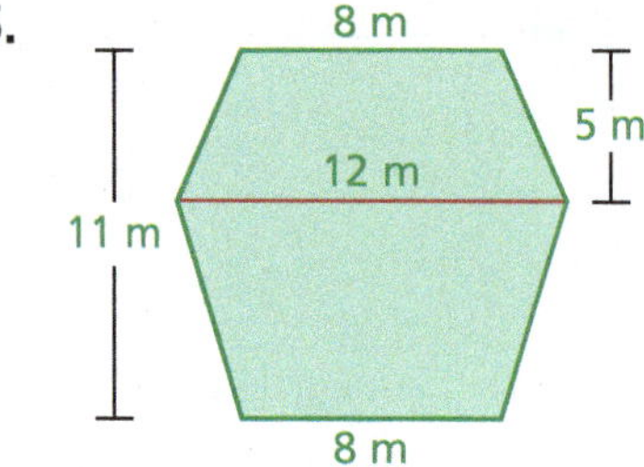

6. 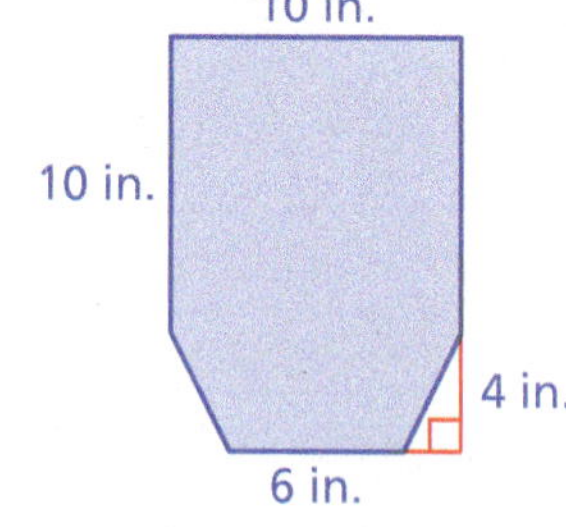

Self-Assessment for Concepts & Skills

Solve each exercise. Then rate your understanding of the success criteria in your journal.

7. **WRITING** Explain how to use the area of a parallelogram to find the area of a trapezoid.

8. **MP REASONING** What measures do you need to find the area of a kite?

FINDING AREA Find the area of the figure.

9. 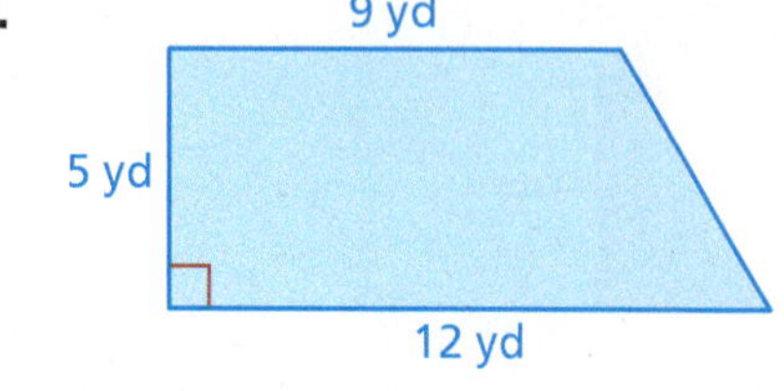

10. 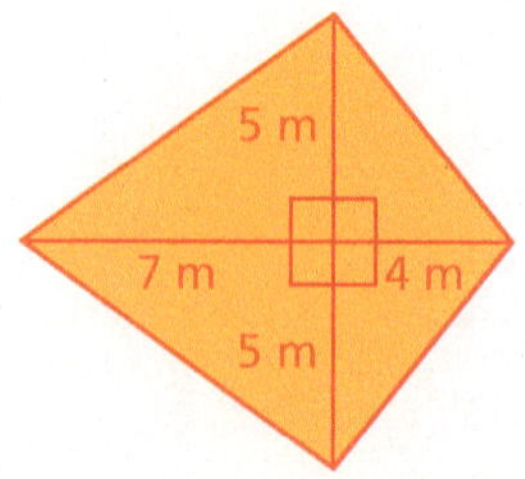

Laurie's Notes

EXAMPLE 3

- ? "Which shapes can you separate the figure into?" *Sample answer:* a rectangle and a trapezoid "What are the dimensions of the rectangle?" The length is 6 inches and the width is 4 inches. "What are the dimensions of the trapezoid?" The bases are 4 inches and 8 inches, and the height is 2 inches.
- Write the formula for the area of each shape, substitute the known values, and perform the computations. Don't forget to add the areas of the parts to find the total area and use appropriate units.
- ? "Can the figure be decomposed a different way? Explain." Have students show different methods.
- If time allows, work through different methods so that students understand the area of the figure will not change.
- Students are working on the third success criterion.
- If time allows, have students look back at Section 7.2 Example 3 and justify the answer using a trapezoid in their calculations.

Try It

- **Neighbor Check:** Have students work independently and then have their neighbors check their work. Have students discuss any discrepancies.
- In Exercise 5, notice that the two trapezoids are not congruent. Ask students to find the height of each one. If they struggle, have them make an exact copy on grid paper and label the dimensions. They can count the grid lines to verify that the heights are different.

Self-Assessment for Concepts & Skills

- Have students work independently. Give them time to write their answers for Exercises 7 and 8. These will provide insight into students' understanding of trapezoids and kites.
- Exercises 9 and 10 are accessible to all students.
- All four success criteria are being assessed. Use *Fist of Five* to check students' understanding.

ELL Support

Provide students with extra support and language practice by having them work in pairs. Monitor discussions of Exercises 7 and 8. Then check comprehension of Exercises 9 and 10 by having each pair display their answers on a whiteboard for your review.

The Success Criteria Self-Assessment chart can be found in the *Student Journal* or online at *BigIdeasMath.com*.

Extra Example 3

Find the area of the figure.

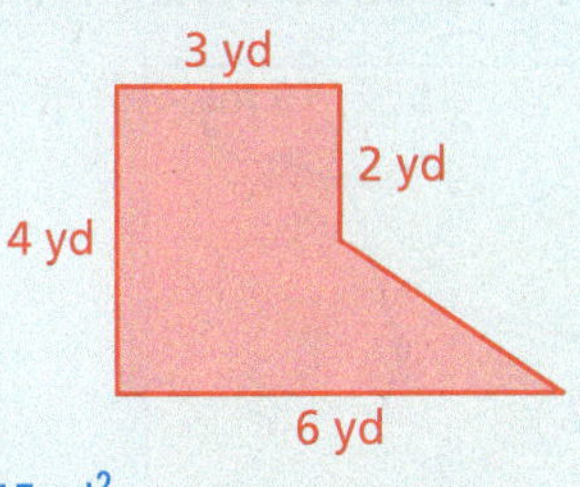

15 yd^2

Try It

5. 110 m^2
6. 132 $in.^2$

Self-Assessment for Concepts & Skills

7. *Sample answer:* A trapezoid with bases b_1 and b_2 and height h has half the area as a parallelogram with base $b_1 + b_2$ and height h.
8. the diagonal lengths
9. 52.5 yd^2
10. 55 m^2

Extra Example 4

A trapezoid can be used to approximate the shape of Smyth County, Virginia. The population is about 31,000. About how many people are there per square mile?

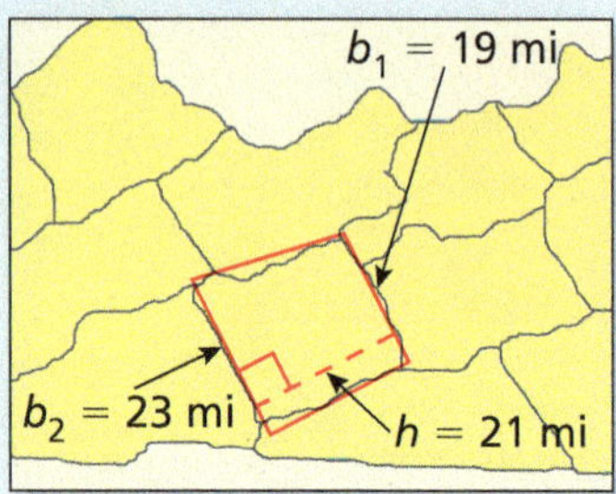

about 70 people per square mile

Laurie's Notes

EXAMPLE 4

- Students will use the area of a trapezoid to divide whole numbers where the remainder is not zero. Discuss with students that in the context of the problem, the nearest whole number is an appropriate answer. Have students use long division to find the quotient. In a future course, students will study decimal remainders.
- This is an example of finding population density. Help students think about the size of 1 square mile. Relate it to a physical location in your area that students are familiar with. In Scott County, there are approximately 42 people living in every square mile.
- **MP1 Make Sense of Problems and Persevere in Solving Them:** Students look for an entry point and plan a solution pathway which is defined in the example. They use diagrams to help define the problem and ask if the answer makes sense, which can be completed as shown in the Check Reasonableness note.
- **Extension:** Although the county you live and/or teach in may not be similar to a common geometric figure, you can use the land areas and population estimates at *quickfacts.census.gov/gfd/index.html.*

Self-Assessment for Problem Solving

11. 40%

12. $346.50

Self-Assessment for Problem Solving

- Students should work independently and show their work. It is important to provide time in class for problem solving, so that students become comfortable with the problem-solving plan.
- Exercise 11 has a height that is also a side of the trapezoid. You may need to ask guiding questions to help students identify the height.
- Students are assessing their understanding of the last three success criteria.
- When finished, have students *Turn and Talk* to discuss their answers and methods. Students should correct any mistakes they find.

The Success Criteria Self-Assessment chart can be found in the *Student Journal* or online at *BigIdeasMath.com.*

Learning Target

Find areas of trapezoids, kites, and composite figures.

Success Criteria

- Explain how the area of a parallelogram is used to find the area of a trapezoid.
- Decompose trapezoids and kites into smaller shapes.
- Use decomposition to find the area of a figure.
- Use the bases and the height of a trapezoid to find its area.

Closure

- Draw the figure on the board. Explain that a diagonal of the trapezoid has been drawn.

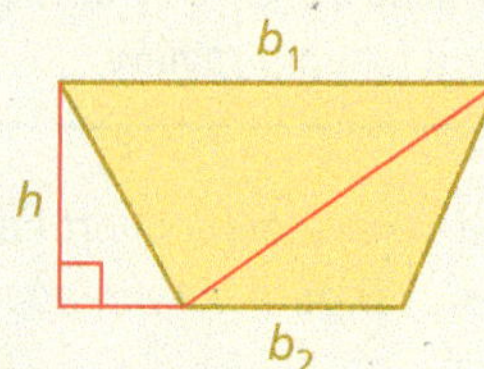

- Have students explain to a partner how they might derive the formula for the area of a trapezoid from this figure. *Sample answer:* The sum of the areas of the triangles is $\frac{1}{2}b_1h + \frac{1}{2}b_2h$. Using the Distributive Property, $\frac{1}{2}b_1h + \frac{1}{2}b_2h = \frac{1}{2}h(b_1 + b_2)$.

EXAMPLE 4 Modeling Real Life

You can use a trapezoid to approximate the shape of Scott County, Virginia. The population is about 22,100. About how many people are there per square mile?

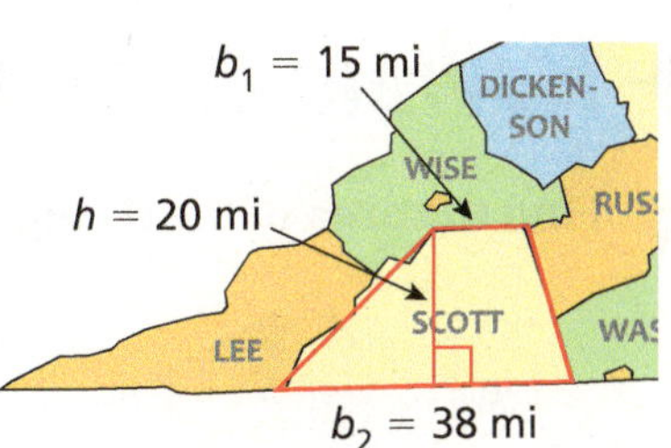

Understand the problem.

You are given the population and the dimensions of a county shaped like a trapezoid. You are asked to find the number of people per square mile.

Make a plan.

Use the formula for the area of a trapezoid to find the area of Scott County. Then divide the population by the area to find the number of people per square mile.

Solve and check.

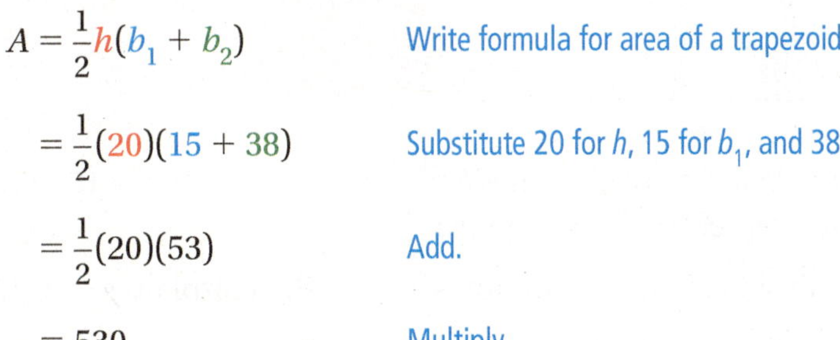

$$A = \frac{1}{2}h(b_1 + b_2)$$ Write formula for area of a trapezoid.

$$= \frac{1}{2}(20)(15 + 38)$$ Substitute 20 for h, 15 for b_1, and 38 for b_2.

$$= \frac{1}{2}(20)(53)$$ Add.

$$= 530$$ Multiply.

The area of Scott County is about 530 square miles.

So, there are about $\frac{22{,}100 \text{ people}}{530 \text{ mi}^2} \approx 42$ people per square mile.

Check Reasonableness

Round the population to 20,000 and the area to 500 square miles to obtain an estimate that is simpler to calculate.

$20{,}000 \div 500 = 40$

The answer is reasonable because

$40 \approx 42$. ✓

Self-Assessment for Problem Solving

Solve each exercise. Then rate your understanding of the success criteria in your journal.

11. **DIG DEEPER!** An archaeologist estimates that the manuscript shown was originally a rectangle with a length of 20 inches. Estimate the percent of the fragment that is missing.

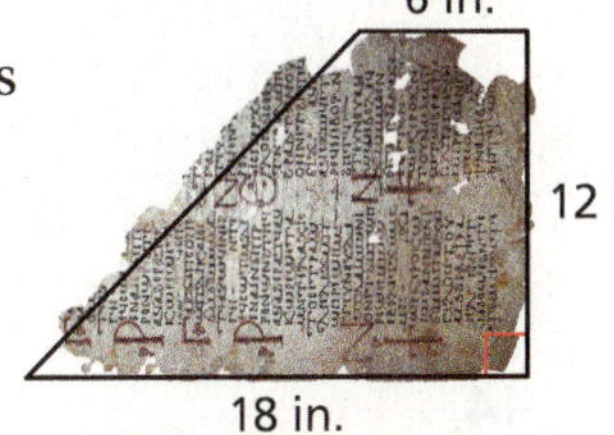

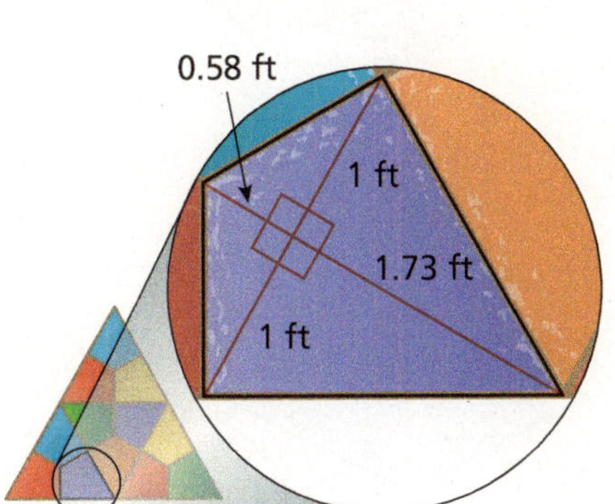

12. The stained-glass window is made of identical kite-shaped glass panes. The approximate dimensions of one pane are shown. The glass used to make the window costs \$12.50 per square foot. Find the total cost of the glass used to make the window.

7.3 Practice

Review & Refresh

Find the area of the triangle.

1. 7 in.; 18 in.

2. 6.5 km; 8 km

3. 4 ft; $12\frac{1}{2}$ ft

Classify the quadrilateral.

4.

5.

6.

7. On a normal day, 12 airplanes arrive at an airport every 15 minutes. Which rate does *not* represent this situation?

   A. 24 airplanes every 30 minutes
   B. 4 airplanes every 5 minutes
   C. 6 airplanes every 5 minutes
   D. 48 airplanes each hour

Concepts, Skills, & Problem Solving

MP **USING TOOLS** **Find the area of the trapezoid by forming a parallelogram.** (See Exploration 1, p. 297.)

8. 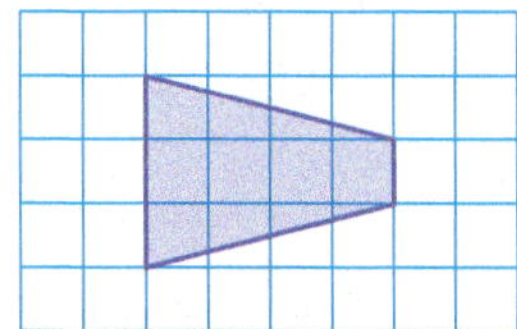

9. 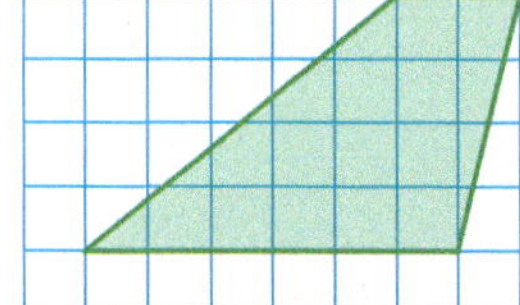

10. 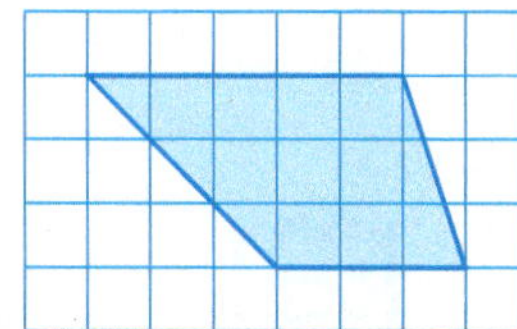

FINDING AREA **Use decomposition to find the area of the figure.**

11. 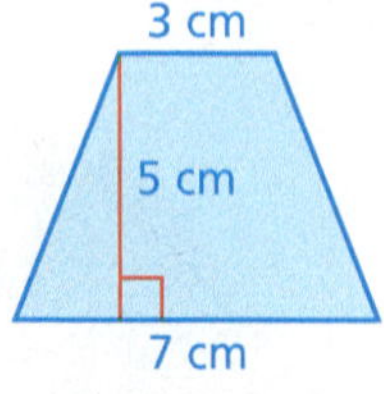

12. 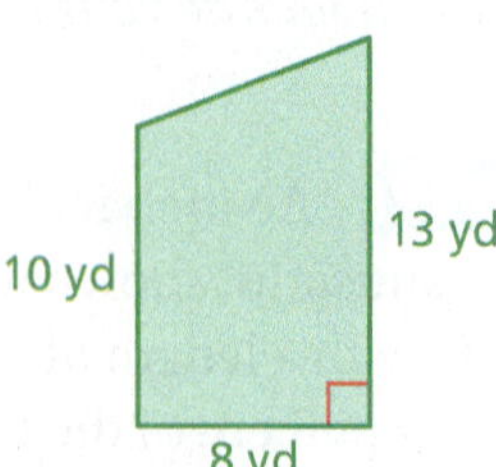

13. 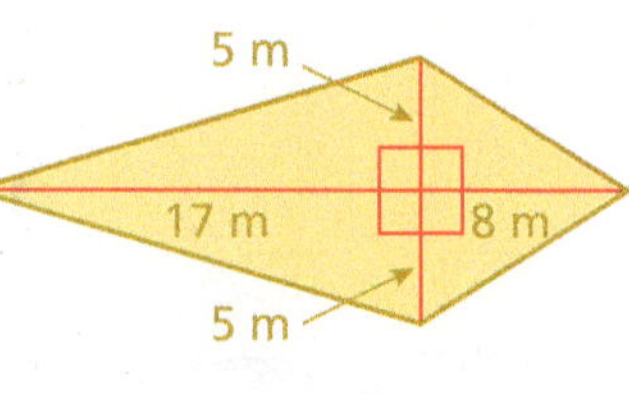

14. 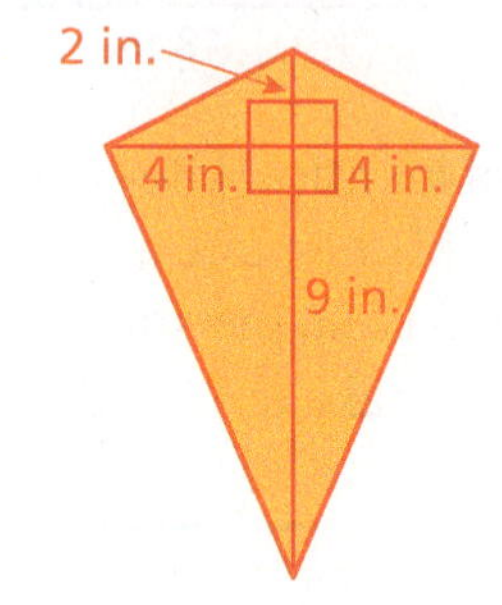

15. 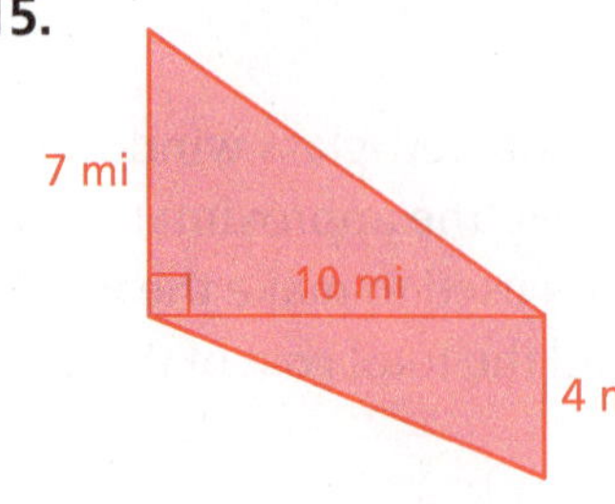

16. 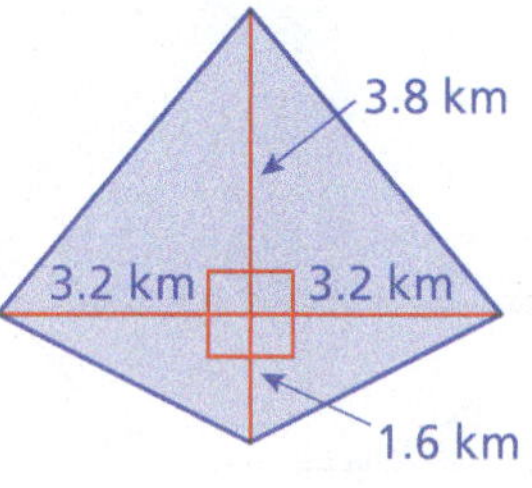

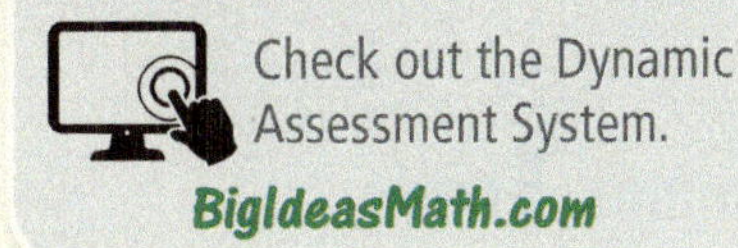

Assignment Guide and Concept Check

Scaffold assignments to support all students in their learning progression. The suggested assignments are a starting point. Continue to assign additional exercises and revisit with spaced practice to move every student toward proficiency.

Level	Assignment 1	Assignment 2
Emerging	3, 6, 7, 8, 10, 11, 14, 17, 22	12, 13, 20, 21, 25, 28, 33
Proficient	3, 6, 7, 9, 10, 12, 13, 18, 23	20, 21, 26, 29, 31, 32, 33
Advanced	3, 6, 7, 10, 15, 16, 19, 20, 24	27, 30, 31, 32, 33, 34, 35

- Assignment 1 is for use after students complete the Self-Assessment for Concepts & Skills.
- Assignment 2 is for use after students complete the Self-Assessment for Problem Solving.
- The red exercises can be used as a concept check.

Review & Refresh Prior Skills

Exercises 1–3 Finding the Area of a Triangle
Exercises 4–6 Classifying Quadrilaterals
Exercise 7 Comparing Rates

Common Errors

- **Exercises 8–10** Students may not count grid lines correctly. Often they will count points versus the segments between the points. When this happens the bases and the heights will be one greater than they should be.

Review & Refresh

1. 63 in.^2
2. 26 km^2
3. 25 ft^2
4. rectangle
5. trapezoid
6. parallelogram
7. C

Concepts, Skills, & Problem Solving

8. 8 units^2
9. 16 units^2
10. 12 units^2
11. 25 cm^2
12. 92 yd^2
13. 125 m^2
14. 44 in.^2
15. 55 mi^2
16. 17.28 km^2

Concepts, Skills, & Problem Solving

17. 28 $in.^2$

18. 10 cm^2

19. 105 ft^2

20. no; Area $= \frac{1}{2}(8)(6 + 14) = 80 \text{ m}^2$

21. 16 ft^2

22. 220.5 ft^2

23. 20 $units^2$

24. 32 $units^2$

25. 20 km

26. 25 yd

27. 4 mm

Common Errors

- **Exercises 17–19** Students may forget to multiply by $\frac{1}{2}$. Tell students to write out the formula for the area of a trapezoid and then identify the value of each variable before substituting.

FINDING AREA Find the area of the trapezoid.

17.

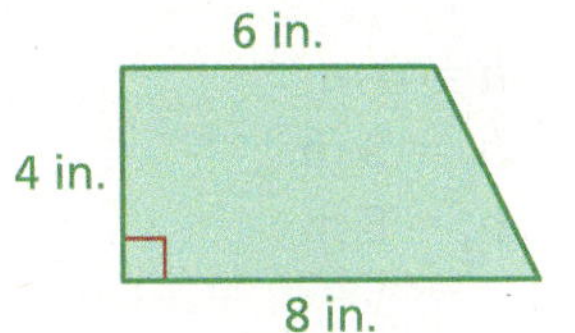

18.

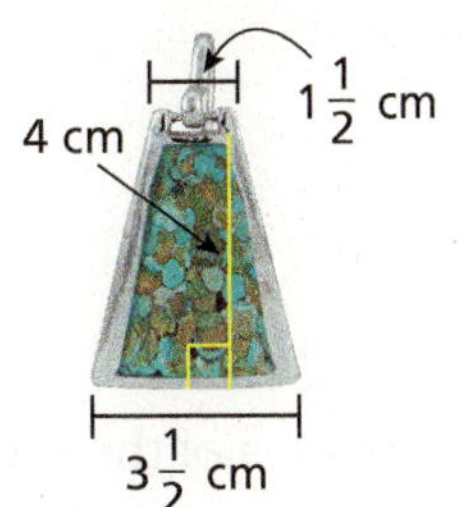

19.

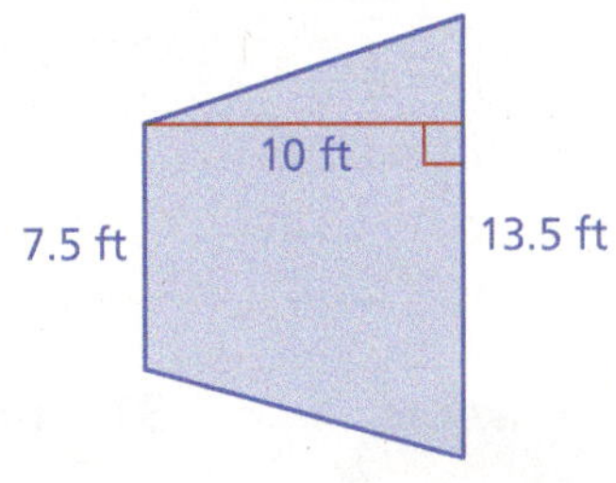

20. **MP YOU BE THE TEACHER** Your friend finds the area of the trapezoid. Is your friend correct? Explain your reasoning.

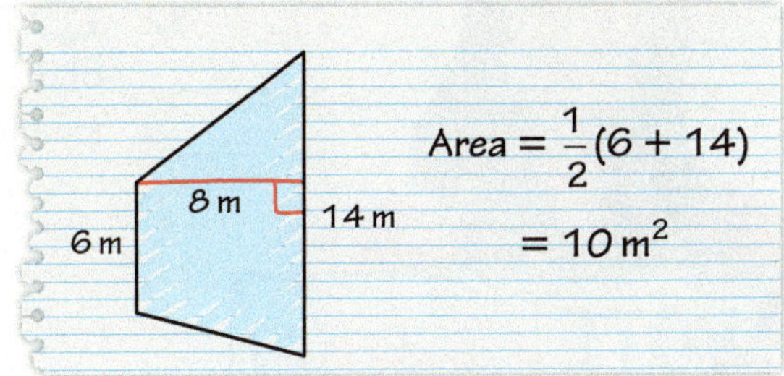

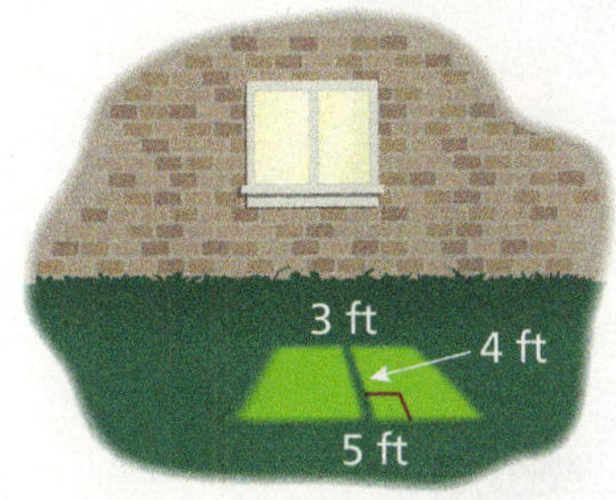

21. **MP MODELING REAL LIFE** Light shines through a window. What is the area of the trapezoid-shaped region created by the light?

COMPOSITE FIGURES Find the area of the figure.

22.

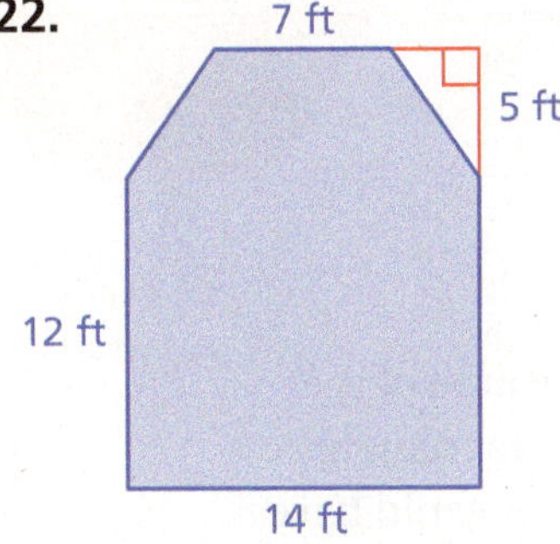

23.

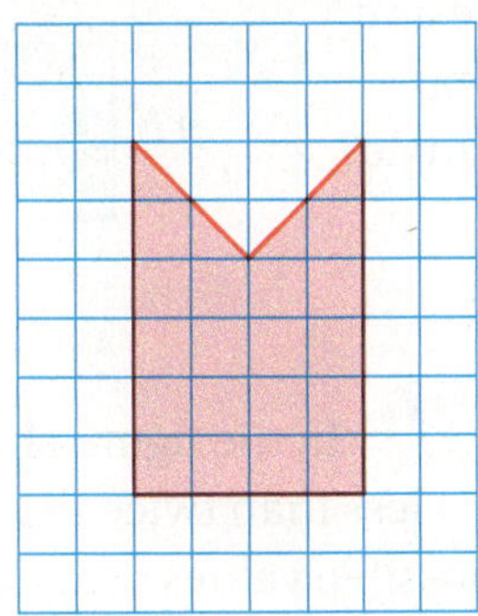

24.

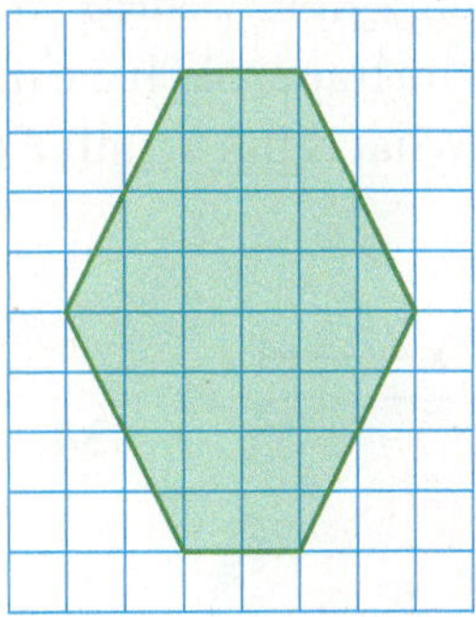

FINDING A MISSING DIMENSION Find the height of the trapezoid.

25. Area = 180 km^2

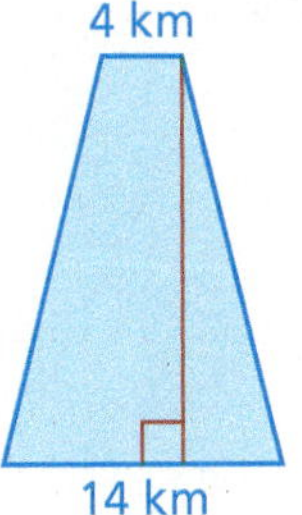

26. Area = 600 yd^2

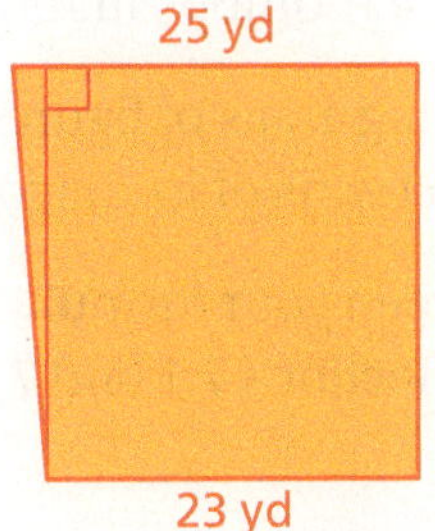

27. Area = $21\frac{1}{5}\text{ mm}^2$

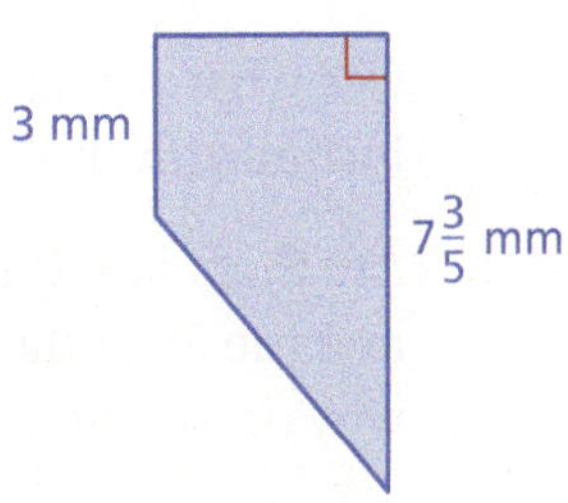

FINDING AREA **Find the area (in square feet) of a trapezoid with height h and bases b_1 and b_2.**

28. $h = 6$ in.
$b_1 = 9$ in.
$b_2 = 12$ in.

29. $h = 12$ yd
$b_1 = 5$ yd
$b_2 = 7$ yd

30. $h = 6$ m
$b_1 = 3$ m
$b_2 = 8$ m

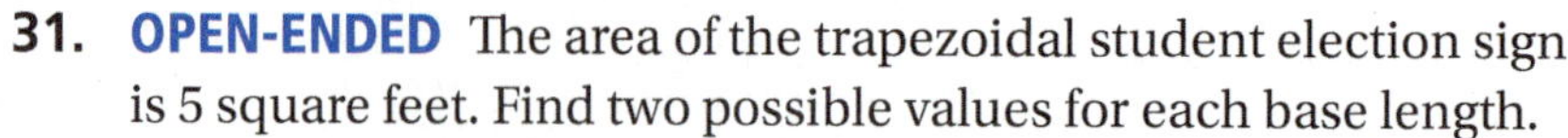

31. **OPEN-ENDED** The area of the trapezoidal student election sign is 5 square feet. Find two possible values for each base length.

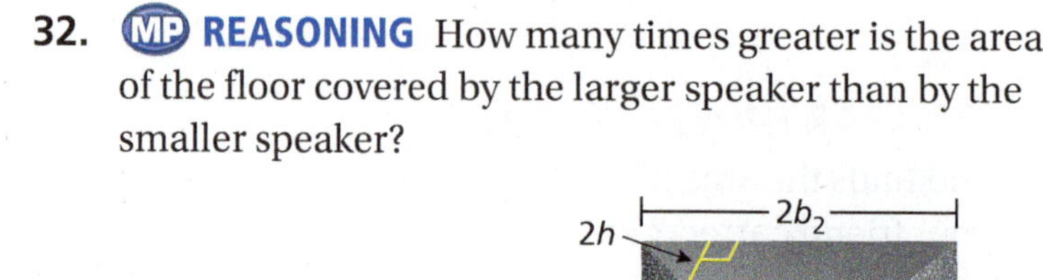

32. **MP REASONING** How many times greater is the area of the floor covered by the larger speaker than by the smaller speaker?

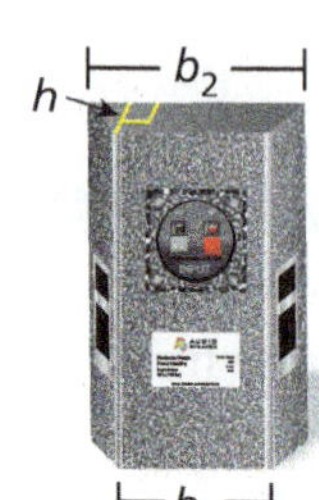

33. **MP REASONING** The rectangle and the trapezoid have the same area. What is the length ℓ of the rectangle?

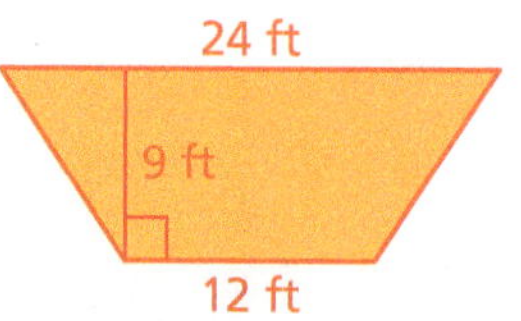

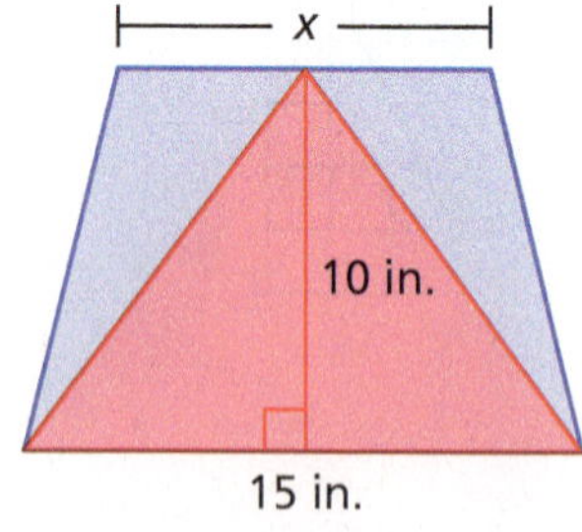

34. **DIG DEEPER!** In the figure shown, the area of the trapezoid is less than twice the area of the triangle. Find the possible values of x. Can the trapezoid have the same area as the triangle? Explain your reasoning.

35. **MP STRUCTURE** In Section 7.1 Exercise 34 and Section 7.2 Exercise 29, you wrote a formula for the area of a rhombus in terms of its diagonals.

a. Use what you know about finding areas of figures to write a formula for the area of a kite in terms of its diagonals.

b. Are there any similarities between your formula in part (a) and the formula you found in Sections 7.1 and 7.2? Explain why or why not.

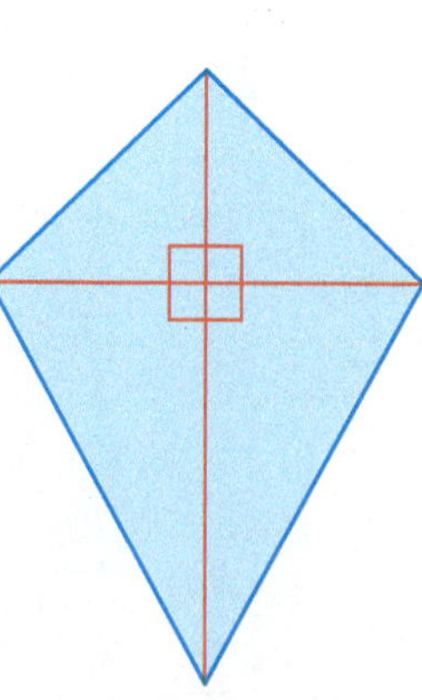

Common Errors

- **Exercises 28–30** Students may substitute the height for one of the bases. Tell students to write out the formula for the area of a trapezoid and then identify the value of each variable before substituting.

Mini-Assessment

Find the area of the figure.

1.

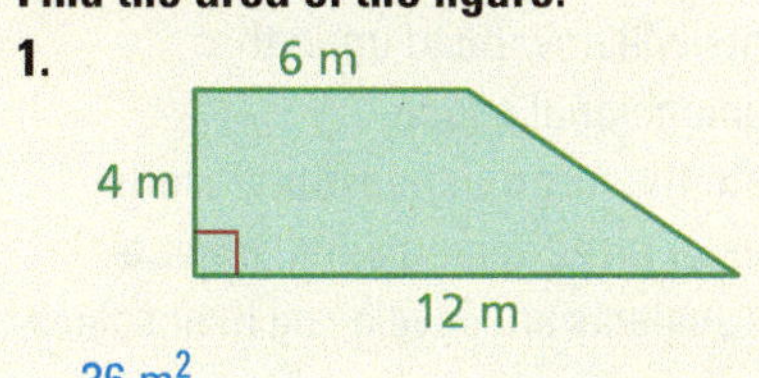

36 m^2

2.

7 in.
8 in.
8 in.
14 in.

168 in.^2

3.

2 yd
8 yd
6 yd

32 yd^2

4.

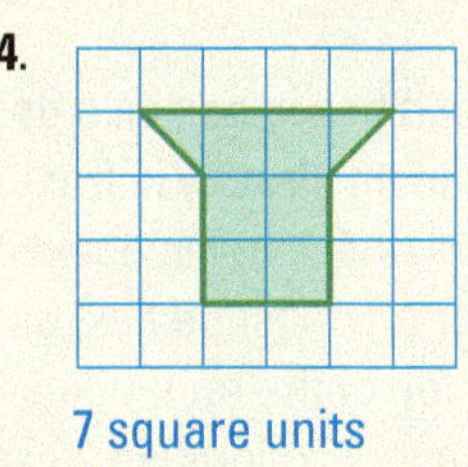

7 square units

5. Find the area of the trapezoid-shaped mirror.

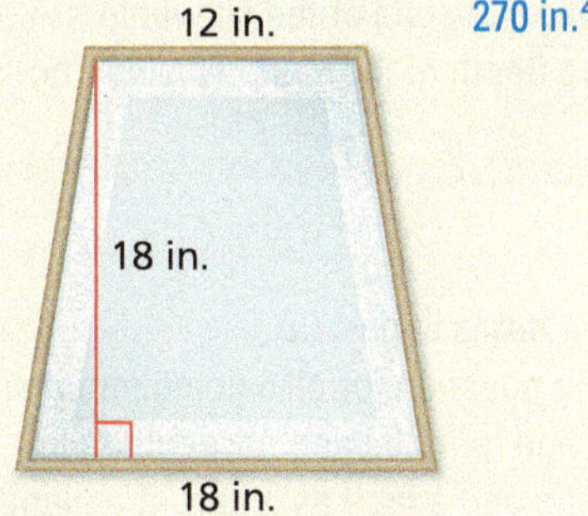

270 in.^2

Section Resources

Surface Level	Deep Level
Resources by Chapter • Extra Practice • Reteach • Puzzle Time Student Journal • Self-Assessment • Practice Differentiating the Lesson Tutorial Videos Skills Review Handbook Skills Trainer	Resources by Chapter • Enrichment and Extension Graphic Organizers Dynamic Assessment System • Section Practice
Transfer Level	
Dynamic Assessment System • Mid-Chapter Quiz	Assessment Book • Mid-Chapter Quiz

Concepts, Skills, & Problem Solving

28. $\frac{7}{16} \text{ ft}^2$

29. 648 ft^2

30. about 355.03 ft^2 or about 366.67 ft^2

31. *Sample answers:* $b_1 = 2$ ft, $b_2 = 3$ ft; $b_1 = 1.5$ ft, $b_2 = 3.5$ ft

32. 4

33. 18 ft

34. x must be greater than 0 and less than 15; no; x would be 0.

35. **a.** $A = \frac{1}{2}ab$, where a and b are the diagonal lengths

b. yes; *Sample answer:* The formulas are the same.

Learning Target

Describe and draw three-dimensional figures.

Success Criteria

- Find the numbers of faces, edges, and vertices of a three-dimensional figure.
- Draw prisms and pyramids.
- Draw the front, side, and top views of a three-dimensional figure.

Warm Up

Cumulative, vocabulary, and prerequisite skills practice opportunities are available in the *Resources by Chapter* or at *BigIdeasMath.com.*

ELL Support

Explain that students will learn about prisms in this lesson. Explain that a flat side of a prism is called a *face*. The meaning of *face* in mathematics is different than its meaning in everyday language. In everyday language, a face is the front of a person's head from the forehead to the chin.

Exploration 1

a. face: a flat surface of a prism; edge: a line segment where two faces intersect; vertex: a point where edges intersect

b. See Additional Answers.

Exploration 2

a–d. See Additional Answers.

Laurie's Notes

STATE STANDARDS
Preparing for 6.G.A.4

Preparing to Teach

- In the previous course, students studied two-dimensional figures and began to look at three-dimensional figures. Students will now build upon that knowledge to visualize and draw in three-dimensional space.
- Spatial reasoning allows students to navigate the three-dimensional world and make sense of two-dimensional pictures of three-dimensional objects.
- **MP5 Use Appropriate Tools Strategically:** As students are developing their spatial and visual skills, having cubes to manipulate and view is very helpful. The diagrams in the book are two-dimensional representations of three-dimensional figures.

Motivate

- Place a cube-shaped tissue box on a desk. Ask students to describe what they see when standing directly in front of the cube (front view), to the side of the cube (side view), and looking down on the cube (top view).
- Place a rectangular **prism** (shoe box) on the desk. Describe all three views.
- Place the cube on top of the rectangular prism to create a **solid** that is similar to the one shown in the Exploration 2 example at the left.
- Have students describe all three views. Students need to ignore the difference in depth when describing a solid from one of the viewpoints and focus on the surface they see, not the depth of the solid. This can be confusing to students.

Exploration 1

- Ensure that students correctly identify the terms in part (a).
- In part (b), make sure students answer the question for all 6 combinations: line and line, plane and plane, and plane and line (parallel and perpendicular). It is vital they think of an **edge** as a part of a line and a **face** as a part of a plane.
- Students will likely say that lines are parallel in three dimensions if they do not intersect, however, the lines must also lie in the same plane. Allow them to struggle with this and be incorrect at first. Then tell them that lines that do not intersect in three dimensions and are in different planes are called *skew lines*.
- To get students away from only considering planes in which the faces of the prism lie, ask if the "top" edge of one of the faces is parallel to the "bottom" edge of the opposite face. Because a plane is not drawn through those edges, they may think they are skew. Students need to visualize a plane crossing through the prism diagonally that contains both lines. This is an important preview of slicing three-dimensional figures with planes (for the next course).

Exploration 2

- **MP5 Use Appropriate Tools Strategically:** If possible, give each pair of students 6 cubes. To see each view, students need to be at "eye level" with the solid.
- **Teaching Tip:** Ask, "If you paint the top of part (a), what shapes do you paint?" 3 squares Repeat this strategy for each view.
- Generally, the side view is most challenging to draw. Depending on perspective, the front and side view may be switched (the top view is unique).
- When discussing volume, explain that parts (a) and(c) have cubes behind cubes that support the top cubes.

7.4 Three-Dimensional Figures

Learning Target: Describe and draw three-dimensional figures.

Success Criteria:
- I can find the numbers of faces, edges, and vertices of a three-dimensional figure.
- I can draw prisms and pyramids.
- I can draw the front, side, and top views of a three-dimensional figure.

EXPLORATION 1 Exploring Faces, Edges, and Vertices

Work with a partner. Use the rectangular prism shown.

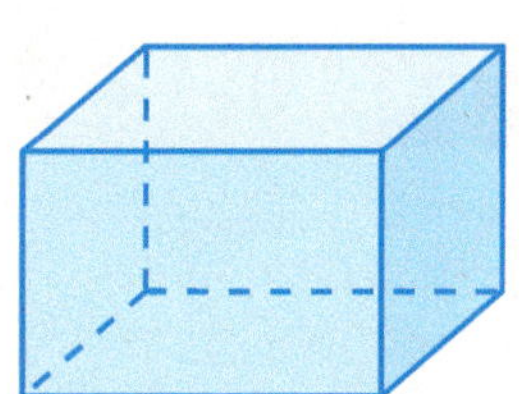

a. Prisms have *faces*, *edges*, and *vertices*. What does each of these terms mean?

b. What does it mean for lines or planes to be parallel or perpendicular in three dimensions? Use drawings to identify one pair of each of the following.

- parallel faces
- parallel edges
- edge parallel to a face
- perpendicular faces
- perpendicular edges
- edge perpendicular to a face

Math Practice

View as Components

What are the different parts of a solid? How can you use these parts to help you draw a solid?

EXPLORATION 2 Drawing Views of a Solid

Work with a partner. Draw the front, side, and top views of each stack of cubes. Then find the number of cubes in the stack. An example is shown at the left.

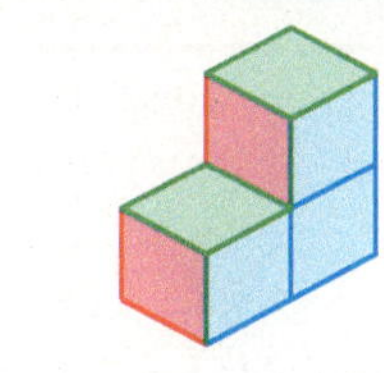

front side top

Number of cubes: 3

a.

b.

c.

d.

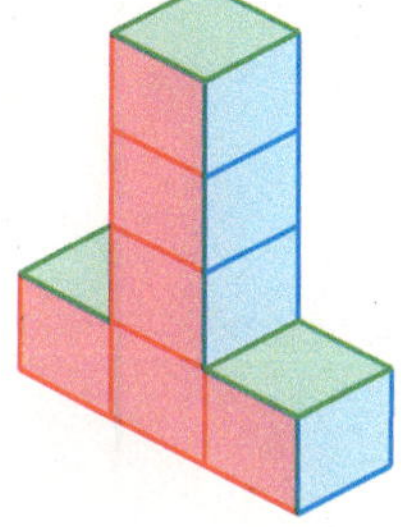

7.4 Lesson

Key Vocabulary
solid, *p. 306*
polyhedron, *p. 306*
face, *p. 306*
edge, *p. 306*
vertex, *p. 306*
prism, *p. 306*
pyramid, *p. 306*

A **solid** is a three-dimensional figure that encloses a space. A **polyhedron** is a solid whose *faces* are all polygons.

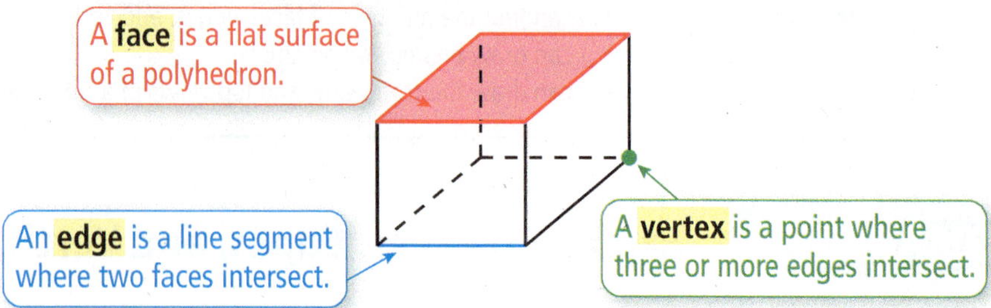

EXAMPLE 1 Finding the Numbers of Faces, Edges, and Vertices

Find the numbers of faces, edges, and vertices of the solid.

The solid has 1 face on the bottom, 1 face on the top, and 4 faces on the sides.

The faces intersect at 12 different line segments.

The edges intersect at 8 different points.

 So, the solid has 6 faces, 12 edges, and 8 vertices.

Try It

1. Find the numbers of faces, edges, and vertices of the solid.

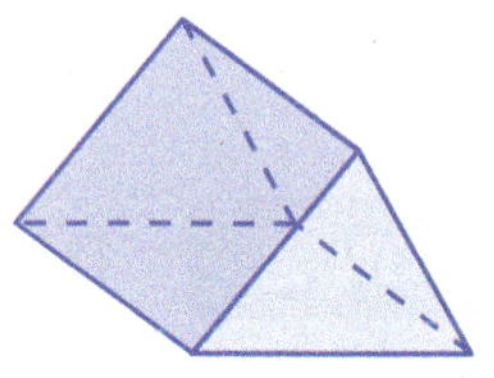

Key Ideas

Prisms

A **prism** is a polyhedron that has two parallel, identical *bases*. The *lateral faces* are parallelograms.

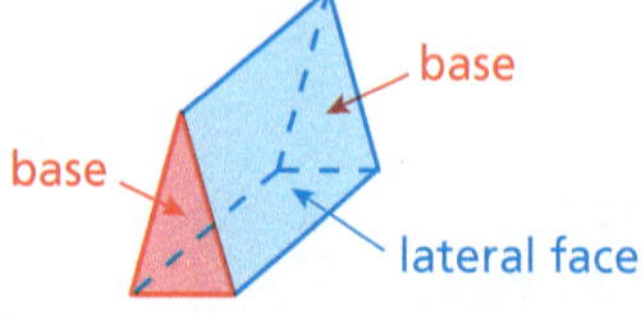

Triangular Prism

Pyramids

A **pyramid** is a polyhedron that has one base. The lateral faces are triangles.

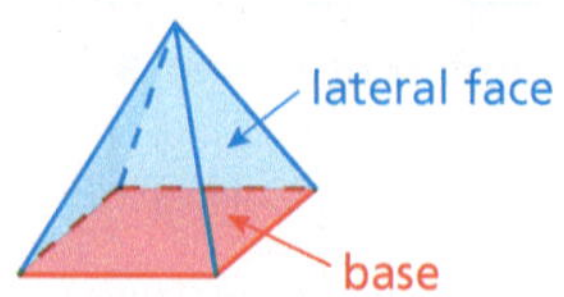

Rectangular Pyramid

The shape of the base tells the name of the prism or the pyramid.

Multi-Language Glossary at *BigIdeasMath.com*

Laurie's Notes

Scaffolding Instruction

- Students are moving from visualizing and discussing solids to drawing and analyzing prisms and pyramids.
- **Emerging:** Students may need practice using the vocabulary or visualizing and drawing three-dimensional figures. Examples 1 and 2 are specific to those skills.
- **Proficient:** Students understand and use three-dimensional terms with confidence. These students can complete Try It Exercises 2 and 3 before using the Self-Assessment exercises to check their understanding.

Discuss

- Review and discuss the vocabulary terms. Relate them to Exploration 1. Have students give examples of **polyhedrons** and describe them using precise language. Ask students if the **solids** have any common attributes.
- Point out that the dashed lines in the figure represent the edges that cannot be seen from the given perspective.

EXAMPLE 1

? "How many faces are there? Describe them." 6; top, bottom, 4 sides

? "How many edges are there? Describe them." 12; 4 around the top, 4 around the bottom, and 4 around the sides

? "How many vertices are there and where are they located?" 8; 4 on the top and 4 on the bottom

- **MP7 Look for and Make Use of Structure:** Repeat the example for a prism with bases that are not quadrilaterals. Students should recognize that the number of faces is 2 more than the number of edges on the base. The number of vertices is twice the number of edges on the base. The number of edges is 3 times the number of edges on the base.

◉ Students are reinforcing the first success criterion.

Try It

- **Neighbor Check:** Have students work independently and then have their neighbors check their work. Have students discuss any discrepancies.

Key Ideas

- The point of the vocabulary is not to memorize definitions, but to have a sense as to the attributes of each solid. This will help in generalizing surface area and volume formulas later.
- Mention to students that **prisms** and **pyramids** have a qualifying name, given by the type of base. For example, a triangular prism has two bases that are triangles.
- **Common Error:** Students often think that the face that is "on the bottom" is the base. In a prism, the bases are the two parallel, congruent faces. In a pyramid, the base is the face that is not a lateral face. The solid does not need to be oriented so that it is resting on a base. Demonstrate this with several solids.

Scaffold instruction to support all students in their learning. Learning is individualized and you may want to group students differently as they move in and out of these levels with each skill and concept. Student self-assessment and feedback help guide your instructional decisions about how and when to layer support for all students to become proficient learners.

Extra Example 1

Find the numbers of faces, edges, and vertices of the solid.

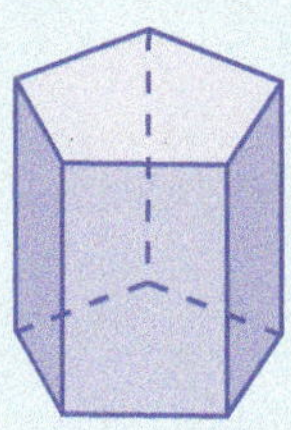

7 faces, 15 edges, 10 vertices

ELL Support

Have students practice language by working in pairs to complete Try It Exercise 1. Have one partner ask the other, "How many faces are there?" After the partner answers, have them switch roles to ask about the numbers of edges and vertices.

Beginner: State the numbers.

Intermediate: Answer with simple sentences such as, "There are five."

Advanced: Answer with detailed sentences such as, "I counted five faces on the solid."

Try It

1. 5 faces, 9 edges, 6 vertices

Extra Example 2

a. Draw a hexagonal prism

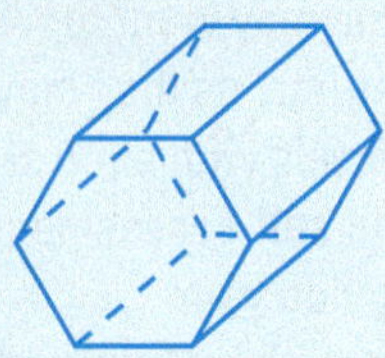

b. Draw a rectangular pyramid.

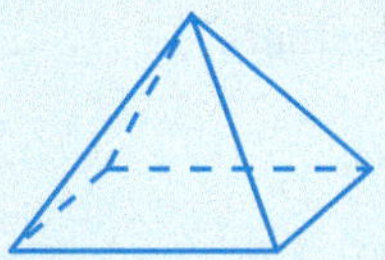

Try It

2.

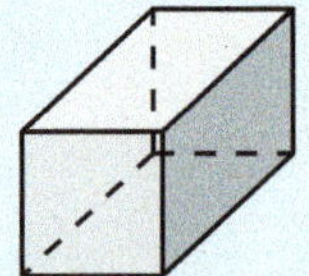

3.

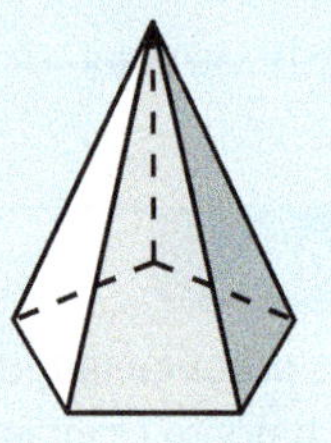

Self-Assessment
for Concepts & Skills

4. 4 faces, 6 edges, 4 vertices

5.

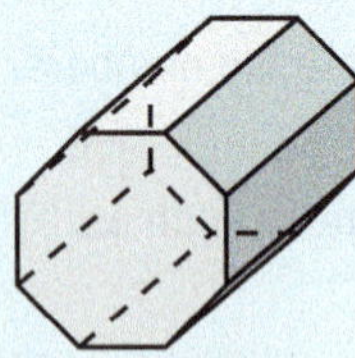

6.

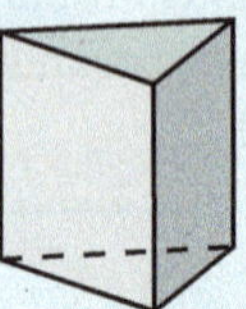

The other three figures are pyramids.

Laurie's Notes

EXAMPLE 2

- Demonstrate how to sketch each solid.
- Drawings of solids may differ based on perspective. For instance, in part (b), the point in Step 1 could be placed below the triangle, or different lines in Step 3 could be dashed. Each would offer a different perspective of the same figure.

Try It

- Give students time to practice sketching the solids.
- Ask volunteers to share their sketches at the board or document camera.
- **Thumbs Up:** Have students assess their understanding of the second success criterion.

Self-Assessment for Concepts & Skills

- Have students complete the exercises independently.
- Exercise 5 gives students a chance to demonstrate their expertise in drawing a three-dimensional figure.
- When all students are finished, have volunteers share their drawings for Exercise 5. If students are still struggling to draw solids, encourage them to keep practicing. Persevering will bring results.
- Ask students to justify their choices for Exercise 6 and listen for mathematical vocabulary in their analyses of prisms versus pyramids.
- **MP6 Attend to Precision:** As students explain their reasoning, they use a standardized language so they communicate precisely.
- Have students use *Thumbs Up* to indicate their understanding of the first two success criteria.

ELL Support

Check understanding of Exercises 4 and 5 by having students use whiteboards to display their answers for your review. Have students work in groups to write out their reasoning for Exercise 6. Then have each group present their reasoning to the class.

The Success Criteria Self-Assessment chart can be found in the *Student Journal* or online at *BigIdeasMath.com*.

EXAMPLE 2 Drawing Solids

a. Draw a rectangular prism.

Step 1: Draw identical rectangular bases.

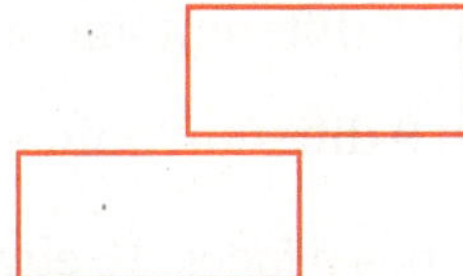

Step 2: Connect corresponding vertices.

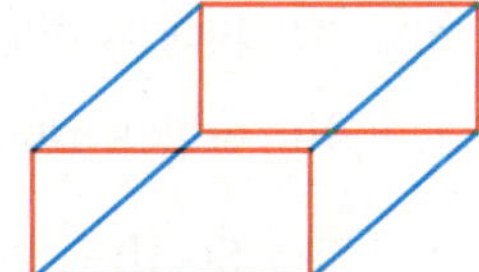

Step 3: Change any *hidden* lines to dashed lines.

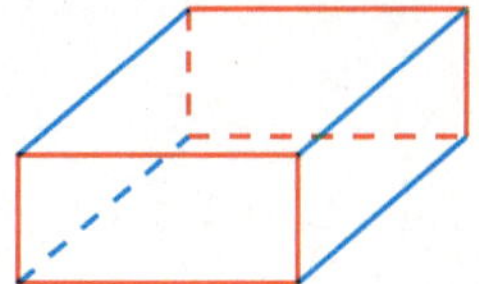

b. Draw a triangular pyramid.

Step 1: Draw a triangular base and a point.

Step 2: Connect the vertices of the triangle to the point.

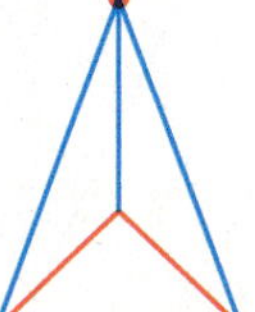

Step 3: Change any *hidden* lines to dashed lines.

Try It **Draw the solid.**

2. square prism

3. pentagonal pyramid

Self-Assessment for Concepts & Skills

Solve each exercise. Then rate your understanding of the success criteria in your journal.

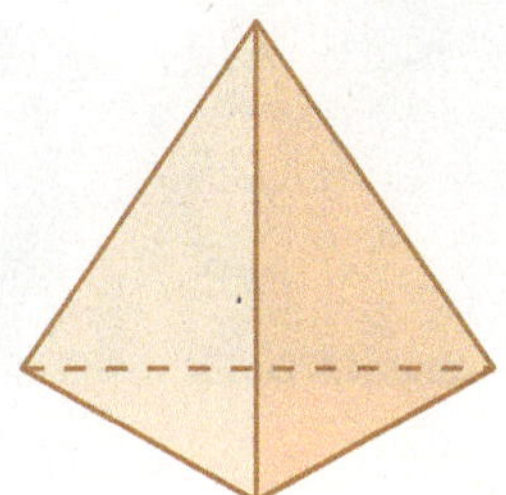

4. FACES, EDGES, AND VERTICES Find the numbers of faces, edges, and vertices of the solid at the left.

5. DRAWING A SOLID Draw an octagonal prism.

6. WHICH ONE DOESN'T BELONG? Which figure does *not* belong with the other three? Explain your reasoning.

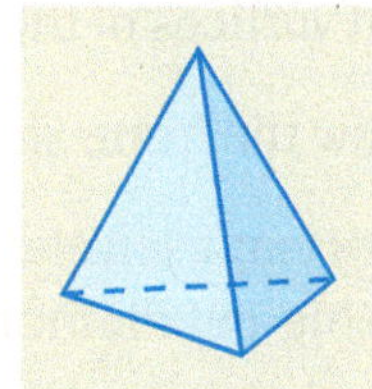

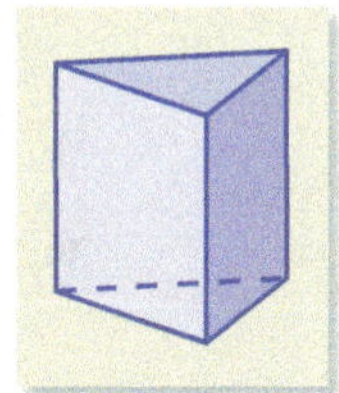

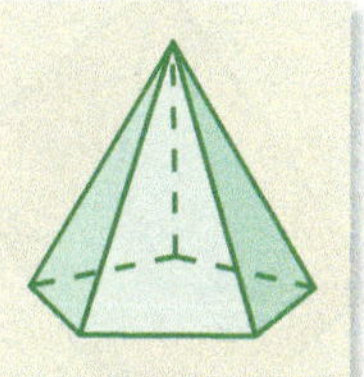

EXAMPLE 3 Modeling Real Life

a. Find the numbers of faces, edges, and vertices of the table-cut diamond.

The diamond has 1 face on the top and 8 faces on the sides.

The faces intersect at 16 different line segments.

The edges intersect at 9 different points.

So, the diamond has 9 faces, 16 edges, and 9 vertices.

b. Draw the front, side, and top views of the diamond.

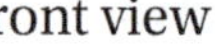

Front view   Side view   Top view

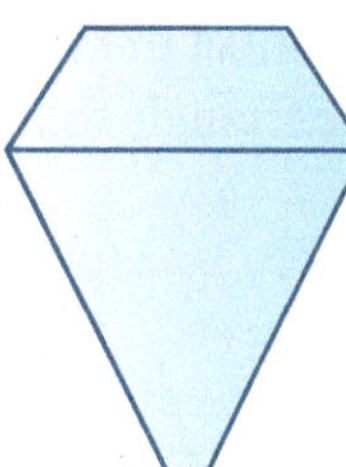

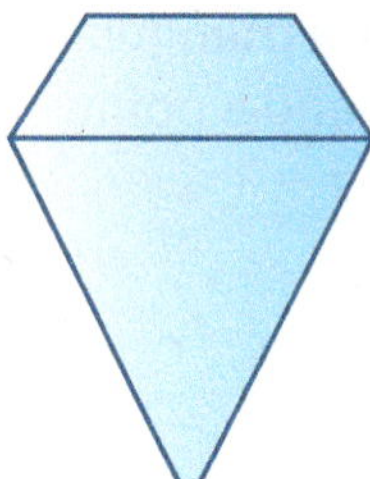

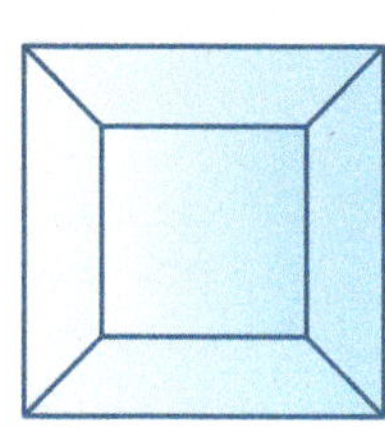

Self-Assessment for Problem Solving

Solve each exercise. Then rate your understanding of the success criteria in your journal.

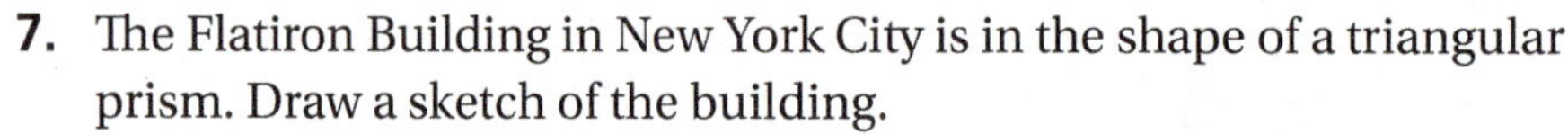

7. The Flatiron Building in New York City is in the shape of a triangular prism. Draw a sketch of the building.

8. The Pyramid of the Niches is in El Tajín, an archaeological site in Veracruz, Mexico. Draw the front, side, and top views of the pyramid. Explain.

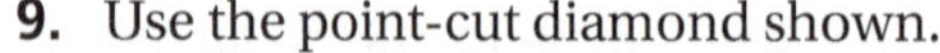

9. Use the point-cut diamond shown.

   a. Find the numbers of faces, edges, and vertices of the diamond.

   b. Draw the front, side, and top views of the diamond.

   c. How can a jeweler transform the point-cut diamond into a table-cut diamond as in Example 3?

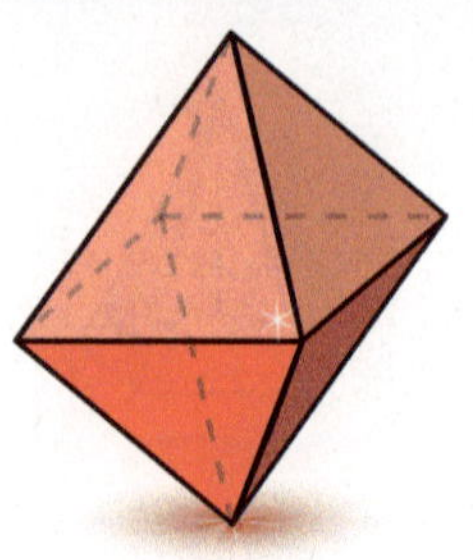

Laurie's Notes

EXAMPLE 3

- This example connects to Exploration 2.
- Show the diagram of the table-cut diamond. If you have models of this particular diamond, pass them around for students to "see" how a two-dimensional drawing represents a three-dimensional solid.
- Have students work through the example in groups. Encourage students to use correct vocabulary as they discuss the solid. Words such as *intersect, parallel, triangle*, and *trapezoid* may enter conversations.

? As you listen to conversations, you may need to ask questions to guide students' thinking. "Does that edge have any other points of intersection? Where? How do you know that this face is a trapezoid? Are any faces parallel? If so, which ones?"

Self-Assessment for Problem Solving

- Students may benefit from trying the exercises independently and then working with peers to refine their work. It is important to provide time in class for problem solving, so that students become comfortable with the problem-solving plan.
- Have students compare their sketches for Exercises 7 and 8 with partners. Encourage discussion of how the sketches were completed and why each view is a particular shape. Discuss any remaining disagreements as a class.
- After completing Exercise 9, have students compare answers. Invite students to share their drawings for part (b) at the board. Have a class discussion about Exercise 9(c). Students should describe cutting through the top of the diamond, parallel to the plane where the two pyramids meet, to create a square top view.

The Success Criteria Self-Assessment chart can be found in the *Student Journal* or online at *BigIdeasMath.com*.

Closure

- **Teaching Strategy:** Draw the three views shown and have students draw the solid they represent.

top

front

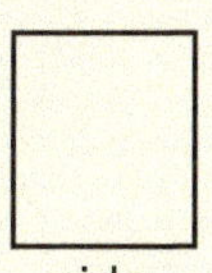
side

Sample answer:

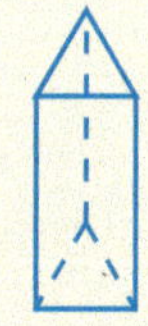

- "Can you prove that your drawing is accurate for the given faces? Explain." Listen to explanations and view their methods of proof.

Teaching Strategy

Asking students to work backwards requires higher cognitive demand. Solving a problem after practicing many similar examples develops the skill, but students need to understand meaning and the structure of the mathematics. You want students to work at levels of synthesis and evaluation to develop higher-order thinking.

Extra Example 3

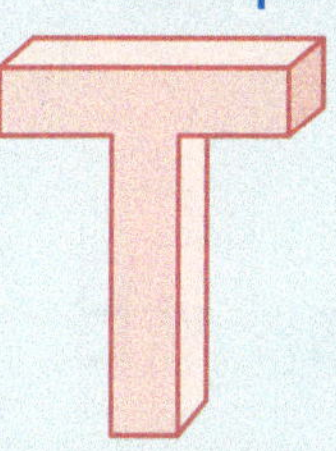

a. Find the numbers of faces, edges, and vertices of the solid. 10 faces, 24 edges, 16 vertices

b. Draw the front, side, and top views of the solid.

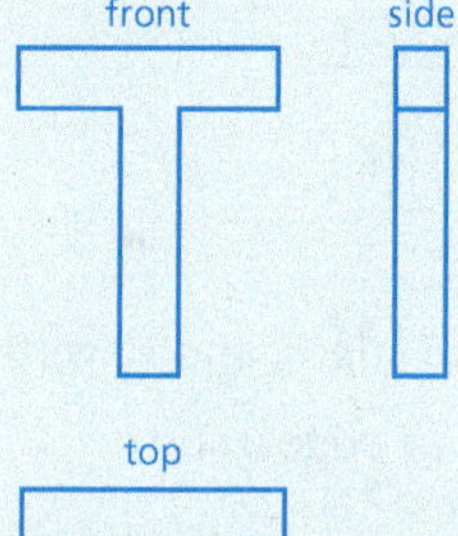

Self-Assessment for Problem Solving

7–9. See Additional Answers.

Learning Target

Describe and draw three-dimensional figures.

Success Criteria

- Find the numbers of faces, edges, and vertices of a three-dimensional figure.
- Draw prisms and pyramids.
- Draw the front, side, and top views of a three-dimensional figure.

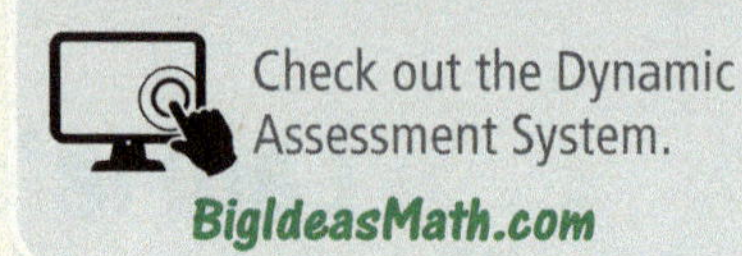

Review & Refresh

1. 15 ft^2
2. 18 km^2
3. 108 m^2
4. 24
5. 75
6. 352
7. 210
8. 36
9. 40
10. 70

Concepts, Skills, & Problem Solving

11. front: 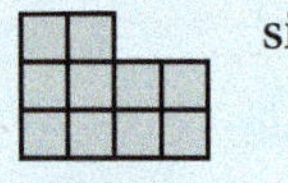 side: top: 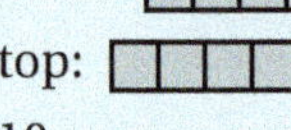
10

12. front: 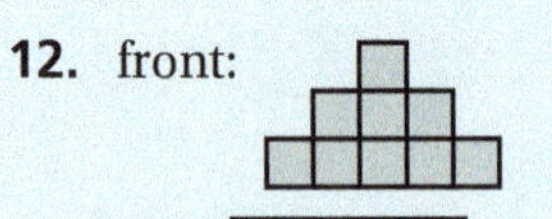 side: top: 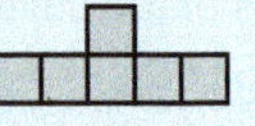
9

13. front: 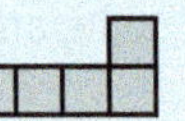
side:
top: 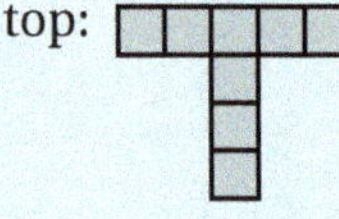
9

14. 7 faces, 15 edges, and 10 vertices
15. 10 faces, 24 edges, and 16 vertices
16. 7 faces, 12 edges, and 7 vertices
17. 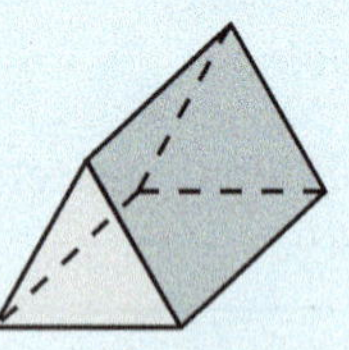
18. 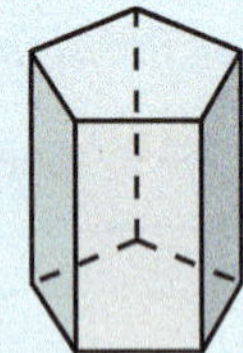
19. 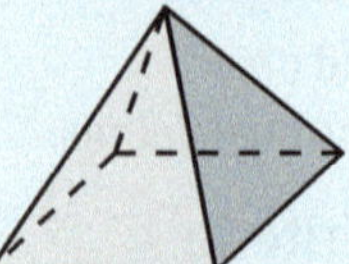
20. 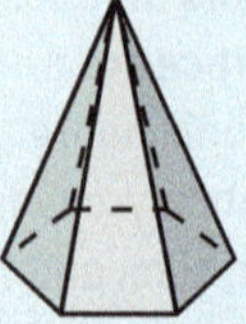
21. 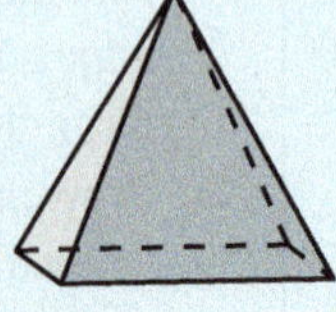
22. See Additional Answers.

Assignment Guide and Concept Check

Scaffold assignments to support all students in their learning progression. The suggested assignments are a starting point. Continue to assign additional exercises and revisit with spaced practice to move every student toward proficiency.

Level	Assignment 1	Assignment 2
Emerging	2, 3, 7, 10, 12, 14, 17, 19, 25	13, 16, 18, 21, 24, 27, 29
Proficient	2, 3, 7, 10, 13, 15, 17, 20, 26	16, 18, 21, 24, 27, 29, 33
Advanced	2, 7, 10, 13, 15, 16, 18, 20, 28	22, 27, 30, 31, 32, 33, 34

- Assignment 1 is for use after students complete the Self-Assessment for Concepts & Skills.
- Assignment 2 is for use after students complete the Self-Assessment for Problem Solving.
- The red exercises can be used as a concept check.

Review & Refresh Prior Skills

Exercises 1 and 2 Finding the Area of a Trapezoid
Exercise 3 Finding Area by Decomposition
Exercises 4–7 Finding the LCM
Exercises 8–10 Using a Tape Diagram

Common Errors

- **Exercises 17–20** Students may mix up the different types of solids. Remind them of the definitions and provide a few real-life examples of each solid.

7.4 Practice

Review & Refresh

Find the area of the figure.

1. 6 ft, 3 ft, 4 ft

2. 5 km, 3 km, 7 km

3. 6 m, 9 m, 9 m, 6 m

Find the LCM of the numbers.

4. 8, 12 **5.** 15, 25 **6.** 32, 44 **7.** 3, 7, 10

A bucket contains stones and seashells. You are given the number of seashells in the bucket and the ratio of stones to seashells. Find the number of stones in the bucket.

8. 18 seashells; 2 to 1 **9.** 30 seashells; 4 : 3 **10.** 40 seashells; 7 : 4

Concepts, Skills, & Problem Solving

DRAWING VIEWS OF A SOLID **Draw the front, side, and top views of the stack of cubes. Then find the number of cubes in the stack.** (See Exploration 2, p. 305.)

11. 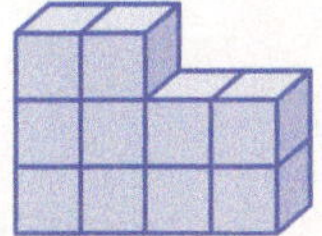

12. 

13. 

FACES, EDGES, AND VERTICES **Find the numbers of faces, edges, and vertices of the solid.**

14. 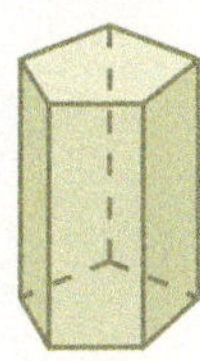

15. 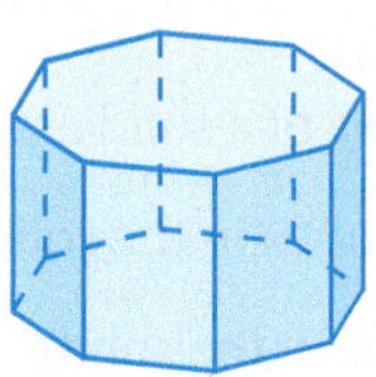

16. 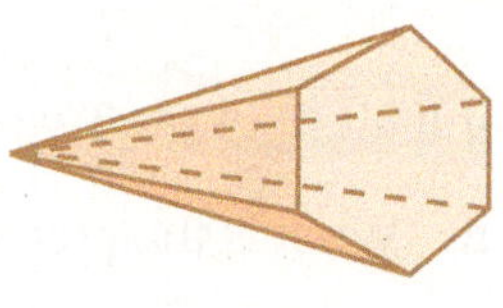

DRAWING SOLIDS **Draw the solid.**

17. triangular prism **18.** pentagonal prism

19. rectangular pyramid **20.** hexagonal pyramid

21. MP **MODELING REAL LIFE** The Pyramid of Cestius in Rome, Italy, is in the shape of a square pyramid. Draw a sketch of the pyramid.

22. **RESEARCH** Use the Internet to find a picture of the Washington Monument. Describe its shape.

DRAWING VIEWS OF A SOLID **Draw the front, side, and top views of the solid.**

23. 

24. 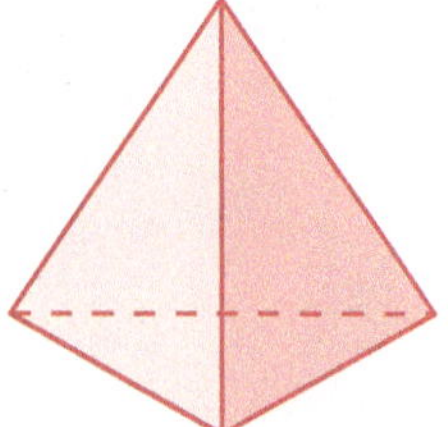

25. 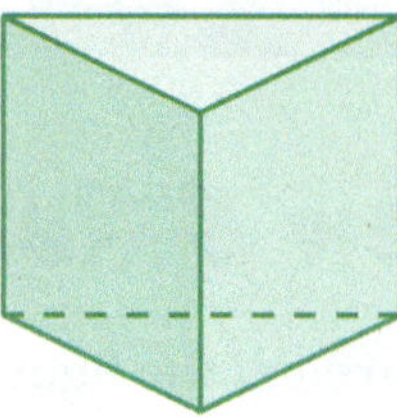

26. 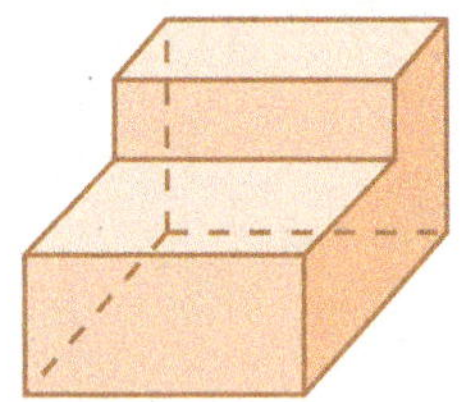

27. 

28. 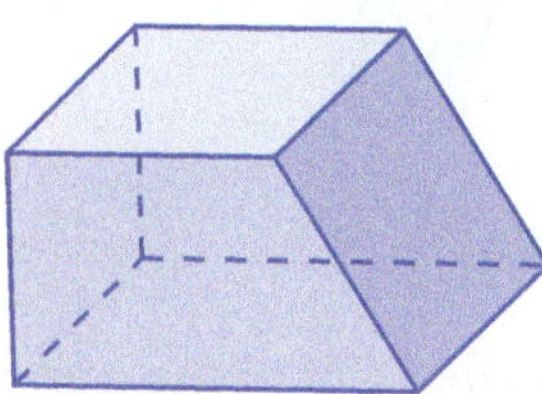

DRAWING SOLIDS **Draw a solid with the following front, side, and top views.**

29. 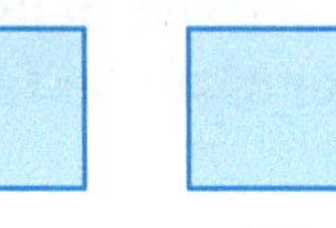

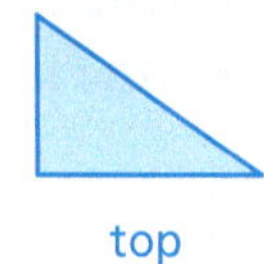

30. 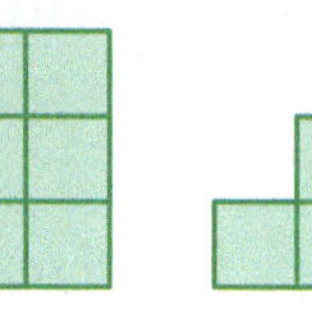

31. MP **MODELING REAL LIFE** Design and draw a house. Name the different solids that you can use to make a model of the house.

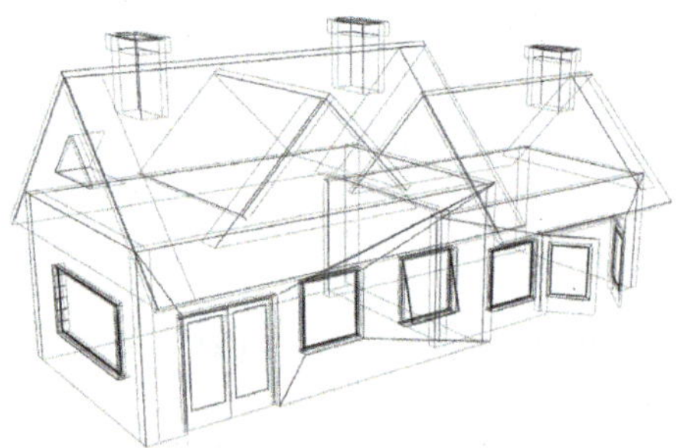

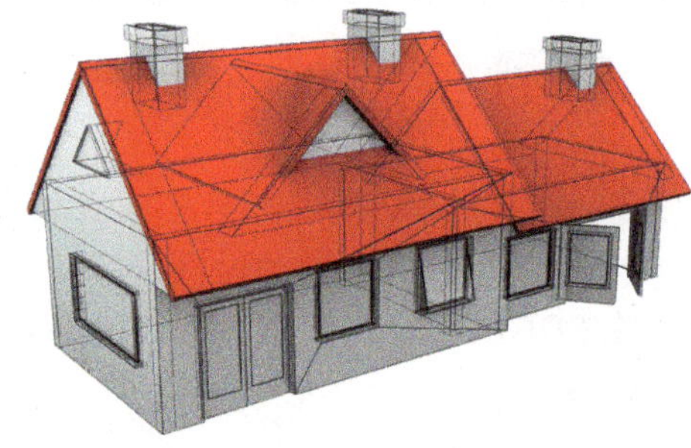

32. **DIG DEEPER!** Two of the three views of a solid are shown.

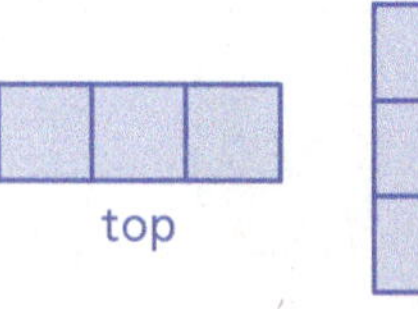

a. What is the greatest number of cubes in the solid?

b. What is the least number of cubes in the solid?

c. Draw the front views of both solids in parts (a) and (b).

33. **OPEN-ENDED** Draw two different solids with five faces.

a. Write the numbers of vertices and edges for each solid.

b. Explain how knowing the numbers of edges and vertices helps you draw a three-dimensional figure.

34. **CRITICAL THINKING** The base of a pyramid has n sides. Find the numbers of faces, edges, and vertices of the pyramid. Explain your reasoning.

Common Errors

- **Exercises 23–28** Students may have difficulty visualizing the front, side, and top views of the solid. Create paper objects for those who are struggling to draw the different sides of the solid.
- **Exercises 29 and 30** Students may not be able to see how the shapes go together. Have them cut out pieces of paper or use blocks to model the solid.

Mini-Assessment

1. Find the numbers of faces, edges, and vertices of the solid.

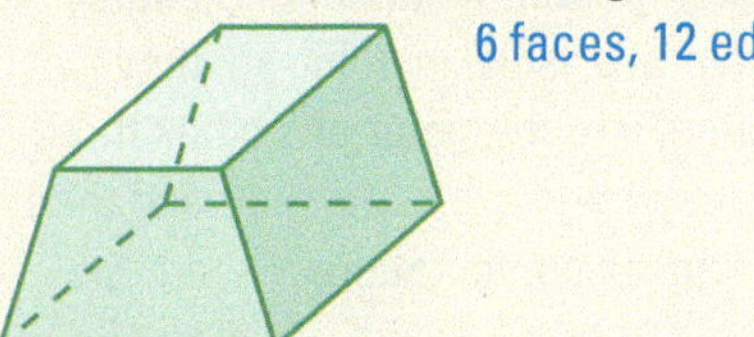

6 faces, 12 edges, 8 vertices

2. Draw a hexagonal prism.

3. Draw a triangular pyramid.

4. You and a friend attend a birthday party.

a. Find the numbers of faces, edges, and vertices of the cake.
6 faces, 12 edges, 8 vertices

b. Draw the front, side, and top views of the birthday cake.

Section Resources

Surface Level	Deep Level
Resources by Chapter • Extra Practice • Reteach • Puzzle Time Student Journal • Self-Assessment • Practice Differentiating the Lesson Tutorial Videos Skills Review Handbook Skills Trainer	Resources by Chapter • Enrichment and Extension Graphic Organizers Dynamic Assessment System • Section Practice

Concepts, Skills, & Problem Solving

23. front: side: top:

24. front: side: top:

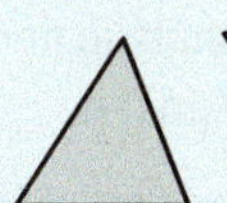

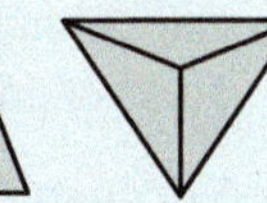

25. See Additional Answers.

26. front: side: top:

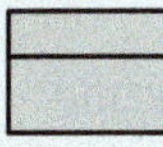

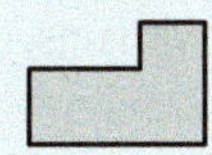

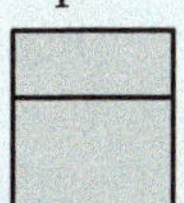

27. front: side:

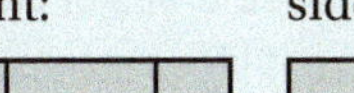

top:

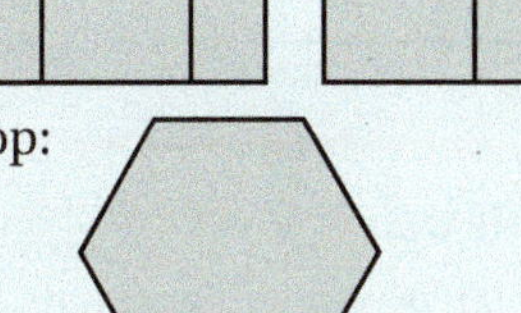

28. front: side

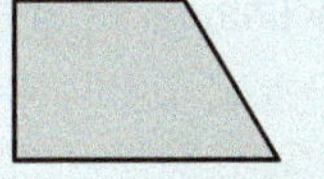

top:

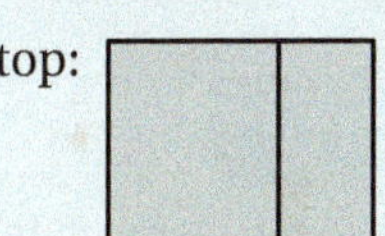

29.

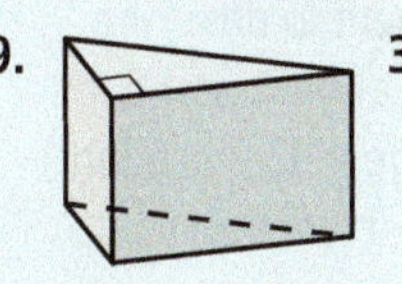

30.

31. *Answer should include, but is not limited to:* an original drawing of a house; a description of any solids in the drawing

32. a. 9 b. 5

c. greatest: least:

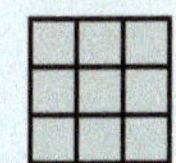

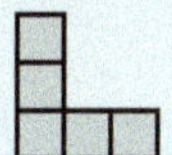

33. See Additional Answers.

34. $(n + 1)$ faces, $2n$ edges, $(n + 1)$ vertices; n lateral faces and 1 base, n edges at sides of base and n edges between lateral sides, n vertices of the base and 1 vertex at the top

Laurie's Notes

Learning Target

Represent prisms using nets and use nets to find surface areas of prisms.

Success Criteria

- Draw nets to represent prisms.
- Use nets to find surface areas of prisms.
- Use a formula to find the surface area of a cube.
- Apply surface areas of prisms to solve real-life problems.

Warm Up

Cumulative, vocabulary, and prerequisite skills practice opportunities are available in the *Resources by Chapter* or at *BigIdeasMath.com.*

ELL Support

Students may be familiar with the word *net*. Ask them to describe what they know about nets. Then point to the image in Exploration 1 and explain that it is a net in mathematics. A net is a two-dimensional representation of a three-dimensional solid.

Exploration 1

a. rectangular prism

b. 228 units^2

Exploration 2

a. 78 units^2;
$2(3 \times 3) + 4(3 \times 5) = 78$

b. 84 units^2;
$3 \times 6 + 4 \times 6 + 5 \times 6 + 2\left(\frac{1}{2}\right)(3 \times 4) = 84$

Preparing to Teach

- After naming attributes and drawing prisms in the previous section, students will now find surface areas of rectangular and triangular prisms.
- **MP8 Look for and Express Regularity in Repeated Reasoning:** Students will find the area of the entire surface of several prisms. In doing so, they may discover an efficient method. For instance, a rectangular prism has three pairs of congruent faces. Finding the area of one from each pair and then doubling is more efficient than completing six computations.

Motivate

- Hold up two different rectangular prisms made of cardboard, one clearly larger than the other.
- ? "Which box required more cardboard to make it? How do you know?" Listen for explanations that refer to finding the area of each face, adding all the areas, and then repeating the process for the other box.
- Review vocabulary associated with prisms, including *base* and *lateral face*.
- Point out that prisms are named by the shapes of their bases. For instance, a triangular prism has triangular bases.
- **Note:** *Lateral surface area* will be taught in the next course.

Exploration 1

- **Teaching Tip:** To avoid having scraps of paper on the floor, tape plastic bags to desks around the room. Make sure there is a bag close to each group.
- To copy the figure correctly, students need to determine the dimensions of each face. This process helps develop the concept of **surface area** of a solid.
- If time permits, ask students questions about the prism they folded.
- ? **Extension:** Display a **net** for a triangular prism. Complete parts (a) and (b), asking questions as before. Then ask, "How are the two solids different? the same?" The bases are different shapes; They are both prisms.

Exploration 2

- **Scaffolding:** If time is a concern, have half the class work on part (a) and the other half work on part (b).
- **Teaching Tip:** Refer to the faces as the *surface*, so students are finding the area of the surface. This leads into the definition of *surface area* in the lesson.
- Some students have well-defined spatial sense and can "see" all the surfaces that they need to consider, while others may want to look at the prisms unfolded. These drawings can be challenging. Going from a solid to the two-dimensional representation is different than the reverse. If students are having trouble, suggest that they begin with one face and sketch it. Then move to a second face that shares an edge with the first face. The two faces are either both lateral, or one is a lateral face and the other is a base.
- Have students share their methods and solutions.

7.5 Surface Areas of Prisms

Learning Target: Represent prisms using nets and use nets to find surface areas of prisms.

Success Criteria:
- I can draw nets to represent prisms.
- I can use nets to find surface areas of prisms.
- I can use a formula to find the surface area of a cube.
- I can apply surface areas of prisms to solve real-life problems.

EXPLORATION 1 Using Grid Paper to Construct a Solid

Work with a partner. Copy the figure shown below onto grid paper.

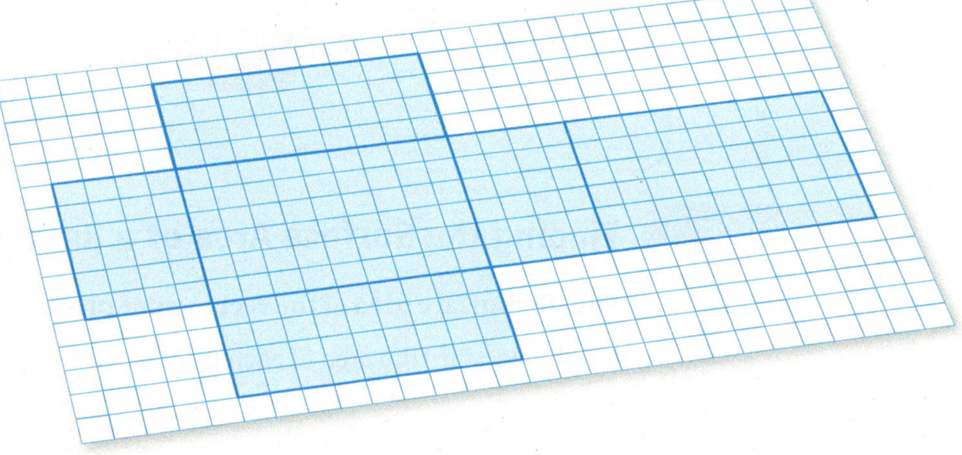

a. Cut out and fold the figure to form a solid. What type of solid does the figure form?

b. What is the area of the entire surface of the solid?

EXPLORATION 2 Finding the Area of the Entire Surface

Math Practice

Repeat Calculations

When finding the area of the entire surface, what calculations do you repeat?

Work with a partner. Find the area of the entire surface of each solid. Explain your reasoning.

a.

b.

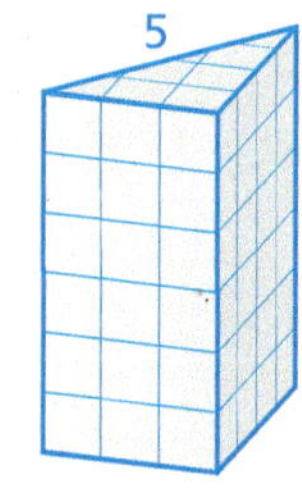

7.5 Lesson

Key Vocabulary
surface area, *p. 312*
net, *p. 312*

The **surface area** of a solid is the sum of the areas of all of its faces. You can use a two-dimensional representation of a solid, called a **net**, to find the surface area of the solid. Surface area is measured in *square units.*

Net of a Rectangular Prism

A *rectangular prism* is a prism with rectangular bases.

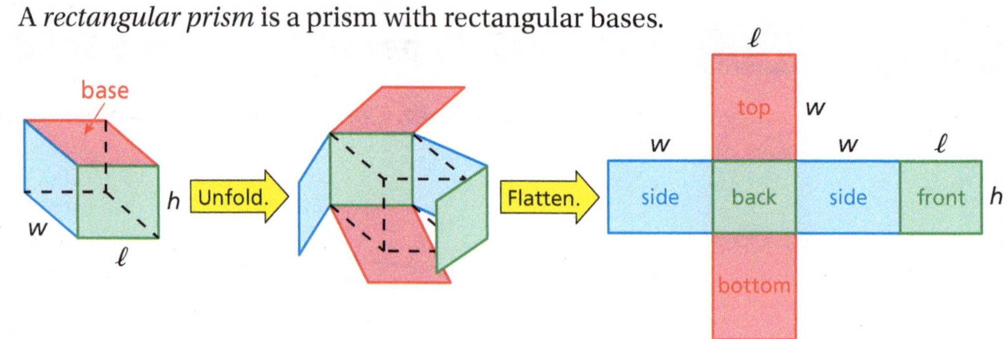

EXAMPLE 1 Finding the Surface Area of a Rectangular Prism

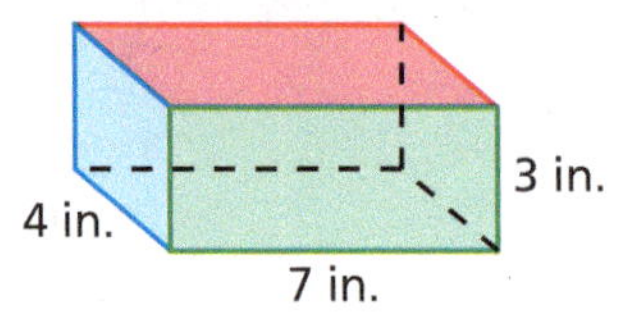

Find the surface area of the rectangular prism.

Use a net to find the area of each face.

Top: $7 \cdot 4 = 28$
Bottom: $7 \cdot 4 = 28$
Front: $7 \cdot 3 = 21$
Back: $7 \cdot 3 = 21$
Side: $4 \cdot 3 = 12$
Side: $4 \cdot 3 = 12$

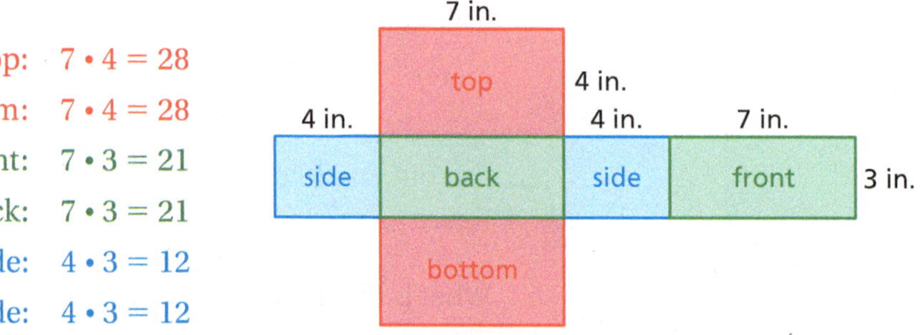

Find the sum of the areas of the faces.

$$\text{Surface Area} = \text{Area of top} + \text{Area of bottom} + \text{Area of front} + \text{Area of back} + \text{Area of a side} + \text{Area of a side}$$

$$S = 28 + 28 + 21 + 21 + 12 + 12 = 122$$

So, the surface area is 122 square inches.

Try It **Find the surface area of the rectangular prism.**

1.

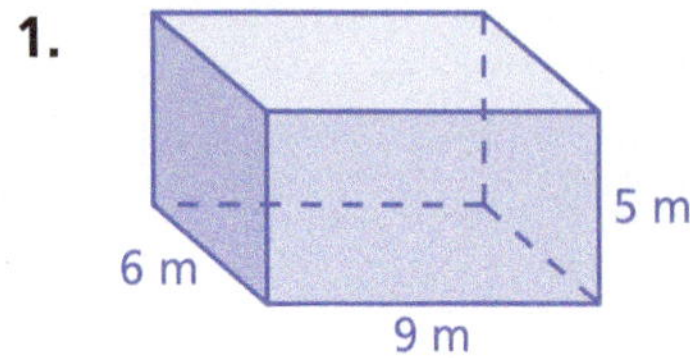

2.

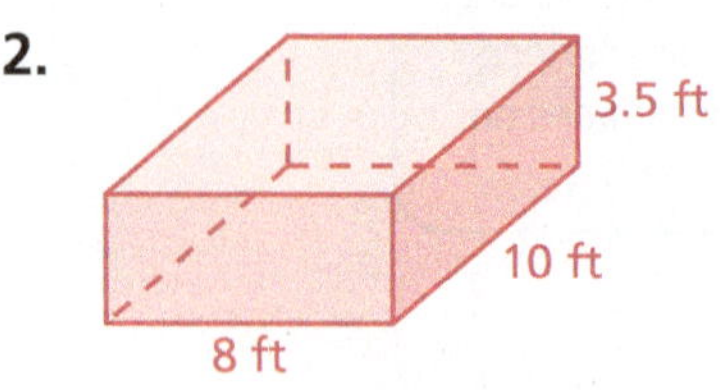

Laurie's Notes

Scaffolding Instruction

- Visualizing three dimensions from a two-dimensional representation is a skill that students need to practice. A net is one way to visualize a solid. It allows students a view of all faces, so they can find the area of all the surfaces and deduce a practical formula.
- **Emerging:** Students need practice visualizing the diagram of all faces to realize that opposite faces are congruent in a rectangular prism. They may need to fold nets into prisms to conceptualize the transition from two dimensions to three dimensions. The examples will lead them through this process.
- **Proficient:** Many of these students can visualize the net without the drawing. They understand the development of finding the surface area of a prism using a net. Review the formula for finding the surface area of a cube and then have students complete the Try It exercises. Students can use the Self-Assessment exercises to assess their understanding.

Discuss

- Define **surface area** and **net**.
- Remind students that square units are used to label surface area.

Key Idea

- Write the Key Idea.
- **Teaching Strategy:** Display cardboard prisms that have been folded and assembled. Ask students to visualize and describe the cardboard nets that result when the prisms are "unfolded."
- Unfold the prisms so that students can see the net of the prism.

EXAMPLE 1

? Hold a cardboard box and ask, "How can you find the total amount of cardboard used to make this box?" Find the sum of the areas of the faces.

- **MP8 Look for and Express Regularity in Repeated Reasoning:** Work through the example as shown. Students may find it easier to consider the three pairs of opposite faces instead of finding the area of each of the six faces separately.

? "What units are used to label surface area?" square units

◉ This example formalizes the launch of the second success criterion.

Try It

- **Turn and Talk:** Have students work independently on the exercises. Then have students discuss their answers with a partner and look for errors.
- In Exercise 2, verify that students complete the decimal computations correctly. Using prior skills within different contexts builds fluency. Remind students that there are many instances in which surface areas involve fractions and decimals.

Scaffold instruction to support all students in their learning. Learning is individualized and you may want to group students differently as they move in and out of these levels with each skill and concept. Student self-assessment and feedback help guide your instructional decisions about how and when to layer support for all students to become proficient learners.

Teaching Strategy

Students need to see and touch physical models whenever possible. Using three-dimensional models helps students imagine the solids that are represented in two dimensions. They can identify lateral faces and bases. Students can also determine parallel and perpendicular faces, which are difficult to see in two-dimensional drawings. Nets are another model students can use to view three dimensions in two dimensions.

Extra Example 1

Find the surface area of the rectangular prism.

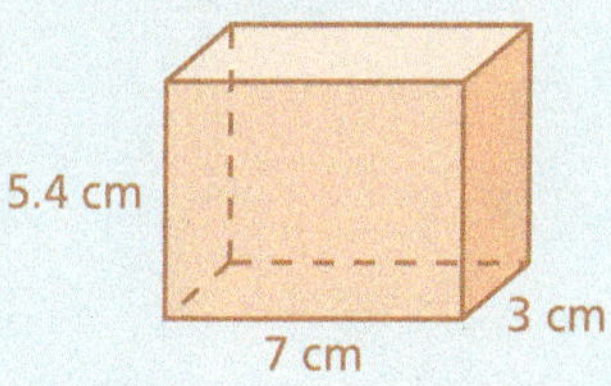

150 cm^2

Try It

1. 258 m^2
2. 286 ft^2

Laurie's Notes

Key Idea

- Write the Key Idea and draw the net.
- **Teaching Strategy:** Have a net available as a visual, whether it is a cardboard box or a triangular prism made from polygon frames.
- Discuss with students that a triangular prism has two opposite faces that are triangles and the rest of the faces are rectangles.

EXAMPLE 2

- Note that the net is a visual reminder to find the area of each face. Color-coding the face helps students keep track of their work.
- ? "How many faces does a triangular prism have?" 5
- ? "How do you find the area of a triangle?" $A = \frac{1}{2}bh$
- Encourage students to write a verbal model for the surface area of the prism and then substitute the areas of the faces as they are computed.

Try It

- **MP6 Attend to Precision:** Students may forget to include the area of one or more of the faces when finding the surface area.
- Exercise 3 involves a right triangle. Some students may need to be reminded that one side is the base and the one side is the height.

ELL Support

After demonstrating Example 2, have students practice language by working in groups to complete the exercises. Model guiding questions such as: How many faces does the prism have? What is the area of the base? Monitor student discussions. Expect students at different language levels to perform as described.

Beginner: State the answers to the guiding questions using numbers.

Intermediate: State the answers to the guiding questions using phrases such as, "five sides."

Advanced: State the answers to the guiding questions using sentences such as, "There are five sides."

Extra Example 2

Find the surface area of the triangular prism.

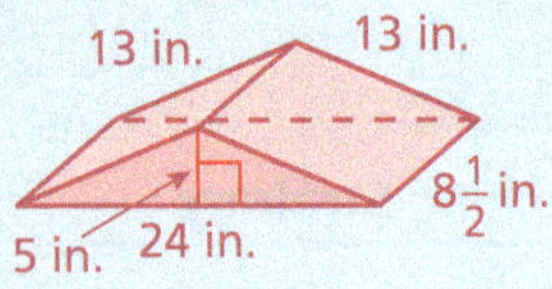

545 in.^{2}

Try It

3. 60 yd^2
4. 420 m^2

Net of a Triangular Prism

A *triangular prism* is a prism with triangular bases.

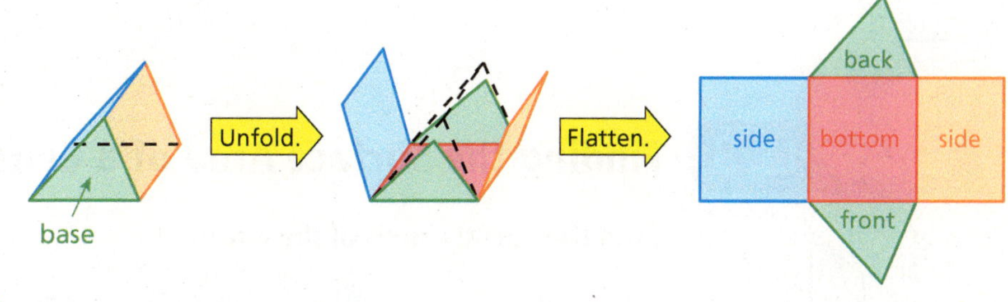

EXAMPLE 2 Finding the Surface Area of a Triangular Prism

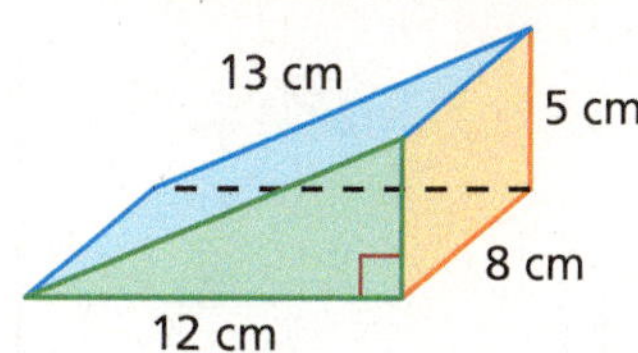

Find the surface area of the triangular prism.

Use a net to find the area of each face.

Bottom: $12 \cdot 8 = 96$

Front: $\frac{1}{2} \cdot 12 \cdot 5 = 30$

Back: $\frac{1}{2} \cdot 12 \cdot 5 = 30$

Side: $13 \cdot 8 = 104$

Side: $8 \cdot 5 = 40$

13 cm
5 cm
13 cm
back
12 cm
side
bottom
side
8 cm
front

Find the sum of the areas of the faces.

Surface Area	=	Area of bottom	+	Area of front	+	Area of back	+	Area of a side	+	Area of a side
S	=	96	+	30	+	30	+	104	+	40
	= 300									

So, the surface area is 300 square centimeters.

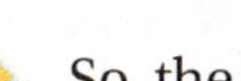

Find the surface area of the triangular prism.

3.

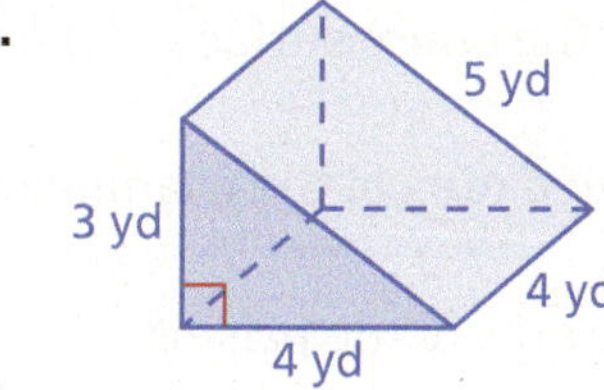

4.

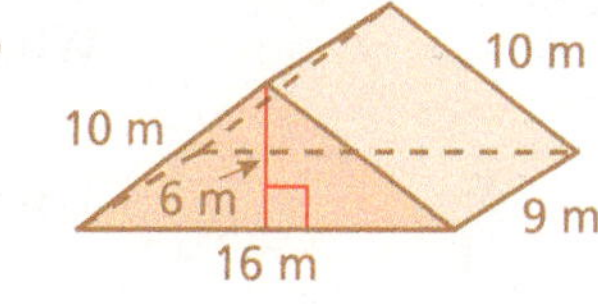

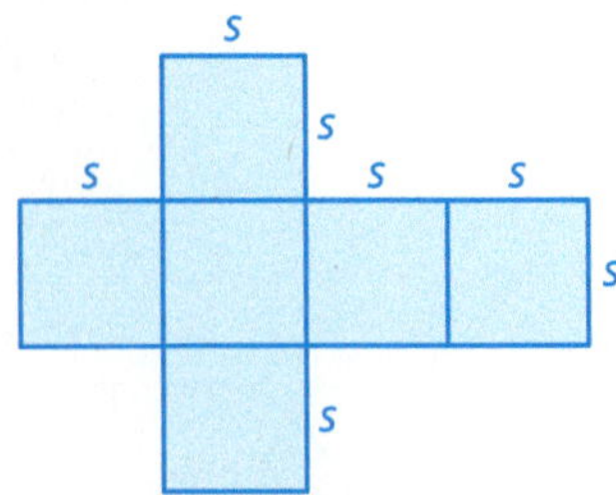

When all the edges of a rectangular prism have the same length s, the rectangular prism is a cube. The net of a cube shows that each of the 6 identical square faces has an area of s^2. So, a formula for the surface area of a cube is

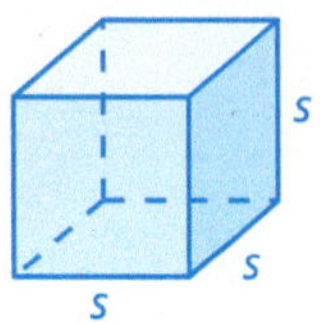

$S = 6s^2$. Formula for surface area of a cube

EXAMPLE 3 Finding the Surface Area of a Cube

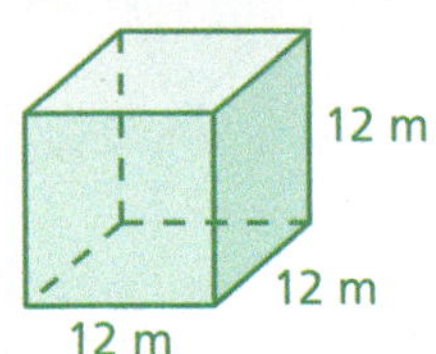

Find the surface area of the cube.

$S = 6s^2$	Write formula for surface area of a cube.
$= 6(12)^2$	Substitute 12 for s.
$= 6(144)$	Evaluate power.
$= 864$	Multiply.

The surface area of the cube is 864 square meters.

Try It **Find the surface area of the cube.**

5. 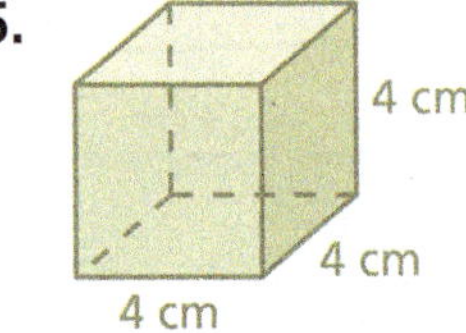

6. 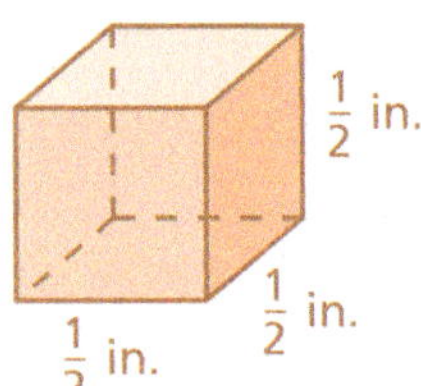

Self-Assessment for Concepts & Skills

Solve each exercise. Then rate your understanding of the success criteria in your journal.

7. **FINDING SURFACE AREA** Find the surface area of a cube with edge lengths of 9 centimeters.

8. **DIFFERENT WORDS, SAME QUESTION** Which is different? Find "both" answers.

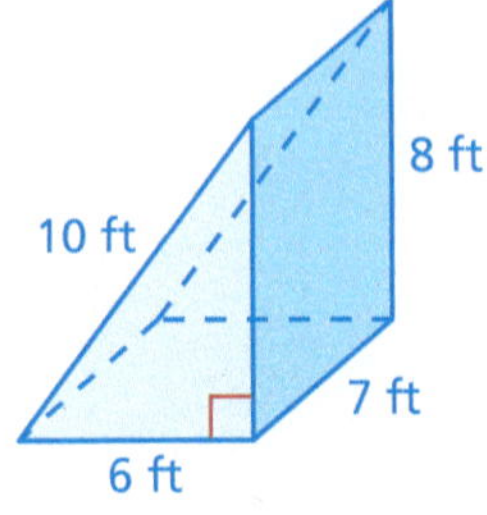

What is the sum of the areas of all of the faces of the prism?

What is the area of the entire surface of the prism?

What is the combined area of the triangular faces of the prism?

What is the surface area of the prism?

Laurie's Notes

Discuss

- Hold up a cube-shaped object (a die) and ask students to name the solid. *Rectangular prism* and *square prism* are correct, but you want students to state the most specific name, *cube*.
- Have students sketch a net for a cube on grid paper. Solicit volunteers to share their nets. They won't all look like the one in the book. The squares can be oriented differently and still form a cube.
- ? "What can you tell me about the edges of the figure in your net?" They are all the same length.
- Ask students to discuss how they can find the surface area of a cube. Some students will recognize that all six faces are congruent and each area is s^2. Although they can add the areas of the six faces, encourage students to find the area of a single face and then multiply by 6. This is the most efficient method and represents the formula.

EXAMPLE 3

- Write the formula for the surface area of a cube: $S = 6s^2$.
- Substitute for the variable and work through the problem as shown.

Try It

- **MP8 Look for and Express Regularity in Repeated Reasoning:** After discovering the formula for the surface area of a cube, students will see how efficiently they can find the surface area of a cube compared to the surface area of a rectangular prism.
- In Exercise 6, verify that students complete the fraction computations correctly.
- Check that students are using square units in their answers.

Self-Assessment for Concepts & Skills

- **Attend to Precision:** These exercises emphasize the importance of knowing mathematical terms and formulas.
- **Neighbor Check:** Have students work independently and then have their neighbors check and discuss their work.
- For Exercise 8, listen to students' reasoning to gain insight into their understanding of the surface area of a prism.
- Students are assessing their understanding of the first three success criteria.

ELL Support

Have students work in pairs to complete Exercise 7 and display their answers on whiteboards for your review. Group two pairs to discuss Exercise 8 and monitor discussions, providing support as needed.

The Success Criteria Self-Assessment chart can be found in the *Student Journal* or online at *BigIdeasMath.com*.

Extra Example 3

Find the surface area of the cube.

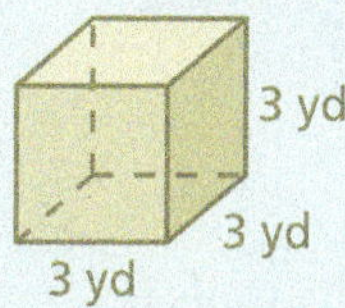

54 yd^2

Try It

5. 96 cm^2
6. $1\frac{1}{2}$ in.^{2}

Self-Assessment for Concepts & Skills

7. 486 cm^2
8. What is the combined area of the triangular faces of the prism?; 48 ft^2; 216 ft^2

Extra Example 4

What is the least amount of material needed to make a box in the shape of a rectangular prism with a length of 18 inches, a width of 16 inches, and a height of 14 inches? 1528 in.^{2}

Self-Assessment for Problem Solving

9. 72 cm^2
10. 10; The area of the walls is 560 square feet.
11. 10 cm

Learning Target

Represent prisms using nets and use nets to find surface areas of prisms.

Success Criteria

- Draw nets to represent prisms.
- Use nets to find surface areas of prisms.
- Use a formula to find the surface area of a cube.
- Apply surface areas of prisms to solve real-life problems.

Laurie's Notes

EXAMPLE 4

- Show the picture of the gold-wrapped prism. Ask students what it may be and why it is wrapped in a reflective gold material. After several guesses, explain that it is a space telescope in the shape of a prism.
- Have a volunteer read the problem aloud.
- ? "How can you find the least amount of MLI needed?" Listen for answers that define the surface area of the prism. "Why might you want to know the least amount needed?" *Sample answer:* To purchase the least amount of material required because the material is probably expensive.
- Have students work in pairs to solve the problem. Check their answers for square units.
- Select volunteers to show different methods of solving. Students may use nets, verbal models, or double the nonparallel face areas.
- Point out the Check Reasonableness note.

Self-Assessment for Problem Solving

- Allow time in class for students to practice using the problem-solving plan. Remember, some students may only be able to complete the first step.
- Students will encounter rectangular and triangular prisms in real life. These problems show several contexts associated with surface area.
- **MP1 Make Sense of Problems and Persevere in Solving Them:** Students analyze information, find entry points, and make plans based on their understanding of prisms. Mathematically proficient students check their answers for reasonableness.
- ? In Exercise 10, ask, "Is there a difference between *finding the least number of pints of paint needed* and *finding the least amount of paint needed*?" Discuss how changing the wording may change the answer.
- Have students use *Thumbs Up* to indicate their understanding of finding surface areas of prisms to solve real-life problems.

The Success Criteria Self-Assessment chart can be found in the *Student Journal* or online at *BigIdeasMath.com.*

Closure

? Tell students that you are mailing a gift to a friend. You need to place it in a box (rectangular prism) that has whole-number dimensions and meets the following specifications:

- the length is between 2 inches and 8 inches,
- the width is between 2 inches and 6 inches,
- the height is between 6 inches and 12 inches, and
- the surface area is between 128 square inches and 160 square inches.

"Find a set of possible dimensions for the box. What might the gift be?" *Sample answer:* 5 in. $\times$ 3 in. $\times$ 7 in.; a candle

EXAMPLE 4 Modeling Real Life

Space instruments are often wrapped in gold-colored multi-layer insulation (MLI) to reflect radiation from the Sun. What is the least amount of MLI needed to wrap an instrument in the shape of a rectangular prism with a length of 5 feet, a width of 5 feet, and a height of 3 feet?

Draw the prism. The least amount of MLI needed is represented by the surface area of the prism. Use a net to find the surface area.

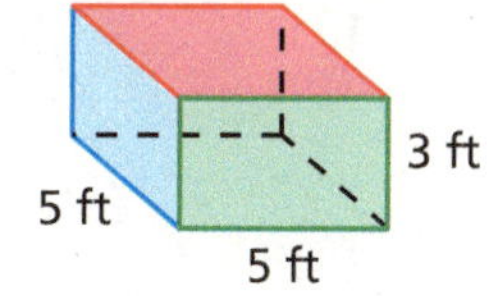

Top: $5 \cdot 5 = 25$

Bottom: $5 \cdot 5 = 25$

Front: $5 \cdot 3 = 15$

Back: $5 \cdot 3 = 15$

Side: $5 \cdot 3 = 15$

Side: $5 \cdot 3 = 15$

5 ft
top
5 ft
5 ft
5 ft
5 ft
side
back
side
front
3 ft
bottom

$S = 25 + 25 + 15 + 15 + 15 + 15 = 110$

So, the least amount of MLI needed is 110 square feet.

Check Reasonableness The surface area of a 5 ft × 5 ft × 3 ft prism should be less than the surface area of a 5 ft × 5 ft × 5 ft cube. The cube has a surface area of $6(5)^2 = 150$ square feet. Because $110\text{ ft}^2 < 150\text{ ft}^2$, the answer is reasonable. ✓

Find General Methods

What is the surface area of a rectangular prism with length ℓ, width w, and height h? Explain your reasoning.

Self-Assessment for Problem Solving

Solve each exercise. Then rate your understanding of the success criteria in your journal.

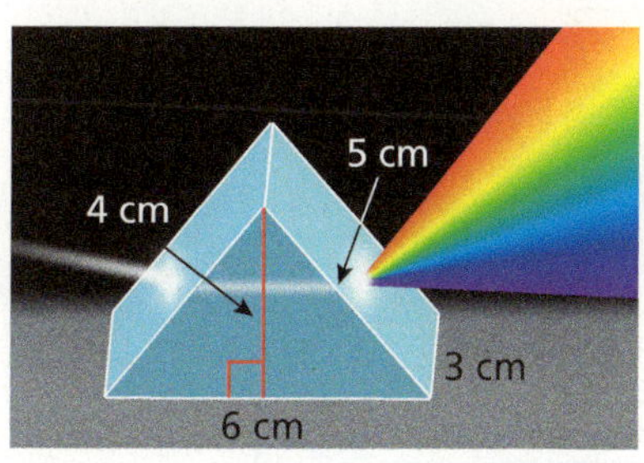

9. Light shines through a glass prism and forms a rainbow. What is the surface area of the prism?

10. One pint of chalkboard paint covers 60 square feet. What is the least number of pints of paint needed to paint the walls of a room in the shape of a rectangular prism with a length of 15 feet, a width of 13 feet, and a height of 10 feet? Explain.

11. **DIG DEEPER!** A flexible *metamaterial* is developed for use in robotics and prosthetics. A block of metamaterial is in the shape of a cube with a surface area of 600 square centimeters. What is the edge length of the block of metamaterial?

7.5 Practice

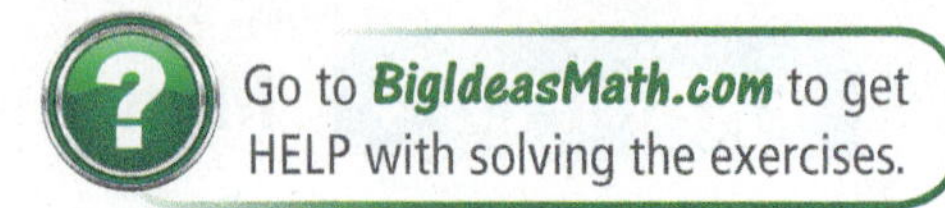

Review & Refresh

Draw the front, side, and top views of the solid.

1. 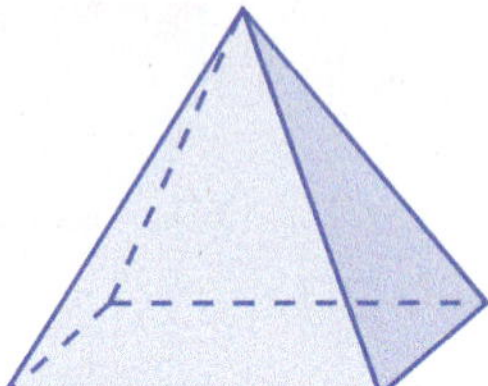

2. 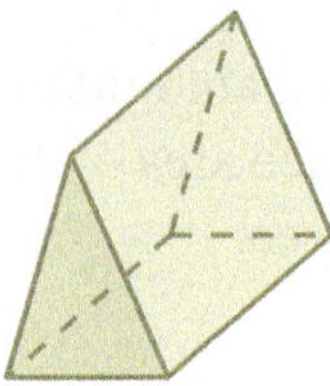

3. 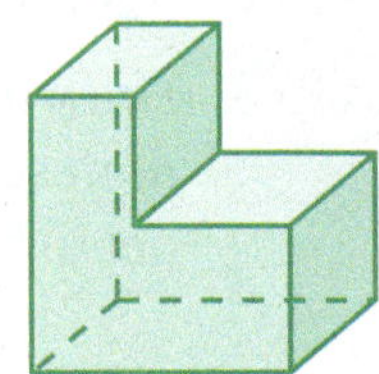

Find the GCF of the numbers.

4. 18, 72

5. 44, 110

6. 78, 93

7. 60, 96, 156

Solve the equation.

8. $s - 5 = 12$

9. $x + 9 = 20$

10. $48 = 6r$

11. $\frac{m}{5} = 13$

Divide.

12. $496 \div 16$

13. $765 \div 45$

14. $1173 \div 23$

Concepts, Skills, & Problem Solving

USING TOOLS **Use a net to find the area of the entire surface of the solid. Explain your reasoning.** (See Exploration 2, p. 311.)

15. 

16. 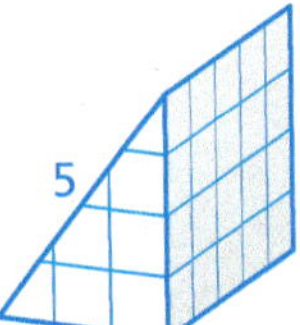

17. 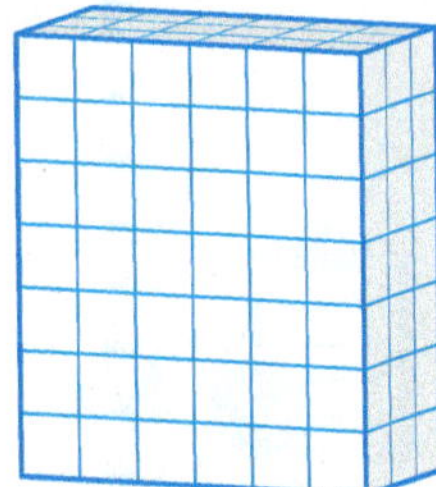

FINDING SURFACE AREA **Find the surface area of the rectangular prism.**

18. 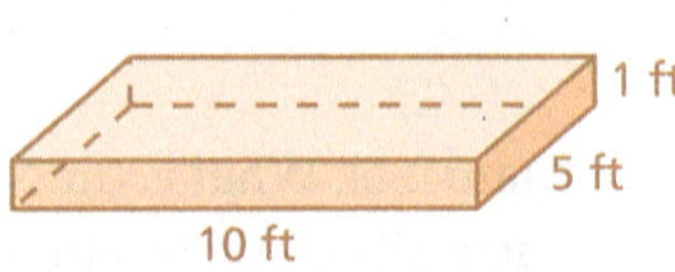

19. 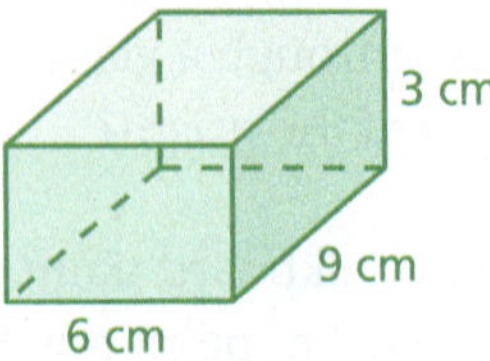

20. 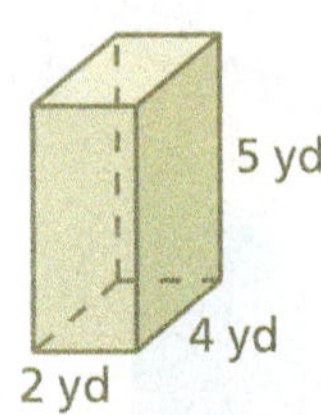

21. 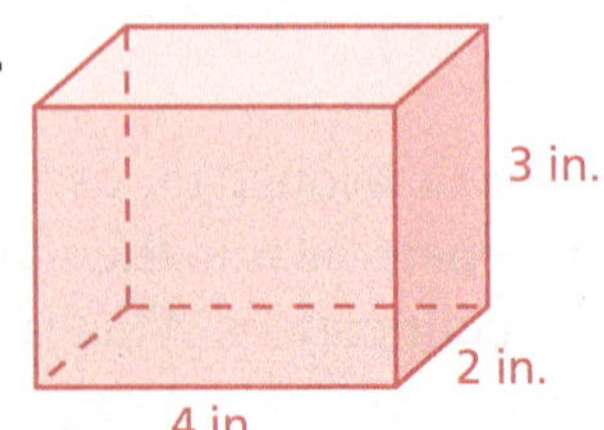

22. 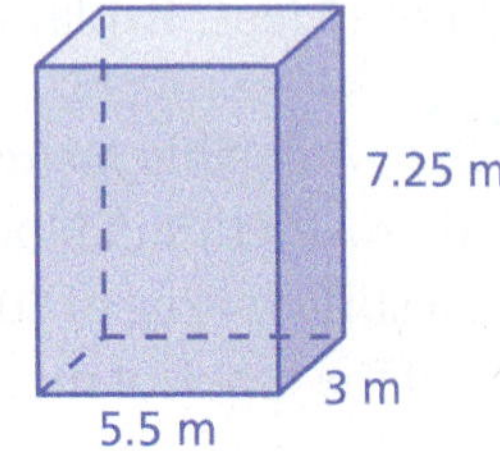

23. 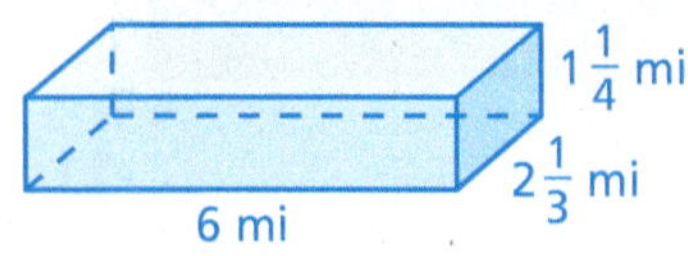

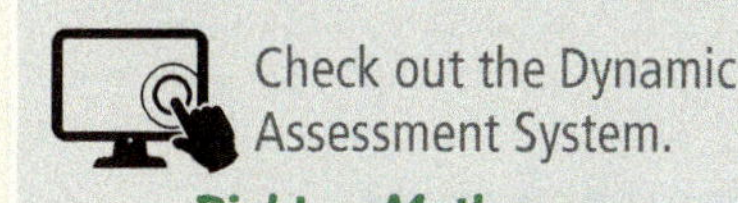

Assignment Guide and Concept Check

Scaffold assignments to support all students in their learning progression. The suggested assignments are a starting point. Continue to assign additional exercises and revisit with spaced practice to move every student toward proficiency.

Level	Assignment 1	Assignment 2
Emerging	1, 7, 9, 11, 14, 16, 21, 22, 24, 25, 32	30, 31, 35, 36, 39, 40
Proficient	1, 7, 9, 11, 14, 16, 19, 22, 25, 26, 33, 36	31, 37, 38, 39, 40, 41
Advanced	1, 7, 9, 11, 14, 16, 19, 23, 27, 29, 34, 36	31, 38, 39, 40, 41, 42

- Assignment 1 is for use after students complete the Self-Assessment for Concepts & Skills.
- Assignment 2 is for use after students complete the Self-Assessment for Problem Solving.
- The red exercises can be used as a concept check.

Review & Refresh Prior Skills

Exercises 1–3 Drawing Views of a Solid
Exercises 4–7 Finding the GCF
Exercises 8–11 Solving Equations
Exercises 12–14 Dividing Whole Numbers

Common Errors

- **Exercises 18–23** Students may find the area of only three faces instead of all six. Remind them that each face is paired with another. Show students the net of a rectangular solid to remind them of the six faces.

Review & Refresh

1. front: side: top:
2. front: side: top:
3. front: side: top:
4. 18
5. 22
6. 3
7. 12
8. $s = 17$
9. $x = 11$
10. $r = 8$
11. $m = 65$
12. 31
13. 17
14. 51

Concepts, Skills, & Problem Solving

15. 94 units^2; $2(5)(3) + 2(4)(3) + 2(4)(5) = 94$
16. 72 units^2; $2\left(\frac{1}{2}\right)(4)(3) + (5)(3) + (5)(4) + (5)(5) = 72$
17. 162 units^2; $2(3)(7) + 2(6)(7) + 2(3)(6) = 162$
18. 130 ft^2
19. 198 cm^2
20. 76 yd^2
21. 52 in.^{2}
22. 156.25 m^2
23. $48\frac{5}{6}$ mi^2

Concepts, Skills, & Problem Solving

24. 132 cm^2
25. 740 m^2
26. 828 in.^2
27. 17.6 ft^2
28. 57.1 mm^2
29. 324 m^2
30. 448 in.^2; It is the surface area of the box.
31. 136 ft^2
32. 216 km^2
33. $\frac{2}{3} \text{ ft}^2$
34. 181.5 yd^2
35. 294 cm^2
36. no; $S = 12h + 18$

Common Errors

- **Exercises 24–29** Students may forget to count the surface area of the top and bottom faces. Remind them that they must count all of the faces, which includes the top and bottom as well as the sides.

FINDING SURFACE AREA **Find the surface area of the triangular prism.**

24.

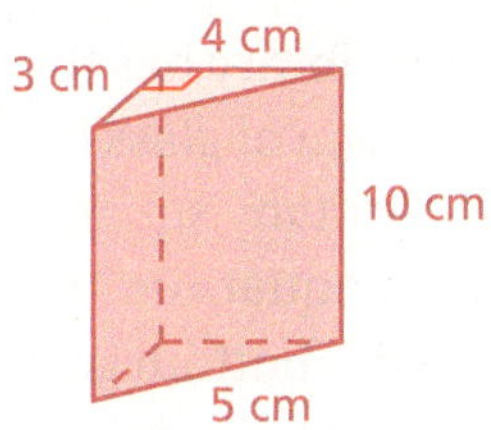

25.

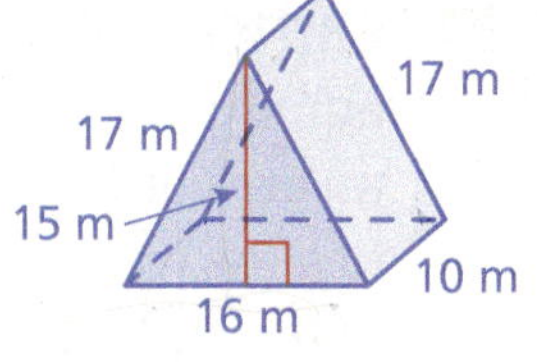

26.

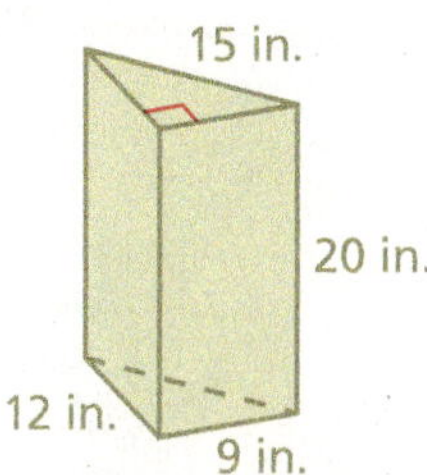

27.

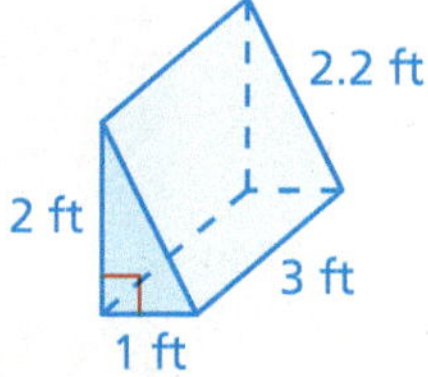

28.

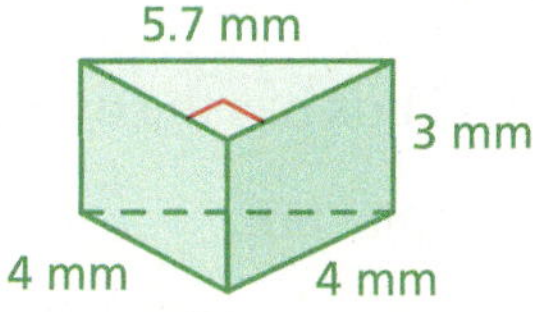

29.

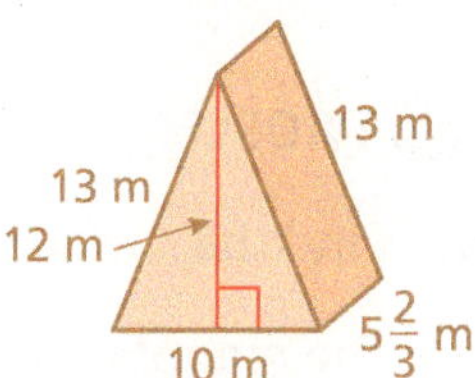

30. **MP MODELING REAL LIFE** A gift box in the shape of a rectangular prism measures 8 inches by 8 inches by 10 inches. What is the least amount of wrapping paper needed to wrap the gift box? Explain.

31. **MP MODELING REAL LIFE** What is the least amount of fabric needed to make the tent?

FINDING SURFACE AREA **Find the surface area of the cube.**

32.

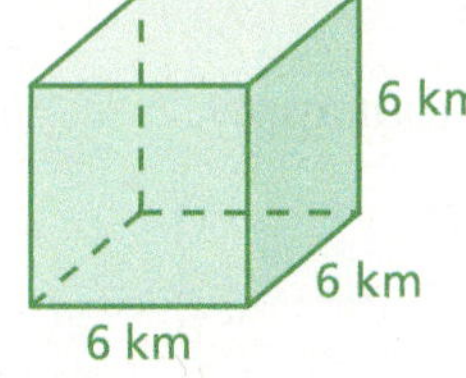

33.

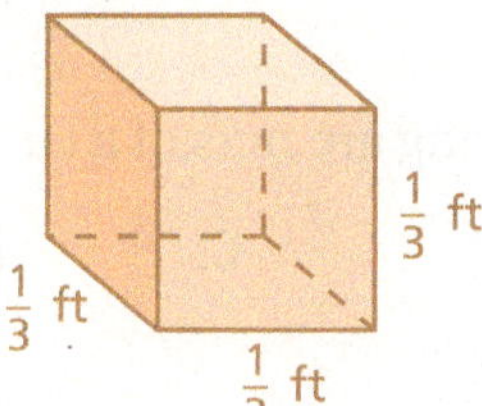

34.

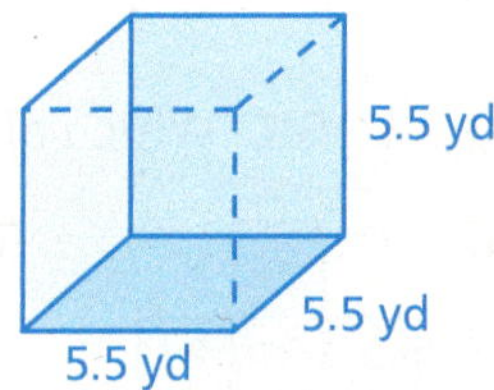

35. **MP MODELING REAL LIFE** A piece of dry ice is in the shape of a cube with edge lengths of 7 centimeters. Find the surface area of the dry ice.

36. **MP YOU BE THE TEACHER** Your friend finds the surface area of the prism. Is your friend correct? Explain your reasoning.

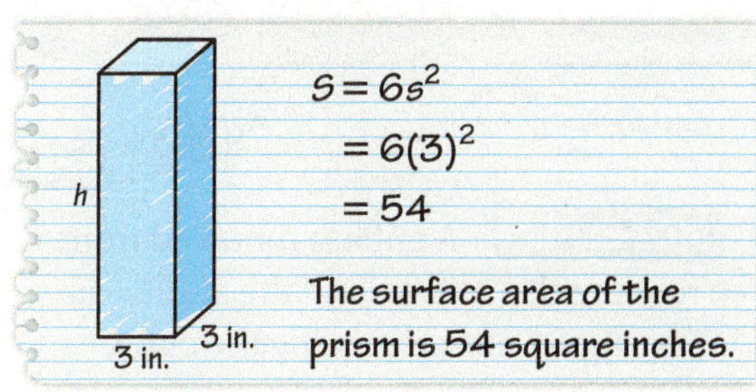

37. **CRITICAL THINKING** A public library has the aquarium shown. The front piece of glass has an area of 24 square feet. How many square feet of glass were used to build the aquarium? (The top of the aquarium is open and the bottom is glass.)

38. **MP PROBLEM SOLVING** A cereal box has the dimensions shown.

   a. Find the surface area of the cereal box.

   b. The manufacturer decides to decrease the size of the box by reducing each of the dimensions by 1 inch. Find the decrease in surface area.

39. **MP REASONING** The material used to make a storage box costs $1.25 per square foot. The boxes have the same volume. Which box might a company prefer to make? Explain your reasoning.

	Length	Width	Height
Box 1	20 in.	6 in.	4 in.
Box 2	15 in.	4 in.	8 in.

40. **MP LOGIC** Which of the following are nets of a cube? Select all that apply.

A. 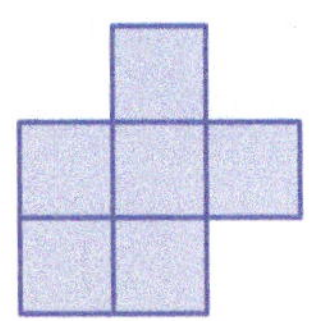

B. 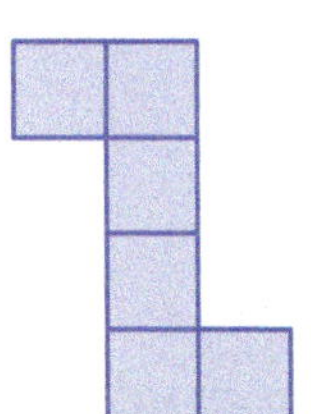

C. 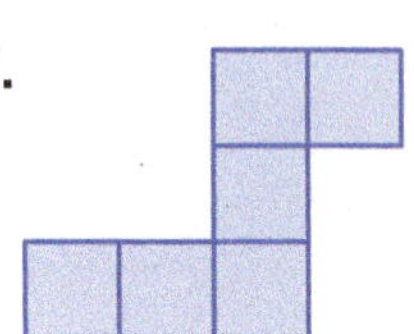

D. 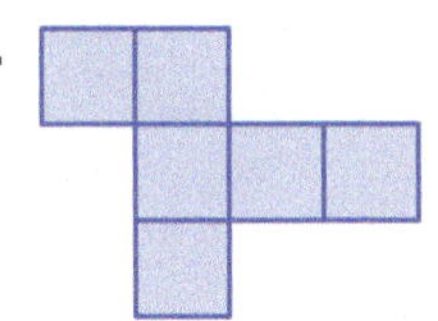

$25\frac{1}{12}$ ft

5 ft

25 in.

25 ft

41. **MP MODELING REAL LIFE** A quart of stain covers 100 square feet. How many quarts should you buy to stain the wheelchair ramp? (Assume you do not have to stain the bottom of the ramp.)

42. **DIG DEEPER!** A cube is removed from a rectangular prism. Find the surface area of the figure after removing the cube.

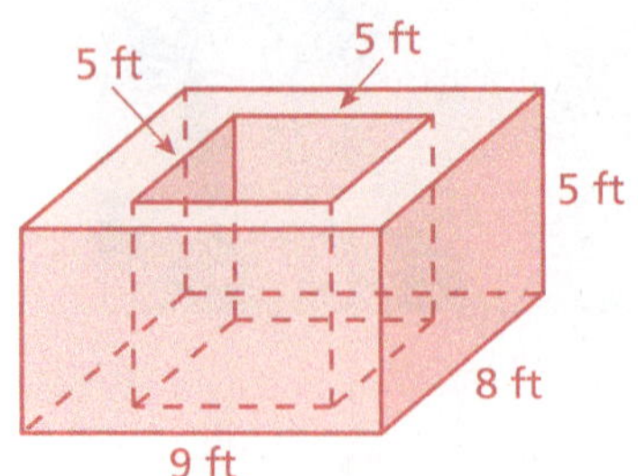

Common Errors

- **Exercise 37** Students may include the top of the aquarium when finding the square feet of glass used to build the aquarium. Remind students that the top of the aquarium is open.

Mini-Assessment

1. Find the surface area of the rectangular prism.

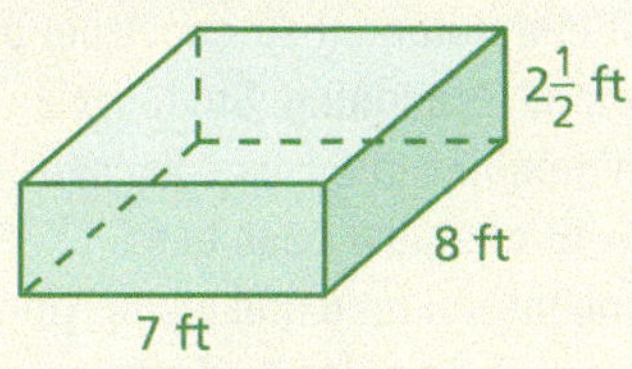

187 ft^2

2. Find the surface area of the triangular prism.

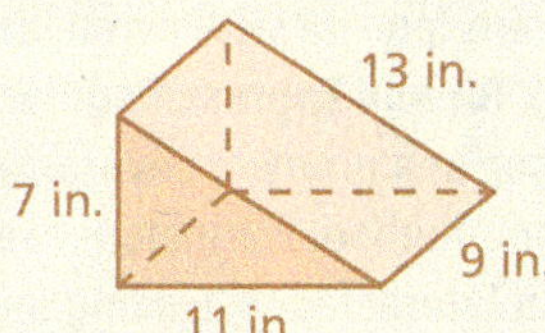

356 in.^{2}

3. Find the surface area of the cube.

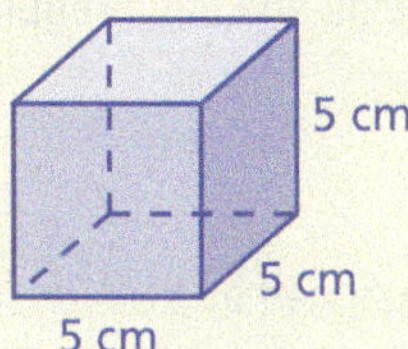

150 cm^2

4. What is the least amount of wrapping paper needed to cover the box?

22 ft^2

Section Resources

Surface Level	Deep Level
Resources by Chapter • Extra Practice • Reteach • Puzzle Time Student Journal • Self-Assessment • Practice Differentiating the Lesson Tutorial Videos Skills Review Handbook Skills Trainer	Resources by Chapter • Enrichment and Extension Graphic Organizers Dynamic Assessment System • Section Practice

Concepts, Skills, & Problem Solving

37. 83 ft^2

38. **a.** 384 in.^{2}

b. 94 in.^{2}

39. box 2; It should cost less to make.

40. B, D

41. 2 qt

42. 364 ft^2

Learning Target

Represent pyramids using nets and use nets to find surface areas of pyramids.

Success Criteria

- Draw nets to represent pyramids.
- Use nets to find surface areas of pyramids.
- Apply surface areas of pyramids to solve real-life problems.

Warm Up

Cumulative, vocabulary, and prerequisite skills practice opportunities are available in the *Resources by Chapter* or at *BigIdeasMath.com.*

ELL Support

Ask students to share what they know about pyramids, outside of math. Have them give specific examples, if they know of any. Share pictures of pyramids from Egypt and Mexico. Discuss how these are similar to and different from the mathematical definition of a pyramid. Guide students to recognize that the sides of pyramids in Egypt and Mexico are not flat surfaces and they do not always converge at a single vertex.

Exploration 1

a. square pyramid

b. 132 units^2

Exploration 2

a. 33 units^2;

$3 \cdot 3 + 4 \cdot \left(\frac{1}{2}\right) \cdot 3 \cdot 4 = 33$

b. 75 units^2;

$5 \cdot 5 + 4 \cdot \left(\frac{1}{2}\right) \cdot 5 \cdot 5 = 75$

Laurie's Notes

Preparing to Teach

- Prior work with areas of triangles, areas of squares, and surface areas of prisms provides the foundation for finding the surface area of a pyramid. Most students are familiar with pyramids but do not understand their constructions.
- **MP8 Look for and Express Regularity in Repeated Reasoning:** Students will find surface areas of several pyramids. In doing so, they may discover an efficient method. For instance, a pyramid with a regular base has congruent lateral faces. Finding the area of one lateral face and multiplying by the number of lateral faces is more efficient than completing multiple computations.
- **Note:** Pyramids are named by their base shapes and they all have triangular lateral faces. All pyramids in this section are right pyramids and have regular bases (squares and triangles only).

Motivate

- Show a picture of the Louvre pyramid in Paris. It was designed by I.M. Pei, as the Louvre's main entrance, which is used to handle the enormous number of visitors on an everyday basis.
- I.M. Pei also designed the East Building of the National Gallery of Art in Washington, D.C. and the Rock and Roll Hall of Fame in Cleveland, Ohio.

Exploration 1

- **Teaching Tip:** Again, tape bags to desks around the room for easy cleanup.
- To copy the figure correctly, students need to determine the base and height of each triangular face. In this exploration, the base of the pyramid is a square, which means that all of the triangles are congruent.

? **MP3 Construct Viable Arguments and Critique the Reasoning of Others:** If time permits, ask students questions about the pyramid they folded.

- "If you know the shape of the base, what do you know about the total number of faces?" The total number of faces is one more than the number of sides of the base.
- "If you know the shape of the base, what do you know about the total number of edges?" The total number of edges is twice the number of sides of the base.
- "If you know the shape of the base, what do you know about the total number of vertices?" The total number of vertices is one more than the number of sides of the base.
- If time allows, ask students to describe or draw a net for a triangular pyramid.

Exploration 2

- **Scaffolding:** If time is a concern, have half the class work on part (a) and the other half work on part (b).
- Some students have well-defined spatial sense and can "see" all the surfaces that they need to consider, while others may want to use a net. Going from a solid to the two-dimensional representation can be challenging.
- Although there are different two-dimensional representations (nets) that can be drawn for each pyramid, it is likely that students will draw a template similar to Exploration 1. If time permits, investigate other nets.

7.6 Surface Areas of Pyramids

Learning Target: Represent pyramids using nets and use nets to find surface areas of pyramids.

Success Criteria:
- I can draw nets to represent pyramids.
- I can use nets to find surface areas of pyramids.
- I can apply surface areas of pyramids to solve real-life problems.

EXPLORATION 1 Using a Net to Construct a Solid

Work with a partner. Copy the net shown below onto grid paper.

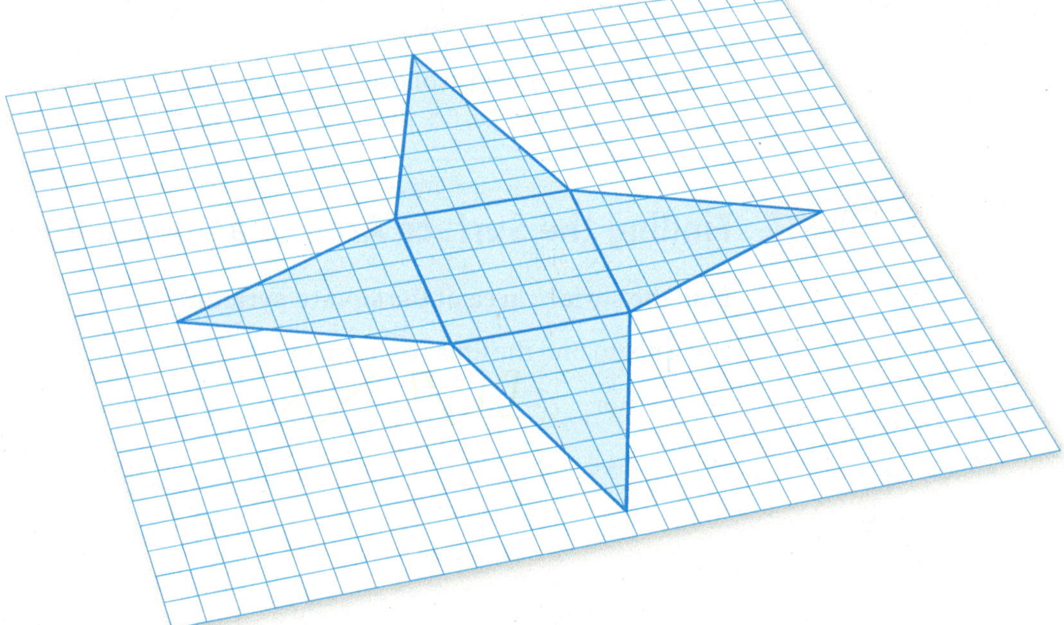

a. Cut out and fold the net to form a solid. What type of solid does the net form?

b. What is the surface area of the solid?

EXPLORATION 2 Finding Surface Areas of Solids

Math Practice

Analyze Givens
What information can you determine from the diagram? How does this help you find the surface area of the solid?

Work with a partner. Find the surface area of each solid. Explain your reasoning.

a.

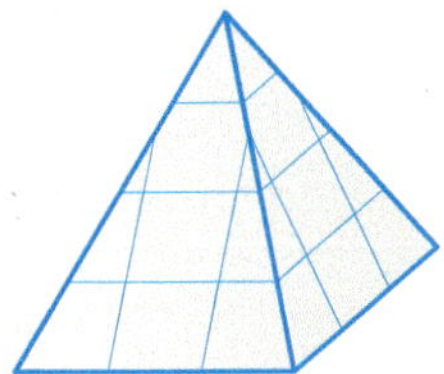

b.

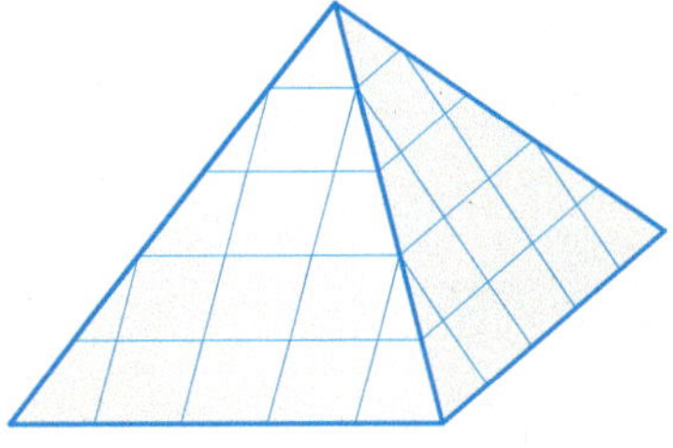

7.6 Lesson

Key Idea

Net of a Pyramid

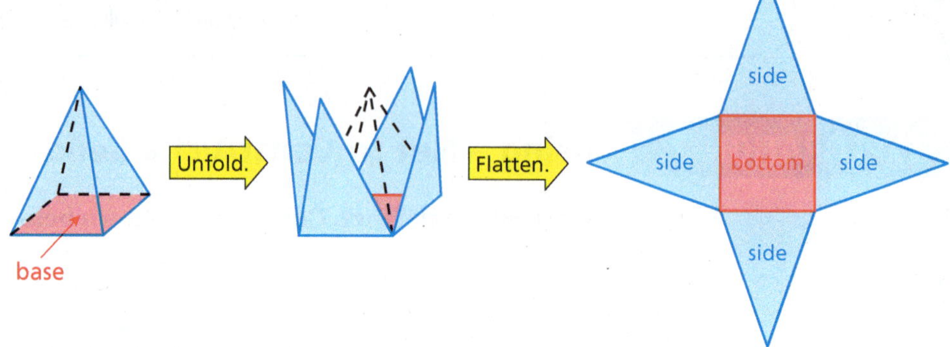

In this book, the base of every pyramid is either a square or an equilateral triangle. So, the lateral faces are identical triangles.

Remember

A *square pyramid* is a pyramid with a square base. A *triangular pyramid* is a pyramid with a triangular base.

EXAMPLE 1 Finding the Surface Area of a Square Pyramid

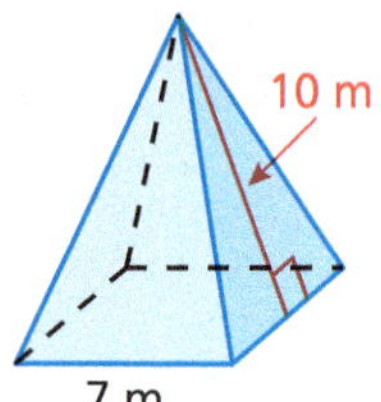

Find the surface area of the square pyramid.

Use a net to find the area of each face.

Bottom: $7 \cdot 7 = 49$

Side: $\frac{1}{2} \cdot 7 \cdot 10 = 35$

Side: $\frac{1}{2} \cdot 7 \cdot 10 = 35$

Side: $\frac{1}{2} \cdot 7 \cdot 10 = 35$

Side: $\frac{1}{2} \cdot 7 \cdot 10 = 35$

Find the sum of the areas of the faces.

Surface Area = Area of bottom + Area of a side + Area of a side + Area of a side + Area of a side

$S = 49 + 35 + 35 + 35 + 35 = 189$

So, the surface area is 189 square meters.

Math Practice

Look for Patterns

How can you find the surface area of a square pyramid by calculating the area of only two of its faces?

Try It **Find the surface area of the square pyramid.**

1.

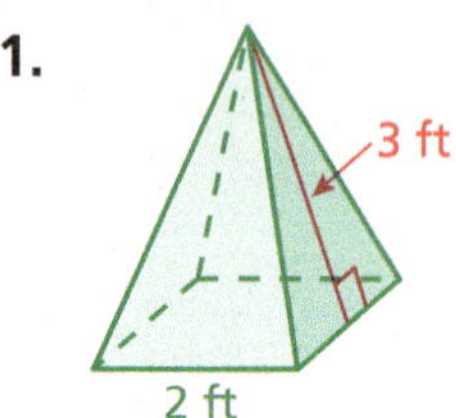

2.

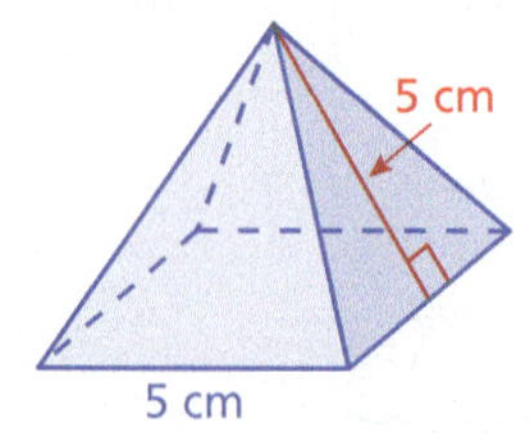

Laurie's Notes

Scaffolding Instruction

- Nets and verbal models provide the basis for students to make conjectures about algorithms for finding the surface area of each type of pyramid.
- **Emerging:** Students rely on a net or find the area of each face separately. The examples provide practice with visual and verbal models. Provide repetition so that students can begin generalizing the process.
- **Proficient:** Students can visualize the unseen sides and find their areas efficiently. Have students demonstrate their understanding by completing the Self-Assessment exercises.

Key Idea

- Having physical models of a square pyramid and a triangular pyramid to refer to is helpful.
- Notice that the base and lateral faces are labeled as *bottom* and *side* when the pyramid is unfolded as a net.
- **Note:** Because the net shown is for a square pyramid, create a paper triangular pyramid to demonstrate how it unfolds.

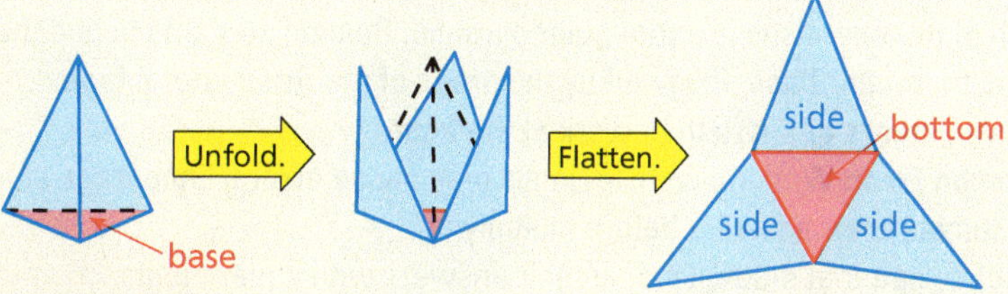

EXAMPLE 1

? "How can you find the surface area of this square pyramid?" Find the area of the bottom and each of the sides, and then add them together.

- **Common Error:** In using the area formula for a triangle, the $\frac{1}{2}$ often produces a computational mistake. Remind students that they can change the order of the factors (Commutative Property). Rewriting the problem as $\frac{1}{2} \cdot 10 \cdot 7$ allows them to work with whole numbers: $\frac{1}{2} \cdot 10 \cdot 7 = 5 \cdot 7 = 35$.
- **MP8 Look for and Express Regularity in Repeated Reasoning:** Students may ask about the repeated steps of finding the area of each lateral face. Encourage them to look for a more efficient method: surface area = area of bottom + 4(area of a side).
- Remind students to label their answers with square units.

ELL Support

After demonstrating Example 1, have students practice language by working in pairs to complete Try It Exercises 1 and 2. Model guiding questions such as: How many sides are there? What is the area of the bottom? the side? Monitor student discussions. Expect students at different language levels to state the answers to the guiding questions as described.

Beginner: Use numbers.

Intermediate: Use phrases such as, "five sides."

Advanced: Use sentences such as, "There are five sides."

Scaffold instruction to support all students in their learning. Learning is individualized and you may want to group students differently as they move in and out of these levels with each skill and concept. Student self-assessment and feedback help guide your instructional decisions about how and when to layer support for all students to become proficient learners.

Teaching Strategy

There are many websites that allow students to investigate three-dimensional solids in ways that physical models cannot. Solids may be turned so that students see it from different perspectives, or they may be colored, unfolded, and then put back together again! Share these websites with students so that they can further investigate solids in class or during their own time.

Extra Example 1

Find the surface area of the square pyramid.

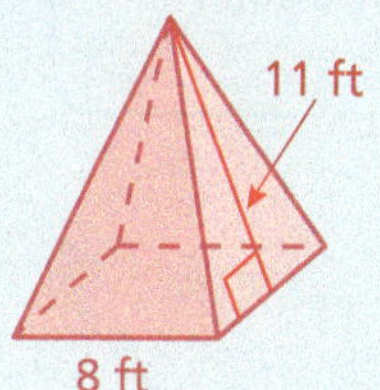

240 ft^2

Try It

1. 16 ft^2
2. 75 cm^2

Extra Example 2

Find the surface area of the triangular pyramid.

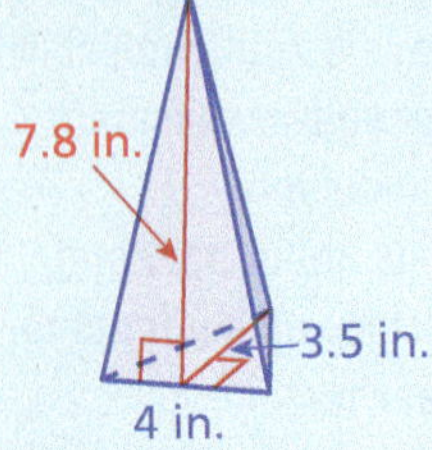

53.8 in.^{2}

Try It

3. 10.7 cm^2
4. 129.6 in.^{2}

ELL Support

Have students work in groups to complete the Self-Assessment for Concepts & Skills exercises. Monitor discussions of Exercise 5. Have each group collaborate to write their explanation and then present it to the class. Then have each group display their answers for Exercises 6 and 7 on a whiteboard.

Self-Assessment for Concepts & Skills

5. Find the sum of the areas of the faces.
6. 105 yd^2
7. 111.6 m^2

Laurie's Notes

EXAMPLE 2

- Drawing the net is an important step. It allows the dimensions to be labeled in a way that can be seen.
- Remind students that the base of a triangular pyramid in this section is assumed to be an equilateral triangle because of the statement in the Key Idea. Otherwise, they could not find the surface area of this pyramid.
- Ask students to estimate the area of the base before computing: $\frac{1}{2} \cdot 6 \cdot 5 = 15$ square feet.
- **MP8 Look for and Express Regularity in Repeated Reasoning:** Students may ask about the repeated steps of finding the area of each lateral face. Ask if the more efficient method from Example 1 still works. Listen for reasoning about the number of lateral faces being different, so the formula for a triangular pyramid is surface area = area of bottom + 3(area of a side).
- Students are continuing to work on the second success criterion.

Try It

- Each of the exercises is a triangular pyramid. Remind students to find the area of the triangular base, followed by the areas of the three lateral faces.
- Ask volunteers to share their work at the board.
- **Common Error:** Working with decimals may cause errors. Encourage students to estimate their answers before multiplying.
- Check to see that students label their answers with square units.

Self-Assessment for Concepts & Skills

- Students should work independently on these exercises. They are demonstrating their progress with the first two success criteria.
- **MP6 Attend to Precision:** In Exercise 5, the explanations will reveal students' grasp of finding the surface area of a pyramid. Students should use mathematical language to describe their methods effectively.
- Exercises 6 and 7 require the skills that students have acquired from the examples. They will find the surface area of both a square pyramid and a triangular pyramid.
- Have students share their answers and discuss any differences.

The Success Criteria Self-Assessment chart can be found in the *Student Journal* or online at *BigIdeasMath.com.*

EXAMPLE 2 Finding the Surface Area of a Triangular Pyramid

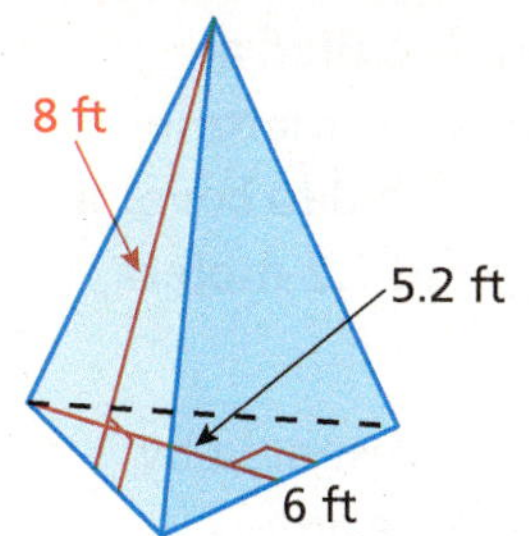

Find the surface area of the triangular pyramid.

Use a net to find the area of each face.

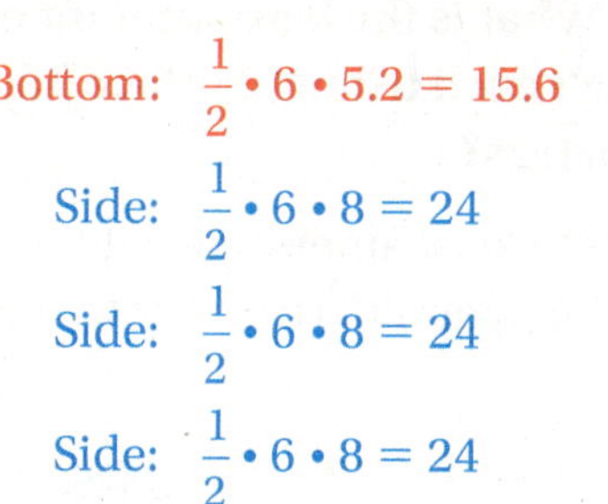

Bottom: $\frac{1}{2} \cdot 6 \cdot 5.2 = 15.6$

Side: $\frac{1}{2} \cdot 6 \cdot 8 = 24$

Side: $\frac{1}{2} \cdot 6 \cdot 8 = 24$

Side: $\frac{1}{2} \cdot 6 \cdot 8 = 24$

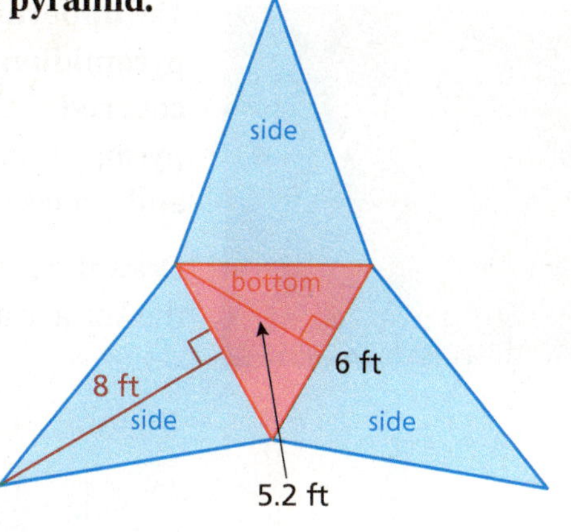

Find the sum of the areas of the faces.

$$\text{Surface Area} = \text{Area of bottom} + \text{Area of a side} + \text{Area of a side} + \text{Area of a side}$$

$$S = 15.6 + 24 + 24 + 24$$

$$= 87.6$$

So, the surface area is 87.6 square feet.

Try It **Find the surface area of the triangular pyramid.**

3.

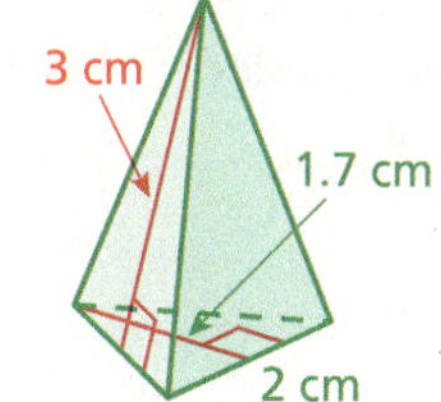

4.

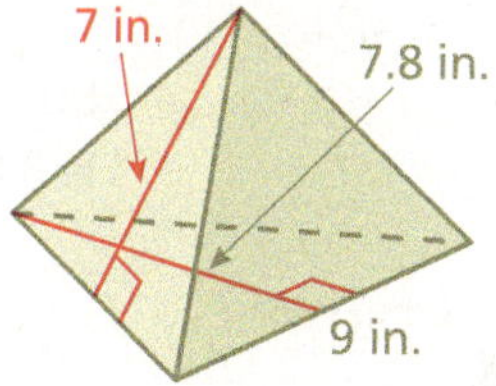

Self-Assessment for Concepts & Skills

Solve each exercise. Then rate your understanding of the success criteria in your journal.

5. MP **PRECISION** Explain how to find the surface area of a pyramid.

FINDING SURFACE AREA **Find the surface area of the pyramid.**

6.

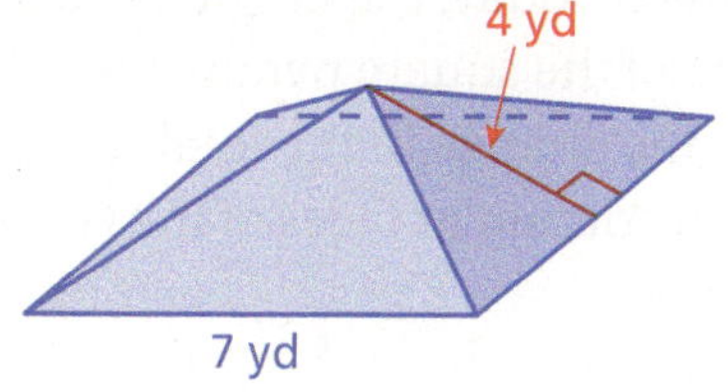

7.

7 m

6.9 m

8 m

EXAMPLE 3 Modeling Real Life

The uppermost piece of an ancient Egyptian pyramid is called a pyramidion. These square pyramid-shaped pieces were sometimes covered with gold. What is the least amount of gold needed to cover a pyramidion in which each triangular face has a height of 1.2 meters and a base of 1.5 meters?

Draw the pyramid. The least amount of gold needed is represented by the surface area of the pyramid. Use a net to find the surface area.

Bottom: $1.5 \cdot 1.5 = 2.25$

Side: $\frac{1}{2} \cdot 1.5 \cdot 1.2 = 0.9$

Side: $\frac{1}{2} \cdot 1.5 \cdot 1.2 = 0.9$

Side: $\frac{1}{2} \cdot 1.5 \cdot 1.2 = 0.9$

Side: $\frac{1}{2} \cdot 1.5 \cdot 1.2 = 0.9$

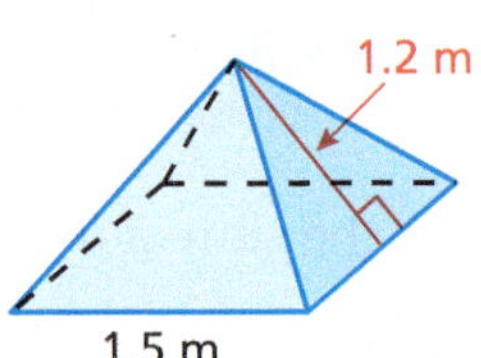

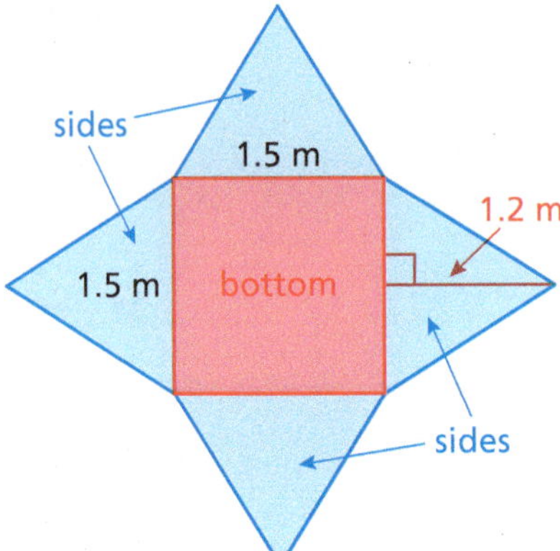

$$S = 2.25 + 0.9 + 0.9 + 0.9 + 0.9 = 5.85$$

So, the least amount of gold needed is 5.85 square meters.

Self-Assessment for Problem Solving

Solve each exercise. Then rate your understanding of the success criteria in your journal.

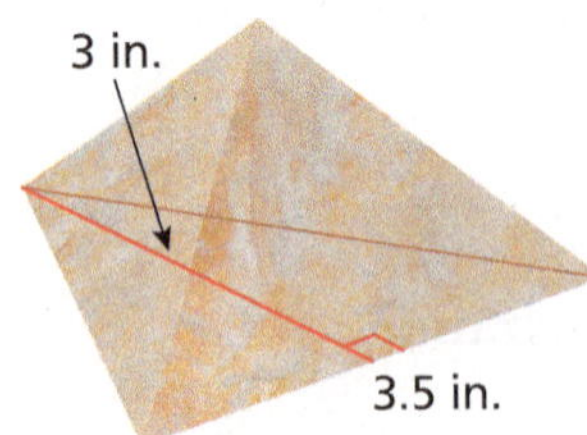

Surface Area = 15.75 in.^{2}

8. A salt lamp is shaped like a triangular pyramid. Find the area of each triangular face.

9. Originally, each triangular face of the Great Pyramid of Giza had a height of 612 feet and a base of 756 feet. Today, the height of each triangular face of the square pyramid is 592 feet. Find the change in the total surface area of the four triangular faces of the Great Pyramid of Giza.

Laurie's Notes

EXAMPLE 3

- Show students the picture of the pyramidion. Tell them that a pyramidion is a piece of an Egyptian pyramid. Most that remain are made of black granite; however, some were made of limestone. Ancient accounts often refer to them covered with gold, particularly the ones of the Great Pyramids.
- ? "Where do you think you would find a pyramidion?" *Sample answer:* at the top of a pyramid
- Select a volunteer to read the problem aloud.
- ? "The special placement of a pyramidion meant that it was sometimes covered in gold. How can you find the least amount of gold to cover it?" Listen for answers that define the surface area of the pyramid.
- Have students work in pairs to solve the problem. Then have pairs use their nets and work to justify their answers to the class.
- **MP1 Make Sense of Problems and Persevere in Solving Them:** Some students may find the total area of *only* the lateral faces because the base is not visible when the pyramidion is placed at the top of a pyramid. Mention that this is the *lateral surface area*, which will be introduced in the next course. The lateral surface area is an acceptable answer, as long as students' explanations support their work. Others may say that the problem asks for the amount to cover the pyramidion and does not exclude any faces. The total surface area is also an acceptable answer. Students are thinking deeply about the problem and defending their approaches.

Self-Assessment for Problem Solving

- Students are assessing their understanding of the third success criterion. It is important to provide time in class for problem solving, so that students become comfortable with the problem-solving plan.
- Exercise 8 is an opportunity for students to analyze information from a picture and apply their knowledge of surface area of a triangular pyramid. Encourage students to estimate the answer first.
- **MP4 Model with Mathematics:** Encourage students to analyze the information given in Exercise 9 and determine if it makes sense to find the lateral surface area or the total surface area in the context of the situation.
- Select volunteers to share their work for each exercise at the board.

The Success Criteria Self-Assessment chart can be found in the *Student Journal* or online at *BigIdeasMath.com.*

Closure

- **Quick Write:** How is finding the surface area of a pyramid different from finding the surface area of a prism?
  Remind students to write their main ideas first and then elaborate if they have time.

Extra Example 3

A student is creating a square pyramid-shaped clay model. What is the least amount of varnish needed to cover the clay model in which each triangular face has a height of 7 inches and a base of 5 inches? 95 in.^{2}

Self-Assessment for Problem Solving

8. 3.5 in.^{2}
9. 30,240 ft^2

Learning Target

Represent pyramids using nets and use nets to find surface areas of pyramids.

Success Criteria

- Draw nets to represent pyramids.
- Use nets to find surface areas of pyramids.
- Apply surface areas of pyramids to solve real-life problems.

Review & Refresh

1. $82\ ft^2$
2. $540\ cm^2$
3. $384\ in.^2$
4. C
5. B
6. D
7. A
8. 68%
9. 95%
10. 687.5%
11. 0.75%

Concepts, Skills, & Problem Solving

12. $160\ units^2$; $8 \cdot 8 + 4 \cdot \left(\frac{1}{2}\right) \cdot 8 \cdot 6 = 160$
13. $133\ units^2$; $7 \cdot 7 + 4 \cdot \left(\frac{1}{2}\right) \cdot 7 \cdot 6 = 133$
14. $171\ units^2$; $9 \cdot 9 + 4 \cdot \left(\frac{1}{2}\right) \cdot 9 \cdot 5 = 171$
15. $119\ in.^2$
16. $172.8\ yd^2$
17. $552\ cm^2$
18. $224.4\ ft^2$
19. $195.6\ in.^2$
20. $55\ m^2$

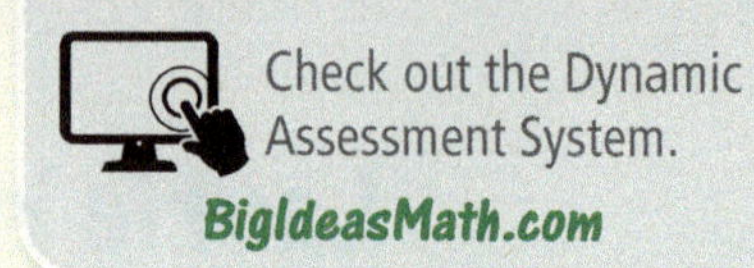

Assignment Guide and Concept Check

Scaffold assignments to support all students in their learning progression. The suggested assignments are a starting point. Continue to assign additional exercises and revisit with spaced practice to move every student toward proficiency.

Level	Assignment 1	Assignment 2
Emerging	2, 4, 5, 6, 7, 11, 12, 15, 18	14, 16, 21, 25
Proficient	2, 4, 5, 6, 7, 11, 14, 17, 20	21, 22, 23, 24, 25, 26
Advanced	2, 4, 5, 6, 7, 11, 14, 16, 19	22, 23, 24, 25, 26, 27

- Assignment 1 is for use after students complete the Self-Assessment for Concepts & Skills.
- Assignment 2 is for use after students complete the Self-Assessment for Problem Solving.
- The red exercises can be used as a concept check.

Review & Refresh Prior Skills

Exercises 1–3 Finding the Surface Area of a Prism
Exercises 4–7 Simplifying Expressions
Exercises 8–11 Writing Fractions as Percents

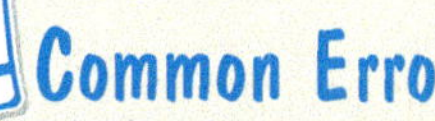

Common Errors

- **Exercises 15–20** Students may forget to include the area of the base when finding the surface area. Remind them that when asked to find the surface area, the base is included.
- **Exercises 15–20** Students may add the wrong number of lateral face areas to the area of the base. Remind students that the number of sides of the base determines how many triangles make up the lateral surface area.
- **Exercises 18–20** Students may forget to multiply by $\frac{1}{2}$ when finding the area of the base triangle. Remind students that the formula for the area of a triangle is $A = \frac{1}{2}bh$.

7.6 Practice

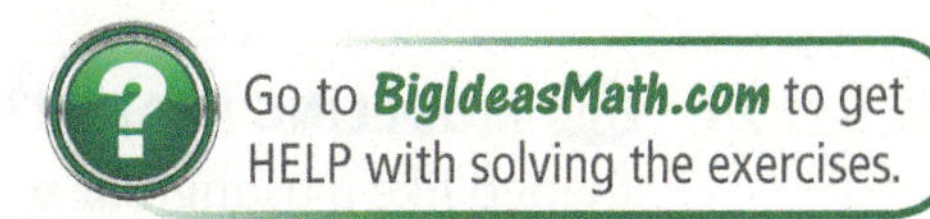

Review & Refresh

Find the surface area of the prism.

1. 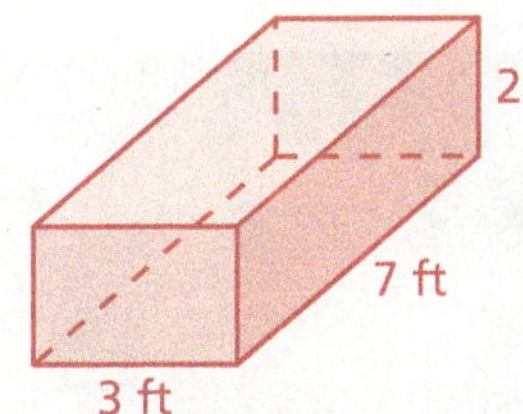

2. 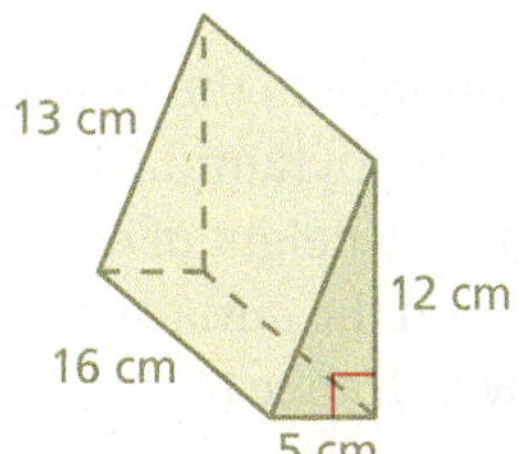

3. 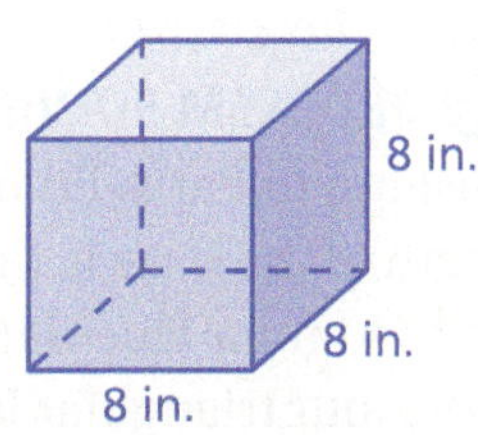

Match the expression with an equivalent expression.

4. $3(4n + 2)$
5. $6(2n + 3)$
6. $4(3n + 4)$
7. $12(n + 1)$

A. $2(6n + 6)$
B. $12n + 18$
C. $2(6n + 3)$
D. $12n + 16$

Write the fraction or mixed number as a percent.

8. $\frac{17}{25}$
9. $\frac{19}{20}$
10. $6\frac{7}{8}$
11. $\frac{3}{400}$

Concepts, Skills, & Problem Solving

MP USING TOOLS **Use a net to find the surface area of the solid. Explain your reasoning.** (See Exploration 2, p. 319.)

12. 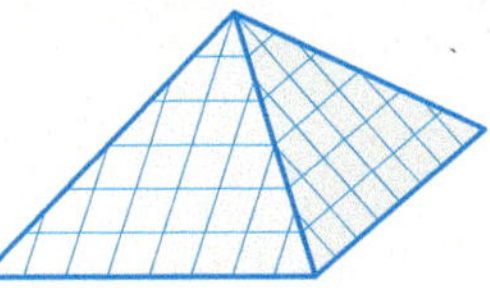

13. 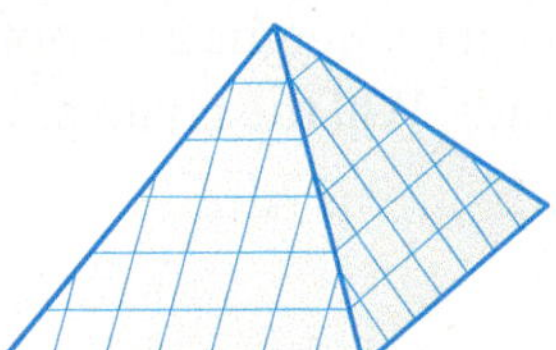

14. 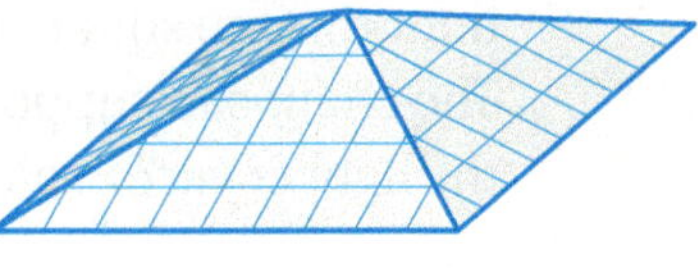

FINDING SURFACE AREA **Find the surface area of the pyramid.**

15. 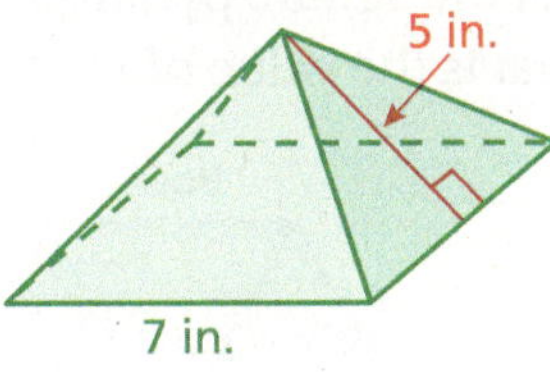

16. 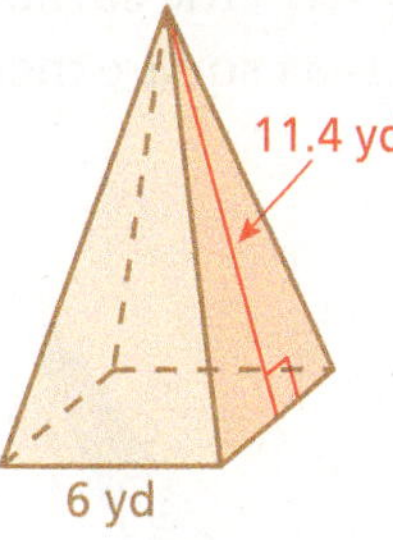

17. 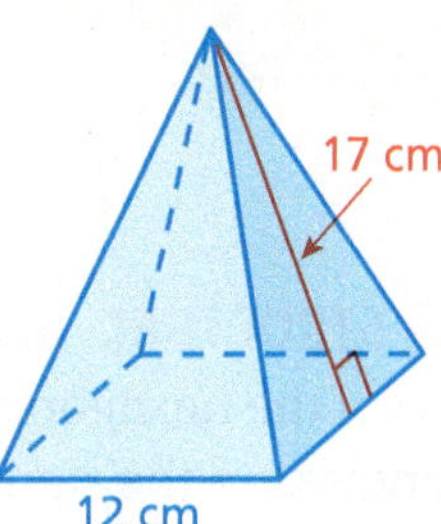

18. 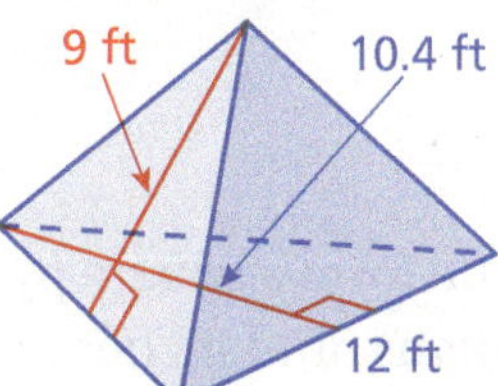

19. 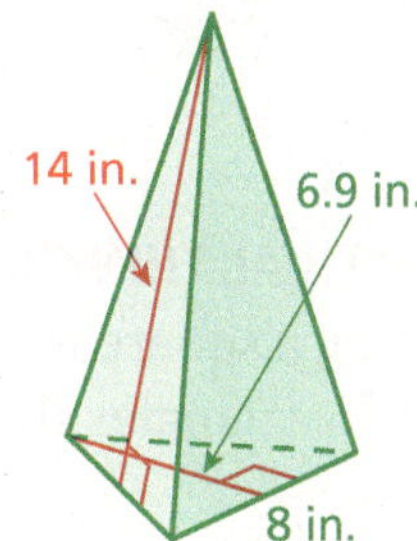

20. 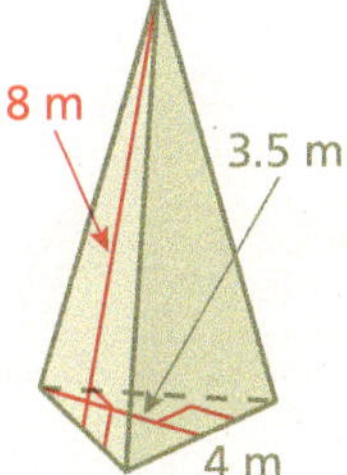

21. **MP MODELING REAL LIFE** A paperweight is shaped like a triangular pyramid. Find the surface area of the paperweight.

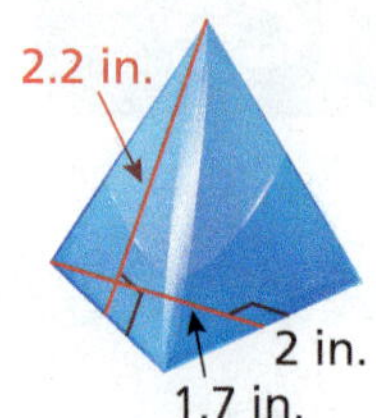

22. **MP PROBLEM SOLVING** The entrance to the Louvre Museum in Paris, France, is a square pyramid. The side length of the base is 116 feet, and the height of one of the triangular faces is 91.7 feet. Find the surface area of the four triangular faces of the entrance to the Louvre Museum.

23. **MP MODELING REAL LIFE** A silicon wafer is textured to minimize light reflection. This results in a surface made up of square pyramids. Each triangular face of one of the pyramids has a base of 5 micrometers and a height of 5.6 micrometers. Find the surface area of the pyramid, including the base.

24. **MP REASONING** A hanging light cover made of glass is shaped like a square pyramid. The cover does not have a bottom. One square foot of the glass weighs 2.45 pounds. The chain can support 35 pounds. Will the chain support the light cover? Explain.

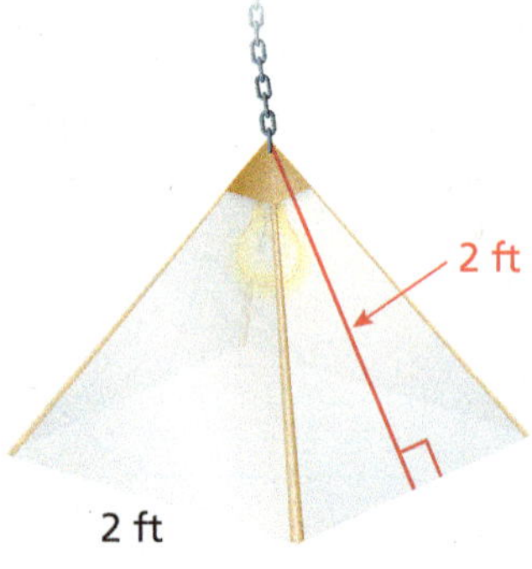

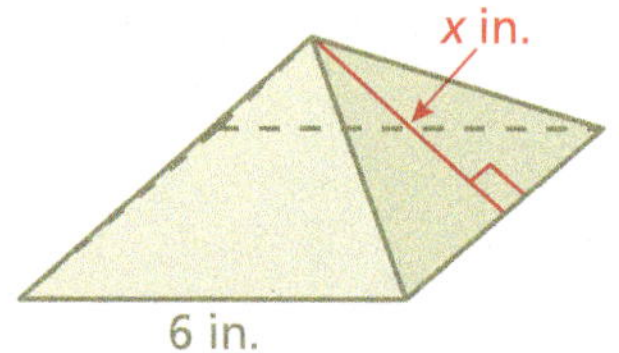

25. **GEOMETRY** The surface area of the square pyramid shown is 84 square inches. What is the value of x?

26. **MP STRUCTURE** In the diagram of the base of the hexagonal pyramid, all the triangles are the same. Find the surface area of the hexagonal pyramid.

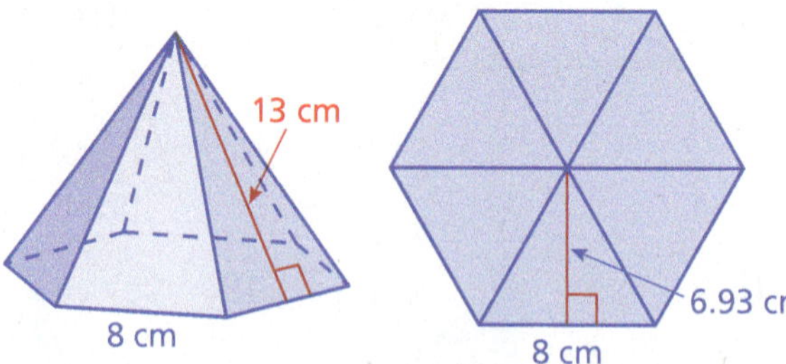

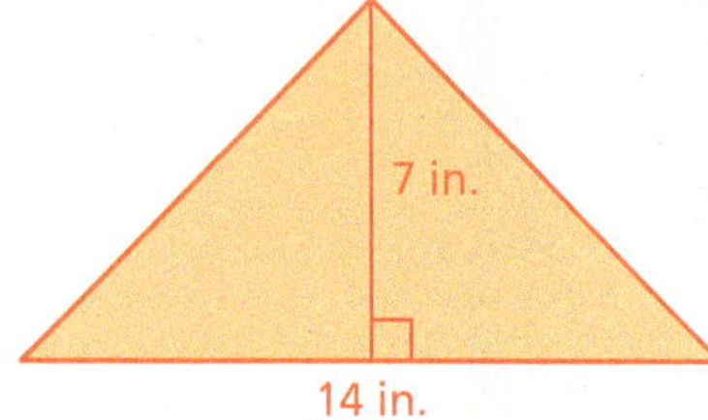

27. **CRITICAL THINKING** Can you form a square pyramid using a square with side lengths of 14 inches and four of the triangles shown? Explain your reasoning.

Mini-Assessment

Find the surface area of the pyramid.

1.

231 cm²

2.

114.24 m²

3.

114.6 in.²

4.

79.58 ft²

5. A fishing sinker is shaped like a square pyramid. Each triangular face has a height of 1.2 inches and a base of 0.5 inch. Find the surface area of the fishing sinker. 1.45 in.²

Section Resources

Surface Level	Deep Level
Resources by Chapter • Extra Practice • Reteach • Puzzle Time Student Journal • Self-Assessment • Practice Differentiating the Lesson Tutorial Videos Skills Review Handbook Skills Trainer	Resources by Chapter • Enrichment and Extension Graphic Organizers Dynamic Assessment System • Section Practice

Concepts, Skills, & Problem Solving

21. 8.3 in.²
22. 21,274.4 ft²
23. 81 micrometers²
24. yes; The weight of the glass is 19.6 pounds.
25. 4
26. 478.32 cm²
27. no; You can place the four triangles on top of the square and it covers the entire square. But when you lift up the triangles, they do not touch. So, they do not form a pyramid.

Learning Target

Find volumes and missing dimensions of rectangular prisms.

Success Criteria

- Use a formula to find the volume of a rectangular prism.
- Use a formula to find the volume of a cube.
- Use the volume of a rectangular prism and two of its dimensions to find the other dimension.
- Apply volumes of rectangular prisms to solve real-life problems.

Warm Up

Cumulative, vocabulary, and prerequisite skills practice opportunities are available in the *Resources by Chapter* or at *BigIdeasMath.com.*

ELL Support

Ask students to recall information they learned about volume from the Chapter Exploration. What does the word *volume* refer to outside of math? Students may say loudness or one of a series of books or recordings. Remind students that in math, volume is a measure of the space occupied by a three-dimensional figure.

Exploration 1

a. The volume of each prism is $\frac{1}{24}$ unit^3; There are 24 identical prisms in the unit cube.

b. See Additional Answers.

c. *Sample answer:* Divide a unit cube into 2, 2, and 4 parts, use 3 of them to form the given prism.

d. See Additional Answers.

Laurie's Notes

Preparing to Teach

- Finding surface areas in the previous sections lead into another measurement, volume. Although students found volumes of rectangular prisms in the previous course, they will now involve fractional and decimal dimensions.
- **MP3 Construct Viable Arguments and Critique the Reasoning of Others:** The learning target is to find volumes and missing dimensions of rectangular prisms. As students make conjectures in the exploration, they will see the connection to the volume formula. Students should be expected to listen carefully and critique the reasoning of their classmates.

Motivate

- Hold up a variety of common containers and ask what is commonly found inside each one. Examples: egg carton (12 eggs), playing cards box (52 cards), crayon box (8 crayons).
- Discuss with students these examples of volume. Each container is filled with objects of the same size. How many eggs fit in the egg carton? How many cards fit in the cards box? How many crayons fit in the crayon box? Because the units are different (eggs, cards, crayons), you cannot compare the volumes.

Exploration 1

- **Teaching Tip:** Make a unit cube out of poster board or construction paper. It is important that it not look like a cubic foot or a cubic inch, so that students are simply thinking of a unit cube as having all edges equal in length.
- Say, "This is a unit cube."
- In part (a), students need to know how many identical prisms are in the unit cube. Tell them to think about how many prisms are in each layer.
- **MP3 Construct Viable Arguments and Critique the Reasoning of Others:** Ask volunteers to share their reasoning for part (a). Most students will say that there are 24 identical prisms, so each prism has a **volume** of $\frac{1}{24}$ cubic unit.
- Help students see the connection between the denominators of the dimensions in part (b) and the numbers of equal parts in part (a).
- Say, "The width of the prism is $\frac{3}{4}$ unit, so think of it as three of four equal parts. Each part is $\frac{1}{4}$-unit long." Use this strategy for the halves and thirds.
- Students can sketch lines parallel to the edges of the prism in part (b) to reveal the smaller prisms, which have the same dimensions as those in part (a). The volume of each smaller rectangular prism is $\frac{1}{24}$ cubic unit.

  There are 18 smaller prisms, so the volume of this prism is $\frac{18}{24}$, or $\frac{3}{4}$ cubic unit.
- **MP3 Construct Viable Arguments and Critique the Reasoning of Others:**

  When students finish part (c), ask volunteers to explain how they found the volume.
- In part (d), have each pair check the examples of another pair.

7.7 Volumes of Rectangular Prisms

Learning Target: Find volumes and missing dimensions of rectangular prisms.

Success Criteria:
- I can use a formula to find the volume of a rectangular prism.
- I can use a formula to find the volume of a cube.
- I can use the volume of a rectangular prism and two of its dimensions to find the other dimension.
- I can apply volumes of rectangular prisms to solve real-life problems.

Recall that the **volume** of a three-dimensional figure is a measure of the amount of space that it occupies. Volume is measured in *cubic units*.

EXPLORATION 1 Using a Unit Cube

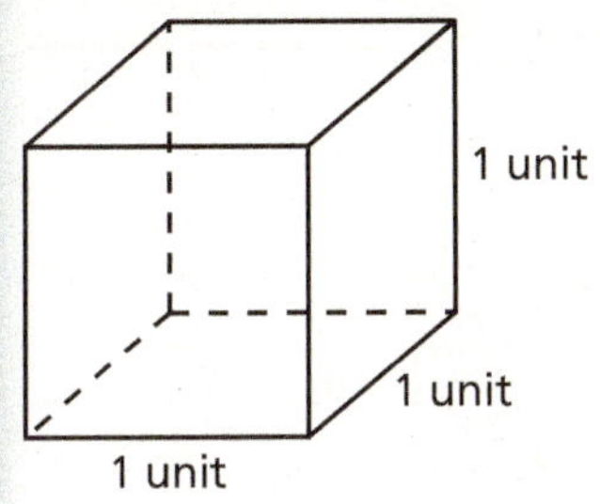

Work with a partner. A *unit cube* is a cube with an edge length of 1 unit. The parallel edges of the unit cube have been divided into 2, 3, and 4 equal parts to create smaller rectangular prisms that are identical.

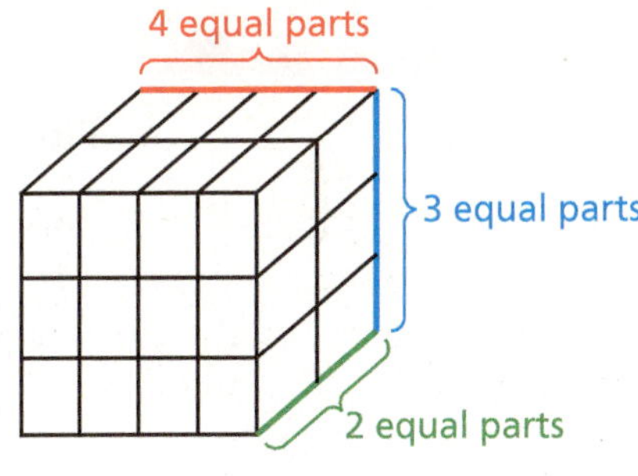

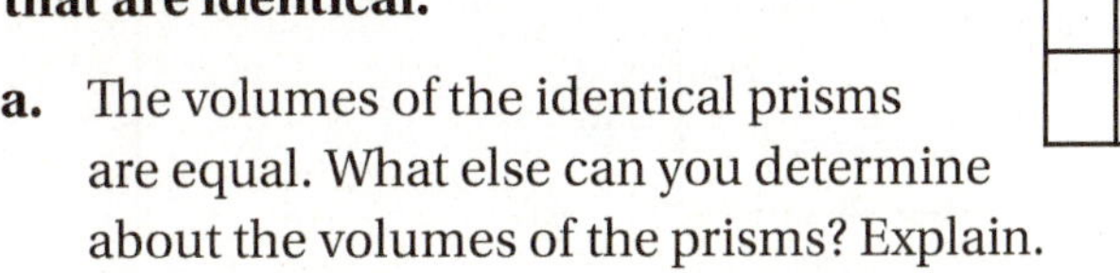

a. The volumes of the identical prisms are equal. What else can you determine about the volumes of the prisms? Explain.

b. Use the identical prisms in part (a) to find the volume of the prism below. Explain your reasoning.

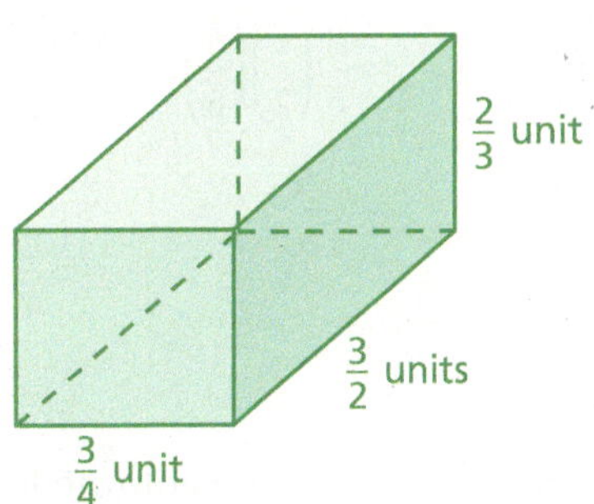

c. How can you use a unit cube to find the volume of the prism below? Explain.

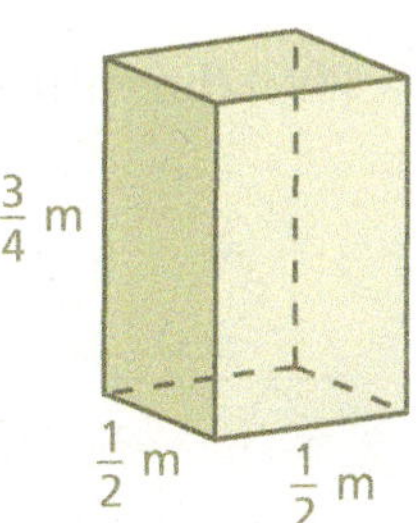

d. Do the formulas $V = Bh$ and $V = \ell wh$ work for rectangular prisms with fractional edge lengths? Give examples to support your answer.

Math Practice

Communicate Precisely

In part (c), explain why you decided to divide the unit cube in the way you did.

7.7 Lesson

Key Vocabulary
volume, *p. 325*

Key Idea

Volume of a Rectangular Prism

Words The volume V of a rectangular prism is the product of the area of the base and the height of the prism.

Algebra $V = Bh$ or $V = \ell wh$

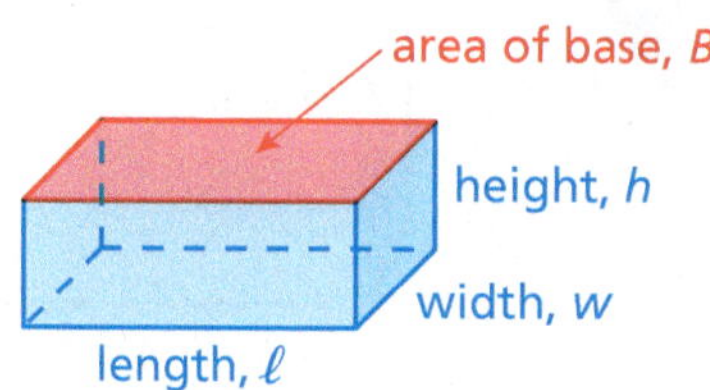

When a rectangular prism is a cube with an edge length of s, you can also use the formula $V = s^3$ to find the volume V of the cube.

EXAMPLE 1 Finding Volumes of Rectangular Prisms

Find the volume of each prism.

a.

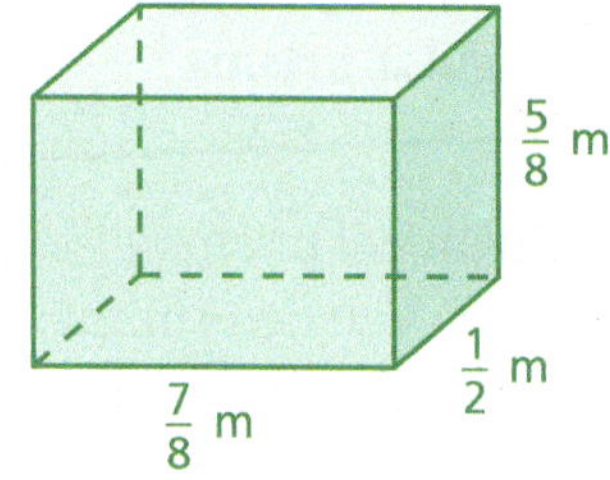

$$V = \ell wh$$
$$= \frac{7}{8}\left(\frac{1}{2}\right)\left(\frac{5}{8}\right)$$
$$= \frac{35}{128}$$

So, the volume is $\frac{35}{128}$ cubic meter.

b.

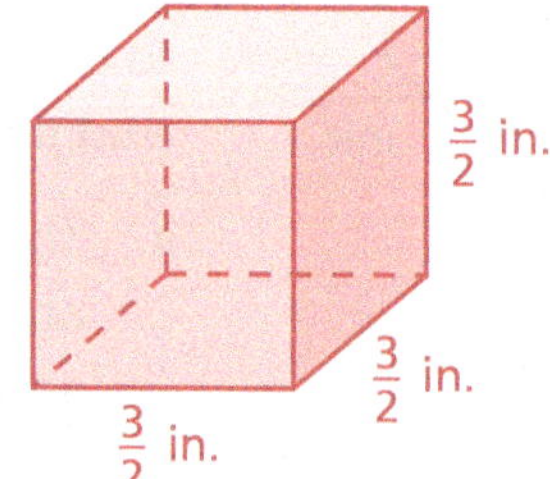

$$V = s^3$$
$$= \left(\frac{3}{2}\right)^3$$
$$= \frac{3}{2}\left(\frac{3}{2}\right)\left(\frac{3}{2}\right)$$
$$= \frac{27}{8}, \text{ or } 3\frac{3}{8}$$

So, the volume is $3\frac{3}{8}$ cubic inches.

Math Practice

Repeat Calculations

In Example 1(b), do you get the same answer when you use the formula $V = \ell wh$ to find the volume? Explain why or why not.

Try It **Find the volume of the prism.**

1.

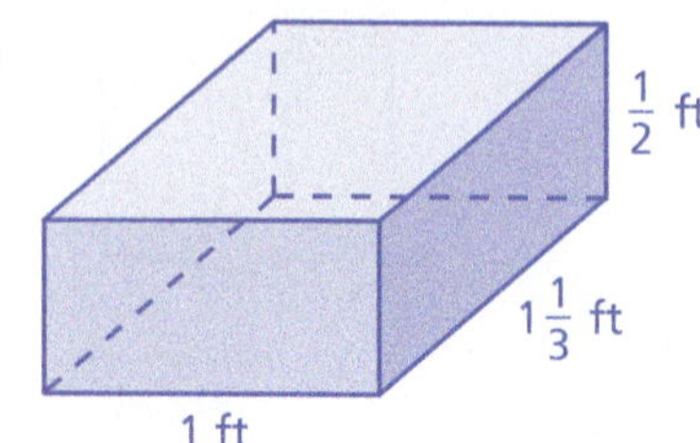

2.

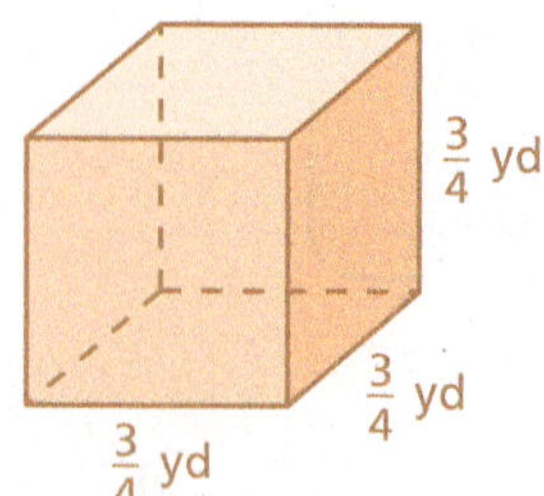

Laurie's Notes

Scaffolding Instruction

- The exploration introduced parts of cubic units. Now students see that volumes of prisms may be measured in tenths, sixteenths, or any fractional part of a cubic unit.
- **Emerging:** Students may find understanding the structure of prisms with fractional dimensions challenging. The examples and exercises provide practice finding volumes of prisms that have fractional dimensions.
- **Proficient:** Students progressed from whole-number dimensions to fractional dimensions seamlessly. They are confident in solving equations and can proceed to the Self-Assessment exercises.

Scaffold instruction to support all students in their learning. Learning is individualized and you may want to group students differently as they move in and out of these levels with each skill and concept. Student self-assessment and feedback help guide your instructional decisions about how and when to layer support for all students to become proficient learners.

Key Idea

? "Why is it called a *rectangular prism*?" Because the bases are rectangles.

- Write the formula for the **volume** of a rectangular prism in words and symbols.
- **Note:** Although any variable can be used to represent any unknown number, it is helpful if the variable reminds you of its meaning. B (area of the base) is capitalized to prevent confusion with b (base length) from other formulas.
- Point out and discuss the formula for the volume of a cube with an edge length of s.

EXAMPLE 1

- Write the formula for volume and substitute the value of each dimension.
- Note that parentheses are used to denote multiplication.
- After students work through each problem, ask them to use their hands to demonstrate the size of a cubic meter and a cubic inch.

? "How different are the two units?" Answers will vary.

Try It

? "In Exercise 1, can the 1 foot and $\frac{1}{2}$ foot dimensions be the length and width, and the $1\frac{1}{3}$ foot dimension be the height? Explain." Yes, the bases of the prism would be the 1 foot by $\frac{1}{2}$ foot faces.

◉ Students are working towards the first two success criteria.

? **Extension:** Point out that in Exercise 2, all of the dimensions are in yards. Then ask, "What would the dimensions be if they were labeled in feet?" $\frac{9}{4}$, or $2\frac{1}{4}$ feet "How would you find the volume?" $\left(\frac{9}{4}\right)^3$ "What units would be in the answer?" cubic feet

ELL Support

Have students work in pairs to discuss and complete Try It Exercises 1 and 2. Remind them of the types of guiding questions they used to discuss the Try It exercises in previous sections. Monitor discussion and expect students at different language levels to perform as described.

Beginner: State the answers to the guiding questions using numbers.

Intermediate: State the answers to the guiding questions using phrases.

Advanced: State the answers to the guiding questions using sentences and describe the process used to find the volume.

Extra Example 1

Find the volume of each prism.

a.

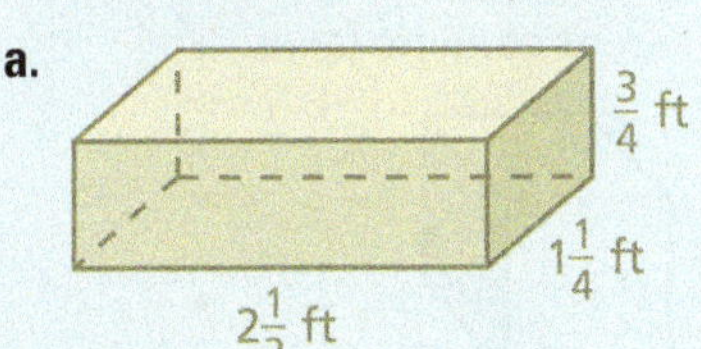

$2\frac{11}{32}$ ft^3

b.

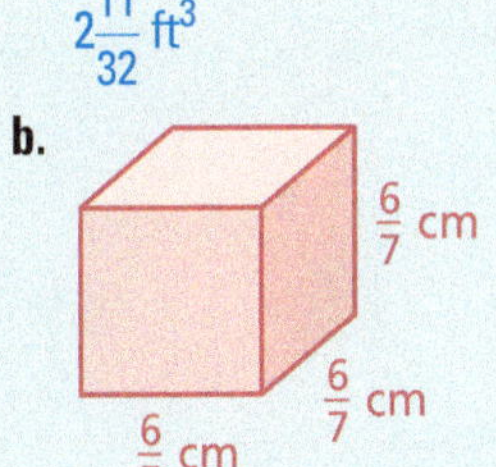

$\frac{216}{343}$ cm^3

Try It

1. $\frac{2}{3}$ ft^3
2. $\frac{27}{64}$ yd^3

Extra Example 2

An MP3 player has a length of 4 centimeters, a width of 0.6 centimeter, and a volume of 21.6 cubic centimeters. Find the height of the MP3 player. 9 cm

Try It

3. $\ell = 6$ in.
4. $w = 12\frac{1}{2}$ cm

Self-Assessment for Concepts & Skills

5. The volume of an object is the amount of space it occupies. The surface area of an object is the sum of the areas of all its faces.
6. 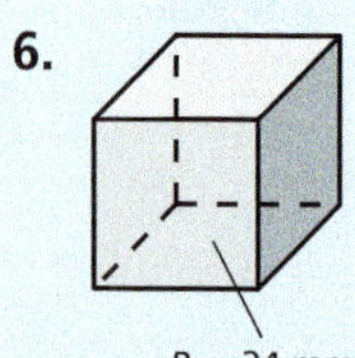

6 mm
7. $\frac{15}{64}$ m^3
8. $\frac{343}{1000}$ in.^{3}

Laurie's Notes

EXAMPLE 2

- Students are beginning to work on the third success criterion.
- Students solved equations in the previous chapter, so they should not have trouble with this problem. Using the properties of equality to solve for a missing dimension exemplifies the connection between algebraic skills and geometric formulas. Remind students to simplify both sides of an equation before using properties.
- ? "What is known in this problem?" volume, length, and width "What are you trying to find?" height
- ? "Is the answer reasonable? Explain." yes; Answers will vary.

Try It

- **Neighbor Check:** Have students work independently and then have their neighbors check their work. Have students discuss any discrepancies.

Self-Assessment for Concepts & Skills

- Have students complete the exercises independently and then discuss their solutions in a group. Students are assessing their progress with the first three success criteria.
- **MP6 Attend to Precision:** Listen to students' explanations for Exercise 5. They should communicate their thoughts using precise language when comparing the measurements.
- Exercise 6 assesses students' understanding of the alternate formula, $V = Bh$. Check students' work for solving equations.

ELL Support

Allow students extra support and language practice by working in pairs to complete the exercises. Monitor discussions of Exercise 5, and then review it as a class. Check understanding of Exercises 6–8 by having each pair display their answers on a whiteboard for your review.

The Success Criteria Self-Assessment chart can be found in the *Student Journal* or online at *BigIdeasMath.com.*

EXAMPLE 2 Finding a Missing Dimension of a Rectangular Prism

Volume = 1792 in.^{3}

Find the height of the computer tower.

$V = \ell wh$	Write formula for volume.
$1792 = 16(7)h$	Substitute values.
$1792 = 112h$	Simplify.
$\frac{1792}{112} = \frac{112h}{112}$	Division Property of Equality
$16 = h$	Simplify.

So, the height of the computer tower is 16 inches.

Try It Find the missing dimension of the prism.

3. Volume = 72 in.^{3}

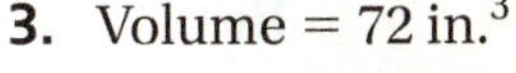

4. Volume = 1375 cm^3

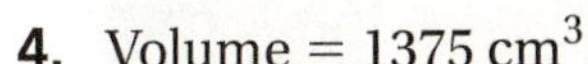

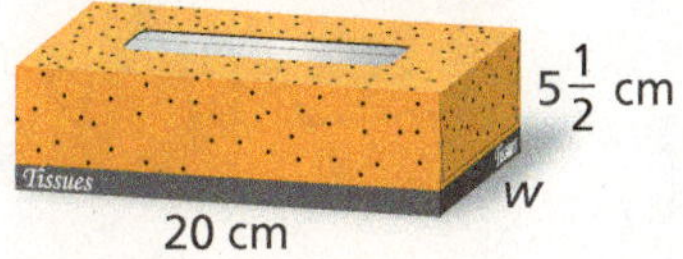

Self-Assessment for Concepts & Skills

Solve each exercise. Then rate your understanding of the success criteria in your journal.

5. **CRITICAL THINKING** Explain how volume and surface area are different.

6. **FINDING A MISSING DIMENSION** The base of a rectangular prism has an area of 24 square millimeters. The volume of the prism is 144 cubic millimeters. Make a sketch of the prism. Then find the height of the prism.

FINDING VOLUME Find the volume of the prism.

7.

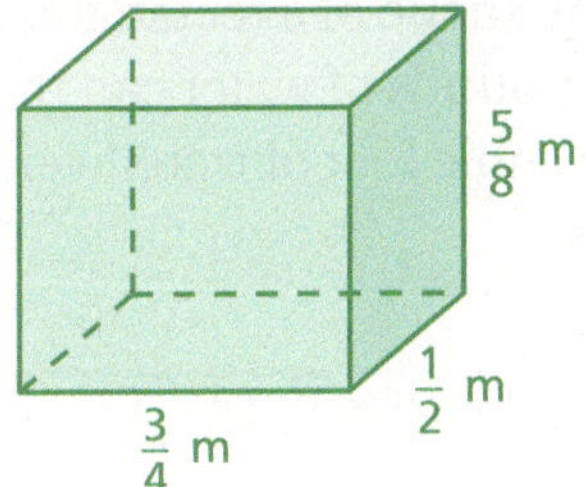

8.

$\frac{7}{10}$ in.

$\frac{7}{10}$ in.

$\frac{7}{10}$ in.

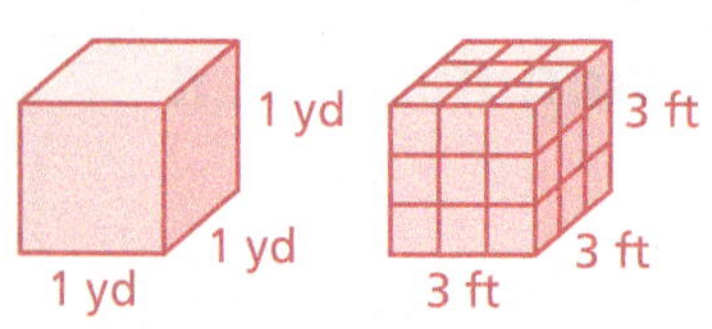

When finding volumes, you may need to convert cubic units. The diagrams at the left show that there are 27 cubic feet per cubic yard.

$$1 \text{ yd}^3 = (1 \text{ yd})(1 \text{ yd})(1 \text{ yd}) = (3 \text{ ft})(3 \text{ ft})(3 \text{ ft}) = 27 \text{ ft}^3$$

You can use a similar procedure to convert other cubic units.

EXAMPLE 3 Modeling Real Life

The dump truck shown delivers dirt for $18 per cubic yard. About how much does a full load of dirt cost?

Find the volume of a full load of dirt in cubic feet.

$$V = \ell wh \quad \text{Write formula for volume.}$$
$$= 17(8)\left(4\frac{3}{4}\right) \quad \text{Substitute values.}$$
$$= 646 \quad \text{Multiply.}$$

A full load of dirt is 646 cubic feet. Because $1 \text{ yd}^3 = 27 \text{ ft}^3$, convert the volume to cubic yards using a conversion factor.

$$646 \text{ ft}^3 = 646 \text{ ft}^3 \times \frac{1 \text{ yd}^3}{27 \text{ ft}^3} \approx 24 \text{ yd}^3$$

So, a full load of dirt costs about $24 \text{ yd}^3 \times \frac{\$18}{1 \text{ yd}^3} = \$432$.

Self-Assessment for Problem Solving

Solve each exercise. Then rate your understanding of the success criteria in your journal.

9. **DIG DEEPER!** The shark cage is in the shape of a rectangular prism and has a volume of 315 cubic feet. Find a set of reasonable dimensions for the base of the cage. Justify your answer.

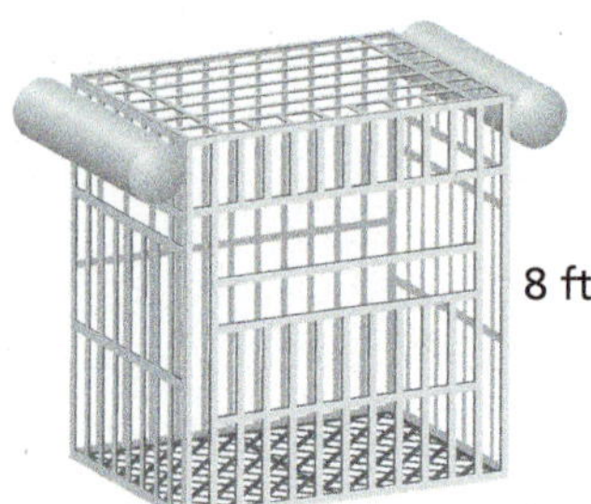

10. The hot tub is in the shape of a rectangular prism. How many pounds of water can the hot tub hold? One cubic foot of water weighs about 62.4 pounds.

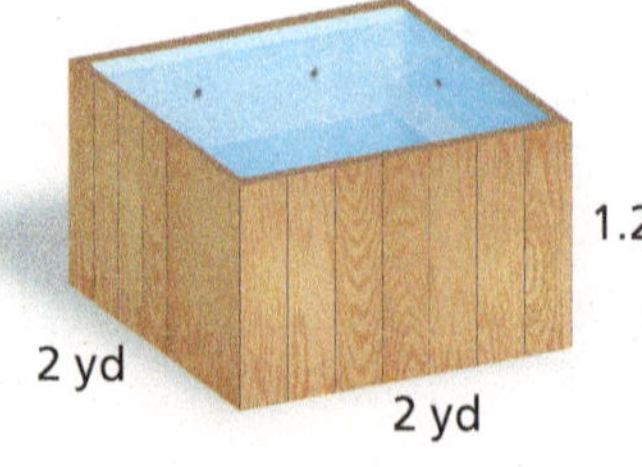

Laurie's Notes

EXAMPLE 3

- It may be helpful to sketch and label the dump truck in a horizontal position.
- **MP6 Attend to Precision:** Note the use of dimensional analysis to show that the final answer has units of dollars.
- The answer is estimated due to rounding the cubic yards. Approximations for real-world situations are common. In real life, the truck would not be *exactly* full. Students' answers should be close.
- **Another Method:** Students may convert each dimension first and then find the volume but fractions make it more difficult. For example: $\frac{17}{3}\text{ yd}\left(\frac{8}{3}\text{ yd}\right)\left(\frac{19}{12}\text{ yd}\right) = \frac{2584}{108}$, or $\frac{646}{27}\text{ yd}^3 \approx 24\text{ yd}^3$, so the answer would be the same when multiplied by $\frac{\$18}{1\text{ yd}^3}$.
- Students may reason that because each cubic yard is \$18 and there are 27 cubic feet per cubic yard, each cubic foot is $\frac{2}{3}$ of a dollar. Students can then multiply the volume in cubic feet (646 ft^3) by $\frac{2}{3}$ to get $\$430\frac{2}{3}$.
- Either alternate method can be used as a check for reasonableness.

Self-Assessment for Problem Solving

- It is important to provide time in class for problem solving, so that students become comfortable with the problem-solving plan. Keep in mind that some students may only be ready for the first step.
- **MP2 Reason Abstractly and Quantitatively:** Exercise 10 is a multi-step problem. It is the first problem in this section involving decimals, but students should be able to solve just as they have with fractions and whole numbers. Remind students of Example 3 and to consider units.
- Students are assessing their understanding of the fourth success criterion.

The Success Criteria Self-Assessment chart can be found in the *Student Journal* or online at *BigIdeasMath.com.*

Closure

Open-Ended Question: Tell students that you are mailing a gift to a friend. You need to place it in a box (rectangular prism) that meets the following specifications:

- the length is between 1 foot and 2 feet,
- the width is between 0.5 foot and 2 feet, and
- the volume is 2.25 cubic feet.

"Find a possible height for the box. Justify your answer." *Sample answer:* 2 feet; The length is 1.5 feet and the width is 0.75 foot.

Formative Assessment Tip

Open-Ended Question

This technique allows you to determine the breadth and depth of students' understanding of a concept. *Open-Ended Questions* require students to think, persevere, and justify the answer. When there are many possible answers, *Open-Ended Questions* offer accessibility and deeper thinking.

Extra Example 3

In Example 3, the length of the dump truck is 22 feet. About how much does a full load of dirt cost? \$558

Self-Assessment for Problem Solving

9. *Sample answer:* 7 ft by $5\frac{5}{8}$ ft; $7 \cdot 5\frac{5}{8} \cdot 8 = 315$
10. about 8424 lb

Learning Target

Find volumes and missing dimensions of rectangular prisms.

Success Criteria

- Use a formula to find the volume of a rectangular prism.
- Use a formula to find the volume of a cube.
- Use the volume of a rectangular prism and two of its dimensions to find the other dimension.
- Apply volumes of rectangular prisms to solve real-life problems.

Review & Refresh

1. 51 ft^2
2. 74.25 m^2
3. 533 yd^2
4. $8 + x$; 10
5. $y - 9$; 3

Concepts, Skills, & Problem Solving

6. $\frac{1}{16} \text{ unit}^3$
7. $\frac{1}{18} \text{ unit}^3$
8. $\frac{1}{75} \text{ unit}^3$
9. $\frac{3}{10} \text{ in.}^3$
10. $1\frac{5}{16} \text{ cm}^3$
11. $\frac{8}{125} \text{ ft}^3$
12. $\frac{15}{16} \text{ m}^3$
13. $3\frac{1}{8} \text{ cm}^3$
14. $12\frac{1}{2} \text{ m}^3$

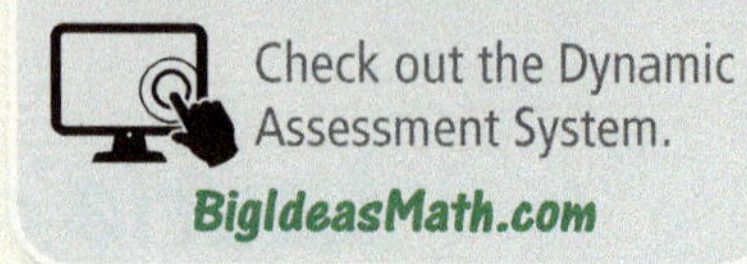

Assignment Guide and Concept Check

Scaffold assignments to support all students in their learning progression. The suggested assignments are a starting point. Continue to assign additional exercises and revisit with spaced practice to move every student toward proficiency.

Level	Assignment 1	Assignment 2
Emerging	3, 5, 7, 9, 11, 15	8, 10, 12, 16, 18, 22
Proficient	3, 5, 8, 11, 12, 16	13, 17, 18, 19, 20, 22, 24
Advanced	3, 5, 8, 11, 14, 17	16, 18, 19, 21, 22, 23, 24

- Assignment 1 is for use after students complete the Self-Assessment for Concepts & Skills.
- Assignment 2 is for use after students complete the Self-Assessment for Problem Solving.
- The red exercises can be used as a concept check.

Review & Refresh Prior Skills

Exercises 1–3 Finding the Surface Area of a Pyramid
Exercises 4 and 5 Writing Expressions and Evaluating Expressions

Common Errors

- **Exercises 9–14** Students may write the units incorrectly, often writing square units instead of cubic units. Remind them that volume has cubic units because there are three dimensions.

7.7 Practice

Find the surface area of the pyramid.

1. 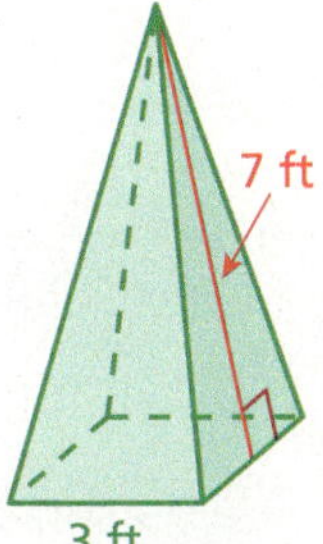

2. 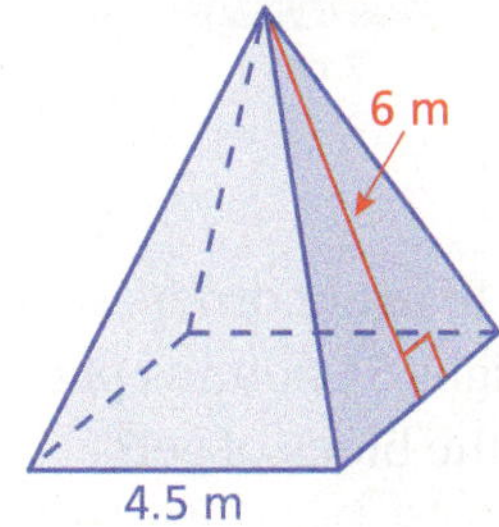

3. 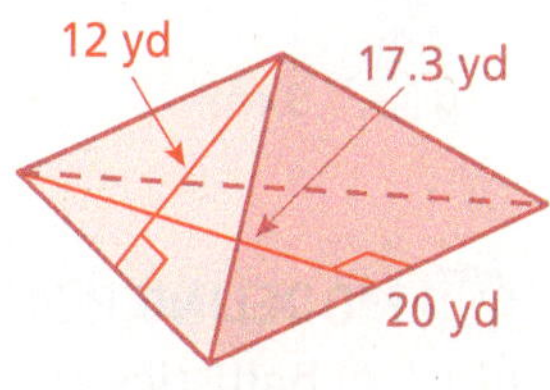

Write the phrase as an expression. Then evaluate the expression when $x = 2$ and $y = 12$.

4. 8 more than a number x

5. the difference of a number y and 9

Concepts, Skills, & Problem Solving

STRUCTURE **The unit cube is divided into identical rectangular prisms. What is the volume of one of the identical prisms?** (See Exploration 1, p. 325.)

6. 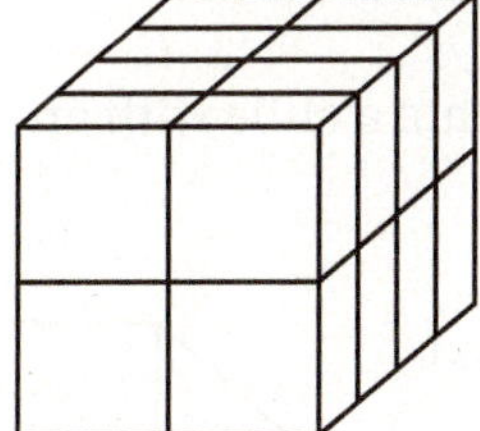

7. 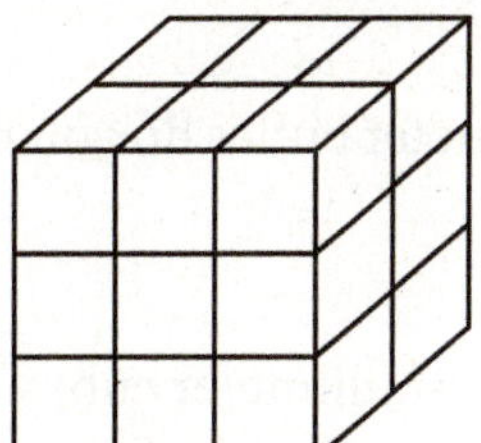

8. 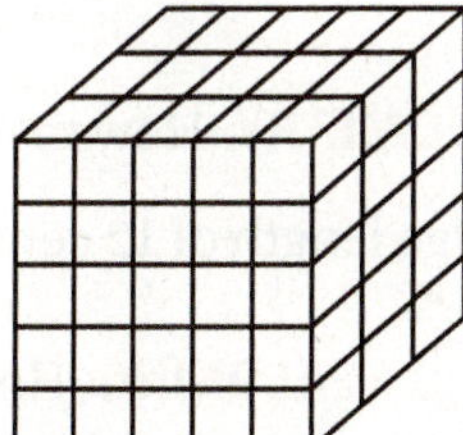

FINDING VOLUME **Find the volume of the prism.**

9. 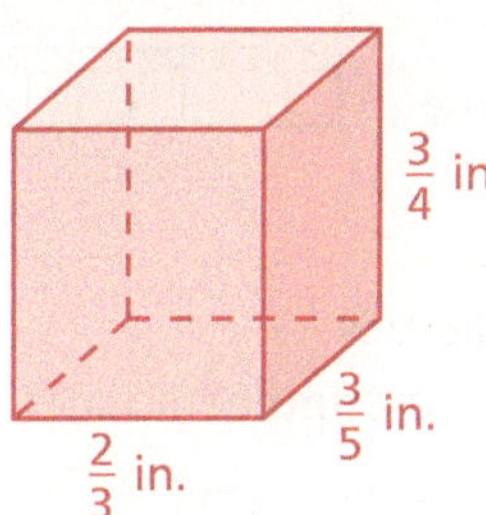

10. 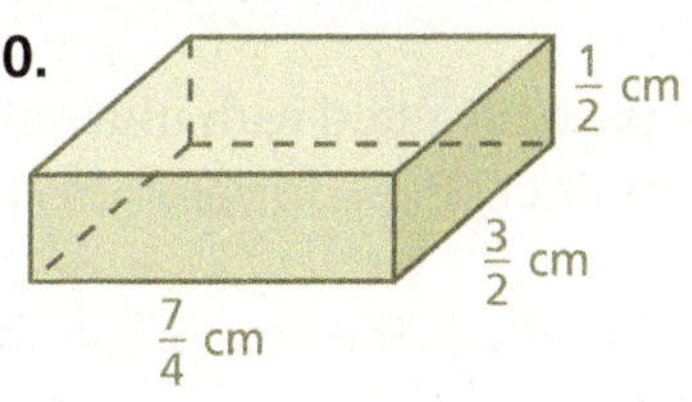

11. 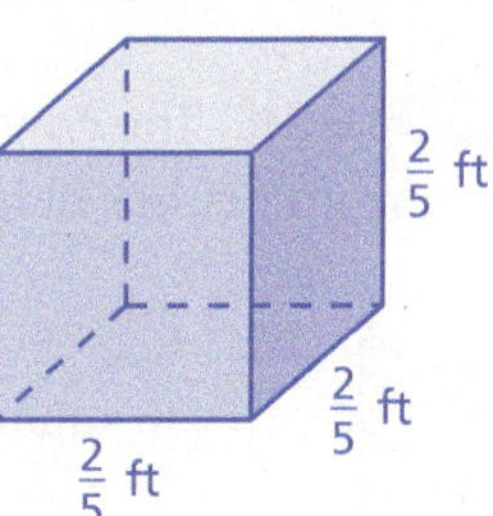

12. 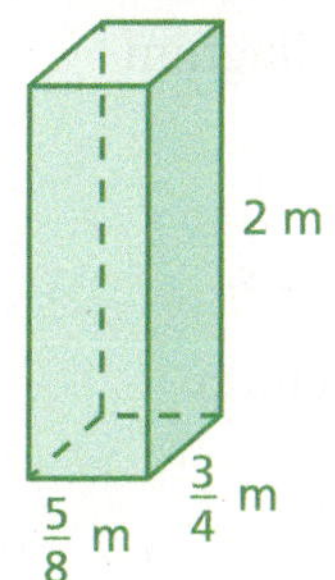

13. 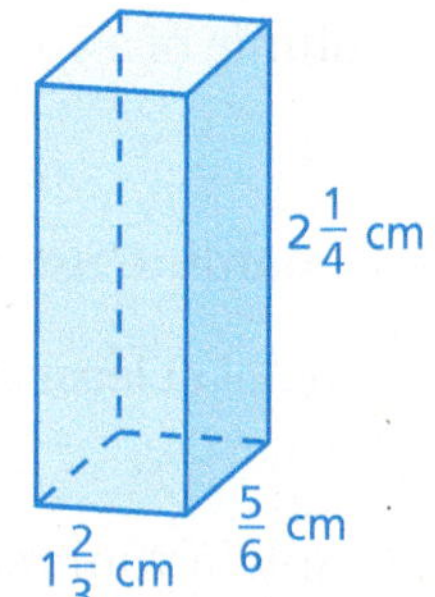

14. 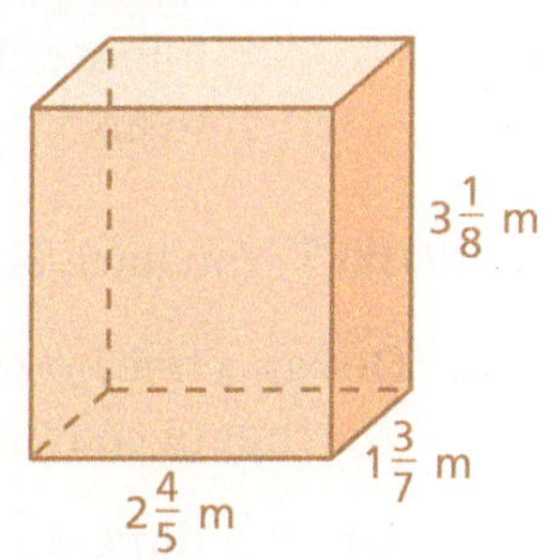

FINDING A MISSING DIMENSION **Find the missing dimension of the prism.**

15. Volume $= 1620\text{ cm}^3$

16. Volume $= 220.5\text{ cm}^3$

17. Volume $= 532\text{ in.}^3$

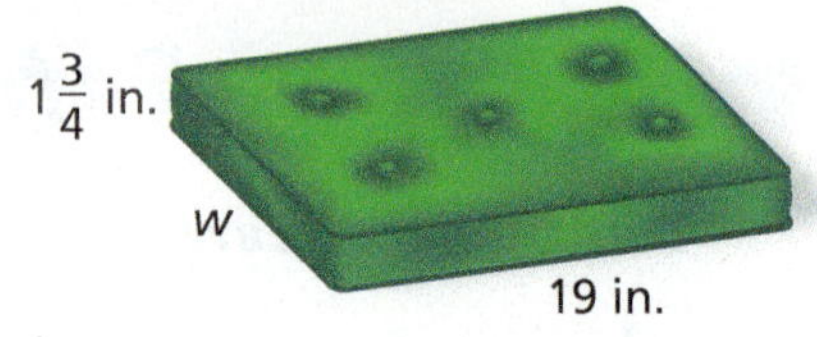

18. **MP MODELING REAL LIFE** An FBI agent orders a block of ballistics gel. The gel weighs 54 pounds per cubic foot. What is the weight of the block of gel?

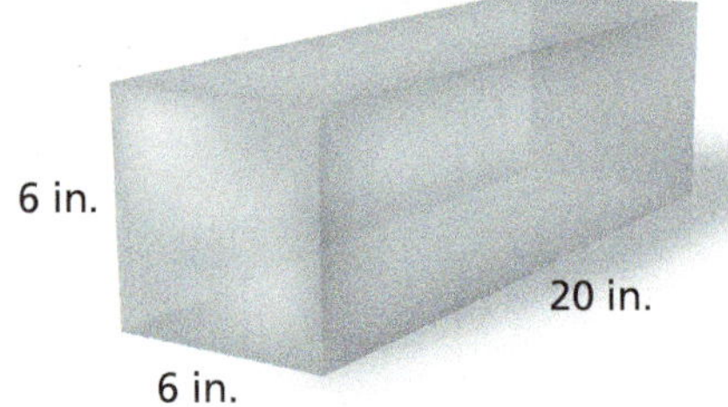

19. **MP MODELING REAL LIFE**

a. Estimate the amount of casserole left in the dish.

b. Will the casserole fit in the storage container? Explain your reasoning.

20. **GEOMETRY** How many $\frac{3}{4}$-centimeter cubes do you need to create a cube with an edge length of 12 centimeters?

21. **MP REASONING** How many one-millimeter cubes do you need to fill a cube that has an edge length of 1 centimeter? How can this result help you convert a volume from cubic millimeters to cubic centimeters? from cubic centimeters to cubic millimeters?

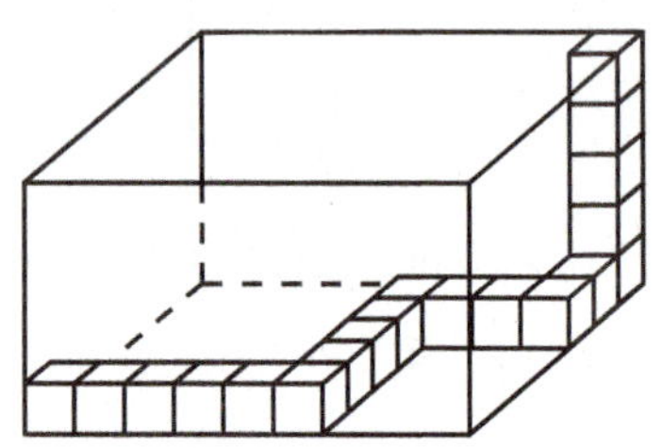

22. **MP LOGIC** The container is partially filled with unit cubes. How many unit cubes fit in the container? Explain your reasoning.

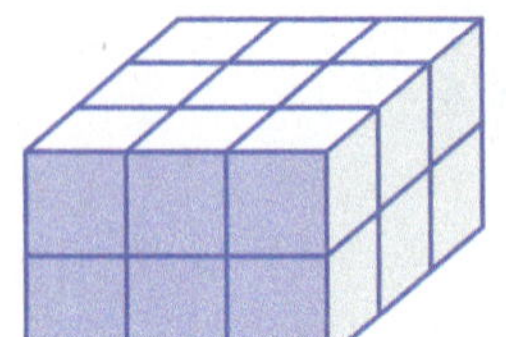

23. **MP PROBLEM SOLVING** The area of the shaded face is 96 square centimeters. What is the volume of the rectangular prism?

24. **DIG DEEPER!** Is the combined volume of a 4-foot cube and a 6-foot cube equal to the volume of a 10-foot cube? Use a diagram to justify your answer.

25. **PROJECT** You have 1400 square feet of boards to use for a new tree house.

a. Design a tree house that has a volume of at least 250 cubic feet. Include sketches of your tree house.

b. Are your dimensions reasonable? Explain your reasoning.

Mini-Assessment

Find the volume of the prism.

1.

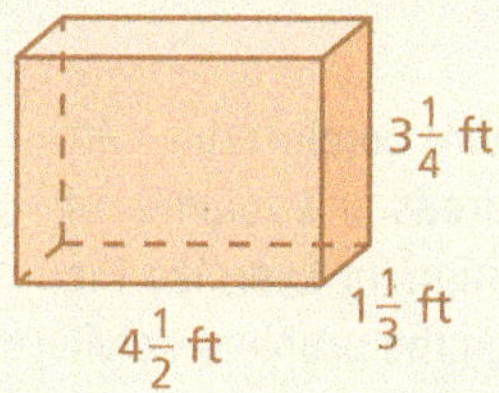

$19\frac{1}{2}$ ft^3

2.

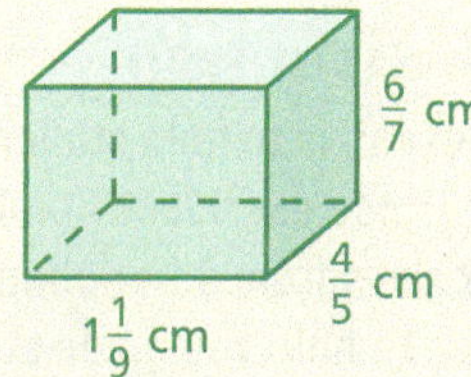

$\frac{16}{21}$ cm^3

3.

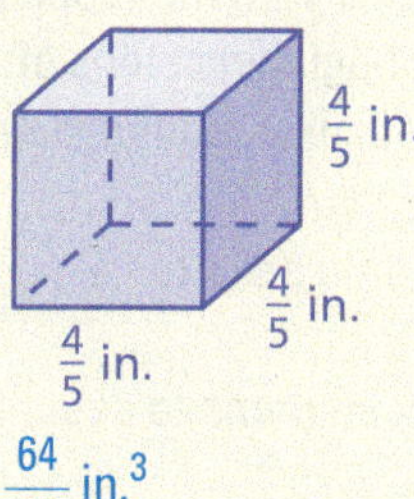

$\frac{64}{125}$ in.^{3}

4. The volume of the cell phone is 75 cubic centimeters. Find the height of the cell phone. Round your answer to the nearest tenth.

1.6 cm

Section Resources

Surface Level	Deep Level
Resources by Chapter • Extra Practice • Reteach • Puzzle Time Student Journal • Self-Assessment • Practice Differentiating the Lesson Tutorial Videos Skills Review Handbook Skills Trainer	Resources by Chapter • Enrichment and Extension Graphic Organizers Dynamic Assessment System • Section Practice
Transfer Level	
Dynamic Assessment System • End-of-Chapter Quiz	Assessment Book • End-of-Chapter Quiz

Concepts, Skills, & Problem Solving

15. $h = 20$ cm
16. $w = 4.5$ cm
17. $w = 16$ in.
18. 22.5 lb
19. a. *Sample answer:* 297 in.^{3}
    b. no; The container only holds 196 cubic inches.
20. 4096
21. 1000; Multiply by the conversion factor $\frac{1 \text{ cm}^3}{1000 \text{ mm}^3}$;
    Multiply by the conversion factor $\frac{1000 \text{ mm}^3}{1 \text{ cm}^3}$.
22. 315; $9 \cdot 7 \cdot 5 = 315$
23. 1152 cm^3
24. no;

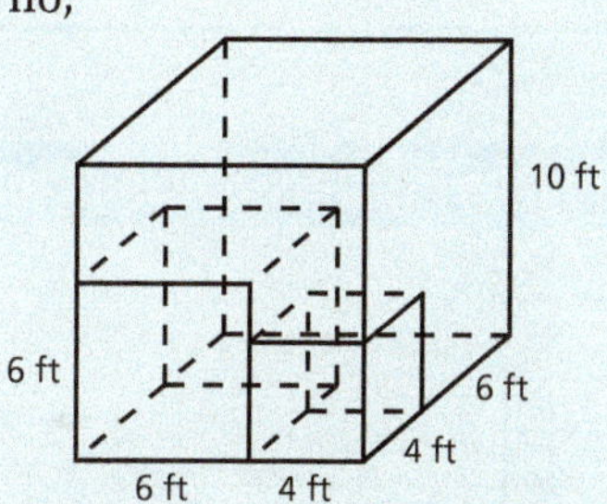

25. *Answers should include, but not limited to:*
    a. a sketch of a tree house that has a surface area of at most 1400 square feet and a volume of at least 250 cubic feet
    b. For the dimensions to be reasonable, the tree house should be able to fit people and fit in a tree.

Skills Needed

Exercise 1

- Finding the Volume of a Rectangular Prism
- Writing Fractions as Percents

Exercise 2

- Finding the Surface Area of a Prism
- Graphing Equations
- Writing Equations in Two Variables

Exercise 3

- Finding a Missing Dimension
- Solving Equations

ELL Support

Explain that a toy chest is a box in which toys can be stored. The word *chest* may refer to a person's upper body or different types of containers that hold things, such as a treasure chest or a chest of drawers.

Using the Problem-Solving Plan

1. 28%
2. 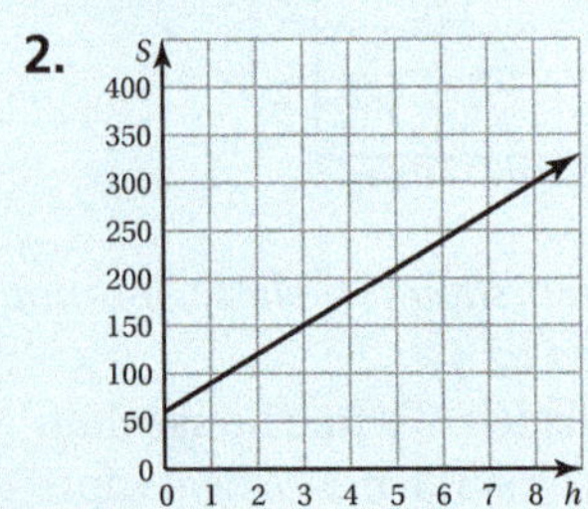

   $6\frac{2}{3}$ m
3. 15 in.

Performance Task

The *STEAM Video Performance Task* provides the opportunity for additional enrichment and greater depth of knowledge as students explore the mathematics of the chapter within a context tied to the chapter STEAM Video. The performance task and a detailed scoring rubric are provided at *BigIdeasMath.com*.

Laurie's Notes

Scaffolding Instruction

- The goal of this lesson is to help students become more comfortable with problem solving. These exercises combine surface areas and volumes of prisms with prior skills from other chapters. The solution for Exercise 1 is worked out below, to help you guide students through the problem-solving plan. Use the remaining class time to have students work on the other exercises.
- **Emerging:** The goal for these students is to feel comfortable with the problem-solving plan. Allow students to work in pairs to write the beginning steps of the problem-solving plan for Exercise 2. Keep in mind that some students may only be ready to do the first step.
- **Proficient:** Students may be able to work independently or in pairs to complete Exercises 2 and 3.
- Visit each pair to review their plan for each problem. Ask students to describe their plans.

Using the Problem-Solving Plan

Exercise 1

Understand the problem. You know the shape and the dimensions of the two swimming pools. You are asked to find the amount of water in the smaller pool as a percent of the amount of water in the larger pool.

Make a plan. First, find the volume of each pool. Then represent the amount of water in the smaller pool as a fraction of the amount of water in the larger pool. Find an equivalent fraction whose denominator is 100 to find the percent.

Solve and check. Use the plan to solve the problem. Then check your solution.

- Use the formula for the volume of a rectangular prism to find the volume of each pool.

  Larger Pool: $V = \ell wh = (50)(25)(3) = 3750$

  Smaller Pool: $V = \ell wh = (25)(21)(2) = 1050$

  So, the volume of the larger pool is 3750 m^3 and the volume of the smaller pool is 1050 m^3.
- Represent the amount of water in the smaller pool as a fraction of the amount of water in the larger pool: $\frac{1050}{3750} = \frac{1050 \div 150}{3750 \div 150} = \frac{7}{25}$.
- Write $\frac{7}{25}$ as a percent: $\frac{7}{25} = \frac{7 \times 4}{25 \times 4} = \frac{28}{100} = 28\%$.

  So, the amount of water in the smaller pool is 28% of the amount of water in the larger pool.
- **Check:** Verify the answer by finding 28% of the amount of water in the larger pool.

  28% of 3750 = 0.28 × 3750 = 1050 ✓

7 Connecting Concepts

Using the Problem-Solving Plan

1. A sports complex has two swimming pools that are shaped like rectangular prisms. The amount of water in the smaller pool is what percent of the amount of water in the larger pool?

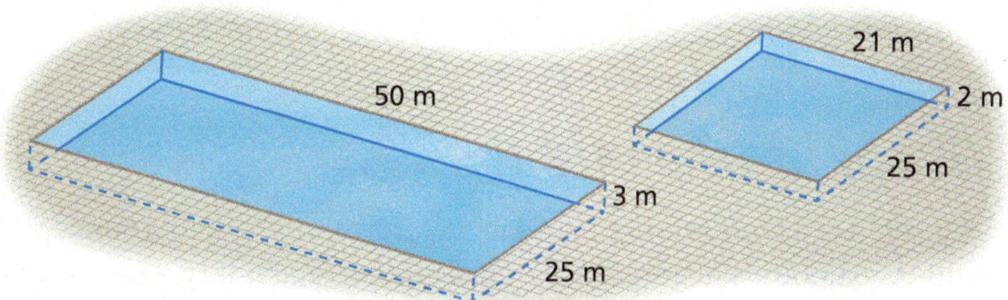

Understand the problem. You know the shape and the dimensions of the two swimming pools. You are asked to find the amount of water in the smaller pool as a percent of the amount of water in the larger pool.

Make a plan. First, find the volume of each pool. Then represent the amount of water in the smaller pool as a fraction of the amount of water in the larger pool. Find an equivalent fraction whose denominator is 100 to find the percent.

Solve and check. Use the plan to solve the problem. Then check your solution.

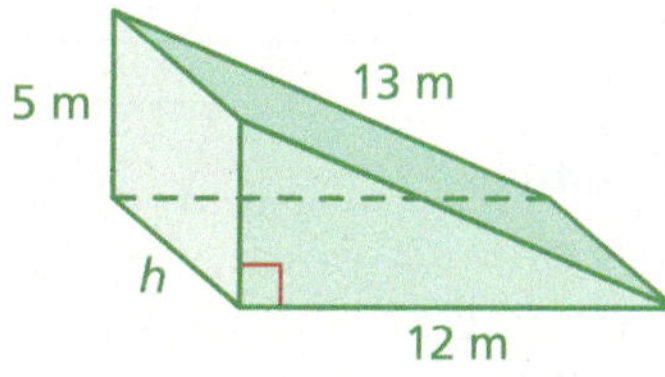

2. Use a graph to represent the relationship between the surface area S (in square meters) and the height h (in meters) of the triangular prism. Then find the height when the surface area is 260 square meters.

3. A toy company sells two different toy chests. The toy chests have different dimensions, but the same volume. What is the width w of Toy Chest 2?

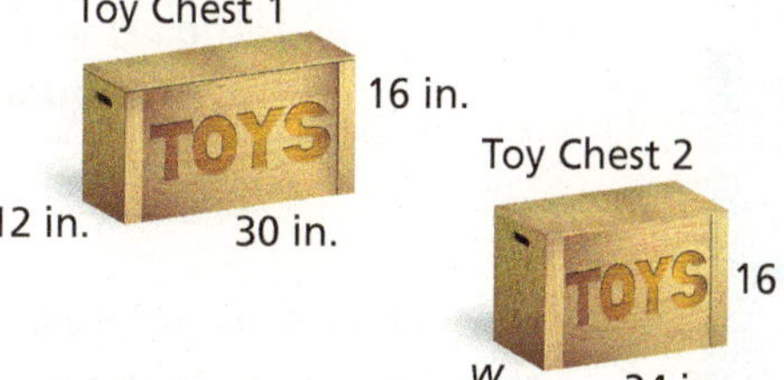

Performance Task

Maximizing the Volumes of Boxes

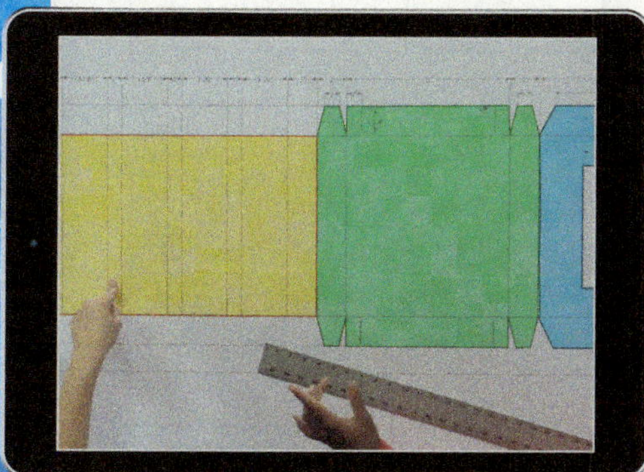

At the beginning of this chapter, you watched a STEAM Video called "Packaging Design." You are now ready to complete the performance task related to this video, available at ***BigIdeasMath.com***. Be sure to use the problem-solving plan as you work through the performance task.

7 Chapter Review

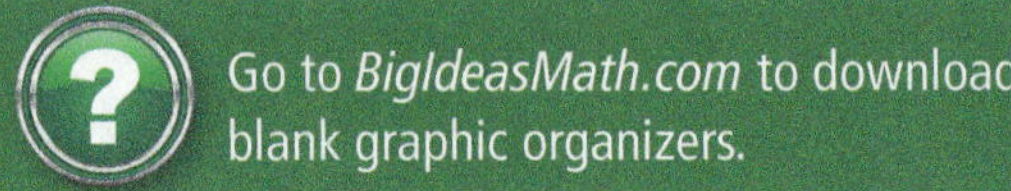

Review Vocabulary

Write the definition and give an example of each vocabulary term.

polygon, *p. 285*	solid, *p. 306*	vertex, *p. 306*	surface area, *p. 312*
composite figure, *p. 294*	polyhedron, *p. 306*	prism, *p. 306*	net, *p. 312*
kite, *p. 298*	face, *p. 306*	pyramid, *p. 306*	volume, *p. 325*
	edge, *p. 306*		

Graphic Organizers

You can use a **Four Square** to organize information about a concept. Each of the four squares can be a category, such as definition, vocabulary, example, non-example, words, algebra, table, numbers, visual, graph, or equation. Here is an example of a Four Square for the ***area of a parallelogram***.

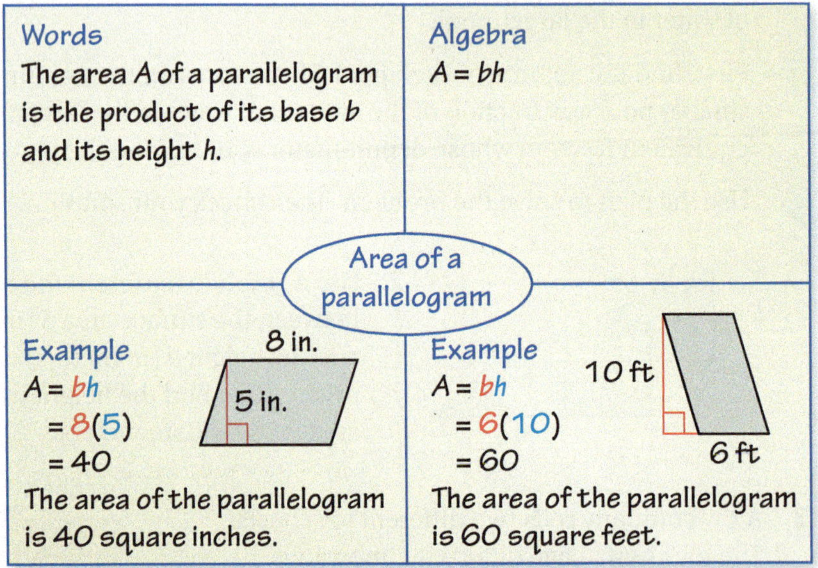

Choose and complete a graphic organizer to help you study the concept.

1. area of a triangle
2. area of a trapezoid
3. area of a composite figure
4. polyhedron
5. surface area of a prism
6. surface area of a pyramid
7. volume of a rectangular prism

"Here is my **Four Square** to organize information about rattlesnakes. How do you like it?"

Review Vocabulary

- As a review of the chapter vocabulary, have students revisit the vocabulary section in their *Student Journals* to fill in any missing definitions and record examples of each term.

Graphic Organizers

Sample answers:

1.

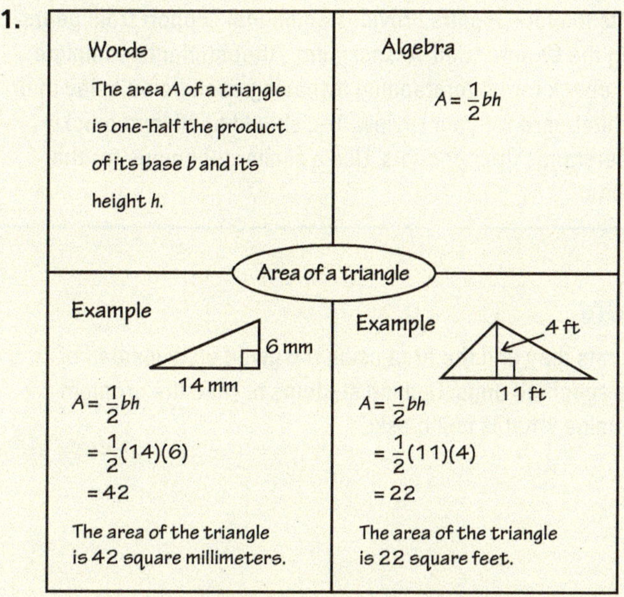

2.

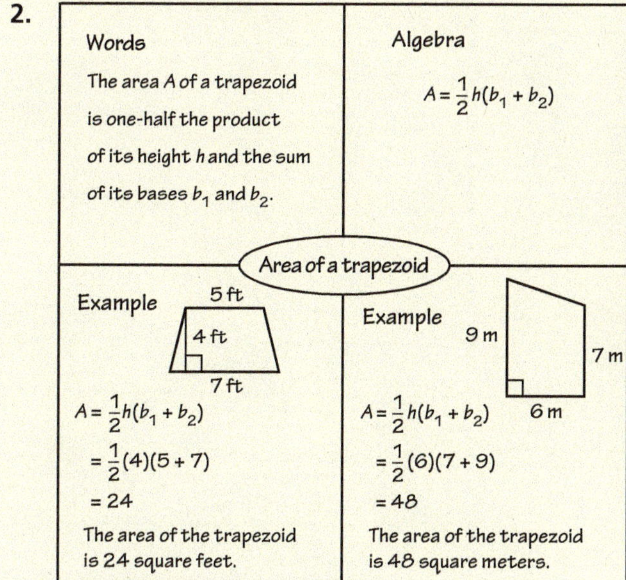

3–7. Answers at *BigIdeasMath.com.*

List of Organizers

Available at *BigIdeasMath.com*
Definition and Example Chart
Example and Non-Example Chart
Four Square
Information Frame
Summary Triangle

About this Organizer

A **Four Square** can be used to organize information about a concept. Students write the concept in the oval. Then students use each of the four squares surrounding the oval to represent a related category. Related categories may include: definition, vocabulary, example, non-example, words, algebra, table, numbers, visual, graph, or equation. Encourage students to use categories that will help them study the concept. Students can place their Four Squares on note cards to use as a quick study reference.

Chapter Self-Assessment

1. 500 yd^2
2. 242 mm^2
3. 45 cm^2
4. 864 $in.^2$
5. 14 ft
6. 1.5 m
7. *Sample answer:*

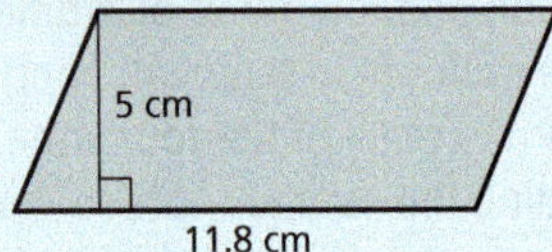

Chapter Self-Assessment

The Success Criteria Self-Assessment chart can be found in the *Student Journal* or online at *BigIdeasMath.com.*

ELL Support

Allowing students to work in pairs provides additional support from peers while completing the Chapter Self-Assessment. After students complete the first section, check for understanding by having each pair display their answers on a whiteboard for your review. You should be able to quickly assess who understands the concepts. Use a similar technique for the remaining sections.

Common Errors

- **Exercise 4** Students may find the area using the given units instead of converting to the specified units. Remind students to read the problem carefully to determine what is being asked.

Chapter Self-Assessment

As you complete the exercises, use the scale below to rate your understanding of the success criteria in your journal.

1	2	3	4
I do not understand.	I can do it with help.	I can do it on my own.	I can teach someone else.

7.1 Areas of Parallelograms *(pp. 285–290)*

Learning Target: Find areas and missing dimensions of parallelograms.

Find the area of the parallelogram.

1. 20 yd, 25 yd

2. 22 mm, 11 mm

3. 9 cm, 5 cm

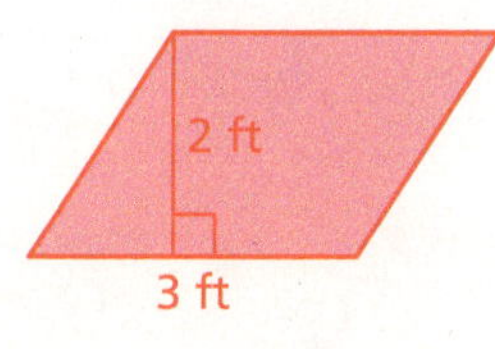

4. Find the area (in square inches) of the parallelogram.

5. The billboard shown is in the shape of a parallelogram with a base of 48 feet. What is the height of the billboard?

6. The freeway noise barrier shown is made of identical parallelogram-shaped sections. The area of each section is 7.5 square meters, and the height of the barrier is 5 meters. How many meters wide is each section of the noise barrier?

7. Draw a parallelogram that has an area between 58 and 60 square centimeters.

7.2 Areas of Triangles (pp. 291–296)

Learning Target: Find areas and missing dimensions of triangles, and find areas of composite figures.

Find the area of the triangle.

8.

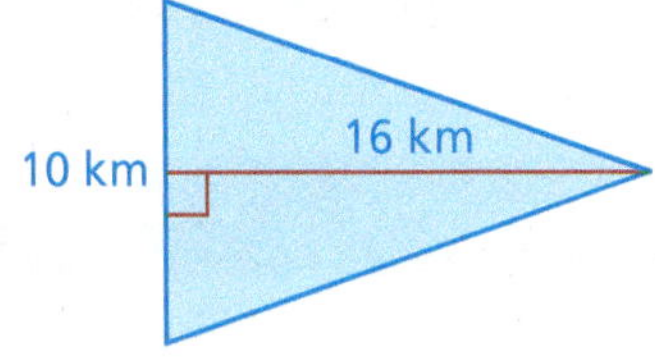

9.

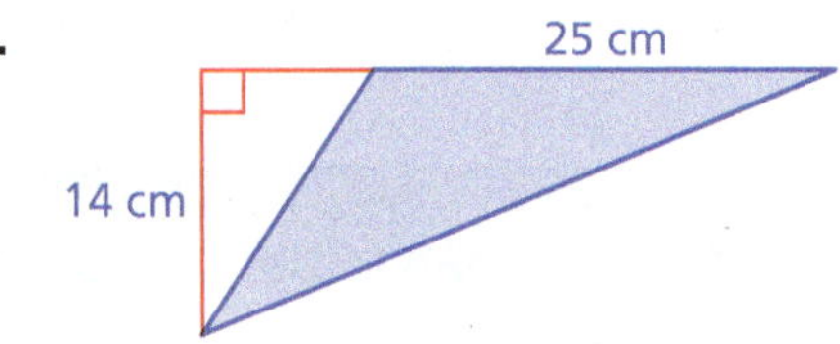

Find the missing dimension of the triangle.

10. Area = 35 mi²

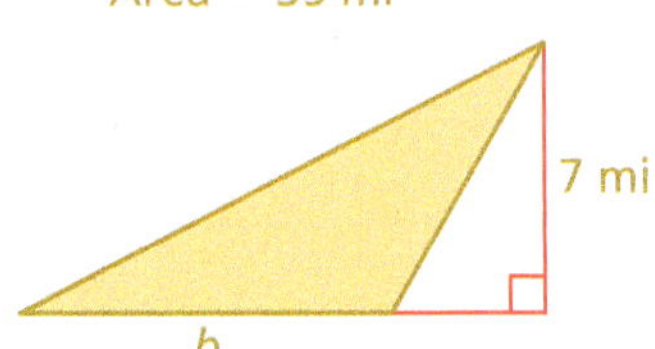

11. Area = 5 cm²

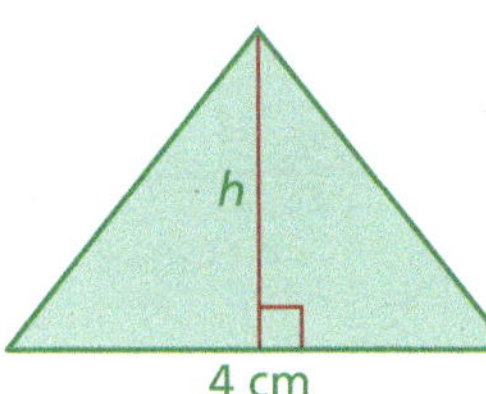

Find the area of the figure.

12.

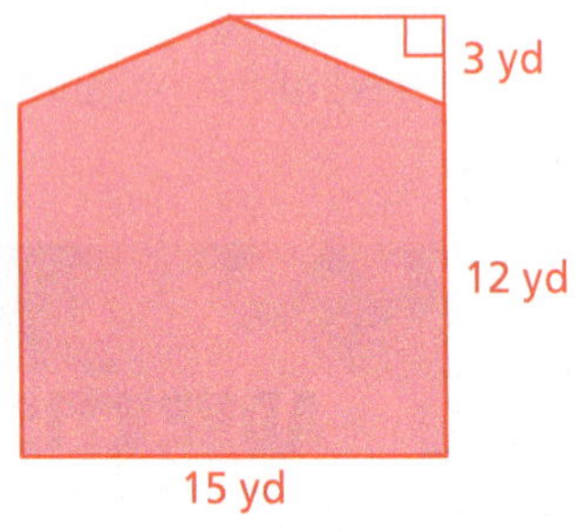

13.

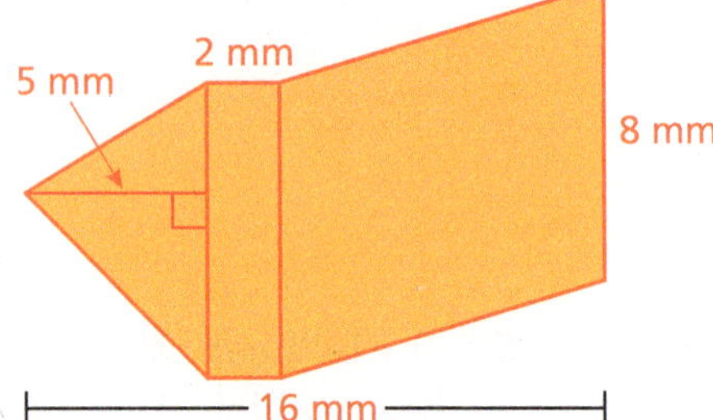

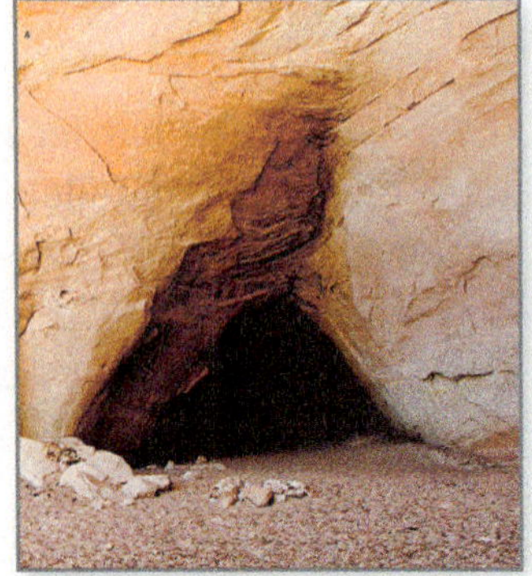

14. Draw a composite figure that has an area less than 35 square inches.

15. The triangle-shaped entrance to the cavern is $2\frac{1}{2}$ feet tall and 4 feet wide. What is the area of the entrance?

- **Exercises 8 and 9** Students may multiply the base and the height and forget to multiply by $\frac{1}{2}$. Tell students to write the formula and then identify the value of each variable before substituting.
- **Exercises 12 and 13** Students may forget to include one or more parts of the composite figure or may include a part more than once. Tell them to draw and label each part, find the area of each part, and then add the areas of the parts to find the area of the composite figure.

Chapter Self-Assessment

8. 80 km^2

9. 175 cm^2

10. $b = 10$ mi

11. $h = 2.5$ cm

12. 202.5 yd^2

13. 108 mm^2

14. *Sample answer:*

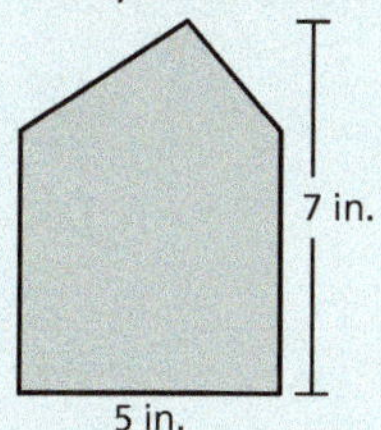

15. 5 ft^2

Chapter Self-Assessment

16. 300 in.^2

17. 105 m^2

18. 6 in.^2

19. 49 mi^2

20. 76 ft^2

21. 120 cm^2

22. 90 in.^2

23. 636 in.^2

24. 80,000 cm^2

Common Errors

- **Exercises 17–19** Students may forget to multiply by $\frac{1}{2}$ or substitute the height for one of the bases. Tell students to write out the formula for the area of a trapezoid and then identify the value of each variable before substituting.

7.3 Areas of Trapezoids and Kites *(pp. 297–304)*

Learning Target: Find areas of trapezoids, kites, and composite figures.

16. Use decomposition to find the area of the kite.

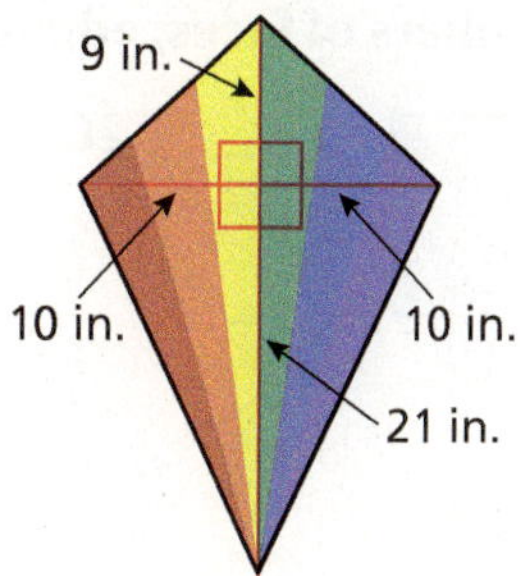

Find the area of the trapezoid.

17.

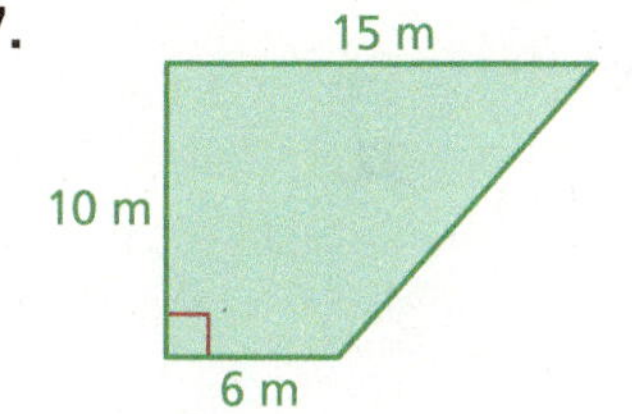

18.

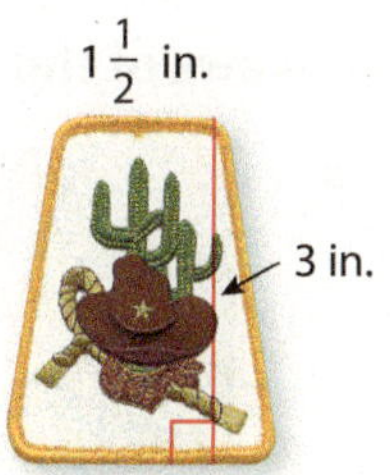

19.

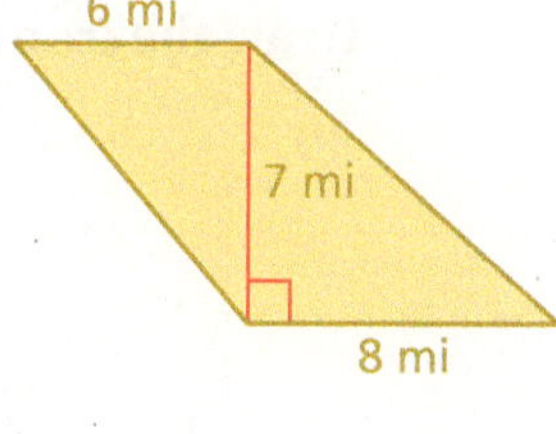

Find the area of the figure.

20.

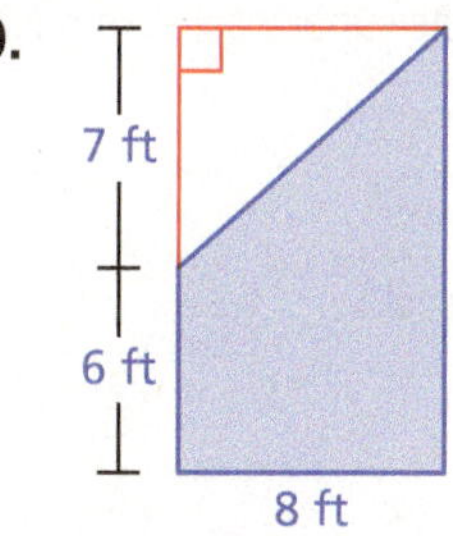

21.

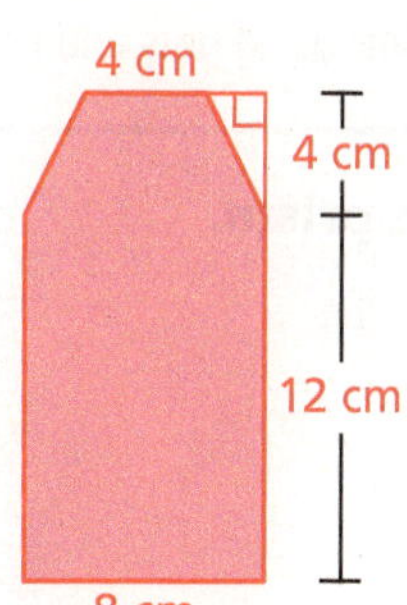

22.

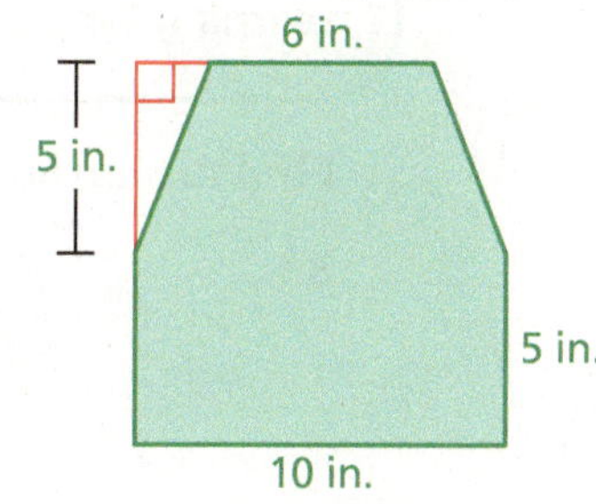

24 in.
6 in.
14 in.
54 in.

23. You are creating a design for the side of the soapbox car. How much area do you have for the design?

24. Find the area (in square centimeters) of a trapezoid with a height of 2 meters and base lengths of 3 meters and 5 meters.

7.4 Three-Dimensional Figures (pp. 305–310)

Learning Target: Describe and draw three-dimensional figures.

Find the numbers of faces, edges, and vertices of the solid.

25. 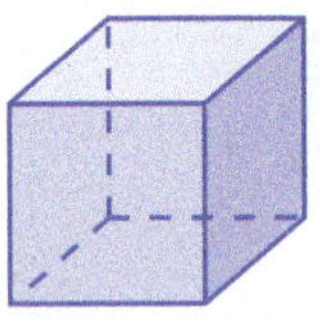

26. 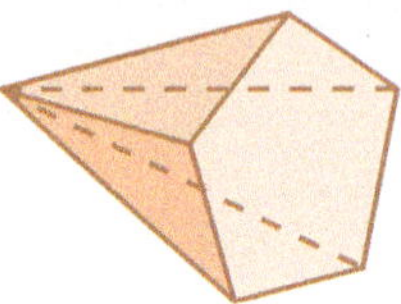

27. 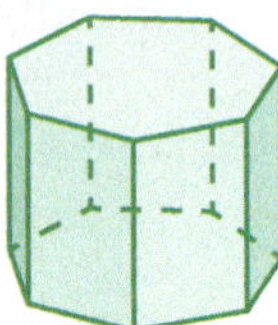

Draw the solid.

28. square pyramid

29. hexagonal prism

Draw the front, side, and top views of the solid.

30. 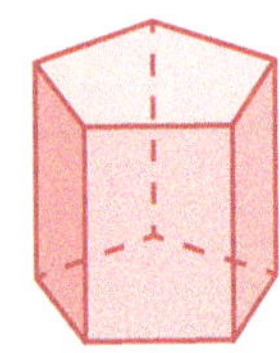

31. 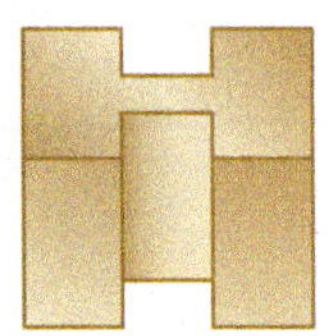

32. 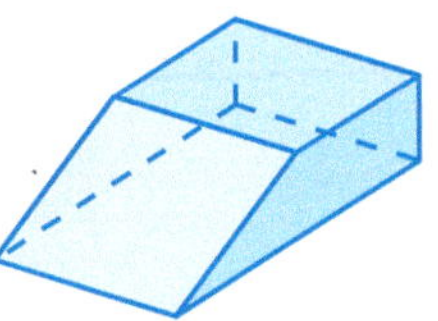

7.5 Surface Areas of Prisms (pp. 311–318)

Learning Target: Represent prisms using nets and use nets to find the surface areas of prisms.

Find the surface area of the prism.

33. 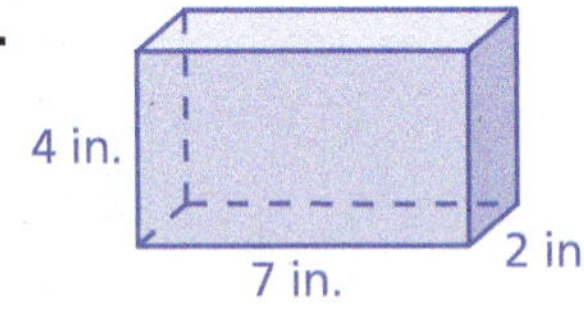

34. 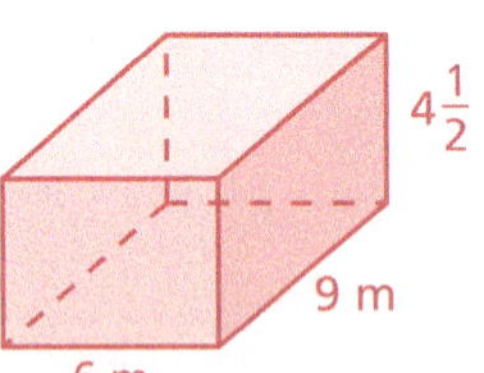

35. 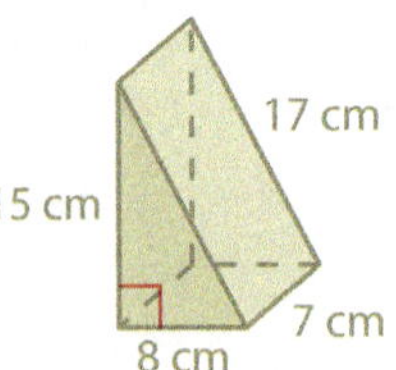

36. 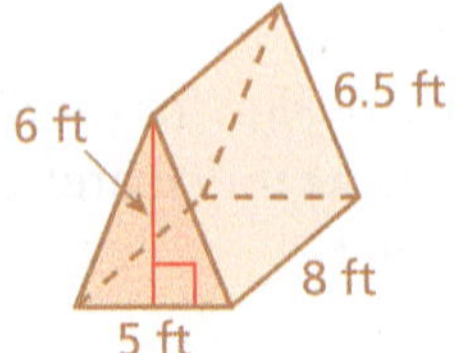

37. 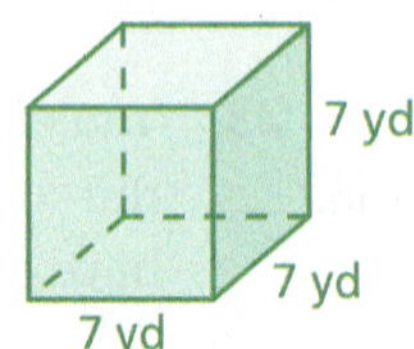

38. 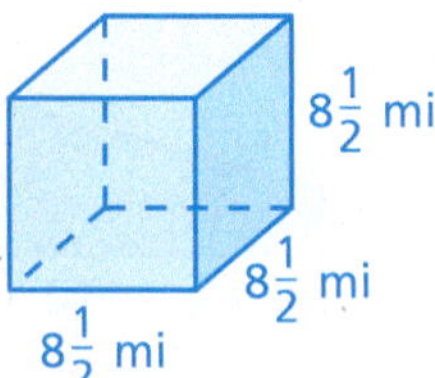

39. One quart of water-resistant paint covers 75 square feet. A swimming pool is in the shape of a rectangular prism with a length of 20 feet, a width of 10 feet, and a height of 5 feet. How many quarts should you buy to paint the swimming pool with two coats of paint?

Common Errors

- **Exercises 28 and 29** Students may mix up the different types of solids. Remind them of the definitions and provide a few real-life examples of each solid.
- **Exercises 30–32** Students may have difficulty visualizing the front, side, and top views of the solid. Create paper objects for those who are struggling to draw the different sides of the solid.
- **Exercises 33 and 34** Students may find the area of only three faces instead of all six. Remind them that each face is paired with another. Show students the net of a rectangular solid to remind them of the six faces.
- **Exercise 39** Students may include the top of the pool as part of the area that needs to be painted. Remind students that the top of the pool is open and will not be painted.

Chapter Self-Assessment

25. 6 faces, 12 edges, 8 vertices

26. 6 faces, 10 edges, 6 vertices

27. 9 faces, 21 edges, 14 vertices

28. 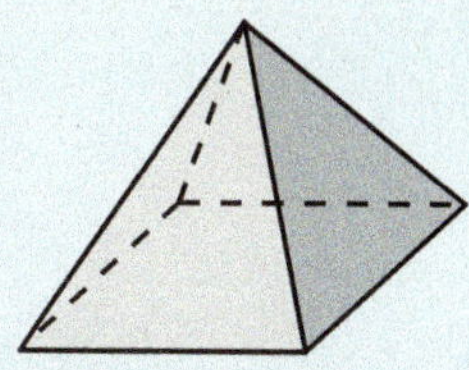

29. 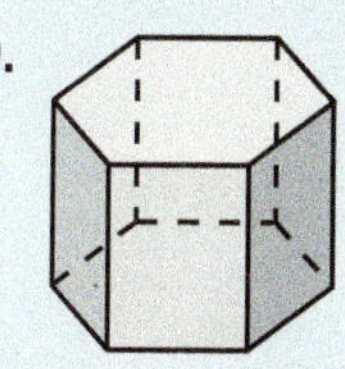

30. front: 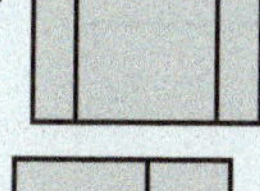

side: 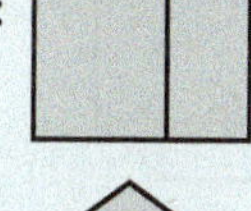

top: 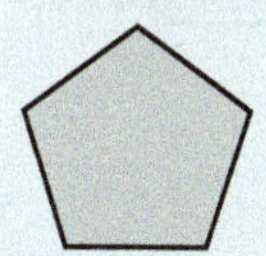

31. front: 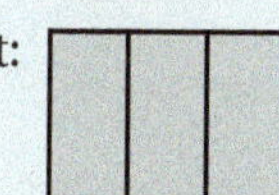

side: 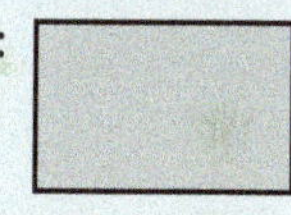

top: 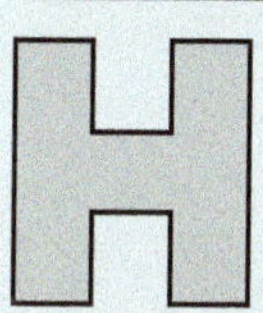

32. front:

side: 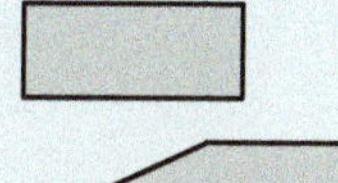

top: 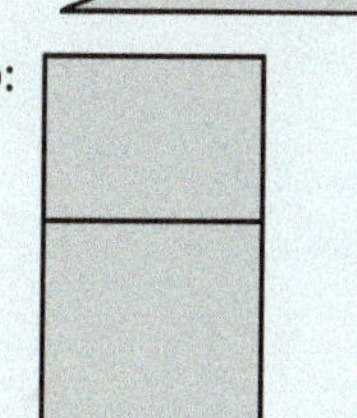

33. 100 in.^2 **34.** 243 m^2

35. 400 cm^2 **36.** 174 ft^2

37. 294 yd^2 **38.** $433\frac{1}{2} \text{ mi}^2$

39. 14

Chapter Self-Assessment

40. 533 yd^2

41. 147.6 m^2

42. 180.6 cm^2

43. 80 in.^2

44. 5 ft^3

45. $\frac{11}{18} \text{ cm}^3$

46. $\frac{27}{512} \text{ in.}^3$

47. 7.5 ft

48. $162\frac{1}{2}$

49. *Sample answer:*

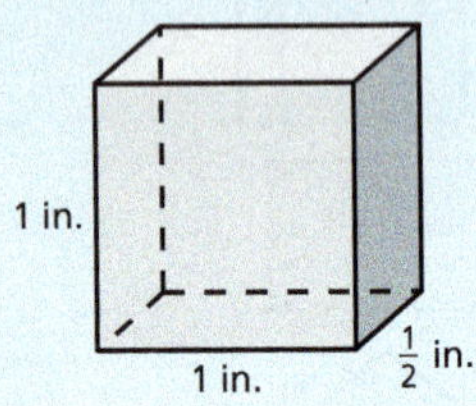

Common Errors

- **Exercises 40–43** Students may forget to include the area of the base when finding the surface area. Remind them that when asked to find the surface area, the base is included.
- **Exercises 40–43** Students may add the wrong number of lateral face areas to the area of the base. Remind students that the number of sides of the base determines how many triangles make up the lateral surface area.
- **Exercises 44–46** Students may write the units incorrectly, often writing square units instead of cubic units. Remind them that volume has cubic units because there are three dimensions.

Chapter Resources

Surface Level	Deep Level
Resources by Chapter • Extra Practice • Reteach • Puzzle Time Student Journal • Practice • Chapter Self-Assessment Differentiating the Lesson Tutorial Videos Skills Review Handbook Skills Trainer Game Library	Resources by Chapter • Enrichment and Extension Graphic Organizers Game Library
Transfer Level	
STEAM Video Dynamic Assessment System • Chapter Test	Assessment Book • Chapter Tests A and B • Alternative Assessment • STEAM Performance Task

7.6 Surface Areas of Pyramids (pp. 319–324)

Learning Target: Represent pyramids using nets and use nets to find the surface areas of pyramids.

Find the surface area of the pyramid.

40.

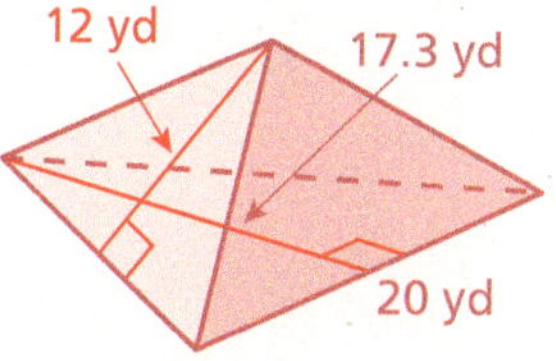

41.

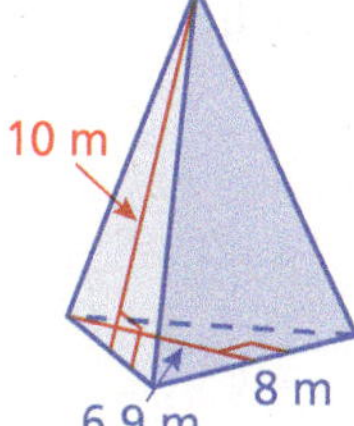

42.

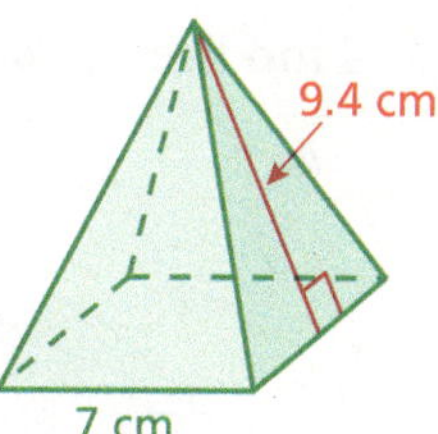

43. You make a square pyramid for a school project. Find the surface area of the pyramid.

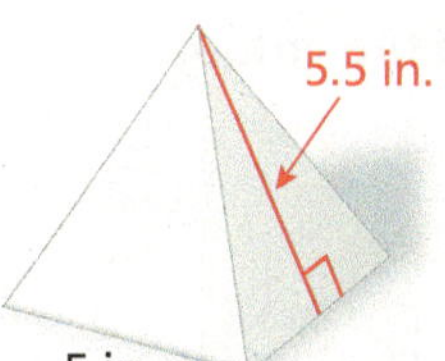

7.7 Volumes of Rectangular Prisms (pp. 325–330)

Learning Target: Find volumes and missing dimensions of rectangular prisms.

Find the volume of the prism.

44.

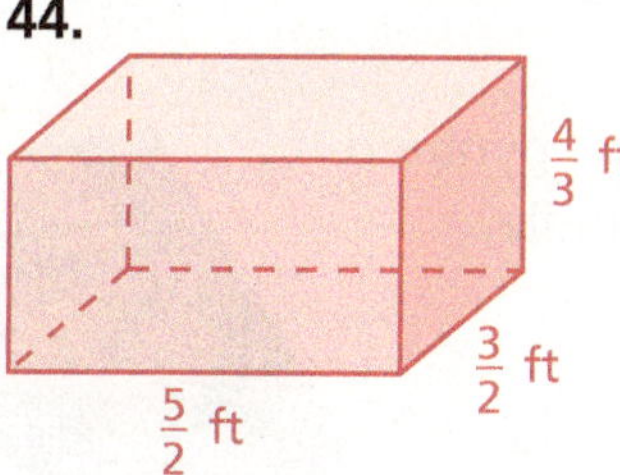

45.

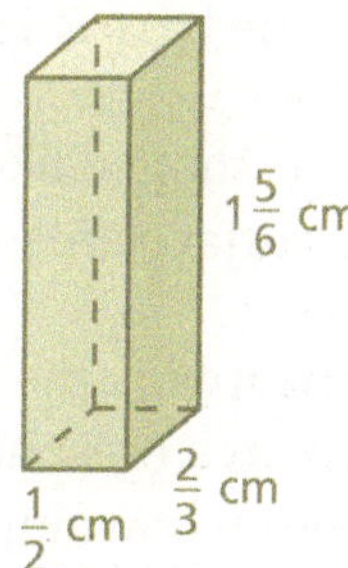

46.

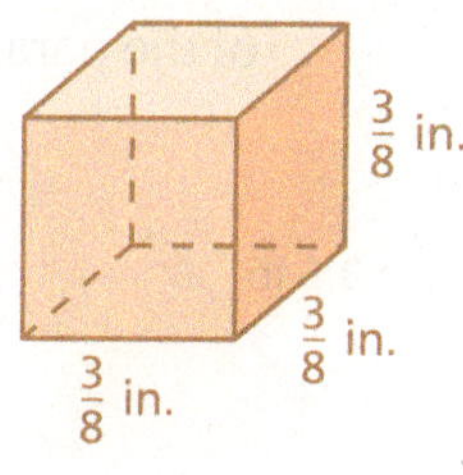

47. The prism has a volume of 150 cubic feet. Find the length of the prism.

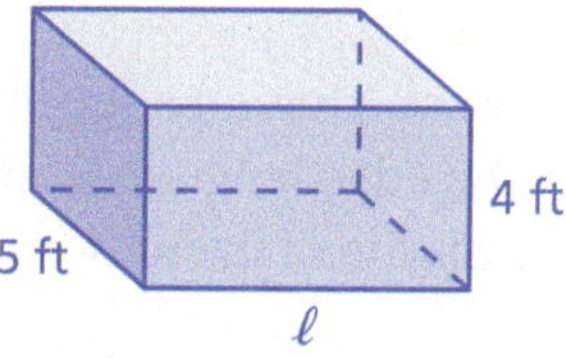

48. How many cubic inches of tissues can the box hold?

49. Draw a rectangular prism that has a volume less than 1 cubic inch.

7 Practice Test

Find the area of the figure.

1. 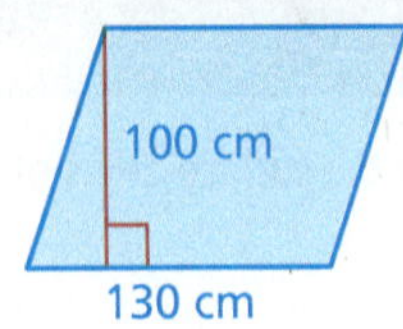

2. 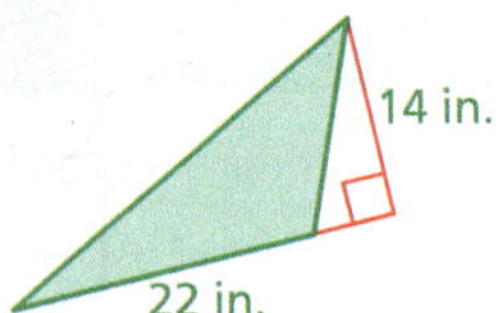

3. 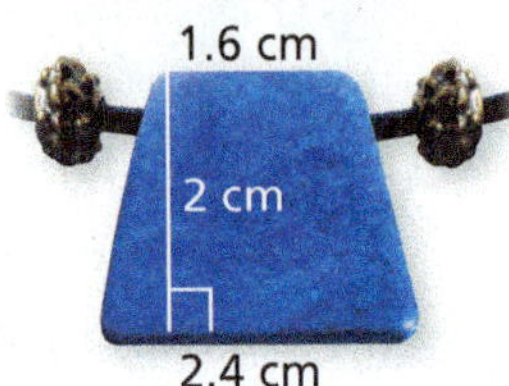

Find the surface area of the solid.

4. 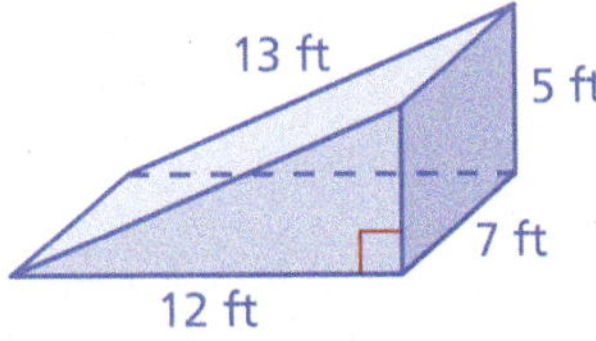

5. 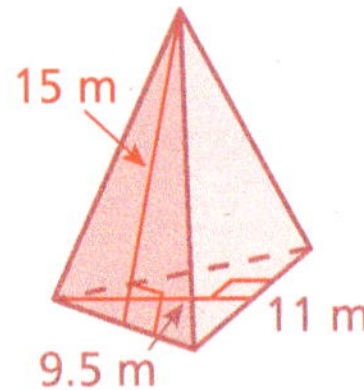

Find the volume of the prism.

6. 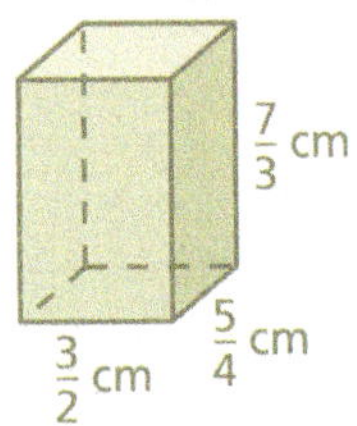

7. 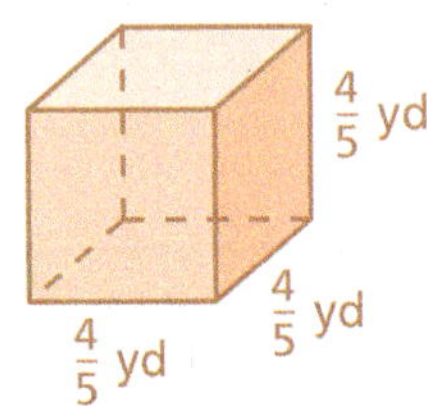

8. Draw an octagonal prism.

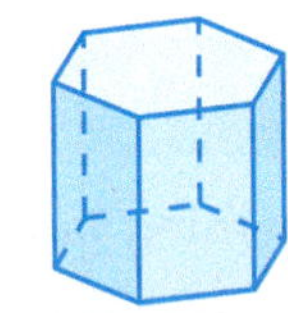

9. Find the numbers of faces, edges, and vertices of the solid.

10. The area of a parallelogram is 156 square meters. What is the height of the parallelogram when the base is 13 meters?

11. A candle is shaped like a square pyramid. Find the surface area of the candle.

3.6 in.

4 in.

12. You are wrapping the boxed DVD collection as a present. What is the least amount of wrapping paper needed to wrap the box?

13. A cube has an edge length of 4 inches. You double the edge lengths. How many times greater is the volume of the new cube?

14. The Pentagon in Arlington, Virginia, is the headquarters of the U.S. Department of Defense. The building's center contains a pentagon-shaped courtyard with an area of about 5 acres. Find the land areas (in square feet) of the courtyard and the building.

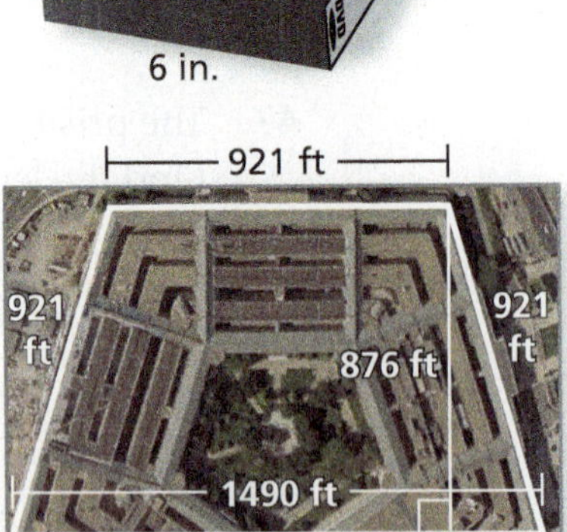

Practice Test Item References

Practice Test Questions	Section to Review
1, 10	7.1
2	7.2
3, 14	7.3
8, 9	7.4
4, 12	7.5
5, 11	7.6
6, 7, 13	7.7

Test-Taking Strategies

Remind students to quickly look over the entire test before they start so that they can budget their time. This test is very visual and requires students to remember many terms. It might be helpful for them to jot down some of the terms on the back of the test before they start. It is very important for students to use the **Stop** and **Think** strategy for each question. When students hurry on a test involving area, surface area, and volume, they may use the wrong formula. Encourage students to write the formula first and then substitute the values for the variables.

Common Errors

- **Exercises 1–3** Students may use the wrong formula. Tell students to write the formula and then identify the value of each variable before substituting.
- **Exercise 2** Students may multiply the base and the height and forget to multiply by $\frac{1}{2}$. Tell students to write the formula and then identify the value of each variable before substituting.
- **Exercises 3 and 14** Students may substitute the height for one of the bases. Tell students to write out the formula for the area of a trapezoid and then identify the value of each variable before substituting.
- **Exercises 6 and 7** Students may write the units incorrectly, often writing square units instead of cubic units. Remind them that volume has cubic units because there are three dimensions.

Practice Test

1. $13{,}000\ \text{cm}^2$
2. $154\ \text{in.}^2$
3. $4\ \text{cm}^2$
4. $270\ \text{ft}^2$
5. $299.75\ \text{m}^2$
6. $\frac{35}{8}\ \text{cm}^3$, or $4\frac{3}{8}\ \text{cm}^3$
7. $\frac{64}{125}\ \text{yd}^3$
8. *Sample answer:*

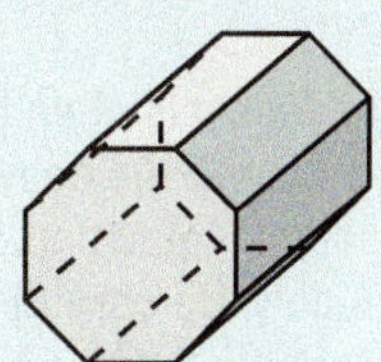

9. 8 faces, 18 edges, 12 vertices
10. 12 m
11. $44.8\ \text{in.}^2$
12. $138\ \text{in.}^2$
13. 8
14. about $217{,}800\ \text{ft}^2$, about $1{,}242{,}263\ \text{ft}^2$

Test-Taking Strategies

Available at *BigIdeasMath.com*

After Answering Easy Questions, Relax

Answer Easy Questions First

Estimate the Answer

Read all Choices before Answering

Read Question before Answering

Solve Directly or Eliminate Choices

Solve Problem before Looking at Choices

Use Intelligent Guessing

Work Backwards

About this Strategy

When taking a timed test, it is often best to skim the test and answer the easy questions first. Read each question carefully and thoroughly. Be careful that you record your answer in the correct position on the answer sheet.

Cumulative Practice

1. B
2. H
3. C
4. F

Item Analysis

1. **A.** The student does not interpret the remainder as needing another lifeboat.

B. Correct answer

C. The student adds the remainder (21) to the quotient (33).

D. The student divides 4971 by 15 instead of 150.

2. **F.** The student does not follow the order of operations; adding 6 to $3 \cdot 4^2$ before dividing 6 by 2.

G. The student does not follow the order of operations; adding 6 to 4^2 before multiplying and dividing.

H. Correct answer

I. The student does not follow the order of operations; evaluating the expression as $[(3 \cdot 4)^2 + 6] \div 2$.

3. **A.** The student multiplies the volume by $\frac{1}{2}$.

B. The student calculates the surface area instead of the volume.

C. Correct answer

D. The student multiplies the volume by 2.

4. **F.** Correct answer

G. The student incorrectly adds 60 and $8y$ to get $68y$.

H. The student interchanges the coefficient and the constant.

I. The student adds 8 and y together instead of multiplying them.

7 Cumulative Practice

Test-Taking Strategy
Answer Easy Questions First

What is the area of the nacho chip that has a base of 2 centimeters and a height of 4 centimeters?
Ⓐ 2 cm^2 Ⓑ 4 cm^2 Ⓒ 6 cm^2 Ⓓ 8 cm^2

I love easy questions!

"Scan the test and answer the easy questions first. You know that the area of a triangle is one-half times the product of its base and its height."

1. A cruise ship is carrying a total of 4971 people. Each lifeboat can hold a maximum of 150 people. What is the minimum number of lifeboats needed to evacuate everyone on the cruise ship?

A. 33 lifeboats **B.** 34 lifeboats

C. 54 lifeboats **D.** 332 lifeboats

2. Which number is equivalent to the expression?

$$3 \cdot 4^2 + 6 \div 2$$

F. 27 **G.** 33

H. 51 **I.** 75

3. What is the volume of the package?

A. 240 in.^3 **B.** 376 in.^3

C. 480 in.^3 **D.** 960 in.^3

4. A housing community started with 60 homes. In each of the following years, 8 more homes were built. Let y represent the number of years that have passed since the first year, and let n represent the number of homes. Which equation describes the relationship between n and y?

F. $n = 8y + 60$ **G.** $n = 68y$

H. $n = 60y + 8$ **I.** $n = 60 + 8 + y$

5. What is the value of m that makes the equation true?

$$4m = 6$$

6. What is the surface area of the square pyramid?

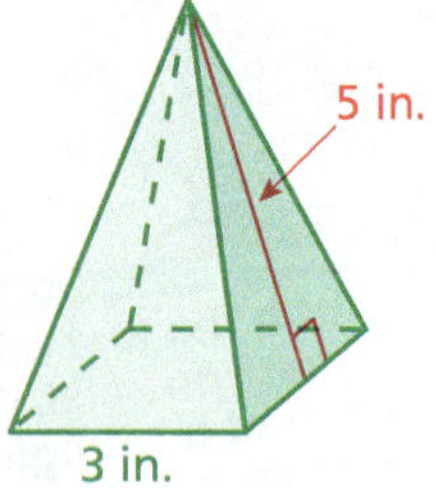

A. 30 in.^{2} B. 31.5 in.^{2}

C. 39 in.^{2} D. 69 in.^{2}

7. A wooden box has a length of 12 inches, a width of 6 inches, and a height of 8 inches.

Think Solve Explain

Part A Draw and label a rectangular prism with the dimensions of the wooden box.

Part B What is the surface area, in square inches, of the wooden box? Show your work.

Part C You have a two-fluid ounce sample of wood stain that covers 900 square inches. Is this enough to give the entire box two coats of stain? Show your work and explain your reasoning.

8. On Saturday, you earned \$35 mowing lawns. This was x dollars more than you earned on Thursday. Which expression represents the amount, in dollars, you earned mowing lawns on Thursday?

F. $35x$ G. $x + 35$

H. $x - 35$ I. $35 - x$

Item Analysis (continued)

5. **Gridded Response:** Correct answer: 1.5, or $\frac{3}{2}$

   Common error: The student subtracts 4 from 6 and gets an answer of 2.

6. **A.** The student does not include the area of the base.

   B. The student includes the areas of only three triangular faces instead of four triangular faces.

   C. Correct answer

   D. The student does not multiply by $\frac{1}{2}$ when determining the area of each triangular face.

7. **4 points** The student's work and explanations demonstrate a thorough understanding of the shape and attributes of a rectangular prism. The student draws and correctly labels the dimensions of the box and calculates the surface area as 432 square inches. The student explains why the two-fluid ounce sample of stain is enough for two coats. The student provides accurate work with clear and complete explanations.

   3 points The student's work and explanations demonstrate an essential but less than thorough understanding of the shape and attributes of a rectangular prism.

   2 points The student's work and explanations demonstrate a partial but limited understanding of the shape and attributes of a rectangular prism.

   1 point The student's work and explanations demonstrate a very limited understanding of the shape and attributes of a rectangular prism.

   0 points The student provides no response, a completely incorrect or incomprehensible response, or a response that demonstrates insufficient understanding of the shape and attributes of a rectangular prism.

8. **F.** The student misinterprets *more than* as meaning multiplication.

   G. The student misinterprets the problem; thinking that more is earned on Thursday than Saturday.

   H. The student subtracts in the wrong order and writes an expression that represents $35 less than the difference of the amounts earned on Thursday and Saturday.

   I. Correct answer

Cumulative Practice

5. 1.5, or $\frac{3}{2}$

6. C

7. *Part A*

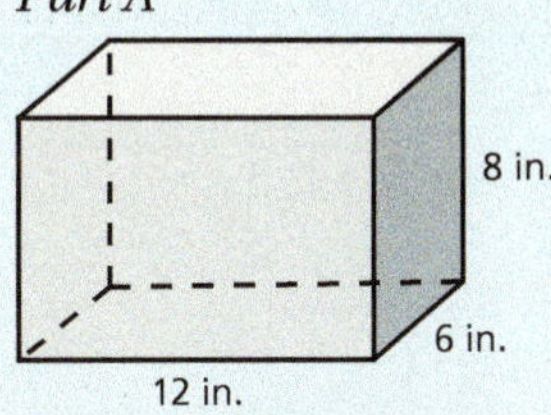

   Part B 432 in.^2

   Part C yes; $900 \div 432 \approx 2.1$

8. I

Cumulative Practice

9. 20

10. C

11. H

12. C

Item Analysis (continued)

9. Gridded Response: Correct answer: 20

Common error: The student multiplies 5 by 8 to get 40 and forgets to multiply by $\frac{1}{2}$.

10. **A.** The student multiplies by the reciprocal of the dividend instead of multiplying by the reciprocal of the divisor.

B. The student multiplies the fractions instead of dividing.

C. Correct answer

D. The student multiplies by both the reciprocal of the dividend and the reciprocal of the divisor instead of only multiplying by the reciprocal of the divisor.

11. **F.** The student incorrectly identifies the description as the formula for the area of a rectangle.

G. The student incorrectly identifies the description as the formula for the area of a parallelogram.

H. Correct answer

I. The student incorrectly identifies the description as the formula for the area of a triangle.

12. **A.** The student finds the number of ounces for 1 bag instead of 21 bags.

B. The student adds 15 to 6 to get 21 bags and then adds 15 to 150 to get 165 ounces.

C. Correct answer

D. The student finds the number of ounces for 24 bags instead of 21 bags.

9. What is the area, in square yards, of the triangle?

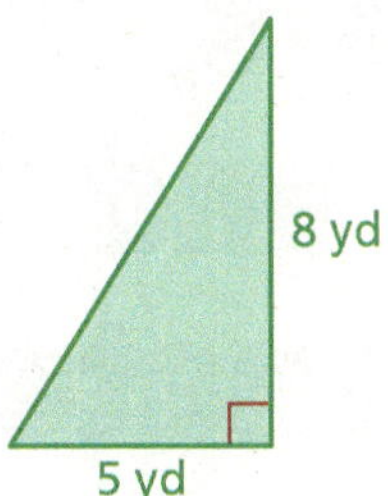

10. Which expression is equivalent to $\frac{12}{35}$?

A. $\frac{5}{6} \div \frac{2}{7}$

B. $\frac{2}{7} \div \frac{6}{5}$

C. $\frac{2}{7} \div \frac{5}{6}$

D. $\frac{5}{6} \div \frac{7}{2}$

11. The description below represents the area of which polygon?

"one-half the product of its height and the sum of its bases"

F. rectangle

G. parallelogram

H. trapezoid

I. triangle

12. What is the missing quantity in the double number line?

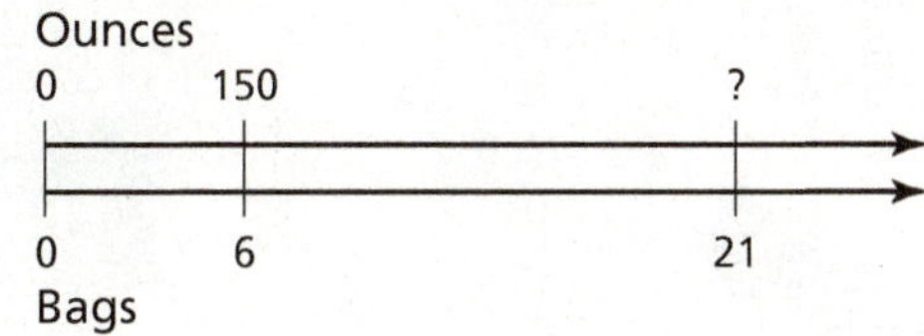

A. 25 ounces

B. 165 ounces

C. 525 ounces

D. 600 ounces

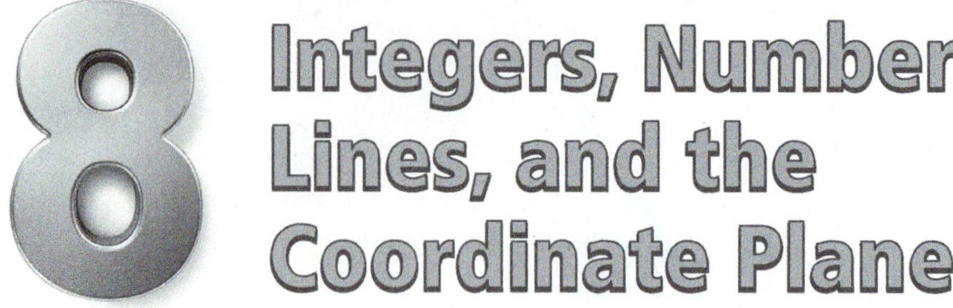

8 Integers, Number Lines, and the Coordinate Plane

Chapter Learning Target:
Understand integers.

Chapter Success Criteria:
- I can write integers to represent quantities.
- I can describe quantities.
- I can order and compare quantities.
- I can apply integers to model real-life problems.

STEAM Video: "Designing a CubeSat"

Laurie's Notes

Chapter 8 Overview

This chapter brings together and extends two areas of previous study, the number system and work with equations. Students' understanding of decimals and fractions is applied to negative quantities and their understanding of equations is applied to inequalities. Computations with negative rational numbers will be introduced in the next course.

Recognizing that there is such a thing as negative numbers is not difficult for students to accept. However, understanding that negative numbers can represent quantities that have opposite directions or values is more difficult and representing negative numbers on a number line is often the most challenging. Temperatures and elevations are familiar applications for students and both are typically represented in a vertical form. When rational numbers are represented on a horizontal number line, students can become very confused.

A common error that students often make when scaling a number line is shown.

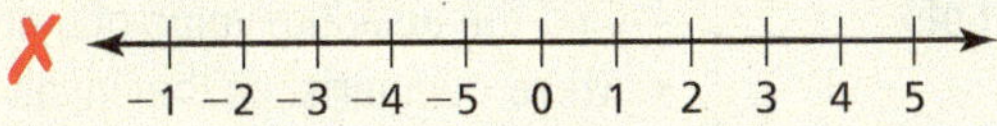

Drawing a number line on paper allows you to fold the number line at 0, helping students to develop an understanding of the symmetric nature of integers. It also serves as an informal introduction to absolute value later in the chapter. Representing integers and rational numbers on a number line helps students visualize and make sense of how to compare and order these numbers.

Absolute value is introduced next, defining $|a|$ as the distance between the number and 0. Students will often say, "Just make the number positive," which does not help them interpret absolute value as a magnitude when a contextual problem involves a negative quantity.

There are two lessons on graphing in the coordinate plane, a topic most students really enjoy. Earlier in the course, students learned to plot ordered pairs in the first quadrant and with the introduction of negative numbers students can now plot in all four quadrants.

The last two lessons in the chapter connect earlier work with solving equations to solving inequalities. Students have little difficulty applying the techniques they learned for solving equations to solving inequalities. It is important for students to recognize that inequalities, such as $x < 4$, have an infinite number of solutions that can be represented on a number line.

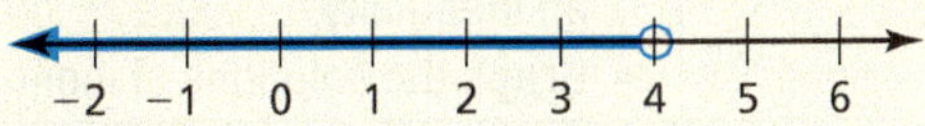

Suggested Pacing

Chapter Opener	1 Day
Section 1	2 Days
Section 2	2 Days
Section 3	2 Days
Section 4	2 Days
Section 5	2 Days
Section 6	2 Days
Section 7	3 Days
Section 8	3 Days
Connecting Concepts	1 Day
Chapter Review	1 Day
Chapter Test	1 Day
Total Chapter 8	22 Days
Year-to-Date	130 Days

Chapter Learning Target

Understand integers.

Chapter Success Criteria

- Write integers to represent quantities.
- Describe quantities.
- Order and compare quantities.
- Apply integers to model real-life problems.

Chapter 8 Learning Targets and Success Criteria

Section	Learning Target	Success Criteria
8.1 Integers	Understand the concept of negative numbers and that they are used along with positive numbers to describe quantities.	• Write integers to represent quantities in real life. • Graph integers on a number line. • Find the opposite of an integer. • Apply integers to model real-life problems.
8.2 Comparing and Ordering Integers	Compare and order integers.	• Explain how to determine which of two integers is greater. • Order a set of integers from least to greatest. • Interpret statements about order in real-life problems.
8.3 Rational Numbers	Compare and order rational numbers.	• Explain the meaning of a rational number. • Graph rational numbers on a number line. • Determine which of two rational numbers is greater. • Order a set of rational numbers from least to greatest.
8.4 Absolute Value	Understand the concept of absolute value.	• Find the absolute value of a number. • Make comparisons that involve absolute values of numbers. • Apply absolute value in real-life problems.
8.5 The Coordinate Plane	Plot and reflect ordered pairs in all four quadrants of a coordinate plane.	• Identify ordered pairs in a coordinate plane. • Plot ordered pairs in a coordinate plane and describe their locations. • Reflect points in the x-axis, the y-axis, or both axes. • Apply plotting points in all four quadrants to solve real-life problems.
8.6 Polygons in the Coordinate Plane	Draw polygons in the coordinate plane and find distances between points in the coordinate plane.	• Draw polygons in the coordinate plane. • Find distances between points in the coordinate plane with the same x-coordinates or the same y-coordinates. • Find horizontal and vertical side lengths of polygons in the coordinate plane. • Draw polygons in the coordinate plane to solve real-life problems.
8.7 Writing and Graphing Inequalities	Write inequalities and represent solutions of inequalities on number lines.	• Write word sentences as inequalities. • Determine whether a value is a solution of an inequality. • Graph the solutions of inequalities.
8.8 Solving Inequalities	Write and solve inequalities.	• Apply the properties of inequality to generate equivalent inequalities. • Solve inequalities using addition or subtraction. • Solve inequalities using multiplication or division. • Write and solve inequalities that represent real-life problems.

Progressions

Through the Grades		
Grade 5	**Grade 6**	**Grade 7**
• Generate numerical patterns, identify the relationship, and form ordered pairs. • Compare decimals to the thousandths place. • Graph ordered pairs in the first quadrant of the coordinate plane.	• Describe quantities with positive and negative numbers. • Graph ordered pairs in all four quadrants of the coordinate plane. • Order integers and absolute value numbers. • Write and solve one-step inequalities. • Represent constraints with inequalities. • Draw polygons in the coordinate plane.	• Add, subtract, multiply, and divide rational numbers. • Convert a rational number to a decimal using long division. • Solve two-step inequalities involving integers and rational numbers.

Through the Chapter								
Standard	**8.1**	**8.2**	**8.3**	**8.4**	**8.5**	**8.6**	**8.7**	**8.8**
6.NS.C.5 Understand that positive and negative numbers are used together to describe quantities having opposite directions or values; use positive and negative numbers to represent quantities in real-world contexts, explaining the meaning of 0 in each situation.	●		★					
6.NS.C.6a Recognize opposite signs of numbers as indicating locations on opposite sides of 0 on the number line; recognize that the opposite of the opposite of a number is the number itself, e.g., $-(-3) = 3$, and that 0 is its own opposite.	●		★					
6.NS.C.6b Understand signs of numbers in ordered pairs as indicating locations in quadrants of the coordinate plane; recognize that when two ordered pairs differ only by signs, the locations of the points are related by reflections across one or both axes.					★			
6.NS.C.6c Find and position integers and other rational numbers on a horizontal or vertical number line diagram; find and position pairs of integers and other rational numbers on a coordinate plane.	●	●	●		★			
6.NS.C.7a Interpret statements of inequality as statements about the relative position of two numbers on a number line diagram.		●	★					
6.NS.C.7b Write, interpret, and explain statements of order for rational numbers in real-world contexts.		●	★					
6.NS.C.7c Understand the absolute value of a rational number as its distance from 0 on the number line; interpret absolute value as magnitude for a positive or negative quantity in a real-world situation.				★				
6.NS.C.7d Distinguish comparisons of absolute value from statements about order.				★				
6.NS.C.8 Solve real-world and mathematical problems by graphing points in all four quadrants of the coordinate plane. Include use of coordinates and absolute value to find distances between points with the same first coordinate or the same second coordinate.					●	★		
6.EE.B.5 Understand solving an equation or inequality as a process of answering a question: which values from a specified set, if any, make the equation or inequality true? Use substitution to determine whether a given number in a specified set makes an equation or inequality true.							●	★
6.EE.B.6 Use variables to represent numbers and write expressions when solving a real-world or mathematical problem; understand that a variable can represent an unknown number, or, depending on the purpose at hand, any number in a specified set.							●	★
6.EE.B.8 Write an inequality of the form $x > c$ or $x < c$ to represent a constraint or condition in a real-world or mathematical problem. Recognize that inequalities of the form $x > c$ or $x < c$ have infinitely many solutions; represent solutions of such inequalities on number line diagrams.							●	★
6.G.A.3 Draw polygons in the coordinate plane given coordinates for the vertices; use coordinates to find the length of a side joining points with the same first coordinate or the same second coordinate. Apply these techniques in the context of solving real-world and mathematical problems.						★		

Key: ▲ = preparing ★ = complete ● = learning ■ = extending

STEAM Video

1. *Sample answer:* astronomy, meteorology
2. *Sample answer:* It takes more force to reach orbit than stay in orbit.
3. *Sample answer:* It would fall apart or not function properly.

Performance Task

Sample answer: The CubeSat needs to be able to withstand different conditions and function properly.

Mathematical Practices

Students have opportunities to develop aspects of the mathematical practices throughout the chapter. Here are some examples.

1. **Make Sense of Problems and Persevere in Solving Them**
   8.2 Math Practice note, *p. 353*
2. **Reason Abstractly and Quantitatively**
   8.2 Exercise 34, *p. 356*
3. **Construct Viable Arguments and Critique the Reasoning of Others**
   8.7 Exercise 49, *p. 389*
4. **Model with Mathematics**
   8.8 Exercise 39, *p. 397*
5. **Use Appropriate Tools Strategically**
   8.2 Math Practice note, *p. 351*
6. **Attend to Precision**
   8.6 Exercise 41, *p. 382*
7. **Look for and Make Use of Structure**
   8.5 Exercise 69, *p. 375*
8. **Look for and Express Regularity in Repeated Reasoning**
   8.1 Exercise 42, *p. 350*

Laurie's Notes

STEAM Video

Before the Video

- To introduce the STEAM Video, read aloud the first paragraph of Designing a CubeSat. Then discuss the picture of the CubeSat and its dimensions.

During the Video

- In this video, Tony is designing a CubeSat.
- ? Pause the video at 1:38 and ask, "What conditions does Tony need to consider when designing his CubeSat? " *Sample answers:* launch forces, temperature, pressure
- Watch the remainder of the video.

After the Video

- ? "What are g-forces?" the measure of how heavy you feel
- Have students work with a partner to answer Questions 1–3.
- As students discuss and answer the questions, listen for understanding of how inequalities relate to real life.

Performance Task

- Use this information to spark students' interest and promote thinking about real-life problems.
- ? Ask, "Why might g-force, pressure, and temperature be important considerations for making your decision?"
- After completing the chapter, students will have gained the knowledge needed to complete "Launching a CubeSat."

STEAM Video

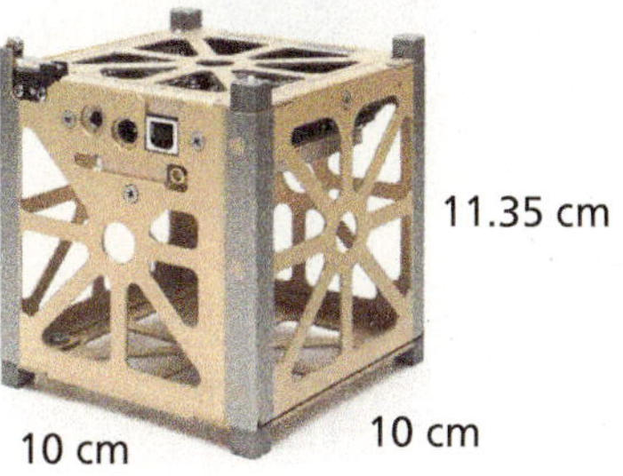

Designing a CubeSat

A *CubeSat* is a type of miniature satellite that is used for space research. Each CubeSat has the dimensions shown and a mass of no more than 1.33 kilograms.

Watch the STEAM Video "Designing a CubeSat." Then answer the following questions.

1. For what fields of study do you think CubeSats can be used?

2. Tony says g-forces are a measure of how heavy you feel. The table shows the g-forces on a CubeSat at three points in time. Why can g-forces be as high as 6 during a rocket launch and as low as 0 in space?

Time	Before launch	During launch	After entering space
G-Force	1	6	0

3. What would happen to a CubeSat that cannot withstand a g-force of 6? a g-force of 0?

Performance Task

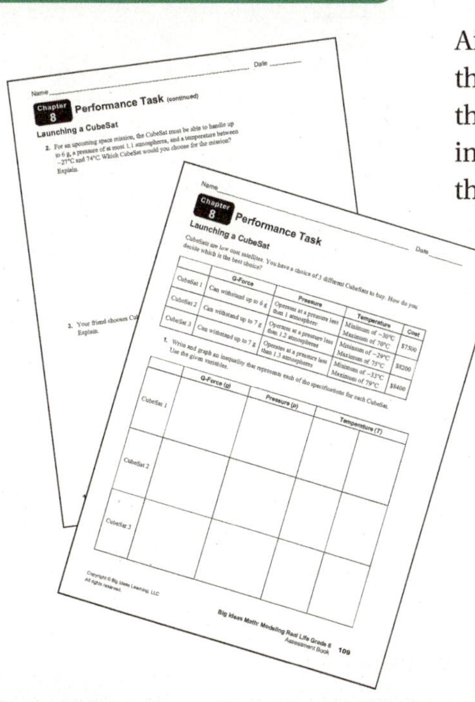

Name ________ Date ________

Chapter 8 **Performance Task** (continued)

Launching a CubeSat

2. For an upcoming space mission, the CubeSat must be able to handle up to 6 g, a pressure of at most 1.1 atmospheres, and a temperature between −27°C and 74°C. Which CubeSat would you choose for the mission? Explain.

3. Your friend chooses Cu... Explain.

Name ________ Date ________

Chapter 8 **Performance Task**

Launching a CubeSat

CubeSats are low cost satellites. You have a choice of 3 different CubeSats to buy. How do you decide which is the best choice?

	G-Force	Pressure	Temperature	Cost
CubeSat 1	Can withstand up to 6 g	Operates at a pressure less than 1 atmosphere	Minimum of −30°C Maximum of 70°C	$7500
CubeSat 2	Can withstand up to 7 g	Operates at a pressure less than 1.2 atmospheres	Minimum of −29°C Maximum of 75°C	$8200
CubeSat 3	Can withstand up to 7 g	Operates at a pressure less than 1.3 atmospheres	Minimum of −33°C Maximum of 79°C	$8400

1. Write and graph an inequality that represents each of the specifications for each CubeSat. Use the given variables.

	G-Force (g)	Pressure (p)	Temperature (T)
CubeSat 1			
CubeSat 2			
CubeSat 3			

Big Ideas Math: Modeling Real Life Grade 6
Assessment Book 109

Launching a CubeSat

After completing this chapter, you will be able to use the concepts you learned to answer the questions in the *STEAM Video Performance Task*. You will be given information about three different types of Cubesats that you can purchase.

CubeSat 1: $7500

CubeSat 2: $8200

CubeSat 3: $8400

You will determine which of the three CubeSats is the best option for a mission. Why might g-force, pressure, and temperature be important considerations for making your decision?

Getting Ready for Chapter 8

Chapter Exploration

1. Work with a partner. Plot and connect the points to make a picture.

1(6, 9) **2**(4, 11) **3**(2, 12) **4**(0, 11) **5**(−2, 9)
6(−6, 2) **7**(−9, 1) **8**(−11, −3) **9**(−7, 0) **10**(−5, −1)
11(−5, −5) **12**(−4, −8) **13**(−6, −10) **14**(−3, −9) **15**(−3, −10)
16(−4, −11) **17**(−4, −12) **18**(−3, −11) **19**(−2, −12) **20**(−2, −11)
21(−1, −12) **22**(−1, −11) **23**(−2, −10) **24**(−2, −9) **25**(1, −9)
26(2, −8) **27**(2, −10) **28**(1, −11) **29**(1, −12) **30**(2, −11)
31(3, −12) **32**(3, −11) **33**(4, −12) **34**(4, −11) **35**(3, −10)
36(3, −8) **37**(4, −6) **38**(6, 0) **39**(9, −3) **40**(9, −1)
41(8, 1) **42**(5, 3) **43**(3, 6) **44**(3, 7) **45**(4, 8)

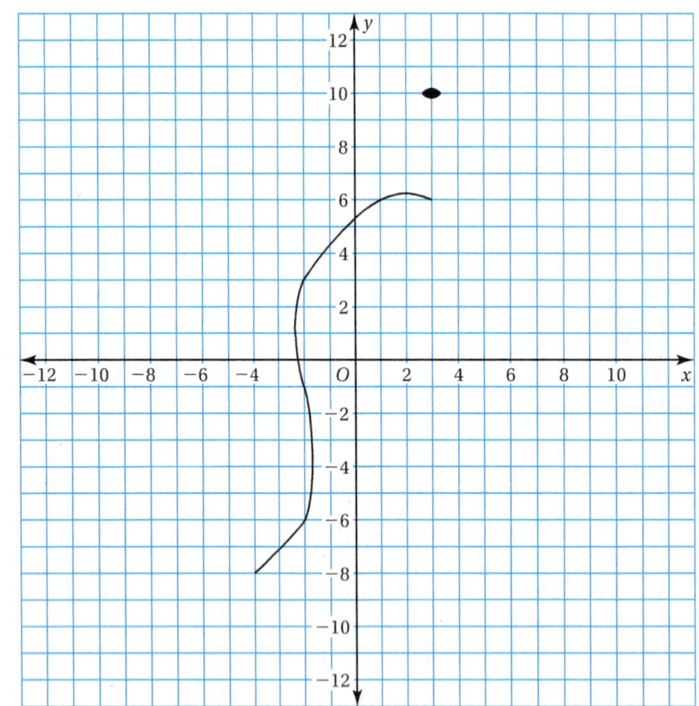

2. Create your own "dot-to-dot" picture. Use at least 20 points.

Vocabulary

The following vocabulary terms are defined in this chapter. Think about what each term might mean and record your thoughts.

negative numbers opposites inequality quadrants

Laurie's Notes

Chapter Exploration

- Students should be familiar with plotting points in the first quadrant of the coordinate plane.
- **Note:** Students have not yet plotted negative numbers in a coordinate plane, so this page may be challenging. You may need to tell them that negative x-coordinates are plotted to the left of the y-axis and negative y-coordinates are plotted below the x-axis.
- You may need to show students how to plot a point in each of the four quadrants of the coordinate plane. Examples: $(2, 3)$, $(-2, 3)$, $(-2, -3)$, and $(2, -3)$.
- Allow students to work in pairs to complete the exercises.
- Ask volunteers to share their "dot-to-dot" pictures from Exercise 2.
- **Extension:** Have each pair write the coordinates of their "dot-to-dot" picture on a piece of paper and then exchange papers with another pair. Have each pair plot the other pair's points to make a picture.

Vocabulary

- These terms represent some of the vocabulary that students will encounter in Chapter 8. Discuss the terms as a class.
- Where have students heard the term *inequality* outside of a math classroom? In what contexts? Students may not be able to write the actual definition, but they may write phrases associated with *inequality*.
- Allowing students to discuss these terms now will prepare them for understanding the terms as they are presented in the chapter.
- When students encounter a new definition, encourage them to write in their *Student Journals*. They will revisit these definitions during the Chapter Review.

ELL Support

Explain the relationship between the terms *negative numbers* and *opposites*. Positive numbers are greater than 0. Negative numbers are less than 0. Opposites are two numbers that are the same distance from 0 on a number line but on opposite sides of 0. Write "inequality" on the board with a slash after the prefix *in*– (in/equality). Say, "The prefix *in*– comes from the Latin language. When *in*– is at the beginning of a word, it often means "not." Equality means that two quantities are the same or equivalent. Inequality means that two quantities are *not* the same or *not* equivalent. The prefix *in*– makes the meaning of the word the opposite of equality.

Topics for Review

- Comparing Numbers
- Evaluating Expressions
- Graphing Ordered Pairs in the First Quadrant
- Ordering Decimals
- Ordering Fractions
- Place Value
- Writing and Solving One-Step Equations

Chapter Exploration

1. See Additional Answers.
2. Check students' work.

Learning Target

Understand the concept of negative numbers and that they are used along with positive numbers to describe quantities.

Success Criteria

- Write integers to represent quantities in real life.
- Graph integers on a number line.
- Find the opposite of an integer.
- Apply integers to model real-life problems.

Warm Up

Cumulative, vocabulary, and prerequisite skills practice opportunities are available in the *Resources by Chapter* or at *BigIdeasMath.com*.

ELL Support

Explain that the temperatures in the exploration use the Fahrenheit scale, which is the standard in the United States. Many students will be familiar with the Celsius scale. Explain that 0°C is the freezing point of water and 100°C is the boiling point of water. The equivalents on the Fahrenheit scale are 32°F and 212°F. To convert from Fahrenheit to Celsius: subtract 32 and then multiply by $\frac{5}{9}$.

Exploration 1

a. See Additional Answers.

b. *Sample answer:* All temperatures are greater than or equal to 0°F.

c. *Sample answer:* It is colder than 0°F; −2°F; elevation, banking

d. *Sample answer:* on a horizontal number line

Laurie's Notes

Preparing to Teach

- Students will build upon their experiences with finding non-negative numbers on a horizontal or vertical number line to develop the number line to the left of 0 or below 0.
- This is the beginning of students' formal introduction to integers, so they need opportunities to appreciate the negative numbers that surround them but perhaps have not been named. Negative numbers are represented in situations such as temperatures, ocean floor measurements, banking, and well-drilling.
- **MP5 Use Appropriate Tools Strategically:** It is important for students to create a number line and then represent integers on the number line. A physical model that can be folded at 0 helps students to develop an understanding of the symmetric nature of integers.

Motivate

- Ask 7 volunteers to hold onto a piece of rope. They should be equally spaced. Ask the person in the middle to hold a card with the number 0 written on it.
  - Say, "If you are 2 people away from 0, raise your hand."
  - Say, "If you are 3 people away from 0, raise your hand."
- Now hand the card with the number 1 written on it to the person on the right of the person holding the 0 card.
  - Say, "If you are the number −1, raise your hand."
  - Say, "If you are the number 3, raise your hand."
  - Say, "Keep your hand in the air if you are the least of the two numbers."
  - Repeat the instructions to compare 2 and 3, and to compare −2 and −3.
- This gives students a strong visual image of how a number line looks and where positive and negative numbers are located.

Exploration 1

- This exploration requires basic familiarity of different climate zones within the United States.
- ? "Do you think time of year has any bearing on the temperature readings? Explain." yes; Temperatures change through the seasons of the year.
- ? "What is the warmest (coldest) temperature you've experienced?" This will begin a discussion that will likely lead to a temperature below 0°F.
- After partners discuss part (b), have them share with another pair.
- Listen as students discuss part (c). Allow volunteers to share with the class.
- **Discuss:** Students are familiar with whole numbers, fractions, and decimals. Ask them what other types of numbers there are.
- ? In part (d), students may represent temperatures on a horizontal number line. Draw one on the board to match the vertical one. Ask, "Which is colder, 10°F or −9°F? −16°F or −15°F?" −9°F; −16°F "How can you tell?" *Sample answer:* The temperature farthest to the left or down a number line is the coldest.
- **Common Error:** It is very common for students to incorrectly place the negative numbers by starting with −1 to the left as shown.

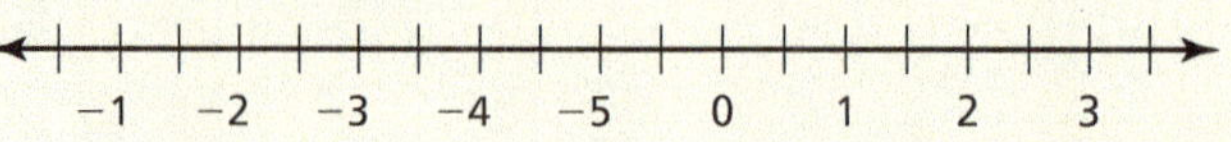

8.1 Integers

Learning Target: Understand the concept of negative numbers and that they are used along with positive numbers to describe quantities.

Success Criteria:
- I can write integers to represent quantities in real life.
- I can graph integers on a number line.
- I can find the opposite of an integer.
- I can apply integers to model real-life problems.

EXPLORATION 1 Reading and Describing Temperatures

Work with a partner. The thermometers show the temperatures in four cities.

Honolulu, Hawaii	***Anchorage, Alaska***
Death Valley, California	***Seattle, Washington***

a. Match each temperature with its most appropriate location.

i.

°F
120
110
100
90
80
70
60
50
40
30
20
10
0
−10
−20
−30
−40

ii.

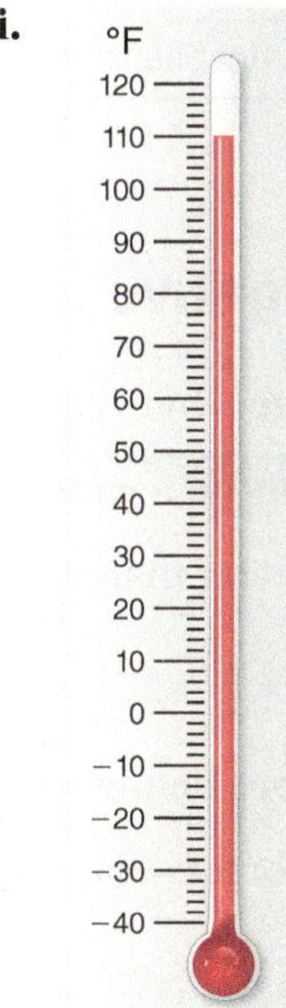

iii.

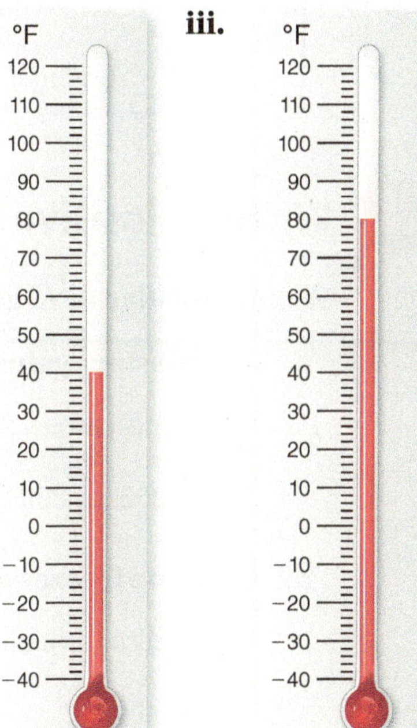

iv.

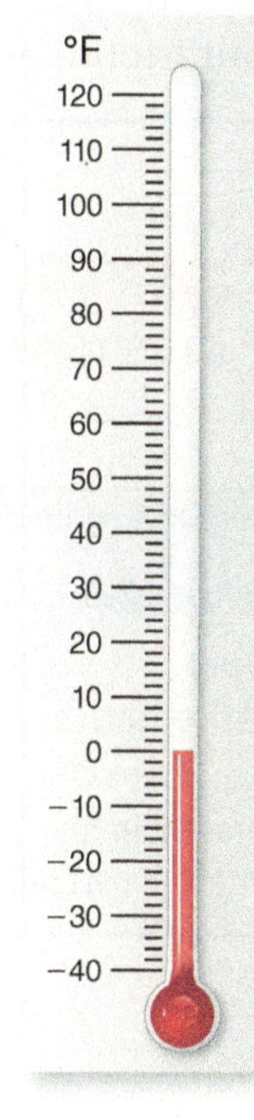

b. What do all of the temperatures have in common?

c. What does it mean for a temperature to be *below* zero? Provide an example. Can you think of any other situations in which numbers may be less than zero?

d. The thermometers show temperatures on a vertical number line. How else can you represent numbers less than zero? Provide an example.

> **Math Practice**
>
> **Maintain Oversight**
>
> How does this exploration help you extend your knowledge of number systems?

8.1 Lesson

Key Vocabulary
positive numbers, *p. 346*
negative numbers, *p. 346*
opposites, *p. 346*
integers, *p. 346*

Positive numbers are greater than 0. They can be written with or without a positive sign (+).

$+1 \qquad 5 \qquad +20 \qquad 10{,}000$

Negative numbers are less than 0. They are written with a negative sign (−).

$-1 \qquad -5 \qquad -20 \qquad -10{,}000$

Two numbers that are the same distance from 0 on a number line, but on opposite sides of 0, are called **opposites**. The opposite of 0 is 0.

The Meaning of a Word

Opposite

When you sit across from your friend at the lunch table, you sit **opposite** your friend.

Key Idea

Integers

Words **Integers** are the set of whole numbers and their opposites.

Graph

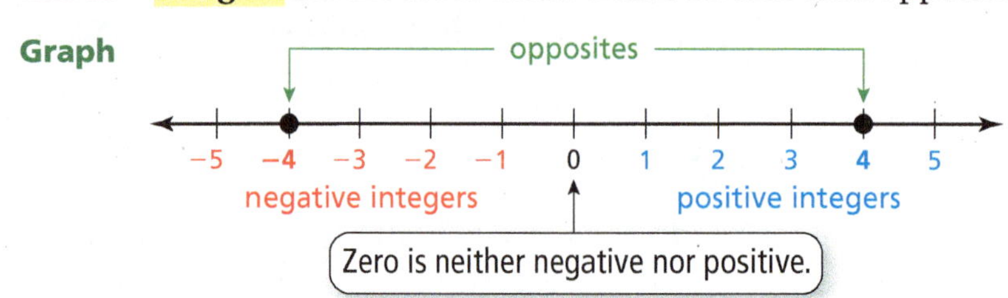

EXAMPLE 1 Writing Positive and Negative Integers

Write a positive or negative integer that represents each situation.

a. A contestant gains 250 points on a game show.

Gains indicates a number greater than 0. So, use a positive integer.

▶ +250, or 250

b. Gasoline freezes at 40 degrees below zero.

Below zero indicates a number less than 0. So, use a negative integer.

▶ −40

Math Practice

Apply Mathematics

What does −250 represent in the context in part (a)?

Try It **Write a positive or negative integer that represents the situation.**

1. A hiker climbs 900 feet up a mountain.
2. You have a debt of $24.
3. A student loses 5 points for not showing work on a quiz.
4. A savings account earns $10.

Multi-Language Glossary at *BigIdeasMath.com*

Laurie's Notes

Scaffolding Instruction

- As students begin to see negative numbers on a number line, they will also start to question how to write, graph, and use negative numbers.
- **Emerging:** Students may incorrectly label negative numbers to the left of 0 or struggle with the concept of a measure that is less than 0. The examples will help students master the success criteria.
- **Proficient:** Students have an understanding of negative numbers from the exploration. Have students review the Key Idea and then proceed to the Self-Assessment exercises.

Key Idea

- Define **integers**. Make it clear to students that there are three types of integers: positive integers, negative integers, and 0. Zero is neither positive nor negative.
- Remind students that whole numbers are 0, 1, 2, 3, . . .
- Draw a number line, using two colors to differentiate positive and negative integers.
- **MP5 Use Appropriate Tools Strategically**: Have students draw a number line with integers to the left and right of 0. They can use a ruler or grid paper to equally space the tick marks. Then have students fold the number line around 0 so that the lines and tick marks overlap. This will provide a kinesthetic method of understanding opposites and the symmetry about 0.
- Point out The Meaning of a Word to provide another view of opposite.

EXAMPLE 1

- Discuss each part of the example. The context for each part should be familiar to students.
- Point out that the + sign is optional in writing a positive number. It generally is not written.
- **MP6 Attend to Precision:** Students should use correct language in stating the integers. In part (b), they should say, "negative forty." If students say "minus forty," remind students that minus is an operation.

Try It

- **Neighbor Check:** Have students work independently and then have their neighbors check their work. Have students discuss any discrepancies.

? **Extension:** "What is the opposite of each situation?" *Sample answers:* The hiker descends 900 feet down a mountain; You have a credit of $24; A student gains 5 points for showing work on a quiz; $10 is withdrawn from a savings account.

Scaffold instruction to support all students in their learning. Learning is individualized and you may want to group students differently as they move in and out of these levels with each skill and concept. Student self-assessment and feedback help guide your instructional decisions about how and when to layer support for all students to become proficient learners.

Extra Example 1

Write a positive or negative integer that represents each situation.

a. A balloon floats 7 feet above the ground. 7

b. An anchor is 15 feet underwater. −15

ELL Support

Allow students to work in groups to practice language as they complete Try It Exercises 1–4. Expect students at different language levels to perform as described.

Beginner: Write the numbers.

Intermediate: State the numbers. For example, "positive nine hundred."

Advanced: Identify key words that signal positive or negative, such as *earns* and *debt*.

Try It

1. 900
2. −24
3. −5
4. 10

Teaching Strategy

Visual models are important tools for presenting integers. Physically placing numbers on horizontal and vertical number lines helps students to "see" the numbers, directions, increments, and relative positions.

Extra Example 2

Graph each integer and its opposite.

a. 4

b. −10

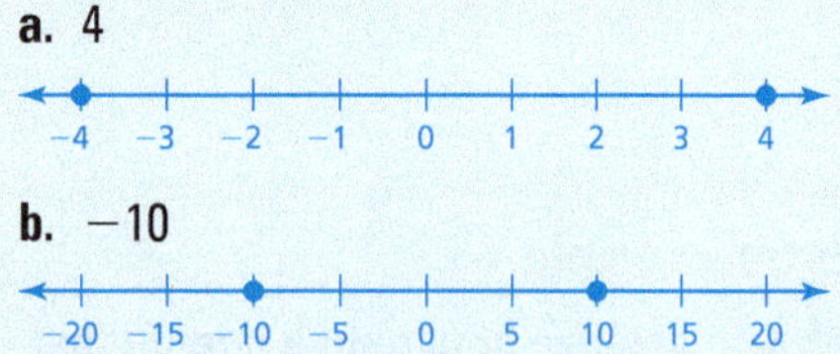

Try It

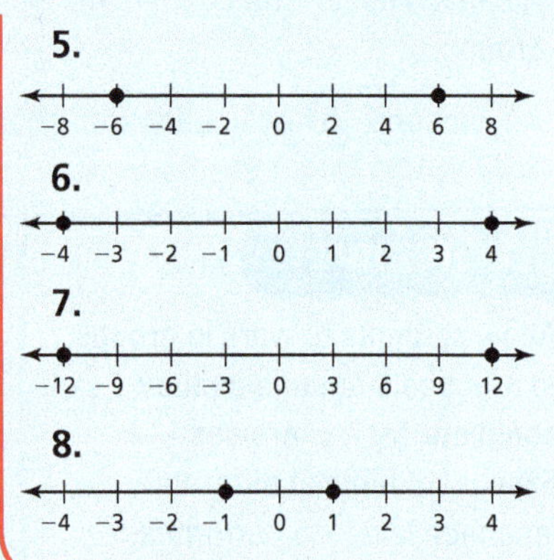

Self-Assessment for Concepts & Skills

9. 78 **10.** −3750

11.

12.

13.

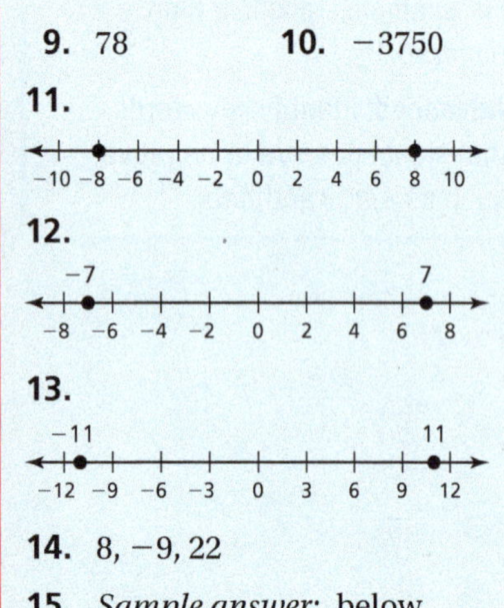

14. 8, −9, 22

15. *Sample answer:* below, under, lose

16. a negative integer; a positive integer; zero

Laurie's Notes

EXAMPLE 2

- "What is the opposite of 5?" −5 "What is the opposite of −13?" 13
- **Teaching Strategy:** Have students create a number line for each part and then graph both integers using closed circles.
- **Common Error:** When asked to graph the numbers −2 and 2, students may draw a number line and label −2, 0, and 2 as shown and write nothing else.

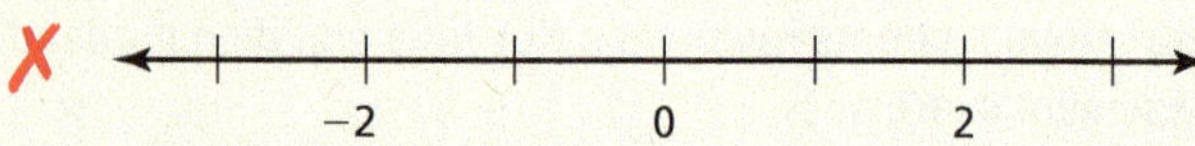

Make it clear to students that they should decide on a scale and then put a closed circle on the number line to graph a number.

- "What number is halfway between a number and its opposite?" 0
- **MP6 Attend to Precision:** Discuss the Reading note. Remind students that −2 is read "negative two" or "the opposite of two." It should not be read as "minus two." Minus is an operation.
- This example represents the second and third success criteria.

Try It

- **Think-Pair-Share:** Students should read each exercise independently and then work in pairs to complete the exercises. Then have each pair compare their answers with another pair and discuss any discrepancies.

Self-Assessment for Concepts & Skills

- These exercises ask students to know the definition of integers, why integers are used, how to graph integers, and when integers model a situation. This fundamental understanding of the set of integers is the foundation for the rest of the chapter and further work with the set of rational numbers.
- Have students work on these exercises independently, so that you and the students know where they are on the continuum of the success criteria.
- Have students share answers with a partner and discuss any discrepancies. Exercises 9–14 are objective and easily assessed. Listen to conversations about Exercises 15 and 16. Select volunteers to share different responses with the class. Ask students if there are any answers that should be revised.

ELL Support

Allow students to work in pairs on Exercises 9–14. Have each pair display their answers on a whiteboard for your review. Have two pairs form a group to discuss Exercises 15 and 16. Monitor discussions and provide support as needed.

The Success Criteria Self-Assessment chart can be found in the *Student Journal* or online at *BigIdeasMath.com*.

EXAMPLE 2 Graphing Integers

Graph each integer and its opposite.

a. 3

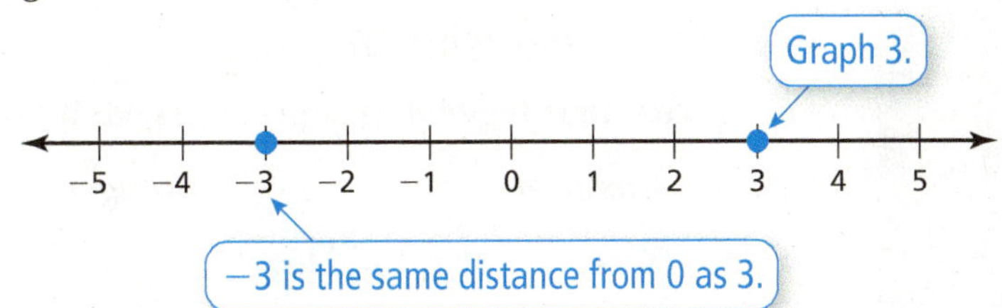

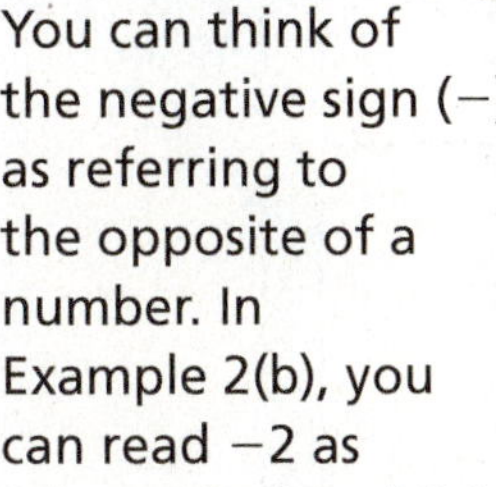

You can think of the negative sign (−) as referring to the opposite of a number. In Example 2(b), you can read −2 as "the opposite of 2."

b. −2

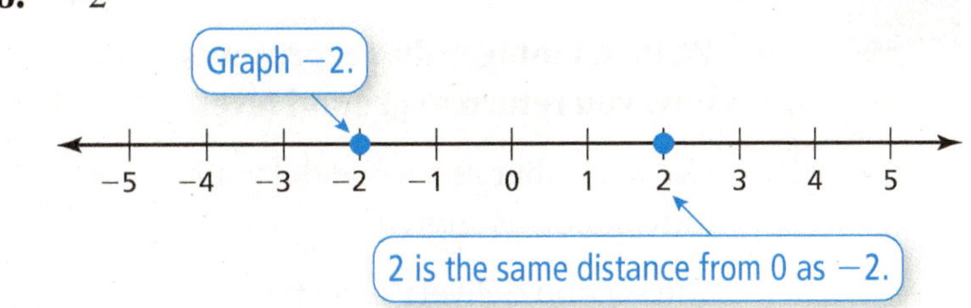

Try It **Graph the integer and its opposite.**

5. 6 **6.** −4 **7.** −12 **8.** 1

Self-Assessment for Concepts & Skills

Solve each exercise. Then rate your understanding of the success criteria in your journal.

WRITING INTEGERS **Write a positive or negative integer that represents the situation.**

9. A baseball is thrown at a speed of 78 miles per hour.

10. A submarine is 3750 feet below sea level.

GRAPHING INTEGERS **Graph the integer and its opposite.**

11. 8 **12.** −7 **13.** 11

14. **VOCABULARY** Which of the following numbers are integers?

$$8, -4.1, -9, \frac{1}{6}, 1.75, 22$$

15. **VOCABULARY** List three words or phrases used in real life that indicate negative integers.

16. **WRITING** Describe the opposite of a positive integer, the opposite of a negative integer, and the opposite of zero.

EXAMPLE 3 Modeling Real Life

You deliver flowers to an office building. You enter at ground level and go down 2 floors to make the first delivery. Then you go up 7 floors to make the second delivery.

a. Write an integer that represents each position.

Position	*Integer*
You enter at ground level.	0
You go down 2 floors.	−2
You go up 7 floors.	+7

b. Write an integer that represents how you return to ground level.

Use a number line to model your movement, as shown.

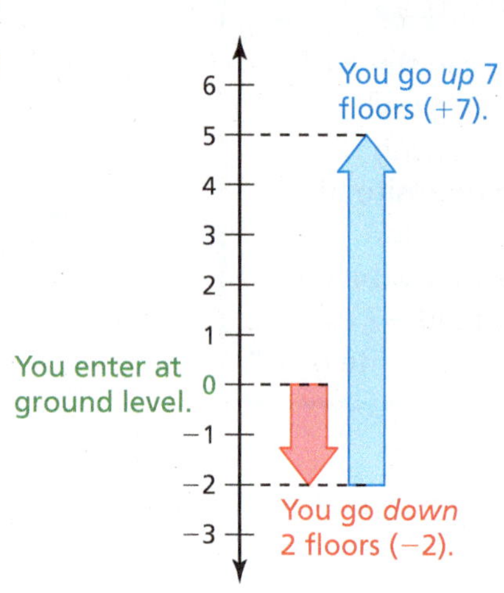

The second delivery is on the fifth floor. You must go down 5 floors to return to ground level.

The integer representing "down 5 floors" is −5.

Self-Assessment for Problem Solving

Solve each exercise. Then rate your understanding of the success criteria in your journal.

17. The world record for scuba diving is 332 meters below sea level. Write an integer that represents a new world record. Explain.

18. The indoor and outdoor temperatures are shown. The freezing point of water is 32°F. Write integers that represent how each temperature must change to reach the freezing point of water. Explain.

19. An *ion* is an atom that has a positive or negative electric charge. When an ion has more protons than electrons, it has a positive charge. When an ion has fewer protons than electrons, it has a negative charge. Explain what it means for an atom to have an electric charge of zero.

Laurie's Notes

EXAMPLE 3

- Draw a vertical number line on the board as a visual aid for students as you work through this problem.
- **FYI:** Students may ask if underground floors are really numbered using negative numbers. It is most common to use a letter, such as L or P, to denote a lower level or a parking level.

Self-Assessment for Problem Solving

- The goal for all students is to feel comfortable with the problem-solving plan. It is important for students to problem-solve in class, where they may receive support from you and their peers. Keep in mind that some students may only be ready for the first step.
- After completing the exercises independently, have students share their thinking with the class. Listen for different methods.

MP6 Attend to Precision: When students fully achieve the success criteria of this section, they not only answer the problems correctly, but they also communicate and justify their mathematical thinking.

Extension: "How far is −3°F from 0°F?" 3°F "How far is 32°F from 0°F?" 32°F "What is the temperature change from −3°F to the freezing point of water?" 35°F It is important to continuously make connections to further the study of integers.

The Success Criteria Self-Assessment chart can be found in the *Student Journal* or online at *BigIdeasMath.com*.

Closure

- **Exit Ticket:** Graph each integer on the same number line and write a context for each: −6 and 4.

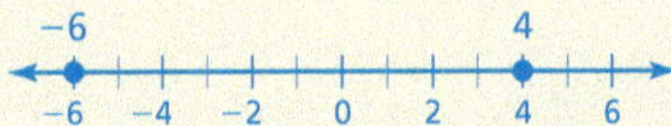

Sample answers: A student misses 6 questions on a quiz; There are 4 new students in the class.

Extra Example 3

At the end of the first round of a game, you have 10 points. You gain 4 points in the second round. In the third round, you lose 7 points.

a. Write an integer that represents each round.

You have 10 points. 10
You gain 4 points. +4
You lose 7 points. −7

b. After the fourth round, your score is 10 points. Write an integer that represents how many points you received in the fourth round. +3

Self-Assessment for Problem Solving

17. *Sample answer:* −338; A depth of 338 meters is below a depth of 332 meters.

18. indoor: −36; outdoor: 7; *Sample answer:* 68°F is 36°F above freezing, 25°F is 7°F below freezing.

19. The atom has the same number of protons and electrons.

Learning Target

Understand the concept of negative numbers and that they are used along with positive numbers to describe quantities.

Success Criteria

- Write integers to represent quantities in real life.
- Graph integers on a number line.
- Find the opposite of an integer.
- Apply integers to model real-life problems.

Review & Refresh

1. $\frac{3}{20}$ mm^3
2. $\frac{3}{8}$ yd^3
3. 8 ft^3
4. $4(m + 8)$
5. $2(9z - 11)$
6. $2(19x + 40)$
7. $3(14n - 9s)$
8. B

Concepts, Skills, & Problem Solving

9. *Sample answer:* losing 6 points on a test
10. *Sample answer:* adding 12 members to a club
11. *Sample answer:* diving 45 feet below the surface
12. -3
13. -6
14. 15
15. 600
16. -42
17. 37,500
18. 17
19. -56
20. -350
21. 5
22. 120
23. 83; -47

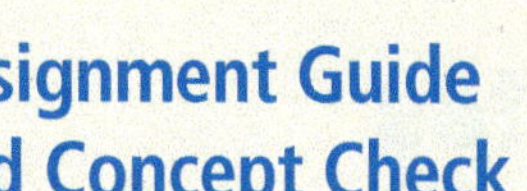

Assignment Guide and Concept Check

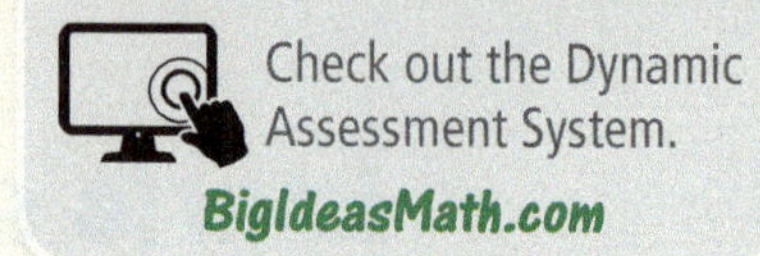

Scaffold assignments to support all students in their learning progression. The suggested assignments are a starting point. Continue to assign additional exercises and revisit with spaced practice to move every student toward proficiency.

Level	Assignment 1	Assignment 2
Emerging	3, 7, 8, 9, 13, 14, 24, 27, 36	10, 16, 22, 23, 28, 37, 38, 39, 40, 41
Proficient	3, 7, 8, 9, 16, 18, 28, 29, 36	10, 23, 34, 37, 38, 39, 40, 41, 43
Advanced	3, 7, 9, 11, 16, 18, 34, 35, 36	23, 37, 38, 39, 40, 41, 42, 43

- Assignment 1 is for use after students complete the Self-Assessment for Concepts & Skills.
- Assignment 2 is for use after students complete the Self-Assessment for Problem Solving.
- The red exercises can be used as a concept check.

Review & Refresh Prior Skills

Exercises 1–3 Finding the Volume of a Rectangular Prism
Exercises 4–7 Factoring Algebraic Expressions
Exercise 8 Converting Measures

Common Errors

- **Exercises 12–21** Students may use the wrong sign when writing the integer. Tell them to look for key words, such as *rise* and *fall*, to help them determine the sign.

8.1 Practice

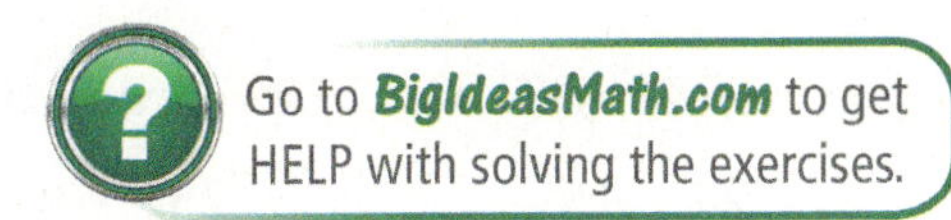

Review & Refresh

Find the volume of the prism.

1. $\frac{3}{8}$ mm, $\frac{1}{2}$ mm, $\frac{4}{5}$ mm

2. $\frac{3}{4}$ yd, $\frac{5}{8}$ yd, $\frac{4}{5}$ yd

3.

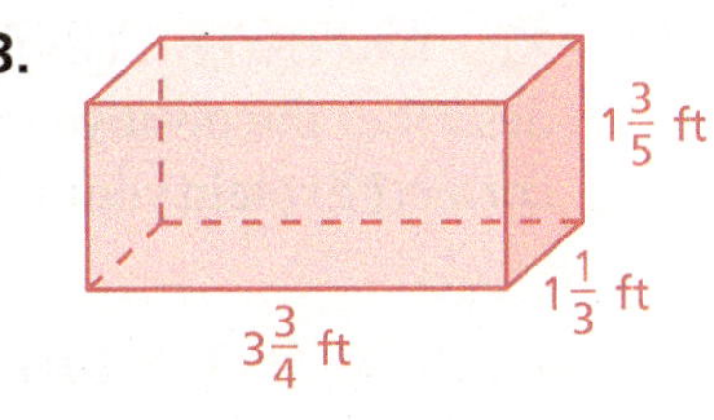

Factor the expression using the GCF.

4. $4m + 32$
5. $18z - 22$
6. $38x + 80$
7. $42n - 27s$

8. The height of a statue is 276 inches. What is the height of the statue in meters? Round your answer to the nearest hundredth.

A. 1.09 m **B.** 7.01 m **C.** 108.66 m **D.** 701.04 m

Concepts, Skills, & Problem Solving

OPEN-ENDED **Describe a situation that can be represented by the integer.** (See Exploration 1, p. 345.)

9. -6
10. 12
11. -45

WRITING INTEGERS **Write a positive or negative integer that represents the situation.**

12. A football team loses 3 yards.
13. The temperature is 6 degrees below zero.
14. You earn $15 raking leaves.
15. A person climbs 600 feet up a mountain.
16. You withdraw $42 from an account.
17. An airplane climbs to 37,500 feet.
18. The temperature rises 17 degrees.
19. You lose 56 points in a video game.
20. A ball falls 350 centimeters.
21. You receive 5 bonus points in class.

22. **MP MODELING REAL LIFE** On December 17, 1903, the Wright brothers accomplished the first powered flight. The plane traveled a distance of 120 feet. Write this distance as an integer.

23. **MP MODELING REAL LIFE** A stock market gains 83 points. The next day, the stock market loses 47 points. Write each amount as an integer.

GRAPHING INTEGERS **Graph the integer and its opposite.**

24. -5	**25.** -8	**26.** 14	**27.** 9
28. -14	**29.** 20	**30.** -26	**31.** 18
32. 30	**33.** -150	**34.** -32	**35.** 400

36. **MP YOU BE THE TEACHER** Your friend describes the positive integers. Is your friend correct? Explain your reasoning.

The positive integers are 0, 1, 2, 3, ...

USING A NUMBER LINE **Identify the integer represented by the point on the number line.**

37. A	**38.** B	**39.** C	**40.** D

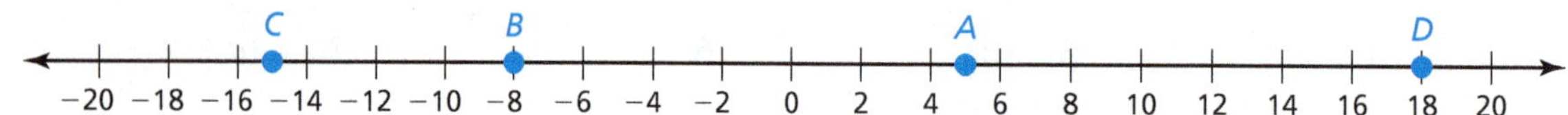

41. **DIG DEEPER!** Low tide, represented by the integer -1, is 1 foot below the average water level. High tide is 5 feet higher than low tide.

a. What does 0 represent in this situation?

b. Write an integer that represents the average water level relative to high tide.

42. **MP REPEATED REASONING** Consider an integer n.

a. Is the opposite of n always less than 0? Explain your reasoning.

b. What can you conclude about the opposite of the opposite of n? Justify your answer.

c. Describe the meaning of $-[-(-n)]$. What is it equal to?

43. **MP NUMBER SENSE** In a game of tug-of-war, a team wins by pulling the flag over its goal line. The flag begins at 0. During a game, the flag moves 8 feet to the right, 12 feet to the left, and 13 feet back to the right. Did a team win? Explain. If not, what does each team need to do in order to win?

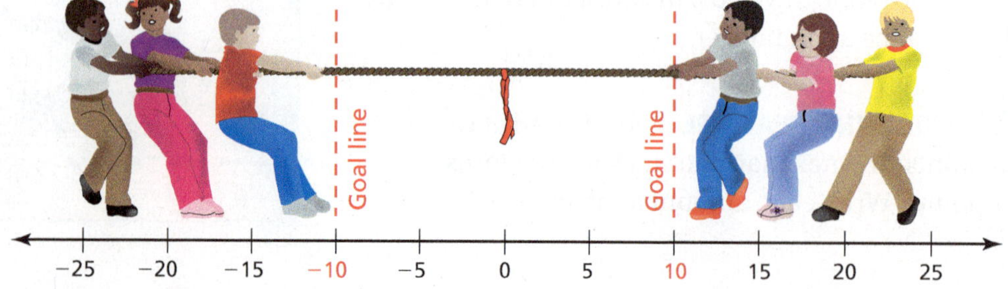

Common Errors

- **Exercises 24–35** Students may think that *opposites* are only negative numbers. For example, a student may think that the opposite of −3 is −3 and the opposite of 3 is −3. Remind them that the opposite of a negative number is positive.

Mini-Assessment

Write a positive or negative integer that represents the situation.

1. A fish is 12 meters underwater. −12
2. You deposit $25 into your savings account. 25

Graph the integer and its opposite.

3. 7

4. −15

5. While playing a game, you move 6 steps forward and then 10 steps backward. Write each number of steps as an integer. 6; −10

Section Resources

Surface Level	Deep Level
Resources by Chapter • Extra Practice • Reteach • Puzzle Time Student Journal • Self-Assessment • Practice Differentiating the Lesson Tutorial Videos Skills Review Handbook Skills Trainer	Resources by Chapter • Enrichment and Extension Graphic Organizers Dynamic Assessment System • Section Practice

Concepts, Skills, & Problem Solving

24.

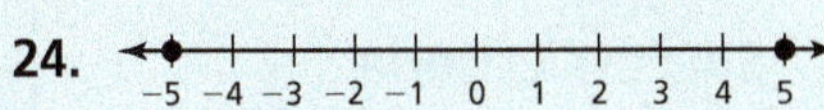

25.

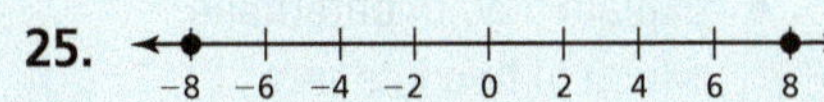

26. −14, 14; −12 −8 −4 0 4 8 12

27. −12 −9 −6 −3 0 3 6 9 12

28. −14, 14; −16 −12 −8 −4 0 4 8 12 16

29. −20 −10 0 10 20

30. −26, 26; −24 −12 0 12 24

31. −18 −12 −6 0 6 12 18

32. −40 −30 −20 −10 0 10 20 30 40

33. −150 −100 −50 0 50 100 150

34. −32, 32; −30 −20 −10 0 10 20 30

35. −400 −200 0 200 400

36. no; *Sample answer:* 0 is neither positive nor negative.

37. 5

38. −8

39. −15

40. 18

41. a. the average water level

    b. −4

42. a. no; *Sample answer:* The opposite of −6 is 6.

    b. It is n; The opposite of n is $-n$ and the opposite of $-n$ is n.

    c. $-[-(-n)]$ is the opposite of the opposite of $-n$; $-n$

43. no; The flag starts at 0, moves to 8, left to −4, and right to 9; The left team would need to pull the flag 19 feet. The right team would need to pull the flag 1 foot.

Learning Target

Compare and order integers.

Success Criteria

- Explain how to determine which of two integers is greater.
- Order a set of integers from least to greatest.
- Interpret statements about order in real-life problems.

Warm Up

Cumulative, vocabulary, and prerequisite skills practice opportunities are available in the *Resources by Chapter* or at *BigIdeasMath.com.*

ELL Support

Review the comparative and superlative adjectives *greater* and *greatest.* Great means "big." When comparing two numbers, you add *–er* to make *greater.* To identify the number in a group of numbers that has the most value, you add *–est* to make *greatest.* These are regular endings to make comparative and superlative adjectives; however, some adjectives have irregular forms. For example, *less* and *least* are comparative and superlative forms of *little*, which is the opposite of *big.*

Exploration 1

a. See Additional Answers.

b. rocket topping sequence complete, launch control system enabled, launch verification, main engine start, boosters ignite, rocket clears launchpad tower

c. Check students' work.

Laurie's Notes

STATE STANDARDS
6.NS.C.6c, 6.NS.C.7a, 6.NS.C.7b

Preparing to Teach

- Now that students can use integers to represent a situation, they will extend that understanding to comparing and ordering. For example, -8 may mean that a student owes \$8 or an account is overdrawn by \$8, but is -12 better or worse in this scenario? Where is -12 located on the number line?
- **MP5 Use Appropriate Tools Strategically:** A physical model of a number line that can be folded at 0 helps students to develop an understanding of the symmetric nature of integers, review opposites, and serves as an informal introduction to absolute value later in the chapter.

Motivate

- **Teaching Strategy:** Place a piece of masking tape on the floor to represent a number line. Identify the location of 0 by having a student stand at 0.
- Have two more students stand at two other integers. Have the students change their locations several times to represent the following scenarios: two positive integers, one positive integer and one negative integer, both negative integers, and a pair of opposites.

Exploration 1

- **MP4 Model with Mathematics:** Discuss with students that even though negative numbers are *not* read as "minus 3," it is common language at a space launch to use the phrase "minus 3" instead of "negative 3."
- **MP2 Reason Abstractly and Quantitatively:** In part (a), students need to make sense of the problem and decide what they will choose to represent 0 and why. They need to conclude that liftoff represents 0.
- Tell students to not label every integer between -110 and 6. Every other integer or every third or fifth integer can be labeled.
- To make the list for part (b), students should first locate the events at appropriate points on the number line. Students can place a closed circle on the number line and a letter above it that corresponds to one of the six events. Let rocket clears launchpad tower = A, launch verification = B, and so on.
- **Extension:** If you have a long piece of rope, you can have students *act out* the number line. Two students stretch the rope across the front of the classroom. Six students *locate themselves* on the rope number line. Hang a large paper clip to identify zero. Then students place themselves in approximately the correct location.
- **Research:** Part (c) is most easily accomplished in a library or computer lab.
- Discuss the order of the events. Those that are *before* launch should be to the left of 0.

8.2 Comparing and Ordering Integers

Learning Target: Compare and order integers.

Success Criteria:
- I can explain how to determine which of two integers is greater.
- I can order a set of integers from least to greatest.
- I can interpret statements about order in real-life problems.

EXPLORATION 1 Seconds to Liftoff

Work with a partner. You are listening to a command center before the liftoff of a rocket.

You hear the following:

> **"T minus 10 seconds . . . go for main engine start . . . T minus 9 . . . 8 . . . 7 . . . 6 . . . 5 . . . 4 . . . 3 . . . 2 . . . 1 . . . we have liftoff."**

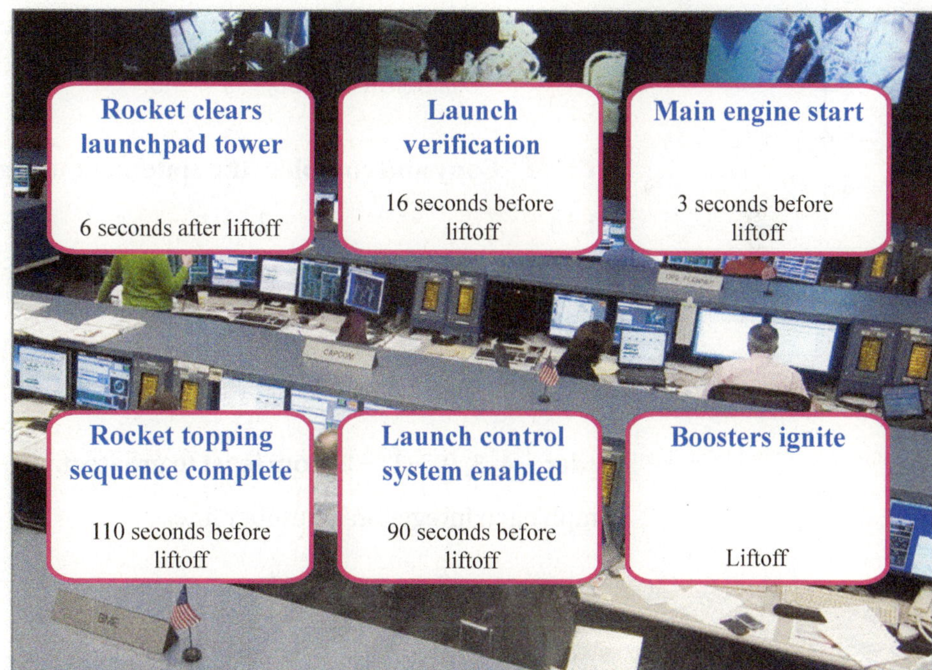

a. Represent these events on a number line.

b. List the events in the order they occurred. Explain your reasoning.

c. Extend the number line in part (a) to show events in an astronaut's day. Include at least five events before liftoff and at least five events after liftoff. Use the Internet or another reference source to gather information.

Math Practice

Use Other Resources

Which sources would give you the most accurate information? How do you know you can trust the information you find?

8.2 Lesson

Recall that on a horizontal number line, numbers to the left are less than numbers to the right. Numbers to the right are greater than numbers to the left.

On a vertical number line, numbers below are less than numbers above. Numbers above are greater than numbers below.

EXAMPLE 1 Comparing Integers

a. Compare 2 and −6.

Graph each number on a horizontal number line.

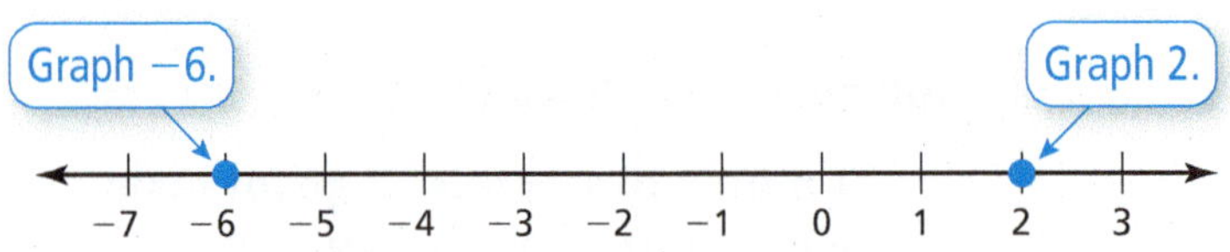

▶ 2 is to the right of −6. So, 2 > −6.

b. Compare −5 and −3.

Graph each number on a vertical number line.

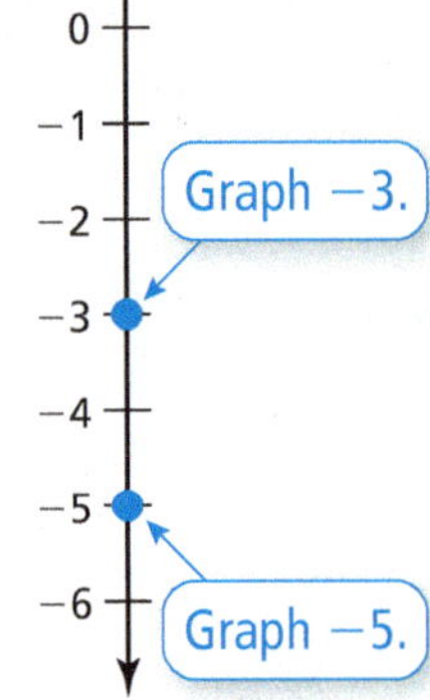

▶ −5 is below −3. So, −5 < −3.

Try It **Copy and complete the statement using < or >.**

1. 0 ▭ −4 **2.** −5 ▭ 5 **3.** −8 ▭ −7

EXAMPLE 2 Ordering Integers

Order −4, 3, 0, −1, −2 from least to greatest.

Graph each integer on a number line.

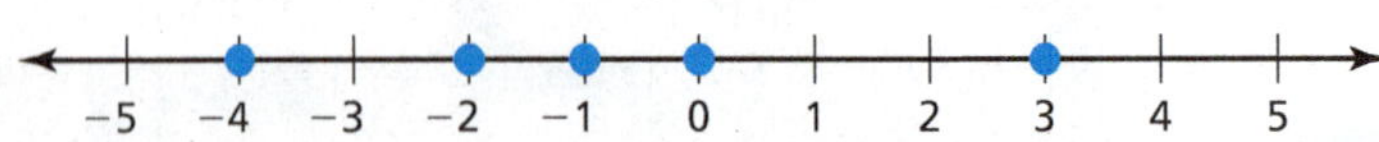

Write the integers as they appear on the number line from left to right.

▶ So, the order from least to greatest is −4, −2, −1, 0, 3.

Try It **Order the integers from least to greatest.**

4. −2, −3, 3, 1, −1 **5.** 4, −7, −8, 6, 1

Laurie's Notes

Scaffolding Instruction

- In the exploration, students explored a real-life application of integers and gained an intuitive understanding of comparing integers.
- **Emerging:** Students may create incorrect number lines or only compare without considering the signs of the integers. For instance, students may say −7 is larger than 3. The examples provide additional practice comparing integers on a number line.
- **Proficient:** Students view integers as the distance from 0 in a negative or positive direction. They understand that numbers to the left (or below) are less than numbers to the right (or above). They can go through Example 3 and then proceed to the Self-Assessment for Concepts & Skills exercises.

EXAMPLE 1

- For part (a), draw a number line and graph 2 and −6.
- Discuss with students that 0 does not have to be in the middle of the number line. Sometimes number lines do not show 0.
- **Big Idea:** The farther to the left on the number line, the less the number becomes. The farther to the right on the number line, the greater the number becomes.
- ? **Extension:** "How far are 2 and −6 from 0?" 2 is 2 units from 0 and −6 is 6 units from 0.
- For part (b), draw a vertical number line and graph −5 and −3.
- ? **Extension:** "How far are −5 and −3 from 0?" −5 is 5 units from 0 and −3 is 3 units from 0.

Try It

- Check students' answers for Exercise 3. Comparing two negative numbers is a difficult concept for some students. Encourage them to graph the numbers on a number line.

EXAMPLE 2

- Draw a number line and graph the integers. Discuss with students the difference between labeling the number line with integers and graphing integers with closed circles.

Try It

- **Turn and Talk:** Have students discuss their answers with a partner. As they compare their work, encourage them to look at their number lines to resolve any disagreements.

ELL Support

Allow students to work in pairs to complete Try It Exercises 4 and 5. Have one student ask the other, "What is the order from least to greatest?" Then have partners reverse roles.

Beginner: Write the numbers in order.

Intermediate: State the numbers in order.

Advanced: Use a complete sentence to describe the order of the numbers, such as, "The order from least to greatest is..."

Scaffold instruction to support all students in their learning. Learning is individualized and you may want to group students differently as they move in and out of these levels with each skill and concept. Student self-assessment and feedback help guide your instructional decisions about how and when to layer support for all students to become proficient learners.

Teaching Strategy

A floor number line allows students to be physical about placing points on a number line. Students will notice others' locations on the number line and determine who represents the greatest number. A floor number line can also be used to find opposites and order numbers.

Extra Example 1

a. Compare −3 and 6. $-3 < 6$

b. Compare −1 and −2. $-1 > -2$

Try It

1. > **2.** <

3. <

Extra Example 2

Order −3, 9, 0, −7, 1 from least to greatest. −7, −3, 0, 1, 9

Try It

4. $-3, -2, -1, 1, 3$

5. $-8, -7, 1, 4, 6$

Extra Example 3

A number is greater than -7 and less than 3. What is the least possible integer value of this number?

A. -8 **B.** -6 **C.** 0 **D.** 1

B

Try It

6. -7

Self-Assessment
for Concepts & Skills

7. $-4, -1, 3, 5, 6$

8. $-9, -7, -2, 0, 8$

9. *Sample answer:* Use a number line.

10. a.

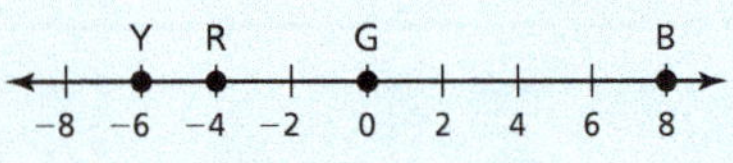

b. Write the integers as they appear on the horizontal number line from left to right or on the vertical number line from bottom to top.

11. a is less than b; a is to the left of b.

Laurie's Notes

EXAMPLE 3

- Drawing a number line and plotting the answers is helpful for students.
- Discuss with students that the phrase *greater than -8 and less than 0* does not include the integers -8 and 0.
- **Common Error:** Students will often say -7 is the greatest integer between -8 and 0. They are still uncertain of comparing negative integers. Remind students to use a number line to compare the integers. They should recognize that -1 is to the right of -7, so -1 is greater than -7.

Try It

- Ask students to share their reasoning for Exercise 6.

Self-Assessment for Concepts & Skills

- **MP5 Use Appropriate Tools Strategically:** Determining the placement of an integer on a number line and gauging its value compared to others are important skills. Students will need these skills as they progress through the study of integers.
- Students should work on the exercises independently to assess their progress with the first two success criteria. Then have students *Turn and Talk* to discuss their answers.
- Many students may use number lines to answer Exercises 7 and 8. Others may be able to "see" the relationship without using a tool.
- Look at students' work for Exercise 10 to check that students can move from horizontal to vertical number lines with ease.
- Listen to discussions surrounding Exercise 11, which requires critical thinking and conceptual understanding. Have students share their reasoning with the class.

ELL Support

Allow students to work in pairs on Exercises 7, 8, and 10. Check comprehension by having each pair display their answers on a whiteboard for your review. Have pairs discuss and answer Exercises 9 and 11 and then compare their answers with another pair. Each group must come to agreement if their answers differ. Monitor discussions and provide support.

The Success Criteria Self-Assessment chart can be found in the *Student Journal* or online at *BigIdeasMath.com.*

EXAMPLE 3 Reasoning with Integers

A number is greater than -8 and less than 0. What is the greatest possible integer value of this number?

A. -10 **B.** -7 **C.** -1 **D.** 2

Math Practice

Find Entry Points

Which choices can be eliminated by looking at the number line? Explain your reasoning.

The number is greater than -8 and less than 0. So, the number must be to the right of -8 and to the left of 0 on a horizontal number line.

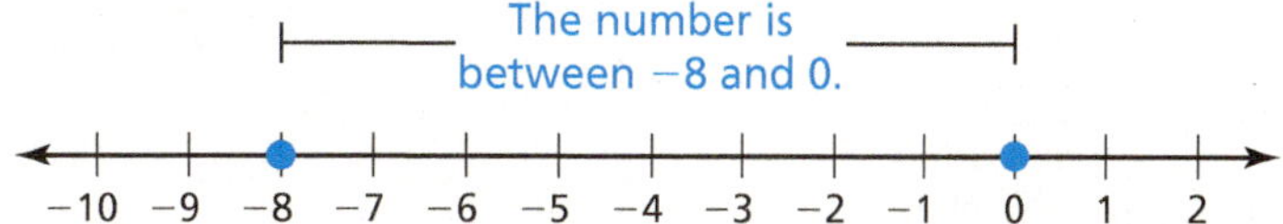

The greatest possible integer value between -8 and 0 is the integer farthest to the right on the number line between these values, which is -1.

So, the correct answer is **C**.

Try It

6. In Example 3, what is the least possible integer value of the number?

Self-Assessment for Concepts & Skills

Solve each exercise. Then rate your understanding of the success criteria in your journal.

ORDERING INTEGERS **Order the integers from least to greatest.**

7. $6, -4, -1, 3, 5$

8. $-7, -9, 0, 8, -2$

9. **WRITING** Explain how to determine which of two integers is greater.

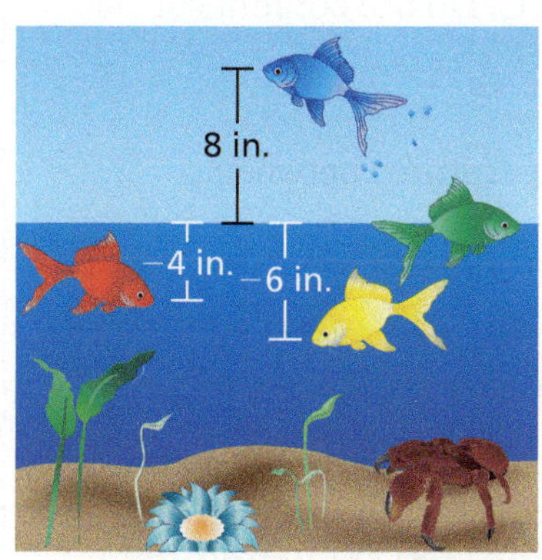

10. **MP REASONING** The positions of four fish are shown.

a. Use red, blue, yellow, and green dots to graph the positions of the fish on a horizontal number line and a vertical number line.

b. Explain how to use the number lines from part (a) to order the positions from least to greatest.

11. **MP NUMBER SENSE** a and b are negative integers. Compare a and b. Explain your reasoning.

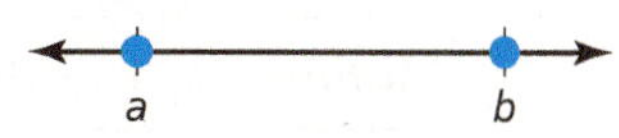

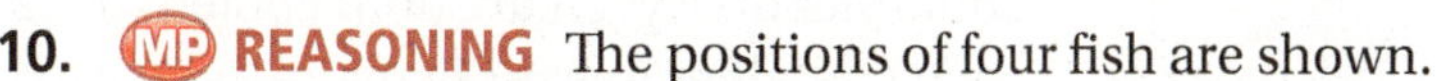

EXAMPLE 4 Modeling Real Life

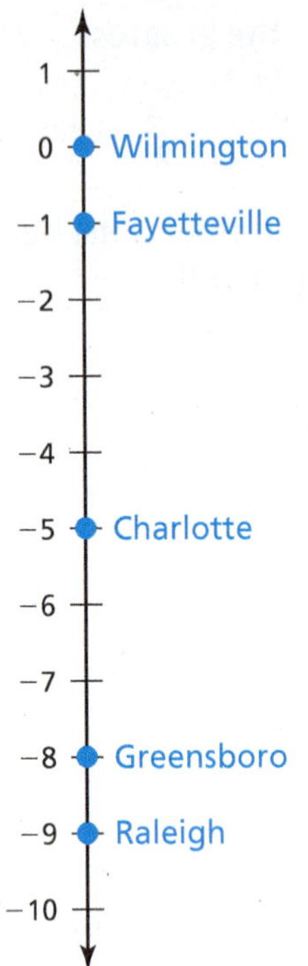

The diagram shows the coldest recorded temperatures for several cities in North Carolina.

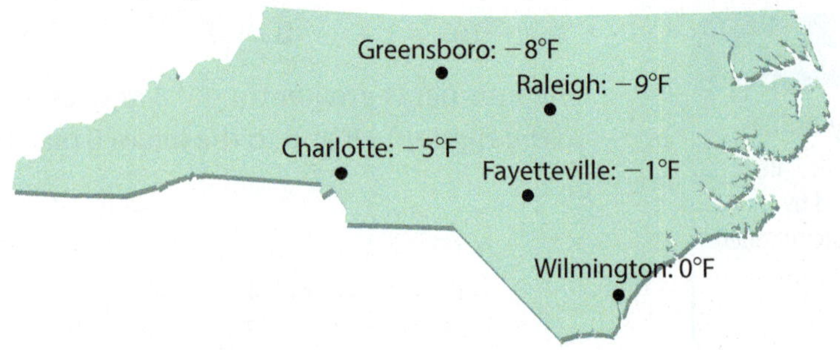

a. **Which city has the coldest recorded temperature?**

Graph each integer on a vertical number line.

−9 is the lowest on the number line. So, Raleigh has the coldest recorded temperature.

b. **Has a negative Fahrenheit temperature ever been recorded in Wilmington? Explain.**

The coldest recorded temperature in Wilmington is 0°F, which is greater than every negative Fahrenheit temperature. So, a negative Fahrenheit temperature has never been recorded in Wilmington.

Self-Assessment for Problem Solving

Solve each exercise. Then rate your understanding of the success criteria in your journal.

12. The freezing temperature of nitrogen is −210°C, and the freezing temperature of oxygen is −219°C. A container of nitrogen and a container of oxygen are both cooled to −215°C. Do the contents of each container freeze? Explain.

13. DIG DEEPER! Complete the table with temperatures between −10°C and 10°C so that

- one day had only positive temperatures,
- one day had only negative temperatures, and
- three days could have had both positive and negative temperatures.

Daily High Temperatures			Daily Low Temperatures	
Monday	Tuesday	Wednesday	Thursday	Friday
°C	°C	°C	°C	°C

Laurie's Notes

EXAMPLE 4

- Students should notice that all of the temperatures are negative, with the exception of Wilmington.
- ◉ This example provides practice for the third success criterion.
- **Extension:** Have students research the coldest and warmest recorded temperatures for their town or city.

Self-Assessment for Problem Solving

- Students may benefit from trying the exercises independently and then working in groups to discuss their work. It is important to provide time in class for problem solving, so that students become comfortable with the problem-solving plan.
- As students work independently, make sure that they are writing explanations. Writing the explanations will focus students' thinking and cement understanding.
- If time allows, discuss Exercises 35 and 36 in the Practice exercises. These are great statements to analyze in groups.

The Success Criteria Self-Assessment chart can be found in the *Student Journal* or online at *BigIdeasMath.com*.

Closure

- **Exit Ticket:** Explain why $2 > -42$. 2 is to the right of -42 on the number line

Extra Example 4

In Example 4, Wilmington recorded a new record low last night. The new record low is greater than the record low in Greensboro. What integers can represent the new record low in Wilmington?
$-7, -6, -5, -4, -3, -2, -1$

Self-Assessment for Problem Solving

12. no; $-215 > -219$

13. *Sample answer:* $-1, 3, 4, 2, -8$

Learning Target

Compare and order integers.

Success Criteria

- Explain how to determine which of two integers is greater.
- Order a set of integers from least to greatest.
- Interpret statements about order in real-life problems.

Review & Refresh

1. 83
2. -17
3. 75
4. -250
5. B
6. $1\frac{4}{5}$
7. $1\frac{1}{5}$
8. $\frac{1}{12}$
9. $\frac{1}{14}$

Concepts, Skills, & Problem Solving

10. *Sample answer:* start rocket topping sequence; occurs before rocket topping sequence complete
11. *Sample answer:* test controls; occurs before rocket topping sequence complete
12. *Sample answer:* rocket reaches 1000 feet; occurs after rocket clears launchpad
13. $>$
14. $<$
15. $>$
16. $>$
17. $<$
18. $>$
19. $<$
20. $>$
21. no; $-3 < -1$
22. yes; The reasoning is correct.
23. $-3, -1, 0, 2, 3$
24. $-4, -3, -2, 1, 2$
25. $-4, -3, -2, 3, 4$
26. $-11, -9, -4, 3, 5$
27. $-13, -3, 0, 4, 8$
28. $-7, -4, 2, 3, 6$
29. $-16, -8, 1, 7, 12$
30. $-50, -30, -10, 10, 30$
31. $-20, -10, -5, 15, 25$

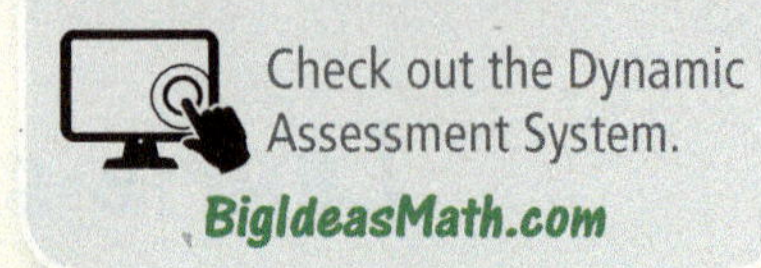

Assignment Guide and Concept Check

Scaffold assignments to support all students in their learning progression. The suggested assignments are a starting point. Continue to assign additional exercises and revisit with spaced practice to move every student toward proficiency.

Level	Assignment 1	Assignment 2
Emerging	4, 5, 9, 10, 13, 15, 19, 21, 23, 25	20, 22, 30, 32, 33, 37, 38
Proficient	4, 5, 9, 10, 14, 15, 18, 21, 24, 28	19, 22, 30, 32, 33, 35, 36, 37, 38
Advanced	4, 5, 9, 11, 14, 18, 19, 21, 26, 30	22, 33, 34, 35, 36, 37, 38, 39, 40

- Assignment 1 is for use after students complete the Self-Assessment for Concepts & Skills.
- Assignment 2 is for use after students complete the Self-Assessment for Problem Solving.
- The red exercises can be used as a concept check.

Review & Refresh Prior Skills

Exercises 1–4 Writing Integers
Exercise 5 Finding the Area of a Trapezoid
Exercises 6–9 Dividing Fractions

Common Errors

- **Exercises 23–31** Students may ignore the signs of the integers and order them incorrectly. Encourage students to use a number line to help order the integers.

8.2 Practice

Go to **BigIdeasMath.com** to get HELP with solving the exercises.

Review & Refresh

Write a positive or negative integer that represents the situation.

1. You walk up 83 stairs.
2. A whale is 17 yards below sea level.
3. An organization receives a $75 donation.
4. A rock falls 250 feet off a cliff.
5. What is the area of the trapezoid?

   A. 6.3 ft^2 **B.** 44.1 ft^2

   C. 50.4 ft^2 **D.** 88.2 ft^2

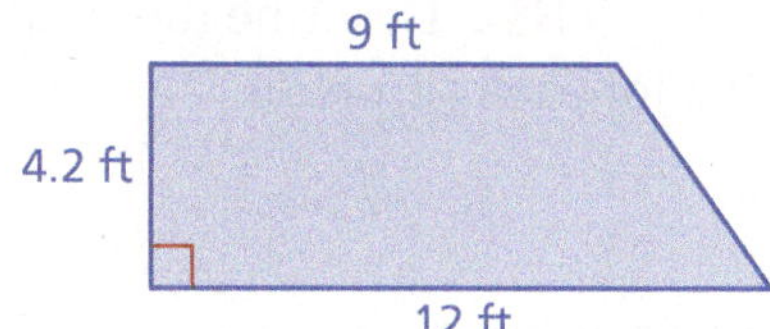

Divide. Write the answer in simplest form.

6. $\frac{1}{5} \div \frac{1}{9}$
7. $\frac{2}{5} \div \frac{1}{3}$
8. $\frac{1}{4} \div 3$
9. $\frac{4}{7} \div 8$

Concepts, Skills, & Problem Solving

OPEN-ENDED **Name an event that could occur at the given time (in seconds) in Exploration 1. Describe when the event occurs in the order of events from the exploration.** (See Exploration 1, p. 351.)

10. -300
11. -150
12. 10

COMPARING INTEGERS **Copy and complete the statement using < or >.**

13. 3 ▭ 0
14. -2 ▭ 0
15. 6 ▭ -6
16. 3 ▭ -4
17. -1 ▭ 4
18. -7 ▭ -8
19. -3 ▭ -2
20. -5 ▭ -10

YOU BE THE TEACHER **Your friend compares two integers. Is your friend correct? Explain your reasoning.**

21. Compare -3 and -1.

    $3 > 1$. So, $-3 > -1$.

22. Compare -7 and -3.

    Because -7 is to the left of -3 on a number line, $-7 < -3$.

ORDERING INTEGERS **Order the integers from least to greatest.**

23. 0, -1, 2, 3, -3
24. -4, -2, -3, 2, 1
25. -2, 3, -3, -4, 4
26. 5, -11, -9, 3, -4
27. -3, 8, 4, 0, -13
28. -7, 2, 6, -4, 3
29. 12, -8, -16, 7, 1
30. 10, -10, 30, -30, -50
31. -5, 15, -10, -20, 25

32. MP **MODELING REAL LIFE** An archaeologist discovers the two artifacts shown.

    a. What integer represents ground level?

    b. A dinosaur bone is 42 centimeters below ground level. Is it deeper than both of the artifacts? Explain.

33. MP **REASONING** A number is between −2 and −10. What is the least possible integer value of this number? What is the greatest possible integer value of this number?

34. MP **NUMBER SENSE** Describe the locations of the integers m and n on a number line for each situation.

    a. $m < n$ b. $m > n$ c. $n > m$ d. $n < m$

CRITICAL THINKING Tell whether the statement is *always*, *sometimes*, or *never* true. Explain.

35. A positive integer is greater than its opposite.

36. An integer is less than its opposite and greater than 0.

37. MP **MODELING REAL LIFE** The table shows the highest and lowest elevations for five states.

    a. Order the states by their highest elevations, from least to greatest.

    b. Order the states by their lowest elevations, from least to greatest.

    c. What does the lowest elevation for Florida represent?

State	Highest Elevation (feet)	Lowest Elevation (feet)
Arkansas	2753	55
California	14,494	−282
Florida	345	0
Louisiana	535	−8
Tennessee	6643	178

38. MP **NUMBER SENSE** Point A is on a number line halfway between −17 and 5. Point B is halfway between Point A and 0. What integer does Point B represent?

39. MP **REASONING** Eleven Fahrenheit temperatures are shown on a map during a weather report. When the temperatures are ordered from least to greatest, the middle temperature is below 0°F. Do you know exactly how many of the temperatures are represented by negative numbers? Explain.

40. **PUZZLE** Nine students each choose one integer. Here are seven of them:

    5, −8, 10, −1, −12, −20, and 1.

    a. When all nine integers are ordered from least to greatest, the middle integer is 1. Describe the integers chosen by the other two students.

    b. When all nine integers are ordered from least to greatest, the middle integer is −3. Describe the integers chosen by the other two students.

Mini-Assessment

Copy and complete the statement using < or >.

1. -7 ▢ 7 $-7 < 7$

2. -3 ▢ -4 $-3 > -4$

Order the integers from least to greatest.

3. $-8, 4, -1, -2, 1$ $-8, -2, -1, 1, 4$

4. $0, 5, -3, -5, -9$ $-9, -5, -3, 0, 5$

5. In miniature golf, the person with the least score wins. You have a score of -5 and your friend has a score of -6. Who is the winner? your friend

Section Resources

Surface Level	Deep Level
Resources by Chapter • Extra Practice • Reteach • Puzzle Time Student Journal • Self-Assessment • Practice Differentiating the Lesson Tutorial Videos Skills Review Handbook Skills Trainer	Resources by Chapter • Enrichment and Extension Graphic Organizers Dynamic Assessment System • Section Practice

Concepts, Skills, & Problem Solving

32. a. 0

    b. no; $-42 > -44$

33. -9; -3

34. a. m is to the left of n.

    b. m is to the right of n.

    c. n is to the right of m.

    d. n is to the left of m.

35. always; Positive integers are greater than negative integers.

36. never; If an integer is less than its opposite, it must be a negative integer, which is never greater than 0.

37. a. Florida, Louisiana, Arkansas, Tennessee, California

    b. California, Louisiana, Florida, Arkansas, Tennessee

    c. sea level

38. $B = -3$

39. no; In order for the median to be below 0°F, at least 6 of the temperatures must be below 0°F.

40. a. Both integers are greater than or equal to 1.

    b. One of the integers is -3 and the other integer is less than or equal to -3.

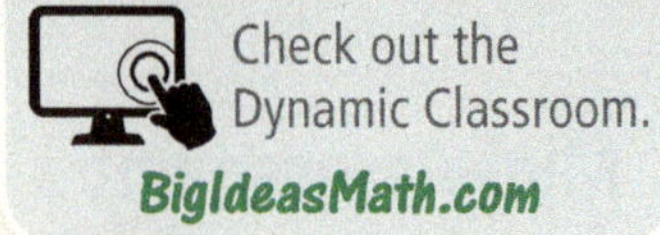

Laurie's Notes

STATE STANDARDS
6.NS.C.5, 6.NS.C.6a, 6.NS.C.6c, 6.NS.C.7a, 6.NS.C.7b

Learning Target

Compare and order rational numbers.

Success Criteria

- Explain the meaning of a rational number.
- Graph rational numbers on a number line.
- Determine which of two rational numbers is greater.
- Order a set of rational numbers from least to greatest.

Warm Up

Cumulative, vocabulary, and prerequisite skills practice opportunities are available in the *Resources by Chapter* or at *BigIdeasMath.com*.

ELL Support

Explain that in everyday language the word *rational* means "reasonable or sensible." In math, it has a special meaning. It describes a set of numbers that includes integers, fractions, and decimals.

Exploration 1

See Additional Answers.

Preparing to Teach

- Earlier in the course, students practiced converting between mixed numbers and improper fractions, using inequality signs, and comparing fractions and decimals. Students will now compare and order **rational numbers**. The number line is still an efficient introductory tool.
- **MP6 Attend to Precision:** Mathematically proficient students are able to communicate precisely to others. In open-ended questions that have more than one possible answer, expect students to be attentive to all students offering solutions. The process students use to arrive at an answer may differ and students should listen critically to the explanations offered.

Motivate

- Place a piece of masking tape on the floor for a number line.
- Have volunteers hold index cards with 0, $\frac{1}{4}$, $\frac{1}{2}$, $\frac{3}{4}$, or 1 written on them and stand at the correct places on the number line.
- Say, "Reading left to right, $0 < \frac{1}{4} < \frac{1}{2} < \frac{3}{4} < 1$."

? Use a marker to write a negative sign in front of all the numbers except 0. "Are the numbers still in the correct order as you look at the number line? Explain." No, 0 and -1 need to swap and $-\frac{1}{4}$ and $-\frac{3}{4}$ need to swap.

- **Big Idea:** Students need to remember that the farther to the right a number is on the number line, the greater it is. Likewise, the farther to the left a number is on the number line, the less it is.

Exploration 1

? "What type of numbers are the A.M. events? the P.M. events?" negative numbers; positive numbers

- **Common Error**: When locating negative fractions, students often move left to right instead of right to left. For example, students may incorrectly place $-8\frac{3}{4}$ (take photograph) closer to -8 than -9. Help students start at -8 and move $\frac{3}{4}$ of the way towards -9.
- "Explain how you wrote 6:20 P.M. as a mixed number and how you located it on the number line." Listen for an explanation that includes $\frac{20}{60} = \frac{1}{3}$ hour, so *float in the cabin* is $\frac{1}{3}$ beyond 6 on the number line.
- Discuss the Math Practice note.

8.3 Rational Numbers

Learning Target: Compare and order rational numbers.

Success Criteria:
- I can explain the meaning of a rational number.
- I can graph rational numbers on a number line.
- I can determine which of two rational numbers is greater.
- I can order a set of rational numbers from least to greatest.

EXPLORATION 1 Locating Fractions on a Number Line

Work with a partner. Represent the events on a number line using a fraction or a mixed number.

a. Radio Transmission: 11:30 A.M.

b. Space Walk: 7:30 P.M.

c. Physical Exam: 4:45 A.M.

d. Take Photograph: 3:15 A.M.

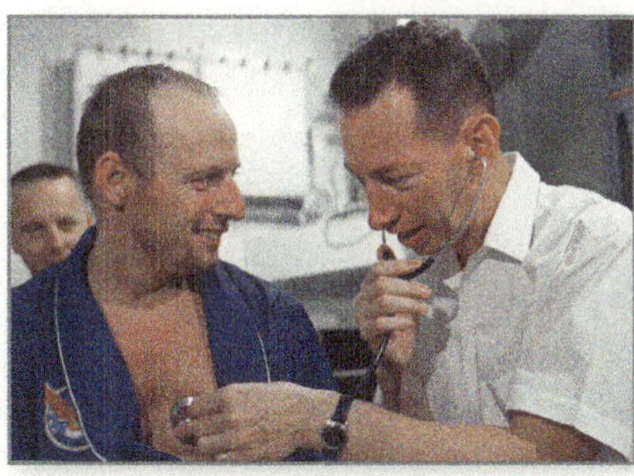

e. Float in the Cabin: 6:20 P.M.

f. Eat Dinner: 8:40 P.M.

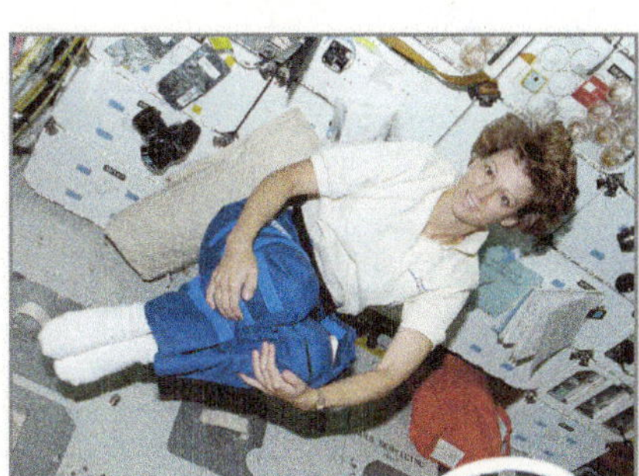

Math Practice

Label Axes

How can you graph *negative* fractions and mixed numbers on a number line?

8.3 Lesson

Key Vocabulary
rational number, *p. 358*

Integers, fractions, and decimals make up the set of *rational numbers*. A **rational number** is a number that can be written as $\frac{a}{b}$, where a and b are integers and $b \neq 0$.

EXAMPLE 1 Graphing Rational Numbers

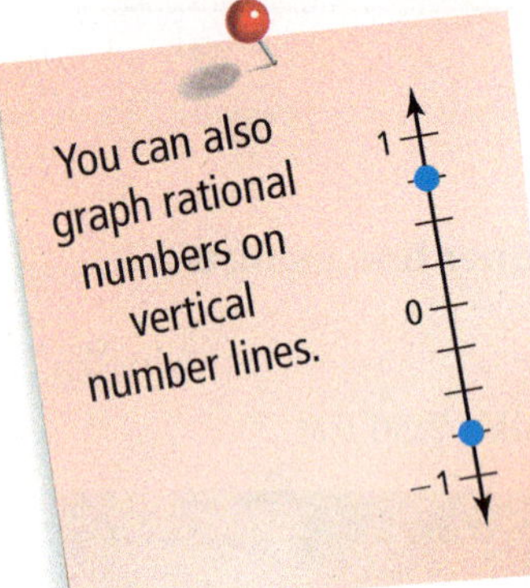

Graph each number and its opposite.

a. $\frac{3}{4}$

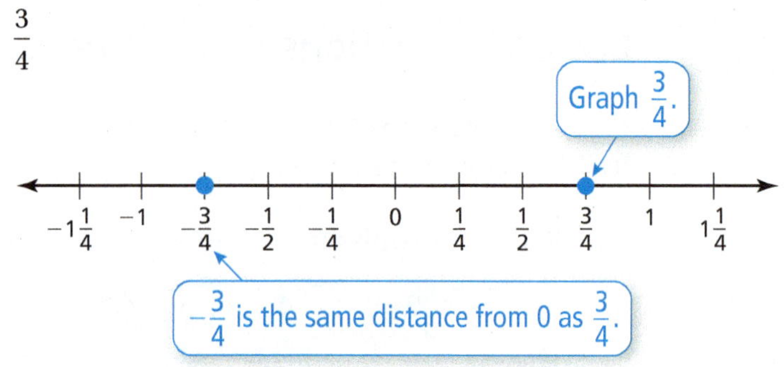

b. -1.6

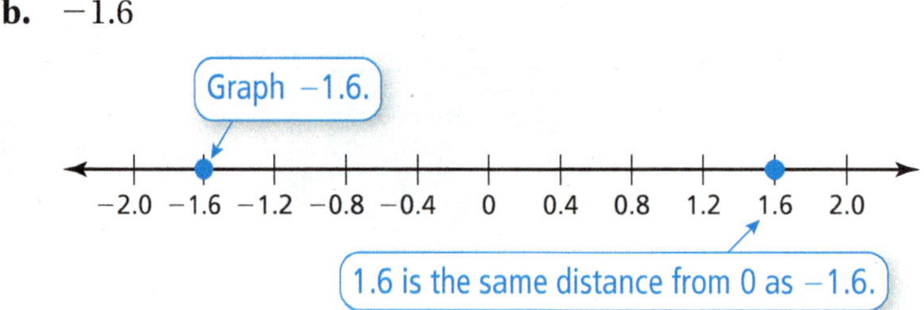

Try It **Graph the number and its opposite.**

1. $2\frac{1}{2}$ **2.** $-\frac{4}{5}$ **3.** -3.5 **4.** 5.25

EXAMPLE 2 Comparing Fractions and Mixed Numbers

a. Compare $-\frac{1}{2}$ and $-\frac{3}{4}$.

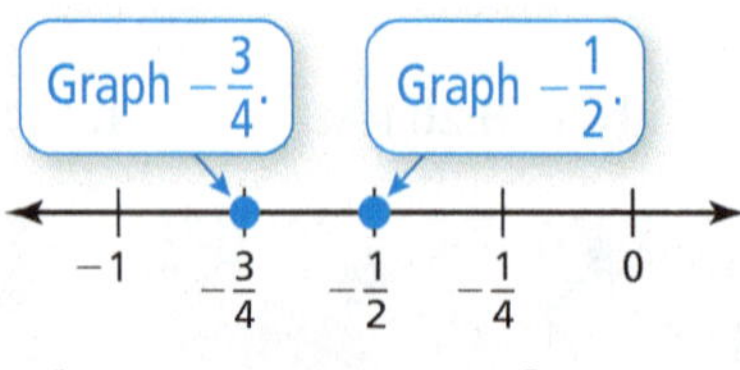

$-\frac{1}{2}$ is to the right of $-\frac{3}{4}$.

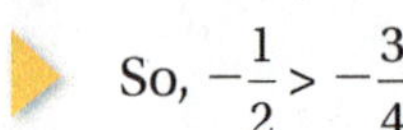
So, $-\frac{1}{2} > -\frac{3}{4}$.

b. Compare $-4\frac{5}{6}$ and $-4\frac{1}{6}$.

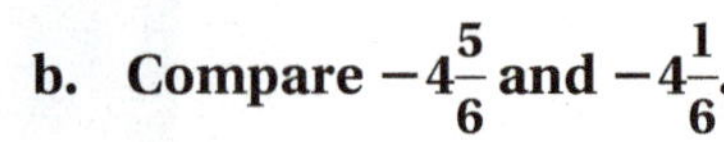

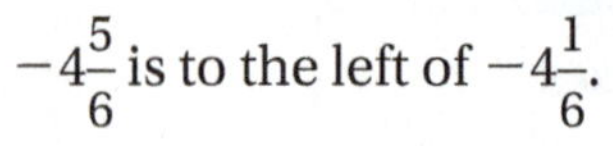

$-4\frac{5}{6}$ is to the left of $-4\frac{1}{6}$.

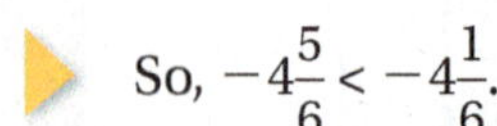
So, $-4\frac{5}{6} < -4\frac{1}{6}$.

Try It **Copy and complete the statement using < or >.**

5. $-\frac{4}{7}$ ▭ $-\frac{1}{7}$ **6.** $-1\frac{2}{3}$ ▭ $-1\frac{5}{6}$

Laurie's Notes

Scaffolding Instruction

- Students are activating prior knowledge of placing fractions and decimals on a number line. They will link this skill with placing integers on a number line from Section 8.1.
- **Emerging:** Students struggle with placement of negative numbers and understanding that −7.2 is smaller than −2.7 or −7.1. Students need the practice provided in the examples.
- **Proficient:** Students showed understanding of rational numbers and their order in the exploration. They can evaluate their understanding by completing the Self-Assessment exercises.

EXAMPLE 1

- Remind students that rational numbers can be positive, negative, or zero.

? "In part (a), how far is each number from 0?" $\frac{3}{4}$ unit

- **MP6 Attend to Precision:** Students may incorrectly believe that the opposite of a number is negative. If the original number is negative, its opposite is positive. *Opposite* does not mean negative.

Teaching Strategy

Number lines provide a visual and a physical path to understanding the order of numbers. Practice with this tool helps students explain and visualize number placement. Use both horizontal and vertical number lines to benchmark numerical values and provide a continuum for counting fractional quantities in positive and negative directions.

Try It

- **Teaching Strategy:** Have students work in pairs. One student can make a horizontal number line and the other student can make a vertical number line. Pairs compare the two models and then switch models for each exercise.

EXAMPLE 2

- Remind students that for negative numbers, you work from right to left.

? "Which number is farther from 0, $-4\frac{5}{6}$ or $-4\frac{1}{6}$?" $-4\frac{5}{6}$

Try It

- **Think-Pair-Share:** Students should read each exercise independently and then work in pairs to complete the exercises. Then have each pair compare their answers with another pair and discuss any discrepancies.

ELL Support

Have students work in pairs to discuss and complete Try It Exercises 5 and 6. Have one student ask the other to describe the relationship between the numbers. Then have partners reverse roles.

Beginner: Write the symbol.

Intermediate/Advanced: State the relationship using a sentence. For example, "Negative four-sevenths is less than negative one-seventh."

Scaffold instruction to support all students in their learning. Learning is individualized and you may want to group students differently as they move in and out of these levels with each skill and concept. Student self-assessment and feedback help guide your instructional decisions about how and when to layer support for all students to become proficient learners.

Extra Example 1

Graph each number and its opposite.

a. $1\frac{1}{3}$

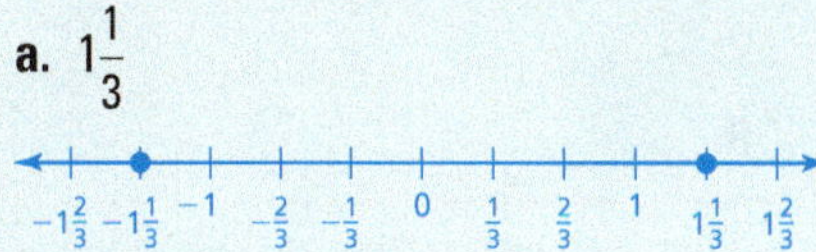

b. −0.7

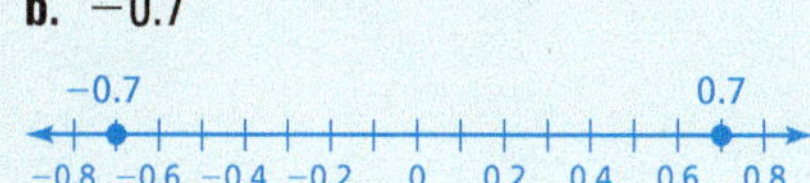

Try It

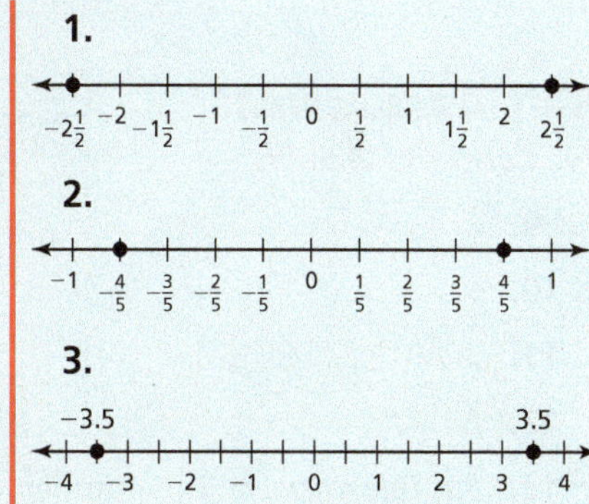

4. See Additional Answers.

Extra Example 2

a. Compare $-\frac{5}{8}$ and $-\frac{3}{8}$. $-\frac{5}{8} < -\frac{3}{8}$

b. Compare $-2\frac{2}{3}$ and $-3\frac{1}{3}$. $-2\frac{2}{3} > -3\frac{1}{3}$

Try It

5. <

6. >

Extra Example 3

a. Compare -0.3 and -1.2. $-0.3 > -1.2$

b. Compare -2.7 and -2.07. $-2.7 < -2.07$

Try It

7. <

8. >

Self-Assessment
for Concepts & Skills

9. <

10. >

11. >

12. A

13. *Sample answer:* The number can be written as a fraction.

Laurie's Notes

EXAMPLE 3

- **MP6 Attend to Precision:** Use correct language in reading the decimals: "negative two and three tenths" and "negative one and five tenths."
- **Teaching Tip:** In part (b), to help students compare decimals with different place values, write trailing zeros as shown.

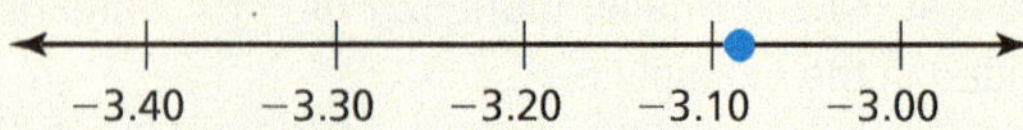

It is not obvious to all students that -3.1 is equivalent to -3.10, or in words, *negative three and one tenth* is equivalent to *negative three and ten hundredths.* The trailing zeros help students recognize where -3.08 is in relation to -3.1 (or -3.10).

Try It

- **Think-Pair-Share:** Students should read each exercise independently and then work in pairs to complete the exercises. Then have each pair compare their answers with another pair and discuss any discrepancies.

Self-Assessment for Concepts & Skills

- Have students work independently as they assess their progress with the first three success criteria. Then students can complete a *Neighbor Check* to compare answers and discuss differences.
- If students are struggling, encourage them to draw number lines.
- Listen to students' discussions of Exercises 9–12 to know if placement of rational numbers is making sense to them. When locating negative fractions, are students avoiding moving from left to right?
- **MP1 Make Sense of Problems and Persevere in Solving Them**: Mathematically proficient students make use of tools and diagrams, such as number lines, to investigate numerical relationships. They appreciate different solution methods and use other students' explanations to increase their own understanding. Allow time for students to persevere!
- Have students use *Fist of Five* to indicate their understanding of comparing rational numbers. You should be able to quickly evaluate where your students are in their journey towards the learning target.

ELL Support

Provide students with extra support and language practice by having them work in pairs. Check comprehension of Exercises 9–11 by using a thumbs up or down to indicate *greater than* or *less than.* Check comprehension of Exercise 12 by having students hold up 1 finger for A, 2 fingers for B, or 3 fingers for C. Discuss Exercise 13 as a class.

The Success Criteria Self-Assessment chart can be found in the *Student Journal* or online at *BigIdeasMath.com.*

EXAMPLE 3 Comparing Decimals

a. Compare −2.3 and −1.5.

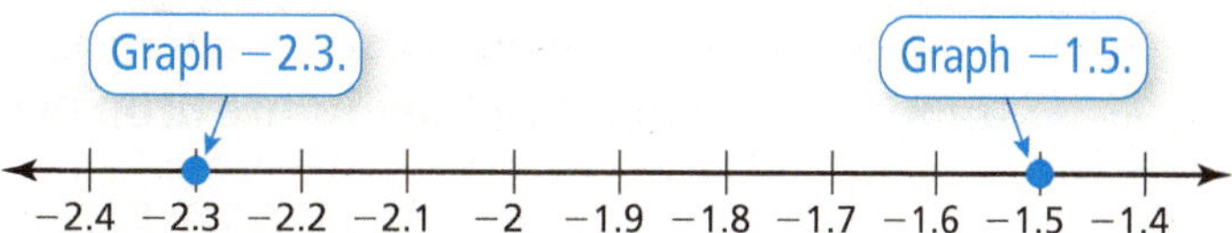

−2.3 is to the left of −1.5.

 So, $-2.3 < -1.5$.

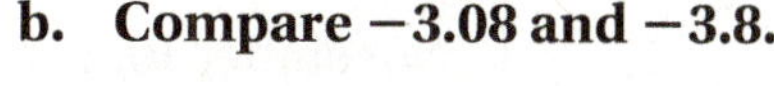

b. Compare −3.08 and −3.8.

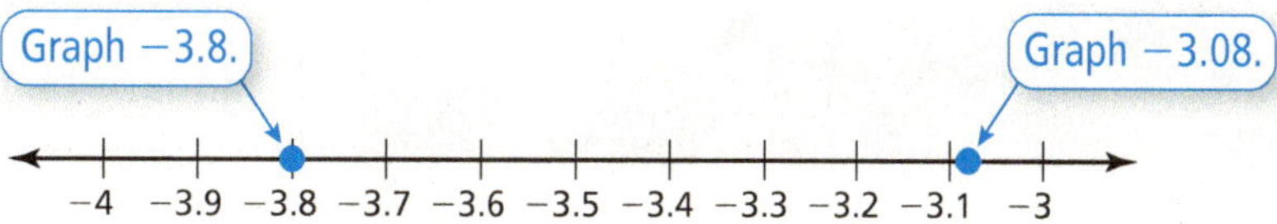

−3.08 is to the right of −3.8.

 So, $-3.08 > -3.8$.

Math Practice

Construct Arguments

Compare any positive number to any negative number. Explain your reasoning.

Try It **Copy and complete the statement using < or >.**

7. -0.5 ☐ 0.3

8. -6.5 ☐ -6.75

Self-Assessment for Concepts & Skills

Solve each exercise. Then rate your understanding of the success criteria in your journal.

COMPARING RATIONAL NUMBERS **Copy and complete the statement using < or >.**

9. $-\frac{2}{3}$ ☐ $-\frac{5}{9}$

10. $-2\frac{1}{4}$ ☐ $-2\frac{3}{8}$

11. -1.7 ☐ -2.4

12. MP **NUMBER SENSE** Which statement is *not* true?

A. On a number line, $-2\frac{1}{6}$ is to the left of $-2\frac{2}{3}$.

B. $-2\frac{2}{3}$ is less than $-2\frac{1}{6}$.

C. On a number line, $-2\frac{2}{3}$ is to the left of $-2\frac{1}{6}$.

13. **WRITING** Explain how to determine whether a number is a rational number.

EXAMPLE 4 Modeling Real Life

A *Chinook wind* is a warm mountain wind that can cause rapid temperature changes. The table shows three of the greatest temperature drops ever recorded after a Chinook wind occurred. On which date did the temperature drop the fastest? Explain.

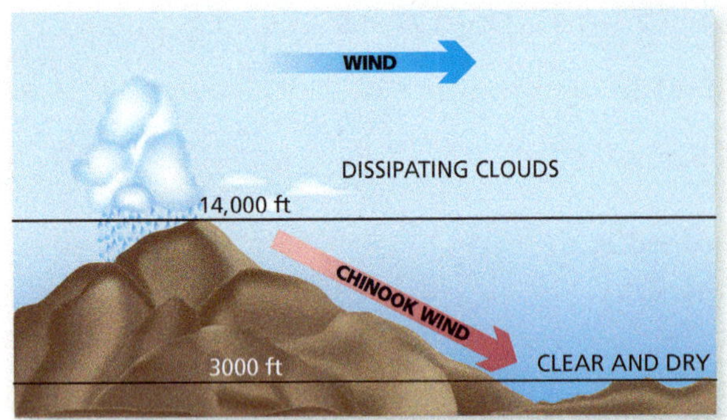

Date	Temperature Change
January 10, 1911	$-3\frac{1}{10}$°F per minute
November 10, 1911	$-\frac{5}{8}$°F per minute
January 22, 1943	$-2\frac{1}{5}$°F per minute

Graph the numbers on a number line.

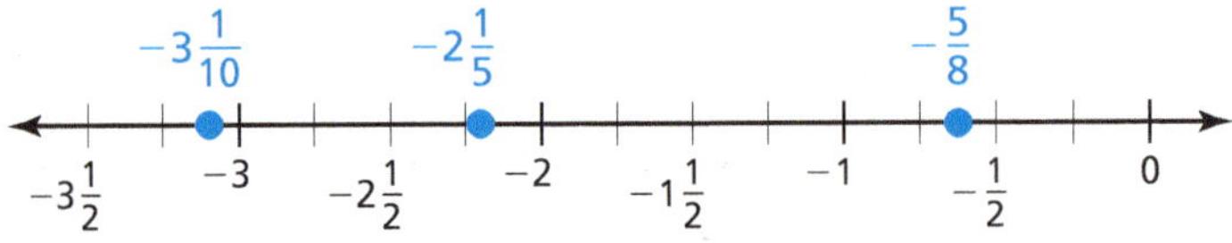

$-3\frac{1}{10}$ is farthest to the left.

So, the temperature dropped the fastest on January 10, 1911.

Self-Assessment for Problem Solving

Solve each exercise. Then rate your understanding of the success criteria in your journal.

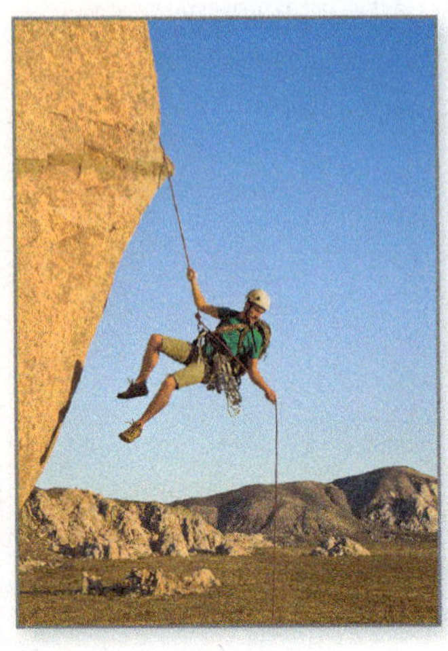

14. You and your friend rappel down a cliff. Your friend descends 0.11 mile and then waits for you to catch up. You descend and your current change in elevation is -0.12 mile. Have you reached your friend? Explain.

15. The table shows the changes in the value of a stock over a period of three days. On which day does the value of the stock change the most? Explain your reasoning.

Day	1	2	3
Change (dollars)	-0.42	0	-0.45

Laurie's Notes

EXAMPLE 4

- Even though the numbers can be compared without graphing on a number line, it is good reinforcement of estimating the location of the numbers.

? "Refer to the diagram. Between which two tick marks is $-\frac{5}{8}$ located? $-2\frac{1}{5}$? $-3\frac{1}{10}$?" $-\frac{3}{4}$ and $-\frac{1}{2}$; $-2\frac{1}{4}$ and -2; $-3\frac{1}{4}$ and -3

- Explain that even though $-3\frac{1}{10}$ is the least of the three numbers, it has the greatest distance from zero (absolute value), so it represents the fastest drop in temperature.
- Absolute value has not been formally defined, yet students intuitively understand that because $3\frac{1}{10} > 2\frac{1}{5} > \frac{5}{8}$, the opposite of each of these numbers is $-3\frac{1}{10} < -2\frac{1}{5} < -\frac{5}{8}$. Remind students of folding the number line at 0 and matching the opposites.

Students are working on the fourth success criterion.

Self-Assessment for Problem Solving

- Students may benefit from trying the exercises independently and then working with peers to refine their work. It is important to provide time in class for problem solving, so that students become comfortable with the problem-solving plan.
- Encourage students to draw number lines to help visualize the problems. Remind them to look for key words such as *descends*.
- Ask students to share their work and reasoning. There may be a variety of methods and students will benefit from hearing alternate reasoning as they persevere in problem solving.

Students are assessing their understanding of the last three success criteria within the context of real-life problems.

The Success Criteria Self-Assessment chart can be found in the *Student Journal* or online at *BigIdeasMath.com*.

Closure

- **Exit Ticket:** Which is greater, $-1\frac{2}{5}$ or $-1\frac{3}{4}$? Explain. $-1\frac{2}{5}$; It is farther to the right on a number line.

Extra Example 4

The daily water level relative to a dock is recorded for three straight days at the same time. On which day was the water level lowest? Explain.

Day	Water Level (meters)
Mon	$-\frac{19}{20}$
Tues	$-1\frac{1}{5}$
Wed	$-1\frac{3}{10}$

Wednesday; Because $-1\frac{3}{10}$ is farthest to the left on a number line.

Self-Assessment for Problem Solving

14. yes; $-0.12 < -0.11$
15. 3; *Sample answer:* -0.45 is farthest from 0.

Learning Target

Compare and order rational numbers.

Success Criteria

- Explain the meaning of a rational number.
- Graph rational numbers on a number line.
- Determine which of two rational numbers is greater.
- Order a set of rational numbers from least to greatest.

Review & Refresh

1. <	**2.** >
3. >	**4.** >
5. D	**6.** 60
7. 75	**8.** 175
9. 70	**10.** 1.59
11. 0.042	**12.** 17.9598
13. 25.69661	

Concepts, Skills, & Problem Solving

14.

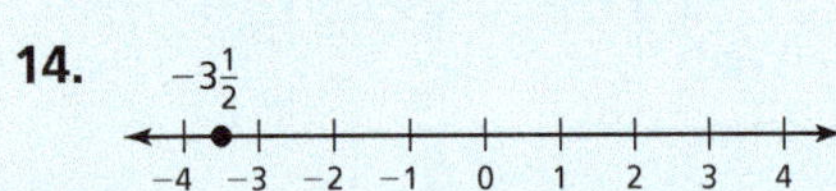

15.

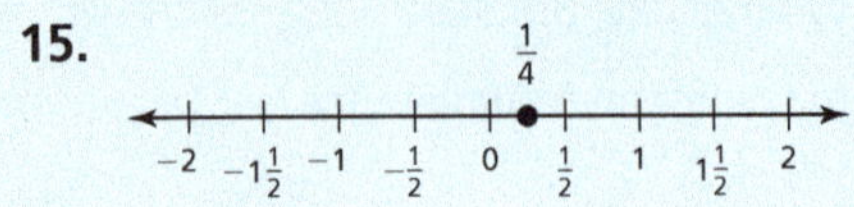

16.

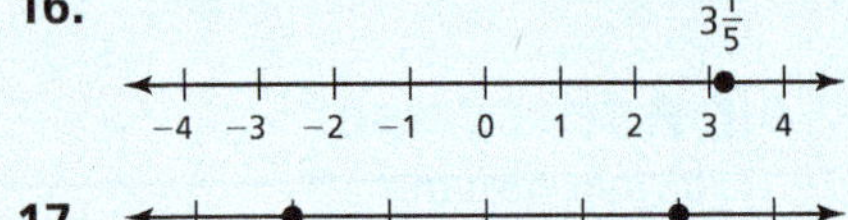

17. −1 $-\frac{2}{3}$ $-\frac{1}{3}$ 0 $\frac{1}{3}$ $\frac{2}{3}$ 1

18.

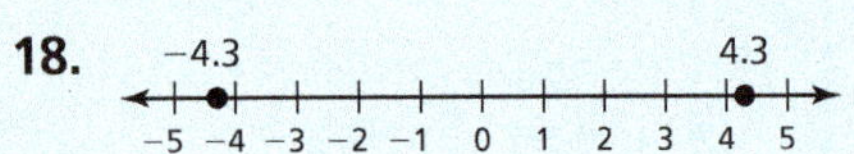

19.

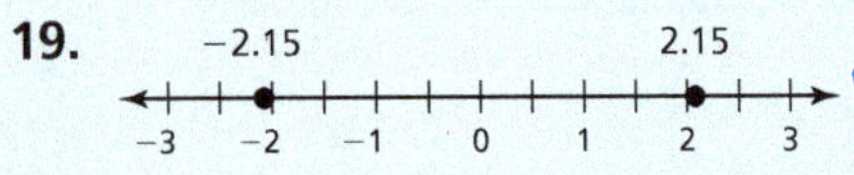

20.

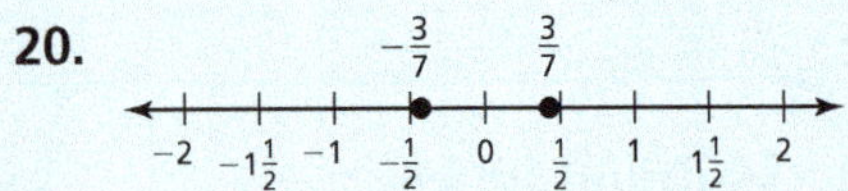

21.

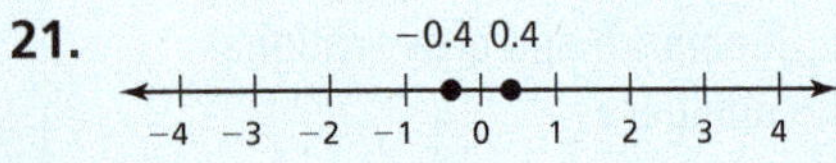

22.

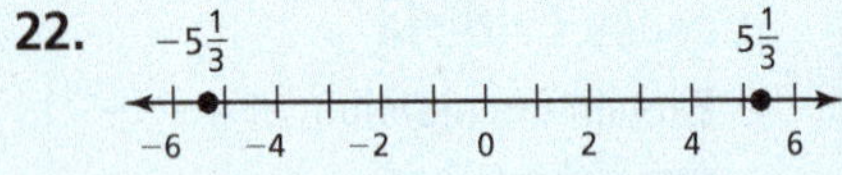

23.

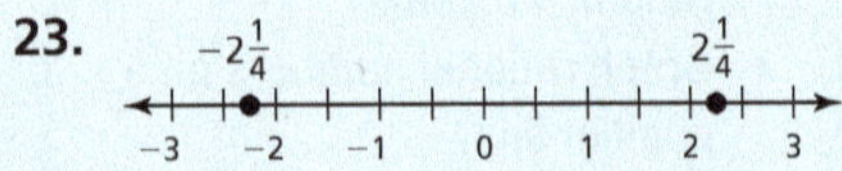

24. $-5\frac{3}{10}$ $5\frac{3}{10}$ (−6 −4 −2 0 2 3 6)

25. >	**26.** <
27. <	**28.** <
29. <	**30.** >
31. <	**32.** >
33. >	

34–39. See Additional Answers.

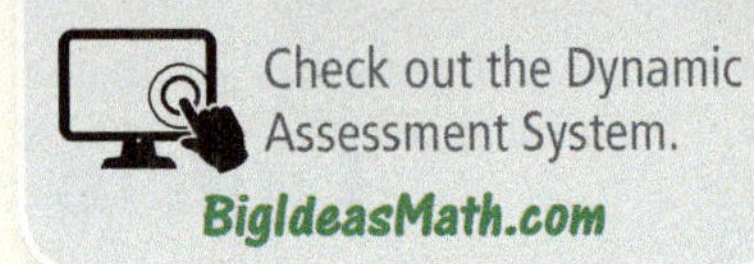

Assignment Guide and Concept Check

Scaffold assignments to support all students in their learning progression. The suggested assignments are a starting point. Continue to assign additional exercises and revisit with spaced practice to move every student toward proficiency.

Level	Assignment 1	Assignment 2
Emerging	2, 5, 8, 9, 13, 14, 17, 18, 25, 27, 30, 35, 37	29, 33, 36, 39, 40, 41, 42, 43
Proficient	2, 5, 8, 9, 13, 15, 18, 22, 26, 28, 30, 35, 38	40, 41, 42, 43
Advanced	2, 5, 8, 9, 13, 16, 19, 24, 26, 28, 33, 35, 39	42, 43, 44, 45

- Assignment 1 is for use after students complete the Self-Assessment for Concepts & Skills.
- Assignment 2 is for use after students complete the Self-Assessment for Problem Solving.
- The red exercises can be used as a concept check.

Review & Refresh Prior Skills

Exercises 1–4 Comparing Integers
Exercise 5 Comparing Rates
Exercises 6–9 Finding the Whole
Exercise 10 Multiplying Decimals and Whole Numbers
Exercises 11–13 Multiplying Decimals

Common Errors

- **Exercises 25–39** Students may ignore the signs of the numbers and order the numbers incorrectly. Encourage students to use a number line to determine which number is farthest to the right.
- **Exercises 37–39** Students may place the fractions in the wrong order. Encourage students to find a common denominator before ordering.

8.3 Practice

Review & Refresh

Copy and complete the statement using < or >.

1. 5 ▭ 8 **2.** -4 ▭ -7 **3.** 2 ▭ -5 **4.** 0 ▭ -3

5. You pay \$48 for 8 pounds of chicken. Which is an equivalent rate?

A. \$44 for 4 pounds **B.** \$28 for 4 pounds

C. \$15 for 3 pounds **D.** \$30 for 5 pounds

Find the whole.

6. 40% of what number is 24? **7.** 12% of what number is 9?

8. 48% of what number is 84? **9.** 140% of what number is 98?

Multiply.

10. 0.53×3 **11.** 0.06×0.7 **12.** 3.7×4.854 **13.** 2.9×8.8609

Concepts, Skills, & Problem Solving

MP USING TOOLS **Use a fraction or a mixed number to represent the time on a number line. Let 0 represent noon.** (See Exploration 1, p. 357.)

14. 8:30 A.M. **15.** 12:15 P.M. **16.** 3:12 P.M.

GRAPHING RATIONAL NUMBERS **Graph the number and its opposite.**

17. $\frac{2}{3}$ **18.** -4.3 **19.** 2.15 **20.** $-\frac{3}{7}$

21. -0.4 **22.** $5\frac{1}{3}$ **23.** $-2\frac{1}{4}$ **24.** $-5\frac{3}{10}$

COMPARING RATIONAL NUMBERS **Copy and complete the statement using < or >.**

25. $-3\frac{1}{3}$ ▭ $-3\frac{2}{3}$ **26.** $-\frac{1}{2}$ ▭ $-\frac{1}{6}$ **27.** $-\frac{3}{4}$ ▭ $\frac{5}{8}$

28. $-2\frac{2}{3}$ ▭ $-2\frac{1}{2}$ **29.** $-1\frac{5}{6}$ ▭ $-1\frac{3}{4}$ **30.** -4.6 ▭ -4.8

31. -0.12 ▭ -0.05 **32.** 2.41 ▭ -3.16 **33.** -3.524 ▭ -3.542

ORDERING RATIONAL NUMBERS **Order the numbers from least to greatest.**

34. $1.3, -2, -1.8, 0, -1.75$ **35.** $-4, -4.35, -4.9, -5, -4.3$

36. $1.6, 1.2, 0, 0.8, -0.1$ **37.** $-\frac{1}{2}, \frac{1}{8}, \frac{3}{4}, -1, -\frac{1}{4}$

38. $-2\frac{3}{10}, -2\frac{2}{5}, -2, -2\frac{1}{2}, -3$ **39.** $-\frac{1}{20}, -\frac{5}{8}, 0, -1, -\frac{3}{4}$

40. MP **MODELING REAL LIFE** In rough water, a small sand dollar burrows $-\frac{1}{2}$ centimeter into the sand. A larger sand dollar burrows $-1\frac{1}{4}$ centimeters into the sand. Which sand dollar burrowed deeper?

41. MP **MODELING REAL LIFE** Two golfers calculate their average scores relative to par over several rounds of golf. Golfer A has an average score of $-1\frac{1}{4}$. Golfer B has an average score of $-1\frac{3}{8}$. Who has the lesser average score?

42. MP **MODELING REAL LIFE** The *apparent magnitude* of a star measures how bright the star appears as seen from Earth. The brighter the star, the lesser the number. Which star is the brightest?

Star	Alpha Centauri	Antares	Canopus	Deneb	Sirius
Apparent Magnitude	−0.27	0.96	−0.72	1.25	−1.46

43. MP **REASONING** The daily water level relative to the pier is recorded for seven straight days at a tide station on the Big Marco River in Florida. On which days is the water level higher than on the previous day? On which days is it lower? Explain.

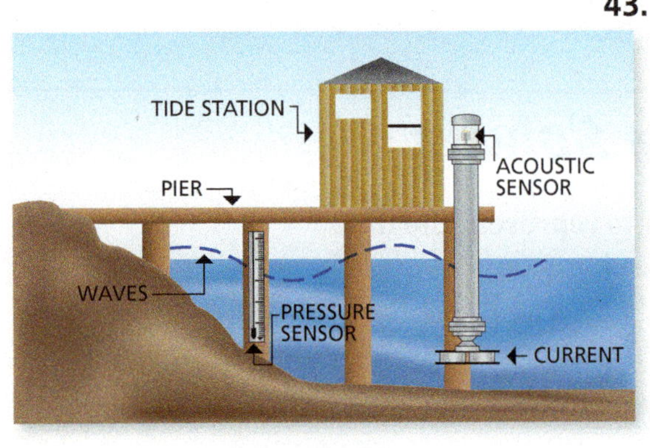

Day	Sun	Mon	Tues	Wed	Thurs	Fri	Sat
Water Level (feet)	$-\frac{3}{25}$	$-\frac{7}{20}$	$-\frac{27}{50}$	$-\frac{13}{20}$	$-\frac{16}{25}$	$-\frac{53}{100}$	$-\frac{1}{3}$

44. **DIG DEEPER!** A guitar tuner allows you to tune a guitar string to its correct pitch. The units on a tuner are measured in *cents*. The units tell you how far the string tone is above or below the correct pitch.

Guitar String	6	5	4	3	2	1
Number of Cents Away from the Correct Pitch	−0.3	1.6	−2.3	2.8	2.4	−3.6

a. What number on the tuner represents a correctly tuned guitar string?

b. Which strings have a pitch below the correct pitch?

c. Which string has a pitch closest to its correct pitch?

d. Which string has a pitch farthest from its correct pitch?

e. The tuner is rated to be accurate to within 0.5 cent of the true pitch. Which string could possibly be correct? Explain your reasoning.

45. MP **NUMBER SENSE** What integer values of x make the statement $-\frac{3}{x} < -\frac{x}{3}$ true?

Mini-Assessment

1. Graph -1.2 and its opposite.

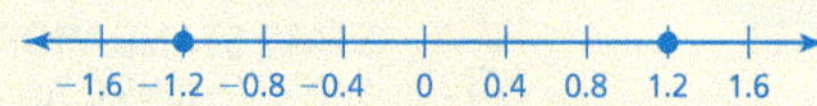

Copy and complete the statement using < or >.

2. -0.06 ▭ -0.1 $-0.06 > -0.1$

3. $-1\frac{1}{2}$ ▭ $-1\frac{1}{3}$ $-1\frac{1}{2} < -1\frac{1}{3}$

4. Order $1\frac{1}{3}, -\frac{5}{6}, 0, -\frac{2}{3}, -1$ from least to greatest. $-1, -\frac{5}{6}, -\frac{2}{3}, 0, 1\frac{1}{3}$

5. In a pond, a school of bass is $-2\frac{1}{3}$ feet from the surface of the pond. A school of trout is $-2\frac{3}{4}$ feet from the surface of the pond. Which school of fish is farther from the surface of the pond? school of trout

Section Resources

Surface Level	Deep Level
Resources by Chapter • Extra Practice • Reteach • Puzzle Time Student Journal • Self-Assessment • Practice Differentiating the Lesson Tutorial Videos Skills Review Handbook Skills Trainer	Resources by Chapter • Enrichment and Extension Graphic Organizers Dynamic Assessment System • Section Practice

Concepts, Skills, & Problem Solving

40. the larger sand dollar

41. Golfer B

42. Sirius

43. Higher on: Thursday, Friday, Saturday;
Lower on: Monday, Tuesday, Wednesday;
$-\frac{3}{25} > -\frac{7}{20} > -\frac{27}{50} > -\frac{13}{20}$,
$-\frac{13}{20} < -\frac{16}{25} < -\frac{53}{100} < -\frac{1}{3}$

44. a. 0
b. 1, 4, and 6
c. 6
d. 1
e. 6; $-0.5 < -0.3 < 0$

45. 1, 2, and any integer less than -3

Learning Target

Understand the concept of absolute value.

Success Criteria

- Find the absolute value of a number.
- Make comparisons that involve absolute values of numbers.
- Apply absolute value in real-life problems.

Warm Up

Cumulative, vocabulary, and prerequisite skills practice opportunities are available in the *Resources by Chapter* or at *BigIdeasMath.com*.

Teaching Strategy

Students may benefit from using a more robust number line made of clothesline. Make card tents with numbers to slide along the number line. This larger model is a great visual and physical teaching tool.

ELL Support

Explain that in everyday language the word *absolute* can be used in many ways. For example, absolute can be used to add emphasis or to describe unlimited power. In math, *absolute value* is the distance between a number and 0 on a number line. Both 10 and −10 have an absolute value of 10.

Exploration 1

a. 0; *Sample answer:* Find the distance of each object from sea level.

b–c. See Additional Answers.

Laurie's Notes

Preparing to Teach

- Students have compared and ordered rational numbers and will now use that understanding to discuss their distances from zero (**absolute value**).

Motivate

- **Teaching Strategy:** Have two students stand at the front of the room holding a piece of clothesline (or string) between them. Share that the distance between the two students is 10 units.
- Hold a piece of paper with the number 0 written on it and position yourself at various points along the line, so that the students have various values.
  - ? "If [Student A] is 3, what number is [Student B]?" −7 "Who is closer to me?" Student A "How far away from me is each person?" 3 units and 7 units
  - ? "If [Student A] is 5, what number is [Student B]?" −5 "Who is closer to me?" neither "How far away from me is each person?" 5 units
  - ? "If [Student A] is 8, what number is [Student B]?" −2 "Who is closer to me?" Student B "How far away from me is each person?" 8 units and 2 units
- ? Without the clothesline, ask, "What numbers are 4 units from 0?" 4 and −4
- Discuss positive and negative directions from 0 on a number line. For instance, it is possible to be 5 units from 0 in either direction.
- Attach the clothesline (or string) in the front of the room with the zero in place, so you can refer to it throughout the lesson.

Exploration 1

- ? "What does 500 feet below sea level mean?" 500 feet below the surface of the water. Remind students that if distances are below sea level, the numbers will be negative.
- After students have finished part (a), discuss their explanations.
- To support discussion, you can create a vertical model, using masking tape (placed on the wall) and index cards with the names of the objects written on them. Deciding on an appropriate scale and placing the cards in approximately the correct positions is a good exercise for students.
- ? "Which objects are closest to sea level?" bald eagle and leatherback turtle "Which objects are closest together?" leatherback turtle and U.S.S. Dolphin
- ? "As objects descend into the water, how do their elevations change?" Listen for language suggesting that the distances from sea level increase but the numbers are negative.
- **MP3 Construct Viable Arguments and Critique the Reasoning of Others:** In part (c), students will have different ways of explaining how far a vessel traveled. Elicit different methods from students. Knowing that their answers are correct, students are more apt to share their reasoning with classmates.
- ? **Extension:** Tell students the end location and how far the vessel moved. "Where did it start?" Listen for answers above and below the end location.

8.4 Absolute Value

Learning Target: Understand the concept of absolute value.

Success Criteria:
- I can find the absolute value of a number.
- I can make comparisons that involve absolute values of numbers.
- I can apply absolute value in real-life problems.

EXPLORATION 1 Comparing Positions of Objects

Work with a partner. The diagram shows the positions of several objects.

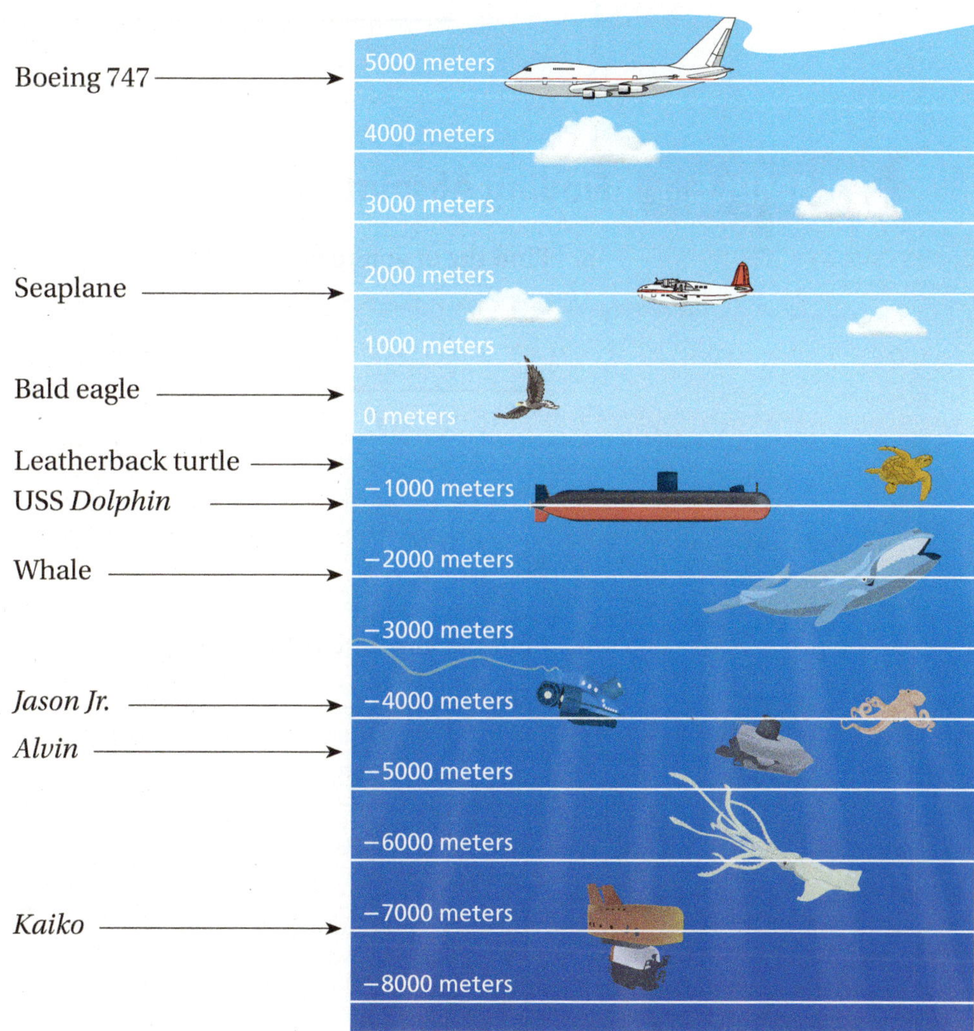

a. What integer represents sea level? How can you compare the positions of objects relative to sea level?

b. Which pairs of objects are the same distance from sea level? How do you know?

c. The vessels *Kaiko*, *Alvin*, and *Jason Jr.* move to be the same distance from sea level as the Boeing 747. About how many meters did each vessel travel?

Math Practice

Understand Quantities

What do positive numbers represent in the problem? What do negative numbers represent?

8.4 Lesson

Key Vocabulary
absolute value, *p. 364*

Key Idea

Absolute Value

Words The **absolute value** of a number is the distance between the number and 0 on a number line. The absolute value of a number a is written as $|a|$.

Numbers $|-2| = 2$ $|2| = 2$

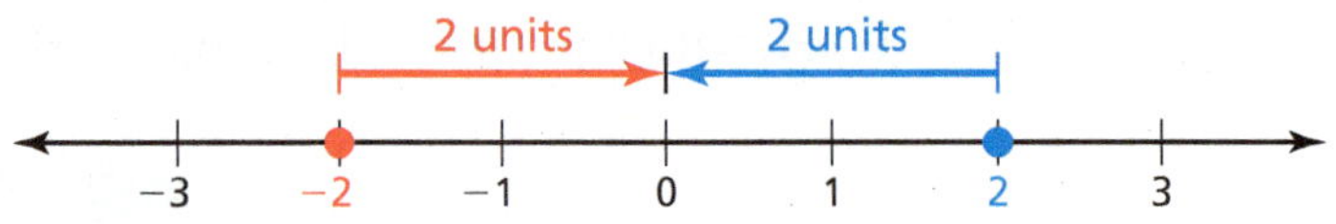

EXAMPLE 1 Finding Absolute Value

a. Find the absolute value of 3.

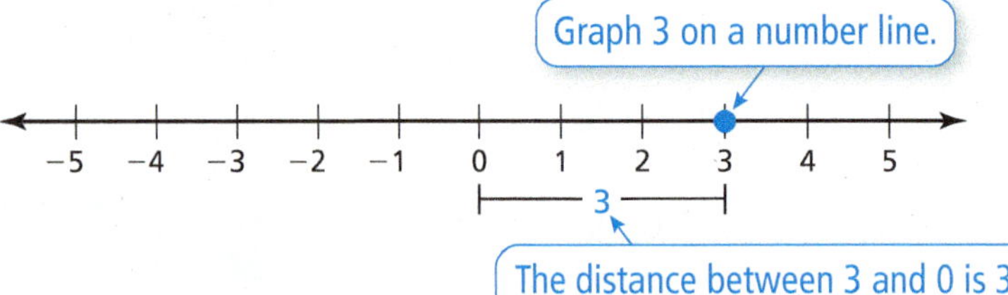

So, $|3| = 3$.

b. Find the absolute value of $-2\frac{1}{2}$.

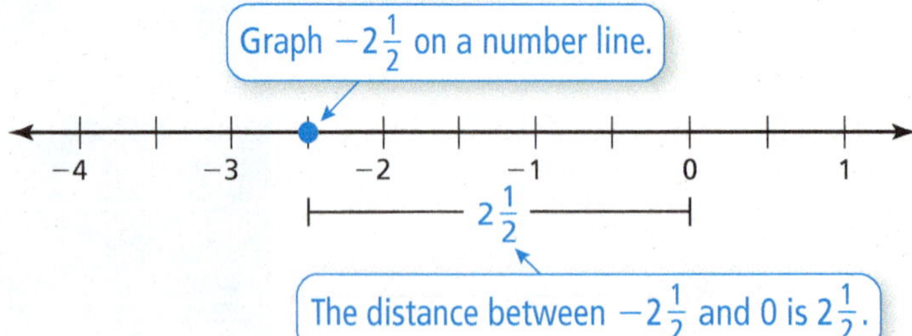

So, $\left|-2\frac{1}{2}\right| = 2\frac{1}{2}$.

Try It **Find the absolute value.**

1. $|8|$
2. $|-6|$
3. $|0|$
4. $\left|\frac{1}{4}\right|$
5. $\left|-7\frac{1}{3}\right|$
6. $|-12.9|$

Multi-Language Glossary at *BigIdeasMath.com*

Laurie's Notes

Scaffolding Instruction

- Students need to understand the relationships between position on a number line, distance from zero, and the absolute value of a number. Be sure to clarify the difference between the *opposite* and the *absolute value* of a number.
- **Emerging:** Students may be struggling with finding distances from zero, finding distances from other numbers, or placing negative numbers on a number line. These students will benefit from guided instruction for the examples.
- **Proficient:** Students showed evidence of understanding absolute value in the exploration. Review the Key Idea and then have students proceed to Try It Exercises 7–10.

Key Idea

- Write the Key Idea on the board.
- $|a|$ is read, "the absolute value of *a*."
- Stress that the **absolute value** of a number is the *distance* between the number and 0. Distance is a positive number or 0. Although directed distances are addressed in science, the concept of distance here is that it is a positive number or 0.
- **MP6 Attend to Precision:** Students may incorrectly say, "Absolute value just makes the number positive." Be sure that students correctly refer to the absolute value of a number as the distance the number is from 0.
- Point out that when you write the notation for the absolute value, it means to take the absolute value of the number inside the symbols.

EXAMPLE 1

- Work through each part to help students gain understanding of the first success criterion.
- **Common Misconception:** Students may say, "Absolute values are always positive." This statement can cause problems when students find $|0|$, which is 0.
- **Extension:** "What is the absolute value of -6.4?" 6.4
- Remind students that the position of a number is its location on a number line, such as -4. The distance from 0 to -4 is 4, because distance cannot be a negative number of units. The absolute value of -4 is 4, because absolute value is the distance between the number and 0.

Try It

- **Common Error:** Students may incorrectly find that the absolute value of a negative number is negative.

Scaffold instruction to support all students in their learning. Learning is individualized and you may want to group students differently as they move in and out of these levels with each skill and concept. Student self-assessment and feedback help guide your instructional decisions about how and when to layer support for all students to become proficient learners.

Extra Example 1

a. Find the absolute value of -8. 8

b. Find the absolute value of 3.3. 3.3

ELL Support

Have students practice language by working in pairs to complete Try It Exercises 1–6. Have one student ask the other, "What is the absolute value?" Have students switch roles for each exercise.

Beginner: Write the absolute value.

Intermediate: State the absolute value. For example, "eight."

Advanced: Answer using a complete sentence. For example, "The absolute value of eight is eight."

Try It

1. 8
2. 6
3. 0
4. $\frac{1}{4}$
5. $7\frac{1}{3}$
6. 12.9

Laurie's Notes

Extra Example 2

a. Compare $|-10|$ and 4. $|-10| > 4$

b. Compare 4.3 and $|-4.3|$. $4.3 = |-4.3|$

Try It

7. >
8. <
9. <
10. =

Self-Assessment for Concepts & Skills

11. >
12. <
13. <
14. What integer is 3 units to the left of 0?; -3; 3

EXAMPLE 2

- Explain that one way to compare numbers is to graph the numbers on a number line. The farther to the right a number is, the greater it is. The farther to the left a number is, the less it is. You may want to use the clothesline to demonstrate.

? "What is $|-5|$?" 5

- **Common Error:** Students may graph $|-5|$ at -5. Explain that you find the absolute value of the number first and then graph it.
- Note that it is also correct to conclude that $|-5| > 2$ and $-1 < |3.5|$.

Try It

Think-Pair-Share: Students should read the exercises independently and then work in pairs to complete the exercises. Then have each pair compare their answers with another pair and discuss any discrepancies. Students are progressing towards the second success criterion.

Self-Assessment for Concepts & Skills

Students have been practicing the first two success criteria and can now assess themselves in those areas.

- As students work, notice their proficiency with Exercise 14. Remind them that they can use a number line as an aid. Later, you may want to group those who struggled with Exercise 14 for a short reteaching of the different words used to denote numbers and their opposites.
- **Teaching Strategy:** After students complete the exercises independently, they can discuss their answers with a partner. Select a few students to explain their reasoning using the clothesline at the front of the class.

ELL Support

Allow students to work in pairs. Check comprehension of Exercises 11–13 by using thumbs up for *greater than*, thumbs down for *less than*, or thumbs sideways for *equal to*. Have two pairs form a group to discuss and answer Exercise 14. Have each group present their responses to the class.

The Success Criteria Self-Assessment chart can be found in the *Student Journal* or online at *BigIdeasMath.com*.

EXAMPLE 2 Comparing Values

a. Compare 2 and $|-5|$.

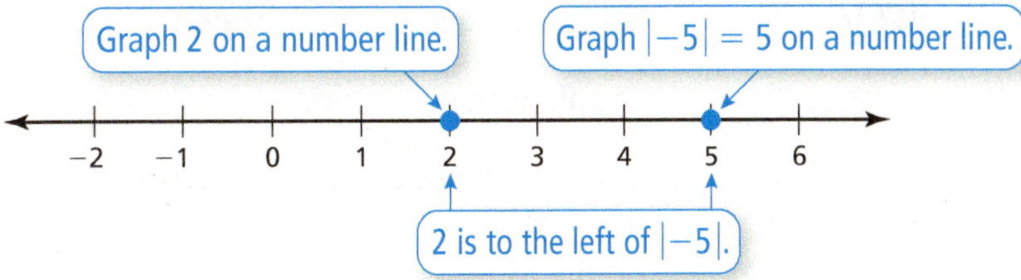

So, $2 < |-5|$.

b. Compare $|3.5|$ and -1.

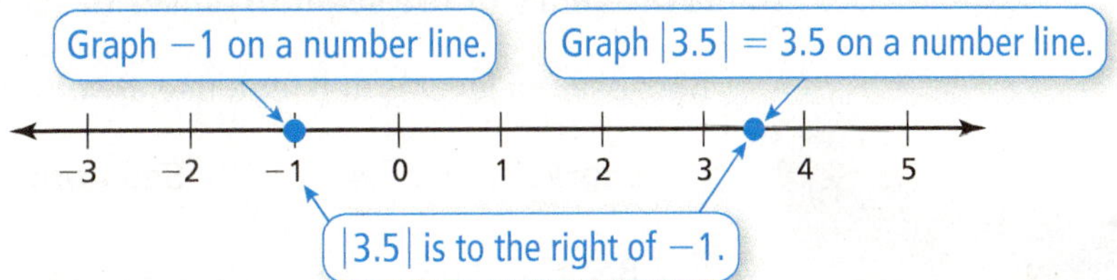

So, $|3.5| > -1$.

Try It **Copy and complete the statement using <, >, or =.**

7. $|-4|$ ▭ -2

8. -5 ▭ $|5|$

9. $|9|$ ▭ 10

10. 3.9 ▭ $|-3.9|$

Self-Assessment for Concepts & Skills

Solve each exercise. Then rate your understanding of the success criteria in your journal.

COMPARING VALUES **Copy and complete the statement using <, >, or =.**

11. $|-6|$ ▭ 3

12. $|-3.5|$ ▭ 4

13. $3\frac{1}{2}$ ▭ $\left|-4\frac{3}{4}\right|$

14. DIFFERENT WORDS, SAME QUESTION Which is different? Find "both" answers.

How far is -3 from 0?

What integer is 3 units to the left of 0?

What is the absolute value of -3?

What is the distance between -3 and 0?

EXAMPLE 3 Modeling Real Life

Animal	Elevation (feet)
Shark	−4
Sea lion	5
Seagull	56
Shrimp	−65
Turtle	−22

The table shows the elevations of several animals.

a. Which animal is the deepest? Explain.

Graph each elevation.

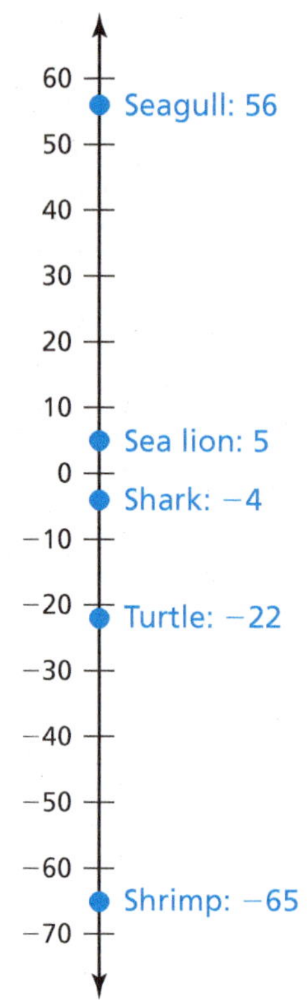

The lowest elevation represents the animal that is the deepest. The integer that is lowest on the number line is −65.

So, the shrimp is the deepest.

b. Is the shark or the sea lion closer to sea level?

Because sea level is at 0 feet, use absolute values.

Shark: $|-4| = 4$ **Sea lion:** $|5| = 5$

Because 4 is less than 5, the shark is closer to sea level than the sea lion.

Self-Assessment for Problem Solving

Solve each exercise. Then rate your understanding of the success criteria in your journal.

15. Describe the position of an object in your classroom using a negative rational number. Then describe the position of a second object using a positive rational number. Which number has a greater absolute value? What does this mean?

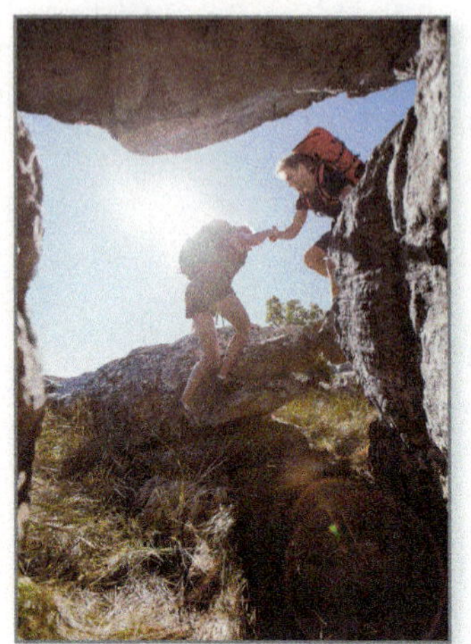

16. **DIG DEEPER!** The table shows the elevations of several checkpoints along a hiking trail.

Checkpoint	1	2	3	4	5
Elevation (feet)	110	38	−24	12	−142

a. Which checkpoint is farthest from sea level?

b. Which checkpoint is closest to sea level?

c. Between which pairs of checkpoints must you reach sea level? Could you reach sea level between any other pair of checkpoints? Explain your reasoning.

Laurie's Notes

EXAMPLE 3

- Discuss the number line. Make sure students observe that, for instance, −22 is below −20. It is not uncommon for students to graph −22 above −20 because 22 is above 20.
- Work through each part of the problem knowing that students are practicing the third success criterion.
- Make a connection to the exploration, in which the term *absolute value* was not used.
- **Extension:** "Is the seagull or the shrimp closer to sea level? Explain." seagull; Because $|56|$ is less than $|-65|$.

Self-Assessment for Problem Solving

- Students may benefit from trying the exercises independently and then working with a partner to refine their work. It is important to provide time in class for problem solving, so that students become comfortable with the problem-solving plan.
- Listen to students' explanations as you circulate. Select a few students with varied reasoning to share with the class and invite students to ask questions.
- **MP6 Attend to Precision:** When justifying their answers, students need to have a command of the terms *absolute value, position,* and *rational.* Listen to their explanations and notice if the students listening understand as well. Part (c) of Exercise 16 requires students to think logically and be able to relate their ideas to others.
- Students are assessing their understanding of the third success criterion.

The Success Criteria Self-Assessment chart can be found in the *Student Journal* or online at *BigIdeasMath.com.*

Closure

- **Exit Ticket:** Order the values from least to greatest.

$|-12|, -8, -10, |6|, |-4|$ $\quad -10, -8, |-4|, |6|, |-12|$

Extra Example 3

The table shows the elevations of a bird and a fish. Is the bird or the fish closer to sea level?

Animal	Elevation (ft)
Bird	10
Fish	−9

fish

Self-Assessment for Problem Solving

15. Answers will vary. Listen for students to identify one object, then a second object above the first.

16. **a.** 5

b. 4

c. 2 and 3, 3 and 4, 4 and 5; yes; You could reach sea level between checkpoints 1 and 2. The trail could go below sea level and come back up to 38.

Learning Target

Understand the concept of absolute value.

Success Criteria

- Find the absolute value of a number.
- Make comparisons that involve absolute values of numbers.
- Apply absolute value in real-life problems.

Review & Refresh

1. $-3.2, -1.8, -1.3, 0.6, 2.4$
2. $-1.5, -0.3, 0, 0.7, 2.2$
3. $\frac{1}{4}, \frac{1}{2}, \frac{2}{3}, \frac{3}{4}, 2$
4. $-2\frac{3}{4}, -2\frac{1}{2}, \frac{1}{5}, \frac{4}{5}, 1\frac{2}{5}$
5. 

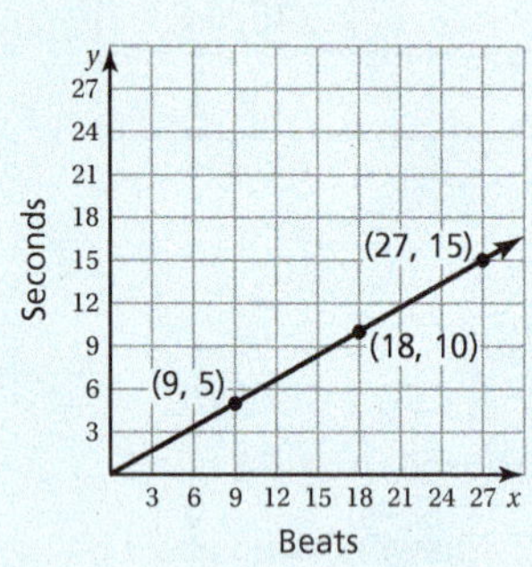

6. See Additional Answers.
7. 13
8. 1
9. 4
10. 40

Concepts, Skills, & Problem Solving

11. dolphin; $|-22| > |-13|$
12. seagull; $|12| > |-4|$
13. shark; $|-40| > |32|$
14. 2
15. 23
16. 11
17. 68
18. 8.35
19. $\frac{1}{6}$
20. 14.06
21. $\frac{5}{8}$
22. $3\frac{2}{5}$
23. 1.026
24. $1\frac{1}{3}$
25. 6.308
26. $-10, 10$
27. no; $|14| = 14$
28. <
29. =
30. >
31. <
32. >
33. >
34. >
35. <
36. <

Check out the Dynamic Assessment System.
BigIdeasMath.com

Assignment Guide and Concept Check

Scaffold assignments to support all students in their learning progression. The suggested assignments are a starting point. Continue to assign additional exercises and revisit with spaced practice to move every student toward proficiency.

Level	Assignment 1	Assignment 2
Emerging	2, 4, 6, 9, 12, 14, 20, 27, 29, 30, 31, 38	18, 19, 24, 26, 32, 34, 37, 39, 42, 46
Proficient	2, 4, 6, 9, 12, 18, 19, 26, 27, 29, 31, 32, 40	24, 25, 35, 36, 37, 41, 43, 45, 46, 47, 48, 49, 50, 51
Advanced	2, 4, 6, 9, 13, 20, 22, 26, 27, 34, 35, 36, 41	37, 44, 45, 46, 47, 48, 49, 50, 52, 53

- Assignment 1 is for use after students complete the Self-Assessment for Concepts & Skills.
- Assignment 2 is for use after students complete the Self-Assessment for Problem Solving.
- The red exercises can be used as a concept check.

Review & Refresh Prior Skills

Exercises 1–4 Ordering Rational Numbers
Exercises 5 and 6 Graphing Ratio Relationships
Exercises 7–10 Evaluating Expressions

Common Errors

- **Exercises 14–25** Students may think the absolute value of a number is its opposite. For example, students may think $|8| = -8$. Use a number line to remind students that absolute value is a number's distance from zero, so it is always a positive number or zero.
- **Exercises 28–36** Students may ignore the absolute value bars when comparing values. Encourage students to graph the values on a number line, as shown in Example 3, to help them correctly compare the values.

8.4 Practice

Go to **BigIdeasMath.com** to get HELP with solving the exercises.

Review & Refresh

Order the numbers from least to greatest.

1. 2.4, −3.2, −1.8, 0.6, −1.3
2. −0.3, 0.7, −1.5, 0, 2.2
3. $\frac{3}{4}, \frac{1}{2}, \frac{2}{3}, 2, \frac{1}{4}$
4. $\frac{1}{5}, 1\frac{2}{5}, -2\frac{3}{4}, \frac{4}{5}, -2\frac{1}{2}$

Represent the ratio relationship using a graph.

5.

Beats	9	18	27
Seconds	5	10	15

6.

Yogurt (ounces)	7	14	21
Granola (ounces)	3	6	9

Evaluate the expression when $a = 2$, $b = 5$, and $c = 8$.

7. $5 + c$
8. $b - 4$
9. $\frac{c}{a}$
10. $b \cdot c$

Concepts, Skills, & Problem Solving

COMPARING POSITIONS OF OBJECTS **Tell which object is farther from sea level. Explain your reasoning.** (See Exploration 1, p. 363.)

11. Scuba diver: −15 m
    Dolphin: −22 m
12. Seagull: 12 m
    School of fish: −4 m
13. Shark: −40 m
    Flag on a ship: 32 m

FINDING ABSOLUTE VALUE **Find the absolute value.**

14. $|-2|$
15. $|23|$
16. $|11|$
17. $|-68|$
18. $|-8.35|$
19. $\left|\frac{1}{6}\right|$
20. $|14.06|$
21. $\left|-\frac{5}{8}\right|$
22. $\left|-3\frac{2}{5}\right|$
23. $|1.026|$
24. $\left|1\frac{1}{3}\right|$
25. $|-6.308|$

26. **MP REASONING** Write two integers that have an absolute value of 10.

27. **MP YOU BE THE TEACHER** Your friend finds the absolute value of 14. Is your friend correct? Explain your reasoning.

COMPARING VALUES **Copy and complete the statement using <, >, or =.**

28. $6 \; \square \; |-8|$
29. $|-3| \; \square \; 3$
30. $|-4.3| \; \square \; 3.4$
31. $\frac{1}{5} \; \square \; \left|-\frac{2}{9}\right|$
32. $|-0.05| \; \square \; 0$
33. $|-5.5| \; \square \; |-3.1|$
34. $\frac{3}{4} \; \square \; \left|-\frac{2}{5}\right|$
35. $|-6.8| \; \square \; |8.25|$
36. $-12 \; \square \; |12|$

37. MP **MODELING REAL LIFE** The table shows the change in the balance of a bank account after each of three transactions. Which transaction has the greatest effect on the balance of the account? Which transaction has the least effect on the balance of the account?

Transaction	Change (dollars)
1	14.72
2	−15.36
3	−38.75

ORDERING VALUES **Order the values from least to greatest.**

38. $5, 0, |-1|, |4|, -2$

39. $|-3|, |5|, -3, -4, |-4|$

40. $10, |-6|, 9, |3|, -11, 0$

41. $-18, |30|, -19, |-22|, -20, |-18|$

SIMPLIFYING EXPRESSIONS **Simplify the expression.**

42. $-|2|$

43. $-|6|$

44. $-|-1|$

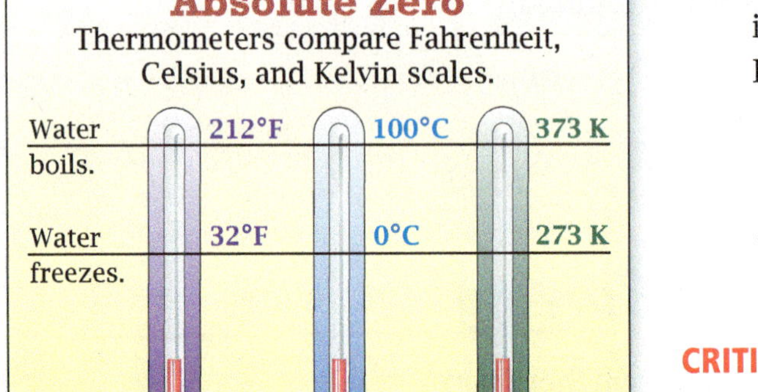

45. MP **REASONING** The coldest possible temperature is called *absolute zero*. It is represented by 0 K on the Kelvin temperature scale.

   a. Which temperature is closer to 0 K: 32°F or −50°C?

   b. What do absolute values and temperatures on the Kelvin scale have in common?

CRITICAL THINKING **Tell whether the statement is *always*, *sometimes*, or *never* true. Explain.**

46. The absolute value of a number is greater than the number.

47. The absolute value of a negative number is positive.

48. The absolute value of a positive number is its opposite.

MATCHING **Match the account balance with the debt that it represents. Explain your reasoning.**

49. account balance = −\$25

50. account balance < −\$25

51. account balance > −\$25

A. debt > \$25

B. debt = \$25

C. debt < \$25

52. MP **PATTERNS** A *palindrome* is a word or sentence that reads the same forward as it does backward.

   a. Graph and label the following points on a number line: $A = -2$, $C = -1$, $E = 0$, $R = -3$. Then, using the same letters as the original points, graph and label the absolute value of each point on the *same* number line.

   b. What word do the letters spell? Is this a palindrome?

   c. Assign letters to points on a number line to make up your own palindrome using the process in part (a).

53. **CRITICAL THINKING** Find values of x and y so that $|x| < |y|$ and $x > y$.

For Your Information

- **Exercise 45** The Kelvin temperature scale does not use a degree symbol.
- **Exercise 52** Spaces and punctuation can be adjusted in a palindrome.

Common Errors

- **Exercises 38–41** Students may ignore the absolute value bars when ordering values. Encourage students to graph the values on a number line, as shown in Example 3, to help them correctly order the values.
- **Exercises 42 and 43** Students may misinterpret the opposite of an absolute value as the absolute value of the opposite. For example, they may think $-|2| = |-2|$, so $-|2| = 2$. Remind students to use the order of operations and that absolute value bars are a grouping symbol.
- **Exercise 44** Students may treat the absolute value bars as parentheses and write $-|-1| = 1$. Remind students that $-|-1|$ is read as "the opposite of the absolute value of negative 1" and that they should find the absolute value first.

Mini-Assessment

Find the absolute value.

1. $|-83|$ 83
2. $|38|$ 38

Copy and complete the statement using <, >, or =.

3. -2 ▢ $|-3|$ $-2 < |-3|$
4. 8 ▢ $|-8|$ $8 = |-8|$
5. The freezing point of airplane fuel is $-53°C$ and the freezing point of candle wax is $55°C$. Which is closer to the freezing point of water, $0°C$? the freezing point of airplane fuel

Section Resources

Surface Level	Deep Level
Resources by Chapter • Extra Practice • Reteach • Puzzle Time Student Journal • Self-Assessment • Practice Differentiating the Lesson Tutorial Videos Skills Review Handbook Skills Trainer	Resources by Chapter • Enrichment and Extension Graphic Organizers Dynamic Assessment System • Section Practice
Transfer Level	
Dynamic Assessment System • Mid-Chapter Quiz	Assessment Book • Mid-Chapter Quiz

Concepts, Skills, & Problem Solving

37. 3; 1
38. $-2, 0, |-1|, |4|, 5$
39. $-4, -3, |-3|, |-4|, |5|$
40. $-11, 0, |3|, |-6|, 9, 10$
41. $-20, -19, -18, |-18|, |-22|, |30|$
42. -2
43. -6
44. -1
45. **a.** $-50°C$

    b. neither can be negative
46. sometimes; If the number is negative then its absolute value is greater, but if the number is positive or zero then it is equal to its absolute value.
47. always; The absolute value is the positive distance from zero on a number line.
48. never; The absolute value of a positive number is the number itself.
49. B; You owe \$25, so debt = \$25.
50. A; You owe more than \$25, so debt > \$25.
51. C; You owe less than \$25, so debt < \$25.
52. **a.**

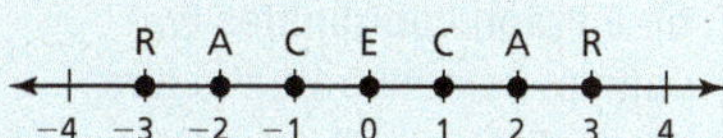

    b. racecar; yes

    c. *Sample answer:*

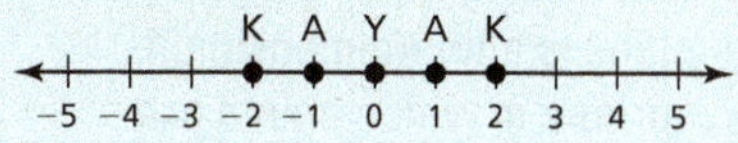

53. *Sample answer:* $x = -2, y = -3$

Laurie's Notes

STATE STANDARDS
6.NS.C.6b, 6.NS.C.6c,
6.NS.C.8

Learning Target

Plot and reflect ordered pairs in all four quadrants of a coordinate plane.

Success Criteria

- Identify ordered pairs in a coordinate plane.
- Plot ordered pairs in a coordinate plane and describe their locations.
- Reflect points in the x-axis, the y-axis, or both axes.
- Apply plotting points in all four quadrants to solve real-life problems.

Warm Up

Cumulative, vocabulary, and prerequisite skills practice opportunities are available in the *Resources by Chapter* or at *BigIdeasMath.com*.

ELL Support

Remind students that the words *coordinate* and *plane* have multiple meanings. When you match clothing colors, you coordinate clothes. A point on a graph coordinates two values. Demonstrate the two pronunciations of *coordinate* and have students repeat. Students may know a plane as a vehicle that flies. In math, a coordinate plane is a two-dimensional surface in which points are plotted. They may know the word *plot* as a story line from Language Arts. In math, it means to draw points in a coordinate plane.

Exploration 1

a–c. See Additional Answers.

Preparing to Teach

- In the previous course and in Section 6.4, students plotted ordered pairs in the first quadrant. Students will expand this prior knowledge and their understanding of plotting rational numbers on horizontal and vertical number lines to plot ordered pairs in all four quadrants of a coordinate plane.
- **MP7 Look for and Make Use of Structure:** Mathematically proficient students make use of patterns when plotting ordered pairs. Students recognize the relationship between plotting (a, b), $(a, -b)$, $(-a, b)$, and $(-a, -b)$.
- The Motivate and Exploration introduce the first three success criteria.

Motivate

- **Teaching Strategy:** Create a coordinate grid on the floor. Use two strips of masking tape laid perpendicular to one another. Use a thick marker to mark the axes, leaving 1–1.5 feet between each label. Write each of the following points on a large piece of paper: $(3, 2)$, $(-3, 2)$, $(-3, -2)$, $(3, -2)$.
- Ask four students to volunteer. Have each student start at the origin and face towards the positive y-axis. Give the following directions:
  - **Student 1:** Move 3 spaces to the right and forward 2 spaces.
  - **Student 2:** Move 3 spaces to the left and forward 2 spaces.
  - **Student 3:** Move 3 spaces to the left and back 2 spaces.
  - **Student 4:** Move 3 spaces to the right and back 2 spaces.
- ? "What figure is formed if you connect each student in order with a piece of string?" a rectangle
- ? "Which direction did I ask the students to move first?" left or right (x) "Which direction did I ask the students to move second?" forward or backward (y) Stress that the order in which you plot points is important.

Exploration 1

- ? As you circulate, ask, "How can you include negative numbers on the x-axis? the y-axis?" *Sample answers:* Extend the x-axis line to the left as a horizontal number line; Extend the y-axis line below as a vertical number line.
- You may need to remind students of how they graphed negative numbers on both horizontal and vertical number lines.
- **Common Error:** Students may interchange the x- and y-coordinates.
- If the **coordinate plane** on the floor isn't visible to all students, draw a coordinate plane on the board. Part (b) contains important concepts for students to discover as they look at each region of the coordinate plane.
- In part (c), students begin exploring reflections in the coordinate plane. Make sure students realize there are reflections in more than one direction. Listen to their reasoning. You want students to see the relationships between the coordinates when the ordered pair is reflected into another **quadrant**.
- ? **Extension:** "What real-life situations use coordinates to locate points?" *Sample answers:* maps, board games (Battleship), longitude and latitude.

8.5 The Coordinate Plane

Learning Target: Plot and reflect ordered pairs in all four quadrants of a coordinate plane.

Success Criteria:
- I can identify ordered pairs in a coordinate plane.
- I can plot ordered pairs in a coordinate plane and describe their locations.
- I can reflect points in the x-axis, the y-axis, or both axes.
- I can apply plotting points in all four quadrants to solve real-life problems.

EXPLORATION 1 Extending the Coordinate Plane

Work with a partner. Previously, you plotted points with positive coordinates in a coordinate plane like the one shown at the right.

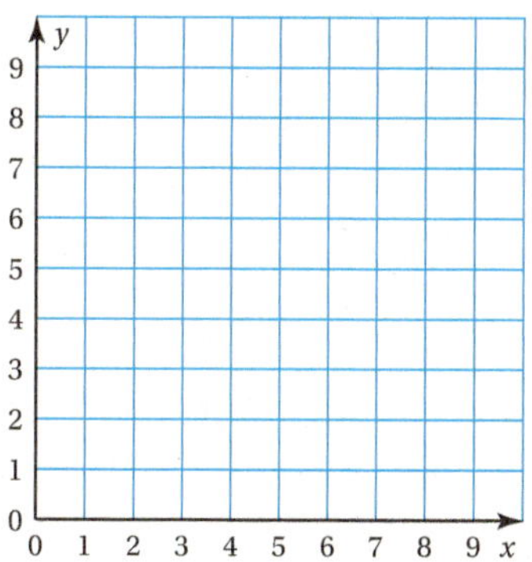

a. You can also plot points in which one or both of the coordinates are negative numbers. Create ordered pairs with different combinations of positive and negative coordinates, as described below. Then plot the ordered pairs and explain how you extended the coordinate plane shown.

(positive, positive) (negative, positive)

(negative, negative) (positive, negative)

b. How many regions of the coordinate plane are created by the x-axis and y-axis? What do the points in each of these regions have in common?

c. The photo shows the *reflection*, or mirror image, of a mountain in a lake. When you fold the photo on its axis, the mountain and its reflection align.

Plot a point and its *reflection* in one of the axes. Explain your reasoning. What do you notice about the coordinates of the points?

Math Practice

Check Progress
How can you check your progress to make sure you are reflecting your point correctly?

8.5 Lesson

Key Vocabulary
coordinate plane, *p. 370*
origin, *p. 370*
quadrants, *p. 370*

Previously, you plotted points with positive coordinates. Now, you will plot points with positive and negative coordinates.

The Coordinate Plane

A **coordinate plane** is formed by the intersection of a horizontal number line and a vertical number line. The number lines intersect at the **origin** and separate the coordinate plane into four regions called **quadrants**.

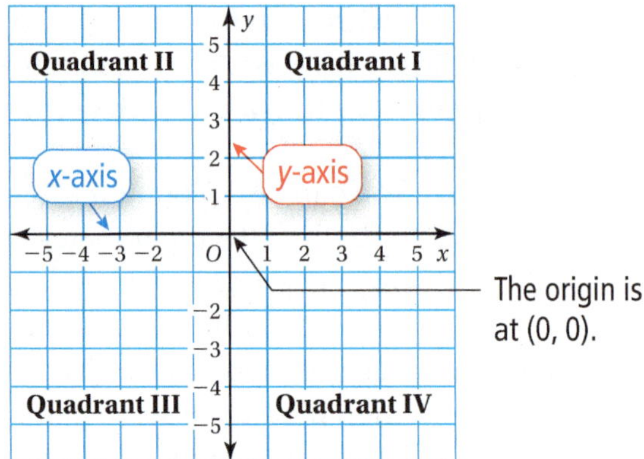

An *ordered pair* is used to locate a point in a coordinate plane.

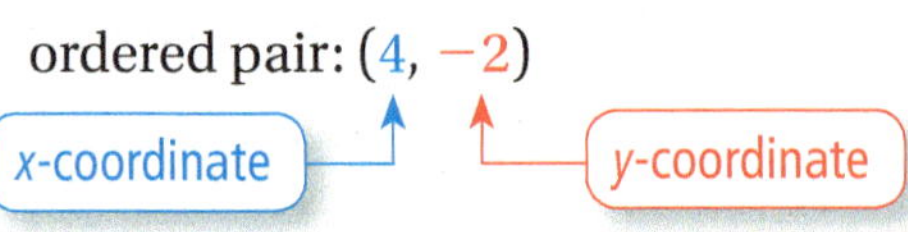

EXAMPLE 1 Identifying an Ordered Pair

Which ordered pair corresponds to Point T?

A. $(-3, -3)$ **B.** $(-3, 3)$

C. $(3, -3)$ **D.** $(3, 3)$

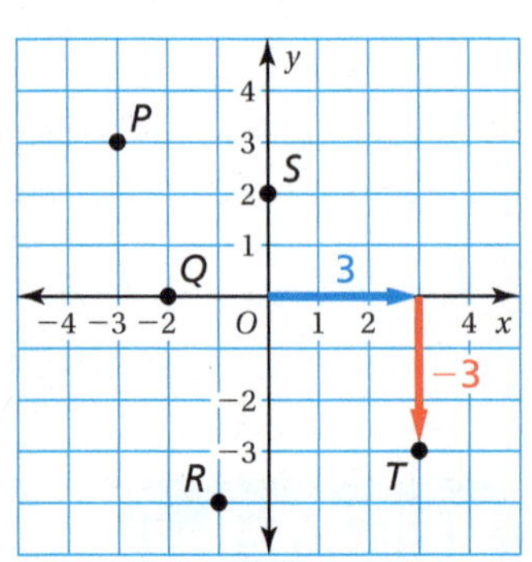

Point T is 3 units to the right of the origin and 3 units down. So, the x-coordinate is 3 and the y-coordinate is -3.

The ordered pair $(3, -3)$ corresponds to Point T. The correct answer is **C**.

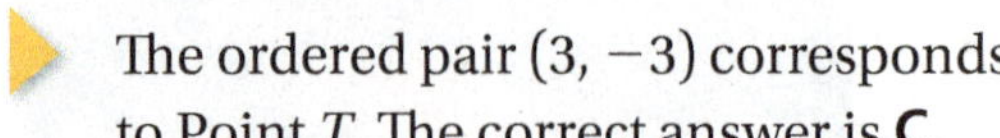

Use the graph in Example 1 to write an ordered pair corresponding to the point.

1. Point P **2.** Point Q **3.** Point R **4.** Point S

Laurie's Notes

Scaffolding Instruction

- As you formalize vocabulary surrounding the coordinate plane, students will investigate characteristics of ordered pairs and useful applications.
- **Emerging:** Students may confuse the *x*- and *y*-coordinates or have difficulty generalizing the signs of the ordered pairs in the four quadrants. The examples offer more practice with the first three success criteria.
- **Proficient:** Students can identify and plot ordered pairs. They can use their understanding of the coordinate plane to predict positions after reflections. After reviewing the Key Idea, have students proceed to the Self-Assessment exercises.

Key Idea

- It is important to have a model of the coordinate *grid* versus only a model of scaled axes. The grid is essential in helping students understand that a point is plotted by moving in two directions (horizontal and vertical). You may want to project a coordinate grid, if possible, on the wall or board.
- Use the model of the coordinate grid to identify important vocabulary: **coordinate plane**, **origin**, **quadrants**, *x*-axis, *y*-axis, and ordered pair.
  - **MP6 Attend to Precision**: These terms will be used throughout students' future mathematics courses. Students need to be comfortable using these terms, so that they become a staple in mathematical discussions.
- **Connections:** To help students remember which way is horizontal, hold your arms out horizontally and relate them to the horizon. Origin means "where something starts." If your students have played the game of *four square*, relate the quadrants to the four square court.
- Stress that the ordered pairs (2, 4) and (4, 2) are not the same. The order matters and the ordered pairs are always (*x*, *y*).

EXAMPLE 1

- The colored arrows on the diagram will help students plot in the *x*-direction first, followed by the *y*-direction.
- **Teaching Strategy:** If students are having difficulty, place a piece of paper with a "*T*" written on it on the floor coordinate grid at (3, −3). Have a volunteer stand at the origin facing the positive *y*-axis and ask others to give directions, similar to the Motivate, to guide the volunteer to the "*T*." Students should say, "move 3 spaces to the right and back 3 spaces."

Try It

- Ask if there are any questions. Then have students work independently to write the ordered pairs for the remaining points, *P*, *Q*, *R*, and *S*. Ask volunteers to present their answers to the class.

ELL Support

Have students practice language by working in pairs to complete Try It Exercises 1–4. Have one student ask the other to describe the location of the points. Have partners alternate roles for each exercise.

Beginner: Write the ordered pair.

Intermediate/Advanced: Answer using phrases such as, "negative three, three."

Scaffold instruction to support all students in their learning. Learning is individualized and you may want to group students differently as they move in and out of these levels with each skill and concept. Student self-assessment and feedback help guide your instructional decisions about how and when to layer support for all students to become proficient learners.

Teaching Strategy

A floor coordinate grid allows students to be physical in plotting points. Students will recognize the order of plotting points and use that order to direct the movement of others. A floor coordinate grid can also be used to find reflections of points. This larger model is a great visual and kinesthetic teaching tool.

Extra Example 1

Which ordered pair corresponds to Point *P*?

A. (−3, −2) **B.** (−3, 2)

C. (−2, −3) **D.** (−2, 3)

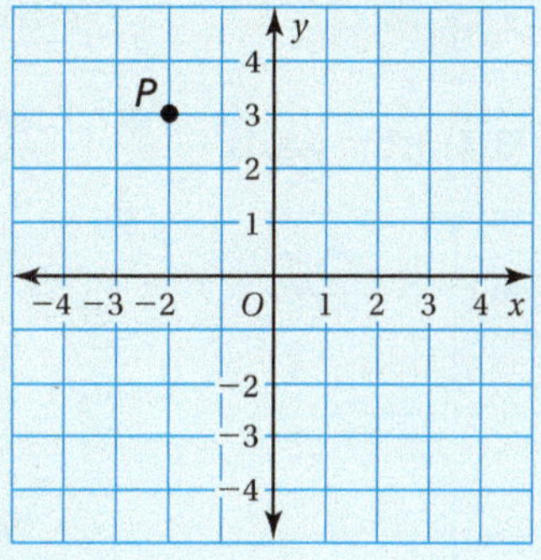

D

Try It

1. (−3, 3)
2. (−2, 0)
3. (−1, −4)
4. (0, 2)

Extra Example 2

Plot **(a)** (2, −1.5) and **(b)** $\left(-2\frac{1}{2}, -3\right)$ in a coordinate plane. Describe the location of each point.

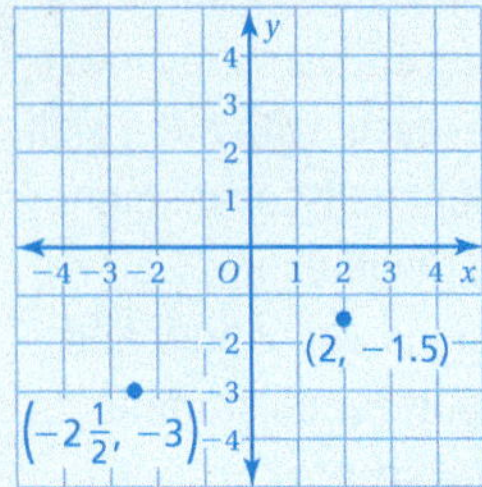

(2, −1.5) is in Quadrant IV; $\left(-2\frac{1}{2}, -3\right)$ is in Quadrant III.

Try It

5–8. See Additional Answers for graph.

5. Quadrant IV

6. *x*-axis

7. Quadrant III

8. Quadrant II

Extra Example 3

a. Reflect (−2, −1) in the *x*-axis.

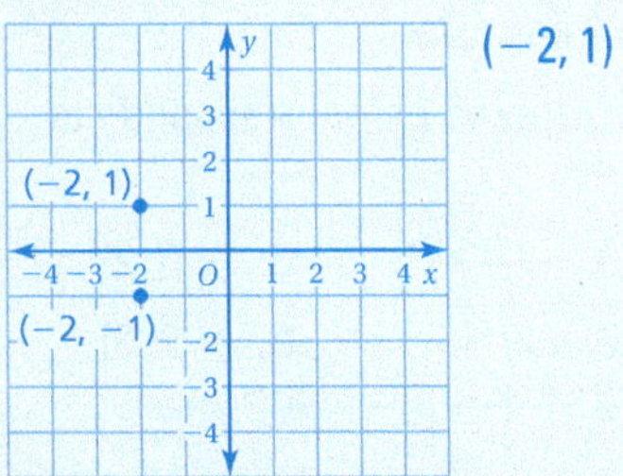

(−2, 1)

b. Reflect (3, 4) in the *y*-axis.

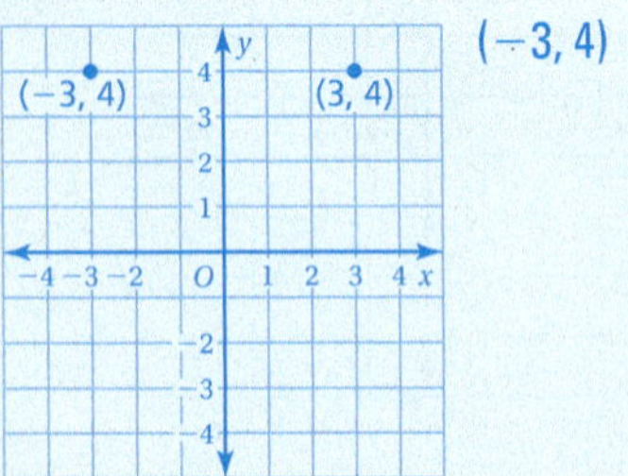

(−3, 4)

Try It

9.	**a.** (3, 2)	**b.** (−3, −2)
10.	**a.** (4, 0)	**b.** (−4, 0)
11.	**a.** (−5, −1.5)	**b.** (5, 1.5)

Laurie's Notes

EXAMPLE 2

? Ask questions about how to position the point in part (a):
- "What is the *x*-coordinate?" −2 "How far horizontally, and in which direction, do you move from (0, 0)?" 2 units left
- "What is the *y*-coordinate?" 3 "How far vertically, and in which direction, do you move from (−2, 0)?" 3 units up

- **Common Error:** Students often plot points on the axes incorrectly. Make sure the plotted point in part (b) is (0, −3.5).
- Explain to students that ordered pairs are in one of the four quadrants, on an axis, or at the origin. The ordered pair in part (b) is on an axis, not in a quadrant.

Try It

- **Common Error:** Students may move the wrong direction, or mix up the *x*- and *y*-coordinates and plot the wrong point.

Key Idea

- **Common Error:** Students think that when you take the opposite of a number, it becomes negative. If the original number is negative, the opposite is positive.

EXAMPLE 3

? "Which quadrant is (−2, 4) in?" Quadrant II "If you reflect (−2, 4) in the *x*-axis, which quadrant is the reflection in?" Quadrant III

- Because (−2, 4) is 4 units above the *x*-axis, its reflection will be 4 units below the *x*-axis. Plot (−2, −4).
- Work through part (b) as shown.

Try It

- **Think-Pair-Share**: Have students complete the exercise independently. Then have students share and discuss their graphs with a partner.
- Students should graph each exercise on a different coordinate grid. If there is a disagreement, students can fold their graphs along the axis to verify their answers.

EXAMPLE 2 Plotting Ordered Pairs

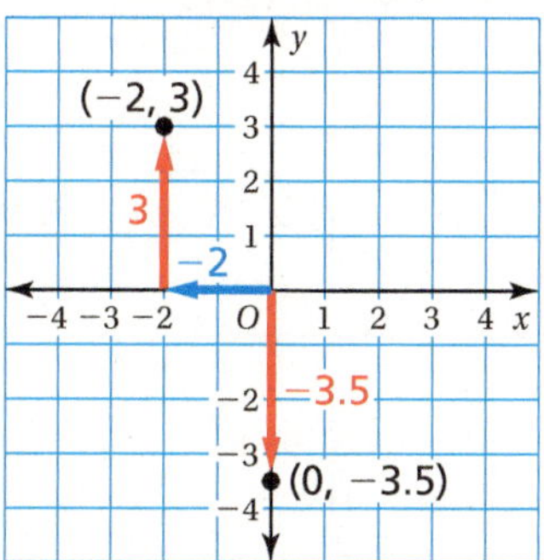

Plot (a) (−2, 3) and (b) (0, −3.5) in a coordinate plane. Describe the location of each point.

a. Start at the origin. Move 2 units left and 3 units up. Then plot the point.

▶ The point is in Quadrant II.

b. Start at the origin. Move 3.5 units down. Then plot the point.

▶ The point is on the y-axis.

Try It **Plot the ordered pair in a coordinate plane. Describe the location of the point.**

5. (3, −1) **6.** (−5, 0) **7.** (−2.5, −1) **8.** $\left(-1\frac{1}{2}, \frac{1}{2}\right)$

Key Idea

Math Practice

Use Clear Definitions

What are the *lines of reflection* in the Key Idea?

Reflecting a Point in the Coordinate Plane

- To reflect a point in the x-axis, use the same x-coordinate and take the opposite of the y-coordinate.
- To reflect a point in the y-axis, use the same y-coordinate and take the opposite of the x-coordinate.

EXAMPLE 3 Reflecting Points in One Axis

a. Reflect (−2, 4) in the x-axis.

Plot (−2, 4).

To reflect (−2, 4) in the x-axis, use the same x-coordinate, −2, and take the opposite of the y-coordinate. The opposite of 4 is −4.

▶ So, the reflection of (−2, 4) in the x-axis is (−2, −4).

b. Reflect (−3, −1) in the y-axis.

Plot (−3, −1).

To reflect (−3, −1) in the y-axis, use the same y-coordinate, −1, and take the opposite of the x-coordinate. The opposite of −3 is 3.

▶ So, the reflection of (−3, −1) in the y-axis is (3, −1).

Try It **Reflect the point in (a) the x-axis and (b) the y-axis.**

9. (3, −2) **10.** (4, 0) **11.** (−5, 1.5)

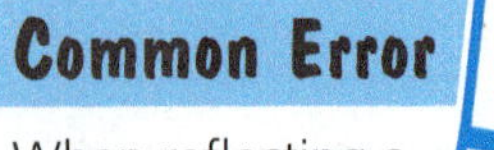

EXAMPLE 4 Reflecting a Point in Both Axes

Reflect (2, 1) in the x-axis followed by the y-axis.

Step 1: Plot (2, 1).

Step 2: Reflect (2, 1) in the x-axis.
Use the same x-coordinate, 2, and take the opposite of the y-coordinate. The opposite of 1 is −1.

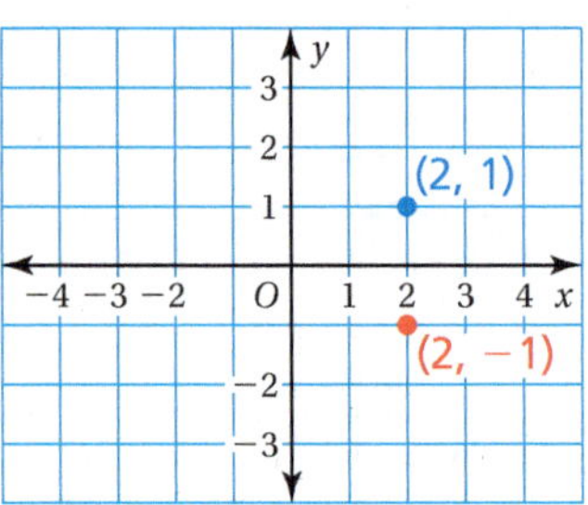

The reflection of (2, 1) in the x-axis is (2, −1).

Common Error

When reflecting a second time, be sure to use the reflected point and not the original point.

Step 3: Reflect (2, −1) in the y-axis.
Use the same y-coordinate, −1, and take the opposite of the x-coordinate. The opposite of 2 is −2.

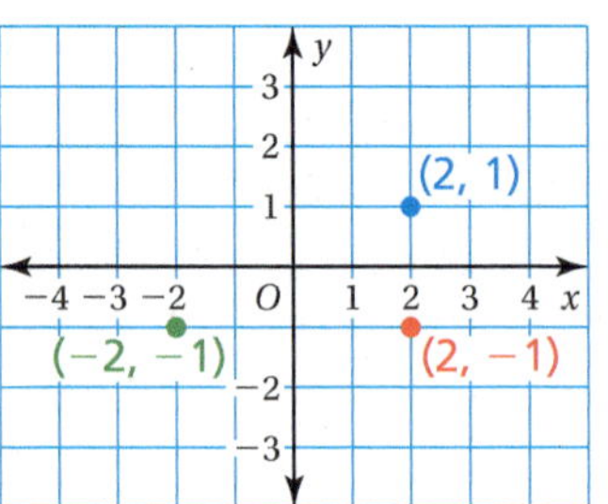

The reflection of (2, −1) in the y-axis is (−2, −1).

So, the reflection of (2, 1) in the x-axis followed by the y-axis is (−2, −1).

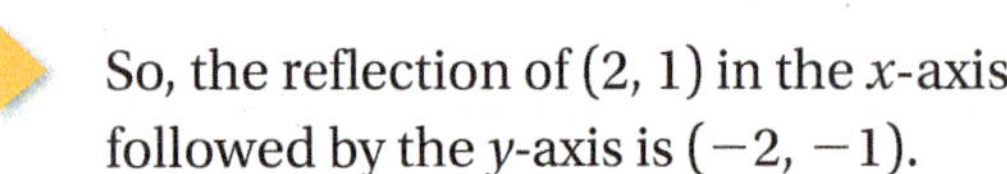

Try It **Reflect the point in the x-axis followed by the y-axis.**

12. (3, 2) **13.** (−1, 2) **14.** (−4, −3) **15.** (5, −2.5)

Self-Assessment for Concepts & Skills

Solve each exercise. Then rate your understanding of the success criteria in your journal.

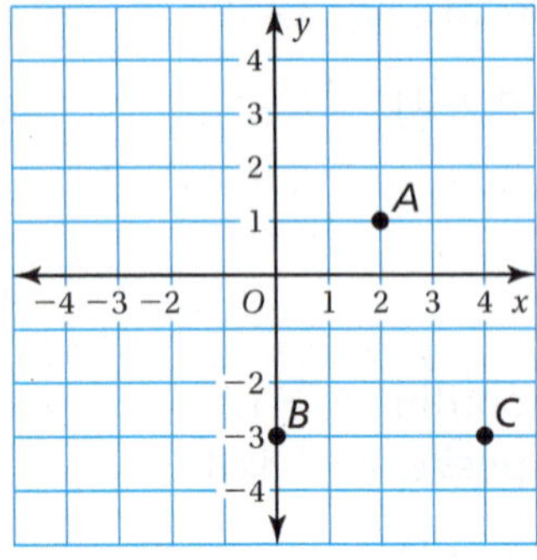

WRITING ORDERED PAIRS **Write an ordered pair corresponding to the point shown in the coordinate plane.**

16. Point A **17.** Point B **18.** Point C

PLOTTING ORDERED PAIRS **Plot the ordered pair in a coordinate plane. Describe the location of the point.**

19. $J(2, 5)$ **20.** $K(4, -6)$ **21.** $L\left(-3, -2\frac{1}{2}\right)$

REFLECTING POINTS **Reflect the point in the given axis or axes.**

22. (9, 8); x-axis **23.** (−7, 3); y-axis

24. (6, −4); x-axis then y-axis **25.** (2.5, −4); y-axis then x-axis

Laurie's Notes

EXAMPLE 4

- **MP8 Look for and Express Regularity in Repeated Reasoning:** When students reflect a point in one axis followed by the other axis, they must repeat their thinking.
- ? "Which quadrant is the point (2, 1) in?" Quadrant I
- ? "What is the reflection of (2, 1) in the x-axis?" (2, −1)
- At this point, tell students that they are reflecting (2, −1) in the y-axis and not the original point (2, 1).
- ? "What is the reflection of (2, −1) in the y-axis?" (−2, −1)
- ? **Extension (MP7 Look for and Make Use of Structure):** "If you reflect (2, 1) in the y-axis followed by the x-axis, will you end at the same location as in the example? In other words, does the order in which you complete the reflections matter?" yes; No, the order doesn't matter because you end at the same location.
- Be sure to point out the Common Error note.

Try It

- Have students complete the exercises independently. Then have students share and discuss their graphs with a group. As students discuss and analyze answers in groups, they are progressing with the third success criterion.
- Students should graph each exercise on a different coordinate grid. Students can color-code their answers—one color for reflecting in the x-axis and another color for reflecting in the y-axis. If there are any disagreements, students can fold their graphs along the axes to verify their answers.

Self-Assessment for Concepts & Skills

- Independent work is needed for students to gauge their individual progress with coordinate planes.
- Students are assessing their understanding of the hierarchy of ordered pairs skills—identifying, plotting, and reflecting—the first three success criteria.
- Watch for students' correct placement of the fractional coordinate in Exercise 21.
- For Exercises 22–25, some students will use coordinate grids to create the reflections, while others may be able to visualize the movement. Allow them to work at their own levels.

The Success Criteria Self-Assessment chart can be found in the *Student Journal* or online at *BigIdeasMath.com*.

Extra Example 4

Reflect (−2, −4) in the x-axis followed by the y-axis.

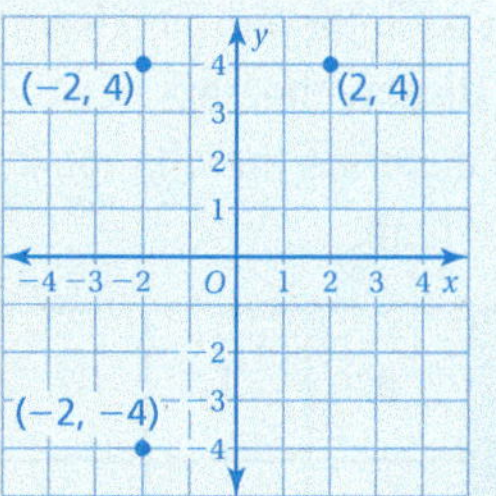

(2, 4)

Try It

12. (−3, −2) **13.** (1, −2)

14. (4, 3) **15.** (−5, 2.5)

ELL Support

Have students work in pairs to complete the Self-Assessment for Concepts & Skills exercises and display their answers for your review. For Exercises 19–25, have each pair display their graphs on a whiteboard or have each of seven pairs display an answer to a different problem on boards around the classroom. Discuss the graphs.

Self-Assessment for Concepts & Skills

16. (2, 1) **17.** (0, −3)

18. (4, −3)

19–21. See Additional Answers for graph.

19. Quadrant I

20. Quadrant IV

21. Quadrant III

22. (9, −8) **23.** (7, 3)

24. (−6, 4) **25.** (−2.5, 4)

Extra Example 5

The table shows the hourly temperatures on a winter morning from 6 A.M. to 11 A.M. Display the data in a line graph. Then describe the change in temperature over time.

Hours after 6 A.M., x	0	1	2
Temperature, y	$-2°C$	$-5°C$	$-1°C$
Hours after 6 A.M., x	3	4	5
Temperature, y	2°C	5°C	10°C

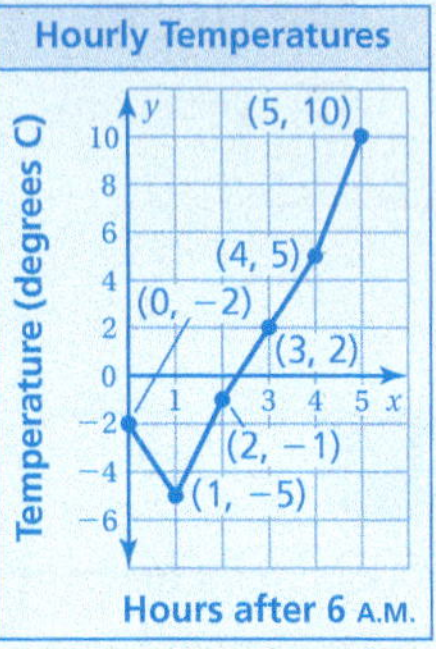

The hourly temperatures decrease from 6 A.M. to 7 A.M. and then increase from 7 A.M. to 11.A.M.

Self-Assessment for Problem Solving

26–27. See Additional Answers.

Learning Target

Plot and reflect ordered pairs in all four quadrants of a coordinate plane.

Success Criteria

- Identify ordered pairs in a coordinate plane.
- Plot ordered pairs in a coordinate plane and describe their locations.
- Reflect points in the x-axis, the y-axis, or both axes.
- Apply plotting points in all four quadrants to solve real-life problems.

Laurie's Notes

EXAMPLE 5

- Ask students to describe the types of graphs with which they are familiar.
- Define a *time series graph*: a line graph that connects ordered pairs to show patterns and trends in data over a period of time
- ? "What do the x-coordinates represent?" numbers of hours after midnight
- ? "What do the y-coordinates represent?" temperatures
- Write the data from the table as ordered pairs.
- ? "What does (5, −4) represent?" At 5:00 A.M., the temperature was −4°F.
- ? "The x-coordinates are all positive, and the y-coordinates are positive and negative. Which quadrants will the graph be in?" Quadrants I and IV
- Draw and label the axes so that the context is known.
- Plot the ordered pairs. Connect the ordered pairs with line segments. The segments allow the trend in the data to be more obvious.
- **MP3 Construct Viable Arguments and Critique the Reasoning of Others & MP6 Attend to Precision:** Ask students to make observations about the graph. Students should offer adequate detail in their observations. For instance, it is not sufficient to simply say, "The graph goes down, then up." Observations should give details and reference the context.
- After you model making a detailed observation, give students time to brainstorm with their neighbors about other observations.
- **Extension:** Record additional data for temperatures prior to midnight. Ask students what changes need to be made to the graph.

Self-Assessment for Problem Solving

- Allow time in class for students to practice using the problem-solving plan. Remember, some students may only be able to complete the first step.
- ◉ The first three success criteria and their applications to real-life situations lay the foundation for problem solving. There are many real-life situations that can be defined by a coordinate grid. Students will make this connection when solving these problems.
- **MP1 Make Sense of Problems and Persevere in Solving Them**: Students are transferring data from one model (a table) to another (a line graph) and then analyzing the display. The line graph helps students conceptualize and solve problems.

The Success Criteria Self-Assessment chart can be found in the *Student Journal* or online at *BigIdeasMath.com*.

Closure

- Plot (− 3, 4).
  (a) Reflect (−3, 4) in the x-axis. (−3, −4)
  (b) Reflect (−3, 4) in the y-axis. (3, 4)
  (c) If these are three vertices of a rectangle, where is the fourth vertex located? Explain. (3, −4); The fourth vertex can be found by reflecting (−3, −4) in the y-axis or reflecting (3, 4) in the x-axis.

You can use line graphs to display data that are collected over a period of time. Graphing and connecting the ordered pairs can show patterns or trends in the data. This type of line graph is also called a *time series graph.*

EXAMPLE 5 Modeling Real Life

A blizzard hits a town at midnight. The table shows the hourly temperatures from midnight to 8:00 A.M. Display the data in a line graph. Then describe the change in temperature over time.

Hours after Midnight, x	0	1	2	3	4	5	6	7	8
Temperature, y	7°F	5°F	3°F	0°F	−1°F	−4°F	−5°F	−2°F	2°F

Write the ordered pairs.

(0, 7) (1, 5) (2, 3)

(3, 0) (4, −1) (5, −4)

(6, −5) (7, −2) (8, 2)

Plot and label the ordered pairs. Then connect the ordered pairs with line segments.

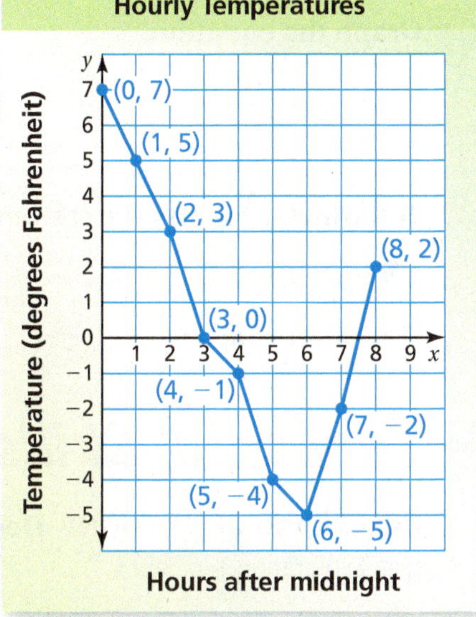

The hourly temperatures decrease from midnight to 6:00 A.M. and then increase from 6:00 A.M. to 8:00 A.M.

Self-Assessment for Problem Solving

Solve each exercise. Then rate your understanding of the success criteria in your journal.

26. At a park, the welcome center is located at (0, 0), the theater is located at (2, 4), and the restrooms are located at (−4.5, 6). The snack bar is exactly halfway between the welcome center and the theater. Graph each location in a coordinate plane.

27. The table shows the elevations of a submarine each hour from noon to 5:00 P.M. Display the data in a line graph. Then describe the change in elevation over time.

Hours after Noon, x	0	1	2	3	4	5
Elevation (kilometers), y	−4.5	−3	−2.5	−2	−3.5	−4

8.5 Practice

Go to **BigIdeasMath.com** to get HELP with solving the exercises.

Review & Refresh

Find the absolute value.

1. $|35|$ **2.** $|-18|$ **3.** $|4.7|$ **4.** $\left|-6\frac{7}{12}\right|$

5. What is the ratio of ducks to swans?

A. 4 : 9 **B.** 4 : 5

C. 5 : 4 **D.** 5 : 9

Graph the equation.

6. $y = 8x$ **7.** $y = 3x + 7$ **8.** $y = \frac{2}{5}x + 2$

Tell which property the statement illustrates.

9. $(2 \cdot p) \cdot 3 = 2 \cdot (p \cdot 3)$ **10.** $m + 0 = m$

11. $w \cdot 1 = w$ **12.** $15 + k = k + 15$

Concepts, Skills, & Problem Solving

DESCRIBING REFLECTIONS **Describe the reflection shown in the image.** (See Exploration 1, p. 369.)

13.

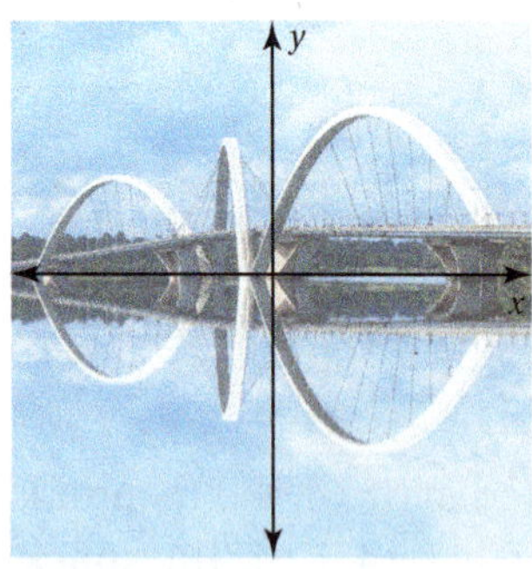

14.

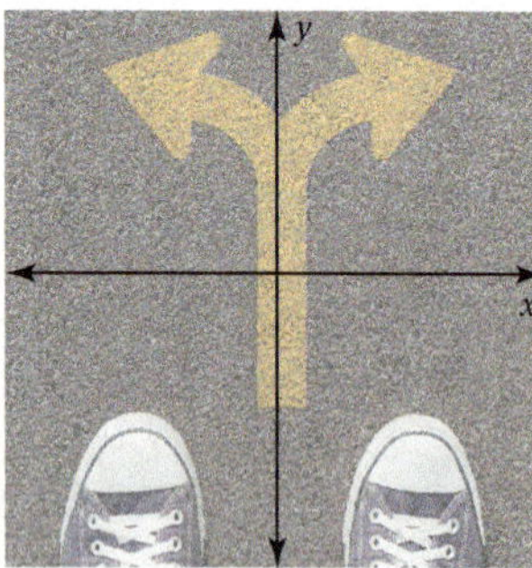

15.

WRITING ORDERED PAIRS **Write an ordered pair corresponding to the point.**

16. Point A **17.** Point B

18. Point C **19.** Point D

20. Point E **21.** Point F

22. Point G **23.** Point H

24. Point I **25.** Point J

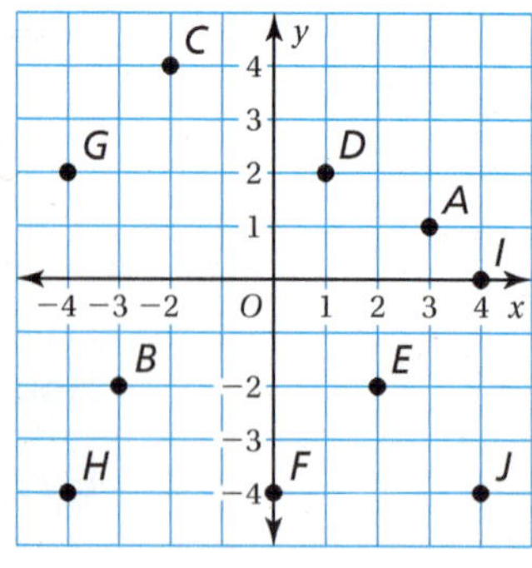

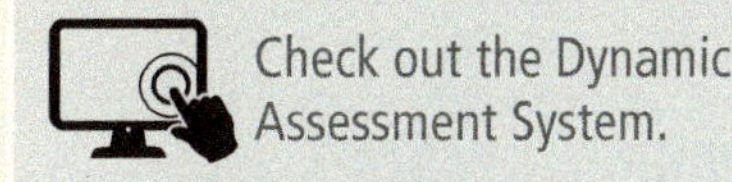

Assignment Guide and Concept Check

Scaffold assignments to support all students in their learning progression. The suggested assignments are a starting point. Continue to assign additional exercises and revisit with spaced practice to move every student toward proficiency.

Level	Assignment 1	Assignment 2
Emerging	4, 5, 8, 9, 14, 17, 19, 21, 27, 29, 37, 45, 47, 57, 59	20, 22, 28, 33, 38, 39, 40, 44, 65, 70, 76, 79
Proficient	4, 5, 8, 9, 14, 18, 20, 24, 30, 36, 54, 55, 60, 65, 69, 70	38, 39, 40, 41, 42, 43, 44, 68, 72, 75, 76, 77, 78, 79, 80
Advanced	4, 5, 8, 9, 15, 18, 20, 24, 30, 36, 54, 56, 66, 68, 69	38, 39, 41, 42, 43, 67, 72, 75, 76, 77, 78, 80, 81, 82

- Assignment 1 is for use after students complete the Self-Assessment for Concepts & Skills.
- Assignment 2 is for use after students complete the Self-Assessment for Problem Solving.
- The red exercises can be used as a concept check.

Review & Refresh Prior Skills

Exercises 1–4 Finding Absolute Value
Exercise 5 Writing Ratios
Exercises 6–8 Graphing Equations
Exercises 9–12 Identifying Properties

Common Errors

- **Exercises 16–25** Students may write the y-coordinate first and then the x-coordinate for the ordered pair. Remind students that the x-coordinate must come before the y-coordinate in the ordered pair.

Review & Refresh

1. 35 **2.** 18

3. 4.7 **4.** $6\frac{7}{12}$

5. C

6.

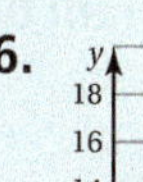

7.

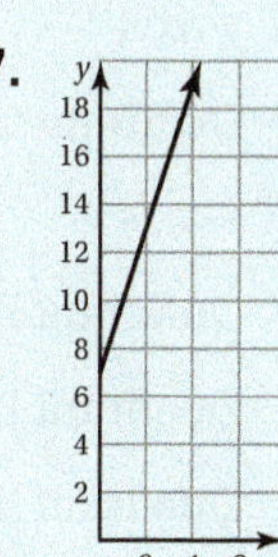

8.

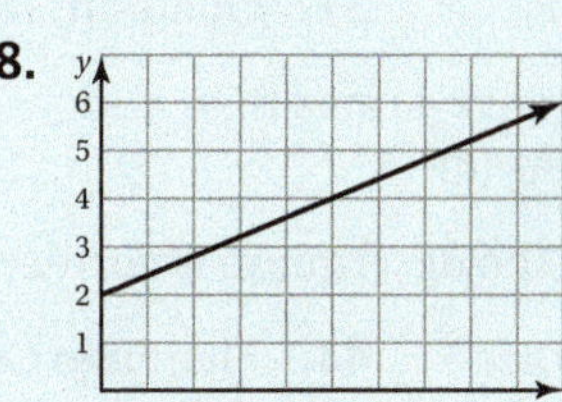

9. Associative Property of Multiplication

10. Addition Property of Zero

11. Multiplication Property of One

12. Commutative Property of Addition

Concepts, Skills, & Problem Solving

13. reflection in the x-axis

14. reflection in the y-axis

15. reflection in the x-axis

16. (3, 1) **17.** (−3, −2)

18. (−2, 4) **19.** (1, 2)

20. (2, −2) **21.** (0, −4)

22. (−4, 2) **23.** (−4, −4)

24. (4, 0) **25.** (4, −4)

Concepts, Skills, & Problem Solving

26–37. See Additional Answers for graph.

26. Quadrant I **27.** Quadrant II

28. y-axis **29.** Quadrant IV

30. Quadrant III

31. x-axis **32.** x-axis

33. Quadrant IV

34. Quadrant IV

35. Quadrant II

36. x-axis **37.** Quadrant III

38. no; move 4 units right and 5 units up

39. yes; The description is correct.

40. Reptiles **41.** Flamingo Café

42. no; *Sample answer:* Quadrant III

43. *Sample answer:* $(5, -1), (5, -2)$

44. Safari Africa

45. **a.** $(3, -2)$ **b.** $(-3, 2)$

46. **a.** $(-4, -4)$ **b.** $(4, 4)$

47. **a.** $(-5, 6)$ **b.** $(5, -6)$

48. **a.** $(4, 7)$ **b.** $(-4, -7)$

49. **a.** $(-9, -3)$ **b.** $(9, 3)$

50. **a.** $(6, 2)$ **b.** $(-6, -2)$

51. **a.** $(0, 1)$ **b.** $(0, -1)$

52. **a.** $(-8, 0)$ **b.** $(8, 0)$

53. **a.** $(-3.5, -2)$ **b.** $(3.5, 2)$

54. **a.** $(2.5, -4.5)$ **b.** $(-2.5, 4.5)$

55. **a.** $\left(-5\frac{1}{2}, -3\right)$ **b.** $\left(5\frac{1}{2}, 3\right)$

56. **a.** $\left(\frac{1}{4}, \frac{7}{8}\right)$ **b.** $\left(-\frac{1}{4}, -\frac{7}{8}\right)$

57. $(-4, -5)$ **58.** $(1, -7)$

59. $(2, 2)$ **60.** $(-6, 7)$

61. $(8, -8)$ **62.** $(-5, -9)$

63. $(0, 2)$ **64.** $(9, 0)$

65. $(-6.5, 10.5)$ **66.** $(0.4, -0.7)$

67. $\left(-\frac{1}{3}, \frac{2}{3}\right)$ **68.** $\left(1\frac{2}{5}, 1\frac{4}{5}\right)$

69. See Additional Answers.

Common Errors

- **Exercises 26–37** Students may plot the x-coordinate vertically instead of horizontally and the y-coordinate horizontally instead of vertically. Remind students that x is horizontal and y is vertical.
- **Exercises 45–56** In part (a), students may take the opposite of the x-coordinate instead of the y-coordinate. In part (b), students may take the opposite of the y-coordinate instead of the x-coordinate. Their answers for parts (a) and (b) will be switched. Remind students that to reflect in the x-axis, they need to take the opposite of the y-coordinate. Remind students that to reflect in the y-axis, they need to take the opposite of the x-coordinate.

PLOTTING ORDERED PAIRS **Plot the ordered pair in a coordinate plane. Describe the location of the point.**

26. $K(4, 3)$ **27.** $L(-1, 2)$ **28.** $M(0, -6)$ **29.** $N(3, -7)$

30. $P(-5, -9)$ **31.** $R(8, 0)$ **32.** $S(-1.5, 0)$ **33.** $T(3.5, -1.5)$

34. $U(2, -4)$ **35.** $V(-4, 1)$ **36.** $W\left(2\frac{1}{2}, 0\right)$ **37.** $Z(-4, -5)$

MP YOU BE THE TEACHER **Your friend describes how to plot the point. Is your friend correct? Explain your reasoning.**

38. To plot (4, 5), start at (0, 0) and move 4 units up and 5 units right.

39. To plot (−6, 3), start at (0, 0) and move 6 units left and 3 units up.

MP MODELING REAL LIFE **In Exercises 40–44, use the map of the zoo.**

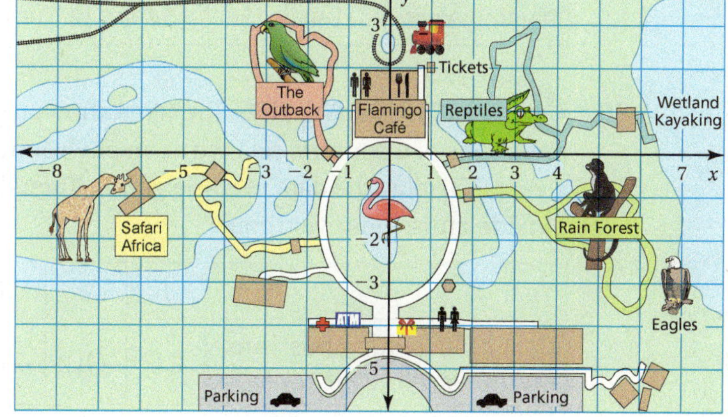

40. Which exhibit is located at (2, 1)?

41. Name an attraction on the positive y-axis.

42. Is parking available in Quadrant II? If not, name a quadrant in which you can park.

43. Write two different ordered pairs that represent the location of the Rain Forest.

44. Which exhibit is closest to (−8, −3)?

REFLECTING POINTS IN ONE AXIS **Reflect the point in (a) the x-axis and (b) the y-axis.**

45. $(3, 2)$ **46.** $(-4, 4)$ **47.** $(-5, -6)$ **48.** $(4, -7)$

49. $(-9, 3)$ **50.** $(6, -2)$ **51.** $(0, -1)$ **52.** $(-8, 0)$

53. $(-3.5, 2)$ **54.** $(2.5, 4.5)$ **55.** $\left(-5\frac{1}{2}, 3\right)$ **56.** $\left(\frac{1}{4}, -\frac{7}{8}\right)$

REFLECTING POINTS IN BOTH AXES **Reflect the point in the x-axis followed by the y-axis.**

57. $(4, 5)$ **58.** $(-1, 7)$ **59.** $(-2, -2)$ **60.** $(6, -7)$

61. $(-8, 8)$ **62.** $(5, 9)$ **63.** $(0, -2)$ **64.** $(-9, 0)$

65. $(6.5, -10.5)$ **66.** $(-0.4, 0.7)$ **67.** $\left(\frac{1}{3}, -\frac{2}{3}\right)$ **68.** $\left(-1\frac{2}{5}, -1\frac{4}{5}\right)$

69. **MP STRUCTURE** Reflect a point in the x-axis followed by the y-axis. Then reflect the original point in the y-axis followed by the x-axis. Do you get the same results? Explain.

MP REASONING **Describe the possible location(s) of the point (x, y).**

70. $x > 0, y > 0$ **71.** $x < 0, y < 0$ **72.** $x > 0, y < 0$

73. $x > 0$ **74.** $y < 0$ **75.** $x = 0, y = 0$

CRITICAL THINKING **Tell whether the statement is *always*, *sometimes*, or *never* true. Explain your reasoning.**

76. The x-coordinate of a point on the x-axis is zero.

77. The y-coordinates of points in Quadrant III are positive.

78. The x-coordinate of a point in Quadrant II has the same sign as the y-coordinate of a point in Quadrant IV.

79. **MP MODELING REAL LIFE** The table shows the number of people who participate in a blood drive each year for 9 years. Display the data in a line graph. Then describe the change in the number of participants over time.

Year, x	1	2	3	4	5	6	7	8	9
Participants, y	140	136	134	132	131	135	136	142	145

80. **MP MODELING REAL LIFE** The table shows the amount of carbon dioxide emissions of a country, relative to an environmental standard, each year for 7 years. Display the data in a line graph. Then describe the change in carbon dioxide emissions over time.

Year, x	1	2	3	4	5	6	7
Carbon Dioxide Emissions (millions of metric tons), y	0.6	−0.2	−1.2	1.2	0.8	1	−0.6

81. **MP PATTERNS** The table shows the total miles run through each of 18 weeks for a marathon training program.

Week	1	2	3	4	5	6	7	8	9
Total Miles	22	46	72	96	124	151	181	211	244

Week	10	11	12	13	14	15	16	17	18
Total Miles	279	317	357	397	437	473	506	530	544

a. Create a table for the distance run during each week of training.

b. Display the data from part (a) in a line graph.

c. Explain the pattern shown in the graph.

82. **MP LOGIC** Two points are plotted in the coordinate plane. Plot each of the following ordered pairs in the same coordinate plane.

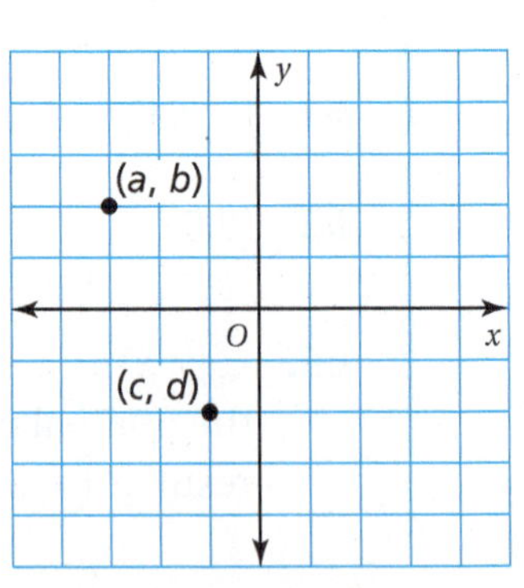

a. $P(a, -b)$ **b.** $Q(-a, b)$ **c.** $R(c, -d)$

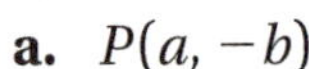

d. $S(-c, -d)$ **e.** $T(c, -a)$ **f.** $U(-d, -b)$

Common Errors

- **Exercise 76** Students may not think about the origin, which is the reason the statement is *sometimes* true. Tell students to think about the *x*-axis as a number line and ask if there is any place where *x* is 0.

Mini-Assessment

The points *A*(−2, 3), *B*(4, 3), *C*(−2, −4), and *D*(4, −4) represent the vertices of a garden.

1. Plot the ordered pairs in a coordinate plane.

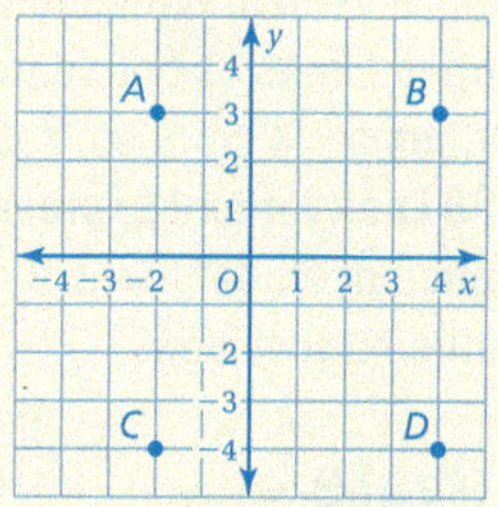

2. Describe the location of each point. *A*: Quadrant II, *B*: Quadrant I, *C*: Quadrant III, *D*: Quadrant IV

3. Reflect (2, −3) in the *x*-axis. (2, 3)

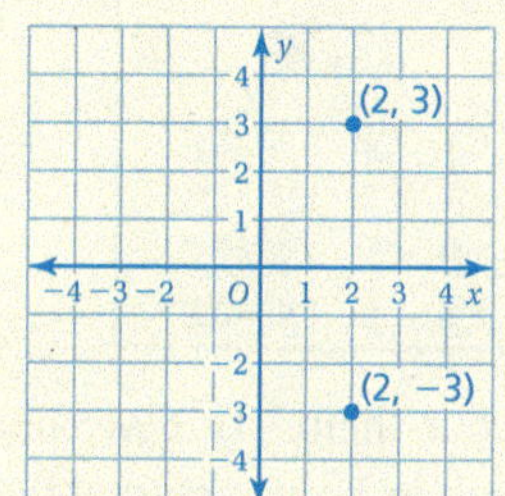

4. Reflect (4, 3) in the *y*-axis. (−4, 3)

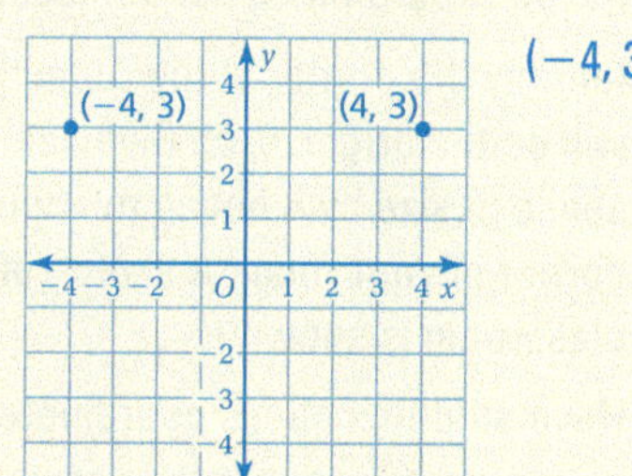

5. Reflect (2, −2) in the *x*-axis followed by the *y*-axis. (−2, 2)

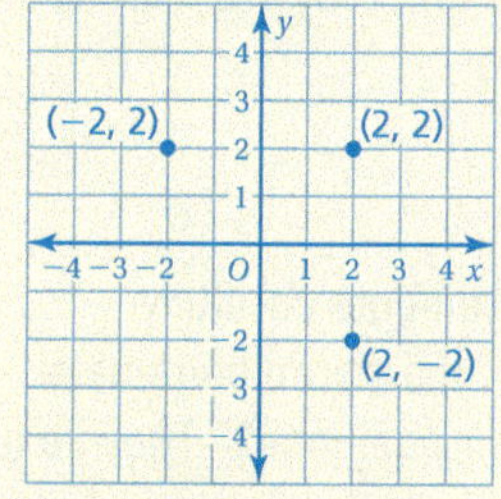

Section Resources

Surface Level	Deep Level
Resources by Chapter • Extra Practice • Reteach • Puzzle Time Student Journal • Self-Assessment • Practice Differentiating the Lesson Tutorial Videos Skills Review Handbook Skills Trainer	Resources by Chapter • Enrichment and Extension Graphic Organizers Dynamic Assessment System • Section Practice

Concepts, Skills, & Problem Solving

70. Quadrant I
71. Quadrant III
72. Quadrant IV
73. Quadrant I, Quadrant IV, or the positive *x*-axis
74. Quadrant III, Quadrant IV, or the negative *y*-axis
75. origin
76. sometimes; It is true only for (0, 0).
77. never; All points in Quadrant III have negative *y*-coordinates.
78. always; The *x*-coordinate of a point in Quadrant II is negative, and so is the *y*-coordinate of a point in Quadrant IV.
79. 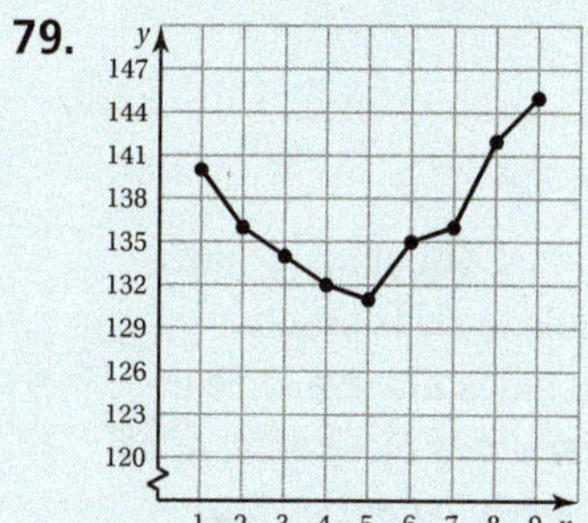

    decreased from year 1 to year 5 and increased from year 5 to year 9
80. 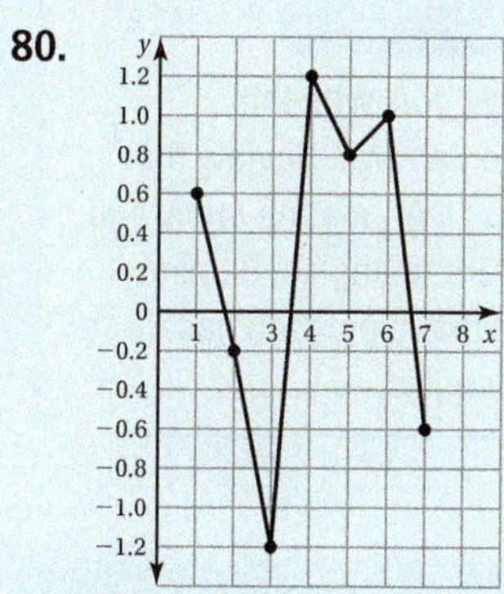

    decreased from year 1 to 3, year 4 to year 5, and year 6 to year 7; increased from year 3 to year 4, year 5 to year 6

81–82. See Additional Answers.

Laurie's Notes

STATE STANDARDS
6.NS.C.8, 6.G.A.3

Learning Target

Draw polygons in the coordinate plane and find distances between points in the coordinate plane.

Success Criteria

- Draw polygons in the coordinate plane.
- Find distances between points in the coordinate plane with the same *x*-coordinates or the same *y*-coordinates.
- Find horizontal and vertical side lengths of polygons in the coordinate plane.
- Draw polygons in the coordinate plane to solve real-life problems.

Warm Up

Cumulative, vocabulary, and prerequisite skills practice opportunities are available in the *Resources by Chapter* or at *BigIdeasMath.com*.

ELL Support

Write *poly/gon*, with the separation shown. Review that the prefix *poly–* means *many* and *–gon* refers to angles. Remind students that a polygon has three or more angles.

Exploration 1

a. See Additional Answers.

b. *Sample answer:* It is a right triangle.

c. yes; yes; *Sample answer:* side lengths, perimeter, and area of the rectangle, area of the trapezoid

Preparing to Teach

- Students will extend their new understanding of graphing points in all four quadrants to drawing polygons in the coordinate plane. Finding areas using graphed lines as boundaries is a foundational concept for higher-level mathematics courses. You are setting the stage for students' future success!
- **MP8 Look for and Express Regularity in Repeated Reasoning:** Mathematically proficient students recognize patterns and make connections among mathematical ideas.

Motivate

- ❓ "Who has played the game of *Battleship* before?" Chances are most students have or will have familiarity with it.
- Tell them that you have hidden something in the classroom. It's their job to guess "coordinates" of the location.
- Identify the corner of the room that will be the origin (0, 0). Give some sense of size by labeling the opposite corner of your room. A sketch of my classroom is shown.

(20, 14)

(0, 0)

- Have students guess coordinates of the location of your "hide." This will allow you to review concepts necessary for this lesson, such as how to start at the origin (0, 0) and locate an ordered pair.
- To make the hunt move quicker, you can tell students that they are "hot" or "cold" so that students make more educated guesses!

Exploration 1

- In part (a), advise students to read the bulleted requirements carefully.
- ❓ To prompt students who are struggling to begin, ask, "If ordered pairs have the same *x*-coordinates, what do you know about their positions?" They lie on the same vertical line. "If ordered pairs have the same *y*-coordinates, what do you know about their positions?" They lie on the same horizontal line.
- ❓ "How many quadrants will you be using?" 2
- Ask students to explain why their three ordered pairs meet the requirements.
- In part (b), tell students to identify their polygons using specific names: right, (scalene or isosceles) triangle. Allow time for students to share their triangles with the class.
- ❓ "Can you find the area of your triangle?" yes "How can you find the area?" *Sample answers:* You can count and approximate the number of squares or use the base and height in the area formula.
- ❓ "How can you find the lengths of the height and the base?" Count the squares vertically and horizontally. "Can you find the length of the diagonal side?" no
- ❓ "Does it matter that the figure has negative coordinates? Explain." No, distance is a measurable quantity and must be positive.
- ❓ "Can using absolute value help you determine the lengths of the height and the base?" Discuss the Math Practice note with students.

8.6 Polygons in the Coordinate Plane

Learning Target: Draw polygons in the coordinate plane and find distances between points in the coordinate plane.

Success Criteria:
- I can draw polygons in the coordinate plane.
- I can find distances between points in the coordinate plane with the same x-coordinates or the same y-coordinates.
- I can find horizontal and vertical side lengths of polygons in the coordinate plane.
- I can draw polygons in the coordinate plane to solve real-life problems.

EXPLORATION 1 Drawing Polygons in the Coordinate Plane

Work with a partner.

a. Write three ordered pairs that meet the following requirements. Then plot the ordered pairs in a coordinate plane, like the one shown.

- Two of the ordered pairs have the same x-coordinates.
- Two of the ordered pairs have the same y-coordinates.
- Two of the points are in the same quadrant. The other point is in a different quadrant.

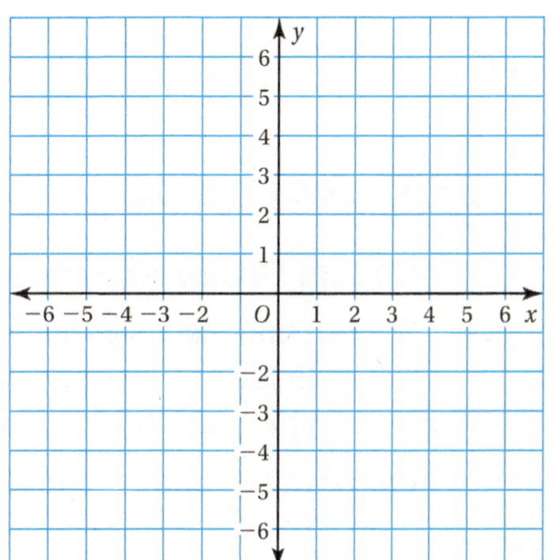

b. The points represent the vertices of a polygon. What conclusions can you make about the polygon?

c. Can you plot another point to form a rectangle? a trapezoid? If so, what measures of the quadrilateral can you calculate?

Math Practice

Find General Methods

How can you use absolute values of coordinates to find lengths of horizontal and vertical line segments in the coordinate plane?

8.6 Lesson

You can use ordered pairs to represent vertices of polygons. To draw a polygon in a coordinate plane, plot and connect the vertices.

EXAMPLE 1 Drawing a Polygon in a Coordinate Plane

The vertices of a quadrilateral are $A(-1, 1)$, $B(0, 6)$, $C(4, 5)$, and $D(5, -2)$. Draw the quadrilateral in a coordinate plane.

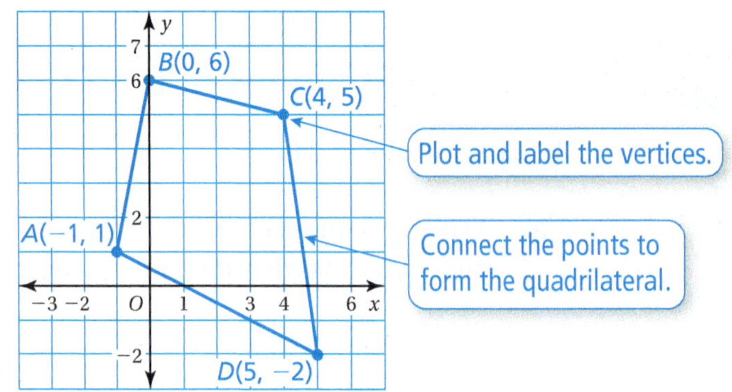

After you plot the vertices, connect them *in order* to draw the polygon.

Try It **Draw the polygon with the given vertices in a coordinate plane.**

1. $A(0, 0)$, $B(5, 7)$, $C(4, -3)$
2. $W(4, 4)$, $X(7, 4)$, $Y\left(2\frac{1}{2}, -2\right)$, $Z\left(-\frac{1}{2}, -2\right)$

Key Idea

Finding Distances between Points in a Coordinate Plane

You can find distances between points in a coordinate plane with the same x-coordinates or the same y-coordinates using the absolute values of the coordinates that are different.

Points in the same quadrant:

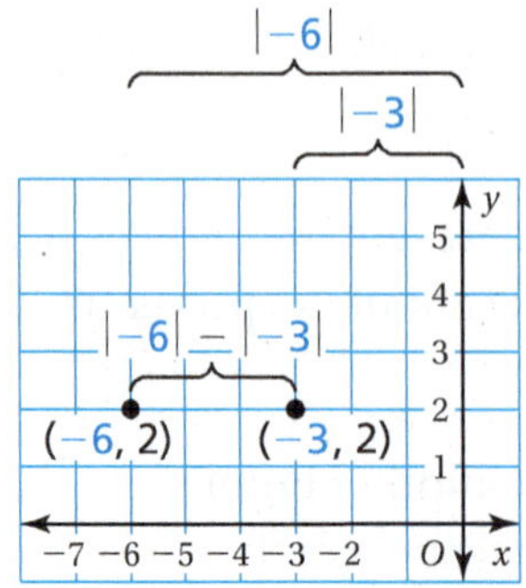

Points in different quadrants:

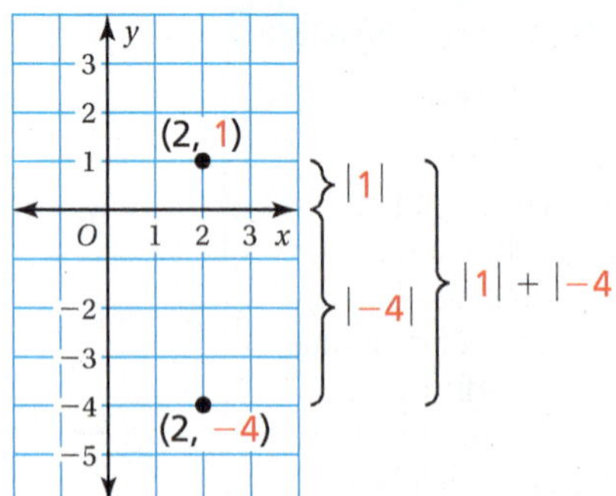

When finding distances between points in the same quadrant, be sure to subtract the lesser absolute value from the greater absolute value.

Laurie's Notes

Scaffolding Instruction

- In this section, geometry and algebra join with work in the number system to solve mathematical problems. The solutions may require expressions or equations for situations that are based on geometric models and formulas.
- **Emerging:** Students may confuse the *x*- and *y*-coordinates when finding vertical and horizontal distances, or they may want to count the squares for measuring distance instead of adding or subtracting absolute values. The examples provide additional practice with these skills.
- **Proficient:** Students can identify ordered pairs that lie on vertical or horizontal lines of the coordinate grid. They understand how the points relate to measuring distances and can find distances by adding or subtracting absolute values. After completing Try It Exercises 3 and 4, students can check their understanding using the Self-Assessment exercises.

EXAMPLE 1

- This example continues with the first success criterion.
- **No-Hands Questioning:** "Can you determine the perimeter of this quadrilateral without using a tool such as a ruler? Explain." No, the sides are neither horizontal nor vertical, so their lengths cannot be counted.
- **Extension:** Ask four students to place a finger in a floor coordinate plane to represent each of the four points. Give them a long piece of string and ask students to find a way to find the perimeter without using a measuring tool.
  - Students can hold the string to outline the perimeter and mark the end of the perimeter on the string. Then they can place the string on horizontal or vertical grid lines to count the number of units in the perimeter.

Try It

- Students should use a different coordinate plane for each exercise.
- Have volunteers share their polygons with the class. Have students identify the types of polygons they plotted.

ELL Support

Have students work in groups to complete Try It Exercises 1 and 2. Expect students at different language levels to perform as described.

Beginner: Plot the points and draw the polygon.

Intermediate: Describe the polygon.

Advanced: Explain the process they used to draw the polygon.

Key Idea

- Write the Key Idea and sketch examples of both cases.
- When points are in the same quadrant, find the *difference* of the absolute values of the coordinates that are different. When points are in different quadrants, find the *sum* of the absolute values of the coordinates that are different. Point out the push-pin note.
- Students can count units to *verify* distances and to build confidence in the algorithm, but encourage students to add or subtract the absolute values to prepare for coordinates containing rational numbers.

Scaffold instruction to support all students in their learning. Learning is individualized and you may want to group students differently as they move in and out of these levels with each skill and concept. Student self-assessment and feedback help guide your instructional decisions about how and when to layer support for all students to become proficient learners.

Formative Assessment Tip

No-Hands Questioning

Typically when you ask a question there are hands that immediately go up, often the same hands each time. Some students need a longer time to process a question and think through their responses. This technique instructs students not to put their hands in the air when the question is posed. You can then use *Popsicle Sticks* to call on students or purposely call on those students whose voices you do not hear enough. The questions posed during *No-Hands Questioning* should require more than simple responses.

Extra Example 1

The vertices of a quadrilateral are $A(-4, 5)$, $B(-1, 4)$, $C(1, 1)$, and $D(-5, -2)$. Draw the quadrilateral in a coordinate plane.

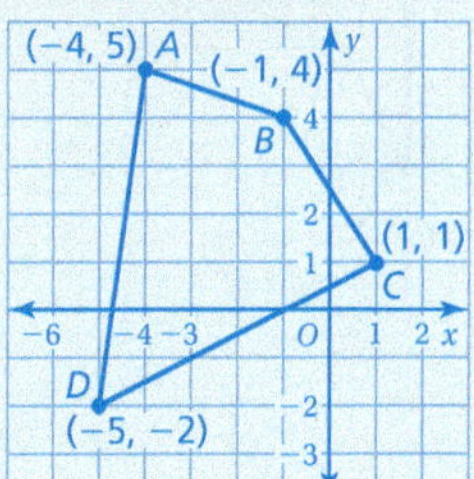

Try It

1–2. See Additional Answers.

Extra Example 2

a. Find the distance between $(-2, -5)$ and $(-2, 1)$. 6

b. Find the distance between $(-4.5, 2)$ and $(-7, 2)$. 2.5

Try It

3. 4

4. 7

Self-Assessment
for Concepts & Skills

5.

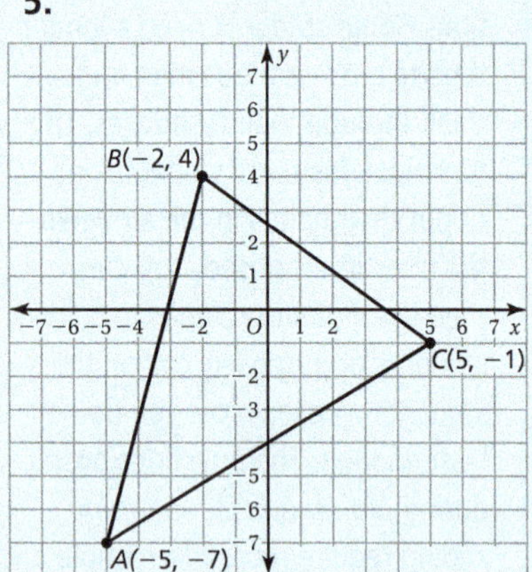

6.

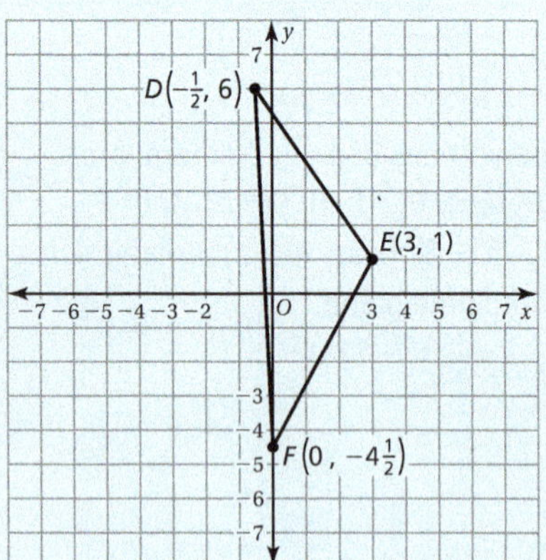

7. 2

8. 9

9. $(-7, -1)$, $(-7, 4)$; The distance between these two points is 5, the others have a distance of 6.

Laurie's Notes

EXAMPLE 2

- Students explored the second success criterion and will continue working towards it in this example. Some students may need more practice than others in finding distances.
- If students finish this example quickly, ask them to find the vertical or horizontal distance between two points that contain fractions. Students need to generalize the process, so that it doesn't matter what kind of numbers are given. They can use the same methods for all types of coordinates.
- **MP7 Look for and Make Use of Structure:** Mathematically proficient students recognize that vertical segments have the same x-coordinates and horizontal segments have the same y-coordinates. Some students may simply say, "the points are up and down" or "the points are straight across from one another." These are good first observations about their locations; however, focus their attention to recognizing that the points are on vertical or horizontal lines from the ordered pairs. This is the first step to using only ordered pairs to find distances.

Try It

- **Think-Pair-Share:** Students should read each exercise independently and then work in pairs to complete the exercises. Then have each pair compare their answers with another pair and discuss any discrepancies.

Self-Assessment for Concepts & Skills

- This independent work assesses students' progress with the first two success criteria.
- **MP6 Attend to Precision:** Proficient students are careful in their work and communication. In Exercises 5 and 6, check that students plot and label the points accurately. Labels can be a critical part of solving a problem and may cause students to make an unwanted detour.
- Watch for students who draw a coordinate grid and count units. At this point, students should plot or visualize the points and then add or subtract the absolute values of the coordinates.
- **Common Error:** In Exercise 9, students may say that there is not just one pair of points that doesn't belong because two pairs have the same x-coordinates and the other two have the same y-coordinates. Encourage students to continue investigating until they find something that only one pair of points can claim.

ELL Support

Have students work in pairs to complete the exercises. Then have two pairs come together to compare answers and reconcile any differences. Monitor discussions and provide support as needed.

The Success Criteria Self-Assessment chart can be found in the *Student Journal* or online at *BigIdeasMath.com*.

EXAMPLE 2 Finding Distances between Points

a. Find the distance between (−3, −5) and (2, −5).

Plot the points.

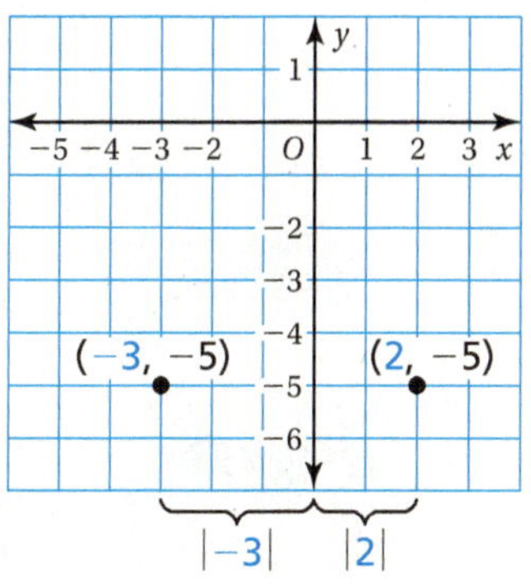

The points are in different quadrants and have the same y-coordinates. The distance between the points is the sum of the absolute values of the x-coordinates.

$$|-3| + |2| = 3 + 2 = 5$$

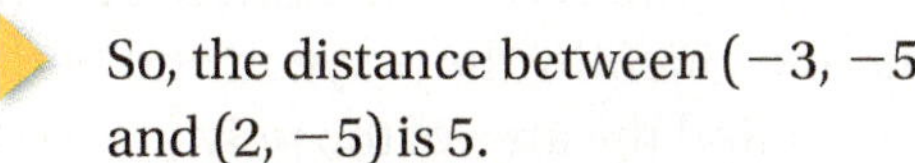

So, the distance between (−3, −5) and (2, −5) is 5.

b. Find the distance between (3, −2.5) and (3, −5).

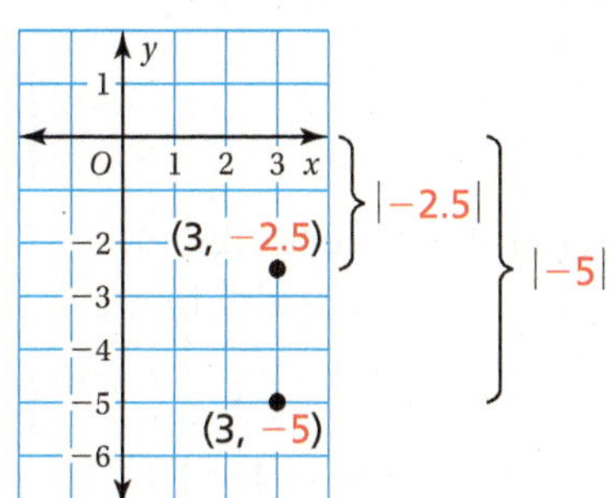

Plot the points.

The points are in the same quadrant and have the same x-coordinates. The distance between the points is the difference of the absolute values of the y-coordinates.

$$|-5| - |-2.5| = 5 - 2.5 = 2.5$$

So, the distance between (3, −2.5) and (3, −5) is 2.5.

Try It **Find the distance between the points.**

3. (−6, 6.5), (−2, 6.5) **4.** (−4, 2), (−4, −5)

Self-Assessment for Concepts & Skills

Solve each exercise. Then rate your understanding of the success criteria in your journal.

DRAWING A POLYGON **Draw the polygon with the given vertices in a coordinate plane.**

5. $A(-5, -7), B(-2, 4), C(5, -1)$ **6.** $D\left(-\frac{1}{2}, 6\right), E(3, 1), F\left(0, -4\frac{1}{2}\right)$

FINDING DISTANCES **Find the distance between the points.**

7. (2, 7), (2, 9) **8.** (−3, −8), (6, −8)

9. WHICH ONE DOESN'T BELONG? Which pair of points does *not* belong with the other three? Explain your reasoning.

(−2, 5), (4, 5)

(6, −3), (6, 3)

(−7, −1), (−7, 4)

(2, −1), (−4, −1)

EXAMPLE 3 Modeling Real Life

An archaeologist divides an area using a coordinate plane in which the coordinates are measured in meters. The vertices of a secret chamber are $(-8, 10)$, $(4, 10)$, $(4, 2)$, and $(-8, 2)$. Find the perimeter and the area of the secret chamber.

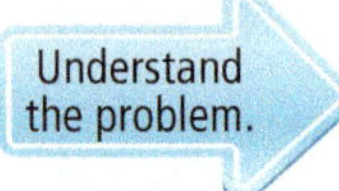

You are given the vertices of a secret chamber. You are asked to find the perimeter and the area of the chamber.

Make a plan.

Plot and connect the vertices to draw the polygon that represents the secret chamber. Identify the polygon and find its dimensions. Then find the perimeter and the area of the polygon.

Solve and check.

Draw the polygon.

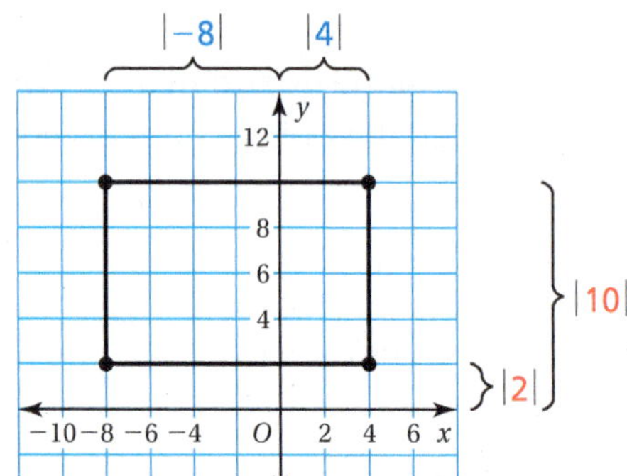

The secret chamber is rectangular. Find the length and the width of the rectangle.

Length: $|-8| + |4| = 8 + 4 = 12$

Width: $|10| - |2| = 10 - 2 = 8$

Another Method Each grid square has an area of $2^2 = 4$ square meters. The secret chamber consists of 24 grid squares. So, the area is $24(4) = 96$ square meters. ✓

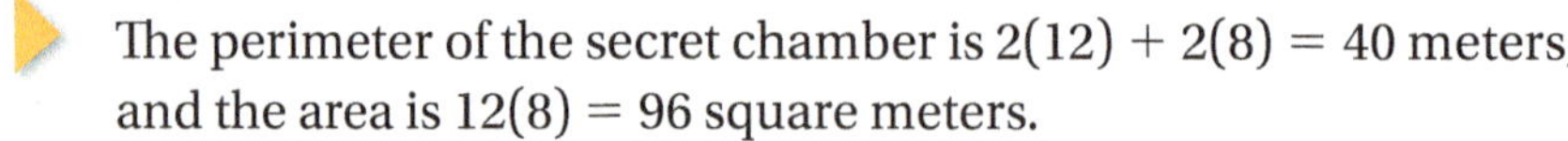

The perimeter of the secret chamber is $2(12) + 2(8) = 40$ meters, and the area is $12(8) = 96$ square meters.

Self-Assessment for Problem Solving

Solve each exercise. Then rate your understanding of the success criteria in your journal.

10. A digital map of your hometown is shown in a coordinate plane in which the coordinates are measured in miles. The map shows your house at $(-2, -7)$, your school at $(5, -7)$, and your friend's house at $(-2, 1)$. How far is your house from your school? How far is your house from your friend's house?

11. You design a tree house using a coordinate plane in which the coordinates are measured in feet. The vertices of the floor are $(-2, -3)$, $(-2, 4)$, $(5, 4)$, and $(5, -3)$. Find the perimeter (in yards) and the area (in square yards) of the floor.

Laurie's Notes

EXAMPLE 3

- **FYI:** An *archaeologist* studies ancient ruins and objects to learn about people and cultures.
- Point out that the absolute values for the length come from the *x*-coordinates and the absolute values for the width come from the *y*-coordinates. The absolute values represent the distance from the axis.
- Remind students to consider the scale of the axes, if they count units to find the dimensions. Counting units can be used to check the perimeter.
- **Note:** You can also use (−8, 2) and (4, 2) to find the length and (−8, 10) and (−8, 2) to find the width.
- Ask students to explain why you add the absolute values to find the length (points are in different quadrants), but subtract to find the width (points are in the same quadrant).
- Explain to students that even though two of the ordered pairs are in Quadrant II, where *x*-coordinates are negative, the dimensions are positive.
- Ask students to identify which parts of the problem align to the third success criterion and which parts align to the fourth success criterion.
- Refer students to the Another Method note. Students may have creative ways to solve the problem. Ask volunteers to explain other methods.
- **Extension:** Compare this problem to part (b) of the exploration. Say, "This problem asks you to find the perimeter of a polygon in a coordinate plane. Could you have found the perimeter in the exploration? Explain." No, in the exploration, the triangle had a diagonal side that could not be measured precisely.

Self-Assessment for Problem Solving

- After independent work on these exercises, allow students to share their results with a partner and discuss any differences. It is important to provide time in class for problem solving, so that students become comfortable with the problem-solving plan.
- **Common Error**: In Exercise 11, students may not recognize that although the coordinates are measured in feet, they need to find the answers in yards and square yards. Remind students to read the problem carefully to determine what is being asked.
- Although these are introductory problems, it is easy to see how cartography and architecture projects are based on grids.
- **Thumbs Up:** Ask students to assess their understanding of the third and fourth success criteria.

The Success Criteria Self-Assessment chart can be found in the *Student Journal* or online at *BigIdeasMath.com*.

Closure

- Plot a rectangle with a perimeter of 20. What are the coordinates? *Sample answer:* (1, 2), (7, 2), (7, 6), (1, 6) Have students share their answers.

Extra Example 3

An interior designer maps out a room design using a coordinate plane in which the coordinates are measured in meters. The vertices of the room are (−3, 2), (5, 2), (5, −3), and (−3, −3). Find the perimeter and the area of the room.
26 meters; 40 m^2

Self-Assessment for Problem Solving

10. 7 mi; 8 mi

11. $9\frac{1}{3}$ yd; $5\frac{4}{9}$ yd^2

Learning Target

Draw polygons in the coordinate plane and find distances between points in the coordinate plane.

Success Criteria

- Draw polygons in the coordinate plane.
- Find distances between points in the coordinate plane with the same *x*-coordinates or the same *y*-coordinates.
- Find horizontal and vertical side lengths of polygons in the coordinate plane.
- Draw polygons in the coordinate plane to solve real-life problems.

Review & Refresh

1. (1, 4)
2. (−2, 2)
3. (−4, −1)
4. (3, −3)
5. 0.62
6. 0.07
7. 1.33
8. 0.0045
9. 8

Concepts, Skills, & Problem Solving

10. 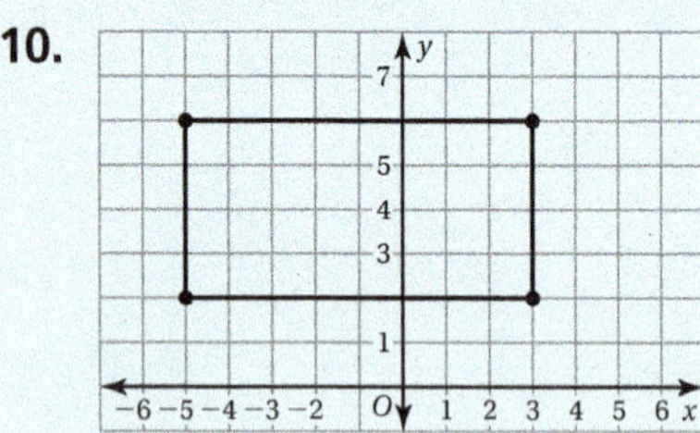

11. 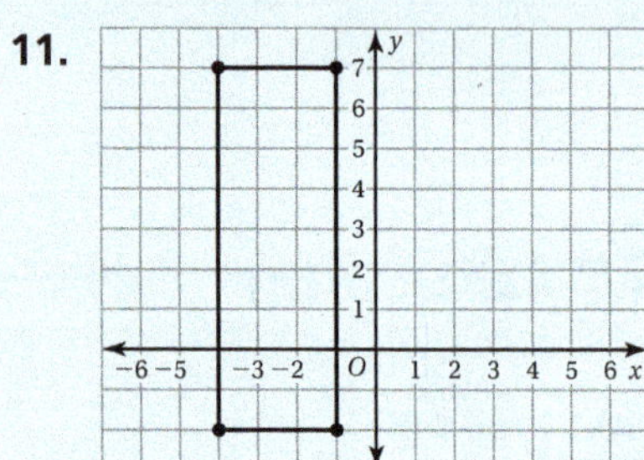

12. 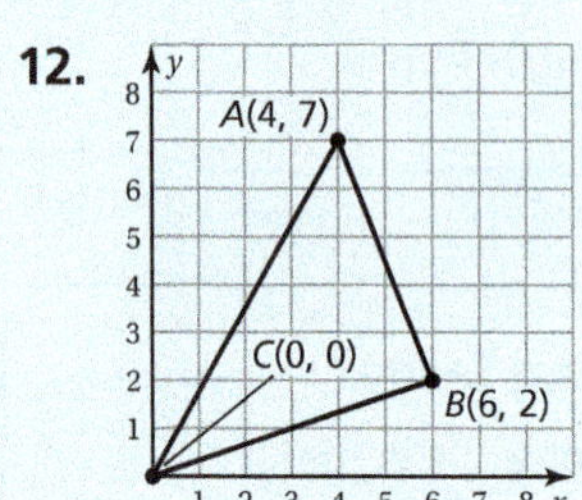

13. 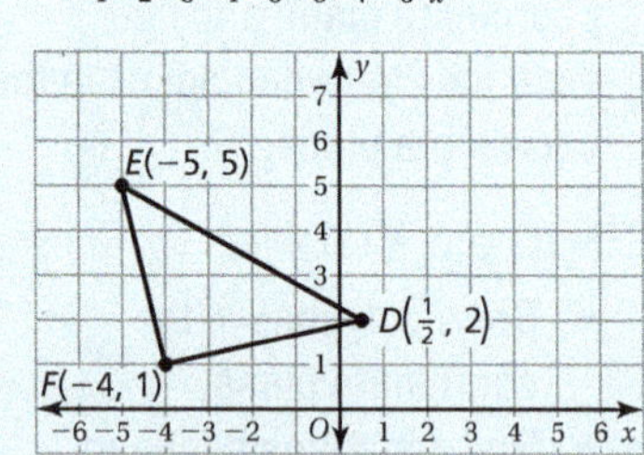

14–17. See Additional Answers.

18. no; A should be at (3, −1), not (3, 1).

19. 5
20. 6
21. 2
22. 11
23. 15
24. 14
25. 8.5
26. 7.5
27. 8.75

Assignment Guide and Concept Check

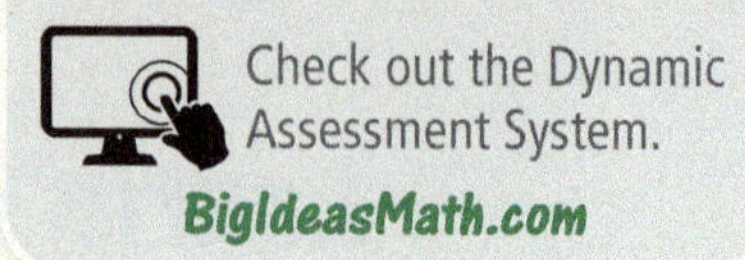

Scaffold assignments to support all students in their learning progression. The suggested assignments are a starting point. Continue to assign additional exercises and revisit with spaced practice to move every student toward proficiency.

Level	Assignment 1	Assignment 2
Emerging	4, 7, 8, 9, 10, 12, 15, 18, 19, 21	16, 22, 25, 28, 32, 35, 36, 37
Proficient	4, 7, 8, 9, 10, 13, 14, 18, 20, 22	17, 27, 30, 32, 33, 34, 35, 36, 37, 39
Advanced	4, 7, 8, 9, 11,16, 17, 18, 26, 27	31, 33, 34, 35, 36, 38, 40, 41

- Assignment 1 is for use after students complete the Self-Assessment for Concepts & Skills.
- Assignment 2 is for use after students complete the Self-Assessment for Problem Solving.
- The red exercises can be used as a concept check.

Review & Refresh Prior Skills

Exercises 1–4 Writing Ordered Pairs
Exercises 5–8 Writing Percents as Decimals
Exercise 9 Using a Tape Diagram

Common Errors

- **Exercises 13, 14, and 17** The fractions in the coordinates may confuse students. Refresh the concept of graphing a coordinate involving a fraction.

8.6 Practice

Review & Refresh

Write an ordered pair corresponding to the point.

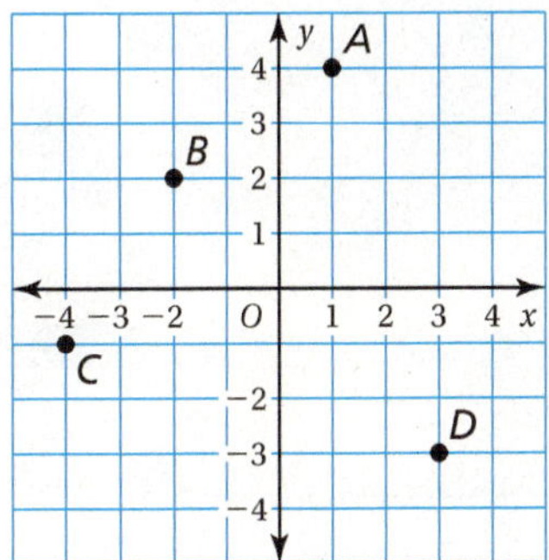

1. Point A
2. Point B
3. Point C
4. Point D

Write the percent as a decimal.

5. 62%
6. 7%
7. 133%
8. 0.45%

9. The tape diagram represents the ratio of the time you spend online to the time your friend spends online. You are online for 6 hours. How many hours does your friend spend online?

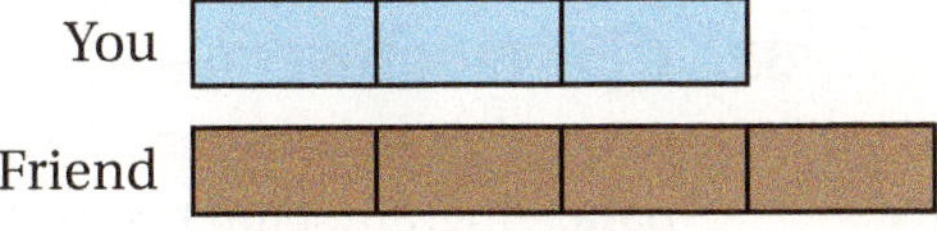

Concepts, Skills, & Problem Solving

MP STRUCTURE **Plot the ordered pairs in a coordinate plane. Then plot another point to form a rectangle.** (See Exploration 1, p. 377.)

10. (3, 2), (3, 6), (−5, 2)
11. (−4, 7), (−1, 7), (−4, −2)

DRAWING A POLYGON **Draw the polygon with the given vertices in a coordinate plane.**

12. $A(4, 7), B(6, 2), C(0, 0)$
13. $D\left(\frac{1}{2}, 2\right), E(-5, 5), F(-4, 1)$
14. $G\left(1\frac{1}{2}, 4\right), H\left(1\frac{1}{2}, -8\right), J(5, -8), K(5, 4)$
15. $L(-3, 2), M(-3, 5), N(2, 2), P(2, -1)$
16. $Q(0, 4), R(-3, 8), S(-7, 4), T(-1, -2), U(7, -2)$
17. $V(-4, -2), W\left(-3, 3\frac{1}{2}\right), X\left(2, 3\frac{1}{2}\right), Y(4, 0), Z(1, -4)$
18. **MP YOU BE THE TEACHER** Your friend draws a triangle with vertices $A(3, -1)$, $B(4, 3)$, and $C(-1, 2)$. Is your friend correct? Explain your reasoning.

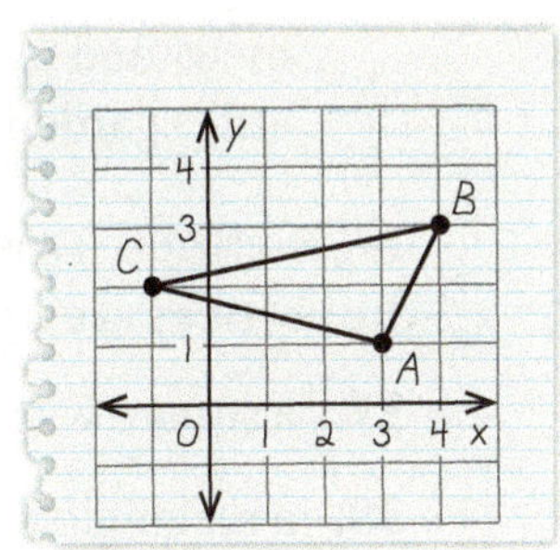

FINDING DISTANCES **Find the distance between the points.**

19. (4, 6), (9, 6)
20. (5, 10), (5, 4)
21. (3, 0), (3, −2)
22. (5, −2), (−6, −2)
23. (−1, 12), (−1, −3)
24. (−7, 8), (7, 8)
25. (−6, 5), (−6, −3.5)
26. (−2.5, 3), (5, 3)
27. (4.5, −1.5), (4.5, 7.25)

GEOMETRY Find the perimeter and the area of the polygon with the given vertices.

28. $C(1, 1), D(1, 4), E(4, 4), F(4, 1)$

29. $J(-1, -2), K(-6, -2), L(-6, -8), M(-1, -8)$

30. $N(-4, 2), P(5, 2), Q(5, 5), R(-4, 5)$

31. $S(-11, -8), T(-11, 0), U(0, 0), V(0, -8)$

32. MP **MODELING REAL LIFE** The coordinates of several stars drawn in a coordinate plane are $(8, 0)$, $(7, -3)$, $(3, -2.5)$, $(3.5, 0.5)$, $(-1, 3)$, $(-3, 5)$, and $(-7, 6)$. Plot the locations of the stars. Draw a constellation by connecting the points.

33. MP **STRUCTURE** The coordinate plane shows three vertices of a parallelogram. Find two possible points that could represent the fourth vertex.

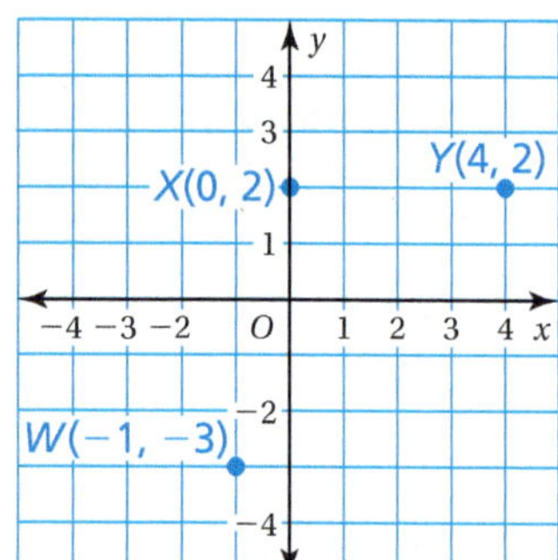

34. MP **PROBLEM SOLVING** Polygon $JKLMNP$ represents a bus route. Each grid square represents 9 square miles. What is the shortest distance, in miles, from Station P to Station L using the bus route? Explain.

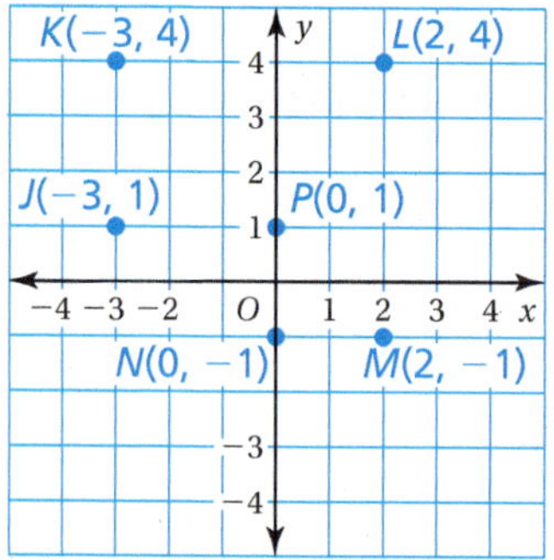

35. MP **MODELING REAL LIFE** In a topographical map of a city, the vertices of the city limits are $A(-7, 3)$, $B(1, 3)$, $C(1, -4)$, $D(-3, -1.5)$, and $E(-7, -1.5)$. The coordinates are measured in miles. What is the area of the city?

36. **DIG DEEPER!** A map shows that the vertices of a backyard are $W(-100, -70)$, $X(-100, 0)$, $Y(0, 0)$, and $Z(-60, -70)$. The coordinates are measured in feet. The line segment XZ separates the backyard into a lawn and a garden. How many times larger is the lawn than the garden?

OPEN-ENDED Draw a polygon with the given conditions in a coordinate plane where the vertices are not all in the same quadrant.

37. a square with a perimeter of 20 units

38. a rectangle with a perimeter of 18 units

39. a rectangle with an area of 24 units^2

40. a triangle with an area of 15 units^2

41. MP **PRECISION** The vertices of a rectangle are $(1, 0)$, $(1, a)$, $(5, a)$, and $(5, 0)$. The vertices of a parallelogram are $(1, 0)$, $(2, b)$, $(6, b)$, and $(5, 0)$. The values of a and b are both positive and $a > b$. Which polygon has a greater area? Explain.

Common Errors

- **Exercises 28–31** Students may confuse perimeter and area. Have them write the formulas and then substitute the values. Students should also include "units" or "square units" as a part of their answers.
- **Exercise 34** Students may be confused by the statement, "Each grid square represents 9 square miles." Help students realize that if 1 grid square is 9 square miles, then 1 unit length is 3 miles.

Mini-Assessment

1. The vertices of a polygon are $A(-3, 2)$, $B(-4, -2)$, $C(3, -3)$, and $D(4, 0)$. Draw the quadrilateral in a coordinate plane.

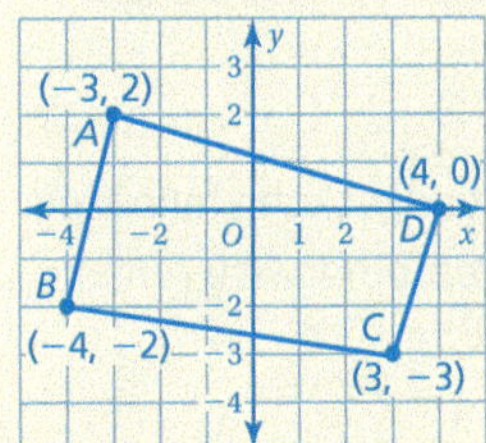

Find the distance between the points.

2. (5, 7), (5, −2) 9
3. (−8, 3.5), (−5, 3.5) 3
4. In a grid of the swimming area at a beach, the vertices are (1, −1), (1, 5), (−4, 5), and (−4, −1). The coordinates are measured in meters. Find the perimeter and the area of the swimming area. 22 m; 30 m^2

Section Resources

Surface Level	Deep Level
Resources by Chapter • Extra Practice • Reteach • Puzzle Time Student Journal • Self-Assessment • Practice Differentiating the Lesson Tutorial Videos Skills Review Handbook Skills Trainer	Resources by Chapter • Enrichment and Extension Graphic Organizers Dynamic Assessment System • Section Practice

Concepts, Skills, & Problem Solving

28. 12 units; 9 units^2
29. 22 units; 30 units^2
30. 24 units; 27 units^2
31. 38 units; 88 units^2
32. See Additional Answers.
33. *Sample answer:* (3, −3); (−5, −3)
34. 27 miles; Traveling from Station *P* to *N* to *M* to *L* is 27 miles. Traveling from Station *P* to *J* to *K* to *L* is 33 miles.
35. 41 mi^2
36. 2.5 times larger
37. *Sample answer:*

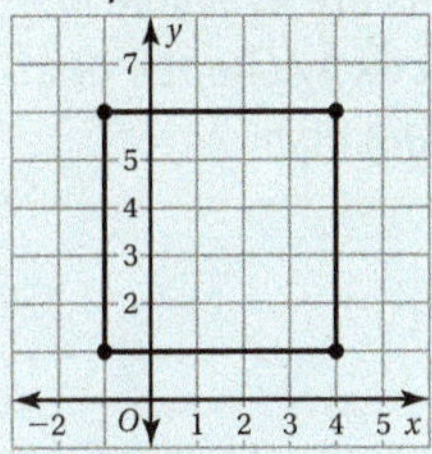

38. *Sample answer:*

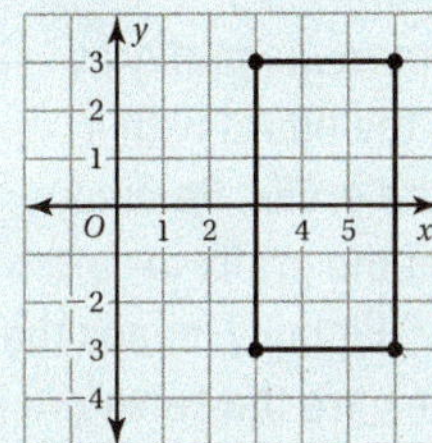

39. *Sample answer:*

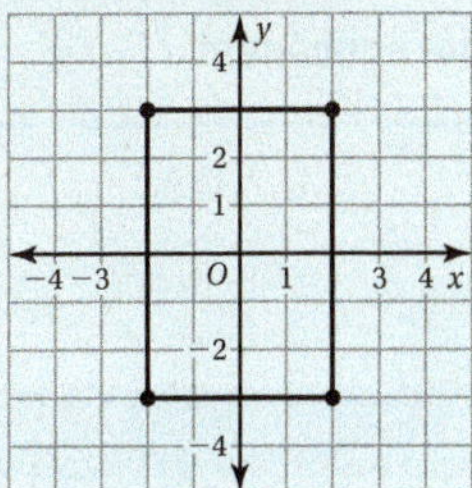

40. See Additional Answers.
41. rectangle; *Sample answer:* Each base is 4 units and the heights are *a* units and *b* units.

Learning Target

Write inequalities and represent solutions of inequalities on number lines.

Success Criteria

- Write word sentences as inequalities.
- Determine whether a value is a solution of an inequality.
- Graph the solutions of inequalities.

Warm Up

Cumulative, vocabulary, and prerequisite skills practice opportunities are available in the *Resources by Chapter* or at *BigIdeasMath.com*.

ELL Support

Review the term *inequality* by writing it on the board with a slash after the prefix. Remind students that the prefix *in–* often means "not." Equality means that two quantities are the same or equivalent. Inequality means that two quantities are *not* the same and are *not* equivalent.

Exploration 1

a. any number greater than 3; 3 or any number greater than 3; 3 or any number less than 3; any number less than 3

b. *Sample answer:* Shade the values to the left or right of 3.

Laurie's Notes

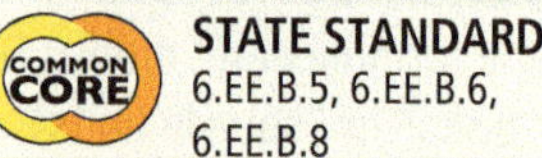

STATE STANDARDS
6.EE.B.5, 6.EE.B.6, 6.EE.B.8

Preparing to Teach

- Students have used inequality vocabulary and symbols (<, >) for the past few years. Now they will add two more symbols: ≤ and ≥. Students will learn their meanings and consider inequalities with more depth.
- **MP6 Attend to Precision:** Mathematically proficient students can state clearly the meanings of the symbols they use. Symbols used in this lesson include <, ≤, >, and ≥. Proficient students understand the difference between $x > 4$ and $x \geq 4$.

Motivate

? As a quick introduction to the vocabulary in this section, ask the following questions. Each student stands up if the answer is *yes*, otherwise remain seated. The corresponding inequalities are provided.
  - "Is your birth month before May?" $m < 5$ or $m \leq 4$
  - "Is your height more than 5 feet?" $h > 5$
  - "Do you have at most 1 sibling?" $x \leq 1$
  - "Do you have at least 1 pet?" $p \geq 1$
- For each question, students should observe that not all students who stand up have the same "answer." For instance, birth months of 1, 2, 3, and 4 all satisfy the first question. Students should also note the numbers that do not work.

Exploration 1

- The exploration introduces all the success criteria.
- Students must read each statement and decide which numbers make sense in the problem. You may want to complete this exploration with larger groups of students or as a class. Every student should have a chance to "be" a number.
- Students may need additional examples of contexts where *at most* and *at least* are used. For instance, "You may have *at most* 2 apples." Or, " You must read *at least* 20 pages." Ask students for more examples and discuss their meanings.

? "In the first statement of part (a), can your class start 30 minutes late? 3 minutes late? 5.5 minutes late?" yes; no; yes

? "How many solutions does the first statement have?" Students might not know the word *infinite*, but they should be able to describe the concept. If students only consider whole-number solutions, bring up rational numbers.

- **Big Idea:** When giving additional numbers that make the statement true, students must consider the context of the problem. For instance, in the last statement, it may not make sense to have a negative number of points.

? "Can you think of a scenario in which fractional numbers are *not* appropriate?" *Sample answer:* You catch at least 7 fish.

- **MP6 Attend to Precision:** Discuss the Math Practice note with students. Students often confuse the **inequality** symbols. I have a poster in my room with the symbols and their translations for students to refer to.
- Have students discuss part (b) with their partners and then share their ideas with the class. Do the graphs they propose include all possible answers?

8.7 Writing and Graphing Inequalities

Learning Target: Write inequalities and represent solutions of inequalities on number lines.

Success Criteria:
- I can write word sentences as inequalities.
- I can determine whether a value is a solution of an inequality.
- I can graph the solutions of inequalities.

EXPLORATION 1 Understanding Inequality Statements

Work with a partner. Create a number line on the floor with both positive and negative integers.

a. For each statement, stand at a number on your number line that makes the statement true. On what other numbers can you stand?

- Class starts more than 3 minutes late.

- You need at least 3 peaches for a recipe.

- The temperature is at most 3 degrees Celsius.

- After playing a video game for 5 minutes, you have fewer than 3 points.

b. How can you represent the solutions of each statement in part (a) on a number line?

Math Practice

State the Meaning of Symbols

You know the inequality symbols $<$ and $>$. What do the symbols $\leq$ and $\geq$ mean?

8.7 Lesson

Key Vocabulary

inequality, *p. 384*
solution of an inequality, *p. 385*
solution set, *p. 385*
graph of an inequality, *p. 386*

An **inequality** is a mathematical sentence that compares expressions. It contains the symbols $<$, $>$, $\leq$, or $\geq$. To write a word sentence as an inequality, look for the following phrases to determine where to place the inequality symbol.

Inequality Symbols				
Symbol	$<$	$>$	$\leq$	$\geq$
Key Phrases	• is less than • is fewer than	• is greater than • is more than	• is less than or equal to • is at most • is no more than	• is greater than or equal to • is at least • is no less than

EXAMPLE 1 Writing Inequalities

Write each word sentence as an inequality.

a. A number c is less than -4.

A number c | is less than | -4.

c $\quad$ $<$ $\quad$ -4

An inequality is $c < -4$.

b. A number k plus 5 is greater than or equal to 8.

A number k plus 5 | is greater than or equal to | 8.

$k + 5$ $\quad$ $\geq$ $\quad$ 8

An inequality is $k + 5 \geq 8$.

c. Four times a number q is at most 16.

Four times a number q | is at most | 16.

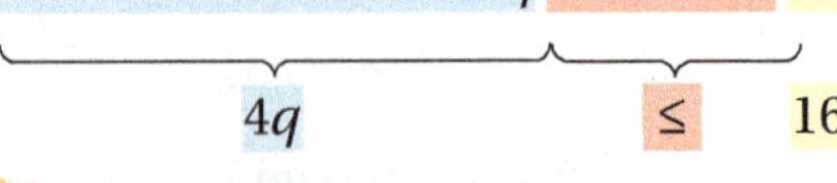

$4q$ $\quad$ $\leq$ $\quad$ 16

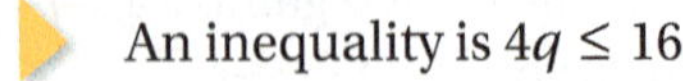

An inequality is $4q \leq 16$.

Try It **Write the word sentence as an inequality.**

1. A number n is greater than 1.
2. Twice a number p is fewer than 7.
3. A number w minus 3 is less than or equal to 10.
4. A number z divided by 2 is at least -6.

Laurie's Notes

Scaffolding Instruction

- In the exploration, different contexts were used to investigate inequalities. Now students will formalize their understanding by translating words into mathematical inequalities, checking solutions of inequalities, and graphing inequalities.
- **Emerging:** Students confuse terms, such as *at least* or *at most*, with the incorrect inequality symbol or have difficulty translating word sentences to a graph. The examples provide practice representing inequalities in both forms.
- **Proficient:** Students understand the table of inequality symbols and have shown competency in translating from words and symbols to graphs. They can work on Try It Exercises 8–11 before moving on to the Self-Assessment exercises.

Discuss

- Discuss the definition of **inequality** and the vocabulary associated with each symbol. If there is not a similar chart hanging in your room, have students copy the chart.

EXAMPLE 1

- If possible, change color as you work through the problems. This will help students view the different components of writing an inequality.
- Work through each part. Note that you are *not* solving the inequalities.
- In part (a), you may want to discuss the difference between the phrases *less than* and *is less than*. If the problem was written as "a number c less than -4," it would represent the expression $-4 - c$.
- Part (c) will be the most challenging. Students may struggle with determining the correct inequality symbol for *at most*. Give them a context to relate to such as, "The wait time to enter is at most 16 minutes." This will help students translate the words using the correct inequality symbol ($\leq$).

Try It

- **Think-Pair-Share:** Students should read each exercise independently and then work in pairs to complete the exercises. Then have each pair compare their answers with another pair and discuss any discrepancies.
- Ask volunteers to write their inequalities on the board.

? "In Exercise 4, the inequality is $\frac{z}{2} \geq -6$. Can $z = 4$?" yes "How do you know?" $4 \div 2 = 2$, which is greater than -6. "Can $z = 0$?" yes "How do you know?" $0 \div 2 = 0$, which is greater than -6.

Scaffold instruction to support all students in their learning. Learning is individualized and you may want to group students differently as they move in and out of these levels with each skill and concept. Student self-assessment and feedback help guide your instructional decisions about how and when to layer support for all students to become proficient learners.

Extra Example 1

Write each word sentence as an inequality.

a. A number t is no more than 7. $t \leq 7$

b. The difference of a number p and 3 is at least 10. $p - 3 \geq 10$

c. One-fourth of a number x is greater than 2. $\frac{1}{4}x > 2$

Try It

1. $n > 1$
2. $2p < 7$
3. $w - 3 \leq 10$
4. $\frac{z}{2} \geq -6$

Extra Example 2

Tell whether the given value is a solution of the inequality.

a. $d - 5 \le 7$; $d = 9$ yes

b. $4y \ge 24$; $y = 6$ yes

c. $\frac{m}{5} < 6$; $m = 30$ no

Try It

5. no

6. yes

7. no

Laurie's Notes

Discuss

- **Vocabulary:** Explain the vocabulary terms **solution of an inequality** and **solution set**.
- **Representation:** Discuss the notation used to show that 8 is *not* less than or equal to 7 ($8 \not\le 7$).
- Use the examples in the table to show the substitution for the value of the variable. If the inequality statement is true, the value of the variable is a solution, otherwise it is not a solution.

EXAMPLE 2

- Work through each part as shown.
- **MP6 Attend to Precision:** In each part, the *value of the variable is substituted* for the variable. Avoid using language such as, "Plug in the number for *x*."
- Note that in part (c), 5 is greater than or equal to 5.

? **Extension:** "Is 15 a solution of the inequality $5 > \frac{z}{3}$? Explain." No, 5 is not greater than 5.

Try It

- **Neighbor Check:** Have students work independently and then have their neighbors check their work. Have students discuss any discrepancies.

ELL Support

Have students work in pairs to discuss and complete Exercises 5–7. Have one student ask the other, "Is 3 a solution?" Then have students switch roles.

Beginner: Write the answer and state "yes" or "no."

Intermediate: Use a sentence to answer such as, "Three is a solution."

Advanced: Explain why 3 is or is not a solution.

A **solution of an inequality** is a value that makes the inequality true. An inequality can have more than one solution. The set of all solutions of an inequality is called the **solution set**.

Value of x	$x + 3 \le 7$	Is the inequality true?
3	$3 + 3 \overset{?}{\le} 7$ $6 \le 7$ ✓	yes
4	$4 + 3 \overset{?}{\le} 7$ $7 \le 7$ ✓	yes
5	$5 + 3 \overset{?}{\le} 7$ $8 \nleq 7$ ✗	no

Reading

The symbol $\nleq$ means *is not less than or equal to.*

EXAMPLE 2 Checking Solutions

Tell whether the given value is a solution of the inequality.

a. $x + 1 > 7;\ x = 8$

$x + 1 > 7$ — Write the inequality.

$8 + 1 \overset{?}{>} 7$ — Substitute 8 for x.

$9 > 7$ ✓ — Add. 9 is greater than 7.

 So, 8 is a solution of the inequality.

b. $7y < 27;\ y = 4$

$7y < 27$ — Write the inequality.

$7(4) \overset{?}{<} 27$ — Substitute 4 for y.

$28 \nless 27$ ✗ — Multiply. 28 is *not* less than 27.

 So, 4 is *not* a solution of the inequality.

c. $5 \ge \frac{z}{3};\ z = 15$

$5 \ge \frac{z}{3}$ — Write the inequality.

$5 \overset{?}{\ge} \frac{15}{3}$ — Substitute 15 for z.

$5 \ge 5$ ✓ — Divide. 5 is greater than or equal to 5.

 So, 15 is a solution of the inequality.

Try It **Tell whether 3 is a solution of the inequality.**

5. $b + 4 < 6$ **6.** $9 - n \ge 6$ **7.** $10 \le 18 \div x$

The **graph of an inequality** shows all the solutions of the inequality on a number line. An open circle, ○, is used when a number is *not* a solution. A closed circle, ●, is used when a number is a solution. An arrow to the left or right shows that the graph continues in that direction.

EXAMPLE 3 Graphing an Inequality

Reading

The inequality $g > 2$ is the same as $2 < g$.

Graph $g > 2$.

Use an open circle because 2 is *not* a solution.

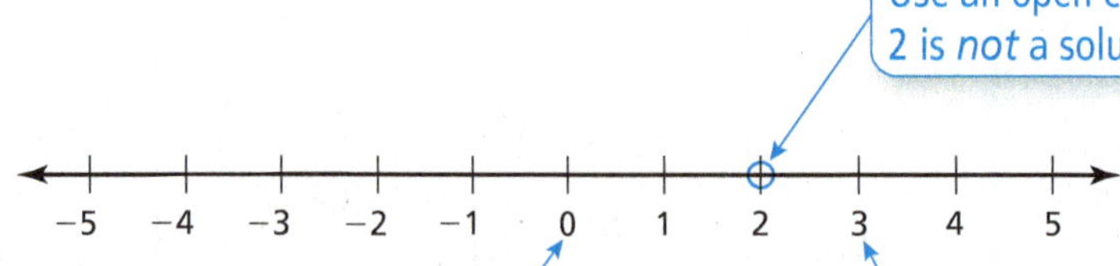

Test a number to the left of 2. $g = 0$ is *not* a solution.

Test a number to the right of 2. $g = 3$ is a solution.

Shade the number line on the side where you found the solution. Every number on the shaded arrow is a solution of the inequality. So, there are *infinitely many* solutions.

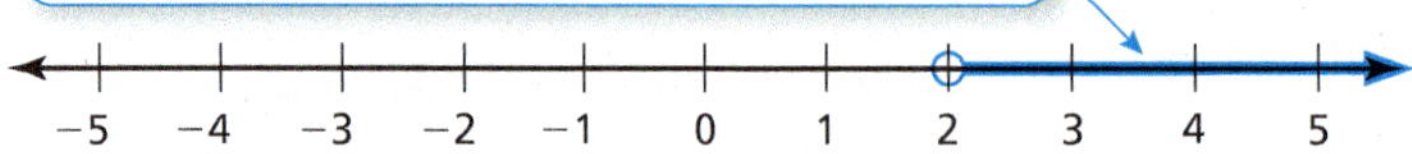

Try It **Graph the inequality on a number line.**

8. $a < 4$ **9.** $f \leq 7$ **10.** $n > 0$ **11.** $-3 \leq p$

Self-Assessment for Concepts & Skills

Solve each exercise. Then rate your understanding of the success criteria in your journal.

12. DIFFERENT WORDS, SAME QUESTION Which is different? Write "both" inequalities.

A number n is at most 3.	A number n is no more than 3.
A number n is less than or equal to 3.	A number n is at least 3.

CHECKING SOLUTIONS **Tell whether the given value is a solution of the inequality.**

13. $p + 5 \leq 12; p = 6$ **14.** $w - 12 < 4; w = 16$

GRAPHING AN INEQUALITY **Graph the inequality on a number line.**

15. $n > 8$ **16.** $q \leq -4$ **17.** $5 < s$

Laurie's Notes

Discuss

- **Vocabulary:** Explain the vocabulary term **graph of an inequality.**
- Discuss the difference between $x > 5$ and $x \geq 5$. Remind students that they know how to describe the difference in words. Now you want to show them the differences when you graph the solution of each.
- Describe the difference between an open circle and a closed circle.
- Graph $x > 5$ and $x \geq 5$.

EXAMPLE 3

- Work through the example. Use the language of *test point* to describe how to determine which side of the boundary point ($g = 2$) to shade.
- **Summarize:** Shading on the number line indicates a solution of the inequality, such as $g = 3$. No shading on the number line indicates that the number is not a solution, such as $g = 0$.
- Be sure to discuss the Reading note with students, as they will encounter inequalities with the variable on the right side of the inequality symbol in the Try It exercises. It is very common for students to graph this type of inequality incorrectly. They will often shade in the wrong direction.

Try It

- **Whiteboards:** Students should work with partners. Have partners complete the exercises independently and then display their graphs simultaneously.
- Check students' graphs in Exercise 11. Students tend to think that the variable must be on the left side of an inequality. Remind students to rewrite or read the inequality for understanding. In other words, if -3 is less than any number p represents, then p must be greater than or equal to -3. So, the solution is -3 or any number greater than -3.

Self-Assessment for Concepts & Skills

- Students should work independently to gauge their progress on meeting the success criteria. Then have students compare their answers with a neighbor. This should prompt beneficial discussion.
- Exercise 12 provides insight into students' understanding of phrases that represent inequalities.
- Check students' graphs of Exercise 17. Listen for conversations about the variable being on the right side of the inequality symbol and how the inequality is read.

ELL Support

Proceed as described in Laurie's Notes for the exercises, but allow students to work in pairs instead of independently. Where instruction indicates that students should compare answers, have two pairs come together.

The Success Criteria Self-Assessment chart can be found in the *Student Journal* or online at *BigIdeasMath.com*.

Extra Example 3

Graph $h \leq 5$.

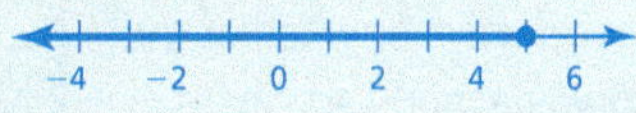

Try It

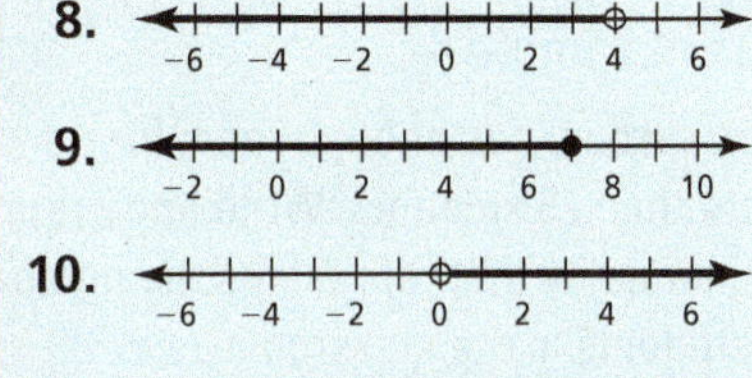

Self-Assessment for Concepts & Skills

12. A number n is at least 3; $n \geq 3$; $n \leq 3$
13. yes
14. no
15. 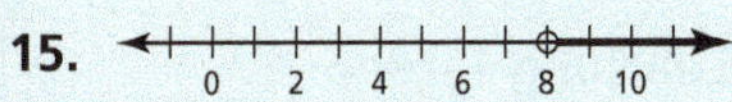

16. 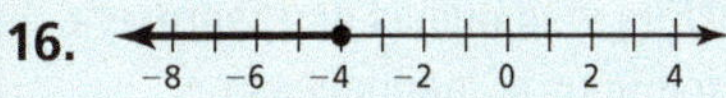

17. 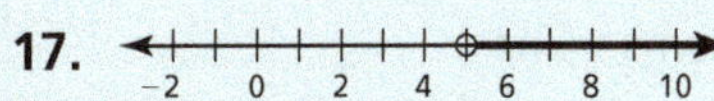

Formative Assessment Tip

Point of Most Significance

This technique is the opposite of *Muddiest Point*. Students are asked to identify the most significant idea, learning, or concept they gained in the lesson. Students reflect on the lesson and identify the key example, problem, or point that contributed to their attainment of the learning target. It is important to know whether the lesson was effective or whether the lesson should be modified. Share with students what you learn from their reflections. Students will take reflections more seriously if they see that you value and use them.

Extra Example 4

A classroom has enough room for no more than 25 students. Write and graph an inequality that represents the number of students in the classroom. $s \le 25$

Self-Assessment for Problem Solving

18. See Additional Answers.

19. yes; *Sample answer:* Halfway up the building is 190 feet, so you can control the drone up to $190 + 200 = 390$ feet.

20. $19.95x > 89.95$

Learning Target

Write inequalities and represent solutions of inequalities on number lines.

Success Criteria

- Write word sentences as inequalities.
- Determine whether a value is a solution of an inequality.
- Graph the solutions of inequalities.

Laurie's Notes

EXAMPLE 4

- All three success criteria can play a part in modeling real-life situations.
- You may need to explain that *up to and including* means the same as *less than or equal to*.
- **Common Misconception:** Students may think that 0 must be included on the number line and that 0 must be centered. In this example, students use a scale on the number line that is not in increments of 1 and is not centered at 0.
- Have students work with a partner on this problem. Then have students share their inequalities and checks using a test point that is in the shaded part of the number line.
- **Note**: Some contextual problems will be restricted to only positive numbers, however, students are not asked to work with compound inequalities in this course. Students may recognize that a solution set is restricted to only positive numbers, but they are not expected to reflect that in their inequalities.
- ? Stop and ask students, "What was the *Point of Most Significance* in this lesson?"

Self-Assessment for Problem Solving

- Students may benefit from trying the exercises independently and then working with peers to refine their work. It is important to provide time in class for problem solving, so that students become comfortable with the problem-solving plan.
- Explaining answers provides feedback to both you and the student about his or her level of understanding. These exercises ask students to represent inequalities algebraically, graphically, and verbally. Students need to justify their mathematical reasoning and make real-life decisions based upon the mathematics.
- Students are applying their understanding of all three success criteria.

The Success Criteria Self-Assessment chart can be found in the *Student Journal* or online at *BigIdeasMath.com*.

Closure

- Write the word sentence as an inequality. Then graph the inequality on a number line.
- A number a is greater than 2. $a > 2$

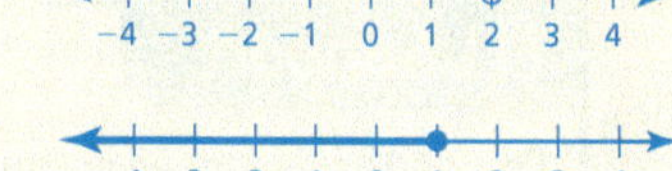

- A number b is less than or equal to 1. $b \le 1$

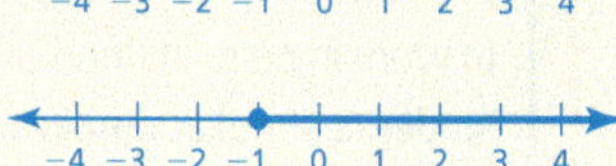

- A number x is at least −1. $x \ge -1$

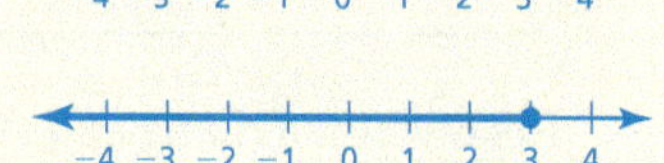

- A number y is at most 3. $y \le 3$

−4 −3 −2 −1 0 1 2 3 4

EXAMPLE 4 Modeling Real Life

The NASA *Solar Probe Plus* can withstand temperatures up to and including 2600°F. Write and graph an inequality that represents the temperatures the probe can withstand.

Words	temperatures	up to and including	2600°F
Variable	Let t be the temperatures (in degrees Fahrenheit) that the probe can withstand.		
Inequality	t	$\leq$	2600

An inequality is $t \leq 2600$.

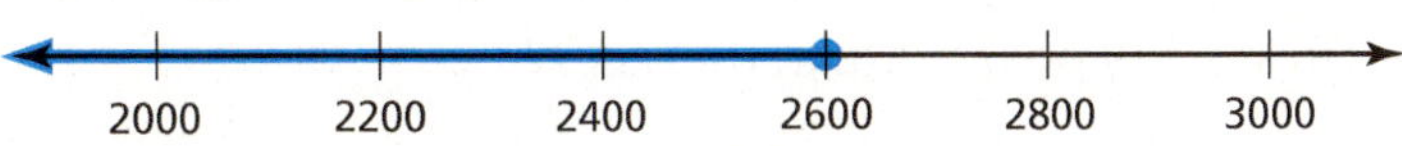

Check The graph shows that 2000°F is a solution. Check this in the inequality.

$$t \leq 2600$$

$$2000 \leq 2600 \checkmark$$

Self-Assessment for Problem Solving

Solve each exercise. Then rate your understanding of the success criteria in your journal.

18. To obtain a babysitting license, you still need to train for at least 6 hours and 45 minutes. Describe the amounts of time that you can train and still not obtain a license. Use a graph to justify your answer.

19. **DIG DEEPER!** The farthest away a drone can fly is 200 meters. A building is 380 meters tall. You control the drone from a floor that is halfway to the top of the building. Can the drone reach the top of the building? Explain your reasoning.

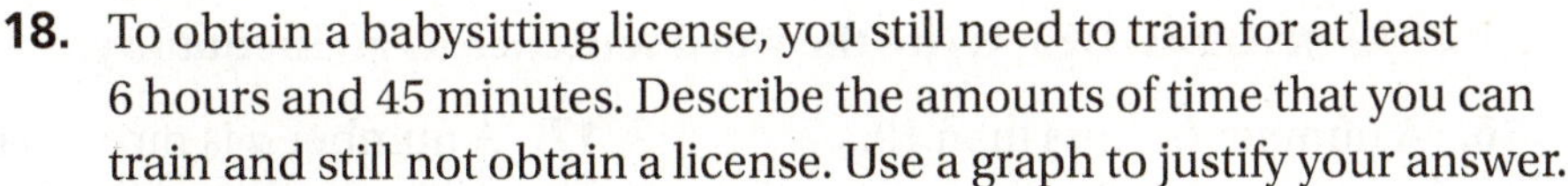

20. Each visit to a water park costs \$19.95. An annual pass to the park costs \$89.95. Write an inequality that represents the numbers of times you would need to visit the park for the pass to be a better deal.

8.7 Practice

Go to **BigIdeasMath.com** to get HELP with solving the exercises.

Review & Refresh

Find the distance between the points.

1. (2, 8), (6, 8)
2. (−5, 9), (7, 9)
3. (−3, 6), (−3, −2)

Solve the equation. Check your solution.

4. $x + 3 = 12$
5. $x - 6 = 8$
6. $\frac{t}{12} = 4$
7. $8x = 72$

8. A stack of boards is 24 inches high. The thickness of each board is $\frac{3}{8}$ inch. How many boards are in the stack?

   A. $\frac{1}{9}$ **B.** $\frac{1}{6}$ **C.** 9 **D.** 64

Find the area of the parallelogram.

9. 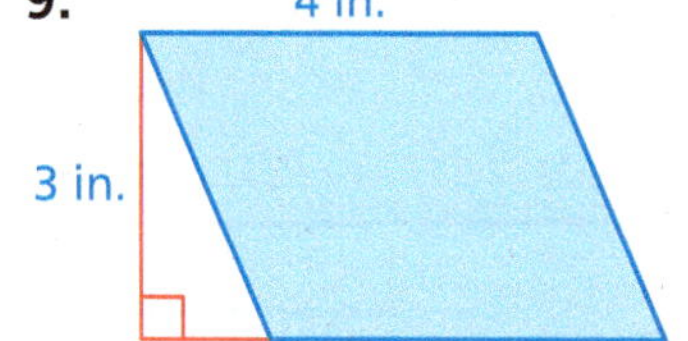

10. 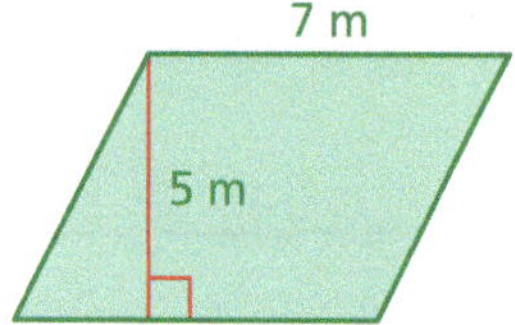

11. 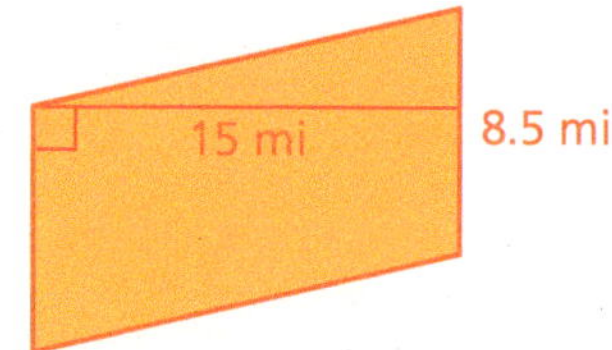

Concepts, Skills, & Problem Solving

UNDERSTANDING INEQUALITY STATEMENTS **Choose a number that makes the statement true. What other numbers make the statement true?** (See Exploration 1, p. 383.)

12. You are less than 3 miles from home.
13. You need at least $5 for lunch.
14. You buy more than 2 movie tickets.
15. A game lasts no more than 10 minutes.

WRITING INEQUALITIES **Write the word sentence as an inequality.**

16. A number k is less than 10.
17. A number a is more than 6.
18. A number z is fewer than $\frac{3}{4}$.
19. A number b is at least −3.
20. One plus a number y is no more than −13.
21. A number x divided by 3 is at most 5.

CHECKING SOLUTIONS **Tell whether the given value is a solution of the inequality.**

22. $x - 1 \le 7;\ x = 6$
23. $y + 5 < 13;\ y = 17$
24. $3z > 6;\ z = 3$
25. $6 \le \frac{b}{2};\ b = 10$
26. $c + 2.5 < 4.3;\ c = 1.8$
27. $a \le 0;\ a = -5$

Assignment Guide and Concept Check

Scaffold assignments to support all students in their learning progression. The suggested assignments are a starting point. Continue to assign additional exercises and revisit with spaced practice to move every student toward proficiency.

Level	Assignment 1	Assignment 2
Emerging	3, 7, 8, 11, 12, 17, 19, 23, 24, 28, 29, 30, 31, 33, 35	21, 26, 40, 41, 44, 48, 49, 50, 51
Proficient	3, 7, 8, 11, 13, 18, 19, 22, 25, 28, 29, 30, 31, 40, 41	26, 43, 44, 48, 49, 51, 52, 54, 55, 56
Advanced	3, 7, 8, 11, 15, 18, 21, 25, 26, 28, 29, 30, 31, 42, 43	46, 48, 49, 52, 53, 54, 55, 56, 57, 58

- Assignment 1 is for use after students complete the Self-Assessment for Concepts & Skills.
- Assignment 2 is for use after students complete the Self-Assessment for Problem Solving.
- The red exercises can be used as a concept check.

Review & Refresh Prior Skills

Exercises 1–3 Finding Distances between Points
Exercises 4–7 Solving Equations
Exercise 8 Dividing Fractions
Exercises 9–12 Finding the Area of a Parallelogram

Common Errors

- **Exercises 16–21** Students may struggle with knowing which symbol to use in the inequality. Encourage students to put the word sentence into a real-life context or to use the table in the lesson that explains which symbol matches each phrase.
- **Exercises 22–27** Students may try to perform operations on both sides of the inequality (often not the same operation) to get both sides to be the same answer. Remind students that they are checking to see if the value of the variable makes the inequality true, so they are simplifying one side of the inequality and comparing the result to the other side.

Review & Refresh

1. 4
2. 12
3. 8
4. $x = 9$
5. $x = 14$
6. $t = 48$
7. $x = 9$
8. D
9. 12 in.^{2}
10. 35 m^2
11. 127.5 mi^2

Concepts, Skills, & Problem Solving

12. any number less than 3
13. 5 or any number greater than 5
14. any number greater than 2
15. 10 or any number less than 10
16. $k < 10$
17. $a > 6$
18. $z < \frac{3}{4}$
19. $b \geq -3$
20. $1 + y \leq -13$
21. $\frac{x}{3} \leq 5$
22. yes
23. no
24. yes
25. no
26. no
27. yes

Concepts, Skills, & Problem Solving

28. B **29.** A

30. D **31.** C

32. −2 0 2 4 6 8 10

33. −4 0 4 8 12 16 20

34. −6 −4 −2 0 2 4 6

35. −3 −2 −1 0 1 2 3

36. $-\frac{4}{9}$ $-\frac{2}{9}$ 0 $\frac{2}{9}$ $\frac{4}{9}$ $\frac{6}{9}$ $\frac{8}{9}$

37. −6 −4 −2 0 2 4 6

38. −6 −4 −2 0 2 4 6

39. −6 −4 −2 0 2 4 6

40. −3 −2 −1 0 1 2 3

41. −3 −2 −1 0 1 2 3

42. −1.8 −1.6 −1.4 −1.2 −1.0 −0.8 −0.6

43. $\frac{4}{3}$ $\frac{5}{3}$ $\frac{6}{3}$ $\frac{7}{3}$ $\frac{8}{3}$ $\frac{9}{3}$ $\frac{10}{3}$

44. $x < 1$; A number x is less than 1.

45. $x \leq 1$; A number x is at most 1.

46. $x \geq -4$; A number x is at least -4.

47. $x > 0$; A number x is more than 0.

48. yes; The graph is correct.

49. no; The graph shows $x < -1$, not $x > -1$.

50. $f > 2252.4$ m;

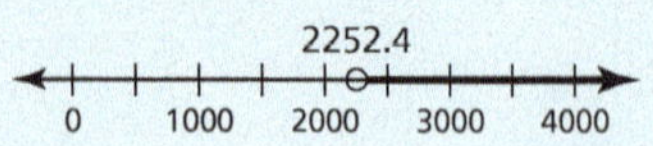

51. **a.** $b \leq 3$;

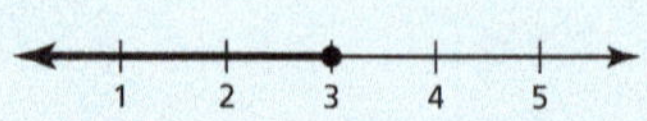

b. $\ell \geq 18$;

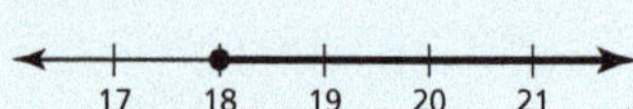

Common Errors

- **Exercises 28–31** Students may mix up open and closed circles when matching. Remind students that an open circle means the number is not included and a closed circle means that the number is included.
- **Exercises 32–43** Students may shade the number line in the wrong direction. This often happens when the variable is on the right side of the inequality. Remind students to use test points to the left and right of the boundary point to determine which direction to shade the number line.
- **Exercises 32–43** Students may draw a closed circle instead of an open circle and vice versa. Remind students that an open circle means the number is not included and a closed circle means the number is included.
- **Exercise 51** Students may mix up the inequalities given in the word problem. Remind students to read carefully and encourage them to write word sentences for the given information.

MATCHING Match the inequality with its graph.

28. $x \geq -2$ **29.** $x < -2$ **30.** $x > -2$ **31.** $x \leq -2$

A. −3 −2 −1 0 1 2 3

B. −3 −2 −1 0 1 2 3

C. −3 −2 −1 0 1 2 3

D. −3 −2 −1 0 1 2 3

GRAPHING AN INEQUALITY Graph the inequality on a number line.

32. $a > 4$ **33.** $n \geq 8$ **34.** $3 \geq x$ **35.** $y < \frac{1}{2}$

36. $x < \frac{2}{9}$ **37.** $-3 \geq c$ **38.** $m > -5$ **39.** $0 \leq b$

40. $1.5 > f$ **41.** $t \geq -\frac{1}{2}$ **42.** $p > -1.6$ **43.** $\frac{7}{3} \geq z$

OPEN-ENDED Write an inequality and a word sentence that represent the graph.

44. −3 −2 −1 0 1 2 3

45.

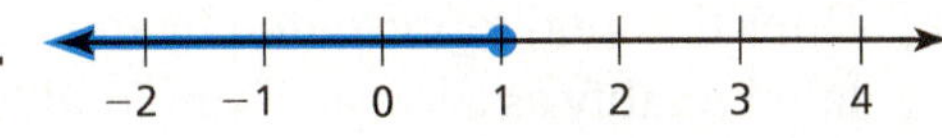

46. −6 −4 −2 0 2 4 6

47.

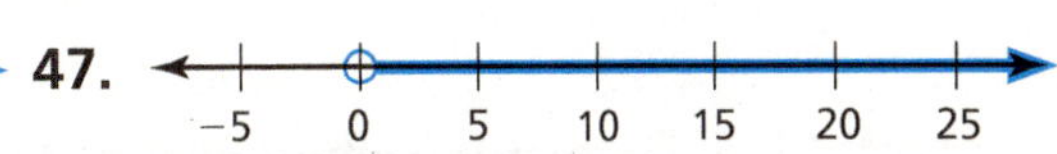

MP YOU BE THE TEACHER Your friend graphs the inequality. Is your friend correct? Explain your reasoning.

48.

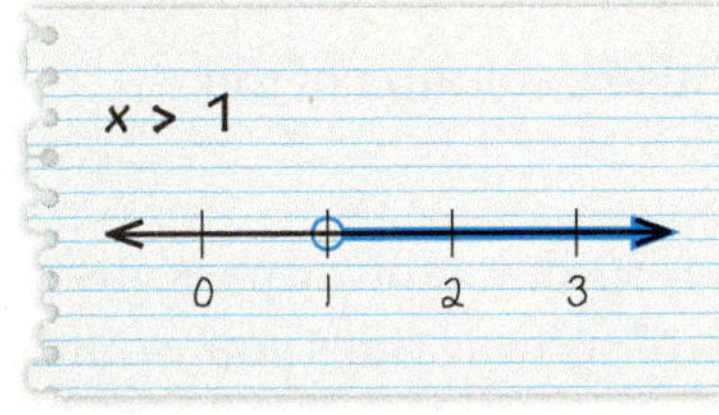

49.

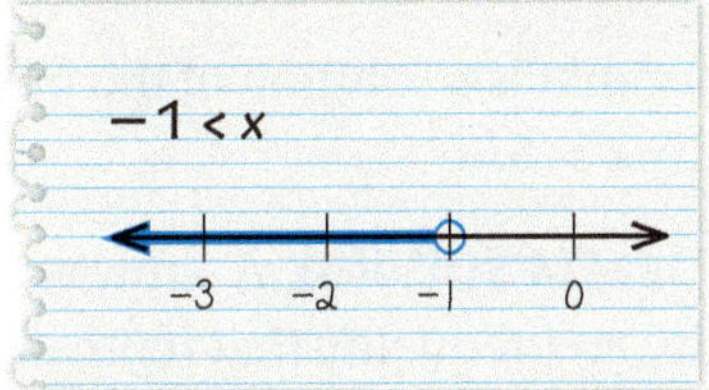

50. **MP MODELING REAL LIFE** The world record for the farthest flight by hoverboard is 2252.4 meters. Write and graph an inequality that represents the distances that would set a new world record.

51. **MP MODELING REAL LIFE** You are fishing and are allowed to keep at most 3 striped bass. Each striped bass must be no less than 18 inches long.

a. Write and graph an inequality that represents the numbers of striped bass you are allowed to keep.

b. Write and graph an inequality that represents the lengths of striped bass you are allowed to keep.

52. **MP REASONING** You have \$33. You want to buy a necklace and one other item from the list.

Item	Price (with tax)
T-shirt	\$15
Book	\$20
Sunglasses	\$13
Necklace	\$16

a. Write an inequality that represents the situation.

b. Can the other item be a T-shirt? Explain.

c. Can the other item be a book? Explain.

53. **MP LOGIC** For a food to be labeled *low sodium*, there must be no more than 140 milligrams of sodium per serving.

a. Write and graph an inequality that represents the amount of sodium in a low-sodium serving.

b. Write and graph an inequality that represents the amount of sodium in a serving that does *not* qualify as low sodium.

c. Does the food represented by the nutrition facts label qualify as a low-sodium food? Explain.

Nutrition Facts

4 servings per container

Serving size ½ cup (114g)

Amount per serving	
Calories	**90**
	% Daily Value*
Total Fat 3g	5%
Saturated Fat 0g	0%
Cholesterol 0mg	0%
Sodium 300mg	13%
Total Carbohydrate 13g	4%
Dietary Fiber 3g	12%
Sugars 3g	
Protein 3g	
Vitamin A 80% •	Vitamin C 60%
Calcium 4 % •	Iron 4%

CRITICAL THINKING Determine whether the statement is *always*, *sometimes*, or *never* true. Explain your reasoning.

54. A number that is a solution of the inequality $x > 5$ is also a solution of the inequality $x \geq 5$.

55. A number that is a solution of the inequality $5 \leq x$ is also a solution of the inequality $x > 5$.

56. **MP PROBLEM SOLVING** A subway ride costs \$1.50. A 30-day subway pass costs \$36. Write an inequality that represents the numbers of subway rides you would need to take for the pass to be a better deal.

57. **MP PROBLEM SOLVING** Fifty people are seated in a movie theater. The maximum capacity of the theater is 425 people. Write an inequality that represents the numbers of additional people who can be seated.

58. **CRITICAL THINKING** The map shows the elevations above sea level for an area of land.

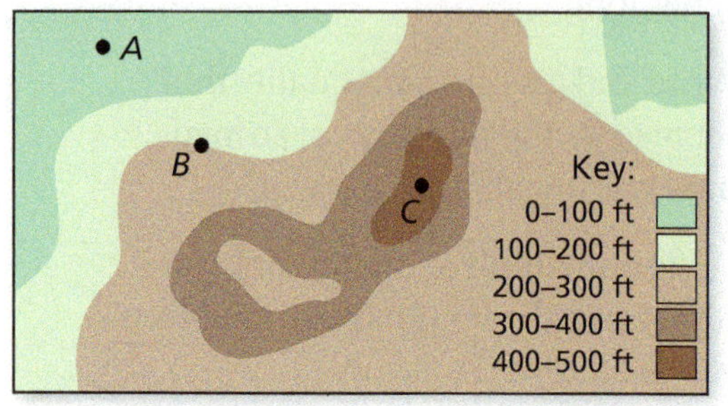

a. Graph the possible elevations of A. Write the set of elevations as two inequalities.

b. Graph the possible elevations of C. How can you write this set of elevations as a single inequality? Explain.

c. What is the elevation of B? Explain.

For Your Information

- **Exercise 58** Part (b) introduces the concept of compound inequalities.

Mini-Assessment

Write the word sentence as an inequality.

1. A number b is at least 5. $b \geq 5$
2. Twice a number s is less than 15. $2s < 15$

Tell whether the given value is a solution of the inequality.

3. $3x > 16$; $x = 6$ yes
4. $12 - n \geq 5$; $n = 8$ no
5. No more than 10 people will go to the movies. Write and graph an inequality to represent the number of people that go to the movies. $x \leq 10$

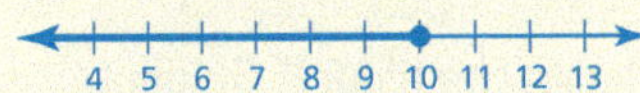

Section Resources

Surface Level	Deep Level
Resources by Chapter • Extra Practice • Reteach • Puzzle Time Student Journal • Self-Assessment • Practice Differentiating the Lesson Tutorial Videos Skills Review Handbook Skills Trainer	Resources by Chapter • Enrichment and Extension Graphic Organizers Dynamic Assessment System • Section Practice

Concepts, Skills, & Problem Solving

52. a. $x \leq 17$

b. yes; $15 \leq 17$

c. no; $20 > 17$

53. a. $s \leq 140$;

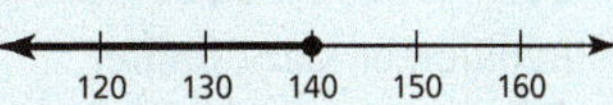

b. $s > 140$;

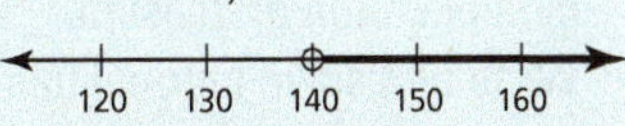

c. no; There are 300 milligrams of sodium in one serving, which is greater than 140.

54. always; A number that is greater than 5 is always greater than or equal to 5.

55. sometimes; The only time this is not true is if $x = 5$.

56. $1.50x > 36$

57. $p + 50 \leq 425$

58. a. $e \geq 0, e \leq 100$

b. $400 \leq e \leq 500$; The elevation is between 400 feet and 500 feet.

c. 200 feet; B falls on the border of two ranges of elevation:
$100 \leq e \leq 200$
$200 \leq e \leq 300$
The only elevation that is a solution of both inequalities is 200 feet.

Learning Target

Write and solve inequalities.

Success Criteria

- Apply the properties of inequality to generate equivalent inequalities.
- Solve inequalities using addition or subtraction.
- Solve inequalities using multiplication or division.
- Write and solve inequalities that represent real-life problems.

Warm Up

Cumulative, vocabulary, and prerequisite skills practice opportunities are available in the *Resources by Chapter* or at *BigIdeasMath.com*.

ELL Support

Students may be familiar with the word *property* as it describes objects or real estate that people own. Explain that in mathematics, a property is a rule that states characteristics, traits, or attributes. For example, the properties of inequality provide rules that can be applied to inequalities.

Exploration 1

a. *Sample answer:* Replace the equal sign with a greater than sign.

b. $x > 8$; *Sample answer:* Subtract 4 from 12 and from $x + 4$.

c. $4x < 20$; *Sample answer:* $x < 5$

Laurie's Notes

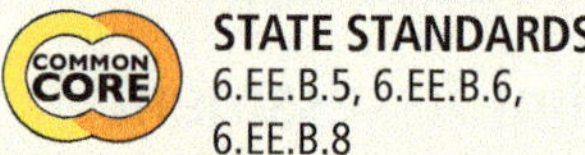

STATE STANDARDS
6.EE.B.5, 6.EE.B.6, 6.EE.B.8

Preparing to Teach

- Students are connecting their prior knowledge of solving one-step equations to solving one-step inequalities.
- As students analyze tape diagrams, they can apply their skills of writing and graphing inequalities to solving them.

Motivate

? Ask a series of questions that suggest the properties of inequality that will be used today. Samples:
  - "I am older than each of you. In 3 years, who will be older?" Students should recognize that adding 3 years to each age does not change the fact that you are older than your students.
  - "A 2D movie ticket costs less than a 3D movie ticket. If both prices double, which ticket is cheaper?" Students should recognize that doubling each price does not change the fact that a 2D movie ticket is cheaper than a 3D movie ticket.
- This introduction helps to create context for the properties of inequality.

Exploration 1

◎ This exploration introduces the first three success criteria.

- Students should be comfortable using tape diagrams from modeling equations. Have pairs discuss and answer part (a). Select volunteers to share.

? "How can you change the original tape diagram to represent the new relationship?" Make the x part longer.

? "In part (b), how does the first tape diagram change into the second tape diagram?" $4 + 8$ is substituted for 12 "What happens to the 4s in the last tape diagram?" 4 is subtracted from both tapes. "What does the last tape diagram represent?" The solution of the inequality ($x > 8$). "What numbers are solutions of the inequality?" numbers greater than 8 "What numbers are *not* solutions of the inequality?" numbers less than or equal to 8

? "In part (c), can you tell just by looking at the tape diagram if it represents a *less than* or *greater than* situation? Explain." Allow pairs to discuss before responding. Listen for students recognizing that the tapes are not the same length, so the tape diagram must represent an inequality.

- Have pairs complete part (c) and share their ideas with the class. Control the sequence of responses to lead up to a well-defined conclusion.
- **MP6 Attend to Precision**: Mathematically proficient students communicate using correct mathematical vocabulary. In their discussions, students assign meaning to both symbols (inequality signs) and tools (tape diagrams).

8.8 Solving Inequalities

Learning Target: Write and solve inequalities.

Success Criteria:
- I can apply the properties of inequality to generate equivalent inequalities.
- I can solve inequalities using addition or subtraction.
- I can solve inequalities using multiplication or division.
- I can write and solve inequalities that represent real-life problems.

EXPLORATION 1 Using Tape Diagrams

Work with a partner. In Section 6.2 Exploration 1, the tape diagram below was used to model the equation $x + 4 = 12$.

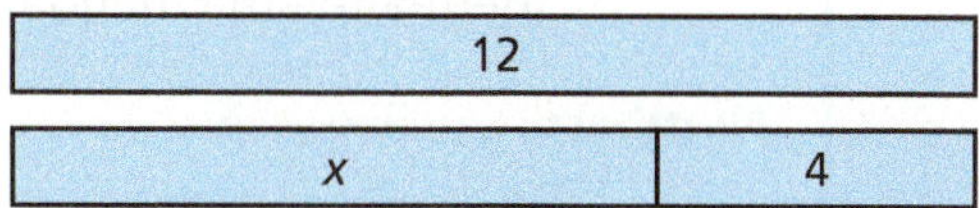

a. Suppose that $x + 4$ is greater than 12. How can you change the equation to represent the new relationship between $x + 4$ and 12?

b. A student finds the possible values of x using the tape diagrams below. What is the solution? How can you find the solution algebraically?

> **Math Practice**
>
> **Interpret a Solution**
>
> How is the solution in part (b) different from the solution of an equation?

c. Describe the relationship between $4x$ and 20 as shown by the tape diagram below. What can you conclude about x?

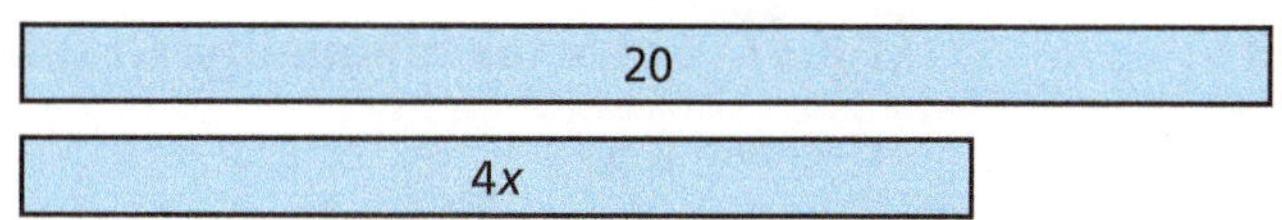

8.8 Lesson

You can solve inequalities the same way you solve equations. Use inverse operations to get the variable by itself.

Addition Property of Inequality

Words When you add the same number to each side of an inequality, the inequality remains true.

Numbers

$$\begin{array}{rr} 3 < & 5 \\ +2 & +2 \\ \hline 5 < & 7 \end{array}$$

Algebra

$$\begin{array}{rr} x - 4 > & 5 \\ +4 & +4 \\ \hline x > & 9 \end{array}$$

Subtraction Property of Inequality

Words When you subtract the same number from each side of an inequality, the inequality remains true.

Numbers

$$\begin{array}{rr} 3 < & 5 \\ -2 & -2 \\ \hline 1 < & 3 \end{array}$$

Algebra

$$\begin{array}{rr} x + 4 > & 5 \\ -4 & -4 \\ \hline x > & 1 \end{array}$$

These properties are also true for ≤ and ≥.

EXAMPLE 1 Solving Inequalities Using Addition or Subtraction

a. Solve $x - 3 > 1$. Graph the solution.

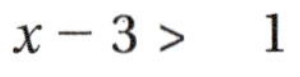

$x - 3 > 1$ Write the inequality.

Undo the subtraction. → $+3 \quad +3$ Addition Property of Inequality

$x > 4$ Simplify.

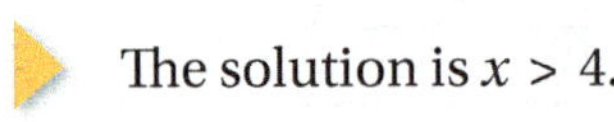

The solution is $x > 4$.

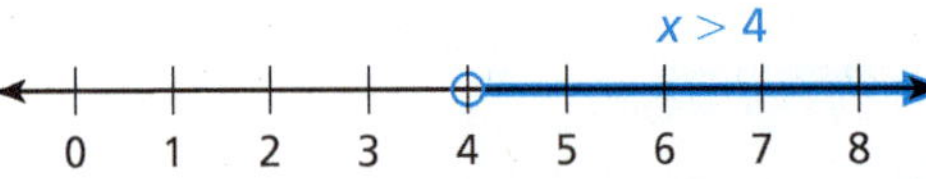

b. Solve $15 \geq 6 + h$. Graph the solution.

$15 \geq 6 + h$ Write the inequality.

Undo the addition. → $-6 \quad -6$ Subtraction Property of Inequality

$9 \geq h$ Simplify.

The solution is $h \leq 9$.

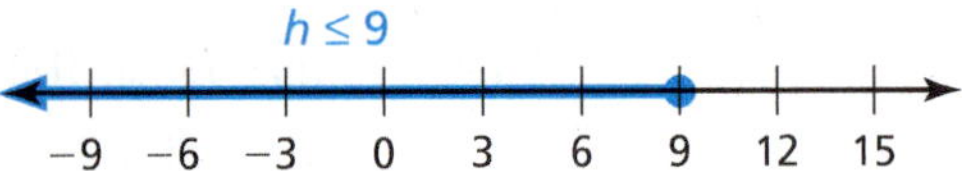

Math Practice

Communicate Precisely

Explain why $h \leq 9$ is the same as $9 \geq h$.

Try It **Solve the inequality. Graph the solution.**

1. $x - 2 < 3$

2. $10 \geq z - 1$

3. $y + 2 \geq 17$

Laurie's Notes

Scaffolding Instruction

- Students go from *exploring* solutions of inequalities to *applying* properties of inequalities to solve algebraically and graphically.
- **Emerging:** Students may not have a mental picture of the solution for a specific inequality that is greater or less than a certain number. They may have difficulty working with an inequality in which the variable is on the right side. The examples provide practice using properties to solve inequalities.
- **Proficient:** Students intuitively visualize the solutions of inequalities and have mastered writing word sentences as inequalities. After reviewing the Key Ideas, they can proceed to the Self-Assessment exercises.
- **MP5 Use Appropriate Tools Strategically:** A number line can help students visualize the results of solving an inequality. Students know what the graph of $x \geq 6$ looks like. Seeing the graph of the solution to the inequality $x + 2 \geq 6$ helps students verify that $x = 4$ is a solution, but all values less than 4 are not. Students test values on either side of the boundary point to determine where to shade the number line.

Scaffold instruction to support all students in their learning. Learning is individualized and you may want to group students differently as they move in and out of these levels with each skill and concept. Student self-assessment and feedback help guide your instructional decisions about how and when to layer support for all students to become proficient learners.

Key Ideas

- Refer to the push-pin note. Point out that the properties of inequality correspond to the properties of equality. When using properties of inequality, there is no need to temporarily replace the inequality symbol with an equal sign.
- Remind students to line up their inequality symbols as they solve vertically.
- **Teaching Tip:** Students may want to solve the inequalities in their heads and resist writing their work down. Remind students that you are helping them develop good problem-solving techniques. The problems will become more involved later and students need to know how to record the process.
- **Note:** Applying the properties also results in equivalent inequalities. For example, if $x + 5 > 9$, then $x + 2 > 6$ and $x > 4$ are equivalent inequalities.

EXAMPLE 1

? In part (a), ask, "How do you graph $x > 4$?" open circle at 4, shade to the right of 4 "How do you know which side of the boundary point ($x = 4$) to shade?" test values on each side of 4 "Why is there an open circle?" 4 is not a solution.

? "Is $15 \geq 6 + h$ equivalent to $15 \geq h + 6$? Explain." Yes, addition is commutative. "Is $15 \geq 6 + h$ equivalent to $6 + h \leq 15$? Explain." Yes, if $a \geq b$, then $b \leq a$.

- Students can solve an equivalent inequality or the original inequality.
- Note the last step in part (b) involves rewriting the solution so the variable is on the left side of the inequality symbol.
- **Big Idea:** The solution $h \leq 9$ means that all numbers less than or equal to 9 are solutions. The graph conveys this idea with the left-pointing arrow and the use of negative numbers.

Extra Example 1

a. Solve $5 \leq x - 4$. Graph the solution.

$9 \leq x$ or $x \geq 9$;

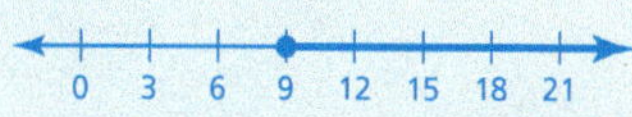

b. Solve $n + 7 < 8$. Graph the solution.

$n < 1$;

−4 −3 −2 −1 0 1 2 3 4

Try It

1. $x < 5$;

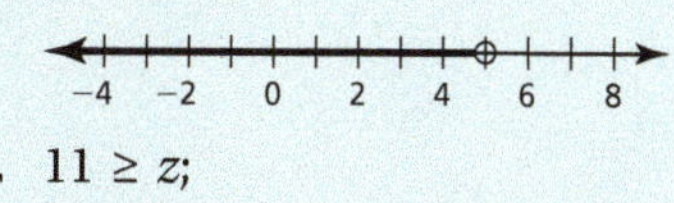

2. $11 \geq z$;

3. $y \geq 15$;

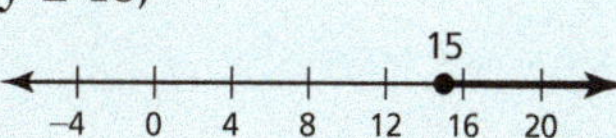

Extra Example 2

a. Solve $8h < 56$. Graph the solution.

$h < 7$;

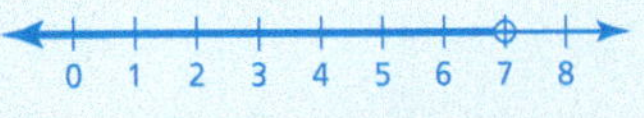

b. Solve $4 \geq r \div 2$. Graph the solution.

$8 \geq r$ or $r \leq 8$;

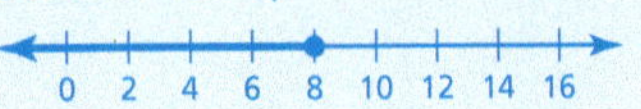

Try It

4. $p \geq 6$;

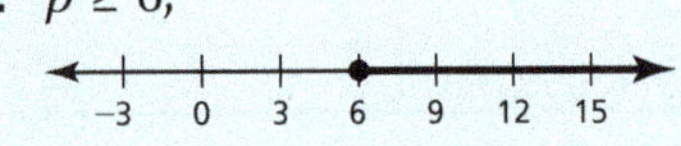

5. $7 < s$;

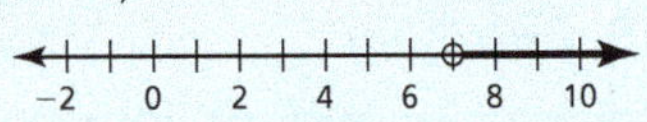

6. $k \leq 3$;

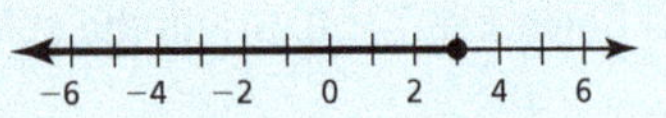

Laurie's Notes

Key Ideas

- Discuss the Words, Numbers, and Algebra.
- Remind students that solving inequalities is similar to solving equations.
- The inequalities solved in this lesson do *not* involve multiplying or dividing by a negative quantity. This type of inequality is taught in a future course.
- Tell students that they are working on the first and third success criteria.

EXAMPLE 2

- Work through each part as shown.
- ? "How do you graph $x < 10$?" open circle at 10, shade to the left of 10
- ? "How do you know which side of the boundary point ($x = 10$) to shade?" test values on each side of 10 "Why is the circle open?" 10 is not a solution.
- **MP5 Use Appropriate Tools Strategically:** In checking their solutions, have students check numbers on either side of the open (or closed) circle.
- ? "How do you undo a multiplication inequality?" divide
- ? "Why is the circle in part (b) closed?" 8 is a solution.
- Discuss with students the scale used for the graph in part (b). Remind them that it is not necessary to use increments of 1 on a number line.

Try It

- **Think-Pair-Share**: Students should read each exercise independently and then work in pairs to complete the exercises. Then have each pair compare their answers with another pair and discuss any discrepancies.
- Note that division in Exercise 4 is represented differently than the division in Exercise 5.
- **Common Error**: In Exercise 5, because the variable is on the right, it is common for students to shade the wrong side of the inequality when graphing.

ELL Support

Have students work in groups to discuss and complete Exercises 4–6. Monitor discussions and expect students at different language levels to perform as described.

Beginner: Write the solution.

Intermediate: State the solution. For example, "p is greater than or equal to six."

Advanced: Guide other students through the process of solving the inequality.

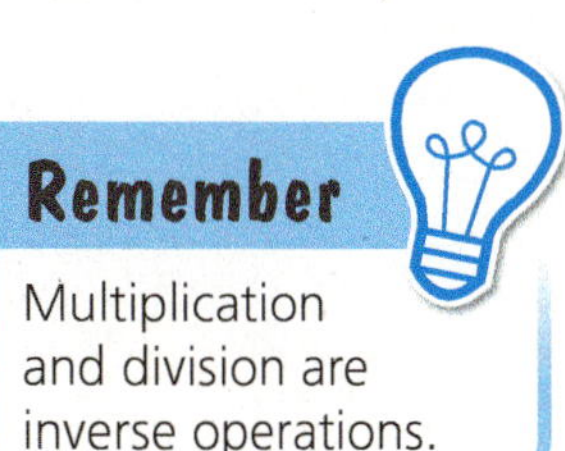

Key Ideas

Multiplication Property of Inequality

Words When you multiply each side of an inequality by the same *positive* number, the inequality remains true.

Numbers

$$8 > 6$$
$$8 \times 2 > 6 \times 2$$
$$16 > 12$$

Algebra

$$\frac{x}{4} < 2$$
$$\frac{x}{4} \cdot 4 < 2 \cdot 4$$
$$x < 8$$

Division Property of Inequality

Words When you divide each side of an inequality by the same *positive* number, the inequality remains true.

Numbers

$$8 > 6$$
$$8 \div 2 > 6 \div 2$$
$$4 > 3$$

Algebra

$$4x < 8$$
$$\frac{4x}{4} < \frac{8}{4}$$
$$x < 2$$

These properties are also true for $\leq$ and $\geq$.

EXAMPLE 2 Solving Inequalities Using Multiplication or Division

a. Solve $\frac{x}{5} < 2$. Graph the solution.

$\frac{x}{5} < 2$ — Write the inequality.

Undo the division. → $\frac{x}{5} \cdot 5 < 2 \cdot 5$ — Multiplication Property of Inequality

$x < 10$ — Simplify.

The solution is $x < 10$.

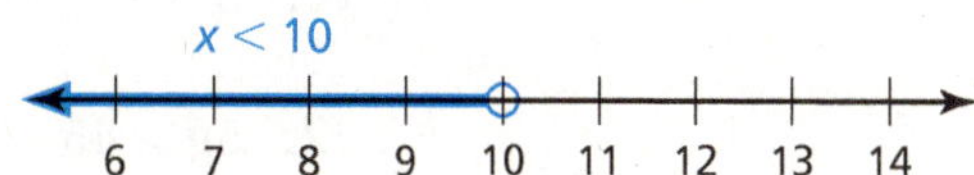

b. Solve $4n \geq 32$. Graph the solution.

$4n \geq 32$ — Write the inequality.

Undo the multiplication. → $\frac{4n}{4} \geq \frac{32}{4}$ — Division Property of Inequality

$n \geq 8$ — Simplify.

The solution is $n \geq 8$.

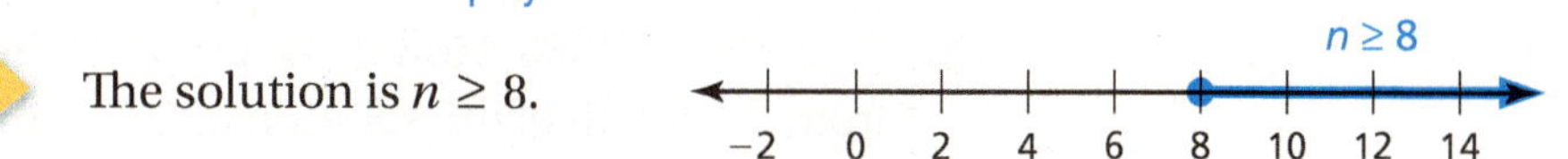

Try It **Solve the inequality. Graph the solution.**

4. $p \div 3 \geq 2$

5. $1 < \frac{s}{7}$

6. $11k \leq 33$

EXAMPLE 3 Solving an Inequality Using a Reciprocal

Solve $\frac{2x}{3} \le 4$. Graph the solution.

$$\frac{2x}{3} \le 4 \qquad \text{Write the inequality.}$$

$$\frac{2}{3}x \le 4 \qquad \text{Rewrite } \frac{2x}{3} \text{ as } \frac{2}{3}x.$$

Multiply each side by the reciprocal of $\frac{2}{3}$.

$$\frac{3}{2} \cdot \frac{2}{3}x \le \frac{3}{2} \cdot 4 \qquad \text{Multiplication Property of Inequality}$$

$$x \le 6 \qquad \text{Simplify.}$$

 The solution is $x \le 6$.

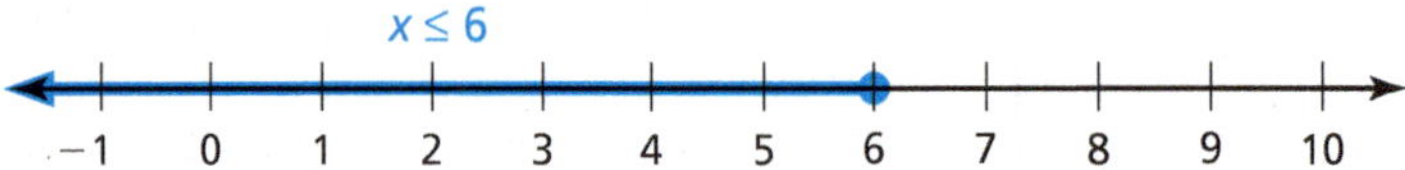

Try It **Solve the inequality. Graph the solution.**

7. $\frac{3}{2}m > 1$ **8.** $\frac{3}{5}q \le 6$ **9.** $5 > \frac{5t}{6}$

Self-Assessment for Concepts & Skills

Solve each exercise. Then rate your understanding of the success criteria in your journal.

SOLVING INEQUALITIES **Solve the inequality. Graph the solution.**

10. $n + 6 < 10$

11. $h - 13 \ge 7$

12. $5g > 45$

13. $\frac{3}{4}k \le 6$

14. OPEN-ENDED Write an inequality that the graph represents. Then use the Addition Property of Inequality to write another inequality that the graph represents.

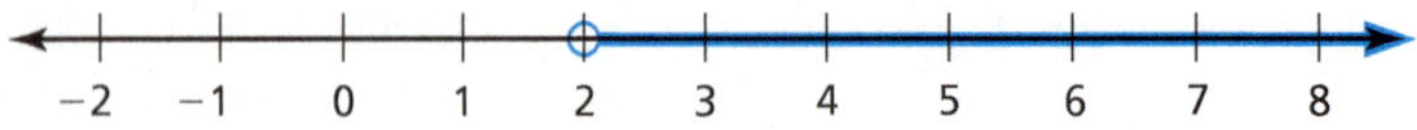

15. MP **REASONING** How is the graph of the solution of $2x \ge 10$ different from the graph of the solution of $2x = 10$?

16. OPEN-ENDED Write two inequalities that have the same solution set: one that you can solve using division and one that you can solve using subtraction.

Laurie's Notes

Discuss

- Remind students of multiplying by reciprocals to solve equations. Explain that now they will multiply by reciprocals to solve inequalities.
- Remind students that they have been using inverse operations to solve inequalities. If $4x$ is on one side of an inequality, then students need to divide by 4 or multiply by $\frac{1}{4}$ (the reciprocal of 4). Either method will work. Ask students which method they prefer and why.

EXAMPLE 3

- **Note**: Point out that $\frac{2x}{3}$ can be written as $\frac{2}{3}x$, as shown in the second step. Students may not need to perform this step to see that they need to multiply by $\frac{3}{2}$, but it can be helpful.
- When the coefficient is $\frac{2}{3}$, it means the variable is multiplied by 2 and divided by 3. To "undo" the operations, students need to divide by 2 and multiply by 3. Because dividing by 2 is the same as multiplying by $\frac{1}{2}$, the operations can be combined as multiplying by $\frac{3}{2}$.
- Remind students to multiply both sides of the inequality by the reciprocal.
- Ask students to explain how to graph the solution.

Try It

- **Think-Pair-Share**: Students should read each exercise independently and then work in pairs to complete the exercises. Then have each pair compare their answers with another pair and discuss any discrepancies.
- Exercise 9 is written with the variable on the right side. Students may avoid making a graphing mistake by rewriting the solution as $t < 6$.

Self-Assessment for Concepts & Skills

- Allow time for students to complete the exercises independently.
- Exercises 14–16 provide insight into students' understanding of inequalities.
- Have students trade the inequalities they wrote for Exercises 14 and 16, and then solve the inequalities to see if they agree with the writers' answers. Students are assessing their progress with the first three success criteria.

The Success Criteria Self-Assessment chart can be found in the *Student Journal* or online at *BigIdeasMath.com*.

Extra Example 3

Solve $\frac{3b}{4} > 6$. Graph the solution.

$b > 8$;

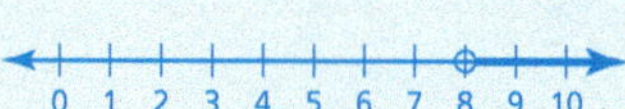

Try It

7. See Additional Answers.

8. $q \leq 10$;

9. $6 > t$;

ELL Support

Have students work in pairs to complete the Self-Assessment for Concepts & Skills exercises. For Exercises 10–13, have each pair display their graphs on a whiteboard for your review or have each of four pairs display an answer to a different problem on boards around the classroom. Discuss the graphs. Have pairs discuss and answer Exercises 14–16 and then compare their answers with another pair and reconcile any disagreements.

Self-Assessment for Concepts & Skills

10. $n < 4$;

11. $h \geq 20$;

12. $g > 9$;

13. $k \leq 8$;

14. *Sample answer:* $x > 2$; $x - 1 > 1$

15–16. See Additional Answers.

Extra Example 4

A one-day ticket to an amusement park costs \$32.50. A season pass to the amusement park costs \$227.50. When is the season pass a better deal?

$32.5n > 227.50$; $n > 7$; When you visit the amusement park more than 7 days in a season.

Self-Assessment
for Problem Solving

17. $x + 24 \geq 40$; $x \geq 16$

18. **a.** at least 30 students

b. The number of students must be a multiple of 5.

Formative Assessment Tip

I Used to Think... But Now I Know

This technique asks students to consider how their thinking about a concept or skill has changed from the beginning of instruction to the end of instruction. This can be done orally or in writing. It is important for students to be able to self-assess and reflect on their own learning. Use this technique at the end of the formal lesson. If time permits, have students discuss with one another or the whole class how their understanding developed and/or changed.

Learning Target

Write and solve inequalities.

Success Criteria

- Apply the properties of inequality to generate equivalent inequalities.
- Solve inequalities using addition or subtraction.
- Solve inequalities using multiplication or division.
- Write and solve inequalities that represent real-life problems.

Laurie's Notes

EXAMPLE 4

- Review the problem-solving plan with students.
- ? Discuss how multiple-day bus passes and one-way rides work.
  - "How many rides can you take with a 30-day bus pass?" unlimited
  - "If you take 42 rides using a 30-day pass, what is the cost per ride? Explain." \$1.00; Divide the cost of a 30-day pass by the number of rides.
  - "If you take 42 rides and pay separately each time, what is the total cost? Explain." \$73.50; Multiply the number of rides by the cost of a one-way ride.
- ? "How many rides do you need to take before the cost of the one-way ride is at least as expensive as the 30-day pass?" Set up the inequality and solve.
- **Estimate**: Encourage students to estimate: $42 \div 1.75$ is approximately $42 \div 2 = 21$.
- **MP3 Construct Viable Arguments and Critique the Reasoning of Others**: Mathematically proficient students take into account the context of the problem. Students should consider the number of times a person needs to ride a bus in a 30-day period when deciding whether a 30-day pass saves money.
- Discuss the Check note with students.

Self-Assessment for Problem Solving

- Allow time in class for students to practice using the problem-solving plan. Remember, some students may only be able to complete the first step.
- Encourage students to read the problems carefully. There are terms, such as *additional*, *at least*, and *possible*, which are critical to solving the problems.
- **MP1 Make Sense of Problems and Persevere in Solving Them**: I tell my students to read the problem and then read the problem again. Too often students ask for assistance before making an honest effort to understand the problem. Make students try independently before you help them or they help each other.
- Read students' responses for Exercise 18 and pay attention to their reasoning.
- Students are assessing their progress on the last success criterion.

The Success Criteria Self-Assessment chart can be found in the *Student Journal* or online at *BigIdeasMath.com*.

Closure

- **I Used to Think... But Now I Know:** Take time for students to reflect on their current understanding of solving inequalities. Make sure that students include all four operations in their reflections.

EXAMPLE 4 Modeling Real Life

A one-way bus ride costs \$1.75. A 30-day bus pass costs \$42. When is the 30-day pass a better deal?

You are given the cost of a one-way bus ride and the cost of a 30-day bus pass. You are asked to determine when the pass is a better deal.

For the pass to be a better deal, the total cost of one-way bus rides in a 30-day period must be greater than the cost of the pass. Use a verbal model to write an inequality. Then solve the inequality.

Verbal Model	Cost of a one-way ride (dollars)	•	Number of one-way rides	>	Cost of a 30-day bus pass (dollars)
Variable	Let r be the number of one-way rides.				
Inequality	1.75	•	r	>	42

$1.75r > 42$ — Write the inequality.

$\frac{1.75r}{1.75} > \frac{42}{1.75}$ — Division Property of Inequality

$r > 24$ — Simplify.

So, the 30-day pass is a better deal when you take more than 24 one-way rides in a 30-day period.

Check Verify that 23 one-way rides are less than \$42 and 25 one-way rides are greater than \$42.

$23(1.75) = \$40.25$ ✓

$25(1.75) = \$43.75$ ✓

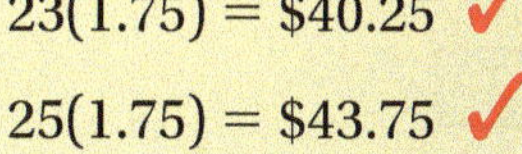

Self-Assessment for Problem Solving

Solve each exercise. Then rate your understanding of the success criteria in your journal.

17. A small pizza costs \$4.50, and a salad costs \$3.75. You plan to buy two small pizzas and four salads. Write and solve an inequality to find the additional amounts you can spend to get free delivery.

18. **DIG DEEPER!** Students at a playground are divided into 5 groups with at least 6 students in each group.

a. Find the possible numbers of students at the playground.

b. Suppose the students are divided into 5 *equal* groups. How does this change your answer in part (a)?

8.8 Practice

Review & Refresh

Tell whether the given value is a solution of the inequality.

1. $n + 4 > 15;\ n = 9$
2. $s - 12 \le 8;\ s = 20$
3. $\frac{z}{4} \ge 7;\ z = 32$
4. $6g < 48;\ g = 8$

Find the area of the triangle.

5. 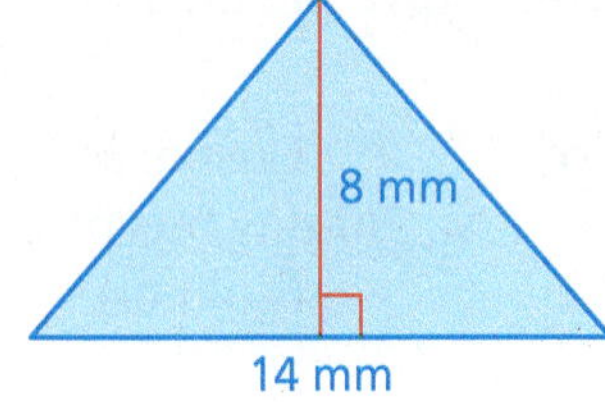

6. 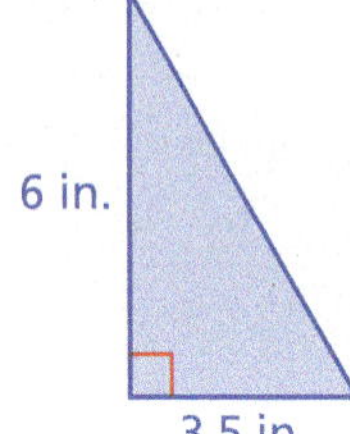

7. 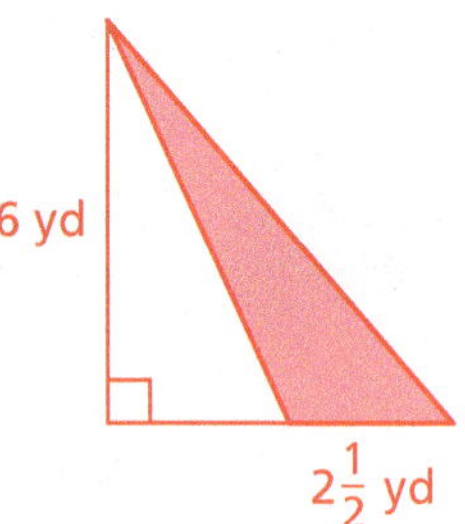

Write the product as a power.

8. 7×7
9. $12 \times 12 \times 12 \times 12$
10. $1.4 \times 1.4 \times 1.4$

Concepts, Skills, & Problem Solving

MP **USING TOOLS** **Describe the relationship shown by the tape diagram. What can you conclude about x?** (See Exploration 1, p. 391.)

11.
9
1 | 2x

12. 
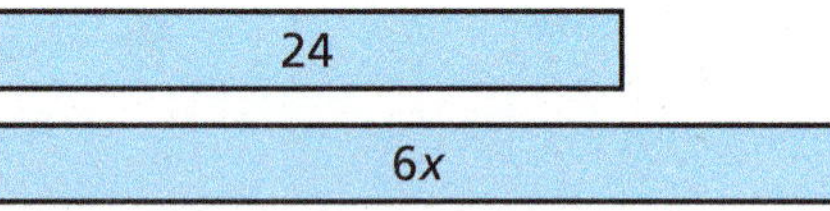

SOLVING INEQUALITIES **Solve the inequality. Graph the solution.**

13. $x - 4 < 5$
14. $5 + h > 7$
15. $3 \ge y - 2$
16. $y - 21 < 85$
17. $18 > 12 + x$
18. $\frac{m}{8} < 4$
19. $n \div 6 > 2$
20. $12x < 96$
21. $\frac{1}{11}c \ge 9$
22. $8 \cdot w \le 72$
23. $7.2 < x + 4.2$
24. $12.7 \ge s - 5.3$
25. $\frac{3}{4} \le \frac{1}{2} + n$
26. $7.5p \le 45$
27. $\frac{5}{9}v \le 45$
28. $\frac{5x}{8} \ge 30$

MP **YOU BE THE TEACHER** **Your friend solves the inequality. Is your friend correct? Explain your reasoning.**

29. 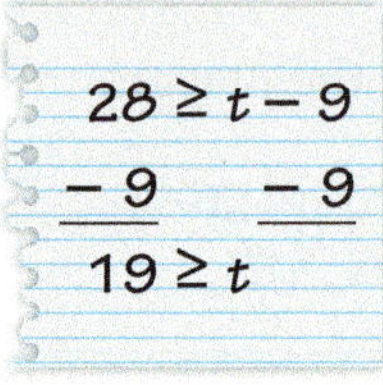

30.
$\frac{x}{6} \le 30$

$\frac{x}{6} \cdot 6 \le 30 \cdot 6$

$x \le 180$

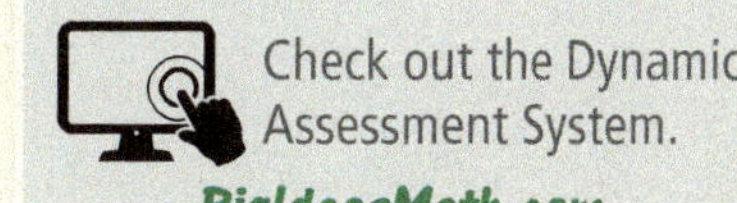

Assignment Guide and Concept Check

Scaffold assignments to support all students in their learning progression. The suggested assignments are a starting point. Continue to assign additional exercises and revisit with spaced practice to move every student toward proficiency.

Level	Assignment 1	Assignment 2
Emerging	3, 7, 9, 11, 13, 17, 18, 20, 29, 30, 45	25, 27, 31, 33, 36, 37, 39, 48, 53, 60
Proficient	3, 7, 9, 11, 14, 16, 18, 22, 29, 30, 44	25, 27, 32, 34, 37, 38, 39, 40, 42, 48, 50, 52, 54, 61
Advanced	3, 7, 9, 11, 24, 25, 26, 28, 29, 30, 48	34, 35, 39, 41, 42, 43, 49, 50, 52, 58, 59, 63

- Assignment 1 is for use after students complete the Self-Assessment for Concepts & Skills.
- Assignment 2 is for use after students complete the Self-Assessment for Problem Solving.
- The red exercises can be used as a concept check.

Review & Refresh Prior Skills

Exercises 1–4 Checking Solutions of Inequalities
Exercises 5–7 Finding the Area of Triangle
Exercises 8–10 Writing Expressions as Powers

Common Errors

- **Exercises 13–28** Students may use the same operation instead of the inverse operation to solve. Simplify the inequality on the board to demonstrate that this will not work. Remind students to check their answers in the original inequality.

Review & Refresh

1. no
2. yes
3. yes
4. no
5. 56 mm^2
6. 10.5 in.^{2}
7. $7\frac{1}{2}$ yd^2
8. 7^2
9. 12^4
10. 1.4^3

Concepts, Skills, & Problem Solving

11. $2x + 1 < 9$; x is less than 4
12. $6x > 24$; x is greater than 4
13. $x < 9$;
14. $h > 2$; 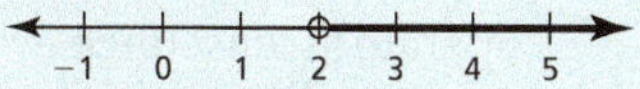
15. $5 \geq y$; 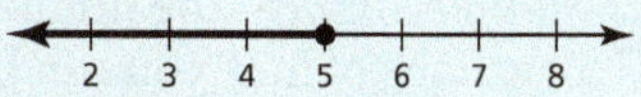
16. $y < 106$;
17. $6 > x$; 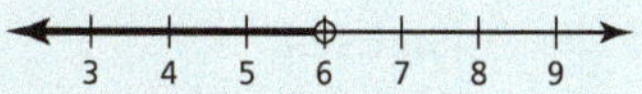
18. $m < 32$;
19. $n > 12$; 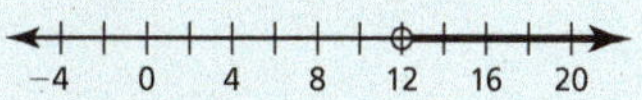
20. $x < 8$;
21. $c \geq 99$; 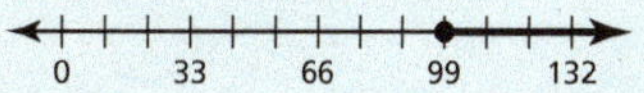
22. $w \leq 9$; 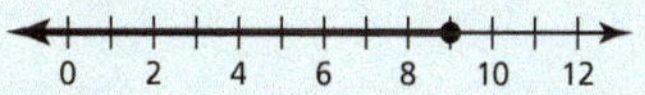
23. $3 < x$;
24. $18 \geq s$;

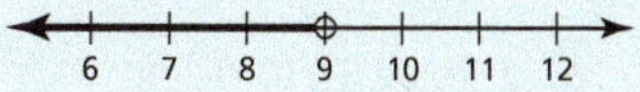

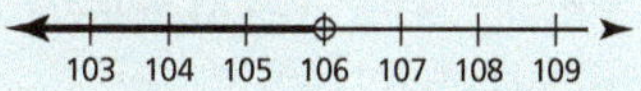

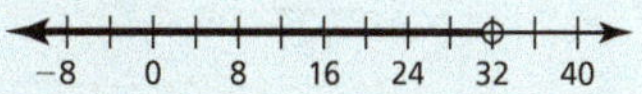

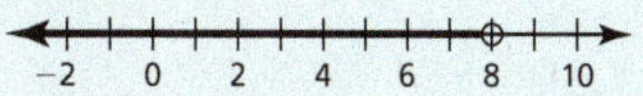

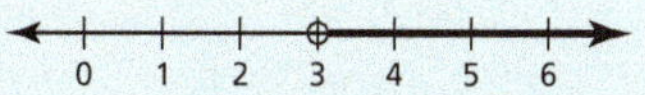

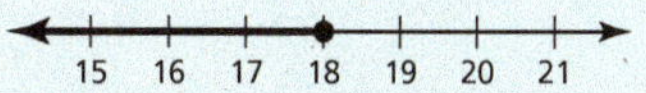

25–29. See Additional Answers.

30. yes; The solution is correct.

Concepts, Skills, & Problem Solving

31. $p + 5 < 17; p < 12$

32. $b - 3 > 15; b > 18$

33. $8n < 72; n < 9$

34. $t \div 32 \leq 4.25; t \leq 136$

35. $225 \geq \frac{3}{4}w; 300 \geq w$

36. $22 + x \leq 40; x \leq 18$ lb

37. $x + 18.99 \leq 24; x \leq \$5.01$

38. $8x < 168; x < 21$ ft

39. when visiting more than 4 times in a year; $\$30 < \$7.50x$ when $4 < x$

40. **a.** at least 1250 rides

b. no; The ride would need to operate at least once every 35 seconds.

41. *Sample answer:* the number of gallons of milk you can buy with \$20; the length of a park that has an area of at least 500 square feet

42. no solution; A number is never less than itself.

WRITING INEQUALITIES **Write the word sentence as an inequality. Then solve the inequality.**

31. Five more than a number p is less than 17.

32. Three less than a number b is more than 15.

33. Eight times a number n is less than 72.

34. A number t divided by 32 is at most 4.25.

35. 225 is no less than $\frac{3}{4}$ times a number w.

36. MP **MODELING REAL LIFE** Your carry-on bag can weigh at most 40 pounds. Write and solve an inequality that represents how much more weight you can add to the bag and still meet the requirement.

37. MP **MODELING REAL LIFE** It costs $\$x$ for a round-trip bus ticket to the mall. You have \$24. Write and solve an inequality that represents how much money you can spend for the bus ticket and still have enough to buy a hat that costs \$18.99.

38. **GEOMETRY** The length of a rectangle is 8 feet, and its area is less than 168 square feet. Write and solve an inequality that represents the possible widths of the rectangle.

39. MP **MODELING REAL LIFE** A ticket to a dinosaur exhibit costs \$7.50. A one-year pass to the exhibit costs \$30. When is the one-year pass a better deal? Explain.

Park Hours
10:00 A.M.–10:00 P.M.

40. MP **REASONING** A thrill ride at an amusement park holds a maximum of 12 people per ride.

a. Find the possible numbers of rides needed for 15,000 people.

b. Is it reasonable for 15,000 people to ride the thrill ride in one day? Explain.

41. **OPEN-ENDED** Give an example of a real-life situation in which you can list all the solutions of an inequality. Give an example of a real-life situation in which you cannot list all the solutions of an inequality.

42. MP **LOGIC** Describe the solution of $7x < 7x$. Explain your reasoning.

43. **MP NUMBER SENSE** The possible values of x are given by $x - 3 \geq 2$. What is the least possible value of $5x$?

SOLVING INEQUALITIES **Solve the inequality. Graph the solution.**

44. $x + 9 - 3 \leq 14$

45. $44 > 7 + s + 26$

46. $6.1 - 0.3 \geq c + 1$

47. $2n < 4.6 \times 12$

48. $32 \geq 2h + 6h$

49. $2\frac{2}{5}b - 1\frac{3}{10}b \leq 6\frac{3}{5}$

50. **MP PROBLEM SOLVING** The high score for a video game is 36,480. Your current score is 34,280. Each dragonfly you catch is worth 1 point. You also get a 1000-point bonus for reaching 35,000 points. Find the possible numbers of dragonflies you can catch to earn a new high score.

51. **MP REASONING** A winning football team more than doubled the offensive yards gained by its opponent. The opponent gained 272 offensive yards. The winning team had 80 offensive plays. Find the possible numbers of yards per play for the winning team. Justify your answer.

52. **DIG DEEPER!** You complete two events of a triathlon. Your goal is to finish with an overall time of less than 100 minutes.

a. Find the possible numbers of minutes you can take to finish the running event and still meet your goal.

b. The running event is 3.1 miles long. Estimate how many minutes it would take you to run 3.1 miles. Would this time allow you to reach your goal? Explain your reasoning.

Triathlon

Event	Your Time (minutes)
Swimming	18.2
Biking	45.4
Running	?

SOLVING INEQUALITIES **Graph the numbers that are solutions of both inequalities.**

53. $x + 7 > 9$ and $8x \leq 64$

54. $z - 3 \leq 8$ and $6z < 72$

55. $w + 5 \geq 8$ and $4w > 20$

56. $g - 6 \leq 1$ and $3g \geq 21$

57. $2.7 + k \geq 5.3$ and $0.8k \leq 3.36$

58. $p + \frac{3}{4} < 3$ and $\frac{1}{4}p > \frac{3}{8}$

59. **MP PROBLEM SOLVING** You are selling items from a catalog for a school fundraiser. Find the range of sales that will earn you at least \$40 and at most \$50.

CRITICAL THINKING **Let $a > b > 0$ and $x > y > 0$. Tell whether the statement is *always* true. Explain your reasoning.**

60. $a + x > b + y$

61. $a - x > b - y$

62. $ax > by$

63. $\frac{a}{x} > \frac{y}{b}$

Common Errors

- **Exercises 53–58** Students may not understand how to graph two inequalities together. Encourage them to draw the graph for each inequality separately, one above the other, and remove the parts that do not overlap.

Mini-Assessment

Solve the inequality. Graph the solution.

1. $x + 9 \le 15$ $x \le 6$

2. $4.7 > z - 2.3$ $7 > z$ or $z < 7$

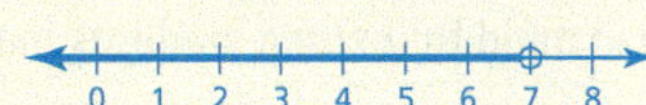

3. $\frac{r}{3} \ge 2$ $r \ge 6$

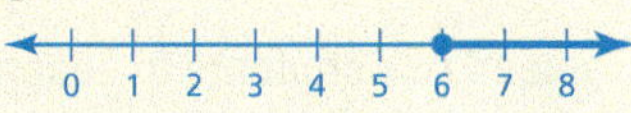

4. $25 < 5g$ $5 < g$ or $g > 5$

5. You have 70 DVDs. The DVD cabinet you own holds 150 DVDs. Write and solve an inequality to represent how many more DVDs you can buy and fit into the cabinet. $70 + x \le 150$; $x \le 80$ DVDs

Section Resources

Surface Level	Deep Level
Resources by Chapter • Extra Practice • Reteach • Puzzle Time Student Journal • Self-Assessment • Practice Differentiating the Lesson Tutorial Videos Skills Review Handbook Skills Trainer	Resources by Chapter • Enrichment and Extension Graphic Organizers Dynamic Assessment System • Section Practice
Transfer Level	
Dynamic Assessment System • End-of-Chapter Quiz	Assessment Book • End-of-Chapter Quiz

Concepts, Skills, & Problem Solving

43. 25

44. $x \le 8$;

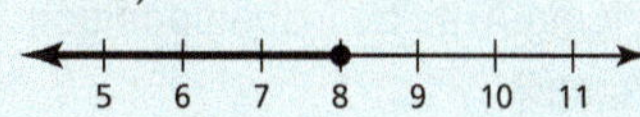

45. $11 > s$;

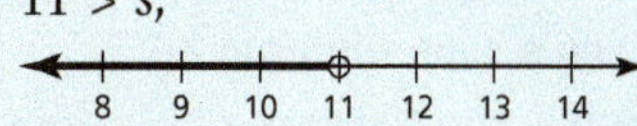

46. $4.8 \ge c$;

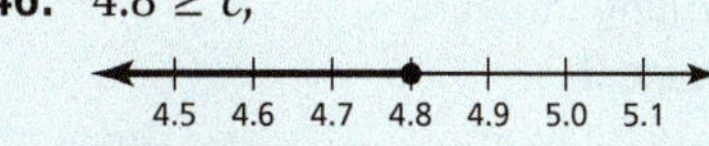

47. $n < 27.6$;

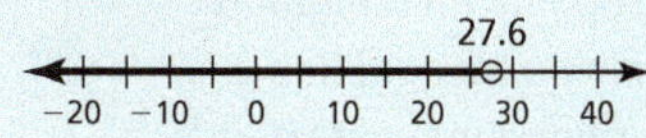

48. $4 \ge h$;

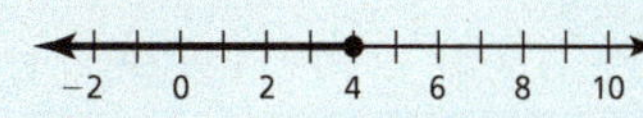

49. $b \le 6$;

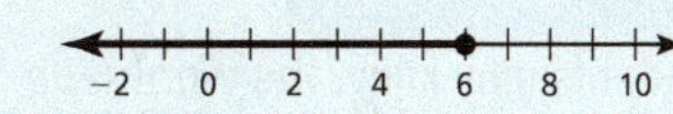

50. $d > 1200$

51. $x > 6.8$; $80x > 2 \cdot 272$ when $x > 6.8$.

52. a. $x < 36.4$

    b. *Sample answer:* 25 minutes; yes; $25 < 36.4$

53. −2 0 2 4 6 8 10

54.

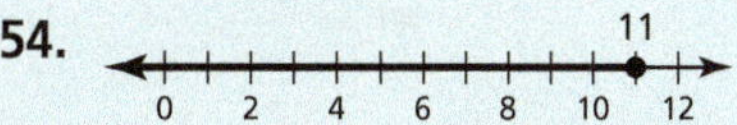

55. −2 0 2 4 6 8 10

56.

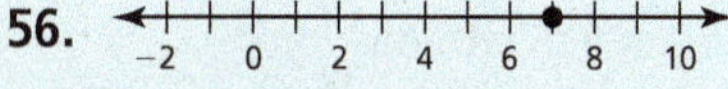

57. 2.6 3.0 3.4 3.8 4.2 4.6

58. $0 \ \frac{1}{4} \ \frac{1}{2} \ \frac{3}{4} \ 1 \ \frac{5}{4} \ \frac{3}{2} \ \frac{7}{4} \ 2 \ \frac{9}{4} \ \frac{5}{2} \ \frac{11}{4} \ 3$

59. $x \ge 400$ and $x \le 500$

60. yes; $a > b$ and $x > y$

61. no; *Sample answer:* $a = 9$, $b = 8$, $x = 3$, $y = 2$; $a - x = 6$, $b - y = 6$; so, $a - x = b - y$.

62. yes; $a > b$ and $x > y$

63. See Additional Answers.

Skills Needed

Exercise 1

- Converting Measures
- Drawing a Polygon in a Coordinate Plane
- Finding Area by Decomposition

Exercise 2

- Evaluating Expressions
- Using a Tape Diagram
- Writing Expressions
- Writing Integers

Exercise 3

- Finding the Percent of a Number
- Graphing an Inequality
- Solving Inequalities
- Writing Inequalities

ELL Support

Students may know the word *tape* as a school supply. Point out that in Exercise 2 a tape diagram is not related to this kind of tape. It is similar to a tape measure, which allows a person to compare amounts represented by lengths. You may also want to discuss banking and the use of a savings account.

Using the Problem-Solving Plan

1. 0.46875 yd^2, or $\frac{15}{32} \text{ yd}^2$
2. $-\$40$; 6 months; $240 - 40m = 0$ when $m = 6$
3. 0 20 40 60 80 100 120 140 160 180 200

Performance Task

The *STEAM Video Performance Task* provides the opportunity for additional enrichment and greater depth of knowledge as students explore the mathematics of the chapter within a context tied to the chapter STEAM Video. The performance task and a detailed scoring rubric are provided at *BigIdeasMath.com.*

Laurie's Notes

Scaffolding Instruction

- The goal of this lesson is to help students become more comfortable with problem solving. These exercises combine graphing in the coordinate plane, area, and inequalities with prior skills from other chapters. The solution for Exercise 1 is worked out below to help you guide students through the problem-solving plan. Use the remaining class time to have students work on the other exercises.
- **Emerging:** The goal for these students is to feel comfortable with the problem-solving plan. Allow students to work in pairs to write the beginning steps of the problem-solving plan for Exercise 2. Keep in mind that some students may only be ready to do the first step.
- **Proficient:** Students may be able to work independently or in pairs to complete Exercises 2 and 3.
- Visit each pair to review their plan for each problem. Ask students to describe their plans.

Using the Problem-Solving Plan

Exercise 1

Understand the problem. You know the vertices of your kite design in a coordinate plane, where the coordinates are measured in inches. You are asked to find the least number of square yards of fabric needed to make the kite.

Make a plan. First, draw a diagram of the design in a coordinate plane. Then decompose the figure into two triangles to find the area of the kite in square inches. Finally, convert the area from square inches to square yards.

Solve and check. Use the plane to solve the problem. Then check your solution.

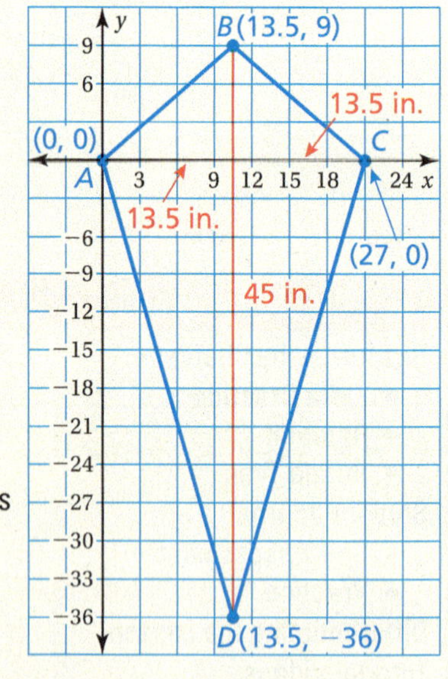

- Draw a diagram of the design in a coordinate plane and decompose the figure into two triangles.
- Find the sum of areas of the two triangles.

$$A = \frac{1}{2}(45)(13.5) + \frac{1}{2}(45)(13.5)$$
$$= 303.75 + 303.75$$
$$= 607.5 \text{ in.}^2$$

So, the area of the kite is 607.5 square inches.

- Convert the area from square inches to square yards.

$$1 \text{ yd}^2 = (1 \text{ yd})(1 \text{ yd}) = (3 \text{ ft})(3 \text{ ft})$$
$$= (36 \text{ in.})(36 \text{ in.}) = 1296 \text{ in.}^2$$

$$607.5 \text{ in.}^2 = 607.5 \text{ in.}^2 \times \frac{1 \text{ yd}^2}{1296 \text{ in.}^2} = 0.46875 \text{ yd}^2$$

So, the least amount of fabric needed is 0.46875 square yard.

- **Check:** Count the grid squares to estimate the area in square inches. There are about 68 grid squares. Each grid square represents $(3 \text{ in.})(3 \text{ in.}) = 9 \text{ in.}^2$ and $68 \times 9 = 612 \text{ in.}^2$, which is about 607.5 in.^2 ✓

Connecting Concepts

Using the Problem-Solving Plan

1. You use a coordinate plane to design a kite for a competition. The vertices of the design are $A(0, 0)$, $B(13.5, 9)$, $C(27, 0)$, and $D(13.5, -36)$. The coordinates are measured in inches. Find the least number of square yards of fabric you need to make the kite.

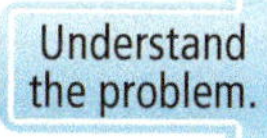

You know the vertices of your kite design in a coordinate plane, where the coordinates are measured in inches. You are asked to find the least number of square yards of fabric needed to make the kite.

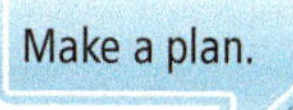

First, draw a diagram of the design in a coordinate plane. Then decompose the figure into two triangles to find the area of the kite in square inches. Finally, convert the area from square inches to square yards.

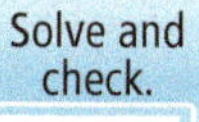

Use the plan to solve the problem. Then check your solution.

2. You have \$240 in a savings account. You deposit \$60 per month. The tape diagram represents the ratio of money deposited to money withdrawn each month. Find the monthly change in your account balance. How long will it take for the account to have a balance of \$0? Justify your answer.

Money Deposited	▭	▭	▭		
Money Withdrawn	▭	▭	▭	▭	▭

3. A cord made of synthetic fiber can support 630 pounds, which is at least 450% of the weight that can be supported by a cord made of steel. Graph the possible weights that can be supported by the steel cord.

Performance Task

Launching a CubeSat

At the beginning of this chapter, you watched a STEAM Video called "Designing a CubeSat." You are now ready to complete the performance task related to this video, available at ***BigIdeasMath.com***. Be sure to use the problem-solving plan as you work through the performance task.

Review Vocabulary

Write the definition and give an example of each vocabulary term.

positive numbers, *p. 346*
negative numbers, *p. 346*
opposites, *p. 346*
integers, *p. 346*
rational number, *p. 358*
absolute value, *p. 364*
coordinate plane, *p. 370*
origin, *p. 370*
quadrants, *p. 370*
inequality, *p. 384*
solution of an inequality, *p. 385*
solution set, *p. 385*
graph of an inequality, *p. 386*

Graphic Organizers

You can use a **Summary Triangle** to explain a concept. Here is an example of a Summary Triangle for ***integers***.

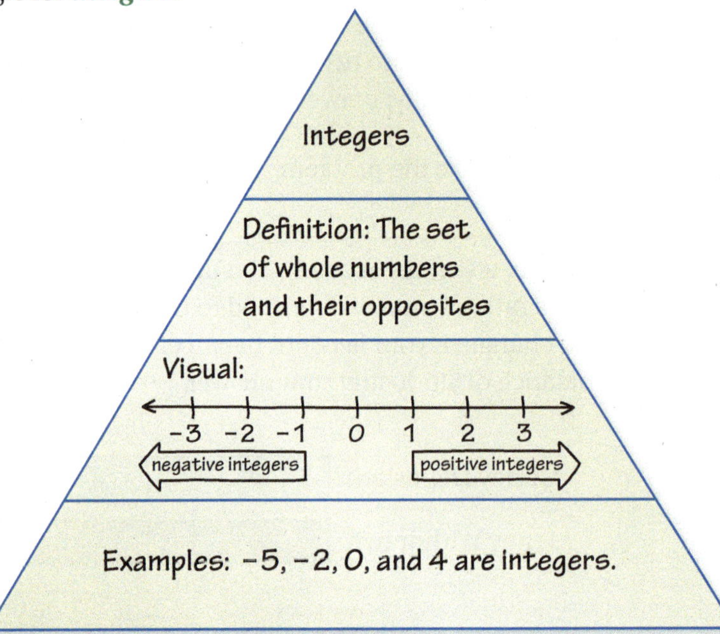

Choose and complete a graphic organizer to help you study the concept.

1. opposites
2. rational number
3. absolute value
4. coordinate plane
5. inequalities
6. solving inequalities using addition or subtraction
7. solving inequalities using multiplication or division

"I'm posting my new Summary Triangle on my daily blog. Do you think it will get me more hits?"

Review Vocabulary

- As a review of the chapter vocabulary, have students revisit the vocabulary section in their *Student Journals* to fill in any missing definitions and record examples of each term.

Graphic Organizers

Sample answers:

1.

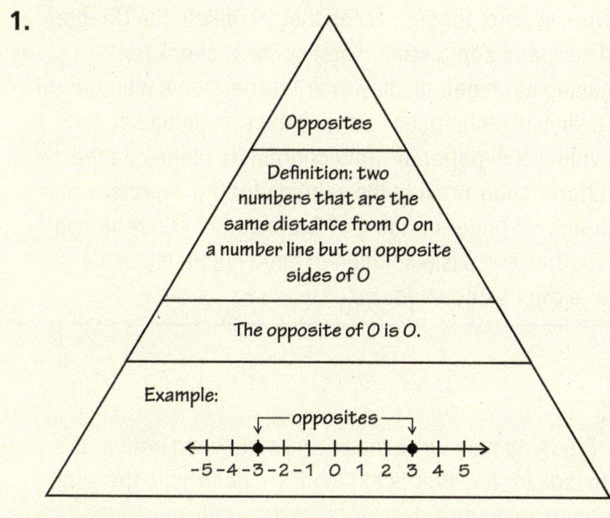

2.

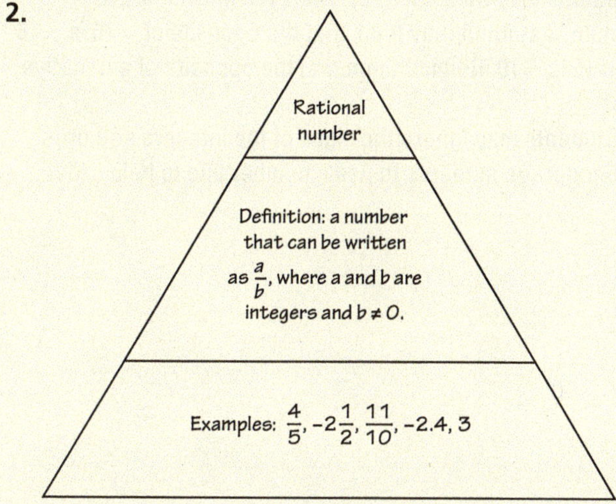

3.

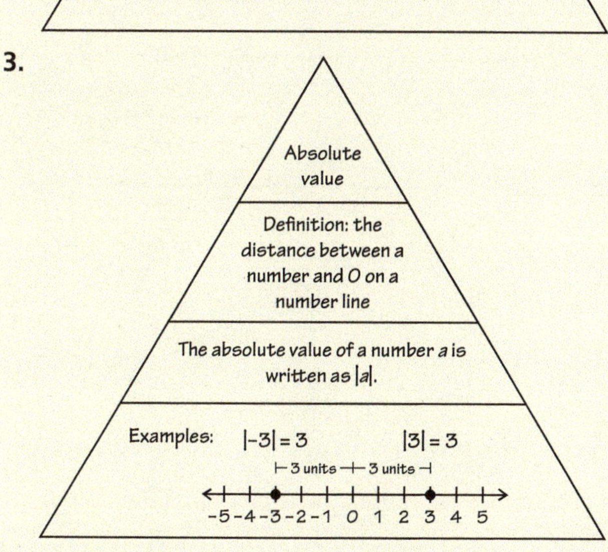

4–7. Answers at *BigIdeasMath.com.*

List of Organizers

Available at *BigIdeasMath.com*
Definition and Example Chart
Example and Non-Example Chart
Four Square
Information Frame
Summary Triangle

About this Organizer

A **Summary Triangle** can be used to explain a concept. Typically, the Summary Triangle is divided into 3 or 4 parts. Students write related categories in the middle part(s). Related categories may include: procedure, explanation, description, definition, theorem, or formula. In the bottom part, students write an example to illustrate the concept. A Summary Triangle can be used as an assessment tool, in which students complete the missing parts. Students may also place their Summary Triangles on note cards to use as a quick study reference.

Chapter Self-Assessment

1. −8
2. 12
3. 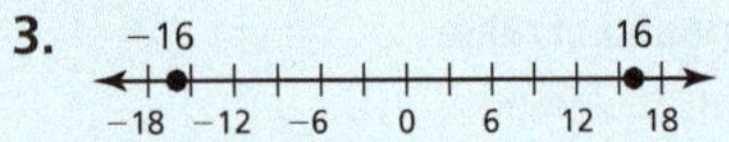

4. 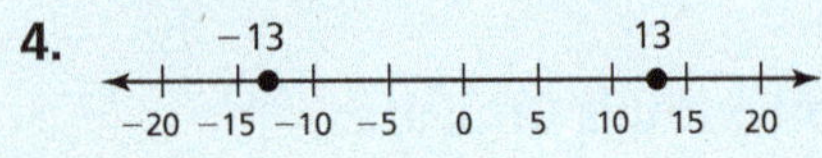

5. −4 −3 −2 −1 0 1 2 3 4
6. −150 −100 −50 0 50 100 150
7. 1
8. 10
9. 7
10. −6
11. >
12. <
13. >
14. −5, −3, −1, 2, 4
15. −20, −10, 5, 10, 15
16. −12, −8, −7, 2, 9
17. −12°C, −7°C, −3°C, 0°C, 8°C
18. 3; 1 or 2; *Sample answer:* The two integers greater than 1 are positive, the two integers less than 1 are negative or zero.

Chapter Self-Assessment

The Success Criteria Self-Assessment chart can be found in the *Student Journal* or online at *BigIdeasMath.com*.

ELL Support

Allow students to work in pairs for support as they complete the Chapter Self-Assessment. After pairs complete the first section, check for understanding by having each pair display their answers on a whiteboard for your review. Use similar techniques to check the remaining sections. For Section 8.5, provide graph paper or draw coordinate planes on the board and have a different pair provide the solution for the exercises that require graphing. Check for understanding of Exercises 77–79 by having students indicate whether $x = 8$ is a solution of each inequality using a thumbs up for *yes* or a thumbs down for *no*.

Common Errors

- **Exercises 1 and 2** Students may write the wrong sign when writing the integer. Tell them to look for key words to help them determine the sign.
- **Exercises 3–6** Students may think that *opposites* are only negative numbers. For example, a student may think that the opposite of −16 is −16 and the opposite of 16 is −16. Remind them that the opposite of a negative number is positive.
- **Exercises 11–16** Students may ignore the signs of the integers and order them incorrectly. Encourage students to use a number line to help order the integers.

Chapter Self-Assessment

As you complete the exercises, use the scale below to rate your understanding of the success criteria in your journal.

1	2	3	4
I do not understand.	I can do it with help.	I can do it on my own.	I can teach someone else.

8.1 Integers *(pp. 345–350)*

Learning Target: Understand the concept of negative numbers and that they are used along with positive numbers to describe quantities.

Write a positive or negative integer that represents the situation.

1. An elevator goes down 8 floors.

2. You earn \$12.

Graph the integer and its opposite.

3. -16

4. 13

5. 4

6. -100

Identify the integer represented by the point on the number line.

7. A

8. B

9. C

10. D

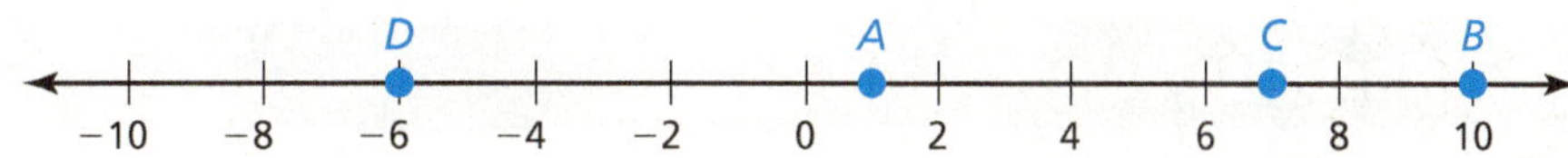

8.2 Comparing and Ordering Integers *(pp. 351–356)*

Learning Target: Compare and order integers.

Copy and complete the statement using < or >.

11. $4 \ \square \ -7$

12. $-1 \ \square \ 0$

13. $-5 \ \square \ -8$

Order the integers from least to greatest.

14. $-5, 4, 2, -3, -1$

15. $5, -20, -10, 10, 15$

16. $-7, -12, 9, 2, -8$

17. Order the temperatures $-3°C$, $8°C$, $-12°C$, $-7°C$, and $0°C$ from coldest to warmest.

18. Your teacher writes five different integers on a note card that are between -10 and 14. When the integers are ordered from least to greatest, the middle number is 1. How many of the integers are positive? negative? Explain.

8.3 Rational Numbers (pp. 357–362)

Learning Target: Compare and order rational numbers.

Graph the number and its opposite.

19. $-\frac{2}{5}$ **20.** $1\frac{3}{4}$ **21.** -1.2 **22.** 2.75

Copy and complete the statement using < or >.

23. $-2\frac{1}{6}$ ☐ $-2\frac{5}{6}$ **24.** $-\frac{1}{3}$ ☐ $-\frac{1}{8}$ **25.** -3.27 ☐ -2.68

Order the numbers from least to greatest.

26. $-2.04, -3, -2.4, -2.19, -5.8$ **27.** $-3\frac{7}{8}, 4, -3\frac{3}{4}, \frac{1}{2}, \frac{1}{6}$

28. Write a number that is greater than -7.81 and less than -7.

29. A dog buries a bone $-1\frac{5}{6}$ inches into the dirt. The dog buries a larger bone $-1\frac{3}{4}$ inches into the dirt. Which bone is buried deeper?

8.4 Absolute Value (pp. 363–368)

Learning Target: Understand the concept of absolute value.

Find the absolute value.

30. $|-8|$ **31.** $|13|$ **32.** $\left|3\frac{6}{7}\right|$ **33.** $|-1.34|$

Copy and complete the statement using <, >, or =.

34. $|-2|$ ☐ 2 **35.** $|4.4|$ ☐ $|-2.8|$ **36.** $\left|\frac{1}{6}\right|$ ☐ $\left|-\frac{2}{9}\right|$

Order the values from least to greatest.

37. $-15, |-21|, |19|, -20, 25$ **38.** $0, |-1|, -2, |2|, -3$

39. Simplify $-|-35|$.

40. The latitude of Erie, Pennsylvania, is 42.129. The latitude of Sydney, Australia, is -33.865. Positive values of latitude are north of the equator, negative values of latitude are south of the equator, and the latitude of the equator is 0. Which city is closest to the equator?

Common Errors

- **Exercises 26 and 27** Students may ignore the signs of the numbers and order the numbers incorrectly. Encourage students to use a number line to determine which number is farthest to the right.
- **Exercises 24 and 27** Students may place the fractions in the wrong order. Encourage students to find a common denominator before ordering.
- **Exercises 30–33** Students may think the absolute value of a number is its opposite. For example, students may think $|8| = -8$. Use a number line to remind students that absolute value is a number's distance from zero, so it is always a positive number or zero.
- **Exercises 34–38** Students may ignore the absolute value bars when comparing or ordering values. Encourage students to graph the values on a number line to help them correctly compare or order the values.

Chapter Self-Assessment

19. 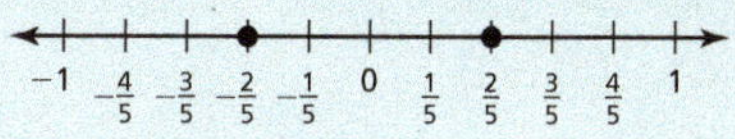

20. 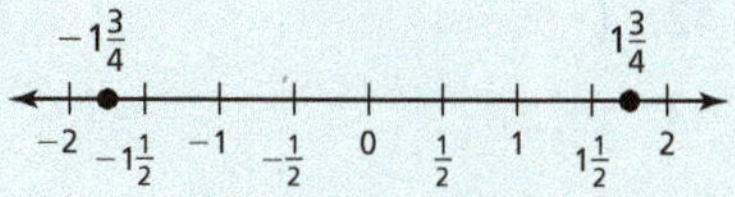

21. 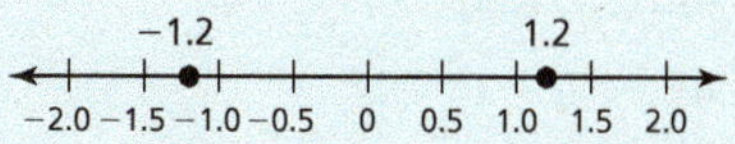

22. 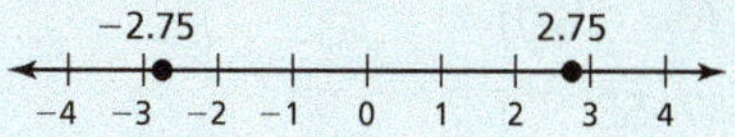

23. >

24. <

25. <

26. $-5.8, -3, -2.4, -2.19, -2.04$

27. $-3\frac{7}{8}, -3\frac{3}{4}, \frac{1}{6}, \frac{1}{2}, 4$

28. *Sample answer:* -7.5

29. smaller bone

30. 8

31. 13

32. $3\frac{6}{7}$

33. 1.34

34. =

35. >

36. <

37. $-20, -15, |19|, |-21|, 25$

38. $-3, -2, 0, |-1|, |2|$

39. -35

40. Sydney, Australia

Chapter Self-Assessment

41. (0, −2)

42. (−2, −4)

43. (5, 2)

44. (−1, 3)

45. (3, −4)

46. (1, 0)

47–50.

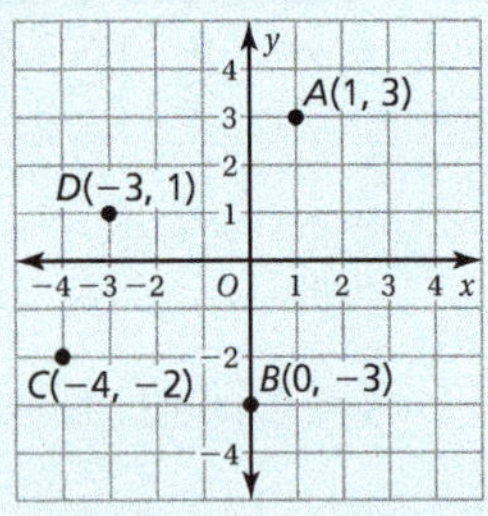

47. Quadrant I

48. *y*-axis

49. Quadrant III

50. Quadrant II

51. **a.** (4, −1)

b. (−4, 1)

52. **a.** (−2, −3)

b. (2, 3)

53. **a.** (2, 5)

b. (−2, −5)

54. **a.** (−3.5, 2.5)

b. (3.5, −2.5)

55. (−1, −2)

56. (4, −6)

57. (−3, 4)

58. (3, 3)

59. **a.** drugstore

b. hospital

c. Quadrant II

d. *Sample answer:* (−1, −3), (−2, −3)

e. post office

60. (2, 2)

61. (3, 9)

Common Errors

- **Exercises 47–50** Students may write the *y*-coordinate first and then the *x*-coordinate for the ordered pair. Remind students that the *x*-coordinate must come before the *y*-coordinate in the ordered pair.
- **Exercises 51–54** In part (a), students may take the opposite of the *x*-coordinate instead of the *y*-coordinate. In part (b), students may take the opposite of the *y*-coordinate instead of the *x*-coordinate. Their answers for parts (a) and (b) will be switched. Remind students that to reflect in the *x*-axis, they need to take the opposite of the *y*-coordinate. Remind students that to reflect in the *y*-axis, they need to take the opposite of the *x*-coordinate.

8.5 The Coordinate Plane (pp. 369–376)

Learning Target: Plot and reflect ordered pairs in all four quadrants of a coordinate plane.

Write an ordered pair corresponding to the point.

41. Point J **42.** Point K

43. Point L **44.** Point M

45. Point N **46.** Point P

Plot the ordered pair in a coordinate plane. Describe the location of the point.

47. $A(1, 3)$ **48.** $B(0, -3)$

49. $C(-4, -2)$ **50.** $D(-3, 1)$

Reflect the point in (a) the x-axis and (b) the y-axis.

51. $(4, 1)$ **52.** $(-2, 3)$

53. $(2, -5)$ **54.** $(-3.5, -2.5)$

Reflect the point in the x-axis followed by the y-axis.

55. $(1, 2)$ **56.** $(-4, 6)$

57. $(3, -4)$ **58.** $(-3, -3)$

59. Use the map of the town.

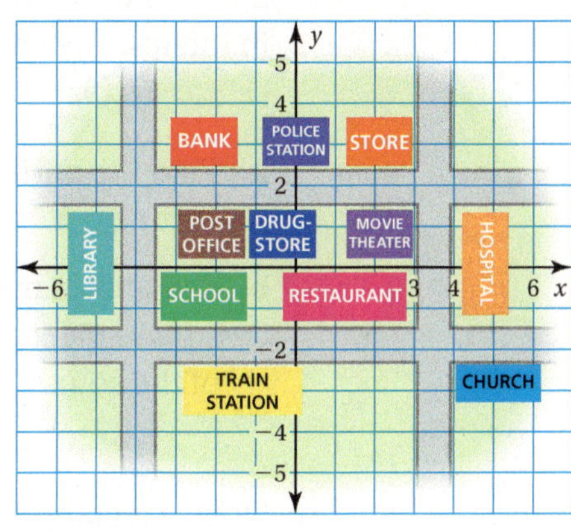

- **a.** Which building is located at $(-1, 1)$?
- **b.** Name a building on the positive x-axis.
- **c.** In which quadrant is the bank located?
- **d.** Write two different ordered pairs that represent the location of the train station.
- **e.** You can find the original location of the movie theater by reflecting its location in the y-axis. What building is now in that location?

60. Name the ordered pair that is 5 units right and 2 units down from $(-3, 4)$.

61. A point is reflected in the x-axis. The reflected point is $(3, -9)$. What is the original point?

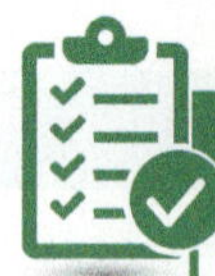

8.6 Polygons in the Coordinate Plane (pp. 377–382)

(pp. 377–382)

Learning Target: Draw polygons in the coordinate plane and find distances between points in the coordinate plane.

Draw the polygon with the given vertices in a coordinate plane.

62. $A(3, 2)$, $B(4, 7)$, $C(6, 0)$

63. $A(1, 2)$, $B(1, -7)$, $C(5, -7)$, $D(8, 2)$

64. $E\left(-1, -3\frac{1}{2}\right)$, $F(1, 0)$, $G(-2, 0)$, $H\left(-4, -3\frac{1}{2}\right)$

Find the distance between the points.

65. $(4, -2)$, $(4, -5)$

66. $(7, 2)$, $(-4, 2)$

67. $(-1, 6)$, $(-1, -3)$

68. $(-5, -8)$, $(-9, -8)$

Find the perimeter and the area of the polygon with the given vertices.

69. $T(2, 7)$, $U(2, 9)$, $V(5, 9)$, $W(5, 7)$

70. $P(4, -3)$, $Q(4, 2)$, $R(9, 2)$, $S(9, -3)$

71. $W(-12, -2)$, $X(-12, 13)$, $Y(5, 13)$, $Z(5, -2)$

72. You design the quilt shown using a coordinate plane in which the coordinates are measured in inches. The vertices of the quilt are $(-3, 5)$, $(-3, -7)$, $(9, 5)$, and $(9, -7)$.

a. Find the perimeter and the area of the quilt.

b. The quilt is made of identical-sized square pieces. What is the area of one of the square pieces?

73. Draw a rectangle with a perimeter of 14 units in a coordinate plane where the vertices are in two quadrants.

74. Draw a triangle with an area of 21 square units in a coordinate plane where the vertices are not all in the same quadrant.

Common Errors

- **Exercises 69–71** Students may confuse perimeter and area. Have them write the formulas and then substitute the values. Students should also include "units" or "square units" as a part of their answers.

Chapter Self-Assessment

62. B(4, 7), A(3, 2), C(6, 0)

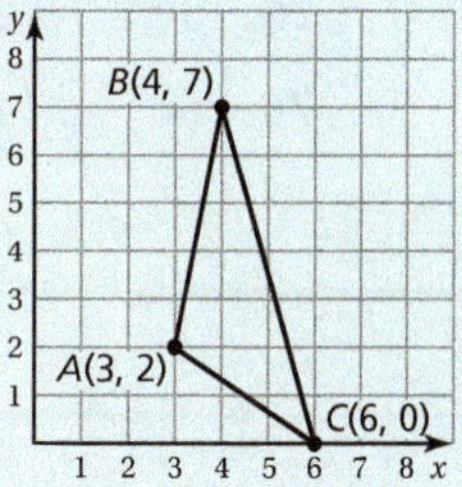

63. A(1, 2), D(8, 2), B(1, −7), C(5, −7)

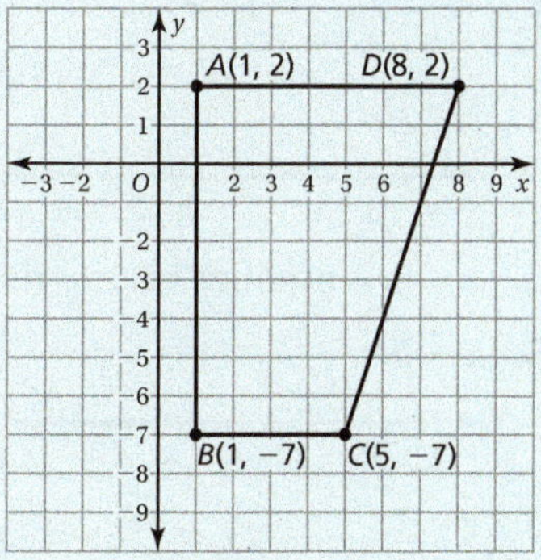

64. G(−2, 0), F(1, 0), $E\left(-1, -3\frac{1}{2}\right)$, $H\left(-4, -3\frac{1}{2}\right)$

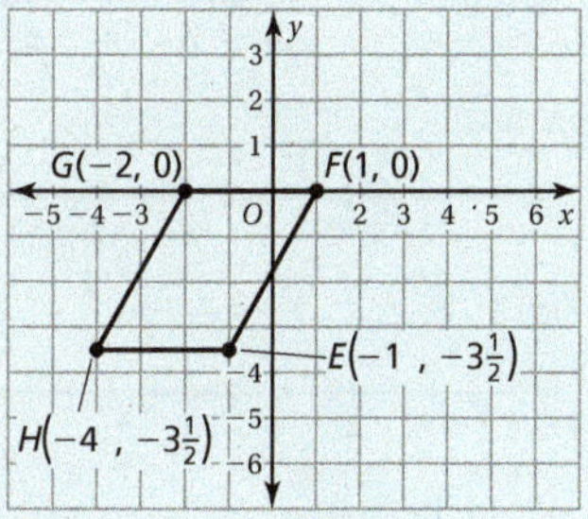

65. 3 **66.** 11

67. 9 **68.** 4

69. 10 units; 6 units^2

70. 20 units; 25 units^2

71. 64 units; 255 units^2

72. **a.** 48 in.; 144 in.^{2}

b. 9 in.^{2}

73. *Sample answer:*

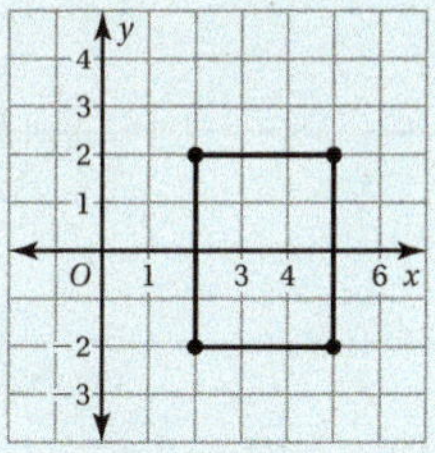

74. *Sample answer:*

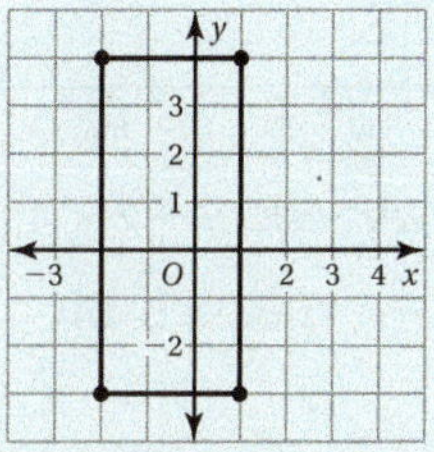

Chapter Self-Assessment

75. $m < 5$ **76.** $3h \geq -12$

77. yes **78.** no

79. yes

80. 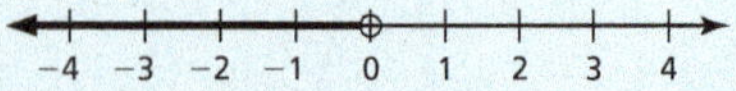

81. 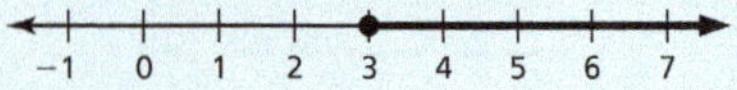

82. 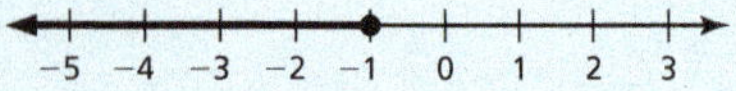

83. $s \leq 35$;

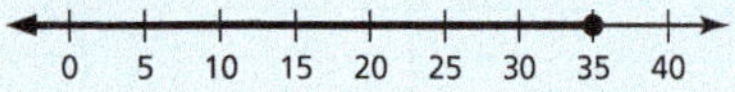

84. $x < 3$; A number x is less than 3.

85. $x > 2$;

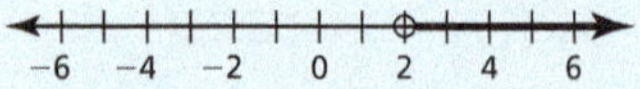

86. $y \geq 1$;

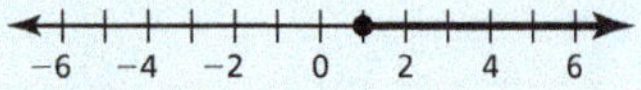

87. $k \leq 7$;

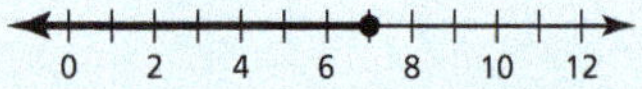

88. $n \geq 7$;

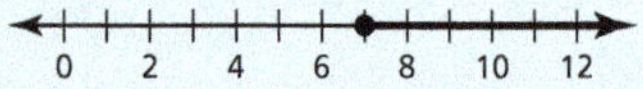

89. $x > 13$;

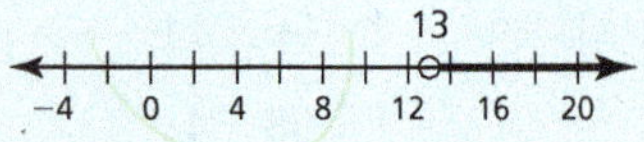

90. $x < 8$;

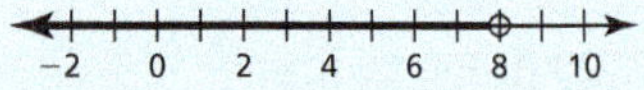

91. $n \geq 8$;

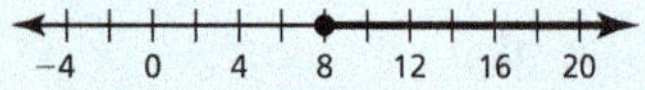

92. $p > 4$;

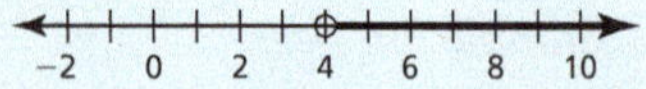

93. $s < 4$;

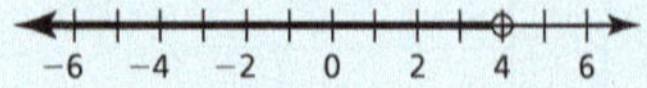

94. $x \leq 6$;

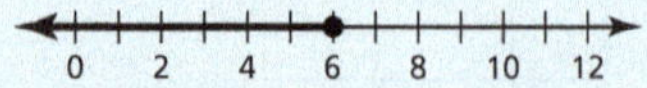

95. See Additional Answers.

96. $k < 55$;

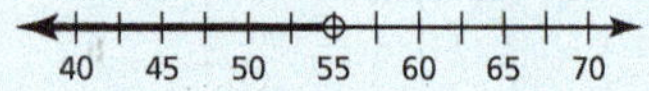

97. *Sample answer:* $x + 2 < 4$; $3x < 6$

98. $s \leq \$9$ **99.** $s \leq 13$

Common Errors

- **Exercises 77–79** Students may try to perform operations on both sides of the inequality (often not the same operation) to get both sides to be the same answer. Remind students that they are checking to see if the value of the variable makes the inequality true, so they are simplifying one side of the inequality and comparing the result to the other side.
- **Exercises 80–82** Students may shade the number line in the wrong direction. This often happens when the variable is on the right side of the inequality. Remind students to use test points to the left and right of the boundary point to determine which direction to shade the number line.
- **Exercises 80–82** Students may draw a closed circle instead of an open circle and vice versa. Remind students that an open circle means the number is not included and a closed circle means the number is included.
- **Exercises 85–96** Students may use the same operation instead of the inverse operation to solve. Simplify the inequality on the board to demonstrate that this will not work. Remind students to check their answers in the original inequality.

Chapter Resources

Surface Level	Deep Level
Resources by Chapter • Extra Practice • Reteach • Puzzle Time Student Journal • Practice • Chapter Self-Assessment Differentiating the Lesson Tutorial Videos Skills Review Handbook Skills Trainer Game Library	Resources by Chapter • Enrichment and Extension Graphic Organizers Game Library
Transfer Level	
STEAM Video Dynamic Assessment System • Chapter Test	Assessment Book • Chapter Tests A and B • Alternative Assessment • STEAM Performance Task

8.7 Writing and Graphing Inequalities (pp. 383–390)

Learning Target: Write inequalities and represent solutions of inequalities on a number line.

Write the word sentence as an inequality.

75. A number m is less than 5.

76. Three times a number h is at least -12.

Tell whether $x = 8$ is a solution of the inequality.

77. $\frac{x}{2} \geq 3$

78. $13 - x > 5$

79. $19 > 2x$

Graph the inequality on a number line.

80. $x < 0$

81. $a \geq 3$

82. $n \leq -1$

83. The speed limit on a road is 35 miles per hour. Write and graph an inequality that represents the legal speeds on the road.

84. Write an inequality and a word sentence that represent the graph.

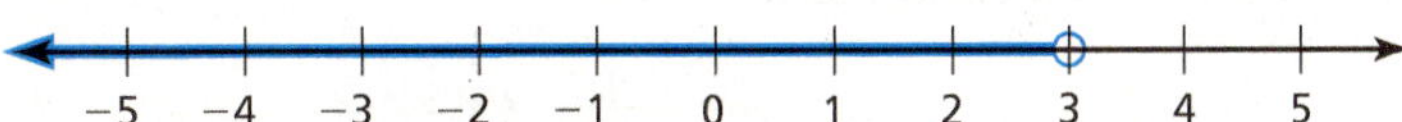

8.8 Solving Inequalities (pp. 391–398)

Learning Target: Write and solve inequalities.

Solve the inequality. Graph the solution.

85. $x + 1 > 3$

86. $y + 8 \geq 9$

87. $k - 7 \leq 0$

88. $9n \geq 63$

89. $24 < 11 + x$

90. $x \div 2 < 4$

91. $4 \leq n - 4$

92. $10p > 40$

93. $s - 1.5 < 2.5$

94. $\frac{5}{3}x \leq 10$

95. $\frac{1}{4} + m \leq \frac{1}{2}$

96. $\frac{3}{11}k < 15$

97. Write two inequalities that have the same solution set and can be solved using different operations.

98. You have \$15 to spend on a ticket to a movie and snacks. Find the possible amounts you can spend on snacks.

99. You want to use a square section of your yard for a chicken pen. You have at most 52 feet of fencing to form the pen. Find the possible lengths of each side of the chicken pen.

8 Practice Test

Order the values from least to greatest.

1. 0, −2, 3, 1, −4

2. −8, $|-3|$, $|5|$, 4, −5

3. −2.46, −2.5, −2, 1, −2.293

Graph the number and its opposite.

4. 23

5. $-1\frac{1}{3}$

Find the absolute value.

6. $|7|$

7. $|-11|$

Copy and complete the statement using <, >, or =.

8. $-\frac{2}{3}$ ▭ $-\frac{3}{5}$

9. 2.5 ▭ $|2.5|$

Plot the ordered pair in a coordinate plane. Describe the location of the point.

10. $J(4, 0)$

11. $L(1.5, -3.5)$

12. $M(-2, -3)$

13. Reflect $(-5, 1)$ in (a) the x-axis, (b) the y-axis, and (c) the x-axis followed by the y-axis.

Graph the inequality on a number line.

14. $x \geq 5$

15. $m \leq -2$

Solve the inequality. Graph the solution.

16. $x - 3 < 7$

17. $12 \geq n + 6$

18. $\frac{4}{3}b \leq 12$

19. $72 < 12p$

20. A hurricane has wind speeds that are greater than or equal to 74 miles per hour. Write an inequality that represents the possible wind speeds during a hurricane.

21. Two vertices of a triangle are $F(1, -4)$ and $G(6, -4)$. Find two possible points that represent the third vertex so that the triangle has an area of 20 square units.

22. The table shows the melting points (in degrees Celsius) of several elements. Compare the melting point of mercury to the melting point of each of the other elements.

Element	Mercury	Radon	Bromine	Cesium	Francium
Melting Point (°C)	−38.83	−71	−7.2	28.5	27

23. A map shows the vertices of a campsite are (25, 10), (25, −5), (−5, −5), and (−5, 10). The vertices of your tent are (0, −3), (0, 6), (10, 6), and (10, −3). The coordinates are measured in feet. What percent of the campsite is *not* covered by your tent?

Practice Test Item References

Practice Test Questions	Section to Review
4	8.1
1	8.2
3, 5, 8, 22	8.3
2, 6, 7, 9	8.4
10, 11, 12, 13	8.5
21, 23	8.6
14, 15, 20	8.7
16, 17, 18, 19	8.8

Test-Taking Strategies

Remind students to quickly look over the entire test before they start so that they can budget their time. On this test, it is very important for students to use the **Stop** and **Think** strategy. When students hurry on a test dealing with positive and negative numbers, they often make "sign errors." Encourage students to represent problems with a number line, if appropriate, to ensure that they think through the process. When working with inequalities, students need to write all numbers and variables clearly. Some numbers and variables are easy to confuse. Have students pay close attention to 6, *s*, 4, 9, 7, and *x*. Remind students to line up terms in each step and to not crowd their work.

Common Errors

- **Exercises 1–3** Students may ignore the signs of the numbers and order the numbers incorrectly. Encourage students to use a number line to determine which number is farthest to the right.
- **Exercises 4 and 5** Students may think that *opposites* are only negative numbers. Remind them that the opposite of a negative number is positive.
- **Exercises 10–12** Students may plot the *x*-coordinate vertically instead of horizontally and the *y*-coordinate horizontally instead of vertically. Remind students that *x* is horizontal and *y* is vertical.
- **Exercises 14 and 15** Students may shade the number line in the wrong direction. This often happens when the variable is on the right side of the inequality. Remind students to use test points to the left and right of the boundary point to determine which direction to shade the number line.

Practice Test

1. $-4, -2, 0, 1, 3$
2. $-8, -5, |-3|, 4, |5|$
3. $-2.5, -2.46, -2.293, -2, 1$
4. 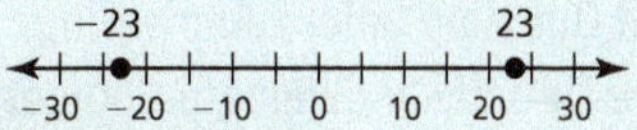

−23
23
−30 −20 −10 0 10 20 30

5. 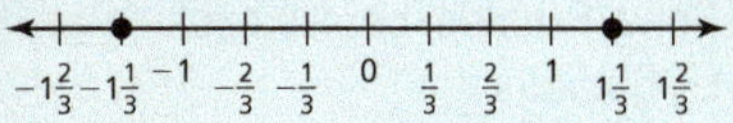
6. 7
7. 11
8. <
9. =

10–12. 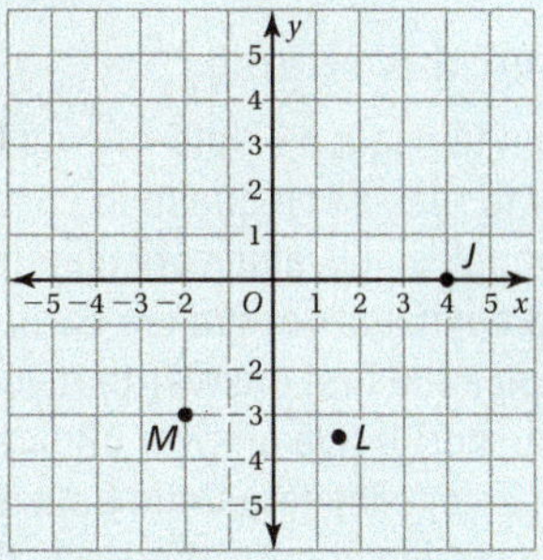

y
x
O
M
L
J

10. x-axis
11. Quadrant IV
12. Quadrant III
13. a. $(-5, -1)$
    b. $(5, 1)$
    c. $(5, -1)$
14. 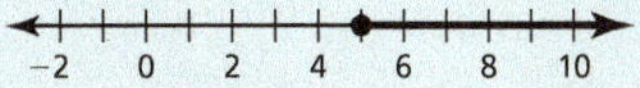

−2 0 2 4 6 8 10

15. 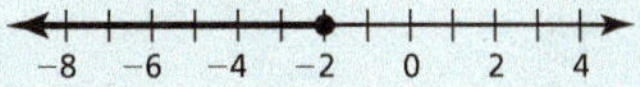

−8 −6 −4 −2 0 2 4

16. $x < 10$;
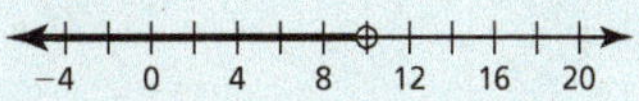

−4 0 4 8 12 16 20

17. $n \le 6$;
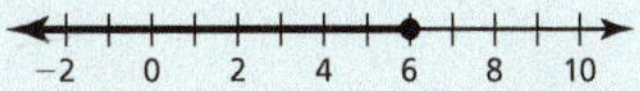

−2 0 2 4 6 8 10

18. $b \le 9$;
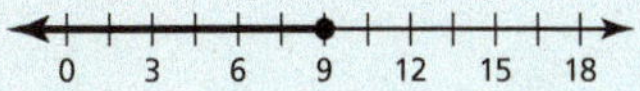

0 3 6 9 12 15 18

19. $6 < p$
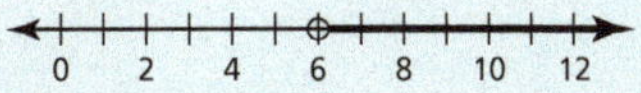

0 2 4 6 8 10 12

20. $w \ge 74$
21. *Sample answer:* $(1, 4), (6, 4)$
22. Mercury has a higher melting point than Radon and a lower melting point than Bromine, Cesium, and Francium.
23. 80%

Test-Taking Strategies

Available at *BigIdeasMath.com*

After Answering Easy Questions, Relax

Answer Easy Questions First

Estimate the Answer

Read All Choices before Answering

Read Question before Answering

Solve Directly or Eliminate Choices

Solve Problem before Looking at Choices

Use Intelligent Guessing

Work Backwards

About this Strategy

When taking a multiple-choice test, be sure to read each question carefully and thoroughly. It is also very important to read each answer choice carefully. Do not pick the first answer that you think is correct! If two answer choices are the same, eliminate them both. Unless the question states otherwise, there can only be one correct answer.

Cumulative Practice

1. C
2. G
3. 12
4. D
5. F

Item Analysis

1. **A.** The student does not follow the correct order of operations; adding $3c$ to $5b$ and then subtracting this sum from $8a$.

   B. The student substitutes 5 for c and 4 for b.

   C. Correct answer

   D. The student makes two-digit numbers out of the coefficients and the variables, such as 86 instead of 8(6).

2. **F.** The student incorrectly thinks that points in Quadrant II have negative y-coordinates.

   G. Correct answer

   H. The student incorrectly thinks that points in Quadrant II have negative y-coordinates. The student also reverses the x- and y-coordinates.

   I. The student reverses the x- and y-coordinates.

3. **Gridded Response:** Correct answer: 12
   Common error: The student adds 6 to both sides of the equation instead of subtracting 6 from both sides and incorrectly thinks $a = 24$.

4. **A.** The student ignores the signs of the numbers.

   B. The student incorrectly thinks $|4| = -4$.

   C. The student ignores the absolute value bars.

   D. Correct answer

5. **F.** Correct answer

   G. The student uses the formula for the area of a triangle $\left(A = \frac{1}{2}bh\right)$ instead of the formula for the area of a parallelogram ($A = bh$).

   H. The student subtracts 15 from 90 instead of dividing 90 by 15.

   I. The student multiplies 90 by 15 instead of dividing.

Cumulative Practice

1. What is the value of the expression when $a = 6$, $b = 5$, and $c = 4$?

$$8a - 3c + 5b$$

A. 11 **B.** 53

C. 61 **D.** 107

2. Point P is plotted in the coordinate plane.

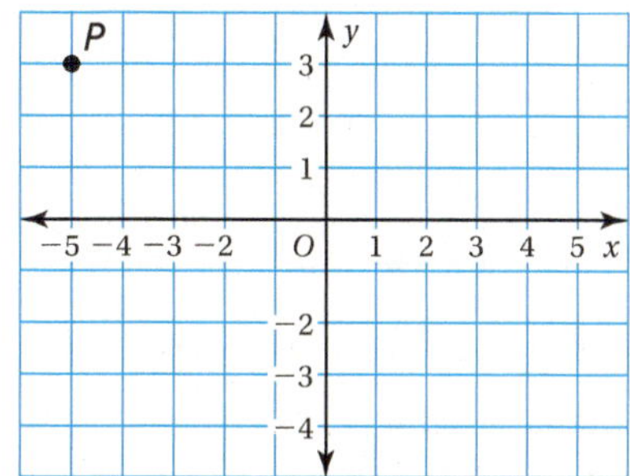

What are the coordinates of point P?

F. $(-5, -3)$ **G.** $(-5, 3)$

H. $(-3, -5)$ **I.** $(3, -5)$

3. What is the value of a that makes the equation true?

$$a + 6 = 18$$

4. Which list of values is in order from least to greatest?

A. $2, |-3|, |4|, -6$ **B.** $-6, |4|, 2, |-3|$

C. $-6, |-3|, 2, |4|$ **D.** $-6, 2, |-3|, |4|$

5. What is the height of the parallelogram?

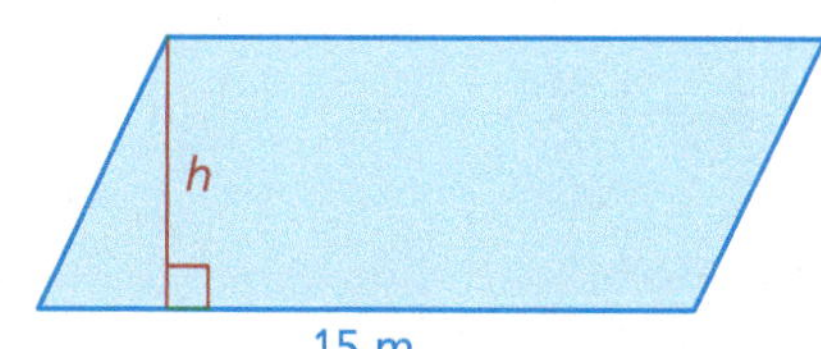

F. 6 meters

G. 12 meters

H. 75 meters

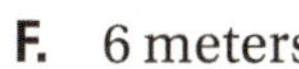

I. 1350 meters

6. Which property is illustrated by the statement?

$$4 + (6 + n) = (4 + 6) + n$$

A. Associative Property of Addition **B.** Commutative Property of Addition

C. Associative Property of Multiplication **D.** Distributive Property

7. Which number line shows the graph of $x \geq 5$?

F. 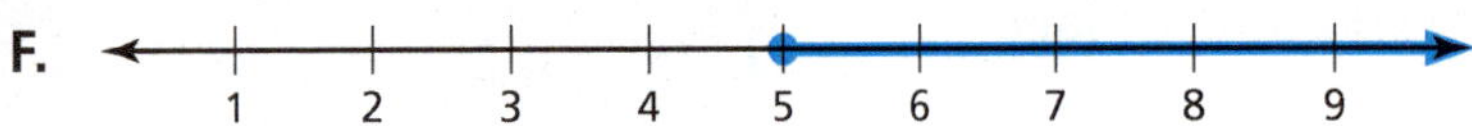

G. 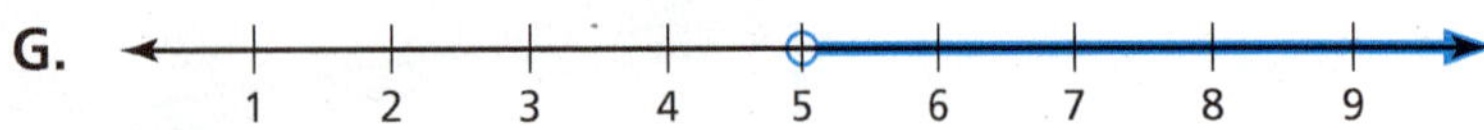

H.
1 2 3 4 5 6 7 8 9

I. 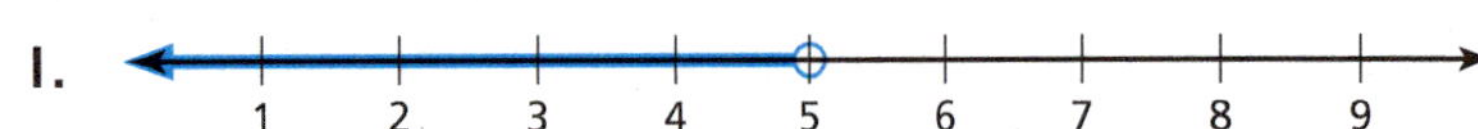

8. Which number is the greatest?

A. $\frac{7}{8}$ **B.** 0.86

C. $\frac{22}{25}$ **D.** 85%

9. What is the area of the shaded region?

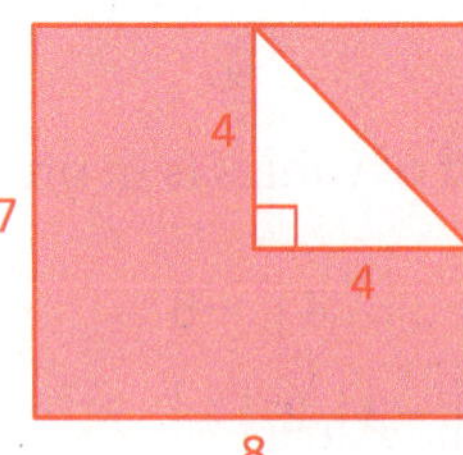

F. 23 units^2 **G.** 40 units^2

H. 48 units^2 **I.** 60 units^2

10. Write 23.5% as a decimal.

Item Analysis (continued)

6. **A.** Correct answer

   B. The student misidentifies the property as the Commutative Property of Addition.

   C. The student misidentifies the property as the Associative Property of Multiplication.

   D. The student misidentifies the property as the Distributive Property.

7. **F.** Correct answer

   G. The student uses an open circle instead of a closed circle.

   H. The student shades in the wrong direction on the number line.

   I. The student uses an open circle instead of a closed circle and shades in the wrong direction on the number line.

8. **A.** The student thinks $\frac{7}{8}$ is greater than $\frac{22}{25}$.

   B. The student thinks 0.86 is greater than $\frac{22}{25}$.

   C. Correct answer

   D. The student thinks 85% is 85.

9. **F.** The student adds the four numbers in the figure.

   G. The student does not multiply by $\frac{1}{2}$ when finding the area of the triangle, gets 16 square units for the area of the triangle, and then subtracts 16 square units from 56 square units.

   H. Correct answer

   I. The student thinks the composite figure can be divided into two rectangles, one 7 units $\times$ 4 units and the other 8 units $\times$ 4 units.

10. **Gridded Response:** Correct answer: 0.235
    Common error: The student removes the percent symbol but does not divide by 100 and gets 23.5.

Cumulative Practice

6. A
7. F
8. C
9. H
10. 0.235

Cumulative Practice

11. *Part A* and *Part B*

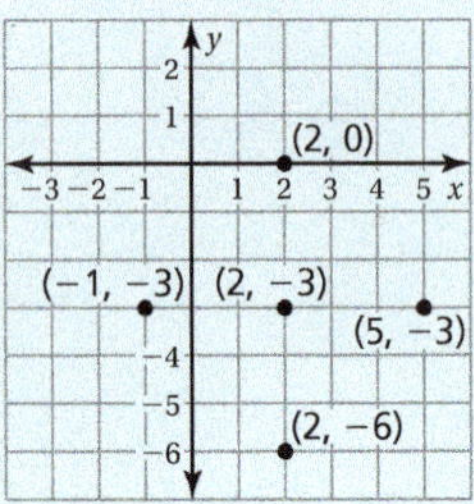

12. C

13. G

14. D

Item Analysis (continued)

11. **2 points** The student's work demonstrates a thorough understanding of plotting points in all four quadrants of the coordinate plane. The student correctly plots and labels points at $(2, -3)$, $(2, -6)$, $(-1, -3)$, $(2, 0)$, and $(5, -3)$.

1 point The student's work demonstrates a partial but limited understanding of plotting points in all four quadrants of the coordinate plane. The student shows some knowledge of how to plot points but does not successfully plot all points.

0 points The student provides no response, a completely incorrect or incomprehensible response, or a response that demonstrates insufficient understanding of plotting points in all four quadrants of the coordinate plane.

12. **A.** The student only finds the length.

B. The student adds the length and width.

C. Correct answer

D. The student multiplies the length and width.

13. **F.** The student thinks the pieces on the top and bottom must be across from one another.

G. Correct answer

H. The student thinks the question asks for which net forms a cube.

I. The student thinks the pieces on the top and bottom must be across from one another.

14. **A.** The student multiplies both sides of the equation by $\frac{3}{4}$ instead of $\frac{4}{3}$ and incorrectly thinks $y = 9$.

B. The student subtracts $\frac{3}{4}$ from both sides of the equation instead of multiplying both sides by $\frac{4}{3}$ and incorrectly thinks $y = 11\frac{1}{4}$.

C. The student adds $\frac{3}{4}$ to both sides of the equation instead of multiplying both sides by $\frac{4}{3}$ and incorrectly thinks $y = 12\frac{3}{4}$.

D. Correct answer

11. Use grid paper to complete the following.

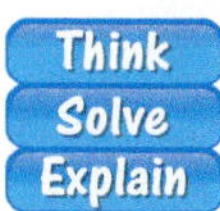

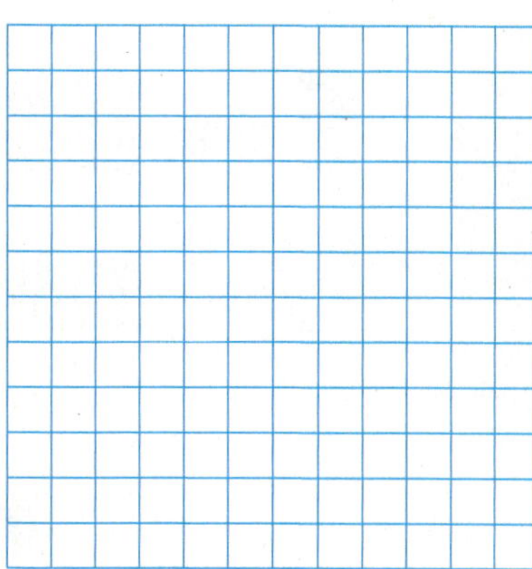

Part A Draw an x-axis and a y-axis of a coordinate plane. Then plot and label the point $(2, -3)$.

Part B Plot and label *four* points that are 3 units away from $(2, -3)$.

12. What is the perimeter of the rectangle with the vertices shown below?

$$A(-4, -1), B(-4, 7), C(1, 7), D(1, -1)$$

A. 8 units

B. 13 units

C. 26 units

D. 40 units

13. Which net does *not* form a cube?

F.

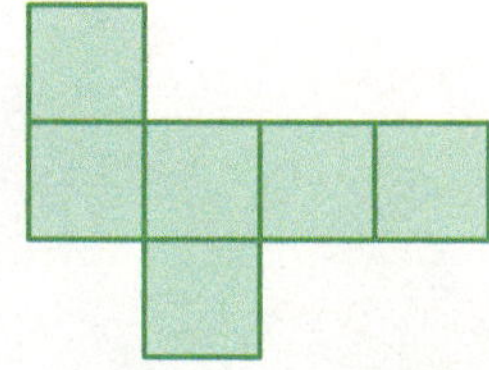

G.

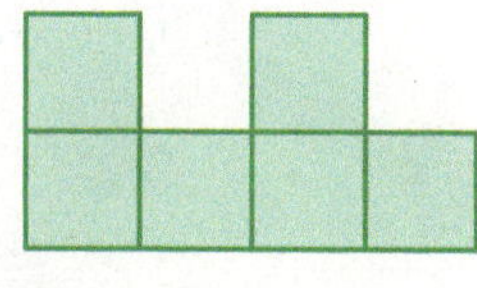

H.

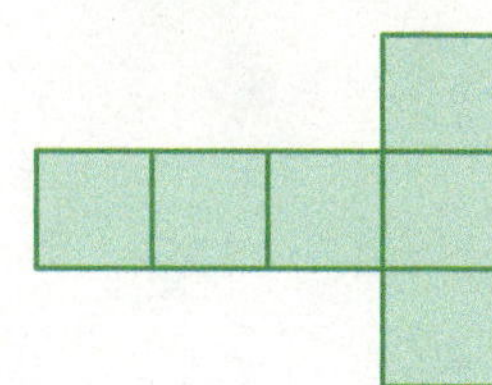

I.

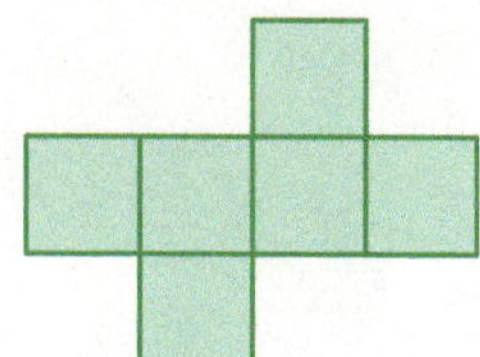

14. Which value of y makes the equation true?

$$\frac{3}{4}y = 12$$

A. 9

B. $11\frac{1}{4}$

C. $12\frac{3}{4}$

D. 16

9 Statistical Measures

9.1 Introduction to Statistics

9.2 Mean

9.3 Measures of Center

9.4 Measures of Variation

9.5 Mean Absolute Deviation

Chapter Learning Target:
Understand statistical measures.

Chapter Success Criteria:
- I can construct a data set.
- I can explain how a data set can be interpreted.
- I can find and interpret the measures of center and the measures of variation for a data set.
- I can compare the measures of center and the measures of variation for data sets.

Laurie's Notes

Chapter 9 Overview

The last two chapters of this course focus on the data and statistics strand. Although students have read information from data displays throughout this course, significant analysis of a data set has been left for this chapter.

Students first need to understand what a statistical question is. "What video game did you play last night?" is not a statistical question. "What video games did students in your math class play last night?" is a statistical question about categorical data. You expect a variety of answers. "How many video games were played by students in your math class last night?" is a statistical question about numeric data. You expect a variety of answers and you are interested in the *distribution* and *tendency* of those answers.

Data related to *what video games were played* can be displayed in a bar graph or pictograph, two displays students should be familiar with. Data related to *how many video games were played* can be displayed in a dot plot (or line plot), where a number line is used to show the number of times each value in a data set occurs. A dot plot shows the *spread* and the *distribution* of a data set.

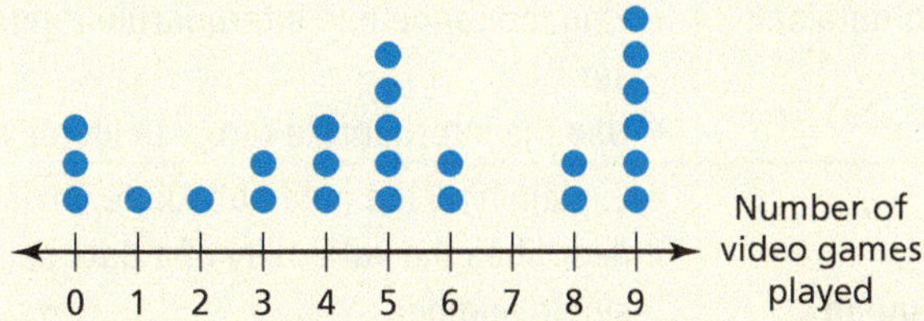

The data collected to answer the question, "How many video games were played by students in your math class last night?" can be described by its center, spread, and overall shape. A measure of center summarizes all of the values in a data set with a single number and describes *the typical value of a data set.* Measures of center include mean, median, and mode. A measure of variation describes *the variability of a data set* with a single number. Measures of variation include range, interquartile range, and mean absolute deviation.

Describing the overall shape of the data display and examining any gaps or outliers is further analysis that you want students to do. For the data set displayed in the dot plot, imagine that another data value is added for a student that played 25 video games last night. You want students to understand how that one data value, an outlier, can affect the measures of center and measures of variation.

Overarching goals of the chapter are for students to develop an understanding of statistical variability and to be able to summarize and describe the distribution of a data set. It is also important to remember the context in which the data was gathered. The set of data for the number of video games played last night may be different if it was gathered during summer vacation versus a weeknight during the school year.

Additional data displays for numeric data sets are presented in the next chapter.

Suggested Pacing

Chapter Opener	1 Day
Section 1	2 Days
Section 2	1 Day
Section 3	1 Day
Section 4	2 Days
Section 5	2 Days
Connecting Concepts	1 Day
Chapter Review	1 Day
Chapter Test	1 Day
Total Chapter 9	12 Days
Year-to-Date	142 Days

Chapter Learning Target

Understand statistical measures.

Chapter Success Criteria

- Construct a data set.
- Explain how a data set can be interpreted.
- Find and interpret the measures of center and the measures of variation for a data set.
- Compare the measures of center and the measures of variation for data sets.

Chapter 9 Learning Targets and Success Criteria

Section	Learning Target	Success Criteria
9.1 Introduction to Statistics	Identify statistical questions and use data to answer statistical questions.	• Recognize questions that anticipate a variety of answers. • Construct and interpret a dot plot. • Use data to answer a statistical question.
9.2 Mean	Find and interpret the mean of a data set.	• Explain how the mean summarizes a data set with a single number. • Find the mean of a data set. • Use the mean of a data set to answer a statistical question.
9.3 Measures of Center	Find and interpret the median and mode of a data set.	• Explain how the median and mode summarize a data set with a single number. • Find the median and mode of a data set. • Explain how changes to a data set affect the measures of center. • Use a measure of center to answer a statistical question.
9.4 Measures of Variation	Find and interpret the range and interquartile range of a data set.	• Explain how the range and interquartile range describe the variability of a data set with a single number. • Find the range and interquartile range of a data set. • Use the interquartile range to identify outliers.
9.5 Mean Absolute Deviation	Find and interpret the mean absolute deviation of a data set.	• Explain how the mean absolute deviation describes the variability of a data set with a single number. • Find the mean absolute deviation of a data set. • Compare data sets using the mean absolute deviation to draw conclusions.

Progressions

Through the Grades		
Grade 5	**Grade 6**	**Grade 7**
• Use line plots to solve problems involving operations on fractions.	• Recognize statistical questions as ones anticipating variability. • Understand that data used to answer statistical questions has a distribution that can be described by center and spread. • Recognize that a measure of center for a numerical data set summarizes all of its values with a single number, and a measure of variation describes how its values vary with a single number • Display data on number lines, including dot plots, stem-and-leaf plots, histograms, and box-and-whisker plots. • Use measures of center to summarize all of the values in a data set with a single number, and use measures of variation to summarize how all the values in a data set vary with a single number.	• Understand representative samples (random samples) and populations. • Use samples to draw inferences about populations. • Compare two populations from random samples using measures of center and variability.

Through the Chapter					
Standard	**9.1**	**9.2**	**9.3**	**9.4**	**9.5**
6.SP.A.1 Recognize a statistical question as one that anticipates variability in the data related to the question and accounts for it in the answers.	★				
6.SP.A.2 Understand that a set of data collected to answer a statistical question has a distribution, which can be described by its center, spread, and overall shape.	●	●	●	●	●
6.SP.A.3 Recognize that a measure of center for a numerical data set summarizes all of its values with a single number, while a measure of variation describes how its values vary with a single number.		●	●	●	★
6.SP.B.4 Display numerical data in plots on a number line, including dot plots, histograms, and box plots.	●				
6.SP.B.5a Summarize numerical data sets in relation to their context, such as by reporting the number of observations.	●	★			
6.SP.B.5b Summarize numerical data sets in relation to their context, such as by describing the nature of the attribute under investigation, including how it was measured and its units of measurement.	★				
6.SP.B.5c Summarize numerical data sets in relation to their context, such as by giving quantitative measures of center (median and/or mean) and variability (interquartile range and/or mean absolute deviation), as well as describing any overall pattern and any striking deviations from the overall pattern with reference to the context in which the data were gathered.		●	●	●	●

Key

▲ = preparing ★ = complete

● = learning ■ = extending

STEAM Video

1. *Sample answer:* The Earth rotates on a tilted axis.
2. *Sample answer:* 633 min

Performance Task

Sample answer: They are planning a vacation.

Mathematical Practices

Students have opportunities to develop aspects of the mathematical practices throughout the chapter. Here are some examples.

1. **Make Sense of Problems and Persevere in Solving Them**
   9.3 Exercise 37, *p. 432*
2. **Reason Abstractly and Quantitatively**
   9.5 Math Practice note, *p. 439*
3. **Construct Viable Arguments and Critique the Reasoning of Others**
   9.3 Exercise 19, *p. 430*
4. **Model with Mathematics**
   9.2 Exercise 23, *p. 424*
5. **Use Appropriate Tools Strategically**
   9.1 Math Practice note, *p. 413*
6. **Attend to Precision**
   9.3 Math Practice note, *p. 428*
7. **Look for and Make Use of Structure**
   9.4 Exercise 29, *p. 438*
8. **Look for and Express Regularity in Repeated Reasoning**
   9.5 Math Practice note, *p. 440*

Laurie's Notes

STEAM Video

Before the Video

- To introduce the STEAM Video, read aloud the first paragraph of Daylight in the Big City and discuss the questions with your students.
- ? "How can you use averages to compare the amounts of daylight in different cities? Can you think of any other real-life situations where averages are useful?"

During the Video

- The video shows Robert and Tory discussing changes in the amount of daylight of several big cities.
- ? Pause the video at 1:16 and ask, "Which North American cities are Robert and Tory discussing?" New York, Mexico City, and Los Angeles
- ? "Where are most big cities located?" Asia
- Watch the remainder of the video.

After the Video

- ? "How did Robert and Tory find the average difference between the shortest day and the longest day of a big city?" They found the mean of the differences.
- ? "What is the average difference with the outlier?" 238 minutes, or about 4 hours
- ? "What is the average difference without the outlier?" 222 minutes
- Have students work with a partner to answer Questions 1 and 2.
- As students discuss and answer the questions, listen for understanding of how averages and range apply to real-life situations.

Performance Task

- Use this information to spark students' interest and promote thinking about real-life problems.
- ? Ask, "Why might someone be interested in the amounts of daylight throughout the year in a city?"
- After completing the chapter, students will have gained the knowledge needed to complete "Which Measure of Center Is Best: Mean, Median, or Mode?"

STEAM Video

Daylight in the Big City

Averages can be used to compare different sets of data. How can you use averages to compare the amounts of daylight in different cities? Can you think of any other real-life situations where averages are useful?

Watch the STEAM Video "Daylight in the Big City." Then answer the following questions.

1. Why do different cities have different amounts of daylight throughout the year?

2. Robert's table includes the difference of the greatest amount of daylight and the least amount of daylight in Lagos, Nigeria, and in Moscow, Russia.

   Lagos: 44 minutes

   Moscow: 633 minutes

   Use these values to make a prediction about the difference of the greatest amount of daylight and the least amount of daylight in a city in Alaska.

Performance Task

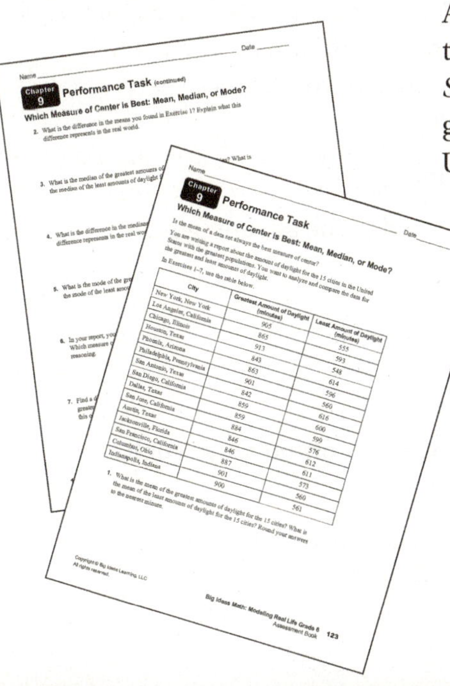

Name _______ Date _______

Chapter 9 **Performance Task** (continued)

Which Measure of Center Is Best: Mean, Median, or Mode?

2. What is the difference in the means you found in Exercise 1? Explain what this difference represents in the real world.

3. What is the median of the greatest amounts of ... What is the median of the least amounts of daylight ...

4. What is the difference in the medians ... difference represents in the real wo...

5. What is the mode of the gre... the mode of the least amou...

6. In your report, you ... Which measure o... reasoning.

7. Find a d... greate... this o...

Name _______ Date _______

Chapter 9 **Performance Task**

Which Measure of Center Is Best: Mean, Median, or Mode?

Is the mean of a data set always the best measure of center?

You are writing a report about the amount of daylight for the 15 cities in the United States with the greatest populations. You want to analyze and compare the data for the greatest and least amounts of daylight.

In Exercises 1–7, use the table below.

City	Greatest Amount of Daylight (minutes)	Least Amount of Daylight (minutes)
New York, New York	905	555
Los Angeles, California	865	593
Chicago, Illinois	913	548
Houston, Texas	843	614
Phoenix, Arizona	863	596
Philadelphia, Pennsylvania	901	560
San Antonio, Texas	842	616
San Diego, California	859	600
Dallas, Texas	859	599
San Jose, California	884	576
Austin, Texas	846	612
Jacksonville, Florida	846	611
San Francisco, California	887	573
Columbus, Ohio	901	560
Indianapolis, Indiana	900	561

1. What is the mean of the greatest amounts of daylight for the 15 cities? What is the mean of the least amounts of daylight for the 15 cities? Round your answers to the nearest minute.

Big Ideas Math: Modeling Real Life Grade 6
Assessment Book 123

Which Measure of Center Is Best: Mean, Median, or Mode?

After completing this chapter, you will be able to use the concepts you learned to answer the questions in the *STEAM Video Performance Task*. You will be given the greatest and least amounts of daylight in the 15 cities in the United States with the greatest populations.

	Greatest	Least
New York:	905 minutes	555 minutes
Los Angeles:	865 minutes	593 minutes
Chicago:	913 minutes	548 minutes

You will determine which measure of center best represents the data. Why might someone be interested in the amounts of daylight throughout the year in a city?

Getting Ready for Chapter 9

Chapter Exploration

Work with a partner. Write the number of letters in each of your first names on the board.

1. Write all of the numbers on a piece of paper. The collection of numbers is called *data*.
2. Talk with your partner about how you can organize the data. What conclusions can you make about the numbers of letters in the first names of the students in your class?
3. Draw a grid like the one shown below. Then use the grid to draw a graph of the data.

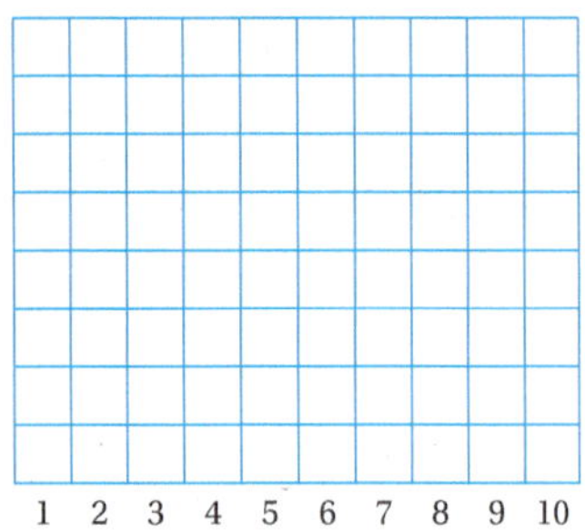

4. **THE CENTER OF THE DATA** Use the graph of the data in Exercise 3 to answer the following.
   a. Is there one number that occurs more than any of the other numbers? If so, write a sentence that interprets this number in the context of your class.
   b. Complete the sentence, "In my class, the average number of letters in a student's first name is __________." Justify your reasoning.
   c. Organize your data using a different type of graph. Describe the advantages or disadvantages of this graph.

Vocabulary

The following vocabulary terms are defined in this chapter. Think about what each term might mean and record your thoughts.

statistical question	measure of center	measure of variation
mean	median	range

Laurie's Notes

Chapter Exploration

- Students should be familiar with making line (dot) plots, bar graphs, double bar graphs, and picture graphs (pictographs) from previous courses.
- Ask students where they have heard the term *data* before. Students may not know the formal definition, but they have likely heard data referenced in sports, advertisements, and other real-life contexts.
- Have partners complete Exercises 1 and 2. Ask students to share their conclusions with the class.
- After students complete Exercise 4, discuss each part as a class.
- For part (c), have each pair compare their graph with another pair and discuss the advantages and disadvantages of both. Then have each group display both of their graphs to the class. Discuss the similarities and differences of all the graphs.

ELL Support

Explain that phonetic languages, such as English, use letters to represent sounds. The letters of the English alphabet were originally used by the Romans to write the Latin language. Some phonetic languages, such as Russian and Arabic, use different types of letters, not Roman letters. Non-phonetic languages use different writing systems. For instance, the Chinese language uses characters to express complete words. Students whose first languages do not use Roman letters have had their names translated into the English writing system. Have these students write their names in their original languages and compare them to their names in English. You could have students find the average number of letters in a student's first name from different language groups and compare that number to the number found in Exercise 4(b).

Vocabulary

- These terms represent some of the vocabulary that students will encounter in Chapter 9. Discuss the terms as a class.
- Where have students heard the term *range* outside of a math classroom? In what contexts? Students may not be able to write the actual definition, but they may write phrases associated with *range*.
- Allowing students to discuss these terms now will prepare them for understanding the terms as they are presented in the chapter.
- When students encounter a new definition, encourage them to write in their *Student Journals*. They will revisit these definitions during the Chapter Review.

Topics for Review

- Analyzing Double Bar Graphs
- Making Line Plots
- Operations with Decimals
- Ordering Decimals

Chapter Exploration

1. Check students' work.
2. Answers will vary. Listen for students to mention ideas such as lowest and highest numbers, numbers that occur most often, and numbers that look to be in the middle of the data set.
3. Check students' work.
4. (a)–(c). Check students' work.

Learning Target

Identify statistical questions and use data to answer statistical questions.

Success Criteria

- Recognize questions that anticipate a variety of answers.
- Construct and interpret a dot plot.
- Use data to answer a statistical question.

Warm Up

Cumulative, vocabulary, and prerequisite skills practice opportunities are available in the *Resources by Chapter* or at *BigIdeasMath.com*.

ELL Support

Explain that statistics is the science of collecting, organizing, analyzing, and interpreting data. The data is often collected from a smaller group and then applied to a larger group. For example, if there are 10,000 voters and 1,000 people are polled, you can predict the election results based on the results of the poll. You assume that the percent of people voting for a particular candidate in the smaller group will be similar to the larger group. The word *statistics* is related to the word *state*. In its early use, the term *statistics* was used to describe information about states.

Exploration 1

a. *Sample answer:* 66

b. Check students' work.

c. See Additional Answers.

Exploration 2

a. 1 and 4; 2 and 3

b. *Sample answer:* 2 and 3; The answers will vary.

Laurie's Notes

STATE STANDARDS
6.SP.A.1, 6.SP.A.2, 6.SP.B.4, 6.SP.B.5a, 6.SP.B.5b

Preparing to Teach

- Dot plots and ratio tables are important data displays that students already have in their toolkits. In this section, students will analyze data in these displays to answer statistical questions.
- **MP3 Construct Viable Arguments and Critique the Reasoning of Others:** Mathematically proficient students make conjectures and justify their explanations or conclusions to others. At this point, students should understand the need to give logical support for their statements.

Motivate

- Give each student a sticky note.
- ? "How many times have you eaten pizza in the last month? If you can't remember, an estimate is fine. Write your answer on the sticky note."
- Use student responses to make a line plot on the board.
- Draw a horizontal number line with a scale to fit the range of the data. Have students place their sticky notes above the appropriate values.
- ? "What can you infer from this display?" Answers will vary.

Exploration 1

- This exploration provides some groundwork for **statistics**: students are collecting, analyzing, and interpreting data to answer a question.
- Provide directions for finding your pulse: face the palm of one of your hands upward, place the tips of your fingers on your wrist below the base of your thumb, and press lightly until you feel the pulsing beneath your fingers.
- If unsuccessful, students can try at the elbow, neck, or foot, as described.
- Have students count the number of beats for 10 seconds and then use a ratio table to find the number of beats per minute.
- If there are fewer than 15 students in the class, you may want to include data from another class. Encourage students to use a line plot to organize the data, so they can see the spread of the data.
- **MP3 Construct Viable Arguments and Critique the Reasoning of Others:** In part (c), students understand that they can describe a set of values using only one number. Students should explain why they chose the value they did.

Exploration 2

- ? "How many of you have answered a survey?" Answers will vary.
- ? "Does everyone answer the same on a survey?" no "Why?" *Sample answer:* Surveys are designed to gather information that varies from person to person.
- For a *factual* question such as "How many states are in the United States?" there is one correct answer, and the answer does not vary across respondents. For a ***statistical* question** such as "How much does a movie ticket cost?" answers may vary across respondents.
- **MP3 Construct Viable Arguments and Critique the Reasoning of Others:** Ask students to explain the difference between a statistical question and a factual question. *Sample answer:* A statistical question has answers that vary.

9.1 Introduction to Statistics

Learning Target: Identify statistical questions and use data to answer statistical questions.

Success Criteria:
- I can recognize questions that anticipate a variety of answers.
- I can construct and interpret a dot plot.
- I can use data to answer a statistical question.

EXPLORATION 1 Using Data to Answer a Question

Work with a partner.

a. Use your pulse to find your heart rate in beats per minute.

Places to check your pulse:
- on your wrist
- inside your elbow
- on the side of your neck
- on top of your foot

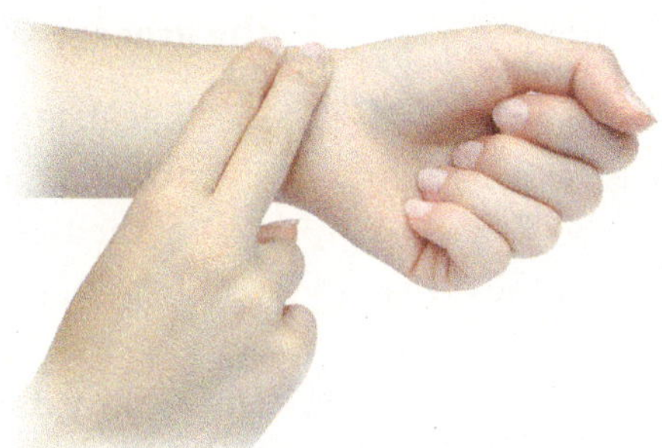

Math Practice

Use Technology to Explore

How can you use technology to show the spread of the data?

b. Collect the recorded heart rates of the students in your class, including yourself. How spread out are the data? Use a diagram to justify your answer.

c. MP **REASONING** How would you answer the following question by using only one value? Explain your reasoning.

"What is the heart rate of a sixth-grade student?"

EXPLORATION 2 Identifying Types of Questions

Work with a partner.

a. Answer each question on your own. Then compare your answers with your partner's answers. For which questions should your answers be the same? For which questions might your answers be different?

1. How many states are in the United States?
2. How much does a movie ticket cost?
3. What color fur do bears have?
4. How tall is your math teacher?

b. **CONJECTURE** Some of the questions in part (a) are considered *statistical* questions. Which ones are they? Explain.

9.1 Lesson

Key Vocabulary
statistics, *p. 414*
statistical question, *p. 414*

Statistics is the science of collecting, organizing, analyzing, and interpreting data. A **statistical question** is one for which you do not expect to get a single answer. Instead, you expect a variety of answers, and you are interested in the *distribution* and *tendency* of those answers.

EXAMPLE 1 Identifying Statistical Questions

Determine whether the question is a statistical question. Explain.

a. How many countries start with the letter Z?

Because there is only one answer, it is not a statistical question.

b. How much do bags of pretzels cost at the grocery store?

Because you can anticipate that the prices will vary, it is a statistical question. The table at the right may represent prices of several bags of pretzels at a grocery store.

Prices	
\$0.99	\$2.99
\$1.99	\$2.99
\$1.99	\$4.29

c. How many days does your school have off for spring break this year?

Because there is only one answer, it is not a statistical question.

d. What are the hair colors of students in your class?

Because you can anticipate that the colors will vary, it is a statistical question. The table below may represent hair colors of several students in a class.

Hair Colors	
Brown	Red
Black	Blonde
Blonde	Pink
Red	Brown

Try It **Determine whether the question is a statistical question. Explain.**

1. What types of cell phones do students have in your class?
2. How many desks are in your classroom?
3. How much do virtual-reality headsets cost?
4. How many minutes are in your lunch period?

Multi-Language Glossary at BigIdeasMath.com

Laurie's Notes

Scaffolding Instruction

- After exploring statistical questions, students will use the formal definition to identify them. Students will also analyze data to answer statistical questions.
- **Emerging:** Students may have difficulty distinguishing statistical questions from factual questions, or they may need more practice creating and analyzing dot plots. Students should continue to practice these skills in the examples.
- **Proficient:** Students can identify statistical questions. They can also create dot plots to analyze data and answer statistical questions. Have students assess their understanding using the Self-Assessment exercises.

Discuss

? "What do you know about the word *statistics*?" Answers will vary.

- Define **statistics** and relate it to the answers given by students.
- Define **statistical question** and relate it to the explorations. You are interested in the distribution and tendency of the answers.
- Ask whether "How many times have you eaten pizza in the last month?" from the Motivate is a statistical question.

EXAMPLE 1

- As in Exploration 2, this example provides practice with the first success criterion.
- Work through each part and have students explain their reasoning.
- Discuss the difference between data that is numerical (quantitative data) and data that is categorical (qualitative data). Answers to "How much do bags of pretzels cost at the grocery store?" are numerical, but answers to "What are the hair colors of students in your class?" are categorical.

Try It

- **Neighbor Check:** Have students work independently and then have their neighbors check their work. Have students discuss any discrepancies.

ELL Support

Allow students to work in pairs to complete Exercises 1–4. Have two pairs compare their answers and discuss their reasoning. Expect students at different language levels to perform as described.

Beginner: Determine whether the question is a statistical question.

Intermediate: Explain why a question is or is not a statistical question.

Advanced: Explain their reasoning and help guide the discussion.

Scaffold instruction to support all students in their learning. Learning is individualized and you may want to group students differently as they move in and out of these levels with each skill and concept. Student self-assessment and feedback help guide your instructional decisions about how and when to layer support for all students to become proficient learners.

Extra Example 1

Determine whether the question is a statistical question. Explain.

a. What are the favorite sports of students in your class? Because you can anticipate that the sports will vary, it is a statistical question.

b. How many states start with the letter N? Because there is only one answer, it is not a statistical question.

c. How many meters are in a kilometer? Because there is only one answer, it is not a statistical question.

d. How many letters are in the first names of students in your class? Because you can anticipate that the numbers will vary, it is a statistical question.

Try It

1. yes; The answers will vary.
2. no; There is only one answer.
3. yes; The answers will vary.
4. no; There is only one answer.

Laurie's Notes

Extra Example 2

The dot plot shows the heights of sixth-grade students in a gym class.

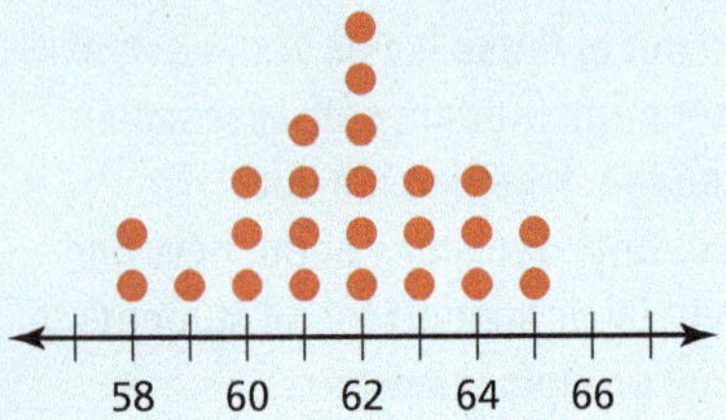

a. Find and interpret the number of data values on the dot plot. 24; There are 24 students in the gym class.

b. How can you collect these data? What are the units? Use a measuring tape; inches

c. Write a statistical question that you can answer using the dot plot. Then answer the question. *Sample answer:* How tall are the students in the gym class? Most of the students are about 62 inches tall.

Try It

5. a. 20; There were 20 students in the race.

b. Time the students using a stopwatch; seconds (in tenths)

c. See Additional Answers.

ELL Support

Allow students to work in groups to complete the Self-Assessment for Concepts & Skills exercises. Monitor discussions and provide help as needed. Have each group present their answers and discuss each answer as a class.

Self-Assessment for Concepts & Skills

6–7. See Additional Answers.

Discuss

- Review and discuss *dot plots.* Tell students that the line plot from the Motivate can be called a dot plot.
- Numerical data that is collected from a statistical question can be displayed in a dot plot. Explain that if you cannot quantify the answers to a question, the results cannot be displayed in a dot plot. The answers must be measurable.
  - For example, "How many times have you eaten pizza in the last month?" is measurable, but "What is your favorite pizza topping?" is *not* measurable and cannot be displayed in a dot plot.
- ? "What does each dot on a dot plot represent?" a data value
- ? "How can you tell how many data values were collected?" count the dots
- ? "What do you think *spread* and *distribution* mean?" Guide student responses to defining spread as a measure of variability that describes how similar or varied the data values are, and distribution as the arrangement and frequency of the data values.

EXAMPLE 2

- This is a nice example of a vertical dot plot.
- Thermometers are not scaled as shown. This is done for illustrative purposes.
- **MP5 Use Appropriate Tools Strategically:** The units of temperature are not specified, but students should be familiar with Fahrenheit and Celsius thermometers. Ask students which units are reasonable for the given context.
- Ask students whether they think they could use negative values in a dot plot (e.g., negative temperatures, golf scores).
- In part (a), ask how a conversion factor is used to convert days into weeks. Select a volunteer to show his or her work on the board.
- In part (c), help students understand that a survey question is *not* a statistical question. For example, "How old are you?" is a survey question used to gather data for the statistical question, "How old are the students in your school?"
- "What is the daily high temperature in August?" is an example of a statistical question that does not have a single answer. The temperatures are spread out from 80°F to 87°F with two peaks occurring at 81°F and 86°F.

Try It

- The units of time are not specified, but students should know that reasonable units for this exercise would be seconds.

Self-Assessment for Concepts & Skills

- Students are assessing their understanding of all the success criteria.
- In Exercise 6, students reveal their understanding of statistical questions by creating an example and a non-example. In doing so, they demonstrate their understanding of the definition and the common characteristics of statistical questions.

The Success Criteria Self-Assessment chart can be found in the *Student Journal* or online at *BigIdeasMath.com.*

A *dot plot* uses a number line to show the number of times each value in a data set occurs. Dot plots show the *spread* and the *distribution* of a data set.

EXAMPLE 2 Using a Dot Plot

You record the high temperature every day while at summer camp in August. Then you create the vertical dot plot.

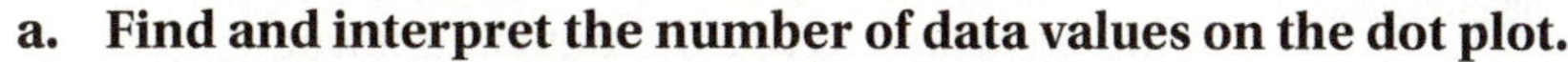

a. Find and interpret the number of data values on the dot plot.

There are 28 data values on the dot plot. So, you were at camp 28 days, or 4 weeks.

b. How can you collect these data? What are the units?

You can collect these data with a thermometer. The units are degrees Fahrenheit (°F).

c. Write a statistical question that you can answer using the dot plot. Then answer the question.

One possible statistical question is,

"What is the daily high temperature in August?"

The high temperatures are spread out with about half of the temperatures around 81°F and half of the temperatures around 86°F.

Try It

5. Repeat parts (a)–(c) using the dot plot below that shows the times of students in a 100-meter race.

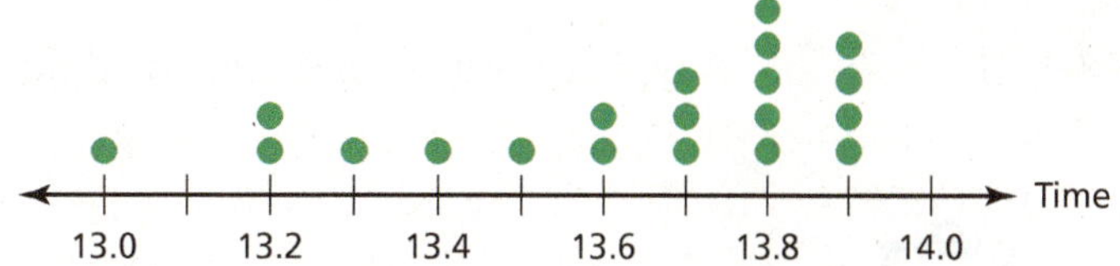

Self-Assessment for Concepts & Skills

Solve each exercise. Then rate your understanding of the success criteria in your journal.

6. VOCABULARY What is a statistical question? Give an example and a non-example.

7. OPEN-ENDED Write and answer a statistical question using the dot plot. Then find and interpret the number of data values.

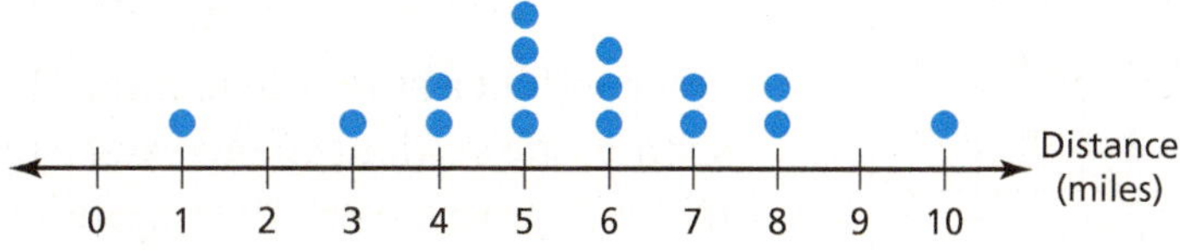

EXAMPLE 3 Modeling Real Life

Your teacher asks you, "What is the mass of a typical mouse?" You conduct a science experiment on house mice. Use the data in the table to answer the question.

Masses (grams)			
20	19	21	20
18	20	27	21
28	23	20	19
20	21	18	27
19	22	21	20

Understand the problem.

You know the masses of several mice. You are asked to use the data to answer a statistical question.

Make a plan.

Display the data in a dot plot. Identify any clusters, peaks, or gaps in the data. Then use the distribution of the data to answer the question.

Solve and check.

Draw a number line that includes the least value, 18, and the greatest value, 28. Then place a dot above the number line for each data value.

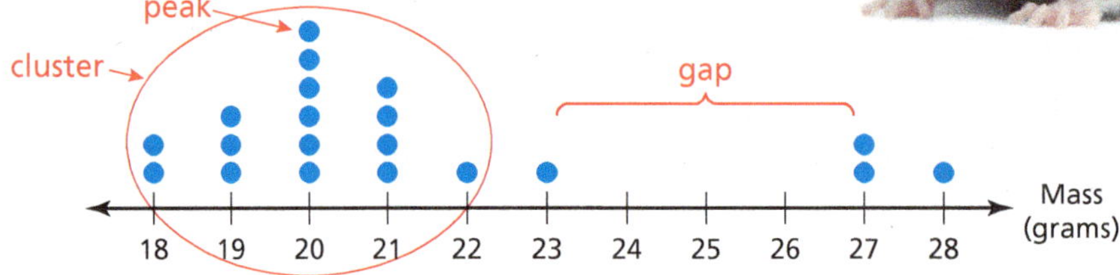

Most of the data are clustered around 20. There is a peak at 20 and a gap between 23 and 27.

A typical mouse has a mass of about 20 grams.

Check Reasonableness

65% of the mice have a mass of 19, 20, or 21 grams. So, it is reasonable to say that a typical mouse has a mass of about 20 grams. ✓

Self-Assessment for Problem Solving

Solve each exercise. Then rate your understanding of the success criteria in your journal.

8. You record the amount of snowfall each day for several days. Then you create the dot plot.

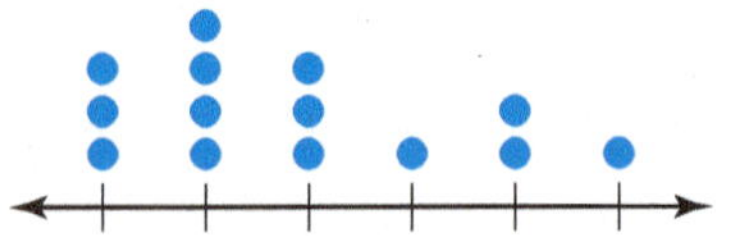

a. Find and interpret the number of data values on the dot plot.

b. How can you collect these data? What are the units?

c. Write a statistical question that you can answer using the dot plot. Then answer the question.

9. You conduct a survey to answer, "How many hours does a typical sixth-grade student spend exercising during a week?" Use the data in the table to answer the question.

Hours of Exercise				
5	1	5	3	5
4	5	2	5	4
3	4	6	5	6

Laurie's Notes

Discuss

- The terms *cluster*, *peak*, and *gap* describe the distribution of data. A cluster is when several data points lie in a small interval. A peak is the data value that occurs most often in an interval. A gap is an interval with no data. A data set can have *zero*, *one*, or *more* clusters, peaks, or gaps.

EXAMPLE 3

? "What is the least mass of the mice?" 18 grams "What is the greatest mass of the mice?" 28 grams
- Draw a number line with whole numbers from 18 to 28. Do not skip 24, 25, and 26. These numbers must be included to see the gap in the data.
- Have students describe the dot plot in terms of clusters, peaks, and gaps.

? Ask the original (statistical) question, "What is the mass of a typical mouse?" Remind students that they are estimating the answer based on the dot plot. Then discuss the Check Reasonableness note.

Formative Assessment Tip

Paired Verbal Fluency (PVF)
This technique is used between two partners where each person takes a turn speaking, uninterrupted, for a specified period of time. The roles reverse and the listener then speaks, uninterrupted, for the same amount of time. Verbalizing their understanding and being attentive listeners will activate student thinking and should help identify areas of difficulty or uncertainty.
Paired Verbal Fluency can be used at the beginning, middle, or end of instruction. Used at the beginning of instruction, students share their prior knowledge about a particular topic, skill, or concept. Used at the end of instruction, students reflect on learning that occurred during the lesson or at the end of a connected group of lessons.

Self-Assessment for Problem Solving

- Have students complete the exercises independently to assess their understanding of the success criteria. It is important to provide time in class for problem solving, so that students become comfortable with the problem-solving plan.
- **Paired Verbal Fluency:** Ask students to discuss their answers. Encourage students to use precise vocabulary: gaps, peaks, clusters, data value, spread, dot plot, statistical question.

The Success Criteria Self-Assessment chart can be found in the *Student Journal* or online at *BigIdeasMath.com*.

Closure

- Write a statistical question that you can answer using the dot plot made with sticky notes at the beginning of class. Then answer the question. *Sample answer:* How many times a month does a typical sixth-grade student eat pizza?; Answers will vary.

Extra Example 3

Your teacher asks you, "What is the weight of a typical cat?" You conduct a science experiment on cats. Use the data in the table to answer the question.

Weights (pounds)			
10	7	8	12
8	9	10	20
9	11	10	11
15	18	12	13
10	14	19	10

A typical cat weighs about 10 pounds.

Self-Assessment for Problem Solving

8. a. 14; recorded snowfall in 14 days
   b. *Sample answer:* Use a yardstick to measure new snowfall; *Sample answer:* inches
   c. *Sample answer:* What is the amount of snowfall that was recorded each day during these days?; On most days during the recording period there were between 1 and 3 inches of snowfall.
9. about 5

Learning Target

Identify statistical questions and use data to answer statistical questions.

Success Criteria

- Recognize questions that anticipate a variety of answers.
- Construct and interpret a dot plot.
- Use data to answer a statistical question.

Review & Refresh

1. $x > 24$

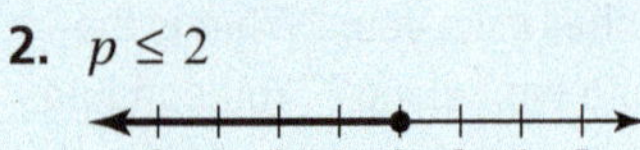

2. $p \leq 2$
3. $9 > k$
4. $m \geq 36$
5. yes
6. no
7. yes
8. D
9. $0.2, 24\%, \frac{1}{4}, 0.32, \frac{7}{20}$
10. $\frac{3}{4}, 78\%, 85\%, \frac{7}{8}, 0.88$

Concepts, Skills, & Problem Solving

11. 12; yes
12. *Sample answer:* 2; no
13. *Sample answer:* 9th; no
14. 100; yes
15. yes; The answers will vary.
16. no; There is only one answer.
17. yes; The answers will vary.
18. yes; The answers will vary.
19. a. 18; 18 players are on the team
    b. *Sample answer:* Use a tape measure; inches
    c. *Sample answer:* "What are the heights of players on an NBA championship team?"; The heights are spread out, but most of the heights (in inches) are in the mid-to-low 80s.

Assignment Guide and Concept Check

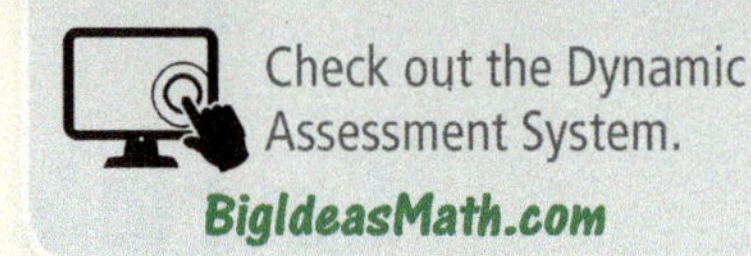

Check out the Dynamic Assessment System.
BigIdeasMath.com

Scaffold assignments to support all students in their learning progression. The suggested assignments are a starting point. Continue to assign additional exercises and revisit with spaced practice to move every student toward proficiency.

Level	Assignment 1	Assignment 2
Emerging	1, 4, 7, 8, 10, 11, 12, 15, 16, 19, 23	18, 20, 21, 24, 29
Proficient	1, 4, 7, 8, 10, 13, 14, 16, 18, 19, 23, 29	17, 20, 22, 24, 25, 27
Advanced	1, 4, 7, 8, 10, 13, 14, 16, 18, 20, 24, 29	22, 25, 26, 27, 28, 30

- Assignment 1 is for use after students complete the Self-Assessment for Concepts & Skills.
- Assignment 2 is for use after students complete the Self-Assessment for Problem Solving.
- The red exercises can be used as a concept check.

Review & Refresh Prior Skills

Exercises 1–4 Solving Inequalities
Exercises 5–7 Identifying Solutions
Exercise 8 Reflecting Points in One Axis
Exercises 9 and 10 Ordering Numbers

Common Errors

- **Exercise 19** Students will have to use reasonableness to determine a method for collecting the data and the units of measurement used. For instance, it is not reasonable for the units to be in feet.

9.1 Practice

Review & Refresh

Solve the inequality. Graph the solution.

1. $x - 16 > 8$
2. $p + 6 \leq 8$
3. $54 > 6k$
4. $\frac{m}{12} \geq 3$

Tell whether the ordered pair is a solution of the equation.

5. $y = 4x$; (2, 8)
6. $y = 3x + 5$; (3, 15)
7. $y = 6x - 15$; (4, 9)

8. A point is reflected in the x-axis. The reflected point is (4, −3). What is the original point?

   A. (−3, 4) **B.** (−4, 3) **C.** (−4, −3) **D.** (4, 3)

Order the numbers from least to greatest.

9. 24%, $\frac{1}{4}$, 0.2, $\frac{7}{20}$, 0.32
10. $\frac{7}{8}$, 85%, 0.88, $\frac{3}{4}$, 78%

Concepts, Skills, & Problem Solving

IDENTIFYING TYPES OF QUESTIONS Answer the question. Tell whether your answer should be the same as your classmates'. (See Exploration 2, p. 413.)

11. How many inches are in 1 foot?
12. How many pets do you have?
13. On what day of the month were you born?
14. How many senators are in Congress?

IDENTIFYING STATISTICAL QUESTIONS Determine whether the question is a statistical question. Explain.

15. What are the eye colors of sixth-grade students?
16. At what temperature (in degrees Fahrenheit) does water freeze?
17. How many pages are in the favorite books of students your age?
18. How many hours do sixth-grade students use the Internet each week?
19. **MP MODELING REAL LIFE** The vertical dot plot shows the heights of the players on a recent NBA championship team.

    a. Find and interpret the number of data values on the dot plot.

    b. How can you collect these data? What are the units?

    c. Write a statistical question that you can answer using the dot plot. Then answer the question.

20. **MP MODELING REAL LIFE** The dot plot shows the lengths of earthworms.

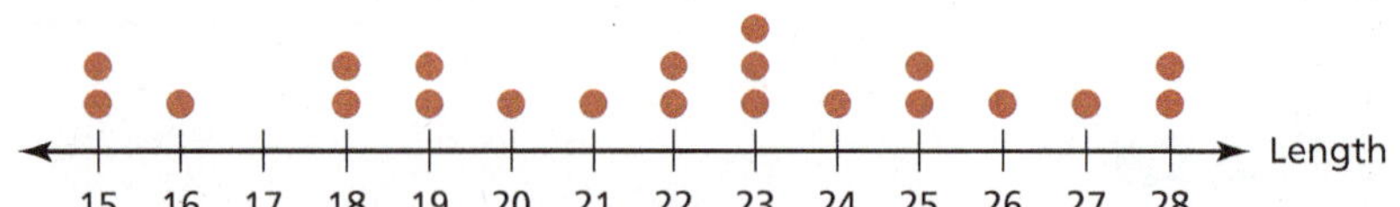

a. Find and interpret the number of data values on the dot plot.

b. How can you collect these data? What are the units?

c. Write a statistical question that you can answer using the dot plot. Then answer the question.

DESCRIBING DATA **Display the data in a dot plot. Identify any clusters, peaks, or gaps in the data.**

21.

Camper Registrations				
21	25	25	22	21
23	24	26	25	16
24	26	22	25	22

22.

Test Scores				
85	80	83	90	88
82	83	81	80	89
89	84	86	87	83

INTERPRETING DATA **The dot plot shows the speeds of cars in a traffic study. Estimate the speed limit. Explain your reasoning.**

23.

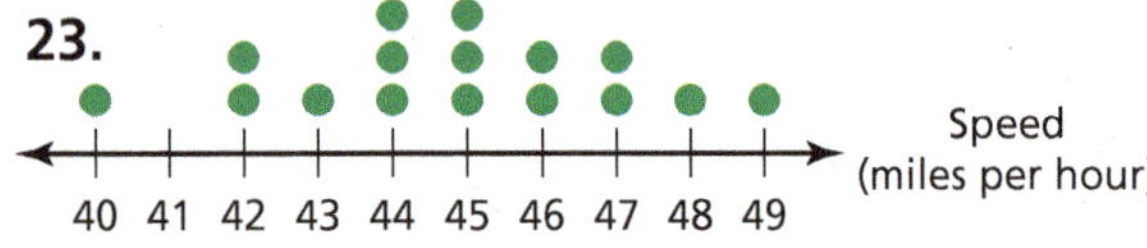

24.

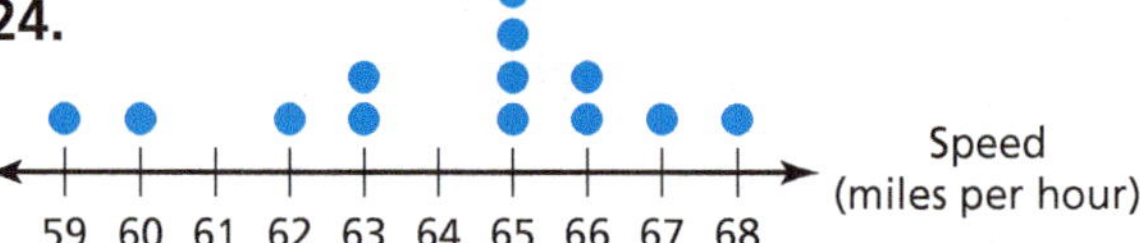

Hours of Homework			
2	4	3	2
1	2	2	1
2	3	5	2

25. **MP MODELING REAL LIFE** You conduct a survey to answer, "How many hours does a sixth-grade student spend on homework during a school night?" The table shows the results.

a. Is this a statistical question? Explain.

b. Identify any clusters, peaks, or gaps in the data.

c. Use the distribution of the data to answer the question.

RESEARCH **Use the Internet to research and identify the method of measurement and the units used when collecting data about the topic.**

26. wind speed

27. amount of rainfall

28. earthquake intensity

29. **MP REASONING** Write a question about letters in the English alphabet that is *not* a statistical question. Then write a question about letters that is a statistical question. Explain your reasoning.

30. **MP REASONING** A bar graph shows the favorite colors of 30 people. Does it make sense to describe clusters in the data? peaks? gaps? Explain.

Common Errors

- **Exercise 20** Students will have to use reasonableness to determine a method for collecting the data and the units of measurement used. For instance, it is not reasonable for the units to be in feet.
- **Exercises 21 and 22** Students may miss gaps in the data because they include only data values along the number line for the dot plot. Remind students to include all the integers from the least data value to the greatest data value along the number line.

Mini-Assessment

You conduct a survey to answer, "How many hours of television does a typical sixth-grade student watch in a week?" The table shows the results.

Time Spent Watching TV (hours)					
5	7	10	10	13	14
14	6	17	18	5	11
12	10	11	12	12	13
15	17	18	11	18	11
13	12	13	12	12	

1. Is this a statistical question? Explain. Because you can anticipate that the number of hours will vary, it is a statistical question.
2. Display the data in a dot plot.

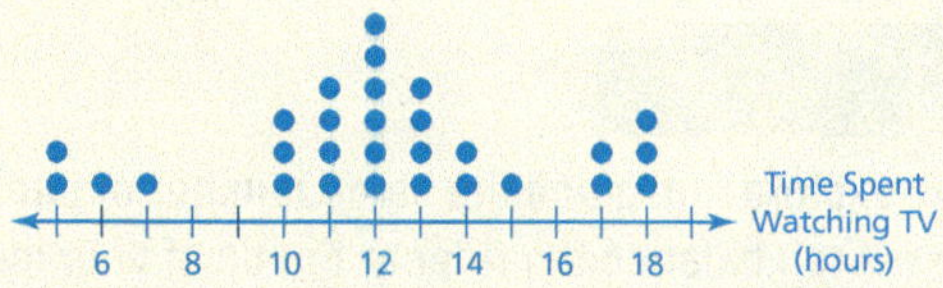

3. Identify any clusters, peaks, or gaps in the data. Most of the data are clustered around 12. There is a peak at 12. There are gaps between 7 and 10 and between 15 and 17.
4. Use the distribution of the data to answer the question. Most students spend 12 hours each week watching television.

Section Resources

Surface Level	Deep Level
Resources by Chapter • Extra Practice • Reteach • Puzzle Time Student Journal • Self-Assessment • Practice Differentiating the Lesson Tutorial Videos Skills Review Handbook Skills Trainer	Resources by Chapter • Enrichment and Extension Graphic Organizers Dynamic Assessment System • Section Practice

Concepts, Skills, & Problem Solving

20. **a.** 21; There are 21 earthworms

b. *Sample answer:* Use a centimeter ruler; centimeters

c. *Sample answer:* "What is the length of an earthworm?"; The lengths are spread out pretty evenly from 15 centimeters to 28 centimeters.

21–22. See Additional Answers.

23. *Sample answer:* 45 mi/h; Most of the data cluster around 45 and 45 miles per hour is a common speed limit.

24. *Sample answer:* 65 mi/h; Most of the data cluster around 65 and 65 miles per hour is a common speed limit.

25. **a.** yes; It is a statistical question because you would anticipate variability in the hours spent on homework each night by students.

b. Most of the hours cluster around 2. The peak is 2. There is no gap.

c. Most students spend between 1 and 3 hours on homework during a school night.

26. *Sample answer:* anemometer; miles per hour

27. *Sample answer:* rain gauge; inches

28. *Sample answer:* Richter scale; magnitude

29. *Sample answer:* "How many letters are there in the English alphabet?"; "How many letters are there in a word?"; The number of letters in the English alphabet is fixed but different words will have different numbers of letters.

30. no; yes; yes; The order of the colors can vary, so clusters do not mean anything, but peaks and gaps can show the most and least popular colors.

Learning Target

Find and interpret the mean of a data set.

Success Criteria

- Explain how the mean summarizes a data set with a single number.
- Find the mean of a data set.
- Use the mean of a data set to answer a statistical question.

Warm Up

Cumulative, vocabulary, and prerequisite skills practice opportunities are available in the *Resources by Chapter* or at *BigIdeasMath.com*.

ELL Support

Students may know the word *mean* as it applies to the way someone is acting. Explain that in math, mean refers to a type of average and *not* a type of action. Mean will be described in detail in the lesson.

Exploration 1

a. 4; yes; *Sample answer:* There are the same number of tokens on either side of the balance point of 4.

b. 6; no; *Sample answer:* There are many more tokens to the left of 6.

Exploration 2

a. 4; *Sample answer:* Everyone has the same number of tokens.

b. Divide the total number of tokens by 6 people.

c. *Sample answer:* How many tokens do people bring to the batting cages?

Laurie's Notes

STATE STANDARDS
6.SP.A.2, 6.SP.A.3, 6.SP.B.5a, 6.SP.B.5c

Preparing to Teach

- As students continue to analyze data, they will summarize a set of data with a single value (the mean) and use that value to answer a statistical question.
- **MP2 Reason Abstractly and Quantitatively:** Students will use counters to develop the concept of a mean abstractly. Then they will use quantitative reasoning to determine the mathematical processes for finding a mean.

Motivate

- Use 24 pennies or counters and sort them into 3 stacks of height 3, 7, and 14. Ask how to find the *average* number of pennies in a stack.
- Ask a volunteer to show how it can be done. Perhaps the student will "share" some pennies among the stacks. The stacks will even out to 8 per stack, which is the **mean**.
- **Big Idea:** Finding the mean of a data set is a sharing process. By summing the data set and then dividing by the number of data values you even out the data, so they are all the same.
- Start with the 3 unequal stacks of pennies and model the process of finding the mean: combine the pennies and then divide them into 3 equal stacks.

Exploration 1

- To introduce this exploration, place the same number of pennies at each end of a 12-inch ruler. Then balance the ruler at the tip of your index finger.
- ? "Why is the ruler balanced?" The finger is in the center, and the weight is the same at each end.
- ? "What will happen if more pennies are added to one end but not the other end?" The ruler will become unbalanced, and the pennies will fall.
- ? Probe at the idea of a balancing point. Ask, "How far from the center of the ruler are the piles of pennies?" *Sample answer:* 5 inches "Will the ruler be balanced if I place the pennies at the 5-inch and 7-inch marks? at the 4-inch and 9-inch marks?" yes; no
- Have students work through both parts of the exploration with partners.
- **MP3 Construct Viable Arguments and Critique the Reasoning of Others:** Have a class discussion about how students decided where on the number line the data set is balanced. Students may start to talk about a *fair share* process, that is, an "equal dividing" of the data.
- Each part of the exploration can be modeled using a ruler and some pennies.

Exploration 2

- **MP5 Use Appropriate Tools Strategically:** Students can use counters to physically model the sharing process.
- Six volunteers can model this exploration. Have them talk aloud as they share the counters evenly. Relate this to balancing the pennies on a ruler.
- Encourage students to discuss their questions and reasoning for part (c).
- **Extension:** Ask students how they would share three more tokens.

9.2 Mean

Learning Target: Find and interpret the mean of a data set.

Success Criteria:
- I can explain how the mean summarizes a data set with a single number.
- I can find the mean of a data set.
- I can use the mean of a data set to answer a statistical question.

EXPLORATION 1 Finding a Balance Point

Work with a partner. The diagrams show the numbers of tokens brought to a batting cage. Where on the number line is the data set *balanced*? Is this a good representation of the average? Explain.

a.

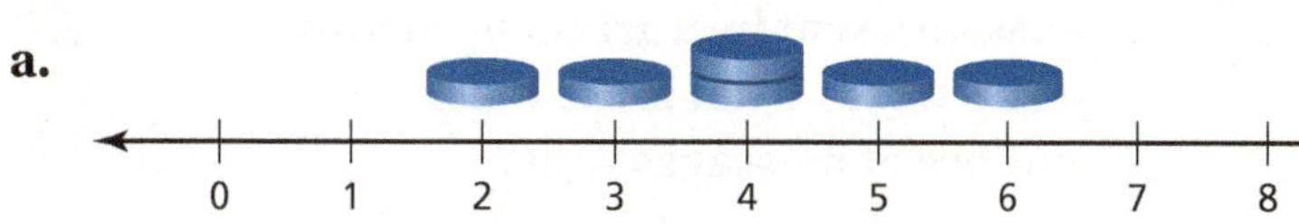

b.

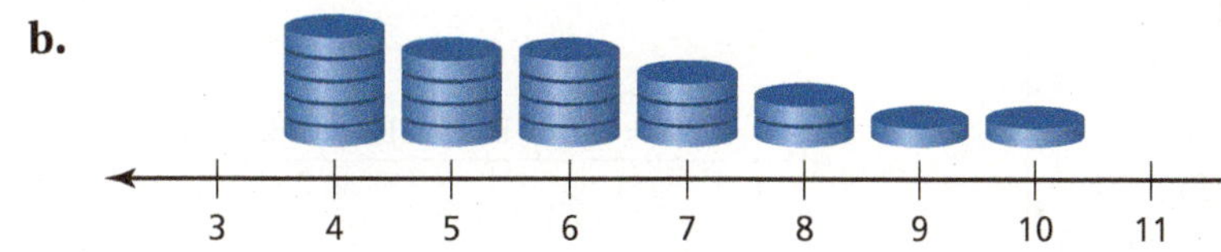

EXPLORATION 2 Finding a Fair Share

Work with a partner. One token lets you hit 12 baseballs in a batting cage. The table shows the numbers of tokens six friends bring to the batting cage.

Tokens					
John	Lisa	Miguel	Matt	Cheryl	Anika
6	3	4	5	2	4

a. Regroup the tokens so that everyone has the same amount. How many times can each friend use the batting cage? Explain how this represents a "fair share."

b. How can you find the answer in part (a) algebraically?

c. Write a statistical question that can be answered using the value in part (a).

Math Practice

Apply Mathematics

What does it mean for data to have an average? Describe a real-life situation where it is helpful to determine an average value.

9.2 Lesson

Key Vocabulary
mean, *p. 420*
outlier, *p. 422*

Key Idea

Mean

Words The **mean** of a data set is the sum of the data divided by the number of data values. The mean is a type of average.

Numbers **Data:** 8, 5, 6, 9 **Mean:** $\frac{8+5+6+9}{4} = \frac{28}{4} = 7$

4 data values

EXAMPLE 1 Finding the Mean

Text Messages Sent
Mark: 120
Laura: 95
Stacy: 101
Josh: 125
Kevin: 82
Maria: 108
Manny: 90

The table shows the numbers of text messages sent by a group of friends over 1 week. What is the mean number of messages sent?

A. 100 **B.** 102

C. 103 **D.** 104

$$\text{Mean} = \frac{120 + 95 + 101 + 125 + 82 + 108 + 90}{7}$$

sum of the data

number of values

$$= \frac{721}{7}$$ Add values in numerator.

$$= 103$$ Divide.

The mean number of text messages sent is 103. The correct answer is **C**.

Try It **Find the mean of the data.**

1.

Dog Weights (pounds)
Sparky: 18
Spot: 9
Rover: 60
Newton: 89
Diego: 44
Ruby: 13
Mookie: 54
Fido: 45

2.

Airbag Backpack Costs				
\$600	\$450	\$350	\$650	\$800
\$300	\$550	\$500	\$600	\$750

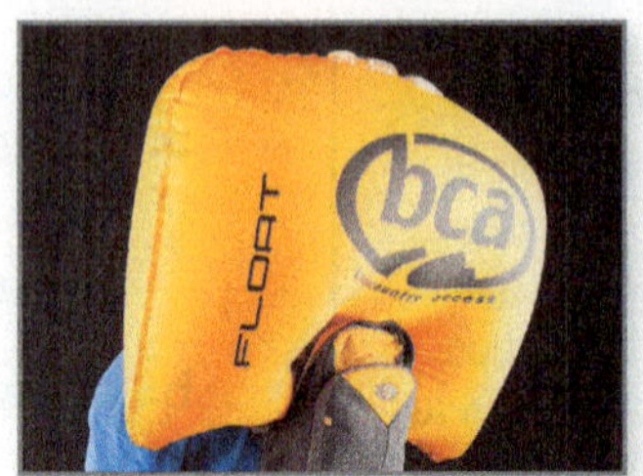

Laurie's Notes

Scaffolding Instruction

- Students move from visually approximating the *typical* quantity in a data set to formally finding the mean and examining its relation to the data.
- **Emerging:** Students may have difficulty visualizing where a data set is *balanced* or understanding how finding the *fair share* leads to the formula for mean. These students will benefit from the additional practice provided in the examples.
- **Proficient:** Students are comfortable with division and make the connection between the *fair share* process and the formula for finding the mean. After reviewing the Key Idea, students can use the Self-Assessment exercises to assess their understanding of the success criteria.

Key Idea

- There are three *measures of central tendency* or *averages*. This lesson is about the **mean**. The next section introduces two other measures of central tendency, the median and the mode.
- Write the Key Idea.
- Discuss the Numbers. For the data values of 8, 5, 6, and 9, the mean is somewhere between the low (5) and high (9) data values. After sharing some from the 9 to the 5 and some from the 8 to the 6, the mean is 7.

EXAMPLE 1

? "What is the greatest value?" 125 "What is the least value?" 82

? "What do you know about the mean?" It is a number between 82 and 125.

- Work through the problem as shown.

? "Is 103 a reasonable answer?" yes "How can you tell?" 103 falls between 82 (the low) and 125 (the high).

- **Caution:** If students use a calculator and enter all the operations in one step, they must remember to place the numerator in parentheses and then divide by the denominator: $\frac{(120 + 95 + 101 + 125 + 82 + 108 + 90)}{7} = 103$.

Try It

- **Think-Pair-Share:** Students should review each data set independently and estimate the means. Then have students work in pairs to find the means and compare their answers to their estimates. Have each pair compare their answers with another pair.

◉ Students are working on the first two success criteria.

ELL Support

Allow students to work in groups to complete Try It Exercises 1 and 2. Provide guiding questions: What is the sum? By what number is the sum divided? What is the mean? Monitor discussions and provide support as needed. Expect students to perform as described.

Beginner: Use numbers to answer the guiding questions.

Intermediate: Use simple sentences to answer the guiding questions.

Advanced: Use detailed sentences to answer the guiding questions and help guide discussion.

Scaffold instruction to support all students in their learning. Learning is individualized and you may want to group students differently as they move in and out of these levels with each skill and concept. Student self-assessment and feedback help guide your instructional decisions about how and when to layer support for all students to become proficient learners.

Extra Example 1

The table shows the numbers of pictures taken by a group of friends over 1 week. What is the mean number of pictures taken?

Pictures Taken
Jessica: 30
Susan: 81
Steven: 50
Jacob: 24
Pablo: 15
Sarah: 64

A. 38 **B.** 44
C. 52 **D.** 53

B

Try It

1. 41.5 lb
2. \$555

Extra Example 2

The monthly rainfall amounts (in inches) for two cities over a five-month period are given. Compare the mean monthly rainfalls.

City A: 2.5, 4.3, 4.8, 2.7, 1.2

City B: 1.7, 4.1, 5.5, 3.2, 0.5

Because 3.1 is greater than 3, City A averaged more rainfall.

Try It

3. no; City A will still average more rainfall.

Self-Assessment
for Concepts & Skills

4. no; Dividing the sum of the data by the number of data values to find the mean does not necessarily result in one of the data values.
5. *Sample answer:* The mean describes the values when the data is evenly distributed.
6. *Sample answer:* the first data set generally has higher values than the second
7. The mean of Data set A is greater than the mean of Data set B.

Laurie's Notes

EXAMPLE 2

? "Which city is represented by the dark green bar?" City A

? "In what month was the rainfall the same in the two cities?" February

- Work through the computation for each city and determine which city had the greater average rainfall.

Try It

- Have students work in pairs to complete the exercise. Listen to discussions and make notes about the order in which you want to call on students. Select students to share their reasoning by sequencing responses, starting with the more elementary and leading to the more profound.

Formative Assessment Tip

Always-Sometimes-Never True (AT-ST-NT)

This strategy is useful in assessing whether students overgeneralize or under generalize a particular concept. When answering, a student should be asked to justify his or her answer and other students listening should critique the reasoning.

AT-ST-NT statements help students practice the habit of checking validity when a statement (or conjecture) is made. Are there different cases that need to be checked? Is there a counterexample that would show the conjecture to be false? To develop these statements for a lesson, consider the common errors or misconceptions that students have relating to the success criteria of the lesson. Allow private think time before students share their thinking with partners or the whole class.

Self-Assessment *for Concepts & Skills*

- Students' answers will provide information about their progress with the first two success criteria. Students should work independently so they can assess their own understanding.
- Use *Always-Sometimes-Never True* to discuss Exercise 4. Students should explain their reasoning and give examples.
- For Exercise 7, consider allowing students to use calculators, so that the process of dividing does not impede their ability to find the mean.

ELL Support

Allow students to work in pairs to complete the exercises. Then have each pair discuss their answers with another pair. Each group should come to agreement if their answers differ. Monitor discussions and provide support.

The Success Criteria Self-Assessment chart can be found in the *Student Journal* or online at *BigIdeasMath.com*.

EXAMPLE 2 Comparing Means

The double bar graph shows the monthly rainfall amounts for two cities over a six-month period. Compare the mean monthly rainfalls.

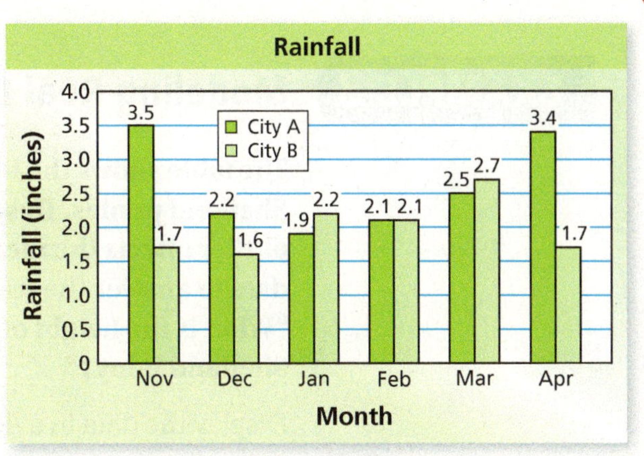

City A mean: $\dfrac{3.5 + 2.2 + 1.9 + 2.1 + 2.5 + 3.4}{6} = \dfrac{15.6}{6} = 2.6$

City B mean: $\dfrac{1.7 + 1.6 + 2.2 + 2.1 + 2.7 + 1.7}{6} = \dfrac{12}{6} = 2$

 Because 2.6 is greater than 2, City A averaged more rainfall.

Try It

3. **WHAT IF?** The monthly rainfall in May was 0.5 inch in City A and 2 inches in City B. Does this affect your answer in Example 2? Explain.

Self-Assessment for Concepts & Skills

Solve each exercise. Then rate your understanding of the success criteria in your journal.

4. **MP NUMBER SENSE** Is the mean always equal to a value in the data set? Explain.

5. **WRITING** Explain why the mean describes a typical value in a data set.

6. **MP NUMBER SENSE** What can you determine when the mean of one data set is greater than the mean of another data set? Explain your reasoning.

7. **COMPARING MEANS** Compare the means of the data sets.

   Data set A: 43, 32, 16, 41, 24, 19, 30, 27

   Data set B: 44, 18, 29, 24, 36, 22, 26, 21

An **outlier** is a data value that is much greater or much less than the other values. When included in a data set, it can affect the mean.

EXAMPLE 3 Modeling Real Life

The table shows the heights of several Shetland ponies. Describe how the outlier affects the mean. Then use the data to answer the statistical question, "What is the height of a typical Shetland Pony?"

Shetland Pony Heights (inches)				
40	37	39	40	42
38	38	37	28	40

Display the data in a dot plot to see the distribution of the data.

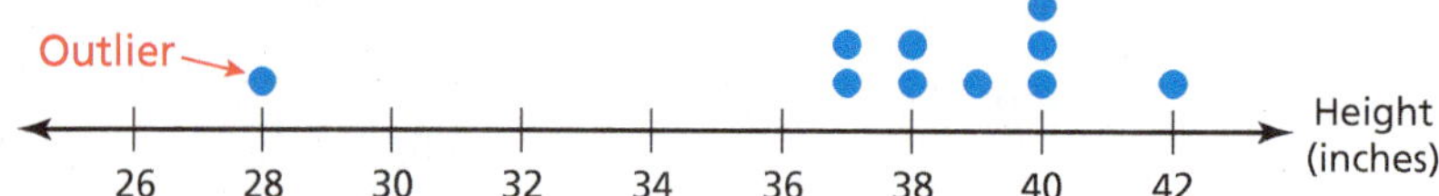

The height of 28 inches is much less than the other heights. So, it is an outlier. Find the mean with and without the outlier.

Mean with outlier:

$$\frac{40 + 37 + 39 + 40 + 42 + 38 + 38 + 37 + 28 + 40}{10} = \frac{379}{10} = 37.9$$

Mean without outlier:

$$\frac{40 + 37 + 39 + 40 + 42 + 38 + 38 + 37 + 40}{9} = \frac{351}{9} = 39$$

With the outlier, the mean is less than all but three of the heights. Without the outlier, the mean better represents the heights. So, the height of a typical Shetland pony is about 39 inches.

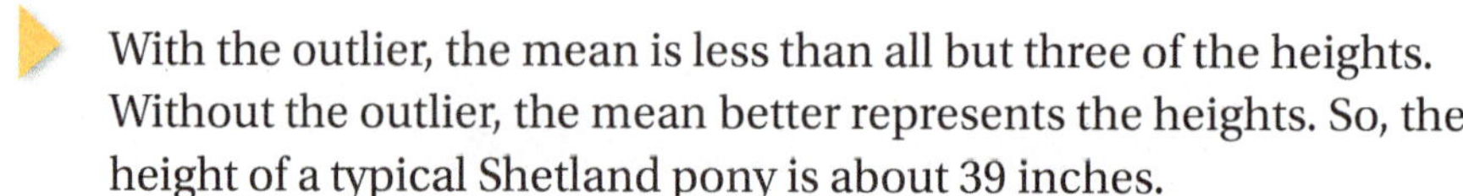

Self-Assessment for Problem Solving

Solve each exercise. Then rate your understanding of the success criteria in your journal.

8. **DIG DEEPER!** The monthly numbers of customers at a store in the first half of a year are 282, 270, 320, 351, 319, and 252. The monthly numbers of customers in the second half of the year are 211, 185, 192, 216, 168, and 144. Find and interpret the difference of the means of the data sets.

Tournament Finishes			
5	1	2	5
21	2	8	3
1	5	9	10
3	4	8	9

9. The table shows tournament finishes for a golfer. What place does the golfer typically finish in tournaments? Explain how you found your answer.

Laurie's Notes

EXAMPLE 3

- Have students read and discuss the definition of an **outlier**. In this section, students will identify outliers visually. In Section 9.4, they will use a formula.
- Ask students to examine the height of each pony.
- ? "Is there one pony that is noticeably different in size from the others? Describe how you can tell." Yes, there is one pony that is 28 inches in height. This pony is much shorter than the other ponies.
- **Multiple Representations:** Some students will be able to find the outlier simply by reading through the table. Others may struggle to find the outlier. Have these students graph the heights in a dot plot as shown. This will visually reinforce why 28 inches is an outlier.
- ? Calculate the mean of the data with the outlier. Then ask, "Are any of the ponies exactly 37.9 inches tall?" no "How many ponies are taller than the mean?" There are 7 ponies taller than the mean.
- ? "Does the mean represent the height of a typical Shetland Pony well?" no
- Calculate the mean *without* the outlier.
- **Common Error**: Some students may forget to subtract 1 from the total number of data values when removing the outlier. Remind students that they are using one less value, so the denominator should decrease by 1.
- ⦿ "Which mean better describes the height of a typical Shetland Pony?" 39 inches Students are using the mean to answer a statistical question.
- **Big Idea:** An outlier that is very low compared to the rest of the data values will cause the mean to be too low. By removing the outlier, you can calculate a mean that better demonstrates the average of the data.
- ? **MP2 Reason Abstractly and Quantitatively:** "What effect would an extremely tall pony have on the mean?" It would cause the mean to be too high. "What could you do to correct this?" You could remove the outlier and calculate a mean without it.
- **Always-Sometimes-Never True:** "All data values are used to find the mean of a set of data." sometimes true; If there are outliers, then you may remove those values.

Self-Assessment for Problem Solving

- Students may benefit from trying the exercises independently and then working with peers to refine their work. It is important to provide time in class for problem solving, so that students become comfortable with the problem-solving plan.
- ⦿ Students are assessing their understanding of the last two success criteria.

The Success Criteria Self-Assessment chart can be found in the *Student Journal* or online at *BigIdeasMath.com*.

Closure

- **Exit Ticket:** How could you find the time it takes a typical student in your school to commute from home to school? *Sample answer:* You could conduct a survey to see how long it takes each student in a class to commute from home to school. Then find the mean of the collected data.

Extra Example 3

The table shows the weights of several kittens. Describe how the outlier affects the mean. Then use the data to answer the statistical question, "What is the weight of a typical kitten?"

Kitten Weights (pounds)				
4.5	5.7	4.4	4.45	5.5
5.6	4.7	4.9	7.25	5

With the outlier, the mean is greater than six of the weights. Without the outlier, the mean better represents the weights; The weight of a typical kitten is about 4.97 pounds.

Self-Assessment for Problem Solving

8. 113; The mean number of monthly customers is greater in the first half of the year by 113 customers.
9. 5; *Sample answer:* The average finish for the golfer was 5th place after removing the outlier, 21st place.

Learning Target

Find and interpret the mean of a data set.

Success Criteria

- Explain how the mean summarizes a data set with a single number.
- Find the mean of a data set.
- Use the mean of a data set to answer a statistical question.

Review & Refresh

1. yes; The answers will vary.
2. no; There is only one answer.
3. no; There is only one answer.
4. yes; The answers will vary.
5. $\frac{21}{25}$
6. $\frac{71}{100}$
7. $3\frac{53}{100}$
8. $\frac{1}{500}$
9. 1.3
10. 14.56
11. 4.2
12. 24.8

Concepts, Skills, & Problem Solving

13. 12
14. 1
15. 2
16. 3
17. 103
18. 16
19. a. yes; The answers will vary.
    b. 3.45 minutes

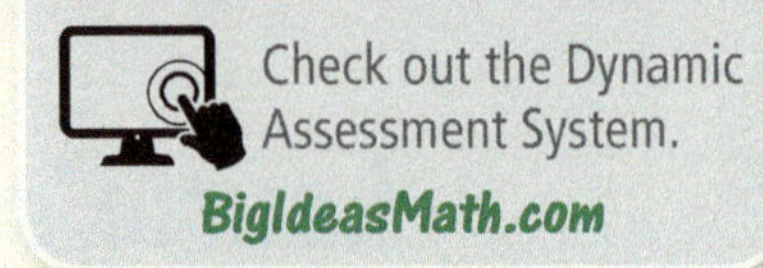

Assignment Guide and Concept Check

Scaffold assignments to support all students in their learning progression. The suggested assignments are a starting point. Continue to assign additional exercises and revisit with spaced practice to move every student toward proficiency.

Level	Assignment 1	Assignment 2
Emerging	3, 4, 5, 7, 8, 10, 11, 13, 15, 16	14, 17, 18, 19, 20, 22, 24
Proficient	3, 4, 5, 7, 8, 10, 11, 13, 16, 17, 21	18, 19, 20, 22, 23, 24
Advanced	3, 4, 5, 7, 8, 10, 11, 14, 17, 18, 21	20, 22, 23, 24, 25, 26

- Assignment 1 is for use after students complete the Self-Assessment for Concepts & Skills.
- Assignment 2 is for use after students complete the Self-Assessment for Problem Solving.
- The red exercises can be used as a concept check.

Review & Refresh Prior Skills

Exercises 1–4 Identifying Statistical Questions
Exercises 5–8 Writing Percents as Fractions
Exercises 9 and 10 Dividing Decimals by Whole Numbers
Exercises 11 and 12 Dividing Decimals

Common Errors

- **Exercises 15–18** Students may find the sum of the data values and then incorrectly divide by the maximum data value. Remind students to divide by the total number of data values to find the mean. Tell students it is as though they are dividing the total evenly among the number of groups that there are. For example, the mean number of pets owned describes how many pets each person would have if all the pets were divided evenly among each person.

9.2 Practice

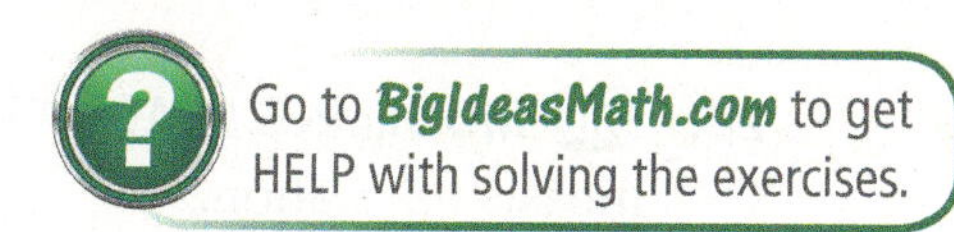

Review & Refresh

Determine whether the question is a statistical question. Explain.

1. How tall are sixth-grade students?
2. How many minutes are in 1 year?
3. How many counties are in Tennessee?
4. What is a student's favorite sport?

Write the percent as a fraction or mixed number in simplest form.

5. 84%
6. 71%
7. 353%
8. 0.2%

Divide. Check your answer.

9. $11.7 \div 9$
10. $5\overline{)72.8}$
11. $6.8\overline{)28.56}$
12. $93 \div 3.75$

Concepts, Skills, & Problem Solving

FINDING A FAIR SHARE **Regroup the amounts so that each person has the same amount. What is the amount?** (See Exploration 2, p. 419.)

13. Dollars brought by friends to a fair: 11, 12, 12, 12, 12, 12, 13
14. Tickets earned by friends playing an arcade game: 0, 0, 0, 1, 1, 2, 3

FINDING THE MEAN **Find the mean of the data.**

15.

Pets Owned	
Brandon	I
Jill	III
Mark	II
Nicole	IIII
Steve	0

16.

Brothers and Sisters	
Amanda	🯅
Eve	🯅 🯅 🯅 🯅 🯅
Joseph	🯅 🯅 🯅 🯅
Michael	🯅 🯅

17.

Sit-Ups		
108	85	94
103	112	115
98	119	126
105	82	89

18.

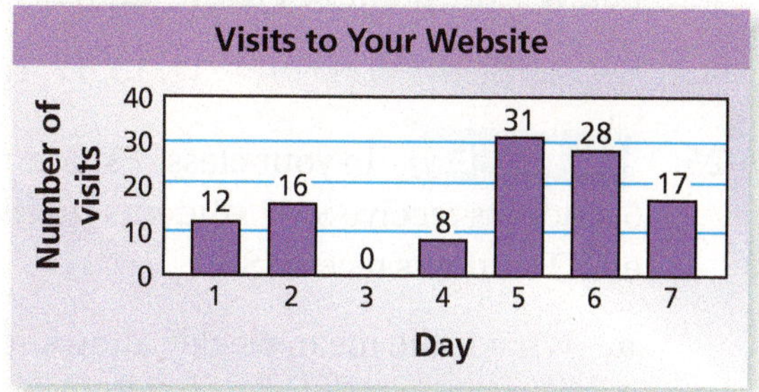

19. **MODELING REAL LIFE** You and your friends are watching a television show. One of your friends asks, "How long are the commercial breaks during this show?"

Break Times (minutes)				
4.2	3.5	4.55	2.75	2.25

a. Is this a statistical question? Explain.

b. Use the mean of the values in the table to answer the question.

20. **MP MODELING REAL LIFE** The table shows the monthly rainfall amounts at a measuring station.

Month	Jan	Feb	Mar	Apr	May	Jun	Jul	Aug	Sep	Oct	Nov	Dec
Rainfall (inches)	2.22	1.51	1.86	2.06	3.48	4.47	3.37	5.40	5.45	4.34	2.64	2.14

a. What is the mean monthly rainfall?

b. Compare the mean monthly rainfall for the first half of the year with the mean monthly rainfall for the second half of the year.

21. **OPEN-ENDED** Create two different data sets that have six values and a mean of 21.

22. **MP MODELING REAL LIFE** The bar graph shows your cell phone data usage for five months. Describe how the outlier affects the mean. Then use the data to answer the statistical question, "How much cell phone data do you use in a month?"

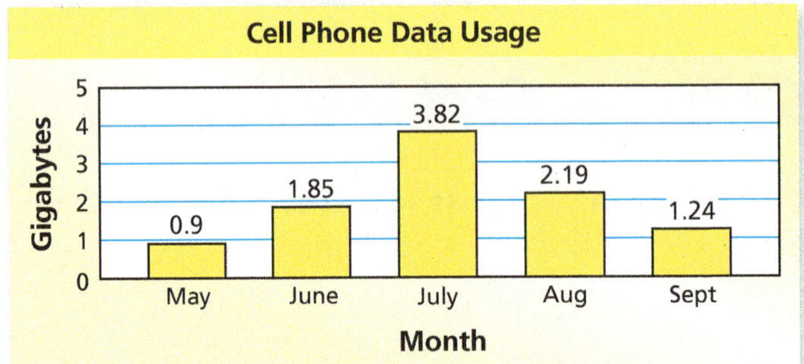

23. **MP MODELING REAL LIFE** The table shows the heights of the volleyball players on two teams. Compare the mean heights of the two teams. Do outliers affect either mean? Explain.

	Player Heights (inches)											
Dolphins	59	65	53	56	58	61	64	68	51	56	54	57
Tigers	63	68	66	58	54	55	61	62	53	70	64	64

24. **MP REASONING** Use a dot plot to explain why the mean of the data set below is the point where the data set is balanced.

11, 13, 17, 15, 12, 18, 12

25. **DIG DEEPER!** In your class, 7 students do not receive a weekly allowance, 5 students receive \$3, 7 students receive \$5, 3 students receive \$6, and 2 students receive \$8.

a. What is the mean weekly allowance? Explain how you found your answer.

b. A new student who joins your class receives a weekly allowance of \$3.50. Without calculating, explain how this affects the mean.

26. **MP PRECISION** A collection of 8 geodes has a mean weight of 14 ounces. A different collection of 12 geodes has a mean weight of 9 ounces. What is the mean weight of the 20 geodes? Explain how you found your answer.

Common Errors

- **Exercise 23** Students may have difficulty finding outliers just by looking at the table. Tell students to graph the values in a dot plot to make outliers appear more obvious.

Mini-Assessment

Find the mean of the data.

1. 2, 5, 7, 2, 4 4
2. 35, 56, 41, 59, 37, 48, 53 47
3.

Questions Answered
Matt: 22
Wendy: 29
Eva: 18
Tommy: 31

25 questions

4. The table shows the weekly allowances of several sixth-grade students. Describe how the outlier affects the mean. Then use the data to answer the statistical question, "What is the weekly allowance of a typical sixth-grade student?"

Weekly Allowance (dollars)			
0	5	10	5
8	0	30	10

With the outlier, the mean is greater than five of the weekly allowances. Without the outlier, the mean better represents the weekly allowances; The weekly allowance of a typical sixth-grade student is about $5.43.

Section Resources

Surface Level	Deep Level
Resources by Chapter • Extra Practice • Reteach • Puzzle Time Student Journal • Self-Assessment • Practice Differentiating the Lesson Tutorial Videos Skills Review Handbook Skills Trainer	Resources by Chapter • Enrichment and Extension Graphic Organizers Dynamic Assessment System • Section Practice

Concepts, Skills, & Problem Solving

20. **a.** 3.245 in.

    b. The first half of the year had a lower mean rainfall than the second half of the year.

21. *Sample answer:* 20, 21, 21, 21, 21, 22; 20, 20.5, 20.5, 21.5, 21.5, 22

22. The outlier caused the mean to be about 0.455 gigabyte more; 1.545 gigabytes

23. The Tigers' mean height is greater; no; neither data set has outliers.

24. 11 12 13 14 15 16 17 18

    The sum of the distances from the mean, 14, to points above the mean is 8, and the sum of the distances from the mean to points below the mean is 8. These sums are equal, so the mean is the point where the data set is balanced.

25. **a.** $3.50; Divide $84 by 24 people.

    b. *Sample answer:* The class mean will not change since the new student's weekly allowance is the same as the mean.

26. 11 oz; The total weight is $8(14) + 12(9) = 220$. So, the mean weight is $\frac{220}{20}$.

Learning Target

Find and interpret the median and mode of a data set.

Success Criteria

- Explain how the median and mode summarize a data set with a single number.
- Find the median and mode of a data set.
- Explain how changes to a data set affect the measures of center.
- Use a measure of center to answer a statistical question.

Warm Up

Cumulative, vocabulary, and prerequisite skills practice opportunities are available in the *Resources by Chapter* or at *BigIdeasMath.com*.

ELL Support

Explain that the words *median* and *mode* each have multiple meanings. In math, each word describes a type of measure of center. In everyday language, *median* often refers to the middle strip of land that divides a road. Mode usually means a style, method, manner, or approach.

Exploration 1

a. Check students' work.

b. Check students' work.

c. *Sample answer:* To find the median, the data strip was folded in half, displaying the middle number. To find the mode, the repetitions of the numbers were counted.

d. *Sample answer:* They are representations of the central value (median) and the peaked values (modes).

Laurie's Notes

STATE STANDARDS
6.SP.A.2, 6.SP.A.3, 6.SP.B.5c

Preparing to Teach

- Just as proficiency with division helps students to find the mean of a set of data, proficiency with ordering and organizing data makes finding the median and mode more manageable. The ability to see data at a glance forms a common-sense view of the measures of center.
- **MP5 Use Appropriate Tools Strategically:** Sorting data from least to greatest in a table or organizing data in a dot plot can help students determine the median and mode of a set of data more efficiently.

Motivate

? Ask a few questions that do not necessarily need to be answered. The questions are intended to get students thinking about another type of average (the mode).

- "What is the most common (average) color of car in the parking lot?"
- "What is the typical (average) eye color of students in the class?"
- "What is the typical (average) style of shoe worn by students in the class?"

Exploration 1

- **Discuss:** The mean is not the only way to describe a data set. The mean is one of many types of averages used in statistics. Two more averages are the **median** and **mode**. Tell students that they will work with these today.
- Let students freely choose the names of 15 people, as long as they can spell the names correctly. People from the past are fair game. Do not count the space between first and last names when completing part (a).
- Have strips of grid paper available with 15 boxes for part (b). Students should use all 15 numbers, even if they are repeated.
- After students finish the exploration, ask a volunteer to describe what the median of a data set is. The student may fail to mention that the data needs to be ordered from least to greatest. Discuss whether the middle value in the student's *original* list of 15 values is the median. Most likely it is not.
- Ask students to share how they found the median in part (c). Some students may have placed a finger on each end of the strip and moved both fingers at the same time towards the center. Others may have folded the strip in half and identified the crease as the median.
- Students may ask how to find median if there is an even number of values. This is explained in the Key Ideas.
- After discussing mode as an average of a data set, relate it to the Motivate questions that used terminology such as *common* and *typical*.
- **Always-Sometimes-Never True:** "The median is a value in the data set." sometimes true; If there is an even number of values, then the median may or may not be a value in the data set. "If a data set has a mode, it is a value in the data set." always true; The mode is the value(s) that occurs most often, so it must be in the data set.

9.3 Measures of Center

Learning Target: Find and interpret the median and mode of a data set.

Success Criteria:
- I can explain how the median and mode summarize a data set with a single number.
- I can find the median and mode of a data set.
- I can explain how changes to a data set affect the measures of center.
- I can use a measure of center to answer a statistical question.

EXPLORATION 1 Finding the Median

Work with a partner.

a. Write the total numbers of letters in the first and last names of 15 celebrities, historical figures, or people you know. One person is already listed for you.

Person	Number of Letters in First and Last Name
Abraham Lincoln	14

b. Order the values in your data set from least to greatest. Then write the data on a strip of grid paper with 15 boxes.

Math Practice

Use a Graph

How can you use a dot plot to find the mode?

c. The *middle value* of the data set is called the *median.* The value (or values) that occur most often is called the *mode.* Find the median and the mode of your data set. Explain how you found your answers.

d. Why are the median and the mode considered averages of a data set?

9.3 Lesson

Key Vocabulary
measure of center, *p. 426*
median, *p. 426*
mode, *p. 426*

A **measure of center** is a measure that describes the typical value of a data set. The mean is one type of measure of center. Here are two others.

Key Ideas

Median

Words Order the data. For a set with an odd number of values, the **median** is the middle value. For a set with an even number of values, the **median** is the mean of the two middle values.

Numbers **Data:** 5, 8, 9, 12, 14 The median is 9.

Data: 2, 3, 5, 7, 10, 11 The median is $\frac{5+7}{2} = 6$.

Mode

Words The **mode** of a data set is the value or values that occur most often. Data can have one mode, more than one mode, or no mode. When all values occur only once, there is no mode.

Numbers **Data:** 11, 13, 15, 15, 18, 21, 24, 24

The modes are 15 and 24.

The mode is the only measure of center that you can use to describe a set of data that is *not* made up of numbers.

EXAMPLE 1 Finding the Median and Mode

Bowling Scores				
120	135	160	125	90
205	160	175	105	145

Find the median and mode of the bowling scores.

90, 105, 120, 125, 135, 145, 160, 160, 175, 205 Order the data.

Median: $\frac{135 + 145}{2} = \frac{280}{2} = 140$ Add the two middle values and divide by 2.

Mode: 90, 105, 120, 125, 135, 145, 160, 160, 175, 205

The value 160 occurs most often.

The median is 140. The mode is 160.

Try It **Find the median and mode of the data.**

1. 20, 4, 17, 8, 12, 9, 5, 20, 13

2. 100, 75, 90, 80, 110, 102

Laurie's Notes

Scaffolding Instruction

- Finding median and mode is fairly easy for students, but their depth of understanding is apparent when students analyze the best measure of center, describe the effect of an outlier, and explain how changes to a data set affect the measures of center.
- **Emerging:** Students can find the median and mode, but they may need practice using these statistics in different situations and choosing a measure of center to represent a data set. Students may benefit from guided instruction with the examples.
- **Proficient:** Students understand the meaning of median and mode, find them efficiently, and can apply them in different situations. Have students check their progress using the Try It exercises before completing the Self-Assessment exercises.

Scaffold instruction to support all students in their learning. Learning is individualized and you may want to group students differently as they move in and out of these levels with each skill and concept. Student self-assessment and feedback help guide your instructional decisions about how and when to layer support for all students to become proficient learners.

Key Ideas

- Define **measure of center**. The three types (mean, median, and mode) describe the typical value of a data set.
- Write the Key Ideas.
- Discuss the **median** and **mode** and how each is determined.
- **FYI:** The median household income in the U.S. is $55,775 (U.S. Census Bureau 2015). Discuss with students that this means half of all households have an income greater than the median and half have an income less than the median.
- To help students remember the difference between mean and median, tell them to think about the median on a highway.
- Point out the push-pin note. The mode is the only measure of center that can be used to describe non-numeric data sets, such as the responses to the questions in the Motivate.

EXAMPLE 1

? "What is the first step in finding the median?" order the data

- **Common Error:** Students forget to arrange the data in order before finding the median.
- **Note:** Sorting the data also makes it easier to determine the mode(s).
- **Connection:** Adding two middle values and dividing by 2 is the same as finding the mean of the middle two data values.
- **Extension:** If time permits, find the mean (142). Discuss the three measures of center found and if all are representative of the data.

? **Extension:** "Is it possible for the median and the mode to be the same?" yes

◉ Students are working on the first two success criteria.

Extra Example 1

Find the median and mode of the test scores.

Test Scores			
95	80	85	86
89	100	95	

median = 89; mode = 95

Try It

- After completing the exercises, ask students to explain how to find the median for a data set.

Try It

1. median = 12; mode = 20
2. median = 95; no mode

Extra Example 2

The list shows the favorite colors for students in a class. Organize the data in a table. Then find the mode.

blue, green, purple, blue, green, pink, purple, blue, green, purple, blue, blue, green, pink, blue, blue, green, blue, green

Color	Number of Students
Blue	8
Green	6
Pink	2
Purple	3

mode: blue

Try It

3. yes; Comedy and horror are both modes now that horror has the same number of votes as comedy.

Extra Example 3

Seven competitors stack 85, 70, 60, 12, 88, 85, and 62 cups in a cup-stacking competition. Find the mean, median, and mode of the data with and without the outlier. Which measure does the outlier affect the most?

With outlier: mean = 66, median = 70, mode = 85;
Without outlier: mean = 75, median = 77.5, mode = 85;
mean

Try It

4. With outlier:
mean = 18 min,
median = 12.5 min,
mode = 10 min;
Without outlier:
mean = 12.6 min,
median = 10 min,
mode = 10 min;
mean

Laurie's Notes

EXAMPLE 2

- Remind students of the push-pin note on page 426.
- **MP5 Use Appropriate Tools Strategically:** Counting the number of each type of movie in the list and then organizing the data in a table is an effective way to determine the mode for a non-numeric data set.

Try It

- Have students share their thoughts about this problem in groups. Listen to their explanations.
- Students are beginning to consider how changes to a data set affect the measures of center.

EXAMPLE 3

- ? "Why is 2 an outlier?" The competitor with 2 bugs ate much less than the other competitors.
- ? "Which of the three measures does the outlier impact the most?" the mean
- ? "Why did the median change when the outlier was removed?" There was an odd number of data values before removing the outlier, so the median was the middle number. After removing the outlier, there is an even number of data values and the median of the two middle values is not the same as the median of the original data set.
- ? "Why does the outlier affect the mean more than the median?" *Sample answer:* Because the middle values of the ordered data are relatively close, so removing the outlier does not change the median as much.
- ? "Why does the outlier affect the mean more than the mode?" *Sample answer:* Because 2 is not the mode of the original data set, so removing it does not affect the mode.
- **Big Idea:** Typically, the mean of a data set is affected the most by an outlier.
- ? **Extension:** "If the outlier of a data set is a greatest value, what effect does it have on the mean?" The mean with the outlier is greater than the mean without the outlier.

Try It

- Exercise 4 will take time for students to complete. They could work with partners.

ELL Support

Have students work in pairs to discuss and complete Exercise 4. Expect students to perform as described.

Beginner: State the numbers.

Intermediate: Use phrases to describe each measure of center.

Advanced: Use sentences to describe each measure of center and guide discussion.

EXAMPLE 2 Finding the Mode

The list shows the favorite types of movies for students in a class. Organize the data in a table. Then find the mode.

Favorite Types of Movies		
Comedy	Drama	Horror
Horror	Drama	Horror
Comedy	Comedy	Action
Action	Comedy	Action
Horror	Drama	Comedy
Comedy	Comedy	Horror
Horror	Comedy	Action
Horror	Action	Drama

Type	Number of Students
Action	5
Comedy	8
Drama	4
Horror	7

Comedy received the most votes.

So, the mode is comedy.

Try It

3. One member of the class was absent and ends up voting for horror. Does this change the mode? Explain.

EXAMPLE 3 Removing an Outlier

Seven competitors eat 26, 33, 34, 2, 32, 34, and 42 bugs in a bug-eating competition. Find the mean, median, and mode of the data with and without the outlier. Which measure does the outlier affect the most?

The competitor with 2 bugs ate much less than any other competitor. So, the outlier is 2.

	Mean	Median	Mode
With Outlier	29	33	34
Without Outlier	33.5	33.5	34

Removing the outlier increases the mean more than the median. The mode is not affected.

So, the mean is affected the most by the outlier.

Try It

4. The times (in minutes) it takes six students to travel to school are 8, 10, 10, 15, 20, and 45. Find the mean, median, and mode of the data with and without the outlier. Which measure does the outlier affect the most?

EXAMPLE 4 Changing the Values of a Data Set

The prices of six video games at an online store are shown in the table. The price of each game increases by $4.98 when a shipping charge is included. How does this increase affect the mean, median, and mode?

Video Game Prices	
$53.42	$35.69
$18.99	$25.13
$27.97	$53.42

Make a new table by adding $4.98 to each price. Then find the mean, median, and mode of both data sets.

Video Game Prices with Shipping Charge	
$58.40	$40.67
$23.97	$30.11
$32.95	$58.40

	Mean	Median	Mode
Original Price	35.77	31.83	53.42
Price with Shipping Charge	40.75	36.81	58.4

Compare the measures of center of both data sets.

Mean: $40.75 - 35.77 = 4.98$

Median: $36.81 - 31.83 = 4.98$

Mode: $58.4 - 53.42 = 4.98$

Math Practice

Communicate Precisely

Explain why the measures of centers increased by the same amount as each data value.

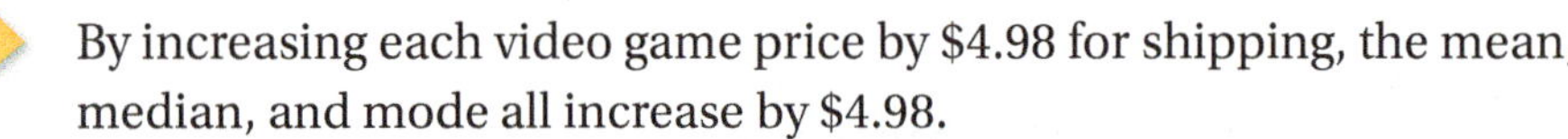

By increasing each video game price by $4.98 for shipping, the mean, median, and mode all increase by $4.98.

Try It

5. **WHAT IF?** The store decreases the price of each video game by $3. How does this decrease affect the mean, median, and mode?

Self-Assessment for Concepts & Skills

Solve each exercise. Then rate your understanding of the success criteria in your journal.

6. **FINDING MEASURES OF CENTER** Consider the data set below.

   15, 18, 13, 11, 12, 21, 9, 11

   a. Find the mean, median, and mode of the data.

   b. Each value in the data set is decreased by 7. How does this change affect the mean, median, and mode?

7. **WRITING** Explain why a typical value in a data set can be described by the median or the mode.

Laurie's Notes

EXAMPLE 4

- This example shows how the mean, median, and mode change when every data value increases by the same amount.
- ? You can introduce the idea of changing the values of a data set by saying, "When I graded your tests for Chapter 8, I computed the mean, median, and mode of the scores for the class. How would those three averages change if I gave everyone 3 bonus points?" They will each increase by 3 points.
- Like the 3 bonus points, in Example 4 a shipping charge of $4.98 is added to each price. Ask a student to read the problem.
- Give students time to compute the mean, median, and mode of the original set of data. Remind them to sort the data before finding the median.
- ? "How does the cost of each video game change when you include shipping?" The total cost of each game increases by $4.98.
- Give students time to compute the mean, median, and mode of the new set of data.
- ? "How do the mean, median, and mode change?" They each increase by $4.98.
- **Big Idea:** When all values of a data set increase by an amount n, the mean, median, and mode will each increase by n.
- **Extension:** If time permits, you could explore what happens to the mean, median, and mode when all the prices increase by 10%.

Try It

Students are continuing to work on the third success criterion.

Self-Assessment for Concepts & Skills

Students are assessing their understanding of the first three success criteria. They are summarizing their understanding of the measures of center and justifying their answers.

- Look at students' explanations in Exercise 7 to check their understanding.

ELL Support

Have students work in pairs to complete Exercise 6 and display the mean, median, and mode for parts (a) and (b) on a whiteboard for your review. Have each pair check comprehension of Exercise 7 by discussing their answer with another pair to reach an agreement. Monitor discussions and provide support. Have groups present their answers to the class.

The Success Criteria Self-Assessment chart can be found in the *Student Journal* or online at *BigIdeasMath.com*.

Extra Example 4

The prices of six digital e-readers at an online store are shown in the table. The price of each e-reader increases by $6.27 when a shipping charge is included. How does this increase affect the mean, median, and mode?

e-Reader Prices	
$59.99	$128.99
$69.99	$99.99
$159.99	$128.99

The mean, median, and mode all increase by $6.27.

Try It

5. The mean, median, and mode all decrease by $3.

Self-Assessment for Concepts & Skills

6. a. mean = 13.75; median = 12.5; mode = 11

   b. The mean, median, and mode all decrease by 7.

7. *Sample answer:* The median describes the central data point and the mode describes the peak of the data.

Extra Example 5

The data are the prices of several different pairs of jeans. Use the data to answer the statistical question, "How much does a pair of jeans cost?"

$32	$50	$19	$25
$27	$45	$46	$34
$120	$20	$25	$31

A pair of jeans costs about $31.50.

Teaching Strategy

Research has shown that it is beneficial for students to spend time comparing and contrasting similar methods. Each student should draw upon his or her own knowledge and then listen to the reasoning of others to increase their understanding of different methods. Students will begin to see splinters of differences in similar ideas, which will help guide their decisions in future problem solving.

Self-Assessment for Problem Solving

8–9. See Additional Answers.

10. 1700 pounds

Learning Target

Find and interpret the median and mode of a data set.

Success Criteria

- Explain how the median and mode summarize a data set with a single number.
- Find the median and mode of a data set.
- Explain how changes to a data set affect the measures of center.
- Use a measure of center to answer a statistical question.

Laurie's Notes

EXAMPLE 5

- **Discuss:** When you shop for climbing shoes, there is a range of prices in the store. How do you decide what the *typical* price is of the climbing shoes?
- ? As you work through the example, ask, "How do you find the mean of a set of data?" Add the data values and divide by the number of values. "How do you find the median of a set of data?" Order the data and find the middle value or the mean of the two middle values. "How do you find the mode of a set of data?" Find the most frequent value.
- Note that by sorting the data values first, the mode is easier to identify.
- ? In analyzing the data, ask, "Why is the mean so high?" Because 142 is an outlier. "What affect does the outlier have on the mean?" The mean with the outlier is greater than the mean without the outlier.
- **MP6 Attend to Precision**: The units (dollars) are not written in the computations for the mean, median, and mode; however, mathematically proficient students will consider the units when discussing the values of the measures of center.
- ? **Extension:** "If you ask what the average employee salary is at a local discount store, would you rather have the manager tell you the mean or the median? Explain." *Sample answer:* median; The mean would include outliers in upper management, so the mean will likely be greater than most of the data.

Self-Assessment for Problem Solving

- Allow time in class for students to practice using the problem-solving plan. Remember, some students may only be able to complete the first step.
- Students are assessing their understanding of the last three success criteria. Mathematically proficient students understand that outliers can greatly affect measures of center.
- **MP1 Make Sense of Problems and Persevere in Solving Them**: Mathematically proficient students analyze statistical questions and use tools (e.g., tables, dot plots) to help organize the information. As changes to a data set occur, students weigh their options and determine which measure of center best answers the statistical question.
- **Teaching Strategy:** After completing the exercises, have students compare their answers and discuss any differences. Students should justify their answers to one another.
- In this era of technology and instantaneous information, students need to understand how to answer statistical questions, so that they can evaluate the validity of statistics.

The Success Criteria Self-Assessment chart can be found in the *Student Journal* or online at *BigIdeasMath.com*.

Closure

- **Writing Prompt:** To determine the median of one dozen data values…

EXAMPLE 5 Modeling Real Life

Use the data to answer the statistical question, "How much do climbing shoes cost?"

Find the mean, median, and mode of the data. Then answer the question by creating a dot plot to determine which measure best represents the data.

Mean: $\frac{40 + 51 + 142 + 68 + 57 + 40 + 65 + 85}{8} = \frac{548}{8} = 68.5$

Median: 40, 40, 51, 57, 65, 68, 85, 142 Order the data.

$$\frac{57 + 65}{2} = \frac{122}{2} = 61$$

Mode: 40, 40, 51, 57, 65, 68, 85, 142 The value 40 occurs most often.

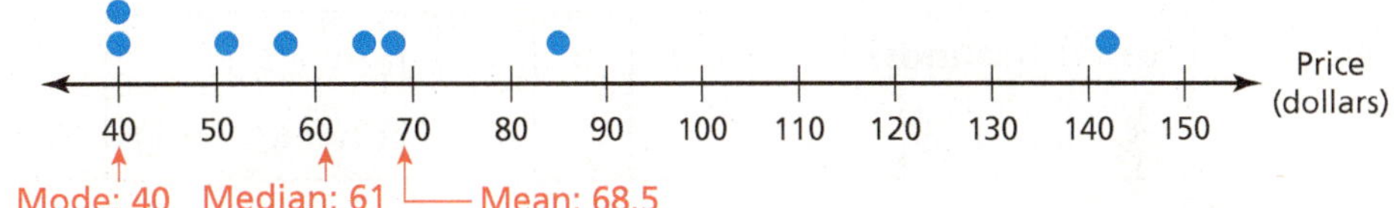

The mode is less than most of the data, and the mean is greater than most of the data. The median best represents the data. So, climbing shoes cost about $61.

Self-Assessment for Problem Solving

Solve each exercise. Then rate your understanding of the success criteria in your journal.

8. How does removing the outlier affect your answer in Example 5?

9. It takes 10 contestants on a television show 43, 41, 62, 40, 44, 43, 44, 46, 45, and 41 seconds to cross a canyon on a zipline. Find the mean, median, and mode of the data with and without the outlier. Which measure does the outlier affect the most?

10. The table shows the weights of several great white sharks. Use the data to answer the statistical question, "What is the weight of a great white shark?"

Great White Shark Weights (pounds)			
1700	1500	1700	2100
1600	1700	1900	3900
1700	2200	1800	1600

9.3 Practice

Review & Refresh

Find the mean of the data.

1. 1, 5, 8, 4, 5, 7, 6, 6, 2, 3
2. 9, 12, 11, 11, 10, 7, 4, 8
3. 26, 42, 31, 50, 29, 37, 44, 31
4. 53, 45, 43, 55, 28, 21, 61, 29, 24, 40, 27, 42
5. A shelf in your room can hold at most 30 pounds. There are 12 pounds of books already on the shelf. Which inequality represents the numbers of pounds you can add to the shelf?

   A. $x < 18$ **B.** $x \geq 18$ **C.** $x \leq 42$ **D.** $x \leq 18$

Find the missing values in the ratio table. Then write the equivalent ratios.

6.

Turkey (pounds)	1	2	3
Price (dollars)	5.50		

7.

Guests	5	30	6
Cost (dollars)	100		

Find the surface area of the prism.

8.

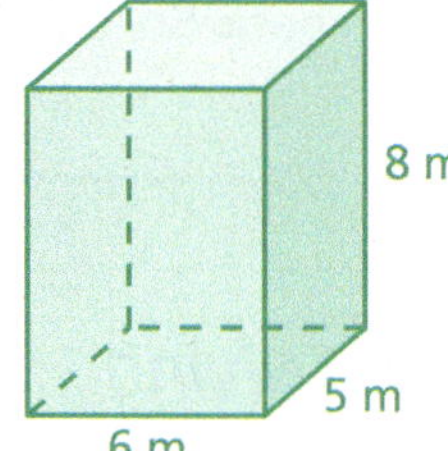

9.

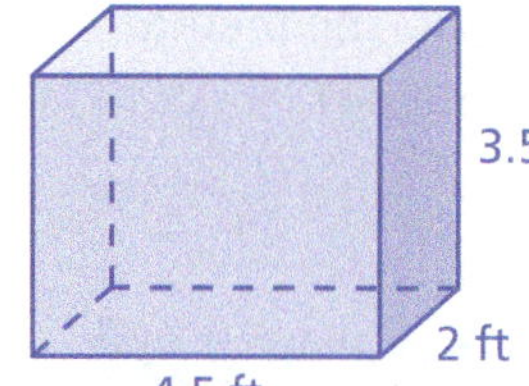

10.

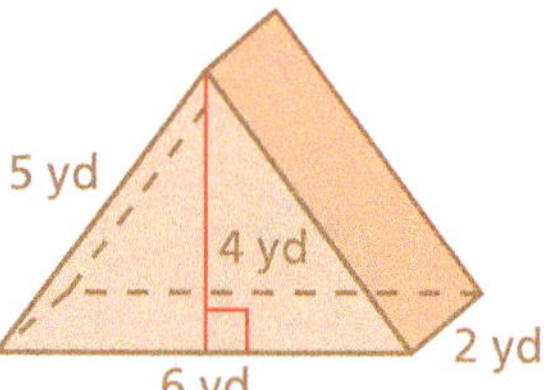

Concepts, Skills, & Problem Solving

FINDING THE MEDIAN **Use grid paper to find the median of the data.** (See Exploration 1, p. 425.)

11. 9, 7, 2, 4, 3, 5, 9, 6, 8, 0, 3, 8
12. 16, 24, 13, 36, 22, 26, 22, 28, 25

FINDING THE MEDIAN AND MODE **Find the median and mode of the data.**

13. 3, 5, 7, 9, 11, 3, 8
14. 14, 19, 16, 13, 16, 14
15. 93, 81, 94, 71, 89, 92, 94, 99
16. 44, 13, 36, 52, 19, 27, 33
17. 12, 33, 18, 28, 29, 12, 17, 4, 2
18. 55, 44, 40, 55, 48, 44, 58, 67
19. **MP YOU BE THE TEACHER** Your friend finds the median of the data. Is your friend correct? Explain your reasoning.

    The median is 58.

    63, 55, 49, 58, 50, 59, 51

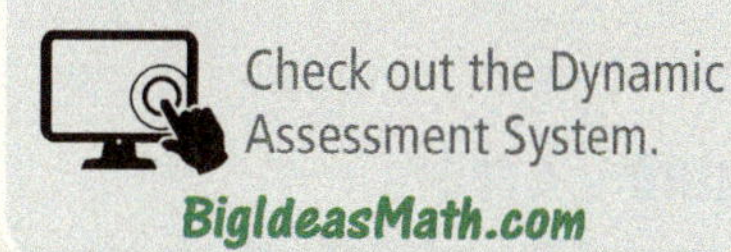

Assignment Guide and Concept Check

Scaffold assignments to support all students in their learning progression. The suggested assignments are a starting point. Continue to assign additional exercises and revisit with spaced practice to move every student toward proficiency.

Level	Assignment 1	Assignment 2
Emerging	4, 5, 6, 9, 10, 11, 13, 15, 19, 20, 27, 31	16, 17, 21, 22, 23, 25, 28, 39
Proficient	4, 5, 6, 9, 10, 12, 14, 16, 19, 21, 28, 32	18, 22, 23, 25, 29, 30, 35, 38, 39
Advanced	4, 5, 6, 9, 10, 12, 16, 18, 19, 21, 29, 34	22, 24, 30, 35, 36, 37, 38, 39, 40

- Assignment 1 is for use after students complete the Self-Assessment for Concepts & Skills.
- Assignment 2 is for use after students complete the Self-Assessment for Problem Solving.
- The red exercises can be used as a concept check.

Review & Refresh Prior Skills

Exercises 1–4 Finding the Mean
Exercise 5 Solving Inequalities
Exercises 6 and 7 Completing Ratio Tables
Exercises 8–10 Finding the Surface Area of a Prism

Common Errors

- **Exercises 13–18** Students may try to identify the median without ordering the data first. Remind students that it is essential to order the data first and then find the median. This makes finding the mode more efficient as well.

Review & Refresh

1. 4.7
2. 9
3. 36.25
4. 39
5. D
6. 11.00, 16.50; 1 : 5.5, 2 : 11, 6 : 16.5
7. 600, 120; 5 : 100, 30 : 600, 6 : 120
8. 236 m^2
9. 63.5 ft^2
10. 56 yd^2

Concepts, Skills, & Problem Solving

11. 5.5
12. 24
13. median = 7; mode = 3
14. median = 15; modes = 14, 16
15. median = 92.5; mode = 94
16. median = 33; no mode
17. median = 17; mode = 12
18. median = 51.5; modes = 44, 55
19. no; The data were not ordered from least to greatest.

Concepts, Skills, & Problem Solving

20. black, blue
21. singing
22. no; only the mode can describe a set of data that is not made up of numbers.
23. mean = 7.61; median = 7.42; no mode
24. mean = $6\frac{3}{8}$; median = $6\frac{3}{16}$; mode = $6\frac{5}{8}$
25. mean = 2.7; median = 2.6; mode = 2.2
26. With outlier: mean = 48.5, median = 53, no mode; Without outlier: mean = 53, median = 54, no mode; mean
27. With outlier: mean = 103, median = 85, mode = 85; Without outlier: mean = 85, median = 85, mode = 85; mean
28. With outlier: mean = 38, median = 35, modes = 23, 45; Without outlier: mean = 33, median = 27, modes = 23, 45; median
29. With outlier: mean = 101, median = 102, mode = 110; Without outlier: mean = 105.625, median = 106, mode = 110; mean
30. **a.** mean = \$1794; median = \$1790; mode = \$1940

    b. mean = \$1883.70; median = \$1879.50; mode = \$2037; The mean, median, and mode all increased by 5%.

    c. The mean, median, and mode of annual salaries are 12 times the mean, median, and mode of the monthly salaries.

31–34. See Additional Answers.

Common Errors

- **Exercises 20 and 21** Students may make an educated guess of which color or act appears the most, instead of organizing the data. Remind students of the importance of organizing data. It not only helps them find the mode but also helps answer questions such as "How many students wore black?"
- **Exercises 26–29** When finding the mean of a set of data after removing an outlier, students may forget to subtract one from the denominator. Remind students that when the outlier is removed, there is one less data value.
- **Exercises 31–34** Students may only find the mean, median, and mode instead of making a dot plot before deciding which measure of center is the best representative. Even if students are correct, encourage them to make dot plots to check their answers. Creating a visual of the data helps students to explain why that measure of center is the best representative.

FINDING THE MODE **Find the mode of the data.**

20.

Shirt Colors		
Black	Blue	Red
Pink	Black	Black
Gray	Green	Blue
Blue	Blue	Red
Yellow	Blue	Blue
Black	Orange	Black
Black		

21.

Talent Show Acts		
Singing	Dancing	Comedy
Singing	Singing	Dancing
Juggling	Dancing	Singing
Singing	Poetry	Dancing
Comedy	Magic	Dancing
Poetry	Singing	Singing

22. **MP REASONING** In Exercises 20 and 21, can you find the mean and median of the data? Explain.

FINDING MEASURES OF CENTER **Find the mean, median, and mode of the data.**

23. 4.7, 8.51, 6.5, 7.42, 9.64, 7.2, 9.3

24. $8\frac{1}{2}, 6\frac{5}{8}, 3\frac{1}{8}, 5\frac{3}{4}, 6\frac{5}{8}, 5\frac{1}{4}, 10\frac{5}{8}, 4\frac{1}{2}$

25. **MP MODELING REAL LIFE** The weights (in ounces) of several moon rocks are shown in the table. Find the mean, median, and mode of the weights.

Moon Rock Weights (ounces)		
2.2	2.2	3.2
2.4	2.8	3.4
2.6	3.0	2.5

REMOVING AN OUTLIER **Find the mean, median, and mode of the data with and without the outlier. Which measure does the outlier affect the most?**

26. 45, 52, 17, 63, 57, 42, 54, 58

27. 85, 77, 211, 88, 91, 84, 85

28. 23, 73, 45, 27, 23, 25, 43, 45

29. 101, 110, 99, 100, 64, 112, 110, 111, 102

30. **MP REASONING** The table shows the monthly salaries for employees at a company.

Monthly Salaries (dollars)				
1940	1660	1860	2100	1720
1540	1760	1940	1820	1600

a. Find the mean, median, and mode of the data.

b. Each employee receives a 5% raise. Find the mean, median, and mode of the data with the raise. How does this increase affect the mean, median, and mode of the data?

c. How are the mean, median, and mode of the monthly salaries related to the mean, median, and mode of the annual salaries?

CHOOSING A MEASURE OF CENTER **Find the mean, median, and mode of the data. Choose the measure that best represents the data. Explain your reasoning.**

31. 48, 12, 11, 45, 48, 48, 43, 32

32. 12, 13, 40, 95, 88, 7, 95

33. 2, 8, 10, 12, 56, 9, 5, 2, 4

34. 126, 62, 144, 81, 144, 103

35. **MP MODELING REAL LIFE** The weather forecast for a week is shown. Which measure of center best represents the high temperatures? the low temperatures? Explain your reasoning.

	Sun	Mon	Tue	Wed	Thu	Fri	Sat
High	90°F	91°F	89°F	97°F	101°F	99°F	91°F
Low	74°F	78°F	77°F	77°F	83°F	78°F	72°F

36. **RESEARCH** Find the costs of 10 different boxes of cereal. Choose one cereal whose cost will be an outlier.

a. Which measure of center does the outlier affect the most? Justify your answer.

b. Use the data to answer the statistical question, "How much does a box of cereal cost?"

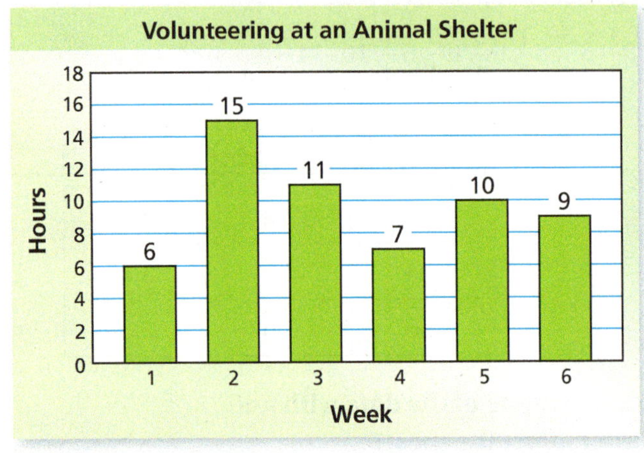

37. **MP PROBLEM SOLVING** The bar graph shows the numbers of hours you volunteered at an animal shelter. What is the minimum number of hours you need to volunteer in the seventh week to justify that you volunteered an average of 10 hours per week for the 7 weeks? Explain your answer using measures of center.

38. **MP REASONING** Why is the mode the least frequently used measure of center to describe a data set? Explain.

39. **DIG DEEPER!** The data are the prices of several fitness wristbands at a store.

$130 $170 $230 $130

$250 $275 $130 $185

ON SALE NOW!

NOW ONLY $130

a. Does the price shown in the advertisement represent the prices well? Explain.

b. Why might the store use this advertisement?

c. In this situation, why might a person want to know the mean? the median? the mode? Explain.

40. **CRITICAL THINKING** The expressions $3x$, $9x$, $4x$, $23x$, $6x$, and $3x$ form a data set. Assume $x > 0$.

a. Find the mean, median, and mode of the data.

b. Is there an outlier? If so, what is it?

Mini-Assessment

Find the median and mode of the data.

1. 56, 27, 35, 27, 44, 25 median = 31; mode = 27
2. 65, 2, 23, 41, 11, 7, 55 median = 23; no mode
3. The table shows the numbers of times you win playing a video game.

Mon	Tues	Wed	Thu	Fri	Sat
2	10	12	14	2	11

a. Find the mean, median, and mode of the data. Choose the measure that best represents the data. Explain your reasoning. mean = 8.5; median = 10.5; mode = 2; *Sample answer:* The median is best because the mean and mode are less than most of the data.

b. You win 33 times on Sunday. Find the mean, median, and mode of the data with this outlier. Which measure does the outlier affect the most? mean = 12; median = 11; mode = 2; mean

Section Resources

Surface Level	Deep Level
Resources by Chapter • Extra Practice • Reteach • Puzzle Time Student Journal • Self-Assessment • Practice Differentiating the Lesson Tutorial Videos Skills Review Handbook Skills Trainer	Resources by Chapter • Enrichment and Extension Graphic Organizers Dynamic Assessment System • Section Practice
Transfer Level	
Dynamic Assessment System • Mid-Chapter Quiz	Assessment Book • Mid-Chapter Quiz

Concepts, Skills, & Problem Solving

35. *Sample answer:* Both the median and mode are the best measures for the high temperatures; Both the mean and median are the best measures for the low temperatures; Median and mode were chosen for high temperatures because they are both close to most of the values. Mean and median were chosen for the low temperatures because there were two modes.

36. Answers will vary. Students should list 10 cereal unit prices including one outlier. Part (a) should identify and justify which measure is most affected by the outlier and identify the outlier. The mean, median, and mode should be calculated for comparison. Part (b) should answer the question using the data and the measures of center.

37. 10; you need to work 12 more hours to make the mean 10 hours but only 10 more hours to make the median and mode 10 hours.

38. *Sample answer:* A mode can be an unreliable measure of a data set because there can be no mode or more than one mode.

39. **a.** no; The price is the mode, but it is the lowest price. Most fitness wristbands cost more.

b. By advertising the lowest price, they are likely to draw more customers to the store.

c. *Sample answer:* Knowing all the measures can help you know whether the store has many models in your price range.

40. **a.** mean = $8x$; median = $5x$; mode = $3x$

b. yes; $23x$

Learning Target

Find and interpret the range and interquartile range of a data set.

Success Criteria

- Explain how the range and interquartile range describe the variability of a data set with a single number.
- Find the range and interquartile range of a data set.
- Use the interquartile range to identify outliers.

Warm Up

Cumulative, vocabulary, and prerequisite skills practice opportunities are available in the *Resources by Chapter* or at *BigIdeasMath.com.*

ELL Support

Help students understand the meaning of *interquartile* by examining its parts. The prefix *inter–* means "among," the root word *quart* refers to one-fourth (as in *quart* and *quarter*), and the suffix *–ile* means "relating to." The term *interquartile range* describes the spread of the data in the second and third quarters of a data set. Explain that *variation* refers to the distribution of a data set.

Exploration 1

a. *Sample answer:* The lowest score is 75% and the highest score is 96%. Most of the students scored closer to 96% than to 75%.

b–c. See Additional Answers

Exploration 2

a–c. See Additional Answers.

Laurie's Notes

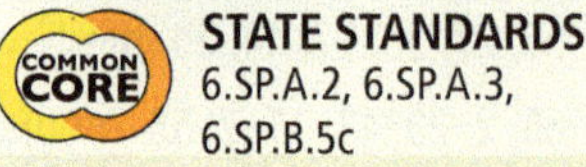

Preparing to Teach

- Students have used tables, dot plots, and formulas to examine central tendency. Now they will examine the spread of a data set and measures of variation. Students will also be introduced to several new vocabulary terms.
- **MP8 Look for and Express Regularity in Repeated Reasoning:** In the previous section, students may have found the median for a data set by folding strips of grid paper. Students can now make a second fold to divide the data into 4 equal parts to create a visual representation for finding the quartiles.

Motivate

- Write the word *range* on the board and ask what it means.
- Allow discussion of the many meanings. In this lesson, the **range** is the difference between the greatest and least values in a data set. The range is a single number that describes the spread of the data.
- Give an example: "The range of ages at the dance is 5 years."
- Say, "You have been studying measures of center. Now you will explore several ways to measure variation."

Exploration 1

- Ask a volunteer to read the situation aloud. Have partners complete part (a).
- ? "Do you know how many students scored either of these two grades?" no
- ? "Without knowing the average score, what can you conclude about your exam score?" Students should reason that their scores are at least 75% and no more than 96%. They may also suggest that their scores are closer to the higher end of the range because of the second statement.
- **MP3 Construct Viable Arguments and Critique the Reasoning of Others:** Ask students to share and compare dot plots and explain their reasoning for each one. Each unique plot should have 24 dots.

Exploration 2

- Begin with a discussion about trips the students have made.
- In part (b), listen to students' observations. Are students noticing: any clusters or gaps? the data trend toward more states or fewer states? the spread of the data? the location of the median?
- **MP8 Look for and Express Regularity in Repeated Reasoning:** In part (c), students can use a strip of grid paper to find the *middle half*. They fold once to divide the 22 data values into two halves of 11 values. They fold again to find the median of the lower half (the **first quartile**, 2) and the median of the upper half (the **third quartile**, 10).
- ? "What fraction of the data values are in each part?" about $\frac{1}{4}$
- Have students share their descriptions of the *middle half* in a class discussion.
- Point out that the **quartiles** may or may not be values in the data set. In this case, the second quartile (the median) is not, but the other two are.

9.4 Measures of Variation

Learning Target: Find and interpret the range and interquartile range of a data set.

Success Criteria:
- I can explain how the range and interquartile range describe the variability of a data set with a single number.
- I can find the range and interquartile range of a data set.
- I can use the interquartile range to identify outliers.

EXPLORATION 1 Interpreting Statements

Math Practice

Analyze Givens

How can you use the given information to determine how spread out the data are?

Work with a partner. There are 24 students in your class. Your teacher makes the following statements.

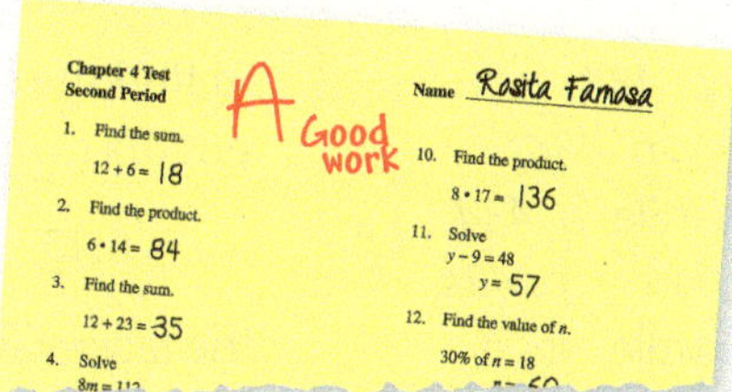

- *"The exam scores range from 75% to 96%."*
- *"Most of the students received high scores."*

a. What does each statement mean? Explain.

b. Use your teacher's statements to make a dot plot that can represent the distribution of the exam scores of the class.

c. Compare your dot plot with other groups'. How are they alike? different?

EXPLORATION 2 Grouping Data

Work with a partner. The numbers of U.S. states visited by students in a sixth-grade class are shown.

Numbers of States Visited

1	7	5	2	4	18	1	6
11	6	3	20	2	7	1	8
10	2	12	5	3	21		

a. Represent the data using a dot plot. Between what values do the data range?

b. Use the dot plot to make observations about the data.

c. How can you describe the *middle half* of the data?

9.4 Lesson

A **measure of variation** is a measure that describes the distribution of a data set. A simple measure of variation to find is the *range*. The **range** of a data set is the difference of the greatest value and the least value.

Key Vocabulary

measure of variation, p. 434
range, p. 434
quartiles, p. 434
first quartile, p. 434
third quartile, p. 434
interquartile range, p. 434

EXAMPLE 1 Finding the Range

The table shows the lengths of several Burmese pythons captured for a study. Find and interpret the range of the lengths.

Lengths (feet)	
18.5	8
11	10
14	15.5
12.5	6.25
16.25	5

To find the least and the greatest values, order the lengths from least to greatest.

5, 6.25, 8, 10, 11, 12.5, 14, 15.5, 16.25, 18.5

The least value is 5. The greatest value is 18.5.

So, the range of the lengths is 18.5 − 5 = 13.5 feet. This means that the lengths vary by no more than 13.5 feet.

Try It

1. The ages of people in line for a roller coaster are 15, 17, 21, 32, 41, 30, 25, 52, 16, 39, 11, and 24. Find and interpret the range of the ages.

Key Ideas

Quartiles

The **quartiles** of a data set divide the data into four equal parts. Recall that the median (second quartile) divides the data set into two halves.

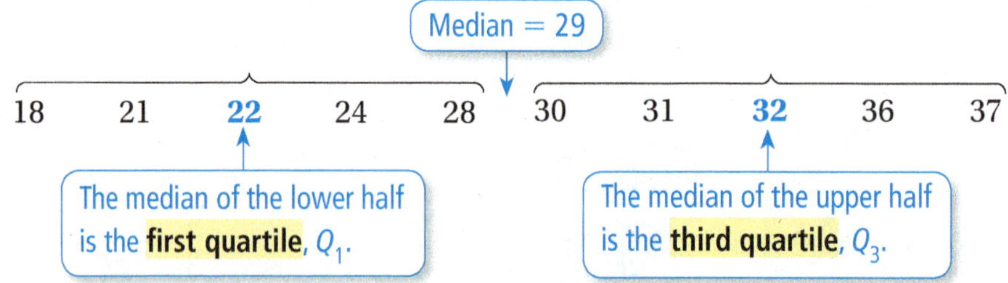

Reading

The first quartile can also be called the *lower quartile*. The third quartile can also be called the *upper quartile*.

Interquartile Range (IQR)

The difference of the third quartile and the first quartile is called the **interquartile range**. The IQR represents the range of the middle half of the data and is another measure of variation.

18 21 22 24 28 30 31 32 36 37

$$\begin{aligned}\text{IQR} &= Q_3 - Q_1 \\ &= 32 - 22 \\ &= 10\end{aligned}$$

Multi-Language Glossary at BigIdeasMath.com

Laurie's Notes

Scaffolding Instruction

- After exploring and generalizing the spread of data, students will focus on using specific measures of variation to describe the spread of data.
- **Emerging:** Students understand measures of central tendency (averages) but find the concept of variation somewhat confusing. These students need practice finding and interpreting quartiles, interquartile range, and outliers. Provide guided instruction for the examples.
- **Proficient:** Although students understand range and general descriptions of data distribution, interquartile range and using the interquartile range to find outliers are new to all students. Review the Key Ideas and provide guided instruction for Examples 2 and 3.

EXAMPLE 1

- In finding the range, ordering the data helps to ensure that you find the least and greatest data values correctly.
- **MP4 Model with Mathematics:** To interpret the range of 13.5 feet, state what it means in the context of the problem: "The lengths vary by no more than 13.5 feet."

Try It

- Check that students give both the range and the interpretation of what the range means in the context of the problem.
- **Common Error:** Students may write the range as an interval, 11–52 people, rather than as a distance between the greatest and least values.

Teaching Strategy

Visual models are helpful tools but physical methods extend students' understanding even further. Students can use strips of grid paper to see where the data values are located on a number line. Then fold once to find the median and again to find the quartiles. Students will recognize that about 25% of the data values are in each section and the difference between two adjacent quarters of the data is typically *not* 25% of the range!

Key Ideas

- **Teaching Strategy:** Fold a strip of grid paper twice and say, "The folds corresponded to the **quartiles** of the data."
- Explain that the median of the lower half is called the **first quartile** (Q_1) and the median of the upper half is the **third quartile** (Q_3). The overall median is also known as the *second quartile* (Q_2). Point out the Reading note.
- Define and discuss the **interquartile range** (IQR), which measures the spread of the middle 50% of the data. Because the IQR tends to ignore outliers, it may give a clearer picture of a data set than the range.

? **MP2 Reason Abstractly and Quantitatively:** "What fraction or percent of the data set is within the IQR?" about 50% or about $\frac{1}{2}$ "What fraction or percent is greater than the third quartile?" about 25% or about $\frac{1}{4}$

Scaffold instruction to support all students in their learning. Learning is individualized and you may want to group students differently as they move in and out of these levels with each skill and concept. Student self-assessment and feedback help guide your instructional decisions about how and when to layer support for all students to become proficient learners.

Extra Example 1

The table shows the lengths of great white sharks at a local aquarium. Find and interpret the range of the lengths.

Lengths (feet)	
15	16.5
14	18
19	15
17.5	16
14	15.5

The range of the lengths is 5 feet, which means that the lengths vary by no more than 5 feet.

ELL Support

After discussing Example 1, have students work in pairs to discuss and complete Try It Exercise 1. Expect students to perform as described.

Beginner: Calculate the range and state the number.

Intermediate: Use a simple sentence to state the range.

Advanced: Use a detailed sentence to state and interpret the range and guide discussion.

Try It

1. 41 yr; The ages of people in line vary by no more than 41 years.

Extra Example 2

The numbers of pages in eight different sixth-grade math textbooks are shown below. Find and interpret the interquartile range of the data.

560, 532, 466, 728, 636, 512, 698, 444

178 pages; The middle half of the numbers of pages vary by no more than 178 pages.

Try It

2. 38 pages; The middle half of the numbers of pages vary by no more than 38.

Self-Assessment
for Concepts & Skills

3. *Sample answer:* Range describes the spread of the numbers in that set. Interquartile range describes the spread of the numbers in the middle half of the data set.
4. What is the range of the data?; 20; 12

Laurie's Notes

EXAMPLE 2

- Ask a volunteer to read the problem aloud.
- **MP7 Look for and Make Use of Structure:** Ask students how they can use the structure of the dot plot to find the mode.
- Some students will use the dot plot to find the quartiles without rewriting the data set in an ordered list. Suggest that they will make fewer errors when they rewrite the data.
- Write the list and show the location of the median (Q_2).
- ? "How do you find the first quartile, (Q_1)?" Find the median of the lower half.
- ? "How do you find the third quartile (Q_3)?" Find the median of the upper half.
- Remind students to never include the median in the lower half or the upper half of data. This way they will know how to handle a data set with an odd number of data.
- Find the interquartile range (IQR). Interpret what it means in the context of the problem.

Try It

- Remind students not to include the median in the lower half or the upper half of the data.
- **Neighbor Check:** Have students work independently and then have their neighbors check their work. Have students discuss any discrepancies.

Self-Assessment for Concepts & Skills

- As students complete these exercises independently, look for their understanding of the first success criterion, particularly in their explanations for Exercise 3.
- Some students may want to use grid paper to find the quartiles and that is okay. As they continue practicing this skill, students will understand how counting the data values is a more efficient method.

ELL Support

To provide support and language practice, have students work in pairs to complete the exercises. Then have pairs compare their answers and discuss their methods with a group.

The Success Criteria Self-Assessment chart can be found in the *Student Journal* or online at *BigIdeasMath.com*.

EXAMPLE 2 Finding the Interquartile Range

The dot plot shows the top speeds of 12 sports cars. Find and interpret the interquartile range of the data.

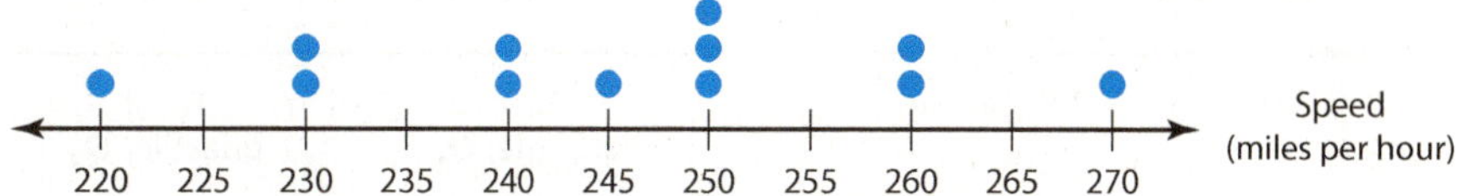

Order the speeds from slowest to fastest. Find the quartiles.

Median: $\frac{245 + 250}{2} = 247.5$

220 230 230 240 240 245 250 250 250 260 260 270

Q_1: $\frac{230 + 240}{2} = 235$

Q_3: $\frac{250 + 260}{2} = 255$

So, the interquartile range is $255 - 235 = 20$. This means that the middle half of the speeds vary by no more than 20 miles per hour.

Try It

2. The data are the number of pages in each of an author's novels. Find and interpret the interquartile range of the data.

356, 364, 390, 468, 400, 382, 376, 396, 350

Self-Assessment for Concepts & Skills

Solve each exercise. Then rate your understanding of the success criteria in your journal.

3. WRITING Explain why the variability of a data set can be described by the range or the interquartile range.

4. DIFFERENT WORDS, SAME QUESTION Which is different? Find "both" answers.

53, 47, 60, 45, 62, 59, 65, 50, 56, 48

What is the interquartile range of the data shown?

What is the range of the data shown?

What is the range of the middle half of the data shown?

What is $Q_3 - Q_1$ for the data shown?

You can use the quartiles and the interquartile range to check for outliers.

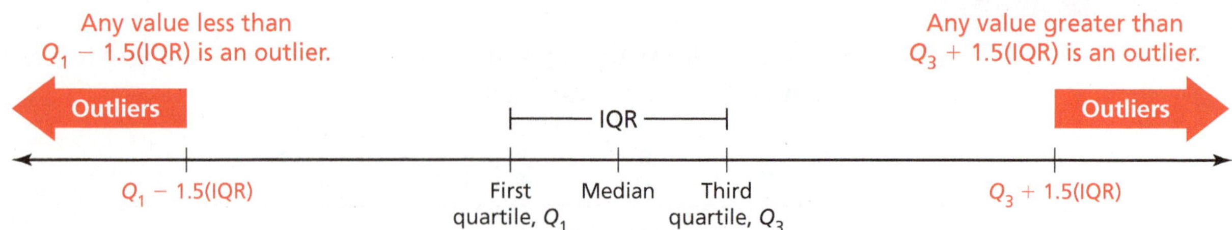

EXAMPLE 3 Modeling Real Life

Bugs Eaten			
26	34	32	42
33	2	34	

Section 9.3 Example 3 identifies 2 as an outlier of the data in the table shown. Use the IQR to determine whether it is the only outlier.

Order the data values from least to greatest. Find the quartiles.

2 26 32 33 34 34 42

$Q_1 = 26$ Median $= 33$ $Q_3 = 34$

The IQR is $34 - 26 = 8$. Use the IQR to find the outlier boundaries.

$$Q_1 - 1.5(\text{IQR}) = 26 - 1.5(8) = 14 \qquad Q_3 + 1.5(\text{IQR}) = 34 + 1.5(8) = 46$$

The only data value less than 14 is 2. There are no data values greater than 46. So, the only outlier is 2.

Self-Assessment for Problem Solving

Solve each exercise. Then rate your understanding of the success criteria in your journal.

Distances (feet)			
$13\frac{1}{2}$	$21\frac{1}{2}$	21	$16\frac{3}{4}$
$10\frac{1}{4}$	19	32	$26\frac{1}{2}$
29	$16\frac{1}{4}$	$28\frac{1}{2}$	$18\frac{1}{2}$

5. The table shows the distances traveled by a paper airplane. Find and interpret the range and interquartile range of the distances.

6. The table shows the years of teaching experience of math teachers at a school. How do the outlier or outliers affect the variability of the data?

Teaching Experience (years)	5	10	7	8	10
	11	22	8	6	35

Laurie's Notes

Discuss

- You can use quartiles and the IQR to check for outliers. An outlier is any data value that is more than 1.5(IQR) below Q_1 or above Q_3. The boundaries are $Q_1 - 1.5(\text{IQR})$ and $Q_3 + 1.5(\text{IQR})$ as shown on the number line at the top of the page.
- Compare checking for outliers by using the IQR formulas with using the definition of an outlier as a *data value that is much greater or much less than other values*. Before students were making an educated guess. Now they can prove that a data value is an outlier using a formula.

EXAMPLE 3

- Work through the problem to prove that 2 is the only outlier in the data set from Section 9.3 Example 3.
- ⦿ To provide additional practice with the third success criterion, you could have students check Example 2 for outliers (there are none) or return to Section 9.2 Example 3 and Section 9.3 Example 5 to prove the outliers in those data sets.

Self-Assessment for Problem Solving

- Students may benefit from trying the exercises independently and then working with peers to refine their work. It is important to provide time in class for problem solving, so that students become comfortable with the problem-solving plan.
- ⦿ Students are assessing their understanding of all three success criteria. Not only do the exercises ask students to use their data skills, but they also probe for understanding of the measures of variation.

The Success Criteria Self-Assessment chart can be found in the *Student Journal* or online at *BigIdeasMath.com*.

Closure

- Give an example of a data set with 6 data values that has a median of 20 and a range of 20. *Sample answer:* 4, 5, 18, 22, 23, 24

Extra Example 3

Check for outliers in the data set in Extra Example 2. There are no books with fewer than 222 pages or more than 934 pages, so the data set has no outliers.

Self-Assessment for Problem Solving

5. range $= 21\frac{3}{4}$ ft; The distances traveled by the paper airplane vary by no more than $21\frac{3}{4}$ feet; IQR $= 11$ ft; The middle half of the distances traveled by the paper airplane vary by no more than 11 feet.
6. The outliers increase the range by 24 and increase the interquartile range by 0.5.

Learning Target

Find and interpret the range and interquartile range of a data set.

Success Criteria

- Explain how the range and interquartile range describe the variability of a data set with a single number.
- Find the range and interquartile range of a data set.
- Use the interquartile range to identify outliers.

1. mean = 7.1; median = 7; mode = 4
2. mean = 77; median = 78; no mode
3. mean = 16; median = 16; modes = 15, 17
4. mean = 23; median = 22; no mode
5. >
6. <
7. >
8. >
9. $480\ \text{mm}^2$
10. $110\ \text{in.}^2$
11. $96.6\ \text{ft}^2$

12. *Sample answer:*

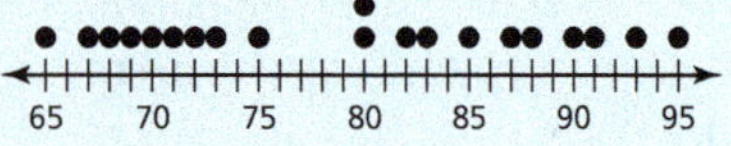

13. *Sample answer:*

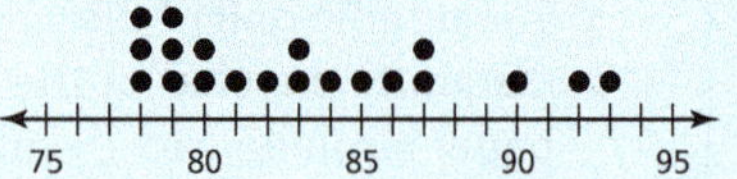

14. 7
15. 33
16. 12
17. 23
18. 57
19. 7.3
20. no; The data were not ordered from least to greatest.
21. 5
22. 3.5
23. 7
24. 8
25. 11
26. 10

Check out the Dynamic Assessment System.
BigIdeasMath.com

Assignment Guide and Concept Check

Scaffold assignments to support all students in their learning progression. The suggested assignments are a starting point. Continue to assign additional exercises and revisit with spaced practice to move every student toward proficiency.

Level	Assignment 1	Assignment 2
Emerging	4, 6, 10, 11, 12, 15, 17, 20, 21, 23	19, 24, 27, 28, 30, 31
Proficient	4, 6, 10, 11, 12, 14, 16, 20, 24, 25	19, 26, 27, 28, 30, 31, 33
Advanced	4, 6, 10, 11, 12, 18, 19, 20, 24, 26	28, 29, 30, 31, 32, 33, 34

- Assignment 1 is for use after students complete the Self-Assessment for Concepts & Skills.
- Assignment 2 is for use after students complete the Self-Assessment for Problem Solving.
- The red exercises can be used as a concept check.

Review & Refresh Prior Skills

Exercises 1–4 Finding Measures of Center
Exercises 5–8 Comparing Integers
Exercises 9–11 Finding the Surface Area of a Pyramid

Common Errors

- **Exercises 14–19** Students may write the range as an interval, such as 4–9, rather than as the distance between the greatest and least values, 5. Emphasize that the range is a value, not an interval.
- **Exercises 21–26** Students may include the median in the two halves of data when finding the quartiles. Remind students never to include the median in the upper or lower half of the data.

9.4 Practice

Review & Refresh

Find the mean, median, and mode of the data.

1. 4, 8, 11, 6, 4, 5, 9, 10, 10, 4
2. 74, 78, 86, 67, 80
3. 15, 18, 17, 17, 15, 16, 14
4. 31, 14, 18, 26, 17, 32

Copy and complete the statement using < or >.

5. $6 \ \square \ -7$
6. $-3 \ \square \ 0$
7. $14 \ \square \ -14$
8. $8 \ \square \ -10$

Find the surface area of the pyramid.

9. 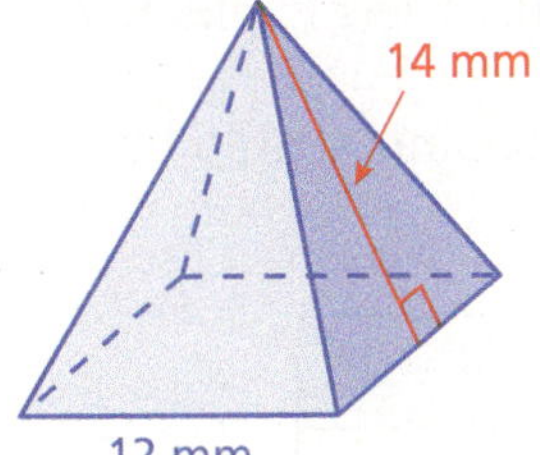

10. 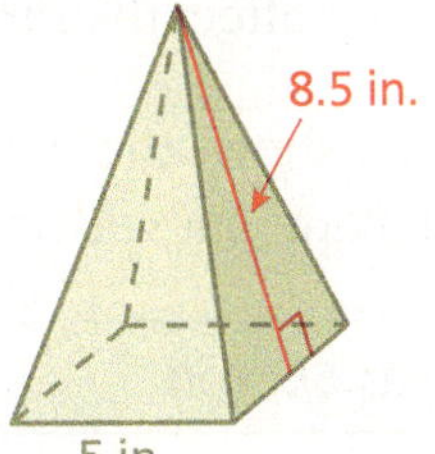

11. 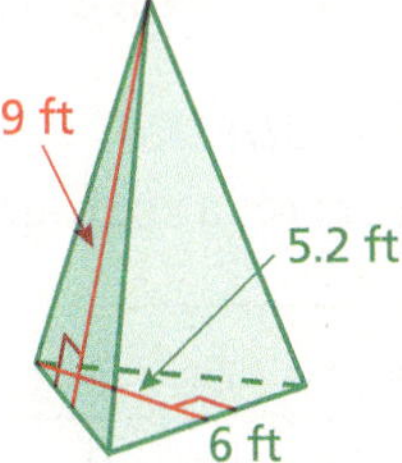

Concepts, Skills, & Problem Solving

INTERPRETING STATEMENTS **There are 20 students in your class. Your teacher makes the two statements shown. Use your teacher's statements to make a dot plot that can represent the distribution of the scores of the class.** (See Exploration 1, p. 433.)

12. *"The quiz scores range from 65% to 95%."*
"The scores were evenly spread out."

13. *"The project scores range from 78% to 93%."*
"Most of the students received low scores."

FINDING THE RANGE **Find the range of the data.**

14. 4, 8, 2, 9, 5, 3
15. 28, 42, 36, 23, 14, 47, 40
16. 26, 21, 27, 33, 24, 29
17. 52, 40, 49, 48, 62, 54, 44, 58, 39
18. 133, 117, 152, 127, 168, 146, 174
19. 4.8, 5.5, 4.2, 8.9, 3.4, 7.5, 1.6, 3.8

20. **MP YOU BE THE TEACHER** Your friend finds the range of the data. Is your friend correct? Explain your reasoning.

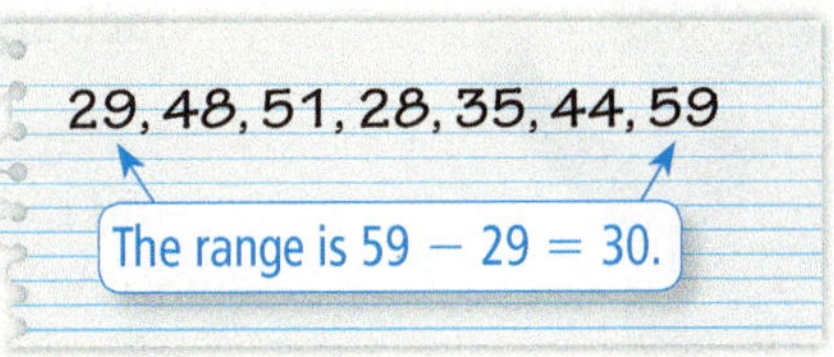

FINDING THE INTERQUARTILE RANGE **Find the interquartile range of the data.**

21. 4, 6, 4, 2, 9, 1, 12, 7
22. 18, 22, 15, 16, 15, 13, 19, 18
23. 40, 33, 37, 54, 41, 34, 27, 39, 35
24. 84, 75, 90, 87, 99, 91, 85, 88, 76, 92, 94
25. 132, 127, 106, 140, 158, 135, 129, 138
26. 38, 55, 61, 56, 46, 67, 59, 75, 65, 58

27. MP **MODELING REAL LIFE** The table shows the number of tornadoes in Alabama each year for several years. Find and interpret the range and interquartile range of the data. Then determine whether there are any outliers.

Numbers of Tornadoes			
65	32	54	23
55	145	37	80
94	42	69	77

28. **WRITING** Consider a data set that has no mode. Which measure of variation is greater, the range or the interquartile range? Explain your reasoning.

29. MP **STRUCTURE** Is it possible for the range of a data set to be equal to the interquartile range? Explain your reasoning.

30. MP **REASONING** How does an outlier affect the range of a data set? Explain.

31. MP **MODELING REAL LIFE** The table shows the numbers of points scored by players on a sixth-grade basketball team in a season.

Points Scored					
21	53	74	82	84	93
103	108	116	122	193	

a. Find the range and interquartile range of the data.

b. Identify the outlier(s) in the data set. Find the range and interquartile range of the data set without the outlier(s). Which measure does the outlier or outliers affect more?

32. **DIG DEEPER!** Two data sets have the same range. Can you assume that the interquartile ranges of the two data sets are about the same? Give an example to justify your answer.

33. MP **MODELING REAL LIFE** The tables show the ages of the finalists for two reality singing competitions.

a. Find the mean, median, range, and interquartile range of the ages for each show. Compare the results.

b. A 21-year-old is voted off Show A, and the 36-year-old is voted off Show B. How do these changes affect the measures in part (a)? Explain.

Ages for Show A	
18	17
15	21
22	16
18	28
24	21

Ages for Show B	
21	20
23	13
15	18
17	22
36	25

34. **OPEN-ENDED** Create a set of data with 7 values that has a mean of 30, a median of 26, a range of 50, and an interquartile range of 36.

Common Errors

- **Exercise 28** Students may fail to realize that the range must be greater than the IQR. Point out that for the range and the IQR to be equal, either each data value must be the same, or all of the data values consist of only two different numbers. In both cases, the data set will have a mode. Otherwise, the quartiles must be between the least and greatest data values.

Mini-Assessment

Find the range and the interquartile range of the data. Determine whether there are any outliers.

1. 8, 9, 1, 5, 5, 7, 9, 12, 15 range = 14; IQR = 5.5; no outliers
2. 43, 25, 39, 45, 57, 44, 48 range = 32; IQR = 9; outlier = 25
3. 110, 115, 116, 118, 121 range = 11; IQR = 7; no outliers
4. 359, 496, 482, 456, 498 range = 139; IQR = 89.5; no outliers

Section Resources

Surface Level	Deep Level
Resources by Chapter • Extra Practice • Reteach • Puzzle Time Student Journal • Self-Assessment • Practice Differentiating the Lesson Tutorial Videos Skills Review Handbook Skills Trainer	Resources by Chapter • Enrichment and Extension Graphic Organizers Dynamic Assessment System • Section Practice

Concepts, Skills, & Problem Solving

27. range = 122; The numbers of tornados in Alabama for several years vary by no more than 122; IQR = 39; The middle half of the numbers of tornados in Alabama vary by no more than 39; outlier = 145
28. range; The range is the difference between the greatest value and the least value. The interquartile range is the range of the middle half of the data.
29. yes; *Sample answer:* If all the data values in the set were the same number, the range and interquartile range would be the same.
30. *Sample answer:* An outlier increases the range of a data set because there is a wider spread between the greatest and least values.
31. **a.** range = 172 points; IQR = 42 points

    b. 193 points; range = 101 points; IQR = 34 points; range
32. no; Example: Data set 1: 1, 5, 6, 6, 6, 7, 11; range = 10, IQR = 2; Data set 2: 1, 2, 2, 6, 10, 10, 11; range = 10, IQR = 8
33. See Additional Answers.
34. *Sample answer:* 10, 14, 20, 26, 30, 50, 60

Laurie's Notes

STATE STANDARDS
6.SP.A.2, 6.SP.A.3, 6.SP.B.5c

Preparing to Teach

- Students began working with measures of variation in the last section. They will now add another measure of variation–the mean absolute deviation (MAD). Students will use their understanding of the mean to find another single number that describes the variability of a data set.
- **MP2 Reason Abstractly and Quantitatively:** For a set of data values, students will compute how much each value deviates from the mean, sum all the deviations, divide by the number of values, and then interpret the meaning.

Motivate

- Write the number 20 on a piece of paper. Fold it and place it on a front desk before students enter the classroom.
- Give each student two number cubes. Tell them that you wrote a special number on the piece of paper. Whoever rolls a total closest to the special number in three rolls of the number cubes is the "Big Kahuna" of the day! My students love that title, but you can use something different.
- Each student records three rolls of the cubes and finds the sum.
- Reveal your special number. One or more students may hit 20.
- For several of the totals that are not 20, say, "You were off, or *deviated*, from 20 by *x*." Do this for numbers less than 20 and numbers greater than 20.

Exploration 1

? "What will be your first step in part (a)?" Find the mean.
- Give partners time to work through part (a). Students may ask what part (a) means and how to find the amount of deviation. Tell them to recall how much they deviated from the special number in the Motivate.
- Before beginning part (b), have partners discuss the Math Practice note.
- Allow students the freedom to organize their data and deviations as they choose. If students are struggling, suggest that they make a table.

? "Overall, do you think the exam scores are *close* to the mean or *far away* from the mean?" Some students may think the scores are close to the mean, while others may not. Some students may observe that no student failed.

? "What is the median?" 89 "What is the mode?" 80, 89, and 96
- Remind students that unlike the median, the mean does not necessarily divide the data set into two sets with the same number of values.
- Before part (c), have students find the sum of the deviations below the mean and the sum of the deviations above the mean. It should not be surprising that the sums are equal. Relate this equality to the mean as a *balance point*.
- In part (c), students are finding the **mean absolute deviation** and what it represents. Listen to students' discussion and help them reach a consensus.

? **MP3 Construct Viable Arguments and Critique the Reasoning of Others**: In discussing part (d), listen for the idea that a smaller value means the data are close together. "What would it mean if the value you found was far from 0? Explain." Listen for the idea that a larger value means the data are spread out.

Learning Target

Find and interpret the mean absolute deviation of a data set.

Success Criteria

- Explain how the mean absolute deviation describes the variability of a data set with a single number.
- Find the mean absolute deviation of a data set.
- Compare data sets using the mean absolute deviation to draw conclusions.

Warm Up

Cumulative, vocabulary, and prerequisite skills practice opportunities are available in the *Resources by Chapter* or at *BigIdeasMath.com*.

ELL Support

Explain that *deviant* describes something that is not normal (out of the ordinary) and is related to the word *deviation*. In mathematics, a deviation is the amount a value or measurement differs from a fixed value such as the mean.

Exploration 1

a. 76; 89; *Sample answer:* The difference between 76 and the mean is the highest and the difference between 89 and the mean is the lowest.

b. Ben: 1; Emma: 2; Jeremy: 8; Pete: 8; Malik: 8; Omar: 7; Hong: 8; Rob: 4; Amy: 2; Sue: 12; Dan: 6; Lucy: 1; Priya: 4; Heather: 3

c. 5.286; *Sample answer:* Average deviation from the mean for each student

d. *Sample answer:* The values in the data set are close to the mean.

9.5 Mean Absolute Deviation

Learning Target: Find and interpret the mean absolute deviation of a data set.

Success Criteria:
- I can explain how the mean absolute deviation describes the variability of a data set with a single number.
- I can find the mean absolute deviation of a data set.
- I can compare data sets using the mean absolute deviation to draw conclusions.

The Meaning of a Word ▶ Deviate

When you **deviate** from something, you stray or depart from the normal course of action.

EXPLORATION 1 Finding Distances from the Mean

Work with a partner. The table shows the exam scores of 14 students in your class.

Exam Scores					
Ben	89	Omar	95	Dan	94
Emma	86	Hong	96	Lucy	89
Jeremy	80	Rob	92	Priya	84
Pete	80	Amy	90	Heather	85
Malik	96	Sue	76		

a. Which exam score *deviates* the most from the mean? Which exam score *deviates* the least from the mean? Explain how you found your answers.

b. How far is each data value from the mean?

c. Divide the sum of the values in part (b) by the number of values. In your own words, what does this represent?

d. MP **REASONING** In a data set, what does it mean when the value you found in part (c) is close to 0? Explain.

Math Practice

Use Operations

What operation can you use to find the distance from the mean? Explain.

9.5 Lesson

Key Vocabulary
mean absolute deviation, *p. 440*

Another measure of variation is the *mean absolute deviation.* The **mean absolute deviation** is an average of how much data values differ from the mean.

Key Idea

Finding the Mean Absolute Deviation (MAD)

Step 1: Find the mean of the data.

Step 2: Find the distance between each data value and the mean.

Step 3: Find the sum of the distances in Step 2.

Step 4: Divide the sum in Step 3 by the total number of data values.

EXAMPLE 1 Finding the Mean Absolute Deviation

Find and interpret the mean absolute deviation of the data.

1, 2, 2, 2, 4, 4, 4, 5

Step 1: Mean $= \frac{1+2+2+2+4+4+4+5}{8} = \frac{24}{8} = 3$

Step 2: You can use a dot plot to organize the data. Replace each dot with its distance from the mean.

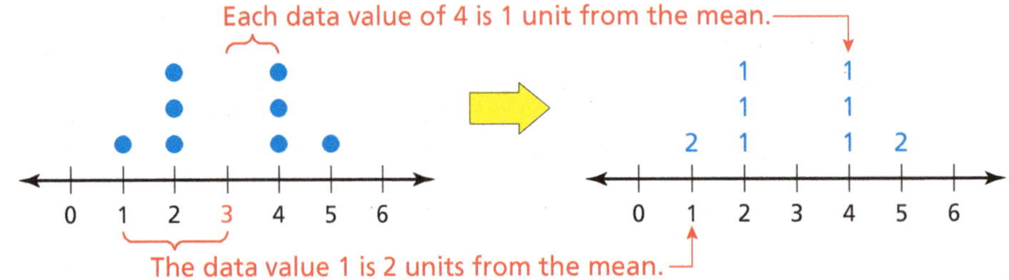

Step 3: The sum of the distances is $2+1+1+1+1+1+1+2 = 10$.

Step 4: The mean absolute deviation is $\frac{10}{8} = 1.25$.

So, the data values differ from the mean by an average of 1.25.

Math Practice

Maintain Oversight

When each data value in Example 1 increases by 5, do you need to repeat Steps 1–4 to find the mean absolute deviation? Explain your reasoning.

Try It

1. Find and interpret the mean absolute deviation of the data.

   5, 8, 8, 10, 13, 14, 16, 22

Laurie's Notes

Scaffolding Instruction

- Students have investigated the mean absolute deviation (MAD) and developed a conceptual understanding using a data set. Now they will learn the formal definition of the MAD and use the MAD to describe the spread of data.
- **Emerging:** Students can find measures of central tendency but need guided instruction with measures of variation, especially the MAD. These students will benefit from the practice provided in the examples.
- **Proficient:** Students understand the difference between measures of central tendency and measures of variability. They can use range, IQR, and outliers to describe the distribution of a data set. Before completing the Self-Assessment exercises, have students review the Key Idea and Example 2.

Key Idea

- Write the steps for finding the **mean absolute deviation** (MAD).
- **Note:** The steps use *distance* rather than *deviation*. See the Teacher Note in Example 1.

EXAMPLE 1

? "What is the first step?" Find the mean of the 8 data values.

? "What is the second step?" Find the distance between each data value and the mean.

- **MP5 Use Appropriate Tools Strategically:** A dot plot is a helpful tool for organizing the data. It can be used to record the distance each data value is from the mean. A dot plot also helps students to see the mean as the *balance point* of the data set.
- **Teacher Note:** In Step 2, notice that the *deviations* on the left side of the mean are negative: $1 - 3 = -2$, $2 - 3 = -1$, and so on. Students have not performed operations with negative numbers yet. This is why *distance* is used instead of *absolute deviation*. Students can simply count how far away each value is from the mean without performing integer operations.
- Continue to work through the problem as shown.
- The mean absolute deviation is 1.25, which is the average of how much data values differ from the mean of 3.

Try It

- **Neighbor Check:** Have students work independently and then have their neighbors check their work. Have students discuss any discrepancies.

◉ Students are continuing to practice the first two success criteria.

Scaffold instruction to support all students in their learning. Learning is individualized and you may want to group students differently as they move in and out of these levels with each skill and concept. Student self-assessment and feedback help guide your instructional decisions about how and when to layer support for all students to become proficient learners.

Extra Example 1

Find and interpret the mean absolute deviation of the data.

5, 5, 5, 6, 7, 7, 7, 9, 9, 10

1.4; The data values differ from the mean by an average of 1.4.

ELL Support

Have students practice language by working in pairs to complete Try It Exercise 1. Expect students to perform as described.

Beginner: Calculate and state the MAD.

Intermediate: State the MAD using a simple sentence.

Advanced: State the MAD using a detailed sentence and guide discussion.

Try It

1. 4.25; The data values differ from the mean by an average of 4.25.

Extra Example 2

The numbers of interceptions thrown by a quarterback in six seasons are shown. Find the mean, median, and mean absolute deviation of the data.

Quarterback A: 11, 9, 19, 14, 15, 13

mean = 13.5; median = 13.5; MAD = 2.5

Try It

2. The mean absolute deviation will decrease; The distance between the new value and the mean is less than the mean absolute deviation of 2.4.

Self-Assessment
for Concepts & Skills

3. *Sample answer:* The mean absolute deviation measures the average difference of the values from the mean value.
4. 4; The data values differ from the mean by an average of 4.
5. mean; It is a measure of center. All the other measures are measures of variation.

Laurie's Notes

EXAMPLE 2

- Ask a volunteer to read the problem aloud. Be sure that students understand the context. Pitchers want a low number of runs scored against them and coaches want consistent performances from pitchers.
- ? "What is the mean for Pitcher A?" 3.5 runs
- ? "What is the median for Pitcher A?" 4 runs
- ? "What can you conclude about Pitcher A from the mean and median?" On average, Pitcher A allows about 3.5 or 4 runs per start.
- **MP5 Use Appropriate Tools Strategically:** A dot plot is again used to organize the data. It is then modified to record the distance of each data value from the mean.
- ? "After finding the distance between each data value and the mean, what else must you do to find the mean absolute deviation?" Find the sum of the differences and divide by the number of games (10).
- Students are continuing to progress with finding the mean absolute deviation of a data set.

Try It

- ? "Without completing any computations, how do you expect the pitcher's statistics to change (if at all)?" Have students share their thoughts with a neighbor. Select volunteers to share their ideas with the class. Can they prove their conjectures with computations?
- **Think-Pair-Share:** After students have had individual time to read and consider this exercise, they can discuss and complete the problem with a partner. Encourage students to use precise language.

Self-Assessment for Concepts & Skills

- Look carefully at students' answers to the exercises. These will provide insight into their understanding of the difference between measures of central tendency and measures of variability.
- After completing the exercises, ask volunteers to share their thoughts with the class. Allow students to ask questions to clarify their understanding of the first two success criteria.

ELL Support

To provide support and language practice, have students work in pairs. For Exercises 4 and 5, have each pair display their answers on a whiteboard for your review. Then have two pairs form a group to discuss their answers for Exercise 3 and share with the class.

The Success Criteria Self-Assessment chart can be found in the *Student Journal* or online at *BigIdeasMath.com*.

EXAMPLE 2 Finding the Mean Absolute Deviation

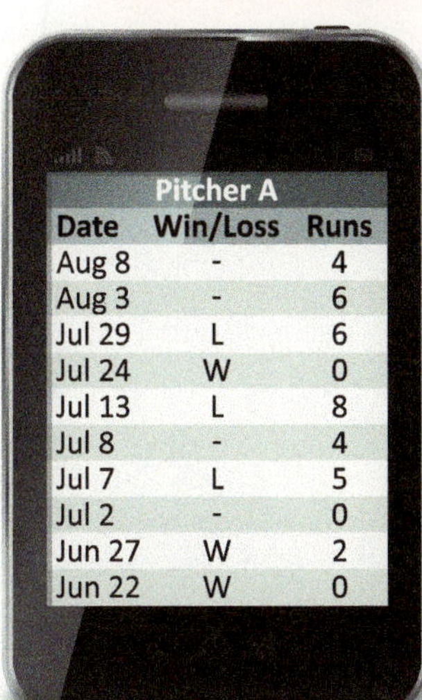

Pitcher A		
Date	Win/Loss	Runs
Aug 8	-	4
Aug 3	-	6
Jul 29	L	6
Jul 24	W	0
Jul 13	L	8
Jul 8	-	4
Jul 7	L	5
Jul 2	-	0
Jun 27	W	2
Jun 22	W	0

The smartphone shows the numbers of runs allowed by a pitcher in his last 10 starts. Find the mean, median, and mean absolute deviation of the data.

Order the runs allowed:

0, 0, 0, 2, 4, 4, 5, 6, 6, 8.

$\text{Mean} = \frac{35}{10} = 3.5$ $\quad$ $\text{Median} = \frac{4+4}{2} = 4$

Mean absolute deviation:

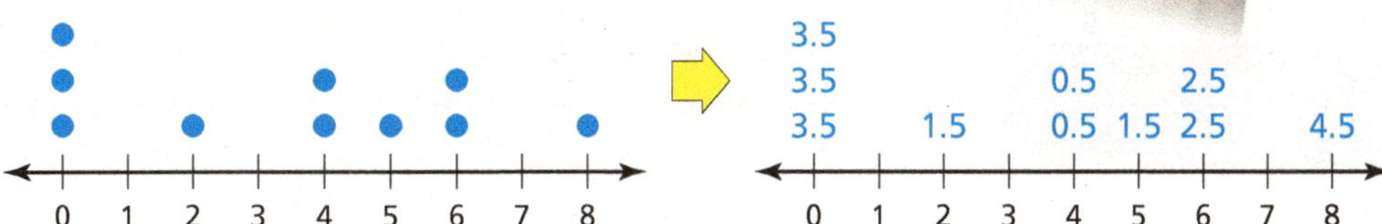

The mean absolute deviation is $\frac{24}{10} = 2.4$.

▶ The mean is 3.5, the median is 4, and the mean absolute deviation is 2.4.

Try It

2. **WHAT IF?** The pitcher allows 4 runs in the next game. How would you expect the mean absolute deviation to change? Explain.

Self-Assessment for Concepts & Skills

Solve each exercise. Then rate your understanding of the success criteria in your journal.

3. **WRITING** Explain why the variability of a data set can be described by the mean absolute deviation.

4. **FINDING THE MEAN ABSOLUTE DEVIATION** Find and interpret the mean absolute deviation of the data.

   8, 12, 4, 3, 14, 1, 9, 13

5. **WHICH ONE DOESN'T BELONG?** Which one does *not* belong with the other three? Explain your reasoning.

   range $\quad$ interquartile range

   mean $\quad$ mean absolute deviation

EXAMPLE 3 Modeling Real Life

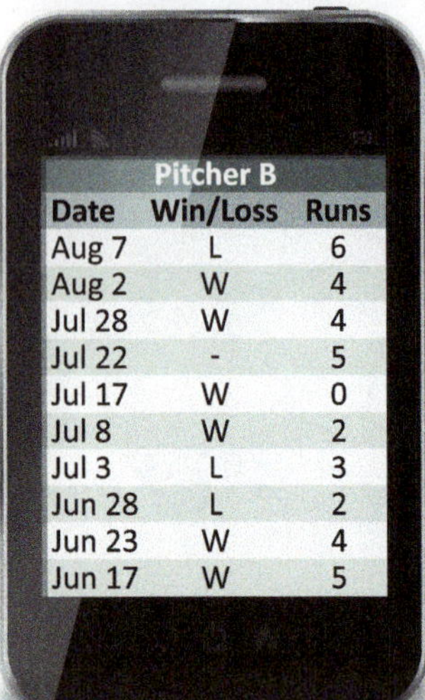

Find the mean, median, and mean absolute deviation of the numbers of runs allowed by Pitcher B in his last 10 starts. Which measure can you use to distinguish these data from the data in Example 2? What can you conclude?

Order the runs allowed for Pitcher B: 0, 2, 2, 3, 4, 4, 4, 5, 5, 6.

$$\text{Mean} = \frac{35}{10} = 3.5 \qquad \text{Median} = \frac{4+4}{2} = 4$$

Mean absolute deviation:

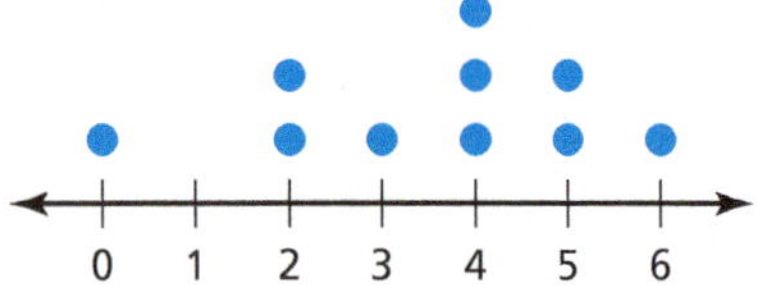

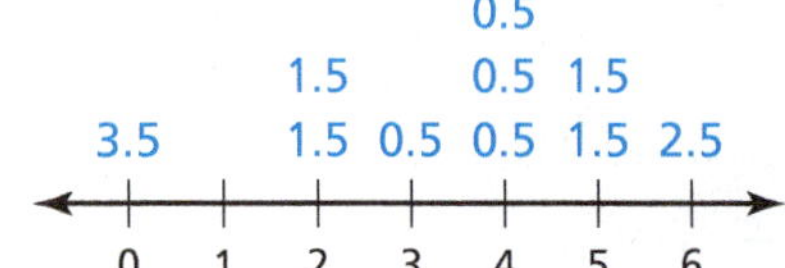

The mean absolute deviation is $\frac{14}{10} = 1.4$.

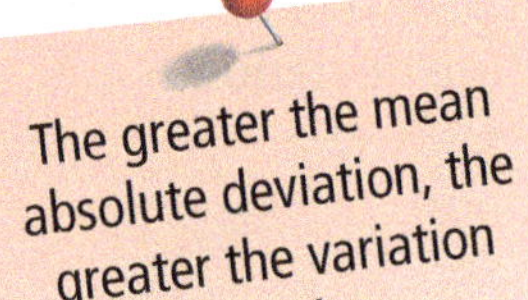

You cannot use the measures of center to distinguish the data because they are the same for each data set. The measure of variation, MAD, is 2.4 for Pitcher A and 1.4 for Pitcher B. This indicates that the data for Pitcher B has less variation.

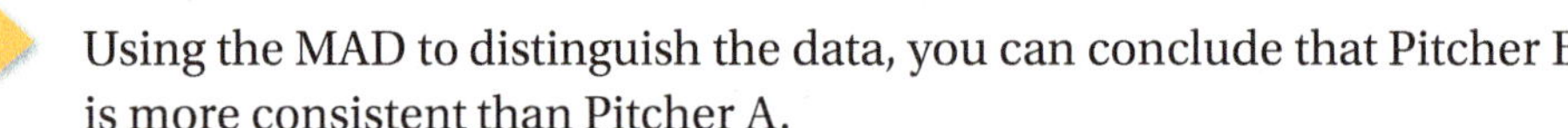

Using the MAD to distinguish the data, you can conclude that Pitcher B is more consistent than Pitcher A.

Self-Assessment for Problem Solving

Solve each exercise. Then rate your understanding of the success criteria in your journal.

Tiger Sharks	
Allison	3
Fito	6
Chuck	5
Sumila	4
Lauren	4
Antonio	2

Bear Cats	
Cherie	6
Carlos	1
Dominic	4
Jack	1
Gloria	8
Hannah	4

6. The tables show the numbers of questions answered correctly by members of two teams on a game show. Compare the mean, median, and mean absolute deviation of the numbers of correct answers for each team. What can you conclude?

7. The data set shows the numbers of books that students in your book club read last summer.

   8, 6, 11, 12, 14, 12, 11, 6, 15, 9, 7, 10, 9, 13, 5, 8

   A new student who read 18 books last summer joins the club. Is 18 an outlier? How does including this value in the data set affect the measures of center and variation? Explain.

Laurie's Notes

EXAMPLE 3

- As students consider Pitcher B's statistics, ask if they notice anything interesting. You may receive a variety of answers, such as both pitchers won their first two games or Pitcher B won more games than Pitcher A.
- After a few minutes, ask students if they wonder about anything related to the pitchers. Students may say: Which pitcher has the best average? Which pitcher is the most consistent? Guide students to questions involving the statistical measurements they have been studying.
- After discussing the problem, repeat the process used in Example 2 for Pitcher B.

? "How do Pitcher B's measures of center compare to Pitcher A's?" They are the same.

? "If the mean and median are the same, why are the dot plots different?" *Sample answer:* Pitcher A has a greater mean absolute deviation than Pitcher B, so his data is more spread out on the dot plot.

- **MP3 Construct Viable Arguments and Critique the Reasoning of Others**: Listen for an explanation that states that the mean absolute deviation (MAD) is less for Pitcher B, so there is less variation for him as a pitcher in the last 10 starts. Point out the push-pin note.

Formative Assessment Tip

Talk Moves

This technique helps facilitate classroom discussion. Prompt students to answer a question and provide adequate *Wait Time* for students to respond. After a student shares an answer, repeat the answer to emphasize and clarify what the student said. Leave room for the student to agree, disagree, or elaborate by saying, "So you are saying _____. Do I have that right?" Then ask a student to restate what another student has said to ensure that students are listening carefully. Continue asking students to evaluate, critique, and use the responses and strategies.

Self-Assessment for Problem Solving

- Allow time in class for students to practice using the problem-solving plan. Remember, some students may only be able to complete the first step.
- These exercises assess students' understanding of the success criteria, as well as their understanding of measures of central tendency and other measures of variation. Students need to see the "big picture" of statistical questions.
- Use *Talk Moves* to discuss students' answers.

The Success Criteria Self-Assessment chart can be found in the *Student Journal* or online at *BigIdeasMath.com*.

Closure

- Explain how the range and the mean absolute deviation are similar. Explain how they are different. *Sample answer:* The range and the mean absolute deviation both measure the variability of a data set. The range is determined using only two values of the data set, while the mean absolute deviation is determined using all values of the data set.

Extra Example 3

The numbers of interceptions thrown by Quarterback B in six seasons are shown. Find the mean, median, and mean absolute deviation of the data. Which measure can you use to distinguish these data from the data in Extra Example 2? What can you conclude?

Quarterback B: 12, 19, 7, 15, 8, 20

mean = 13.5; median = 13.5; MAD = 4.5; MAD; The data for Quarterback A has less variation.

Self-Assessment for Problem Solving

6. *Sample answer:* Both teams had the same mean and median, but the Tiger Sharks had a lower MAD than the Bear Cats, meaning their numbers of questions answered correctly has less variation.
7. no; The range increased by 3. The modes stayed the same. The mean, median, IQR, and MAD all increased slightly. The value 18 is on one end of the data set but is not an outlier, so the range is the only measure that is affected much.

Learning Target

Find and interpret the mean absolute deviation of a data set.

Success Criteria

- Explain how the mean absolute deviation describes the variability of a data set with a single number.
- Find the mean absolute deviation of a data set.
- Compare data sets using the mean absolute deviation to draw conclusions.

Review & Refresh

1. range = 22; IQR = 13

2. range = 26; IQR = 15.5

3.
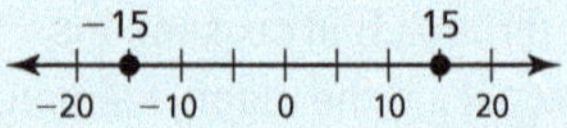

4.
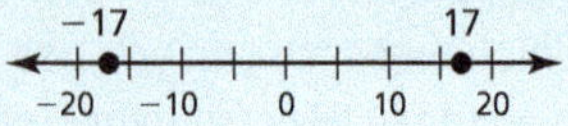

5.
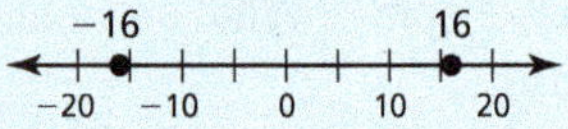

6.
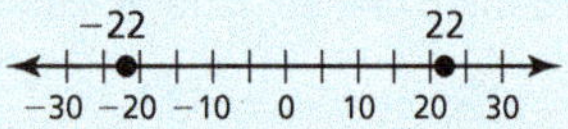

7. faces: 7; edges: 15; vertices: 10

8. $17 + q = 40$

9. $14s = 49$

10. $b - 9 = 32$

11. $\frac{36}{g} = 9$

Concepts, Skills, & Problem Solving

12. 2.8 yr

13. $7.20

14. 6; The values differ from the mean by an average of 6.

15. 4; The values differ from the mean by an average of 4.

16. 8.75; The values differ from the mean by an average of 8.75.

17. 4.4; The values differ from the mean by an average of 4.4.

18. 26; The values differ from the mean by an average of 26.

19. 2; The values differ from the mean by an average of 2.

20. $\frac{3}{20}$; The values differ from the mean by an average of $\frac{3}{20}$.

21. 1.45; The values differ from the mean by an average of 1.45.

22. yes; The calculations were done correctly.

Check out the Dynamic Assessment System.
BigIdeasMath.com

Assignment Guide and Concept Check

Scaffold assignments to support all students in their learning progression. The suggested assignments are a starting point. Continue to assign additional exercises and revisit with spaced practice to move every student toward proficiency.

Level	Assignment 1	Assignment 2
Emerging	2, 5, 6, 7, 11, 12, 15, 17, 22	20, 21, 23, 24, 25, 29
Proficient	2, 5, 6, 7, 11, 13, 16, 18, 22	20, 21, 23, 24, 25, 27, 28, 29
Advanced	2, 5, 6, 7, 11, 13, 18, 20, 22	21, 23, 25, 26, 27, 28, 29, 30

- Assignment 1 is for use after students complete the Self-Assessment for Concepts & Skills.
- Assignment 2 is for use after students complete the Self-Assessment for Problem Solving.
- The red exercises can be used as a concept check.

Review & Refresh Prior Skills

Exercises 1 and 2 Finding the Range and Finding the Interquartile Range
Exercises 3–6 Graphing Integers
Exercise 7 Finding Faces, Edges, and Vertices
Exercises 8–11 Writing Equations in One Variable

Common Errors

- **Exercises 12 and 13** Students may find the distance from the median instead of the mean. Remind students to read the problem carefully.
- **Exercises 14–21** Students may find the mean absolute deviation using the median instead of the mean. Remind students that the MAD measures the variation from the mean.

9.5 Practice

Review & Refresh

Find the range and interquartile range of the data.

1. 23, 45, 39, 34, 28, 41, 26, 33
2. 63, 53, 48, 61, 69, 63, 57, 72, 46

Graph the integer and its opposite.

3. −15
4. 17
5. 16
6. −22

7. Find the numbers of faces, edges, and vertices of the solid.

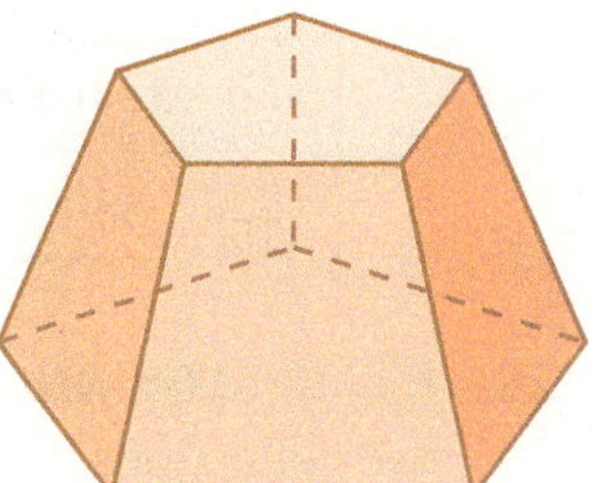

Write the word sentence as an equation.

8. 17 plus a number q is 40.
9. The product of a number s and 14 is 49.
10. The difference of a number b and 9 is 32.
11. The quotient of 36 and a number g is 9.

Concepts, Skills, & Problem Solving

FINDING DISTANCES FROM THE MEAN **Find the average distance of each data value in the set from the mean.** (See Exploration 1, p. 439.)

12. Model years of used cars on a lot: 2014, 2006, 2009, 2011, 2005
13. Prices of kites at a shop: \$7, \$20, \$9, \$35, \$12, \$15, \$7, \$10, \$20, \$25

FINDING THE MEAN ABSOLUTE DEVIATION **Find and interpret the mean absolute deviation of the data.**

14. 69, 51, 71, 77, 71, 80, 75, 63, 73
15. 94, 86, 95, 99, 88, 90
16. 46, 54, 43, 57, 50, 62, 78, 42
17. 25, 28, 20, 22, 32, 28, 35, 34, 30, 36
18. 101, 115, 124, 125, 173, 165, 170
19. 1.1, 7.5, 4.9, 0.4, 2.2, 3.3, 5.1
20. $\frac{1}{4}, \frac{5}{8}, \frac{3}{8}, \frac{3}{4}, \frac{1}{2}$
21. 4.6, 8.5, 7.2, 6.6, 5.1, 6.2, 8.1, 10.3

22. **MP YOU BE THE TEACHER** Your friend finds and interprets the mean absolute deviation of the data set 35, 40, 38, 32, 42, and 41. Is your friend correct? Explain your reasoning.

$$\text{Mean} = \frac{35 + 40 + 38 + 32 + 42 + 41}{6} = 38$$

$$\text{MAD} = \frac{3 + 2 + 0 + 6 + 4 + 3}{6} = 3$$

So, the data values differ from the mean by an average of 3.

23. MP **MODELING REAL LIFE** The data set shows the admission prices at several glass-blowing workshops.

$20, $20, $16, $12, $15, $25, $11

Find and interpret the range, interquartile range, and mean absolute deviation of the data.

24. MP **MODELING REAL LIFE** The table shows the prices of the five most-expensive and least-expensive dishes on a menu. Find the MAD of each data set. Then compare their variations.

Five Most-Expensive Dishes	Five Least-Expensive Dishes
$28 $30 $28 $39 $25	$7 $7 $10 $8 $12

25. MP **REASONING** The data sets show the years of the coins in two collections.

Your collection: 1950, 1952, 1908, 1902, 1955, 1954, 1901, 1910

Your friend's collection: 1929, 1935, 1928, 1930, 1925, 1932, 1933, 1920

Compare the measures of center and the measures of variation for each data set. What can you conclude?

Movies Watched			
7	5	14	5
6	9	10	12
15	4	5	8
11	10	9	2

26. MP **MODELING REAL LIFE** You survey students in your class about the numbers of movies they watched last month. A new student joins the class who watched 22 movies last month. Is 22 an outlier? How does including this value affect the measures of center and the measures of variation? Explain.

MP **REASONING** **Which data set would have the greater mean absolute deviation? Explain your reasoning.**

27. guesses for number of gumballs in a jar
guesses for number of baseballs in a jar

28. monthly rainfall amounts in a city
monthly amounts of water used in a home

29. MP **REASONING** Range, interquartile range, and mean absolute deviation are all measures of variation. Which measure of variation is most reliable? Explain your reasoning.

30. **DIG DEEPER!** Add and subtract the MAD from the mean in the original data set in Exercise 26.

a. What percent of the values are within one MAD of the mean? two MADs of the mean? Which values are more than twice the MAD from the mean?

b. What do you notice as you get more and more MADs away from the mean? Explain.

Common Errors

- **Exercise 28** Students may be confused about units. Discuss using the correct units for this exercise. Rainfall is most likely measured in inches, while water usage in a home is most likely measured in gallons.

Mini-Assessment

Find and interpret the mean absolute deviation of the data.

1. 7, 9, 10, 12, 12, 13, 14 2; The data values differ from the mean by an average of 2.
2. 40, 8, 29, 9, 41, 30, 45, 42 11.5; The data values differ from the mean by an average of 11.5.
3. 189, 161, 283, 499, 348 102; The data values differ from the mean by an average of 102.
4. The table shows the prices of several earbuds. Find and interpret the mean absolute deviation of the data.

Prices of Earbuds				
$3	$2	$7	$8	$2
$9	$5	$7	$3	$4

2.2; The prices of earbuds differ from the mean by an average of $2.20.

Section Resources

Surface Level	Deep Level
Resources by Chapter • Extra Practice • Reteach • Puzzle Time Student Journal • Self-Assessment • Practice Differentiating the Lesson Tutorial Videos Skills Review Handbook Skills Trainer	Resources by Chapter • Enrichment and Extension Graphic Organizers Dynamic Assessment System • Section Practice
Transfer Level	
Dynamic Assessment System • End-of-Chapter Quiz	Assessment Book • End-of-Chapter Quiz

Concepts, Skills, & Problem Solving

23. range = 14, IQR = 8, MAD = 4; The prices vary by no more than $14, the middle half of the prices vary by no more than $8, and the admission prices differ from the mean price by an average of $4.

24. The MAD of the five most-expensive dishes is 3.6. The MAD of the five least-expensive dishes is 1.76. The MAD of the five least-expensive dishes is much less than the MAD of the five most-expensive dishes.

25. See Additional Answers.

26. yes; $22 > Q_3 + 1.5\text{IQR}$. The range is most affected by including this value. The mode stays the same. The mean, median, IQR, and MAD all increased slightly.

27. *Sample answer:* The MAD for gumballs is greater than the MAD for baseballs. In general, guesses for gumballs will *deviate* more because there are many more in the jar, making it harder to guess and producing a larger range of guesses.

28. See Additional Answers.

29. *Sample answer:* MAD; The range only uses two data values from a set and is greatly affected by outliers. The interquartile range ignores outliers but also only uses two data values from a set. When calculating the mean absolute deviation of a data set, you use all of the values.

30. **a.** 50%; 87.5%; 2 and 15

b. *Sample answer:* A good portion of a data set is within one MAD of the mean and most of the data set is within two MADs of the mean. As you get more and more MADs away from the mean, the percent increases because more and more data are included in the interval.

Skills Needed

Exercise 1

- Finding the Mean
- Finding the Mean Absolute Deviation
- Finding the Median
- Ordering Numbers

Exercise 2

- Finding the Interquartile Range
- Finding the Range
- Using an Equation in Two Variables

ELL Support

You may want to discuss carnival games and ski rentals to familiarize students with the cultural settings of the exercises.

Using the Problem-Solving Plan

1. mean = 8%; median = 7%; MAD = 4%; When a person plays this carnival game, about 7% or 8% of the balloons pop. The data values differ from the mean by an average of 4%.
2. range = \$242; IQR = \$88; outlier = \$264

Performance Task

The *STEAM Video Performance Task* provides the opportunity for additional enrichment and greater depth of knowledge as students explore the mathematics of the chapter within a context tied to the chapter STEAM Video. The performance task and a detailed scoring rubric are provided at *BigIdeasMath.com*.

Laurie's Notes

Scaffolding Instruction

- The goal of this lesson is to help students become more comfortable with problem solving. These exercises combine statistical measures with prior skills from other chapters. The solution for Exercise 1 is worked out below, to help you guide students through the problem-solving plan. Use the remaining class time to have students work on the other exercise.
- **Emerging:** The goal for these students is to feel comfortable with the problem-solving plan. Allow students to work in pairs to write the beginning steps of the problem-solving plan for Exercise 2. Keep in mind that some students may only be ready to do the first step.
- **Proficient:** Students may be able to work independently or in pairs to complete Exercise 2.
- Visit each pair to review their plan for the problem. Ask students to describe their plans.

Using the Problem-Solving Plan

Exercise 1

Understand the problem. You know that each person throws the same number of darts. You are given the portion of balloons popped by each person as a fraction, a decimal, or a percent.

Make a plan. First, write each fraction and each decimal as a percent. Next, order the percents from least to greatest. Then find and interpret the mean, median, and MAD of the data.

Solve and check. Use the plan to solve the problem. Then check your solution.

- Write each fraction and each decimal as a percent.

  $\frac{2}{25} = 8\%, 0.06 = 6\%, \frac{1}{50} = 2\%, 0.12 = 12\%, 0.04 = 4\%$
- Order the percents from least to greatest.

  2%, 4%, 6%, 8%, 12%, 16%
- Find and interpret the mean, median, and MAD of the data.

  $\text{Mean} = \frac{2+4+6+8+12+16}{6} = \frac{48}{6} = 8$

  $\text{Median} = \frac{6+8}{2} + \frac{14}{2} = 7$

  Mean absolute deviation:

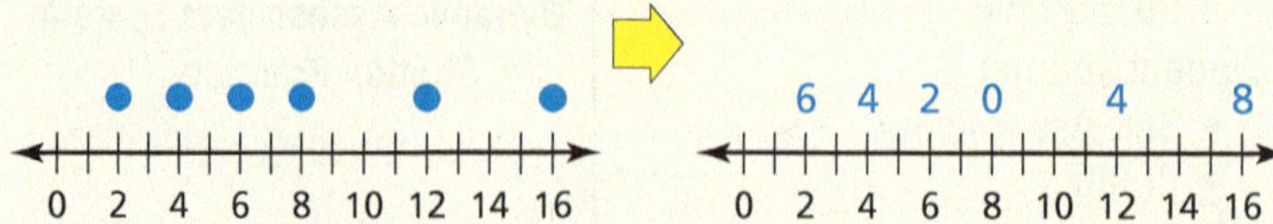

  The mean absolute deviation is $\frac{24}{6} = 4$.

  So, when a person plays this carnival game, about 7% or 8% of the balloons pop. The data values differ from the mean by an average of 4%.
- **Check:** There are no outliers in the data and the mean and median only differ by 1%, so it is reasonable that the MAD is relatively small, 4%. ✓

Connecting Concepts

Using the Problem-Solving Plan

1. Six friends play a carnival game in which a person throws darts at balloons. Each person throws the same number of darts and then records the portion of the balloons that pop. Find and interpret the mean, median, and MAD of the data.

Understand the problem.

You know that each person throws the same number of darts. You are given the portion of balloons popped by each person as a fraction, a decimal, or a percent.

Make a plan.

First, write each fraction and each decimal as a percent. Next, order the percents from least to greatest. Then find and interpret the mean, median, and MAD of the data.

Solve and check.

Use the plan to solve the problem. Then check your solution.

2. The cost c (in dollars) to rent skis at a resort for n days is represented by the equation $c = 22n$. The durations of several ski rentals are shown in the table. Find the range and interquartile range of the costs of the ski rentals. Then determine whether any of the costs are outliers.

Duration of Rentals (days)							
1	5	1	3	1	2	5	4
3	12	1	12	5	7	4	1

Performance Task

Which Measure of Center Is Best: Mean, Median, or Mode?

At the beginning of this chapter, you watched a STEAM Video called "Daylight in the Big City." You are now ready to complete the performance task related to this video, available at ***BigIdeasMath.com***. Be sure to use the problem-solving plan as you work through the performance task.

9 Chapter Review

Go to *BigIdeasMath.com* to download blank graphic organizers.

Review Vocabulary

Write the definition and give an example of each vocabulary term.

statistics, *p. 414*
statistical question, *p. 414*
mean, *p. 420*
outlier, *p. 422*
measure of center, *p. 426*
median, *p. 426*
mode, *p. 426*
measure of variation, *p. 434*
range, *p. 434*
quartiles, *p. 434*
first quartile, *p. 434*
third quartile, *p. 434*
interquartile range, *p. 434*
mean absolute deviation, *p. 440*

Graphic Organizers

You can use a **Definition and Example Chart** to organize information about a concept. Here is an example of a Definition and Example Chart for the vocabulary term ***statistical question*.**

Statistical Question: a question in which you do not expect to get a single answer

Example
What are the heights of sixth-grade students?

Example
What are the ages of people in the auditorium?

Example
What are the numbers of letters in the first names of sixth-grade students?

Choose and complete a graphic organizer to help you study the concept.

1. mean
2. outlier
3. median
4. mode
5. range
6. quartiles
7. interquartile range
8. mean absolute deviation

"Here is my Definition and Example Chart. I'll toss one of my frisbees into the surf and you see if you can fetch it."

Review Vocabulary

- As a review of the chapter vocabulary, have students revisit the vocabulary section in their *Student Journals* to fill in any missing definitions and record examples of each term.

Graphic Organizers

Sample answers:

1. Mean: the sum of the data divided by the number of data value

Example

Find the mean of the data set.
3, 5, 3, 4, 5
Mean $= \frac{3+5+3+4+5}{5} = \frac{20}{5} = 4$

Example

Find the mean of the data set.
4, 9, 11, 22, 15, 14
Mean $= \frac{4+9+11+22+15+14}{6} = \frac{75}{6} = 12.5$

Example

In your class. 4 students do not receive a weekly allowance, 8 students receive $5, 3 students receive $8, and 5 students receive $10. What is the mean weekly allowance?
Mean $= \frac{114}{20} = 5.7$ So, the mean weekly allowance is $5.70.

2. Outlier: a data value that is much greater or much less than the other values

Example

Data: 6, 10, 18, 15, 8, 0, 120, 14
Outlier: 120

Example

Data: 150, 2, 120, 134, 106, 162, 154
Outlier: 2

Example

Prices of Sandals			
$15	$29	$75	$20
$25	$19	$29	$24

Outlier: $75

3. Median: the middle of a data set. For a data set with an odd number of values, the median is the middle value. For a data set with an even number of values, the median is the mean of the two middle values.

Example

Data: 3, 4, 5, 6, 7
Median: 5

Example

Data: 9, 10, 12, 14, 20, 21
Median $= \frac{12+14}{2} = 13$

Example

Prices of Backpacks						
$25	$20	$18	$33	$45	$35	$29

Median: $29

4–8. Answers at *BigIdeasMath.com.*

List of Organizers

Available at *BigIdeasMath.com*

Definition and Example Chart

Example and Non-Example Chart

Four Square

Information Frame

Summary Triangle

About this Organizer

A **Definition and Example Chart** can be used to organize information about a concept. Students fill in the top rectangle with a term and its definition or description. Students fill in the rectangles that follow with examples to illustrate the term. Each sample answer shows three examples, but students can show more or fewer examples.

Definition and Example Charts are useful for concepts that can be illustrated with more than one type of example.

Chapter Self-Assessment

1. no; There is only one answer for the question.
2. yes; The answers will vary.
3. **a.** 20; There are 20 families who live in the city block.

   b. *Sample answer:* How many televisions does a family on the city block have?; Most families on the block have between 1 and 4 televisions.
4. 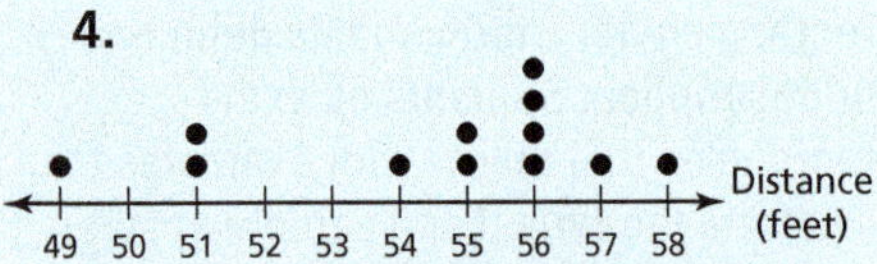

   Most of the data are clustered around 56. There is a peak at 56. There are gaps between 49 and 51 and between 51 and 54.
5. 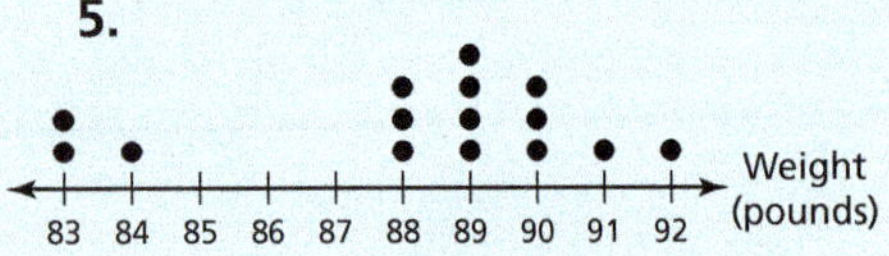

   Most of the data are clustered around 89. There is a peak at 89. There is a gap between 84 and 88.
6. *Sample answer:* 68.44 beats per minute

Chapter Self-Assessment

The Success Criteria Self-Assessment chart can be found in the *Student Journal* or online at *BigIdeasMath.com*.

ELL Support

Allow students to work in pairs for support as they complete the Chapter Self-Assessment. After students complete the first section, check for understanding by having each pair display their answers. For Exercises 1 and 2, have students indicate whether each question is a statistical question using a thumbs up for *yes* or a thumbs down for *no*. Have each pair display their dot plots for Exercises 4 and 5 on a whiteboard for your review. Have students make similar dot plots for Exercise 6 and write their answers. Use similar techniques to check the remaining sections of the Chapter Self-Assessment.

Common Errors

- **Exercises 4 and 5** Students may miss gaps in the data because they include only data values along the number line for the dot plot. Remind students to include all the integers from the least data value to the greatest data value along the number line.

Chapter Self-Assessment

As you complete the exercises, use the scale below to rate your understanding of the success criteria in your journal.

1	2	3	4
I do not understand.	I can do it with help.	I can do it on my own.	I can teach someone else.

9.1 Introduction to Statistics *(pp. 413–418)*

Learning Target: Identify statistical questions and use data to answer statistical questions.

Determine whether the question is a statistical question. Explain.

1. How many positive integers are less than 20?

2. In what month were the students in a sixth-grade class born?

3. The dot plot shows the number of televisions owned by each family on a city block.

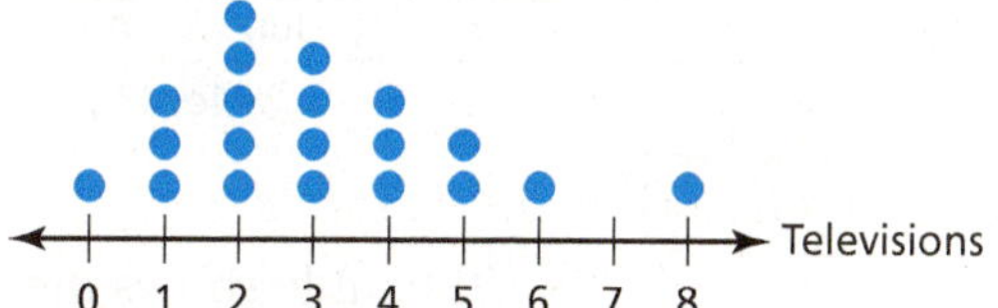

a. Find and interpret the number of data values on the dot plot.

b. Write a statistical question that you can answer using the dot plot. Then answer the question.

Display the data in a dot plot. Identify any clusters, peaks, or gaps in the data.

4.

Distances (feet)			
56	55	56	57
58	54	51	55
51	56	49	56

5.

Weights (pounds)				
83	88	89	90	89
91	89	84	90	92
90	88	89	83	88

6. You conduct a survey to answer, "What is the heart rate of a typical sixth-grade student?" The table shows the results. Use the distribution of the data to answer the question.

Heart Rates (beats per minute)					
68	69	74	68	64	67
66	70	67	68	74	69
68	69	74	70	68	70
70	68	68	69	67	64
69	65	66	68	69	67

9.2 Mean (pp. 419–424)

Learning Target: Find and interpret the mean of a data set.

7. Find the mean of the data.

Boiling Points (°F)	Arsenic	Cadmium	Mercury	Phosphorus	Potassium	Sodium
	1117	1409	675	536	1398	1621

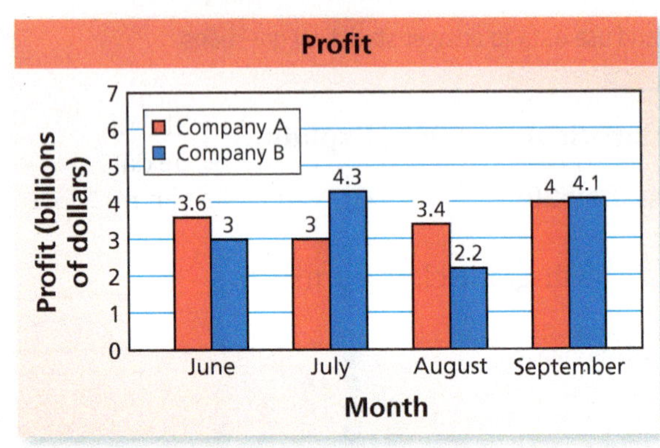

8. The double bar graph shows the monthly profit for two toy companies over a four-month period. Compare the mean monthly profits.

9. The table shows the test scores for a class of sixth-grade students. Describe how the outlier affects the mean. Then use the data to answer the statistical question, "What is the typical test score for a student in the class?"

Test Scores		
91	81	100
72	83	70
85	97	75
80	90	36

9.3 Measures of Center (pp. 425–432)

Learning Target: Find and interpret the median and mode of a data set.

Find the median and mode of the data.

10. 8, 8, 6, 8, 4, 5, 6

11. 24, 74, 61, 29, 38, 27, 68, 54

12. Find the mean, median, and mode of the data set 67, 52, 50, 99, 66, 50, and 57 with and without the outlier. Which measure does the outlier affect the most?

13. The table shows the lengths of several movies. Which measure of center best represents the data? Explain your reasoning.

Movie Lengths (minutes)		
91	112	126
142	113	112
92	144	148

14. Give an example of a data set that does not have a median. Explain why the data set does not have a median.

Common Errors

- **Exercise 7** Students may find the sum of the data values and then incorrectly divide by the maximum data value. Remind students to divide by the total number of data values to find the mean.
- **Exercises 10 and 11** Students may try to identify the median without ordering the data first. Remind students that it is essential to order the data first and then find the median. This makes finding the mode more efficient as well.
- **Exercise 12** When finding the mean of a set of data after removing an outlier, students may forget to subtract one from the denominator. Remind students that when the outlier is removed, there is one less data value.
- **Exercise 13** Students may only find the mean, median, and mode instead of making a dot plot before deciding which measure of center is the best representative. Even if students are correct, encourage them to make dot plots to check their answers. Creating a visual of the data helps students to explain why that measure of center is the best representative.

Chapter Self-Assessment

7. 1126°F

8. Company A averaged more profit than Company B.

9. The outlier lowers the mean by 4 points; *Sample answer:* The typical score for a student in the class is an 80.

10. median = 6; mode = 8

11. median = 46; no mode

12. With outlier: mean = 63, median = 57, mode = 50; Without outlier: mean = 57, median = 54.5, mode = 50; mean

13. median; The mode is less than most of the data, the mean is greater than most of the data.

14. *Sample answer:* the eye colors of the students in the classroom; The median can only be calculated for numerical data sets.

Chapter Self-Assessment

15. 77

16. 87

17. 36.5

18. 66.5

19. range = 12.5 kg; IQR = 7 kg; The weights vary by no more than 12.5 kilograms and the middle half of the weights vary by no more than 7 kilograms; The data set has no outliers.

20. no; *Sample answer:* Set 1: 1, 2, 3, 4, 5, 6; Set 2: 1, 2, 3, 4, 5, 8

21. about 1.3; The shoe sizes differ from the mean size by an average of about 1.3.

22. $26; The prices differ from the mean price by an average of $26.

23. most-expensive MAD = $5.6; least-expensive MAD = $2.4; The five least-expensive manicures have less variance in average price compared to the five most-expensive manicures.

24. yes; The mean, median, IQR, and MAD change slightly. The mode stays the same. The range increases dramatically.

Common Errors

- **Exercises 15 and 16** Students may write the range as an interval, such as 21–98, rather than as the distance between the greatest and least values, 77. Emphasize that the range is a value, not an interval.
- **Exercises 17 and 18** Students may include the median in the two halves of data when finding the quartiles. Remind students never to include the median in the upper or lower half of the data.
- **Exercises 21–23** Students may find the mean absolute deviation using the median instead of the mean. Remind students that the MAD measures the variation from the mean.

Chapter Resources

Surface Level	Deep Level
Resources by Chapter • Extra Practice • Reteach • Puzzle Time Student Journal • Practice • Chapter Self-Assessment Differentiating the Lesson Tutorial Videos Skills Review Handbook Skills Trainer Game Library	Resources by Chapter • Enrichment and Extension Graphic Organizers Game Library
Transfer Level	
STEAM Video Dynamic Assessment System • Chapter Test	Assessment Book • Chapter Tests A and B • Alternative Assessment • STEAM Performance Task

9.4 Measures of Variation (pp. 433–438)

Learning Target: Find and interpret the range and interquartile range of a data set.

Find the range of the data.

15. 45, 76, 98, 21, 52, 39

16. 95, 63, 52, 8, 93, 16, 42, 37, 62

Find the interquartile range of the data.

17. 28, 46, 25, 76, 18, 25, 47, 83, 44

18. 14, 25, 97, 55, 66, 28, 92, 38, 94

19. The table shows the weights of several adult emperor penguins. Find and interpret the range and interquartile range of the data. Then determine whether there are any outliers.

Weights (kilograms)	
25	27
36	23.5
33.5	31.25
30.75	32
24	29.25

20. Two data sets have the same interquartile range. Can you assume that the ranges of the two data sets are about the same? Give an example to justify your answer.

9.5 Mean Absolute Deviation (pp. 439–444)

Learning Target: Find and interpret the mean absolute deviation of a data set.

Find and interpret the mean absolute deviation of the data.

21.

Shoe Sizes			
6	8.5	6	9
10	7	8	9.5

22.

Prices of Tablets (dollars)				
130	150	190	100	175
120	165	140	180	190

23. The table shows the prices of the five most-expensive and least-expensive manicures given by a salon technician on a particular day. Find the MAD of each data set. Then compare their variations.

Five Most-Expensive Manicures	Five Least-Expensive Manicures
\$58 \$52 \$70 \$49 \$56	\$10 \$10 \$15 \$10 \$15

24. You record the lengths of songs you stream. The next song is 276 seconds long. Is 276 an outlier? How does including this value affect the measures of center and the measures of variation? Explain.

Song Lengths (seconds)					
233	219	163	213	224	208
225	220	222	240	228	219
260	249	209	236	206	

Practice Test

Find the mean, median, mode, range, and interquartile range of the data.

1. 5, 6, 4, 24, 10, 6, 9, 8

2. 46, 27, 94, 56, 53, 65, 43

3. 32, 58, 19, 36, 44, 57, 11, 26, 74

4. 36, 24, 49, 32, 37, 28, 38, 40, 39

Find and interpret the mean absolute deviation of the data.

5.

Distances Driven (miles)			
312	286	196	201
158	225	206	192

6.

Prices of Sunglasses (dollars)				
15	8	19	20	18
20	22	14	10	15

7. You conduct a survey to answer, "How many minutes does it take a typical sixth-grade student to run a mile?" The table shows the results. Use the distribution of the data to answer the question.

Times (minutes)			
8.25	9	10.25	8.75
8.5	8.25	9.25	8.5
7.75	8.5	8.75	7.5

Weights (pounds)				
81	81	80	82	81
83	76	83	76	80
75	83	94	82	81

8. The table shows the weights of Alaskan malamute dogs at a veterinarian's office. Which measure of center best represents the weight of an Alaskan malamute? Explain your reasoning.

9. The table shows the numbers of guests at a hotel on different days.

Numbers of Guests					
66	58	90	57	63	55
60	62	56	54	72	

a. Find the range and interquartile range of the data.

b. Use the interquartile range to identify the outlier(s) in the data set. Find the range and interquartile range of the data set without the outlier(s). Which measure did the outlier or outliers affect more?

10. The data sets show the numbers of hours worked each week by two people for several weeks.

Person A: 9, 18, 12, 6, 9, 21, 3, 12

Person B: 12, 18, 15, 16, 14, 12, 15, 18

Compare the measures of center and the measures of variation for each data set. What can you conclude?

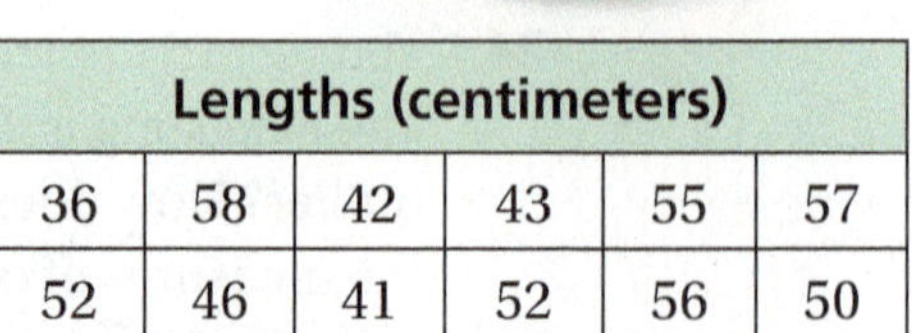

11. The table shows the lengths of several bearded dragons captured for a study. Find the mean, median, and mode of the data in centimeters and in inches. How does converting to inches affect the mean, median, and mode?

Lengths (centimeters)					
36	58	42	43	55	57
52	46	41	52	56	50

Practice Test Item References

Practice Test Questions	Section to Review
7	9.1
1, 2, 3, 4	9.2
1, 2, 3, 4, 8, 11	9.3
1, 2, 3, 4, 9	9.4
5, 6, 10	9.5

Test-Taking Strategies

Remind students to quickly look over the entire test before they start so that they can budget their time. Students should jot down the definitions of mean, median, mode, range, interquartile range, and mean absolute deviation on the back of the test before they start. By doing this, students will not become confused when they are under pressure. Have them use the **Stop** and **Think** strategy before they write their answers.

Common Errors

- **Exercises 1–4** Students may try to identify the median without ordering the data first. Remind students that it is essential to order the data first and then find the median. This makes finding the mode more efficient as well.
- **Exercises 1–4** Students may write the range as an interval, such as 4–24, rather than as the distance between the greatest and least values, 20. Emphasize that the range is a value, not an interval.
- **Exercises 1–4** Students may include the median in the two halves of data when finding the quartiles. Remind students never to include the median in the upper or lower half of the data.
- **Exercises 5 and 6** Students may find the mean absolute deviation using the median instead of the mean. Remind students that the MAD measures the variation from the mean.
- **Exercise 8** Students may only find the mean, median, and mode instead of making a dot plot before deciding which measure of center is the best representative. Even if students are correct, encourage them to make dot plots to check their answers. Creating a visual of the data helps students to explain why that measure of center is the best representative.

Practice Test

1. mean = 9; median = 7; mode = 6; range = 20; IQR = 4
2. mean ≈ 54.86; median = 53; no mode; range = 67; IQR = 22
3. mean ≈ 39.7; median = 36; no mode; range = 63; IQR = 35
4. mean = 35.9; median = 37; no mode; range = 25; IQR = 9.5
5. about 39.3 mi; The distances driven differ from the mean distance by an average of about 39.3 miles.
6. \$3.70; The prices of sunglasses differ from the mean price by an average of \$3.70.
7. about 8.5 minutes
8. The mean, median, and mode are all good representations of the data because they are all about the same.
9. **a.** range = 36 guests; IQR = 10 guests

   b. 90 guests; range = 18; IQR = 7; range
10. Person A's hours: mean = 11.25 h, median = 10.5 h, modes = 9 h, 12 h, range = 18 h, IQR = 7.5 h, MAD = 4.5 h; Person B's hours: mean = 15 h, median = 15 h, modes = 12 h, 15 h, 18 h, range = 6 h, IQR = 4 h, MAD = 1.75 h; *Sample answer:* The measures of center for Person B's hours are greater than the measures of center for Person A's hours. The measures of variation for Person B's hours are less than the measures of variation for Person A's hours.
11. centimeters: mean = 49 cm, median = 51 cm, mode = 52 cm; inches: mean = 19.29 in., median = 20.08 in., mode = 20.47 in.; *Sample answer:* The mean, median, and mode are all divided by 2.54.

Test-Taking Strategies

Available at *BigIdeasMath.com*

After Answering Easy Questions, Relax

Answer Easy Questions First

Estimate the Answer

Read All Choices before Answering

Read Question before Answering

Solve Directly or Eliminate Choices

Solve Problem before Looking at Choices

Use Intelligent Guessing

Work Backwards

About this Strategy

When taking a multiple-choice test, be sure to read each question carefully and thoroughly. Sometimes you may not know the answer. So…guess intelligently! Look at the choices and choose the ones that are reasonable answers.

Cumulative Practice

1. D
2. 16
3. I
4. A

Item Analysis

1. **A.** The student incorrectly associates *rises* with a negative integer.

   B. The student incorrectly associates *ascends* with a negative integer.

   C. The student incorrectly associates *earn* with a negative integer.

   D. Correct answer

2. **Gridded Response:** Correct answer: 16

   Common error: The student multiplies the length and width to get $367\frac{1}{2}$ but forgets to divide 5880 by $367\frac{1}{2}$.

3. **F.** The student multiplies by $\frac{2}{3}$ instead of $\frac{3}{2}$.

   G. The student subtracts $\frac{2}{3}$ instead of multiplying by $\frac{3}{2}$.

   H. The student adds $\frac{2}{3}$ instead of multiplying by $\frac{3}{2}$.

   I. Correct answer

4. **A.** Correct answer

   B. The student does not list the data in order and finds the median using 12 and 3, getting 7.5, which is less than the mean of 8.

   C. The student does not correctly determine that the mode is 10 and instead incorrectly determines a value that is less than 8.

   D. The student does not list the data in order and finds the range using 7 and 6, getting 1, which is less than the mean of 8.

Cumulative Practice

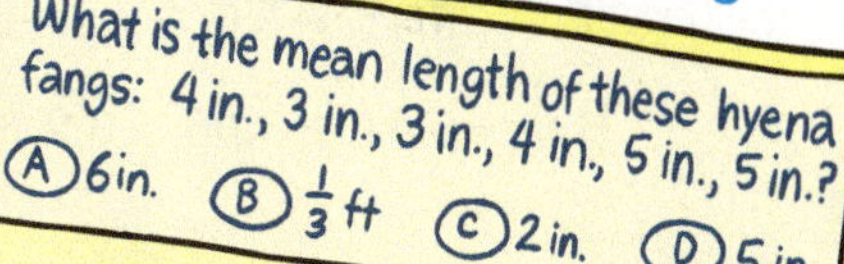

"The mean can't be 6 or 2 or 5 inches. So, you can use intelligent guessing to find that the answer is $\frac{1}{3}$ ft, or 4 in."

1. Which statement can be represented by a negative integer?

A. The temperature rises 15 degrees.

B. A hot-air balloon ascends 450 yards.

C. You earn \$50 completing chores.

D. A submarine submerges 260 feet.

2. What is the height h (in inches) of the prism?

Volume $= 5880$ in.^{3}

3. Which is the solution of the inequality $\frac{2}{3}x < 6$?

F. $x < 4$

G. $x < 5\frac{1}{3}$

H. $x < 6\frac{2}{3}$

I. $x < 9$

4. The number of hours that each of six students spent reading last week is shown in the bar graph.

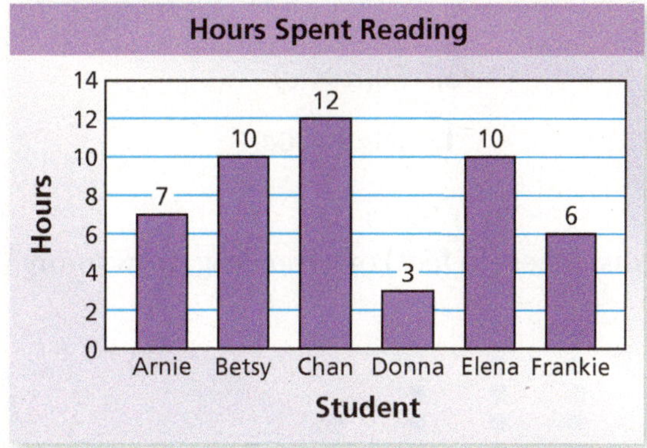

For the data in the bar graph, which measure is the *least*?

A. mean

B. median

C. mode

D. range

5. Which list of numbers is in order from least to greatest?

F. $-5.41, -3.6, -3.2, -3.06, -1$

G. $-1, -3.06, -3.2, -3.6, -5.41$

H. $-5.41, -3.06, -3.2, -3.6, -1$

I. $-1, -3.6, -3.2, -3.06, -5.41$

6. What is the mean absolute deviation of the data shown in the dot plot, rounded to the nearest tenth?

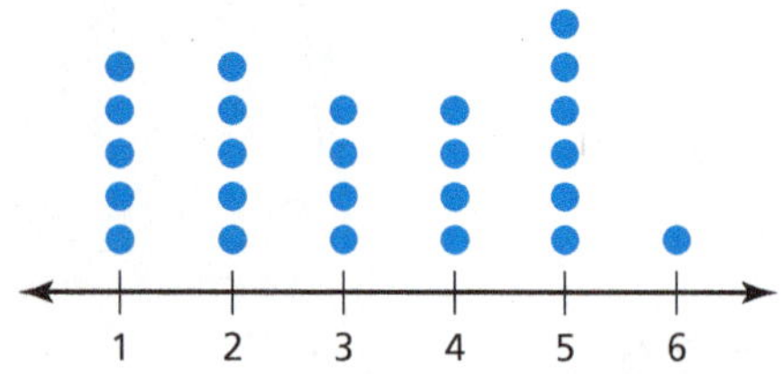

A. 1.4

B. 3

C. 3.2

D. 5

7. A family wants to buy tickets to a theme park. There are separate ticket prices for adults and children.

Roller-Coaster World!

Tickets: \$30 per adult
\$20 per child

Which expression represents the total cost (in dollars) for a adult tickets and c child tickets?

F. $600(a + c)$

G. $50(a \times c)$

H. $30a + 20c$

I. $30a \times 20c$

8. The dot plot shows the leap distances (in feet) of a tree frog. How many leaps were recorded?

0 1 2 3 4 5 6 7 8

Distance (feet)

Item Analysis (continued)

5. **F.** Correct answer

   G. The student orders the numbers from greatest to least.

   H. The student thinks −3.06 is less than −3.6.

   I. The student orders incorrectly.

6. **A.** Correct answer

   B. The student confuses the median for the mean absolute deviation.

   C. The student confuses the mean for the mean absolute deviation.

   D. The student confuses the mode for the mean absolute deviation.

7. **F.** The student multiplies the product of the prices by the sum of the variables.

   G. The student multiplies the sum of the prices by the product of the variables.

   H. Correct answer

   I. The student finds the product instead of the sum.

8. **Gridded Response:** Correct answer: 20

   Common error: The student thinks the question is asking for the range of the leap distances and gets 6.

Cumulative Practice

5. F
6. A
7. H
8. 20

Cumulative Practice

9. C

10. G

11. B

12. *Sample answer:* 2, 3, 9, 10, 11; The median of 9 was used to create the central number of the set, then the rest of the data were created such that the calculated mean was 7.

Item Analysis (continued)

9. **A.** The student uses 0.6 for a instead of 6 and 0.14 for b instead of 14.

B. The student uses 6 for the hundredths digit in $0.8a$ and 14 for the thousandths and ten-thousandths digits in $0.02b$ instead of multiplying the coefficients by the values of the variables, and then finds $0.86 + 0.0214$.

C. Correct answer

D. The student finds the sum of the coefficients and the sum of the values of the variables, and then finds the product of these two sums.

10. **F.** The student does not recognize that the Distributive Property is used to write the expression in the second line.

G. Correct answer

H. The student does not recognize that the Multiplication Property of One is used to find the final answer.

I. The student does not recognize that the Commutative Property of Multiplication is used in the first line.

11. **A.** The student incorrectly thinks that points in Quadrant IV have negative x-coordinates.

B. Correct answer

C. The student incorrectly thinks that points in Quadrant IV have negative x-coordinates. The student also switches the x- and y-coordinates.

D. The student switches the x- and y-coordinates.

12. **2 points** The student's work demonstrates a thorough understanding of analyzing sets of data with respect to the mean and median. The student correctly determines a data set that has a mean of 7 and a median of 9. One possible answer is the data set of 2, 3, 9, 10, and 11. The student clearly explains the steps used and the method is unambiguous. The student correctly shows that the data set has a mean of 7 and a median of 9.

1 point The student's work demonstrates a partial but limited understanding of analyzing sets of data with respect to the mean and median. The student shows some knowledge of how to determine the mean and/or median, but does not successfully answer the question.

0 points The student provides no response, a completely incorrect or incomprehensible response, or a response that demonstrates insufficient understanding of analyzing sets of data with respect to the mean and median.

9. What is the value of the expression when $a = 6$ and $b = 14$?

$$0.8a + 0.02b$$

A. 0.4828 **B.** 0.8814

C. 5.08 **D.** 16.4

10. Which property was *not* used to simplify the expression?

$$\begin{aligned} 0.3 \times y + y \times 0.7 &= y \times 0.3 + y \times 0.7 \\ &= y \times (0.3 + 0.7) \\ &= y \times 1 \\ &= y \end{aligned}$$

F. Distributive Property

G. Associative Property of Addition

H. Multiplication Property of One

I. Commutative Property of Multiplication

11. What are the coordinates of Point P?

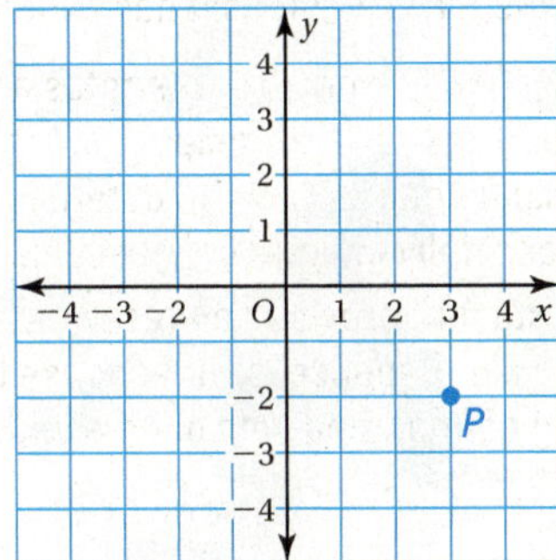

A. $(-3, -2)$ **B.** $(3, -2)$

C. $(-2, -3)$ **D.** $(-2, 3)$

12. Create a data set with 5 numbers that has the following measures.

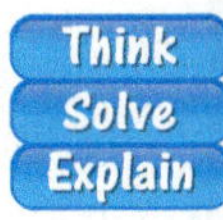

- a mean of 7
- a median of 9

Explain how you created your data set.

10 Data Displays

Chapter Learning Target:
Understand data displays.

Chapter Success Criteria:

- I can construct a data display.
- I can interpret data in a data display.
- I can choose the appropriate measures of center and variation to describe a data set.
- I can compare data sets.

Laurie's Notes

Chapter 10 Overview

This is the last chapter of the book and certainly one of my favorites! Students often feel the same way. They are interested in the variety of data sets and enjoy the opportunity to think about the different ways in which some data sets can be displayed.

Students should have a familiarity with bar graphs, dot plots, line graphs, and pictographs. In this chapter, they will extend their understanding of data displays to stem-and-leaf plots, histograms, and box-and-whisker plots.

Plant Heights

Stem	Leaf
0	1 2 4 5 6 8 9
1	1 1 1 2 3 5
2	2
3	2

Key: 1 | 5 = 15 inches

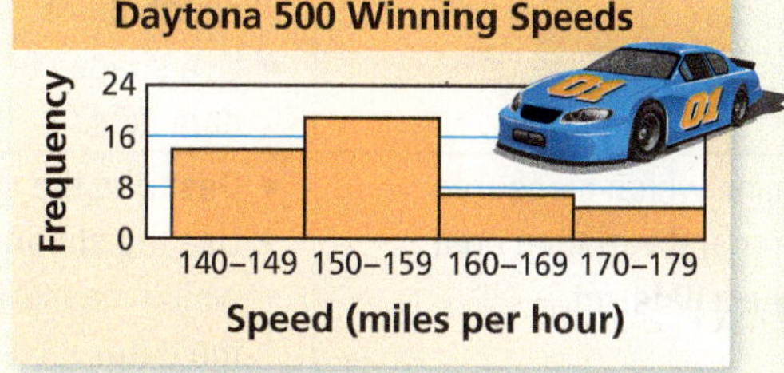

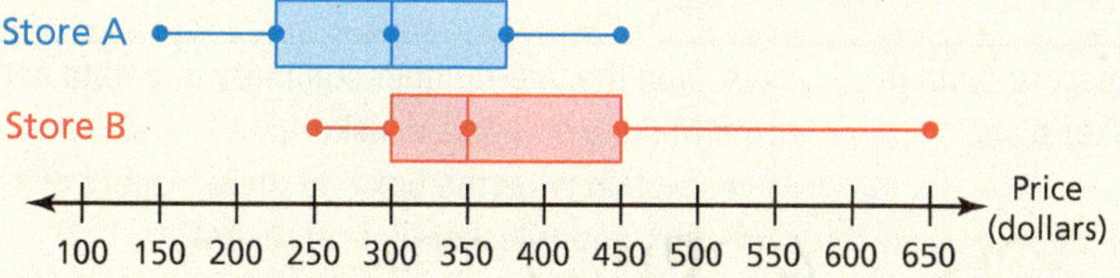

In choosing a type of data display, students must first consider the type of data they have and what would be an appropriate way to display it. The numbers of hours of sleep on seven consecutive nights could be displayed in a dot plot or bar graph, but there would likely be little to describe if it were plotted using any of the new data displays in this chapter. The height (in inches) of students in a class could be plotted in any of the displays.

It is important to remember how the previous chapter is integrated into this chapter. Students should be able to look at the three data displays above and talk about the measures of center, meaning what is the *typical* plant height or the *typical* winning speed at the Daytona 500? Similarly, students should be able to describe the outlier in the plant heights and the range and interquartile range of prices at each store in the box-and-whisker plot. What does the distribution of the data look like? Is it skewed? Is it symmetric?

There are opportunities to use graphing utilities and calculators in completing the work of this chapter. Resources can be found online at *BigIdeasMath.com*.

Suggested Pacing

Chapter Opener	1 Day
Section 1	1 Day
Section 2	2 Days
Section 3	2 Days
Section 4	2 Days
Section 5	2 Days
Connecting Concepts	1 Day
Chapter Review	1 Day
Chapter Test	1 Day
Total Chapter 10	13 Days
Year-to-Date	155 Days

Chapter Learning Target

Understand data displays.

Chapter Success Criteria

- Construct a data display.
- Interpret data in a data display.
- Choose the appropriate measures of center and variation to describe a data set.
- Compare data sets.

Chapter 10 Learning Targets and Success Criteria

Section	Learning Target	Success Criteria
10.1 Stem-and-Leaf Plots	Display and interpret data in stem-and-leaf plots.	• Explain how to choose stems and leaves of a data set. • Make and interpret a stem-and-leaf plot. • Use a stem-and-leaf plot to describe the distribution of a data set.
10.2 Histograms	Display and interpret data in histograms.	• Explain how to draw a histogram. • Make and interpret a histogram. • Determine whether a question can be answered using a histogram.
10.3 Shapes of Distributions	Describe and compare shapes of distributions.	• Explain what it means for a distribution to be skewed left, skewed right, or symmetric. • Use data displays to describe shapes of distributions. • Use shapes of distributions to compare data sets.
10.4 Choosing Appropriate Measures	Determine which measures of center and variation best describe a data set.	• Describe the shape of a distribution. • Use the shape of a distribution to determine which measure of center best describes the data. • Use the shape of a distribution to determine which measure of variation best describes the data.
10.5 Box-and-Whisker Plots	Display and interpret data in box-and-whisker plots.	• Find the five-number summary of a data set. • Make a box-and-whisker plot. • Explain what the box and the whiskers of a box-and-whisker plot represent. • Compare data sets represented by box-and-whisker plots.

Progressions

Through the Grades		
Grade 5	**Grade 6**	**Grade 7**
• Use line plots to solve problems involving operations on fractions.	• Understand that data used to answer statistical questions has a distribution that can be described by center, spread, and shape. • Display data on number lines, including dot plots, stem-and-leaf plots, histograms, and box-and-whisker plots. • Use measures of center to summarize all values in a data set with a single number, and use measures of variation to summarize how all of the values in a data set vary with a single number. • Choose appropriate measures of center and variation based on shape.	• Understand representative samples (random samples) and populations. • Use samples to draw inferences about populations. • Compare two populations from random samples using measures of center and variability.

Through the Chapter					
Standard	**10.1**	**10.2**	**10.3**	**10.4**	**10.5**
6.SP.A.2 Understand that a set of data collected to answer a statistical question has a distribution which can be described by its center, spread, and overall shape.	●		●	●	★
6.SP.B.4 Display numerical data in plots on a number line, including dot plots, histograms, and box plots.		●	●		★
6.SP.B.5c Giving quantitative measures of center (median and/or mean) and variability (interquartile range and/or mean absolute deviation), as well as describing any overall pattern and any striking deviations from the overall pattern with reference to the context in which the data were gathered.					★
6.SP.B.5d Relating the choice of measures of center and variability to the shape of the data distribution and the context in which the data were gathered.				★	

Key

▲ = preparing ★ = complete

● = learning ■ = extending

Laurie's Notes

STEAM Video

Before the Video

- To introduce the STEAM Video, read aloud the first paragraph of Choosing a Dog and discuss the prompt with your students.
- "Describe a real-life situation where knowing an animal's growth rate can be useful."

During the Video

- The video shows Alex and Tony discussing choosing a dog for a pet.
- ? Pause the video at 1:44 and ask, "How much do most dogs weigh when they are born?" less than 1 pound
- ? Continue to play the video until 2:20 and then pause to ask, "What type of data display are Alex and Tory using to organize their data?" a stem-and-leaf plot
- Watch the remainder of the video.

After the Video

- Have students work with a partner to answer Questions 1 and 2.
- As students discuss and answer the questions, listen for understanding of interpreting stem-and-leaf plots.

Performance Task

- Use this information to spark students' interest and promote thinking about real-life problems.
- ? Ask, "Why might someone be interested in knowing the sizes of dogs at a shelter?"
- After completing the chapter, students will have gained the knowledge needed to complete "Classifying Dog Breeds by Size."

STEAM Video

1. *Sample answer:* At 3 months old, most dogs are just under half their adult weight. At 6 months old, most dogs are just over half their adult weight.
2. *Sample answer:* After 9 months, most dog weights will be between 60% and 80% of the dog's adult weight. After 1 year, most dog weights will be between 80% and 90% of the dog's adult weight.

Performance Task

to determine the amount of food needed

Mathematical Practices

Students have opportunities to develop aspects of the mathematical practices throughout the chapter. Here are some examples.

1. **Make Sense of Problems and Persevere in Solving Them**
   10.2 Math Practice note, *p. 464*
2. **Reason Abstractly and Quantitatively**
   10.2 Self-Assessment 5, *p. 466*
3. **Construct Viable Arguments and Critique the Reasoning of Others**
   10.3 Exercise 14, *p. 476*
4. **Model with Mathematics**
   10.4 Exercise 16, *p. 482*
5. **Use Appropriate Tools Strategically**
   10.5 Exercise 35, *p. 490*
6. **Attend to Precision**
   10.2 Math Practice note, *p. 463*
7. **Look for and Make Use of Structure**
   10.5 Exercise 33, *p. 490*
8. **Look for and Express Regularity in Repeated Reasoning**
   10.1 Math Practice note, *p. 460*

STEAM Video

Choosing a Dog

Different animals grow at different rates. Given a group of puppies, describe an experiment that you can perform to compare their growth rates. Describe a real-life situation where knowing an animal's growth rate can be useful.

Watch the STEAM Video "Choosing a Dog." Then answer the following questions.

1. Using Alex and Tony's stem-and-leaf plots below, describe the weights of most dogs at 3 months of age and 6 months of age.

3 months

Stem	Leaf
2	9
3	4
4	0 0 1 2 4 6 7 8 8
5	3

Key: 3 | 4 = 34% of adult weight

6 months

Stem	Leaf
5	7 8
6	1 1 3 4 5 5 5 6 7
7	3

Key: 6 | 4 = 64% of adult weight

2. Make predictions about how the stem-and-leaf plot will look after 9 months and after 1 year.

Performance Task

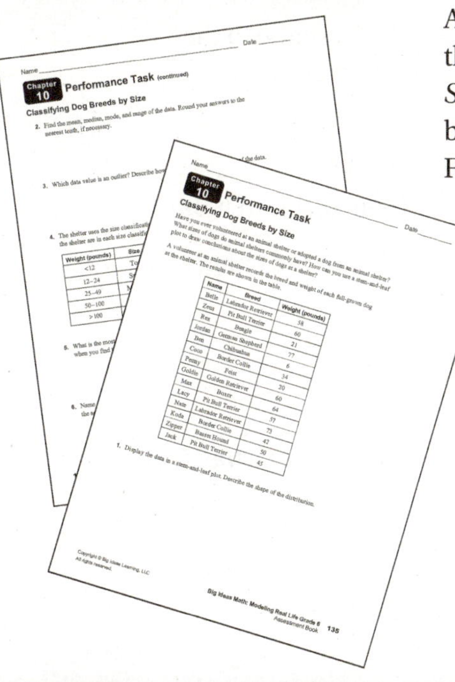

Name ________ Date ________

Chapter 10 **Performance Task**

Classifying Dog Breeds by Size

Have you ever volunteered at an animal shelter or adopted a dog from an animal shelter? What sizes of dogs do animal shelters commonly have? How can you use a stem-and-leaf plot to draw conclusions about the sizes of dogs at a shelter?

A volunteer at an animal shelter records the breed and weight of each full-grown dog at the shelter. The results are shown in the table.

Name	Breed	Weight (pounds)
Belle	Labrador Retriever	58
Zeus	Pit Bull Terrier	60
Rex	Beagle	21
Jordan	German Shepherd	77
Ben	Chihuahua	6
Coco	Border Collie	34
Penny	Feist	20
Goldie	Golden Retriever	60
Max	Boxer	64
Lacy	Pit Bull Terrier	57
Nate	Labrador Retriever	73
Koda	Border Collie	42
Zipper	Basset Hound	50
Jack	Pit Bull Terrier	45

1. Display the data in a stem-and-leaf plot. Describe the shape of the distribution.

Copyright © Big Ideas Learning, LLC All rights reserved.

Big Ideas Math: Modeling Real Life Grade 6 Assessment Book 135

Name ________ Date ________

Chapter 10 **Performance Task** (continued)

Classifying Dog Breeds by Size

2. Find the mean, median, mode, and range of the data. Round your answers to the nearest tenth, if necessary.

3. Which data value is an outlier? Describe how

4. The shelter uses the size classificati the shelter are in each size classific

Weight (pounds)	Size
<12	To
12–24	S
25–49	M
50–100	
>100	

5. What is the most when you find

6. Name the

Classifying Dog Breeds by Size

After completing this chapter, you will be able to use the concepts you learned to answer the questions in the *STEAM Video Performance Task*. You will be given names, breeds, and weights of full-grown dogs at a shelter. For example:

Name	Breed	Weight
Jordan	German shepherd	77 pounds
Ben	Chihuahua	6 pounds
Koda	Border collie	42 pounds

You will use a data display to make conclusions about the sizes of dogs at the shelter. Why might someone be interested in knowing the sizes of dogs at a shelter?

Getting Ready for Chapter 10

Chapter Exploration

Work with a partner. A famous data set was collected in Scotland in the mid-1800s. It contains the chest sizes (in inches) of 5738 men in the Scottish Militia.

Chest Size	Number of Men
33	3
34	18
35	81
36	185
37	420
38	749
39	1073
40	1079
41	934
42	658
43	370
44	92
45	50
46	21
47	4
48	1

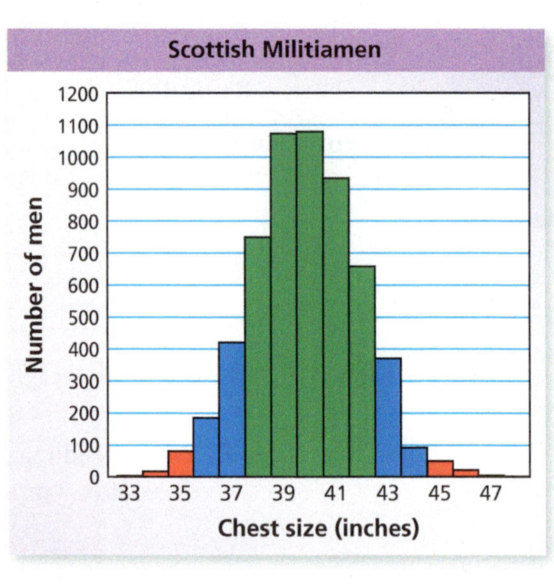

1. Describe the shape of the bar graph shown above.

2. Which of the following data sets have a bar graph that is similar in shape to the bar graph shown above? Assume the sample is selected randomly from the population. Explain your reasoning.

   a. the heights of 500 women
   b. the ages of 500 dogs
   c. the last digit of 500 phone numbers
   d. the weights of 500 newborn babies

3. Describe two other real-life data sets, one that is similar in shape to the bar graph shown above and one that is not.

Vocabulary

The following vocabulary terms are defined in this chapter. Think about what each term might mean and record your thoughts.

stem-and-leaf plot
box-and-whisker plot
frequency table
five-number summary

Laurie's Notes

Chapter Exploration

- Students should be familiar with making dot plots, bar graphs, double bar graphs, and pictographs from the previous chapter and previous courses. They have used data displays to identify clusters, peaks, and gaps in data.
- Have partners complete Exercise 1 and then share their descriptions with the class. Students may say that the sides are "balanced" or "the same." Lead students to describing the shape as almost symmetric.
- After students complete Exercise 2, discuss each sample as a class. Students may have different answers for some of the samples. Listen to students' reasoning to see if their answers are justified.
- For Exercise 3, have each pair share their answers with the class. Allow others to ask questions for clarification.

Vocabulary

- These terms represent some of the vocabulary that students will encounter in Chapter 10. Discuss the terms as a class.
- Where have students heard the term *frequency table* outside of a math classroom? In what contexts? Students may not be able to write the actual definition, but they may write phrases associated with a *frequency table*.
- Allowing students to discuss these terms now will prepare them for understanding the terms as they are presented in the chapter.
- When students encounter a new definition, encourage them to write in their *Student Journals*. They will revisit these definitions during the Chapter Review.

ELL Support

Explain that the bar graph shown is one way to show data (statistical information) visually. Point out that the vocabulary terms name different ways to represent data. Discuss each term and have students guess their meanings based on what they already know. For example, students should understand that in this context a table is a type of chart, not a type of furniture. If they know that the word *frequency* means how often something happens, students should guess that a frequency table shows how often a data value occurs.

Topics for Review

- Analyzing Bar Graphs
- Dot Plots
- Finding Percents
- Interquartile Range
- Measures of Center
- Measures of Variation
- Multiplying Fractions and Whole Numbers
- Ordering Whole Numbers and Integers
- Outliers
- Quartiles

Chapter Exploration

1. *Sample answer:* The shape of the graph looks like a bell curve, centered near the value of 40, with a range of values from 33 to 48.
2. a, d; *Sample answer:* Most of the values will be close to the average of the population.
3. *Sample answer:* similar: shoe size of 1000 males; not similar: household income in the United States

Learning Target

Display and interpret data in stem-and-leaf plots.

Success Criteria

- Explain how to choose stems and leaves of a data set.
- Make and interpret a stem-and-leaf plot.
- Use a stem-and-leaf plot to describe the distribution of a data set.

Warm Up

Cumulative, vocabulary, and prerequisite skills practice opportunities are available in the *Resources by Chapter* or at *BigIdeasMath.com.*

ELL Support

Discuss the meaning of *stem-and-leaf plot* by having students examine each word in the term. They should know that a plot can be a chart in which information is organized. Ask if students know the meanings of *stem* and *leaf.* If necessary, explain their meanings using a simple drawing of a plant. Point to the stem-and-leaf plot of the ages of first ladies and ask students to identify the "stems" and the "leaves."

Exploration 1

a. tens digit of the ages; ones digit of the ages

b. the left column; the right column; *Sample answer:* The right column has more values resembling the leaves on the stems of a plant.

c. See Additional Answers.

d. *Sample answer:* In what age range were there more first ladies, 40s or 50s?

Laurie's Notes

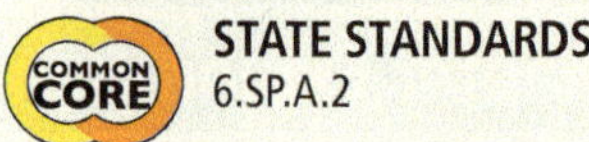

Preparing to Teach

- Students know how to use dot plots to display and analyze data. Now they will add another data display to their toolkits, stem-and-leaf plot.
- **MP4 Model with Mathematics:** Students will construct stem-and-leaf plots to represent and describe features of a data set, including measures of center and measures of variation.

Motivate

- Make a **stem-and-leaf plot** using sticky notes. As students enter, hand each one a sticky note. On the board draw a vertical line and use **stems** of 0, 1, 2, and 3. Ask students to write down the day of the month they were born, making their numbers large and dark enough to be seen from a distance.
- Ask those students born before the 10th of the month to come forward and put their sticky notes in a row adjacent to the stem of 0.
- Repeat for each of the stems; 10th–19th, 20th–29th, and 30th–31st.
- ? "What observations can you make about the data?" Answers will vary. Most likely there are fewer in the 30s; you would expect randomness and balanced distribution over other three stems, but it might not be!
- Do not sort—this will be done later. Explain that now students will explore a new type of plot similar to what they have made with their sticky notes.

Exploration 1

- A stem-and-leaf plot is fairly simple for students to understand. The Motivate should give them a basic understanding of how to construct one.
- **FYI:** The ages given are how old these women were when they *first* became first ladies, which was not always on the day of inauguration.
- For instance, Frances and Grover Cleveland were married on June 2, 1886, during his first term. Also, Woodrow Wilson's second wife, Edith, is not listed. His first wife, Ellen, died while he was in office.
- Students find this data set interesting. Most students know that you must be at least 35 years old to run for president, so they realize that some first ladies were quite young.
- ? "What do the stems represent?" the tens digit of the first ladies' ages
- Note that the **leaves** are in numerical order. Students may not notice this.
- When students have finished, display a completed plot. Have a few students share their answers to part (d). This begins work on the first success criterion.
- **Big Idea:** A stem-and-leaf plot is similar to a dot plot, but the stem-and-leaf plot gives additional information. This stem-and-leaf plot uses the ones digit of the data values instead of dots, so you can see the distribution within each group of ten.
- Return to the sticky note plot from the Motivate. Ask a volunteer to sort the data. Then ask students what descriptors for the data are easy to identify from the stem-and-leaf plot. *Sample answers:* range, median, mode
- **Extension:** Have students research the ages of the presidents on their first inauguration days and make a back-to-back stem-and-leaf plot of the presidents' and first ladies' ages. The distributions are different!

10.1 Stem-and-Leaf Plots

Learning Target: Display and interpret data in stem-and-leaf plots.

Success Criteria:
- I can explain how to choose stems and leaves of a data set.
- I can make and interpret a stem-and-leaf plot.
- I can use a stem-and-leaf plot to describe the distribution of a data set.

EXPLORATION 1 Making a Data Display

Work with a partner. The list below gives the ages of women when they became first ladies of the United States.

THE WHITE HOUSE

WASHINGTON, D.C.

Frances Cleveland - 21	Jacqueline Kennedy - 31
Caroline Harrison - 56	Claudia Johnson - 50
Ida McKinley - 49	Pat Nixon - 56
Edith Roosevelt - 40	Elizabeth Ford - 56
Helen Taft - 47	Rosalynn Carter - 49
Ellen Wilson - 52	Nancy Reagan - 59
Florence Harding - 60	Barbara Bush - 63
Grace Coolidge - 44	Hillary Clinton - 45
Lou Hoover - 54	Laura Bush - 54
Eleanor Roosevelt - 48	Michelle Obama - 45
Elizabeth Truman - 60	Melania Trump - 46
Mamie Eisenhower - 56	

a. The incomplete data display shows the ages of the first ladies in the left column of the list above. What do the numbers on the left represent? What do the numbers on the right represent?

Ages of First Ladies

2	1
3	
4	0 4 7 8 9
5	2 4 6 6
6	0 0

b. This data display is called a *stem-and-leaf plot.* What numbers do you think represent the *stems? leaves?* Explain your reasoning.

c. Complete the stem-and-leaf plot using the remaining ages.

d. MP **REASONING** Write a question about the ages of first ladies that is easier to answer using a stem-and-leaf plot than a dot plot.

Math Practice

Listen and Ask Questions

Listen to other students' questions in part (d) and decide if they make sense. If not, ask for clarification.

10.1 Lesson

Key Vocabulary

stem-and-leaf plot, *p. 458*
stem, *p. 458*
leaf, *p. 458*

The leaves of a stem-and-leaf plot are usually written in ascending order.

Stem-and-Leaf Plots

A **stem-and-leaf plot** uses the digits of data values to organize a data set. Each data value is broken into a **stem** (digit or digits on the left) and a **leaf** (digit or digits on the right).

A stem-and-leaf plot shows how data are distributed.

Stem	Leaf
2	0 0 1 2 5 7
3	1 4 8
4	2
5	8 9

Key: 2|0 = 20

The *key* explains what the stems and leaves represent.

EXAMPLE 1 Making a Stem-and-Leaf Plot

	A	B
1	DATE	MINUTES
2	JULY 9	55
3	JULY 9	3
4	JULY 9	6
5	JULY 10	14
6	JULY 10	18
7	JULY 10	5
8	JULY 10	23
9	JULY 11	30
10	JULY 11	23
11	JULY 11	10
12	JULY 11	2
13	JULY 11	36

Make a stem-and-leaf plot of the lengths of the 12 phone calls.

Step 1: Order the data.

2, 3, 5, 6, 10, 14, 18, 23, 23, 30, 36, 55

Step 2: Choose the stems and the leaves. Because the data values range from 2 to 55, use the *tens* digits for the stems and the *ones* digits for the leaves. Be sure to include the key.

Step 3: Write the stems to the *left* of the vertical line.

Step 4: Write the leaves for each stem to the *right* of the vertical line.

Phone Call Lengths

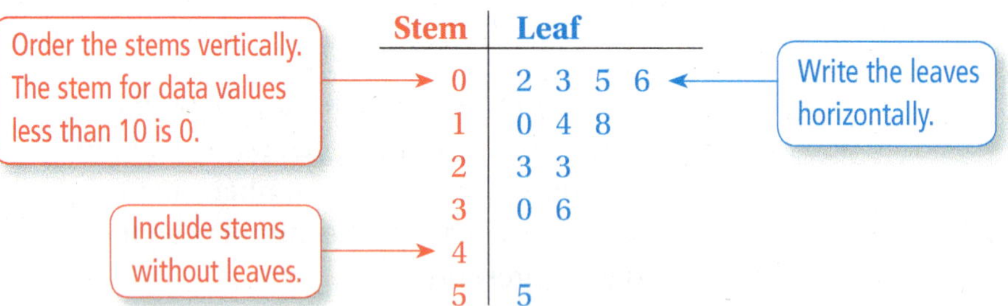

Key: 1|4 = 14 minutes

Try It

1. Make a stem-and-leaf plot of the hair lengths.

Hair Lengths (centimeters)									
5	1	20	12	27	2	30	5	7	38
40	47	1	2	1	32	4	44	33	23

Laurie's Notes

Scaffolding Instruction

- After creating and exploring a stem-and-leaf plot, students will use stem-and-leaf plots to analyze and interpret the data.
- **Emerging:** If students are not completely comfortable analyzing stem-and-leaf plots, they may have difficulty with plots of data that contain large numbers or decimals. The examples offer more practice.
- **Proficient:** Students understand the statistical information that stem-and-leaf plots display. They should complete Try It Exercise 2 before proceeding to the Self-Assessment exercises.

Key Idea

- A common question students ask about **stem-and-leaf plots** is, "What if the data are not two-digit numbers?"
  - If there are three-digit numbers within a small range (e.g., 431–476), the **stem** can be two digits (43, 44, 45, 46, 47).
  - If there are decimals (e.g., 3.4), the stem can be the whole number portion and the **leaf** is the decimal portion.
- Point out the push-pin note. Also point out the key that explains what the stems and leaves represent.

EXAMPLE 1

- By sorting the data first, the leaves are arranged in order when written to the right of the stem.
- **MP6 Attend to Precision:** Discuss with students the need to have a key that describes how to read the data in the plot. Explain the key in the solution.
- **Common Error:** When a data value repeats, remind students that the leaf must be listed again. The number of leaves must equal the number of data values in the set.

? "Describe the stem-and-leaf plot. What does the plot tell you about the data?" *Sample answer:* The data is skewed towards the lower values. It tapers at the upper end. There is a gap from 36 to 55.

- **Big Idea:** Because the stem-and-leaf plot shows how data are distributed, a stem must be included in the plot even if there are no data values in that interval. In this example, the stem of 4 is still included to show the gap in the data. There is no 0 listed in the leaf because that would represent 40!

Try It

- **Think-Pair-Share:** Students should read the exercise independently and then work in pairs to make the stem-and-leaf plot. Have each pair compare their plot with another pair and discuss any discrepancies.
- "Describe what the plot tells you about the data." *Sample answer:* There are some smaller data values and larger data values with few in the middle.
- "Explain why this might be the case." *Sample answer:* Differences between hair lengths of girls and boys.

Scaffold instruction to support all students in their learning. Learning is individualized and you may want to group students differently as they move in and out of these levels with each skill and concept. Student self-assessment and feedback help guide your instructional decisions about how and when to layer support for all students to become proficient learners.

Extra Example 1

Make a stem-and-leaf plot of the lengths (in inches) of the eleven fish.

7, 12, 20, 14, 20, 25, 8, 18, 16, 20, 14

Fish Length

Stem	Leaf
0	7 8
1	2 4 4 6 8
2	0 0 0 5

Key: 1 | 8 = 18 inches

ELL Support

Allow students to work in groups to practice language as they complete Try It Exercise 1. Expect students at different language levels to perform as described.

Beginner: Make a stem-and-leaf plot.

Intermediate: Use simple sentences to describe how to make the stem-and-leaf plot. For example, "Three goes in the stem and zero, two, and eight go in the leaf."

Advanced: Use detailed sentences to describe how to make the stem-and-leaf plot and help guide discussion.

Try It

1. **Hair Length**

Stem	Leaf
0	1 1 1 2 2 4 5 5 7
1	2
2	0 3 7
3	0 2 3 8
4	0 4 7

Key: 1 | 2 = 12 cm

Extra Example 2

Use the stem-and-leaf plot of student quiz scores in Example 2.

a. How many students scored more than 8.5 points? 8

b. How many students scored at most 7.5 points? 3

c. What is the highest quiz score? 10

Try It

2. a. 9 b. 4

Self-Assessment
for Concepts & Skills

3.

Stem	Leaf
0	8 9
1	3 4
2	2 5 9
3	0

Key: $1|3 = 13$

4. From the leaves, you can see where most of the data lies and whether there are many values that are low or high.

5. a. 2

   b. 8

   c. There are a few low values, a few in the middle, but the majority of the values are on the high end.

6. Use 8, 9, 10, 11, and 12 as the stems and the ones digit of the values as the leaves.

Laurie's Notes

EXAMPLE 2

- **Big Idea:** The leaves in a stem-and-leaf plot are sorted from least to greatest. The range can be found quickly, along with the median. To find the median quiz score, alternate counting in from each end of the data (the least and the greatest). Students are working on all three success criteria.
- ? "How many students are represented in the plot?" 18
- ? "What is the median? Explain how you found it." 8.4; There are 18 scores, so the middle will be the average of the 9th and 10th scores, which are both 8.4.

Try It

- Listen to students' discussions of these questions – they will shed light on their understanding of reading and interpreting a stem-and-leaf plot.
- **Extension:** Ask students to describe the plot.

Self-Assessment for Concepts & Skills

- These exercises should be completed independently, so students can assess their understanding of all three success criteria.
- If students have difficulty with Exercise 6, tell them to consider how many digits they have written for the leaves in the examples.
- **Neighbor Check:** After completing the exercise, have students check their work with a neighbor and discuss how to interpret stem-and-leaf plots.

ELL Support

To provide support and language practice, allow students to work in pairs. Have each pair display their stem-an-leaf plot on a whiteboard for your review. Have two pairs discuss their answers to Exercises 4–6. Monitor discussions and provide help as needed. Have each group come to agreement on final answers for their discussion questions.

The Success Criteria Self-Assessment chart can be found in the *Student Journal* or online at *BigIdeasMath.com*.

EXAMPLE 2 Interpreting a Stem-and-Leaf Plot

Quiz Scores

Stem	Leaf
6	6
7	0 5 7 8
8	1 1 3 4 4 6 8 8 9
9	0 2 9
10	0

Key: 9 | 2 = 9.2 points

The stem-and-leaf plot shows student quiz scores. (a) How many students scored less than 8 points? (b) How many students scored at least 9 points? (c) How are the data distributed?

a. There are five scores less than 8 points: 6.6, 7.0, 7.5, 7.7, and 7.8.

Five students scored less than 8 points.

b. There are four scores of at least 9 points: 9.0, 9.2, 9.9, and 10.0.

Four students scored at least 9 points.

c. There are few low quiz scores and few high quiz scores. So, most of the scores are in the middle, from 8.1 to 8.9 points.

Try It

2. Use the grading scale at the right.

A: 9.0–10.0
B: 8.0–8.9
C: 7.0–7.9
D: 6.0–6.9
F: 5.9 and below

a. How many students received a B on the quiz?

b. How many students received a C on the quiz?

Self-Assessment for Concepts & Skills

Solve each exercise. Then rate your understanding of the success criteria in your journal.

3. MAKING A STEM-AND-LEAF PLOT Make a stem-and-leaf plot of the data values 14, 22, 9, 13, 30, 8, 25, and 29.

4. WRITING How does a stem-and-leaf plot show the distribution of a data set?

Stem	Leaf
0	2 3
1	
2	1 6
3	0 4 6
4	4 5 8 8 9

Key: 4 | 8 = 48

5. MP REASONING Consider the stem-and-leaf plot shown.

a. How many data values are at most 10?

b. How many data values are at least 30?

c. How are the data distributed?

6. CRITICAL THINKING How can you display data whose values range from 82 through 129 in a stem-and-leaf plot?

EXAMPLE 3 Modeling Real Life

The stem-and-leaf plot shows the heights of several houseplants. Use the data to answer the question, "What is a typical height of a houseplant?"

Plant Heights

Stem	Leaf
0	1 2 4 5 6 8 9
1	1 1 1 2 3 5
2	2
3	2

Key: 1 | 5 = 15 inches

Find the mean, median, and mode of the data. Use the measure that best represents the data to answer the statistical question.

Mean: $\frac{162}{15} = 10.8$

Median: 11

Mode: 11

The mean is slightly less than the median and mode, but all three measures can be used to represent the data.

So, the typical height of a houseplant is about 11 inches.

Math Practice

Find General Methods

Explain to a classmate how to use an ordered stem-and-leaf plot to find the median of a data set.

Self-Assessment for Problem Solving

Solve each exercise. Then rate your understanding of the success criteria in your journal.

7. Work with a partner. Use two number cubes to conduct the following experiment. Then use a stem-and-leaf plot to organize your results and describe the distribution of the data.

- Toss the cubes and find the product of the resulting numbers. Record your results.
- Repeat this process 30 times.

8. The stem-and-leaf plot shows the weights (in pounds) of several puppies at a pet store. Use the data to answer the question, "How much does a puppy at the pet store weigh?"

Puppy Weights

Stem	Leaf
0	8
1	2 5 7 8
2	4 4
3	1

Key: 2 | 4 = 24 pounds

Laurie's Notes

EXAMPLE 3

- Ask, "What are you looking for when asked to find the *typical* height of a house plant?" A measure of central tendency: mean, median, or mode.
- "Can you find the mean, median, and mode from a stem-and-leaf plot?" yes Have students explain how to find each. Remind students that they found these in the previous chapter.
  - For the mode, students should identify the value(s) that appears the most.
  - For the median, students may alternate counting in from each end of the data or they may recognize that because there are 15 data values they can count to the 8th value because there are 7 values on either side of it.
  - For the mean, students should add all the values they read from the plot and divide by the total number of data values.
- "Which measure best represents the data? Explain." any; Because they all round to 11.
- "Are there any outliers? Explain." 32; The interquartile range is 8 and $13 + 1.5(8) = 25$ and $32 > 25$.
- **MP8 Look for and Express Regularity in Repeated Reasoning:** If time allows, have students repeat their calculations without the outlier. Ask them to explain how the outlier affects the mean, median, and mode.

Self-Assessment for Problem Solving

- Allow time in class for students to practice using the problem-solving plan. Remember, some students may only be able to complete the first step.
- As students work on these exercises, they are assessing their understanding of interpreting a stem-and-leaf plot and using it to describe the distribution of a data set.
- **Teaching Strategy:** Have students work with a partner. In Exercise 7, they will roll number cubes and record the products of the resulting numbers. Each student should make a stem-and-leaf plot of the data values. Then have students compare their plots with their partners. Allow time for discussion and revision. Partners should reach agreement for the description of the distribution of the data.
- **Teaching Strategy:** Partners should review the stem-and-leaf plot in Exercise 8 and then find all three measures of center before agreeing upon a single answer. This exercise assesses students' ability to read, interpret, and analyze the distribution of data in a stem-and-leaf plot.

The Success Criteria Self-Assessment chart can be found in the *Student Journal* or online at *BigIdeasMath.com*.

Closure

- Explain how a stem-and-leaf plot is similar to a bar graph and how it differs from a bar graph. *Sample answer:* A stem-and-leaf plot shows the frequency of different intervals for the data as well as displaying the distribution of the data, similar to a bar graph. All of the data values are displayed in a stem-and-leaf plot, but not in a bar graph.

Extra Example 3

The stem-and-leaf plot shows the lengths of several cats. Use the data to answer the question, "What is a typical length of a cat?"

Cat Lengths

Stem	Leaf
0	9
1	0 2 4 4 6 8 8 8 9
2	0 1 1 3 4
3	1

Key: 1 | 6 = 16 inches

about 18 inches

Teaching Strategy

Encourage an atmosphere in which incorrect answers are viewed as opportunities to learn. Provide chances for students to refine their answers after mathematical discussion and contemplation. The initial solution should be considered a rough draft and with more discourse and attempts, students revise and improve their responses.

Self-Assessment for Problem Solving

7. Check students' work.
8. See Additional Answers.

Learning Target

Display and interpret data in stem-and-leaf plots.

Success Criteria

- Explain how to choose stems and leaves of a data set.
- Make and interpret a stem-and-leaf plot.
- Use a stem-and-leaf plot to describe the distribution of a data set.

Review & Refresh

1. MAD = 2; The data values differ from the mean by an average of 2.
2. MAD = 6.6; The data values differ from the mean by an average of 6.6.
3. MAD = 9; The data values differ from the mean by an average of 9.
4. MAD = 6.5; The data values differ from the mean by an average of 6.5.
5. $5n + 40$
6. $7y - 42$
7. $28b + 42$
8. $99 + 11s$
9. $p = 24$
10. $g = 4\frac{2}{3}$
11. $d = 12$
12. $z = 15$

Concepts, Skills, & Problem Solving

13. *Sample answer:* How many times did 40 or more customers visit the store?
14. *Sample answer:* How many times did the person receive less than 60 text messages?
15. **Books Read**

Stem	Leaf
0	9
1	5 7 9
2	0 5 6 6 9
3	1 2
4	0

Key: 1 | 5 = 15 books

16. **Hours Online**

Stem	Leaf
0	0 2 6 8
1	2 2 4 5 7 8
2	1 4

Key: 2 | 1 = 21 hours

17–20. See Additional Answers.

Assignment Guide and Concept Check

Scaffold assignments to support all students in their learning progression. The suggested assignments are a starting point. Continue to assign additional exercises and revisit with spaced practice to move every student toward proficiency.

Level	Assignment 1	Assignment 2
Emerging	2, 7, 11, 13, 14, 16, 17, 21	19, 20, 22, 23, 24, 25, 26, 27
Proficient	2, 7, 11, 13, 16, 17, 21, 26	19, 20, 22, 23, 24, 25, 27, 28
Advanced	2, 7, 11, 14, 19, 20, 21, 26	22, 23, 24, 25, 27, 28

- Assignment 1 is for use after students complete the Self-Assessment for Concepts & Skills.
- Assignment 2 is for use after students complete the Self-Assessment for Problem Solving.
- The red exercises can be used as a concept check.

Review & Refresh Prior Skills

Exercises 1–4 Finding the Mean Absolute Deviation
Exercises 5–8 Simplifying Expressions
Exercises 9–12 Solving Equations

Common Errors

- **Exercises 15–20** Students may forget to include the numbers that have zeros in the ones place in the leaf part of the plot. Remind students that they should be able to read the numbers in the data set by reading the stem *and* leaf.
- **Exercises 15–20** Students may not include repeats of numbers. Remind students that the plot represents all of the data values, so they should be able to count the values in the leaf part and have all of the data accounted for.
- **Exercises 15–20** Students may forget to include stems that have no data values. Reminds students of Example 1. It is necessary to include the stems with no data to help answer questions about the data set.

10.1 Practice

Go to **BigIdeasMath.com** to get HELP with solving the exercises.

Review & Refresh

Find and interpret the mean absolute deviation of the data.

1. 8, 6, 8, 5, 3, 10, 11, 5, 7

2. 55, 46, 39, 62, 55, 51, 48, 60, 39, 45

3. 37, 54, 41, 18, 28, 32

4. 12, 25, 8, 22, 6, 1, 10, 4

Use the Distributive Property to simplify the expression.

5. $5(n+8)$ **6.** $7(y-6)$ **7.** $14(2b+3)$ **8.** $11(9+s)$

Solve the equation.

9. $\frac{p}{3}=8$ **10.** $28=6g$ **11.** $3d \div 4 = 9$ **12.** $10=\frac{2z}{3}$

Concepts, Skills, & Problem Solving

MP REASONING **Write a question that is easier to answer using the stem-and-leaf plot than a dot plot.** (See Exploration 1, p. 457.)

13. **Numbers of Customers**

Stem	Leaf
1	2 3 6 7
2	0 1 1 3 3 8 8
3	2 3 4 4 5 5 6 9 9
4	0 1 1 2 4 6 7 8 9 9

Key: 1 | 3 = 13 customers

14. **Text Messages Received**

Stem	Leaf
4	0 0 2 6 6 9
5	1 1 3 3 7 7 7 9 9 9
6	1 2 2 5 5 6 7 8 8
7	0 2 2 3 4

Key: 5 | 1 = 51 text messages

MAKING A STEM-AND-LEAF PLOT **Make a stem-and-leaf plot of the data.**

15.

Books Read			
26	15	20	9
31	25	29	32
17	26	19	40

16.

Hours Online			
8	12	21	14
18	6	15	24
12	17	2	0

17.

Test Scores (%)				
87	82	95	91	69
88	68	87	65	81
97	85	80	90	62

18.

Points Scored				
58	50	42	71	75
45	51	43	38	71
42	70	56	58	43

19.

Bikes Sold			
78	112	105	99
86	96	115	100
79	81	99	108

20.

Minutes in Line			
4.0	2.6	1.9	3.1
3.6	2.2	2.7	3.8
1.6	2.0	3.1	2.9

21. **MP YOU BE THE TEACHER** Your friend makes a stem-and-leaf plot of the data. Is your friend correct? Explain your reasoning.

51, 25, 47, 42, 55, 26, 50, 44, 55

Stem	Leaf
2	5 6
4	2 4 7
5	0 1 5 5

Key: 4|2 = 42

MP MODELING REAL LIFE **The stem-and-leaf plot shows the numbers of confirmed cases of a virus in 15 countries.**

22. How many of the countries have more than 60 confirmed cases?

23. Find the mean, median, mode, range, and interquartile range of the data.

24. How are the data distributed?

25. Which data value is an outlier? Describe how the outlier affects the mean.

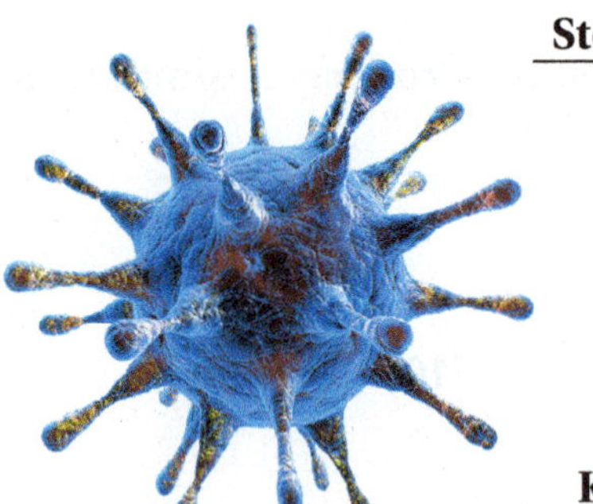

Stem	Leaf
4	1 1 3 3 5
5	0 2 3 4
6	2 3 3 7
7	5
8	
9	7

Key: 5|0 = 50 cases

26. **MP REASONING** Each stem-and-leaf plot below has a mean of 39. Without calculating, determine which stem-and-leaf plot has the lesser mean absolute deviation. Explain your reasoning.

Stem	Leaf
2	3 7
3	0 2 6 9
4	1 2 5 8
5	1 4

Key: 4|1 = 41

Stem	Leaf
2	2 4 5 8 9
3	3 8
4	5
5	3 6 7 8

Key: 5|3 = 53

27. **DIG DEEPER!** The stem-and-leaf plot shows the daily high temperatures (in degrees Fahrenheit) for the first 15 days of June.

Stem	Leaf
6	7 8
7	0 0 3 4 6 8 9
8	2 3 6 7 8 9

Key: 6|7 = 67°F

a. When you include the daily high temperatures for the rest of the month, the mean absolute deviation increases. Draw a stem-and-leaf plot that could represent all of the daily high temperatures for the month.

b. Use your stem-and-leaf plot from part (a) to answer the question, "What is a typical daily high temperature in June?"

28. **CRITICAL THINKING** The back-to-back stem-and-leaf plot shows the 9-hole golf scores for two golfers. Only one of the golfers can compete in a tournament as your teammate. Use measures of center and measures of variation to support choosing either golfer.

Rich		Will
7 5	3	
8 5 4 3 2 1	4	2 3 4 4 6 7 7 8 9
5 0	5	0

Key: 1|4|2 = 41 and 42 strokes

Common Errors

- **Exercises 23 and 25** Students may need to be reminded of the definitions for some of the terms so that they can answer the questions. Give an example of each term and how to find it using a stem-and-leaf plot.

Mini-Assessment

The table shows the numbers of hours 15 students were online this week.

Hours Online				
21	14	8	13	17
18	9	12	7	21
15	12	21	15	7

1. Make a stem-and-leaf plot of the data.

Stem	Leaf
0	7 7 8 9
1	2 2 3 4 5 5 7 8
2	1 1 1

Key: 1|8 = 18 hours

2. Find the mean, median, mode, and range of the data. mean = 14 h; median = 14 h; mode = 21 h; range = 14 h
3. How are the data distributed? Most of the scores are in the 10s.

Section Resources

Surface Level	Deep Level
Resources by Chapter • Extra Practice • Reteach • Puzzle Time Student Journal • Self-Assessment • Practice Differentiating the Lesson Tutorial Videos Skills Review Handbook Skills Trainer	Resources by Chapter • Enrichment and Extension Graphic Organizers Dynamic Assessment System • Section Practice

Concepts, Skills, & Problem Solving

21. no; The stem of 3 should be included.
22. 6
23. mean = 56.6 cases; median = 53 cases; modes = 41 cases, 43 cases, 63 cases; range = 56 cases; IQR = 20 cases
24. Most of the data are in the 40s, 50s, and 60s.
25. 97 cases; It increases the mean.
26. The left plot; The left plot has the lesser mean absolute deviation because it has more values closer to the mean.
27. **a.** See Additional Answers.
    b. *Sample answer:* about 77°F
28. *Sample answer:* You would choose Rich because he has the lowest individual scores and the lowest average score. You would choose Will because his scores are less variable showing he is more consistent.

Laurie's Notes

Learning Target

Display and interpret data in histograms.

Success Criteria

- Explain how to draw a histogram.
- Make and interpret a histogram.
- Determine whether a question can be answered using a histogram.

Warm Up

Cumulative, vocabulary, and prerequisite skills practice opportunities are available in the *Resources by Chapter* or at *BigIdeasMath.com*.

ELL Support

Explain that the suffix *–gram* comes from the Greek language and indicates a drawing or visual representation. Ask students if they are familiar with other words that include this root (e.g., telegram and diagram). A telegram is the written representation of information sent by telegraph and a diagram is an explanatory drawing. Have students guess what *histogram* might mean. It is believed that Karl Pearson, who first used the term *histogram*, intended it to mean "historical diagram." A histogram is a bar graph that shows the frequencies of data values in intervals of the same size.

Exploration 1

a. Check students' work.

b. Check students' work.

c–d. See Additional Answers.

Preparing to Teach

- Students will use their understanding of statistics to connect frequency tables and stem-and-leaf plots to histograms.
- **MP4 Model with Mathematics:** Students will construct histograms to represent data sets. Such graphical representations enable students to describe features of data sets.

Motivate

- Ask if students have ever made paper airplanes. If so, how long did their planes usually stay in flight before crashing?

Exploration 1

- This exploration allows students to collect their own data. It is always more engaging and interesting for students to work with data they generate.
- Use scrap paper and allow only one sheet per student. They need to think before they fold! Instructions for the construction are given.
- **Management Tip:** Lay tape measures out in a parallel fashion about 6 feet apart on the soccer field or other school grounds.
- Two students at a time fly their planes. They make a quick read of distance to the nearest foot and relay their distances to their partners who record them.
- If needed, review how to round to the nearest foot before going outside.
- Students continue in pairs until all have completed 20 trials. The pilot and recorder switch roles and repeat the process.
- To save time, you could decrease the number of trials from 20 to 10, but remember that a larger data set is often better for drawing conclusions.
- **Safety:** Students should fly their planes in the same direction so that no one is accidentally hit in the face.
- **Management Tip:** You may choose to complete this exploration inside. If so, it is helpful to mark the floor prior to the start of the exploration. For instance, have students measure and mark distances 2 feet apart. When students test their planes, they only have to measure between the marks. This will also allow students to review their measuring skills.
- Once the data is collected, complete part (c) inside. To save time, do not have students do any conversions to total inches. The intervals are generally a width of about 2 feet. Ask students to define *intervals*.

? Ask probing questions such as, "What intervals make sense in this scenario? Why are the intervals the same size? How can you write the intervals in the **frequency table**?" Select a pair of students to explain their frequency table.

- **MP6 Attend to Precision:** Students have fun folding and flying the airplane, but don't forget the mathematics. Raw data does not tell much of a story until it is organized in some fashion.
- Guide students to displaying their data in a **histogram**. They are not likely to know the terminology, but they can think of it in terms of a bar graph in which each category is an interval.

? Ask, "What is the range?" Answers will vary. "Where are the mean, median, and mode located in the table and graph?" Answers will vary.

- **Note:** You may want to have students save their data for later explorations.

10.2 Histograms

Learning Target: Display and interpret data in histograms.

Success Criteria:
- I can explain how to draw a histogram.
- I can make and interpret a histogram.
- I can determine whether a question can be answered using a histogram.

EXPLORATION 1 Performing an Experiment

Work with a partner.

a. Make the airplane shown from a single sheet of $8\frac{1}{2}$-by-11-inch paper. Then design and make your own paper airplane.

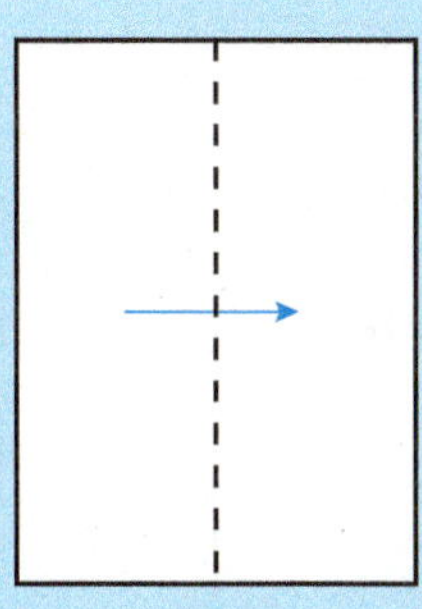

1. Fold in half. Then unfold.

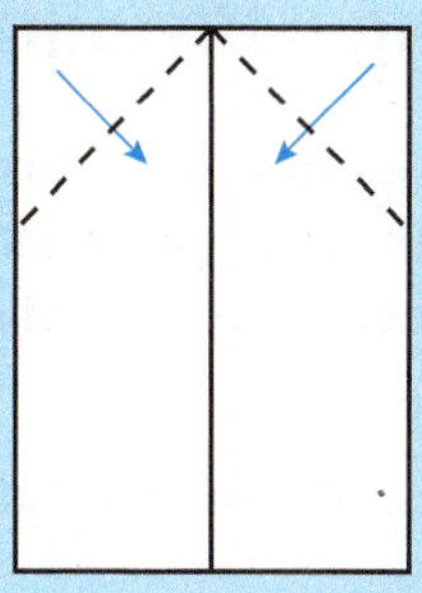

2. Fold corners.

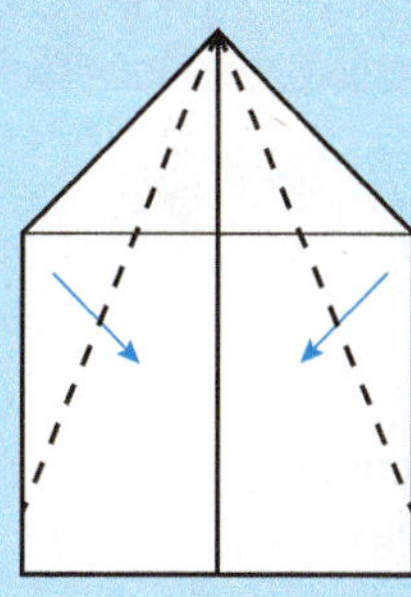

3. Fold corners again.

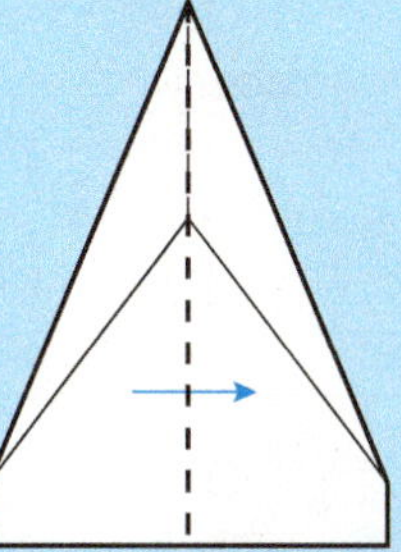

4. Fold in half.

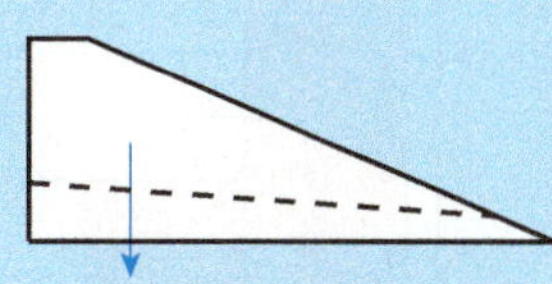

5. Fold wings out on both sides.

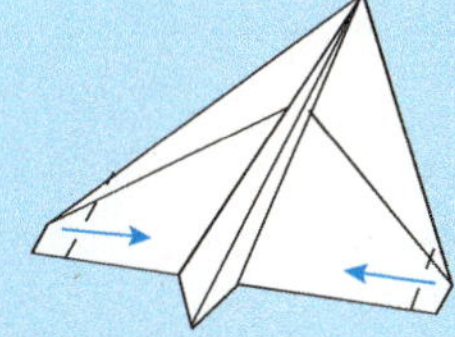

6. Fold wing edges up.

Math Practice

Specify Units
What units will you use to measure the distance flown? Will the units you use affect the results in your frequency table? Explain.

b. MP **PRECISION** Fly each airplane 20 times. Keep track of the distance flown each time.

c. A **frequency table** groups data values into intervals. The **frequency** is the number of values in an interval. Use a frequency table to organize the results for each airplane.

d. **MODELING** Represent the data in the frequency tables graphically. Which airplane flies farther? Explain your reasoning.

10.2 Lesson

Key Vocabulary
frequency table, *p. 463*
frequency, *p. 463*
histogram, *p. 464*

Key Idea

Histograms

A **histogram** is a bar graph that shows the frequencies of data values in intervals of the same size.

The height of a bar represents the frequency of the values in the interval.

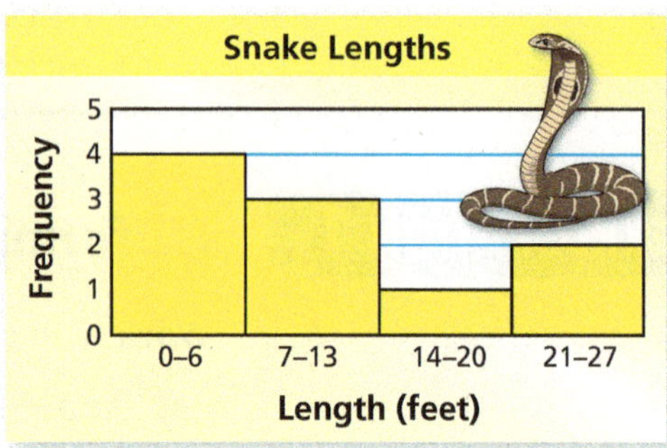

EXAMPLE 1 **Making a Histogram**

Math Practice

Make a Plan
In Example 1, it may be difficult or impossible to record the numbers of laps completed by every person at the pool. What factors might affect the accuracy of your data? How can you ensure that you collect truthful data?

The frequency table shows the numbers of laps that people in a swimming class completed today. Display the data in a histogram.

Number of Laps	Frequency
1–3	11
4–6	4
7–9	0
10–12	3
13–15	6

Step 1: Draw and label the axes.

Step 2: Draw a bar to represent the frequency of each interval.

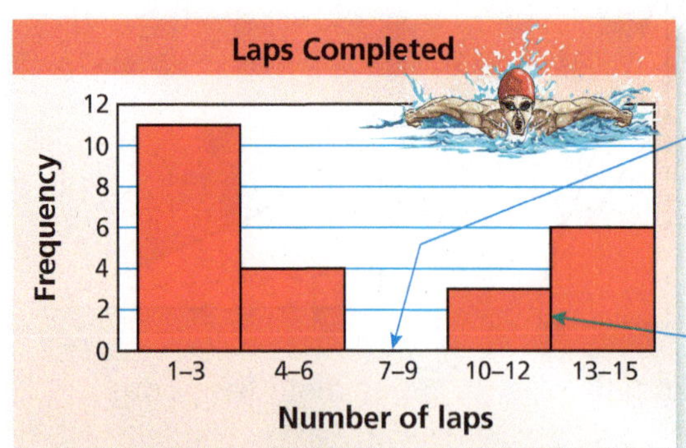

Include any interval with a frequency of 0. The bar height is 0.

There is no space between the bars of a histogram.

Try It

1. The frequency table shows the ages of people riding a roller coaster. Display the data in a histogram.

Age	10–19	20–29	30–39	40–49	50–59
Frequency	16	11	5	2	4

Laurie's Notes

Scaffolding Instruction

- Students will build upon their prior knowledge of data displays to make and interpret histograms. They will also use histograms to answer statistical questions.
- **Emerging:** Students who have difficulty identifying intervals or interpreting the meaning of data displays will benefit from guided practice for the examples.
- **Proficient:** Students who show understanding of frequency tables and making a histogram may proceed to Example 3. Check that students understand a circle graph and its relationship to a histogram. Then have these students proceed to the Self-Assessment exercises.
- If students did not make a histogram in the exploration, they should review the Key Idea and Example 1 first.

Key Idea

- Students have constructed bar graphs. A **histogram** is a particular type of bar graph where the data is numeric and the data is grouped into intervals of equal size. A *bar graph* includes categorical data (e.g., favorite vegetable) and numeric data.
- ? Use the histogram shown to ask questions, checking students' understanding of how to read a histogram.
    - "How many snakes were measured?" 10
    - "How many snakes measured at 6 or fewer feet?" 4
    - "How many snakes were 10 feet long?" cannot determine

EXAMPLE 1

- The intervals for the histogram have been pre-determined. The size of each interval is 3. Students should notice the pattern in the right-end values of the intervals: 3, 6, 9, 12, 15.
- Labeling the axes often presents a challenge for students. Students may write a number below the hash mark instead of writing an interval between the hash marks.
- Explain that no space is left between the bars because the intervals are continuous.
- Remind students that the axes are labeled and the histogram is given a title explaining what the data is about.
- Ask questions about the completed histogram.

Try It

- Students should recognize that the data is about people ages 10 to 59. It would not be correct to leave a gap for people ages 0 to 9.
- Ask a volunteer to share his or her histogram at the board or under a document camera.

Scaffold instruction to support all students in their learning. Learning is individualized and you may want to group students differently as they move in and out of these levels with each skill and concept. Student self-assessment and feedback help guide your instructional decisions about how and when to layer support for all students to become proficient learners.

Extra Example 1

The frequency table shows the numbers of T-shirts each person in a class owns. Display the data in a histogram.

T-shirts	Frequency
1–4	3
5–8	6
9–12	13
13–16	0
17–20	4

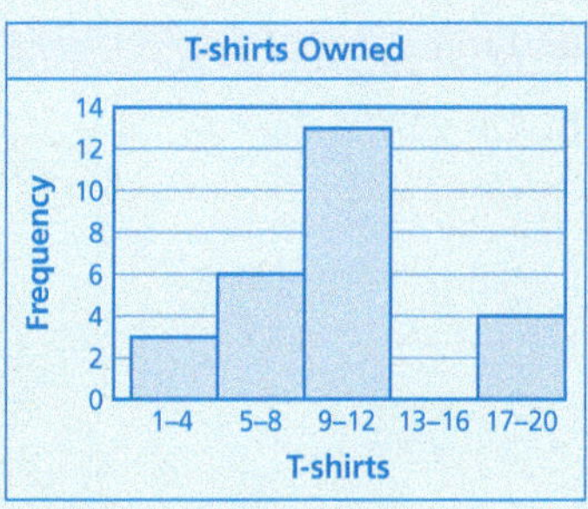

1.

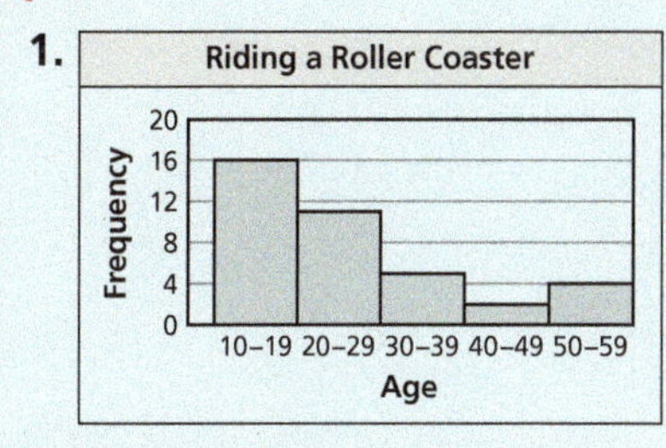

Extra Example 2

The histogram shows the numbers of different instruments each member of a jazz band can play.

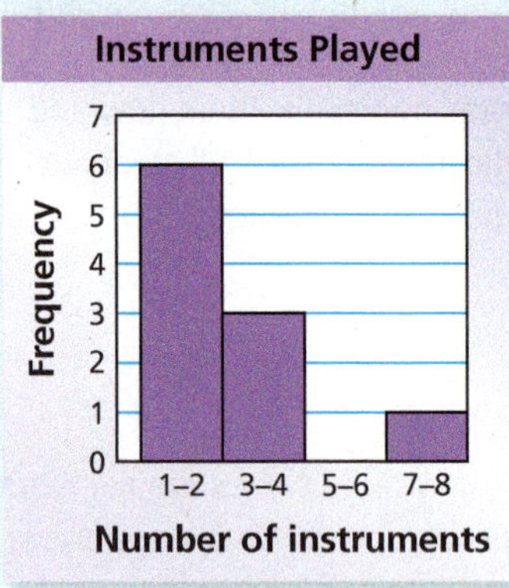

a. Which interval contains the most data values? 1–2

b. How many band members can play more than 2 instruments? 4

c. How many band members can play at most 2 instruments? 6

Try It

2. a. 11

b. 18

Laurie's Notes

EXAMPLE 2

- The focus of this example is to interpret information given in a histogram. Review the vocabulary *less than, at least, at most,* and *more than.*
- In addition to the questions posed, ask students to describe the distribution of the data. Also ask about the number of races shown in the graph.

◉ **MP3 Construct Viable Arguments and Critique the Reasoning of Others:** Listen to students' reasoning as they interpret the histogram. Encourage other students to listen carefully and critique the reasoning of their classmates.

Try It

- This graph is almost symmetric. Ask students what it means for a graph to be symmetric.

ELL Support

Discuss the meanings of *at least* and *less than.* Allow students to work in pairs to complete Try It Exercise 2. Provide questions for their discussions as they interpret the histogram: What do the time intervals represent? What does *Frequency* represent?

Beginner: Write the numbers that answer the questions.

Intermediate: State the numbers that answer the questions.

Advanced: Use complete sentences to answer the questions. For example, "Eleven students slept at least eight hours."

EXAMPLE 2 Using a Histogram

The histogram shows winning speeds at the Daytona 500.
(a) Which interval contains the most data values?
(b) How many of the winning speeds are less than 140 miles per hour?
(c) How many of the winning speeds are at least 160 miles per hour?

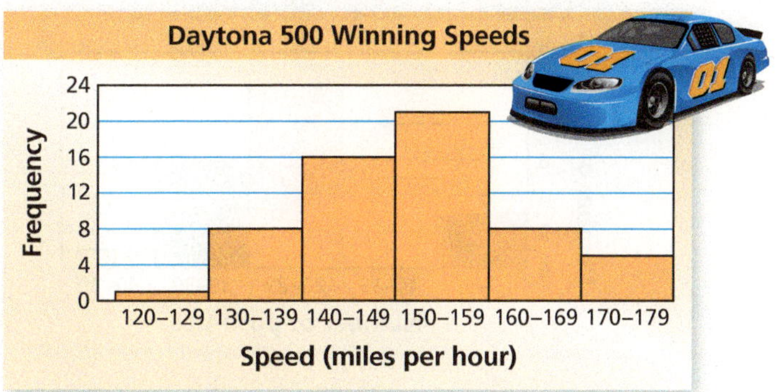

a. The interval with the tallest bar contains the most data values.

So, the 150 – 159 miles per hour interval contains the most data values.

b. One winning speed is in the 120 – 129 miles per hour interval, and eight winning speeds are in the 130 – 139 miles per hour interval.

So, $1 + 8 = 9$ winning speeds are less than 140 miles per hour.

c. Eight winning speeds are in the 160 – 169 miles per hour interval, and five winning speeds are in the 170 – 179 miles per hour interval.

So, $8 + 5 = 13$ winning speeds are at least 160 miles per hour.

Try It

2. The histogram shows the numbers of hours that students in a class slept last night.

a. How many students slept at least 8 hours?

b. How many students slept less than 12 hours?

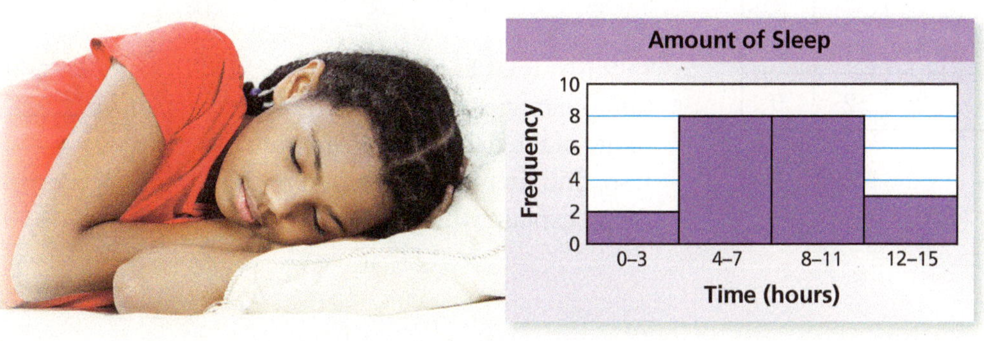

EXAMPLE 3 Comparing Data Displays

The data displays show how many push-ups students in a class completed for a physical fitness test. Which data display can you use to find how many students are in the class? Explain.

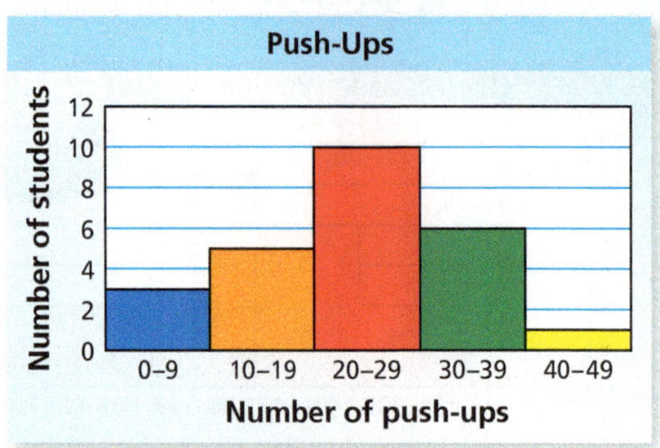

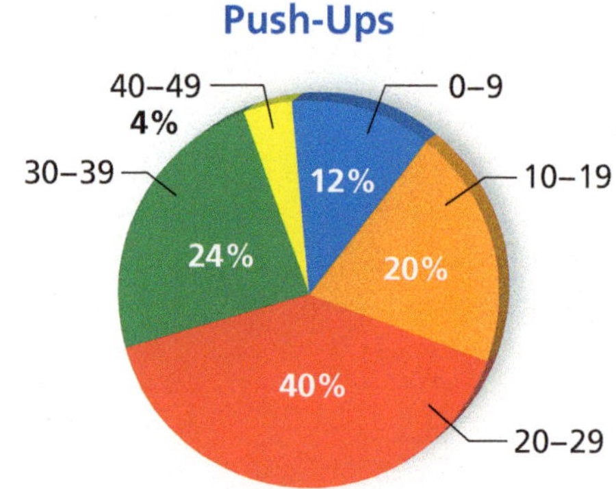

You can use the histogram because it shows the number of students in each interval. The sum of these values represents the number of students in the class. You cannot use the circle graph because it does not show the number of students in each interval.

Try It

3. Which data display should you use to describe the portion of the entire class that completed 30 − 39 push-ups? Explain.

Self-Assessment for Concepts & Skills

Solve each exercise. Then rate your understanding of the success criteria in your journal.

Numbers of Siblings			
0	2	3	6
3	2	1	2
1	4	0	3
7	3	1	5
4	3	2	0

4. **MAKING A HISTOGRAM** The table shows the numbers of siblings of students in a class.

   a. Display the data in a histogram.

   b. Explain how you chose reasonable intervals for your histogram in part (a).

5. **MP NUMBER SENSE** Can you find the range and the interquartile range of the data in the histogram? If so, find them. If you cannot find them, explain why not.

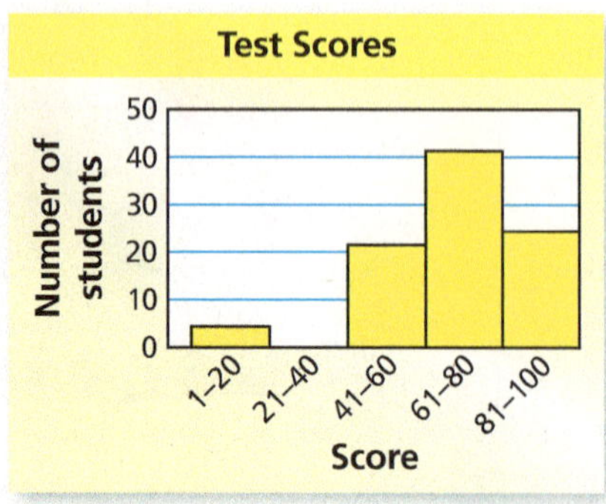

Laurie's Notes

EXAMPLE 3

? "When the sections of a circle graph are labeled with percents, what do you know about the sum of these percents?" They add up to the whole amount, 100% of the data.

- **Connection:** Students should recognize that the colors in each data display represent the same interval of push-ups. Completing 20–29 push-ups was the most frequent amount completed by students. The histogram shows that there were 10 students who completed 20–29 push-ups, which represents 40% of the class.

? "Could the data set have a mode? Explain." It is possible, but you cannot tell for sure. Neither data display gives individual values.

Try It

- **Turn and Talk:** Partners should discuss their reasoning for choosing a data display and reach a consensus.
- Have students share their reasoning with the entire class.

Self-Assessment for Concepts & Skills

- Exercise 4 gives students their first opportunity to determine the size of the intervals. After completing this exercise, have students share their histograms and reasoning for their choices of interval size. There is more than one possibility.
- **MP1 Make Sense of Problems and Persevere in Solving Them:** The size of the interval influences the shape of the histogram. Too many or too few intervals may mean that some features of the data go unnoticed.
- Exercise 5 provides insight into students' understanding of a histogram and their awareness of the information that it provides. After completing this exercise, have students discuss why a histogram is useful.

Students are assessing all of the success criteria.

ELL Support

Allow students to work in pairs. Have pairs display their histograms on whiteboards for your review. Have one pair present their answer for Exercise 4(b) to a second pair. Then have the second pair present their answer for Exercise 5. Encourage students to ask questions to clarify understanding. Provide support as needed.

The Success Criteria Self-Assessment chart can be found in the *Student Journal* or online at *BigIdeasMath.com*.

Extra Example 3

In Example 3, which data display can you use to compare the number of students that completed 10–19 push-ups with the number of students that completed 20–29 push-ups? Explain.

both; The 20–29 interval bar height is two times taller than the 10–19 interval bar height in the histogram, and the percent of the 20–29 section is twice the percent of the 10–19 section in the circle graph. So, twice as many students completed 20–29 push-ups as 10–19 push-ups.

Try It

3. circle graph; it shows the portion relative to the entire class

Self-Assessment for Concepts & Skills

4. a.

Students' Siblings

Number of siblings	Frequency
0–1	6
2–3	9
4–5	3
6–7	2

b. *Sample answer:* The intervals show the distribution of the data clearly.

5. no; You only know what interval each of the data values falls into, not the specific data values.

Extra Example 4

Which statements *cannot* be made using the data displays in Example 3?

A. Three students completed at most 9 push-ups.

B. Everyone in the class completed at least 1 push-up.

C. Twenty percent of the class completed at most 19 push-ups.

D. More than $\frac{1}{2}$ of the class completed 20 or more push-ups.

B and C

Self-Assessment for Problem Solving

6. a. 2–3 rebounds

b. 12 **c.** 25%

7. See Additional Answers.

Formative Assessment Tip

Every Graph Tells a Story

This open-ended technique reveals how students make sense of a graph. Give students a graph of a data set with labeled axes and a missing title. Then ask students to provide a story (or scenario) that makes sense for the data. As they create their situations, students should also consider statements and conclusions that can be made using the graph.

Learning Target

Display and interpret data in histograms.

Success Criteria

- Explain how to draw a histogram.
- Make and interpret a histogram.
- Determine whether a question can be answered using a histogram.

Laurie's Notes

EXAMPLE 4

- **MP3 Construct Viable Arguments and Critique the Reasoning of Others:** Ask different students to read each statement and explain whether or not it can be made using one of the data displays.

? "Can you determine how many students completed 15 push-ups from either data display? Explain." No, the histogram only tells how many students completed 10-19 push-ups and the circle graph tells the percent of students who completed 10-19 push-ups.

- Justify to students that you can add percents using fractions: $\frac{24}{100} + \frac{4}{100} = \frac{28}{100} = 28\%$

Self-Assessment for Problem Solving

- Students are assessing their progress with the last two success criteria. They may benefit from trying the exercises independently and then working with peers to refine their work. It is important to provide time in class for problem solving, so that students become comfortable with the problem-solving plan.
- **MP1 Make Sense of Problems and Persevere in Solving Them:** As students read and comprehend the words in the problems, they must also read and comprehend the histogram. Students' understanding of this visual display and their analyses allow them to answer questions and draw conclusions.

The Success Criteria Self-Assessment chart can be found in the *Student Journal* or online at *BigIdeasMath.com*.

Closure

- **Every Graph Tells a Story:** Display the histogram. Ask students to create a frequency table, a scenario, and a title for the histogram. Then ask students to write two statements that can be made using the graph.

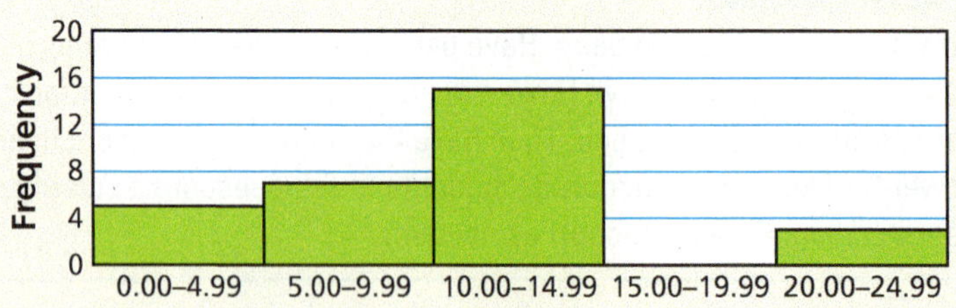

Dollars	Frequency
0.00–4.99	5
5.00–9.99	7
10.00–14.99	15
15.00–19.99	0
20.00–24.99	3

Sample answers: The data represents the costs of menu items at a restaurant; Costs of Menu Items; Five menu items cost less than \$5.00, and most menu items cost at least \$10.00 and at most \$14.99.

- Ask volunteers share their scenarios, titles, and statements with the class.

EXAMPLE 4 Modeling Real Life

Which statements *cannot* be made using the data displays in Example 3?

A. Twelve percent of the class completed 9 push-ups.

B. Five students completed at least 10 and at most 19 push-ups.

C. At least one student completed more than 39 push-ups.

D. Less than $\frac{1}{4}$ of the class completed 30 or more push-ups.

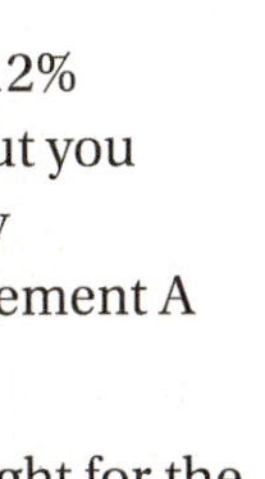

The circle graph shows that 12% completed 0–9 push-ups, but you cannot determine how many completed exactly 9. So, Statement A cannot be made.

In the histogram, the bar height for the 10–19 interval is 5, and the bar height for the 40–49 interval is 1. So, Statements B and C can be made.

The circle graph shows that 24% completed 30–39 push-ups, and 4% completed 40–49 push-ups. So, 24% + 4% = 28% completed 30 or more push-ups. Because $\frac{1}{4}$ = 25% and 28% > 25%, Statement D cannot be made.

The correct answers are **A** and **D**.

Self-Assessment for Problem Solving

Solve each exercise. Then rate your understanding of the success criteria in your journal.

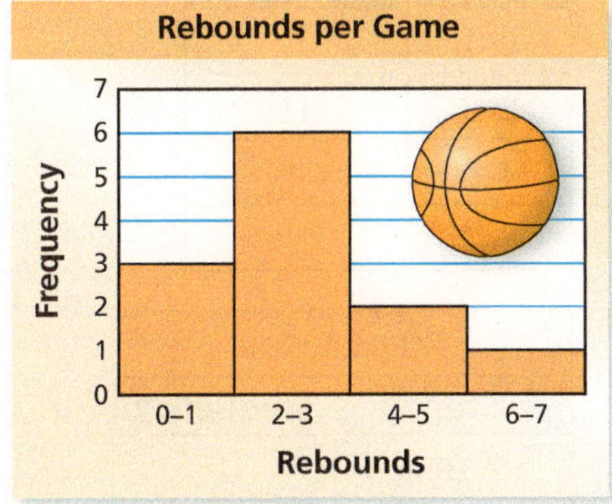

6. The histogram shows the numbers of rebounds per game for a middle school basketball player in a season.

a. Which interval contains the most data values?

b. How many games did the player play during the season?

c. In what percent of the games did the player have 4 or more rebounds?

7. Determine whether you can make each statement by using the histogram in the previous exercise. Explain.

a. The basketball player had 2 rebounds in 6 different games.

b. The basketball player had more than 1 rebound in 9 different games.

10.2 Practice

Review & Refresh

Make a stem-and-leaf plot of the data.

1.

Blog Posts			
7	5	12	4
20	11	9	15
4	8	6	12

2.

Social Media Comments			
4	18	1	32
10	36	16	7
44	3	7	15

Find the percent of the number.

3. 25% of 180
4. 30% of 90
5. 16% of 140
6. 64% of 80
7. What is the least common multiple of 7 and 12?

A. 28 **B.** 42 **C.** 84 **D.** 168

Concepts, Skills, & Problem Solving

MAKING A FREQUENCY TABLE **Organize the data using a frequency table.** (See Exploration 1, p. 463.)

8.

Members of Book Clubs			
6	17	13	19
13	9	18	24
11	15	21	14

9.

Points Scored				
42	45	57	39	55
38	48	36	48	46
51	29	45	54	42

MAKING A HISTOGRAM **Display the data in a histogram.**

10.

States Visited	
States	Frequency
1–5	12
6–10	14
11–15	6
16–20	3

11.

Chess Team	
Wins	Frequency
10–13	3
14–17	4
18–21	4
22–25	2

12.

Movies Watched	
Movies	Frequency
0–1	5
2–3	11
4–5	8
6–7	1

13.

Ages of Celebrities	
Ages	Frequency
10–19	2
20–29	6
30–39	8
40–49	4

14.

Shoes Owned	
Pairs of Shoes	Frequency
1–3	3
4–6	8
7–9	10
10–12	0
13–15	2

15.

Steps Taken	
Steps	Frequency
0–1999	1
2000–3999	4
4000–5999	9
6000–7999	12
8000–9999	11

Assignment Guide and Concept Check

Scaffold assignments to support all students in their learning progression. The suggested assignments are a starting point. Continue to assign additional exercises and revisit with spaced practice to move every student toward proficiency.

Level	Assignment 1	Assignment 2
Emerging	2, 5, 7, 8, 10, 11, 12, 16, 18	9, 13, 14, 15, 17, 19, 20, 21, 25
Proficient	2, 5, 7, 9, 11, 12, 13, 16, 18	14, 15, 17, 19, 20, 21, 22, 23, 25
Advanced	2, 5, 7, 9, 13, 14, 15, 16, 18	17, 19, 20, 21, 22, 23, 25

- Assignment 1 is for use after students complete the Self-Assessment for Concepts & Skills.
- Assignment 2 is for use after students complete the Self-Assessment for Problem Solving.
- The red exercises can be used as a concept check.

Review & Refresh Prior Skills

Exercises 1 and 2 Making a Stem-and-Leaf Plot
Exercises 3–6 Finding the Percent of a Number
Exercise 7 Finding the LCM

- **Exercises 10–15** Students may struggle with determining how to scale the vertical axis of the histogram. Remind students to use consistent intervals and to base their decisions on the frequency of the data. For example, if there is a high frequency, they should count by 5s or 10s, but if there is a low frequency, they should count by 1s or 2s.

Review & Refresh

1. **Blog Posts**

Stem	Leaf
0	4 4 5 6 7 8 9
1	1 2 2 5
2	0

Key: 2 | 3 = 23 blog posts

2. **Social Media Comments**

Stem	Leaf
0	1 3 4 7 7
1	0 5 6 8
2	
3	2 6
4	4

Key: 2 | 3 = 23 comments

3. 45
4. 27
5. 22.4
6. 51.2
7. C

8. *Sample answer:*

Interval	Tally	Total
0–9	II	2
10–19	~~IIII~~ III	8
20–29	II	2

9. *Sample answer:*

Interval	Tally	Total
20–29	I	1
30–39	III	3
40–49	~~IIII~~ II	7
50–59	IIII	4

10. 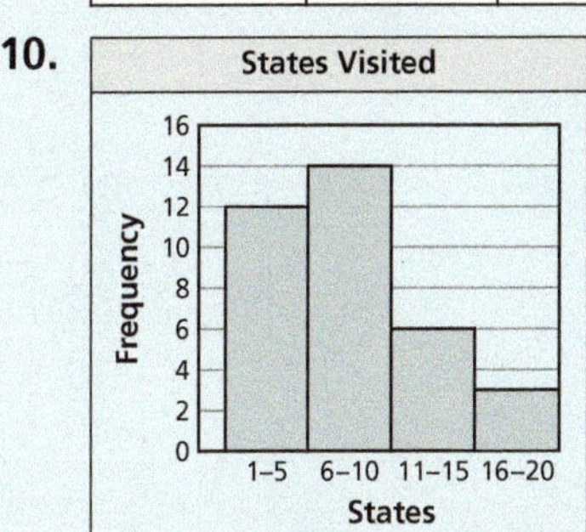

11–15. See Additional Answers.

Concepts, Skills, & Problem Solving

16. no; There should not be any space between the bars of the histogram.

17. **a.** 4–5 magazines read

b. 20 students

c. 85%

18. no; The frequency is the number of songs not the percent of songs.

19. **a.** no; The histogram shows that only one state fell in the interval of 40%–44.9%. This state did not necessarily have 40% of possible voters vote.

b. yes; 36 states are between 50% and 64.9%.

c. no; The 55%–59.9% interval has the highest frequency, but does not necessarily contain the mode of the data.

Common Errors

- **Exercise 17** Students may say that the interval 0–1 has the fewest data values, but it is really 4–5. To help students answer this question, ask them to label each interval with the frequency of that interval. Writing the frequency helps students to read the histogram.

16. MP **YOU BE THE TEACHER** Your friend displays the data in a histogram. Is your friend correct? Explain your reasoning.

Snow Days per School	
Snow Days	**Frequency**
0–1	9
2–3	6
4–5	2
6–7	1

17. MP **MODELING REAL LIFE** The histogram shows the numbers of magazines read last month by the students in a class.

a. Which interval contains the fewest data values?

b. How many students are in the class?

c. What percent of the students read fewer than six magazines?

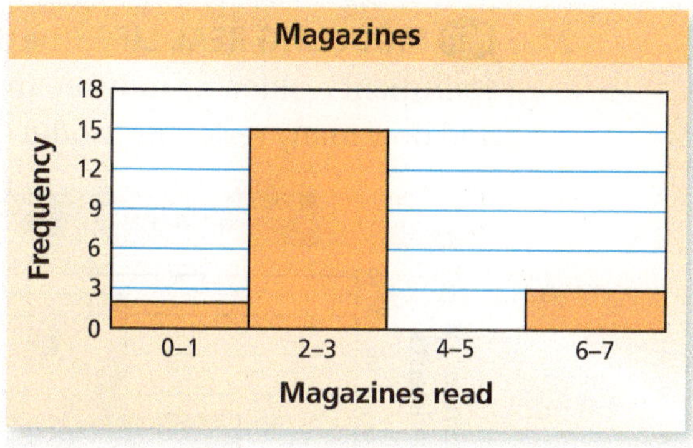

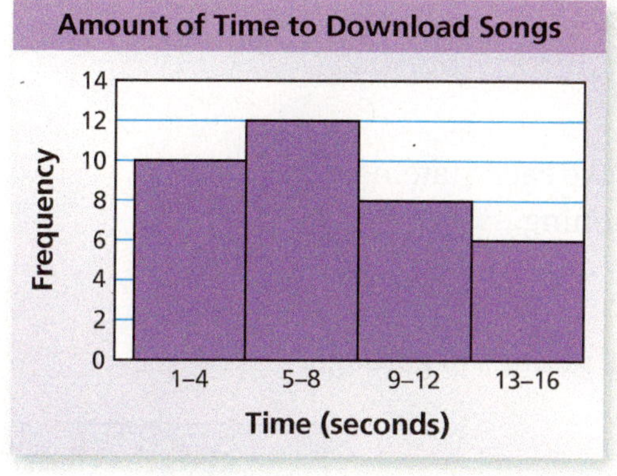

18. MP **YOU BE THE TEACHER** Your friend interprets the histogram. Is your friend correct? Explain your reasoning.

19. MP **REASONING** The histogram shows the percent of the voting-age population in each state who voted in a presidential election. Explain whether the graph supports each statement.

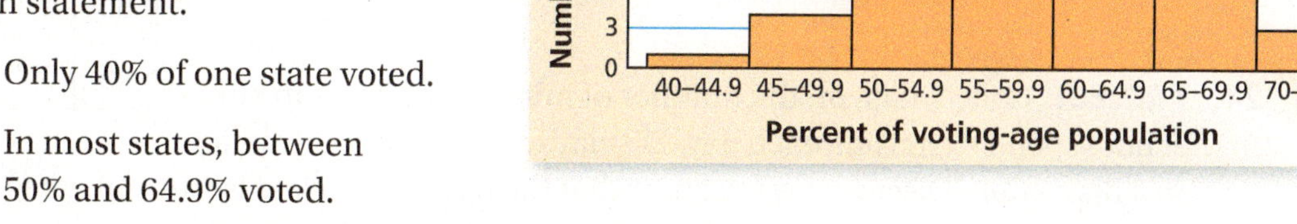

a. Only 40% of one state voted.

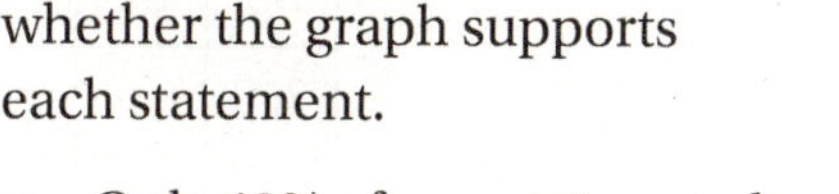

b. In most states, between 50% and 64.9% voted.

c. The mode of the data is between 55% and 59.9%.

20. **MP PROBLEM SOLVING** The histograms show the areas of counties in Pennsylvania and Indiana. Which state do you think has the greater area? Explain.

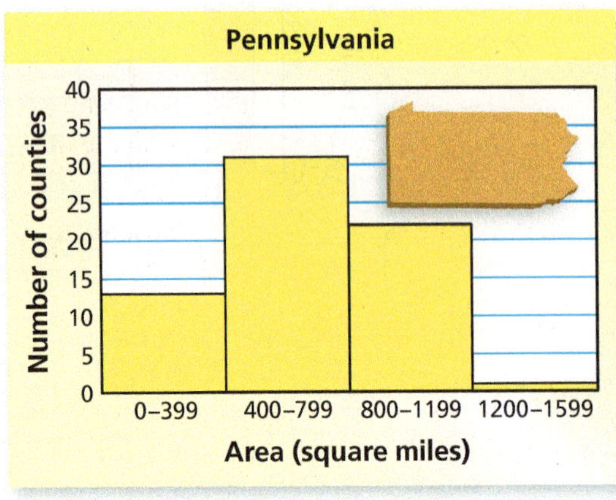

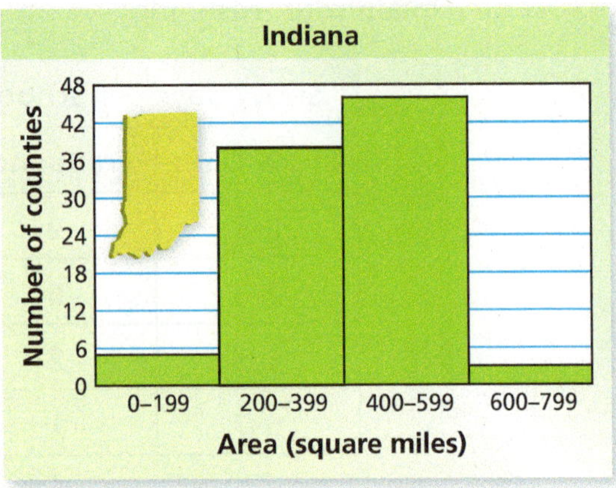

21. **MP MODELING REAL LIFE** The data displays show how many pounds of garbage apartment residents produced in 1 week. Which data display can you use to find how many residents produced more than 25 pounds of garbage? Explain.

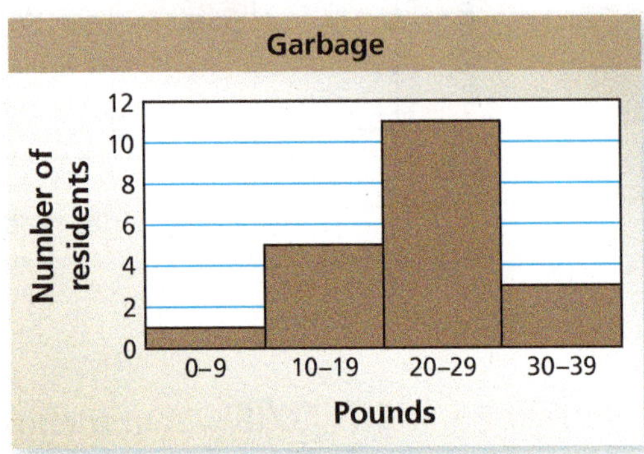

Garbage

Stem	Leaf
0	9
1	0 5 8 8 9
2	1 2 5 5 6 7 7 7 9 9 9
3	2 3 3

Key: 1 | 5 = 15 pounds

22. **MP REASONING** Determine whether you can make each statement by using the data displays in Exercise 21. Explain your reasoning.

a. One resident produced 10 pounds of garbage.

b. Twelve residents produced between 20 and 29 pounds of garbage.

23. **DIG DEEPER!** The table shows the lengths of some whales in a marine sanctuary.

a. Make a histogram of the data starting with the interval 51–55.

b. Make another histogram of the data using a different-sized interval.

c. Compare and contrast the two histograms.

Lengths (feet)				
81	88	57	82	70
71	51	82	77	79
83	80	54	80	81
59	84	75	76	68
83	78	55	67	85
85	77	73	78	79

24. **PROJECT** Collect data on the number of minutes students in your school spend exercising each day. Display and interpret the data in a histogram. Discuss ways to know that the data you collect is truthful data.

25. **MP LOGIC** Can you find the mean or the median of the data in Exercise 17? Explain.

For Your Information

- **Exercise 20** Pennsylvania has a total area of 46,055 square miles. Indiana has a total area of 36,418 square miles.

Common Errors

- **Exercise 20** Students may only look at the frequency for each graph and say that Indiana has the greater area. Encourage students to look at the intervals as well. The two graphs are drawn using different intervals, so they cannot be compared strictly by the heights of the bars.

Mini-Assessment

The table shows the numbers of songs downloaded last month by your friends.

Songs Downloaded	
Songs	Frequency
0–1	4
2–3	12
4–5	8
6–7	5

1. Display the data in a histogram.

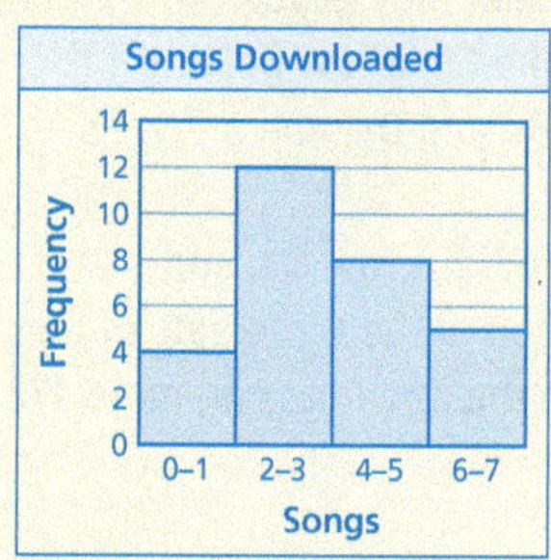

2. Which interval contains the most data values? 2–3
3. Which interval contains the fewest data values? 0–1
4. What is the difference between the 2–3 and 4–5 intervals? 4

Section Resources

Surface Level	Deep Level
Resources by Chapter • Extra Practice • Reteach • Puzzle Time Student Journal • Self-Assessment • Practice Differentiating the Lesson Tutorial Videos Skills Review Handbook Skills Trainer	Resources by Chapter • Enrichment and Extension Graphic Organizers Dynamic Assessment System • Section Practice
Transfer Level	
Dynamic Assessment System • Mid-Chapter Quiz	Assessment Book • Mid-Chapter Quiz

Concepts, Skills, & Problem Solving

20. Pennsylvania; You can see from the intervals and frequencies that Pennsylvania counties are greater in area, which makes up for it having fewer counties.

21. stem-and-leaf plot; You need to know the specific data values, the intervals in the histogram do not give enough information.

22. a. yes; The stem-and-leaf plot shows that 10 pounds is a data value.

    b. no; Both displays show that 11 residents produced between 20 and 29 pounds of garbage.

23. a.

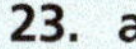

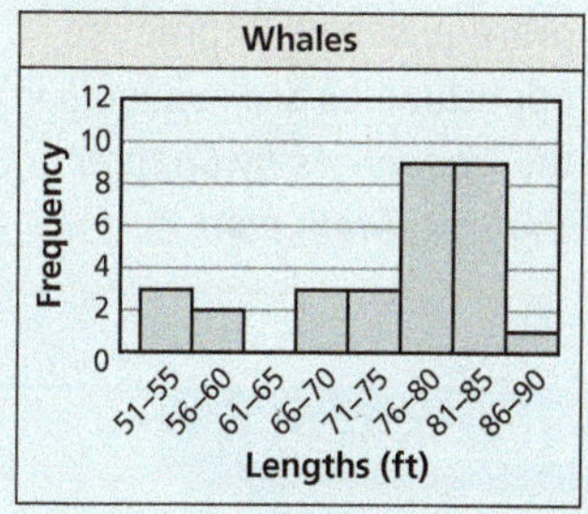

b.

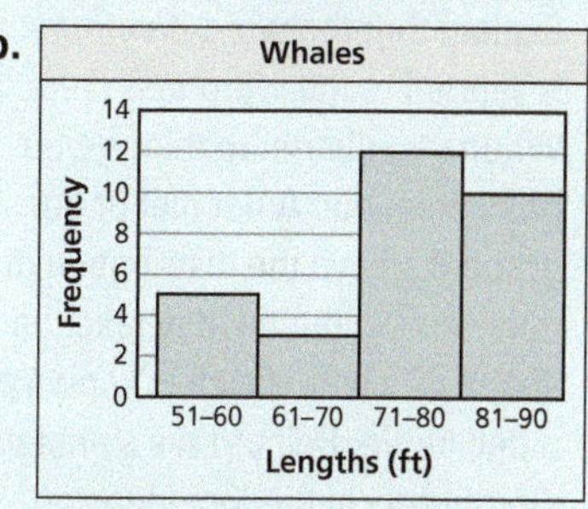

c. *Sample answer:* The second histogram has four intervals and it does not have a gap as in the first histogram.

24. Answers will vary. *Sample answer:* High outliers may indicate false data.

25. no; You only know what interval each of the data values falls into, not the specific values

Learning Target

Describe and compare shapes of distributions.

Success Criteria

- Explain what it means for a distribution to be skewed left, skewed right, or symmetric.
- Use data displays to describe shapes of distributions.
- Use shapes of distributions to compare data sets.

Warm Up

Cumulative, vocabulary, and prerequisite skills practice opportunities are available in the *Resources by Chapter* or at *BigIdeasMath.com.*

ELL Support

Explain that the word *distribution* is related to the word *distribute.* When you distribute things, you pass them out. A dot plot or bar graph displays the distribution of data. A distribution may take the shape of a bell, which is known as a bell curve. Point to the symmetric distribution in the Key Ideas on page 472 to illustrate a bell curve. Explain that most of the data falls in the middle of a bell curve.

Exploration 1

a. See Additional Answers.

b. *Sample answer:* Most of the data are between 0 and 2 with a peak at 1. There are no gaps and the data extends to 7; It has a peak so it is not flat like the last digit plot from part (a). The peak is not in the middle of the data so it does not look like the first digit plot from part (a).

Laurie's Notes

Preparing to Teach

- Students have used dot plots and histograms to display and analyze data. They will now use the shapes of these displays to compare data sets.
- **MP3 Construct Viable Arguments and Critique the Reasoning of Others:** Students will describe the shape of a distribution and make a connection to the measures of center and variation studied in Chapter 9.

Motivate

- **Story Time:** Tell students that yesterday, in the teacher's lounge, three teachers were describing the results of a recent test they gave.
  - **Teacher A:** Lots of high scores; As and Bs, some Cs, a few Ds, and 1 F.
  - **Teacher B:** Lots of average scores; Cs, some Bs and Ds, and a few Fs and As.
  - **Teacher C:** Lots of low scores; Ds and Fs, some Cs, a few Bs, and 1 A.
- Ask students to quickly sketch a histogram for each of the three sets of test scores. Sketches should be similar to the ones in the Key Ideas on page 472.

Exploration 1

- Discuss the meaning of *skewed.* Look around the classroom for an example of something that is skewed and something that is symmetrical.
- Review lines of symmetry to extend students' knowledge of symmetric shapes. Also, review the discussion in Section 9.1 regarding the basic characteristics of a distribution, such as peaks, gaps, and clusters.
- **Discuss:** Have partners read part (a). Then say, "Before you describe the shapes, you need to create displays of the data sets. What type of display should you use? Why?" If students choose a histogram, ask them to describe the intervals they will use. "Will a histogram provide the information you need?" no Lead students to choose dot plots for their displays, so they can see the distributions.
- Discuss telephone numbers. The area code and exchanges for a particular area are not randomly distributed. The last digits of the given telephone numbers, which can be considered random, are evenly distributed. So, the dot plot appears flat or rectangular.
- A contact list will have a limited number of exchanges, so the dot plot will look different than that of last digits. Some numbers (0, 1, 2, 3, and 9 in this exploration) do not appear at all, but it is symmetric.
- In part (b), "What does an age of 0 mean?" a fairly new cell phone
- **MP3 Construct Viable Arguments and Critique the Reasoning of Others:** Listen to student reasoning as they compare the shapes of the two distributions.
- "How do you know that the distribution for ages of cell phones is skewed?" *Sample answer:* The distribution has a slanted direction.
- Students should save their work. This data will be used again in Section 10.4.

10.3 Shapes of Distributions

Learning Target: Describe and compare shapes of distributions.

Success Criteria:
- I can explain what it means for a distribution to be skewed left, skewed right, or symmetric.
- I can use data displays to describe shapes of distributions.
- I can use shapes of distributions to compare data sets.

Math Practice

Apply Mathematics

How can the word *skewed* be applied in mathematics?

The Meaning of a Word ▶ Skewed

When something is **skewed**, it has a slanted direction or position.

EXPLORATION 1 Describing Shapes of Distributions

Work with a partner. The lists show the first three digits and last four digits of several phone numbers in the contact list of a cell phone.

538-
438-
664-
761-
868-
735-
694-
599-
725-
556-
555-
456-
736-
664-
576-

664-
664-
538-
855-
664-
538-
654-
654-
725-
538-
799-
764-
664-
664-
725-

a. Compare and contrast the distribution of the last digit of each phone number to the distribution of the first digit of each phone number. Describe the shapes of the distributions.

b. Describe the shape of the distribution of the data in the table below. Compare it to the distributions in part (a).

Ages of Cell Phones (years)					
0	1	0	6	4	0
2	3	5	1	1	2
0	1	2	3	1	0
0	0	1	1	1	1
7	1	4	2	2	2

-7253
-7290
-7200
-1192
-1142
-3500
-2531
-2079
-5897
-5341
-1392
-5406
-7875
-7335
-0494

-8678
-2063
-2911
-2103
-4328
-7826
-7957
-7246
-2119
-7845
-1109
-9154
-9018
-2184
-2367

10.3 Lesson

You can use dot plots and histograms to identify shapes of distributions.

If all the dots of a dot plot or bars of a histogram are about the same height, then the distribution is a *flat*, or *uniform*, distribution. A uniform distribution is also symmetric.

Symmetric and Skewed Distributions

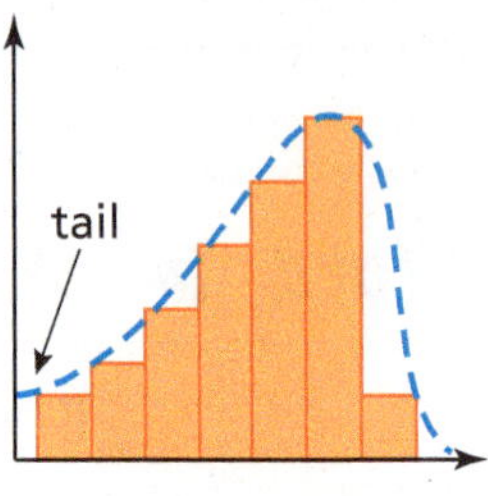

Skewed left

- The "tail" of the graph extends to the left.
- Most data are on the right.

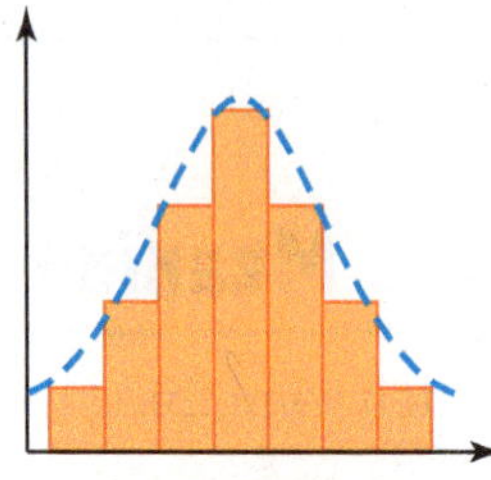

Symmetric

- The left side of the graph is a mirror image of the right side of the graph.

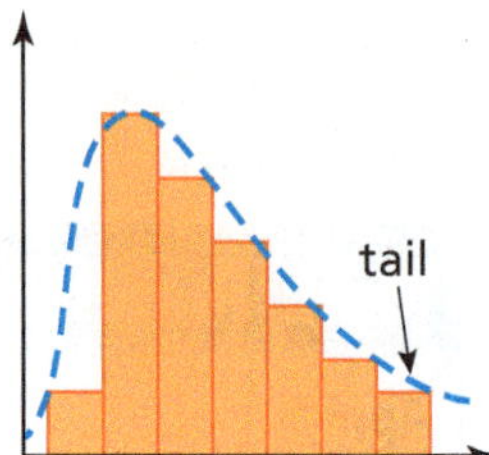

Skewed right

- The "tail" of the graph extends to the right.
- Most data are on the left.

EXAMPLE 1 Describing Shapes of Distributions

Describe the shape of each distribution.

a. Daily Snowfall Amounts

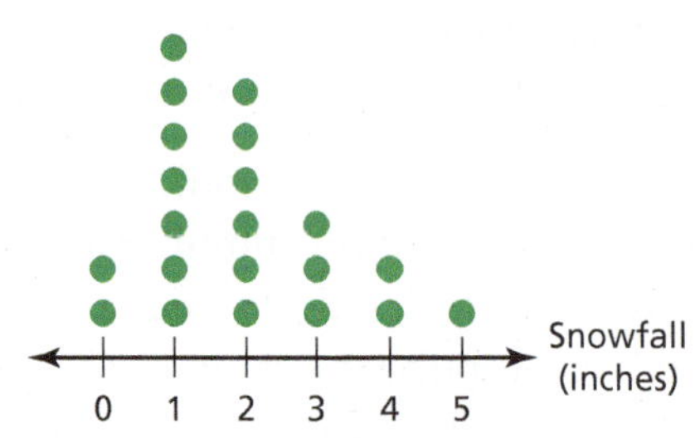

Most of the data are on the left, and the tail extends to the right.

So, the distribution is skewed right.

b.

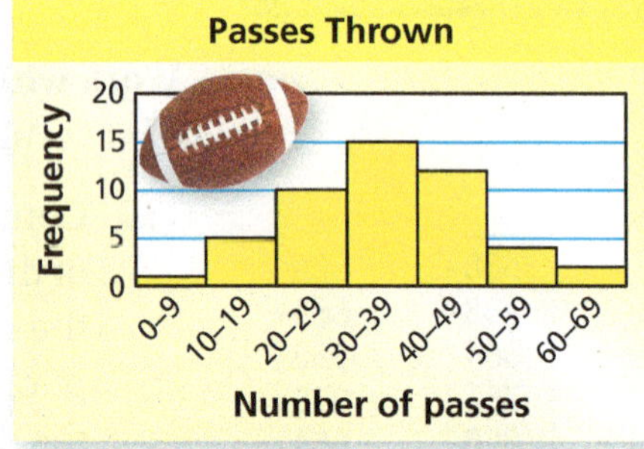

The left side of the graph is approximately a mirror image of the right side of the graph.

So, the distribution is symmetric.

Try It

1. Describe the shape of the distribution.

Daily Spam Emails Received

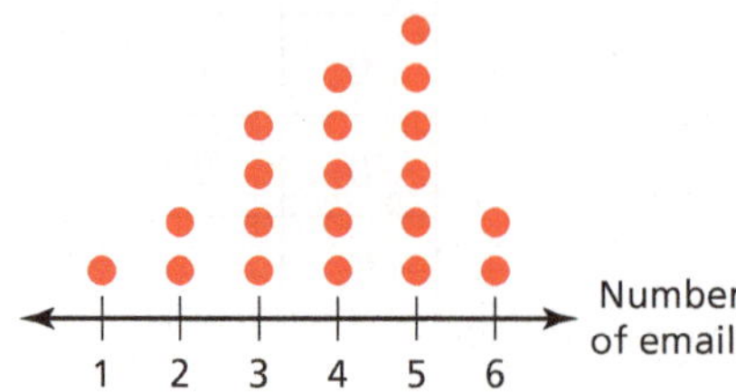

Laurie's Notes

Scaffolding Instruction

- After exploring shapes of distribution, students will use precise language to describe data displays and analyze the displays to compare sets of data.
- **Emerging:** Students may not understand when to use dot plots or histograms for data sets. They may have difficulty recognizing the skewed direction from the shape. The examples provide more practice.
- **Proficient:** Students are comfortable with the new language and they can correctly identify the shapes of distributions. They can also use the shapes to compare data sets and draw conclusions. Have students self-assess using the Self-Assessment exercises.

Key Ideas

- Draw a sketch of each type of distribution and label it: skewed left, symmetric, and skewed right.
- Connect the distributions to the test score descriptions in the Motivate.
- Explain that a dashed line can be drawn to help identify the greatest frequency and to help highlight the basic shape of a distribution.

? "Do all distributions fall into one of these three categories?" No, there are many different types of distributions.

- Skewed left is also called *negatively* skewed and skewed right is also called *positively* skewed. This may help students remember by relating skewness to the number line: the negative direction is to the left and the positive direction is to the right.

EXAMPLE 1

? "How many days are represented by the distribution in part (a)?" 21

- **MP4 Model with Mathematics:** Ask students to make a statement about the data represented by the histogram in part (b). *Sample answer:* Between 30 and 39 passes are typically thrown.

Try It

- **Neighbor Check:** Have students work independently and then have their neighbors check their work. Have students discuss any discrepancies.
- If time allows, ask questions about the mean, median, mode, and number of data values.
- **Extension:** Have students use the data they gathered about paper airplanes in Section 10.2 Exploration 1 to create a dot plot. Then ask students to determine mean, median, mode, and any outliers. If some students only have their frequency tables, they can borrow data from their partners.

ELL Support

Have students practice language by working in pairs to complete Try It Exercise 1. Have students discuss the questions: What does the graph show? What do the numbers along the bottom represent? What does each dot represent? What is the shape of the distribution?

Beginner: State one-word answers or phrases.

Intermediate: State phrases or simple sentences.

Advanced: State complete sentences.

Scaffold instruction to support all students in their learning. Learning is individualized and you may want to group students differently as they move in and out of these levels with each skill and concept. Student self-assessment and feedback help guide your instructional decisions about how and when to layer support for all students to become proficient learners.

Extra Example 1

Describe the shape of each distribution.

a. **Monthly Rainfall Amounts**

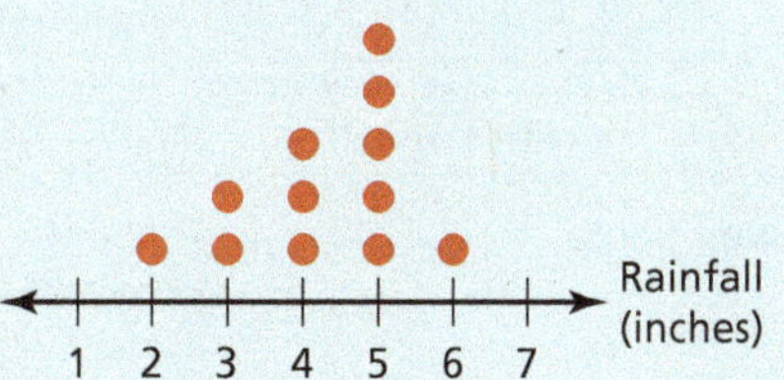

skewed left

b.

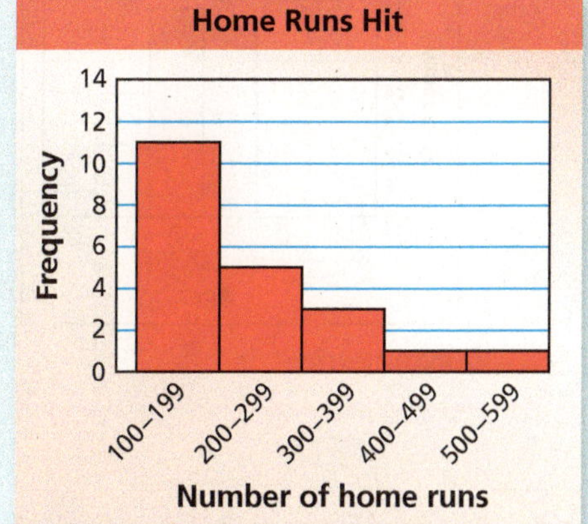

skewed right

Try It

1. skewed left

Extra Example 2

The frequency table shows the quiz scores (in percent) in a science class. Display the data in a histogram. Then describe the shape of the distribution.

Scores (percent)	Frequency
75–79	4
80–84	11
85–89	7
90–94	6
95–100	4

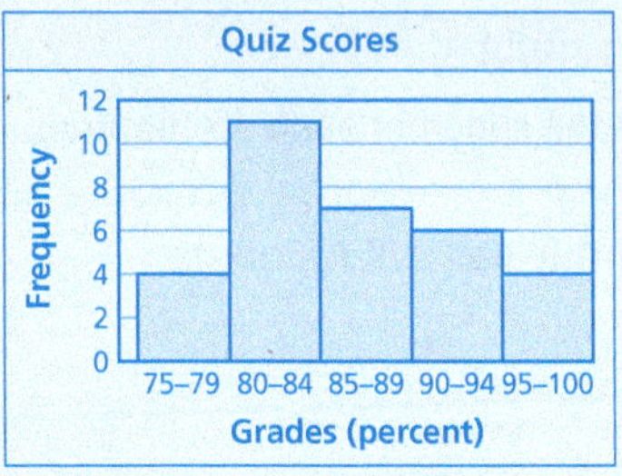

skewed right

Try It

2.

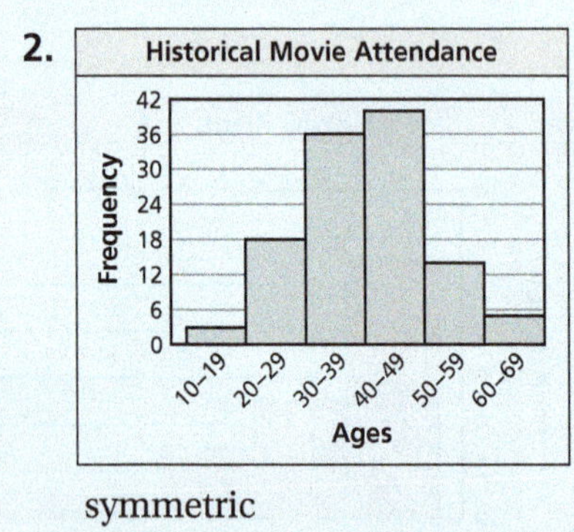

symmetric

Self-Assessment for Concepts & Skills

3–4. See Additional Answers.

5. the last histogram; It is skewed to the right, while the other three histograms are close to symmetric.

Laurie's Notes

EXAMPLE 2

- This is a good review of drawing a histogram. The intervals are given, which are often difficult for students to determine.
- Ask a volunteer to read the values in the frequency table as you write them. Have students describe the process for creating the histogram.
- Ask a few students to do their work on transparencies if a document camera is not available.

Try It

- After students have finished, ask a volunteer to share his or her histogram at the board or under a document camera.

Self-Assessment for Concepts & Skills

- Students are independently checking their progress with the first two success criteria.
- Carefully read students' answers to Exercises 3 and 4 to see if they correlate. Do students know the definitions? Can they apply their understanding to describe a data display? If one or both answers are wrong, you may want to have a reteaching station for those students the next day.
- **MP3 Construct Viable Arguments and Critique the Reasoning of Others:** Students compare the histograms in Exercise 5 to determine which one doesn't belong. As students defend their answers, listen for appropriate justifications and precise vocabulary.

ELL Support

Allow students to work in groups. Make sure there is at least one student with advanced language skills in each group. Have each group present one of their answers to the class. Provide support and guidance as needed during presentations.

The Success Criteria Self-Assessment chart can be found in the *Student Journal* or online at *BigIdeasMath.com.*

EXAMPLE 2 Describing the Shape of a Distribution

Ages	Frequency
10–13	1
14–17	3
18–21	7
22–25	12
26–29	20
30–33	18
34–37	3

The frequency table shows the ages of people watching a comedy in a theater. Display the data in a histogram. Then describe the shape of the distribution.

Draw and label the axes. Then draw a bar to represent the frequency of each interval.

Most of the data are on the right, and the tail extends to the left.

So, the distribution is skewed left.

Try It

2. The frequency table shows the ages of people watching a historical movie in a theater. Display the data in a histogram. Describe the shape of the distribution.

Ages	10–19	20–29	30–39	40–49	50–59	60–69
Frequency	3	18	36	40	14	5

Self-Assessment for Concepts & Skills

Solve each exercise. Then rate your understanding of the success criteria in your journal.

3. WRITING Explain in your own words what it means for a distribution to be (a) skewed left, (b) symmetric, and (c) skewed right.

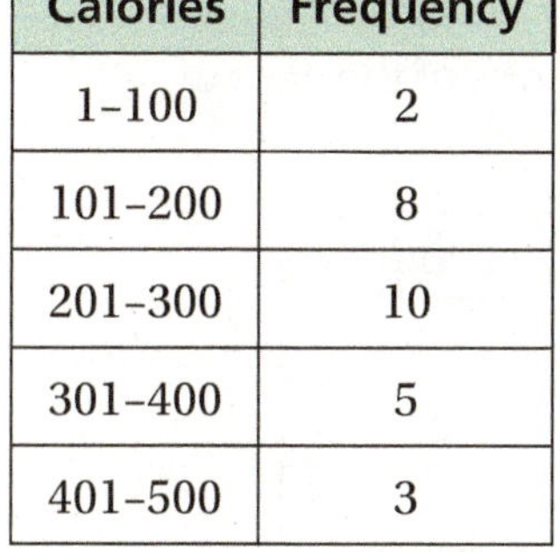

Calories	Frequency
1–100	2
101–200	8
201–300	10
301–400	5
401–500	3

4. DESCRIBING A DISTRIBUTION Display the data shown in a histogram. Describe the shape of the distribution.

5. WHICH ONE DOESN'T BELONG? Which histogram does *not* belong with the other three? Explain your reasoning.

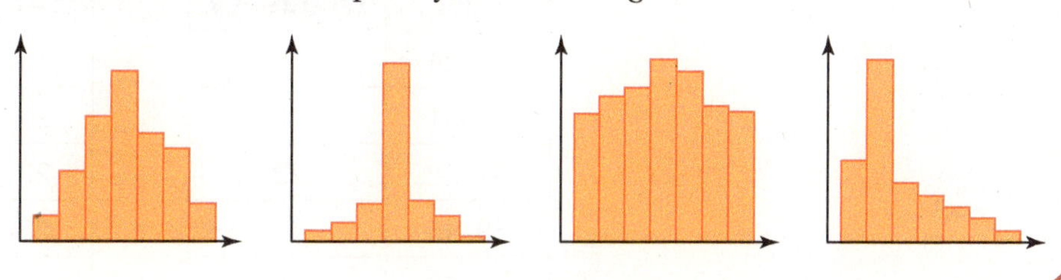

EXAMPLE 3 Modeling Real Life

The histogram shows the ages of people watching an animated movie in the same theater as in Example 2. Which movie has an older audience?

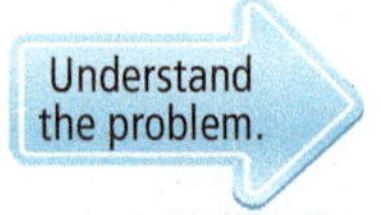

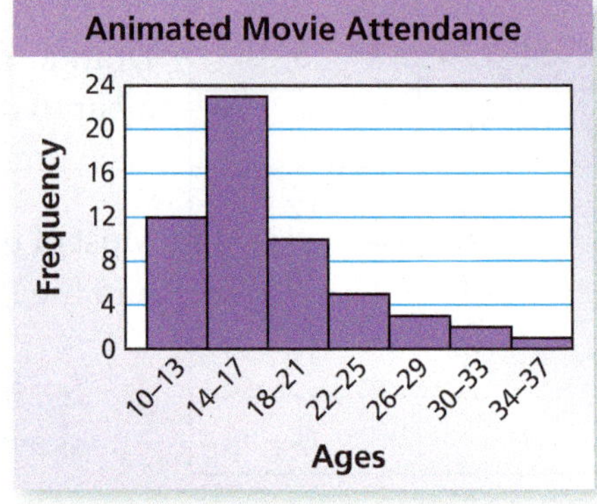

You are given histograms that display the ages of people watching two movies. You are asked to determine which movie has an older audience.

Use the intervals and distributions of the data to determine which movie has an older audience.

Solve and check.

The intervals in the histograms are the same. Most of the data for the animated movie are on the left, while most of the data for the comedy are on the right. This means that the people watching the comedy are generally older than the people watching the animated movie.

So, the comedy has an older audience.

Check Reasonableness The movies have similar attendance. However, only 4 people watching the comedy are 17 or under. A total of 35 people watching the animated movie are 17 or under. So, it is reasonable to conclude that the comedy has an older audience. ✓

Self-Assessment for Problem Solving

Solve each exercise. Then rate your understanding of the success criteria in your journal.

Visitors	Aurora	Grover
1–20	3	6
21–40	5	11
41–60	6	7
61–80	10	4
81–100	7	3

6. The frequency table shows the numbers of visitors each day to parks in Aurora and Grover in one month. Which park generally has more daily visitors? Justify your answer.

7. **DIG DEEPER!** The frequency tables below show the ages of guests on two cruises. Can you make accurate comparisons of the ages of the guests? Explain your reasoning.

Ages	Frequency
18–24	26
25–31	26
32–38	22
39–45	14
46–52	8

Ages	Frequency
18–22	16
23–27	22
28–32	26
33–37	20
38–42	12

Laurie's Notes

Formative Assessment Tip

Wait Time
Wait Time is the interval between a question being posed and a student (or teacher) response. Silence can be uncomfortable in a classroom, but research has shown that increasing *Wait Time* increases class participation and answers become more detailed. For complex, higher-order thinking questions, increased *Wait Time* is necessary. With increased participation, you will learn more about your students' progress and learning.

EXAMPLE 3

- **Note:** This histogram is similar to the histogram in Example 2 in that they have the same age intervals; however, they represent the attendance of two very different types of movies.
- Discuss the data represented in this histogram.
- ? You may have to remind students that they considered movie attendance in Example 2 with very different results. "Why do you think the histograms are so different?" *Sample answer:* They are very different types of movies. Give sufficient *Wait Time* before asking volunteers to share their ideas.
- ◎ "Describe the shape of this distribution." skewed right "What does that mean?" Most of the data are on the left.
- **MP3 Construct Viable Arguments and Critique the Reasoning of Others:** The explanations that students offer provide additional practice with constructing viable arguments.
- Discuss the Check Reasonableness note.

✓ Self-Assessment for Problem Solving

- The goal for all students is to feel comfortable with the problem-solving plan. It is important for students to problem-solve in class, where they may receive support from you and their peers. Keep in mind that some students may only be ready for the first step.
- ◎ As students assess their understanding of the last two success criteria, they are given opportunities to analyze a single data display and compare two sets of data.
- Although students may want to just consider the frequency tables, they should create histograms and analyze the distribution shapes.
- **Popsicle Sticks:** After completing the exercises, select students to share their graphs and explanations.

The Success Criteria Self-Assessment chart can be found in the *Student Journal* or online at *BigIdeasMath.com*.

Closure

- Sketch a dot plot that has a symmetric distribution and a mean of 4.
  Sample answer:

0 1 2 3 4 5 6 7 8

Extra Example 3

The histogram shows the quiz scores (in percent) in a social studies class in the same school as in Extra Example 2. Which class has better grades?

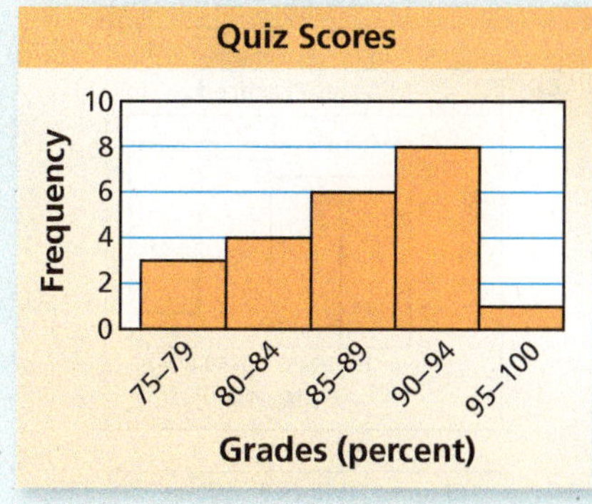

the social studies class

Self-Assessment for Problem Solving

6. Aurora; The intervals in the frequency table are the same, and Aurora has most of their data values at the high end of the visitors intervals. Grover has most of their data values at the low end of the visitors intervals.
7. no; The intervals are not the same.

Learning Target

Describe and compare shapes of distributions.

Success Criteria

- Explain what it means for a distribution to be skewed left, skewed right, or symmetric.
- Use data displays to describe shapes of distributions.
- Use shapes of distributions to compare data sets.

Review & Refresh

1\.

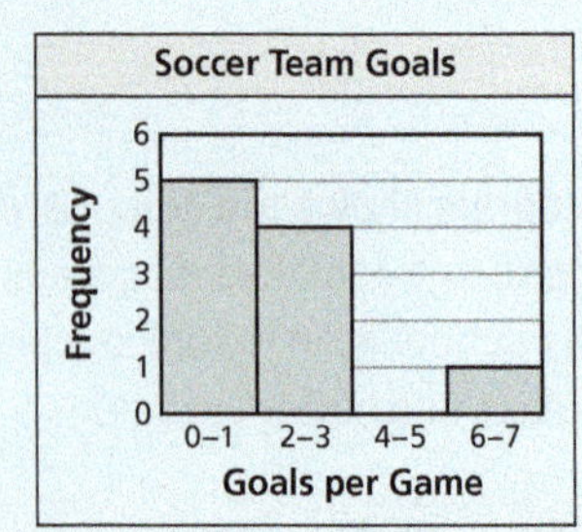

2\.

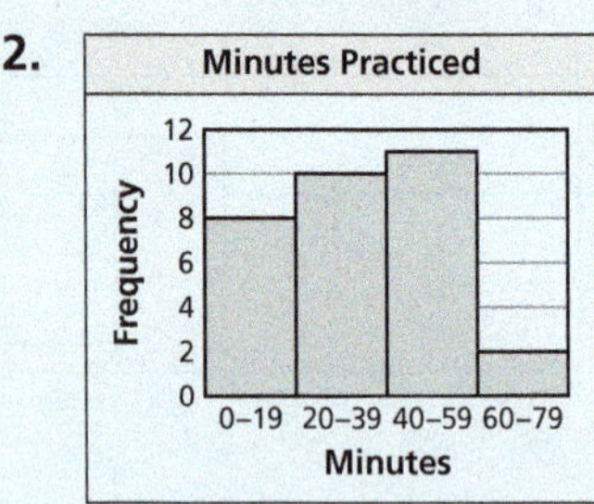

3\.

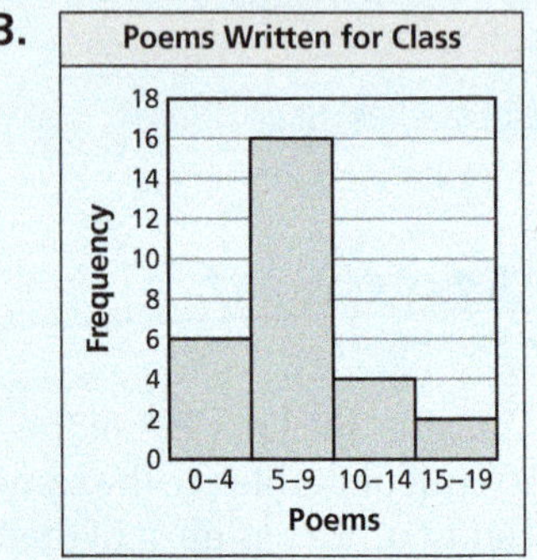

4. $25 per day
5. 40 km/hr

Concepts, Skills, & Problem Solving

6. skewed right
7. flat
8. skewed left
9. symmetric
10. skewed right
11. skewed left

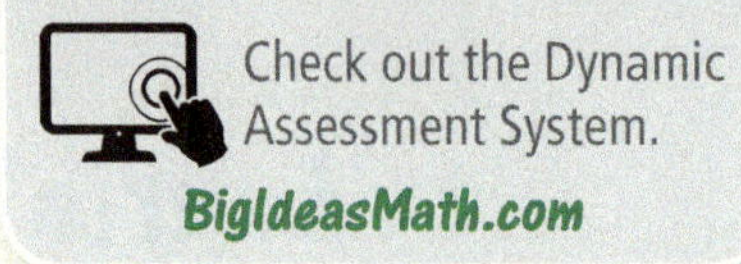

Assignment Guide and Concept Check

Scaffold assignments to support all students in their learning progression. The suggested assignments are a starting point. Continue to assign additional exercises and revisit with spaced practice to move every student toward proficiency.

Level	Assignment 1	Assignment 2
Emerging	3, 5, 6, 9, 11	8, 10, 12, 13, 14
Proficient	3, 5, 7, 8, 9, 10, 13, 14	11, 12, 15, 16
Advanced	3, 5, 7, 8, 9, 11, 13, 14	12, 15, 16, 17

- Assignment 1 is for use after students complete the Self-Assessment for Concepts & Skills.
- Assignment 2 is for use after students complete the Self-Assessment for Problem Solving.
- The red exercises can be used as a concept check.

Review & Refresh Prior Skills

Exercises 1–3 Making a Histogram

Exercises 4 and 5 Finding a Unit Rate

Common Errors

- **Exercises 6–11** Students may confuse *skewed left* and *skewed right*. Point out that the tail of the graph of a distribution determines the direction. That is, in a skewed left distribution, the tail extends to the left, and in a skewed right distribution, the tail extends to the right.

10.3 Practice

Review & Refresh

Display the data in a histogram.

1.

Goals per Game	
Goals	**Frequency**
0–1	5
2–3	4
4–5	0
6–7	1

2.

Minutes Practiced	
Minutes	**Frequency**
0–19	8
20–39	10
40–59	11
60–79	2

3.

Poems Written for Class	
Poems	**Frequency**
0–4	6
5–9	16
10–14	4
15–19	2

Write a unit rate for the situation.

4. $200 per 8 days

5. 60 kilometers for every 1.5 hours

Concepts, Skills, & Problem Solving

DESCRIBING SHAPES OF DISTRIBUTIONS **Describe the shape of the distribution of the data in the table.** (See Exploration 1, p. 471.)

6.

Miles Run per Day										
1	4	2	0	3	2	1	2	4	2	3
2	1	6	3	2	4	0	5	3	1	5

7.

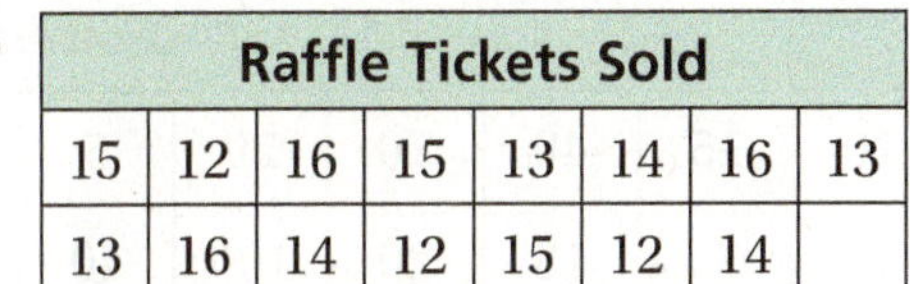

Raffle Tickets Sold							
15	12	16	15	13	14	16	13
13	16	14	12	15	12	14	

DESCRIBING SHAPES OF DISTRIBUTIONS **Describe the shape of the distribution.**

8.

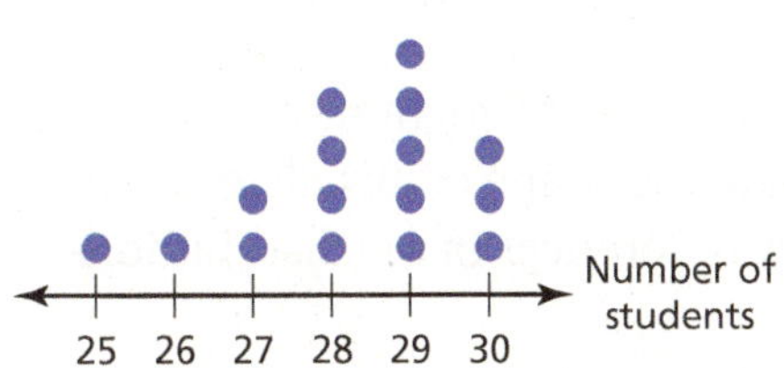

9.

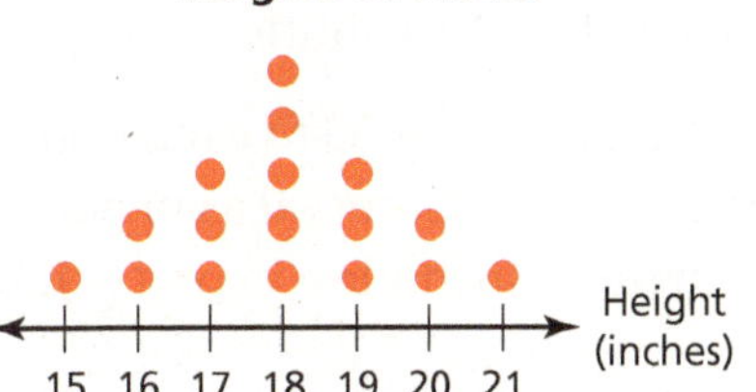

10.

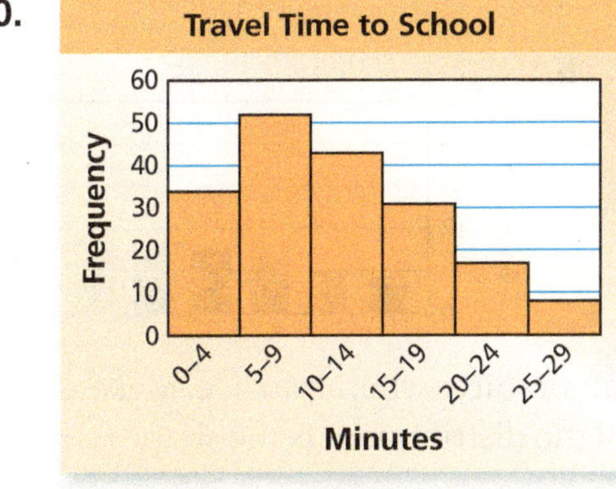

11.

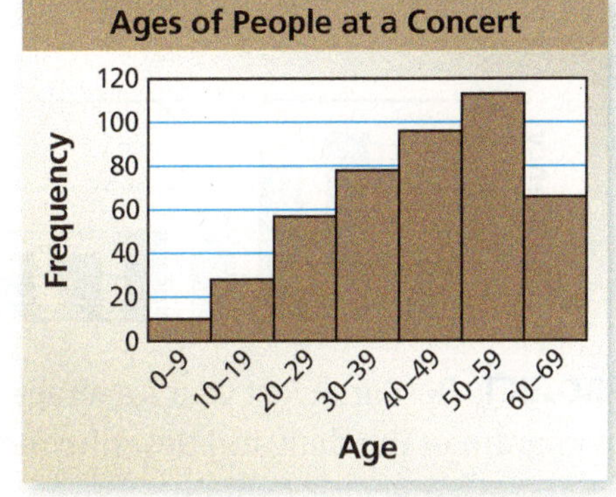

12. MP **MODELING REAL LIFE** The frequency table shows the years of experience for the medical staffs in Jones County and Pine County. Display the data for each county in a histogram. Which county's medical staff has less experience? Explain.

Years of Experience	0–3	4–7	8–11	12–15	16–19	20–23	24–27
Frequency for Jones County	7	15	17	12	8	5	3
Frequency for Pine County	3	5	9	14	10	6	2

13. MP **REASONING** What is the shape of the distribution of the restaurant waiting times? Explain your reasoning.

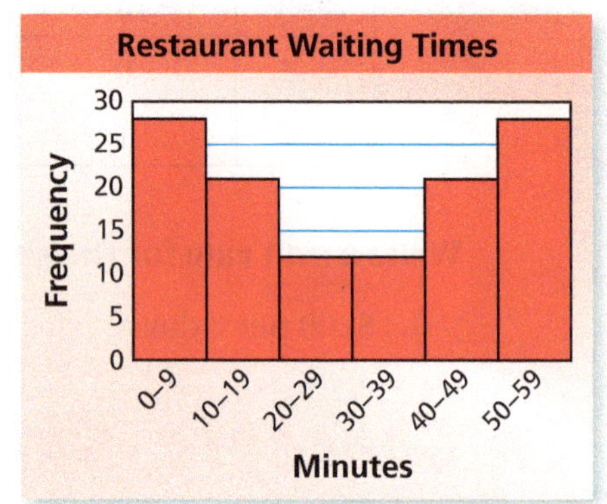

14. MP **LOGIC** Are all distributions either approximately symmetric or skewed? Explain. If not, give an example.

15. MP **REASONING** Can you use a stem-and-leaf plot to describe the shape of a distribution? Explain your reasoning.

16. **DIG DEEPER!** The table shows the donation amounts received by a charity in one day.

Donations (dollars)												
20	15	40	70	20	5	25	50	47	20	62	55	40
10	50	18	20	100	40	80	60	20	80	3	30	50
25	30	10	33	20	50	7	35	40	25	70		

a. Make a histogram of the data starting with the interval 0–14. Describe the shape of the distribution.

b. A company adds \$5 to each donation. Make another histogram starting with the same interval as in part (a). Compare the shape of this distribution with the distribution in part (a). Explain any differences in the distributions.

17. **CRITICAL THINKING** Describe the shape of the distribution of each bar graph. Match the letters A, B, and C with the mean, the median, and the mode of each data set. Explain your reasoning.

a.

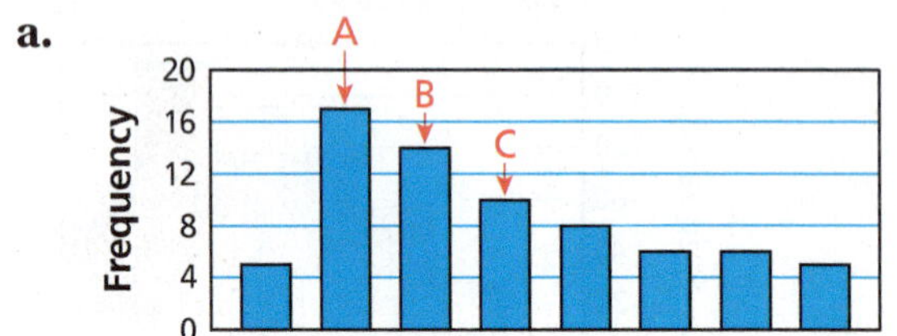

b.

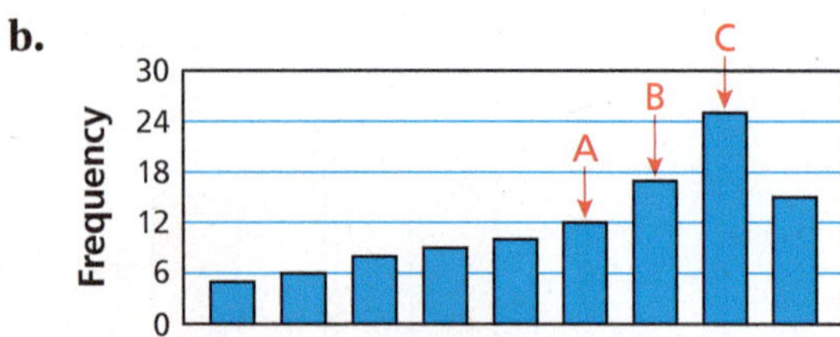

18. **PROJECT** Research last year's average daily temperatures where you live. Make a histogram of the data and describe the shape of the distribution. Is the shape what you expected? Explain.

Mini-Assessment

The frequency table shows the ages of people in attendance at a baseball game.

Ages	Frequency
0–9	25
10–19	30
20–29	58
30–39	60
40–49	32
50–59	21
60–69	16
70–79	8
80–89	4

1. Display the data in a histogram.

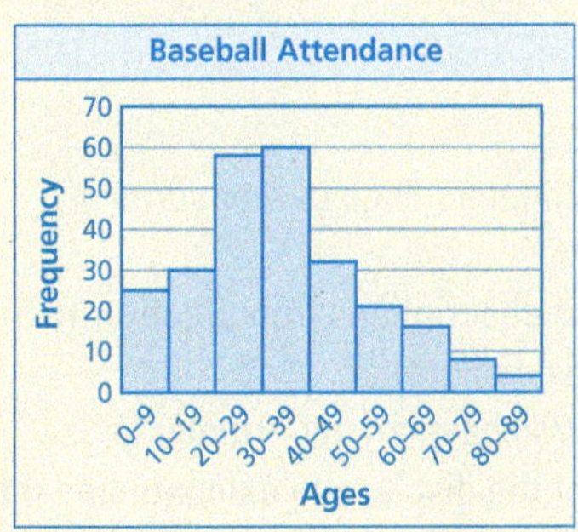

2. Describe the shape of the distribution. skewed right

Section Resources

Surface Level	Deep Level
Resources by Chapter • Extra Practice • Reteach • Puzzle Time Student Journal • Self-Assessment • Practice Differentiating the Lesson Tutorial Videos Skills Review Handbook Skills Trainer	Resources by Chapter • Enrichment and Extension Graphic Organizers Dynamic Assessment System • Section Practice

Concepts, Skills, & Problem Solving

12. See Additional Answers.

13. symmetric; The data on the left are a mirror image of the data on the right.

14. no; Distribution can have any shape.

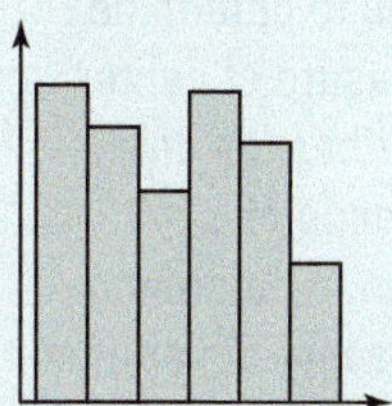

15. yes; *Sample answer:* When the stem-and-leaf plot has most of its values on the bottom, the distribution is skewed left because when the data are placed in a dot plot or histogram, most of the data values will be on the right. When the stem-and-leaf plot is a mirror image on the top and bottom for the numbers of values, the distribution is symmetric. When the stem-and-leaf plot has most of its values on the top, the distribution is skewed right because when the data is placed in a dot plot or histogram, most of the data values will be on the left.

16. See Additional Answers.

17. **a.** skewed right; A: Mode, B: Median, C: Mean; *Sample answer:* A is the value with the highest frequency, about half of the data are to the left of B and about half are to the right of B

b. skewed left; A: Mean, B: Median, C: Mode; *Sample answer:* C is the value with the highest frequency, about half of the data are to the left of B and about half are to the right of B

18. Check students' work.

Laurie's Notes

Learning Target

Determine which measures of center and variation best describe a data set.

Success Criteria

- Describe the shape of a distribution.
- Use the shape of a distribution to determine which measure of center best describes the data.
- Use the shape of a distribution to determine which measure of variation best describes the data.

Warm Up

Cumulative, vocabulary, and prerequisite skills practice opportunities are available in the *Resources by Chapter* or at *BigIdeasMath.com*.

ELL Support

Discuss the meaning of the word *measure.* Ask students what they measure and how they measure. Students may say weight, height, or cooking ingredients. Ask if they would use a scale or tape measure to measure height. Explain that measures of center and variation are measures of statistical information. Point out that just as you choose an appropriate tool for measuring in daily life, you choose an appropriate measure of center and variation to measure data.

Exploration 1

a–c. See Additional Answers.

Preparing to Teach

- In the previous section, students learned to describe and compare shapes of distributions. These foundational skills allow students to use the shape of a distribution to choose the most appropriate measures to describe the center and variation.
- **MP4 Model with Mathematics:** Students will represent sets of data in histograms and dot plots to analyze the shapes of the distributions. They will use their analyses to summarize numerical data sets in relation to their contexts.

Motivate

- ? How many states does [insert your state] border?" Answers will vary.
- ? "How many states border 0 or 1 other states? Explain." 3; Hawaii and Alaska border 0 other states and Maine borders 1 other state.
- Explain that one of the examples in today's lesson will explore a data set involving state borders.

Exploration 1

- Review how to find mean and median and the meanings of *measures of center* and *measures of variation*.
- Students should use their data displays and descriptions from Section 10.3 Exploration 1 to answer the questions in this exploration.
- With two very different dot plots, students will have an opportunity to use trends, numbers, and the physical outline of the displays to estimate and make connections to the statistical measures. Encourage different types of learners to share their strategies with the class.
- Encourage students to recognize and use shortcuts to find the means. For the set of first digits, ask whether anyone can tell "by inspection" that the mean is 6. Have a student explain to the entire class.
- ? "How can you find the median in a dot plot?" Because the data values in a dot plot are in order, students should describe moving from the least and greatest numbers toward the center of the distribution.
- In answering part (b), students may notice that the mean and median of the first digits are equal. If students are stuck trying to come up with an answer, then suggest that the mean uses all of the data values in its calculation, so it could be considered more reliable.
- ◉ For the ages of cell phones, the median and mode are both 1 and most of the data are clustered around 1. The mean is more affected by the outliers than the median, so the median should be used. Students are working on the second success criterion.
- Student answers to part (b) will influence their answers to part (c).
- ◉ To help students with part (c), review interquartile range and mean absolute deviation from Chapter 9. Students are now working on the third success criterion.
- Discuss the Math Practice note.

10.4 Choosing Appropriate Measures

Learning Target: Determine which measures of center and variation best describe a data set.

Success Criteria:
- I can describe the shape of a distribution.
- I can use the shape of a distribution to determine which measure of center best describes the data.
- I can use the shape of a distribution to determine which measure of variation best describes the data.

EXPLORATION 1 Using Shapes of Distributions

Work with a partner.

a. In Section 10.3 Exploration 1(a), you described the distribution of the first digits of the numbers at the right. In Exploration 1(b), you described the distribution of the data set below.

538-	664-
438-	664-
664-	538-
761-	855-
868-	664-
735-	538-
694-	654-
599-	654-
725-	725-
556-	538-
555-	799-
456-	764-
736-	664-
664-	664-
576-	725-

Ages of Cell Phones (years)					
0	1	0	6	4	0
2	3	5	1	1	2
0	1	2	3	1	0
0	0	1	1	1	1
7	1	4	2	2	2

What do you notice about the measures of center, measures of variation, and the shapes of the distributions? Explain.

b. Which measure of center best describes each data set? Explain your reasoning.

c. Which measure of variation best describes each data set? Explain your reasoning.

Math Practice

Construct Arguments

Explain why the shapes of the distributions in Exploration 1 affect which measures best describe the data.

10.4 Lesson

You can use a measure of center and a measure of variation to describe the distribution of a data set. The shape of the distribution can help you choose which measures are the most appropriate to use.

Key Idea

Choosing Appropriate Measures

The mean absolute deviation (MAD) uses the mean in its calculation. So, when a data distribution is *symmetric,*

- use the mean to describe the center and
- use the MAD to describe the variation.

The interquartile range (IQR) uses quartiles in its calculation. So, when a data distribution is *skewed,*

- use the median to describe the center and
- use the IQR to describe the variation.

EXAMPLE 1 Choosing Appropriate Measures

Bordering States	Frequency
0–1	3
2–3	13
4–5	21
6–7	11
8–9	2

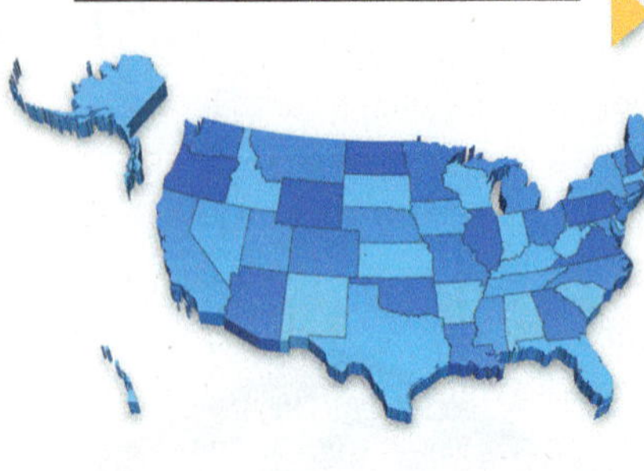

The frequency table shows the number of states that border each state in the United States. What are the most appropriate measures to describe the center and the variation?

To see the distribution of the data, display the data in a histogram.

The left side of the graph is approximately a mirror image of the right side of the graph. The distribution is symmetric.

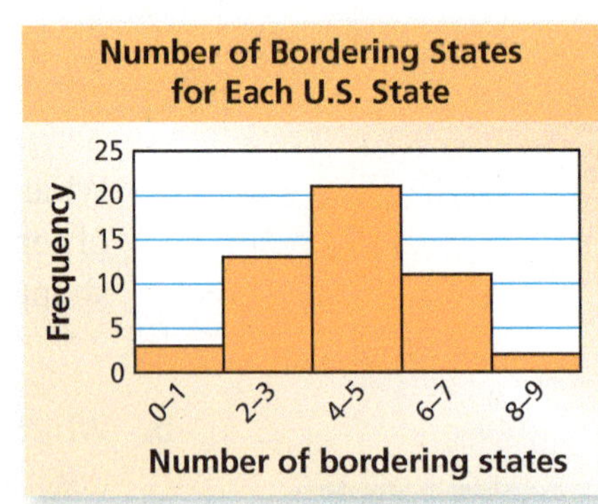

So, the mean and the mean absolute deviation are the most appropriate measures to describe the center and the variation.

Try It

1. The frequency table shows the gas mileages of several motorcycles made by a company. What are the most appropriate measures to describe the center and the variation?

Mileage (miles per gallon)	40–44	45–49	50–54	55–59	60–64	65–69
Frequency	2	1	6	8	10	3

Laurie's Notes

Scaffolding Instruction

- As students continue to analyze, describe, and compare sets of data, they will become more proficient with making sense of data.
- **Emerging:** Students may have difficulty transferring their knowledge of data displays to determining which measures of center and variation best describe a data set. These students will benefit from guided instruction for the examples.
- **Proficient:** Students can view a data display and visualize which measures of center and variation best describe the data set. Have students complete Try It Exercises 1 and 2 before moving on to the Self-Assessment exercises.

Key Idea

- Write the Key Idea. In choosing the appropriate measures, first determine the shape of the distribution, symmetric or skewed. Students should know that the shape does not need to be either of these, but only these types of shapes are considered here.
- **MP2 Reason Abstractly and Quantitatively:** Discuss how outliers can affect mean and median. Both symmetric and skewed distributions can have outliers.

EXAMPLE 1

? "Where does [insert your state] fall in the frequency table?" Answers will vary.

? "How many values does the data set have?" 50

- **FYI:** Tennessee and Missouri both border 8 other states.
- Study the frequency table and ask students to predict the shape of the distribution to be skewed or symmetric. Students should recognize that the data is symmetric.
- Have students construct the histogram. Ask students if they still agree with the predicted shape.

? "What are the most appropriate measures to describe the center and variation? Explain." mean and mean absolute deviation; The distribution is symmetric.

- **MP2 Reason Abstractly and Quantitatively:** Students should be able to explain why it is not possible to find exact values of the mean and the mean absolute deviation for the data.

Try It

- **Think-Pair-Share:** Students should read the exercise independently and then work in pairs to solve the problem. Have each pair compare their answers with another pair and discuss any discrepancies.

Extra Example 1

The frequency table shows the gas mileages of several vehicles made by a company. What are the most appropriate measures to describe the center and the variation?

Mileage (miles per gallon)	Frequency
15–17	2
18–20	4
21–23	3
24–26	2
27–29	1

median and interquartile range

ELL Support

Have students work in groups to discuss Try It Exercise 1. Provide guiding questions as they discuss the data: What does the top row of information show? What does each number in the bottom row indicate? How do you graph the information? How is the data distributed? What is the most appropriate measure of center? What is the most appropriate measure of variation?

Beginner: Draw the graph and write the answers to the problem.

Intermediate: Use simple sentences to answer the guiding questions. For example, "The top row shows the miles per gallon."

Advanced: Use detailed sentences to answer the guiding questions and help guide discussion.

Try It

1. median and IQR

Extra Example 2

The dot plot shows the average numbers of hours students in a class exercise each day. Describe the center and the variation of the data set.

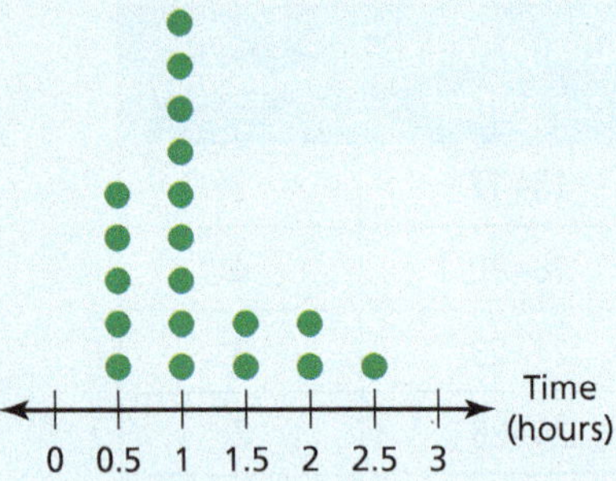

The data are centered around 1 hour. The middle half of the data varies by no more than 1 hour.

Try It

2. The data values are centered around 5 hours. The data values differ from the mean by an average of 1.2 hours.

Self-Assessment for Concepts & Skills

3. *Sample answer:*

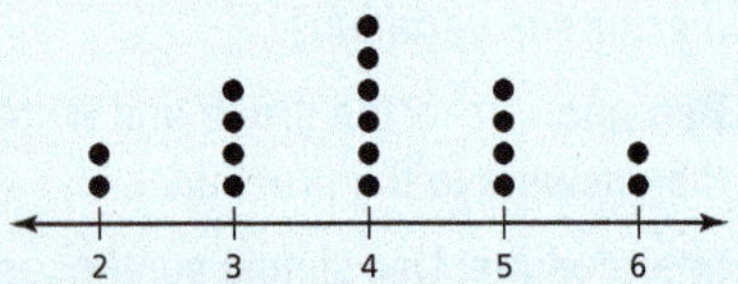

4. median and IQR; data are skewed left; median = 40, IQR = 12
5. mean and MAD; data are symmetric; mean = 14, MAD = 2.5
6. See Additional Answers.

Laurie's Notes

EXAMPLE 2

- "What is the average number of hours of sleep you get each night?" Answers will vary.
- Sketch the dot plot shown.
- "How many students does this plot represent?" 19 "What is the range?" 4 hours "What is the mode?" 9 hours
- "What are the most appropriate measures to describe the center and variation? Explain." median and interquartile range; Because the data distribution is skewed.
- Work through the steps in finding the median and the interquartile range. Summarize the results as shown.

Try It

- **Neighbor Check:** Have students work independently and then have their neighbors check their work. Have students discuss any discrepancies.
- If students also displayed the data in a histogram, have them share their graphs with other students by using a document camera. Have students discuss which data display is better suited for determining the most appropriate measures of center and variation. Students may choose either one for different reasons.

Self-Assessment for Concepts & Skills

- Students' responses to Exercise 3 give you a glimpse into the depth of understanding your students have about data analysis.
- Look for a relationship between students' responses to Exercises 4, 5, and 6. Are they in agreement?
- Students are assessing their progress with all of the success criteria.

ELL Support

Allow students to work in pairs. Have pairs display their dot plots on whiteboards for your review. Have two pairs compare their answers for Exercises 4–6. Monitor discussions and provide support as needed. Have each group reach a consensus for their final answers. Then review the answers to each exercise as a class.

The Success Criteria Self-Assessment chart can be found in the *Student Journal* or online at *BigIdeasMath.com*.

EXAMPLE 2 Describing a Data Set

The dot plot shows the average numbers of hours students in a class sleep each night. Describe the center and the variation of the data set.

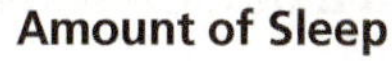

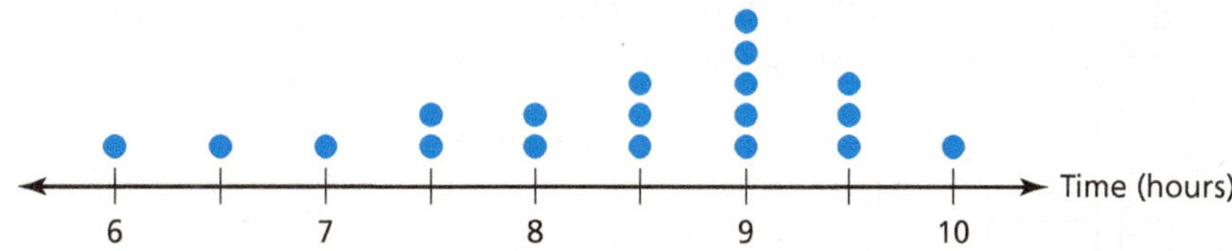

Most of the data values are on the right, clustered around 9, and the tail extends to the left. The distribution is skewed left, so the median and the interquartile range are the most appropriate measures to describe the center and the variation.

The median is 8.5 hours. The first quartile is 7.5, and the third quartile is 9. So, the interquartile range is $9 - 7.5 = 1.5$ hours.

The data are centered around 8.5 hours. The middle half of the data varies by no more than 1.5 hours.

Try It

Weekly Gym Time

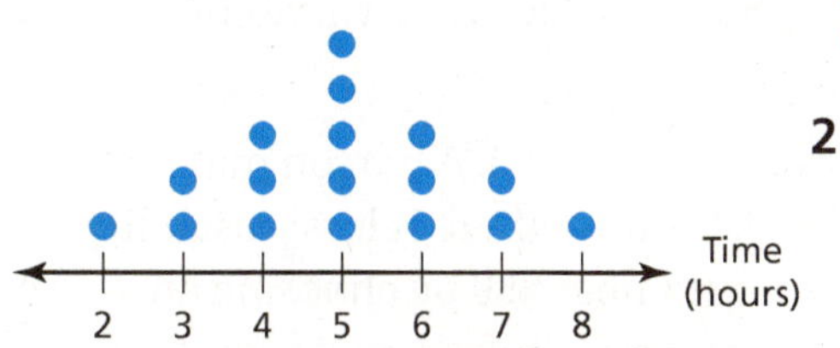

2. The dot plot shows the numbers of hours people spent at the gym last week. Describe the center and the variation of the data set.

Self-Assessment for Concepts & Skills

Solve each exercise. Then rate your understanding of the success criteria in your journal.

3. **OPEN-ENDED** Construct a dot plot for which the mean is the most appropriate measure to describe the center of the distribution.

CHOOSING APPROPRIATE MEASURES **Choose the most appropriate measures to describe the center and the variation. Explain your reasoning. Then find the measures you chose.**

4.

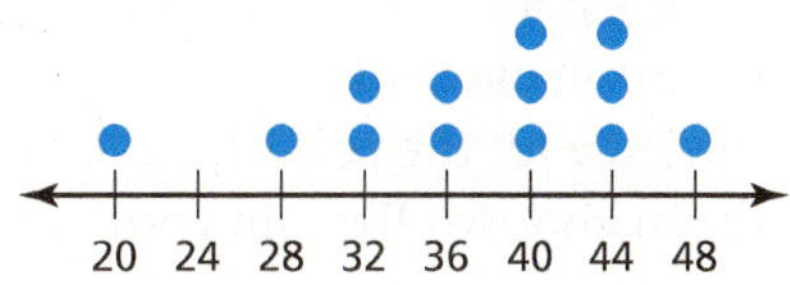

5.

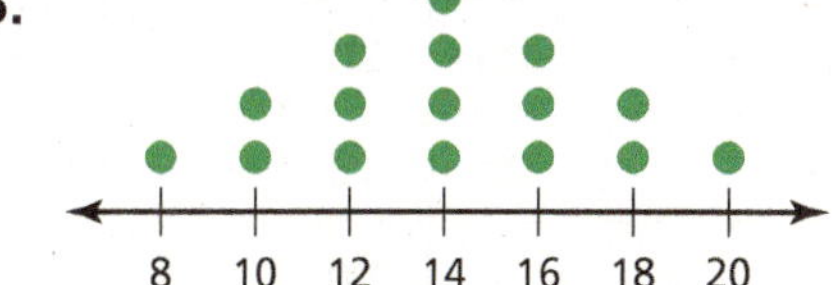

6. **WRITING** Explain why the most appropriate measures to describe the center and the variation of a data set are determined by the shape of the distribution.

EXAMPLE 3 Modeling Real Life

Basket A	
$70	$40
$60	$90
$10	$0
$70	$40
$30	$100
$50	$60
$40	$50
$60	$30

Basket B	
$45	$30
$45	$55
$55	$40
$50	$60
$45	$50
$55	$55
$60	$45
$40	$70

Two baskets each have 16 envelopes with money inside, as shown in the tables. How much does a typical envelope in each basket contain? Why might a person want to pick from Basket B instead of Basket A?

To answer each question, display the data in dot plots to see the distributions of the data.

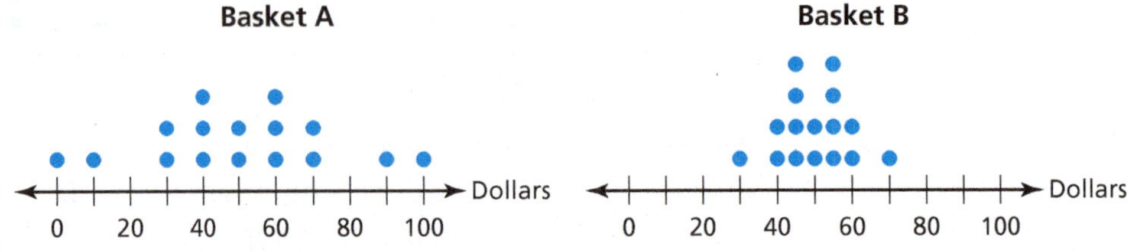

In each graph, the left side is a mirror image of the right side. Because both distributions are symmetric, the mean and the mean absolute deviation are the most appropriate measures to describe the center and the variation.

The mean of each data set is $\frac{800}{16} = \$50$. The MAD of Basket A is $\frac{320}{16} = \$20$, and the MAD of Basket B is $\frac{120}{16} = \$7.50$. So, Basket A has more variability.

A typical envelope in each basket contains about $50. A person may choose from Basket B instead of Basket A because there is less variability. This means it is more likely to get an amount near $50 by choosing an envelope from Basket B than by choosing an envelope from Basket A.

Self-Assessment for Problem Solving

Solve each exercise. Then rate your understanding of the success criteria in your journal.

7. Why might a person want to pick from Basket A instead of Basket B in Example 3? Explain your reasoning.

8. In a video game, two rooms each have 12 treasure chests containing gold coins. The tables show the numbers of coins in each chest. You pick one chest and are rewarded with the coins inside. From which room would you choose? Explain your reasoning.

Room A	
5	25
30	45
20	15
50	20
25	30
10	25

Room B	
25	15
30	20
5	10
20	50
45	5
25	50

9. Create a dot plot of the numbers of pets that students in your class own. Describe the center and the variation of the data set.

Laurie's Notes

Formative Assessment Tip

3-Read Modeling
This technique helps students make sense of word problems by focusing their attention on understanding the situation rather than finding the answer. The *problem stem* (the word problem without the question) is read three times with a different goal each time. First, read the problem stem to the class and ask, "What is this situation about?" Second, lead students in a choral read or have students read the problem stem to a partner. Then ask, "What quantities and units are involved?" Third, ask students to think about what is missing while they choral or partner read. Then ask, "What mathematical questions could you ask about this situation?" After each question is shared, ask, "Can this question be answered with the given information?" Discuss why or why not. Then have students work in groups to solve a question based on the problem stem. You can assign a specific question or allow groups to choose.

EXAMPLE 3

- In this example, students will use the shape of a distribution to determine which measures of center and variation best describe the data set. Students will apply the learning target to analyze a real-life situation.
- **3-Read Modeling:** Read the problem stem and table.
- Draw the dot plots and ask students which basket they would prefer to choose the envelope from. Have students explain their choices. Listen for descriptions of clusters, gaps, spread, and likelihood.
- ? "What do the dot plots have in common?" *Sample answer:* They are both symmetric and they have the same number of data values.
- Have students calculate the mean and the mean absolute deviation of each data set. Students should recognize that the data for Basket A are more spread out than Basket B, so it makes sense that Basket A has more variability.

Self-Assessment for Problem Solving

- **MP5 Use Appropriate Tools Strategically:** In Exercise 8, encourage students to use a dot plot or a histogram to display the data.
- Ask each student how many pets he or she owns. Record their answers on the board so students can use the data for Exercise 9.
- When students finish the exercises, have them share their thinking about Exercises 7 and 8.

The Success Criteria Self-Assessment chart can be found in the *Student Journal* or online at *BigIdeasMath.com.*

Closure

- **Exit Ticket:** Summarize how to use the shape of a distribution to choose the most appropriate measures to describe the center and the variation. When the data is symmetric, use the mean and the mean absolute deviation. When the data is skewed, use the median and interquartile range.

Extra Example 3

Two boxes each have 10 gift certificates inside, as shown in the tables. How much is a typical gift certificate in each box worth? Why might a person want to pick from Box A instead of Box B?

Box A	
$10	$20
$20	$15
$15	$20
$25	$20
$30	$25

Box B	
$15	$5
$15	$35
$25	$20
$15	$20
$25	$25

Box A: $20, Box B: $20; Because Box A has less variability.

Self-Assessment for Problem Solving

7. Basket A contains a few envelopes with more money in them compared to Basket B.
8. *Sample answer:* A person may choose Room A because there is less variability in Room A's treasure chests compared to Room B.
9. Check students' work.

Learning Target

Determine which measures of center and variation best describe a data set.

Success Criteria

- Describe the shape of a distribution.
- Use the shape of a distribution to determine which measure of center best describes the data.
- Use the shape of a distribution to determine which measure of variation best describes the data.

Review & Refresh

1. skewed left
2. skewed right
3. median = 70; $Q_1 = 65.5$; $Q_3 = 75$; IQR = 9.5
4. median = 37.5; $Q_1 = 30$; $Q_3 = 44$; IQR = 14
5. $2\frac{1}{5}$
6. $5\frac{6}{7}$
7. $2\frac{1}{8}$
8. $\frac{8}{75}$

Concepts, Skills, & Problem Solving

9. mean = 7; median = 7.5; The distribution is skewed left, so the median is the most appropriate measure of center.
10. mean = 26; median = 26; The distribution is symmetric, so the mean is the most appropriate measure of center.
11. median and IQR
12. mean and MAD
13. mean and MAD
14. median and IQR

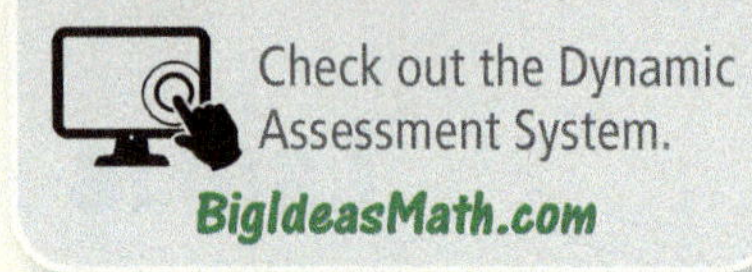

Assignment Guide and Concept Check

Scaffold assignments to support all students in their learning progression. The suggested assignments are a starting point. Continue to assign additional exercises and revisit with spaced practice to move every student toward proficiency.

Level	Assignment 1	Assignment 2
Emerging	1, 2, 4, 7, 9, 11, 13	12, 14, 15, 16, 17, 18, 19
Proficient	1, 2, 4, 7, 10, 11, 13	12, 14, 15, 16, 17, 18, 19
Advanced	1, 2, 4, 7, 10, 12, 14	16, 17, 18, 19, 20, 21

- Assignment 1 is for use after students complete the Self-Assessment for Concepts & Skills.
- Assignment 2 is for use after students complete the Self-Assessment for Problem Solving.
- The red exercises can be used as a concept check.

Review & Refresh Prior Skills

Exercises 1 and 2 Describing Shapes of Distributions
Exercises 3 and 4 Finding the Interquartile Range
Exercises 5–8 Dividing With Mixed Numbers

Common Errors

- **Exercises 9–14** Students may mix up the appropriate measures for symmetric and skewed data distributions and then use the wrong measures to describe the center and the variation. Remind students to use the mean and MAD to describe symmetric distributions and use the median and IQR to describe skewed distributions.

10.4 Practice

Review & Refresh

Describe the shape of the distribution.

1.

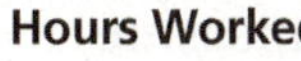

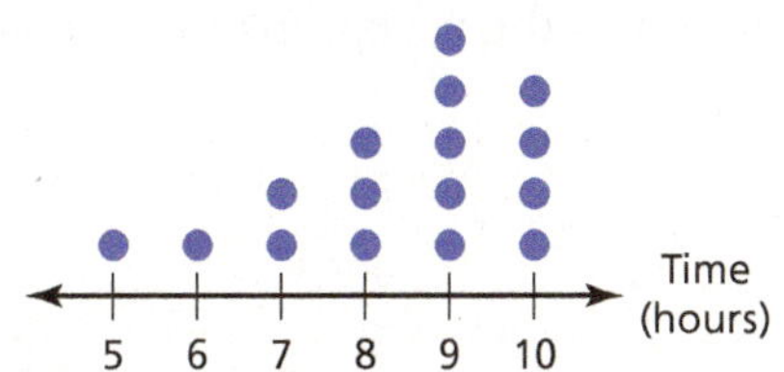

2.

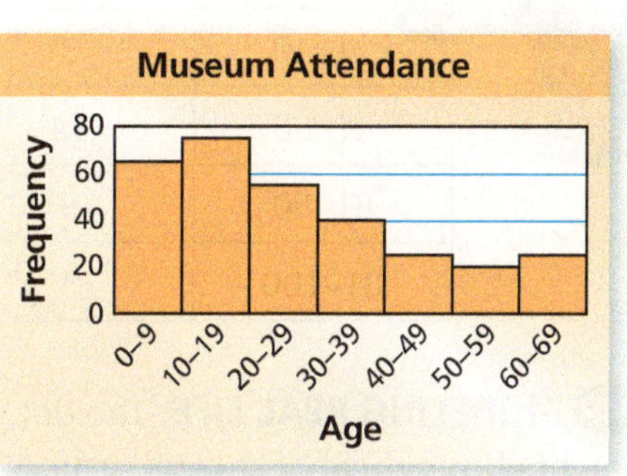

Find the median, first quartile, third quartile, and interquartile range of the data.

3. 68, 74, 67, 72, 63, 70, 78, 64, 76

4. 39, 48, 33, 24, 30, 44, 36, 41, 28, 53

Divide. Write the answer in simplest form.

5. $4\frac{2}{5} \div 2$

6. $5\frac{1}{8} \div \frac{7}{8}$

7. $2\frac{3}{7} \div 1\frac{1}{7}$

8. $\frac{4}{5} \div 7\frac{1}{2}$

Concepts, Skills, & Problem Solving

USING SHAPES OF DISTRIBUTIONS **Find the mean and the median of the data set. Which measure of center best describes the data set? Explain your reasoning.** (See Exploration 1, p. 477.)

9. 9, 3, 7, 7, 9, 2, 8, 9, 6, 7, 8, 9

10. 24, 25, 27, 27, 23, 29, 26, 26, 26, 25, 28

CHOOSING APPROPRIATE MEASURES **Choose the most appropriate measures to describe the center and the variation.**

11.

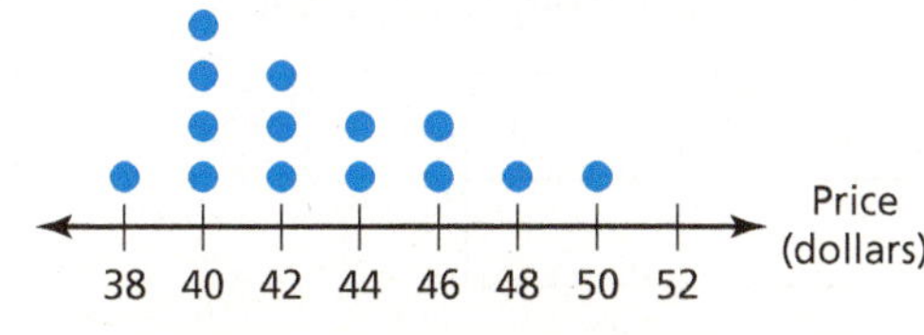

12. Time Volunteering

Time (hours): 2, 3, 4, 5, 6, 7, 8, 9

13.

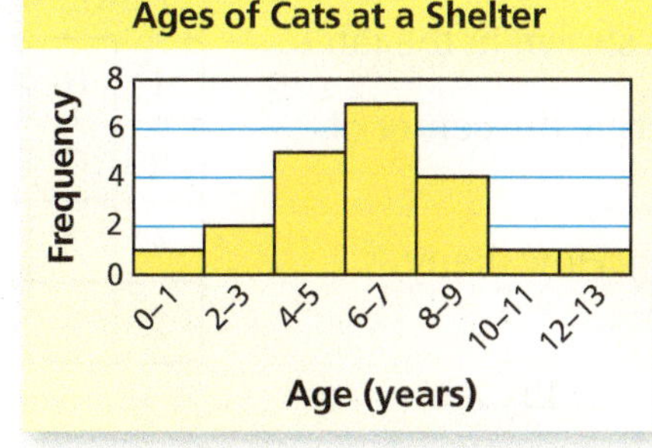

14.

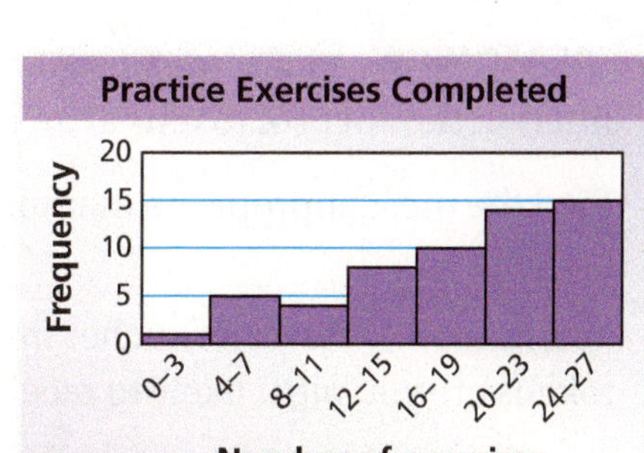

15. **DESCRIBING DATA SETS** Describe the centers and the variations of the data sets in Exercises 11 and 12.

Eggs (thousands)	Frequency
1–20	5
21–40	8
41–60	14
61–80	9
81–100	3

16. **MP MODELING REAL LIFE** The frequency table shows the numbers of eggs laid by several octopi. What are the most appropriate measures to describe the center and the variation? Explain your reasoning.

17. **MP MODELING REAL LIFE** The dot plot shows the vertical jump heights (in inches) of several professional athletes. Describe the center and the variation of the data set.

Height	Dots
37	●
36	
35	●
34	●●
33	●
32	●●
31	●●●
30	●●●●
29	●●●
28	●●
27	●
26	●
25	
24	●

18. **OPEN-ENDED** Describe a real-life situation where the median and the interquartile range are likely the best measures of center and variation to describe the data. Explain your reasoning.

Pile A	
5	7
4	3
6	4
5	6
4	6
3	5
5	7

Pile B	
7	5
5	2
3	8
5	6
5	4
0	8
2	10

19. **MP PROBLEM SOLVING** You play a board game in which you draw from one of two piles of cards. Each card has a number that says how many spaces you will move your piece forward on the game board. The tables show the numbers on the cards in each pile. From which pile would you choose? Explain your reasoning.

20. **DIG DEEPER!** The frequency table shows the numbers of words that several students can form in 1 minute using the letters P, S, E, D, A. What are the most appropriate measures to describe the center and variation? Can you find the exact values of the measures of center and variation for the data? Explain.

Number of Words	1–3	4–6	7–9	10–12	13–15
Frequency	7	9	5	3	1

21. **MP REASONING** A bag contains 20 vouchers that can be redeemed for different numbers of tokens at an arcade, as shown in the table.

Numbers of Tokens				
1	10	2	1	4
9	3	10	2	3
4	2	1	4	1
2	1	10	3	7

a. Find the most appropriate measure to describe the center of the data set.

b. You randomly select a voucher from the bag. How many tokens are you most likely to receive? Explain.

c. Are your answers in parts (a) and (b) the same? Explain why or why not.

Mini-Assessment

The dot plot shows the average numbers of minutes students in a class exercise each day.

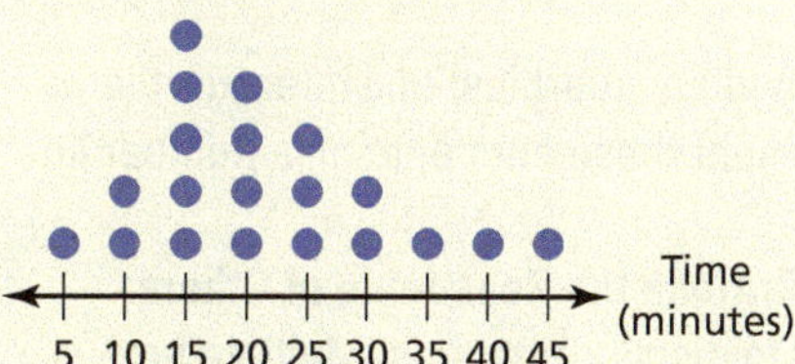

1. What are the most appropriate measures to describe the center and the variation? median and interquartile range
2. Describe the center and the variation of the data set. The data are centered around 20 minutes. The middle half of the data varies by no more than 12.5 minutes.

Section Resources

Surface Level	Deep Level
Resources by Chapter • Extra Practice • Reteach • Puzzle Time Student Journal • Self-Assessment • Practice Differentiating the Lesson Tutorial Videos Skills Review Handbook Skills Trainer	Resources by Chapter • Enrichment and Extension Graphic Organizers Dynamic Assessment System • Section Practice

Concepts, Skills, & Problem Solving

15. Exercise 11: The price of jeans is centered around 42 dollars and the middle half of the prices vary by no more than 6 dollars; Exercise 12: The time spent volunteering centered around approximately 5.78 hours and the values differ from the average by about 1.47 hours.
16. mean and MAD; The distribution is symmetric so mean and MAD would be the most appropriate.
17. The typical vertical jump height is about 30.45 inches. The data values differ from the mean by an average of about 2.31 inches.
18. *Sample answer:* The distribution of household income in the United States. The data values for this distribution will be skewed to the right, indicating that median and IQR will be the most appropriate.
19. *Sample answer:* Pile A; Pile A has less variability than Pile B.
20. median and IQR; no; *Sample answer:* You only know what interval each of the data values falls into, not the specific data values.
21. a. median = 3 tokens

    b. *Sample answer:* You will be most likely to pick a voucher for 1 token because that is the mode.

    c. no; *Sample answer:* In part (a), the most appropriate measure to describe the center was found. In part (b), the number of tokens that appears most was found.

Learning Target

Display and interpret data in box-and-whisker plots.

Success Criteria

- Find the five-number summary of a data set.
- Make a box-and-whisker plot.
- Explain what the box and the whiskers of a box-and-whisker plot represent.
- Compare data sets represented by box-and-whisker plots.

Warm Up

Cumulative, vocabulary, and prerequisite skills practice opportunities are available in the *Resources by Chapter* or at *BigIdeasMath.com*.

ELL Support

Draw a simple representation of a cat or dog's face with whiskers projecting. Point to the whiskers and ask students to name them. Provide support if they are unfamiliar with the word. Ask a volunteer to draw a box. Then ask students to guess what they think a box-and-whisker plot might look like.

Exploration 1

a. *Sample answer:* The rectangle from 8 to 17 represents the "box"; The line segments from 2 to 8 and 17 to 19 represent the "whiskers" because they look like whiskers coming off the box.

b. 2: least value; 8: first quartile; 14: median; 17: third quartile; 19: greatest value

c. See Additional Answers.

d. Check students' work.

Laurie's Notes

STATE STANDARDS
6.SP.A.2, 6.SP.B.4, 6.SP.B.5c

Preparing to Teach

- Students should know how to find the median, quartiles, and interquartile range of a data set. They will now represent these concepts on a number line using a box-and-whisker plot.
- **MP3 Construct Viable Arguments and Critique the Reasoning of Others:** Students create box-and-whisker plots to display data sets. Multiple box-and-whisker plots can be displayed on the same number line, so students are asked to construct viable arguments in comparing data sets.

Motivate

- The physical involvement of making a human **box-and-whisker plot** makes a lasting impression on students.
- **Preparation:** Give each student a paper with a large number written on it. Include an outlier or two on one end of the data.

? "What is the first step in analyzing data?" sort the data

- Students should stand up and sort themselves. Have the median, the first and third quartiles, and the least and greatest data values take one step forward. If there is an even number of data values, the middle two students must figure out how to represent their mean and take a step also. These students represent the **five-number summary**. All other students go back to their seats.
- Make a number line on the floor. Position the five key values. Use string to form a segment from the student representing the first (or lower) quartile to the student representing the least value. Do the same for the third (or upper) quartile and the greatest value. Have the students representing the first and third quartiles hold wrapping paper between them to represent the box. The student(s) representing the median should take his or her place in front of the wrapping paper. Say, "This is a box-and-whisker plot!"
- **MP2 Reason Abstractly and Quantitatively:** Discuss features of the plot. If the plot includes an outlier, the length of the string becomes an instant topic of conversation. Students recognize that the same number of data values is being represented by each whisker, yet the lengths of string are very different.

Exploration 1

- Explain that a box-and-whisker plot is a data display that is generally used for very large data sets. Not every value is plotted, but characteristics of the data set are still conveyed. For instance, the results of a state test for all sixth-grade students could be displayed using a box-and-whisker plot.
- **Big Idea:** The five numbers graphed summarize the entire data set. The least and greatest values are the boundaries. The median separates the data into two parts. The first quartile is the median of the lower half. The third quartile is the median of the upper half. The box encloses the middle 50% of the data.

? **MP2 Reason Abstractly and Quantitatively:** "What percent of the data is represented by each whisker?" 25% "How many data values are in each whisker?" 6 These questions allow students to reason quantitatively.

- For part (d), collect students' papers and write the numbers on the board.

10.5 Box-and-Whisker Plots

Learning Target: Display and interpret data in box-and-whisker plots.

Success Criteria:
- I can find the five-number summary of a data set.
- I can make a box-and-whisker plot.
- I can explain what the box and the whiskers of a box-and-whisker plot represent.
- I can compare data sets represented by box-and-whisker plots.

EXPLORATION 1 Drawing a Box-and-Whisker Plot

Work with a partner. Each student in a sixth-grade class is asked to choose a number from 1 to 20. The results are shown below.

Numbers Chosen			
4	5	14	16
5	16	17	8
18	13	17	18
17	14	19	11
15	8	2	18
13	19	8	7

a. The *box-and-whisker plot* below represents the data set. Which part represents the *box*? the *whiskers*? Explain.

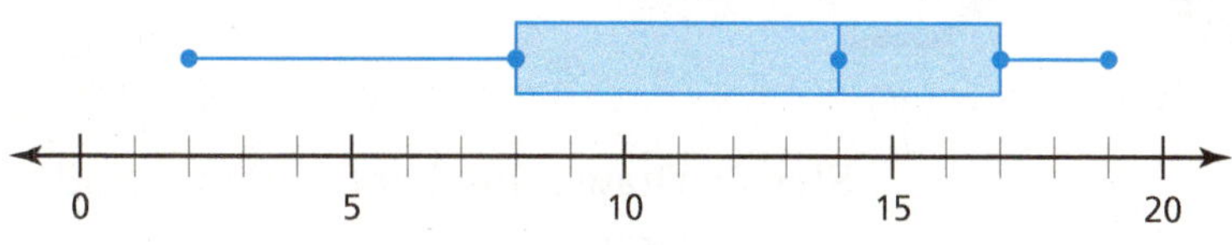

Math Practice

View as Components
What do the different components of a box-and-whisker plot represent?

b. What does each of the five plotted points represent?

c. In your own words, describe what a box-and-whisker plot is and what it tells you about a data set.

d. Conduct a survey in your class. Have each student write a number from 1 to 20 on a piece of paper. Collect all of the data and draw a box-and-whisker plot that represents the data. Compare the data with the box-and-whisker plot in part (a).

10.5 Lesson

Key Vocabulary
box-and-whisker plot, p. 484
five-number summary, p. 484

Key Idea

Box-and-Whisker Plot

A **box-and-whisker plot** represents a data set along a number line by using the least value, the greatest value, and the quartiles of the data. A box-and-whisker plot shows the *variability* of a data set.

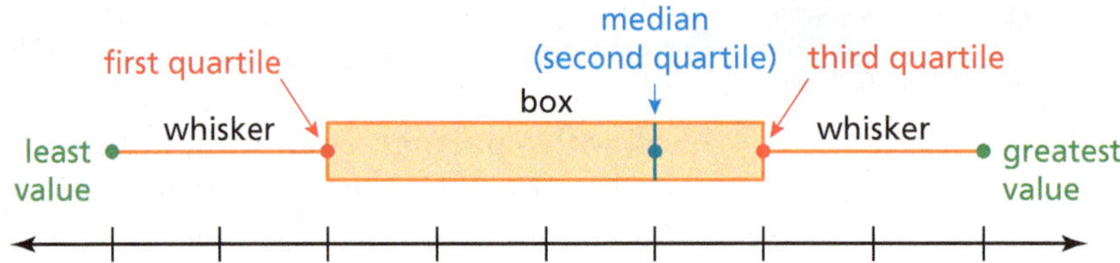

The five numbers that make up the box-and-whisker plot are called the **five-number summary** of the data set.

EXAMPLE 1 Making a Box-and-Whisker Plot

Make a box-and-whisker plot for the ages (in years) of the spider monkeys at a zoo.

15, 20, 14, 38, 30, 36, 30, 30, 27, 26, 33, 35

Step 1: Order the data. Find the quartiles.

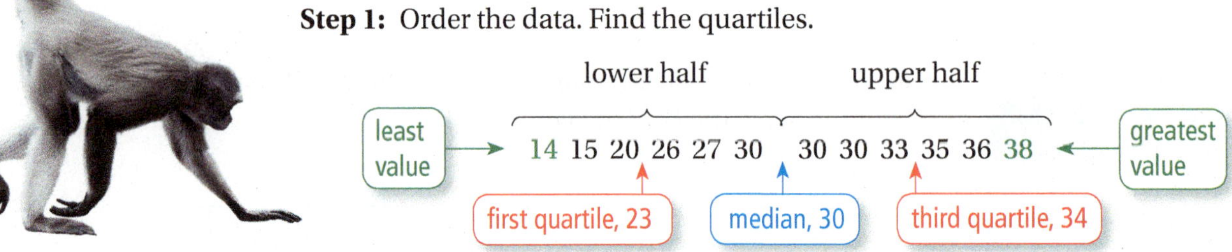

Step 2: Draw a number line that includes the least and greatest values. Graph points above the number line that represent the five-number summary.

Step 3: Draw a box using the quartiles. Draw a line through the median. Draw whiskers from the box to the least and the greatest values.

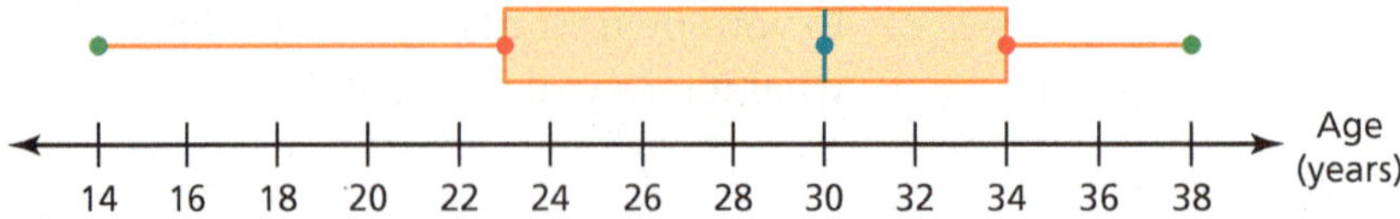

Try It

1. A group of friends spent 1, 0, 2, 3, 4, 3, 6, 1, 0, 1, 2, and 2 hours online last night. Make a box-and-whisker plot for the data.

Multi-Language Glossary at BigIdeasMath.com

Laurie's Notes

Scaffolding Instruction

- Throughout this chapter, students have analyzed data in many ways. They know how to find the five numbers that make up a box-and-whisker plot, but the actual display is new. After some experience constructing and interpreting a box-and-whisker plot, students will appreciate its usefulness when analyzing large data sets and comparing two or more data sets.
- **Emerging:** Students have difficulty either using the five key values to create a box-and-whisker plot or interpreting the information displayed in a box-and-whisker plot. The examples will give students more practice with both skills.
- **Proficient:** Students can find the five numbers that make up a box-and-whisker plot. They may relate the shape of a distribution to how the data are distributed in the box-and-whisker plot. This display is new to students, so have them complete the Try It exercises before using the Self-Assessment exercises to check their own understanding.

Key Idea

- Define a **box-and-whisker plot**. Draw the sample plot and discuss the process and vocabulary.
- **Discuss:** The box-and-whisker plot shows the *variability* of the data. Refer to this idea when working through each example.

EXAMPLE 1

- Point out that ordering the data from least to greatest makes it possible to find the least value, greatest value, and quartiles.

? "How many data values are there?" 12 "When there are 12 data values, how do you find the median?" Find the mean of the 6th and 7th data values.

- There are six data values in the lower half and six data values in the upper half. The first quartile and third quartile are the mean of the middle two data values in each half.

Try It

- Students are working on the first two success criteria.
- **Common Error:** Students may forget to order the data before creating the box-and-whisker plot.

ELL Support

Have students practice language by working in pairs to complete Try It Exercise 1. Provide guiding questions: How will you organize the data? What values form the box? What values form the left whisker? the right whisker?

Beginner: Draw the box-and-whisker plot.

Intermediate: Use simple sentences to answer the guiding questions such as, "Order the numbers."

Advanced: Use detailed sentences to answer the guiding questions and help guide discussion.

Scaffold instruction to support all students in their learning. Learning is individualized and you may want to group students differently as they move in and out of these levels with each skill and concept. Student self-assessment and feedback help guide your instructional decisions about how and when to layer support for all students to become proficient learners.

Extra Example 1

Make a box-and-whisker plot for the numbers of text messages received over several days.

32, 18, 11, 28, 42, 33, 40, 21, 37, 24

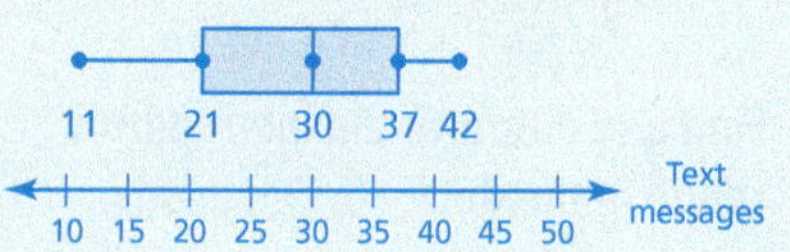

Try It

1.

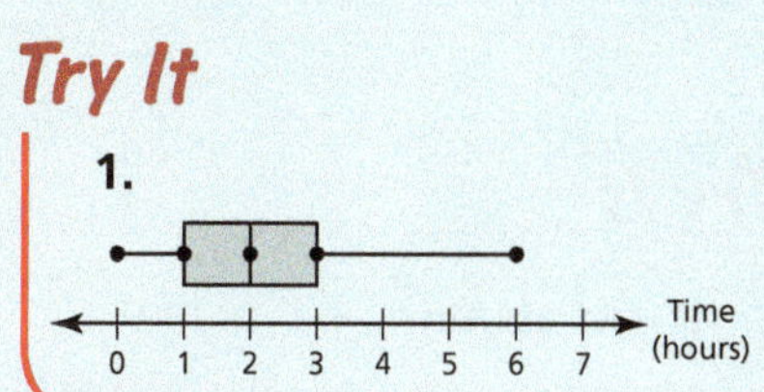

Laurie's Notes

Discuss

- Students need to understand how data are distributed in a box-and-whisker plot so that they can interpret the spread of the data.
- The five key values plotted in a box-and-whisker plot divide the data into four parts.
- ? "What fraction of the data in the box are to the left of the median? to the right?" about $\frac{1}{4}$; about $\frac{1}{4}$
- Relate the parts of the box-and-whisker plot to benchmark percents (e.g., 25%, 50%, 75%) of the data values.
- Relate the definition of interquartile range to the box-and-whisker plot, indicating that it represents the "length" of the box. Discuss the push-pin note.

EXAMPLE 2

- **FYI:** Body Mass Index (BMI) is a numerical value determined using a person's weight and height. BMI can be used to screen for health problems.
- ? "Do you know from the box-and-whisker plot how many students are in the class?" no
- It is important for students to remember that you cannot determine the number of data points from a given box-and-whisker plot. You can only determine the five-number summary points and of those, only two *must* be values in the data set (the least value and greatest value).
- ? "What is the range of the data and what does it mean in the context of the problem?" $28 - 17 = 11$; This means that the difference between the highest and lowest BMIs is 11.
- ? "What does the length of each part of the box-and-whisker plot tell you about the distribution of the data?" *Sample answers:* About 25% of the BMIs are between 17 and 19, about 50% are between 19 and 22, and about 25% are between 22 and 28.
- In part (c), students should focus on the middle half of the data (the box).
- It may be difficult for some students to understand that one part of the box-and-whisker plot can be much shorter than another part. For example, the lower quarter (the left whisker) of the data range from 17 to 19, while the upper quarter (the right whisker) of the data range from 22 to 28.

Try It

- **MP3 Construct Viable Arguments and Critique the Reasoning of Others:** Ask different students to explain their answers. Then ask other students to critique their reasoning. Listen for correct language and valid arguments.
- **Common Error:** Students may read the box-and-whisker plot incorrectly and find the range instead of the interquartile range.
- Students are working on the third success criterion.

Extra Example 2

The box-and-whisker plot shows the times that students in a gym class spent on an obstacle course.

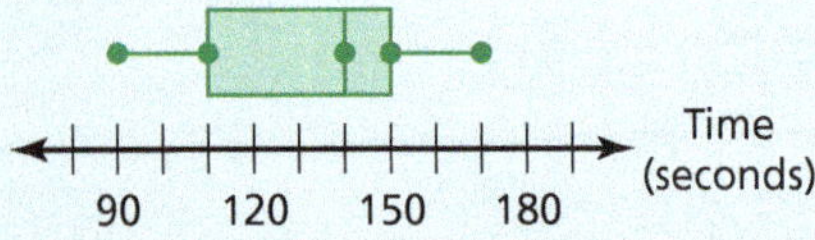

a. What fraction of the class spent 110 seconds or less on the obstacle course? about $\frac{1}{4}$

b. Are the data more spread out below the first quartile or above the third quartile? Explain. neither; Both whiskers are the same length.

c. Find and interpret the interquartile range of the data. 40; The middle half of the students' times varies by no more than 40 seconds.

Try It

2. **a.** about $\frac{3}{4}$

   b. neither; The data are evenly spread out below and above the median.

   c. 80 ft; The middle half of the heights varies by no more than 80 feet.

The figure shows how data are distributed in a box-and-whisker plot.

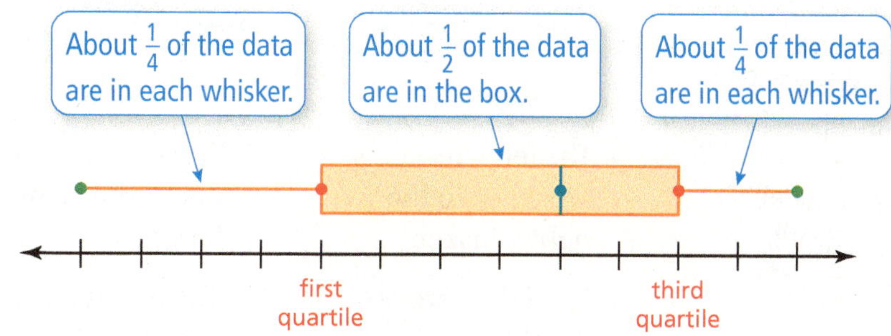

A long whisker or box indicates that the data are more spread out.

EXAMPLE 2 Analyzing a Box-and-Whisker Plot

The box-and-whisker plot shows the body mass index (BMI) of a sixth-grade class.

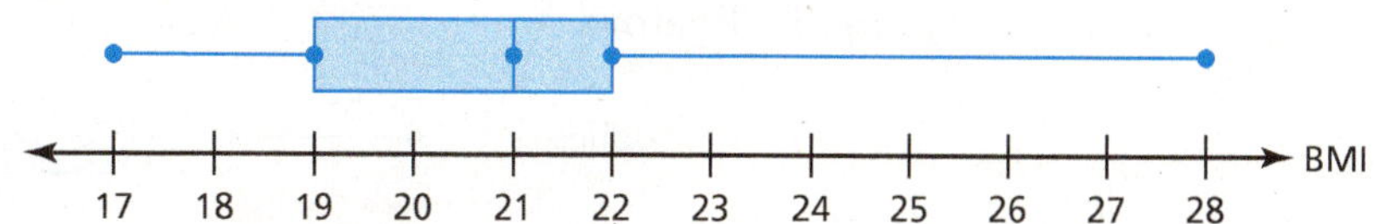

a. What fraction of the students have a BMI of at least 22?

The right whisker represents students who have a BMI of at least 22.

So, about $\frac{1}{4}$ of the students have a BMI of at least 22.

b. Are the data more spread out below the first quartile or above the third quartile? Explain.

The right whisker is longer than the left whisker.

So, the data are more spread out above the third quartile than below the first quartile.

c. Find and interpret the interquartile range of the data.

interquartile range = third quartile − first quartile

$= 22 - 19 = 3$

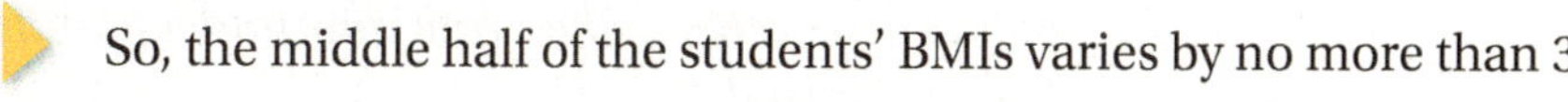

So, the middle half of the students' BMIs varies by no more than 3.

Try It

2. The box-and-whisker plot shows the heights of the roller coasters at an amusement park. (a) What fraction of the roller coasters are between 120 feet tall and 220 feet tall? (b) Are the data more spread out below or above the median? Explain. (c) Find and interpret the interquartile range of the data.

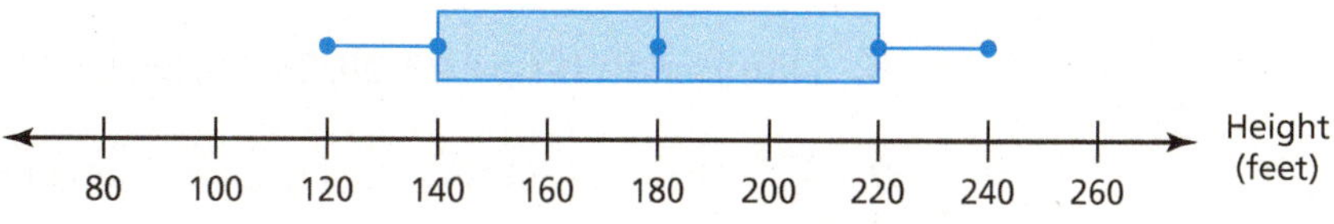

If you can draw a line through the median of a box-and-whisker plot, and each side is a mirror image of the other, then the distribution is symmetric.

A box-and-whisker plot also shows the shape of a distribution.

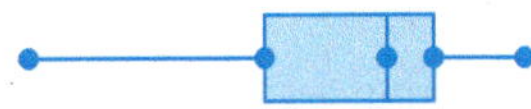

Skewed left

- The left whisker is longer than the right whisker.
- Most data are on the right.

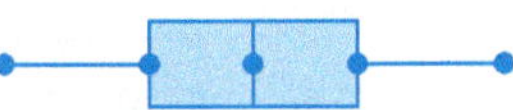

Symmetric

- The whiskers are about the same length.
- The median is in the middle of the box.

Skewed right

- The right whisker is longer than the left whisker.
- Most data are on the left.

EXAMPLE 3 Identifying Shapes of Distributions

The double box-and-whisker plot represents the life spans of crocodiles and alligators at a zoo. Identify the shape of the distribution of the life spans of alligators.

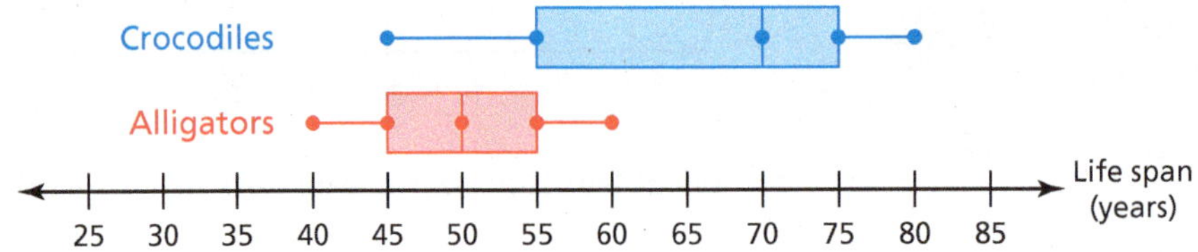

For alligator life spans, the whisker lengths are equal. The median is in the middle of the box. The left side of the box-and-whisker plot is a mirror image of the right side of the box-and-whisker plot.

So, the distribution is symmetric.

Try It

3. Identify the shape of the distribution of the life spans of crocodiles.

Self-Assessment for Concepts & Skills

Solve each exercise. Then rate your understanding of the success criteria in your journal.

4. **VOCABULARY** Explain how to find the five-number summary of a data set.

MAKING A BOX-AND-WHISKER PLOT Make a box-and-whisker plot for the data. Identify the shape of the distribution.

5. Ticket prices (dollars): 39, 42, 40, 47, 38, 39, 44, 55, 44, 58, 45

6. Number of sit-ups: 20, 20, 23, 25, 25, 26, 27, 29, 30, 30, 32, 34, 37, 38

7. **MP NUMBER SENSE** In a box-and-whisker plot, what fraction of the data is greater than the first quartile?

Laurie's Notes

Discuss

- Have students sketch each of these box-and-whisker plots. Discuss what the shape of the plot implies about the distribution of the data.
- ? "If the box-and-whisker plots represent the prices of jeans at three different stores and the range is the same for all three plots, what does the shape tell you about the distribution of the prices at all three stores?" Listen for student understanding of the spread of the data, referencing percentages and relative price.
- Discuss why the push-pin note is true.

EXAMPLE 3

- One advantage of a box-and-whisker plot is that multiple data sets can be shown in the same display, as with double bar graphs and double line graphs. The data sets can also have different numbers of data values.
- Ask students what they notice about the box-and-whisker plot for alligator life spans. Some students will mention that the median is in the middle of the box or that the whiskers are the same length.
- ? "What do these features tell you about the shape of the distribution?" It is symmetric.
- Students are continuing to work on the third success criterion.

Try It

- **Neighbor Check:** Have students work independently and then have their neighbors check their work. Have students discuss any discrepancies.
- **MP7 Look for and Make Use of Structure:** Ask students to explain how the shape of a distribution in a box-and-whisker plot is related to the shape of the distribution in a histogram or dot plot.

Self-Assessment for Concepts & Skills

As students individually assess their progress with the success criteria, they should see the growth of their understanding; from finding a five-number summary to creating a box-and-whisker plot to analyzing the shape of a distribution.

ELL Support

Allow students to work in pairs. Have each pair display their answers to Exercises 5 and 6 on a whiteboard for your review. Ask volunteers to present their answers for Exercises 4 and 7 and then discuss as a class.

The Success Criteria Self-Assessment chart can be found in the *Student Journal* or online at *BigIdeasMath.com*.

Extra Example 3

The box-and-whisker plot represents the prices of basketballs at a store. Identify the shape of the distribution.

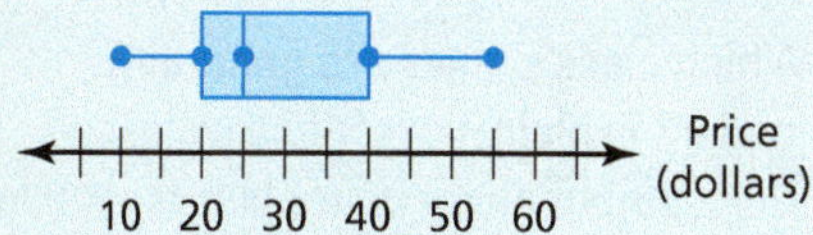

skewed right

Try It

3. skewed left

Self-Assessment for Concepts & Skills

4. Order the data. The first number is the *least value* and the last number is the *greatest value*. The middle value is the *median*. The middle value of the lower half of the data is the *first quartile*. The middle value of the upper half of the data is *third quartile*.
5. See Additional Answers.
6.

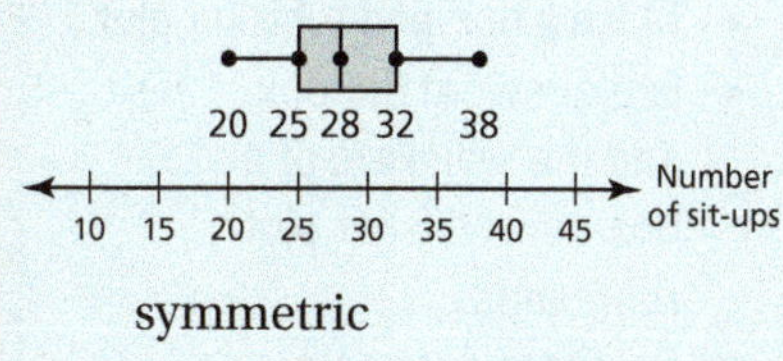

symmetric

7. $\frac{3}{4}$

Extra Example 4

The double box-and-whisker plot represents the times (in minutes) it takes students in your gym class and your friend's gym class to run 1 mile.

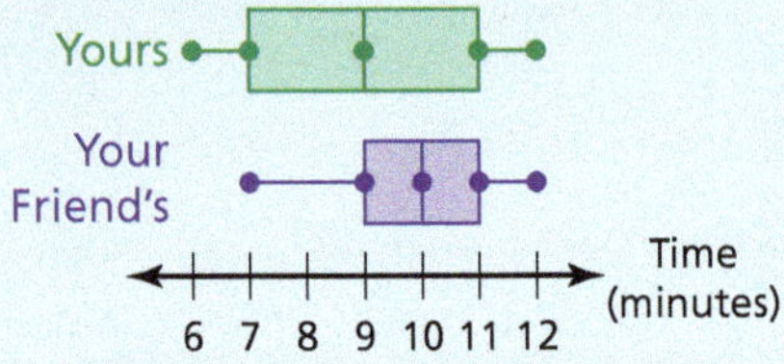

a. Which class's times are more spread out. Explain. your class; The box for your class is longer, so the interquartile range is greater. The range of times for your class is also greater than the range of times for your friend's class.

b. Which class's times are generally longer? Explain. your friend's class; The distribution for your class is symmetric with about one-half of the times above 9 minutes. The distribution for your friend's class is skewed left with about three-fourths of the times above 9 minutes.

Self-Assessment for Problem Solving

8. See Additional Answers.
9. Check students' work.

Learning Target

Display and interpret data in box-and-whisker plots.

Success Criteria

- Find the five-number summary of a data set.
- Make a box-and-whisker plot.
- Explain what the box and the whiskers of a box-and-whisker plot represent.
- Compare data sets represented by box-and-whisker plots.

Laurie's Notes

Formative Assessment Tip

KNWS Chart

This technique helps guide students through solving a word problem. Students complete a chart with the following columns as they work through the word problem.

K: What do you *know*? N: What is *not* important?
W: *What* is the problem asking? S: What *strategy* can you use?

Students can use their *KNWS Charts* to discuss and compare solving strategies with a partner. This technique helps students organize their thoughts and provides an effective process for problem solving.

EXAMPLE 4

- Model solving each part using a *KNWS Chart*. A sample for part (a) is shown.

K	N	W	S
• least values • first quartiles • medians • third quartiles • greatest values	• the picture	• To find which store's prices are more spread out.	• Identify the data set with the greater variability: IQR and range.

- Students should recognize that because they do not know individual data points, they cannot find the MAD.
- In part (b), a student might comment that a high price in Store B could be the reason for it being skewed. Without the outlier it could be symmetric.
- **MP2 Reason Abstractly and Quantitatively:** Supplement the discussion in part (b) with quantitative comparisons. For instance, about 50% of the prices in Store A are as low as, or lower than, the lowest 25% of the prices in Store B.
- If students are struggling to compare data sets, you can conduct a similar comparison using the distributions in Example 3.

Self-Assessment for Problem Solving

- Allow time in class for students to practice using the problem-solving plan. Remember, some students may only be able to complete the first step.
- For Exercise 9, students need lists of the heights of the boys and girls in the class. Help students create these lists on the board.
- If students struggle with Exercise 8, allow them to work on Exercise 9 in pairs. Then have partners revisit Exercise 8 and make changes as needed.

The Success Criteria Self-Assessment chart can be found in the *Student Journal* or online at *BigIdeasMath.com*.

Closure

- **Exit Ticket:**
  - How does an outlier affect a box-and-whisker plot? *Sample answer:* It increases the length of one of the whiskers.
  - Explain why two data sets of different sizes can be plotted as box-and-whisker plots on the same number line. Box-and-whisker plots show the distribution of the data, not the individual data points.

EXAMPLE 4 Modeling Real Life

The double box-and-whisker plot represents the prices of snowboards at two stores.

Store A

Store B

100 150 200 250 300 350 400 450 500 550 600 650

Price (dollars)

a. Which store's prices are more spread out? Explain.

Both boxes appear to be the same length. So, the interquartile range of each data set is equal. The range of the prices in Store B, however, is greater than the range of the prices in Store A.

 So, the prices in Store B are more spread out.

b. Which store's prices are generally higher? Explain.

For Store A, the distribution is symmetric with about one-half of the prices above \$300.

For Store B, the distribution is skewed right with about three-fourths of the prices above \$300.

 So, the prices in Store B are generally higher.

Math Practice

Justify Conclusions

Use the five-number summary for each data set to justify the solutions in parts (a) and (b).

Self-Assessment for Problem Solving

Solve each exercise. Then rate your understanding of the success criteria in your journal.

Test Scores	
75	65
64	79
100	75
94	52
73	80

Test Scores	
56	70
47	100
83	44
45	58
54	30

8. The tables at the left show the test scores of two sixth-grade achievement tests. The same group of students took both tests. The students took one test in the fall and the other in the spring.

a. Analyze each distribution. Then compare and contrast the test results.

b. Which table likely represents the results of which test? Explain your reasoning.

9. Make a box-and-whisker plot that represents the heights of the boys in your class. Then make a box-and-whisker plot that represents the heights of the girls in your class. Compare and contrast the distributions.

10.5 Practice

Go to **BigIdeasMath.com** to get HELP with solving the exercises.

Review & Refresh

Choose the most appropriate measures to describe the center and the variation.

1.

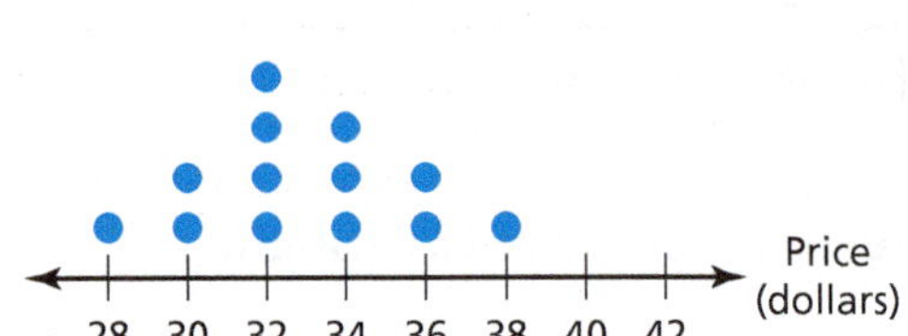

2.

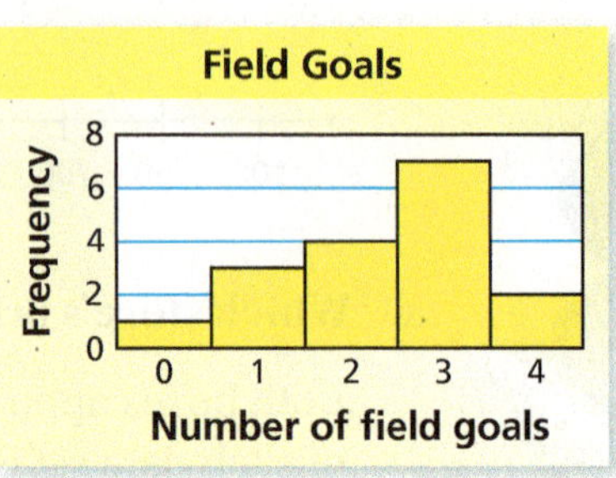

Copy and complete the statement using < or >.

3. $-\frac{2}{3} \;\square\; -\frac{3}{4}$ **4.** $-2\frac{1}{5} \;\square\; -2\frac{1}{6}$ **5.** $-5.3 \;\square\; -5.5$

Factor the expression using the GCF.

6. $42 + 14$ **7.** $12x - 18$ **8.** $28n + 20$ **9.** $60g - 25h$

Concepts, Skills, & Problem Solving

COMPARING DATA **Compare the data in the box-and-whisker plots.** (See Exploration 1, p. 483.)

10.

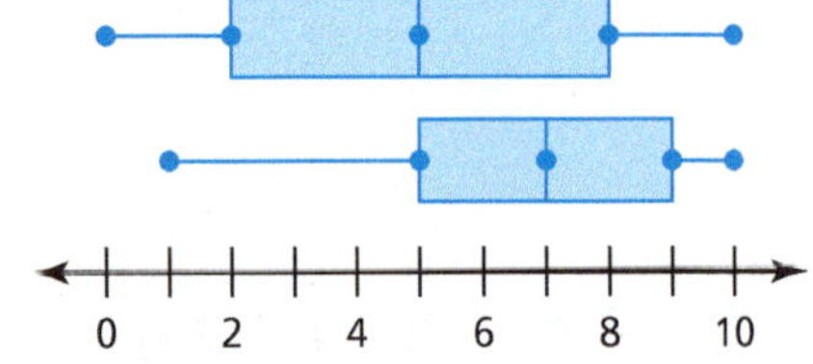

11.

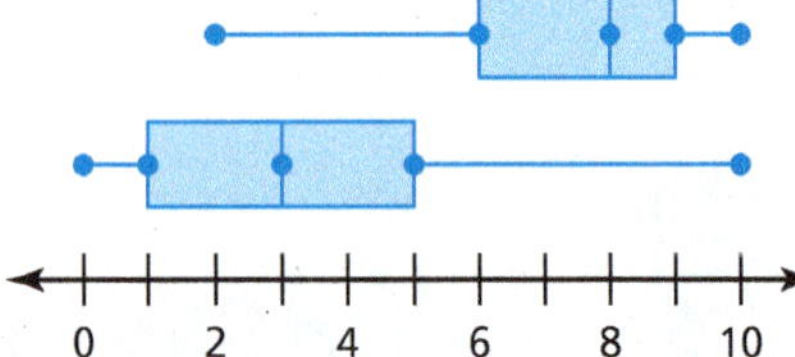

MAKING A BOX-AND-WHISKER PLOT **Make a box-and-whisker plot for the data.**

12. Ages of teachers (in years): 30, 62, 26, 35, 45, 22, 49, 32, 28, 50, 42, 35

13. Quiz scores: 8, 12, 9, 10, 12, 8, 5, 9, 7, 10, 8, 9, 11

14. Donations (in dollars): 10, 30, 5, 15, 50, 25, 5, 20, 15, 35, 10, 30, 20

15. Science test scores: 85, 76, 99, 84, 92, 95, 68, 100, 93, 88, 87, 85

16. Shoe sizes: 12, 8.5, 9, 10, 9, 11, 11.5, 9, 9, 10, 10, 10.5, 8

17. Ski lengths (in centimeters): 180, 175, 205, 160, 210, 175, 190, 205, 190, 160, 165, 195

18. MP **YOU BE THE TEACHER** Your friend makes a box-and-whisker plot for the data shown. Is your friend correct? Explain your reasoning.

2, 6, 4, 3, 7, 4, 6, 9, 6, 8, 5, 7

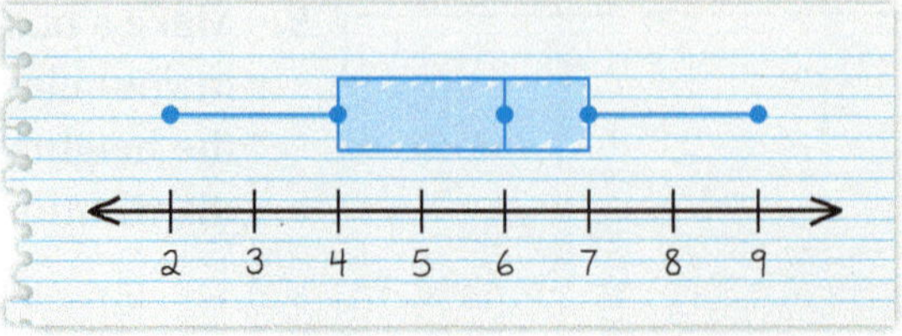

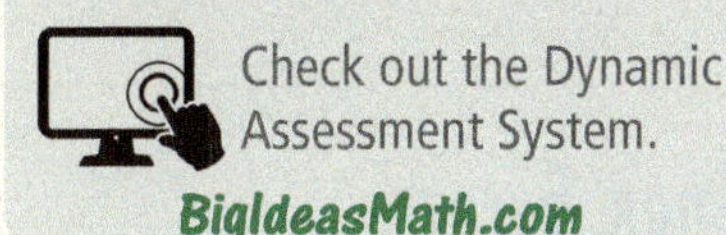

Assignment Guide and Concept Check

Scaffold assignments to support all students in their learning progression. The suggested assignments are a starting point. Continue to assign additional exercises and revisit with spaced practice to move every student toward proficiency.

Level	Assignment 1	Assignment 2
Emerging	2, 3, 5, 6, 9, 10, 13, 15, 18, 20, 23, 25	16, 19, 21, 24, 26, 27, 28
Proficient	2, 3, 5, 6, 9, 11, 12, 14, 18, 20, 24, 26	16, 19, 21, 22, 27, 28, 30, 31, 34
Advanced	2, 3, 5, 6, 9, 11, 16, 17, 18, 20, 24, 26	21, 22, 27, 30, 31, 32, 33, 34, 35

- Assignment 1 is for use after students complete the Self-Assessment for Concepts & Skills.
- Assignment 2 is for use after students complete the Self-Assessment for Problem Solving.
- The red exercises can be used as a concept check.

Review & Refresh Prior Skills

Exercises 1 and 2 Choosing Appropriate Measures
Exercises 3–5 Comparing Rational Numbers
Exercise 6 Factoring Numerical Expressions
Exercises 7–9 Factoring Algebraic Expressions

Common Errors

- **Exercises 12–17** Students may have difficulty creating the box-and-whisker plots. Remind them of the five-number summary of a data set.

Review & Refresh

1. mean and MAD
2. median and IQR
3. >
4. <
5. >
6. $14(3 + 1)$
7. $6(2x - 3)$
8. $4(7n + 5)$
9. $5(12g - 5h)$

Concepts, Skills, & Problem Solving

10. *Sample answer:* The top plot has a distribution that is symmetric while the bottom plot has a distribution that is skewed to the left. The top plot has more variability in its scores as the range and interquartile range are higher compared to the bottom plot. The bottom plot has a higher median and quartile values in comparison to the top plot.

11. *Sample answer:* The top plot has a distribution that is skewed left while the bottom plot has a distribution that is skewed right. The top plot has less variability in its scores within its quartiles compared to the bottom plot. The bottom plot has a lower median and quartile values in comparison to the top plot.

12–14. See Additional Answers.

15.

68 84.5 87.5 94 100
65 70 75 80 85 90 95 100 Score

16.

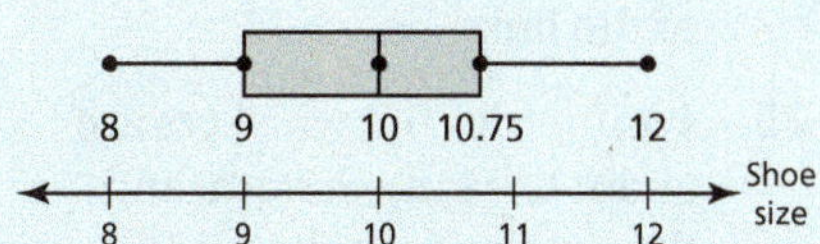

17. See Additional Answers.

18. yes; The five-number summary is correct and the plot is drawn correctly.

Concepts, Skills, & Problem Solving

19.

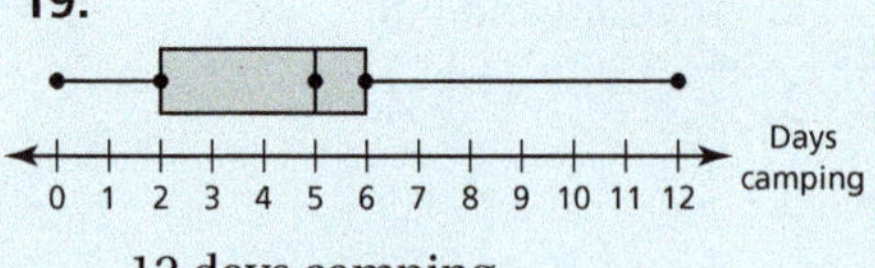

12 days camping

20. **a.** about $\frac{1}{2}$

b. above the third quartile; The right whisker is longer.

c. 150 gallons; The middle half of the data varies by no more than 150 gallons.

21. **a.** about 75%

b. above 345 meters; The right whisker is longer.

c. 84.5 m; The middle half of the data varies by no more than 84.5 meters.

22. **a.** See Additional Answers.

b. *Sample answer:* dot plot: advantages: gives the overall shape of the distribution; disadvantages: a lot of work to plot a very large set of numbers; box-and-whisker plot: advantages: handles large data sets easily and details of the distribution can be found; disadvantages: exact values cannot be obtained.

23. skewed left; The left whisker is longer than the right whisker, and most of the data are on the right.

24. symmetric; The whiskers are about the same length, and the median is in the middle of the box.

25. symmetric; The whiskers are about the same length, and the median is in the middle of the box.

26. skewed right; The right whisker is longer than the left whisker, and most of the data are on the left.

Common Errors

- **Exercises 19–21** Students may confuse the range and interquartile range of a data set. Remind them of these definitions.
- **Exercises 23–26** When identifying the shape of the distribution, students may confuse the meanings of skewed left and skewed right. Tell them that the shape is determined by the longer whisker.

19. **MP MODELING REAL LIFE** The numbers of days 12 friends went camping during the summer are 6, 2, 0, 10, 3, 6, 6, 4, 12, 0, 6, and 2. Make a box-and-whisker plot for the data. What is the range of the data?

20. **ANALYZING A BOX-AND-WHISKER PLOT** The box-and-whisker plot represents the numbers of gallons of water needed to fill different types of dunk tanks offered by a company.

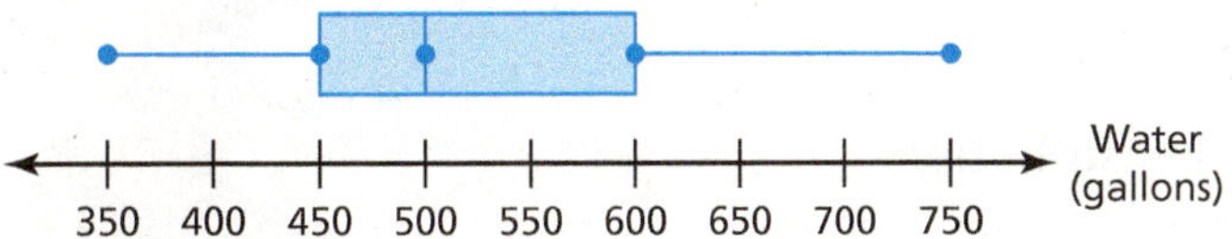

a. What fraction of the dunk tanks requires at least 500 gallons of water?

b. Are the data more spread out below the first quartile or above the third quartile? Explain.

c. Find and interpret the interquartile range of the data.

21. **MP MODELING REAL LIFE** The box-and-whisker plot represents the heights (in meters) of the tallest buildings in Chicago.

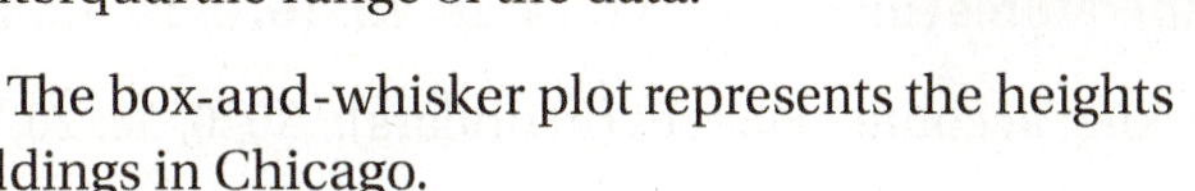

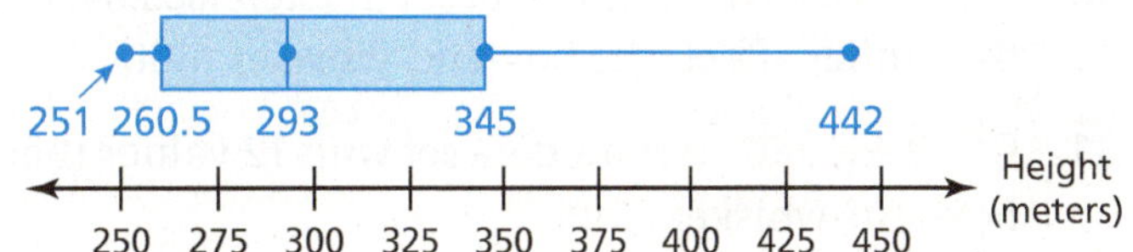

a. What percent of the buildings are no taller than 345 meters?

b. Is there more variability in the heights above 345 meters or below 260.5 meters? Explain.

c. Find and interpret the interquartile range of the data.

22. **CRITICAL THINKING** The numbers of spots on several frogs in a jungle are shown in the dot plot.

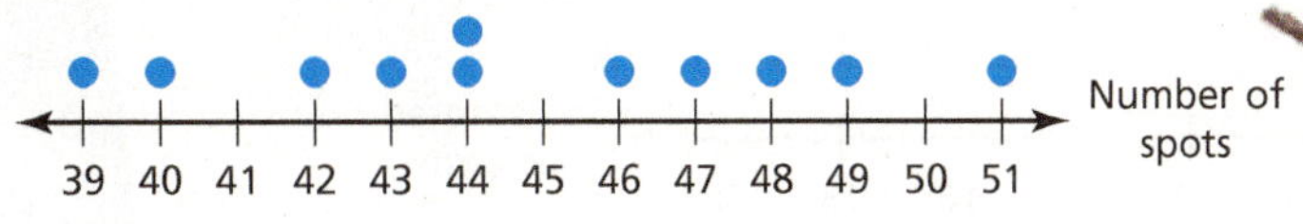

a. Make a box-and-whisker plot for the data.

b. Compare the dot plot and the box-and-whisker plot. Describe the advantages and disadvantages of each data display.

SHAPES OF BOX-AND-WHISKER PLOTS **Identify the shape of the distribution. Explain.**

23. 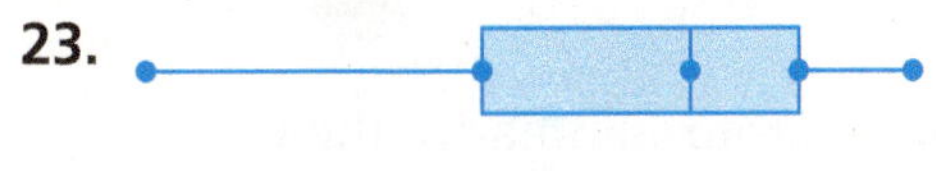

24. 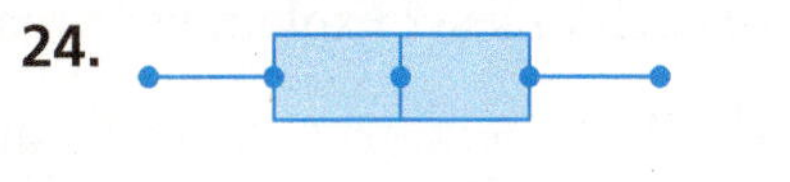

25. 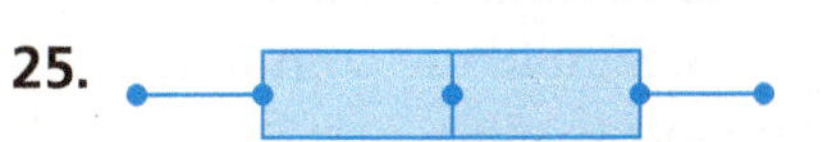

26. 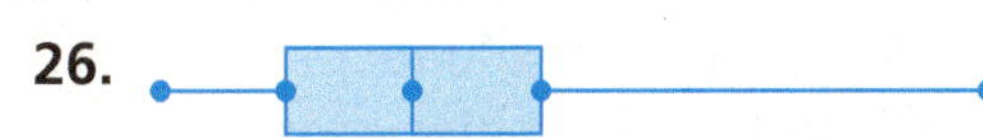

27. **MP MODELING REAL LIFE** The double box-and-whisker plot represents the start times of recess for classes at two schools.

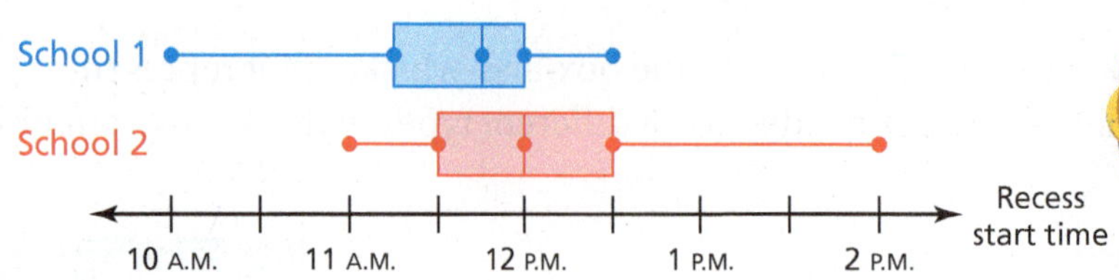

a. Identify the shape of each distribution.

b. Which school's start times for recess are more spread out? Explain.

c. You randomly pick one class from each school. Which class is more likely to have recess before lunch? Explain.

MAKING A BOX-AND-WHISKER PLOT **Make a box-and-whisker plot for the data.**

28. Temperatures (in °C): 15, 11, 14, 10, 19, 10, 2, 15, 12, 14, 9, 20, 17, 5

29. Checking account balances (in dollars): 30, 0, 50, 20, 90, −15, 40, 100, 45, −20, 70, 0

30. **MP REASONING** The data set in Exercise 28 has an outlier. Describe how removing the outlier affects the box-and-whisker plot.

31. **OPEN-ENDED** Write a data set with 12 values that has a symmetric box-and-whisker plot.

32. **CRITICAL THINKING** When does a box-and-whisker plot *not* have one or both whiskers?

33. **MP STRUCTURE** Draw a histogram that could represent the distribution shown in Exercise 25.

34. **DIG DEEPER!** The double box-and-whisker plot represents the goals scored per game by two lacrosse teams during a 16-game season.

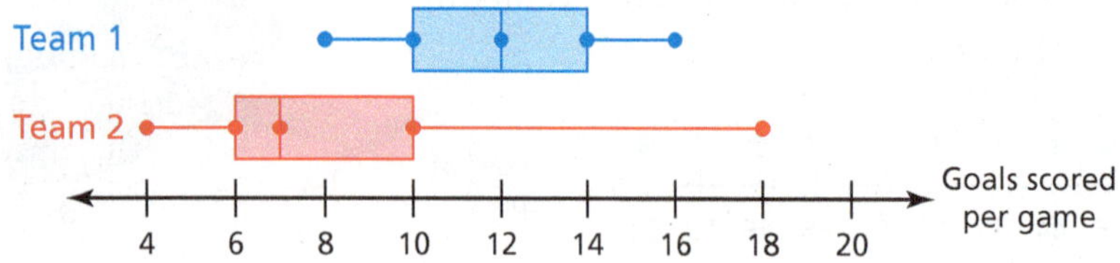

a. Which team is more consistent? Explain.

b. Team 1 played Team 2 once during the season. Which team do you think won? Explain.

c. Can you determine the number of games in which Team 2 scored 10 goals or less? Explain your reasoning.

35. **MP CHOOSE TOOLS** A market research company wants to summarize the variability of the SAT scores of graduating seniors in the United States. Should the company use a stem-and-leaf plot, a histogram, or a box-and-whisker plot? Explain.

Mini-Assessment

The list represents the numbers of DVDs owned by the students in your class.

25, 31, 27, 36, 19, 22, 20, 24, 30, 32, 29, 27

1. Make a box-and-whisker plot for the data.

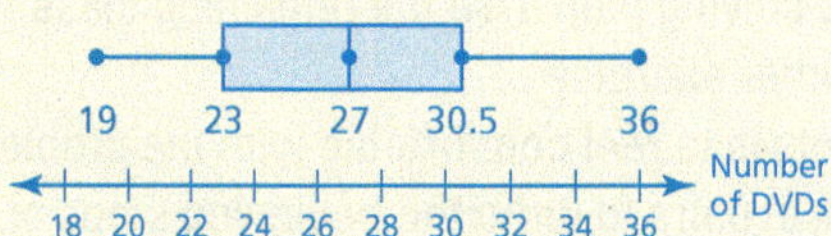

2. What is the range of the data? 17
3. What fraction of students owns at least 23 DVDs? $\frac{3}{4}$
4. Find and interpret the interquartile range of the data. 7.5; The middle half of the numbers of DVDs owned varies by no more than 7.5.

Section Resources

Surface Level	Deep Level
Resources by Chapter • Extra Practice • Reteach • Puzzle Time Student Journal • Self-Assessment • Practice Differentiating the Lesson Tutorial Videos Skills Review Handbook Skills Trainer	Resources by Chapter • Enrichment and Extension Graphic Organizers Dynamic Assessment System • Section Practice
Transfer Level	
Dynamic Assessment System • End-of-Chapter Quiz	Assessment Book • End-of-Chapter Quiz

27. **a.** School 1 is skewed left and School 2 is skewed right.

b. School 2; The range and the IQR of School 2 are greater than those of School 1.

c. class from School 1; At any time School 1 has more data on the left than School 2.

28–30. See Additional Answers.

31. *Sample answer:* 10, 15, 20, 20, 25, 30, 30, 35, 40, 40, 45, 50

32. When the least value and the first quartile are equal, there is no whisker on the left. When the greatest value and the third quartile are equal, there is no whisker on the right.

33. *Sample answer:*

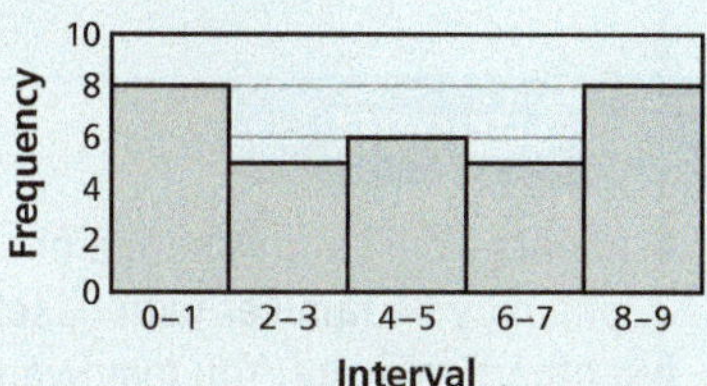

34. **a.** Team 1; The range and IQR are both smaller for Team 1 than for Team 2.

b. Team 1; In 75% of the games, Team 1 scored 10 goals or more. However, Team 2 scored 10 goals or less in 75% of the games.

c. yes; Team 2 played 16 games and they scored 10 or fewer goals in 75% of those games. So, 75% of 16 games is 12 games.

35. *Sample answer:* box-and-whisker plot; A stem-and-leaf plot of a large data set would be impractical. The size of the display would be massive and difficult to use. While a histogram can show the variability of a data set, it is not as accurate and obvious as a box-and-whisker plot due to intervals and bar size.

Skills Needed

Exercise 1

- Choosing Appropriate Measures
- Identifying Shapes of Box-and-Whisker Plots
- Making a Box-and-Whisker Plot
- Writing Ordered Pairs

Exercise 2

- Finding the Interquartile Range
- Finding the Mean
- Finding the Mean Absolute Deviation
- Finding the Range
- Making a Histogram

Exercise 3

- Choosing Appropriate Measures
- Describing Data Sets
- Describing Shapes of Distributions
- Finding the Volume of a Rectangular Prism

ELL Support

Students from Latin America or Japan may be familiar with baseball, but others may not. You may want to discuss its basics. Explain that the location of a pitch determines if it is a *ball* or a *strike*. For a pitch to be a strike it must be between the knees and armpits of the batter and over home plate.

Using the Problem-Solving Plan

1–2. See Additional Answers.

3. symmetric; mean and MAD

Performance Task

The *STEAM Video Performance Task* provides the opportunity for additional enrichment and greater depth of knowledge as students explore the mathematics of the chapter within a context tied to the chapter STEAM Video. The performance task and a detailed scoring rubric are provided at *BigIdeasMath.com.*

Laurie's Notes

Scaffolding Instruction

- The goal of this lesson is to help students become more comfortable with problem solving. These exercises combine data displays with prior skills from other chapters. The solution for Exercise 1 is worked out below, to help you guide students through the problem-solving plan. Use the remaining class time to have students work on the other exercises.
- **Emerging:** The goal for these students is to feel comfortable with the problem-solving plan. Allow students to work in pairs to write the beginning steps of the problem-solving plan for Exercise 2. Keep in mind that some students may only be ready to do the first step.
- **Proficient:** Students may be able to work independently or in pairs to complete Exercises 2 and 3.
- Visit each pair to review their plan for each problem. Ask students to describe their plans.

Using the Problem-Solving Plan

Exercise 1

Understand the problem. You know the locations of the pitches. You are asked to find the location of a typical pitch in the at-bat.

Make a plan. First, use the coordinates of the pitches to create two data sets, one for the x-coordinates of the pitches and one for the y-coordinates of the pitches. Next, make a box-and-whisker plot for each data set. Then use the most appropriate measure of center for each data set to find the location of a typical pitch.

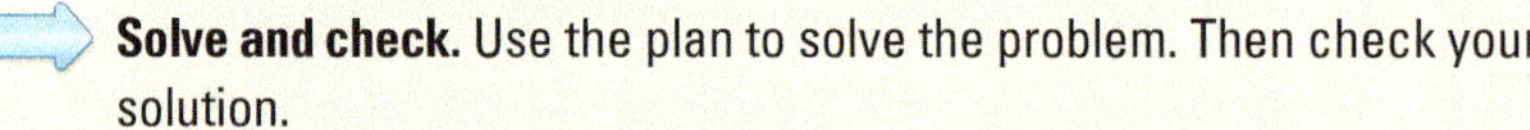

Solve and check. Use the plan to solve the problem. Then check your solution.

- Use the coordinates of the pitches to create two data sets.
  x-coordinates: 2, 2, 2, 4, 6, 6, 6, 8, 8, 10, 10, 16, 22, 24
  y-coordinates: 0, 2, 2, 4, 6, 6, 6, 8, 10, 12, 12, 18, 22, 28
- Make a box-and-whisker plot for each data set.

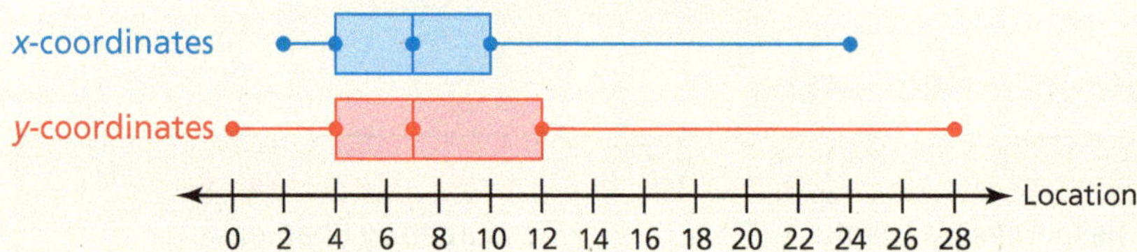

- Find the location of a typical pitch.
  In both distributions, the right whiskers are longer than the left whiskers. Because both distributions are skewed right, the median is the most appropriate measure to describe the center.
  The median of the x-coordinates is 7. The median of the y-coordinates is 7. So, a typical pitch is located at (7, 7).
- **Check:** Use the means to check reasonableness.

  The mean of the x-coordinates (without outliers 22 and 24) is $\frac{80}{12} \approx 7$ and the mean of the y-coordinates (without the outlier 28) is $\frac{108}{13} \approx 8$. So, (7, 7) is a reasonable location. ✓

10 Connecting Concepts

Using the Problem-Solving Plan

1. The locations of pitches in an at-bat are shown in the coordinate plane, where the coordinates are measured in inches. Describe the location of a typical pitch in the at-bat.

Understand the problem. You know the locations of the pitches. You are asked to find the location of a typical pitch in the at-bat.

Make a plan. First, use the coordinates of the pitches to create two data sets, one for the x-coordinates of the pitches and one for the y-coordinates of the pitches. Next, make a box-and-whisker plot for each data set. Then use the most appropriate measure of center for each data set to find the location of a typical pitch.

Solve and check. Use the plan to solve the problem. Then check your solution.

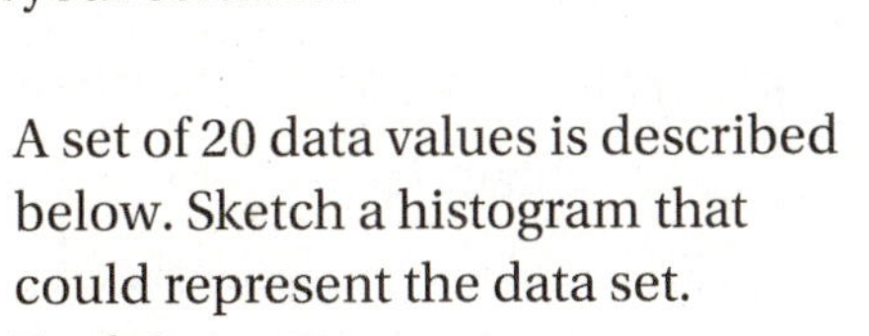

2. A set of 20 data values is described below. Sketch a histogram that could represent the data set. Explain.

- least value: 10
- third quartile: 34
- first quartile: 25
- greatest value: 48
- mean: 29
- MAD: 7

SHIPPING RATES

Dimensions	Price
$5 \times 5 \times 4$	\$6.80
$8 \times 5 \times 3$	\$8.30
$9 \times 8 \times 5$	\$9.75
$10 \times 6 \times 6$	\$10.75
$10 \times 10 \times 4$	\$10.75
$8 \times 7 \times 5$	\$10.75
$12 \times 10 \times 3$	\$11.25
$15 \times 10 \times 3$	\$12.25
$12 \times 12 \times 5$	\$17.40

3. The chart shows the dimensions (in inches) of several flat-rate shipping boxes. Each box is in the shape of a rectangular prism. Describe the distribution of the volumes of the boxes. Then find the most appropriate measures to describe the center and the variation of the volumes.

Performance Task

Classifying Dog Breeds by Size

At the beginning of this chapter, you watched a STEAM Video called "Choosing a Dog." You are now ready to complete the performance task related to this video, available at ***BigIdeasMath.com***. Be sure to use the problem-solving plan as you work through the performance task.

Review Vocabulary

Write the definition and give an example of each vocabulary term.

stem-and-leaf plot, *p. 458*
stem, *p. 458*
leaf, *p. 458*
frequency table, *p. 463*
frequency, *p. 463*
histogram, *p. 464*
box-and-whisker plot, *p. 484*
five-number summary, *p. 484*

Graphic Organizers

You can use an **Information Frame** to help you organize and remember concepts. Here is an example of an Information Frame for the vocabulary term ***histogram***.

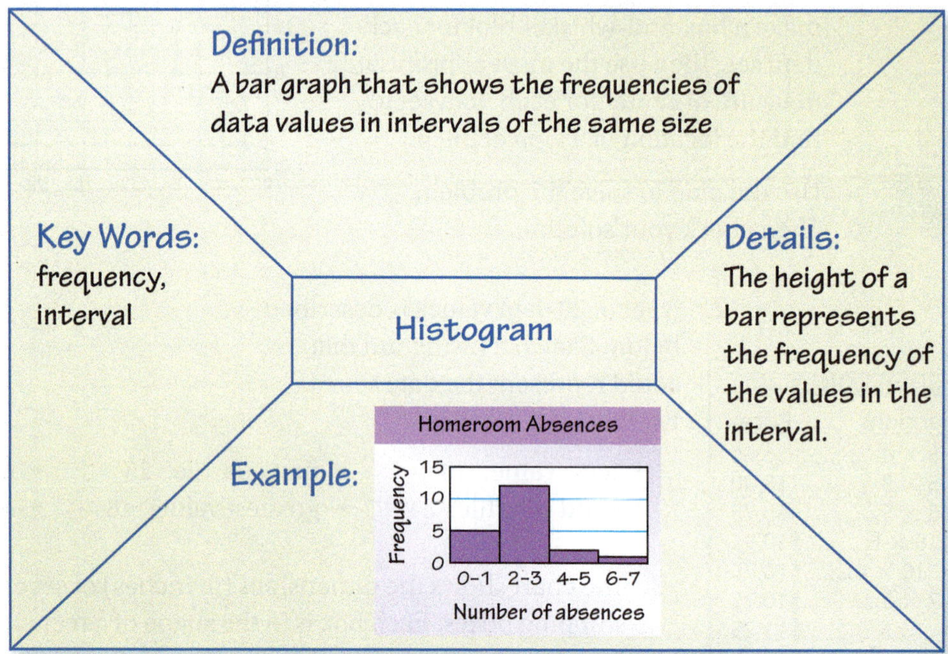

"I finished my Information Frame about dog sweaters. Why don't you make your information frame about barn cats?"

Choose and complete a graphic organizer to help you study the concept.

1. stem-and-leaf plot
2. frequency table
3. shapes of distributions
4. box-and-whisker plot

Review Vocabulary

- As a review of the chapter vocabulary, have students revisit the vocabulary section in their *Student Journals* to fill in any missing definitions and record examples of each term.

Graphic Organizers

Sample answers:

1. 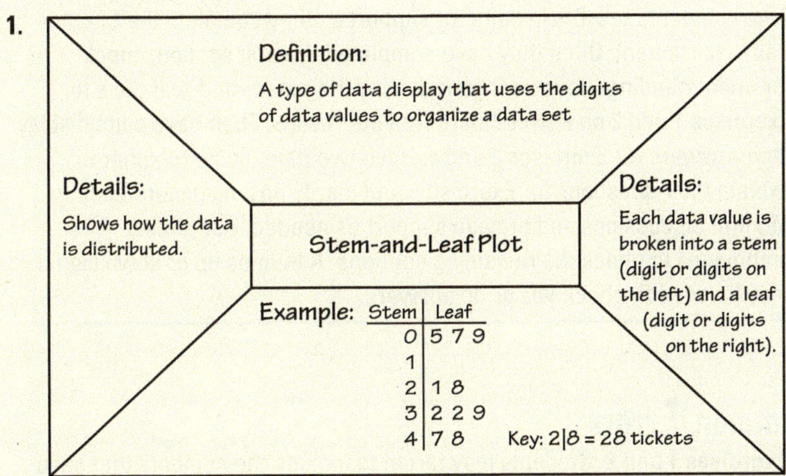

2. 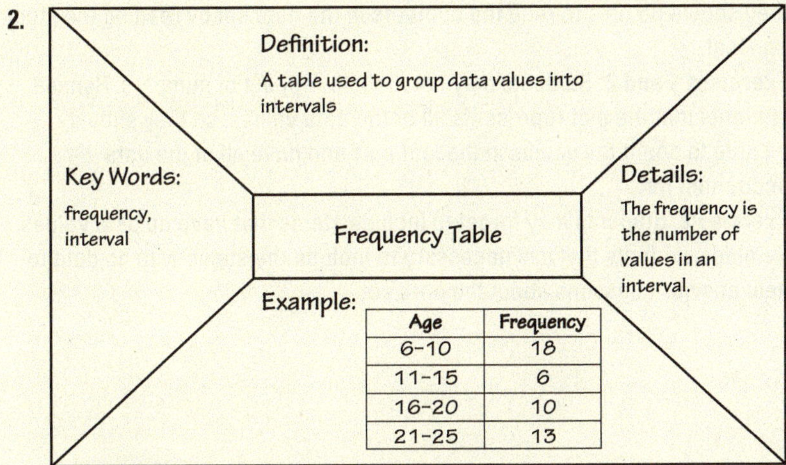

3. 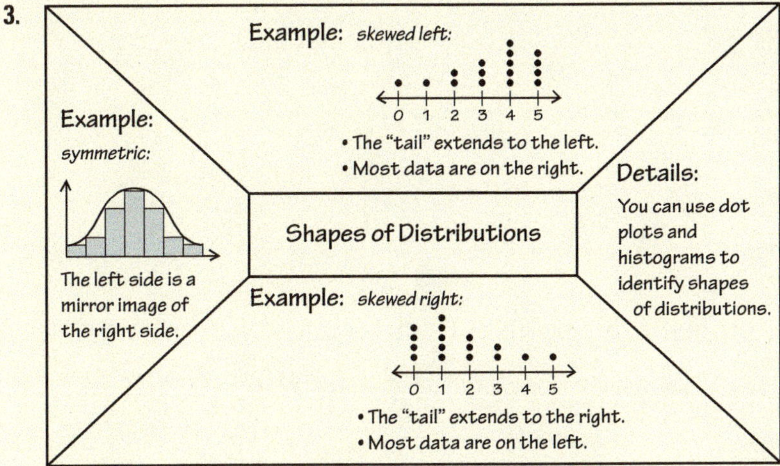

4. Answer at *BigIdeasMath.com*.

List of Organizers

Available at *BigIdeasMath.com*
Definition and Example Chart
Example and Non-Example Chart
Four Square
Information Frame
Summary Triangle

About this Organizer

An **Information Frame** can be used to help students organize and remember concepts. Students write the concept in the middle rectangle. Then students write related categories in the spaces around the rectangle. Related categories may include: words, numbers, algebra, example, definition, non-example, visual, procedure, details, or vocabulary. Students can place their Information Frames on note cards to use as a quick study reference.

Chapter Self-Assessment

1. **Hats Sold Each Day**

Stem	Leaf
0	5 8 9
1	2 2 3 4 5 8
2	1 5
3	0

Key: 2 | 1 = 21 hats

2. **Ages of Park Volunteers**

Stem	Leaf
1	3 3 5 7 9
2	0 1
3	
4	0 8
5	2 5
6	0

Key: 1 | 3 = 13 years old

3. **a.** 10

   b. mean = 87 lb;
   median = 85 lb;
   mode = 85 lb;
   range = 26 lb;
   IQR = 15 lb

   c. The weights are spread out from 76 pounds to 102 pounds with peaks at 76, 85, and 96 pounds and gaps from 89 to 93 pounds and from 96 to 102 pounds.

4. *Sample answer:* 24; The mean, median, and mode are all the same value, so any one of them could be used to answer the question.

5. *Sample answer:* How many songs were downloaded daily?

Chapter Self-Assessment

The Success Criteria Self-Assessment chart can be found in the *Student Journal* or online at *BigIdeasMath.com.*

ELL Support

Allow students to work in pairs for support as they complete the Chapter Self-Assessment. Once they have completed the first section, check for understanding. Have each pair display their stem-and-leaf plots for Exercises 1 and 2 on a whiteboard for your review. Then have pairs display their answers for Exercises 3 and 4. Have two pairs come together to explain their questions for Exercise 5 and clarify any misunderstandings. Monitor discussions and provide support as needed. Use similar techniques to check the remaining sections. A thumbs up or down signal may be used to check *yes* or *no* answers.

Common Errors

- **Exercises 1 and 2** Students may forget to include the numbers that have zeros in the ones place in the leaf part of the plot. Remind students that they should be able to read the numbers in the data set by reading the stem *and* leaf.
- **Exercises 1 and 2** Students may not include repeats of numbers. Remind students that the plot represents all of the data values, so they should be able to count the values in the leaf part and have all of the data accounted for.
- **Exercise 2** Students may forget to include stems that have no data values. Reminds students that it is necessary to include the stems with no data to help answer questions about the data set.

Chapter Self-Assessment

As you complete the exercises, use the scale below to rate your understanding of the success criteria in your journal.

1	2	3	4
I do not understand.	I can do it with help.	I can do it on my own.	I can teach someone else.

10.1 Stem-and-Leaf Plots (pp. 457–462)

Learning Target: Display and interpret data in stem-and-leaf plots.

Make a stem-and-leaf plot of the data.

1.

Hats Sold Each Day			
5	18	12	15
21	30	8	12
13	9	14	25

2.

Ages of Park Volunteers			
13	17	40	15
48	21	19	52
13	55	60	20

3. The stem-and-leaf plot shows the weights (in pounds) of yellowfin tuna caught during a fishing contest.

Stem	Leaf
7	6 6 8
8	0 2 5 5 5 7 9
9	3 5 6 6
10	2

Key: 8 | 5 = 85 pounds

a. How many tuna weigh less than 90 pounds?

b. Find the mean, median, mode, range, and interquartile range of the data.

c. How are the data distributed?

4. The stem-and-leaf plot shows the body mass index (BMI) for adults at a recreation center. Use the data to answer the question, "What is the typical BMI for an adult at the recreation center?" Explain.

Stem	Leaf
1	6 8 9
2	0 2 3 4 4 5 7 9
3	0 5

Key: 2 | 7 = 27

5. Write a statistical question that can be answered using the stem-and-leaf plot.

Songs Downloaded per Day

Stem	Leaf
0	0 2 4 5 6 6 6 7 8
1	3 4 8 9
2	
3	2

Key: 1 | 9 = 19 songs

10.2 Histograms (pp. 463–470)

Learning Target: Display and interpret data in histograms.

Display the data in a histogram.

6.

Heights of Gymnasts	
Heights (inches)	**Frequency**
50–54	1
55–59	8
60–64	5
65–69	2

7.

Minutes Studied	
Minutes	**Frequency**
0–19	5
20–39	9
40–59	12
60–79	3

8. The histogram shows the number of crafts each member of a craft club made for a fundraiser.

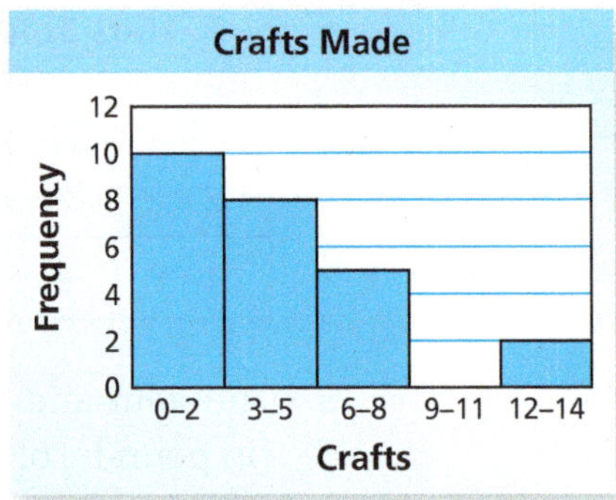

a. Which interval contains the most data values?

b. How many members made at least 6 crafts?

c. Can you use the histogram to determine the total number of crafts made? Explain.

10.3 Shapes of Distributions (pp. 471–476)

Learning Target: Describe and compare shapes of distributions.

9. Describe the shape of the distribution.

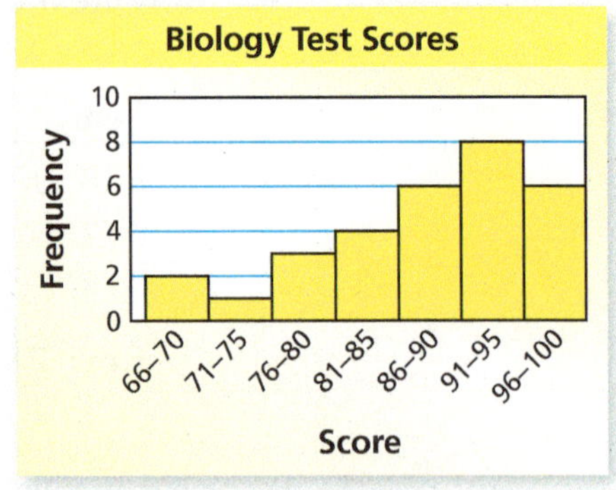

10. The frequency table shows the math test scores for the same class of students as Exercise 9. Display the data in a histogram. Which test has higher scores?

Score	66–70	71–75	76–80	81–85
Frequency	1	5	10	8

Score	86–90	91–95	96–100
Frequency	2	2	2

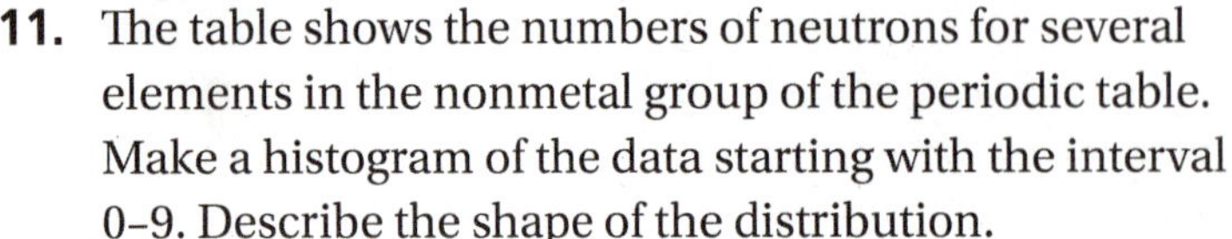
11. The table shows the numbers of neutrons for several elements in the nonmetal group of the periodic table. Make a histogram of the data starting with the interval 0–9. Describe the shape of the distribution.

Number of Neutrons			
0	45	16	8
7	6	16	

Common Errors

- **Exercises 6 and 7** Students may struggle with determining how to scale the vertical axis of the histogram. Remind students to use consistent intervals and to base their decisions on the frequency of the data. For example, if there is a high frequency, they should count by 5s or 10s, but if there is a low frequency, they should count by 1s or 2s.
- **Exercises 9 and 11** Students may confuse *skewed left* and *skewed right*. Point out that the tail of the graph of a distribution determines the direction. That is, in a skewed left distribution, the tail extends to the left, and in a skewed right distribution, the tail extends to the right.

Chapter Self-Assessment

6.

Heights of Gymnasts

Frequency: 0, 2, 4, 6, 8, 10

50–54 55–59 60–64 65–69

Heights (in.)

7.

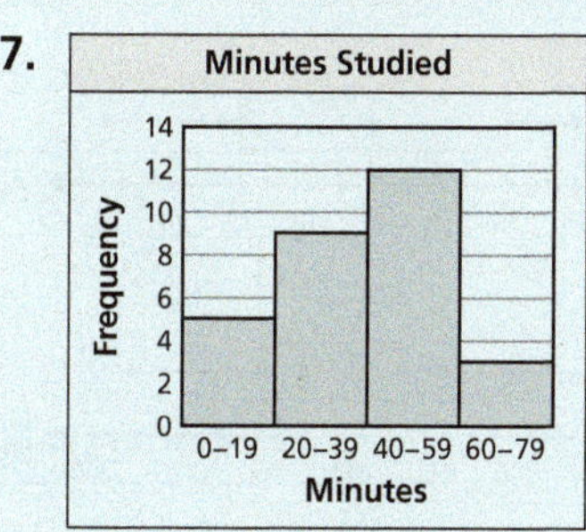

8. **a.** 0–2 crafts

b. 7

c. no; *Sample answer:* In a histogram, you can only tell the intervals that the data values are contained in, not the exact values.

9. skewed left

10.

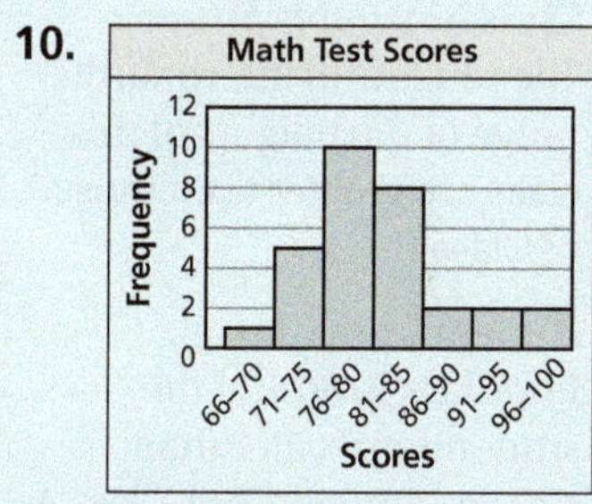

biology

11.

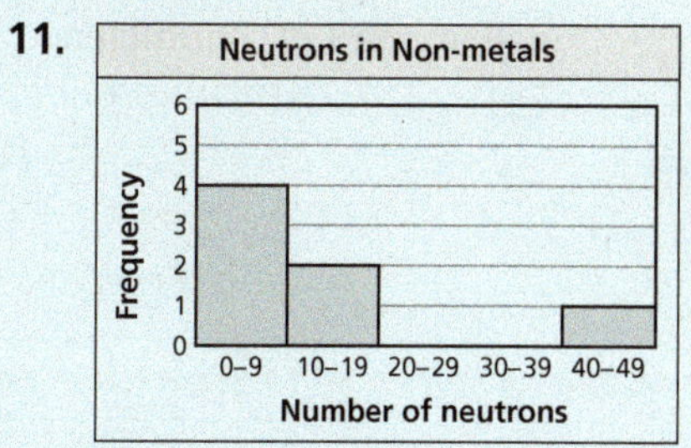

skewed right

Chapter Self-Assessment

12. median and IQR

13. mean and MAD

14. The students' heights center around 60 inches. The heights differ from the average height by an average of $\frac{8}{9}$ inch.

15.

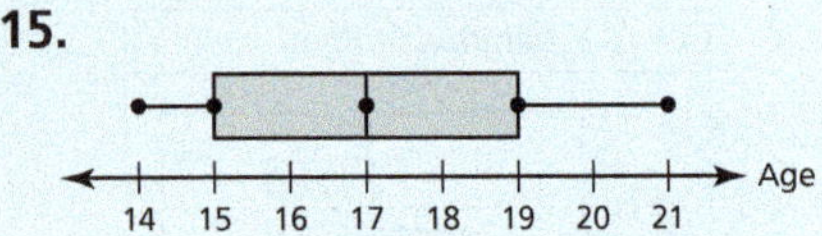

16.

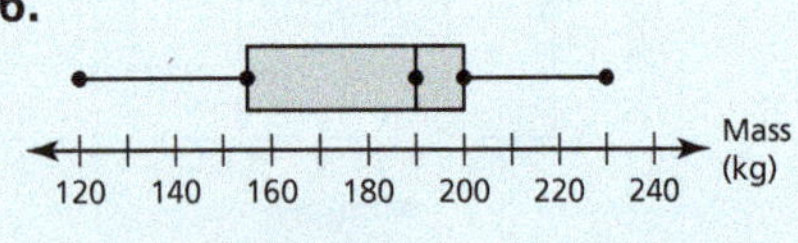

17. a. about 50%

b. longer than 130 minutes; the right whisker is longer

c. 20 minutes; The middle half of the data vary by no more than 20 minutes.

18. a. Class A: skewed left; Class B: symmetric

b. Class A; *Sample answer:* The range and interquartile range of the heights of this class are greater than those of Class B.

c. student from Class B; For Class B, 50% of the students are taller than 170 centimeters. For Class A only 25% of the students are taller than 170 centimeters.

Common Errors

- **Exercise 14** Students may mix up the appropriate measures for symmetric and skewed data distributions and then use the wrong measures to describe the center and the variation. Remind students to use the mean and MAD to describe symmetric distributions and use the median and IQR to describe skewed distributions.
- **Exercises 15 and 16** Students may have difficulty creating the box-and-whisker plots. Remind them of the five-number summary of a data set.
- **Exercise 17** Students may confuse the range and interquartile range of a data set. Remind them of these definitions.
- **Exercise 18** When identifying the shape of the distribution, students may confuse the meanings of skewed left and skewed right. Tell them that the shape is determined by the longer whisker.

Chapter Resources

Surface Level	Deep Level
Resources by Chapter • Extra Practice • Reteach • Puzzle Time Student Journal • Practice • Chapter Self-Assessment Differentiating the Lesson Tutorial Videos Skills Review Handbook Skills Trainer Game Library	Resources by Chapter • Enrichment and Extension Graphic Organizers Game Library
Transfer Level	
STEAM Video Dynamic Assessment System • Chapter Test	Assessment Book • Chapter Tests A and B • Alternative Assessment • STEAM Performance Task

10.4 Choosing Appropriate Measures (pp. 477–482)

Learning Target: Use the shape of the distribution of a data set to determine which measures of center and variation best describe the data.

Choose the most appropriate measures to describe the center and the variation.

12.

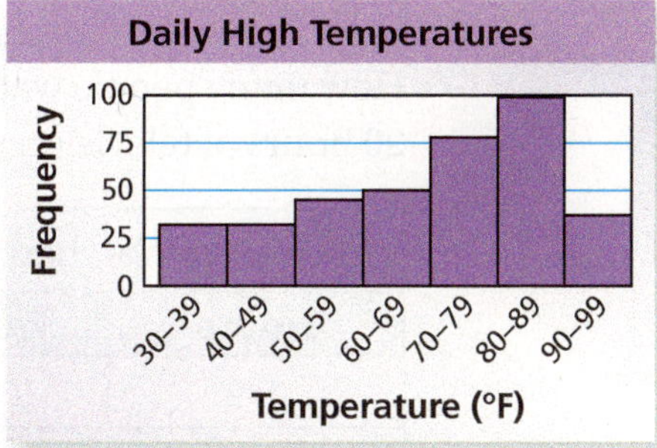

13.

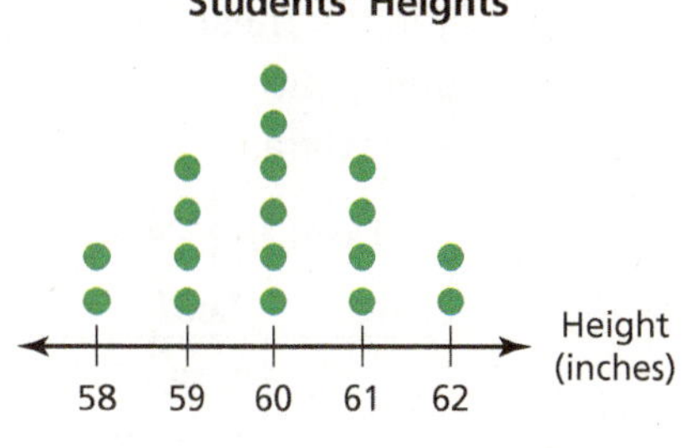

14. Describe the center and the variation of the data set in Exercise 13.

10.5 Box-and-Whisker Plots (pp. 483–490)

Learning Target: Display and interpret data in box-and-whisker plots.

Make a box-and-whisker plot for the data.

15. Ages of volunteers at a hospital:
14, 17, 20, 16, 17, 14, 21, 18

16. Masses (in kilograms) of lions:
120, 200, 180, 150, 200, 200, 230, 160

17. The box-and-whisker plot represents the lengths (in minutes) of movies being shown at a theater.

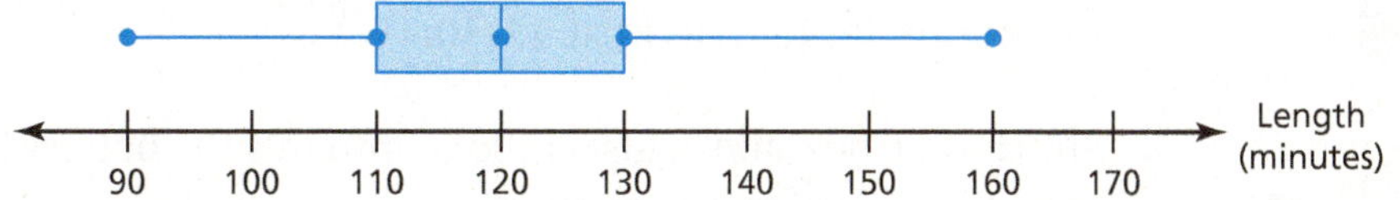

a. What percent of the movies are no longer than 120 minutes?

b. Is there more variability in the movie lengths longer than 130 minutes or shorter than 110 minutes? Explain.

c. Find and interpret the interquartile range of the data.

18. The double box-and-whisker plot represents the heights of students in two math classes.

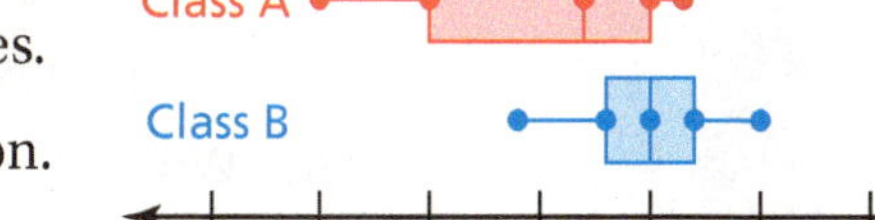

a. Identify the shape of each distribution.

b. Which class has heights that are more spread out? Explain.

c. You randomly pick one student from each class. Which student is more likely to be taller than 170 centimeters? Explain.

10 Practice Test

Make a stem-and-leaf plot of the data.

1.

Quiz Scores (%)			
96	88	80	72
80	94	92	100
76	80	68	90

2.

Songs Downloaded Each Day				
45	31	29	38	38
67	40	62	45	60
40	39	60	43	48

3. Find the mean, median, mode, range, and interquartile range of the data.

Cooking Time

Stem	Leaf
3	5 8
4	0 1 8
5	0 4 4 4 5 9
6	0

Key: 4 | 1 = 41 minutes

4. Display the data in a histogram. How many people watched less than 20 hours of television per week?

Television Watched per Week	
Hours	**Frequency**
0–9	14
10–19	16
20–29	10
30–39	8

5. The dot plot shows the numbers of glasses of water that the students in a class drink in one day.

a. Describe the shape of the distribution.

b. Choose the most appropriate measures to describe the center and the variation. Find the measures you chose.

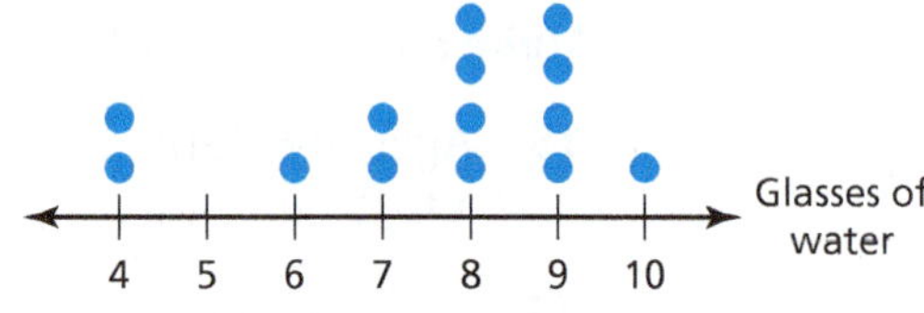

6. Make a box-and-whisker plot for the lengths (in inches) of fish in a pond: 12, 13, 7, 8, 14, 6, 13, 10.

7. The double box-and-whisker plot compares the battery lives (in hours) of two brands of cell phones.

Brand A
Brand B
9 9.5 10 10.5 11 11.5 12 12.5 13 13.5 14
Battery life (hours)

a. What is the range of the upper 75% of battery life for each brand of cell phone?

b. Which brand of cell phone typically has a longer battery life? Explain.

c. In the box-and-whisker plot, there are 190 cell phones of Brand A that have at most 10.5 hours of battery life. About how many cell phones are represented in the box-and-whisker plot for Brand A?

Practice Test Item References

Practice Test Questions	Section to Review
1, 2, 3	10.1
4	10.2
5	10.3
5	10.4
6, 7	10.5

Test-Taking Strategies

Remind students to quickly look over the entire test before they start so that they can budget their time. On this test, students are asked to display as well as analyze data. It can be difficult for students to determine how to begin. Remind students to use the **Stop** and **Think** strategy before they write their answers.

Common Errors

- **Exercises 1 and 2** Students may forget to include the numbers that have zeros in the ones place in the leaf part of the plot. Remind students that they should be able to read the numbers in the data set by reading the stem *and* leaf.
- **Exercises 1 and 2** Students may not include repeats of numbers. Remind students that the plot represents all of the data values, so they should be able to count the values in the leaf part and have all of the data accounted for.
- **Exercise 2** Students may forget to include stems that have no data values. Reminds students that it is necessary to include the stems with no data to help answer questions about the data set.
- **Exercise 5** Students may confuse *skewed left* and *skewed right*. Point out that the tail of the graph of a distribution determines the direction. That is, in a skewed left distribution, the tail extends to the left, and in a skewed right distribution, the tail extends to the right.
- **Exercise 5** Students may mix up the appropriate measures for symmetric and skewed data distributions and then use the wrong measures to describe the center and the variation. Remind students to use the mean and MAD to describe symmetric distributions and use the median and IQR to describe skewed distributions.
- **Exercise 6** Students may have difficulty creating the box-and-whisker plot. Remind them of the five-number summary of a data set.

Practice Test

1. **Quiz Scores**

Stem	Leaf
6	8
7	2 6
8	0 0 0 8
9	0 2 4 6
10	0

Key: 7 | 2 = 72%

2. **Songs Downloaded Each Day**

Stem	Leaf
2	9
3	1 8 8 9
4	0 0 3 5 5 8
5	
6	0 0 2 7

Key: 4 | 0 = 40 Songs

3. mean = 49 min;
median = 52 min;
mode = 54 min;
range = 25 min;
IQR = 14 min

4. 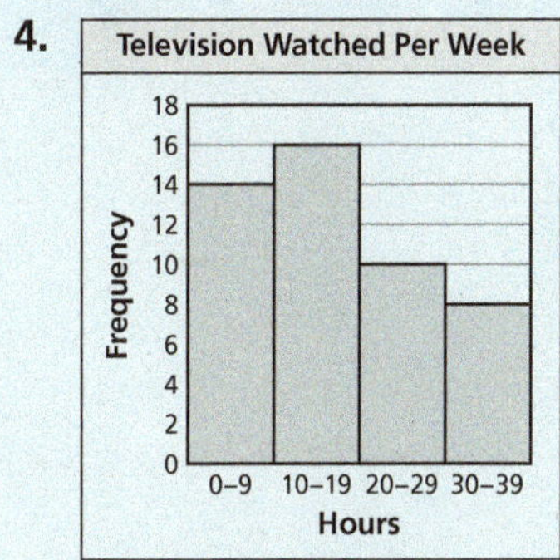

30

5. **a.** skewed left

b. median and IQR;
median = 8 glasses,
IQR = 2 glasses

6. 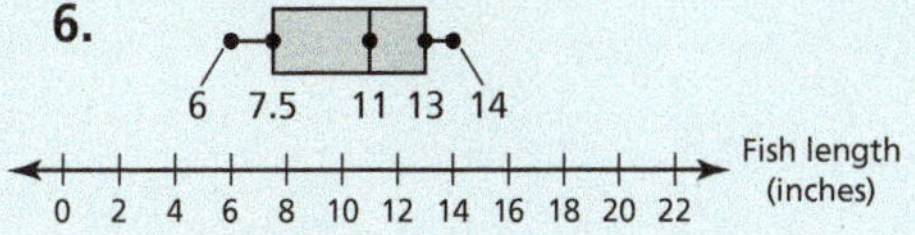

7. **a.** Brand A: 3.5 h; Brand B: 2.7 h

b. Brand A; Brand A has a higher mean, greatest value, and first and third quartile.

c. 760

Test-Taking Strategies

Available at *BigIdeasMath.com*
After Answering Easy Questions, Relax
Answer Easy Questions First
Estimate the Answer
Read All Choices before Answering
Read Question before Answering
Solve Directly or Eliminate Choices
Solve Problem before Looking at Choices
Use Intelligent Guessing
Work Backwards

About this Strategy

When taking a multiple-choice test, be sure to read each question carefully and thoroughly. Look closely for words that change the meaning of the questions, such as *not*, *never*, *all*, *every*, and *always*.

Cumulative Practice

1. D

2. F

3. C

Item Analysis

1. **A.** The student misreads the plot, thinking that the median is the greatest value.

   B. The student misreads the plot, thinking that the right whisker represents 50% of the data.

   C. The student misreads the plot, thinking that the left whisker represents 50% of the data.

   D. Correct answer

2. **F.** Correct answer

   G. The student estimates the mean instead of finding the interquartile range.

   H. The student finds the difference between the greatest value and the interquartile range instead of finding the interquartile range.

   I. The student finds the greatest value instead of the interquartile range.

3. **A.** The student forgets to count the middle integer as negative.

   B. The student incorrectly assumes that all integers to the right of -1 must be positive. One of the integers could be 0, which is neither positive nor negative.

   C. Correct answer

   D. The student incorrectly assumes that all the integers to the right of -1 must be positive. One of the integers could be 0, which is neither positive nor negative.

10 Cumulative Practice

Test-Taking Strategy
Read Question before Answering

Of 2048 cats, how many of them will NOT answer to "Here, kitty kitty"?

Ⓐ 100% Ⓑ 1 Ⓒ $\frac{4098}{2}$ Ⓓ 2048

Hey, it means "free food."

"Be sure to read the question before choosing your answer. You may find a word that changes the meaning."

1. Research scientists are measuring the numbers of days lettuce seeds take to germinate. In a study, 500 seeds were planted. Of these, 473 seeds germinated. The box-and-whisker plot summarizes the numbers of days it took the seeds to germinate. What can you conclude from the box-and-whisker plot?

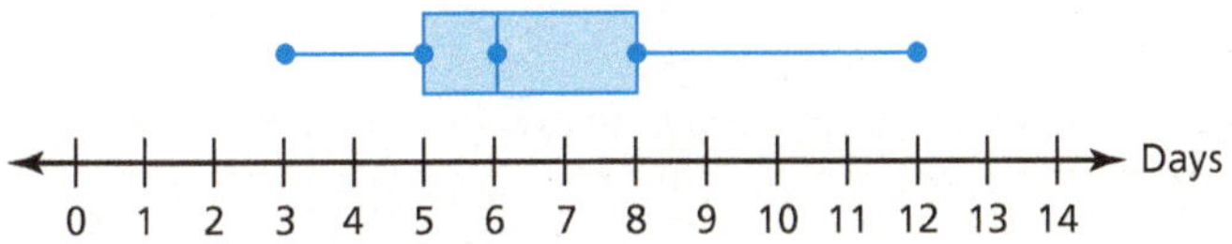

A. The median number of days for the seeds to germinate is 12.

B. 50% of the seeds took more than 8 days to germinate.

C. 50% of the seeds took less than 5 days to germinate.

D. The median number of days for the seeds to germinate was 6.

2. Find the interquartile range of the data.

15 7 5 8 9 20 12 7 11 7 15

F. 8 **G.** 11

H. 12 **I.** 20

3. There are seven different integers in a set. When they are listed from least to greatest, the middle integer is -1. Which statement below must be true?

A. There are three negative integers in the set.

B. There are three positive integers in the set.

C. There are four negative integers in the set.

D. The integer in the set after -1 is positive.

4. What is the mean number of seats?

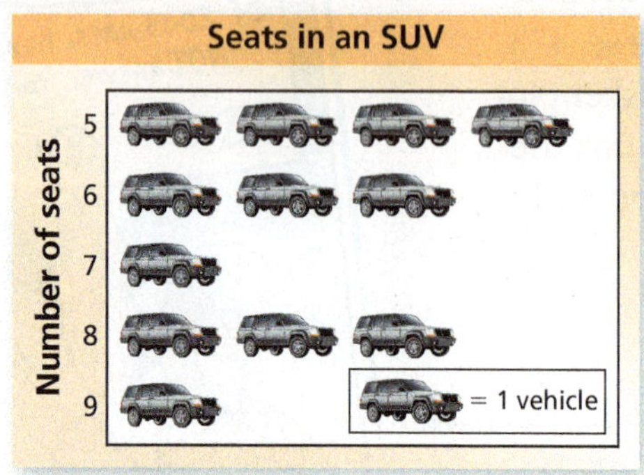

F. 2.4 seats

G. 5 seats

H. 6.5 seats

I. 7 seats

5. On Wednesday, a town received 17 millimeters of rain. This was x millimeters more rain than the town received on Tuesday. Which expression represents the amount of rain, in millimeters, the town received on Tuesday?

A. $17x$

B. $17 - x$

C. $x + 17$

D. $x - 17$

6. One of the leaves is missing in the stem-and-leaf plot.

The median of the data set represented by the stem-and-leaf plot is 38. What is the value of the missing leaf?

Stem	Leaf
1	3 4
2	
3	4 5 7 7 7 ? 9
4	0 1 1 4
5	0 2 3

Key: 1|4 = 14

7. Which property is demonstrated by the equation?

$$723 + (y + 277) = 723 + (277 + y)$$

F. Associative Property of Addition

G. Commutative Property of Addition

H. Distributive Property

I. Addition Property of Zero

Item Analysis (continued)

4. **F.** The student adds the frequencies and divides by 5 to find the mean.

   G. The student finds the mode instead of the mean.

   H. Correct answer

   I. The student chooses the middle number of seats.

5. **A.** The student misinterprets *more rain than* as meaning multiplication.

   B. Correct answer

   C. The student misinterprets the inverse relationship in the problem, thinking that the town received more rain on Tuesday than on Wednesday.

   D. The student subtracts in the wrong order and writes an expression that represents 17 millimeters less rain than the difference of the rain amounts on Tuesday and Wednesday.

6. **Gridded Response:** Correct answer: 7
   Common error: The student thinks that the missing leaf represents the ones digit of the median and gets 8.

7. **F.** The student misidentifies the property as the Associative Property of Addition.

   G. Correct answer

   H. The student misidentifies the property as the Distributive Property.

   I. The student misidentifies the property as the Addition Property of Zero.

Cumulative Practice

4. H

5. B

6. 7

7. G

Cumulative Practice

8. C

9. 14

10. *Part A* 22, 24, 25, 28, 28, 30, 31, 37, 37, 39, 40, 40, 44, 51, 58, 62

Part B 37 yr

Part C

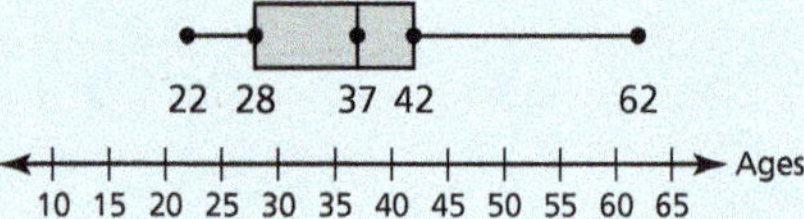

Item Analysis (continued)

8. A. The student thinks mean is mode.

B. The student finds the mean of the four scores (91) and then adds 1 to 92 because 91 is 1 less than 92.

C. Correct answer

D. The student makes an arithmetic error when finding the sum.

9. Gridded Response: Correct answer: 14
Common error: The student only considers the bar immediately to the left of 10 and gets 6.

10. 4 points The student's work demonstrates a thorough understanding of how to make a box-and-whisker plot. The data is ordered correctly. The median (37), first quartile (28), third quartile (42), least value (22), and greatest value (62) are identified correctly and graphed accurately.

3 points The student's work demonstrates an essential but less than thorough understanding of how to make a box-and-whisker plot. For example, the data is ordered correctly and the median is identified, but there may be a small mistake made when finding a quartile or when plotting on the number line.

2 points The student's work demonstrates a partial but limited understanding of how to make a box-and-whisker plot. For example, the data is ordered correctly, but the quartiles are misidentified.

1 point The student's work demonstrates a very limited understanding of how to make a box-and-whisker plot. For example, the only key value that the student can accurately identify is the median.

0 points The student provides no response, a completely incorrect or incomprehensible response, or a response that demonstrates insufficient understanding of how to make a box-and-whisker plot.

8. A student took five tests and had a mean score of 92. Her scores on the first 4 tests were 90, 96, 86, and 92. What was her score on the fifth test?

A. 92 **B.** 93

C. 96 **D.** 98

9. At the end of the school year, your teacher counted the number of absences for each student. The results are shown in the histogram. How many students had fewer than 10 absences?

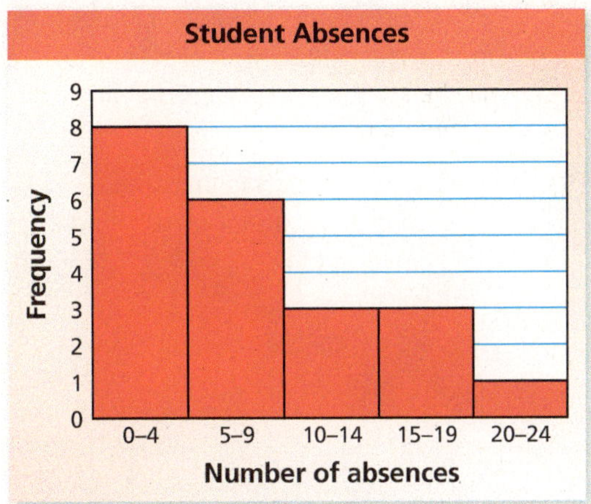

10. The ages of the 16 members of a camera club are listed below.

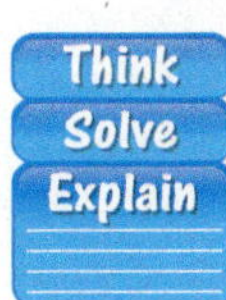

40, 22, 24, 58, 30, 31, 37, 25, 62, 40, 39, 37, 28, 28, 51, 44

Part A Order the ages from youngest to oldest.

Part B Find the median of the ages.

Part C Make a box-and-whisker plot for the ages.

0 10 20 30 40 50 60 70

Additional Answers

Chapter 1

Section 1.1

Exploration 1

Repeated Factors	Using an Exponent	Value
a. 10×10	10^2	100
b. 4×4	4^2	16
c. 6×6	6^2	36
d. $10 \times 10 \times 10$	10^3	1000
e. $100 \times 100 \times 100$	100^3	1,000,000
f. $3 \times 3 \times 3 \times 3$	3^4	81
g. $4 \times 4 \times 4 \times 4 \times 4$	4^5	1024
h. $2 \times 2 \times 2 \times 2 \times 2 \times 2$	2^6	64

Self-Assessment for Concepts & Skills

16. An exponent indicates the number of times the base is used as a factor. A power is the entire expression (base and exponent). A power is a product of repeated factors.

17. no; yes; 10 is not the square of a whole number, so it is not a perfect square. $100 = 10^2$, so it is a perfect square.

Section 1.2

Exploration 2

c. Find the value of the power, then add or subtract.

d. no; $18 \div 3 \cdot 3 = 6 \cdot 3 = 18$ and $18 \div 3^2 = 18 \div 9 = 2$

e. Evaluate powers first.

Section 1.3

Exploration 1

b. $80 = 2 \cdot 2 \cdot 2 \cdot 2 \cdot 5$; $162 = 2 \cdot 3 \cdot 3 \cdot 3 \cdot 3$; $300 = 2 \cdot 2 \cdot 3 \cdot 5 \cdot 5$

c. Answers will vary. Look for students to pick the products with five prime factors. *Sample answer:* The factors are prime.

Review & Refresh

4.

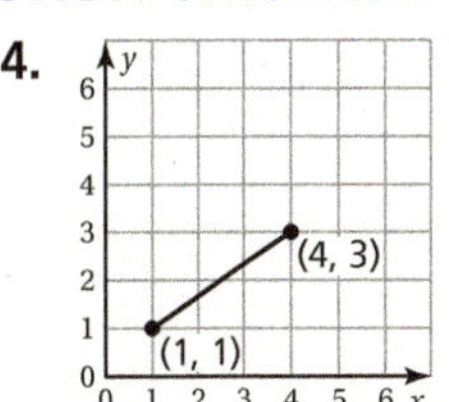

5.

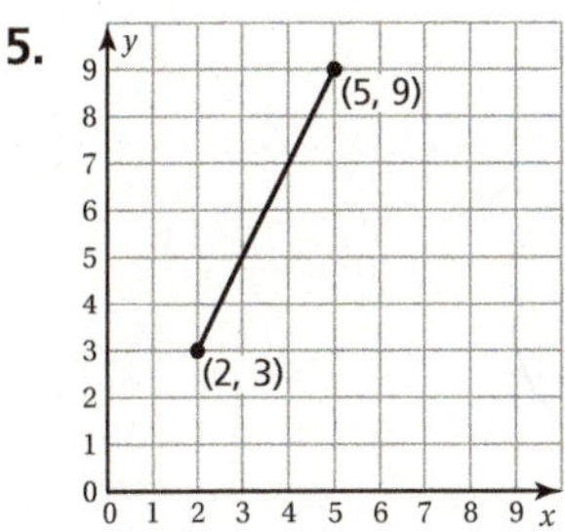

6.

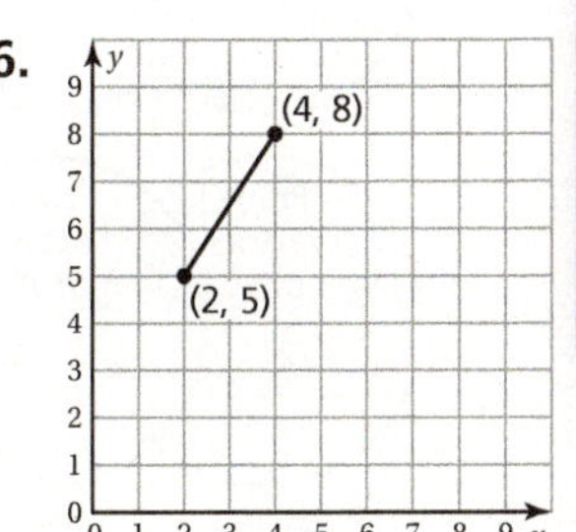

Section 1.4

Exploration 1

a.

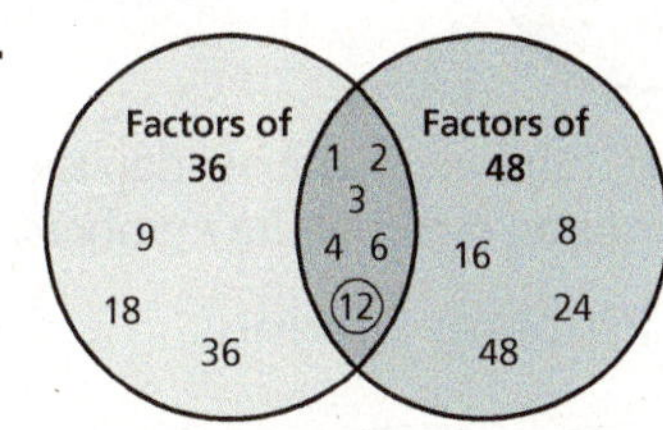

1, 2, 3, 4, 6, 12

b.

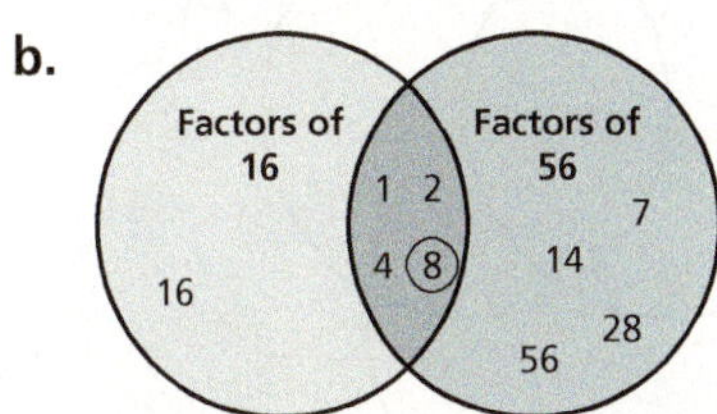

1, 2, 4, 8

c.

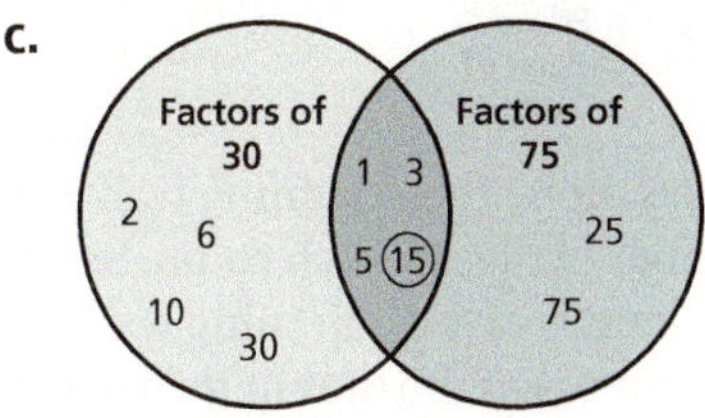

1, 3, 5, 15

d.

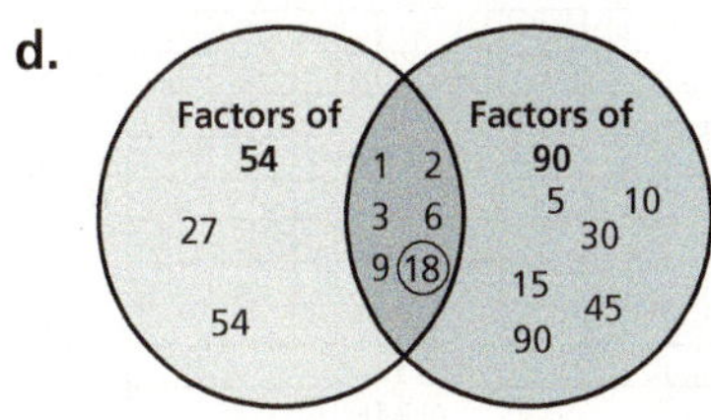

1, 2, 3, 6, 9, 18

Additional Answers

Exploration 2

b.

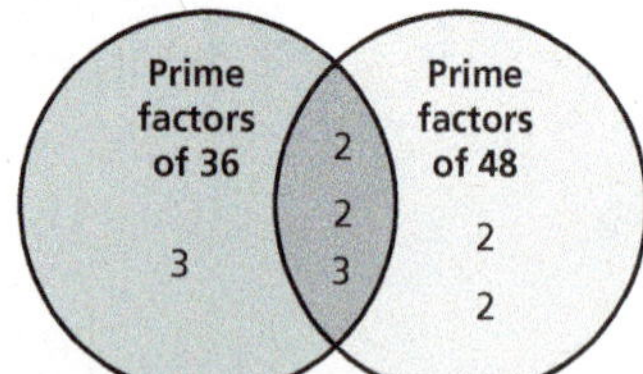

c.

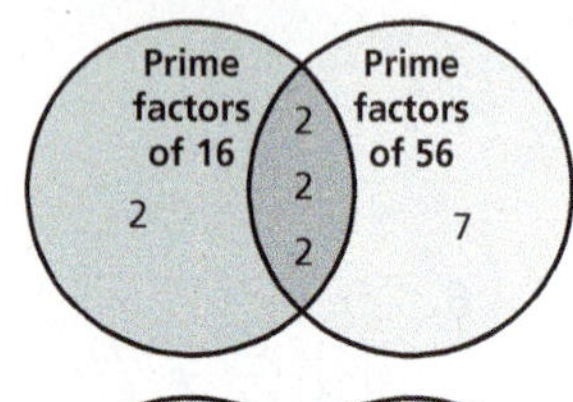

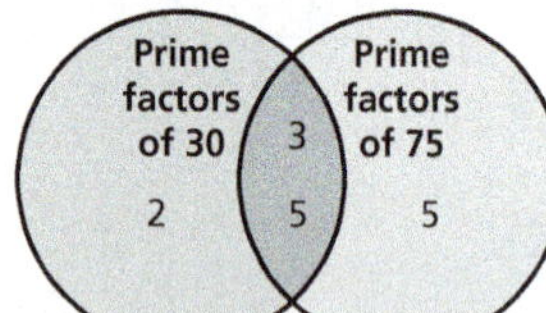

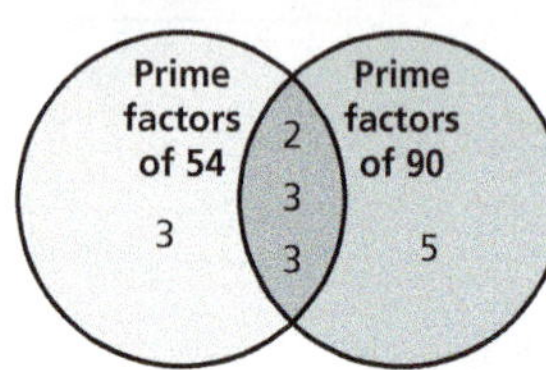

d. The product of the numbers in the overlap is equal to the greatest common factor of the numbers.

Concepts, Skills, & Problem Solving

54. a.

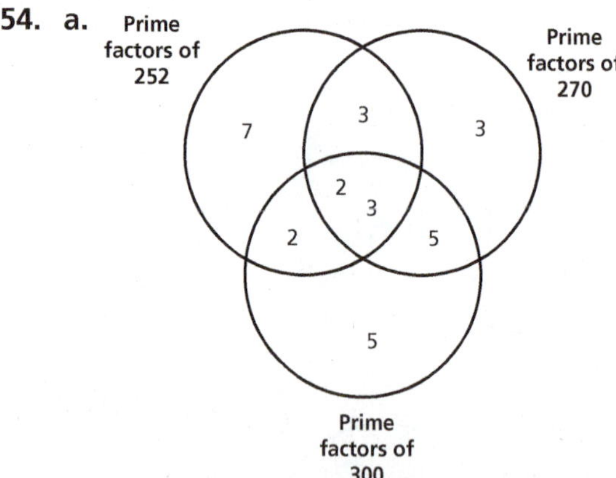

56. The number of tiles along the adjoining wall is a factor of the number of tiles in each room. So, the greatest possible length of the adjoining wall is the GCF of the numbers of the tiles in the rooms. *Sample answer:*

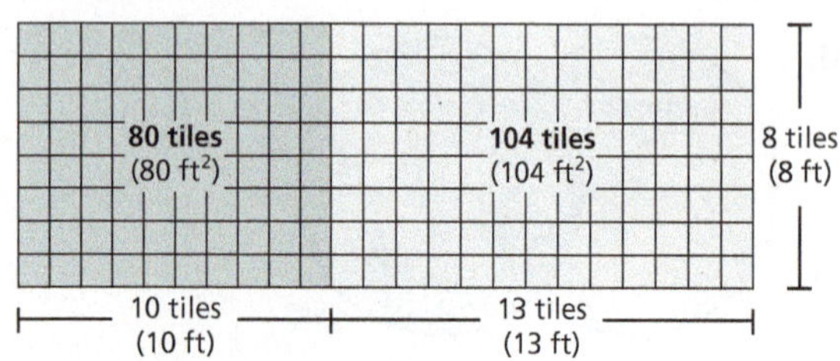

Section 1.5

Exploration 1

a.

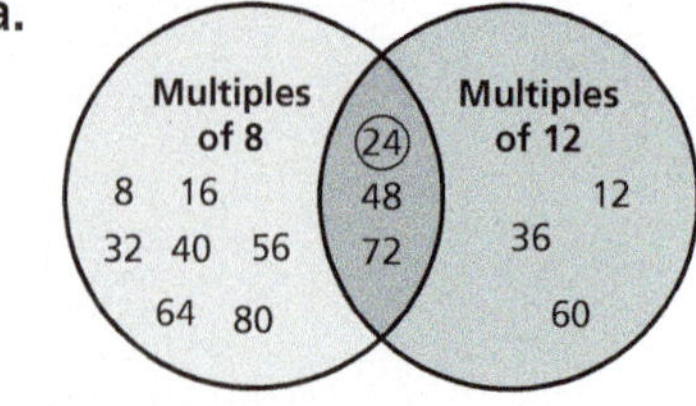

24, 48, 72

b.

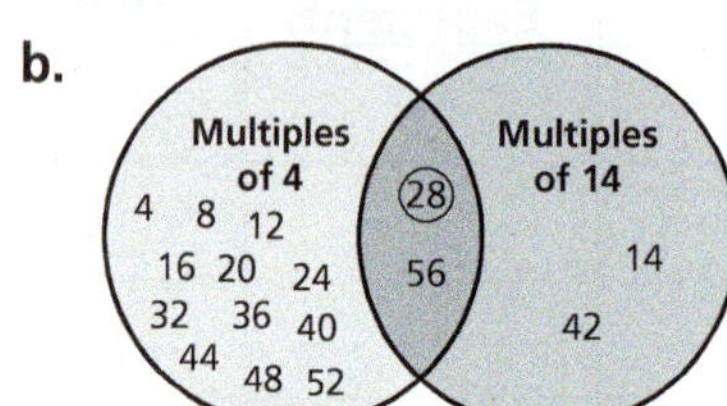

28, 56

c.

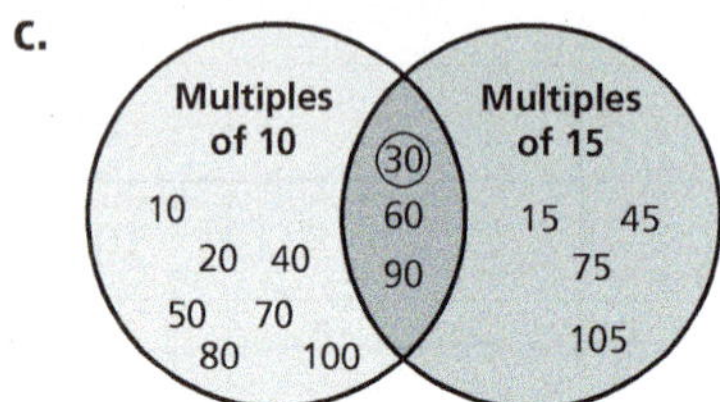

30, 60, 90

d.

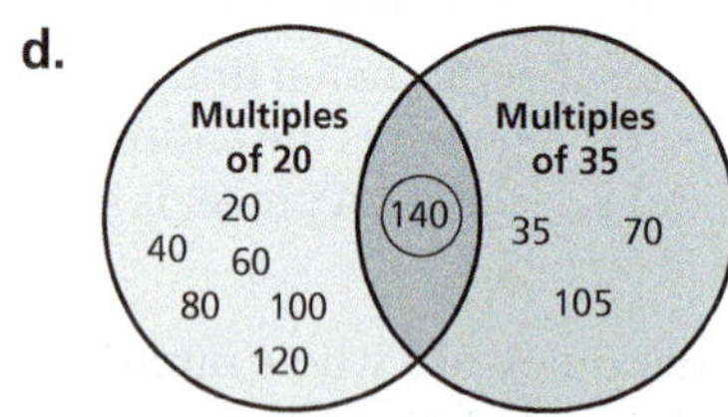

140

Exploration 2

b.

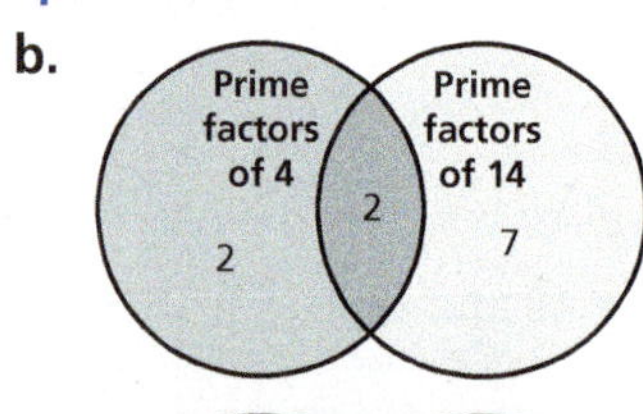

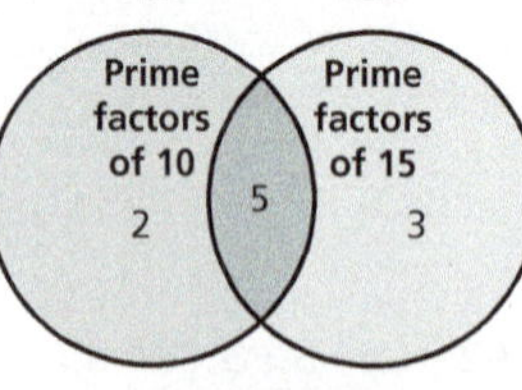

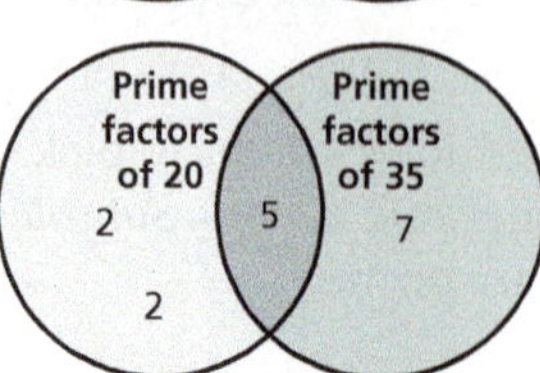

Chapter 2

Section 2.1

Exploration 1

$\frac{2}{6}$ or $\frac{1}{3}$ bottle; *Sample answer:* Shade 2 of the 3 columns of the area model. Then shade 1 of the 2 rows. Write the fraction of the model that is shaded twice.

Review & Refresh

6. $\frac{1}{32}$; *Sample answer:*

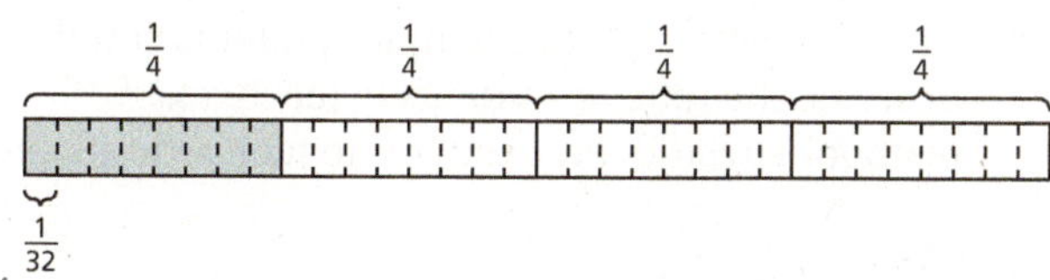

8. $\frac{1}{20}$; *Sample answer:*

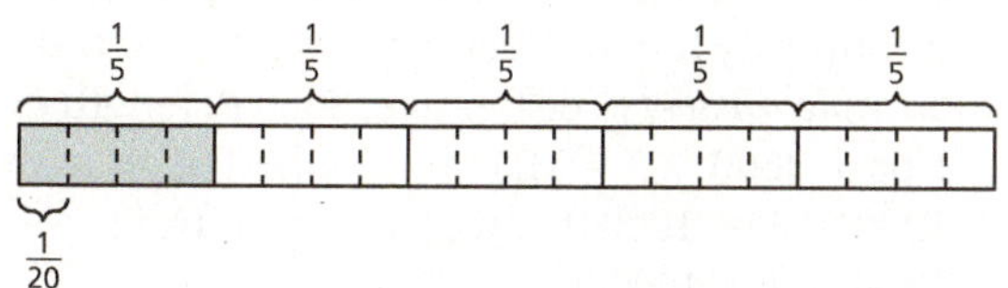

Concepts, Skills, and Problem Solving

69. $9\frac{1}{2} \times 8\frac{3}{4} \times 7\frac{5}{6} = 651\frac{7}{48}$; $1\frac{4}{9} \times 2\frac{5}{8} \times 3\frac{6}{7} = 14\frac{5}{8}$; *Sample answer:* Use the greatest (or least) digits for the whole numbers, then use the remaining digits to form the greatest (or least) fractional parts. Guess and test combinations of whole numbers and fractions to find the greatest (or least) product.

Section 2.2

Try It

6. $1\frac{1}{3}$

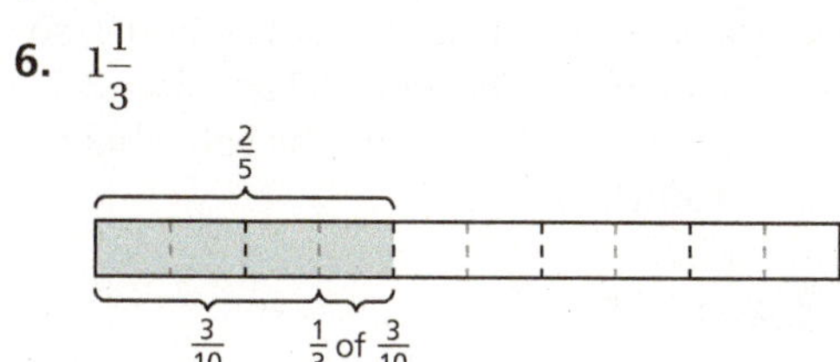

Concepts, Skills, and Problem Solving

53. >; When you divide a fraction by a fraction less than 1, the quotient is greater than the fraction.

54. $\frac{1}{216}$

55. $\frac{1}{144}$

56. $1\frac{1}{6}$

57. 4

58. 2

59. $\frac{5}{6}$

60. $\frac{3}{26}$

61. $\frac{1}{10}$

62. $\frac{2}{3}$

63. when the simplified fraction has a 1 in the numerator; The reciprocal will have a 1 in the denominator.

Section 2.3

Exploration 1

b. *Sample answer:* You ran $\frac{3}{8}$ of a mile yesterday. You ran $2\frac{1}{4}$ miles today. How many times farther did you run today than yesterday? 6

c. *Sample answer:* You have 6 cups of biscuit mix. One batch calls for $1\frac{1}{2}$ cups of mix. How many batches can you make? 4

d. *Sample answer:* A bicycle travels 1 yard when the foot pedal makes $\frac{7}{6}$ rotations. How many yards does the bicycle travel when the foot pedal makes $3\frac{1}{3}$ rotations? $2\frac{6}{7}$ yd

e. *Sample answer:* One batch of punch calls for $1\frac{1}{5}$ pints of cider. How many batches can you make with 5 pints of cider? $4\frac{1}{6}$

f. *Sample answer:* A dump truck holding $3\frac{1}{2}$ tons of sand dumps $2\frac{1}{2}$ tons of sand. What portion of the sand is dumped? $\frac{5}{7}$

g. *Sample answer:* You buy $4\frac{1}{2}$ gallons of paint. It takes $1\frac{1}{2}$ gallons to paint a room. What portion of the paint do you use to paint the room? $\frac{1}{3}$

Section 2.4

Exploration 1

a. 1.1, 0.5; *Sample answer:* $A = 0.3$ and $B = 0.8$

b. 2.24, 0.02; *Sample answer:* $A = 1.11$ and $B = 1.13$

c. 7.6, 0.8; *Sample answer:* $A = 3.4$ and $B = 4.2$

d. 5.1, 0.8; *Sample answer:* $A = 2.15$ and $B = 2.95$

Exploration 2

Write the numbers in the rows of the chart.

a. 18.995 **b.** 15.479

c. 30.102 **d.** 13.801

e. 310.1465 **f.** 1004.90032

Section 2.5

Exploration 1

b. Multiply as with whole numbers; The number of decimal places in each answer is equal to the sum of the number of decimal places in the factors.

c. 0.2475; *Sample answer:* Multiply as with whole numbers, the product has four decimal places.

Concepts, Skills, and Problem Solving

74. a. *Sample answer:*

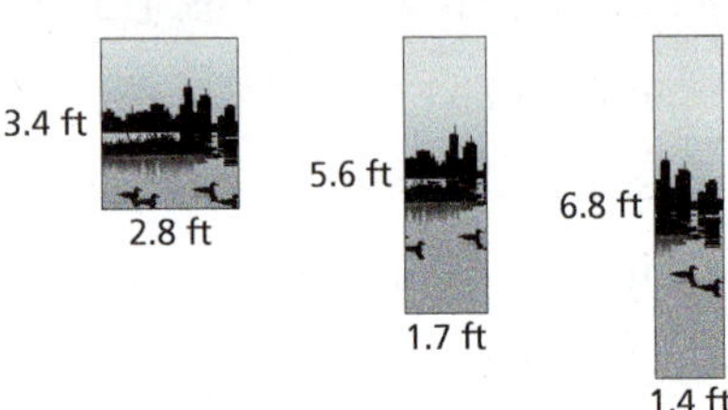

Section 2.6

Exploration 1

a. *Sample answer:* The amount of trash increased each year; The amount of recyclables increased each year; The amount of trash is several times greater than the amount of recyclables; There was 3 times as much trash in 2017 as in 2014; The cleanup started in 2014.

b. *Sample answer:* There was $4970 \div 2130 = 2\frac{1}{3}$ times as much trash and $732 \div 183 = 4$ times as much recyclables collected in 2016 as in 2014.

Section 2.7

Exploration 1

a. i. $0.4 \div 0.8 = 0.5$, $0.4 \div 0.5 = 0.8$; Rewrote $0.8 \times 0.5 = 0.4$.

ii. $0.75 \div 0.5 = 1.5$, $0.75 \div 1.5 = 0.5$; Rewrote $0.5 \times 1.5 = 0.75$.

iii. $1.19 \div 0.7 = 1.7$, $1.19 \div 1.7 = 0.7$; Rewrote $0.7 \times 1.7 = 1.19$.

Chapter 3

Chapter Exploration

14. *Sample answers:*

Y	Y	R	R	R	R	R

R	R	R	Y	R	R	Y
Y	R	R	Y	R	R	R

15. no; $\frac{8}{14} > \frac{9}{17}$; 2

Section 3.1

Exploration 1

a. *Sample answers:* 8 boys and 16 girls; 6 boys and 12 girls; 10 boys and 20 girls

b. Answers will vary. Listen for students to describe the ratio of girls to boys in their class and compare to the 2 : 1 ratio for the science class; no; no; The actual numbers of girls and boys in the science class is not given.

c. Answers will vary. For example, students could describe the ratio of students to teachers, textbooks to students, students to tables/desks, etc.

Section 3.2

Exploration 1

c. Divide the length by the number of parts, then multiply by the number of parts for each trail; *Sample answers:* difference: 3600 ft; length of 1 part: $3600 \div 3 = 1200$ ft, length of beginner trail: $1200 \times 1 = 1200$ ft, length of expert trail: $1200 \times 4 = 4800$ ft

Section 3.3

Exploration 1

a.

Cups	2	4	6	8	10
Calories	180	360	540	720	900

Exploration 2

a.

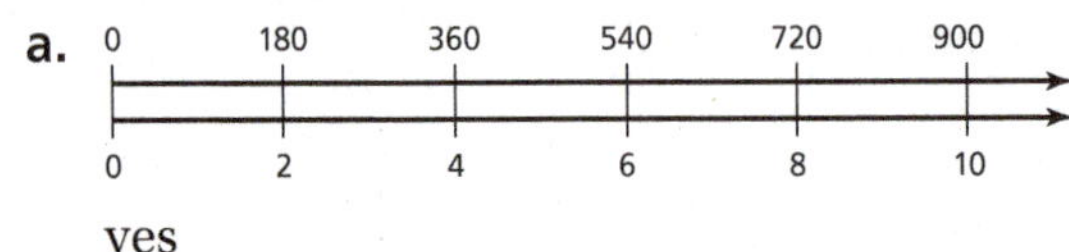

yes

b. *Sample answer:* 3 is halfway between 2 and 4, so find the value halfway between 180 and 360; 3.5 is halfway between 3 and 4, so find the value halfway between 270 and 360.

Section 3.4

Exploration 1

a. *Sample answer:*

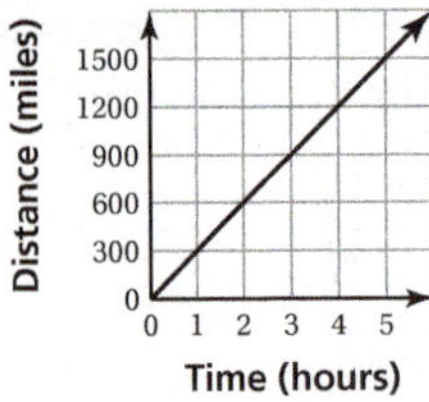

Exploration 2

Sample answer:

Milk (fluid ounces)	0	5	10	15
Cereal (ounces)	0	2	4	6

The blue and red arrows correspond to equivalent ratios of milk to cereal. The green arrows show how to generate an equivalent ratio.

Try It

3. a.

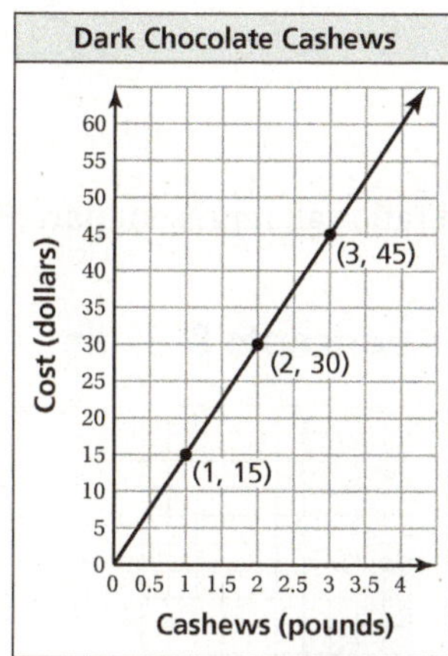

Concepts, Skills, & Problem Solving

13.

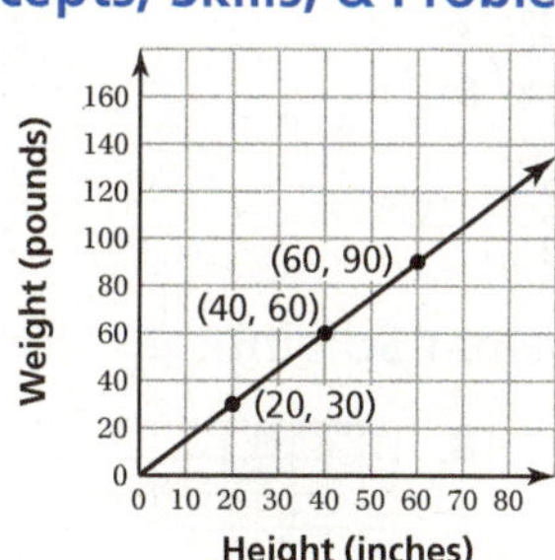

14.

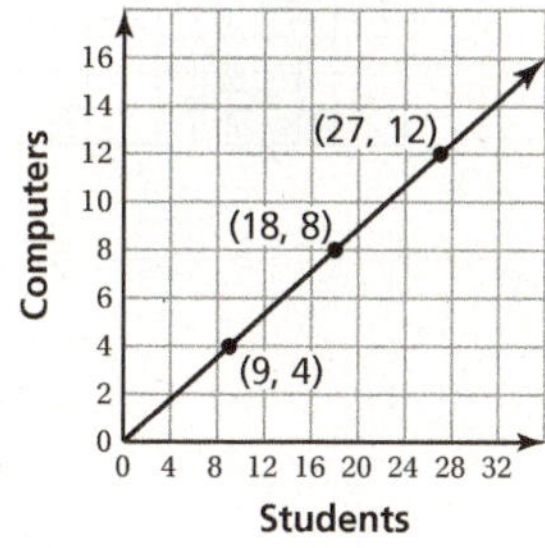

15.

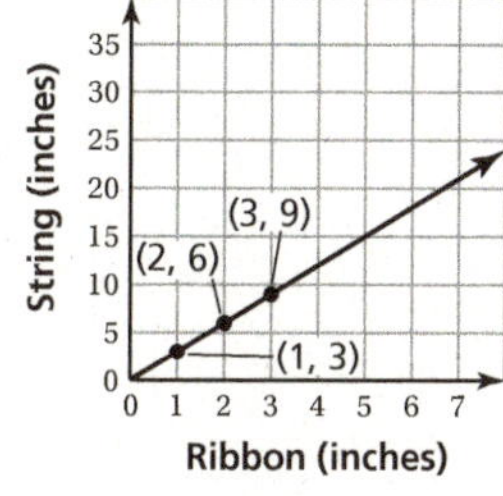

16.

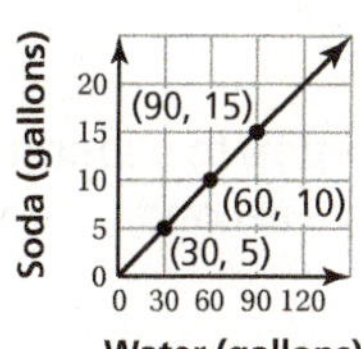

17.

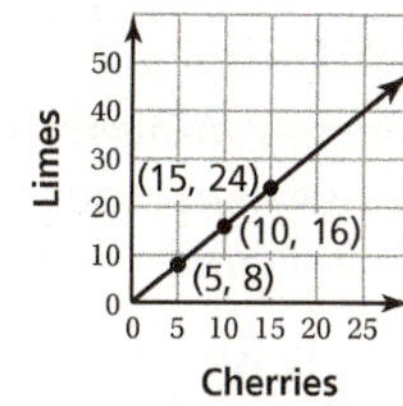

18.

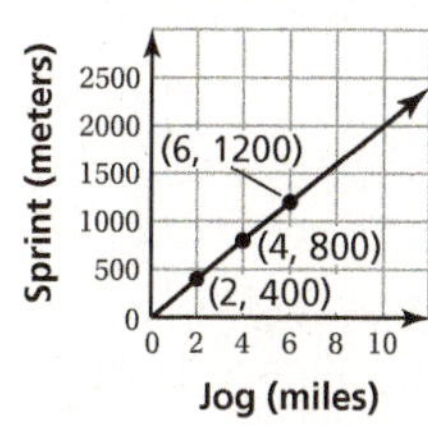

23.

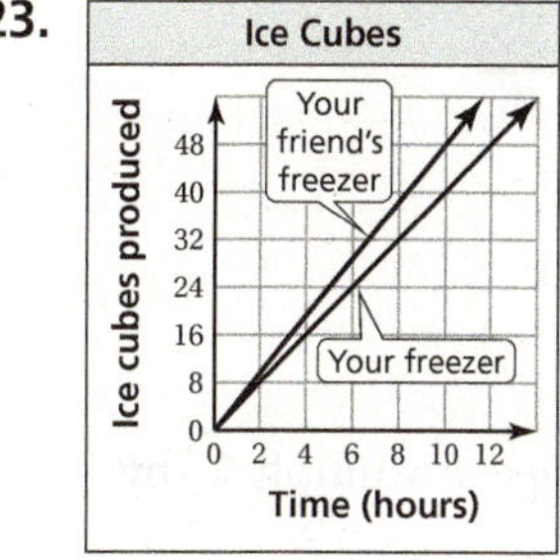

your friend's

25. a. 70

b.

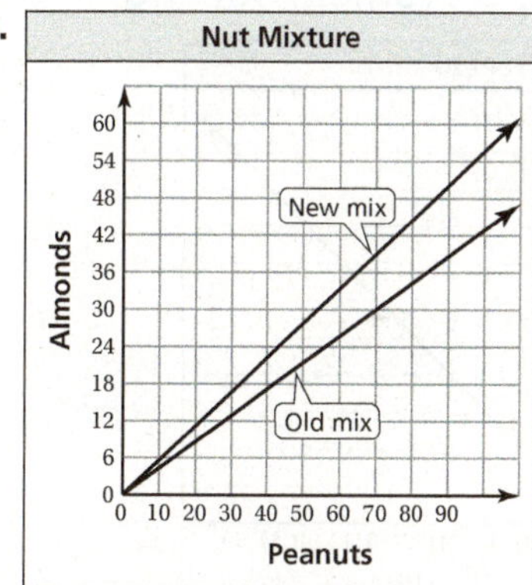

yes; The new mixture is more expensive to make because the new mix has a greater ratio of almonds to peanuts.

Section 3.5

Exploration 1

c.

Multiply the speed by 3.25.

Exploration 2

b. *Sample answer:* Use multiplication to generate equivalent ratios for times of 120 seconds, 150 seconds, and 180 seconds.

Review & Refresh

3.

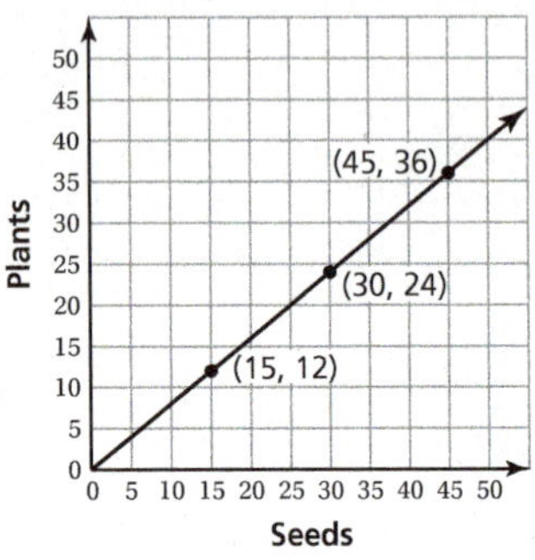

Section 3.6

Exploration 1

c. $20\frac{5}{8}$ L, 3 gal; *Sample answers:* Multiply $3\frac{3}{4}$ by 5.5, and multiply 12 by $\frac{1}{4}$; Graph the ratio relationship.

Concepts, Skills, & Problem Solving

33. a.

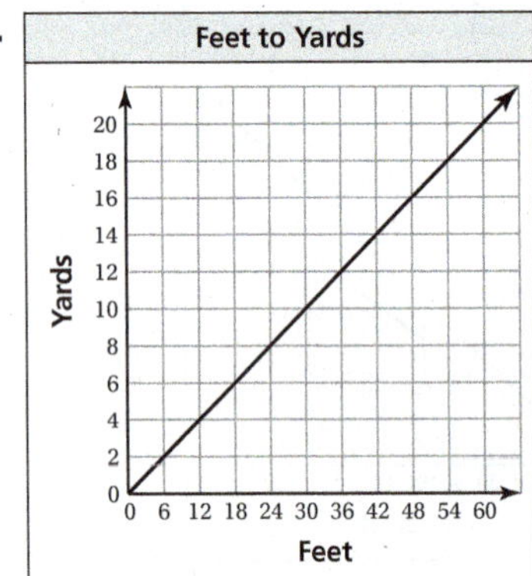

b.

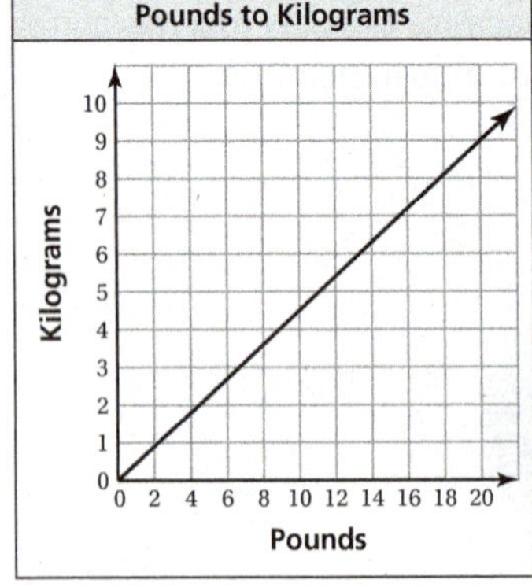

Chapter 4

Section 4.1

Exploration 1

a. 60%; $\frac{60}{100}$; 60 : 100

b. 8%; $\frac{8}{100}$; 8 : 100

c. 51%; $\frac{51}{100}$; 51 : 100

d. 25%; $\frac{25}{100}$; 25 : 100

Percents, fractions, and ratios all represent part of a whole.

Self-Assessment for Concepts & Skills

9. $\frac{2}{5}$; *Sample answer:*

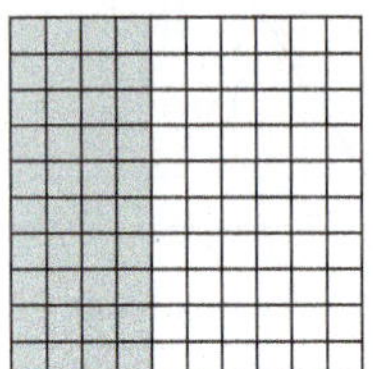

12. *Sample answer:* $\frac{3}{20}, \frac{23}{100}, \frac{1}{8}$

13. yes; $1\frac{1}{4} = \frac{5 \times 25}{4 \times 25} = \frac{125}{100} = 125\%$

Concepts, Skills, & Problem Solving

17.

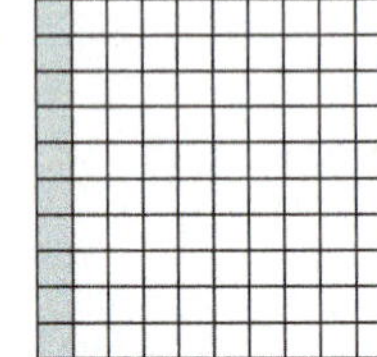

18.

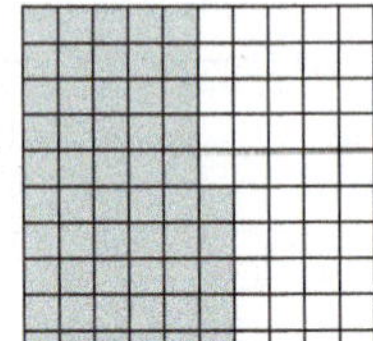

19.

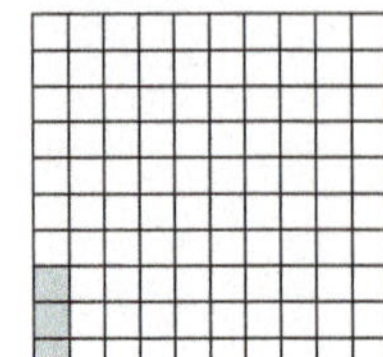

Section 4.2

Try It

2. 0.03

3. 1.07

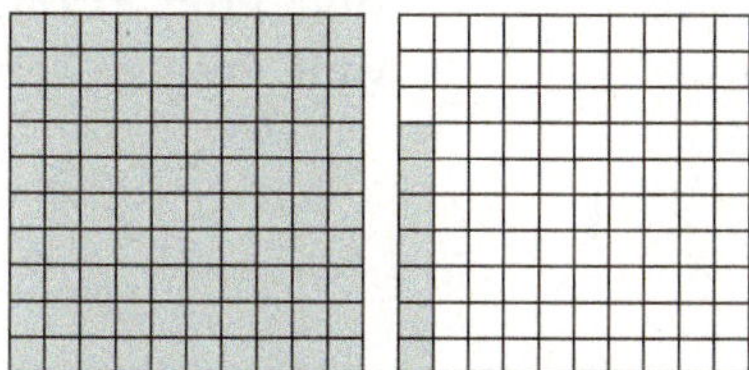

4. 0.925

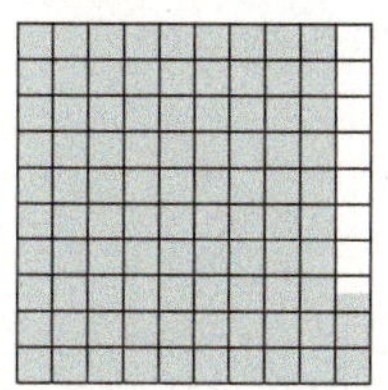

Self-Assessment for Concepts & Skills

10. 0.32

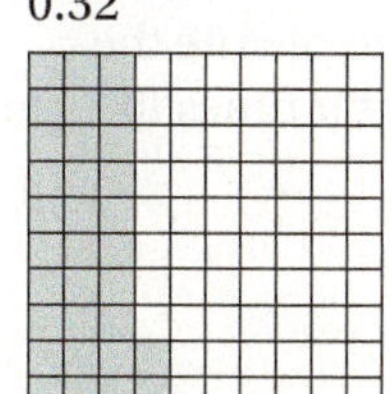

11. 0.545

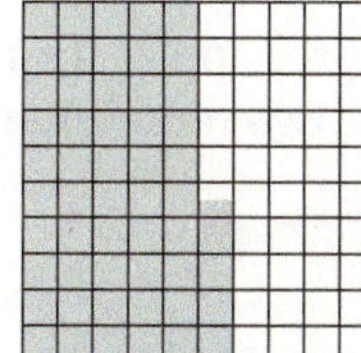

12. 1.08

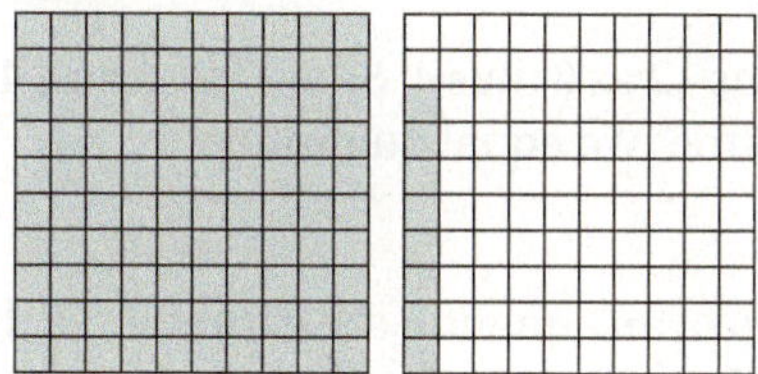

Section 4.3

Exploration 1

a. 0.9%, 0.25, 40%, 0.5

b. 0%, $\frac{1}{20}$, 30%, $\frac{3}{4}$

c. 0.125, $\frac{3}{10}$, 75%, 100%

d. $\frac{1}{100}$, 12.5%, 25%, 1.02

e. 4%, $\frac{1}{8}$, 0.3, 0.75

f. $\frac{9}{10}$, $\frac{51}{50}$, 105%, 1.5

Sample answer: Labeled the number line with fractions, decimals, and percents.

Concepts, Skills, & Problem Solving

32. 26.8%, 2.26, $2\frac{2}{5}$, 2.62, 271%

33. $\frac{21}{50}$, $\frac{87}{200}$, 43.7%, 0.44

34. yes

Section 4.4

Exploration 1

a. above: 25%, $66\frac{2}{3}$%; below: 20, 45;

Sample answer: different percents of 60

b. *Sample answer:*

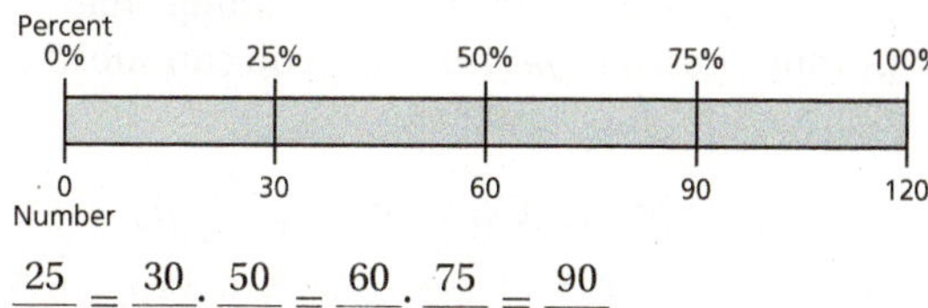

$\frac{25}{100} = \frac{30}{120}$; $\frac{50}{100} = \frac{60}{120}$; $\frac{75}{100} = \frac{90}{120}$

Chapter 5

Section 5.2

Exploration 1

a.

Sandwich	Price (dollars)	Change Received (dollars)
Reuben	6.45	20 − 6.45
BLT	5.25	20 − 5.25
Egg salad	4.65	20 − 4.65
Roast beef	6.75	20 − 6.75

Section 5.3

Exploration 1

a. *Sample answer:*

x	1	2	3	4
$4 + x + 4$	9	10	11	12

x	1	2	3	4
$16x$	16	32	48	64

x	1	2	3	4
$4 \cdot (x \cdot 4)$	16	32	48	64

x	1	2	3	4
$x + 4 + 4$	9	10	11	12

x	1	2	3	4
$x + 8$	9	10	11	12

x	1	2	3	4
$(4 \cdot x) \cdot 4$	16	32	48	64

yes; $4 + x + 4 = x + 4 + 4 = x + 8$;
$16x = 4 \cdot (x \cdot 4) = (4 \cdot x) \cdot 4$

b. Commutative Property of Addition: Changing the order of addends does not change the sum; Commutative Property of Multiplication: Changing the order of factors does not change the product; Associative Property of Addition: Changing the grouping of addends does not change the sum; Associative Property of Multiplication: Changing the grouping of factors does not change the product; yes; *Sample answer:* You can substitute numbers for the variables.

Self-Assessment for Concepts & Skills

7. $(7 + c) + 4 = (c + 7) + 4$ Comm. Prop. of Add.
$= c + (7 + 4)$ Assoc. Prop. of Add.
$= c + 11$ Add 7 and 4.

8. $4(b \cdot 6) = 4(6 \cdot b)$ Comm. Prop. of Mult.
$= (4 \cdot 6)b$ Assoc. Prop. of Mult.
$= 24b$ Multiply 4 and 6.

9. $0 \cdot b \cdot 9 = (0 \cdot b)9$ Assoc. Prop. of Mult.
$= 0 \cdot 9$ Mult. Prop. of Zero
$= 0$ Mult. Prop. of Zero

Concepts, Skills, & Problem Solving

28. $6(2b) = (6 \cdot 2)b$ Assoc. Prop. of Mult.
$= 12b$ Multiply 6 and 2.

29. $7(9w) = (7 \cdot 9)w$ Assoc. Prop. of Mult.
$= 63w$ Multiply 7 and 9.

30. $3.2 + (x + 5.1)$
$= 3.2 + (5.1 + x)$ Comm. Prop. of Add.
$= (3.2 + 5.1) + x$ Assoc. Prop. of Add.
$= 8.3 + x$ Add 3.2 and 5.1.

31. $(0 + a) + 8 = a + 8$ Add. Prop. of Zero

32. $9 \cdot c \cdot 4 = 9 \cdot 4 \cdot c$ Comm. Prop. of Mult.
$= (9 \cdot 4) \cdot c$ Assoc. Prop. of Mult.
$= 36c$ Multiply 9 and 4.

33. $(18.6 \cdot d) \cdot 1 = 18.6 \cdot (d \cdot 1)$ Assoc. Prop. of Mult.
$= 18.6d$ Mult. Prop. of One

34. $\left(3k + 4\frac{1}{5}\right) + 8\frac{3}{5}$
$= 3k + \left(4\frac{1}{5} + 8\frac{3}{5}\right)$ Assoc. Prop. of Add.
$= 3k + 12\frac{4}{5}$ Add $4\frac{1}{5}$ and $8\frac{3}{5}$.

35. $(2.4 + 4n) + 9$
$= (4n + 2.4) + 9$ Comm. Prop. of Add.
$= 4n + (2.4 + 9)$ Assoc. Prop. of Add.
$= 4n + 11.4$ Add 2.4 and 9.

36. $(3s) \cdot 8 = (s \cdot 3) \cdot 8$ Comm. Prop. of Mult.
$= s \cdot (3 \cdot 8)$ Assoc. Prop. of Mult.
$= s \cdot 24$ Multiply 3 and 8.
$= 24s$ Comm. Prop. of Mult.

37. $z \cdot 0 \cdot 12 = (z \cdot 0) \cdot 12$ Assoc. Prop. of Mult.
$= 0 \cdot 12$ Mult. Prop. of Zero
$= 0$ Mult. Prop. of Zero

Section 5.4

Exploration 1

c. To multiply a sum by a number, multiply each term in the sum by the number. *Sample answer:* yes; It is true for the expression in part (a).

Section 5.5

Exploration 1

a. *Sample answer:* $4(2 + 6)$; $8(10 + 7)$; $3(x + 6)$; Use a common factor as the height and find the lengths.

b. *Sample answer:* Use the Distributive Property.

c. Use the Distributive Property to rewrite the expression as the common factor times the sum of the two remaining factors.

Chapter 6

Section 6.2

Exploration 1

b. Step 2 reforms 12 as 8 plus 4, Step 3 subtracts 4 from each of the two equal quantities.

Exploration 2

a. The two sides of an equation are expressions that are equal, or have the same value.

b. Add the same amount of weight to the other side; Subtract the same amount of weight from the other side; When you add or subtract the same amount to each side of an equation, the sides will be equal.

Section 6.3

Exploration 2

b. Triple the weight on the other side; Divide the weight on the other side in half; Do the same thing to each side.

Section 6.4

Try It

7. $c = 8h + 25$

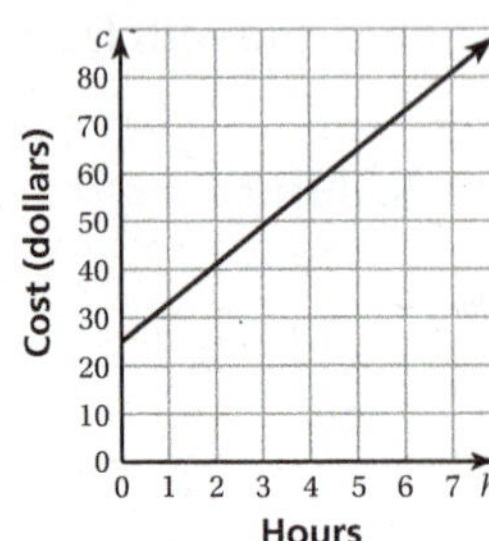

Concepts, Skills, & Problem Solving

48.

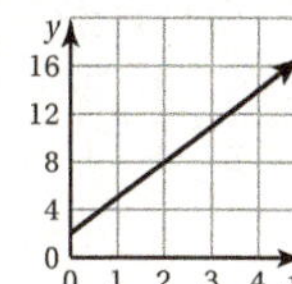

49.

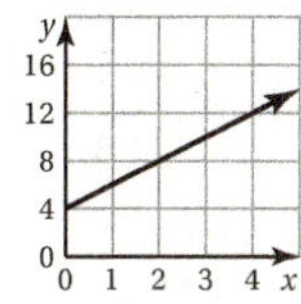

50.

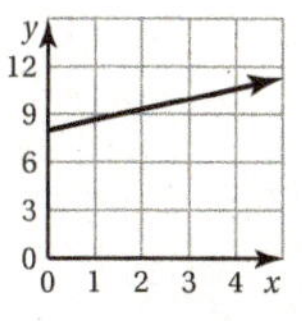

51.

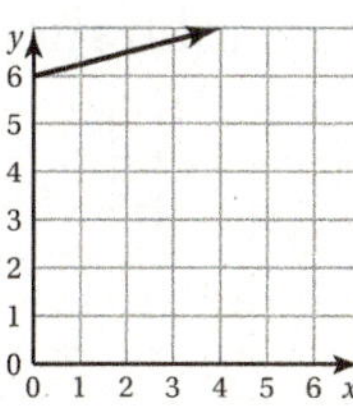

52.

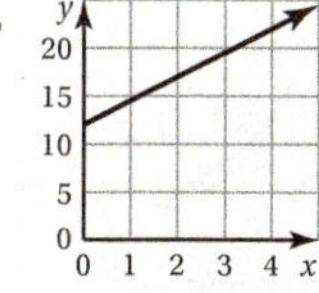

53. $c = 1.5t + 5$

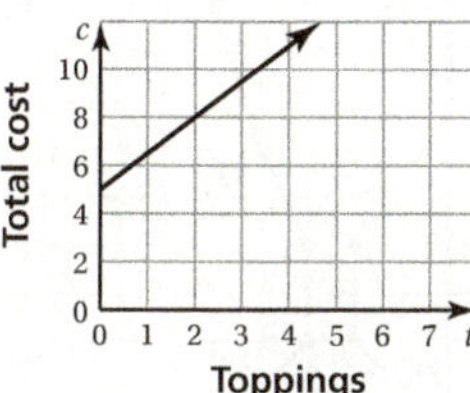

54. $c = 15m + 35$

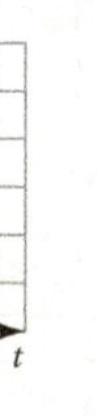

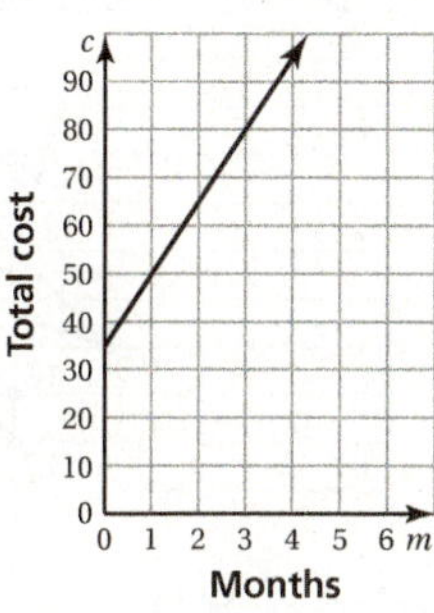

55. **a.** $r = 160 - x$

b. independent variable: x, dependent variable: r

c. 145

60. $d = 240t$

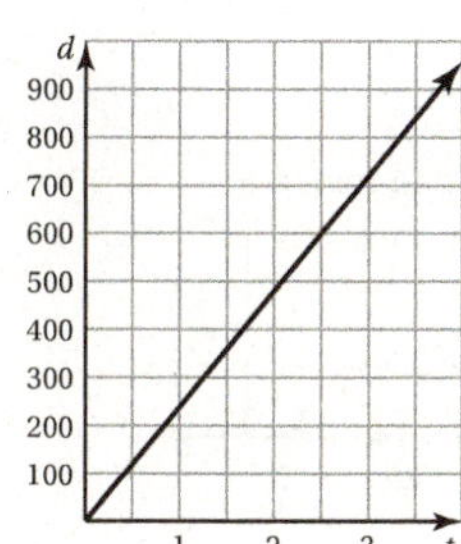

Chapter Self-Assessment

32. $y = 50x$

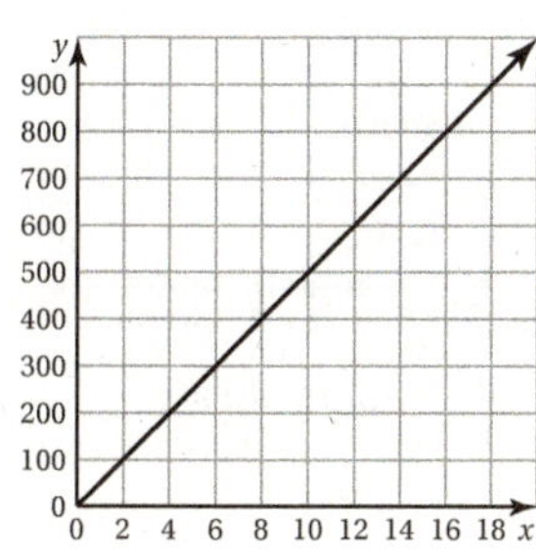

10.5 h

Chapter 7

Section 7.2

Exploration 1

d. no; The area is not changed by how it is calculated.

e. $A = \frac{1}{2}bh$; 15 m^2

Section 7.4

Exploration 1

b. *Sample answer:* Planes are parallel if they never intersect; lines are parallel if they lie on the same plane and do not intersect; a line is parallel to a plane if they never intersect; lines or planes are perpendicular if they meet at a right angle;

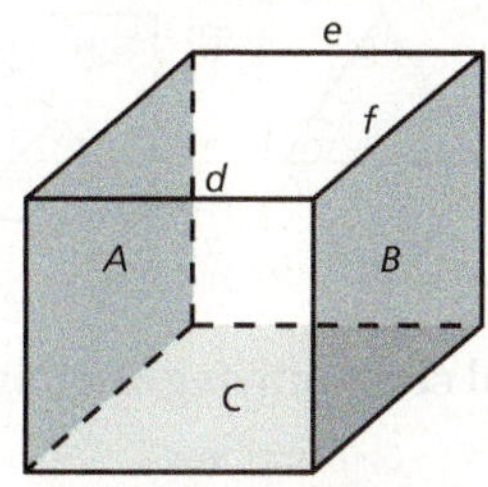

Faces A and B are parallel.
Face C is perpendicular to faces A and B.
Edges d and e are parallel.
Edge f is perpendicular to edges d and e.
Edges d and e are parallel to face C.
Edges d and e are perpendicular to faces A and B.

Exploration 2

a.

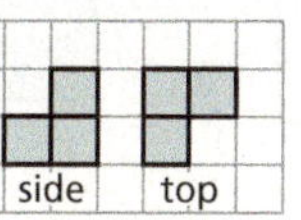

4

b.

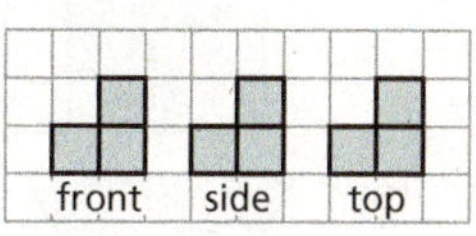

4

c.

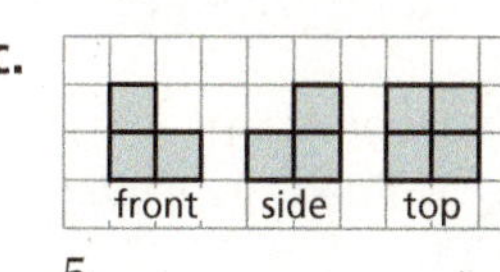

5

d.

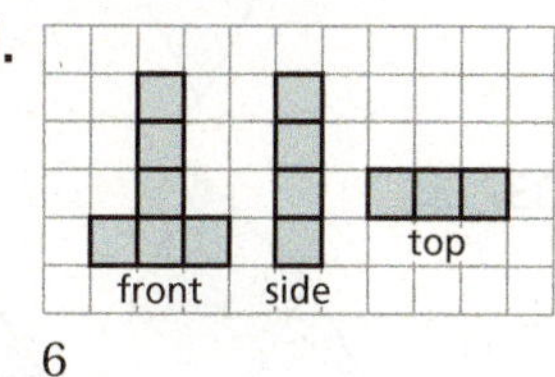

6

Self-Assessment for Problem Solving

7.

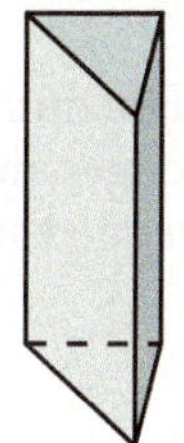

8. front: side:

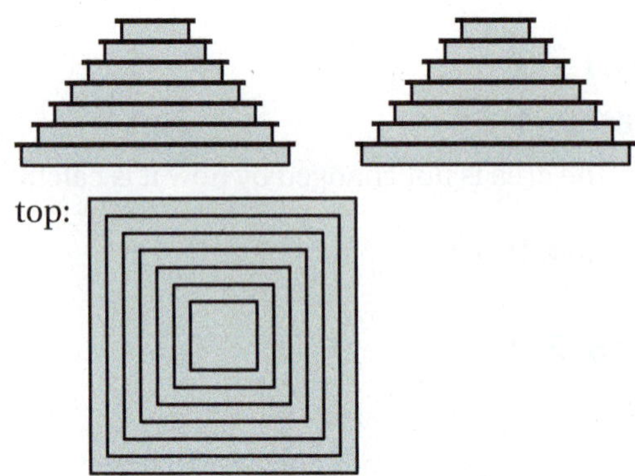

top:

Sample answer: There are 7 levels and the pyramid is probably symmetric.

9. a. 8 faces, 12 edges, 6 vertices

b. front: side: top:

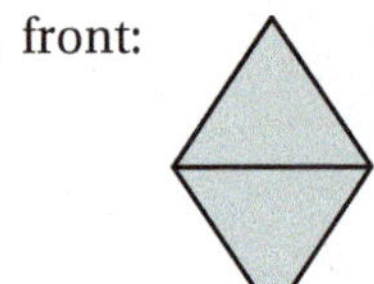

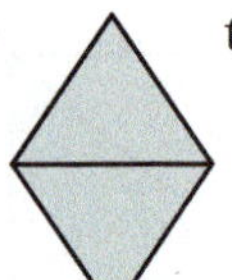

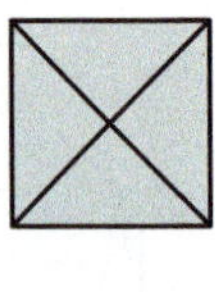

c. Make a flat, horizontal cut removing a square pyramid from the top.

Concepts, Skills, & Problem Solving

22. The Washington Monument is an *obelisk*. It consists of a pyramid sitting on top of a solid that tapers as it rises.

25. front: side:

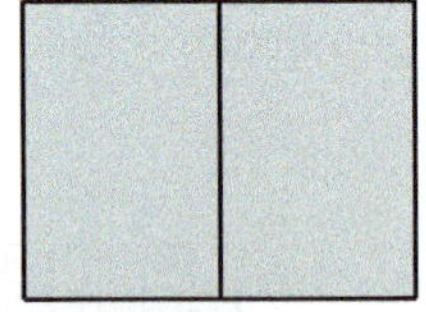

top:

33. a.

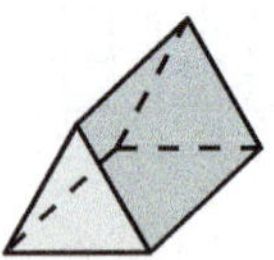

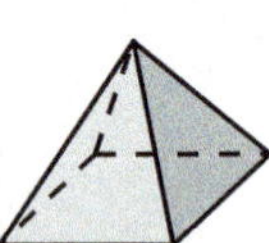

6 vertices
9 edges

5 vertices
8 edges

b. More than one solid can have the same number of faces, so knowing the number of edges and vertices can help you to draw the intended solid.

Section 7.7

Exploration 1

b. $\frac{18}{24}$, or $\frac{3}{4}$ unit^3; The prism can be made of 18 of the prisms from part (a).

d. yes; *Sample answer:* In part (b), $B = \frac{3}{2} \bullet \frac{3}{4} = \frac{9}{8}$, so

$V = Bh = \frac{9}{8} \bullet \frac{2}{3} = \frac{3}{4}$, and $V = \ell wh = \frac{3}{2} \bullet \frac{3}{4} \bullet \frac{2}{3} = \frac{3}{4}$.

Chapter 8

Chapter Exploration

1.

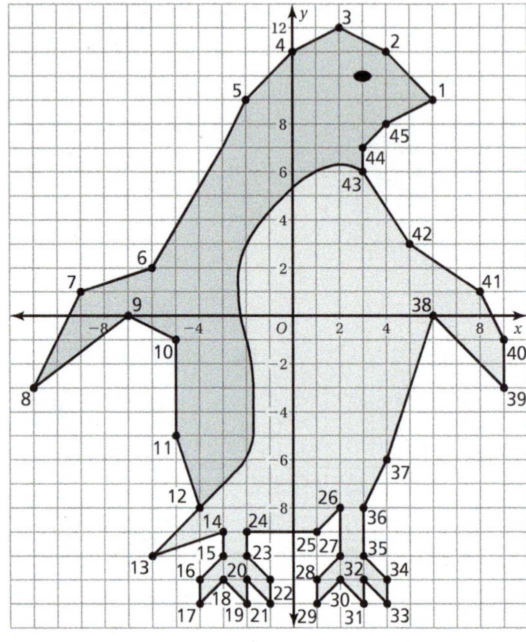

Section 8.1

Exploration 1

a. i: Death Valley, California; ii: Seattle, Washington; iii: Honolulu, Hawaii; iv: Anchorage, Alaska

Section 8.2

Exploration 1

a.

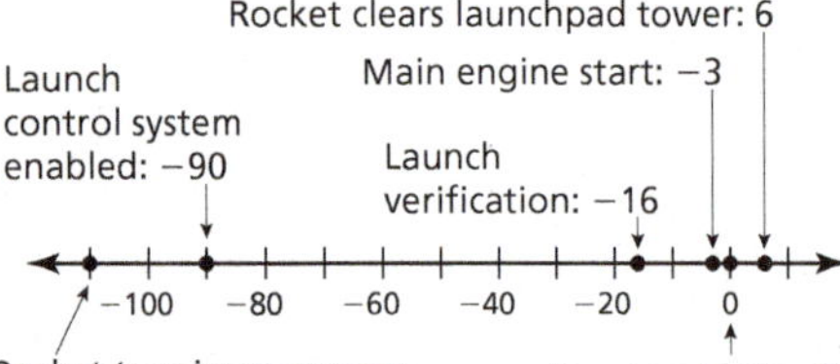

Section 8.3

Exploration 1

Sample answer: Let 0 represent noon.

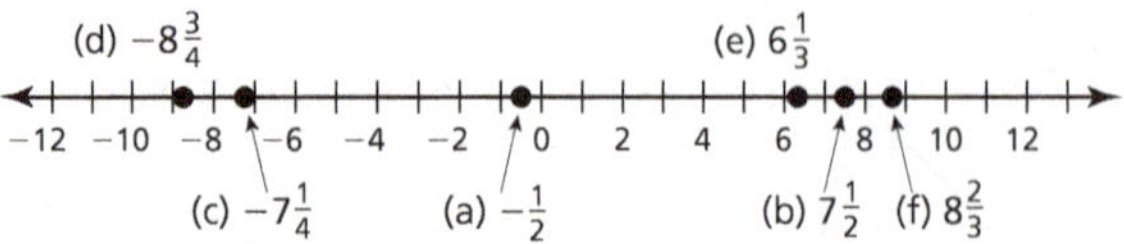

Try It

4. 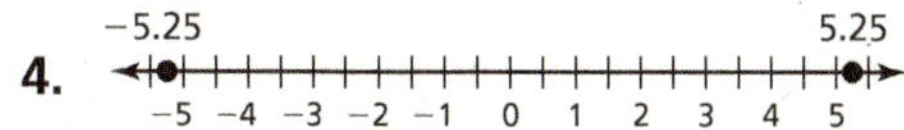

Concepts, Skills, & Problem Solving

34. $-2, -1.8, -1.75, 0, 1.3$

35. $-5, -4.9, -4.35, -4.3, -4$

36. $-0.1, 0, 0.8, 1.2, 1.6$

37. $-1, -\frac{1}{2}, -\frac{1}{4}, \frac{1}{8}, \frac{3}{4}$

38. $-3, -2\frac{1}{2}, -2\frac{2}{5}, -2\frac{3}{10}, -2$

39. $-1, -\frac{3}{4}, -\frac{5}{8}, -\frac{1}{20}, 0$

Section 8.4

Exploration 1

b. *Sample answer:* seaplane and whale; Both are the same distance from sea level.

c. *Kaiko:* up 2000 meters; *Sample answer: Alvin*: down 500 meters; *Jason, Jr.*: down 1100 meters

Review & Refresh

6. 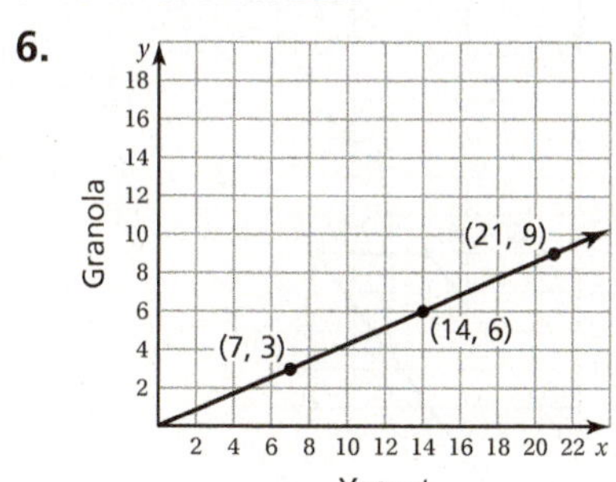

Section 8.5

Exploration 1

a. *Sample answer:*

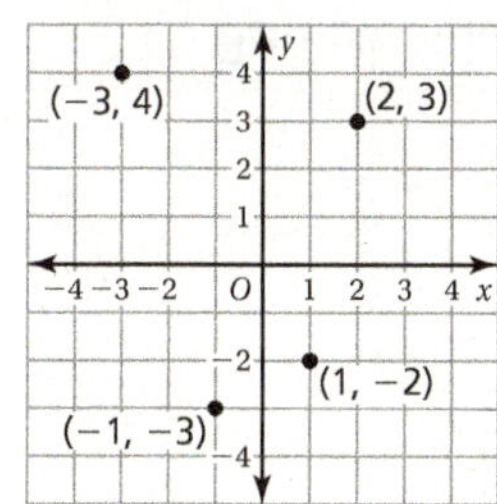

Extend the x- and y-axes to include negative values.

b. 4; The signs of the coordinates are the same within each region.

c. *Sample answer:*

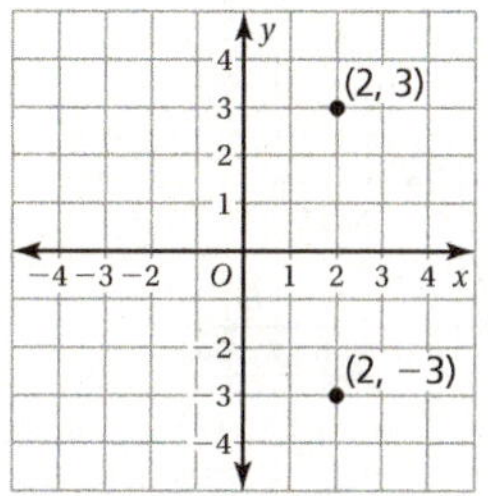

The x-coordinate remains the same, the y-coordinate changes sign.

Try It

5–8. 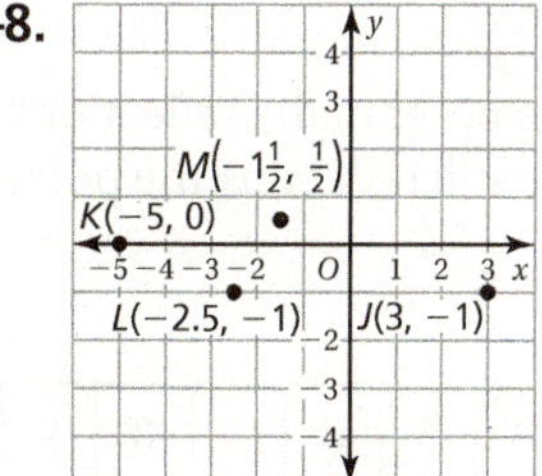

Self-Assessment for Concepts & Skills

19–21. 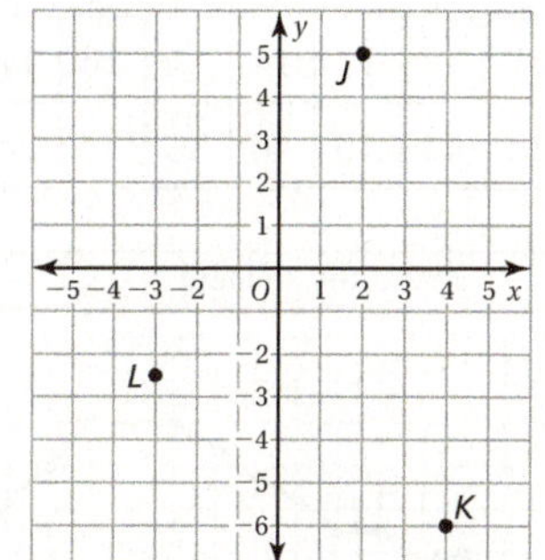

Self-Assessment for Problem Solving

26. 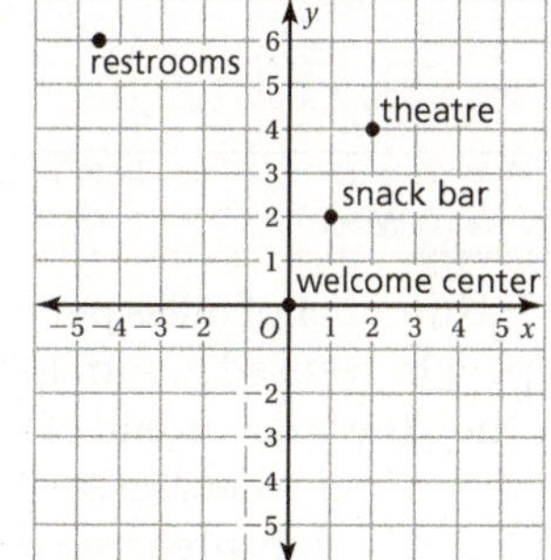

27. 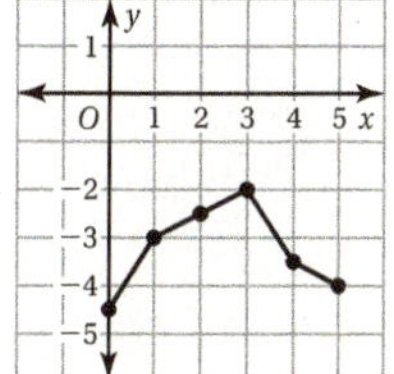

The elevation increased from noon until 3:00 P.M. and decreased from 3:00 P.M. until 5:00 P.M.

Concepts, Skills, & Problem Solving

26–37.

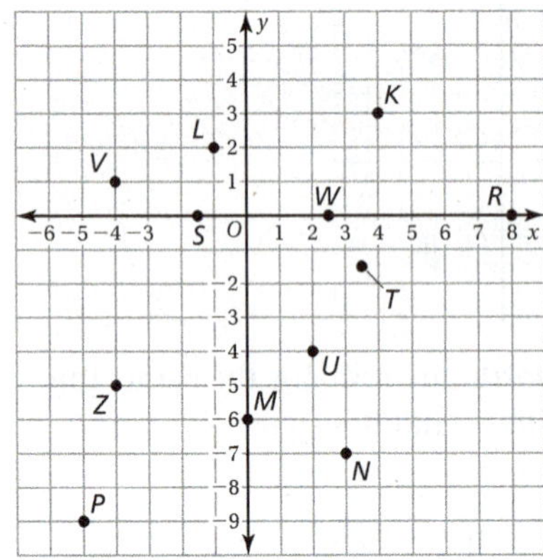

69. yes; *Sample answer:* The order of the reflections does not matter. You are still reflecting the points in both axes.

81. a.

Week	1	2	3	4	5	6	7	8	9
Miles	22	24	26	24	28	27	30	30	33

Week	10	11	12	13	14	15	16	17	18
Miles	35	38	40	40	40	36	33	24	14

b.

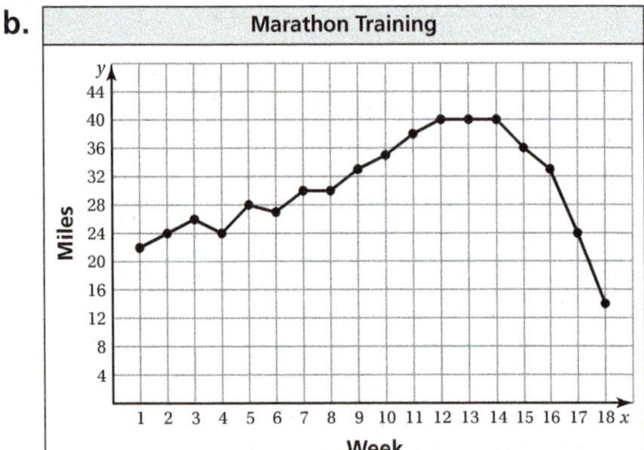

c. *Sample answer:* The number of miles per week increases so that people get used to running longer distances. Then towards the end of the program, the number of miles decreases so that people can recover and be fully prepared for the marathon.

82. a–f.

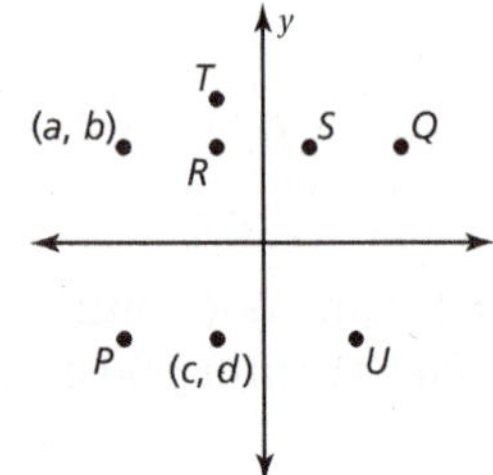

Section 8.6

Exploration 1

a. *Sample answer:*

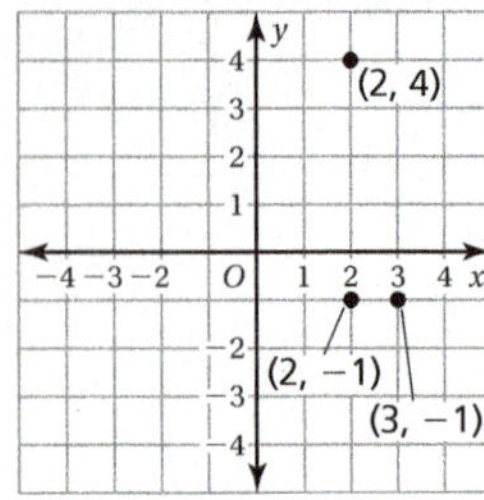

Try It

1.

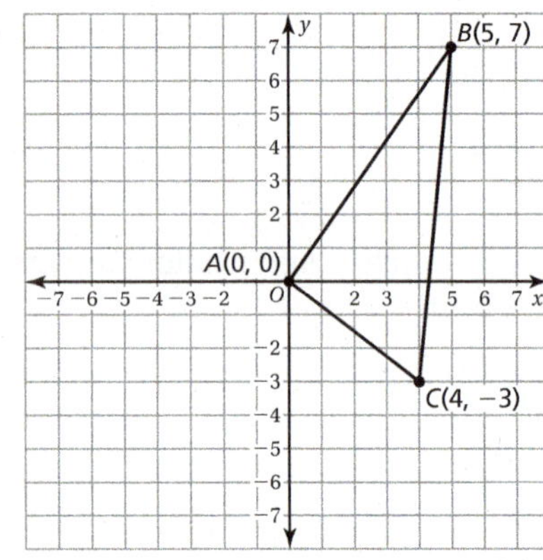

2.

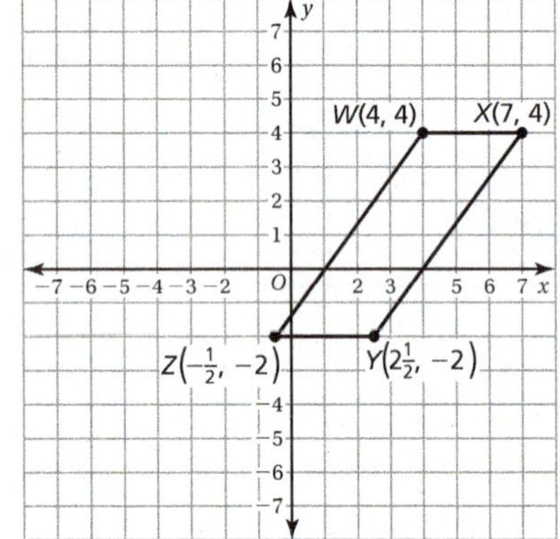

Concepts, Skills, & Problem Solving

14.

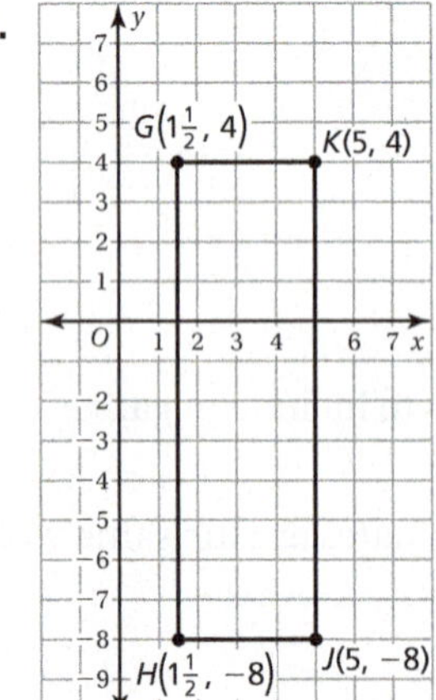

15.

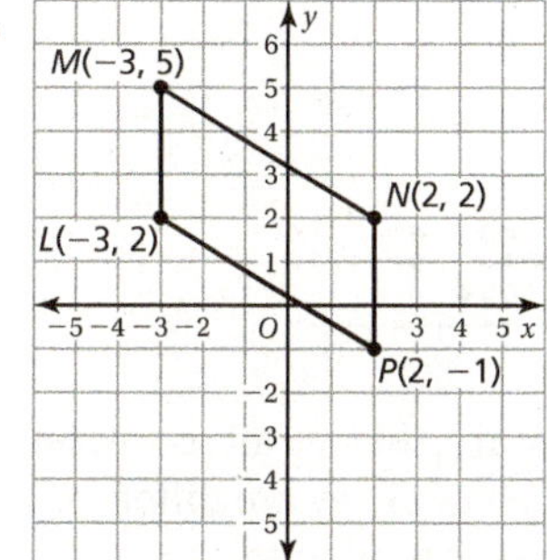

16.

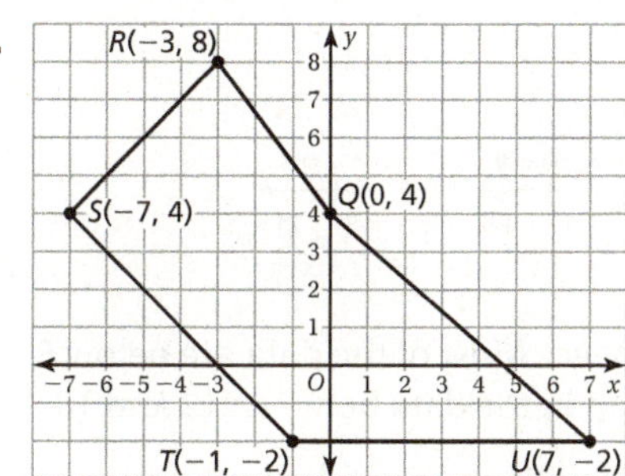

17.

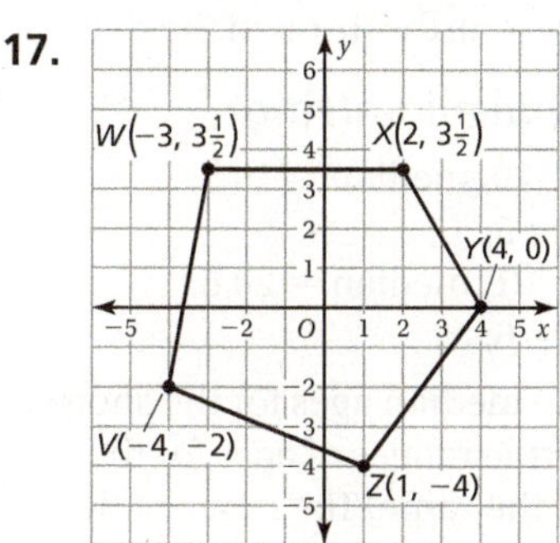

32.

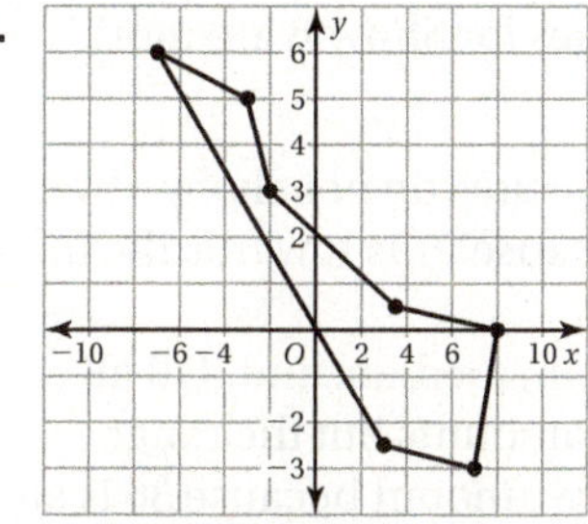

40. *Sample answer:*

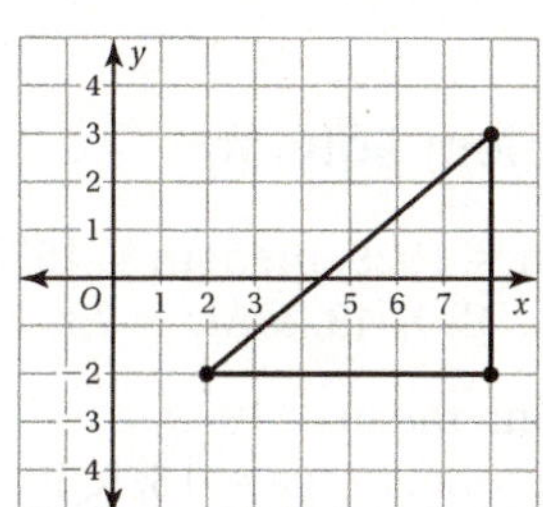

Section 8.7

Self-Assessment for Problem Solving

18. $t < 6\frac{3}{4}$

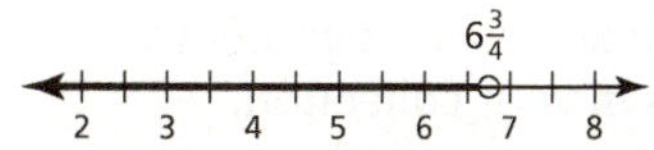

Section 8.8

Try It

7. $m > \frac{2}{3}$;

Self-Assessment for Concepts & Skills

15. The solution of $2x \geq 10$ includes the solution of $2x = 10$, $x = 5$, and all other x values that are greater than 5.

16. *Sample answer:* $x + 4 \geq 12$, $2x \geq 16$

Concepts, Skills, & Problem Solving

25. $\frac{1}{4} \leq n$;

26. $p \leq 6$;

27. $v \leq 81$;

28. $x \geq 48$;

29. no; add 9 to both sides to get $37 \geq t$.

63. no; *Sample answer:* $a = 6$, $b = 5$, $x = 10$, $y = 4$

$$\frac{a}{x} \overset{?}{>} \frac{y}{b}$$

$$\frac{6}{10} \overset{?}{>} \frac{4}{5}$$

$$0.6 \ngtr 0.8$$

Chapter 8 Self-Assessment

95. $m \leq \frac{1}{4}$;

Chapter 9

Section 9.1

Exploration 1

c. *Sample answer:* Find the average; The average represents the center of the data set.

Try It

5. c. *Sample answer:* How long does it take a sixth grade student to run 100 meters? It takes most sixth graders between 13.7 and 13.9 seconds to run 100 meters.

Self-Assessment for Concepts & Skills

6. A statistical question is one for which you do not expect to get a single answer. Instead, you expect a variety of answers, and you are interested in the distribution and tendency of those answers; How old are the teachers in middle school?; How many senators are from our state?

7. *Sample answer:* How many miles did each member of the track team run this weekend?; Most of the members of the track team ran between 4 and 7 miles this weekend; 16; There are 16 members on the track team who ran this weekend.

Concepts, Skills, & Problem Solving

21. 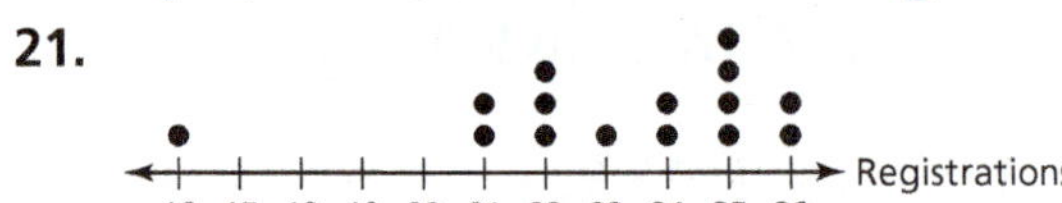

Most of the registrations are in a cluster from 21 to 26. The peak is 25. There is a gap between 16 and 21.

22. 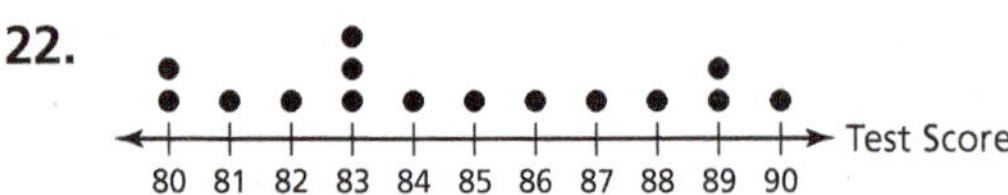

The test scores are spread out pretty evenly with no clusters or gaps. The peak is 83.

Section 9.3

Self-Assessment for Problem Solving

8. The mean lowers from 68.5 to 58, the median lowers from 61 to 57, and the mode remains unchanged at 40. The median will still be the best representative of the data set.

9. With outlier: mean = 44.9 sec, median = 43.5 sec, modes = 41 sec, 43 sec, 44 sec;
Without outlier: mean = 43 sec, median = 43 sec, modes = 41 sec, 43 sec, 44 sec; mean

Concepts, Skills, & Problem Solving

31. mean = 35.875; median = 44; mode = 48; *Sample answer:* The median is best because the mean is less than most of the data and the mode is the greatest value.

32. mean = 50; median = 40; mode = 95; *Sample answer:* The mean is best because the mode is the greatest value and the median is too far from the greater values.

33. mean = 12; median = 8; mode = 2; *Sample answer:* The median is best because the mean is greater than most of the data and the mode is the least value.

34. mean = 110; median = 114.5; mode = 144; *Sample answer:* Either the mean or median is best because the mode is the greatest value.

Section 9.4

Exploration 1

b. *Sample answer:*

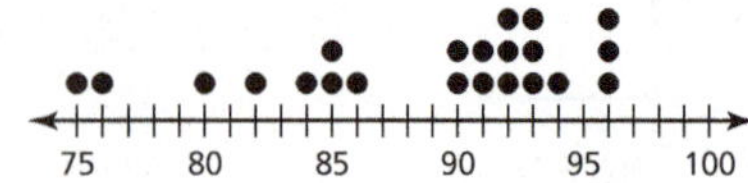

c. *Sample answer:* They are alike as all scores fell between a 75% and a 96%. They are different in where the actual scores are plotted.

Exploration 2

a. 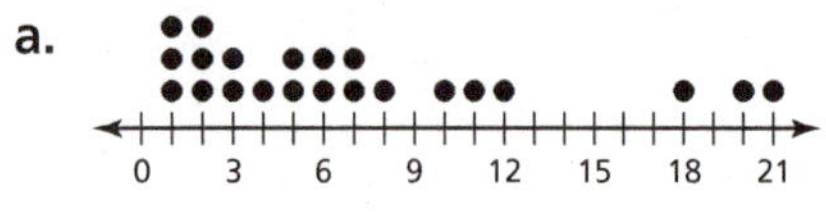

1 and 21

b. *Sample answer:* Most of the data are below 8. There is a gap in the data between 12 and 18.

c. By finding the difference of the numbers that are one-fourth and three-fourths through the data set.

Concepts, Skills, & Problem Solving

33. a. Show A: mean = 20, median = 19.5, range = 13, IQR = 5;
Show B: mean = 21, median = 20.5, range = 23, IQR = 6;

The mean and the median ages for the shows, and the interquartile ranges of ages for the shows, are about the same. The range of the ages for Show A is less than the range for Show B, so the ages for Show B are more spread out.

b. Show A: The measures do not change by a large amount because 21 is towards the middle of the data set.
Show B: The mean, median, and IQR all change by small amounts but the range changes by a large amount because 36 is an outlier of the data set.

Section 9.5

Concepts, Skills, & Problem Solving

25. Your collection: mean = 1929, median = 1930, no mode, range = 54, IQR = 48, MAD = 23.75;

Your friend's collection: mean = 1929, median = 1929.5, no mode, range = 15, IQR = 6, MAD = 3.5;
Sample answer: The measures of center for the data sets are almost identical. But the measures of variation for your friend's coin collection are much less than the measures for your coin collection. This means that the years of the coins in your friend's collection are closer together than the years of the coins in your collection.

28. *Sample answer:* The monthly rainfall amounts in a city will have a higher MAD than the monthly amounts of water used in a home. On average, a home will use close to the same amount of water per month while monthly rainfall amounts can differ greatly from month to month.

Chapter 10

Section 10.1

Exploration 1

c. Ages of First Ladies

Stem	Leaf
2	1
3	1
4	0 4 5 5 6 7 8 9 9
5	0 2 4 4 6 6 6 6 9
6	0 0 3

Self-Assessment for Problem Solving

8. Weights

Stem	Leaf
0	8
1	2 5 7 8
2	4 4
3	1

Key: 2|4 = 24 pounds

about 18 pounds

Concepts, Skills, & Problem Solving

17. Test Scores

Stem	Leaf
6	2 5 8 9
7	
8	0 1 2 5 7 7 8
9	0 1 5 7

Key: 8|1 = 81%

18. Points Scored

Stem	Leaf
3	8
4	2 2 3 3 5
5	0 1 6 8 8
6	
7	0 1 1 5

Key: 3|8 = 38 points

19. Bikes Sold

Stem	Leaf
7	8 9
8	1 6
9	6 9 9
10	0 5 8
11	2 5

Key: 11|2 = 112 bikes

20. Minutes in Line

Stem	Leaf
1	6 9
2	0 2 6 7 9
3	1 1 6 8
4	0

Key: 4|0 = 4.0 minutes

27. a. *Sample answer:*

Stem	Leaf
6	2 5 7 7 8 8 9
7	0 0 0 1 1 3 4 6 8 9
8	2 3 5 5 6 6 7 7 8 8 8 9 9

Key: 6|7 = 67°F

Section 10.2

Exploration 1

c. *Sample answer:*

Distance Traveled	Plane 1 Frequency	Plane 2 Frequency
0.0–1.9	3	2
2.0–3.9	5	2
4.0–5.9	3	3
6.0–7.9	7	6
8.0–9.9	1	2
10 +	1	5

d. *Sample answer:*

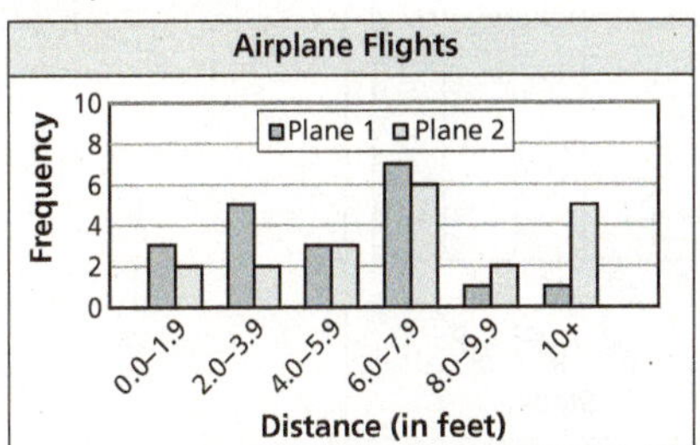

Plane 2; Most of Plane 2 flights were longer than most Plane 1 flights.

Additional Answers

Self-Assessment for Problem Solving

7. a. no; You only know that the player got 2 or 3 rebounds in 6 different games.

   b. yes; The sum of the frequencies excluding the interval 0–1 is 9.

Concepts, Skills, & Problem Solving

11. 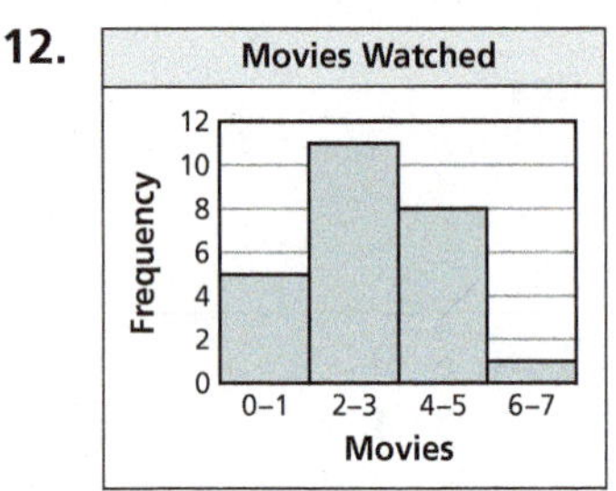

12. 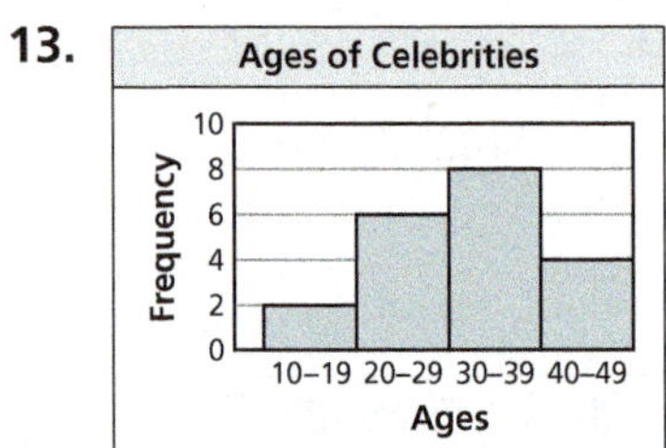

13. 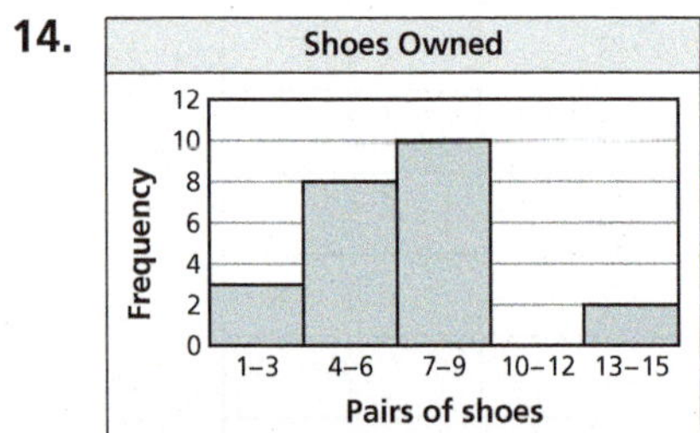

14. Shoes Owned

15. 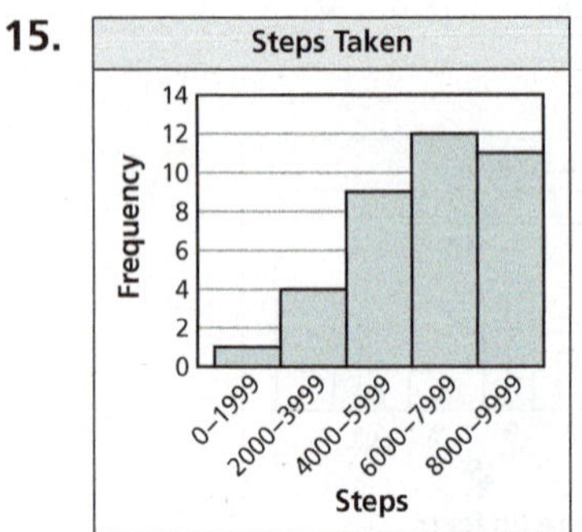

Section 10.3

Exploration 1

a. *Sample answer:* All of the values along the last digit number line have the same number of dots making the distribution look flat. The sets of dots form what looks like a rectangle. The first digit dot plot looks like it peaks at 6. There are the same number of values on each side of the peak. The dots at 4 and 5 match the dots at 8 and 7.

Self-Assessment for Concepts & Skills

3. a. *Sample answer:* Most of the data is on the right side of the graph, and the tail extends to the left.

   b. *Sample answer:* The left side of the graph is a mirror image of the right side of the graph.

   c. *Sample answer:* Most of the data is on the left side of the graph, and the tail extends to the right.

4. 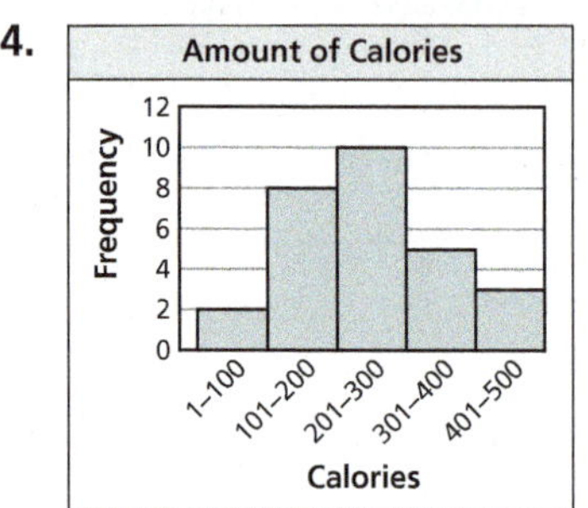

   Sample answer: skewed right

Concepts, Skills, & Problem Solving

12. 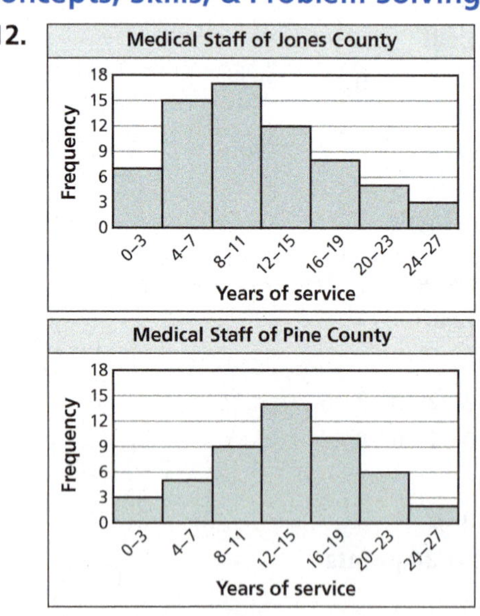

   Jones County; The distribution of Jones County is skewed right, so most of the data values are on the left.

16. a.

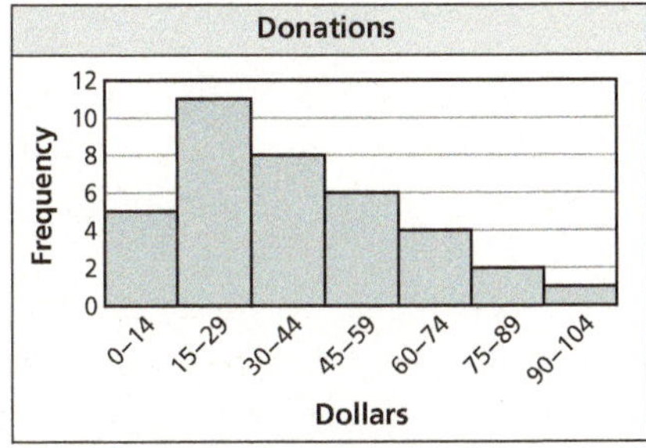

skewed right

b.

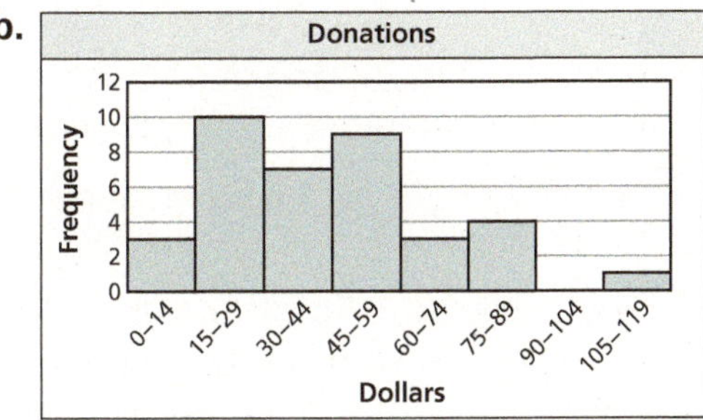

Both distributions are skewed right. The original donation distribution is more skewed right than the distribution when the increases are added to the donations. Some of the data values moved into different intervals when $5 is added to each donation, which is why the distributions are not exactly the same.

Section 10.4

Exploration 1

a. The mean, median, and mode of the first digits are all the same but the mean of the ages is greater than the median and mode of the ages. The range and MAD of the first digits are less than those of the ages but the IQR is greater. The data from the first digits are symmetric while the data for ages are skewed right.

b. *Sample answer:* first digits: mean; The mean is a more reliable measure because it uses all of the data values in its calculation; ages: median; The mode of the data set is 1, and most of the data are clustered around 1. The mean is affected by the outliers.

c. first digits: MAD; *Sample answer:* The mean is used in the calculation of MAD; ages: IQR; *Sample answer:* Quartiles are used in the calculation of IQR.

Self-Assessment for Concepts & Skills

6. *Sample answer:* In symmetric distribution, the mean represents the most typical value in the data set. So, the mean and the MAD are the most appropriate to use. In a skewed distribution, the mean is sensitive to any outliers, being pulled in the direction toward those outliers. Therefore, the median and IQR are the most appropriate to use.

Section 10.5

Exploration 1

c. *Sample answer:* The box-and-whisker plot uses quartiles to divide the data set into four parts; It shows how the data varies in each of those four parts.

Self-Assessment for Concepts & Skills

5.

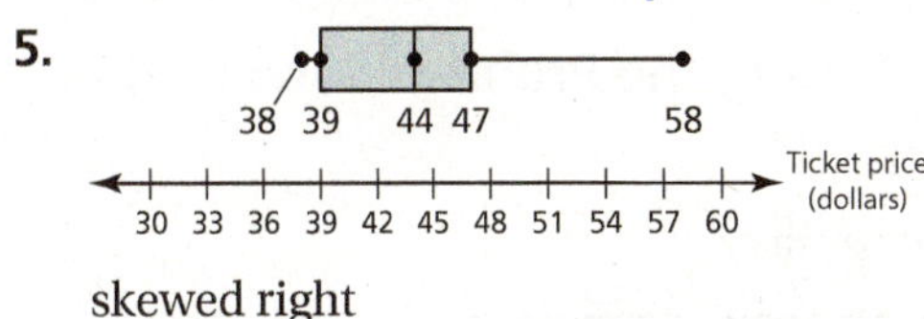

skewed right

Self-Assessment for Problem Solving

8. a. *Sample answer:* Table 1 scores are approximately symmetric. Table 2 scores are skewed right. Table 2 values appear to be lower in almost every category of the five-number summary. Table 1 has smaller values for the range and interquartile range of the distribution so there is less variability.

b. *Sample answer:* Table 1: spring, Table 2: fall; The five-number summary of Table 2 is much lower in every category than those of Table 1. Students taking the test in the spring will usually score better on the exam.

Concepts, Skills, & Problem Solving

12.

13.

14.

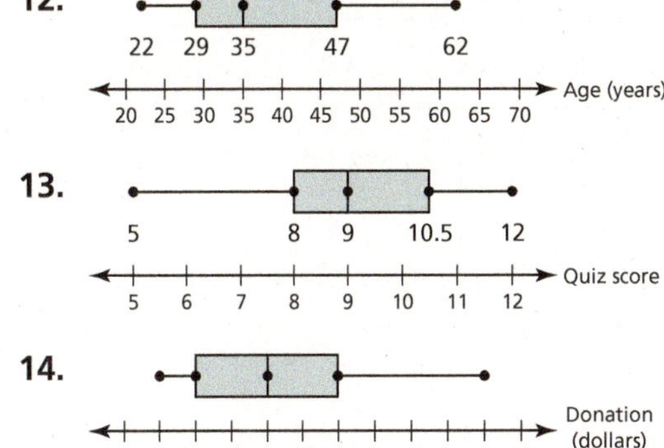

17.

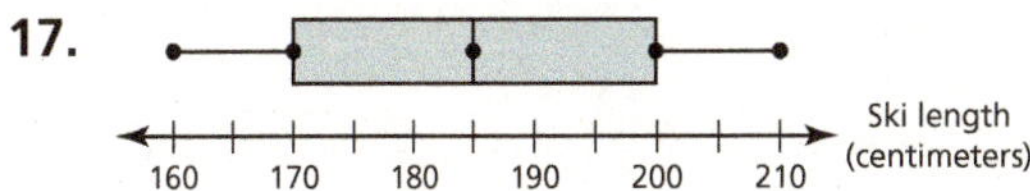

22. a.

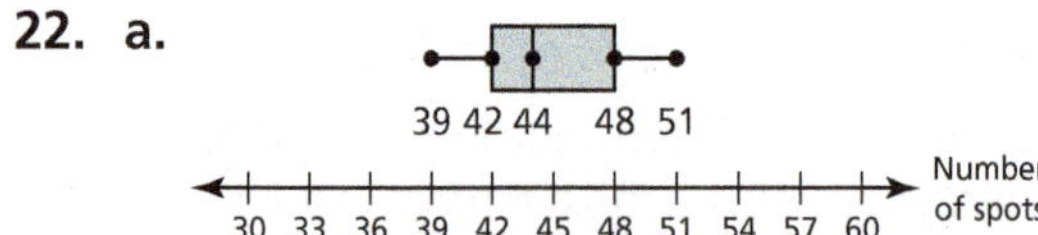

28.

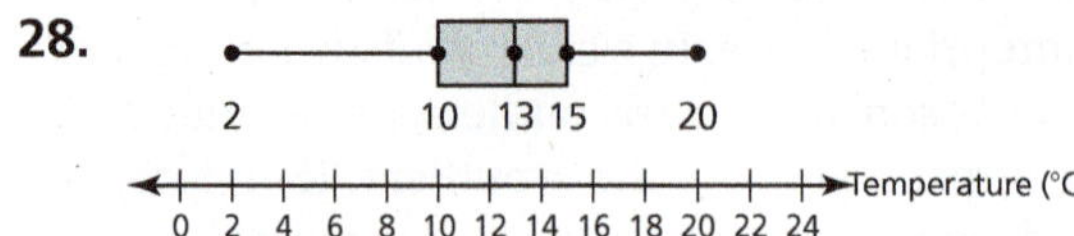

29.

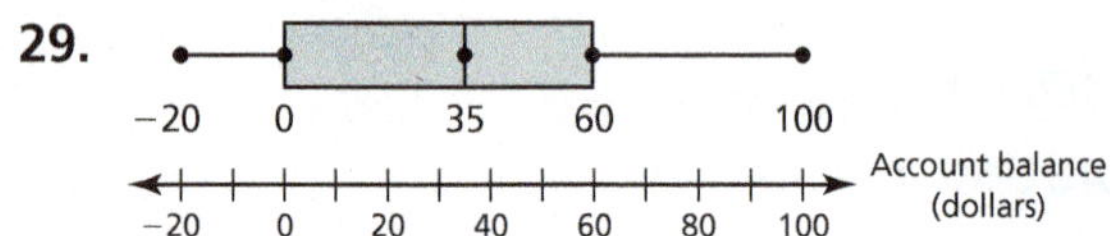

30. The left whisker is shorter, the length of the box is slightly smaller, the least value increased, the median increased, and the first quartile increased. In this case, removing the outlier had no effect on the third quartile and greatest value.

Chapter 10 Using the Problem-Solving Plan

1. (7, 7)

2. *Sample answer:*

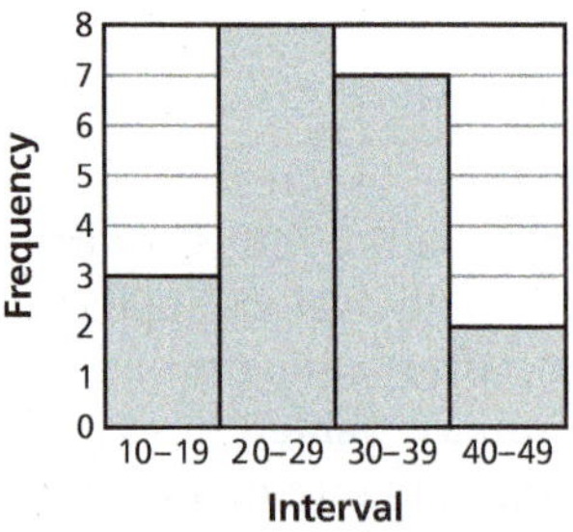

The data values 10, 13, 16, 21, 25, 25, 26, 27, 28, 29, 29, 30, 31, 32, 34, 34, 37, 38, 47, and 48 have the desired measures.

English-Spanish Glossary

English	Spanish
A	
absolute value *(p. 364)* The distance between a number and 0 on a number line; The absolute value of a number a is written as $\|a\|$.	**valor absoluto** *(p. 364)* La distancia entre un número y 0 en una recta numérica; El valor absoluto de un número a es escrito como $\|a\|$.
algebraic expression *(p. 202)* An expression that contains numbers, operations, and one or more variables	**expresión algebraica** *(p. 202)* Una expresión que contiene números, operaciones, y uno o más variables
B	
base (of a power) *(p. 4)* The base of a power is the repeated factor.	**base (de una potencia)** *(p. 4)* La base de una potencia es el factor repetido.
box-and-whisker plot *(p. 484)* A data display that shows the variability of a data set along a number line using the least value, the greatest value, and the quartiles of the data	**diagrama de cajas y bigotes** *(p. 484)* Una presentación de datos que muestra la variabilidad de un conjunto de datos a lo largo de una línea de números usando el valor menor, el valor mayor y los cuartiles de los datos
C	
coefficient *(p. 202)* The numerical factor of a term that contains a variable	**coeficiente** *(p. 202)* El factor numérico de un término que contiene una variable
common factors *(p. 22)* Factors that are shared by two or more numbers	**factores comunes** *(p. 22)* Factores compartidos por dos o más números
common multiples *(p. 28)* Multiples that are shared by two or more numbers	**comunes múltiplos** *(p. 28)* Múltiplos compartidos por dos o más números
composite figure *(p. 294)* A figure made up of triangles, squares, rectangles, and other two-dimensional figures	**figura compuesta** *(p. 294)* Una figura hecha de triángulos, cuadros, rectángulos, y otras figuras bidimensionales
constant *(p. 202)* A term without a variable	**constante** *(p. 202)* Un término que no tiene una variable
conversion factor *(p. 143)* A rate that equals 1	**factor de conversión** *(p. 143)* Una tasa que es igual a 1
coordinate plane *(p. 370)* A plane formed by the intersection of a horizontal number line and a vertical number line	**plano de coordenadas** *(p. 370)* Un plano formado por la intersección de una recta numérica horizontal y una recta numérica vertical

English-Spanish Glossary

D

dependent variable *(p. 266)* The variable that represents the output values of a function

variable dependiente *(p. 266)* La variable que representa los resultados de una función

E

edge *(p. 306)* A line segment where two faces of a polyhedron intersect

arista *(p. 306)* Un segmento de recta donde dos caras de un poliedro se intersecan

equation *(p. 246)* A mathematical sentence that uses an equal sign, =, to show that two expressions are equal

ecuación *(p. 246)* Una oración matemática que usa un signo de igualdad, =, para mostrar que dos expresiones son iguales

equation in two variables *(p. 266)* An equation that represents two quantities that change in relationship to one another

ecuación en dos variables *(p. 266)* Una ecuación que representa dos cantidades que cambian en relación mutua

equivalent expressions *(p. 216)* Expressions with the same value

expresiones equivalentes *(p. 216)* Expresiones con el mismo valor

equivalent rates *(p. 136)* Rates that have the same unit rate

tasas equivalentes *(p. 136)* Tasas que tienen la misma tasa de unidad

equivalent ratios *(p. 109)* Two ratios that describe the same relationship

razones equivalentes *(p. 109)* Dos razones que describen la misma relación

evaluate *(p. 10)* To use the order of operations to find the value of a numerical expression

evaluar *(p. 10)* Usar el orden de operaciones para hallar el valor de una expresión numérica

exponent *(p. 4)* The exponent of a power indicates the number of times the base is used as a factor.

exponente *(p. 4)* El exponente de una potencia indique cuantas veces el base sirve como un factor.

F

face *(p. 306)* A flat surface of a polyhedron

cara *(p. 306)* Una superficie plana de un poliedro

factor pair *(p. 16)* A set of two nonzero factors whose product results in a definite number

par de factor *(p. 16)* Un conjunto de dos factores distintos de cero cuyo producto resulta en un número definido

factor tree *(p. 16)* A diagram used to find the factors of a composite number

árbol de factores *(p. 16)* Un diagrama utilizado para hallar los factores de un número compuesto

factoring an expression *(p. 228)* Writing a numerical expression or algebraic expression as a product of factors

factorizando una expresión *(p. 228)* Escribiendo una expresión numérica o algebraica como un producto de factores

first quartile *(p. 434)* The median of the lower half of a data set; represented by Q_1

primer cuartil *(p. 434)* La mediana de la mitad inferior de un conjunto de datos; representado por Q_1

five-number summary *(p. 484)* The five numbers that make up a box-and-whisker plot

resumen de cinco números *(p. 484)* Los cinco números que componen un diagrama de cajas y bigotes

frequency *(p. 463)* The number of data values in an interval

frecuencia *(p. 463)* El número de valores de datos en un intervalo

frequency table *(p. 463)* A chart that groups data values into intervals

table de frecuencia *(p. 463)* Un gráfico que agrupa valores de datos en intervalos

G

graph of an inequality *(p. 386)* A graph that shows all the solutions of an inequality on a number line

gráfica de una desigualdad *(p. 386)* Una gráfica que muestra todas las soluciones de una desigualdad en una recta numérica

greatest common factor (GCF) *(p. 22)* The greatest of the common factors shared by two or more numbers

máximo factor común (MFC) *(p. 22)* El mayor de los factores comunes compartido por dos o más números

H

histogram *(p. 464)* A bar graph that shows the frequency of data values in intervals of the same size

histograma *(p. 464)* Un gráfico de barras que muestra la frecuencia de valores de datos en intervalos del mismo tamaño

I

independent variable *(p. 266)* The variable that represents the input values of a function

variable independiente *(p. 266)* La variable que representa los valores entradas de una función

inequality *(p. 384)* A mathematical sentence that compares expressions; contains the symbols $<$, $>$, $\leq$, or $\geq$

desigualdad *(p. 384)* Una oración matemática que compara las expresiones; contiene los símbolos $<$, $>$, $\leq$, o $\geq$

integers *(p. 346)* The set of whole numbers and their opposites

números enteros *(p. 346)* El conjunto de números naturales y sus opuestos

interquartile range *(p. 434)* A measure of variation for a data set, which is the difference of the third quartile and the first quartile

rango de intercuartiles *(p. 434)* Una medida de variación para un conjunto de datos, el cual es la diferencia del tercer cuartil y el primer cuartil

inverse operations *(p. 253)* Operations that "undo" each other, such as addition and subtraction, or multiplication and division

operaciones inversas *(p. 253)* Operaciones que deshacer unos de otros, tales como suma y resta, o multiplicación y división

K

kite *(p. 298)* A quadrilateral that has two pairs of adjacent sides with the same length and opposite sides with different lengths

cometa *(p. 298)* Un cuadrilátero que tiene dos pares de lados adyacentes con la misma longitud y lados opuestos con longitudes diferentes

L

leaf *(p. 458)* Digit or digits on the right of a stem-and-leaf plot

hoja *(p. 458)* Dígito o dígitos a la derecha de un digrama de tallo y hojas.

least common multiple (LCM) *(p. 28)* The least of the common multiples shared by two or more numbers

mínimo común múltiplo (MCM) *(p. 28)* El menor de los factores comunes compartido por dos o más números

like terms *(p. 223)* Terms of an algebraic expression that have the same variables raised to the same exponents

términos semejantes *(p. 223)* Términos de una expresión algebraica que tienen las mismas variables elevadas a los mismos exponentes

M

mean *(p. 420)* The sum of the data divided by the number of data values

media *(p. 420)* La suma de los datos dividido por el número de valores de datos

mean absolute deviation (MAD) *(p. 440)* An average of how much data values differ from the mean

desviación media absoluta (MAD) *(p. 440)* Un promedio de cuántos valores de datos difieren de la media

measure of center *(p. 426)* A measure that describes the typical value of a data set

medida de centro *(p. 426)* Una medida que describe el valor típico de un conjunto de datos

measure of variation *(p. 434)* A measure that describes the spread, or distribution, of a data set

medida de variación *(p. 434)* Una medida que describe la extensión, o distribución, de un conjunto de datos

median *(p. 426)* For a data set with an odd number of ordered values, the median is the middle value; For a data set with an even number of ordered values, the median is the mean of the two middle values.

mediana *(p. 426)* Para un conjunto de datos con un número impar de valores ordenados, la mediana es el valor del medio; Para un conjunto de datos con un número par de valores ordenados, la mediana es la media de los dos valores del medio.

metric system *(p. 142)* A decimal system of measurement, based on powers of 10, that contains units for length, capacity, and mass

sistema métrico decimal *(p. 142)* Un sistema de medición, basado en potencias de 10, que incluye unidades para longitud, capacidad, y masa

mode *(p. 426)* The data value or values that occur most often; Data can have one mode, more than one mode, or no mode.

moda *(p. 426)* El valor o valores de datos que ocurre(n) con más frecuencia; Datos pueden tener una moda, más que una moda, o ninguna moda.

multiplicative inverses *(p. 54)* Two numbers whose product is 1

inversos multiplicativos *(p. 54)* Dos números cuyo producto es 1

N

negative numbers *(p. 346)* Numbers that are less than 0

números negativos *(p. 346)* Números que son menos de 0

net *(p. 312)* A two-dimensional representation of a solid

red *(p. 312)* Una representación bidimensional de un sólido

numerical expression *(p. 10)* An expression that contains only numbers and operations

expresión numérica *(p. 10)* Una expresión que contiene solamente números y operaciones

O

opposites *(p. 346)* Two numbers that are the same distance from 0 on a number line, but on opposite sides of 0

opuestos *(p. 346)* Dos números que están a la misma distancia de 0 en una recta numérica, pero en lados opuestos de 0

order of operations *(p. 10)* The order in which to perform operations when evaluating expressions with more than one operation

orden de operaciones *(p. 10)* El orden en el que para realizar operaciones al evaluar expresiones con más de una operación

origin *(p. 370)* The point, represented by the ordered pair (0, 0), where the horizontal and vertical number lines intersect in a coordinate plane

origen *(p. 370)* El punto, representado por el par ordenado (0, 0), donde las rectas numéricas horizontales y verticales se intersecan en un plano de coordenadas

outlier *(p. 422)* A data value that is much greater than or much less than the other values in a data set.

valor atípico *(p. 422)* Una valor de datos que es mucho mayor o mucho menor que los otros valores en un conjunto de datos

P

percent *(p. 164)* The value of a part-to-whole ratio where the whole is 100

porcentaje *(p. 164)* El valor de una razón de número de partes por un entero en donde el entero es 100

perfect square *(p. 5)* The square of a whole number

cuadrado perfecto *(p. 5)* El cuadrado de un número natural

polygon *(p. 285)* A closed figure in a plane that is made up of three or more line segments that intersect only at their endpoints; for example, parallelograms and triangles

polígono *(p. 285)* Una figura cerrada en un plano, hecha de tres o más segmentos de líneas que intersectan solamente à sus puntos finales; por ejemplo, paralelogramos y triángulos

polyhedron *(p. 306)* A solid whose faces are all polygons

poliedro *(p. 306)* Un sólído tridimensional cuyas caras son todas polígonos

positive numbers *(p. 346)* Numbers that are greater than 0

números positivos *(p. 346)* Números que son mayores que 0

power *(p. 4)* A product of repeated factors

potencia *(p. 4)* Un producto de factores repetidos

prime factorization *(p. 16)* Writing a composite number as a product of its prime factors

factorización prima *(p. 16)* Escribir un número compuesto como el producto de sus factores primeros

prism *(p. 306)* A polyhedron that has two parallel, identical bases; The lateral faces are parallelograms.

prisma *(p. 306)* Un poliedro que tiene dos bases idénticas y paralelas; Las caras laterales son paralelogramos.

pyramid *(p. 306)* A polyhedron that has one base; The lateral faces are triangles.

pirámide *(p. 306)* Un poliedro que tiene una base; Las caras laterales son triángulos.

Q

quadrants *(p. 370)* The four regions created by the intersection of the horizontal and vertical number lines in a coordinate plane

cuadrantes *(p. 370)* Las cuatro regiones creadas por la intersección de las rectas numéricas horizontales y verticales en un plano de coordenadas

quartiles *(p. 434)* Values that divide a data set into four equal parts

cuartiles *(p. 434)* Valores que dividen un conjunto de datos en cuatro partes iguales

R

range *(p. 434)* The difference of the greatest value and the least value of a data set

rango *(p. 434)* La diferencia del valor mayor y el valor menor de un conjunto de datos

rate *(p. 136)* A ratio of two quantities using different units

tasa *(p. 136)* Una razón de dos cantidades usando unidades diferentes

ratio *(p. 108)* A comparison of two quantities; The ratio of a to b can be written as $a : b$.

razón *(p. 108)* Una comparación de dos cantidades; La razón de a a b puede escribirse como $a : b$.

ratio table *(p. 122)* A table used to find and organize equivalent ratios

tabla de razones *(p. 122)* Una tabla usada para encontrar y organizar las razones equivalentes

rational number *(p. 358)* A number that can be written as $\frac{a}{b}$ where a and b are integers and $b \neq 0$

número racional *(p. 358)* Un número que puede ser escrito como $\frac{a}{b}$ donde a y b son enteros y $b \neq 0$

reciprocals *(p. 54)* Two numbers whose product is 1

recíprocos *(p. 54)* Dos números cuyo producto es 1

S

solid *(p. 306)* A three-dimensional figure that encloses a space

sólido *(p. 306)* Una figura tridimensional que encierra un espacio

solution *(p. 252)* A value that makes an equation true

solución *(p. 252)* Un valor que hace una ecuación verdadera

solution of an equation in two variables *(p. 266)* An ordered pair (x, y) that makes an equation true

solución de una ecuación en dos variables *(p. 266)* Un par ordenado (x, y) que hace que una ecuación sea verdadera

solution of an inequality *(p. 385)* A value that makes an inequality true

solución de una desigualdad *(p. 385)* Un valor que hace una desigualdad verdadera

solution set *(p. 385)* The set of all solutions of an inequality

conjunto de solución *(p. 385)* El conjunto de todas las soluciones de una desigualdad

statistical question *(p. 414)* A question for which a variety of answers is expected; The interest is in the distribution and tendency of those answers.

pregenta estadística *(p. 414)* Una pregunta para la cual se espera una variedad de repuestas; El interés es en la distribución y la tendencia de aquellas respuestas.

statistics *(p. 414)* The science of collecting, organizing, analyzing, and interpreting data

estadísticas *(p. 414)* La ciencia de recolectar, organizar, analizar e interpretar datos

stem *(p. 458)* Digit or digits on the left of the stem-and-leaf plot

tallo *(p. 458)* Dígito o dígitos a la izquierda de un diagrama de tallo y hojas

stem-and-leaf plot *(p. 458)* A data display that uses the digits of data values to organize a data set; Each data value is broken into a stem (digit or digits on the left) and a leaf (digit or digits on the right).

diagrama de tallo y hojas *(p. 458)* Un representación de datos que usa los dígitos de valores de datos para organizar un conjunto de datos; Cada valor de datos es roto en un tallo (dígito o dígitos a la izquierda) y una hoja (dígito o dígitos a la derecha).

surface area *(p. 312)* The sum of the areas of all the faces of a polyhedron

área de la superficie *(p. 312)* La suma de las áreas de todas las caras de un poliedro

T

term *(p. 202)* A part of an algebraic expression; a number or variable by itself, or the product of numbers and variables

término *(p. 202)* Un component de una expresión algebraica; un número o variable por sí mismo, o el producto de números y variables

third quartile *(p. 434)* The median of the upper half of a data set; represented by Q_3

tercer cuartil *(p. 434)* La mediana de la mitad superior de un conjunto de datos; representado por Q_3

U

unit analysis *(p. 143)* A process used to decide which conversion factor will produce the appropriate units

análisis de unidades *(p. 143)* Un proceso utilizado para decidir qué factor de conversión producirá las unidades apropiadas

unit rate *(p. 136)* A rate that compares a quantity to one unit of another quantity

tasa unitaria *(p. 136)* Una tasa que compara una cantidad a una unidad de otra cantidad

U.S. customary system *(p. 142)* A system of measurement that contains units for length, capacity, and weight

sistema estadounidense *(p. 142)* Un sistema de medición que incluye unidades para longitud, capacidad, y peso

V

value of a ratio *(p. 109)* The number $\frac{a}{b}$ associated with the ratio $a : b$

valor de una razón *(p. 109)* El número $\frac{a}{b}$ asociadas con la razón $a : b$

variable *(p. 202)* A symbol that represents one or more numbers

variable *(p. 202)* Un símbolo que representa a uno o más números

Venn diagram *(p. 21)* A diagram of overlapping circles used to show the relationships between two or more sets

Diagrama de Venn *(p. 21)* Un diagrama de círculos solapados usado para mostrar las relaciones entre dos o más conjuntos

vertex (of a solid) *(p. 306)* A point where three or more edges intersect

vértice (de un sólido) *(p. 306)* Un punto donde tres o más aristas se intersecan

volume *(p. 325)* A measure of the amount of space that a three-dimensional figure occupies; Volume is measured in cubic units such as cubic feet (ft^3) or cubic meters (m^3).

volumen *(p. 325)* Una medida de la cantidad de espacio que una figura tridimensional ocupa; Volumen es medido en unidades cúbicas como pies cúbicos ($pies^3$) o metros cúbicos (m^3).

Index

B

G

H

I

K

L

M

Index

N

O

P

Q

R

Index

S

Credits

Chapter 1

0 *top* zentilia/Shutterstock.com; *bottom* OnstOn/iStock/Getty Images Plus; **1** Ryan McVay/DigitalVision/Getty Images; **2** INTERFOTO/Alamy Stock Photo; **8** WestLight/iStock/Getty Images Plus; **9** manaemedia/iStock/Getty Images Plus; **14** frentusha/iStock/Getty Images Plus; **15** YuriyZhuravov/Shutterstock.com; **16** farbeffekte/Shutterstock.com; **18** *right* studioaraminta/iStock/Getty Images Plus; *left* carlosalvarez/iStock/Getty Images Plus; **20** chinaface/E+/Getty Images; **24** *top* jmatzick/Shutterstock.com; *bottom* Mike Flippo/Shutterstock.com, LauriPatterson/E+/Getty Images; **25** Glenda M. Powers/Shutterstock.com; **26** pialhovik/iStock/Getty Images Plus, cookelma/iStock/Getty Images Plus, CSA-Plastock/iStock/Getty Images Plus, tbd/E+/Getty Images; **29** monkeybusinessimages/iStock/Getty Images Plus; **30** *right* Constantne/iStock/Getty Images Plus; *left* Mlenny/E+/Getty Images; **32** yuyangc/Shutterstock.com; **33** OnstOn/iStock/Getty Images Plus; **35** Wendy Nero/Shutterstock.com; **36** Ioana Drutu/Hemera/Getty Images; **37** *right* hawk111/iStock/Getty Images Plus, IvonneW/iStock/Getty Images Plus; *left* Zimiri/iStock/Getty Images Plus; **38** AnthonyRosenberg/iStock/Getty Images Plus, VitalisG/iStock/Getty Images Plus

Chapter 2

42 *top* zentilia/Shutterstock.com; *bottom* OnstOn/iStock/Getty Images Plus; **43** Blackzheep/iStock/Getty Images Plus; **44** Firmafotografen/iStock/Getty Images Plus; **50** *left* fivespots/Shutterstock.com; *right* bluehand/Shutterstock.com; **57** *top* monkeybusinessimages/iStock/Getty Images Plus; *bottom* PARKJUNGHO/iStock/Getty Images Plus; **60** *left* ©iStockphoto.com/Michael Plumb; *right* g215/Shutterstock.com; **64** *top* ©iStockphoto.com/bonchan; *bottom* Dmytro Aksonov/E+/Getty Images; **66** *top right* AlexLMX/iStock/Getty Images Plus; *center left* damedeeso/iStock/Getty Images Plus, Kuzmik_A/iStock/Getty Images Plus; *bottom right* Romariolen/iStock/Getty Images Plus; **69** bmcent1/iStock/Getty Images Plus; **70** Vacclav/Shutterstock.com; **72** SSSCCC/Shutterstock.com; **77** *top* bagi1998/iStock/Getty Images Plus; *bottom* andrejco/iStock/Getty Images Plus; **78** ©iStockphoto.com/suriyasilsaksom; **79** KENCKOphotography/Shutterstock.com; **81** *top* S.Dashkevych/Shutterstock.com; *bottom* auremar/Shutterstock.com; **83** avid_creative/E+/Getty Images; **84** *top* Nikada/iStock/Getty Images Plus; *bottom* jimfeng/iStock/Getty Images Plus; **86** urfinguss/iStock/Getty Images Plus; **93** dolgachov/iStock/Getty Images Plus; **94** loops7/iStock/Getty Images Plus; **95** *top right* Africa Studio/Shutterstock.com; *center left* swissmediavision/iStock/Getty Images Plus; *bottom left* OnstOn/iStock/Getty Images Plus; **97** *top* kali9/E+/Getty Images; *bottom* MikeyGen73/iStock/Getty Images Plus; **98** *right* elmvilla/iStock/Getty Images Plus; *left* 3DSculptor/iStock/Getty Images Plus; **100** Hstarr/iStock/Getty Images Plus

Chapter 3

104 *top* zentilia/Shutterstock.com; *bottom* OnstOn/iStock/Getty Images Plus; **105** janulla/iStock/Getty Images Plus; **107** *top right* fstop123/iStock/Getty Images Plus; *bottom left* Constantinos/Shutterstock.com; *bottom right* Adyna/DigitalVision Vectors/Getty Images; **108** Vladimir Wrangel/Shutterstock.com; **109** *right* MLB Photos/Contributor/Major League Baseball Platinum/Getty Images; *left* rusm/E+/Getty Images, Tazzy1/iStock/Getty Images Plus; **111** *right* anankkml/iStock/Getty Images Plus; *left* MrPants/iStock/Getty Images Plus; **112** *Exercise 14* Lightspring/Shutterstock.com; *Exercise 12* Constantinos/Shutterstock.com; **113** SpiffyJ/iStock/Getty Images Plus; **114** Route55/iStock/Getty Images Plus; **115** 4x6/iStock/Getty Images Plus; **117** Terryfic3D/iStock/Getty Images Plus; **118** *top* OSTILL/iStock/Getty Images Plus; *bottom* wesvandinter/iStock/Getty Images Plus; **119** yulkapopkova/Vetta/Getty Images; **120** *top left* Lepas/Shutterstock.com; *center right* desert_fox99/iStock/Getty Images Plus; *bottom right* Mirko_Rosenau/iStock/Getty Images Plus, GlobalP/iStock/Getty Images Plus, thawats/iStock/Getty Images Plus, juliaart/iStock/Getty Images Plus; **121** 4kodiak/iStock/Getty Images Plus; **124** Petr Malyshev/Shutterstock.com; **125** *top* Mike Flippo/Shutterstock.com; *bottom* busypix/iStock/Getty Images Plus; **127** *right* GeorgeManga/DigitalVision Vectors/Getty Images; *left* Jacob Wackerhausen/E+/Getty Images; **128** Antagain/iStock/Getty Images Plus; cinoby/iStock/Getty Images Plus; GlobalP/iStock/Getty Images Plus; **129** baibaz/iStock/Getty Images Plus; **132** *top left* ElementalImaging/E+/Getty Images; *bottom right* skodonnell/E+/Getty Images; *bottom left* exopixel/iStock/Getty Images Plus, Givaga/iStock/Getty Images Plus; **134** R. Gino Santa Maria/Shutterstock.com; **135** *top* irmetov/DigitalVision Vectors/Getty Images; *bottom* vita khorzhevska/Shutterstock.com; **137** REUTERS/James Stirton/Handout (AUSTRALIA); **138** *top* Watcha/iStock/Getty Images Plus; *bottom* ©iStockphoto.com/Gord Horne; **140** *top* mvaligursky/GlobalP/iStock/Getty Images Plus; *bottom* FatCamera/iStock/Getty Images Plus; **145** *top* Tom Merton/OJO Images/Getty Images; *bottom* Doug James/Shutterstock.com; **147** Derek Wong/Mackinac Bridge at Sunset in 2008/CC-BY-3.0; **148** *left* DenisTangneyJr/iStock/Getty Images Plus; *right* ©iStockphoto.com/Paul Tessier; **149** *right* Jean Thompson; *center* Barcin/iStock/Getty Images Plus; *bottom* OnstOn/iStock/Getty Images Plus; **151** scanrail/iStock/Getty Images Plus; **152** Marcelo Hom/E+/Getty Images; **153** kentarus/E+/Getty Images; **154** ilbusca/E+/Getty Images; **155** bowdenimages/iStock/Getty Images Plus; **156** ©iStockphoto.com/Ermin Gutenberger; **158** Val_Iva/iStock/Getty Images Plus; blueringmedia/iStock/Getty Images Plus

Chapter 4

160 *top* zentilia/Shutterstock.com; *bottom* OnstOn/iStock/Getty Images Plus; **161** Talaj/iStock/Getty Images Plus; **162** frank600/iStock/Getty Images Plus; **166** Sauliakas/iStock/Getty Images Plus; **168** 4x6/iStock/Getty Images Plus; **172** vvvita/iStock/Getty Images Plus; **174** andyKRAKOVSKI/iStock/Getty Images Plus; **177** 4x6/iStock/Getty Images Plus; **180** ©iStockphoto.com/Eric Isselée; **185** offstocker/iStock/Getty Images Plus; **186** JackF/iStock/Getty Images Plus; **187** *left* LoopAll/iStock/Getty Images Plus; *right* m-gucci/iStock/Getty Images Plus; **188** EMPPhotography/E+/Getty Images; **189** *top* GeorgePeters/E+/Getty Images; *center* Coprid/iStock/Getty Images Plus; *bottom* OnstOn/iStock/Getty Images Plus; **192** pomarinus/E+/Getty Images; **193** BlackJack3D/iStock/Getty Images Plus; **194** fresher/Shutterstock.com

Chapter 5

198 *top* zentilia/Shutterstock.com; *bottom* OnstOn/iStock/Getty Images Plus; **201** *top right* Rawpixel/iStock/Getty Images Plus, Floortje/iStock/Getty Images Plus, esseffe/E+/Getty Images, kreinick/iStock/Getty Images Plus; *center left* pittawut/Shutterstock.com; *center right* Goran Bogicevic/Shutterstock.com; *bottom left* GlobalP/iStock/Getty Images Plus; **205** rgmeier/iStock/Getty Images Plus; **208** Mikalai_Manyshau/iStock/Getty Images Plus, cyano66/iStock/Getty Images Plus, fergregory/iStock/Getty Images Plus, MATJAZ SLANIC/E+/Getty Images, SmallArtFish/iStock/Getty Images Plus, hceliktas/iStock/Getty Images Plus; **212** *top* Kateryna Larina/Shutterstock.com; *bottom* DNY59/iStock/Getty Images Plus; **218** GibsonPictures/E+/Getty Images; **220** Iftodelulian/DigitalVision Vectors/Getty Images; **226** Kandfoto/iStock/Getty Images Plus; **230** *top* Inhabitant/Shutterstock.com; *bottom* Stockbyte/Stockbyte/Getty Images; **233** *top* mediaphotos/iStock/Getty Images Plus; *bottom* OnstOn/iStock/Getty Images Plus; **235** JohnnyGreig/iStock/Getty Images Plus; **237** *right* sidewaysdesign/iStock/Getty Images Plus; *left* liveslow/iStock/Getty Images Plus; **238** *right* Aptyp_koK/Shutterstock.com; *left* Anges van der Logt/Shutterstock.com

Chapter 6

242 *top* zentilia/Shutterstock.com; *bottom* OnstOn/iStock/Getty Images Plus; **243** scotto72/E+/Getty Images; **248** *top* Albert Russ/Shutterstock.com; *bottom* iwka/iStock/Getty Images Plus; **250** *top right* waymoreawesomer/iStock/Getty Images Plus, Zheka-Boss/iStock/Getty Images Plus, clovercity/iStock/Getty Images Plus; *left* ©iStockphoto.com/Kenneth C. Zirkel; **255** *top* alex-mit/iStock/Getty Images Plus; *bottom* ©iStockphoto.com/Jeremy Wee, ©iStockphoto.com/Jan Will; **257** TerryKelly/iStock/Getty Images Plus; **258** Raywoo/Shutterstock.com; **259** ©iStockphoto.com/Vladyslav Otsiatsia; **262** fototrav/iStock Unreleased/Getty Images Plus; **264** *top* monkeybusinessimages/iStock/Getty Images Plus; *bottom* ©iStockphoto.com/Eric Isselée; **266** SerrNovik/iStock/Getty Images Plus; **269** *top* macrovector/iStock/Getty Images Plus; *bottom* bnoragitt/iStock Unreleased/Getty Images Plus; **271** angelinast/iStock/Getty Images Plus; **272** *Exercise 57* d1sk/iStock/Getty Images Plus; *Exercise 59* irmetov/DigitalVision Vectors/Getty Images; **273** *top* imagedepotpro/Vetta/Getty Images; *bottom* OnstOn/iStock/Getty Images Plus; **275** Dmytro Aksonov/E+/Getty Images; **276** *top* Wesley Tolhurst/iStock/Getty Images Plus; *bottom right* Vadim Sadovski/Shutterstock.com; **277** *top left* Siraphol/iStock/Getty Images Plus; *center right* johnkellerman/iStock/Getty Images Plus; *bottom left* Yobro10/iStock/Getty Images Plus; **278** *top* ntzolov/E+/Getty Images; *bottom* ©iStockphoto.com/XiXinXing;

Chapter 7

282 *top* zentilia/Shutterstock.com; *bottom* OnstOn/iStock/Getty Images Plus; **283** *left* iZonda/iStock/Getty Images Plus; *right* Coprid/iStock/Getty Images Plus; **288** fritschk/Shutterstock.com; **T-291** Flatiron Building, NY; **296** Terrance Emerson/Shutterstock.com; **301** jsp/iStock/Getty Images Plus; **304** Kharidehal Abhirama Ashwin /Shutterstock.com; **308** *left* KanKankavee/iStock/Getty Images Plus; *right* gionnixxx/iStock/Getty Images Plus; **309** ©iStockphoto.com/Hedda Gjerpen; **310** *Exercise 23* ©iStockphoto.com/Rich Koele; *Exercise 27* design56/Shutterstock.com; *center* ©iStockphoto.com/rzdeb; **315** Diane Schuster/Fermi Gamma-ray Space Telescope/NASA; **317** Ivo Petkov/iStock/Getty Images Plus; **322** *top* DEA / A. DAGLI ORTI / Contributor; *bottom* Patryk Kosmider/Shutterstock.com; **324** *top right* Tupungato/Shutterstock.com; *center left* scanrail/iStock/Getty Images Plus; **328** ©iStockphoto.com/William Britten; **330** *Exercise 19 left* ©iStockphoto.com/Jill Chen; *Exercise 19 right* ©iStockphoto.com/LongHa2006; **331** OnstOn/iStock/Getty Images Plus; **333** *right* hrstkinkr/iStock/Getty Images Plus; *left* Beeldbewerking/iStock/Getty Images Plus; **334** ncognet0/iStock/Getty Images Plus; **337** Niki Crucillo/Shutterstock.com; **338** *top* ©iStockphoto.com/AlexMax; *center* PeterG/Shutterstock.com; *bottom* U.S. Geological Survey

Chapter 8

342 *top* zentilia/Shutterstock.com; *bottom* OnstOn/iStock/Getty Images Plus; **343** Tal Inbar/Wikipedia; **348** *top* ©iStockphoto.com/Egor Mopanko; *bottom* valdum/iStock/Getty Images Plus; **349** jennyt/Shuttertock.com; **350** catolla/iStock/Getty Images Plus; **351** *top* NASA/Kim Shiflett; *bottom* NASA; **356** Traveladventure/E+/Getty Images; **357** *a.* Astronaut Stephen S. Oswald/NASA; *b.* JSC/NASA; *c.* NASA; *d.* NASA; *e.* Astronaut Eileen M. Collins/NASA; *f.* NASA; **360** gregepperson/iStock/Getty Images Plus; **362** *top* ©iStockphoto.com/jclegg, ©iStockphoto.com/spxChrome, ©iStockphoto.com/Larua Eisenberg; *bottom* adventtr/E+/Getty Images; **366** *top* Shane W Thompson/Shutterstock.com; *bottom* wundervisuals/E+/Getty Images; **369** ©iStockphoto.com/ingmar wesemann; **373** IgorKirillov/iStock/Getty Images Plus; **374** *Exercise 13* rmnunes/iStock/Getty Images Plus; *Exercise 14* BNMK0819/iStock/Getty Images Plus; *Exercise 15* DieterMeyrl/E+/Getty Images; **380** CampPhoto/iStock/Getty Images Plus; **382** vovan13/ iStock/Getty Images Plus; **383** *top* ARSELA/E+/Getty Images; *center* Volosina/ iStock/Getty Images Plus; *bottom* viach80/ iStock/Getty Images Plus; **387** *top left* NASA/Johns Hopkins University Applied Physics Laboratory; *bottom left* cokacoka/iStock/Getty Images Plus; *bottom right* coddy/iStock/Getty Images Plus; **389** ©iStockphoto.com/George Peters; **390** Andrija1/iStock/Getty Images Plus; **395** mladn61/iStock/Getty Images Plus; **397** *top* dodo4466/DigitalVision Vectors/Getty Images; *center* JonathanLesage/iStock/Getty Images Plus; *bottom* Karin Hildebrand Lau/Shutterstock.com; **398** pialhovik/iStock/Getty Images Plus; **399** *top* ElementalImaging/iStock/Getty Images Plus; *bottom* OnstOn/iStock/Getty Images Plus; **404** kastanka/iStock/Getty Images Plus; **406** Harvepino/iStock/Getty Images Plus

Chapter 9

410 *top* zentilia/Shutterstock.com; *bottom* OnstOn/iStock/Getty Images Plus; **411** NASA/Terry Virts; **412** Jupiterimages/PHOTOS.com/Getty Images Plus; **413** *top* LeventeGyori/Shutterstock.com; *bottom* Farinosa/iStock/Getty Images Plus; **414** AnastasiaRasstrigina/iStock/Getty Images Plus; **416** Eric Isselée/Shutterstock.com; **418** bazilfoto/iStock/Getty Images Plus; **419** Rob Byron/Shutterstock.com; **420** *top* bowdenimages/iStock/Getty Images Plus; *bottom* ZargonDesign/iStock Unreleased/Getty Images Plus; **422** ©iStockphoto.com/Eric Isselée; **424** *top* OSTILL/iStock/Getty Images Plus; *bottom* Dash_med/iStock/Getty Images Plus; **425** Hein Nouwens/Shutterstock.com; **427** *right* andresr/E+/Getty Images; *left* only_fabrizio/iStock/Getty Images Plus; **429** USO/iStock/Getty Images Plus; **433** ChrisBoswell/iStock/Getty Images; **435** Charlie Hutton/Shutterstock.com; **438** *top* lvcandy/DigitalVision Vectors/Getty Images; *bottom* ©iStockphoto.com/Jason Lugo; **441** *left* Ganko/Shutterstock.com; *right* Mark Herreid/Shutterstock.com; **442** Ganko/Shutterstock.com; **444** *top* nikolay100//iStock Unreleased/Getty Images Plus; *center* tab62/Shutterstock.com; **445** *top* valentinrussanov/E+/Getty Images; *bottom* OnstOn/iStock/Getty Images Plus; **450** GlobalP/iStock/Getty Images Plus; **451** Six Dun/iStock/Getty Images

Chapter 10

454 *top* zentilia/Shutterstock.com; *bottom* OnstOn/iStock/Getty Images Plus; **T-454** ©iStockphoto.com/susaro; **455** damedeeso/iStock/Getty Images Plus; **457** Elzbieta Szpak/Shutterstock.com; **460** ©iStockphoto.com/Pekka Nikonen; **462** Ralwel/iStock/Getty Images Plus; **464** stockshoppe/Shutterstock.com; **465** *top* ©iStockphoto.com/susaro; *bottom* skynesher/E+/Getty Images; **467** Tomasz Trojanowski/Shutterstock.com; **471** fresher/Shutterstock.com, **474** mmaxer/Shutterstock.com; **476** ranplett/E+/Getty Images; **477** rasslava/iStock/Getty Images Plus; **478** Pingebat/iStock/Getty Images Plus; **480** Allevinatis/iStock/Getty Images Plus; **482** *top left* richcarey/iStock/Getty Images Plus; *center right* Boris Ryaposov/Shutterstock.com; *center left* aphrodite74/E+/Getty Images; **484** JackF/iStock/Getty Images Plus; **485** Sebastian Knight/Shutterstock.com; **487** mountainpix/Shutterstock.com; **489** *top* njpPhoto/iStock Unreleased/Getty Images Plus; *center* Ron_Thomas/E+/Getty Images; *bottom* GlobalP/iStock/Getty Images Plus; **490** *top* zhuda/Shutterstock.com; *bottom* LawrenceSawyer/E+/Getty Images; **491** *top* Rob Marmion/Shutterstock.com; *bottom* OnstOn/iStock/Getty Images Plus; **496** shapecharge/E+/Getty Images

Cartoon illustrations Tyler Stout
Design Elements: ©iStockphoto.com/Gizmo; Songquan Deng/Shutterstock.com; Juksy/iStock/Getty Images Plus

Mathematics Reference Sheet

Conversions

U.S. Customary

1 foot = 12 inches
1 yard = 3 feet
1 mile = 5280 feet
1 acre = 43,560 square feet
1 cup = 8 fluid ounces
1 pint = 2 cups
1 quart = 2 pints
1 gallon = 4 quarts
1 gallon = 231 cubic inches
1 pound = 16 ounces
1 ton = 2000 pounds
1 cubic foot ≈ 7.5 gallons

U.S. Customary to Metric

1 inch = 2.54 centimeters
1 foot ≈ 0.3 meter
1 mile ≈ 1.61 kilometers
1 quart ≈ 0.95 liter
1 gallon ≈ 3.79 liters
1 cup ≈ 237 milliliters
1 pound ≈ 0.45 kilogram
1 ounce ≈ 28.3 grams
1 gallon ≈ 3785 cubic centimeters

Time

1 minute = 60 seconds
1 hour = 60 minutes
1 hour = 3600 seconds
1 year = 52 weeks

Temperature

$C = \frac{5}{9}(F - 32)$

$F = \frac{9}{5}C + 32$

Metric

1 centimeter = 10 millimeters
1 meter = 100 centimeters
1 kilometer = 1000 meters
1 liter = 1000 milliliters
1 kiloliter = 1000 liters
1 milliliter = 1 cubic centimeter
1 liter = 1000 cubic centimeters
1 cubic millimeter = 0.001 milliliter
1 gram = 1000 milligrams
1 kilogram = 1000 grams

Metric to U.S. Customary

1 centimeter ≈ 0.39 inch
1 meter ≈ 3.28 feet
1 kilometer ≈ 0.62 mile
1 liter ≈ 1.06 quarts
1 liter ≈ 0.26 gallon
1 kilogram ≈ 2.2 pounds
1 gram ≈ 0.035 ounce
1 cubic meter ≈ 264 gallons

Number Properties

Commutative Properties of Addition and Multiplication

$a + b = b + a$

$a \cdot b = b \cdot a$

Associative Properties of Addition and Multiplication

$(a + b) + c = a + (b + c)$

$(a \cdot b) \cdot c = a \cdot (b \cdot c)$

Addition Property of Zero

$a + 0 = a$

Multiplication Properties of Zero and One

$a \cdot 0 = 0$

$a \cdot 1 = a$

Multiplicative Inverse Property

$n \cdot \frac{1}{n} = \frac{1}{n} \cdot n = 1, n \neq 0$

Distributive Property:

$a(b + c) = ab + ac$

$a(b - c) = ab - ac$

Properties of Equality

Addition Property of Equality

If $a = b$, then $a + c = b + c$.

Subtraction Property of Equality

If $a = b$, then $a - c = b - c$.

Multiplication Property of Equality

If $a = b$, then $a \cdot c = b \cdot c$.

Division Property of Equality

If $a = b$, then $a \div c = b \div c, c \neq 0$.

Properties of Inequality

Addition Property of Inequality

If $a > b$, then $a + c > b + c$.

Subtraction Property of Inequality

If $a > b$, then $a - c > b - c$.

Multiplication Property of Inequality

If $a > b$ and c is positive, then $a \cdot c > b \cdot c$.

Division Property of Inequality

If $a > b$ and c is positive, then $a \div c > b \div c$.

Perimeter and Area

Square	Rectangle	Parallelogram	Triangle	Trapezoid
s, s	w, ℓ	h, b	h, b	b_1, h, b_2
$P = 4s$ $A = s^2$	$P = 2\ell + 2w$ $A = \ell w$	$A = bh$	$A = \frac{1}{2}bh$	$A = \frac{1}{2}h(b_1 + b_2)$

Surface Area

Prism

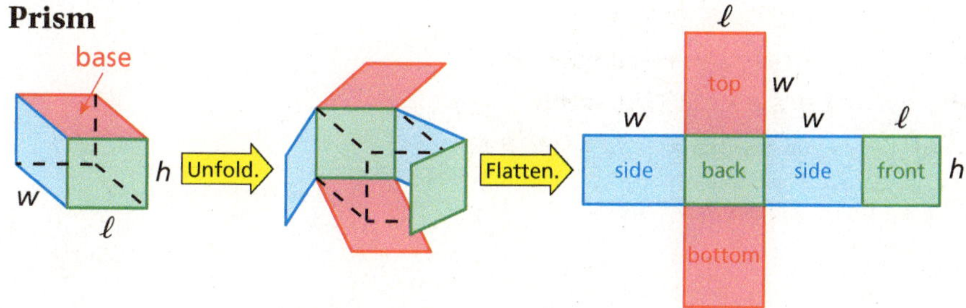

S = areas of bases + areas of lateral faces

Pyramid

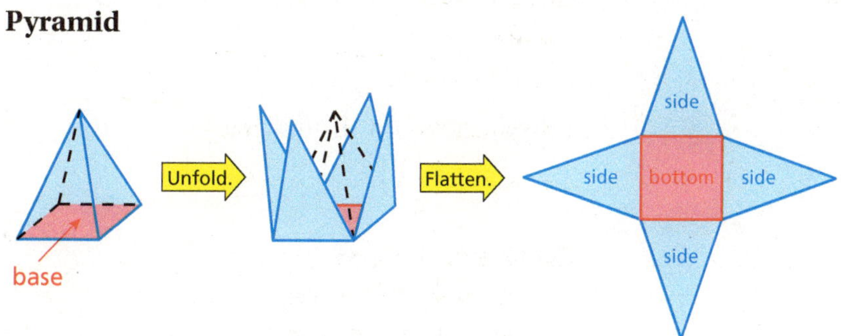

S = area of base + areas of lateral faces

Volume of a Rectangular Prism

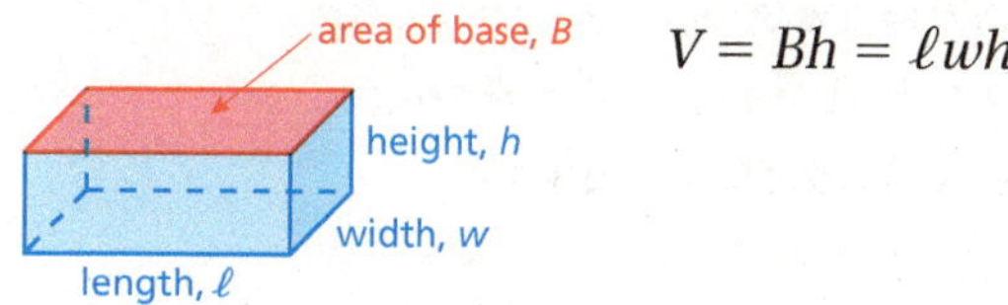

$V = Bh = \ell wh$

The Coordinate Plane

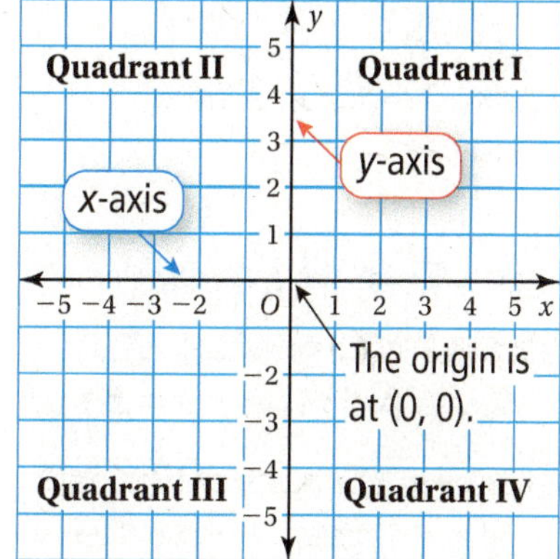